Contemporary Authors®
NEW REVISION SERIES

ISSN 0275-7176

Contemporary

Authors®

**A Bio-Bibliographical Guide to
Current Writers in Fiction, General Nonfiction,
Poetry, Journalism, Drama, Motion Pictures,
Television, and Other Fields**

NEW REVISION SERIES *volume* **138**

THOMSON
GALE

Detroit • New York • San Francisco • San Diego • New Haven, Conn. • Waterville, Maine • London • Munich

THOMSON
GALE

Contemporary Authors, New Revision Series, Vol. 138

Project Editor
Tracey L. Matthews

Editorial
Katy Balcer, Michelle Kazensky, Julie Mellors, Joshua Kondek, Lisa Kumar, Mary Ruby, Maikue Vang

Permissions
Emma Hull, Jacqueline Key, Sue Rudolph

Imaging and Multimedia
Lezlie Light, Michael Logusz

Composition and Electronic Capture
Carolyn Roney

Manufacturing
Drew Kalasky

LIBRARY OF CONGRESS CATALOG CARD NUMBER 81-640179

ISBN 0-7876-7892-9
ISSN 0275-7176

Printed in the United States of America
10 9 8 7 6 5 4 3 2 1

Contents

Preface vii

Product Advisory Board xi

International Advisory Board xii

CA Numbering System and
Volume Update Chart xiii

Authors and Media People
Featured in This Volume xv

Acknowledgments xvii

Author Listings 1

Indexing note: All *Contemporary Authors* entries are indexed in the *Contemporary Authors* cumulative index, which is published separately and distributed twice a year.

As always, the most recent Contemporary Authors cumulative index continues to be the user's guide to the location of an individual author's listing.

Preface

Contemporary Authors (*CA*) provides information on approximately 120,000 writers in a wide range of media, including:

- Current writers of fiction, nonfiction, poetry, and drama whose works have been issued by commercial publishers, risk publishers, or university presses (authors whose books have been published only by known vanity or author-subsidized firms are ordinarily not included)

- Prominent print and broadcast journalists, editors, photojournalists, syndicated cartoonists, graphic novelists, screenwriters, television scriptwriters, and other media people

- Notable international authors

- Literary greats of the early twentieth century whose works are popular in today's high school and college curriculums and continue to elicit critical attention

A *CA* listing entails no charge or obligation. Authors are included on the basis of the above criteria and their interest to *CA* users. Sources of potential listees include trade periodicals, publishers' catalogs, librarians, and other users.

How to Get the Most out of *CA*: Use the Index

The key to locating an author's most recent entry is the *CA* cumulative index, which is published separately and distributed twice a year. It provides access to *all* entries in *CA* and *Contemporary Authors New Revision Series* (*CANR*). Always consult the latest index to find an author's most recent entry.

For the convenience of users, the *CA* cumulative index also includes references to all entries in these Thomson Gale literary series: *African-American Writers, African Writers, American Nature Writers, American Writers, American Writers: The Classics, American Writers Retrospective Supplement, American Writers Supplement, Ancient Writers, Asian American Literature, Authors and Artists for Young Adults, Authors in the News, Beacham's Encyclopedia of Popular Fiction: Analyses, Beacham's Encyclopedia of Popular Fiction: Biography and Resources, Beacham's Guide to Literature for Young Adults, Beat Generation: A Gale Critical Companion, Bestsellers, Black Literature Criticism, Black Literature Criticism Supplement, Black Writers, British Writers, British Writers: The Classics, British Writers Retrospective Supplement, British Writers Supplement, Children's Literature Review, Classical and Medieval Literature Criticism, Concise Dictionary of American Literary Biography, Concise Dictionary of American Literary Biography Supplement, Concise Dictionary of British Literary Biography, Concise Dictionary of World Literary Biography, Contemporary American Dramatists, Contemporary Authors Autobiography Series, Contemporary Authors Bibliographical Series, Contemporary British Dramatists, Contemporary Canadian Authors, Contemporary Dramatists, Contemporary Literary Criticism, Contemporary Novelists, Contemporary Poets, Contemporary Popular Writers, Contemporary Southern Writers, Contemporary Women Dramatists, Contemporary Women Poets, Contemporary World Writers, Dictionary of Literary Biography, Dictionary of Literary Biography Documentary Series, Dictionary of Literary Biography Yearbook, DISCovering Authors, DISCovering Authors 3.0, DISCovering Authors: British Edition, DISCovering Authors: Canadian Edition, DISCovering Authors Modules, Drama Criticism, Drama for Students, Encyclopedia of World Literature in the 20th Century, Epics for Students, European Writers, Exploring Novels, Exploring Poetry, Exploring Short Stories, Feminism in Literature, Feminist Writers, Gay & Lesbian Literature, Guide to French Literature, Harlem Renaissance: A Gale Critical Companion, Hispanic Literature Criticism, Hispanic Literature Criticism Supplement, Hispanic Writers, International Dictionary of Films and Filmmakers: Writers and Production Artists, International Dictionary of Theatre: Playwrights, Junior DISCovering Authors, Latin American Writers, Latin American Writers Supplement, Latino and Latina Writers, Literature and Its Times, Literature and Its Times Supplement, Literature Criticism from 1400-1800, Literature of Developing Nations for Students, Major Authors and Illustrators for Children and Young Adults, Major Authors and Illustrators for Children and Young Adults Supplement, Major 21st Century Writers (eBook version), Major 20th-Century Writers, Modern American Women Writers, Modern Arts Criticism, Modern Japanese Writers, Mystery and Suspense Writers, Native North American Literature, Nineteenth-Century Literature Criticism, Nonfiction Classics for Students, Novels for Students, Poetry Criticism, Poetry for Students, Poets: American and British, Reference Guide to American Literature, Reference Guide to English Literature, Reference Guide to Short Fiction, Reference Guide to World Literature, Science Fiction Writers, Shakespearean Criticism, Shakespeare for Students, Shakespeare's Characters for Students, Short Stories for Students, Short Story Criticism, Something About the Author, Something About the Author Autobiography Series, St. James Guide to Children's Writers, St. James Guide to Crime & Mystery Writers, St. James Guide to Fantasy Writers, St. James Guide to Horror, Ghost & Gothic Writers, St. James Guide to Science Fiction Writers, St. James Guide to Young Adult Writers, Supernatural Fiction*

Writers, Twayne Companion to Contemporary Literature in English, Twayne's English Authors, Twayne's United States Authors, Twayne's World Authors, Twentieth-Century Literary Criticism, Twentieth-Century Romance and Historical Writers, Twentieth-Century Western Writers, William Shakespeare, World Literature and Its Times, World Literature Criticism, World Literature Criticism Supplement, World Poets, World Writing in English, Writers for Children, Writers for Young Adults, and *Yesterday's Authors of Books for Children.*

A Sample Index Entry:

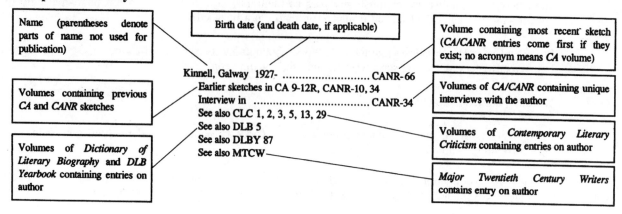

Name (parentheses denote parts of name not used for publication)

Birth date (and death date, if applicable)

Volume containing most recent sketch (*CA/CANR* entries come first if they exist; no acronym means *CA* volume)

Kinnell, Galway 1927- CANR-66
Earlier sketches in CA 9-12R, CANR-10, 34
Interview in CANR-34
See also CLC 1, 2, 3, 5, 13, 29
See also DLB 5
See also DLBY 87
See also MTCW

Volumes containing previous *CA* and *CANR* sketches

Volumes of *Dictionary of Literary Biography* and *DLB Yearbook* containing entries on author

Volumes of *CA/CANR* containing unique interviews with the author

Volumes of *Contemporary Literary Criticism* containing entries on author

Major Twentieth Century Writers contains entry on author

How Are Entries Compiled?

The editors make every effort to secure new information directly from the authors; listees' responses to our questionnaires and query letters provide most of the information featured in *CA*. For deceased writers, or those who fail to reply to requests for data, we consult other reliable biographical sources, such as those indexed in Thomson Gale's *Biography and Genealogy Master Index,* and bibliographical sources, including *National Union Catalog, LC MARC,* and *British National Bibliography.* Further details come from published interviews, feature stories, and book reviews, as well as information supplied by the authors' publishers and agents.

An asterisk (*) at the end of a sketch indicates that the listing has been compiled from secondary sources believed to be reliable but has not been personally verified for this edition by the author sketched.

What Kinds of Information Does An Entry Provide?

Sketches in *CA* contain the following biographical and bibliographical information:

- **Entry heading:** the most complete form of author's name, plus any pseudonyms or name variations used for writing

- **Personal information:** author's date and place of birth, family data, ethnicity, educational background, political and religious affiliations, and hobbies and leisure interests

- **Addresses:** author's home, office, or agent's addresses, plus e-mail and fax numbers, as available

- **Career summary:** name of employer, position, and dates held for each career post; resume of other vocational achievements; military service

- **Membership information:** professional, civic, and other association memberships and any official posts held

- **Awards and honors:** military and civic citations, major prizes and nominations, fellowships, grants, and honorary degrees

- **Writings:** a comprehensive, chronological list of titles, publishers, dates of original publication and revised editions, and production information for plays, television scripts, and screenplays

- **Adaptations:** a list of films, plays, and other media which have been adapted from the author's work

- **Work in progress:** current or planned projects, with dates of completion and/or publication, and expected publisher, when known

- **Sidelights:** a biographical portrait of the author's development; information about the critical reception of the author's works; revealing comments, often by the author, on personal interests, aspirations, motivations, and thoughts on writing

- **Interview:** a one-on-one discussion with authors conducted especially for *CA*, offering insight into authors' thoughts about their craft

- **Autobiographical essay:** an original essay written by noted authors for *CA*, a forum in which writers may present themselves, on their own terms, to their audience

- **Photographs:** portraits and personal photographs of notable authors

- **Biographical and critical sources:** a list of books and periodicals in which additional information on an author's life and/or writings appears

- **Obituary Notices** in *CA* provide date and place of birth as well as death information about authors whose full-length sketches appeared in the series before their deaths. The entries also summarize the authors' careers and writings and list other sources of biographical and death information.

Related Titles in the *CA* Series

Contemporary Authors Autobiography Series complements *CA* original and revised volumes with specially commissioned autobiographical essays by important current authors, illustrated with personal photographs they provide. Common topics include their motivations for writing, the people and experiences that shaped their careers, the rewards they derive from their work, and their impressions of the current literary scene.

Contemporary Authors Bibliographical Series surveys writings by and about important American authors since World War II. Each volume concentrates on a specific genre and features approximately ten writers; entries list works written by and about the author and contain a bibliographical essay discussing the merits and deficiencies of major critical and scholarly studies in detail.

Available in Electronic Formats

GaleNet. *CA* is available on a subscription basis through GaleNet, an online information resource that features an easy-to-use end-user interface, powerful search capabilities, and ease of access through the World-Wide Web. For more information, call 1-800-877-GALE.

Licensing. *CA* is available for licensing. The complete database is provided in a fielded format and is deliverable on such media as disk, CD-ROM, or tape. For more information, contact Thomson Gale's Business Development Group at 1-800-877-GALE, or visit us on our website at www.galegroup.com/bizdev.

Suggestions Are Welcome

The editors welcome comments and suggestions from users on any aspect of the *CA* series. If readers would like to recommend authors for inclusion in future volumes of the series, they are cordially invited to write the Editors at *Contemporary Authors*, Thomson Gale, 27500 Drake Rd., Farmington Hills, MI 48331-3535; or call at 1-248-699-4253; or fax at 1-248-699-8054.

Contemporary Authors Product Advisory Board

The editors of *Contemporary Authors* are dedicated to maintaining a high standard of excellence by publishing comprehensive, accurate, and highly readable entries on a wide array of writers. In addition to the quality of the content, the editors take pride in the graphic design of the series, which is intended to be orderly yet inviting, allowing readers to utilize the pages of *CA* easily and with efficiency. Despite the longevity of the *CA* print series, and the success of its format, we are mindful that the vitality of a literary reference product is dependent on its ability to serve its users over time. As literature, and attitudes about literature, constantly evolve, so do the reference needs of students, teachers, scholars, journalists, researchers, and book club members. To be certain that we continue to keep pace with the expectations of our customers, the editors of *CA* listen carefully to their comments regarding the value, utility, and quality of the series. Librarians, who have firsthand knowledge of the needs of library users, are a valuable resource for us. The *Contemporary Authors* Product Advisory Board, made up of school, public, and academic librarians, is a forum to promote focused feedback about *CA* on a regular basis. The seven-member advisory board includes the following individuals, whom the editors wish to thank for sharing their expertise:

- **Anne M. Christensen,** Librarian II, Phoenix Public Library, Phoenix, Arizona.

- **Barbara C. Chumard,** Reference/Adult Services Librarian, Middletown Thrall Library, Middletown, New York.

- **Eva M. Davis,** Youth Department Manager, Ann Arbor District Library, Ann Arbor, Michigan.

- **Adam Janowski, Jr.,** Library Media Specialist, Naples High School Library Media Center, Naples, Florida.

- **Robert Reginald,** Head of Technical Services and Collection Development, California State University, San Bernadino, California.

- **Stephen Weiner,** Director, Maynard Public Library, Maynard, Massachusetts.

International Advisory Board

Well-represented among the 120,000 author entries published in *Contemporary Authors* are sketches on notable writers from many non-English-speaking countries. The primary criteria for inclusion of such authors has traditionally been the publication of at least one title in English, either as an original work or as a translation. However, the editors of *Contemporary Authors* came to observe that many important international writers were being overlooked due to a strict adherence to our inclusion criteria. In addition, writers who were publishing in languages other than English were not being covered in the traditional sources we used for identifying new listees. Intent on increasing our coverage of international authors, including those who write only in their native language and have not been translated into English, the editors enlisted the aid of a board of advisors, each of whom is an expert on the literature of a particular country or region. Among the countries we focused attention on are Mexico, Puerto Rico, Spain, Italy, France, Germany, Luxembourg, Belgium, the Netherlands, Norway, Sweden, Denmark, Finland, Taiwan, Singapore, Malaysia, Thailand, South Africa, Israel, and Japan, as well as England, Scotland, Wales, Ireland, Australia, and New Zealand. The sixteen-member advisory board includes the following individuals, whom the editors wish to thank for sharing their expertise:

- **Lowell A. Bangerter,** Professor of German, University of Wyoming, Laramie, Wyoming.

- **Nancy E. Berg,** Associate Professor of Hebrew and Comparative Literature, Washington University, St. Louis, Missouri.

- **Frances Devlin-Glass,** Associate Professor, School of Literary and Communication Studies, Deakin University, Burwood, Victoria, Australia.

- **David William Foster,** Regent's Professor of Spanish, Interdisciplinary Humanities, and Women's Studies, Arizona State University, Tempe, Arizona.

- **Hosea Hirata,** Director of the Japanese Program, Associate Professor of Japanese, Tufts University, Medford, Massachusetts.

- **Jack Kolbert,** Professor Emeritus of French Literature, Susquehanna University, Selinsgrove, Pennsylvania.

- **Mark Libin,** Professor, University of Manitoba, Winnipeg, Manitoba, Canada.

- **C. S. Lim,** Professor, University of Malaya, Kuala Lumpur, Malaysia.

- **Eloy E. Merino,** Assistant Professor of Spanish, Northern Illinois University, DeKalb, Illinois.

- **Linda M. Rodríguez Guglielmoni,** Associate Professor, University of Puerto Rico—Mayagüez, Puerto Rico.

- **Sven Hakon Rossel,** Professor and Chair of Scandinavian Studies, University of Vienna, Vienna, Austria.

- **Steven R. Serafin,** Director, Writing Center, Hunter College of the City University of New York, New York City.

- **David Smyth,** Lecturer in Thai, School of Oriental and African Studies, University of London, England.

- **Ismail S. Talib,** Senior Lecturer, Department of English Language and Literature, National University of Singapore, Singapore.

- **Dionisio Viscarri,** Assistant Professor, Ohio State University, Columbus, Ohio.

- **Mark Williams,** Associate Professor, English Department, University of Canterbury, Christchurch, New Zealand.

CA Numbering System and Volume Update Chart

Occasionally questions arise about the *CA* numbering system and which volumes, if any, can be discarded. Despite numbers like "29-32R," "97-100" and "231," the entire *CA* print series consists of only 297 physical volumes with the publication of *CA* Volume 232. The following charts note changes in the numbering system and cover design, and indicate which volumes are essential for the most complete, up-to-date coverage.

CA First Revision
- 1-4R through 41-44R (11 books)
  Cover: Brown with black and gold trim.
  There will be no further First Revision volumes because revised entries are now being handled exclusively through the more efficient *New Revision Series* mentioned below.

CA Original Volumes
- 45-48 through 97-100 (14 books)
  Cover: Brown with black and gold trim.
  101 through 232 (132 books)
  Cover: Blue and black with orange bands.
  The same as previous *CA* original volumes but with a new, simplified numbering system and new cover design.

CA Permanent Series
- *CAP*-1 and *CAP*-2 (2 books)
  Cover: Brown with red and gold trim.
  There will be no further Permanent Series volumes because revised entries are now being handled exclusively through the more efficient *New Revision Series* mentioned below.

CA New Revision Series
- CANR-1 through CANR-138 (138 books)
  Cover: Blue and black with green bands.
  Includes only sketches requiring significant changes; **sketches are taken from any previously published CA, CAP, or CANR volume.**

If You Have:	You May Discard:
CA First Revision Volumes 1-4R through 41-44R and *CA Permanent Series* Volumes 1 and 2	*CA* Original Volumes 1, 2, 3, 4 and Volumes 5-6 through 41-44
CA Original Volumes 45-48 through 97-100 and 101 through 232	**NONE:** These volumes will not be superseded by corresponding revised volumes. Individual entries from these and all other volumes appearing in the left column of this chart may be revised and included in the various volumes of the *New Revision Series*.
CA New Revision Series Volumes *CANR*-1 through *CANR*-138	**NONE:** The *New Revision Series* does not replace any single volume of *CA*. Instead, volumes of *CANR* include entries from many previous *CA* series volumes. All *New Revision Series* volumes must be retained for full coverage.

A Sampling of Authors and Media People
Featured in This Volume

Rita Mae Brown

The founder of several feminist and lesbian activist groups, Brown is considered a pioneer in writing literature featuring lesbian themes and mass market appeal. Rejected by numerous publishers for what they thought was a limited readership, *Rubyfruit Jungle,* Brown's autobiographical tale about lesbian life, has sold over one million copies since its release in 1973. In other popular books, Brown explores family bonds, strong female characters, and sexual stereotypes, frequently in a humorous, irreverent way. The author of historical fiction also, Brown has written a tale about Dolley Madison and how she endured the contradictions in her life as First Lady of the United States. Beginning a mystery series cowritten with her cat, Sneaky Pie, Brown and the feline published their twelfth collaboration, *Whisker of Evil,* in 2004.

Michael Chabon

Arriving onto the American literary scene with his first novel, *The Mysteries of Pittsburgh,* in 1988, Chabon quickly established himself as a young author to watch. After earning several awards for *Wonder Boys,* his 1995 work about a burned-out author, Chabon captured a Pulitzer Prize for *The Amazing Adventures of Kavalier and Clay,* a novel featuring a young author and artist duo in the 1930s and 1940s. Critics commend Chabon for his winding, intricate stories as well as for his adventurous plots and colorful characters. Aiming for a new audience, Chabon's 2002 children's novel, *Summerland,* received wide praise for its depiction of three children and their fantastical adventure to save the world.

(Thelma) Lucille Clifton

The author of poetry and prose for adults and children alike, Clifton has earned numerous accolades for her works that frequently explore the African-American experience. Her many novels are well regarded for their depictions of downtrodden men and women persevering in challenging circumstances, while her poetry wins awards for its sharp, precise images. The author preserves in her stories the lives of everyday men and women, frequently generations from one family, helping readers understand the importance of learning from where one comes. Her 2004 work, *Mercy,* features verse reflecting on family ties, terrorism, and gender.

(Karen) Louise Erdrich

A novelist of Native-American and Germany ancestry, Erdrich is perhaps best known for her series of books depicting life on a fictional Indian reservation in North Dakota. *Love Medicine,* Erdrich's first novel in the loosely-related tales about the Native-American community, introduces a number of characters who seamlessly weave in and out of her subsequent stories. Critics laud Erdrich's decidedly non-linear storytelling technique as well as her ability to show the complicated existence of Native Americans trying to preserve their history, heritage, and lifestyle in the modern world. In her 2004 work *Four Souls,* the author returns to the character Fleur Pillager, originally introduced in *Tracks,* and shares her tale of revenge on the man who tricked her out of her land.

Carlos Fuentes

Considered by many critics to be one of Mexico's finest writers, Fuentes frequently creates stories that are applauded for their innovative narrative style. In his works, Fuentes often writes about the unique blend of Mexican history, being a complex combination of Spanish settlers and native Indian peoples. Part of a wave of Latin American authors receiving much attention for their experimental work in the mid-twentieth century, Fuentes has gained particular attention for his use of magic realism, blurring the lines between reality and fantasy.

Temple Grandin

Though diagnosed with autism at a young age, Grandin has transformed the livestock industry with her inventions that proponents claim provide for more humane treatment of animals. Comparing her own ways in which she senses the outside world with the way animals do, Grandin has developed methods to handle livestock in a way considered gentler and less traumatic for the animals. In addition to her scholarly works on animal behavior, Grandin has written about the acceptance of her ideas in the traditionally male-dominated cattle business, as well as autobiographical works explaining the thought processes, feelings, and world view of the autistic mind.

Alice Hoffman

Hoffman is the author of novels that closely examine interfamily relationships with acute clarity, claim critics. Considered an expert storyteller, Hoffmann explores the lives of her characters, revealing their struggles as they deal with the day-to-day demands of adult life. Finding and becoming comfortable with a place in life is a frequent theme in Hoffman's writing, and the author frequently shares with readers the varied paths her characters take to reach a better understanding of themselves. The author's 2004 *Blackbird House* earned praise from reviewers for its collection of stories revolving around a farmhouse on Cape Cod.

Galway Kinnell

A widely-respected poet and translator, Kinnell is called, by many critics, a major figure in contemporary poetry. The poet's verse covers a wide range of topics, including themes of death, nature, and the self, and reviewers frequently commend Kinnell for his ability to develop intense, uncluttered images in his works. Winner of both a Pulitzer Prize and a National Book Award for his poems, Kinnell continues to publish poems that explore the times and how they relate to the individual.

Peter Matthiessen

Acclaimed for his award-winning books detailing the natural world, Matthiessen is perhaps best known for his 1978 memoir, *The Snow Leopard.* Throughout his works which investigate natural phenomenon around the world, the author seeks to educate the public about the fragile state of many species and ecosystems. Complementing his interest in the wilderness is Matthiessen's literary talents which, according to critics, capture the beauty of nature in clear, colorful prose. The author's fictional works have received much recognition as well, and are noted for their swiftly-paced plots and complex character development. Travelling to the north and south, in 2003 Matthiessen produced both *End of the Earth: Voyages to the White Continent* and *Arctic National Wildlife Refuge: Seasons of Life and Land: A Photographic Journey.*

Timothy Zahn

The author of original science fiction and books based on George Lucas's "Star Wars" series, Zahn examines clashes of cultures in his fiction, often exploring what happens when humans and aliens make contact. Throughout his works, Zahn is known for creating characters who must make difficult decisions and can only survive by using their problem-solving abilities. The author's expansion of the "Star Wars" series also found fans in readers and critics alike, reaching the top of best-seller lists. In his "Star Wars" books, Zahn continues the action where Lucas left off, detailing the further adventures of Luke Skywalker, Han Solo, and Princess Leia. In 2003, Zahn published the first book, *Dragon and Thief,* in the "Dragonback" series, followed by a 2004 installment, *Dragon and Soldier.*

Acknowledgments

Grateful acknowledgment is made to those publishers, photographers, and artists whose work appear with these authors' essays. Following is a list of the copyright holders who have granted us permission to reproduce material in this volume of *CA*. Every effort has been made to trace copyright, but if omissions have been made, please let us know.

Photographs/Art

Robert L. Allen: Allen, portrait. Courtesy of Robert L. Allen. Reproduced by permission.

Nicholson Baker: Baker, photograph. AP/Wide World Photos. Reproduced by permission.

Pickney Benedict: Benedict, author photograph. Photo courtesy of Hollins University. Reproduced by permission.

Robert Olen Butler: Butler, photograph. AP/Wide World Photos. Reproduced by permission.

Ernesto Cardenal: Cardenal, photograph. AP/Wide World Photos. Reproduced by permission.

Michael Chabon: Chabon, photograph. AP/Wide World Photos. Reproduced by permission.

Lucille Clifton: Clifton, photograph by Mark Lennihan. AP/Wide World Photos. Reproduced by permission.

Max Allan Collins: Collins, photograph. AP/Wide World Photos. Reproduced by permission.

Dave Eggers: Eggers, talking to readers at The City Lights Bookstore, photograph by Susan Ragan. AP/Wide World Photos. Reproduced by permission.

Louise Erdrich: Erdrich, photograph by Eric Miller. AP/Wide World Photos. Reproduced by permission.

David French: French, photograph by Cilla Von Tiedemann. Courtesy of David French. Reproduced by permission.

Carlos Fuentes: Fuentes, 2004, photograph. AP/Wide World Photos. Reproduced by permission.

Spalding Gray: Gray, photograph. Frank Capri/Getty Images. Reproduced by permission.

Valiska Gregory: Gregory, photograph by Marshall W. Gregory. Reproduced by permission.

Adele Griffin: Griffin, photograph by John Berg. Courtesy of Adele Griffin. Reproduced by permission.

Judith Guest: Guest, photograph. AP/Wide World Photos. Reproduced by permission.

Jerry B. Jenkins: Jenkins, photograph. AP/Wide World Photos. Reproduced by permission.

Galway Kinnell: Kinnell, photograph. AP/Wide World Photos. Reproduced by permission.

Dean Koontz: Koontz, photograph. AP/Wide World Photos. Reproduced by permission.

Charles Kuralt: Kuralt, photograph by Tim Rue. AP/Wide World. Reproduced by permission.

A

ALAGOA, Ebiegberi Joe 1933-

PERSONAL: Born April 14, 1933, in Nembe, Bayelsa State, Nigeria; son of Joseph Ayibatonye (a chief) and Jane Furombogha (Obasi) Alagoa; married Mercy Gboribusuote Nyananyo, September 26, 1961; children: David Ayibatonye. *Education:* Attended University College (Ibadan, Nigeria); University of London, B.A. (with honors), 1959; American University, certificate in archives administration, 1960; University of Wisconsin, certificate in African studies, 1965, Ph.D., 1966.

ADDRESSES: Office—c/o School of Humanities, University of Port Harcourt, P.O. Box 125, Uniport Post Office, Choba, Port Harcourt, Rivers State, Nigeria; P.O. Box 893, Yenagoa, Bayelsa State, Nigeria; P.O. Box 126, Nembe, Bayelsa State, Nigeria. *E-mail*—kala_joe@yahoo.com.

CAREER: National Archives of Nigeria, Ibadan, began as archivist, became senior archivist, 1959-62; University of Lagos, Lagos, Nigeria, lecturer in African history, 1965-67; University of Ibadan, Ibadan, Nigeria, senior research fellow at Institute of African Studies, 1967-72; University of Lagos, professor of history and director of Centre of Cultural Studies, 1972-77; University of Port Harcourt, Port Harcourt, Rivers State, Nigeria, dean of School of Humanities, 1977-80, deputy vice chancellor, 1980-81, acting vice chancellor, 1982, dean of School of Graduate Studies, 1982-83, 1985-87, chair of faculty of humanities of Niger Delta Research Group, 1990-98. Frobenius Institute, visiting scholar, 1989; Bellagio Study and Conference Center, resident scholar, 1990; Brown University, research scholar, 1993-94. Member of Nigerian National Archives Committee, 1966-70, National Antiquities Commission, 1972-76, National Council for Arts and Culture, 1975-76, 1990-94, Nigerian Television Authority, 1984-86, Nigerian Copyright Council, 1989-93, and Nigerian National Merit Award Board, 1998-2001. Rivers State Council of Arts and Culture, chair, 1972-75; Rivers State Chieftaincy Enquiry, member, 1975; Rivers State Chieftaincy Review Commission, chair, 1975-76; justice of the peace of Bayelsa State, 1999. Rivers State College of Science and Technology, member of council, 1972-75; Niger Delta University, pro-chancellor, 2001.

MEMBER: Historical Society of Nigeria (fellow; president, 1981-83, 1991-94), Nigerian Academy of Letters (fellow), Nigerian Association for Oral History and Tradition (president, 1985-94), American Anthropological Association, Knights of St. Christopher.

AWARDS, HONORS: Fulbright scholar, 1983-84; Rockefeller Foundation scholar, 1990; senior Fulbright scholar, 1993-94; officer, Order of the Niger, 2000.

WRITINGS:

The Small Brave City-State: A History of Nembe-Brass in the Niger Delta, University of Wisconsin Press (Madison, WI), 1964.

Jaja of Opobo: The Slave Who Became a King (juvenile nonfiction), Longman (London, England), 1970.

(With Adadonye Fombo) *A Chronicle of Grand Bonny,* Ibadan University Press (Ibadan, Nigeria), 1972.

A History of the Niger Delta: An Historical Interpretation of Ijo Oral Tradition, Ibadan University Press (Ibadan, Nigeria), 1972.

King Boy of Brass (juvenile nonfiction), Heinemann Educational (London, England), 1975.

(With Nwanna Nzewunwa) *The History of Ogbakiri: An Introduction,* [Port Harcourt, Rivers State, Nigeria], 1980.

The Python's Eye: The Past in the Living Present, [Port Harcourt, Rivers State, Nigeria], 1981.

Sagbe Obasi: Amanyanabo of Okpoama, 1845-1862, [Port Harcourt, Rivers State, Nigeria], 1986.

People of the Fish and Eagle: A History of Okpoama in the Eastern Niger Delta, Isengi Communications (Port Harcourt, Rivers State, Nigeria), 1996.

Okpu: Ancestral Houses in Nembe and European Antiquities on the Brass and Nun Rivers of the Niger Delta, Onyoma Research Publications (Port Harcourt, Rivers State, Nigeria), 2001.

Shorter works include "The Akassa Raid 1895," [Ibadan, Nigeria], 1960; "War Canoe Drums and Topical Songs from Nembe, Rivers State," Rivers State Council for Arts and Culture (Rivers State, Nigeria), 1974; "The Ijaw Nation in the New Millennium," Onyoma Research Publications (Port Harcourt, Rivers State, Nigeria), 1999; and "Beke you mi: Nembe against the British Empire," Onyoma Research Publications (Port Harcourt, Rivers State, Nigeria), 2001. Contributor to books, including *International Handbook of Historical Studies: Contemporary Research and Theory,* edited by G. G. Iggers and H. T. Parker, 1979; *Groundwork of Nigerian History,* edited by O. Ikime, [Ibadan, Nigeria], [Westport, CT], 1980; *UNESCO General History of Africa,* Volume 6, edited by J. F. Ade Ajayi, [California], 1989; *Museums and History in West Africa,* edited by Claude Daniel Ardouin and Emmanuel Arinze, Smithsonian Institution Press (Washington, DC), 2000; and *Ways of the Rivers: Arts and Environment of the Niger Delta,* edited by Martha G. Anderson and Philip M. Peek, Fowler Museum of Cultural History, University of California—Los Angeles (Los Angeles, CA), 2002. Contributor to periodicals, including *Nigerian Heritage, Nigerian Field, Nigerian Archives, Kiabara, Daedalus: Journal of the American Academy of Arts and Sciences,* *New Culture: Review of Contemporary African Arts, Journal of African History, Journal of the Historical Society of Nigeria, Africa,* and *Journal of American Folklore.*

EDITOR:

(With Bolanle Awe, and contributor) *Nigerian Antiquities,* [Ibadan, Nigeria], 1972.

(With Tekena N. Tamuno; and contributor) *Eminent Nigerians of the Rivers State,* Heinemann Educational Books (Ibadan, Nigeria), 1980.

The Teaching of History in African Universities, Association of African Universities (Accra, Ghana), 1981.

(With Kay Williamson) *Ancestral Voices: Oral Historical Texts from Nembe, Niger Delta,* [Port Harcourt, Rivers State, Nigeria], 1981.

More Days, More Wisdom: Nembe Proverbs/Noin nengia bere nengia: Nembe n'akabu, University of Port Harcourt Press (Port Harcourt, Nigeria), 1983.

Tarikh, Volume 8: *Oral Historical Traditions in Africa,* Longman (Ikeja, Nigeria), 1987.

(With F. N. Anozie and Nwanna Nzewunwa) *The Early History of the Niger Delta,* 1988.

(With Tekena N. Tamuno) *The Land and People of Nigeria: Rivers State,* Riverside Communications (Port Harcourt, Rivers State, Nigeria), 1989, revised edition (with Abi A. Derefaka) published as *The Land and People of Rivers State: Eastern Niger Delta,* Onyoma Research Publications (Port Harcourt, Rivers State, Nigeria), 2002.

Oral Tradition and Oral History in Africa and the Diaspora: Theory and Practice, Centre for Black and African Arts and Civilization (Lagos, Nigeria), 1990.

(And contributor) *Dike Remembered, African Reflections on History: Dike Memorial Lectures, 1985-1995,* University of Port Harcourt Press (Port Harcourt, Rivers State, Nigeria), 1998.

A History of the University of Port Harcourt, 1977-1998, University of Port Harcourt Press (Port Harcourt, Rivers State, Nigeria), 1999.

The Land and People of Bayelsa State: Central Niger Delta, Onyoma Research Publications (Port Harcourt, Rivers State, Nigeria), 1999.

Also compiler of "Kien abibi onde fa pugu/Nembe (Ijo) Numerals," Nembe Cultural Association, (Lagos, Nigeria), 1967.

WORK IN PROGRESS: Kaliye Opuye, Opuye Kaliye: A History of Nembe in the Niger Delta; The Practice of History in Africa: A History of African Historiography; The Life and Times of Earnest Sisei Ikoli, Journalist, Nationalist, with John H. Enemugwem; *The Ossomala Kingdom of the Lower Niger and Its Neighbours;* research on drum praise poetry of the Niger Delta, African proverbs, and the ancient Egyptian wisdom literature, and the environment, society, and cultural heritage of the Niger Delta.

SIDELIGHTS: Nigerian historian and educator Ebiegberi Joe Alagoa has written numerous works about his homeland, the Rivers State region of Nigeria. Many of these works deal with history and folklore as incorporated into the oral tradition of Africa. In his 1964 work, *The Small Brave City-State: A History of Nembe-Brass in the Niger Delta,* Alagoa chronicles the history of the Nembe people who have lived near the Brass River estuary of the Niger Delta since the fifteenth century. Drawing on oral sources preserved in the national archives, as well as other published sources, Alagoa describes the social and political organizations, commerce, and politics of the Nembe Brass. He also describes the Akassa War between the Nembe and the British colonial trading company.

Several commentators have praised Alagoa's contribution to the recorded history of Nigeria. Judging Alagoa to be "well equipped to fuse the oral traditions of the Nembe people with the more standard sources," Robert O. Collins, writing in the *American Historical Review,* called the work "first a most useful contribution to the local history of the delta region and second a scholarly addition to the history of Nigeria as a whole." "The chapter on the Akassa War is particularly useful to the African historian," Collins added. In addition, a critic for *Choice* called the work "well written," noting Alagoa's "excellent analysis" of the region's institutions, commenting that it supplements other works on Nigeria.

"Alagoa has written a historical study rather than an ethnography, thus omitting many cultural features which would interest anthropologists," wrote Donald C. Simmons in a review for *American Anthropologist.* "However, anyone interested in the area can glean much background ethnological information from this interesting, well-documented study, whose minor faults are due not to the author but to the paucity of data available for reconstructing Nembe history." The "principal weakness" of *The Small Brave City-State* is Alagoa's "failure to carry the history of Nembe-Brass well into the twentieth century," according to Collins.

For young readers, Alagoa has contributed to the "African Historical Biographies" series of London, England, publisher Heinemann. The goal of this series is to present African history from a native point of view, rather than from the colonial perspective so frequently employed. Thus, *King Boy of Brass* tells the story of a nineteenth-century boy-king of the Niger Delta, who is at first a disappointment to his father, but who redeems himself as a ruler and trader. Abiola Odejide, writing in *Reading Teacher,* mentioned that Alagoa's book turned the reader into a "detached observer, an auditor rather than a vicarious participant of a past experience." "The authors in all the Heinemann series are strongly aware of the historical perspective, leading to an overwhelming factual tone and the relegation of literary quality to the background," stated Odejide. On the other hand, the critic judged Alagoa's 1970 biography, *Jaja of Opobo: The Slave Who Became a King,* to be the more successful of the historian's two juvenile biographies. Because the author fictionalizes the early life of Jaja of Opobo, maintained Odejide, young readers are more likely to become engaged in the work.

BIOGRAPHICAL AND CRITICAL SOURCES:

BOOKS

Ejituwu, Nkparom C., editor, *The Multi-Disciplinary Approach to African History: Essays in Honour of Ebiegberi Joe Alagoa,* University of Port Harcourt Press (Port Harcourt, Rivers State, Nigeria), 1998.

PERIODICALS

American Anthropologist, June, 1965, Donald C. Simmons, review of *The Small Brave City-State: A History of Nembe-Brass in the Niger Delta,* pp. 793-794.
American Historical Review, April, 1965, Robert O. Collins, review of *The Small Brave City-State,* pp. 880-881.

Choice, February, 1965, review of *The Small Brave City-State,* p. 584.

Reading Teacher, March, 1987, Abiola Odejide, review of *King Boy of Brass* and *Jaja of Opobo: The Slave Who Became a King,* pp. 642-643.

*   *   *

ALKIVIADES, Alkis 1953-
(Luke Sharp, a joint pseudonym)

PERSONAL: Born January 13, 1953, in Nicosia, Cyprus; son of Andreas and Anastasia Alkiviades; married Ariane Isabelle Bishop, June 6, 1987. *Ethnicity:* "Greek." *Education:* London School of Oriental and African Studies (London, England), B.A. (with honors), 1975; University of Exeter, postgraduate certificate in education, 1976.

ADDRESSES: Home—Anchor Cottage, Brownshill, Stroud, Gloucestershire GL6 8AG, England. *E-mail*—aalkivia@aol.com.

CAREER: Civil Service Commission, executive officer, 1977-79; Kilburn Skills College, lecturer, 1979-85; London Software Studio, London, England, graphic designer, 1985-87; freelance writer, 1987-91; Micro-Prose Software Ltd., copy writer, 1991-92, communications manager, 1992-95, product information manager, 1995-99; freelance writer, 1999—.

WRITINGS:

The Sports Game, Penguin (New York, NY), 1985.
Star Strider, Penguin (New York, NY), 1986.
(Under joint pseudonym Luke Sharp; with Steve Jackson, Ian Livingstone, and Russ Nicholson) *Steve Jackson and Ian Livingstone Present Chasms of Malice,* Penguin (New York, NY), 1987.
Daggers of Darkness, Penguin (New York, NY), 1988.
(Under joint pseudonym Luke Sharp; with Steve Jackson, Ian Livingstone, and David Gallagher) *Steve Jackson and Ian Livingstone Present Fangs of Fury,* Penguin (New York, NY), 1989.
Dotto and the Pharoah's Mask: An Interactive Connect-the-Dots Adventure, illustrated by Giovanni Caselli, Abrams (New York, NY), 1997.

Dotto and the Minotaur's Maze: An Interactive Connect-the-Dots Adventure, Abrams (New York, NY), 1998.

WORK IN PROGRESS: Passatempo, a novel.

*   *   *

ALLEN, Robert L(ee) 1942-
(Benjamin Peterson)

PERSONAL: Born May 29, 1942, in Atlanta, GA; son of Robert Lee and Sadie (Sims) Allen; married Pamela Parker, August 28, 1965 (divorced); married Janet Carter, 1995; children: (first marriage) Casey Douglass. *Ethnicity:* African-American. *Education:* Attended University of Vienna, 1961-62; Morehouse College, B.S., 1963; graduate study at Columbia University, 1963-64; New School for Social Research, M.A., 1967; University of California—San Francisco, Ph.D., 1983.

ADDRESSES: Home—1034 Vallejo St., San Francisco, CA 94133. *Office*—Black Scholar, P.O. Box 2869, Oakland, CA 94618. *E-mail*—rlallen@berkeley.edu.

CAREER: Department of Welfare, New York, NY, caseworker, 1964-65; reporter for *National Guardian,* 1967-69; San Jose State College (now University), San Jose, CA, began as instructor, became assistant professor of black studies, 1969-72; Mills College, Oakland, CA, began as lecturer, became assistant professor of ethnic studies, 1973-84, head of ethnic studies department, 1981-84; *Black Scholar,* Oakland, CA, associate editor, 1972-74, managing editor, 1974-75, editor, 1975-90, senior editor, 1990—. University of California, Berkeley, CA, visiting professor in African American & ethnic studies department, 1994-2003. Adjunct professor, 2003—. Also general editor of Wild Trees Press, 1984-90. Member of the board of directors of Bay Area Black Journalists, Oakland Men's Project, and San Francisco Book Council.

MEMBER: American Sociological Association, American Historical and Cultural Society, Black World Foundation, Pacific Sociological Association.

AWARDS, HONORS: Merrill grant for Austria, 1961-62; Woodrow Wilson fellowship, 1963-64; Dorothy

Robert L. Allen

Gelgor Prize in New School Social Research, 1967; Guggenheim fellowship, 1977; American Book Award, 1995, for *Brotherman: The Odyssey of Black Men in America.*

WRITINGS:

Black Awakening in Capitalist America, Doubleday (New York, NY), 1969, published as *A Guide to Black Power in America: An Historical Analysis,* Gollanz (London, England), 1970.

Reluctant Reformers: The Impact of Racism on American Social Reform Movements, Howard University Press (Washington, DC), 1974.

The Port Chicago Disaster and Its Aftermath, University of California (San Francisco, CA), 1983, published as *The Port Chicago Mutiny,* Warner (New York, NY), 1989.

(Editor, with Robert Chrisman) *Court of Appeal: The Black Community Speaks Out on the Racial and Sexual Politics of Thomas vs. Hill,* Ballantine Books (New York, NY), 1992.

(Editor, with Herb Boyd) *Brotherman: The Odyssey of Black Men in America,* illustrated by Tom Feelings, One World (New York, NY), 1995.

(With Lee Brown) *Strong in the Struggle: My Life as a Black Labor Activist* (biography of Lee Brown), Rowman & Littlefield (Lanham, MD), 2001.

(With Allene G. Carter) *Honoring Sergeant Carter: Redeeming a Black World War II Hero's Legacy,* Amistad (New York, NY), 2003.

Contributor to *Race, Gender, and Power in America,* edited by Anita Faye Hill and Emma Coleman Jordan, Oxford, 1995; *Readings in Black Political Economy,* edited by John Whitehead and Cobi Kawasi Harris, Kendall/Hunt, 1999; and *The African American Studies Reader,* edited by Nathaniel Norment, Jr., Carolina Academic Press, 2001. Contributor to magazines, sometimes under the pseudonym Benjamin Peterson.

ADAPTATIONS: Port Chicago was adapted as a documentary, television movie, and jazz suite.

SIDELIGHTS: Robert L. Allen once commented, "A recurrent theme in my work is a concern with the role of beliefs and ideologies in the process of social change. I consider myself a materialist sociologist, but I also think that human action is shaped by the subjective understandings that people have of their situations; hence, getting inside the heads of actors, understanding their consciousness, is as important as measuring the social forces that impinge upon them."

For his book *The Port Chicago Disaster and Its Aftermath,* Allen drew upon documents and oral histories he had collected from survivors to describe the events that, according to Allen, "followed the disastrous explosion, at the Port Chicago (California) Naval Ammunition Magazine in July, 1944. After the explosion, fifty black sailors were accused of mutiny when, as part of a larger group, they refused to return to work loading ammunition on ships. (More than three hundred men had been killed in the blast.) The fifty men were court-martialed amid great publicity, convicted, and jailed. A national campaign was organized by the Legal Defense Fund of the National Association for the Advancement of Colored People (NAACP), under the leadership of Thurgood Marshall, to free the men. Eventually, the sentences were set aside and the men were released. The Port Chicago explosion was the worst home-front disaster of World War II, and the trial of the fifty men was the largest mass mutiny trial in U.S. Navy history."

Allen coedited *Brotherman: The Odyssey of Black Men in America,* with Herb Boyd. Containing over one hundred entries, the book is the first anthology devoted exclusively to male African-American writings. Writing in *American Visions,* T. Andreas Spelman considered *Brotherman,* "one of the most comprehensive collections of African American men's writing." While the anthology includes contributions from the famous, including Martin Luther King, Jr., Malcolm X, and Essex Hemphill, *Booklist*'s Greg Burkman observed, "famous individuals don't over-shadow those who are less so" in this "forceful anthology," while a *Publishers Weekly* critic called *Brotherman* "a distinguished addition to black stud-ies."

Honoring Sergeant Carter: Redeeming a Black World War II Hero's Legacy, which Allen coauthored with Carter's daughter-in-law, Allene G. Carter, is "packed with jewels of America's diverse racial and cultural history too often hidden from view," wrote Vernon Ford in a *Booklist* review. With only a few exceptions, African-American soldiers served in segregated units until the latter part of World War II. When, after the Battle of the Bulge, the army allowed the soldiers to volunteer for front-line duty, Eddie Carter was transferred into George Patton's command and fought in one of the first battles to take place on German soil. Single-handedly overtaking enemy machine gun and mortar positions, Carter was said to have fought bravely. He heroically saved the lives of many of his fellow soldiers while suffering great injury himself. He received a Distinguished Service Medal, but did not receive a Medal of Honor, which many felt he justly deserved. In fact, none of the 294 such medals were awarded to any of the 1.2 million African-American soldiers serving in World War II. In response to pressure from veteran's groups, the Army investi-gated Carter's case in 1992.

In the book, the authors suggest that Carter's initial failure to receive a medal was due to the overt racism of some Army officers, Carter's political sympathies, and his vocal objections to the treatment of black soldiers. In 1997, however, President Bill Clinton awarded Carter a posthumous Medal of Honor. Carton's son, Edward III, accepted the medal of behalf of his father, who died in 1963. A *Kirkus Reviews* contributor felt that the authors did "a commendable job of showing just how righteous Carter's cause was, bringing deserved honor to their subject."

BIOGRAPHICAL AND CRITICAL SOURCES:

BOOKS

Contemporary Black Biography, Volume 38, Gale (Detroit, MI), 2003.

PERIODICALS

American Vision, April-May, 1995, T. Andreas Spelman, review of *Brotherman: The Odyssey of Black Men in America,* p. 34.

Black Issues in Higher Education, June 1, 1995, D. Kamili Anderson, review of *Brotherman,* pp. 74-76.

Black Scholar, March-April, 1989, Evelyn C. White, review of *The Port Chicago Mutiny,* pp. 33-35; summer, 1990, "Port Chicago Case Comes before U.S. Congress," pp. 38-40; spring, 1993, review of *The Port Chicago Mutiny,* p. 57; winter, 1995, John Woodford, review of *Brotherman,* pp. 56-58.

Booklist, March 15, 1989, review of *The Port Chicago Mutiny,* p. 93; February 15, 1995, Greg Burkman, review of *Brotherman,* p. 1053; January 1, 2003, Vernon Ford, review of *Honoring Sergeant Carter: Redeeming a Black World War II Hero's Legacy,* p. 838.

Crisis, October, 1995, Malik M. Chaka, review of *Brotherman,* p. 8.

Kirkus Reviews, January 15, 1989, review of *The Port Chicago Mutiny,* p. 93; November 15, 2002, review of *Honoring Sergeant Carter,* p. 1668.

Library Journal, March 1, 1989, Thomas J. Davis, review of *The Port Chicago Mutiny,* p. 78; March 15, 1995, Anita L. Cole, review of *Brotherman,* p. 90.

Michigan Law Review, May, 1990, Derrick A. Bell, review of *The Port Chicago Mutiny,* pp. 1689-1697.

Publishers Weekly, January 13, 1989, review of *The Port Chicago Mutiny,* p. 81; January 23, 1995, review of *Brotherman,* p. 51; December 9, 2002, review of *Honoring Sergeant Carter,* p. 73.

San Francisco Review of Books, 1989, review of *Port Chicago Mutiny,* p. 23.

*   *   *

ANDREWS, Russell
See HANDLER, David

*   *   *

APPLEGATE, K. A.
See APPLEGATE, Katherine (Alice)

APPLEGATE, Katherine (Alice) 1956-
(K. A. Applegate, Katherine Kendall)

PERSONAL: Born 1956, in MI. *Hobbies and other interests:* Playing the cello, travel, reading, gardening, her pet cats.

ADDRESSES: Home—Minneapolis, MN. *Agent*—c/o Scholastic Inc., 555 Broadway, New York, NY 10012. *E-mail*—kaapplcgate@scholastic.com.

CAREER: Freelance writer.

AWARDS, HONORS: Cited among "best new children's book series," *Publishers Weekly,* 1997.

WRITINGS:

"ANIMORPHS" JUVENILE SERIES; UNDER NAME K. A. APPLEGATE

The Invasion, Scholastic, Inc. (New York, NY), 1996.
The Visitor, Scholastic, Inc. (New York, NY), 1996.
The Message, Scholastic, Inc. (New York, NY), 1996.
The Encounter, Demco Media (Madison, WI), 1996.
The Predator, Apple (New York, NY), 1996.
The Capture, Scholastic, Inc. (New York, NY), 1997.
The Stranger, Scholastic, Inc. (New York, NY), 1997.
The Alien, Scholastic, Inc. (New York, NY), 1997.
The Secret, Scholastic, Inc. (New York, NY), 1997.
The Android, Scholastic, Inc. (New York, NY), 1997.
The Forgotten, Scholastic, Inc. (New York, NY), 1997.
The Reaction, Scholastic, Inc. (New York, NY), 1997.
The Andalite Chronicles, Scholastic, Inc. (New York, NY), 1997.
The Change, Scholastic, Inc. (New York, NY), 1997.
The Unknown, Scholastic, Inc. (New York, NY), 1998.
The Warning, Scholastic, Inc. (New York, NY), 1998.
The Underground, Scholastic, Inc. (New York, NY), 1998.
The Hork-Bajir Chronicles, Scholastic, Inc. (New York, NY), 1998.
The Escape, Scholastic, Inc. (New York, NY), 1998.
The Decision, Scholastic, Inc. (New York, NY), 1998.
The Departure, Scholastic, Inc. (New York, NY), 1998.
The Discovery, Scholastic, Inc. (New York, NY), 1998.
The Threat, Demco Media (Madison, WI), 1998.
The Solution, Demco Media (Madison, WI), 1999.

The Pretender, Demco Media (Madison, WI), 1999.
The Suspicion, Demco Media (Madison, WI), 1999.
The Extreme, Little Apple (New York, NY), 1999.
The Attack, Apple (New York, NY), 1999.
The Exposed, Scholastic, Inc. (New York, NY), 1999.
The Experiment, Scholastic, Inc. (New York, NY), 1999.
The Sickness, Scholastic, Inc. (New York, NY), 1999.
The Reunion, Apple (New York, NY), 1999.
The Illusion, Apple (New York, NY), 1999.
The Conspiracy, Apple (New York, NY), 1999.
Enter the Enchanted, Scholastic, Inc. (New York, NY), 1999.
Visser (companion book to *The Hork-Bajir Chronicles*), Scholastic, Inc. (New York, NY), 1999.
The Separation, Gareth Stevens (Milwaukee, WI), 2000.
The Proposal, Gareth Stevens (Milwaukee, WI), 2000.
The Prophecy, Gareth Stevens (Milwaukee, WI), 2000.
The Mutation, Gareth Stevens (Milwaukee, WI), 2000.
The Arrival, Apple (New York, NY), 2000.
The Deception, Apple (New York, NY), 2000.
The Diversion, Apple (New York, NY), 2000.
The Ellimist Chronicles, Apple (New York, NY), 2000.
The Familiar, Apple (New York, NY), 2000.
The Hidden, Apple (New York, NY), 2000.
The Journey, Apple (New York, NY), 2000.
The Other, Apple (New York, NY), 2000.
The Resistance, Apple (New York, NY), 2000.
The Return, Apple (New York, NY), 2000.
The Revelation, Apple (New York, NY), 2000.
The Test, Scholastic, Inc. (New York, NY), 2000.
The Unexpected, Scholastic, Inc. (New York, NY), 2000.
The Weakness, Scholastic, Inc. (New York, NY), 2000.
The Absolute, Scholastic, Inc. (New York, NY), 2001.
The Answer, Apple (New York, NY), 2001.
The Beginning, Apple (New York, NY), 2001.
The Sacrifice, Apple (New York, NY), 2001.

"ANIMORPHS MEGAMORPHS" JUVENILE SERIES

The Andalites Gift, Scholastic, Inc. (New York, NY), 1997.
Animorphs in the Time of the Dinosaurs, Scholastic, Inc. (New York, NY), 1998.
Elfangor's Secret, Apple (New York, NY), 1999.
Back to Before, Apple (New York, NY), 2000.

"BOYFRIENDS AND GIRLFRIENDS" YOUNG ADULT SERIES; REPRINTED AS "MAKING OUT" SERIES

Zoey Fools Around, Harper (New York, NY), 1994.
Don't Tell Zoey, Flare (New York, NY), 1996.
Zoey Speaks Out, Flare (New York, NY), 1996.
Kate Finds Love, Flare (New York, NY), 1997.
Never Trust Lara, Flare (New York, NY), 1997.
Jake Finds Out, Flare (New York, NY), 1998.
Nina Won't Tell, Flare (New York, NY), 1998.
Ben's in Love, Flare (New York, NY), 1998.
What Zoey Saw, Flare (New York, NY), 1998.
Claire Gets Caught, Flare (New York, NY), 1998.
Lucas Gets Hurt, Flare (New York, NY), 1998.
Aisha Goes Wild, Flare (New York, NY), 1999.
Zoey Plays Games, Flare (New York, NY), 1999.
Nina Shapes Up, Camelot (New York, NY), 1999.
Ben Takes a Chance, Flare (New York, NY), 1999.
Claire Can't Lose, Flare (New York, NY), 1999.
Aaron Lets Go, Flare (New York, NY), 1999.
Who Loves Kate, Flare (New York, NY), 1999.
Lara Gets Even, Flare (New York, NY), 1999.
Two-Timing Aisha, Flare (New York, NY), 1999.
Zoey Comes Home, Avon (New York, NY), 2000.
Zoey's Broken Heart, HarperCollins Publishers (New York, NY), 2000.

"EVERWORLD" YOUNG ADULT SERIES; UNDER NAME K. A. APPLEGATE

Search for Senna, Scholastic, Inc. (New York, NY), 1999.
Land of Loss, Scholastic, Inc. (New York, NY), 1999.
Enter the Enchanted, Scholastic, Inc. (New York, NY), 1999.
Realm of the Reaper, Scholastic, Inc. (New York, NY), 1999.
Discover the Destroyer, Scholastic, Inc. (New York, NY), 2000.
Brave the Betrayal, Scholastic, Inc. (New York, NY), 2000.
Fear the Fantastic, Apple (New York, NY), 2000.
Inside the Illusion, Scholastic, Inc. (New York, NY), 2000.
Understand the Unknown, Scholastic, Inc. (New York, NY), 2000.
Entertain the End, Scholastic, Inc. (New York, NY), 2001.

"REMNANTS" JUVENILE SERIES; UNDER NAME K. A. APPLEGATE

Them, Apple (New York, NY), 2001.
Destination Unknown, Apple (New York, NY), 2001.
The Mayflower Project, Apple (New York, NY), 2001.
Isolation, Apple (New York, NY), 2002.
Nowhere Land, Apple (New York, NY), 2002.
No Place like Home, Apple (New York, NY), 2002.
Mother, May I?, Apple (New York, NY), 2002.
Breakdown, Apple (New York, NY), 2002.
Mutation, Apple (New York, NY), 2002.
Survival, Apple (New York, NY), 2003.
Dream Storm, Apple (New York, NY), 2003.
Lost and Found, Apple (New York, NY), 2003.
Begin Again, Apple (New York, NY), 2003.
Aftermath, Apple (New York, NY), 2003.

"SUMMER" SERIES

June Dreams, Archway (New York, NY), 1995.
July's Promise, Archway (New York, NY), 1995.
August Magic, Archway (New York, NY), 1995.
Beaches, Boys, and Betrayal, Archway (New York, NY), 1996.
Sand, Surf, and Secrets, Archway (New York, NY), 1996.
Rays, Romance, and Rivalry, Archway (New York, NY), 1996.
Christmas Special Edition, Archway (New York, NY), 1996.
Spring Break Reunion, Archway (New York, NY), 1996.

BY L. E. BLAIR; TEXT BY KATHERINE APPLEGATE

Horse Fever ("Girl Talk" series), Western Publishing (Racine, WI), 1991.
Family Rules ("Girl Talk" series), Western Publishing (Racine, WI), 1991.
Randy's Big Dream, Western Publishing (Racine, WI), 1992.
Randy and the Great Canoe Race, Western Publishing (Racine, WI), 1992.
Randy and the Perfect Boy, Western Publishing (Racine, WI), 1992.
Randy's Big Chance, Western Publishing (Racine, WI), 1992.

OTHER

(Under pseudonym Katherine Kendall) *The Midas Touch* (adult romance novel), Harlequin Books (New York, NY), 1988.

The Story of Two American Generals: Benjamin O. Davis Jr. and Colin L. Powell (juvenile nonfiction), Dell (New York, NY), 1992.

Disney's The Little Mermaid: The Haunted Palace, illustrated by Philo Barnhart, Disney Press (New York, NY), 1993.

Disney's The Little Mermaid: King Triton, Beware!, illustrated by Philo Barnhart, Disney Press (New York, NY), 1993.

Disney's Christmas with All the Trimmings: Original Stories and Crafts from Mickey Mouse and Friends, illustrated by Phil Wilson, Disney Press (New York, NY), 1994.

The Boyfriend Mix-Up, illustrated by Philo Barnhart, Disney Press (New York, NY), 1994.

Sharing Sam (young adult novel), Bantam (New York, NY), c. 1995.

Disney's Tales from Agrabah: Seven Original Stories of Aladdin and Jasmine, illustrated by Fred Marvin and Jose Cardona, Disney Press (New York, NY), 1995.

(With Nicholas Stephens) *Disney's Climb Aboard if You Dare! Stories from the Pirates of the Caribbean,* illustrated by Roberta Collier-Morales, Disney Press (New York, NY), 1996.

Listen to My Heart ("Love Stories Super" series), Bantam (New York, NY), 1996.

Jack Rabbit and the Beanstalk (picture book), illustrated by Holly Hannon, Inchworm Press (Vancouver, British Columbia, Canada), 1997.

Escape (picture book; "Magic School Bus" series), Scholastic, Inc. (New York, NY), 1998.

The First Journey ("Animorphs Alternamorphs" series), Scholastic, Inc. (New York, NY), 1999.

The Next Passage ("Animorphs Alternamorphs" series), Apple (New York, NY), 2000.

Author of many other juvenile novels, including installments in the "Changes Romance" series, the "Ocean City" series, and the "Sweet Valley Twin" series.

ADAPTATIONS: The "Animorphs" books have been adapted as a television series for Nickelodeon.

SIDELIGHTS: Katherine Applegate, who also writes as K. A. Applegate, has written over one hundred books. While her publications include a romance for the Harlequin line, she has aimed most of her writing at middle-grade readers, penning some titles for the popular "Sweet Valley Twins" series and authoring several books featuring Disney characters. Applegate's most successful venture in juvenile fiction, however, has been her creation of the "Animorph" series. These books, about young adolescents given the power by aliens to "morph" themselves into various animals, have rivaled R. L. Stine's "Goosebumps" series in popularity. Applegate has completed many titles either in the "Animorph" series or related to it; among them are *The Visitor, The Invasion, The Message, The Alien, Animorphs Underground,* and *Animorphs in the Time of the Dinosaurs.* According to Sally Lodge in *Publishers Weekly,* by the late 1990s the series "reside[d] at the top" of that publication's "children's paperback series bestseller list, where booksellers predict it [would] roost for the foreseeable future."

During an interview in *Publishers Weekly,* Applegate told Lodge where her idea for the "Animorph" books originated. "I grew up loving animals and lived with the usual suburban menagerie of dogs, cats, and gerbils," she confided. "I really wanted to find a way to get kids into the heads of various species and decided that a science-fiction premise was the way to do this." She worked up a plan for an entire series—which she initially called "The Changelings"—and submitted it, with rough drafts of chapters for several different novels, to Scholastic, Inc. Picked up by the New York publisher, Applegate's "Animorphs" series received heavy promotion from Scholastic, Inc., and the firm gave the books eye-catching, die-cut covers. But Jean Feiwel, a vice president at Scholastic, Inc., credited Applegate's skill in bringing to life the series' main concept for the success of "Animorphs." Feiwel explained to *Publishers Weekly* that the concept "is absolutely unbelievable but utterly possible. The notion of kids' morphing is also close to adolescent body changes in some ways. It is out of their control," the Scholastic, Inc. staffer continued, "but becomes something quite fabulous—which is what you like to think happens in the process of growing up." Feiwel also noted that while the protagonists of "Animorphs" "may go off to defend the earth against aliens, at the end of the day they still have math homework to do."

One of the earliest novels in the "Animorph" series, *The Message,* centers on a young woman named

Cassie and her decision that she and her friends should change into dolphins in order to come to the rescue of one of the alien groups—the Andalites—who gave them their powers. They must save this victim from another race of aliens, the Yeerks, who wish to invade Earth. Linda Bindner, reviewing *The Message* for *School Library Journal,* had a mixed reaction. Though she felt that the adolescent characters were of the stock variety, Binder praised the authenticity of Cassie's feelings when faced with the responsibility for her friends' safety during the adventure. Bindner also judged that "the descriptions of becoming and living as dolphins and other animals are impressive."

Before embarking on the "Animorphs," Applegate authored a nonfiction work aimed at young people interested in the achievements of African Americans. *The Story of Two American Generals: Benjamin O. Davis Jr. and Colin L. Powell* examines two African Americans who became pioneers in the U.S. Armed Forces. Sheilamae O'Hara, who critiqued the volume for *Booklist,* found it to be somewhat lacking. Though providing basic facts about its two subjects, O'Hara lamented that *The Story of Two American Generals* contains "one-dimensional portraits . . . the humanity never comes through."

Applegate was also selected to write the first novel in Harper's "Boyfriends and Girlfriends" series, *Zoey Fools Around. Zoey Fools Around* is composed of both a normal third-person narrative, and what a *Publishers Weekly* contributor described as "autobiographical fragments" from Zoey herself. Zoey, a senior in high school, has a longtime boyfriend named Jake; they are awaiting their graduation on a small island off the coast of Maine. The balance of the relationships between Zoey, Jake, and their circle of friends is upset when Lucas Cabral returns to their high school after spending two years in a juvenile facility because of his part in a alcohol-related accident that caused the death of Jake's older brother.

Zoey Fools Around also features a subplot revolving around an African-American girl named Aisha, who is frightened of proceeding in a relationship with a boy who might prove her romantic destiny. Complicating matters further is a villainess named Claire, who, in the words of the *Publishers Weekly* reviewer, "is more unhappy and confused than evil." The reviewer cited "better-than-average character development" in predicting that *Zoey Fools Around* would be "likely to hook its intended audience."

Another of Applegate's young adult efforts is *Sharing Sam.* In this novel, Allison is just starting to get to know Sam, the new guy who rides his own Harley Davidson motorcycle to their school in Florida, when she learns that her longtime best friend Izzy has developed brain cancer. Izzy only has a few months of life left to her, and when she begins expressing interest in Sam, Allison decides to put her own desires on hold in favor of making her friend's last days as happy as possible.

Allison manages to talk Sam into dating Izzy; meanwhile, Sam is dealing with the aging process in his much-loved grandfather and trying to face their inevitable parting. A contributor to *Publishers Weekly* praised *Sharing Sam,* observing that "this hokey plot gains some substance from the thoughtful characterizations and the logical, not entirely strife-free way in which the premise is developed."

Applegate discussed her feelings about writing for middle graders with Lodge, calling her audience "the best readers on the planet. They are open-minded, imaginative and willing to embrace ideas." She also revealed that she enjoys the challenges presented to her by "Animorphs," because "a series writer has to develop plotting and pacing that become a well-oiled machine. You don't have the luxury of spending a year on a book and absolutely cannot indulge in writer's block. Yet I knew," Applegate continued, "I had to write in perfect language and choose just the right images, to make sure that my middle readers fell in love with the characters and returned again and again."

BIOGRAPHICAL AND CRITICAL SOURCES:

PERIODICALS

Booklist, April 15, 1992, Sheilamae O'Hara, review of *The Story of Two American Generals: Benjamin O. Davis Jr. and Colin L. Powell;* p. 1532; March 15, 1995, Frances Bradburn, review of *Sharing Sam,* p. 1321; January 1, 1996, Frances Bradburn, review of *See You in September,* p. 813.

Horn Book, January-February, 1998, Christine Heppermann, "Invasion of the 'Animorphs,'" p. 53.

Kirkus Reviews, February 1, 2004, review of *Sharing Sam,* p. 127.

Kliatt, March, 1995, p. 8; November, 1995, p. 21.

Publishers Weekly, February 28, 1994, review of *Zoey Fools Around,* p. 89; December 19, 1994, review of *Sharing Sam,* p. 55; July 10, 1995, review of *July's Promise,* p. 59; November 3, 1997, Sally Lodge, "Scholastic's Animorphs Series Has Legs," p. 36; February 16, 1998, pp. 178-188; June 21, 1999, review of *Search for Senna,* p. 69; February 15, 2004, Rebecca Platzner, review of *Sharing Sam,* p. 1050.

Resource Links, December, 1999, "Animorphs Science Fiction Series: Depart," p. 37.

School Librarian, August, 1997, p. 157; winter, 1999, review of *The Unknown* and *The Escape,* p. 208.

School Library Journal, February, 1995, Judy R. Johnston, review of *Sharing Sam,* p. 112; June, 1997, Linda Bindner, review of *The Message,* p. 114; March, 1996, Susan W. Hunter, review of *Sharing Sam,* p. 218; June, 1997, p. 114.

Voice of Youth Advocates, February, 1996, p. 368; April, 1996, p. 21; April, 1997, p. 21; April, 1999, review of *The Hork-Bajir Chronicle,* p. 44.

ONLINE

Kidsreads.com—K. A. Applegate, http://www.kidsreads.com/ (February 1, 2003).

Scholastic.com—K. A. Applegate, http://www.scholastic.com/ (March 8, 1999; February 1, 2003).*

*   *   *

AXTON, David
See KOONTZ, Dean R(ay)

B

BAIGELL, Matthew 1933-

PERSONAL: Surname is pronounced Bay-*gel;* born April 27, 1933, in New York, NY; married Renee Moses, February 1, 1959; children: Leah, Naomi. *Education:* University of Vermont, B.A., 1954; Columbia University, M.A., 1955; University of Pennsylvania, Ph.D., 1965.

ADDRESSES: Office—Department of Art History, Voorhees Hall, 71 Hamilton St., Rutgers University, New Brunswick, NJ 08903. *E-mail*—baigell@rci. rutgers.edu.

CAREER: Professor of art history. Ohio State University, Columbus, instructor, 1961-65, assistant professor, 1965-67, associate professor of art, 1967-68; Rutgers University, New Brunswick, NJ, associate professor, 1968-72, professor, 1972-78, distinguished professor of art, 1978-2002, professor emeritus, 2002—. *Military service:* U.S. Air Force, 1955-57; became second lieutenant.

MEMBER: College Art Association.

WRITINGS:

A History of American Painting, Praeger (New York, NY), 1971.
(Editor) *A Thomas Hart Benton Miscellany,* State University Press of Kansas (Lawrence, KS), 1971.
The American Scene: American Painting in the 1930s, Praeger (New York, NY), 1974.

Thomas Hart Benton, Abrams (New York, NY), 1974.
Charles Burchfield, Watson-Guptill (New York, NY), 1976.
The Western Art of Frederic Remington, Ballantine (New York, NY), 1976.
Dictionary of American Art, Harper (New York, NY), 1979.
Albert Bierstadt, Watson-Guptill (New York, NY), 1981.
Thomas Cole, Watson-Guptill (New York, NY), 1981.
A Concise History of American Painting and Sculpture, Harper & Row (New York, NY), 1984.
(With others) *Arte Americana, 1930-1970,* Fabbri (Milan, Italy), 1992.
(Editor, with wife, Renee Baigell) *Soviet Dissident Artists: Interviews after Perestroika,* Rutgers University Press (New Brunswick, NJ), 1995.
A Concise History of American Painting and Sculpture, IconEditions (New York, NY), 1996.
Jewish-American Artists and the Holocaust, Rutgers University Press (New Brunswick, NJ), 1997.
Artist and Identity in Twentieth-Century America, Cambridge University Press (New York, NY), 2001.
(With wife, Renee Baigell) *Peeling Potatoes, Painting Pictures: Women Artists in Post-Soviet Russia, Estonia, and Latvia. The First Decade,* Rutgers University Press (New Brunswick, NJ), 2001.
Jewish Artists in New York during the Holocaust Years, Center for Advanced Holocaust Studies (Washington, DC), 2001.
(Editor, with Milly Heyd) *Complex Identities: Jewish Consciousness and Modern Art,* Rutgers University Press (New Brunswick, NJ), 2001.

Contributor to *Nineteenth-Century Painters of the Delaware Valley,* New Jersey State Museum (Trenton,

NJ), 1983; (with Julia Williams) *Artists against War and Fascism: Papers of the First American Artists' Congress,* Rutgers University Press (New Brunswick, NJ), 1986; and *Three Hundred Years of American Painting: The Montclair Art Museum Collection,* Hudson Hills Press, 1989.

SIDELIGHTS: Matthew Baigell has introduced generations of students to the amazing world of art through his more than dozen surveys and studies. In addition to writing noteworthy surveys of American art, Baigell, a long-time professor of art and now professor emeritus at Rutgers University, has studied, written, and edited works dealing with the identity of artists and the social, cultural, and personal contexts in which they work. While Baigell has specialized in American art, in several works he has examined works of a subgroup of American artists—Jewish artists. Among his works are titles about Jewish artists during and after the Holocaust, works by women in countries of the former Soviet Union, and works by modern Jewish artists. When asked why he specialized in American art, Baigell told Aliza Edelman in an interview published at the *Art History* Web site: "The most interesting environment is the one I grew up in, that is, America. I wanted to explore what America was like on a certain cultural level. I was always interested in connecting to an environment that was familiar to me. I do not believe that art comes necessarily just from art but also from some kind of environmental concerns. In order to understand art, you need to understand the environment."

Among Baigell's books are two historical surveys of the American art world, *A History of American Painting* and *The American Scene: American Paintings of the 1930s.* In the first of these works, Baigell chronicles American painting from the 1600s to the late-twentieth century. He characterizes each period by studying prominent American artists whose works represent features of a historical style. Hilton Kramer of the *New York Times Book Review* contended that Baigell's book adheres to "the line of well-established opinion," but a reviewer for the *Times Literary Supplement* observed: "Baigell manages to say something quite individual about most of the major nineteenth-century painters. One feels that the paintings under discussion have been freshly studied before being locked into the inevitable categories." And although some critics found the book too short for a work of scholarship, others recommended it as an introductory reader.

David Gebhard wrote in the *Library Journal,* "For the general reader this book is excellent: [Baigell's] characterizations of the period are well made."

In *The American Scene: American Paintings of the 1930s,* Baigell examines the group of artists that came to be called the American Scene painters. These were a disparate collection of painters who rejected modern European painting styles and developed an indigenous, realistic American art that found expression in scenes of the American landscape and the working class. Except for their mutual interest in painting scenes of American life, this group of artists had little in common. According to James R. Mellow in the *New York Times Book Review,* they manifested no shared style of aesthetics, formed no cohesive program of art, and held no collective motives or ambitions. In the reviewer's opinion, Baigell inherits the inconsistencies of the period in trying to build a clear construct in which to examine the painters; he excludes certain major artists, like Charles Demuth and Edward Hopper, because they do not adhere to his theories on the movement. Mellow commented, "One has the feeling that Professor Baigell wanted to wrap up his subject in a clear and precise pedagogical fashion, but history, with its usual perversity, has presented him with too many loose ends. [He] does little to explain or explore the contradictions of the movement." Still "Baigell makes a useful distinction between the generally apolitical regionalist painters like [Thomas Hart] Benton and [Grant] Wood and the Social Realists, figures like Joe Jones, Philip Evergood, Ben Shahn, whose subject matter tended to suggest political action." On the other hand, Ruth Berenson maintained in the *National Review* that Baigell's "well-illustrated and thoughtfully researched book fills a real need, for the period has been unaccountably neglected by art historians. As the book shows, our view of America has been profoundly affected by images created by American Scene painters."

During his lengthy career, Baigell has been fascinated with issues of artistic identity. After three decades of intermittent work, in 2001 he published the solo essay collection *Artist and Identity in Twentieth-Century America,* which contains seventeen "thought-provoking essays," to quote *Choice* reviewer I. Spalatin. In these essays about the works of such artists as Edward Hopper, Grant Wood, Thomas Hart Benton, Philip Pearlstein, Robert Morris, Richard Estes, Ben Shahn, and Barnett Newmann, Baigell relates their works of art to their social, cultural, and personal contexts, pointing out recurring themes. As Baigell explained, "I grew up hearing about the social view of art, the responsibilities of art and artist to society, and the ways artists reflect various economic and political tendencies in society." Thus in Baigell's analysis of art, the doctrine of social responsibility takes precedence over the form or the view of art for art's sake. Although in essays dating from an earlier period in his life, Baigell used standards of beauty defined by nineteenth-century American writers, in much later essays he employs the ideas of Jacques Derrida, Jean Baudrillard, and Frederic Jameson in determining aesthetic value. Yet Baigell's emphasis on the environment of the artist as the prime factor in his creativity remains a constant. Citing Baigell's "admirable consistency of principle along with an equally admirable flexibility and responsiveness to change," *Art Bulletin* reviewer Sarah Burns praised *Artist and Identity in Twentieth-Century America.* "Baigell never hesitates to criticize moral vacuity or to condemn pretension," she added. "In the end, he rethinks the history of American art."

Several of Baigell's books deal with art in eastern Europe, including the 1995 title *Soviet Dissident Artists: Interviews after Perestroika* and the 2001 work *Peeling Potatoes, Painting Pictures: Women Artists in Post-Soviet Russia, Estonia, and Latvia. The First Decade.* The former came about as a result of the donation of a private collection of paintings by dissident Soviet artists to the Zimmerli Art Museum at Rutgers University. With his wife, Renee, a student of Russian literature, Baigell conducted interviews with the forty-seven artists who had created the newly acquired artworks featured in the book. Free at last to express themselves, these artists discuss not only their styles—which bucked Soviet socialist realism—but their harassment by the Soviet establishment.

After examining the ways by which artists try to define themselves as American, Baigell looked at another subset: Jewish artists. In *Jewish Artists in New York during the Holocaust Years,* published by Center for Advanced Holocaust Studies in 2001, he proposes ways in which such artists as Mane-Katz, Jacques Lipchitz, Marc Chagall, Jack Levine, and Mark Rothko dealt visually with the Holocaust, classifying these representations into four main categories. Baigell grew up in New York during the 1940s and thus had memories that he brought to bear on the study, a fact that Daniel Morris of *American Jewish History* likened

to using Rorschach tests, which "tell us more about Baigell's pysche, and especially his need to believe that important Jewish American modernists did represent the Holocaust, than about the artist under discussion." Morris concluded, "Intriguing as a kind of art historian's psychobiography, the book is not convincing as a work of art history." A book with a much wider focus on Jewish identity is *Complex Identities: Jewish Consciousness and Modern Art,* co-edited with Milly Heyd. In this collection of fifteen essays, the various authors, as the editors explain, deal with "art created by Jewish artists in which one can find some aspect of the Jewish experience, whether religious, cultural, social, or personal." Baigell himself contributed the essay "Jewish American Artists: Identity and Messianism" to this collection, which, in the words of a *Parachute* reviewer, "powerfully demonstrates how the variety of Jewish thought and experience adds beauty and strength to the intrinsic ties between individuals, their history and heritage."

BIOGRAPHICAL AND CRITICAL SOURCES:

BOOKS

Baigell, Matthew, and Milly Heyd, editors, *Complex Identities: Jewish Consciousness and Modern Art,* Rutgers University Press (New Brunswick, NJ), 2001.

PERIODICALS

American Jewish History, September, 2002, Daniel Morris, review of *Jewish Artists in New York: The Holocaust Years,* pp. 329-333.
Art Bulletin, December, 2002, Sarah Burns, review of *Artist and Identity in Twentieth-Century America,* pp. 694-696.
ARTnews, November, 1997, Rex Weil, review of *Jewish-American Artists and the Holocaust,* p. 152.
Burlington Magazine, January, 1987, review of *A Concise History of American Painting and Sculpture,* p. 40.
Choice, March, 1996, review of *Soviet Dissident Artists: Interviews after Perestroika,* p. 1118; February, 1998, review of *Jewish-American Artists and the Holocaust,* p. 980; July-August, 2001, I. Spalatin, review of *Artist and Identity in Twentieth-Century America,* p. 1944.

Christian Century, January 16, 1985, review of *A Concise History of American Painting and Sculpture,* p. 58.

Journal of American History, September, 1987, Joseph Boskin, review of *Artists against War and Fascism: Papers of the First American Artists' Congress,* pp. 550-551.

Library Journal, August, 1971; October 15, 1995, Eric Bryant, review of *Soviet Dissident Artists,* p. 58.

London Review of Books, March 21, 1985, review of *A Concise History of American Painting and Sculpture,* p. 14.

Los Angeles Times, October 7, 1984, Robert L. Pincus, review of *A Concise History of American Painting and Sculpture,* p. 8.

National Review, February 14, 1974.

New York Times Book Review, December 5, 1971; December 1, 1974; April 27, 1986, Hilton Kramer, review of *Artists against War and Fascism,* p. 19.

Parachute, January-March, 2002, review of *Complex Identities: Jewish Consciousness and Modern Art,* p. 116.

Publishers Weekly, November 13, 1995, review of *Soviet Dissident Artists,* p. 56.

Russian Review, October, 1996, Dmitri Shalin, review of *Soviet Dissident Artists,* pp. 709-710.

Shofar, winter, 2003, Carl Belz, review of *Complex Identities,* pp. 187-189.

Slavic and East European Journal, fall, 1997, Tamara Machmut-Jhasi, review of *Soviet Dissident Artists,* pp. 511-513.

Times Literary Supplement, November 9, 1973; March 21, 1980; January 11, 2002, Martha Kapos, review of *Artist and Identity in Twentieth-Century America,* p. 26.

ONLINE

Art History, http://www.arthistory.rutgers.edu/news letter/ (May 14, 2002), Aliza Edelman, "Refocusing and Retirement: An Interview with Professor Matthew Baigell.*"

*   *   *

BAKER, Nicholson 1957-

PERSONAL: Born January 7, 1957, in New York, NY; son of Douglas and Ann (Nicholson) Baker; married Margaret Brentano, 1985; children: Alice, Elias. *Education:* Attended Eastman School of Music, 1974-75; Haverford College, B.A., 1980.

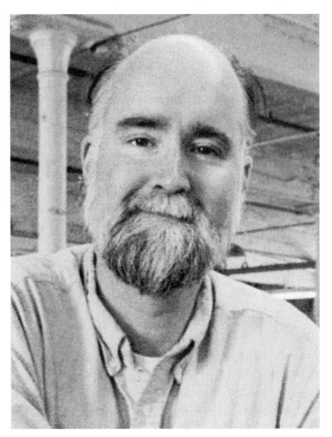

Nicholson Baker

ADDRESSES: Agent—Melanie Jackson Agency, 915 Broadway, Suite 1009, New York, NY 10010.

CAREER: Worked variously as an oil analyst, word processor, and technical writer, 1980-87; full-time writer, 1987—. Founder of the nonprofit organization American Newspaper Repository.

AWARDS, HONORS: National Book Critics Circle Award, 2001, for *Double Fold: Libraries and the Assault on Paper.*

WRITINGS:

NOVELS

The Mezzanine, Weidenfeld & Nicolson (London, England), 1988.

Room Temperature, Grove Weidenfeld (New York, NY), 1990.

Vox, Random House (New York, NY), 1992.

The Fermata, Random House (New York, NY), 1994.

The Everlasting Story of Nory, Random House (New York, NY), 1998.

A Box of Matches, Random House (New York, NY), 2003.

Checkpoint, Knopf (New York, NY), 2004.

Vintage Baker, Vintage Book (New York, NY), 2004.

NONFICTION

U and I, Random House (New York, NY), 1991.

The Size of Thoughts: Essays and Other Lumber, Random House (New York, NY), 1996.

Double Fold: Libraries and the Assault on Paper, Random House (New York, NY), 2001.

Contributor of stories and essays to periodicals, including *Atlantic* and *New Yorker.*

SIDELIGHTS: Critically acclaimed author Nicholson Baker is known for writing comic novels that are essentially plotless. A Baker book, in fact, can consist almost entirely of digression, with virtually no plot, action, dialogue, or characterization. This offbeat approach comes naturally to Baker, although at first he tried to make his work more conventional. "I had a whole elaborate plot worked out with [my first novel]," the author told Harry Ritchie in the London *Sunday Times.* "But I'd start writing, and if the plot were, say, a foot long, I'd find I'd covered an eighth of an inch. So I got rid of the plot. I felt enormous relief that I didn't have to pretend to do something that didn't interest me."

Baker's first novel, *The Mezzanine,* celebrates the trivia of daily existence. The slim volume revolves around the largely uneventful lunch hour of the protagonist, a young office worker named Howie who uses his lunch break to buy shoelaces, eat a hot dog and a cookie, and read from second-century Roman emperor Marcus Aurelius's *Meditations.* "What Howie observes of his equally worn laces—it made the variables of private life seem suddenly graspable and law-abiding—could also be said of Baker's technique," David Dowling wrote in *Contemporary Novelists.* "Whether it is a record player arm, a doorknob, a straw or a shoelace, his disquisitions make one feel the private life matters, can have logic, and even beauty. Sometimes his examinations have the aridity of a

consumer magazine report, but mostly Baker surprises and charms with images which are both ingenious metaphors for the emotional subject, and exact in their own right."

Robert Taylor of the *Boston Globe* noted, "The plot might in summary sound either banal or absurdist, when in fact it is a constant delight." The substance of the novel is derived not from the plot, but from the inner workings of Howie's mind. Through Baker's fascination with minutiae, Howie muses about a myriad of everyday objects and occurrences, including how paper milk cartons replaced glass milk bottles, the miracle of perforation (to which he gives a loving tribute), and the nature of plastic straws, vending machines, paper-towel dispensers, and popcorn poppers.

"What makes Howie's ruminations so mesmerizing is the razor-sharp insight and droll humor with which Mr. Baker illuminates the unseen world," said *New York Times Book Review* contributor Robert Plunket. Barbara Fisher Williamson, writing in *Washington Post Book World,* called Baker's descriptions of ordinary items "verbal ballets of incredible delicacy." Brad Leithauser, in the *New York Review of Books,* cited Baker's precision by quoting a passage from *The Mezzanine:* "The upstairs doorknobs in the house I grew up in were made of faceted glass. As you extended your fingers to open a door, a cloud of flesh-color would diffuse into the glass from the opposite direction. The knobs were loosely seated in their latch mechanism, and heavy, and the combination of solidity and laxness made for a multiply staged experience as you turned the knob: a smoothness that held intermediary tumbleral fallings-into-position. Few American products recently have been able to capture that same knuckly, orthopedic quality." Though some critics considered Baker's technique a gimmick, many praised his mastery of observation. Plunket said *The Mezzanine*'s "135 pages probably contain more insight into life as we live it than anything currently on the best-seller lists." Williamson called it "the most daring and thrilling first novel since John Barth's 1955 *The Floating Opera,* which it somewhat resembles. It is innovative and original. . . . It is wonderfully readable, in fact gripping, with surprising bursts of recognition, humor, and wonder."

Baker wrote *Room Temperature* similarly. Again, the book contains little plot: Mike, the narrator, is feeding his new baby girl. The book takes place during the twenty minutes necessary for the baby, nicknamed the Bug, to finish her bottle. During this time Mike's ruminations include nose-picking, breathing, the comma, childhood, love, and eating peanut butter straight from the jar, digressions that again display what *Washington Post* writer Michael Dirda called a "flair for noticing what we all know but don't quite remember or acknowledge." According to Dirda, *Room Temperature* is like *The Mezzanine* in "its microscopic approach to ordinary life, but is altogether more lighthearted, airier." The phrase "room temperature" describes the feel of the baby's bottle and also Mike's world, that of warm daydreams. Comparing *Room Temperature* with *The Mezzanine, Times Literary Supplement* contributor Lawrence Norfolk said the meanderings in *Room Temperature* are "brought closer to the meditations of the character, becoming credible as part of Mike's psychology rather than his author's cleverness. Not word-play but thought-process." Taylor called the work "a big novel unfolding out of small devices so subtly one is scarcely aware of its magnitude until the final page." Dirda described the book as "less sheerly innovative than its more clinical, austere predecessor, . . . yet nevertheless a real charmer, a breath of fresh air, a show-stopping coloratura aria made up of the quirks of memory and the quiddities of daily life."

Critics have compared Baker's writing, noted for its warmth and power of observation, to that of novelist John Updike, who plays a supporting role in Baker's first nonfiction book, *U and I.* This tribute to Updike is experimental and deliberately nonacademic; early in the book, Baker surprisingly says he has read less than half of Updike's work and does not intend to read any more until he has finished writing *U and I.* Calling his method "memory criticism," Baker strives to discover how Updike truly influenced him only through what he spontaneously remembers and forgets about the author and his work. Lewis Burke Frumkes, in the *New York Times Book Review,* described *U and I* as a "fascinating if unsteady journey of literary analysis and self-discovery, shuttling back and forth between soaring, manic moments of unabashed hero-worship and sober, even critical appraisals of the man who, he says, has haunted, inspired and influenced him beyond any other." *Times Literary Supplement* contributor Galen Strawson, however, maintained that "the *I* engulfs the *U.* In the end, *U and I* is almost all about Baker." Strawson added, "[Baker] has very little of interest to say about Updike." But according to Chicago *Tribune Books* critic Joseph Coates, *U and I* contains "a host of offhand, and sometimes startling, critical observations," making it a "provocative and compelling book for any serious reader of contemporary fiction."

Baker returned to fiction with *Vox* and *The Fermata.* In *Vox,* an *Economist* reviewer wrote, Baker "turns his hand to something that should be really interesting: sex." The story centers on one phone call between a man and a woman. The two characters in this short novel both call an adult party line, then decide to converse privately, a dialogue *Time*'s Richard Stengel called "the ultimate in '90s safe sex: voices, not hands, caress each other." Readers learn very little about the characters, at least physically, as the book focuses only on what these two strangers say to one another. The conversation is sexual in nature, with some critics referring to this novel as soft porn. But Stengel said to call it just that would miss the point. Stengel preferred to call *Vox* "an anatomically correct, technology-assisted love story." He also praised Baker for his obvious love relationship with language. "*Vox* is as much about wordplay," Stengel wrote, "as it is about foreplay."

In *The Fermata,* Baker continues with a discussion of sexuality. In a *Seattle Times* review, Michael Upchurch described this novel as "an X-rated sci-fi fantasy that leaves 'Vox' seeming like mere fiber-optic foreplay." The word *fermata* refers to a so-called fold in time, which the book's socially shy protagonist, Arno Strine, uses to stop time and thus freeze the motions of other characters. Dowling, writing in *Contemporary Novelists,* found the author "freezing" spots of time "so that they, or more precisely those [spots] on the bodies of women in the vicinity, can be examined minutely. The device gives the text its typical baroque lassitude, but the hero, despite protesting: 'My curiosity has more love and tolerance in it than other men's does,' comes across as smug, and his eroticism as unpleasantly voyeuristic." Dowling further faults the narrative for taking an "adolescent male fantasy" approach, but adds that despite these flaws, *The Fermata* "contains some exquisite apercus such as . . . the color of those older Tercels and Civics whose paint had consequently oxidized into state of frescoesque, unsaturated beauty, like M&Ms sucked for a minute and spit back out into the palm for study." However, Upchurch said the novel had an undeniable "warmth and generous spirit," and concluded that *The Fermata* confirmed Baker "as one of our most gifted and original writers."

The Size of Thoughts: Essays and Other Lumber is a collection of essays under the categories of "Thought," "Machinery," "Reading," "Mixed," "Library Science," and "Lumber." Baker examines life's simplicities such as toenail clippers and the all-but-forgotten library index card catalog. Some critics said this collection again exemplifies Baker's passion for language. Jennie Yabroff, writing for the online publication *Hot Wired,* compared Baker to "a hip lit professor who seduces his class into reading deconstructivist criticism by referencing MTV." He "spices up his readings with outrageous metaphors," Yabroff added, to keep his readers involved. Sven Birkerts, for the *New York Times Book Review,* said Baker settles on "something commonplace yet structurally intricate [such as the nail clippers] and then, with magnified detailing and sly humor" proceeds to take his readers into "hitherto unimagined panoramas." His "incessantly effervescing prose," Birkerts wrote, "tunes" the reader's mind.

Baker returned to fiction with his novel *The Everlasting Story of Nory,* which relates the childhood story of Eleanor Winslow, a nine-year-old American girl who attends school in England. Again, Baker manipulates language to set the story apart. Baker demonstrates through his young protagonist, Eric Lorberer wrote in the *Review of Contemporary Fiction,* "how both the scientist and the surrealist inhabit a child's consciousness." Nory entices the reader with her self-defined concepts of the world, her stories, and her own peculiar language in her attempt to find meaning. Carol Herman, in *Insight on the News,* refers to *Nory* as a literary gem that "presents the fears, dreams and ideas of a prepubescent schoolgirl whose preoccupations are more innocent than erotic and as such all the more stunning." Though Baker has a young daughter, Herman found that the author did not write from a father's perspective. Rather, he let Nory speak for herself.

Baker stirred much controversy with *Double Fold: Libraries and the Assault on Paper,* in which he rails against the commonplace destruction of index-card files, newspapers, and other paper documents at many modern libraries across the United States. Although he admits computerized files may be more efficient, the demise of the actual paper products, especially the newspapers and old books, saddens him. According to Margaria Fichtner, writing for the *Knight-Ridder/ Tribune News Service,* Baker blames the loss of "at least 925,000 books," many rare, on modernization. Baker has invested his own money in a non-profit

organization, American Newspaper Repository, through which he attempts to preserve as many old newspapers as he can. In his book, he scolds many large libraries, including the Library of Congress, for their practices. Librarians, such as Francine Fialkoff in her *Library Journal* article, defended such library modernization practices; she said Baker just "doesn't get it." Though Fialkoff bemoaned Baker's negativity, other critics praised him for publicizing the loss of original publications. Baker won the National Book Critics Circle Award for his effort.

In an interview, Baker told Jeffrey Freymann-Weyr of *National Public Radio* that he wrote *A Box of Matches* "only by the light of a fire," because he did not want "to let incandescent light intrude on my consciousness." This 2003 novel focuses on the little things. "I want the books to be about things that you don't notice when you're noticing them," Baker told Freymann-Weyr. Protagonist Emmett, a forty-four-year-old married man, lights a fire every morning, using only one match each time, then sits down to think. He will perform this ceremony for thirty-three days, one day for every match in a box. Emmett, wrote Walter Kirn in the *New York Times Book Review,* is "something of a homebody Thoreau, camped out in the Walden Woods of his own living room." The book captures Emmett's often-funny ruminations. "There is gentle humor at work here," Michael Upchurch wrote for the *Seattle Times.* Some critics have described the humor as melancholic. Someone going through a mid-life crisis worries a lot and reminisces. "There's nothing else like" *A Box of Matches,* wrote Upchurch, except another book by Baker. David Gates in *Newsweek* praised *A Box of Matches* as one of Baker's most "satisfying" books yet.

Baker attracted attention with his next book, *Checkpoint,* which is made up completely of a conversation between two old high school friends, one of whom, Jay, wants to kill President George Bush because of the war in Iraq. The other friend, Ben, tries to talk him out of it. The two friends have not seen each other for many years, and Ben is successful while Jay has lost his job and has become obsessed with his assassination plots. Although Baker has Jay base much of his argument for assassination on real facts about the war, his ideas for completing the task tend to be fantastical. Writing in the *Christian Science Monitor,* Ron Charles noted, "Jay's argument swings wildly from an insane rant to caustic political analysis.

Though most of his weapons—Bush-seeking bullets and a giant uranium ball—are clearly delusional, his final plan is pedestrian and deadly. While largely agreeing with his friend's recitation of Bush's sins, [Ben] struggles to calm [Jay] and get him to abandon his illegal plot." Writing a month before the book appeared in stores, Charles noted that the book could be seen as a threat and lead to Baker being investigated but that the U.S. Justice Department and the FBI would not comment on whether or not Baker was of interest to them. As for Baker, he told David Gates of *Newsweek,* "I don't think I should stand behind any part of the book. These are the miseries, these are the doubts that you have. I had Jay say them as forcefully as I could, because I think the left has to think about this a little more carefully. And it also seemed like, if I'm going to get myself in trouble in a book, why shouldn't I just be indiscriminately outrageous?"

BIOGRAPHICAL AND CRITICAL SOURCES:

BOOKS

Contemporary Novelists, 6th edition, St. James Press (Detroit, MI), 1996.
Saltzman, Arthur M., *Understanding Nicholson Baker,* University of South Carolina Press (Columbia, SC), 1999.

PERIODICALS

America, June 4, 2001, Peter Heinegg, "Bureaucrat, Spare That Book!," p. 27.
Atlantic, January-February, 2003, Thomas Mallon, review of *A Box of Matches,* pp. 190-193.
Booklist, March 15, 1998, Donna Seaman, review of *The Everlasting Story of Nory,* pp. 1178-1179; February 15, 2001, Mark Knoblauch, review of *Double Fold: Libraries and the Assault on Paper,* p. 1087.
Boston Globe, December 14, 1988, Robert Taylor, review of *The Mezzanine;* April 18, 1990, Robert Taylor, review of *Room Temperature,* p. 70.
Christian Science Monitor, July 30, 2004, Ron Charles, "It's Only Fiction, but Is It Legal?," p. 11.
Columbia Journalism Review, July, 2001, James Boylan, review of *Double Fold,* p. 67.
Economist, April 4, 1992, review of *Vox,* p. 109.

Entertainment Weekly, March 11, 1994, p. 28; January 17, 2002, Troy Patterson, review of *A Box of Matches,* p. 85.
Esquire, February, 1994, p. 76.
Guardian (Manchester, England), April 5, 1990.
Harper's Bazaar, February, 1994, p. 84.
Independent (London, England), September 6, 1989.
Insight on the News, August 31, 1998, Carol Herman, review of *The Everlasting Story of Nory,* p. 36.
Knight-Ridder/Tribune News Service, April 11, 2001, Margaria Fichtner, "Writer's Anger Is Painful, and His Book about Library Discards Is Disturbing," p. K4872.
Library Journal, January, 1994, p. 157; May 1, 1998, Kay Hogan, review of *The Everlasting Story of Nory,* p. 135; May 15, 2001, Francine Fialkoff, "Baker's Book Is Half-Baked," p. 102; June 15, 2002, "Baker-Inspired Backlash at LC?," p. 11.
Los Angeles Times, April 19, 1990.
Los Angeles Times Book Review, April 1, 1990, p. 6.
Micrographics and Hybrid Imaging Systems Newsletter, September, 2001, "Fighting Back against the Double Scold," p. 7.
New Republic, May 28, 2001, Alexander Star, review of *Double Fold,* p. 38.
New Statesman, April 6, 1990, p. 38.
Newsweek, April 16, 2001, Malcolm Jones, "Paper Tiger: Taking Librarians to Task," p. 57; January 13, 2002, David Gates, review of *A Box of Matches,* p. 60; August 9, 2004, David Gates, "Target," p. 50.
New York Review of Books, August 17, 1989, Brad Leithauser, review of *The Mezzanine,* p. 15; April 7, 1994, p. 14; June 20, 1996, p. 65.
New York Times Book Review, February 5, 1989, p. 9; April 15, 1990, p. 17; April 14, 1991, Lewis Burke Frumkes, review of *U and I,* p. 12; February 13, 1994, p. 13; April 14, 1996, Sven Birkerts, review of *The Size of Thoughts,* p. 12; February 2, 2003, Walter Kirn, review of *A Box of Matches,* pp. 7, 10.
Observer (London, England), April 1, 1990.
Philadelphia Inquirer, April 15, 1990.
Publishers Weekly, November 29, 1993, p. 52; February 7, 1994, p. 42; March 30, 1998, review of *The Everlasting Story of Nory,* p. 66; April 2, 2001, review of *Double Fold,* p. 53; October 14, 2002, Jeff Zaleski, review of *A Box of Matches,* p. 62.
Review of Contemporary Fiction, fall, 1998, Eric Lorberer, review of *The Everlasting Story of Nory,* p. 242.
San Francisco Chronicle, July 8, 1990, p. 3.

San Jose Mercury News, March 18, 1990, p. 20.

Searcher, June, 2001, review of *Double Fold,* p. 6.

Seattle Times, February 27, 1994, Michael Upchurch, review of *The Fermata,* p. F2; January 12, 2003, Michael Upchurch, review of *A Box of Matches,* p. L10.

Sunday Times (London, England), September 3, 1989; April 8, 1990, p. H8.

Time, February 3, 1992, Richard Stengel, "1-900-Aural Sex," review of *Vox,* p. 59; May 11, 1998, R. Z. Sheppard, review of *The Everlasting Story of Nory,* p. 80.

Times Literary Supplement, September 15, 1989, p. 998; April 27, 1990, Lawrence Norfolk, review of *Room Temperature,* p. 456; April 19, 1991, Galen Strawson, review of *U and I,* p. 20; April 5, 1996, p. 22.

Tribune Books (Chicago, IL), April 28, 1991, Joseph Coates, review of *U and I,* p. 7.

Washington Post, May 7, 1990, Michael Dirda, review of *Room Temperature,* p. C3; September 23, 1990.

Washington Post Book World, November 13, 1988, Barbara Fisher Williamson, review of *The Mezzanine,* p. 7.

Wilson Quarterly, summer, 2001, James Morris, review of "Double Fold," p. 125.

ONLINE

Hot Wired Web site, http://www.hotwired.lycos.com/ (February 15, 2003), Jennie Yabroff, "Lumbering Genius."

National Pubic Radio Web site, http://www.npr.org/ (January 15, 2003), Jeffrey Freymann-Weyr, "Nicholson Baker: A Life in Detail."*

*   *   *

BASRA, Amarjit S(ingh) 1958-

PERSONAL: Born July 13, 1958, in Chiheru, Punjab, India; son of Joginder Singh and Harbans Kaur (Bajwa) Basra; married Ranjit Kaur (a university professor), April 14, 1983; children: Sukhmani Kaur, Nishchayjit Singh. *Ethnicity:* "Sikh." *Education:* Guru Nanak Dev University, B.Sc. (with honors), 1978, M.Sc. (with honors), 1979; Punjab Agricultural University, Ph.D., 1982. *Politics:* "Humanitarian." *Religion:* Sikh. *Hobbies and other interests:* Travel, music, poetry, promotion of world cultures and peace.

ADDRESSES: Office—Department of Botany, Punjab Agricultural University, Ludhiana 141004, Punjab, India; fax: 91-161-400-945.

CAREER: Punjab Agricultural University, Ludhiana, India, assistant professor, 1983-92, associate professor of botany, beginning 1992. University of Western Sydney Hawkesbury, research fellow, 1983-85; Wageningen Agricultural University, senior research fellow, 1989; University of California—Davis, visiting scientist. International Parliament for Safety and Peace, deputy member of assembly.

MEMBER: International Society for Plant Molecular Biology, Society for the Promotion of Plant Science Research (founding member), Indian Society of Developmental Biologists, American Association of Plant Physiologists, Crop Science Society of America, Australian Society of Plant Physiologists.

AWARDS, HONORS: Medal for Young Scientists, Indian National Science Academy, 1987; Rafi Ahmed Kidwai Memorial Prize for Agricultural Research, Indian Council of Agricultural Research, 1988; exchange grant, Rotary International, 1988; decorated knight of the German Lofsensic Order, Templar Order, Order of the Holy Grail, 1992; honorary graduate medal, Antelope Valley College, Lancaster, CA; diplôme d'honneur, Institut des Affaires Internationales, Paris, France.

WRITINGS:

(Editor) *Mechanisms of Plant Growth and Improved Productivity: Modern Approaches,* Marcel Dekker (New York, NY), 1994.

(Editor and contributor) *Stress-Induced Gene Expression in Plants,* Harwood (Chur, Switzerland), 1995.

(Editor) *Seed Quality: Basic Mechanisms and Agricultural Implications,* Food Products Press (Binghamton, NY), 1995.

(Editor, with Ranjit K. Basra) *Mechanisms of Environmental Stress Resistance in Plants,* Harwood Academic (Amsterdam, Netherlands), 1997.

(Editor) *Crop Sciences: Recent Advances,* Food Products Press (New York, NY), 1998.

(Editor) *Cotton Fibers: Developmental Biology, Quality Improvement, and Textile Processing,* Food Products Press (New York, NY), 1999.

(Editor and contributor) *Heterosis and Hybrid Seed Production in Agronomic Crops,* Food Products Press (New York, NY), 1999.

(Editor) *Hybrid Seed Production in Vegetables: Rationale and Methods in Selected Crops,* Food Products Press (New York, NY), 2000.

(Editor) *Crop Responses and Adaptations to Temperature Stress,* Food Products Press (New York, NY), 2000.

(Editor) *Plant Growth Regulators in Agriculture and Horticulture: Their Role and Commercial Uses,* Food Products Press (New York, NY), 2000.

(Editor, with L. S. Randhawa) *Quality Improvement in Field Crops,* Food Products Press (New York, NY), 2002.

Contributor of more than eighty articles to scientific journals, including *Journal of New Seeds.* Founding editor, *Journal of Crop Production,* 1997, and *Journal of Plant Science Research.*

SIDELIGHTS: Amarjit S. Basra once told *CA:* "My primary motivation for writing is to serve the information needs of the plant science community, to advance the knowledge that will improve people's food and livelihood security, and to strive for conservation of global natural resources. I am inspired by a deep, inner need to engage in creative work to produce and synthesize literature of lasting value. The most powerful movers for my writing process are the brilliance and strength of an idea, a clear understanding of the issues involved, stimulating company and environment, and tranquility of mind and nature."

BIOGRAPHICAL AND CRITICAL SOURCES:

PERIODICALS

Choice, January, 1996, L. C. Ewart, review of *Seed Quality: Basic Mechanisms and Agricultural Implications,* p. 816; September, 2001, J. Hancock, review of *Crop Responses and Adaptations to Temperature Stress,* p. 145.

Quarterly Review of Biology, December, 1998, Allen Keast, review of *Crop Sciences: Recent Advances,* p. 509.

Science Books and Films, October, 1998, review of *Crop Sciences,* p. 207.

SciTech Book News, March, 1998, review of *Mechanisms of Environmental Stress Resistance in Plants,* p. 95; June, 1998, review of *Crop Sciences,* p. 102; June, 2001, review of *Plant Growth Regulators in Agriculture and Horticulture: Their Role and Commercial Uses* and *Crop Responses and Adaptations to Temperature Stress,* p. 127.

ONLINE

E-Streams: Electronic Reviews of Science and Technology, http://www.e-streams.com (February, 2001), review of *Hybrid Seed Production in Vegetables: Rationale and Methods in Selected Crops;* (August, 2001), review of *Crop Responses and Adaptations to Temperature Stress.**

*   *   *

BEERS, Mark H. 1954-

PERSONAL: Born April 21, 1954, in Brooklyn, NY. *Education:* Tufts University, B.S., 1978; University of Vermont, M.D., 1982.

ADDRESSES: Home—1903 Walnut St., No. 535, Philadelphia, PA 19103. *Office*—Merck and Co., Inc., BLA-22, P.O. Box 4, West Point, PA 19486-0004. *Agent*—Mel Berger, William Morris Agency, 1350 Avenue of the Americas, New York, NY 10019.

CAREER: Massachusetts General Hospital, Boston, research assistant in developmental biology, 1975-77; New England Medical Center, Boston, MA, intern, 1982-83, assistant in medicine, 1982-84, junior assistant resident, 1983-84; Mount Sinai Hospital, New York, NY, senior assistant resident and assistant in medicine, 1984-85; Beth Israel Hospital, Boston, MA, clinical fellow, 1985-87; University of California, Los Angeles, assistant professor of medicine and medical director of Inpatient Geriatric Unit at university's Medical Center, 1987-92, codirector of Geriatric Review Course, 1990-92, medical director of Home Care Program, 1991-92; Merck and Co., Inc., West Point, PA, associate editor, beginning 1992. Harvard University Medical School, clinical fellow in geriatric medicine and fellow of Program for the Analysis of Clinical Strategies, Division of Aging, 1985-87;

Brigham and Women's Hospital, Boston, MA, clinical fellow, 1985-87; Hebrew Rehabilitation Center for the Aged, Boston, MA, clinical fellow, 1985-87; Jewish Memorial Hospital, Boston, MA, attending physician, 1985-86; RAND Corp., senior natural scientist, 1989-92; California Department of Health, member of Aging Program advisory board, beginning 1989.

MEMBER: American Geriatric Society, Gerontological Society of America (fellow), American College of Physicians (fellow), American Academy of Home Care Physicians, American Society for Clinical Pharmacology and Therapeutics, Massachusetts Medical Society, Alpha Omega Alpha.

AWARDS, HONORS: Charles A. Dana fellowship, 1988-89, advanced fellowship, 1989-90; National Institute on Aging grant, 1990-92; National Quality Scholars Competition Award, 1991.

WRITINGS:

(With I. M. Rollingher) *A Guide to Medications for Older Persons,* University of California (Los Angeles, CA), 1991.

(With S. K. Urice) *Aging in Good Health: A Complete, Essential Medical Guide for Older Men and Women and Their Families,* Pocket Books (New York, NY), 1992.

(Editor) *The Merck Manual of Geriatrics,* Merck Research Laboratories (Whitehouse Station, NJ), c. 1995.

(Editor, with Robert Berkow and Andrew J. Fletcher) *The Merck Manual of Medical Information,* Merck Research Laboratories (Whitehouse Station, NJ), 1997, second edition, 2003, electronic edition published as *The Merck Manual Home Edition,* available at http://www.merck.com/pubs/mmanual/.

(Editor, with Robert Berkow, Robert M. Bogin, and Andrew J. Fletcher) *The Merck Manual of Diagnosis and Therapy: Centennial Edition,* 17th edition, Merck Research Laboratories (Whitehouse Station, NJ), 1999.

Contributor to *The Practice of Geriatrics,* edited by E. Calkins, A. B. Ford, and P. R. Katz, Saunders, 1992. Contributor to medical journals. Member of editorial board, *UCLA Health Insights,* 1988-90, and *Journal of the American Geriatric Society,* beginning 1989.

SIDELIGHTS: A physician specializing in geriatrics, Mark H. Beers has written several books on the subject and has also edited editions of the well-known Merck manuals of medicine. The 1999 edition of *The Merck Manual of Diagnosis and Therapy* is significant in that it marks the one hundredth anniversary since the first edition was published in 1899. The editors included a facsimile of the first edition, which, according to Tony Dajer in *Discover,* offers an interesting opportunity for comparison. The original edition was a mere 192 pages, while the seventeenth edition is a staggering 2,833 pages, clearly demonstrating how far medicine has progressed in terms of the amount of knowledge doctors now have. Dajer further noted that some of the remedies offered by doctors a hundred years ago "were useless, sometimes even lethal." Yet Dajer also commented that there is still a problem today with physicians prescribing drugs that only treat symptoms and that many do not properly diagnose underlying causes of these symptoms. The result is that useless antibiotics are often prescribed for coughs or fevers, and other equally ineffective treatments are made when doctors look for a quick way to relieve a patient's symptoms. "The 1899 Merck Manual offers a wonderful glimpse of where we've been. And, alas, still are," Dajer concluded. In a review of the same book for *Lancet,* John Bignall felt that although the book is "admirably compressed and immaculately edited," it is not longer practical for today's medicine, being too large for a handy reference and too general for the needs of specialists.

The Merck Manual of Medical Information, which draws much of its information from *The Merck Manual of Diagnosis and Therapy,* is a much more useful tool for general reference, according to Martha E. Stone in *Library Journal.* The 2003 edition of this book, which was first published in 1999, was praised by the critic for being more readable than the original, however Stone lamented that the editors sacrificed some scientific terms in favor of colloquial language. Yet Stone concluded that, "Because of its very modest price, as well as its proven track record of excellence, this is a book that every public, school, or consumer health library, regardless of size, would be happy to have in its reference and/or circulating collection."

BIOGRAPHICAL AND CRITICAL SOURCES:

PERIODICALS

Discover, September, 1999, Tony Dajer, review of *The Merck Manual of Diagnosis and Therapy: Centennial Edition,* p. 96.

Lancet, December 18, 1999, John Bignall, "A Centimetre Every Twenty Years," p. 2175.

Library Journal, June 15, 2003, Martha E. Stone, review of *The Merck Manual of Medical Information,* p. 64.

Wall Street Journal, July 17, 1995, Jerry E. Bishop, review of *The Merck Manual of Geriatrics,* p. A8.*

*   *   *

BENEDICT, Pinckney 1964-

Pinckney Benedict

PERSONAL: Born April 12, 1964, in Lewisburg, WV; son of Cleveland Keith (a farmer and politician) and Ann Farrar Arthur Benedict; married Laura Philpot (a writer), 1990; children: Nora, Cleveland. *Education:* Attended a private high school in Pennsylvania; Princeton University, B.A., 1986; University of Iowa, M.F.A., 1988.

ADDRESSES: Office—Hollins University, Roanoke, VA 24020.

CAREER: Writer, 1987—. Hope College, Holland, MI, associate professor of English, 1996-99; Hollins University, Roanoke, VA, associate professor of English, 1999—; Pushcart Anthology Series, contributing editor. Has also taught creative writing at Ohio State University, Oberlin College, The Hill, and Princeton University. Worked as writer for television producer David Milch.

AWARDS, HONORS: Nelson Algren Short Story Award, *Chicago Tribune,* 1986, for the short story "The Sutton Pie Safe"; John Steinbeck Award (Great Britain), 1995, for *Dogs of God;* shortlisted for Hammett Award for Excellence in Crime Writing; Henfield Foundations Transatlantic Review Awards; National Endowment for the Arts grant for outstanding contribution to American literature; *Town Smokes, The Wrecking Yard,* and *Dogs of God* were named Notable Books by *New York Times Book Review.*

WRITINGS:

Town Smokes (stories), Ontario Review Press (New York, NY), 1987.

The Wrecking Yard and Other Stories (stories), Doubleday (New York, NY), 1992.

Dogs of God (novel), Doubleday (New York, NY), 1994.

Four Days (film adaptation of the novel by John Buell), Amerique Films, 1999.

Contributor of stories and nonfiction to publications, including *Ontario Review, Grazia* (Italy), *Gunzo* (Japan), and *The Oxford Book of American Short Stories.* Also author of one-act, full-length, and musical plays.

WORK IN PROGRESS: A screenplay for *Dogs of God* for Gerard de Thame Films, London, England.

SIDELIGHTS: Pinckney Benedict is an award-winning short story writer and novelist whose visceral and often violent tales paint a grim picture of life in the mountainous regions of his native West Virginia. The author grew up on his parents' dairy farm near Lewisberg. While many of his writings depict rugged, backwoods people, Benedict grew up in comfortable circumstances, attending The Hill School near Philadelphia and then going on to Princeton University, where he studied with Joyce Carol Oates. Always fond of reading, his early influences included the sea-adventures of Joseph Conrad and Herman Melville, horror and science fiction by Phillip K. Dick, H. P. Lovecraft, and Stephen King, and the idiosyncratic writing of another West Virginian, Breece D'J Pancake. Pancake's short stories were published after the author took his own life at the age of twenty-seven. They are peopled with working-class Appalachians, struggling to get by. Pancake's stories were a major inspiration to Benedict, and as Brad Vice commented in *Dictionary of Literary Biography,* "It is easy to think of Benedict's early stories in *Town Smokes* as elegies for Pancake. Benedict adopted Pancake's style, marked by its cool, laconic prose and its careful attention to local dialect, making a powerful vehicle for its subject matter, the colorful, often frightening underclass of West Virginia. Soon after the publication of *Town Smokes* in 1987, the author was heralded as the most promising hybrid that gritty minimalist and Southern regionalism had to offer."

Discussing his work with Bruce Weber of *New York Times Book Review,* Benedict commented that "the mountains are pretty wild places," filled with "a lot of very . . . independent people" with "strong personalities." West Virginia's position between the North and South suits Benedict symbolically. "Neither region wants us," Benedict explained to *U.S. News & World Report* contributor Viva Hardigg. "So it does feel like we're sort of a doorway. And that's fine. Because that's the area I like to explore in my work—these places where there's no mainstream to be outside of."

Violence figures prominently in many of the tales collected in *Town Smokes.* Among the characters in these stories are a fifteen-year-old son who despises his father for dying in a lumbering accident, a young man who kills his sick dog with a .45 pistol, and a mother and son who must attempt a night-time rescue of her husband from an enraged moonshiner. "Booze" is a kind of Moby Dick story, with a giant white hog filling in for Melville's whale. Diane McWhorter, writing for the *New York Times Book Review,* praised *Town Smokes* as "an often heart-stopping literary performance." "The assured tone that distinguishes this debut would be remarkable for any author, but it's especially notable given the age of Pinckney Benedict," stated Richard Panek in Chicago *Tribune Books.* "At twenty-three, he has delivered a collection that is almost free of immature material. Aside from one attempt at magical realism that misses, all the stories in *Town Smokes* command respect through their impressive authority." McWhorter added: "Mr. Benedict has taken big risks—

particularly in using a dialect that, failing perfect pitch, would have badly got on one's nerves—and his prose achieves excellent harmony between voice and virtuosity. His lyricism never plays his flinty characters false."

Benedict followed *Town Smokes* with *The Wrecking Yard and Other Stories.* In this collection, Benedict portrays numerous confrontations, including a fight between a rejected lover and a Vietnam veteran gone mad, a carnival worker who electrocutes her lovers, and a rapist being punished at the hands of a vigilante posse. Although there is certainly an element of brutality, the author also shows "a romantic lightheartedness missing in his previous work. Much of the isolation and loneliness that thematically dominated *Town Smokes* is renovated into a sort of comic aggression in *The Wrecking Yard,*" reflected Vice. "Benedict's prose is more polished than in his previous border fiction." Douglas Glover similarly noted in *Tribune Books,* "Benedict's style is laconic and deadpan. He gets comic mileage from the tension between the dry, matter-of-fact way he writes and the terrible and outlandish things he describes." Glover stated that Benedict "is at his best when he ignores the contemporary siren calls of sentimental realism and interpersonal sensitivity and simply lets the violence overflow, propelling the reader into a world of strange and macabre beauty." Vice found that with this collection, Benedict "developed beyond the early influence of Pancake to a form more closely resembling the Gothic stories of Flannery O'Connor or [Eudora] Welty."

Benedict's next published book was his first novel, *Dogs of God.* Set on a remote mountaintop, the book centers on the Tannhauser, a twelve-fingered man who uses enslaved Mexicans to grow marijuana at a strange compound that was previously a military installation, a resort hotel, and a women's prison. Tannhauser calls his kingdom "El Dorado," but he is unaware that the Drug Enforcement Agency is planning a raid, aided by a corrupt local sheriff. Another compelling character is Goody, a boxer who once killed a man in a fixed fight. Goody is forced to fight one of Tannhauser's men as an entertainment for visiting Mafia members. *Dogs of God* ends in a horrific massacre that takes the life of nearly every character. The novel was highly praised by numerous critics. Chris Goodrich, writing in *Los Angeles Times,* called it "about as fine a first novel as one could want." Vice noted that while "the book is set in West Virginia and is written in Benedict's trademark lucid, laconic prose, . . . Benedict's mastery over realistic narrative actually creates a strangely postmodern novel." Alexander Harrison, a writer for *Times Literary Supplement*, found great depth in Benedict's writing, and he particularly pointed out the way in which "the calm, ambiguous tone of Benedict's writing poses questions, not only about his characters but about the wider world from which they seem so cut off." Vice summarized: "[Benedict is] capable of writing prose that is at once simple and spare but also philosophically complicated. There are no easy answers for the poverty-stricken farmers and ridgerunners that populate his stories. Endurance seems to be Benedict's most consistent theme; it is the only virtue in a world where the powers of chance and fate conspire to extinguish both the ignominious and the noble alike."

BIOGRAPHICAL AND CRITICAL SOURCES:

BOOKS

Dictionary of Literary Biography, Volume 244: *American Short-Story Writers since World War II, Fourth Series,* Gale (Detroit, MI), 2001.

PERIODICALS

Appalachian Heritage, fall, 1988, Jim Wayne Miller, "New Generation of Savages Sighted in West Virginia," pp. 28-33.
Appalachian Journal, spring, 1988, Bob Snyder, "Pancake and Benedict," pp. 276-283; fall, 1992, Thomas E. Douglass, interview with Pinckney Benedict, pp. 68-74; winter, 1993, John Alexander Williams, "Unpacking Pinckney in Poland," pp. 162-175; spring, 1998, Angela B. Freeman, "The Origins and Fortunes of Negativity: The West Virginia Worlds of Kromer, Pancake, and Benedict," pp. 244-269.
Bloomsbury Review, May-June 1995, p. 23.
Georgian Review, winter, 1987, pp. 819-826.
Los Angeles Times Book Review, February 2, 1992, p. 6; March 27, 1994, pp. 3, 7.
New Statesman & Society, July 1, 1994, Laurence O'Toole, review of *Dogs of God,* pp. 39-40.
New York Times Book Review, July 12, 1987, Bruce Weber, interview with Pinckney Benedict, pp. 13-14; February 9, 1992, p. 14; February 6, 1994, p. 31.

Novel and Short Story Writers Market, January 1, 2000, Brad Vice, interview with Pinckney Benedict, pp. 35-38.
Publishers Weekly, March 27, 1987, pp. 42-43.
Southern Review, spring, 1994, Michael Griffith, review of *Dogs of God,* p. 379.
Times Literary Supplement, March 6, 1992, p. 21; July 1, 1994, p. 20.
Tribune Books (Chicago, IL), June 1, 1987, p. 3; January 26, 1992, p. 7; February 27, 1994, pp. 3, 11.
U.S. News & World Report, May 16, 1994, Viva Hardigg, interview with Pinckney Benedict, p. 63.
Washington Post, November 2, 1987, pp. C1, C12.*

*   *   *

BIDDULPH, Steve

PERSONAL: Born in Australia; married; wife's name Sharon (a family therapist).

ADDRESSES: Home—New South Wales, Australia. *Office*—c/o Manhood Online, P.O. Box 231, St. Leonards, New South Wales 2065, Australia.

CAREER: Family therapist in Australia, beginning c. 1981. *Manhood Online,* advisor and contributor.

WRITINGS:

NONFICTION

The Secret of Happy Children: A New Guide for Parents, [Australia], 1984, Stein & Day (New York, NY), 1990.
(With wife, Sharon Biddulph) *The Making of Love,* Doubleday (Lane Cove, New South Wales, Australia), 1988, published as *The Secret of a Happy Family: Stay in Love as a Couple through Thick and Thin—and Even with Kids,* Doubleday (Garden City, NY), 1989.
More Secrets of Happy Children, [Australia], 1996, HarperCollins Australia (Pymble, New South Wales, Australia), 1999, Marlowe (New York, NY), 2003.
Raising Boys: Why Boys Are Different—and How to Help Them Become Happy and Well-Balanced Men, Celestial Arts (Berkeley, CA), 1998.

Manhood: An Action Plan for Changing Men's Lives, Celestial Arts (Berkeley, CA), 1999.

(Editor) *Stories of Manhood: Journeys into the Hidden Hearts of Men,* Finch (Sydney, Australia), 2000.

(With Sharon Biddulph) *Love, Laughter, and Parenting: In the Years from Birth to Six,* Dorling Kindersley (New York, NY), 2000.

SIDELIGHTS: Australian author Steve Biddulph has spent many years as a family counselor and has penned several books related to family life. His titles, which have been published in his native country as well as in the United States, include *The Secret of Happy Children: A New Guide for Parents, Raising Boys: Why Boys Are Different—and How to Help Them Become Happy and Well-Balanced Men,* and *Manhood: An Action Plan for Changing Men's Lives.* With his wife Sharon, he is also responsible for *The Secret of a Happy Family: Stay in Love as a Couple through Thick and Thin—and Even with Kids.*

In *The Secret of Happy Children,* Biddulph uses stories from his practice to illustrate parenting techniques. The book has met with generally favorable response, with Virginia Makins in the *Times Educational Supplement* praising the author for his inclusion of "assertiveness training for parents." Reviewers applauded *The Secret of Happy Children* as well, making favorable comparisons to more complicated child-rearing manuals and praising Biddulph's straightforward, clear, and direct approach. The therapist later followed up with *More Secrets of Happy Children,* which also drew positive comments from reviewers.

The Secret of a Happy Family was first published in Australia as *The Making of Love.* Biddulph and his wife, who is also a family therapist, again use stories from their practices to illustrate their advice. They move through all the stages of becoming a family, from early courtship between a man and a woman, to raising children. The pair address conflict resolution, family bonding, and communication skills. Jane Larkin, critiquing *The Secret of a Happy Family* in *Booklist,* judged that "practical guidance is presented in an optimistic and even entertaining fashion."

One of Biddulph's better-known later works is *Raising Boys.* In it, he presents his readers with some of the greater risks facing boys compared to girls, such as learning disabilities, violence, and suicide. Biddulph

also argues that the presence of a good father is essential to a boy's development, asserting that fathers who work more than fifty-five hours a week cannot be good fathers because of their lack of time at home. In addition, he discusses the advantages and disadvantages of involvement in sports—beneficial except when boys become obsessed with winning. A *Publishers Weekly* reviewer described *Raising Boys* as a "highly practical guide" which "offers valuable perspectives to parents of both boys and girls."

Manhood tackles the question of how men have gone wrong in modern civilization and offers suggestions of what can be done to correct their course. The book has been warmly received by critics, therapists, and reviewers alike, and has spawned an online magazine and forum for men, *Manhood Online,* for which Biddulph is an advisor and contributor.

BIOGRAPHICAL AND CRITICAL SOURCES:

PERIODICALS

Booklist, June 1, 1989, Jane Larkin, review of *The Secret of a Happy Family: Stay in Love as a Couple through Thick and Thin—and Even with Kids,* p. 1681.

Library Journal, May 15, 2003, Alice Hershier, review of *More Secrets of Happy Children,* p. 116.

Publishers Weekly, August 3, 1998, review of *Raising Boys: Why Boys Are Different—and How to Help Them Become Happy and Well-Balanced Men,* p. 80.

Times Educational Supplement, May 16, 1986, Virginia Makins, review of *The Secret of Happy Children: A New Guide for Parents,* p. 26.*

*   *   *

BLANCHOT, Maurice 1907-2003

PERSONAL: Born September 22, 1907, in Quain, Saone-et-Loire, France; died, February 20, 2003, in Paris, France. *Education:* Strasbourg University, B.S.; diploma in higher education from the University of Paris, Sorbonne.

CAREER: Journalist, editor, essayist, and novelist. Cofounder of the journal *Le Rempart.*

WRITINGS:

Thomas l'Obscur (novel), Gallimard (Paris, France), 1941, revised edition, 1950, translation by Robert Lamberton published as *Thomas the Obscure,* D. Lewis, 1973.

Aminadab, Gallimard (Paris, France), 1942.

Comment la litterature est-elle possible? (title means "How Is Literature Possible?"), J. Corti, 1942.

Faux Pas, Gallimard (Paris, France), 1943.

L'Arret de mort, Gallimard (Paris, France), 1948, translation by Lydia Davis published as *Death Sentence,* Station Hill (Barrytown, NY), 1978.

Le Tres-Haut (title means "The Almighty"), Gallimard (Paris, France), 1948, translation by Allan Stoekl published as *The Most High,* University of Nebraska Press (Lincoln, NE), 1996.

La Part du feu, Gallimard (Paris, France), 1949, translation by Charlotte Mandell published as *The Work of Fire,* Stanford University Press (Stanford, CA), 1995.

Sade et Restif de la Bretonne, Complexe, 1949.

Lautreamont et Sade avec le texte integral des chants de Maldoror, Editions de Minuit (Paris, France), 1949.

Au moment voulu, Gallimard (Paris, France), 1951, translation by Lydia Davis published as *When the Time Comes,* Station Hill (Barrytown, NY), 1985.

Apres coup precede par Le Ressassement eternal, Editions de Minuit (Paris, France), 1952, translation by Paul Auster published as *Vicious Circles: Two Fictions and "After the Fact,"* Station Hill (Barrytown, NY), 1983.

Celui qui ne m'accompagnait pas, Gallimard (Paris, France), 1953, translation by Lydia Davis published as *The One Who Was Standing Apart from Me,* Station Hill (Barrytown, NY), 1992.

L'Espace litteraire, Gallimard (Paris, France), 1955, translation by Ann Smock published as *The Space of Literature,* University of Nebraska Press (Lincoln, NE), 1982.

Le Dernier Homme, Gallimard (Paris, France), 1957, translation by Lydia Davis published as *The Last Man,* Columbia University Press (New York, NY), 1987.

La Bete de Lascaux, GLM, 1958, enlarged edition, Fata Morgana, 1982.

Le Livre a venir, Gallimard (Paris, France), 1959, translation by Sacha Rabinovitch published as *The Siren's Song: Selected Essays of Maurice Blanchot,* Indiana University Press (Bloomington, IN), 1982.

L'Attente l'oubli, Gallimard (Paris, France), 1962, translation by John Gregg published as *Awaiting Oblivion,* University of Nebraska Press (Lincoln, NE), 1997.

(With Brice Parain, Jean Grenier, and Emmanuel Robles) *Hommage a Albert Camus,* Gallimard (Paris, France), 1967.

L'Entretien infini, Gallimard (Paris, France), 1969, translation by Susan Hanson published as *The Infinite Conversation,* University of Minnesota Press (Minneapolis, MN), 1993.

Pour L'Amitie, Gallimard (Paris, France), 1971, reprinted, Farrago (Paris, France), 2001, translation by Elizabeth Rottenberg published as *Friendship,* Stanford University Press (Stanford, CA) 1997.

La Pas au-dela, Gallimard (Paris, France), 1973, translation by Lycette Nelson published as *The Step Not Beyond,* State University of New York (Albany, NY), 1992.

La Folie du jour, Fata Morgana, 1973, translation by Lydia Davis published as *The Madness of the Day,* Station Hill (Barrytown, NY), 1981.

(Editor, with Francois Larvelle) *Textes pour Emmanuel Levinas,* J. M. Place, 1980.

L'Ecriture du desastre, Gallimard (Paris, France), 1980, translation by Ann Smock published as *The Writing of the Disaster,* University of Nebraska Press (Lincoln, NE), 1986.

The Gaze of Orpheus, and Other Literary Essays, translation by Lydia Davis, edited by P. Adams Sitney, Station Hill (Barrytown, NY), 1981.

De Kafka a Kafka, Gallimard (Paris, France), 1981.

La Bete de Lascoux, Fata Morgana, 1982.

La Communaute inavouable, Editions de Minuit (Paris, France), 1983, translation by Pierre Joris published as *The Unavowable Community,* Station Hill (Barrytown, NY), 1988.

Michel Foucault tel que je l'imagine, illustrated by Jean Ipousteguy, Fata Morgana, 1986, translation by Jeffrey Mehlman published as *Michel Foucault As I Imagine Him,* Zone Editions, 1987.

(With Julien Gracq and J. M. G. Le Clezio) *Sur Lautreamont,* Editions Complexe, 1987.

Joe Bousquet, with an essay by J. Bousquet, illustrated by Pierre Tal Coat, Fata Morgana, 1987.

Michel Foucault as I Imagine Him (printed with Michel Foucault's *Maurice Blanchot: The Thought from Outside*), translated by Jeffrey Mehlman, Zone Books, 1987.

Une voix venue d'ailleurs: sur les poemes de Louis-Rene des Forets, Ulysse, Fin de Siecle, 1992.

Les intellectuels en question: ébauche d'une réflexion, Fourbis (Paris, France), c. 1996.

The Station Hill Blanchot Reader: Fiction & Literary Essays, translated by Lydia Davis, Paul Auster and Robert Lamberton, edited by George Quasha, Station Hill/Barrytown (Barrytown, NY), 1999.

Henri Michaux ou le refus de l'enfermement, Farrago (Tours, France), 1999.

The Instant of My Death = Instant de ma mort (printed with Jacques Derrida's *Demeure: Fiction and Testimony*), translated by Elizabeth Rottenberg, Stanford University Press (Stanford, CA), 2000.

The Book To Come, translated by Charlotte Mandel, Stanford University Press (Stanford, CA), 2002.

Also author of *La Solitude Essentielle;* coauthor of *Misere de la Litterature,* C. Bourgois, 1978. Contributor to periodicals, including *Combat* and *L'Insurge.*

SIDELIGHTS: A profoundly influential figure in contemporary French literature, Maurice Blanchot was self-effacing almost to the point of invisibility. He did not make public appearances or comment on the political issues of the day. In 1982 John Sturrock, appraising a translation of *Le Livre a venir,* titled *The Siren's Song: Selected Essays of Maurice Blanchot,* for the *London Review of Books,* noted that "Blanchot is a name in France, but not a face or a living presence. . . . I do not recall ever having seen a photograph of him, nor—is it possible?—having read an interview with him. . . . Blanchot has an intellectual authority which he forbears conspicuously to use."

He was not always so reticent. Prior to World War II, Blanchot was an outspoken supporter of the right-wing Fascist movement and wrote anti-Semitic articles for such journals as *Combat* and *L'Insurge,* urging revolution against the Popular Front government of Leon Blum. Sturrock quoted an article by Blanchot where he clearly touts terrorism as the route to public salvation. Historical circumstances forced him to reconsider. Germany attacked France in 1940, and Blanchot's Fascism gave way to French nationalism. During the war he actively worked with the French Resistance, switching from the pro-German revolutionary right to the Communist-tinged left he had so recently excoriated. One novel of that era, however, reveals the author's moral ambivalence: *Aminadab,* published in 1942, presents a nightmarish, Kafkaesque

society, a "totalitarian universe characterized by estrangement and the absurd," as a contributor to *Dictionary of Twentieth-Century Culture* noted. "He subsequently called the story 'unfortunate' in its apparent foreshadowings of concentration camps, but his political positions remained ambiguous."

By the end of the war, having published two novels (*Thomas l'Obscur* and *Aminadab*) and two critical works (*Comment la litterature est-elle possible?* and *Faux Pas*), Blanchot seemed to have abandoned politics entirely for a life of letters. For the next half century, he remained personally inconspicuous while building an ever increasing literary reputation, first in France and later abroad. *L'Arret de mort,* the first of Blanchot's works to be widely available in English, is a *recit* (short narrative). This work is an eighty-one-page dramatized philosophical meditation that was published in 1948 and translated three decades later as *Death Sentence.* Reviewing Blanchot's work in the *Dictionary of Literary Biography,* Jeffrey Mehlman called *Death Sentence* "a metaphysical ghost story," in which the narrator concentrates not on the traditional elements of plot, setting, and characterization but rather on the difficulty of the act of writing, on the problems inherent in language as it attempts to convey meaning. Assessing the book in *New Yorker,* John Updike classified it as a "very short novel" and noted the writer's "tortuous, glimmering style," which he found "graceful and maddening, a cascade of mystification bejewelled with melodramatic glances and gothic gewgaws." Sturrock maintained that there are no tricks of syntax in Blanchot, and yet the reader, like the protagonist, is mystified and troubled amidst the nearly imageless, antirealistic verbal universe created by Blanchot.

Mehlman viewed Blanchot's literary ideas as an outgrowth, at least in part, of his wartime renunciation of Fascism that coincided with his conversion from journalism to literature and a subsequent retreat from public stances into philosophical contemplation. Yet Sturrock felt that Blanchot, an atheist existentialist, had clearly been influenced by certain authors and philosophers. The critic commented that an understanding of the writings of the French poet Stephen Mallarme will make the ideological origins of Blanchot's poetry clearer to the reader. Mallarme's attempt to separate the music of poetry from the conventional meanings of its words bears a resemblance to Blanchot's aim in his literary art, which Sturrock explained thus: "It is creation, not representation, a perpetual enigma. The precedence of life over language is reversed." Antoine Compagnon described the writer's ideology further when she wrote in the *Times Literary Supplement* that Blanchot views "literary creation as an experience of limits." She also points out that for Blanchot writing is not a certainty but a necessity.

"Terrifying" is the word used by Irving Malin to describe Blanchot's work in *Awaiting Oblivion*. In a *Review of Contemporary Fiction* piece, Malin assessed the skeletal plot—that of a man and a woman in a hotel-room discussion—and said that the characters "seem to melt into other ghosts," perhaps of themselves, perhaps of others. Then "the author seems to intrude into the text—but isn't the text his own creation?"

Blanchot's other English translated recits include a revised version of *Thomas the Obscure, When the Time Comes, The Madness of the Day,* and *The Last Man.* A reader looking for a coherent story in Blanchot's recits, which are generally regarded as his most mature works, will be disappointed. There is a recurring theme of death, but it poses a dilemma for a writer who regards dying as final and salvation as myth. As Updike pointed out, "though . . . [death] is immense in duration and penetration, because it is nothingness [in Blanchot's view] there is not much to say about it." Nevertheless, death is at the core of Blanchot's fiction. As Francois Collin observed in *Maurice Blanchot et la question de l'ecriture,* "there is no story by Blanchot in which people are not dying, not through a violent accident, but peacefully, through repetition."

The Last Man is set in a hospital or sanitarium where the narrator and a young woman observe an older man, "the professor," who is on the verge of dying. Steven Ungar, writing in the *New York Times Book Review,* noted that here, as in many of Blanchot's texts, "the standard critical approaches do not fully apply; his kind of writing eludes fixed genres and techniques." That statement applies equally well to *Thomas the Obscure* (the recit), *When the Time Comes,* and *The Madness of the Day.*

Blanchot's own critical judgments on literature, which gained him a considerable reputation in France, began to appear in English translation in the 1980s. *The Gaze of Orpheus, and Other Literary Essays* came out in 1981. The title essay, like the myth of Orpheus, suggests, according to Gaetan Picon in *Contemporary French Literature,* that "we cannot look night in the face, that profundity is revealed only if it is concealed." The publication of *The Siren' Song* and *The Space of Literature* introduced Blanchot to a wider English-speaking audience. The critical essays in these collections pose such questions as "What is literature?" and "How is literature possible?" Critics fell that Blanchot seemed more interested in probing the complexities of the questions than in providing answers, and Sturrock noted, "Nothing is to be predicated of the true work of literary art; it simply *is,* as Blanchot likes to repeat." Blanchot "is not generally interested in the content, form, or style of a writer's work," stated Larysa Mykyta in an essay for *Encyclopedia of World Literature,* "but in the paradoxes and ironies of the practice of literature, in the dilemmas and agonies of modern literature that the writer faces."

How, then, does writing get written? Gilbert Sorrentino, writing in the *New York Times Book Review,* quoted Blanchot on the language of literature as "a search for [the] moment which precedes literature." "For Mr. Blanchot," Sorrentino added, "the literature that says 'nothing' permits actuality its hegemony, its existence, its avoidance of the abyss into which a referential language seems to cast it. For him literary language strives to achieve Flaubert's desire, 'a book about nothing.'"

Blanchot assessed one of his contemporaries with *Henri Michaux ou le refuse de l'enfermement.* Michaux, as reclusive and respected as Blanchot himself, died in 1984 having created a literary scandal in the 1950s by subjecting himself to drug-induced hallucinations to inspire his prose. Blanchot appeared to disapprove of such actions—he "analyses the bad infinity to which Michaux has fallen prey in his mescaline writings," noted *Times Literary Supplement* contributor Richard Sieburth. The reviewer pointed out Blanchot's "flinching at Michaux's latent religiosity," but said that at the same time such critiques "belie his fundamental traditionalism, for at base he is accusing Michaux of betraying the disinterested sphere of the aesthetic . . . by his unholy alliance with religion on the one hand and science on the other."

Reviewing *Aminadab* and *Le Tres-Haut* in *The French New Novel* in 1962, Laurent LeSage pointed out that the novel, "as Blanchot makes use of it, is . . .

primarily an investigation of the language phenomenon—its form becomes its content, so to speak."
More than a decade later, Picon, assessing Blanchot's
writing in a broader context of recits and critical
essays, noted that "the attempt to give a precise
explanation of Blanchot's thought makes us run the
risk of misinterpreting it . . . it eludes expression in
words."

Blanchot was one of many great voices of modern
French letters. He had, in Mehlman's words, "made of
his writing a meditation on the problematic being—or
nonbeing—of language, its ultimate incompatibility
with self-consciousness, the exhilarating havoc it
wreaks on any claim to either objective or subjective
identity." In 1999 a collection titled *The Station Hill
Blanchot Reader: Fiction & Literary Essays* paid homage to the author by including several of his best-
known writings. *Review of Contemporary Fiction*
writer Jeffrey DeShell hailed the volume's release as
no less than an event; "this is a magnificent work of
writing, translating, and publishing," DeShell stated.
"As a fiction writer," summed up a *Publishers Weekly*
contributor, "Blanchot is, above all, a great philosopher."

Blanchot died February 20, 2003, in Paris, France.

BIOGRAPHICAL AND CRITICAL SOURCES:

BOOKS

Bruns, Gerald, *Maurice Blanchot: The Refusal of
    Philosophy,* Johns Hopkins University Press
    (Baltimore, MD), 1997.
Collin, Francoise, *Maurice Blanchot et la question de
    l'ecriture,* Gallimard (Paris, France), 1971.
Dictionary of Literary Biography, Volume 72: *French
    Novelists, 1930-1960,* Gale (Detroit, MI), 1988.
Dictionary of Twentieth Century Culture, Volume 2:
    French Culture 1900-1975, Gale (Detroit, MI),
    1995.
*Encyclopedia of World Literature in the Twentieth
    Century,* 3rd edition, St. James Press (Detroit, MI),
    1999.
LeSage, Laurent, *The French New Novel,* Pennsylvania
    State University Press, 1962.
Picon, Gaetan, *Contemporary French Literature,*
    Ungar, 1974.
Sartre, Jean-Paul, *Literary and Philosophical Essays,*
    Criterion, 1955.

PERIODICALS

Choice, October, 1995, N. Lukacher, review of *The
    Work of Fire,* p. 298; October, 2000, N. Lukacher,
    review of *The Instant of My Death,* p. 323; May,
    2003, N. Luckacher, review of *The Book to Come,*
    pp. 1545-1546.
French Review, December, 1994, review of *Une voix
    venue d'ailleurs: sur les poemes de Louis-Rene
    des Forets,* p. 349.
Kirkus Reviews, May 1, 1997, review of *Awaiting
    Oblivion,* p. 679.
Library Journal, August, 1997, Robert Ivey, review *of
    Friendship,* p. 90; March 1, 1999, Ali Houissa,
    review of *The Station Hill Blanchot Reader: Fic-
    tion & Literary Essays,* p. 84.
London Review of Books, August 19, 1982, John
    Sturrock, review of *The Siren's Song: Selected Es-
    says of Maurice Blanchot,* p. 8.
MLN, December, 1998, Bridget Conley, review of
    Friendship, p. 1180.
New Statesman & Society, July 7, 1995, review of
    The Writing of the Disaster, p. 37.
New Yorker, January 11, 1982, John Updike, review of
    Death Sentence, pp. 93-95.
New York Times Book Review, May 25, 1986, p. 23;
    October 11, 1987, p. 56; March 26, 1989, p. 16.
Publishers Weekly, March 8, 1999, review of *The Sta-
    tion Hill Blanchot Reader,* p. 58.
Review of Contemporary Fiction, fall, 1994, Steve
    Dickson, review of *The One Who Was Standing
    Apart from Me,* p. 214; fall, 1996, Marc
    Lowenthal, review of *The Most High,* p. 184; fall,
    1997, Irving Malin, review of *Awaiting Oblivion,*
    p. 228; fall, 1999, Jeffrey DeShell, review of *The
    Station Hill Blanchot Reader,* p. 159.
Sewanee Review, spring, 1996, Wallace Fowlie, review
    of *The Work of Fire.*
Small Press Review, February, 1984, p. 8.
Times Literary Supplement, May 12, 1974, p. 389;
    March 6, 1981, p. 260; December 31, 1982;
    October 27, 1995, Gabriel Josipovici, review of
    The Work of Fire and *The Writing of the Disaster,*
    p. 26; May 1, 1998, Leslie Pindar, review of
    Awaiting Oblivion, p. 6; August 13, 1999, Leslie
    Hill, review of *The Station Hill Blanchot Reader*
    and *Friendship,* p. 24; February 8, 2002, Richard
    Steburth, "Technician of the Sacred," p. 4.
Village Voice Literary Supplement, May, 1982, p. 8.
World Literature Today, autumn, 1981, p. 642; winter,
    1983, p. 103; winter, 1998, Steven Jaron, review

of *Pour l'amitie* and *Les intellectuels en question: Ebauche d'une reflexion*, p. 101.

Yale French Studies, January, 1998, James Swenson, "Revolutionary Sentences," p. 11, Hent De Vries, "'Lapsus Absolu,'" p. 30, Ann Banfield, "The Name of the Subject: The 'Il,'" p. 133, Hans-Jost Frey, "The Last Man and the Reader," p. 252.

ONLINE

Art and Culture, http://www.artandculture.com/ (June 11, 2002).
Maurice Blanchot Resource, http://lists.village.virginia.edu/ (June 11, 2002).

OBITUARIES

PERIODICALS

Art in America, April, 2003, Stephanie Cash, David Ebony, "Obituaries."
New York Times, March 2, 2003, "Maurice Blanchot, 95, Novelist and Essayist," p. 27.*

*   *   *

BOEHM, Herb
    See VARLEY, John (Herbert)

*   *   *

BOJUNGA, Lygia
    See NUNES, Lygia Bojunga

*   *   *

BOJUNGA-NUNES, Lygia
    See NUNES, Lygia Bojunga

*   *   *

BOSWELL, John (Eastburn) 1947-1994

PERSONAL: Born March 20, 1947, in Boston, MA; died of AIDS, December 23, 1994, in New Haven, CT; son of Henry (a U.S. Army officer) and Catherine (Eastburn) Boswell. *Education:* College of William

and Mary, A.B., 1969; Harvard University, M.A., 1971, Ph.D., 1975. *Religion:* Roman Catholic.

CAREER: Yale University, New Haven, CT, assistant professor, 1975-81, associate professor, 1981-82, professor of history, 1982-94, director of graduate studies in history, 1984-86, chairman of history department, 1990-92.

MEMBER: Phi Eta Sigma, Pi Delta Epsilon, Eta Sigma Phi, Phi Beta Kappa.

AWARDS, HONORS: Woodrow Wilson fellowship; Morse fellowship; Frederic G. Melcher Award from the Unitarian Universalist Association, in recognition of an outstanding literary work contributing to religious liberalism, and National Book Award for history, both 1981, for *Christianity, Social Tolerance, and Homosexuality;* honorary master of arts degree from Yale University, 1982; William Clyde deVane Medal from Yale University for teaching and scholarship, 1982; first place in the One Hundred Best Lesbian and Gay Nonfiction Books, Publishing Triangle, 2004, for *Christianity, Social Tolerance, and Homosexuality.*

WRITINGS:

The Royal Treasure: Muslim Communities under the Crown of Aragon in the Fourteenth Century, Yale University Press (New Haven, CT), 1977.
Christianity, Social Tolerance, and Homosexuality: Gay People in Western Europe from the Beginning of the Christian Era to the Fourteenth Century, University of Chicago Press (Chicago, IL), 1980.
The Kindness of Strangers: The Abandonment of Children in Western Europe from Late Antiquity to the Renaissance, Pantheon (New York, NY), 1988.
Same-Sex Unions in Premodern Europe, Villard (New York, NY), 1994.

Contributor of articles to scholarly journals.

SIDELIGHTS: John Boswell stirred controversy in the 1980s and 1990s with two major histories dealing with homosexuality and its place in the Christian West. A professor of history at Yale University, Boswell was best known for his study *Christianity, Social Tolerance, and Homosexuality: Gay People in Western Europe from the Beginning of the Christian Era to the Fourteenth Century,* for which he won the National Book Award in 1981. Educated at the College of William and Mary and at Harvard University, Boswell joined the faculty of Yale University in 1975. At Yale he helped establish the Center for Lesbian and Gay Studies and served as chairperson of the history department from 1990 to 1992. His last work, *Same-Sex Unions in Premodern Europe,* published in 1994—the same year Boswell died of AIDS—proposes that homosexual unions were publicly and liturgically sanctioned during the Middle Ages.

Reviewer Martin Bauml Duberman, writing in *New Republic,* called *Christianity, Social Tolerance, and Homosexuality* "one of the most profound, explosive works of scholarship to appear within recent memory." Offering what critics termed a revolutionary new interpretation of the origins of Christian intolerance of homosexuality, Boswell drew on his knowledge of more than a dozen languages and his broad familiarity with biblical, classical, early Christian, and medieval sources to construct a work that spans fifteen hundred years of European history.

In a *Newsweek* interview, Boswell once described his original motivation to write the book. He recalled that he was still in graduate school when a divinity student friend asked him about the meaning of certain Greek terms in the New Testament that had been translated as references to homosexuals. Consulting texts in the original Greek, Boswell came to his first discovery that the word "homosexual" does not in fact appear in the biblical scriptures. This interpretation aroused skepticism in his friend's seminary class, and it stimulated Boswell's curiosity to the extent that he mounted a full scholarly investigation of Christian attitudes toward homosexuality. Ten years later Boswell's studies culminated in the publication of *Christianity, Social Tolerance, and Homosexuality.*

The author-historian contravenes accepted opinion by asserting that neither Christian doctrine nor religious practice was explicitly anti-homosexual until the late Middle Ages, at which time various secular pressures prompted St. Thomas Aquinas to lead a new evaluation of Church teachings. Boswell buttresses his argument with a detailed etymological analysis of biblical passages commonly interpreted as condemning homosexuality, and he provides a historical survey of

the actual treatment of homosexuals by the Church, civil authority, and general public in Europe from Roman times to the fourteenth century. Boswell's findings are "completely at odds with all our preconceptions about Western civilization," noted *New York Times Book Review* critic Paul Robinson. "But the book's argument is of such richness—its empirical base so broad, its reasoning so fierce—that it succeeds in making one think the unthinkable. It forces us to re-examine even the most fixed notions about our moral and cultural heritage."

There is no passage in the Bible, Boswell declares in *Christianity, Social Tolerance, and Homosexuality,* which "would have categorically precluded homosexual relations among early Christians. . . . At the very most, the effect of Christian Scripture on attitudes toward homosexuality could be described as moot." The author reports that he could discover no extant text or manuscript in either Hebrew, Greek, Syriac, or Aramaic that even contained a word referring specifically to homosexuals, and he argues that the biblical passages traditionally thought to proscribe homosexuality were mistranslated and actually have different meanings. Boswell interprets the sin of the city of Sodom described in the book of Genesis, for example, as inhospitality to strangers, not sodomy. Similarly, the prohibitions in Leviticus, referring to homosexual acts as an abomination and making them a capital offense, reflect Jewish ritual cleanliness concerns, in Boswell's view, rather than a condemnation of homosexuality itself. Even St. Paul's stern censure in Romans, the author asserted, condemns not homosexuals but homosexual acts committed by normally heterosexual persons.

Proceeding from scriptural interpretation to social history, Boswell found a general public tolerance of homosexuality in the Roman world at the beginning of the Christian era in the first two centuries A.D. He argues that while certain early Christian ascetics condemned homosexuality from a general conviction that sexuality should be purely procreative, the broader Christian population did not share this view and tended to regard homosexual attraction as normal. Boswell asserts that certain prominent Church leaders, like St. Paulinus, bishop of Nola, appear to have been openly homosexual yet were revered by the faithful.

Having dismissed early Christian attitudes as a factor, the author suggests that the civil legislation curbing homosexual rights that was adopted in Europe during the fourth through sixth centuries may have an explanation in the increasing ruralization of society as the Roman empire declined. Rural societies, he notes, are structured on family lines and accordingly emphasize procreative sexuality, tending to regard homosexuality as an unwelcome aberration. Homosexual "marriages" were outlawed in 342 A.D. and homosexual activity banned altogether in the remnants of the empire in the sixth century. Little is known of European social life over the next four or five hundred years, but Boswell discovered a new flowering of homosexual culture accompanying renewed urbanization and a revival of classical learning and taste in the early medieval period. "Despite considerable local variation, attitudes toward homosexuality grew steadily more tolerant throughout the early Middle Ages," he writes, as same-sex prostitution and brothels flourished in the urban centers. The years 1050 to 1150 witnessed what the author interprets as an outpouring of popular poetry on homoerotic love themes, much of it written by clerics. Boswell regards the writings and friendships of a number of well-known clerics in the period as clearly homoerotic, and even suggests that St. Anselm, the Archbishop of Canterbury, may himself have had homosexual proclivities. Periodic denunciations of homosexual practices, with demands that clerical offenders be punished, were effectively ignored by popes and bishops, reports Boswell.

Toward the end of the twelfth century, Boswell continues, both civil and ecclesiastical authority turned against homosexuality. The Church's Third Lateran Council of 1179 declared homoerotic acts to be sins against nature and punishable by excommunication. "During the two hundred years from 1150 to 1350, homosexual behavior appears to have changed, in the eyes of the public, from the personal preference of a prosperous minority, satirized and celebrated in popular verse, to a dangerous, antisocial, and severely sinful aberration," he writes. "Between 1250 and 1300, homosexual activity passed from being completely legal in most of Europe to incurring the death penalty in all but a few contemporary legal compilations." Boswell points to several historical developments as possible reasons for the sudden shift in attitude against homosexuality, while noting that contemporary knowledge of the medieval period is still too sketchy "to analyze the causes of this change satisfactorily." In the author's interpretation, an important clue may be found in the general surge of intolerance towards minorities in the thirteenth century, including heretics, Muslims, and Jews, as well as homosexuals. Boswell

suggests that the breakdown of the traditional social order, with attendant political instability, and the rise of the secular state in the High Middle Ages generated new pressures for social conformity and created the repressive apparatus for controlling individual lives. The period witnessed a general systematization of culture and politics that rendered all forms of distinctiveness less acceptable. In addition, the author notes a relationship between the declining fortunes of the Christian crusaders in the Holy Land and the rise in hostility toward infidels and other minorities at home. "This interpretation is presented with vigor and clarity," noted Keith Thomas in the *New York Review of Books*.

In Boswell's view, "The positions of Aquinas and other high medieval theologians regarding homosexuality appear to have been a response more to the pressures of popular antipathy than to the weight of Christian tradition." Aquinas's thirteenth-century argument against homosexuality, which remains one of the Catholic Church's principal teachings on the subject, relied in part on patterns of animal behavior to distinguish what the theologian termed "natural" from "unnatural" pleasures. "Boswell subjects Aquinas's argument *de animalibus* to a merciless, though well deserved, thrashing for its intellectual clumsiness and partiality," remarked Robinson. Boswell concludes that "Aquinas could bring to bear no argument against homosexual behavior which would make it more serious than overeating." The judgment of both ecclesiastical and civil authority, nevertheless, was that sex must be either procreative or immoral, and this also became the dominant popular view well into the modern period.

While commending Boswell for the depth of his scholarship and the originality of his thesis, several critics disagreed with some key interpretations in *Christianity, Social Tolerance, and Homosexuality*. *Commonweal*'s Louis Crompton was unconvinced "that the Bible does not take so negative a stand on homosexuality as is popularly supposed" and judged St. Paul's condemnation in Romans "unambiguous." Peter Linehan of the *Times Literary Supplement* found insufficient evidence for Boswell's suggestion that certain clerical friendships in the twelfth century were homosexual in nature.

Other reviewers were more laudatory in their judgment of *Christianity, Social Tolerance, and Homosexuality. Critic* reviewer Richard Woods, for example, predicted that Boswell's book "will certainly become the standard reference work in the historical study of homosexuality in the Christian era." And Robinson wrote that "Boswell restores one's faith in scholarship as the union of erudition, analysis, and moral vision," adding that the book "sets a standard of excellence that one would have thought impossible in the treatment of an issue so large, uncharted, and vexed."

Boswell dealt with a less-volatile issue in *The Kindness of Strangers: The Abandonment of Children in Western Europe from Late Antiquity to the Renaissance.* This book was inspired by the discovery of an admonition by the early Christian Church for men not to consort with prostitutes. Such a ban was in place not because the deed was considered sinful, but because such customers might risk incest. In other words, child abandonment was common enough that even selling such children directly into prostitution was widespread. For Lawrence Stone, reviewing the book in the *New Republic,* "Boswell's appalling story reminds us that public attitudes toward the treatment of children have changed so dramatically that child abuse by parents today is a major source of public and private concern." Speaking with Alvin P. Sanoff in *U.S. News and World Report,* Boswell once noted that he thought he could "write a little article based on a small amount of anecdotal evidence." He went on to explain, "But as I worked on it, I realized that abandonment of children was a very important demographic phenomenon. In European cities in the eighteenth century, about one out of every three children was abandoned. In southern Italy, the number ran almost as high as fifty percent."

With his final book, the 1994 *Same-Sex Unions in Premodern Europe,* Boswell once again struck on a controversial issue, expanding on his contention in his earlier *Christianity, Social Tolerance, and Homosexuality,* that for over a thousand years the early Catholic Church of Europe actually had rituals for joining same-sex couples, rites suppressed only in later, more homophobic times. In this work Boswell produces such rituals in translation and goes into the history of both heterosexual marriage and same-sex unions from Classical times to the Middle Ages in Europe. Boswell demonstrates that the number of men who actually went through such rituals and set up domestic relationships together was "in significant numbers," according to a reviewer for *Publishers Weekly.* Boswell, further relates that these rituals "were equivalent in meaning

and in form to heterosexual marriages," as Peter Stanford observed in a *New Statesman and Society* review. Stanford also pointed out that Boswell "pithily" demonstrates how marriage has been turned upside down for everyone in the modern world, changing from a matter of property to a matter of love. The same reviewer concluded that Boswell's book was "closely argued, moderately phrased in deference to the prejudices that it may excite, and a model of accessible scholarship."

But Boswell's book did, in fact, excite prejudices and criticism. Philip Lyndon Reynolds, writing in the *Christian Century,* found it a "muddled book" with "very little bearing on the issue of gay union and gay marriage in churches today." Gerald Bray, writing in *Christianity Today,* contended that the liturgies and rituals Boswell alludes to and quotes were in fact intended for ritual brotherhood rather than same-sex unions. In Bray's view, "Boswell quotes what suits his case and does not give an overall picture of human relationships in premodern times." Bray went on to note that "What Boswell has done, though, is remind us of the extent to which the art of friendship, especially male friendship, has been lost." *Commonweal*'s Robert L. Wilken also was of the opinion that such rituals were not a type of gay marriage, but rather "a form of ritualized friendship between males that had been practicing in the Eastern Mediterranean since the time of Homer." Wilken accused Boswell of writing propaganda rather than history. For him Boswell's book "creates a world that never existed, misrepresents Christian practice, and distorts the past. This is a book on a mission, scholarship at the service of social reform, historical learning yoked to a cause, a tract in the cultural wars, and this is in that spirit that it should be read." Similarly, Brent D. Shaw, reviewing the book in the *New Republic,* thought that "a more civil and humane modernity will not be achieved by tendentious misreadings of antiquity."

Other critics were more positive in their judgments of the work. Timothy Perper, for example, writing in *Journal of Sex Research,* called *Same-Sex Unions* "a major work of historiography." Perper further commented, "It is not final nor persuasive in all its details. Those are trivial issues. The crucial point is that texts long hidden in the archives have come to light once more. For that, Boswell's twelve-year odyssey deserves great praise." *Nation*'s Bruce Halsinger observed that "Boswell's careful methodology is obvious in the very structure of the book," and that his findings would "unquestionably challenge a number of cherished assumptions about the nature and history of Christianity." A critic for *Publishers Weekly* had further praise for *Same-Sex Unions,* calling it a "stunning, complex book that is demanding in the brilliance of its scholarship but written with sterling clarity." Ray Olson, writing in *Booklist,* also commended Boswell's "lucidity in writing" and "scrupulous scholarly documentation." Most prophetic of all, in light of the flourishing cultural argument over same-sex unions that was ongoing during the 2000s, was commentary by an *Economist* contributor who noted, "There has been much scholarly fuss over Boswell's work, which will provide fodder for many seminars to come. Even if scholars eventually plump emphatically for Boswell's view—and at present medievalists are testy about it—the large question of whether homosexual marriage is appropriate in modern societies will remain contentious."

BIOGRAPHICAL AND CRITICAL SOURCES:

BOOKS

Boswell, John, *Christianity, Social Tolerance, and Homosexuality: Gay People in Western Europe from the Beginning of the Christian Era to the Fourteenth Century,* University of Chicago Press (Chicago, IL), 1980.

Homosexuality, Intolerance, and Christianity: A Critical Examination of John Boswell's Work, Scholarship Committee, Gay Academic Union (New York, NY), 1981.

PERIODICALS

Advocate, June 22, 2004, "Simply the Best," p. 172.

Booklist, June 1, 1994, Ray Olson, review of *Same-Sex Unions in Premodern Europe,* p. 1735.

Christian Century, January 21, 1981; January 18, 1995, Philip Lyndon Reynolds, review of *Same-Sex Unions in Premodern Europe,* p. 49.

Christianity Today, December 12, 1994, Gerald Bray, review of *Same-Sex Unions in Premodern Europe,* p. 46.

Commonweal, February 27, 1981, Louis Crompton, review of *Christianity, Social Tolerance, and Homosexuality: Gay People in Western Europe from the Beginning of the Christian Era to the Fourteenth Century;* September 9, 1994, Robert L. Wilken, review of *Same-Sex Unions in Premodern Europe,* p. 24.

Critic, November, 1980, Richard Woods, review of *Christianity, Social Tolerance, and Homosexuality.*

Economist, February 11, 1995, review of *Same-Sex Unions in Premodern Europe,* p. 77.

English Historical Review, October, 1981.

Journal of Sex Research, November, 1994, Timothy Perper, review of *Same-Sex Unions in Premodern Europe,* p. 315.

Lambda Book Report, September-October, 1994, John D'Emilio, review of *Same-Sex Unions in Premodern Europe,* p. 14.

Nation, September 5, 1994, Bruce Halsinger, review of *Same-Sex Unions in Premodern Europe,* p. 241.

New Republic, October 18, 1980, Martin Bauml Duberman, review of *Christianity, Social Tolerance, and Homosexuality;* February 27, 1989, Lawrence Stone, review of *The Kindness of Strangers: The Abandonment of Children in Western Europe,* p. 31; July 18, 1994, Brent D. Shaw, review of *Same-Sex Unions in Premodern Europe,* p. 33.

New Statesman and Society, February 24, 1995, Peter Stanford, review of *Same-Sex Unions in Premodern Europe,* p. 53.

Newsweek, September 29, 1980.

New York Review of Books, December 4, 1980, Keith Thomas, review of *Christianity, Social Tolerance, and Homosexuality.*

New York Times Book Review, August 10, 1980, Paul Robinson, review of *Christianity, Social Tolerance, and Homosexuality.*

People, June 27, 1994, Bill Hewitt, review of *Same-Sex Unions in Premodern Europe,* p. 57.

Publishers Weekly, June 6, 1994, review of *Same-Sex Unions in Premodern Europe,* p. 52.

Times Literary Supplement, January 23, 1981, Peter Linehan, review of *Christianity, Social Tolerance, and Homosexuality.*

U.S. News and World Report, March 11, 1981; May 1, 1998, Alvin P. Sanoff, "The Unwanted Children of Times Past."

OBITUARIES

PERIODICALS

Washington Post, December 27, 1994.*

BRACKETT, Peter
  See COLLINS, Max Allan, (Jr.)

*   *   *

BRAUDY, Leo 1941-

PERSONAL: Born June 11, 1941, in Philadelphia, PA; son of Edward and Zelda (Smith) Braudy; married Susan Orr (an editor), August 27, 1964 (divorced December 13, 1973); married Dorothy McGahee (a painter), December 24, 1974. *Education:* Swarthmore College, B.A., 1963; Yale University, M.A., 1964, Ph. D., 1967.

ADDRESSES: Home—207 Woodlawn Rd., Baltimore, MD 21210. *Office*—Department of English, Johns Hopkins University, Baltimore, MD 21218. *Agent*— Maxine Groffsky, 2 Fifth Ave., New York, NY 10011.

CAREER: Yale University, New Haven, CT, instructor in English, 1966-68; Columbia University, New York, NY, assistant professor, 1968-70, associate professor, 1970-73, professor of English, 1973-76; Johns Hopkins University, Baltimore, MD, professor of English, beginning 1977.

MEMBER: Modern Language Association of America, American Society for Eighteenth-Century Studies.

AWARDS, HONORS: Guggenheim fellow, 1971-72; American Council of Learned Societies grant, 1971.

WRITINGS:

Narrative Form in History and Fiction: Hume, Fielding, and Gibbon, Princeton University Press (Princeton, NJ), 1970.
Jean Renoir: The World of His Films, Doubleday (New York, NY), 1972.
(Editor and author of introduction) *Norman Mailer: A Collection of Critical Essays,* Prentice-Hall (Englewood Cliffs, NJ), 1972.
(Editor and author of introduction) *Focus on Shoot the Piano Player,* Prentice-Hall (Englewood Cliffs, NJ), 1972.

The World in a Frame, Doubleday (New York, NY), 1976.
(Editor, with Morris Dickstein, and author of introduction) *Great Film Directors: A Critical Anthology,* Oxford Book Co., 1978.
The Frenzy of Renown: Fame and Its History, Oxford University Press (New York, NY), 1986.
Native Informant: Essays on Film, Fiction, and Popular Culture, Oxford University Press (New York, NY), 1991.
(Editor, with Gerald Mast and Marshall Cohen) *Film Theory and Criticism: Introductory Readings,* Oxford University Press (New York, NY), 1992.
From Chivalry to Terrorism: War and the Changing Nature of Masculinity, Knopf (New York, NY), 2003.

Contributor to books, including *Harvard Guide to Contemporary American Writing,* edited by Daniel Hoffman, Belknap Press of Harvard (Cambridge, MA), 1979.

BIOGRAPHICAL AND CRITICAL SOURCES:

PERIODICALS

Yale Review, winter, 1971.*

*   *   *

BRIGHT, Susannah 1958-
  (Susie Bright)

PERSONAL: Born March 25, 1958, in Arlington, VA; companion of Jon Bailiff; children: Aretha. *Education:* University of California—Santa Cruz, B.A., 1981; also studied women's studies and theatre at California State University—Long Beach. *Religion:* "Raised Catholic."

ADDRESSES: Home—P.O. Box 8377, Santa Cruz, CA 95061. *E-mail*—subscribe@susiebright.com.

CAREER: Author, editor, and performer. Known professionally as Susie Bright. International Socialists, organizer, 1975-77; involved with the underground newspaper the *Red Tide,* c. 1975-77; performance artist in San Francisco, CA, and elsewhere, beginning in the early 1980s; Good Vibrations, clerk, beginning 1981; *On Our Backs* magazine, founder (with others) and manager, 1983, contributing editor and advertising director c. 1983-84, chief editor, 1984-91; *Penthouse Forum,* contributing editor and film columnist, 1987-89; *San Francisco Review of Books,* columnist, 1992-94; member of the advisory board of *OUT!,* 1995; *Penthouse,* contributing fiction editor, 1995-96; University of California—Santa Cruz, instructor, 1995—. Columnist for *Salon* online magazine. Actor in films, including *The Grafenberg Spot* (video), Mitchell Brothers, 1985; *Behind the Green Door, the Sequel* [United States], 1986; *News at 10* (documentary), 1988; *Stripped Bare: Women in the Sex Industry Speak Out,* 1988; *The Virgin Machine* (also known as *Die Jungfrauenmaschine*), Norddeutscher Rundfunk/Hyane Film, 1988; *Kathy* (short film), 1989; *Peril or Pleasure: Feminism and Pornography,* 1989; "Let's Talk about Sex" segment of *Erotique,* Group One Distribution, 1995; (and technical consultant) *Bound,* Gramercy Pictures, 1996; and *The Celluloid Closet* (also known as *Gefangen in der Traumfabrik*), Sony Pictures Classics, 1996; and *Susie Bright, Sex Pest,* (documentary), 1998. Involved in the production of films, including *Clips* and *Suburban Dykes.* Appeared in television specials, including *Reel Sex 8,* HBO, 1994; *Gay and Lesbian Erotica in the U.S.,* BBC; *Susie Bright Live at Bookshop Santa Cruz,* Santa Cruz Community Access Television, 1997; *Crescendo,* Channel 72, 1999; *A Return to Modesty?,* Lifetime Television, 1999; and *Sex in the 20th Century,* History Channel, 2001. Appeared on episodes of television series, including *The Phil Donahue Show,* syndicated, 1991; and *The Joan Rivers Show,* syndicated. Appeared in various stage productions, including *Dress Codes* (solo show), Institute of Contemporary Art, Boston, MA; *Porn I've Known and Loved and Even Been Offended By,* by Roxie Theatre, 1993 and 1995; also appeared in *Girls Gone Bad* and *Knife Paper Scissors,* both produced in the San Francisco, CA, area. Keynote speaker at conferences and delivered the lecture "The Case of Pornography" at the University of California—Santa Barbara Conference on Pornography and Censorship, 1994. Delivered the lecture and film clip presentation "How to Read a Dirty Movie" at various venues, including Cal Arts, Valencia, CA; Stanford University, Palo Alto, CA; San Francisco State University, San Francisco, CA; Roxie Theatre, San Francisco, CA; Dobie Theatre, Austin, TX; Collective for Living Cinema, NY; Massachusetts Institute of Technology (MIT), Cambridge; Nuart Theatre, Los Angeles, CA; Pacific Archive of the

University of California—Berkeley; University of California—Santa Cruz; Castro Theatre, San Francisco, CA; Berlin Lesbian Film Fest, Berlin, Germany; Hamburg Gay Film Festival, Hamburg, Germany; and Virginia Tech, Blacksburg; all 1987-93. Delivered the lecture and film clip presentation *All-Girl Action: The History of Lesbian Erotica* at the Lesbian and Gay Film Festival, Castro Theatre, San Francisco, CA; Gay Film Festival, Music Box Theatre, Chicago, IL; Chatham College, Pittsburgh, PA; Hallwalls, Buffalo, NY; University of Minnesota, Minneapolis; Nuart Theatre, Los Angeles, CA; Amsterdam Gay and Lesbian Film Festival, Amsterdam, the Netherlands; British Film Institute; University of Washington, Seattle; and at the Castro Theatre; all 1989-92. Lecturer of "Sex in Public: Erotic Expression, Censorship, and Sexual Repression" at Hunter College, City University of New York, New York, NY; State University of New York—Binghamton; Brown University, Providence, RI; Harvard University, Cambridge, MA; Amherst College, Amherst, MA; Wesleyan University, Middletown, CT; Cornell University, Ithaca, NY; University of Arkansas, Fayetteville; Yale University, New Haven, CT; Slim's Spoken Word Series, San Francisco, CA; University of Indiana, Bloomington; a Modern Language Association conference; and an American Library Association conference, San Francisco, CA, all 1990-92. Delivered lectures, including "The Bloom in Women's Erotica," Society for the Scientific Study of Sex, Scottsdale, AZ, 1986, and the Institute for the Study of Human Sexuality, San Francisco, CA, 1989; "Sex Educators and Erotica," Society for the Scientific Study of Sex, San Francisco, CA, 1990; "Covering Sex: Sex in the Media," Lesbian/Gay Media Conference, NY, 1993; "Safe Sex for Sex Maniacs," Smith College, Northampton, MA, 1993; "Erotica vs. Pornography," San Francisco Book Fair, San Francisco, CA, 1993 and 1995. Delivered lecture "Sexual State of the Union Address" at the Carnegie-Mellon University, Pittsburgh, PA; University of North Carolina, Chapel Hill; McGill University, Montreal, Quebec, Canada; Florida State University, Gainesville; Alfred U, Alfred, NY; 92nd Street Y, New York, NY; Antioch College, Yellow Springs, OH; Bryn Mawr College, Bryn Mawr, PA; Wesleyan University; Williams College, Williamstown, MA; Vassar College, Poughkeepsie, NY; and Wellesley College, Wellesley, MA; all 1993-95, and at the Women's Live Conference; Smith College, 1997; Tulane University, New Orleans, LA; Northwestern University, Evanston, IL 1998; Carnegie Melon, 1999; Humboldt State University, Arcata, CA; MIT, 2000; Williams College; California State

University at Chico; Ohio State; Carnegie Mellon; all 2003. Delivered lecture (with Molly Katzen and Harriet Lerner) "Food, Sex, and Relationships," Unity Temple, Kansas City, MO, 1996, released as a sound recording (with an interview) by Sounds True, 1997. Conducted workshops, including "Reading, Writing, and Rethinking Erotica: A Creative Writing Workshop for Women," San Francisco, CA, 1993. Also worked as a bookstore clerk, dishwasher, and waiter.

AWARDS, HONORS: Named reason number twenty-four to love America in the article "Recapture the Flag: Sixty-two Reasons to Love America," *Minneapolis City Pages,* 1991; Venus Award, 1997, for *Good Vibrations;* Lambda Literary Award, best photography/art book of the year, 1997, for *Nothing but the Girl; New York Press,* Best of 1998, Best Sex Columnist, for *Salon Magazine*'s "Sexpert Opinion"; Film/Video of the Year Oscar for British TV, 1999, for *Sex Pest;* inducted into the X-Rated Hall of Fame, 2003, and named one of the "one hundred visionaries who could change your life" by the *Utne Reader.*

WRITINGS:

AS SUSIE BRIGHT

(Editor) *Herotica: A Collection of Women's Erotic Fiction,* Down There Press (Burlingame, CA), 1988.
Susie Sexpert's Lesbian Sex World, Cleis Press (Pittsburgh, PA), 1990.
(Editor, with Joani Blank) *Herotica 2: A Collection of Women's Erotic Fiction,* Plume (New York, NY), 1991.
Susie Bright's Sexual Reality: A Virtual Sex World Reader, Cleis Press (Pittsburgh, PA), 1992.
(Editor) *The Best American Erotica,* nine volumes, Macmillan (New York, NY), 1993–2002.
(Author of introduction) Mari Blackman and Trebor Healey, editors, *Beyond Definition,* Manic D Press (San Francisco, CA), 1994.
(Editor) *Herotica 3: An Anthology of Women's Erotic Fiction,* Plume (New York, NY), 1994.
(Editor) *Susie Bright's SexWise: America's X-Rated Intellectual Does Dan Quayle, Catherine MacKinnon, Stephen King, Camille Paglia, Nicholson Baker, Madonna, the Black Panthers, and the GOP,* Cleis Press (Pittsburgh, PA), 1995.

(Editor) *Totally Herotica,* Book-of-the-Month-Club (Garden City, NJ), 1995.
(Editor, with Jill Posener) *Nothing but the Girl: The Blatant Lesbian Image,* Cassell (New York, NY), 1996.
Susie Bright's Sexual State of the Union, Simon & Schuster (New York, NY), 1997.
Full Exposure: Opening Up to Sexually Creativity and Erotic Expression, HarperSanFrancisco (San Francisco, CA), 1999.
How to Write a Dirty Story: Reading, Writing, and Publishing Erotica, Simon & Schuster (New York, NY), 2002.
Mommy's Little Girl: Susie Bright on Sex, Motherhood, Porn, and Cherry Pie, Thunder's Mouth Press (New York, NY), 2003.
(Editor) *The Best American Erotica 2003,* Touchstone (New York, NY), 2003.
(Editor) *The Best American Erotica 2004,* Touchstone (New York, NY), 2004.
(Editor) *Susie Bright Presents: Three the Hard Way,* Touchstone (New York, NY), 2004.

Contributor to books, including *Forbidden Passages,* Cleis Press, 1995; *Surface Tension,* edited by Meg Daly, Simon & Schuster, 1995; and *Virgin Territory,* edited by Shar Rednour, Masquerade Books, 1995. Contributor to periodicals, including the *Advocate, East Bay Express, Elle, Esquire, Future Sex, In These Times, New York Quarterly, New York Times Book Review, On Our Backs Outword, Penthouse, Penthouse Forum, Playboy, Realist, San Francisco Examiner, San Francisco Review of Books, Utne Reader, Village Voice,* and the *Whole Earth Review.* Contributor to and performer in recordings, including *Cyborgasm,* Heydey/Time Warner, 1994, and *The Edge of the Blood,* Heydey/Time Warner, 1995.

PERFORMANCE PIECES FOR THE STAGE; AS SUSIE BRIGHT

(With Honey Lee Cottrell) *How to Read a Dirty Movie,* produced at various venues, 1987–93.
(With Honey Lee Cottrell) *All-Girl Action: The History of Lesbian Erotica,* produced at various venues, 1989–92.

With Caitlin Morgan and Jeanne Gallo, created the stage productions of *Girls Gone Bad* and *Knife Paper Scissors,* both produced in the San Francisco, CA, area.

SCREENPLAYS; AS SUSIE BRIGHT

"Let's Talk about Sex" segment (with Lizzie Borden), *Erotique,* Group One Distribution, 1995.

SIDELIGHTS: A pioneer in creating women's erotica in a variety of media, Susannah Bright, who writes under the name Susie Bright, has achieved wide popularity. She has also earned critical respect for her wit, intelligence, and positive tone. Bright has created and performed in stage productions, edited anthologies featuring women's erotic literature, written books of commentary on sex, appeared on television talk shows and in films, written a screenplay, and has contributed to publications as diverse as *Penthouse Forum,* the *Village Voice,* and the *New York Times Book Review.* Though Bright's ideas sometimes arouse controversy, many critics consider Bright a positive cultural influence. Jonathan Wald, writing in *Gay & Lesbian Biography,* noted that Bright's "candid and insightful attitudes have inspired a new public discussion of eroticism and sex."

Bright was born in Arlington, Virginia, in 1958, but also spent her childhood in parts of California and Canada. She began developing her writing skills in high school when she joined the staff of *Red Tide,* an underground student newspaper. After earning a bachelor's degree at the University of California—Santa Cruz, Bright began working at Good Vibrations, a store specializing in erotic toys, where she organized a feminist erotic video library. At Good Vibrations, Bright also listened to the stories and experiences of customers, amassed a wealth of knowledge on sexual matters, and began to give advice. This experience led her to found and edit *On Our Backs,* a magazine aimed at a lesbian audience. The magazine includes fiction, essays, and photographs on sexual topics.

Bright joined *Penthouse Forum* as a feminist critic of pornographic films. Bright's views about pornography have gotten her into trouble with some feminists who argue that pornography degrades women. Despite these attacks, however, Bright has remained pro-porn. She has criticized the male-dominated pornography business, but she maintains that women have a right to create and enjoy erotic images. Bright has fashioned some of these images herself by contributing to the screenplay for the film *Erotique* and to the production of the films *Clips* and *Suburban Dykes.* She has also appeared in many films relating to sex, including *News at 10* (a documentary), *Stripped Bare: Women in the Sex Industry Speak Out, The Virgin Machine, Peril or Pleasure: Feminism and Pornography, Bound,* and *The Celluloid Closet.*

Bright edited the 1988 *Herotica: A Collection of Women's Erotic Fiction,* a collection of erotic literature written by women. She also edited *Herotica 2: A Collection of Women's Erotic Fiction* with Joani Blank and *Herotica 3: An Anthology of Women's Erotic Fiction.* Pat Murphy, writing in the *Whole Earth Review,* commented that the first *Herotica* is "designed to appeal to a variety of tastes" and deemed it "teasing, comic, and ultimately satisfying." Bright's advice columns for *On Our Backs* were collected and published in *Susie Sexpert's Lesbian Sex World.* This 1990 book is a mixture of advice and cultural commentary on women's sexuality. *Susie Bright's Sexual Reality: A Virtual Sex World Reader* includes pieces on topics such as computer sex, sexuality and pregnancy, date rape, and bisexuality. "Bright is funny, flip, irritating, revealing, and observant," wrote *Booklist* contributor Ryn Etter in a review of *Susie Bright's Sexual Reality,* as the author addresses "the joys, fears, and confusions of gays, lesbians, bis, and straights alike."

In 1993 Bright edited the first volume of the annual anthology *The Best American Erotica* and has edited each volume since. Writing in reference to the 2000 volume in *Lambda Book Report,* Sheryl Fowler remarked, "Perhaps the most surprising thing about this collection is how respectable it is. Real, or apparently real, author names abound, and according to the biographies, erotic writing credits are being placed next to newspaper work and (university) teaching careers." Fowler compared reading erotica to riding a bus: "You're fairly certain it will get you there, you just don't know how fast or in what condition." Fowler went on to say that this anthology "is like traveling by luxury ocean liner, with complimentary champagne, beautiful food, and gorgeous, gorgeous scenery."

A *Kirkus Reviews* contributor praised *The Best American Erotica 2003,* the tenth anniversary edition of the series, saying, "Now that the indefatigable impresario has left behind the focus on fetishism and identity politics that made several of her earlier collections seem pat and mechanical, the twenty-three new stories here are less wide-ranging but more heartfelt and emotionally appealing even for readers who may not be gay, lesbian, transgendered, or sadomasochistic themselves." A *Publishers Weekly* reviewer felt that the "enormous range of subjects and styles is what makes the anthology shine, although some of the stories sacrifice good prose for steamy effects."

Susie Bright's SexWise: America's X-Rated Intellectual Does Dan Quayle, Catherine MacKinnon, Stephen King, Camille Paglia, Nicholson Baker, Madonna, the Black Panthers, and the GOP features pieces about each of the people or groups mentioned in the subtitle. It inspired *New York Times Book Review* contributor Hall Goodman to dub the author "the voice of sweet reason and literacy." *Library Journal* contributor Scott Johnson praised Bright's "sharp, quick, revealing, [and] insightful" writing in *SexWise*. Bright later teamed up with Jill Posener to edit *Nothing but the Girl: The Blatant Lesbian Image* in 1996. The work is "a beautiful, carefully made coffee-table book of erotic images," according to Meryl Altman in the *Women's Review of Books,* "which also gives a clear yet sophisticated history of lesbian-feminist aesthetic politics over the past couple of decades." Altman praised Bright's introduction as well the book's diversity.

The 1997 book *Susie Bright's Sexual State of the Union* is an anthology containing pieces of diverse cultural and political content. In a review of the book, a *Publishers Weekly* contributor stated that "Susie is bright and her knowledge is broad—no one will read this book without learning something." A *Kirkus Reviews* contributor found that the book offers "insight, rendered with soul and humor, on sex and sexual politics," and called its author "an honest spokeswoman for a thoughtful, inclusive politics of liberation."

In reference to Bright's *How to Write a Dirty Story,* a *Publishers Weekly* reviewer remarked that with Bright's extensive experience in the genre, penning a how-to book "is akin to Stephen King or Patricia Cornwell writing about their craft." In the book Bright explains the difference between erotica and porn and discusses the various types of erotica. She recounts each step in writing erotica and discusses how to break into various publishing markets, including finding a literary agent, publishing with small press, or publishing on the Internet. "Despite its far-reaching goals—to encourage more people to write candidly about sex, to

end censorship, and to debunk stereotypes about sex and art—the book is organized handily and is accessible," explained the same *Publishers Weekly* reviewer.

In *Full Exposure* Bright discusses the role sexuality plays in creative expression and the positive effect eroticism has on lives. She contemplates her own "personal erotic identity" and even ventures into childbearing and parenting. Writing in *Library Journal,* Kimberly L. Clarke noted that in the book, "Bright is her usual engaging self, offering lucid meditations— and even wisdom—on one of society's most taboo subjects." Critics appreciated Bright's writing style. A *Publishers Weekly* reviewer described her voice as "earnest, helpful, and American-as-apple-pie even when using profanity to prove points about sexual stereotyping." Another reviewer for the same publication also praised Bright's straightforward approach, noting, "The most refreshing aspect of Bright's breezy, no-holds-barred style is the way she addresses sexual feelings and action in plain English without embarrassment," but voiced that in the end Bright may minimize "more complicated sexual and emotional issues and may seem repetitive to those familiar with her message."

In addition to performing and lecturing throughout the world, Bright has appeared in television specials and on television talk shows, including *The Joan Rivers Show* and *The Phil Donahue Show.* Her impact on contemporary attitudes about sexuality, gender roles, and society reaches a diverse audience. Writing in *Gay & Lesbian Biography,* Jonathan Wald noted that Bright has been identified as "one of America's new powerbrokers of gay clout" by *Newsweek* magazine, while contributors to the *Utne Reader* have included her among the "one hundred visionaries who could change your life." Margot Mifflin, reviewing *Susie Bright's Sexual State of the Union* in the *New York Times Book Review,* observed that "Ms. Bright is the missing link between old-school feminists and their postfeminist heirs. Her writing is sometimes clumsy but generally charming; her ideas are not always profound, but they are often delightfully original."

BIOGRAPHICAL AND CRITICAL SOURCES:

BOOKS

Gay & Lesbian Biography, St. James Press (Detroit, MI), 1997.

PERIODICALS

Advocate, November 16, 1993, p. 92; August 22, 1995, pp. 102-103; November 12, 1996, pp. 65-67; March 4, 1997, pp. 55-56.

Booklist, July, 1992, p. 1902.

Boston Phoenix, December, 1993.

Curve, February, 2004, Rachel Pepper, review of *The Best American Erotica 2004,* p. 44.

Future Sex, May, 1993.

Girljock, summer, 1991.

Globe and Mail (Toronto, Ontario, Canada), November, 1990.

Guardian, April 17, 1999, Julie Burchill, review of *The Best American Erotica 1999,* p. 8.

Impact: New Orleans, September, 1995.

Kirkus Reviews, January 15, 1997, p. 108; September 1, 1999, review of *Full Exposure: Opening Up to Sexually Creativity and Erotic Expression,* p. 118; December 1, 2001, review of *The Best American Erotica,* p. 1623; November 15, 2002, review of *The Best American Erotica 2003: 10th Anniversary Edition,* p. 1636; April 15, 2004, review of *Three the Hard Way,* p. 344.

Lambda Book Report, February, 2000, Sheryl Fowler, "Not Your Mother's Damp Panties," p. 26.

Library Journal, September 15, 1993, p. 108; July, 1995, pp. 104-105; March 1, 1997, p. 91; October 1, 1999, Kimberly L. Clarke, review of *Full Exposure,* p. 118.

Los Angeles Times Magazine, July 24, 1994.

Minneapolis City Pages, July, 1991.

Mother Jones, February-March, 1990.

Nation, March 29, 1993, pp. 418-420.

New Leader, May 19, 1997, pp. 19-22.

New York Observer, April 4, 1994.

New York Times Book Review, July 16, 1995, p. 20; March 23, 1997, p. 16; November 1, 1999, review of *Full Exposure,* p. 44; December 12, 1999, Helen Fisher, "Just Do It: Susie Bright, Who Feels That Sex Gets No Respect, Wants Us to Celebrate Our Libidos," p. 44.

People, November 19, 1996.

Playboy, December, 1993, p. 36.

Publishers Weekly, August 21, 1995, p. 59; August 12, 1996, p. 80; January 13, 1997, p. 61; July 12, 1999, review of *Full Exposure,* p. 84; November 1, 1999, review of *Full Exposure* (audio book), p. 41; January 10, 2000, review of *The Best American Erotica,* p. 46; May 7, 2001, review of *How to Write a Dirty Story,* p. 55; January 21,

2002, review of *The Best American Erotica 2002,* p. 66; December 16, 2002, review of *The Best American Erotica 2003,* p. 44; December 15, 2003, review of *The Best American Erotica 2004,* p. 39.

Rolling Stone, January, 1991.

San Francisco Chronicle, September, 1992; October 7, 2001, Louise Rafkin, "FaceTime," p. 6.

Vanity Fair, February, 1995.

Whole Earth Review, fall, 1986, p. 119; summer, 1992, pp. 97-99.

Windy City Times, June 30, 1994.

Women's Review of Books, March, 1997, pp. 6-8.

ONLINE

Susie Bright Home Page, http://www.susiebright.com (March 22, 2004).*

* * *

BRIGHT, Susie
See BRIGHT, Susannah

* * *

BROWN, Patricia Fortini 1936-

PERSONAL: Born November 16, 1936, in Oakland, CA; daughter of Jack Gino (a chemist) and Mary Lillian (an executive secretary; maiden name, Wells; present surname, Forester) Fortini; married Peter Claus Meyer, May 28, 1957 (divorced August 30, 1978); married Peter Robert Lamont Brown (a historian), August 16, 1980 (divorced July 5, 1989); children: (first marriage) Paul Wells, John Jeffrey. *Ethnicity:* "Caucasian." *Education:* Attended Brigham Young University, 1954-57; University of California at Berkeley, A.B., 1959, M.A., 1978, Ph.D., 1983. *Religion:* Episcopalian.

ADDRESSES: Home—54 Humbert St., Princeton, NJ 08542-3319. *Office*—Department of Art and Archaeology, Princeton University, Princeton, NJ 08544-1018. *E-mail*—pbrown@princeton.edu.

CAREER: State of California, Department of Employment, employment and claims specialist in San Francisco and San Rafael, 1960-65; painter and graphic designer in San Rafael, 1963-76; Mills College, Oakland, CA, lecturer in Italian Renaissance art, spring, 1983; Princeton University, Princeton, NJ, assistant professor, 1983-89, associate professor 1989-97, professor of art and archaeology, 1997—, department chair, 1999-2005; Andrew W. Mellon associate professor in art and archaeology, 1991-95; University of Cambridge, Slade Professor of Fine Arts, 2000; fellow commoner, St. Johns College, Cambridge. Fellow at American Academy in Rome, 1989-90; Guggenheim fellow, 1992-93. Member of San Rafael Cultural Affairs Commission, 1975-77; cocurator of Municipal Art Gallery, Falkirk Community Cultural Center, San Rafael, 1976-77. Member, board of advisors, Center for Advanced Study in the Visual Arts, National Gallery of Art, 2004-07. Former studio artist and graphic designer, 1963-75. Consultant to documentaries; curator of exhibits; presenter at conferences.

MEMBER: College Art Association of America, Renaissance Society of America (member of advisory council; representative of the discipline of the visual arts, 1988-90; member, board of trustees, 1994-96; vice president, 1998-2000; president, 2000-02).

AWARDS, HONORS: Fulbright fellow in Italy, 1980-81; Social Science Research Council fellow, 1980-82; Gladys Krieble Delmas Foundation grant for Venice, 1982, 1998-99; second prize for Premio Salotto Veneto, 1989, for *Venetian Narrative Painting in the Age of Carpaccio;* Rome Prize fellow, 1989-90; Guggenheim fellow, 1989-90; Phyliss Goodhart Gordon Book Prize, 1998, and Charles Rufus Morey Prize finalist, 1999, both for *Venice and Antiquity;* Folger Shakespeare Library Mellon postdoctoral research fellowship, 1998-99.

WRITINGS:

Venetian Narrative Painting in the Age of Carpaccio, Yale University Press (New Haven, CT), 1988.
Venice and Antiquity: The Venetian Sense of the Past, Yale University Press (New Haven, CT), 1996.
Art and Life in Renaissance Venice, Prentice Hall (New York, NY), 1997, published as *Art and Life in Renaissance Venice: A World Apart,* Weidenfeld & Nicolson (London, England), 1997.
Private Lives in Renaissance Venice: Art, Architecture, and the Family, Yale University Press (New Haven, CT), 2004.

Also author of *La pittura nell' eta di Carpaccio: i grandi cicli narrativi,* 1992. Contributor to books, including *Rome: Tradition, Innovation, and Renewal,* edited by Clifford Brown, Chandler Kirwin, and John Osborne, [Florence, Italy], 1989; *St. Augustine in Iconography: History and Legend,* edited by Joseph C. Schoubert and Frederick Van Fleteren, P. Lang (New York, NY), 1999; *Antiquity and Its Interpreters,* edited by Ann Kuttner and others, Cambridge University Press (New York, NY), 2000; *Venice Reconsidered: The History and Civilization of an Italian City-State, 1297-1797,* edited by John Martin and Dennis Romano, Johns Hopkins University Press (Baltimore, MD), 2000; *Macmillan Encyclopedia of Art,* and *Enciclopedia Italiana,* and to various art history journals.

SIDELIGHTS: After reading *Venice & Antiquity: The Venetian Sense of the Past,* one of Patricia Fortini Brown's critically acclaimed art history books, "no one can revisit familiar scenes in Venice . . . without seeing new aspects to the Venetian performance," according to *New York Times Book Review* contributor Gary Wills. Brown analyzes thirteenth- through sixteenth-century Venetian "arts, crafts, and literature to explore . . . 'a Venetian view of time . . . history and . . . historical change,'" noted Mary Morgan Smith in *Library Journal.* "Of all the major medieval cities in Italy, only Venice lacked a classical past. It had no Roman foundations to unearth, build on or celebrate," explained Wills.

Venice & Antiquity presents "themes [that] may not seem either new or profound. But," the reviewer lauded, "she shows, in sensitive detail, how the perpetual reinvention of Venice made the City reinvent the Rome, Constantinople and Jerusalem over against which it was defining itself. This led to a peculiarly shifting and illusionistic view of the past, undergoing subtle changes like the light of the city's own watery atmosphere." Although John Julius Norwich warned in *Observer* that "This book is not an easy read. There were moments when I felt that the author had got a little carried away by her own scholarship and allowed herself to become slightly ponderous," he overwhelmingly praised the work as a "superbly produced and beautifully illustrated book" with virtually no inaccuracies. Norwich maintained that Brown is "alarmingly well-informed" and "writes . . . with fluency and style." In his review, Norwich also positively notes Brown's remarkable first book, *Venetian Narrative Painting in the Age of Carpaccio.*"

In her award-winning *Venetian Narrative Painting in the Age of Carpaccio* "Brown shows how narratives of the lives of saints, miracles, and state processions all yield to the eyewitness style of Gentile Bellini and Vittore Carpaccio," described Thomas D'Evelyn in *Christian Science Monitor.* "Narrative has preoccupied art historians of the Renaissance ever since Vasari recounted his fascination with storytelling pictures in *The Lives of the Artists,* but the very ubiquity of narrative in Renaissance art seems to forestall critical reassessment," wrote a reviewer for *Art Bulletin* who declared *Venetian Narrative Painting in the Age of Carpaccio* to be "a welcome focus on the study of visual narrative in Renaissance art history." Charles Hope praised the book in the *New York Review of Books* for "not just [dealing] very competently with the many specific problems raised by individual works, but also [looking] at more general issues, such as the stylistic origins of the genre." Her work, according to *Times Literary Supplement* contributor David Rosand, "offers a dynamic portrait of a society and its self-imaging." "She has assembled a mass of information, and she has characterized the preoccupations and values of the patrons with skill and sympathy," assessed Hope, qualifying: "But we still need to know much more, not about their piety or their attitudes to Venetian society as a whole, but about their responses to paintings."

Venice is again the focus of *Private Lives in Renaissance Venice: Art, Architecture, and the Family,* as Brown profiles the lives of both the city's wealthiest class as well as its successful merchant or *cittadino* class. The book examines the politics, culture, arts, and architecture of the period, as well as presenting an in-depth look at the lives of some of the most influential women of the day, both courtesans and nobility. Praising *Private Lives* as "that rare thing: a book that will instruct the scholar and delight the general reader,' *Choice* contributor D. Pincus cited the wealth of color illustrations included in the work and dubbed the volume "comprehensive social history at its best." "By focusing on architecture, Brown . . . goes to the heart of Venetian Renaissance culture," Bruce Boucher added in the *New York Times Book Review,* explaining that through her approach, the art historian "traces many paradoxical elements of public and private life back to the consumer society of the late 1500's, which pursued 'an abundance of necessary things.'" Opulence was indeed the order of the day in sixteenth-century Venice, as images of the era's palaces, clothing, textiles, and art will show. Boucher

noted that, through her work, Brown "brings a lost chapter in Venetian history to life through an illuminating selection of images and instances." And, the critic concluded "the curious reader could not wish for a wiser guide."

Brown once told *CA:* "The central concern of my scholarly work has been the manner in which works of art can materialize and 'sum up' significant aspects of the culture in which they were produced. More specifically, I have sought to understand the formal and iconographical qualities of Renaissance art through a study of the perceptual skills, the ideological assumptions, and the social situation that engendered its production. This approach, exemplified by my book, *Venetian Narrative Painting in the Age of Carpaccio,* has been strongly influenced by the particular background out of which I began my academic career.

"After receiving a bachelor of arts degree in political science in 1959, I seriously pursued a career as a studio artist while raising a family. During this period I also became active in historical preservation activities, and in 1976 I began graduate work in the history of art after an interim of about seventeen years away from the academic world.

"While my late reentry into a graduate program presented a number of difficult hurdles—among them, regaining competency in foreign languages and learning how to think, research, and write as a historian—my studio background proved a positive asset. For during my graduate training I was encouraged to develop an interdisciplinary approach that combined my practical experience as a working artist with my earlier interests in history and political theory. The foundation for this approach had been laid in the studio. There I had been in the habit of confronting the work of art as a 'solution': as the end result of a process of problem solving. Thus, while I was learning in the course of my graduate studies to approach art in a consciously analytical, rather than a purely intuitive, manner, the formal analysis of paintings was already a familiar, embedded skill for me.

"Becoming a historian, however, was another matter. It meant a shift in viewpoint to a position opposite to that of the artist: that is, to the position of the original patrons and viewers of the art. Here my earlier interests in political theory and behavior, kept alive in a practical way by my community service, developed into a concern for the broader dynamics of art: its place in a larger social and cultural context of human experience. Essentially, then, I sought to balance in my work the competing claim of the historian and the artist. It is this combination that has challenged me to deal both with the aesthetic and formal elements of works of art and with the contextual concerns of social, political, religious, and cultural history."

BIOGRAPHICAL AND CRITICAL SOURCES:

PERIODICALS

Art Bulletin, March, 1992, pp. 161-62.
Art History, December, 1988.
Choice, November, 1988, p. 474; January, 2005, D. Pincus, review of *Private Lives in Renaissance Venice: Art, Architecture, and the Family,* p. 840.
Christian Science Monitor, September 2, 1988, p. B2.
Library Journal, October 1, 1988, p. 82; February 15, 1997, p. 145.
New York Review of Books, December 22, 1988, p. 42.
New York Times Book Review, April 20, 1997, p. 34; December 4, 2004, Bruce Boucher, review of *Private Lives in Renaissance Venice,* p. 86.
Observer (London, England), February 23, 1997, p. 16.
Times Educational Supplement, October 26, 1990, p. R2.
Times Literary Supplement, October 21, 1988, p. 1178.

*   *   *

BROWN, Rita Mae 1944-

PERSONAL: Born November 28, 1944, in Hanover, PA; adopted daughter of Ralph (a butcher) and Julia Ellen (Buckingham) Brown. *Education:* Attended University of Florida; Broward Junior College, A.A., 1965; New York University, B.A., 1968; New York School of Visual Arts, cinematography certificate, 1968; Institute for Policy Studies, Washington, DC, Ph.D., 1973. *Hobbies and other interests:* Polo, fox hunting, horses, gardening.

ADDRESSES: Home—Charlottesville, VA. *Office*—American Artists Inc., P. O. Box 4671, Charlottesville, VA 22905. *Agent*—The Wendy Weil Agency, 232 Madison Ave., New York, NY 10016.

CAREER: Writer. Sterling Publishing, New York, NY, photo editor, 1969-70; Federal City College, Washington, DC, lecturer in sociology, 1970-71; Institute for Policy Studies, Washington, research fellow, 1971-73; Goddard College, Plainfield, VT, visiting member of faculty in feminist studies, beginning 1973. Founder, Redstockings Radical Feminist Group, National Gay Task Force, National Women's Political Caucus; cofounder, Radical Lesbians; member of board of directors of Sagaris, a feminist school. American Artists Inc., Charlottesville, VA, president, 1980—. Member of literary panel, National Endowment for the Arts, 1978-81; Hemingway judge for first fiction PEN International, 1984; blue ribbon panelist for Prime Time Emmy Awards, 1984, 1986.

MEMBER: PEN International.

AWARDS, HONORS: Shared Writers Guild of America award, 1983, for television special *I Love Liberty;* Emmy Award nominations for *I Love Liberty,* 1982, and *The Long Hot Summer,* ABC mini-series, 1985; Literary Lion Award, New York Public Library, 1986; named Charlottesville Favorite Author.

WRITINGS:

(Translator) *Hrotsvitra: Six Medieval Latin Plays,* New York University Press (New York, NY), 1971.
The Hand That Cradles the Rock (poems), New York University Press (New York, NY), 1971.
Rubyfruit Jungle (novel; also see below), Daughters, Inc. (Plainfield, VT), 1973.
Songs to a Handsome Woman (poems), Diana Press (Baltimore, MD), 1973.
In Her Day (novel), Daughters, Inc. (Plainfield, VT), 1976.
A Plain Brown Rapper (essays), Diana Press (Baltimore, MD), 1976.
Six of One (novel), Harper (New York, NY), 1978.
Southern Discomfort (novel), Harper (New York, NY), 1982.
Sudden Death (novel), Bantam Books (New York, NY), 1983.
High Hearts (novel), Bantam Books (New York, NY), 1986.
The Poems of Rita Mae Brown, Crossing Press (Trumansburg, NY), 1987.

Starting from Scratch: A Different Kind of Writer's Manual (nonfiction), Bantam Books (New York, NY), 1988.

Bingo (novel), Bantam Books (New York, NY), 1988.

(With Sneaky Pie Brown) *Wish You Were Here* (mystery; also see below), Bantam Books (New York, NY), 1990.

(With Sneaky Pie Brown) *Rest in Pieces* (mystery; also see below), Bantam Books (New York, NY), 1992.

Venus Envy (novel), Bantam Books (New York, NY), 1993.

Dolley: A Novel of Dolley Madison in Love and War (novel), Bantam Books (New York, NY), 1994.

(With Sneaky Pie Brown) *Murder at Monticello; or, Old Sins* (mystery; also see below), Bantam Books (New York, NY), 1994.

(With Sneaky Pie Brown) *Pay Dirt; or, Adventures at Ash Lawn,* Bantam Books (New York, NY), 1995.

Riding Shotgun, Bantam Books (New York, NY), 1996.

(With Sneaky Pie Brown) *Murder, She Meowed* (mystery), Bantam Books (New York, NY), 1996.

Rita Will: Memoir of a Literary Rabble-Rouser, Bantam Books (New York, NY), 1997.

(With Sneaky Pie Brown) *Murder on the Prowl,* Bantam Books (New York, NY), 1998.

(With Sneaky Pie Brown) *Cat on the Scent,* Bantam Books (New York, NY), 1998.

Outfoxed, Ballantine Books (New York, NY), 2000.

(With Sneaky Pie Brown) *Pawing through the Past,* illustrated by Itoko Maeno, Bantam Books (New York, NY), 2000.

(With Sneaky Pie Brown) *Claws and Effect,* illustrated by Itoko Maeno, Bantam Books (New York, NY), 2001.

Alma Mater (novel), Ballantine Books (New York, NY), 2001.

(With Sneaky Pie Brown) Catch as Cat Can (mystery), Bantam Books (New York, NY), 2002.

Hotspur (mystery), Ballantine Books (New York, NY), 2002.

(With Sneaky Pie Brown) Tale of the Tip-Off (mystery), Bantam Books (New York, NY), 2003.

Full Cry (mystery), Ballantine Books (New York, NY), 2003.

Wish You Were Here; Rest in Pieces; Murder at Monticello (three "Mrs. Murphy" mysteries in one volume), Wings Books (New York, NY), 2003.

(With Sneaky Pie Brown) *Whisker of Evil* (mystery), Bantam Books (New York, NY), 2004.

Also author or coauthor of eight screenplays, including *Rubyfruit Jungle* (based on novel of same title) and *Slumber Party Massacre;* contributor to script of television special *I Love Liberty,* American Broadcasting Companies, Inc. (ABC), 1982, and author of television filmscripts for *The Long Hot Summer,* a miniseries for National Broadcasting Company, Inc. (NBC), 1985, *The Mists of Avalon,* 1986, *The Girls of Summer,* 1989, *Selma, Lord, Selma,* 1989, *Rich Men, Single Women,* 1989, *Home, Sweet Home,* Columbia Broadcasting System, Inc. (CBS), 1990, and *Graceland,* Napello County Productions, 1992.

SIDELIGHTS: With the 1973 publication of her autobiographical novel *Rubyfruit Jungle,* Rita Mae Brown joined the ranks of those in the forefront of the feminist and gay rights movements. Described by *Ms.* reviewer Marilyn Webb as "an inspiring, bravado adventure story of a female Huck Finn named Molly Bolt," *Rubyfruit Jungle* was at first rejected by editors at the major New York publishing companies due to what they believed to be its lack of mass-market appeal. Eventually published by the small feminist firm Daughters, Inc., it sold an unexpected 70,000 copies. The book's popularity soon brought it to the attention of Bantam Books, which acquired the rights to *Rubyfruit Jungle* in 1977 and printed an additional 300,000 copies. Total sales of the novel number more than one million, and in 1988, Bantam released the book for the first time in hardcover form.

As Webb's comment suggests, *Rubyfruit Jungle* is told in a picaresque, Mark Twain-like fashion, an observation shared by *New Boston Review* critic Shelly Temchin Henze. "Imagine, if you will, Tom Sawyer, only smarter; Huckleberry Finn, only foul-mouthed, female, and lesbian, and you have an idea of Molly Bolt," wrote Henze. Though some adopted *Rubyfruit Jungle* as "a symbol of a movement, a sisterly struggle," the critic continued, the plot of the book is basically that of the "classic American success story." Explained Henze: *Rubyfruit Jungle* "is not about revolution, nor even particularly about feminism. It is about standing on your own two feet, creaming the competition, looking out for Number One." The truly original part of the novel, maintained the critic, is Brown's perspective. "While American heroes may occasionally be women, they may not be lesbian. Or if they are, they had better be discreet or at least miserable. Not Molly. She is lusty and lewd and pursues sex with relentless gusto."

Village Voice reviewer Bertha Harris had a few reservations about the authenticity of Brown's portrayal of lesbian life. "Much of Molly's world seems a cardboard stage set lighted to reveal only Molly's virtues and those characteristics which mark her as the 'exceptional' lesbian," remarked Harris. Nevertheless, Harris went on to state, "it is exactly this quality of *Rubyfruit Jungle* which makes it exemplary (for women) of its kind: an American primitive, whose predecessors have dealt only with male heroes. Although Molly Bolt is not a real woman, she is at least the first real *image* of a heroine in the noble savage, leatherstocking, true-blue bullfighting tradition in this country's literature."

Another *Village Voice* critic, Terry Curtis Fox, viewed *Rubyfruit Jungle* in a somewhat different light. Like Henze, Fox found that Brown relies on a well-known theme for her novel, namely, "sensitive member of outside group heads toward American society and lives to tell the tale." Since this portrayal of resilience and triumph in the face of adversity is so familiar and appealing, maintained the reviewer, "you don't have to be gay or female to identify with Molly Bolt—she is one of the outsiders many of us believe ourselves to be." Furthermore, said Fox, Brown "can laugh at herself as well as at others, and make us laugh, too."

Acutely aware of the fact that humor is a quality seldom found in books dealing with homosexual life, Brown attaches special importance to her ability to make readers laugh, regarding it as a means of overcoming offensive stereotypes. "Most lesbians are thought to be ugly, neurotic and self-destructive and I just am not," she explained in a *New York Times* article. "There's no way they can pass me off that way. I'm not passing myself off as gorgeous, and a bastion of sanity, but I'm certainly not like those gay stereotypes of the miserable lesbian, the poor woman who couldn't get a man and eventually commits suicide. . . . I'm funny. Funny people are dangerous. They knock down barriers. It's hard to hate people when they're funny. I try to be like Flip Wilson, who helped a lot of white people understand blacks through humor. One way or another, I'll make 'em laugh, too."

The novel *Six of One* was Brown's second major breakthrough into the mass-market arena. Based once again on the author's own life as well as on the lives of her grandmother, mother, and aunt, *Six of One*—like *Rubyfruit Jungle*—attempts to make its point

through ribald humor and an emphasis on the poor and uneducated as sources of practical wisdom. The story chronicles the events in a half-Northern, half-Southern, Pennsylvania-Maryland border town from 1909 to 1980, as viewed through the eyes of a colorful assortment of female residents. John Fludas of the *Saturday Review,* noting that *Six of One* is a "bright and worthy successor" to *Rubyfruit Jungle,* wrote that Brown "explores the town's cultural psychology like an American Evelyn Waugh, finding dignity and beauty without bypassing the zany and the corrupt. . . . If at times the comedy veers toward slapstick, and if there are spots when the prose just grazes the beauty of the human moment . . . , the novel loses none of its warmth."

Both Eliot Fremont-Smith and Richard Boeth felt Brown could have done a better job with her material. Commenting in *Village Voice,* for example, Fremont-Smith admitted that *Six of One* "does have a winning cheerfulness," but concluded that "it's mostly just garrulous. . . . As a novel, it doesn't go anywhere; there's no driving edge; and the chatter dissipates. And as a polemical history (the secret and superior dynamics of female relationships), it gives off constant little backfires." *Newsweek* critic Boeth was even less impressed. He stated: "It is a major sadness to report that Brown has made her women [in *Six of One*] not only boring but false. . . . Her only verbal tool is the josh—speech that is not quite witty, sly, wry, sardonic, ironic or even, God help us, clever, but only self-consciously breezy. . . . These aren't human beings talking; it's 310 pages of 'Gilligan's Island.'"

In her *New York Arts Journal* review of *Six of One,* Liz Mednick attributed what some reviewers perceived as characterization problems to Brown's determination "to show how wise, witty, wonderful and cute women really are. Her silent competitor in this game is the masculine standard; her method, systematic oneupmanship. The women in *Six of One* buzz around like furies trying to out-curse, out-class, out-wit, out-smart, out-shout, out-smoke, out-drink, out-read, out-think, out-lech, out-number and outrage every man, dead or alive, in history. Needless to say, ambition frequently leads the author to extremes. . . . As if to insure her success, Brown makes her men as flat as the paper on which they're scrawled. The problem with her men is not even so much that they lack dimension as that they don't quite qualify as male." In short, concluded Mednick, *Six of One* "is less a novel than a wordy costume the author wears to parade herself before her faceless audience. Her heroines are presented not for inspection but as subjects for whom the narrative implicitly demands admiration." *Washington Post Book World* reviewer Cynthia Macdonald, on the other hand, cited *Six of One* as evidence of a welcome change in women's literature. She wrote: "The vision of women we have usually gotten from women novelists is of pain and struggle or pain and passivity; it is seldom joyous and passionate, and almost never funny. And what humor there was has been of the suffering, self-deprecating New York Jewish stand-up comedian type. [This book] is joyous, passionate and funny. What a pleasure! . . . I believe that Brown uses a kind of revisionist history to support her conviction that what was seen in the first half of the twentieth century as the life of women was only what was on the surface, not what was underneath."

Responding to criticism that women of the early 1900s could not possibly have been as liberated—not to mention as raucous—as they are depicted in the novel, Brown told Leonore Fleischer in a *Washington Post Book World* interview: "I grew up with these two almost mythical figures around me, my mother and my aunt, who didn't give a rat's a— what anybody thought. They'd say anything to anybody, and they did as they damn well pleased. We were so poor, who cares what poor people do? Literature is predominantly written by middle-class people for middle-class people and their lives were real different. As a girl, I never saw a woman knuckle under to a man, or a man to a woman, for that matter. . . . The people closest to me were all very dominating characters. The men weren't weak, but somehow the women . . . were the ones you paid attention to."

Though it, too, focuses on the difficulties straight and gay women face in a hypocritical and judgmental society, Brown's novel *Sudden Death* represents what the author herself has termed "a stylistic first for me." Written in an uncharacteristically plain and direct manner, *Sudden Death* examines the "often vicious and cold-blooded" world of women's professional tennis; many readers assume that it more or less chronicles Brown's experiences and observations during her involvement with star player Martina Navratilova. As Brown sees it, however, the book is much more than that: it is the fulfillment of a promise to a dying friend, sportswriter Judy Lacy, who had always wanted to write a novel against the background of women's

tennis. Just prior to her death from a brain tumor in 1980, Lacy extracted a reluctant promise from Brown to write such a novel, even though Brown "didn't think sports were a strong enough metaphor for literature." Judy "tricked me into writing it," explained the author to Fleischer in a *Publishers Weekly* column. "She knew me well enough to know how I'd feel about my promise, that it would be a deathbed promise. . . . I thought about her all the time I was writing it. It was strange to be using material that you felt belonged to somebody else. It's really Judy's book."

For the most part, critics felt that *Sudden Death* has few of the qualities that make *Rubyfruit Jungle* and *Six of One* so entertaining. In the *Chicago Tribune Book World*, for instance, John Blades noted that despite the inclusion of "intriguing sidelights on how [tennis] has been commercialized and corrupted by sponsors, promoters and greedy players," *Sudden Death* "lacks the wit and vitality that might have made it good, unwholesome fun. Brown seems preoccupied here with extraliterary affairs; less interested in telling a story than in settling old scores." Anne Chamberlin commented in the *Washington Post*: "If you thought Nora Ephron's *Heartburn* had cornered the market on true heartbreak, thinly veiled, make room for *Sudden Death*. . . . Don't get mad; get even, as the saying goes, and this novel should bring the score to deuce. It not only chops the stars of women's professional tennis down to size; it tackles the whole pro tennis establishment. . . . Having reduced that tableau to rubble, Brown turns her guns on America's intolerance of lesbians. That's a lot of targets for one bombing run, and all 241 acerbic pages of *Sudden Death* are jammed with as disagreeable a bunch of people doing mean things to each other as you are likely to meet at one time." *Los Angeles Times Book Review* critic Kay Mills felt that the protagonist is characterized so flatly "that one is devoid of sympathy for her when a jealous rival seeks to break her," and Elisabeth Jakab in the *New York Times Book Review* commented that Brown "is not at her best here. The world of tennis does not seem to be congenial terrain for her, and her usually natural and easy style seems cramped. . . . In *Sudden Death* we can almost hear the pieces of the plot clanking into their proper slots." Brown, who says she does not read reviews of her books, is nevertheless aware of the kinds of remarks critics made about *Sudden Death,* to which she responds: "I don't care; it doesn't matter at all; and anyway, I'm already on the next book. . . . I wrote this because Judy asked me to. . . . I learned a lot, but I can't wait to get back on my own territory."

Three years after the publication of *Sudden Death,* Brown produced *High Hearts,* followed by the novel *Bingo* two years later. According to Carolyn See of the *Los Angeles Times, High Hearts* is "a truly wacko novel," while Carolyn Banks of the *Washington Post* called *Bingo* a "pitch for a comic novel, a run-through rather than at something given us at performance level." While neither book achieved the popularity and critical respect of *Rubyfruit Jungle,* both address Brown's familiar themes of feminism and relationships—both homosexual and heterosexual—and satisfied admirers of Brown's glib, often raunchy prose.

In 1990, Brown attempted a literary departure, of sorts. With the "help" of her cat Sneaky Pie Brown, she wrote a mystery titled *Wish You Were Here.* The plot is rather complicated, full of death by cement and train "squishing." At the center of all the mayhem is postmistress Harry and her pets, a cat named Mrs. Murphy and a Welsh Corgi named Tee Tucker. According to See, *Wish You Were Here* is "a carefree canvas for Rita Mae Brown—who remember, has declared independence from the rest of us—to air certain of her own views on the human, feline, and canine condition. . . . Independence is her great thing. And animals, and nature, and a few friends. Not a bad agenda, come to think of it." After this successful attempt at murder mysteries, Brown continued with a second mystery, *Rest in Pieces.* Marilyn Stasio wrote in the *New York Times Book Review* that the gruesome details are not to shock readers: "It is the shattering of [the villagers'] intimacy by acts of violence that Ms. Brown examines so thoughtfully, creating such an enchanting world of Crozet that we shudder to see any more of its citizens in their graves. Or caught with red hands."

Brown resumed her focus on a strong lesbian character in her next novel, *Venus Envy.* Although her forthright treatment of lesbianism first attracted many critics to *Rubyfruit Jungle,* reception of *Venus Envy* was somewhat less enthusiastic. Carla Tomaso, who found Frazier to be another of Brown's loveable, "irreverent individualists," suggested in a *Los Angeles Times Book Review* that Brown's tenth novel, focusing as it does on the importance of self-acceptance and self-love, is too didactic, with the author attempting to pull "too many strings. . . . Brown needs to relax and stop worrying that we won't get the message." R. C. Scott of the *New York Times Book Review* goes even further, stating that the book "forsake[s] character for the naive

and irksome dogma of guilt-free and munificent sex." Nevertheless, *Book* reviewer Diane Salvatore found Brown still capable of acerbic wit, and noted that the message, if somewhat repetitive, is valid.

Brown's 1994 historical work and a product of extensive research, *Dolley: A Novel of Dolley Madison in Love and War,* renewed critical admiration of Brown. The product of eight years of research, *Dolley* stimulated interest in one of America's still-admired though nearly-forgotten women at a time when the current first lady, Hillary Rodham Clinton, was sparking new debates on the roles and rights of presidential wives. A series of journal entries interspersed with third-person chapters, *Dolley* follows history more closely in some areas than others. The connection between the political power-plays, scandals, and infighting during Madison's presidency and contemporary times was not lost on reviewer Roz Spafford, who noted that Washington, during the War of 1812, is "not unfamiliar." The reviewer stated: "Brown successfully brings to life . . . a woman who up to now has not been redeemed by feminist scholarship. . . [and] persuasively highlights the tensions Dolley Madison must have felt: She was closely connected to her Quaker heritage, yet committed to the war effort, strongly anti-slavery but, through her husband, the owner of slaves." *Library Journal* reviewer Mary Ann Parker commented: "Brown knows how to combine the personal and the political in an attractive picture of Dolley."

Since her initial publication of *Rubyfruit Jungle*—which remains her best known work—Brown's identity as a writer has developed several facets. Despite her commitment to depicting gay women in a positive light, she has balked at being labeled a "lesbian writer." In a *Publishers Weekly* interview, she stated: "Calling me a lesbian writer is like calling [James] Baldwin a black writer. I say no; he is not: he is a great writer and that is that. I don't understand people who say Baldwin writes about 'the black experience'—as if it is so different from 'the white experience' that the two aren't even parallel. That is so insulting . . . and I really hate it."

In an essay written for the *Publishers Weekly* column "My Say," Brown elaborated on her opposition to the use of such labels. "Classifying fiction by the race, sex or sex preference of the author is a discreet form of censorship," she maintained. "Americans buy books by convicted rapists, murderers and Watergate conspirators because those books are placed on the bestseller shelf, right out in front where people can see them. Yet novels by people who are not safely white or resolutely heterosexual are on the back shelves, out of sight. It's the back of the bus all over again. Is this not a form of censorship? Are we not being told that some novels are more 'American' than others? That some writers are true artists, while the rest of us are 'spokespersons' for our group? What group? A fiction writer owes allegiance to the English language only. With that precious, explosive tool the writer must tell the *emotional* truth. And the truth surely encompasses the fact that we Americans are female and male; white, brown, black, yellow and red; young, old and in-between; rich and poor; straight and gay; smart and stupid. . . . On the page all humans really are created equal. All stories are important. All lives are worthy of concern and description. . . . Incarcerating authors into types is an act of treason against literature and, worse, an assault on the human heart." Therefore, concluded Brown in her interview, "next time anybody calls me a lesbian writer I'm going to knock their teeth in. I'm a writer and I'm a woman and I'm from the South and I'm alive, and that is that."

BIOGRAPHICAL AND CRITICAL SOURCES:

BOOKS

Contemporary Literary Criticism, Gale (Detroit, MI), Volume 18, 1981, Volume 43, 1987.
Ward, Carol Marie, *Rita Mae Brown,* Twayne (Boston, MA), 1993.

PERIODICALS

Advocate, June 15, 1993, D. B. Atcheson, "Lovely Rita," p. 68.
Best Sellers, February, 1979, May, 1982.
Booklist, August, 1992, Barbara Duree, review of *Rest in Pieces,* p. 1997; February 15, 1993, Marie Kuda, review of *Venus Envy,* p. 1011; March 15, 1994, Marie Kuda, review of *Dolly: A Novel of Dolley Madison in Love and War,* p. 1302; October 1, 1994, Barbara Duree, review of *Murder at Monticello; Or, Old Sins,* p. 241; February 1, 1996, Brad Hooper, review of *Riding Shotgun,* p. 898.

Chicago Tribune Book World, July 4, 1982; July 3, 1983; June 26, 1994, p. 6.
Christian Science Monitor, November 22, 1978.
Detroit Free Press, May 15, 1983.
Detroit News, May 8, 1983.
Globe and Mail (Toronto, Ontario, Canada), May 28, 1988; November 5, 1988.
Kirkus Reviews, January 15, 1996, p. 83.
Lambda Book Report, May, 1993, pp. 13-14.
Library Journal, November 15, 1987, Rosaly Demaios Roffman, "Poems," p. 83; February 1, 1988, Mollie Brodsky, review of *Starting from Scratch: A Different Kind of Writer's Manual,* p. 64; October 15, 1988, Beth Ann Mills, review of *Bingo,* p. 100; November 1, 1990, Rex E. Klett, review of *Wish You Were Here,* p. 128; April 15, 1994, Mary Ann Parker, review of *Dolley,* p. 108; October 15, 1995, Cynthia Johnson, review of *Pay Dirt; or, Adventures at Ash Lawn,* p. 86.
Los Angeles Times, March 10, 1982; April 28, 1986; February 22, 1988; November 10, 1988.
Los Angeles Times Book Review, May 22, 1983; November 27, 1988; April 4, 1993; December 10, 1995, p. 15.
Maclean's, November 13, 1978.
Ms., March, 1974; June, 1974; April, 1977.
Nation, June 19, 1982, Alice Denham, review of *Southern Discomfort,* p. 759.
New Boston Review, April-May, 1979.
Newsweek, October 2, 1978.
New York Arts Journal, November-December, 1978.
New York Times, September 26, 1977.
New York Times Book Review, March 21, 1982, Annie Gottlieb, review of *Southern Discomfort,* p. 10; June 19, 1983, review of *Sudden Death,* p. 12; May 17, 1987, Patricia T. O'Conner, review of *High Hearts,* p. 54; December 20, 1987, p. 13; June 5, 1988, p. 13; September 6, 1992, Marilyn Stasio, review of *Rest in Pieces,* p. 17; June 27, 1993, R. C. Scott, review of *Venus Envy,* p. 18; December 8, 1996, Marilyn Stasio, review of *Murder, She Meowed,* p. 50.
Omni, April, 1988, Marilyn Long, "Paradise Tossed," p. 36; December 16, 1990, p. 33.
People, April 26, 1982, Karen G. Jackovich, "The Unthinkable Rita Mae Brown Spreads around a Little 'Southern Discomfort,'" p. 75; September 6, 1992, p. 17; June 27, 1993, p. 18.
Publishers Weekly, October 2, 1978; February 18, 1983; July 15, 1983; November 20, 1987, John Mutter, review of *The Poems of Rita Mae Brown,* p. 66; December 11, 1987, review of *Starting from*

Scratch, p. 56; September 9, 1988, review of *Bingo,* p. 122; September 21, 1990, review of *Wish You Were Here,* p. 66; June 1, 1992, review of *Rest in Pieces,* p. 54; February 8, 1993, review of *Venus Envy,* p. 76; March 28, 1994, review of *Dolley,* p. 81; August 14, 1995, p. 79; October 16, 1995, review of *Pay Dirt,* p. 44; January 22, 1996, review of *Riding Shotgun,* p. 57; October 14, 1996, "Murder, She Meowed," p. 67.

Quill and Quire, December, 1990, p. 24.

Saturday Review, September 30, 1978.

School Library Journal, April, 1991, Claudia Moore, review of *Wish You Were Here,* p. 153.

Times Literary Supplement, December 7, 1979.

Village Voice, September 12, 1977; October 9, 1978.

Washington Post, May 31, 1983, Anne Chamberlin, review of *Sudden Death,* p. C2; October 27, 1988, p. 11.

Washington Post Book World, October 15, 1978; May 1, 1994.

Wilson Library Bulletin, January, 1991, Kathleen Maio, review of *Wish You Were Here,* p. 113.*

* * *

BUECHNER, (Carl) Frederick 1926-

PERSONAL: Born July 11, 1926, in New York, NY; son of Carl Frederick and Katherine (Kuhn) Buechner; married Judith Friedrike Merck, April 7, 1956; children: Katherine, Dinah, Sharman. *Education:* Lawrenceville School, graduated 1943; Princeton University, A.B., 1948; Union Theological Seminary, B.D., 1958.

ADDRESSES: Home—3572 State Route 315, Pawlet, VT 05761-9753. *Office*—P.O. Box 1145, Pawlet, VT 05761. *Agent*—Lucy Kroll Agency, 390 West End Ave., New York, NY 10024 (drama); Harriet Wasserman, 137 East 36th St., New York, NY 10016.

CAREER: Lawrenceville School, Lawrenceville, NJ, teacher of English, 1948-53; instructor in creative writing, New York University, summers, 1953, 1954; East Harlem Protestant Parish, New York, NY, head of employment clinic, 1954-58; ordained minister of the United Presbyterian Church, 1958; Phillips Exeter Academy, Exeter, NH, chair of department of religion, 1958-60, school minister, 1960-67; writer, 1967—.

William Belden Noble Lecturer, Harvard University, 1969; Russell Lecturer, Tufts University, 1971; Lyman Beecher Lecturer, Divinity School, Yale University, 1976; Harris Lecturer, Bangor Seminary, 1979; Smyth Lecturer, Columbia Seminary, 1981; Zabriskie Lecturer, Virginia Theological Seminary, 1982; Trinity Institute, lecturer, 1990. Guest preacher and lecturer. Trustee, Barlow School, 1965-71; author. *Military service:* U.S. Army, 1944-46.

MEMBER: National Council of Churches (committee on literature, 1954-57), Council for Religion in Independent Schools (regional chair, 1958-63), Foundation for Arts, Religion, and Culture, Presbytery of Northern New England, PEN, Authors Guild, Authors League of America, Century Association, University Club (New York, NY).

AWARDS, HONORS: Irene Glascock Memorial Intercollegiate Poetry Award, 1947; O. Henry Memorial Award, 1955, for short story "The Tiger"; Richard and Hinda Rosenthal Award, 1959, for *The Return of Ansel Gibbs;* National Book Award nomination, 1971, for *Lion Country;* Pulitzer Prize nomination, 1980, for *Godric;* American Academy Award, 1982; D.D. from Virginia Theological Seminary, 1983, Lafayette College, 1984, Cornell College, 1988, Yale University, 1990, and Sewanee University; Litt.D. from Lehigh University.

WRITINGS:

NOVELS

A Long Day's Dying, Knopf (New York, NY), 1950, reprinted, Brook Street Press (Saint Simons Island, GA), 2003.

The Seasons' Difference, Knopf (New York, NY), 1952.

The Return of Ansel Gibbs, Knopf (New York, NY), 1958.

The Final Beast, Atheneum (New York, NY), 1965, reprinted, Harper (San Francisco, CA), 1982.

The Entrance to Porlock, Atheneum (New York, NY), 1970.

Lion Country (also see below; first in "Book of Bebb" tetralogy), Atheneum (New York, NY), 1971.

Open Heart (also see below; second in "Book of Bebb" tetralogy), Atheneum (New York, NY), 1972.

Love Feast (also see below; third in "Book of Bebb" tetralogy), Atheneum (New York, NY), 1974.

Treasure Hunt (also see below; fourth in "Book of Bebb" tetralogy), Atheneum (New York, NY), 1977.

The Book of Bebb (contains *Lion Country, Open Heart, Love Feast,* and *Treasure Hunt*), Atheneum (New York, NY), 1979, reprinted, HarperSanFrancisco (San Francisco, CA), 2001.

Godric, Atheneum (New York, NY), 1980.

Brendan, Atheneum (New York, NY), 1987.

Wizard's Tide: A Story, Harper (New York, NY), 1990.

The Son of Laughter, HarperSanFrancisco (San Francisco, CA), 1993.

On the Road with the Archangel, HarperSanFrancisco (San Francisco, CA), 1997.

The Storm, HarperSanFrancisco (San Francisco, CA), 1998.

NONFICTION

The Magnificent Defeat (meditations), Seabury (New York, NY), 1966.

The Hungering Dark (meditations), Seabury (New York, NY), 1969.

The Alphabet of Grace (theological and autobiographical essays), Seabury (New York, NY), 1970.

Wishful Thinking: A Theological ABC, Harper & Row ((New York, NY), 1973.

The Faces of Jesus, photography by Lee Boltin, Riverwood (Croton-on-Hudson, NY), 1974.

Telling the Truth: The Gospel as Tragedy, Comedy, and Fairy Tale, Harper & Row (San Francisco, CA), 1977.

Peculiar Treasures: A Biblical Who's Who, Harper & Row (San Francisco, CA), 1979.

The Sacred Journey: A Memoir of Early Days (autobiography), Atheneum (New York, NY), 1982.

Now and Then: A Memoir of Vocation (autobiography), Atheneum (New York, NY), 1983.

A Room Called Remember: Uncollected Pieces, HarperSanFrancisco (San Francisco, CA), 1984.

Whistling in the Dark: An ABC Theologized, HarperSanFrancisco (San Francisco, CA), 1988.

Telling Secrets, (autobiography), HarperSanFrancisco (San Francisco, CA), 1991.

The Clown in the Belfry: Writings on Faith and Fiction, HarperSanFrancisco (San Francisco, CA), 1991.

Listening to Your Life: Meditations with Frederick Buechner, HarperSanFrancisco (San Francisco, CA), 1992.

The Longing for Home: Recollections and Reflections (autobiography), HarperSanFrancisco (San Francisco, CA), 1996.

The Eyes of the Heart: A Memoir of the Lost and Found, HarperSanFrancisco (San Francisco, CA), 1999.

Speak What We Feel (Not What We Ought to Say): Reflections on Literature and Faith, HarperSanFrancisco (San Francisco, CA), 2001.

Beyond Words: Daily Readings in the ABC's of Faith, HarperSanFrancisco (New York, NY), 2004.

OTHER

Short stories have been anthologized in *Prize Stories 1955: The O. Henry Awards,* edited by Paul Engle and Hansford Martin, Doubleday (New York, NY), 1955. Contributor to numerous periodicals, including *Poetry* and *Lawrenceville Literary Magazine.*

Collections of Buechner's manuscripts have been established at Princeton University and at Wheaton College, Wheaton, IL.

SIDELIGHTS: Frederick Buechner is a novelist and nonfiction writer whose work as a Presbyterian minister informs his writings. Virtually all of Buechner's books, from his novels to his nonfiction theological "meditations," address moral, ethical, and religious themes.

Two years after graduating from Princeton University, Buechner published his first novel, *A Long Day's Dying.* The book "is a strikingly fine first novel, and it seems entirely safe to say that its publication will introduce a new American novelist of the greatest promise and the greatest talent," wrote C. W. Weinberger in the *San Francisco Chronicle.* "In strict accuracy, it is not proper to refer to Mr. Buechner as being a novelist of great promise, for he has already arrived in superlative fashion."

Buechner's *A Long Day's Dying* is generally considered to be an unusually sensitive and insightful study of various relationships. "Buechner has written a perceptive and often astringently witty study of subtle human relationships and delicate tensions," stated C. J. Rolo in *Atlantic,* "a book which continually reaches for the emotional meanings of the moment." And David Daiches wrote in the *New York Times* that "this first novel by a young man of twenty-three is a remarkable piece of work. There is a quality of civilized perception here, a sensitive and plastic handling of English prose and an ability to penetrate to the evanescent core of a human situation."

Buechner's second novel, *The Seasons' Difference,* was not greeted with the same degree of enthusiasm as *A Long Day's Dying.* For example, Oliver La Farge pointed out in *Saturday Review* that *The Seasons' Difference* "starts with promise. Again and again it looks as if the promise were going to be fulfilled. There are moments when it lights up brightly, and one thinks, at last he has hit his stride—but always, somehow, the light goes out again. It is one of those most tantalizing of all things in writing—a near miss." H. L. Roth wrote in *Library Journal* that Buechner's "emphasis is less on plot than on the development of atmosphere but even that emphasis seems to get lost in an arty attempt at developing a feeling of mysticism."

However, Tangye Lean found Buechner's book "brilliant and closely knit both in its rather overloaded descriptive power and its invention." Writing in *Spectator,* Lean remarked that *The Seasons' Difference* "may be recommended as one of the most distinguished novels that has recently come out of America." And a critic for *U.S. Quarterly Book Review* observed that "the arresting quality of this sensitively and elaborately written novel lies in the delineation of its characters, especially the children, and of their interrelations: adult to adult, child to adult, and child to child." Nevertheless, reasoned Horace Gregory in the *New York Herald Tribune Book Review,* "Buechner probably needs more time to complete his own vision of the world that is glimpsed in certain descriptive passages of [*The Seasons' Difference*]. The promise of his first book is still awaiting its fulfillment."

With his promise not quite fulfilling the initial expectations of critics or readers, Buechner had reached a writer's block. Having moved to New York with two novels completed, he tried to continue writing but found himself considering other careers, according to Philip Yancey in *Books & Culture.* "Uncharacteristically," Yancey wrote, "simply because the building sat a block from his apartment, he began attending the Madison Avenue Presbyterian Church, pastored by the celebrated George Buttrick." Buechner had never attended church regularly until that time, and only occasionally in his childhood. When he heard a sermon delivered in 1952, right around the time of Queen Elizabeth's coronation, Buechner experienced a life-altering revelation. "Buttrick was contrasting Elizabeth's coronation with the coronation of Jesus in the believer's heart, which, he said, should take place among confession and tears," recounted Yancey. Buechner tells the story in *The Alphabet of Grace:* "And then with his head bobbing up and down so that his glasses glittered, he said in his odd, sandy voice, the voice of an old nurse, that the coronation of Jesus took place among confession and tears and then, as God was and is my witness, great laughter, he said. Jesus is crowned among confession and tears and great laughter, and at the phrase great laughter, for reasons that I have never satisfactorily understood, the Great Wall of China crumbled and Atlantis rose up out of the sea, and on Madison Avenue, at 73rd Street, tears leapt from my eyes as though I had been struck across the face." As Yancey pointed out, that was the beginning of Buechner's belief and trust in God. It continued to shape him as an ordained minister, a teacher, and most importantly, as a writer.

"In *The Return of Ansel Gibbs,* Buechner marked a more decisive departure from his earlier manner," wrote Ihab Hassan in *Radical Innocence: Studies in the Contemporary American Novel.* "The book is reasonably forthright; its material, though rich in moral ambiguities, is topical rather than mythic, dramatic more than allusive." An *Atlantic* contributor noted that this book "is quite a departure from [Buechner's] two previous novels, which were open to the charge of preciosity. Now the style is less ornate, the plot straightforward." Richard McLaughlin remarked in the *Springfield Republican* that Buechner's earlier novels "established him as a writer with a distinguished style but a rather narrow range of interests. In [*The Return of Ansel Gibbs*] he explores, with his usual subtlety and feeling for language and moods, a wider, more public domain."

Writing for *Saturday Review,* A. C. Spectorsky commented that "there is a quality of distinction about Frederick Buechner's [*The Return of Ansel Gibbs*] which might best be compared to the gleam of hand-polished old silver. There is about his work some of the charming cultivation of the best of Marquand, and

Cozzens' capacity to make each incident—however casual or trivial in appearance—emerge as meaningful and illuminating."

In 1958, the same year Buechner published *The Return of Ansel Gibbs,* he was ordained a minister of the United Presbyterian Church. For the next several years Buechner performed the duties of school minister at Phillips Exeter Academy while continuing to write his novels. As Elizabeth Janeway explained in the *New York Times:* "Part of Frederick Buechner is a writer of imagination and insight. Part of him is a man with a Christian mission so strong that he decided to enter the Presbyterian ministry. There is no reason why the two shouldn't combine to write excellent and powerful novels."

Not all reviewers have shared Janeway's contention that the ministry and the writing of novels is a likely and acceptable combination. A reviewer for *Publishers Weekly* observed that "to a certain number of critics and reviewers, there is something disconcerting about a minister who can write a novel, containing some vivid sex scenes and a four-letter word or two." Buechner, however, sees no conflict with being a minister and a novelist. He explained in a *Publishers Weekly* interview that, to him, "writing is a kind of ministry." As Buechner once elaborated: "As a preacher I am trying to do many of the same things I do as a writer. In both I am trying to explore what I believe life is all about, to get people to stop and listen a little to the mystery of their own lives. The process of telling a story is something like religion if only in the sense of suggesting that life itself has a plot and leads to a conclusion that makes some kind of sense."

Buechner's first literary work written after his ordination was *The Final Beast.* Published seven years after *The Return of Ansel Gibbs, The Final Beast* displays a shift in theme that a number of reviewers, including Gerald Weales, believed would become more prevalent in future Buechner novels. In the *Reporter,* Weales described the theme as "the possibility of spiritual rebirth." A *Choice* reviewer felt the work marked the beginning of Buechner's "concern with religious belief and the religious life." Charles Dollen remarked in *Best Sellers:* "Despite what might sound like heavy drama in the plot, this [book] is a joyous one and its fictional people are searching for, and finding, real happiness. This is a deeply religious book without the slightest hint of [piety] or sentimentalism."

In 1971 Buechner published *Lion Country,* the first book of a tetralogy that also includes *Open Heart, Love Feast,* and *Treasure Hunt.* Eight years later these four novels were published in one volume titled *The Book of Bebb.* The tetralogy traces the activities and relationships of Leo Bebb, a former Bible salesman, founder of the Church of Holy Love, Incorporated, and of the Open Heart Church, and president of the Gospel Faith College, a religious diploma mill. Buechner did not originally intend to write a follow-up to *Lion Country.* He explained how the series evolved in his introduction to *The Book of Bebb:* "When I wrote the last sentence of *Lion Country,* I thought I had finished with [the characters in the series] for good but soon found out that they were not finished with me. And so it was with the succeeding volumes, at the end of each of which I rang the curtain down only to find that, after a brief intermission, they'd rung it up again."

The Bebb series is considered by some to be Buechner's best work to date. Christopher Lehmann-Haupt wrote in the *New York Times:* "You smile to think how Frederick Buechner keeps getting better with each new novel, for where he was gently amusing in *Lion Country,* he is funny and profound in *Open Heart.*" While numerous elements have been cited as reasons for the popularity of these four novels, most reviewers agree that much of the credit belongs to Buechner's presentation of thought-provoking ideas in a witty manner. A *Times Literary Supplement* contributor commented that Buechner maintains "a strange, serene balancing act which blends successfully satirical talent and the moral purpose." And a *Publishers Weekly* reviewer noted that the way Buechner "writes is special and engaging—serious, comic, with a kind of reverent irreverence for his people and their lives. [He has an] amused and amusing view." Another reviewer for *Publishers Weekly* held up *Lion Country* as a perfect example of a "human comedy of complexity and persuasion." As a *Virginia Quarterly Review* writer remarked: "Urbane, arcane, intelligent, low-keyed comedy is rare enough in these parlous times, but [*Lion Country*] is a choice example certain to appeal to a variety of tastes."

Some reviewers have noted that Buechner's comical sense is especially evident in his handling of religious matters. "This may sound like slapstick [to] suggest that although Mr. Buechner takes bows toward religion he is really more interested in laughs," suggested Michael Mewshaw in the *New York Times Book*

Review, "but throughout the [tetralogy] he is most serious when he is funny, and he has found an inevitable and instructive confusion between wheat and chaff. As the Bible warns, one can't be cut away without injuring the other." And in a review of *Open Heart,* John Skow observed in *Time:* "It is something of a mystery how Buechner has produced a live, warm, wise comic novel. And yet that is exactly what, in all shifty-eyed innocence, he has done. [He] seems to have found an acceptable way to deal with religious mysteries in fiction."

Other reviewers commented similarly that Buechner seems to have mastered a technique for dealing with theological subjects in an entertaining fashion. A *Times Literary Supplement* contributor pointed out: "The fine lucidity of Mr. Buechner's prose, the pure verve of his humour, the grisly authenticity of his characters and settings make this highly elusive, indeed almost deliquescent brand of Christian Philosophy seem not unpalatable but actually convincing." Lehmann-Haupt wrote in the *New York Times* that Buechner's "contrast between the serious and the absurd serves to underline the meaning of both *Love Feast* and the [tetralogy] as a whole: to wit, the message of Jesus Christ may emanate from strange places indeed, but it is the message that matters, not the messenger."

New York Times Book Review contributor Cynthia Ozick believed that the reason the religious messages seem to fit so well into Buechner's novels is that to the author "sacredness lurks effortlessly . . . nearly everywhere; it singles us out." As Buechner himself writes in *The Hungering Dark:* "There is no place or time so lowly and earthbound but that holiness can be there too. And this means that we are never safe, that there is no place where we can hide from God, no place where we are safe from his power . . . to recreate the human heart because it is . . . just where we least expect him where he comes most fully."

"Life is what Buechner is writing about," explained Jonathan Yardley in the *Washington Post Book World.* "Beneath all the antics of Leo Bebb and those who surround him there is a continuing celebration of life and the interrelation of lives. Buechner's people may at first glance seem caricatures, but their robustness is merely humanity magnified." And Thomas Howard remarked in the *New York Times Book Review* that "[Buechner's] vision, then, is that of the poet—the Christian poet. He has articulated what he sees with a

freshness and clarity and energy that hails our stultified imaginations."

Another factor contributing to the success of these novels is Buechner's skill at characterization. "What makes [the 'Leo Bebb' novels] succeed is Buechner's deft placing of all these characters," explained Roger Sale in *Hudson Review,* "keeping them funny or impossible when seen from a distance, then making them briefly very moving when suddenly seen from close up." P. A. Doyle stated in *Best Sellers* that Buechner "grasps each figure firmly and forces it to concrete life. A type of Flannery O'Connor vibrant vividness pervades Bebb . . . and the other principals causing them to pop out most fully alive from the novel[s]." And Sale, writing in another issue of *Hudson Review,* singled out Buechner's treatment of the main character, Leo Bebb, and commented: "The word about Bebb is simple—he lights up every page on which he appears, making each one a joy to read and to anticipate, and of all the characters in American literature, only Hemingway's Bill Gorton rivals him in that respect."

Buechner's skillful use of characters did not end with the Bebb series of novels. Reviewers have cited Buechner's following novel, *Godric,* as still another example of how an effective characterization enriches Buechner's novels. In *Godric,* Buechner tells the story of a twelfth-century Anglo-Saxon saint. Francine Cardman illustrated in *Commonweal:* "Peddler, merchant seaman, pilgrim and perhaps pirate, ultimately hermit; roguist, conniving, irascible, repentant, gentle, fierce: Godric is compelling in his struggle for sanctity. Buechner's retelling draws reader/listener into the world of his words, a world and language so strangely and strongly evocative they would seem to be Godric's own." Noel Perrin remarked in the *Washington Post Book World* that "the old saint [Godric] is so real that it's hard to remember this is a novel. I can think of only one other book like this: Thomas Mann's *The Holy Sinner.* That's the story, taken from medieval legend, of another carnal saint."

Buechner's 1993 novel *The Son of Laughter* again showcased the author's penchant for religious themes—in this case, a novelization of the biblical story of Jacob—and moral issues presented in ambiguous, often comic, tones. In presenting the story of Jacob, Buechner deals with numerous well-known biblical tales, including the stories of Abraham, Sarah, and Isaac—whose name means "laughter." Writing in the *New York Times Book Review*, Lore Dickstein remarked: "Buechner has kept intact all the characters and events, the (unknown) biblical time frame, and much of the tone and cadence of biblical prose. He has altered the sequence of the narrative somewhat, using flashbacks and foreshadowing, but he has omitted nothing." Reviewers noted that in this work, as in his previous novels, Buechner does not offer easy solutions to moral questions. Addressing this issue, Brooke Horvath, in the *Review of Contemporary Fiction*, wrote, "The novel's meditative questioning is often moving. It is also often disturbing." "This question of belief is at the heart of Buechner's work," noted Irving Malin in *Commonweal*. "He makes us wonder about how we can find spiritual truth in the comic incident."

In addition to his novels, Buechner has also written works of nonfiction, including several collections of meditations, religious studies, and autobiographies. Critics have noted that these books are similar in many ways to Buechner novels. As Edmund Fuller wrote in the *New York Times Book Review:* "The same stylistic power, subtlety and originality that have distinguished his novels, from *A Long Day's Dying* to *Open Heart*, lift *Wishful Thinking* far above commonplace religion books nearly to the level of C. S. Lewis's *Screwtape Letters*. An artist is at work here in the vineyard of theology, an able aphorist with a natural gift for gnomics, a wit with wisdom." Reviewing *The Alphabet of Grace*, Thomas Howard wrote in the *New York Times Book Review* that Buechner "takes the common, mundane experiences of daily life and reflects on them," he said. "What he does with his material is what the poets do with theirs: he surprises and delights (and—very softly—teaches) us by giving some shape to apparently random experience by uttering it."

"Novelist Buechner writes about as well as anyone we know of, when it comes to Christian themes today," noted a reviewer for *Christian Century*. In an article on *The Alphabet of Grace*, M. M. Shideler observed in another issue of *Christian Century* that "Buechner's style is by turns meditative, narrative and anecdotal. His manner is honest, sensitive and direct." And N. K. Burger observed in the *New York Times Book Review* that in *The Magnificent Defeat* (Buechner's first book of meditations) Buechner "combines high writing skill with a profound understanding of Christian essentials." Tony Stoneburner wrote in *Christian Century* that

Buechner's collections of meditations "grant relative value to the world, distinguish Christianity and morality, argue the propriety of poetry for discourse about mystery." Commenting on Buechner's second collection, *The Hungering Dark*, Fuller stated in the *New York Times Book Review* that "the touches that distinguish [this book] spring from the fact that in addition to Buechner's role as Presbyterian minister and sometime chaplain, he is also one of the better literary talents of his generation." Fuller went on to say that, "He has artistic as well as pastoral insights into the human soul and also some distinction of style." Reviewing *Telling the Truth: The Gospel as Tragedy, Comedy, and Fairy Tale*, Richard Sistek pointed out that "this is the kind of book that asks for reflection, creativity, and response. With continually changing times and a church in transition, human experience and creativity are sorely needed to make sense out of change, and move forward with hope. The author has challenged me."

Perhaps nowhere else does the reader achieve a real understanding of Buechner, the author and minister, than in his autobiographies. In his introduction to *The Sacred Journey*, Buechner writes: "What I propose to do now is to try listening to my life as a whole, or at least to certain key moments of the first half of my life thus far, for whatever of meaning, of holiness, of God, there may be in it to hear. My assumption is that the story of any one of us is in some measure the story of us all." A *Publishers Weekly* reviewer wrote that in *The Sacred Journey*, Buechner "exemplifies his conviction that God speaks to us not just through sounds but 'through events in all their complexity and variety, through the harmonies and disharmonies and counterpoint of all that happens.'"

Reynolds Price remarked in the *New York Times Book Review* that in *The Sacred Journey*, Buechner "isolates and recreates a few powerfully charged incidents ranging from his early childhood to the time of his decision to enter the ministry." "The heart of this book," Julian N. Hart believed, "is a series of encounters for which 'epiphany,' overworked though it may be, is entirely appropriate." Hart wrote in the *Washington Post Book World* that "the persistent core metaphor is 'journey'; in his case a life-process defined, not merely punctuated, by revelations of what he comes to acknowledge of divine goodness and power."

Now and Then, Buechner's sequel to *The Sacred Journey*, "picks up where the first book ends, with the author's experience of having his life turned upside down while listening to a George Buttrick sermon," recounted Marjorie Casebier McCoy in *Christian Century.* "Part I covers Buechner's years at Union Theological Seminary, where he encountered the theologians and biblical scholars who became his mentors. . . . In Part II Buechner recalls his nine years as a minister and teacher of religion at Phillips Exeter Academy, trying to be an apologist for Christianity against its 'cultured despisers' by presenting the faith 'as appealingly, honestly, relevantly and skillfully as I could,'" she quoted. "Part III begins with Buechner's move to Vermont in 1967, chronicles his struggle to minister through full-time writing and speaking, and provides insights into the development of his subsequent novels and nonfiction."

Buechner's novel *On the Road with the Archangel* is based on the Book of Tobit, which is one of the seven biblical books designated as "Deutero-Canonical" by Catholics. Yet Protestants refer to Tobit and other works, including Esdras, Sirach, and Wisdom, as "the Apocryphal Books"; this alone makes Buechner's choice interesting. Tobit itself is, as Alfred Corn wrote in the *New York Times Book Review,* a sort of historical novel, the only extended first-person narrative in the Old Testament. Written in the second century B.C., its setting is some four centuries earlier, when the Assyrians conquered the northern kingdom of Israel and deported its people (the famous "Lost Tribes of Israel") to the Assyrian capital at Nineveh. There a wealthy and generous figure named Tobit undergoes a series of trials that call to mind those of a more well-known Old Testament figure, Job. Tobit prays for death, while in the town of Ectabana, a beautiful girl named Sarah—plagued by a demon who has killed seven would-be husbands—makes the same request. The angel Raphael hears the prayers of both, and intervenes in their affairs, bringing the two together. The tale ends happily, with Sarah's marriage to Tobit's feckless son Tobias.

"No Job-like depths have been plumbed," in Corn's opinion, "but the conclusion's lightly borne sweetness works to justify the ways of God to man by implying that adversities are sometimes remedied, and that curses can never rival the steadying power given us when we praise being." John Mort in *Booklist* described *On the Road with the Archangel* thus: "Not Buechner's best, but entertaining and wise, even so." W. Dale Brown in *Christian Century* held that "We

have long relied on Frederick Buechner for a good story, and he does not disappoint." Summing up the book, David Stewart wrote in *Christianity Today:* "What it adds up to is an unforgettably funny and lovely picture of unlikely Providence, portraying with extraordinary empathy ordinary, flawed folk who at any given moment have only the vaguest idea of what they are doing, or of the import of their actions for themselves or others," he noted. In the end, Douglas Auchincloss concluded in *Parabola:* "Buechner blesses his readers with two happy endings—one secular and one theological."

In 1998 Buechner published *The Storm,* his fifteenth novel. While some reviewers found it to be his least successful novel, they continued to offer praise for his thoughtful direction and his penchant for offering his readers "the sinful saint," as Gwenette Orr Robertson observed in the *Christian Century.* Maude McDaniel noted in the *World and I:* "Although his nonfiction has always been more satisfying to me, displaying a depth, feeling, and literary virtuosity I do not always find in his storytelling, his fiction often does a grand job of understanding the very real inability among intellectual moderns . . . to commit to religious conviction." The story involves two elderly brothers, Kenzie and Dalton Maxwell, estranged for many years due to a mistake Kenzie made as a volunteer social worker in a New York City shelter for runaways. The theme echoes William Shakespeare's *The Tempest,* with Kenzie working hard to come to terms with his past and the tragedies therein, yet continuing to exercise his control over the lives of those around him. As Bill Ott wrote in *Booklist,* "Faith is at the core of this novel, as it is in much of Buechner's work, but it is an oddly ambiguous, utterly human kind of faith—characterized not by certainty but by good-humored irony, even world-weariness, and above all, by a profound sense of quiet. Kenzie's belief in God translates, in the minutely observed dailiness of his life, into a belief in what he calls Tendresse oblige, and it is that remarkable tenderness, toward people and things, that envelops this tempestuous tale in an irresistible circle of calm."

The Eyes of the Heart: A Memoir of the Lost and Found and *Speak What We Feel (Not What We Ought to Say): Reflections on Literature and Faith* offer further reflections by Buechner. A *Presbyterian Record* reviewer reflected on *The Eyes of the Heart:* "Perhaps following his own dictum that all true theology at its heart is autobiographical, he has produced this fourth volume. But, of course, it is more than a memoir. It is Buechner reflecting on life and the possibility of life after death." Bryce Christensen and Gilbert Taylor wrote in *Booklist* that, "Without ever leaving the magic kingdom of his personal library, the acclaimed author of religious fiction, meditation, and criticism transports us in multiple directions: back in time to witness his grandparents' wedding in Maine; around the world to relive an eventful trip with his wife; and deep into his own dark childhood to comprehend the shock of his alcoholic father's suicide in a fume-filled garage." They concluded saying, "For those unfamiliar with Buechner, these reflections can only awaken desires to explore his other work." In a *Los Angeles Times* review of *Speak What We Feel,* Bernadette Murphy wrote, "This book is a fitting celebration of the grace, courage, honesty, and yes, of the sacredness inherent in remarkable literature."

In all of his writings, the collections of meditations, autobiographical studies, and fiction, Buechner has proven to many his ability to successfully maintain a literary career that reflects his dual roles as author and minister. Max L. Autrey concluded in the *Dictionary of Literary Biography Yearbook:* "Early appraisals of Buechner's work have proved accurate. After producing ten novels and volumes of nonfiction writings, he has demonstrated his right to be listed among such contemporary writers as Mailer, Ellison, Updike, and Barth. Although his literary appeal has been primarily to the intelligentsia, he is now widely recognized as a brilliant, inspirational writer and an original voice."

BIOGRAPHICAL AND CRITICAL SOURCES:

BOOKS

Aldridge, John W., *After the Lost Generation: A Critical Study of the Writers of Two Wars,* McGraw-Hill (New York, NY), 1951.

Buechner, Frederick, *The Hungering Dark,* Seabury (New York, NY), 1969.

Buechner, Frederick, *The Alphabet of Grace,* Seabury (New York, NY), 1970.

Buechner, Frederick, *The Book of Bebb,* Atheneum (New York, NY), 1979.

Buechner, Frederick, *The Sacred Journey: A Memoir of Early Days,* Atheneum (New York, NY), 1982.

Buechner, Frederick, *Now and Then: A Memoir of Vocation,* Atheneum (New York, NY), 1983.

Contemporary Literary Criticism, Gale (Detroit, MI), Volume 2, 1974, Volume 4, 1975, Volume 6, 1976, Volume 9, 1978.

Davies, Marie-Helene, *Laughter in a Genevan Gown: The Works of Frederick Buechner, 1970-1980,* Eerdmans (Grand Rapids, MI), 1983.

Dictionary of Literary Biography Yearbook: 1980, Gale (Detroit, MI), 1981.

Hassan, Ihab, *Radical Innocence: Studies in the Contemporary American Novel,* Princeton University Press (Princeton, NJ), 1961.

PERIODICALS

America, April 14, 1973; December 14, 1974; March 28, 1998, Patricia Allwin DeLeeux, review of *On the Road with the Archangel,* p. 26.

Antioch Review, fall, 1993, p. 659.

Atlantic, February, 1950; March, 1958; September, 1979; December, 1980.

Best Sellers, February 1, 1965; March 1, 1971; February, 1978; December, 1980; June, 1982.

Booklist, October 1, 1997, p. 291; October 1, 1998, John Mort, review of *On the Road with the Archangel,* p. 290; November 15, 1998, Bill Ott, review of *The Storm,* p. 566; October 1, 1999, Bryce Christensen and Gilbert Taylor, review of *The Eyes of the Heart: A Memoir of Lost and Found,* p. 315; October 1, 1999, John Mort and Gilbert Taylor, review of *The Storm,* p. 324; June 1, 2000, Joanne Wilkinson, review of *The Wizard's Tide,* p. 1850; July, 2001, Bryce Christensen, review of *Speak What We Feel (Not What We Ought to Say): Reflections on Literature and Faith,* p. 1969.

Books and Bookmen, March, 1973.

Books & Culture, March-April, 1997, p. 57.

Boston Herald, January 9, 2000, Eric Convey, "Bridging Heaven and Earth—Author Brings Secular Edge to Religious Writing," p. 3.

Choice, September, 1971; June, 1978.

Christian Century, February 9, 1966; April 1, 1970; September 19, 1973; October 13, 1982; March 23, 1983; December 17, 1997, pp. 1203-1204; November 18, 1998, Gwenette Orr Robertson, review of *The Storm,* p. 1097; March 8, 2000, David M. May, review of *The Eyes of the Heart,* p. 283; September 11, 2002, Richard A. Kauffman, interview with Buechner, p. 26.

Christianity Today, February 9, 1998, David Stewart, review of *On the Road with the Archangel,* p. 74; March, 2003, Wendy Murray Zoba, review of *Speak What We Feel,* p. 56.

Commonweal, July, 1971; February 26, 1982; July 16, 1993, p. 27.

Hudson Review, winter, 1972-73; winter, 1974-75.

Library Journal, January 1, 1952; April 15, 1979; October 15, 1997, p. 90.

Los Angeles Times, September 12, 1980; November 15, 1999, review of *The Eyes of the Heart,* p. 54; September 8, 2001, Bernadette Murphy, review of *Speak What We Feel,* p. B18.

National Review, December 20, 1974.

New Republic, January 25, 1975; September 17, 1977.

Newsweek, February 22, 1971; November 10, 1980.

New Yorker, October 21, 1974.

New York Herald Tribune Book Review, January 13, 1952.

New York Review of Books, July 20, 1972.

New York Times, January 8, 1950; February 16, 1958; May 19, 1972; September 25, 1974.

New York Times Book Review, February 20, 1966; March 2, 1969; December 6, 1970; February 14, 1971; June 11, 1972; May 13, 1973; September 22, 1974; October 30, 1977; November 23, 1980; April 11, 1982; September 19, 1993, p. 32; October 26, 1997, p. 23.

Parabola, fall, 1998, Douglas Auchincloss, review of *On the Road with the Archangel,* p. 118.

Presbyterian Record, March, 2001, review of *The Eyes of the Heart: A Memoir of the Lost and Found,* p. 46.

Publishers Weekly, December 28, 1970; March 29, 1971; June 27, 1977; February 12, 1982; November 3, 1997, p. 79; November 8, 1999, review of *The Eyes of the Heart,* p. 54; July 30, 2001, review of *Speak What We Feel (Not What We Ought to Say),* p. 80.

Reporter, September 9, 1965.

Review of Contemporary Fiction, summer, 1994, p. 205.

San Francisco Chronicle, January 22, 1950.

Saturday Review, January 19, 1952.

Saturday Review/Society, July 29, 1972.

Saturday Review/World, October 5, 1974.

Sojourners, May, 2004, review of *Daily Readings in the ABC's of Faith,* p. 38.

Spectator, July 25, 1952.

Springfield Republican, May 11, 1958.

Time, April 12, 1971; July 3, 1972.

Times Literary Supplement, December 29, 1972; May 23, 1975; May 12, 1978; June 13, 1981.

U.S. Quarterly Book Review, June, 1952.

Virginia Quarterly Review, summer, 1971; autumn, 1972.

Washington Post, July 27, 1987.

Washington Post Book World, May 28, 1972; November 3, 1974; November 9, 1980; June 6, 1982; December 7, 1997, p. 12.

World and I, May, 1999, Maude McDaniel, "An Elusive Grace," review of *The Storm,* p. 278.

ONLINE

Pulpit.org, http://www.pulpit.org/ (April, 2002), "Preaching on Hope."

Wheaton College Web site, http://www.wheaton.edu/ (March 31, 2002), "Frederick Buechner."*

*   *   *

BUTLER, Robert Olen (Jr.) 1945-

PERSONAL: Born January 20, 1945, in Granite City, IL; son of Robert Olen (a college professor) and Lucille Frances (an executive secretary; maiden name, Hall) Butler; married Carol Supplee, 1968 (divorced, 1972); married Marilyn Geller (a poet), July 1, 1972 (divorced, 1987); married Maureen Donlan, August 7, 1987 (divorced, 1995); married Elizabeth Dewberry, April 23, 1995; children (second marriage): Joshua Robert. *Education:* Northwestern University, B.S. (summa cum laude; oral interpretation), 1967; University of Iowa, M.A. (playwriting), 1969; postgraduate study at New School for Social Research (now New School University), 1979-81. *Politics:* Independent. *Religion:* Roman Catholic.

ADDRESSES: Office—Department of English, 411-Williams Building, Florida State University, P.O. 1580, Tallahassee, FL 32306-1580.

CAREER: Electronic News, New York, NY, editor/reporter, 1972-73; high school teacher in Granite City, IL, 1973-74; Chicago, IL, reporter, 1974-75; *Energy User News,* New York, NY, editor-in-chief, 1975-85; McNeese State University, Lake Charles, LA, assistant professor, 1985-93, professor of fiction writing, begin-

Robert Olen Butler

ning 1993, then Francis Eppes Professor; Florida State University, Tallahassee, Michael Shaara Chair in Creative Writing. Member of faculty at various writers' conferences, 1988—. *Military service:* U.S. Army, Military Intelligence, 1969-72; served in Vietnam; became sergeant.

MEMBER: PEN.

AWARDS, HONORS: TuDo Chinh Kien Award for Outstanding Contributions to American Culture by a Vietnam Vet, Vietnam Veterans of America, 1987; Emily Clark Balch Award for Best Work of Fiction, *Virginia Quarterly Review,* 1991; Pulitzer Prize for Fiction, Richard and Hilda Rosenthal Foundation Award, American Academy of Arts and Letters, PEN/Faulkner Award nominee, and Notable Book Award, American Library Association, all 1993, all for *A Good Scent from a Strange Mountain;* Guggenheim fellow, 1993; L.H.D., McNeese State University, 1994; National Endowment for the Arts fellow, 1994; Lotos Club Award of Merit, 1996; National Magazine Award for Fiction, 2001.

WRITINGS:

NOVELS

The Alleys of Eden, Horizon Press, 1981.
Sun Dogs, Horizon Press, 1982.
Countrymen of Bones, Horizon Press, 1983.
On Distant Ground, Knopf (New York, NY), 1985.
Wabash, Holt (New York, NY), 1987.
The Deuce, Holt (New York, NY), 1989.
They Whisper, Holt (New York, NY), 1994.
The Deep Green Sea, St. Martin's Press (New York, NY), 1998.
Mr. Spaceman, Grove Press (New York, NY), 2000.
Fair Warning, Atlantic Monthly Press (Boston, MA), 2002.

SHORT STORIES

A Good Scent from a Strange Mountain: Stories, Viking Penguin (New York, NY), 1992.
Tabloid Dreams, Holt (New York, NY), 1996.
Had a Good Time, Grove Press (New York, NY), 2004.

Butler's stories have appeared in *Atlantic Monthly, Esquire, GQ, Harper's, Hudson Review, New Yorker, Paris Review, Ploughshares, Sewanee Review, Virginia Quarterly Review,* and *Zoetrope.*

OTHER

Also author of feature-length screenplays and teleplays for Disney, New Regency, Paramount, Twentieth Century Fox, Universal Pictures Warner Brothers, and Home Box Office.

SIDELIGHTS: Robert Olen Butler is an American writer whose novels and short stories, many of which deal with the legacy of the Vietnam War, have earned the author wide critical acclaim. Butler's first published novel, *The Alleys of Eden,* is the story of an American Army deserter, Cliff, who falls in love with a Vietnamese prostitute, Lanh, and lives with her for four years in the back alleys of Saigon. When Saigon falls to the North Vietnamese in 1975, they manage to escape to the United States, where the contrasts between the American and Vietnamese cultures, as personified by Cliff and Lanh, are brought into focus.

New York Times critic Anatole Broyard praised *The Alleys of Eden,* writing that "Butler seems to have studied and learned from the best masters: his time shifts are reminiscent of Ford Madox Ford." Tom Clark, reviewing in the *Los Angeles Times,* thought: "Butler has an ability to catch tiny shifts of feeling, momentary estrangements, sudden dislocations of mood—a tool as valuable to the novelist as a scalpel to the surgeon." And John Grant, writing in the *Philadelphia Inquirer,* noted that "This excellent novel should be placed alongside such greats as Graham Greene's *The Quiet American.*"

Although set against the background of Vietnam, *The Alleys of Eden* is not primarily a combat novel. The book was described by Marc Leepson in the *Washington Post Book World* as "a unique, haunting story that ultimately serves as a metaphor for the pain and suffering caused by this country's participation in the Vietnam war." Butler's knowledge of Vietnamese culture results from a tour of duty in which he served as a U.S. Army intelligence agent and later, in 1971, as an interpreter for the U.S. advisor to the mayor of Saigon.

The Alleys of Eden, which was written on a lapboard during Butler's daily commutes to work on a train, was rejected twenty-one times before Butler was able to find a publisher who believed it had marketability. One publisher, Methuen, had brought the book as far as the galley stage before getting out of trade-book publishing and canceling its pending list. The book's eventual publication by Horizon Press was greeted by favorable reviews and nominations for respected book awards, including consideration for a Pulitzer Prize.

Sun Dogs, Butler's second novel, centers on the attempts of Wilson Hand, a former prisoner of war turned private investigator, to come to grips with his Vietnam experience and his ex-wife's suicide. Hand, a secondary character in *The Alleys of Eden,* travels to Alaska in search of corporate spies. "It is incredibly exciting to read Butler," reflected Ronald Reed in a *Fort Worth Star-Telegram* review. "Butler is showing himself to be a master stylist. He moves from the most feverish of prose to a flatness and sparseness that is reminiscent of the best of [Raymond] Chandler and [Dashiell] Hammett. And most importantly, he has something to say."

Butler's novel *Countrymen of Bones* "examines the metaphors men find to justify their violence," synopsized *New York Times* critic Broyard. *Countrymen of Bones* relates the efforts of an archaeologist to work an important burial site he has discovered in the New Mexico desert near the end of World War II. The archaeologist is informed by the military and by scientists at Los Alamos that he only has several weeks to complete his work before the site will be destroyed by the testing of the first atomic bomb. "Though *Countrymen of Bones* is a brilliant novel of ideas," added Broyard, "it is never pretentious or didactic. . . . The characters embody and enact—even dance—the author's ideas."

On Distant Ground, published in 1985, concerns an American intelligence officer dealing with the complex moral terrain of the Vietnam War. Captain David Fleming lives by rigid codes and ideals in order to carry out the work of getting information from the enemy. He seems almost an automaton, but one day a prisoner's scrawled graffiti—"hygiene is healthful," written on the wall of the filthy prison—reaches him. Fleming perceives the writer to be a decent and commendable person, and he becomes obsessed with finding and releasing the prisoner, which he eventually does. Taken back to the United States, he is court-martialed. During the proceedings, he realizes that he must have left behind an unborn son in Vietnam. He flees the United States under an assumed name and finds his former lover and his son just a few days before the fall of Saigon.

Butler's fifth novel, *Wabash,* represented a departure for the author, as he turned his attention from the Vietnam War to Depression-era Illinois. Protagonists Jeremy and Deborah Cole struggle to reclaim their marriage in the aftermath of their daughter's death. While attempting to deal with the loss of their child and, seemingly, their love for each other, the Coles engage in fruitless behavior: Jeremy sets out to assassinate the owner of the steel mill where he works, while Deborah writes letters to the rodents inhabiting their house. Eventually, Deborah learns of and then thwarts Jeremy's violent plan, in so doing repairing the physical and emotional link between husband and wife. Reviewers of the novel were mixed in their appraisal of the work, often commending Butler's distinctive prose but calling the plot and character development uneven. Writing in the Chicago *Tribune Books,* Michael Dorris termed the novel "powerful and disturbingly flawed," taking issue in particular with "thin character motivation and a penchant for overblown profundity." A *Publishers Weekly* critic felt that *Wabash* is "beautifully written." Conversely, a *Kirkus Reviews* contributor characterized the plot as "schematic" and "cardboard." While admitting the story's flaws, Dorris concluded that *Wabash* "is a good read, an absorbing, gritty book about people and communities down on their luck."

In his 1989 novel, *The Deuce,* Butler returns to his focus on the Vietnam War. The novel features a sixteen-year-old protagonist, Tony, who is the child of a Vietnamese mother and an American father. Dissatisfied with his sterile suburban life, Tony runs away from his father's New Jersey home to live on the streets of New York City. While trying to come to terms with his life's meaning and direction, Tony has to avoid the clutches of a murderous pederast who is stalking him. As with Butler's previous novels, reviewers called the work ambitious yet flawed. *New York Times Book Review* contributor Scott Spencer, for instance, averred that *The Deuce* is "tensely dramatic." Admitting that Butler sometimes fails in his effort to relate the story from a teenager's viewpoint, Spencer nevertheless remarked that "at its most lucid, the novel speaks directly to us in a voice that is marvelously convincing." James Park Sloan, writing in the Chicago *Tribune Books,* felt that Butler falls short in this regard, "in the process exposing the many pitfalls of a child-narrator and the extraordinary difficulty of writing from within a culture other than one's own." Nevertheless, Sloan commented that the novel "is an intriguing and ambitious piece of work." Concluded Spencer, Butler "has crafted a work of fiction with real narrative energy and cultural sweep."

After producing six well-received but small-selling novels, Butler managed to enter the arena of front-list writers with his 1992 story collection, *A Good Scent from a Strange Mountain,* which was awarded the 1993 Pulitzer Prize for fiction. Set in southern Louisiana, where Butler had moved after he finished *The Deuce,* the fifteen stories in *Good Scent* feature Vietnamese-American characters adjusting to life in America and dealing with their war-ravaged past. In "Love," a nerdish man who spied for the Americans during the war has to deal for the first time with competition for his beautiful wife. During the war, he was able to vanquish all such competitors by turning them in as Viet Cong sympathizers; now in America, he has no such method at his disposal and so resorts to an outlandish voodoo spell to conquer his opponent for his wife's affections. The title story, called "a bril-

liantly told story that I will not soon forget" by *New York Review of Books* contributor Robert Towers, portrays an old Vietnamese man on the verge of death who finds that he is being visited by the ghost of Ho Chi Minh. While passing the time with Ho, the old man realizes that his son-in-law and grandson have helped murder a Vietnamese journalist in New Orleans who was calling for acceptance of their former homeland's Communist government. Echoing Towers in his praise for this story, *Los Angeles Times Book Review* critic Richard Eder remarked, "In a collection so delicate and so strong, the title story stands out as close to magical."

They Whisper, Butler's 1994 novel, recounts the narrator's lifelong passion for women. Ira Holloway, the thirty-five-year-old protagonist, describes his numerous sexual liaisons and his never-ending wonder at the joys of the female body. He also relates his current, dysfunctional marriage to a religion-obsessed woman who demands daily sex to counteract her intense jealousy of other women. Ira's marriage finally unravels when Ira falls in love with another woman. "*They Whisper* conveys my deepest feeling about sexuality, the relationships of men and women, the nature of intimacy—in the sense of secular sacrament. The writing was an act of self-exploration as well as expression," Butler told Sybil S. Steinberg in a *Publishers Weekly* interview.

Reviewers offered differing opinions about *They Whisper.* Commenting in the Chicago *Tribune Books,* Julia Glass praised Butler for once "again tackl[ing] the vagaries of language itself" but criticized the author's treatment of the women in the book: "few of the women we meet seem psychologically distinct, and their soliloquies are mostly indistinguishable in tone from Ira's own voice." While expressing her ambivalence about the novel's ultimate power, Jane Smiley, writing in the *New York Times Book Review,* called the novel "complex and intriguing, . . . many-faceted and fascinating." *Washington Post Book World* contributor Josephine Hart likewise termed *They Whisper* "profound, disturbing and important." While critical of some elements of the novel, Glass concluded that the work is "daring" and an important step "in the ongoing career of a brilliant writer."

Butler followed *Good Scent* with a collection of humorous stories, *Tabloid Dreams,* in which he uses sensationalistic newspaper headlines as jumping-off points for stories about ordinary people. In stories such as "Woman Uses Glass Eye to Spy on Philandering Husband," Butler draws upon both high and low culture to explore issues of cultural exile, loss, hope, and the search for one's self in a consumerist culture. Writing in the *New York Times,* Thomas Mallon compared Butler's sensibility to Flannery O'Connor's and noted, "To call this volume . . . a tour de force would be to reduce something deeply accomplished to a stunt."

In *The Deep Green Sea,* Butler tells of the love story between Tien, a multi-racial Vietnamese woman, and Ben, a forty-eight-year-old Vietnam veteran who returns to Vietnam seeking closure. Though Tien is young enough to be Ben's daughter, the two are immediately drawn to one another. The story is told in alternating "he said/she said" chapters, and encompasses the histories of their respective nations as well as their personal histories. Dwight Gardner, in the *New York Times Book Review,* observed that Butler is perhaps "America's most olfactorily minded novelist . . . he'd rather tell you how a character smells than tell you the color of his eyes." Though admitting that *The Deep Green Sea* falls short of its goal, a *Kirkus Reviews* critic nevertheless finds it "an ambitious, lyrical exploration of the lingering wounds of the Vietnamese war."

The short stories in *Had a Good Time* are based on Butler's collection of vintage postcards from the early decades of the twentieth century. Butler finds the voice of the message on the postcard as interesting as the picture and uses that voice to create the first-person narrative. A *Publishers Weekly* contributor notes that the "stories range in tone and substance, from the humor of 'The Ironworkers' Hayride,' in which a man lusts for a sassy suffragette despite her wooden leg ('her mouth is a sweet painted butterfly'), to the melancholy of 'Carl and I,' about a woman who pines for her consumptive husband ('I breathe myself into my husband's life')." According to a *Kirkus Reviews* contributor, "death haunts every tale. . . . Yet there's delightful humor in stories like . . . 'I Got Married to Milk Can,' about a new bride renouncing her romantic dreams of running off with an artist when he proves to be an 'advanced' painter of the Ash Can school."

Butler once explained of his writing: "I write novels to explore for myself—and to reveal to others—my vision of the fundamental patterns inherent in the flux of experience. These patterns concern man's search for love, kinship, connection, God; man's capacity for desertion, violence, and self-betrayal. But I also write novels to tell stories, a primal human impulse since cave-mouth campfires. I believe that art, to be fully realized, must communicate with as wide a public as possible without losing sight of its deepest truths."

BIOGRAPHICAL AND CRITICAL SOURCES:

BOOKS

Contemporary Literary Criticism, Volume 81, Gale (Detroit, MI), 1994.
Conversations with American Novelists: The Best Interviews from The Missouri Review and the American Audio Prose Library, edited by Kay Bonetti and others, University of Missouri Press (Columbia, MO), 1997.
Trucks, Rob, *The Pleasure of Influence: Conversations with Eleven Contemporary American Male Fiction Writers,* NotaBell Books, 2002.

PERIODICALS

America, May 17, 1997, pp. 8-29.
Antioch Review, spring, 1997, p. 272.
Fort Worth Star-Telegram, November 14, 1982.
Kirkus Reviews, January 15, 1987, p. 74; November 1, 1997; June 1, 2004.
Library Journal, September 1, 1996, p. 212.
London Review of Books, May 12, 1994, p. 24.
Los Angeles Times, February 11, 1982.
Los Angeles Times Book Review, March 29, 1992, p. 3.
Nation, February 27, 1982.
Newsday, March 21, 1982.
New York Review of Books, August 12, 1993, p. 41.
New York Times, November 11, 1981; October 18, 1983; November 3, 1996; January 11, 1998.
New York Times Book Review, January 9, 1983; April 21, 1985; March 15, 1987, p. 16; September 3, 1989, p. 10; February 13, 1994, p. 12.
Philadelphia Inquirer, January 24, 1982.
Publishers Weekly, January 1, 1982; February 11, 1983; December 21, 1984, p. 82; January 16, 1987, p. 62; July 7, 1989, p. 51; January 3, 1994, p. 60; April 12, 2004, p. 34.
St. Louis Post-Dispatch, December 1, 1981.

Times Literary Supplement, December 10, 1993, p. 19; March 18, 1994, p. 14.
Tribune Books (Chicago, IL), March 8, 1987, p. 1; September 24, 1989, p. 7; February 6, 1994, p. 3.
Vogue, February, 1994, p. 122.
Voice of Youth Advocates, December, 1985, p. 318.
Washington Post Book World, April 21, 1985, p. 11; October 1, 1989, p. 6; January 16, 1994, p. 1.
Whole Earth Review, spring, 1994, p. 56.
Writer, April, 1982.
Writer's Digest, January, 1983.

ONLINE

Inside Creative Writing, http://www.fsu.edu/~butler/ (May 9, 2005).
Writers on America, http://usinfo.state.gov/products/ pubs/ (August 3, 2004), Robert Olen Butler, *A Postcard from America.**

* * *

BYER, Kathryn Stripling 1944-

PERSONAL: Born November 25, 1944, in Camilla, GA; daughter of C. M. Stripling (a farmer) and Bernice Stripling (a homemaker; maiden name, Campbell); married James Edwin Byer (a professor), March 22, 1970; children: Corinna Lynette. *Education:* Wesleyan College (Macon, GA), B.A., 1966; University of North Carolina—Greensboro, M.F.A., 1968. *Politics:* Liberal Democrat. *Religion:* "Lapsed Presbyterian."

ADDRESSES: Home—P.O. Box 489, Cullowhee, NC 28723.

CAREER: Writer, poet, and essayist. Western Carolina University, Cullowhee, NC, instructor in English, beginning in 1968; Converse College, Spartanburg, SC, Sara Lura Mathews Self Distinguished Writer-in-Residence, 2004. Has been a poet-in-residence at Western Carolina University and Lenoir Rhyne College. Has been on the faculty of the University of North Carolina—Greensboro's M.F.A. Writing Program.

MEMBER: North Carolina Writers Network.

AWARDS, HONORS: National Endowment for the Arts fellow; Associated Writing Programs Award Series citation, 1986, for *The Girl in the Midst of the Harvest;* North Carolina Arts Council fellow, 1986; Anne Sexton Poetry Award, Boston University's *AGNI* magazine; Lamont Poetry Selection Award, Academy of American Poets, 1992, for *Wildwood Flower;* Thomas Wolfe Literary Award, North Carolina Historical Association; Roanoke-Chowan Award, North Carolina Literary and Historical Association, 1998, and Brockman-Campbell Book Award for best poetry book by a North Carolinian, North Carolina Poetry Society, 1999, both for *Black Shawl;* North Carolina Award in Literature, 2001; *Los Angeles Times* Book Award nomination, 2002, and Southeastern Booksellers Book of the Year Award in poetry, 2003, both for *Catching Light.*

WRITINGS:

Search Party: Poem, drawings by Joyce Sills, Amicae Press (Brooklyn, NY), 1979.
Alma: Poems, drawings by Sharyn Jayne Hyatt, Phoenix Press (Fort Lauderdale, FL), 1983.
The Girl in the Midst of the Harvest, Texas Tech Press (Lubbock, TX), 1986.
Wildwood Flower: Poems, Louisiana State University Press (Baton Rouge, LA), 1992.
Black Shawl: Poems, Louisiana State University Press (Baton Rouge, LA), 1998.
(Author of introduction) Stephen M. Holt, *Late Mowing: Poems and Essays,* Jesse Stuart Foundation (Ashland, KY), 2000.
Catching Light: Poems, Louisiana State University Press (Baton Rouge, LA), 2002.
Wake (chapbook), Spring Street Editions (Sylva, NC), 2003.

Contributor to anthologies, including *The Language They Speak Is Things to Eat: Poems by Fifteen Contemporary North Carolina Poets,* edited by Michael McFee, University of North Carolina Press, 1994; *Dream Garden: The Poetic Vision of Fred Chappell,* edited by Patrick Bizzaro, Louisiana State University Press, 1997; *Bloodroot: Reflections on Place by Appalachian Women Writers,* edited by Joyce Dyer, University Press of Kentucky, 1998; *Gatherings: A Collection of North Carolina Poetry,* Spring Street Editions, 2001; and *Elixir #3,* Elixir Press, 2003. Contributor of poetry and essays to publications such as *Arts Journal, Boston Globe, Hudson Review, Iowa Review, Nimrod, Southern Review, Georgia Review, Greensboro Review, SPR, Shenandoah, Carolina Quarterly,* and the *Asheville Poetry Review.*

SIDELIGHTS: Kathryn Stripling Byer once told *CA:* "When I was growing up in southwest Georgia, I used to go walking in the wide fields near sunset. There I could sing as loud as I wanted and no one was likely to hear but the cows. I could look way beyond the border of oak trees and imagine that the blue massing clouds were mountains, the Blue Ridge, the place my grandmother had wanted to be when she died. She had been born there and had spent most of her girlhood in another mountain range, the Black Hills, growing up as the daughter of an Irish miner and a German painter and schoolmarm turned Presbyterian preacher. The mountains were where she belonged, though she lived most of her adult life in the hot, mosquito-ridden flatlands of tropical Georgia.

"Mountains were where I too belonged, I decided during my sunset ramblings. Because my husband, a Tennessee native, grew up hiking the Great Smoky Mountains and expected me to accompany him on his treks, I soon found my imagination stirred by those trails, the very leaf mold and dirt of them, their shifting light, their windy sounds, their atmosphere of mystery and solitude. The old ballads and lyrics of the region also began to work on my imagination. And the sound of women's voices. Voices that ranged from Emma Bell Miles, whose *Spirit of the Mountains* was the first mountain woman's voice to catch me up in its world, to my friends Willa Mae Pressley and Linda Mathis, both Cullowhee valley natives whose sensitivity to the ambiguities of this region helped draw me into the human reality of the place. And then there was Lee Smith, whose character of Granny Younger in *Oral History* became a guide to the twists and turns of a story-telling that was beginning to fascinate me. These women told me stories, stories of loss, cruelty, disappointments, bitter loves, and 'blood on the moon.' They taught me to sing 'Black Jack Davies' and 'Shady Grove,' to love the names of quilt patterns like 'Heart's Seal' and 'Winding Way,' to relish the saying of particular flowers when I came upon them in the woods—bloodroot, gaywings, trillium.

"Most of my poetry is rooted in the earth of two poetic landscapes, each with its own particular voice and rhythm. One is the flatlands of south Georgia, where I was born and grew up. The other is the mountains of western North Carolina and Tennessee. As far back as I can remember, I heard stories of rugged kinsmen who tilled the land and adventurous kinswomen who took to the Black Hills or the Blue Ridge to find their destiny, to strike it rich digging for the mother lode. I began to see the southern mountains as my destination, and throughout the years I have lived in them, they have provided haven and solitude in which to write about both the southernmost reaches of my memory and the windy places of a solitary woman's imagination. If the Deep South is a dusty plain haunted by childhood, these mountains are a crazy quilt of trails haunted by women's voices. One of those voices, that of a persona I have come to call Alma, has been able to say for me what it must have been like to walk particular traces, stand in particular shadows, singing the old ballads and waiting for something to happen. Not only does she embody for me the spirit of the mountains where I now live, she also seems, in some ancestral way, to be speaking as kinswoman, harking me back to those grandmothers and great-grandmothers whose stories I grew up hearing."

Byer's Alma, who first appeared in her 1983 collection *Alma: Poems,* returns in *Wildwood Flower,* a collection that captures and pays tribute to the voices and ballads of the mountain women of whom the author speaks. *Black Shawl,* the author's next collection, continues in this tone, focusing on the traditions and strength of the women of the southern Appalachian Mountains.

Catching Light, Byer's 2002 poetry collection, is an exploration of the fears of women in their later stages of life, including concerns about aging, death, growing unattractive, and leaving things behind. The first part of the book is a ten-part poem titled "In the Photograph Gallery." In it, Byer presents the character Evelyn, who is based on the subject of a series of photographs that the author saw in City Lights Bookstore in Sylva, North Carolina. The photographs, taken by Louanne Watley, featured an aging artist's model—Betty Bell, or "Evelyn"—and were titled "The Evelyn Series." In *Catching Light,* Evelyn lingers in the gallery where she overhears a frightened little girl who is clutching her mother's skirt ask, "Who is she?," to which her mother replies, "Just a little old lady. That is all she is." Evelyn, however, is revealed to be much more as readers follow her through memories and the circumstances of her life unroll toward death. "I want her to be able to look at what's ahead and spit in its eye,"

Byer told the *Sylva Herald*'s Lynn Hotaling. "Of course she's afraid, but I didn't want her to be spooked."

In an interview with *Smoky Mountain News* contributor Gary Carden, Byer revealed that she "stood there in front of each image, trying to see if a voice would come out of the photos. And it did." She combined this voice with her "own memories and fears, so that in a sense the voices merged or coalesced as the poems took shape." The second part of the book captures the tone of both voices as they explore memory and how an individual is shaped by his or her family. "Poetry is the loss of what you love—of trying to recall the essence of a person or memory," Byer told Lynn Hotaling. The book's third and last part highlights the last moments of Evelyn's life as she waits for death, peering through the open door filled with light, unsure of whether she will walk through it and come out on the other side or disappear altogether. She accepts—and ultimately embraces—death as she makes the conscious decision to rise and walk through the door. "Lightly,/ lightly, I sing to myself,/ shutting the door/ ever after behind me."

Ron Houchin, a reviewer on the *Appalachian Center of Berea College* Web site, wrote "*Catching Light* is a treatise on self-seeing (self-knowledge), catching and holding in the mind those things of being and growing old, about being and aging. . . . *Catching Light* is not death anxiety, letting go of the tight grip on life, or whining about losing one's youthful look in the mirror alone; it is the universal in the individual." Rob Neufeld, in North Carolina's *Asheville Citizen-Times*, praised *Catching Light* and Byer herself, stating, "There is a building vision in Byer's growing body of poetry, which . . . achieves clarity and the other-worldly resonance of old age. And yet she's not near the end. We want to keep following her into the visions."

BIOGRAPHICAL AND CRITICAL SOURCES:

BOOKS

Byer, Kathryn Stripling, *Catching Light: Poems*, Louisiana State University Press (Baton Rouge, LA), 2002.

PERIODICALS

Publishers Weekly, October 5, 1992, review of *Wildwood Flower,* p. 65; October 31, 1994, review of *The Language They Speak Is Things to Eat: Poems by Fifteen Contemporary North Carolina Poets,* p. 55.
Southern Humanities Review, winter, 1994, David Scott Ward, review of *Wildwood Flower,* pp. 105-108.
Women's Review of Books, November, 2002, Doris Davenport, "Light Reading," review of *Catching Light,* pp. 13-14.

ONLINE

Academy of American Poets Web site, http://www.poets.org/ (February 6, 2003), "Kathryn Stripling Byer."
Appalachian Center of Berea College Web site, www.berea.edu/publications/appalachianheritage (April 10, 2003), Ron Houchin, review of *Catching Light.*
Asheville Citizen-Times Web site, http://cgi.citizen-times.com/ (April 19, 2002), Rob Neufeld, "Byer's Poems Enter the Mystery of Old Age."
Cortland Review Web site, http://www.cortlandreview.com/ (August, 2002), "Kathryn Stripling Byer."
Smoky Mountain News Web site, http://www.smokymountainnews.com/ (April 24, 2002), Gary Carden, "Shutting the Door Forever After: Byer's Character Experiences Thoughts on a Life Well Lived."
Sylva Herald Web site, http://www.thesylvaherald.com/ (April 18, 2002), Lynn Hotaling, "Byer's *Catching Light* Searches for Language of Aging."*

C

CARDENAL, Ernesto 1925-

PERSONAL: Born January 20, 1925, in Granada, Nicaragua; son of Rodolfo and Esmerelda (Martinez) Cardenal. *Education:* Attended University of Mexico, 1944-48, and Columbia University, 1948-49. *Politics:* Christian-Marxist.

ADDRESSES: Home—Carretera a Masaya Km. 9 1/2, Apt. A-252, Managua, Nicaragua.

CAREER: Ordained Roman Catholic priest, 1965. Poet and author; formerly Minister of Culture in Nicaragua.

AWARDS, HONORS: Christopher Book Award, 1972, for *The Psalms of Struggle and Liberation;* Premio de la Paz grant, Libreros de la Republica Federal de Alemania, 1980.

WRITINGS:

Ansias lengua de la poesia nueva nicaraguense (poems), [Nicaragua], 1948.

Gethsemani, Ky. (poems), Ecuador 0 Degrees 0' 0", 1960, 2nd edition, with foreword by Thomas Merton, Ediciones La Tertulia (Medellin, Colombia), 1965.

Hora 0 (poems), Revista Mexicano de Literatura, 1960.

Epigramas: Poemas, Universidad Nacional Autonoma de Mexico, 1961.

Ernesto Cardenal

(Translator, with Jose Coronel Urtecho) *Antologia de la poesia Norteamericana,* Aguilar (Madrid, Spain), 1963, Alianza (Madrid, Spain), 1979.

(Translator and editor-at-large, with Jorge Montoya Toro) *Literatura indigena americana: Antologia,* Editorial Universidad de Antioquia (Medellin, Colombia), 1964.

Oracion por Marilyn Monroe, y otros poemas, Ediciones La Tertulia, 1965, reprinted, Editorial Nueva Nicaragua-Ediciones Monimbo, 1985, translation by Robert Pring-Mill published as *Marilyn Monroe and Other Poems,* Search Press, 1975.

El estrecho dudoso (poems), Ediciones Cultura Hispanica (Madrid, Spain), 1966, Editorial Nueva Nicaragua-Ediciones Monimbo, 1985, translation by Tamara R. Williams published as *The Doubtful Strait,* Indiana University Press (Bloomington, IN), 1995.

Antologia de Ernesto Cardenal (poems), Editora Santiago (Santiago, Chile), 1967.

Poemas de Ernesto Cardenal, Casa de las Americas (Havana, Cuba), 1967.

Salmos (poems), Institucion Gran Duque de Alba (Avila, Spain), 1967, Ediciones El Pez y la Serpiente (Managua, Nicaragua), 1975, translation by Emile G. McAnany published as *The Psalms of Struggle and Liberation,* Herder & Herder, 1971, translation, from the sixth edition of 1974, by Thomas Blackburn and others published as *Psalms,* Crossroad Publishing, 1981.

Mayapan (poem), Editorial Alemana (Managua, Nicaragua), 1968.

Homenaje a los indios americanos (poems), Universidad Nacional Autonoma de Nicaragua, 1969, Laia (Madrid, Spain), 1983, translation by Carlos and Monique Altschul published as *Homage to the American Indians,* Johns Hopkins University Press (Baltimore, MD), 1974.

Vida en el Amor (meditations; with foreword by Thomas Merton), Lohle (Buenos Aires), 1970, translation by Kurt Reinhardt published as *To Live Is to Love,* Herder & Herder, 1972, published as *Love,* Search Press, 1974, translation by Dinah Livingstone published as *Love,* Crossroad Publishing, 1981, translation by Mev Puleo published as *Abide in Love,* Orbis Books (Maryknoll, NY), 1995.

La hora cero y otros poemas, Ediciones Saturno, 1971, translation by Paul W. Borgeson and Jonathan Cohen published as *Zero Hour and Other Documentary Poems,* edited by Donald D. Walsh, New Directions (New York, NY), 1980.

Antologia: Ernesto Cardenal, edited by Pablo Antonio Cuadra, Lohle, 1971, 2nd edition, Universidad Centroamericana, 1975.

Poemas, Editorial Leibres de Sinera, 1971.

Poemas reunidos, 1949-1969, Direccion de Cultura, Universidad de Carabobo, 1972.

(And translator) *Epigramas* (with translations from Catullus and Martial), Lohle, 1972.

En Cuba, Lohle, 1972, translation published as *In Cuba,* New Directions (New York, NY), 1974.

Canto nacional, Siglo Veintiuno (Mexico), 1973.

Oraculo sobre Managua, Lohle, 1973.

(Compiler and author of introduction) *Poesia nicaraguense,* Casa de las Americas, 1973, 4th edition, Editorial Nueva Nicaragua, 1981.

Cardenal en Valencia, Ediciones de la Direccion de Cultura, Universidad de Carabobo (Venezuela), 1974.

El Evangelio en Solentiname (also see below), Ediciones Sigueme, 1975, Editorial Nueva Nicaragua-Ediciones Monimbo, 1983, translation by Donald D. Walsh published as *The Gospel in Solentiname,* Orbis Books (Maryknoll, NJ), 1976, published as *Love in Practice: The Gospel in Solentiname,* Search Press, 1977, reprinted in four volumes, Orbis Books (Maryknoll, NJ), 1982.

Poesia escogida, Barral Editores, 1975.

La santidad de la revolucion (title means "The Sanctity of the Revolution"), Ediciones Sigueme, 1976.

Poesia cubana de la revolucion, Extemporaneos, 1976.

Apocalypse, and Other Poems, translated by Thomas Merton, Kenneth Rexroth, Mireya Jaimes-Freyre, and others, New Directions (New York, NY), 1977.

Antologia, Laia (Barcelona, Spain), 1978.

Epigramas, Tusquets (Barcelona, Spain), 1978.

Catulo-Marcial en version de Ernesto Cardenal, Laia, 1978.

Canto a un pais que nace Universidad Autonoma de Puebla, 1978.

Antologia de poesia primitiva, Alianza, 1979.

Nueva antologia poetica, Siglo Veintiuno, 1979.

La paz mundial y la Revolucion de Nicaragua, Ministerio de Cultura, 1981.

Tocar el cielo, Loguez, 1981.

(With Richard Cross) *Nicaraugua: La Guerra de liberacion/der Befreiungskrieg,* Ministerio de Cultura de Nicaragua, c. 1982.

Los campesinos de Solentiname pintan el evangelio, Monimbo, c. 1982.

(Translator from the German) Ursula Schulz, *Tu paz es mi paz,* Editorial Nueva Nicaragua-Ediciones Monimbo, 1982.

(Contributor) *Entrustet Euch!: Für Frieden und volkerverstandigung; Katholiken gegen Faschismus und Krieg* (essays on nuclear disarmament), Rdrberg, 1982.

La democratizacion de la cultura, Ministerio de Cultura, 1982.

Nostalgia del futuro: Pintura y buena noticia en Solentiname, Editorial Nueva Nicaragua, 1982.

Evangelio, pueblo, y arte (selections from *El Evangelio en Solentiname*), Loguez, 1983.

Waslala: Poems, translated by Fidel Lopez-Criado and R. A. Kerr, Chase Avenue Press, 1983.

Antologia: Ernesto Cardenal, Editorial Nueva Nicaragua-Ediciones Monimbo, 1983.

Poesia de la nueva Nicaragua, Siglo Veintiuno, 1983.

The Gospel in Art by the Peasants of Solentiname (translated from *Bauern von Solentiname malen des Evangelium,* selections from *Evangelio en*

Solentiname), edited by Philip and Sally Sharper, Orbis Books (Maryknoll, NJ), 1984.

Vuelos de Victoria, Visor (Madrid, Spain), 1984, Editorial Universitaria, (Leon, Nicaragua), 1987, translation by Marc Zimmerman published as *Flights of Victory: Songs in Celebration of the Nicaraguan Revolution,* Orbis Books (Maryknoll, NJ), 1985.

(Contributor) Teofilo Cabestrero, *Ministros de Dios, ministros del pueblo: Testimonio de tres sacerdotes en el Gobierno Revolucionario de Nicaragua, Ernesto Cardenal, Fernando Cardenal, Miguel d'Escoto,* Ministerio de Cultura, 1985.

Quetzalcoatal, Editorial Nueva Nicaragua-Ediciones Monimbo, 1985.

Nuevo cielo y tierra nueva, Editorial Nueva Nicaragua-Ediciones Monimbo, 1985.

With Walker in Nicaragua and Other Early Poems, 1949-1954, translated by Jonathan Cohen, Wesleyan University Press (Middletown, CT), 1985.

(Compiler and author of introduction) *Antologia: Azarias H. Pallais,* Nueva Nicaragua, 1986.

From Nicaragua with Love: Poems 1979-1986, translated by Jonathan Cohen, City Lights Press, 1986.

Golden UFOs: The Indian Poems/Los Ovnis de oro: poemas indios, translated by Carlos and Monique Altschul, Indiana University Press (Bloomington, IN), 1992.

Cosmic canticle, translated by Jonathan Lyons, Curbstone Press (Willimantic, CT), 1993.

Telescopio en la noche oscura, Trotta (Madrid, Spain), 1993.

El rio San Juan; estrecho dudoso en el centro de American, Latino Editores, 1993.

Antologia nueva, Trotta (Madrid, Spain), 1996.

(Compiler) *Flor y canto: Antologia de poesia nicaraguense* (title means "Flower and Song: Anthology of Nicaraguan Poetry"), Ediciones Centroamericanas Anama (Managua, Nicaragua), 1998.

Vida perdida (title means "Lost Life"), Seix Barral (Barcelona, Spain), 1999.

Los años de Granada: Continuacion de la vida perdida (title means "The Years of Granada: Continuation of the Lost Life"), Ediciones Centroamericanas Anama (Managua, Nicaragua), 2001.

Cincuenta años de esculturas, Anamó Ediciones Centroamericanas (Managua, Nicaragua), 2002.

Las insulas extrañas, Fondo de Cultura Económica (Mexico, D.F.), 2003.

Seis cantigas del contico cosmico, Casa el Vedado (Havana, Cuba), 2003.

Thomas Merton—Ernesto Cardenal. Correspondencia (1959-1968), Trotta (Madrid, Spain), 2004.

Contributor to *Christianismo y revolucion,* Editorial Quetzal (Buenos Aires, Argentina), and *La Batalla de Nicaragua,* Bruguera Mexicana de Ediciones (Mexico).

SIDELIGHTS: Ernesto Cardenal is a major poet of the Spanish language well known in the United States as a spokesman for justice and self-determination in Latin America. Cardenal, who recognizes that poetry and art are closely tied to politics, used his poetry to protest the encroachments of outsiders in Nicaragua and supported the revolution that overthrew Somoza in 1979. Once the cultural minister of his homeland, Cardenal spends much of his time as "a kind of international ambassador," noted Richard Elman in the *Nation.*

Victor M. Valle, writing in the *Los Angeles Times Calendar,* cited Cardenal's statement, "There has been a great cultural rebirth in Nicaragua since the triumph of the revolution. A saving of all of our culture, that which represents our national identity, especially our folklore." Literacy and poetry workshops established throughout the "nation of poets," as it has been known since the early twentieth century, are well attended by people whose concerns had been previously unheard. Most workshops are led by government-paid instructors in cultural centers, while others convene in police stations, army barracks, and workplaces such as sugar mills, Valle reports. In these sessions, Romantic and modern poetry is considered below standard; Cardenal also denigrates socialist realism, which he said "comes from the Stalinist times that required that art be purely political propaganda." The "greatest virtue" of Cardenal's own poems, stated a *Times Literary Supplement* reviewer, "is the indirectness of Cardenal's social criticism, which keeps stridency consistently at bay." In addition, said the reviewer, Cardenal's poems "are memorable and important both for their innovations in technique and for their attitudes." In this way, they are like the works of Ezra Pound, whose aesthetic standards Cardenal promotes.

Review contributor Isabel Fraire demonstrated that there are many similarities between Cardenal's poetry and Pound's. Like Pound, Cardenal borrows the short, epigrammatic form from the masters of Latin poetry Catullus and Martial, whose works he has translated. Cardenal also borrows the canto form invented by Pound to bring "history into poetry" in a manner that preserves the flavor of the original sources—a technique Pablo Neruda employed with success.

Cardenal's use of the canto form "is much more *cant-abile*" than Pound's *Cantos,* said Fraire. "We get passages of a sustained, descriptive lyricism . . . where the intense beauty and harmony of nature or of a certain social order or life style are presented." Pound and Cardenal develop similar themes: "the corrupting effect of moneymaking as the overriding value in a society; the importance of precision and truthfulness in language; the degradation of human values in the world which surrounds us; [and] the search through the past (or, in Cardenal's poetry, in more 'primitive' societies, a kind of contemporary past) for better world-models." Fraire also pointed out an important difference between the two: "Cardenal is rooted in a wider cultural conscience. Where Pound seems to spring up disconnected from his own contemporary cultural scene and to be working against it, Cardenal is born into a ready-made cultural context and shared political conscience. Cardenal's past is common to all Latin Americans. His present is likewise common to all Latin Americans. He speaks to those who are ready and willing to hear him and are likely to agree on a great many points."

Cardenal's early lyrics express feelings of love, social criticism, political passion, and the quest for a transcendent spiritual life. Following his conversion to Christianity in 1956, Cardenal studied to become a priest in Gethsemani, Kentucky, with Thomas Merton, the scholar, poet, and Trappist monk. While studying with Merton, Cardenal committed himself to the practice of nonviolence. He was not allowed to write secular poetry during this period, but kept notes in a journal that later became the poems in *Gethsemani, Ky.* and the spiritual diary in prose, *Vida en el amor.* Cardenal's stay in Kentucky was troubled by illness; he finished his studies in Cuernevaca, Mexico, where he was ordained in 1965. While there, he wrote *El estrecho dudoso* and other epic poems that discuss Central America's history.

Poems collected in *With Walker in Nicaragua and Other Early Poems, 1949-1954* look at the history of Nicaragua which touches upon the poet's ancestry. During the 1800s, the William Walker expedition from the United States tried to make Nicaragua subservient to the Southern Confederacy. According to legend, a defector from that expedition married into Cardenal's family line. Incorporating details from Ephraim George Squier's chronicles of that period, Cardenal's poem "With Walker in Nicaragua" "is tender toward the invaders without being sentimental," Elman observed. "This is political poetry not because it has a particular rhetorical stance but because it evokes the distant as well as the more recent historical roots of the conflict in Central America," Harris Schiff related in the *American Book Review.* The poet identifies with a survivor of the ill-fated expedition in order to express the contrast between the violent attitudes of the outsiders and the beauty of the tropical land they hoped to conquer. "The theme of the gringo in a strange land," as Elman put it, an essentially political topic, is developed frequently in Cardenal's work.

Later poems become increasingly explicit regarding Cardenal's political sympathies. "Zero Hour," for example, is his "single greatest historical poem about gringoism, a patriotic epic of sorts," said Elman. The poem's subject is the assassination of revolutionary leader Cesar Augusto Sandino, who used guerilla tactics against the United States Marines to force them to leave Nicaragua in 1933. "It's a poem of heroic evocation in which the death of a hero is also seen as the rebirth of nationhood: when the hero dies, green herbs rise where he has fallen. It makes innovative use of English and Spanglais and is therefore hard to translate, but . . . it is very much a work of national consciousness and unique poetic expression," Elman related.

Moving further back in time to reclaim a common heritage for his countrymen, Cardenal recaptures the quality of pre-Columbian life in *Homage to the American Indians.* These descriptions of Mayan, Incan, and Nahuatl ways of life present their attractiveness in comparison to the social organization of the present. In these well-crafted and musical poems written at the end of the 1960s, the poet praised "a way of life which celebrates peace above war and spiritual strength above personal wealth. One has a strong sense when reading Cardenal that he is using the American Indian as a vehicle to celebrate those values which are most important to him as a well-educated Trappist monk who has dedicated himself to a life of spiritual retreat," F. Whitney Jones remarked in the *Southern Humanities Review.* That the poems are didactic in no way impedes their effectiveness, say reviewers, who credit the power of the verses to Cardenal's mastery of poetic technique.

The use of Biblical rhetoric and prosody energizes much of Cardenal's poetry. *El estrecho dudoso,* like the Bible, "seeks to convince men that history contains lessons which have a transcendent significance," James J. Alstrum maintained in *Journal of Spanish Studies: Twentieth Century.* Poems in *Salmos,* written in the 1960s, translated and published as *The Psalms of Struggle and Liberation,* echo the forms and the content of the Old Testament psalms. Cardenal's psalms are updated to speak to the concerns of the oppressed in the twentieth century. "The vocabulary is contemporary but the . . . sheer wonder at the workings of the world, is biblical," Jack Riemer observed in *Commonweal.* "Equally memorable are those Psalms in which Cardenal expresses his horror at the cruelty and the brutality of human life. His anguished outcries over the rapaciousness of the greedy and the viciousness of the dictators are the work of a man who has lived through some of the atrocities of this century."

As the conflict between the Nicaraguan people and the Somoza government escalated, Cardenal became convinced that without violence, the revolution would not succeed. "In 1970 he visited Cuba and experienced what he described as 'a second conversion' which led him to formulate his own philosophy of Christian Marxism. In 1977 the younger Somoza destroyed the community at Solentiname and Cardenal became the field chaplain for the Sandinista National Liberation Front," reported Robert Hass in the *Washington Post Book World.* Poems Cardenal wrote during that "very difficult time in his country"—collected in *Zero Hour and Other Documentary Poems*—are less successful than the earlier and later work, says Hass, since "there is a tendency in them to make of the revolution a symbol that answers all questions." Some reviewers have found the resulting combination of Biblical rhetoric and Marxist revolutionary zeal intimidating. For example, Jascha Kessler, speaking on KUSC-FM radio in Los Angeles, California, in 1981, commented, "It is clearly handy to be a trained priest, and to have available for one's poetry the voices of Amos, Isaiah, Hosea and Jeremiah, and to mix prophetic vision with the perspectives of violent revolutionary Marxist ideology. It makes for an incendiary brew indeed. It is not nice; it is not civilized; it is not humane or sceptical or reasonable. But it is all part of the terrible heritage of Central Latin America." Also commenting on *Zero Hour and Other Documentary Poems, American Book Review* contributor Harold Jaffe suggested, "Although the manifest reality of Cardenal's Central America is grim, its future—which to Cardenal is as 'real' as its present—appears eminently hopeful. Furious or revolted as Cardenal is over this or that dread-

ful inequity, he never loses hope. His love, his faith in the disadvantaged, his great good humor, his enduring belief that communism and Christ's communion are at root the same—these extraordinary convictions resound throughout the volume."

"Though Cardenal sees no opposition between Marxism and the radical gospel, neither is he a Moscow-line communist," Mary Anne Rygiel explained in *Southern Humanities Review.* Rygiel cited the poem "Las tortugas" (title means "The Turtles") to demonstrate that Cardenal's reference to "communism" as the order of nature might better be understood as "communalism," a social organization of harmonious interdependence founded on spiritual unity. The poet-priest's social vision stems from his understanding of "the kingdom of God," Lawrence Ferlinghetti noted in *Seven Days in Nicaragua Libre.* "And with [Cardenal's] vision of a primitive Christianity, it was logical for him to add that in his view the Revolution would not have succeeded until there were no more masters and no more slaves. 'The Gospels,' he said, 'foresee a classless society. They foresee also *the withering away of the state*' [Ferlinghetti's emphasis]." In the 1980s, Pope John Paul II reprimanded Cardenal for promoting a liberation theology that the prelate found divergent from Roman Catholicism. Alstrum notes, however, that *El estrecho dudoso* "reaffirms the Judeo-Christian belief that there is an inexorable progression of historical events which point toward the ultimate consummation of the Divine Word. Cardenal himself views his poetry as merely the medium for his hopeful message of the transformation of the old order into a new and more just society in which the utopian dreams and Christian values of men . . . can finally be realized." Cardenal founded the Christian commune Solentiname on an island in Lake Nicaragua near the Costa Rican border to put that dream into practice.

Cardenal's work of several decades reaches its zenith in two collections focusing on his primary subjects: American Indians and Christian Marxism. *Golden UFOs: The Indian Poems/Los ovnis de oro: poemas indios* gathers Cardenal's poetry on North, South, and Central American Indians placed against the background of his Christian-Marxist viewpoint. This reveals "nothing less than an original mythology closely tied to a modern poetics," as Terry O. Taylor noted in *World Literature Today. Cosmic Canticle* unifies Cardenal's cantos written over three decades into a modern epic poem. It covers Nicaraguan and world history from the "Big Bang" through the present-day as Cardenal contemplates political leaders, oppressed peoples, capitalism, and the Nicaraguan Revolution, among other topics.

Some critics feel that the political nature of Cardenal's poetry precludes its appreciation by a sophisticated literary audience. Reviewers responded to the 1966 volume *El estrecho dudoso,* for example, as an attack on the Somoza dynasty while neglecting "the intricate artistry with which Cardenal has intertwined the past and present through myth and history while employing both modern and narrative techniques in his poem," asserted Alstrum. Others point out that Cardenal's work gains importance to the extent that it provides valuable insights into the thinking of his countrymen. Cardenal's poetry, which he read to audiences in the United States during the seventies, was perhaps more informative and accessible than other reports from that region, Kessler concluded in 1981, soon after Nicaraguan revolutionaries ousted the Somoza regime. "It may well be that Cardenal's poems offer us a very clear entrance into the mentality of the men we are facing in the . . . bloody guerilla warfare of Central America," Kessler suggested. More recently, a *New Pages* reviewer commented, "We can learn some contemporary history, [and] discover the feelings and thoughts of the people who were involved in Nicaragua's revolution by reading Cardenal's poems. And once we know what the revolution 'felt' like, we'll be a lot smarter, I believe, than most . . . who . . . make pronouncements about Nicaragua's threat to the free world."

BIOGRAPHICAL AND CRITICAL SOURCES:

BOOKS

Bhalla, Alok, *Latin American Writers: A Bibliography with Critical Biographical Introductions,* Envoy Press, 1987.
Brotherston, Gordon, *Latin American Poetry: Origins and Presence,* Cambridge University Press, 1975.
Cardenal, Ernesto, *Zero Hour and Other Documentary Poems,* edited by Donald D. Walsh, New Directions (New York, NY), 1980.
Contemporary Literary Criticism, Volume 31, Gale (Detroit, MI), 1985.
Ferlinghetti, Lawrence, *Seven Days in Nicaragua Libre,* City Lights Books (San Francisco, CA), 1984.

Mereles Olivera, Sonia, *Cumbres Poeticas Latinoamericanas: Nicanor Parra y Ernesto Cardenal,* Peter Lang, 2003.

PERIODICALS

America, November 6, 1976.
American Book Review, summer, 1978; January, 1982; January-February, 1982; September, 1985.
Booklist, April 1, 1992, p. 1425; December 1, 1993, p. 671; October 15, 1994, p. 394.
Choice, July-August, 1994, p. 1727; October, 1995, p. 299.
Commonweal, September 17, 1971.
Journal of Spanish Studies: Twentieth Century, spring & fall, 1980.
Library Journal, March 15, 1992, p. 91; January, 1994, p. 119.
Los Angeles Times Calendar, January 8, 1984.
Nation, March 30, 1985, p. 372.
National Catholic Reporter, May 27, 1994, p. 28.
New Leader, May 4, 1981.
New Pages, Volume 10, 1986.
New Republic, October 19, 1974; April 9, 1977.
Parnassus, spring-summer, 1976.
Publishers Weekly, November 8, 1993, p. 60; October 31, 1994, p. 54.
Review, fall, 1976.
Small Press, October, 1989, p. 83.
Southern Humanities Review, winter, 1976; winter, 1988.
Stand, autumn, 1991, p. 18.
Times Literary Supplement, July 12, 1974; August 6, 1976; July 14, 1989, p. 779.
Voice Literary Supplement, September, 1982.
Washington Post Book World, June 23, 1985.
World Literature Today, spring, 1983; winter, 1990, p. 80; autumn, 1995, p. 772.

OTHER

Kessler, Jascha, "Ernesto Cardenal: 'Zero Hour and Other Documentary Poems'" (radio broadcast), KUSC-FM, Los Angeles, CA, April 15, 1981.*

*   *   *

CAREY, George Wescott 1933-

PERSONAL: Born November 26, 1933, in Chicago, IL; married Claire Lanur; children: Michelle. *Education:* Northwestern University, B.A.; University of Illinois, M.A.; Indiana University, Ph.D., 1961.

ADDRESSES: Office—Department of Government, Georgetown University, Washington, DC, 20057. *E-mail*—careygw@georgetown.edu.

CAREER: Georgetown University, Washington, DC, professor of government. *Military service:* U.S. Marine Corps, 1955-57.

WRITINGS:

(Selector, with Charles S. Hyneman) *A Second Federalist: Congress Creates a Government* (selections from the Annals of Congress), University of South Carolina Press (Columbia, SC), 1967.

(With Willmoore Kendall) *The Basic Symbols of the American Political Tradition,* Louisiana State University Press (Baton Rouge, LA), 1970, published with new preface, Catholic University of America (Washington, DC), 1995.

(Editor, with George J. Graham, Jr.) *The Post-Behavioral Era: Perspectives on Political Science,* David McKay (New York, NY), 1972.

(Editor, with James V. Schall) *Essays on Christianity and Political Philosophy,* University Press of America (Bryn Mawr, PA), 1984.

(Editor) *Freedom and Virtue: The Conservative/Libertarian Debate,* University Press of America (Lanham, MD), 1984, revised and enlarged edition, ISI Press (Wilmington, DE), 1998.

(Editor) *Order, Freedom, and the Polity: Critical Essays on the Open Society,* University Press of America (Lanham, MD), 1986.

In Defense of the Constitution, James River Press (Cumberland, VA), 1989, revised and enlarged edition, Liberty Press (Indianapolis, IN), 1995.

The Federalist: Design for a Constitutional Republic, University of Illinois Press (Urbana, IL), 1989.

(Editor, with James McClellan) *The Federalist,* Kendall/Hunt Publishing (Dubuque, IA), 1990.

(Editor, with Bruce Frohnen) *Community and Tradition: Conservative Perspectives on the American Experience,* Rowman & Littlefield (Lanham, MD), 1998.

(Editor and author of introduction) *The Political Writings of John Adams,* Regnery Publishing, (Lanham, MD), 2000.

(Coeditor, coauthor of introduction, and contributor of reader's guide and constitutional cross reference and glossary) Alexander Hamilton, *The Federalist: A Collection,* Liberty Fund, (Indianapolis, IN), 2001.

A Student's Guide to American Political Thought, ISI Books (Wilmington, DE), 2004.

Contributor to books, including *Federalism: Infinite Variety in Theory and Practice,* edited by Valerie Earle, F. E. Peacock (Itasca, IL), 1968. Editor of *Political Science Reviewer,* 1973—.

SIDELIGHTS: Political scientist George Wescott Carey has penned or edited several books on the U.S. political system. Most of them examine this system from a conservative or libertarian viewpoint, and concern themselves with attempting to explain the intent of the founding fathers of the United States.

In *The Basic Symbols of the American Political Tradition* Carey and coauthor Willmoore Kendall write that the political tradition accepted as true by many in the legal, political, and academic fields is actually a recent contrivance that strays from the more narrow intent to preserve the right of the people to govern themselves focused on by the authors of the U.S. Constitution. The more modern emphasis on complete equality and complete individual freedom, according to the authors, stems from the time of U.S. President Abraham Lincoln and the famed Gettysburg Address made during the U.S. Civil War. Documents that Carey and Kendall muster in support of their argument include not only the Constitution itself but the Mayflower Compact and the *Federalist Papers.*

Essays on Christianity and Political Philosophy is the published result of a conference on the titled subject at Georgetown University. Since Georgetown is a Roman Catholic institution, it is not unexpected that, according to Robert A. Heineman in *Perspective,* the essayists "are united here in their beliefs that students of political thought should give more attention to the influence of the Catholic Church on the development of the Western political tradition and that the Christian perspective continues to provide a framework for political thought and debate." Coupling his *Modern Age* review of the book with a review of John H. Howard's *Belief, Faith, and Reason,* critic Rene Williamson noted that "practically all of our contributors believe in natural law." Heineman described the volume as "cogent" and "coherent."

In *The Federalist: Design for a Constitutional Republic,* Carey discusses the aims of *The Federalist Papers,* penned pseudonymously by Alexander

Hamilton, James Madison, and John Jay for consideration by the citizens of the then-colony of New York in hopes that it would ratify the newly written U.S. Constitution. Prior interpretation of *The Federalist Papers* generally viewed the publication in the same light that many historians view the Federalist Party, of which Hamilton, Madison, and Jay were considered influential members. The volume and its authors have long had the reputation of being elitist, and of advocating federal power as a means to preserve the power and privilege of upper- and middle-class property owners. Carey states instead that the thrust of the work is actually quite populist, and that "Publius" advocates federal powers—and the checks of the executive and judicial branches on the legislative—in order to protect individuals from the tyranny of particularly powerful groups. Paul Gottfried, critiquing *The Federalist: Design for a Constitutional Republic* in the *National Review,* observed: "I am genuinely impressed by the thoroughness of Mr. Carey's unbiased scholarship," while L. Weinstein in *Choice* concluded that the volume "serves beginners as a useful introduction . . . while for advanced students and informed readers it is a stimulus to reflection and reconsideration."

BIOGRAPHICAL AND CRITICAL SOURCES:

PERIODICALS

Choice, February, 1990, L. Weinstein, review of *The Federalist: Design for a Constitutional Republic,* p. 1010.
Journal of American History, December, 1990, pp. 1003-1004.
Modern Age, spring, 1985, Rene Williamson, review of *Essays on Christianity and Political Philosophy,* pp. 179-181.
National Review, December 31, 1990, Paul Gottfried, review of *The Federalist,* pp. 42, 44.
Perspective, July-August, 1985, Robert A. Heineman, review of *Essays on Christianity and Political Philosophy,* pp. 107-108.

*   *   *

CHABON, Michael 1963-

PERSONAL: Surname is pronounced "shay-bahn"; born 1963, in Washington, DC; son of Robert (a physician, lawyer, and hospital manager) and Sharon (a lawyer) Chabon; married Lollie Groth (a poet;

Michael Chabon

divorced, 1991); married Ayelet Waldman (a writer), 1993; children: (second marriage) Sophie, Ezekiel, Rosie. *Education:* University of Pittsburgh, B.A., 1984; University of California—Irvine, M.F.A.

ADDRESSES: Home—Berkeley, CA. *Agent*—Mary Evans, Inc., 242 East 5th St., New York, NY 10003.

CAREER: Writer and screenwriter.

AWARDS, HONORS: Publishers Weekly Best Books selection, *New York Times* Notable Book selection, both 1995, and Scripter Award, Friends of the University of Southern California Libraries, 2000, all for *Wonder Boys;* O. Henry Award, Third Prize, 1999, for story "Son of the Wolfman"; National Book Critics Circle Award nomination, 2000, short-listed for PEN/ Faulkner Award for fiction, 2001, New York Society Library Award, 2001, Gold Medal, Commonwealth Club of California, 2001, and Pulitzer Prize for fiction, 2001, all for *The Amazing Adventures of Kavalier and Clay.*

WRITINGS:

The Mysteries of Pittsburgh (novel), Morrow (New York, NY), 1988.

A Model World, and Other Stories (includes "The Lost World," "The Little Knife," "More Than Human," and "Blumenthal on the Air"), Morrow (New York, NY), 1991.

Wonder Boys (novel), Villard (New York, NY), 1995.

Werewolves in Their Youth (stories), Random House (New York, NY), 1999.

The Amazing Adventures of Kavalier and Clay (novel), Random House (New York, NY), 2000.

Summerland (novel for children), Hyperion/Miramax (New York, NY), 2002.

The Final Solution: A Story of Detection, Fourth Estate/Harper Collins (New York, NY), 2004.

Also author of screenplays, including *The Gentleman Host, The Martian Agent,* and *The Amazing Spider-Man,* a 2004 sequel to the original movie. Author of introduction to Ben Katchor's *Julius Knipl, Real-Estate Photographer,* Little, Brown (Boston, MA), 1996. Contributor to periodicals, including *Gentlemen's Quarterly, Mademoiselle, New Yorker, New York Times Magazine, Esquire, Playboy, Forward, Paris Review, Civilization,* and *Vogue.* Guest editor of *McSweeney's Mammoth Treasury of Thrilling Tales,* McSweeney's Books (San Francisco, CA), 2002. Contributor to *Fault Lines: Stories of Divorce,* edited by Caitlin Shetterly, Berkley (New York, NY), 2003. Contributor to *Michael Chabon Presents: The Amazing Adventures of the Escapist,* a quarterly comic book based on the character from Chabon's novel *The Amazing Adventures of Kavalier and Clay,* Dark Horse Comics (Milwaukie, OR), 2003.

ADAPTATIONS: Wonder Boys was adapted for film and released by Paramount Studios; *The Amazing Adventures of Kavalier and Clay* has been optioned for a film by Paramount.

WORK IN PROGRESS: A novel, *Hotzeplotz.*

SIDELIGHTS: Michael Chabon is considered by many critics one of the major literary authors of his generation, and with his 2002 novel, *Summerland,* he turned his hand to juvenile fiction, serving up a five-hundred page children's fantasy novel intended to give J. K. Rowling and her "Harry Potter" series a bit of American competition. As Patrick Meanor noted in *Dictionary of Literary Biography,* Chabon "consciously set out to create his own kind of American magical world, combining elements of Native Ameri-

can and Norse myth and folklore." Such a turn to juvenile fiction was all the more surprising, considering that Chabon won the Pulitzer Prize in 2001 for his novel *The Amazing Adventures of Kavalier and Clay,* a book that confirmed the early critical response to his first novel, *The Mysteries of Pittsburgh,* and of his second, the wryly humorous *Wonder Boys.*

Dubbed a "virtuoso" by *Booklist's* Donna Seaman, and a "master stylist" by *Book's* James Sullivan, Chabon has achieved "buzz most writers only dream about," according to Rex Roberts, writing in *Insight on the News.* Such "buzz" has made life easier at the Chabon household, where he and his wife, a writer of mysteries, share parenting duties of their children. The versatile Chabon has, in addition to his novels, penned two short story collections, *A Model World* and *Werewolves in Their Youth,* as well as television pilots, screenplays, and articles.

Chabon was born in Washington, D.C., in 1963, the son of Robert and Sharon Chabon. His father was a physician, lawyer, and hospital manager; his mother later became a lawyer. At the age of six, Chabon and his family moved to the city-in-construction of Columbia, Maryland. They were, as Chabon wrote in "Maps and Legends" on his Web site, "colonists of a dream, immigrants to a new land that as yet existed mostly on paper. More than four-fifths of Columbia's projected houses, office buildings, parks, pools, bike paths, elementary schools and shopping centers had yet to be built; and the millennium of racial and economic harmony that Columbia promised to birth in its theoretical streets and cul-de-sacs was as far from parturition as ever." It was in this never-never land of a city-in-the-making that Chabon came of age. "My earliest memories of Columbia are of the Plan," Chabon wrote, indicating the blueprint for the structure and shape of the city. Hanging a copy of this plan, or map of the projected town, on his wall, Chabon took to studying it as closely as he did the map of Walt Disney's new Magic Kingdom, also thumbtacked nearby. "I glanced up at the map at night as I lay in bed, reading *The Hobbit* or *The Book of Three* or a novel set in Oz. And sometimes I would give it a once over before I set out with my black and white friends for a foray into the hinterlands, to the borders of our town and our imaginations. . . . How fortunate I was to be handed, at such an early age, a map to steer by, however provisional."

A second guidance system for young Chabon was the world of comic books. "I was introduced to them pretty early," Chabon told Scott Tobias in an *Onion* interview, "right around the age of six or so, by my father, who had himself been a devoted reader of comics when he was a child." Chabon's paternal grandfather, a typographer in New York, worked in a plant where they printed comic books and would thus bring home loads of the comics to his son, Chabon's father. Repeating this favor, Robert Chabon introduced his own son to the wonders of DC Comics. Chabon remembered, in his interview with Tobias, the "naive, innocent, primary-colored" nature of these comics, "set in a world with very clear distinctions between good and evil." This was the world of Superman, primarily; as he grew older he sought out the "murkier and more ambiguous" world of the heroes found in Marvel comics. However, by the time he was fourteen or fifteen, he had given up the world of comics, science fiction, and fantasy for more adult, literary fiction, "the stuff my parents would recommend to me that they were enjoying," he told Tobias.

Graduating from high school, Chabon attended the University of Pittsburgh where he earned his undergraduate degree, and then attended the University of California—Irvine, ultimately earning a master's degree in creative writing. During his college years, Chabon expanded on his literally encyclopedic reading. The author has noted that as a child he read the dictionary and encyclopedia for fun; later, he adopted a disparate collection of favorite authors, from Thomas Pynchon to Herman Melville. Writing on his Web site, Chabon lists the writers and works that changed his life, including Jorge Luis Borges and his *Labyrinths,* Gabriel Garcia Marquez and his *Love in the Time of Cholera,* John Cheever's collected stories, Edith Wharton's *The Age of Innocence,* Vladimir Nabokov's *Lolita* and *Pale Fire,* Robert Stone's *Children of the Light,* and F. Scott Fitzgerald's *The Great Gatsby,* among fiction works, and nonfiction works such as Robert Graves's *The White Goddess* and Jan Morris's *Among the Cities.* All of these writers have influenced Chabon in a style of writing that avoids popular minimalism. With more similarity to Marcel Proust than Ernest Hemingway, Chabon has developed a writing style at once expansive and lyric. As he explained to Bob Goodman in an interview in the on-line magazine *Natterbox,* "I'll start writing a sentence with a general idea. I want to say x about this character, and before I know it, it's 135 words long, and I've broken it up with a few parentheticals and something between dashes, and it just happens that way."

Chabon's first book, *The Mysteries of Pittsburgh,* was actually his master's thesis at the University of California—Irvine. Not only did the novel earn him his degree, but also his instructor thought highly enough of it to send the manuscript to his own agent, who quickly found a publisher for it. Upon the publication of the coming-of-age novel *The Mysteries of Pittsburgh* in 1988, Chabon earned recognition as a promising young fiction writer. The story centers on Art Bechstein, who has recently graduated from college and is about to experience what he perceives as the last summer of his youth.

Chabon followed *The Mysteries of Pittsburgh* with *A Model World, and Other Stories,* which includes tales previously published in the *New Yorker.* Many of the stories in this collection involve unrequited love, and five of the tales—collectively termed "The Lost World"—chart the angst of adolescent Nathan Shapiro as he grows from age ten to sixteen. Among these chronicles is "The Little Knife," showing Nathan agonizing over both his parents' antagonistic relationship and the Washington Senators' imminent demise from major-league baseball. In "More Than Human," another tale focusing on Shapiro, the boy must come to terms with his shattered family after his father leaves home. Another story in *A Model World,* "Blumenthal on the Air," centers on an American narrator who marries an Iranian woman simply to provide her with United States citizenship, then finds himself falling in love with her.

In her *New York Times Book Review* appraisal of *A Model World,* Elizabeth Benedict complained that Chabon sometimes uses his polished style as a means of remaining emotionally aloof from his material. "All too often he keeps his distance," she alleged, but she added that even in tales where Chabon remains reserved, he nonetheless manages to produce "fluent, astonishingly vivid prose." Benedict was particularly impressed with "The Lost World" stories, which she lauded for their "breathtaking" descriptive passages. Other tales in the volume, Benedict noted, recalled *The Mysteries of Pittsburgh.* Such stories, the critic affirmed, "have a kaleidoscopic beauty."

Chabon experienced considerable difficulty in following up the success of *The Mysteries of Pittsburgh* and *A Model World.* While living on a large advance from his publisher, he wrote 1,500 pages of what he intended to be his second novel, *Fountain City.* It was,

Chabon told *Los Angeles Times* contributor Erik Himmelsbach, "sort of a map of my brain," and in it, he attempted to express his love for Paris, architecture, baseball, Florida, and more. After four-and-a-half years and four drafts, however, Chabon admitted to himself that he was never going to be able to craft *Fountain City* into a readable book. He explained to Himmelsbach, "Because I had taken that [advance] money, I felt like I couldn't dump the project, even when it was fairly clear to me that it wasn't working."

The *Fountain City* experience was demoralizing, but Chabon eventually turned it to his advantage. In early 1993, he began work on *Wonder Boys* and in less than a year had finished his second novel. *Wonder Boys* is a fast-paced, comic romp that chronicles one long, disastrous weekend in the life of Grady Tripp, a once-lauded writer now burdened with a 2,000-page manuscript he cannot finish. Joseph P. Kahn of the *Boston Globe* called Tripp "an instant classic . . . part Ginger Man, part Garp and altogether brilliantly original." Chabon confided to Lisa See in *Publishers Weekly* that until his wife read the manuscript of *Wonder Boys* and he heard her laughing as she turned the pages, he had no idea that he was writing a comic novel. "To me, Grady has a wry tone, but I felt sad writing about him. In a lot of ways, he is a projection of my worst fears of what I was going to become if I kept working on *Fountain City*." He continued: "To me, the book is about the disappointment of getting older and growing up and not measuring up to what you thought, and the world and the people in it not being what you expected. It's about disillusionment and acceptance." *Wonder Boys* was adapted for a movie starring Michael Douglas as the burnt-out writer.

Library Journal reviewer Joanna M. Burkhardt called the stories in Chabon's 1999 collection *Werewolves in Their Youth* "remarkably crafted." "Brief synopses can't begin to convey the rich texture of Chabon's involved tales," added Donna Seaman in *Booklist*. Failed relationships serve as the recurring theme in the collection's nine stories, all set in the Pacific Northwest. The title story is of two eleven-year-old boys whose games turn extreme. In "The Harris Fetko Story," Harris is a football player in a failing football venture. His father, Norm, a coach who groomed his son to be an athlete, is now selling cars, but dreams of a new sport called "Powerball" that will revive his career. Although father and son have not spoken for years, Norm calls on Harris to be his main attraction.

"When faced with difficult family relations, the protagonists in Michael Chabon's new stories, man and boy alike, harden their hearts and draw into their shells," noted Randall Holdridge in the *Tucson Weekly*. "But vulnerability in these male carapaces, a softness in their hearts, yields compassion at moments of crisis. Usually they pay a high cost in self-sacrifice, but they're rewarded by transfiguring new esteem."

Chabon's next tale, *The Amazing Adventures of Kavalier and Clay,* takes readers into the pulp world of the 1930s and 1940s through the experiences of two Jewish cousins. American Sammy Klayman is an opportunistic young fellow with a real knack for plotting pulp fiction, while Josef Kavalier, a Czech who has fled the Nazis, complements this storytelling talent with his own rare, bold drawing style. Together they create a Harry Houdini-like comic character in a series called *The Escapist,* a superhero who battles World War II enemies on the pages of the comic. Quickly, the cartooning duo become a phenomenal success, but Joe continues to be plagued by guilt and grief over the loss of his family. Finally, he leaves Sammy and his lover to join the Navy. Exploring themes from escapist literature to Golems and beyond, Chabon created, during four years of writing, a huge manuscript that he pared down by two hundred pages before publication. The book became the publishing sensation of the 2000 season.

Reviewing the novel in *Commentary,* John Podhoretz noted that it "combines fable, magical realism, boy's adventure storytelling, Horatio Alger, and mordant humor in an exhilarating stew that also attempts something entirely new in the depiction of the European Jewish catastrophe and the guilt suffered by those who succeeded in escaping it." Podhoretz ultimately felt, however, that while *The Amazing Adventures of Kavalier and Clay* was a "wonderful book," it was still, "despite its scope, a small one." Most other critics offered different opinions. *Booklist's* Seaman thought that Chabon was "equally adept at atmosphere, action, dialogue, and cultural commentary," plumbing the "depths of the human heart" and celebrating "the healing properties of escapism . . . with exuberance and wisdom." Writing in the *World and I,* Tom Deignan called *The Amazing Adventures* a "slam-bang accomplishment, dazzling and profound, cerebral yet wonderfully touching," and went on to proclaim, "Chabon has produced a great and very American novel, which feels both intimate and worldly."

Troy Patterson of *Entertainment Weekly* added to the chorus of praise, noting that Chabon's novel is "a long, lyrical one that's exquisitely patterned rather than grandly plotted, composed with detailed scenes, and spotted with some rapturous passages of analysis." Patterson concluded, "It's like a graphic novel inked in words and starring the author himself in the lead role: Wonder Boy." "Chabon has pulled off another great feat," wrote Susannah Meadows in *Newsweek,* while *Time* critic R. Z. Sheppard characterized the novel as one written with "much imagination, verve and affection." Roberts concluded his review in *Insight on the News* by commenting, "With *Amazing Adventures,* Chabon lives up to his early accolades, and takes a soaring leap into the literary stratosphere." Awards committees offered similar response, as *The Amazing Adventures of Kavalier and Clay* was nominated for both the National Book Award and the PEN/Faulkner Award for fiction before it took the Pulitzer Prize for fiction in 2001.

With his 2002 novel, *Summerland,* Chabon extended his literary ambitions to the world of young-adult literature. The inspiration for this book came from a couple of sources. "It originated in part," Chabon explained to a contributor for *Library Journal,* "with the experience of reading to my kids. . . . A big turning point for me was rereading *Charlotte's Web* and just being blown away again by how beautiful that book is." Combined with this was a youthful ambition he had had to write about American folklore in the same manner as C. S. Lewis and J. R. R. Tolkien had used British folklore as "the backdrops for their works."

Chabon was one of several well-known adult writers to turn his hand to children's books in 2002, and for this "complex, wildly ambitious novel," as *Booklist*'s Brian Wilson described the book, Chabon uses baseball as a symbol or metaphor for life. Eleven-year-old Ethan Feld is perhaps the world's worst baseball player, at least the worst in Clam Island, Washington, where he makes his home. But he and best friends tomboy Jennifer T. Rideout, a Native-American pitcher, and Thor Wignutt, are pressed into service one summer by the sports-loving faeries, the ferishers, to save the world. Coyote, the Native-American trickster, is out to create "Ragged Rock," or the destruction of the world. To this end, he kidnaps Ethan's father, who has invented a mysterious substance that is a universal solvent; Coyote plans to dis-

solve the world away. Ethan—whose mother has died of cancer—along with Jennifer, Thor, and the ferishers, set off on a mission to rescue Ethan's father and secure the fate of the universe. The family Saab—held aloft by a blimp—becomes their ship as they sail through various worlds on their rescue mission. These worlds include Winterland, Summerland, the Middling, and the Gleaming. They play baseball in Summerland and are joined by an unlikely cast of characters, including a talking rat, a former ball player from the Negro leagues, and a Sasquatch named Taffy whom they also rescue. In the end, the fate of the world depends on a baseball game between the villains and this bizarre cast of good guys and girls.

Chabon's first venture into children's books was widely reviewed. A contributor for *Publishers Weekly* felt that Chabon "hits a high-flying home run, creating a vivid fantasy where baseball is king." The same critic further commented that the author "unspools an elaborate yarn in a style that frequently crackles with color and surprise." Similarly, Kimberly L. Paone, writing in *School Library Journal,* thought that Chabon's debut foray into juvenile literature "will enchant its audience." Troy Patterson, writing in *Entertainment Weekly,* noted that Chabon's book "is a baseball novel that gives new meaning to the words fantasy league." Yet Patterson also wondered if *Summerland* were really a children's book. "By calling it such," Patterson observed, "Chabon gives himself prosaic license to indulge in open-hearted hokeyness and reflexive nostalgic revelry."

Laura Miller, writing for *Salon.com,* noted that while *Summerland* "is meant for kids, . . . it's just as rangy, eccentric, dreamy, and funky as [Chabon's] books for adults." However, some other reviewers also noted that the contents of the book might go over the heads of young readers. *Booklist*'s Bill Ott felt that even "committed fantasy buffs . . . will have to bring their A-games if they expect to digest this ingredient-rich plot." Robert Lipsyte, writing in the *New York Times Book Review,* felt that "Chabon drops the ball by giving us a nerdy hero who wins a baseball game in a derivative fantasy world." *Horn Book*'s Peter D. Sieruta also mentioned the "diffuse, somewhat baroque plot," but also went on to observe that "much of the prose is beautifully descriptive as Chabon navigates vividly imagined other worlds and offers up some timeless themes." James Sullivan, reviewing the novel in *Book,* likewise wrote, "Certainly young readers will delight in the author's masterful use of imagery, whatever they make of the story." A critic for *Kirkus Reviews* had less guarded praise for the book, however, declaring that "this raucous, exhilarating, joyful, and above all, fun offering displays an enormous respect for the tradition of great fantasies that come before it."

The versatile Chabon might have a sequel to *Summerland* up his creative sleeve, and most definitely intends to expand his award-winning writing into new directions. As Richard Lacayo noted in *Time* magazine, Chabon wants "literary fiction to enjoy the liberties of fantasy genres like science fiction and horror." Chabon told Lacayo, "I'm not going to become a fantasy writer or a writer of science fiction. But I'm going to ignore the conventions of literary fiction as much as I can. And whatever kind of fiction comes out of that, I'm just going to hope I can bring readers along with me."

BIOGRAPHICAL AND CRITICAL SOURCES:

BOOKS

Contemporary Literary Criticism, Vol. 55, Gale (Detroit, MI), 1989.

Dictionary of Literary Biography, Volume 278: *American Novelists since World War II, Seventh Series,* Gale (Detroit, MI), 2003, pp. 81-90.

Newsmakers, Issue 1, Gale (Detroit, MI), 2003.

PERIODICALS

Advocate, December 19, 2000, p. 62.

Atlanta Journal-Constitution, April 2, 1995, p. M12.

Book, November, 2000, James Sullivan, review of *The Amazing Adventures of Kavalier and Clay,* p. 66; September-October, 2002, James Sullivan, review of *Summerland,* p. 73; November-December, 2002, "Best Children's Book," p. 58.

Booklist, December 15, 1998, Donna Seaman, review of *Werewolves in Their Youth,* p. 726; August, 2000, Donna Seaman, review of *The Amazing Adventures of Kavalier and Clay,* p. 2074; August, 2002, Bill Ott, review of *Summerland,* p. 1884; February 1, 2003, Brian Wilson, review of *Summerland* (audiobook), p. 1006.

Boston Globe, May 14, 1995, Joseph P. Kahn, review of *Wonder Boys,* p. 50; May 22, 1995, p. 30.

Chicago Tribune, April 2, 1995, sec. 14, p. 5.

Commentary, June, 2001, John Podhoretz, review of *The Amazing Adventures of Kavalier and Clay,* p. 68; June, 2003, Sam Munson, "Slices of Life," review of *McSweeney's Mammoth Treasury of Thrilling Tales,* p. 67.

Entertainment Weekly, April 14, 1995, p. 61; September 29, 2000, Troy Patterson, "Comic Genius," p. 123; October 4, 2002, Troy Patterson, "The Natural," p. 146; April 11, 2003, Carina Chocano, "Monster's Ball: Michael Chabon Guest-Edits Dave Eggers' McSweeney's, Producing a Mixed-Bag of Genre Tales," review of *McSweeney's Mammoth Treasury of Thrilling Tales,* p. 80.

Gentlemen's Quarterly, March, 1995, p. 118.

Horn Book, November-December, 2002, Peter D. Sieruta, review of *Summerland,* p. 751.

Insight on the News, February 12, 2001, Rex Roberts, review of *The Amazing Adventures of Kavalier and Clay,* p. 26.

Interview, March, 1988, p. 48.

Kirkus Reviews, November 1, 1998, review of *Werewolves in Their Youth;* September 1, 2002, review of *Summerland,* p. 1305.

Library Journal, January, 1999, Joanna M. Burkhardt, review of *Werewolves in Their Youth,* p. 161; October 15, 2000, p. 100; September 1, 2002, "Ten Books for Fall," pp. 48-52.

Los Angeles Times, June 28, 1988; April 27, 1995, Erik Himmelsbach, "A Life of Wonder and Awe," p. E1; April 17, 2001, p. A16.

Los Angeles Times Book Review, April 17, 1988, Brett Lott, review of *The Mysteries of Pittsburgh,* pp. 1, 11; March 26, 1995, p. 3.

New Republic, June 26, 1995, p. 40.

New Statesman, May 13, 1988, M. George Stevenson, review of *The Mysteries of Pittsburgh,* pp. 34-35.

New Statesman and Society, June 9, 1995, Roz Kaveney, review of *Wonder Boys,* p. 38.

Newsweek, April 10, 1995, pp. 76-77; September 25, 2000, Susannah Meadows, "Golems and Superheroes," p. 69.

New York, April 3, 1988, p. 7; May 2, 1988, p. 30; April 1, 1991, p. 63.

New York Times, March 17, 1995, p. C28; September 21, 2000, p. B10.

New York Times Book Review, April 3, 1988, Alice McDermott, review of *The Mysteries of Pittsburgh,* p. 7; May 26, 1991, Elizabeth Benedict, review of *A Model World, and Other Stories,* p. 7; April 9, 1995, Robert Ward, review of *Wonder Boys,* p. 7;

January 31, 1999, p. 10; September 24, 2000, pp. 8, 9; November 17, 2002, Robert Lipsyte, review of *Summerland*, p. 24.

People Weekly, May 1, 1995, p. 32; June 26, 1995, pp. 63-64; October 14, 2002, Francine Prose, review of *Summerland*, p. 53; December 16, 2002, Galina Espinoza, "Author, Author: She Writes. He Writes. And Both Ayelet Waldman and Michael Chabon Raise the Kids," p. 151.

Publishers Weekly, April 10, 1995, Lisa See, "Michael Chabon: Wonder Boy in Transition," pp. 44-45; November 6, 1995, p. 58; November 23, 1998, review of *Werewolves in Their Youth,* p. 57; August 21, 2000, review of *The Amazing Adventures of Kavalier and Clay,* pp. 44, 45; October 9, 2000, p. 22; June 24, 2002, review of *Summerland,* p. 57; February 24, 2003, review of *McSweeney's Mammoth Treasury of Thrilling Tales,* p. 51.

School Library Journal, Kimberly L. Paone, review of *Summerland,* p. 159.

Time, May 16, 1988, p. 95; April 8, 1991, p. 77; April 10, 1995, John Skow, review of *Wonder Boys,* p. 87; September 25, 2000, R. Z. Sheppard, "Biff! Boom! A Super Novel about the Golden Age of Comics," p. 103; September 23, 2002, Richard Lacayo, "Kids Are Us!," p. 68.

Times Literary Supplement, June 17, 1988, p. 680.

U.S. News and World Report, September 25, 2000, Holly J. Morris, "Smells Like Teen Comics," p. 74.

Village Voice, April 19, 1988, p. 60.

Wall Street Journal, September 22, 2000, p. W13.

Washington Post, June 9, 1995, p. B1.

Washington Post Book World, April 24, 1988, p. 5; April 26, 1991, p. 20; March 19, 1995, p. 3; September 17, 2000, p. X15.

World and I, February, 2001, Tom Deignan, "Playing with Kiddie Dynamite," p. 220.

Writer, August, 2001, p. 15; April, 2002, Kelly Nickell, "The WD Interview: Michael Chabon," pp. 20-21.

ONLINE

Michael Chabon Home Page, http://www.michaelchabon.com/ (August 31, 2003).

Natterbox, http://www.natterbox.com/ (November 22, 2000), Bob Goodman, interview with Chabon.

Onion, http://avclub.theonion.com/ (November 22, 2000), Scott Tobias, interview with Chabon.

Oregon Live, http://www.oregonlive.com/ (February 8, 1999).

Powell's City of Books, http://www.powells.com/ (September 17, 2001), Dave Welch, "Michael Chabon's Amazing Adventures," author interview.

Salon.com, http://www.salon.com/ (February 22, 1999); (October 22, 2002), Laura Miller, "The Lost Adventure of Childhood."

Tucson Weekly, http://www.tucsonweekly.com/ (March 4-10, 1999), Randall Holdridge, review of *Werewolves in Their Youth.**

*   *   *

CHELES, Luciano 1948-

PERSONAL: Born September 7, 1948, in Cairo, Egypt; son of Alberto (a computer engineer) and Agata (di Stefano) Cheles. *Ethnicity:* "White." *Education:* University of Reading, B.A., 1973; University of Wales, certificate in education, 1974; University of Essex, M.Phil., 1980; University of Lancaster, Ph.D., 1990. *Politics:* Labour. *Hobbies and other interests:* Travel, art and design, cinema, classical music, swimming.

ADDRESSES: Office—Department of Italian Studies, University of Poitiers, 86000 Poitiers, France. *E-mail*—cheles@noos.fr.

CAREER: University of Lancaster, Lancaster, England, lecturer, 1978-94, senior lecturer in Italian, beginning 1994; University of Poitiers, Poitiers, France, professor of Italian studies, beginning 1998. Organizer of poster and photographic exhibitions on European propaganda in the twentieth century, 1981—. University of Lyons, visiting professor, 1994-95, 1996, 1997; lecturer on Renaissance art and contemporary propaganda in Italy, France, Germany, and England. Consultant to British Broadcasting Corporation (BBC).

MEMBER: Association for the Study of Modern Italy (member of board of directors, 1992), Society for Italian Studies, Society for Renaissance Studies.

AWARDS, HONORS: Grants from Italian Ministry of Foreign Affairs, 1989, and British Academy, 1990, 1993, 1997; Frontino-Montefeltro Prize, 1992, for *The Studiolo of Urbino: An Iconographic Investigation;* grant from Scouloudi Foundation, 1995.

WRITINGS:

The Studiolo of Urbino: An Iconographic Investigation, Pennsylvania State University Press (University Park, PA), 1986.

(Editor, with Ronald Ferguson and Michalina Vaughan) *Neo-Fascism in Europe,* Longman (New York, NY), 1991, revised edition published as *The Far Right in Western and Eastern Europe,* Longman (New York, NY), 1995.

(Editor, with Lucio Sponza, and contributor) *The Art of Persuasion: Political Communication in Italy from 1945 to the 1900s,* St. Martin's Press (New York, NY), 1999.

Also author of *Grafica utile: l'affiche d'utile publique en Italie.* Contributor to books, including *Atlante de Schifanoia,* edited by Ranieri Varese, Panini (Italy), 1989; and *Letture di storia dell'arte,* edited by Ranieri Varese, Lavoro Editoriale (Italy). Contributor to Italian, French, and German scholarly journals.

SIDELIGHTS: Luciano Cheles once told *CA:* "My two main research areas are Renaissance art and contemporary Italian visual propaganda. I have approached both from the iconographic rather than stylistic standpoint. My main concern has been to investigate the way images are used for manipulative purposes. My book on the *studiolo* of the Ducal Palace of Urbino attempts to show that the room's decorations are a visual panegyric illustrating the political, humanist, and moral aspirations of its dweller and were intended to impress the illustrious visitors to the palace. My research on political posters aims essentially at revealing the visual/verbal rhetoric and subliminal techniques used by the main parties in Italy."

BIOGRAPHICAL AND CRITICAL SOURCES:

PERIODICALS

Historian, spring, 1997, W. Francis Ryan, review of *The Far Right in Western and Eastern Europe,* p. 683.

Times Literary Supplement, June 21, 2002, Peter Burke, review of *The Art of Persuasion: Political Communication in Italy from 1945 to the 1990s,* p. 30.

West European Politics, January, 1998, Noel O'Sullivan, review of *The Far Right in Western and Eastern Europe,* p. 231.*

*   *   *

CLEMENTS, Alan 1948-

PERSONAL: Born Born September 27, 1948, in Warrington, Lancashire, England; son of Frank and Hilda (Webb) Clements; married Susan Mary Northan, June 26, 1971. *Education:* University of Sussex, B.Sc. (electronics; with honors), 1971; Loughborough University, Ph.D., 1976. *Politics:* Socialist. *Religion:* Atheist. *Hobbies and other interests:* Flying as a private pilot, travel, photography, science fiction.

ADDRESSES: Home—12 Merrington Ave., Middlesbrough TS5 8RH, England. *Office*—University of Teeside, Borough Rd., Middlesbrough TS1 3BA, England. *E-mail*—alanclements@ntlworld.com.

CAREER: Department of Electronic Engineering, Loughborough University, research fellow, 1974-76, lecturer, 1976-87, reader in computer science, 1987-92, School of Computing and Mathematics, Motorola Professor, 1992—. Technical Institute of Crete, Greece, visiting professor, 1989-90; *Microprocessors and Microsystems,* associate editor, 1986—; Manchester Metropolitan University, Manchester, England, external examiner for computer science degree, 1990-94; South Bank University, London, England, external examiner, 1991-95; International Institute for Computer Studies, Colombo, Sri Lanka, external examiner, 1992-94; University of Massachusetts, Boston, adjunct professor, 1996-97.

MEMBER: British Computer Society, European Commission, Belgium, (committee member, computer language standards, 1982-84), Microprocessors and Microsystems Design, (member, editorial board, 1988—), IEEE Computer Society (publications board member, 1997—; member of ACM [board of governors], 2001—; chair of international design competition, 2001).

AWARDS, HONORS: National teaching fellowship (United Kingdom), 2002; IEEE Computer Society Undergraduate Teacher of the Year Award, 2002.

WRITINGS:

Microcomputer Design and Construction: Building Your Own System with the Motorola 6800, Prentice-Hall International (London, England), 1982.

The Principles of Computer Hardware, Oxford University Press (Oxford, England), 1985, second revised edition, 2000.

Microprocessor Systems Design: 68000 Software, Hardware, and Interfacing, PWS-Kent (Boston, MA), 1987, second revised edition, 1997.

Microprocessor Interfacing and the 68000: Peripherals and Systems, Wiley (Chichester, England), 1989.

(Editor) *68000 Sourcebook,* McGraw-Hill (London, England), 1990.

(Editor) *Microprocessor Support Chip Sourcebook,* McGraw-Hill (London, England), 1991.

(Editor) *Analog Interface and the DSP Sourcebook,* McGraw-Hill (London, England), 1993.

68000 Family Assemblage Language, PWS Publishing Co. (Boston, MA), 1994.

Author of video script for series *Microprocessor Design,* 1990.

SIDELIGHTS: Alan Clements's contributions to microprocessor design and systems analysis have been significant, especially because they help computer aficionados understand the Motorola 6800 and 68000 series. His first book, *Microcomputer Design and Construction: Building Your Own System with the Motorola 6800,* is aimed at computer-building professionals and graduate students. Although written with the Motorola 6800 in mind, the book applies equally well to other microprocessors. Clements's approach in his book is to take on each component of the microprocessor system one by one, and then to analyze combined components built into a system. The book contends with a wide variety of related topics, including input/output techniques, data bus, memories, system clock circuit, software needs, and multiprocessor systems. In his review of *Microcomputer Design and Construction* for *Science Books and Films,* Ram S. Khare wrote that "Clements succeeds in . . . explain[ing] how to build a microprocessor system."

In 1985 Clements published *The Principles of Computer Hardware,* a work aimed at college students studying computer science or electrical engineering.

The book focuses on such topics as computer arithmetic, logic elements and Boolean algebra, computer memory, computer communications, and the central processing unit. A reviewer for *New Technical Books* thought the text might also be useful to "general readers who want to learn how computers operate."

Microprocessor Interfacing and the 68000: Peripherals and Systems, published in 1989, examines the microprocessor, according to a *New Technical Books* critic, from the standpoint of "peripherals that are connected to it." Topic areas include the modern microcomputer, serial input/output, analog input/output, the real-time clock, the disk drive and its interface, and multiprocessor systems. This book is aimed at students of computer technology or electronic engineers.

Clements told *CA:* "I see my role as an academic author who takes material produced by researchers and presents it in a form that can be assimilated by my students. My goal is to take topics that are traditionally regarded as difficult by students and explain them clearly. Over the past year or so I have been active in the development of the computer architecture curriculum and have attempted to make it more relevant to computer science generally.

"Because my spelling was—and is—rather poor, my school teachers were rather dismissive of my writing. One English teacher said 'Clements, if you ever use a word longer than the indefinite article, look it up in a dictionary.' When I write I sometimes feel that I am doing my best to prove my teachers wrong.

"The main reason that I write is because I am doing something useful and have an effect on those who read my books. When I was involved in pure research, I received little feedback; I was an expert in a topic that I could discuss with very few people. Once I started writing, I received far more feedback from the professors who adopted my books and from the students who used them. I felt that people liked what I was doing and appreciated my efforts. Writing gave me a sense of achievement."

BIOGRAPHICAL AND CRITICAL SOURCES:

PERIODICALS

New Technical Books, November, 1986, p. 643; March-April, 1990, p. 621.
Science Books and Films, May-June, 1983, p. 266.

CLEMENTS, Marcelle 1948-

PERSONAL: Born February 17, 1948, in Paris, France; brought to the United States, 1958; naturalized citizen, 1963; daughter of Leon and Chaja Ruchla (Hechtman) Kleinwecksler; married John Clements, 1968 (divorced, 1972); children: one son. *Education:* Bard College, B.A. (music), 1969.

ADDRESSES: Home—New York, NY. *Agent*—Amanda Urban, International Creative Management, 40 West 57th St., New York, NY 10019.

CAREER: Writer. *Paris Metro* (biweekly, bi-cultural newspaper), Paris, France, writer and contributing editor, until 1978. Trustee, Bard College, 1989, and Corporation of Yaddo; fellow, New York Institute for the Humanities, New York University.

MEMBER: PEN, Authors Guild, Authors League of America, National Writers Union.

AWARDS, HONORS: New York University Institute for the Humanities fellowship, 1992.

WRITINGS:

The Dog Is Us and Other Observations (essays), Viking (New York, NY), 1985.
Rock Me (novel), Simon & Schuster (New York, NY), 1988.
The Improvised Woman: Single Women Reinventing Single Life (nonfiction), Norton (New York, NY), 1998.
Midsummer (novel), Harcourt (New York, NY), 2003.

Contributor to periodicals, including *Rolling Stone, New York Times, Washington Post, Ms., Newsday, Vanity Fair, Esquire,* and *Village Voice.*

SIDELIGHTS: Journalist and novelist Marcelle Clements often writes about recent cultural changes in America and about the lives of characters who are entering mid-life. Influenced by such writers as Emile Zola and Honore de Balzac, her novels *Rock Me* and *Midsummer* are character-driven works that convey much of their stories through dialogue. Her nonfiction books, too, explore issues of social and emotional change.

Clements's first book, *The Dog Is Us and Other Observations,* collects articles the author wrote for such publications as *Rolling Stone* and *Village Voice.* In these pieces, she looks at her own generation—the baby boomers—and traces its ideological progression from the 1960s through the 1980s. According to Martin Kirby in *New York Times Book Review,* the "writings move obsessively between [the] Golden Age and the leaden present" to lament what Clements views as a "loss of intensity, purpose and fulfillment." Citing her essay titled "The Rise of the Mutant Elite," Kirby noted that Clements perceives humanity "as being in a perpetual class war, not the Marxist one between the haves and the have-nots but the one between the kind, sensitive people and the others."

In her title article, Clements examines reasons for the decrease in marijuana usage since the sixties and for the increased popularity of anti-depressants and psychotherapy. Gone are the days, she says, when young people used to sit around, stoned, and laugh at the utter ridiculousness of the pet dog. She suggests that the Eighties' focus on pragmatism, career ambitions, and material gains has destroyed one's ability to relax and enjoy life's simple pleasures. "Now that we're in our mid-thirties," she writes, "what often happens when we get high is that we see the dog again, but now the dog is us. And it's not funny." Nancy Wigston, commending *The Dog Is Us* for the Toronto *Globe and Mail,* stated that "nowhere does the distance traveled by a once-committed generation show itself more clearly." Wigston further observed that, as is representative of her generation, Clements tends to be "obsessively self-referential," but that she is also unusually "witty and articulate."

As Clements explained in the introduction to her book, alienation is a central theme in her articles: "The people I'm speaking of are an increasingly alienated minority. I know their alienation because they are my friends, and they are the people I like to write about. I don't really ever feel comfortable, or safe, with the others. The others frighten me, because I know that among them are those who are capable of callousness, of cruelty, and sometimes of atrocity to defend what they believe they belong to or what belongs to them, and those who will commit any act, no matter how ruthless, to be sure to stay on the winning side. I prefer the other side, though it only occasionally wins. In my writing, what I like to do best is to try to convey pictures from this other side." Clements added that she does not consider alienation to be a necessarily depressing subject. "At least, it's from a struggle against the status quo, and therefore, in my view, ultimately an expression of hope."

Clements's first novel, *Rock Me,* can be viewed as a fictional treatment of the themes explored in *The Dog Is Us.* The main character is Casey, a rock star approaching her forties who is feeling the long-term effects of her early, wild lifestyle. Trying to escape from her life, she takes a trip to Hawaii, where she meets former band-mate Michael and his girlfriend, Leslie. Both Michael and Casie find it difficult to escape their demons while in each other's presence, and Casie, who has always had a difficult time with personal relationships, finds herself lusting after the unavailable Michael. Clements "writes convincingly about the rock and roll subculture's narcissism and offers provocative meditations on love, jealousy and the differences between the '60s and the '80s," concluded Kim Hubbard in a *People Weekly* review, calling the novel "a very promising debut."

Although Clements planned on following *Rock Me* with another novel right away, her next published work was *The Improvised Woman: Single Women Reinventing Single Life,* in which she interviewed over one hundred single women to discuss their views about what it is like to be an unmarried woman in modern America. Her subjects ranged in age from their twenties to their nineties, and included single, widowed, divorced, and never-married women. Some had children; others did not. As Claire Rayner noted in her *New Statesman* review, the book shows that, compared to earlier generations, single women today are more likely to be unmarried by choice rather than widowhood. But while Rayner hoped that Clements would argue for an optimistic message that women no longer need men in their lives in order to feel fulfilled, instead the reviewer felt "disappointed" by the book's disorganization, which in her view conveys no strong single thesis. "It is messy, disorganized and shapeless," Rayner attested, adding that "the text is sprinkled with comments that aspire towards significance but are actually banal." Other reviewers of *The Improvised Woman,* however, found the book enlightening. A *Publishers*

Weekly contributor, noting that Clements is a single mother herself, called the book a "well-grounded, seven-year study, which is sure to be much quoted." *Library Journal* contributor Elizabeth Goeters said the book is useful because it illustrates how attitudes have changed about marriage: "This is one of the most significant cultural changes of the twentieth century." And Mary Carroll asserted in *Booklist* that *The Improvised Woman* is a "lively, provocative analysis of a genuinely new social phenomenon."

Clements admitted to Robert Birnbaum in *Identity Theory* that she tackled *The Improvised Woman,* which took seven years of research and writing to complete, largely because she needed the income while she worked on her second novel. "I needed to support myself . . . but in the end, even financially, it was actually disastrous for me. I balked at writing *The Improvised Woman,* so then I took a long time [writing it]. I spent the advance and I had to do journalism to support the other book. It was insane, and I would never do that again."

Clements's next novel, *Midsummer,* focuses on some of the same themes in *The Improvised Woman.* The book, according to Clements in a *Harcourt Books* online interview, aims "to catch or evoke the moment of the year and also in people's lives when everything seems at its most ripe and beautiful, just before it all turns." *Midsummer* involves six friends from New York City who are all single and, for the most part, in their forties. They converge at a temporarily vacated mansion on the Hudson River for the summer at the invitation of Susie Diamond, a clothing designer who has rented the estate. What follows is an unhurried examination of the lives of these people and their relationships, which are seasoned with sexual tensions that are rarely played out. The characters include Ron, who works as a comedian; Dodge, who is Susie's former lover; Kay, who has suffered a miscarriage; Elise, an artist who has struggled but whose time in the sun may be arriving; and Susie's twenty-three-year-old son, Billy. All the characters are rather self-involved, some to the point of near insanity, which leads the plot toward a startling conclusion.

Birnbaum commented that *Midsummer* has the feel of "a New York book," to which Clements replied: "I think what you say is true, but it also can be thought of as a very French book translated into English. There is a lot of surface language play . . . [and] you can understand the references or just watch the play. I don't think you need to understand all the references. It's a surface and what's going on underneath the dialogue, which I hope emanates from it very clearly, is more important than the specifics. These are characters who obviously are much invested in understanding what is going on in the culture. Even though that inevitably leads them to see that they understand nothing." She continued, "Sometimes I have the fantasy of writing what would be like the Balzac books or the Zola books, a series of interlocking novels about New York and in fact there is a character from my first novel who makes an appearance in this novel, though it's not indicated. They are very much New Yorkers and part of what I was interested in describing was New York."

While some critics appreciated Clements's leisurely stroll amongst these New Yorkers, others could not find a point to the whole exercise. "After a while all this self-pitying navel-gazing by a bunch of self-absorbed New Yorkers gets wearying," complained Wilda Williams in *Library Journal*. Other reviewers, however, enjoyed the ride. Vina Passaro, writing in *O, the Oprah Magazine*, described *Midsummer* as a "fine, graceful" novel, while *Booklist* contributor Deborah Donovan proclaimed that the author "has brilliantly transported a Gatsby-like cast into the twenty-first century." The comment by Donovan was quite observant, as Clements herself told the interviewer for *Harcourt Books*, "When I first began work on this book, I re-read *The Great Gatsby* and originally I had in mind a first-person novel in which the narrator would be describing another, seemingly more attractive person."

As a writer of the baby boomer generation, Clements has continued to be interested in the lives of people in their middle age in her fiction, and of the cultural changes people are living through in her nonfiction. As she told Birnbaum, "I still feel that people now in their forties and fifties and sixties still have an interesting perspective."

BIOGRAPHICAL AND CRITICAL SOURCES:

BOOKS

Clements, Marcelle, *The Dog Is Us and Other Observations*, Viking, (New York, NY), 1985.

PERIODICALS

Booklist, June 1, 1998, Mary Carroll, review of *The Improvised Woman: Single Women Reinventing Single Life,* p. 1681; April 15, 2003, Deborah Donovan, review of *Midsummer,* p. 1447.

Christian Science Monitor, July 22, 1998, Kirsten A. Conover, "Savoring the Single Life," p. B3.

Entertainment Weekly, July 17, 1998, review of *The Improvised Woman,* p. 78.

Globe & Mail (Toronto, Ontario, Canada), April 26, 1986.

Guardian (London, England), February 12, 2000, Vera Rule, review of *The Improvised Woman,* p. 11.

Library Journal, January, 1989, Rosellen Brewer, review of *Rock Me,* p. 100; May 15, 1998, Elizabeth Goeters, review of *The Improvised Woman,* p. 100; June 1, 2003, Wilda Williams, review of *Midsummer,* p. 164.

New Statesman, May 3, 1999, Claire Rayner, review of *The Improvised Woman,* p. 55.

Newsweek, June 22, 1998, Laura Shapiro, "Table for One, Please," p. 81.

New Yorker, August 3, 1998, Daphne Merkin, review of *The Improvised Woman,* p. 74.

New York Times Book Review, March 23, 1986; February 26, 1989, Margot Mifflin, review of *Rock Me,* p. 34; July 26, 1998, Lynn Karpen, review of *The Improvised Woman,* p. 18.

O, the Oprah Magazine, May, 2003, Vina Passaro, "A Midsummer Night's Novel," p. 188.

People Weekly, March 6, 1989, Kim Hubbard, review of *Rock Me,* p. 20.

Publishers Weekly, April 6, 1998, review of *The Improvised Woman,* p. 63.

Rolling Stone, April 20, 1989, review of *Rock Me,* p. 26.

Washington Post, January 25, 1987.

Women's Review of Books, September, 1998, Deborah Solomon Reid, review of *The Improvised Woman,* p. 15.

ONLINE

Harcourt Books Web site, http://www.harcourtbooks.com/ (October 22, 2003), "Interview with Marcelle Clements."

Identity Theory, http://www.identitytheory.com/ (September 9, 2003), Robert Birnbaum, "Marcelle Clements: Author of *Midsummer* Talks with Robert Birnbaum."

Salon.com, http://www.salon.com/books (August 19, 1998), Carolyn McConnell, review of *The Improvised Woman,.**

*   *   *

CLIFTON, (Thelma) Lucille 1936-

PERSONAL: Born June 27, 1936, in Depew, NY; daughter of Samuel Louis, Sr. (a laborer) and Thelma (a laborer; maiden name, Moore) Sayles; married Fred James Clifton (an educator, writer, and artist), May 10, 1958 (died, November 10, 1984); children: Sidney, Fredrica, Channing, Gillian, Graham, Alexia. *Education:* Attended Howard University, 1953-55, and Fredonia State Teachers College (now State University of New York College—Fredonia), 1955.

ADDRESSES: Office—Division of Arts and Letters, St. Mary's College of Maryland, Montgomery Hall #126, St. Mary's City, MD 20686. *Agent*—Marilyn Marlow, Curtis Brown Ltd., 10 Astor Pl., New York, NY 10003. *E-mail*—lclifton@.smcm.edu.

Lucille Clifton

CAREER: New York State Division of Employment, Buffalo, claims clerk, 1958-60; U.S. Office of Education, Washington, DC, literature assistant for Central Atlantic Regional Educational Laboratory, 1969-71; Coppin State College, Baltimore, MD, poet-in-residence, 1974-79; Jirry Moore Visiting Writer, George Washington University, 1982-83; University of California, Santa Cruz, professor of literature and creative writing, 1985-89; St. Mary's College of Maryland, St. Mary's City, MD, Distinguished Professor of Literature, 1989-91, Distinguished Professor of Humanities, 1991—; Hilda C. Landers Chair in the Liberal Arts; Duke University, Durham, NC, Blackburn Professor of Creative Writing; visiting writer, Columbia University School of the Arts, 1995-99; visiting teacher, Memphis State University; visiting poet, St. Edward's University, School of Humanities (Austin, TX), 2000. Woodrow Wilson and Lila Wallace/*Readers Digest* visiting fellowship to Fisk University, Alma College, Albright College, Davidson College, and others. Trustee, Enoch Pratt Free Library, Baltimore. Has made television appearances, including *The Language of Life, The Today Show, Sunday Morning with Charles Kuralt,* Bill Moyers' series, *The Power of the Word,* and *Nightline.*

MEMBER: International PEN, Academy of American Poets (chancellor, 1999—), Poetry Society of America, American Cancer Society, Global Forum Arts Committee, Authors Guild, Authors League of America.

AWARDS, HONORS: Discovery Award, New York YW-YMHA Poetry Center, 1969; *Good Times: Poems* was cited as one of the year's ten best books by the *New York Times,* 1969; Creative Writing Fellowships and awards, National Endowment for the Arts, 1969, 1970, 1972, and 1973; Poet Laureate of the State of Maryland, 1974-85; Juniper Prize, University of Massachusetts Press, 1980; Pulitzer Prize nominations for poetry, 1980, 1987, 1988, and 1991; Coretta Scott King Award, American Library Association, 1984, for *Everett Anderson's Goodbye;* Shestack Poetry Prize, American Poetry Review, 1988; Charity Randall Citation, International Poetry Forum, 1991; Shelley Memorial Prize, Poetry Society of America, 1992; named a "Maryland Living Treasure" and inducted into the Maryland Women's Hall of Fame, 1993; Andrew White Medal, Loyola College of Baltimore, 1993; Cannan Literary Award for Poetry, 1996;

National Book Award nomination, 1996, and Lannan Literary Award for poetry, 1997, both for *The Terrible Stories;* inducted into National Literature Hall of Fame for African American Writers, 1998; Lenore Marshal Poetry Prize and *Los Angeles Times* poetry award, both 1998; Phi Beta Kappa, 1998; Lila Wallace/ *Readers Digest* Award, 1999; National Book Award for poetry, 1999, for *Blessing the Boats: New and Selected Poems, 1988-2000;* Emmy Award, American Academy of Television Arts and Sciences; Fellow, American Academy of Arts and Sciences, 1999; selected as a Literary Lion, New York Public Library; recipient of honorary degrees from Colby College, University of Maryland, Towson State University, Washington College, and Albright College.

WRITINGS:

POETRY

Good Times, Random House (New York, NY), 1969.

Good News about the Earth: New Poems, Random House (New York, NY), 1972.

An Ordinary Woman, Random House (New York, NY), 1974.

Two-Headed Woman, University of Massachusetts Press (Amherst, MA), 1980.

Good Woman: Poems and a Memoir, 1969-1980, BOA Editions (Brockport, NY), 1987.

Next: New Poems, BOA Editions (Brockport, NY), 1987.

Ten Oxherding Pictures, Moving Parts Press (Santa Cruz, CA), 1988.

Quilting: Poems 1987-1990, BOA Editions (Brockport, NY), 1991.

The Book of Light, Copper Canyon Press (Port Townsend, WA), 1993.

The Terrible Stories, BOA Editions (Brockport, NY), 1998.

Blessing the Boats: New and Selected Poems, 1988-2000, BOA Editions (Brockport, NY), 2000.

Mercy: Poems, BOA Editions (Brockport, NY), 2004.

FOR CHILDREN

The Black BCs (alphabet poems), illustrations by Don Miller, Dutton (New York, NY), 1970.

Good, Says Jerome, illustrations by Stephanie Douglas, Dutton (New York, NY), 1973.

All Us Come 'cross the Water, pictures by John Steptoe, Holt (New York, NY), 1973.

Don't You Remember?, illustrations by Evaline Ness, Dutton (New York, NY), 1973.

The Boy Who Didn't Believe in Spring, pictures by Brinton Turkle, Dutton (New York, NY), 1973.

The Times They Used to Be, illustrations by Susan Jeschke, Holt (New York, NY), 1974.

My Brother Fine with Me, illustrations by Moneta Barnett, Holt (New York, NY), 1975.

Three Wishes, illustrations by Stephanie Douglas, Viking (New York, NY), 1976, illustrations by Michael Hays, Delacorte, 1992.

Amifika, illustrations by Thomas DiGrazia, Dutton (New York, NY), 1977.

The Lucky Stone, illustrations by Dale Payson, Delacorte (New York, NY), 1979, Yearling Books Random House (New York, NY), 1986.

My Friend Jacob, illustrations by Thomas DiGrazia, Dutton (New York, NY), 1980.

Sonora Beautiful, illustrations by Michael Garland, Dutton (New York, NY), 1981.

Dear Creator: A Week of Poems for Young People and Their Teachers, illustrations by Gail Gordon Carter, Doubleday (Garden City, NY), 1997.

Clifton's works have been translated into Spanish.

"EVERETT ANDERSON" SERIES; FOR CHILDREN

Some of the Days of Everett Anderson, illustrations by Evaline Ness, Holt (New York, NY), 1970.

Everett Anderson's Christmas Coming, illustrations by Evaline Ness, Holt (New York, NY), 1971, illustrations by Jan Spivey Gilchrist, Holt (New York, NY), 1991.

Everett Anderson's Year, illustrations by Ann Grifalconi, Holt (New York, NY), 1974.

Everett Anderson's Friend, illustrations by Ann Grifalconi, Holt (New York, NY), 1976.

Everett Anderson's 1 2 3, illustrations by Ann Grifalconi, Holt (New York, NY), 1977.

Everett Anderson's Nine Month Long, illustrations by Ann Grifalconi, Holt (New York, NY), 1978.

Everett Anderson's Goodbye, illustrations by Ann Grifalconi, Holt (New York, NY), 1983.

One of the Problems of Everett Anderson, illustrations by Ann Grifalconi, Holt (New York, NY), 2001.

OTHER

(Compiler, with Alexander MacGibbon) *Composition: An Approach through Reading,* Harcourt (New York, NY), 1968.

Generations: A Memoir (prose), Random House (New York, NY), 1976.

Lucille Clifton Reading Her Poems with Comment in the Montpelier Room, October 24, 2002 (sound recoring), Archive of Recorded Poetry and Literature, Library of Congress (Washington, DC), 2002.

The Poet and the Poem from the Library of Congress. Lucille Clifton (sound recording), Archive of Recorded Poetry and Literature, Library of Congress (Washington, DC), 2002.

Contributor to *Poetry of the Negro, 1746-1970,* edited by Langston Hughes and Arna Bontemps, Doubleday (New York, NY), 1970; (with Marlo Thomas and others) *Free to Be . . . You and Me,* McGraw-Hill (New York, NY), 1974; *Free to Be a Family,* 1987; Robert Kapilow's *03: This New Immense Unbound World* (printed music), G. Schirmer (New York, NY), 2003; and other anthologies, including *Norton Anthology of Literature by Women, Coming into the Light,* and *Stealing the Language.* Has made numerous additional sound and video recordings of poetry readings. Contributor of poetry to the *New York Times.* Contributor of fiction to *Negro Digest, Redbook, House and Garden,* and *Atlantic.* Contributor of nonfiction to *Ms.* and *Essence.*

SIDELIGHTS: Poet Lucille Clifton "began composing and writing stories at an early age and has been much encouraged by an ever-growing reading audience and a fine critical reputation," wrote Wallace R. Peppers in a *Dictionary of Literary Biography.* "In many ways her themes are traditional: she writes of her family because she is greatly interested in making sense of their lives and relationships; she writes of adversity and success in the ghetto community; and she writes of her role as a poet."

Clifton's work emphasizes endurance and strength through adversity. Ronald Baughman suggested in his *Dictionary of Literary Biography* essay that Clifton's "pride in being black and in being a woman helps her transform difficult circumstances into a qualified affirmation about the black urban world she portrays." A *Publishers Weekly* critic noted that Clifton "redeems the human spirit from its dark moments. She is among our most trustworthy and gifted poets." Clifton is a Distinguished Professor of Humanities at St. Mary's College of Maryland and a Chancellor of the Academy of American Poets. In addition to her numerous poetry collections, her work is included in many anthologies, and she has written many children's books. Not surprising, Clifton has won numerous literary awards and was the first author to have two books of poetry chosen as finalists for the Pulitzer Prize, *Good Woman: Poems and a Memoir, 1969-1980* and *Next: New Poems.* She served as the state of Maryland's poet laureate from 1974 until 1985, and won the prestigious National Book Award in 1999 for *Blessing the Boats: New and Selected Poems, 1988-2000.* Her poetry has been translated into Norwegian, Spanish, French, Japanese, Hebrew, and other languages.

Clifton is noted for saying much with few words. In a *Christian Century* review of Clifton's work, Peggy Rosenthal noted, "The first thing that strikes us about Lucille Clifton's poetry is what is missing: capitalization, punctuation, long and plentiful lines. We see a poetry so pared down that its spaces take on substance, become a shaping presence as much as the words themselves. . . . She has chosen a minimalist mode that clears out human society's clutter, the mess we've made by identifying ourselves in contending genders, ethnicities, nations. Lightly, as if biting her tongue, with a wise smile, she shows us a radically egalitarian world where no one or no capitalized word lords it over others." In an *American Poetry Review* article about Clifton's work, Robin Becker commented on Clifton's lean style. "Clifton's poetics of understatement—no capitalization, few strong stresses per line, many poems totaling fewer than twenty lines, the sharp rhetorical question—includes the essential only."

Clifton's first volume of poetry, *Good Times,* which was cited by the *New York Times* as one of 1969's ten best books, was described by Peppers as a "varied collection of character sketches written with third person narrative voices." Baughman noted that the poems "attain power not only through their subject matter but also through their careful techniques; among Clifton's most successful poetic devices . . . are the precise evocative images that give substance to her rhetorical statements and a frequent duality of vision that lends complexity to her portraits of place and character." Calling the book's title "ironic," Baughman stated: "Although the urban ghetto can, through its many hardships, create figures who are tough enough to survive and triumph, the overriding concern of this book is with the horrors of the location, with the human carnage that results from such problems as poverty, unemployment, substandard housing, and inadequate education."

In Clifton's second volume of poetry, *Good News about the Earth: New Poems*, "the elusive good times seem more attainable," remarked Baughman, who summarized the three sections into which the book is divided: the first section "focuses on the sterility and destruction of 'white ways,' newly perceived through the social upheavals of the early 1970s"; the second section "presents a series of homages to black leaders of the late 1960s and early 1970s"; and the third section "deals with biblical characters powerfully rendered in terms of the black experience." Harriet Jackson Scarupa noted in *Ms.* that after having read what Clifton says about blackness and black pride, some critics "have concluded that Clifton hates whites. [Clifton] considers this a misreading. When she equates whiteness with death, blackness with life, she says: 'What I'm talking about is a certain kind of white arrogance—and not all white people have it— that is not good. I think airs of superiority are very dangerous. I believe in justice. I try not to be about hatred.'" Writing in *Poetry,* Ralph J. Mills, Jr., said that Clifton's poetic scope transcends the black experience "to embrace the entire world, human and non-human, in the deep affirmation she makes in the teeth of negative evidence."

An Ordinary Woman, Clifton's third collection of poems, "abandons many of the broad racial issues examined in the two preceding books and focuses instead on the narrower but equally complex issues of the writer's roles as woman and poet," according to Baughman. Peppers likewise commented that "the poems take as their theme a historical, social, and spiritual assessment of the current generation in the genealogical line" of Clifton's great-great-grandmother, who had been taken from her home in Dahomey, West Africa, and brought to America in slavery in 1830. Peppers noted that by taking an ordinary experience and personalizing it, "Clifton has elevated the experience into a public confession" which may be shared, and "it is this shared sense of situation, an easy identification between speaker and reader, that heightens the notion of ordinariness and gives . . . the collection an added dimension." Helen Vendler declared in the *New York Times Book Review* that Clifton "recalls for us those bare places we have all waited as 'ordinary women,' with no choices but yes or no, no art, no grace, no words, no reprieve." "Written in

the same ironic, yet cautiously optimistic spirit as her earlier published work," observed Peppers, *An Ordinary Woman* is "lively, full of vigor, passion, and an all-consuming honesty."

In *Generations: A Memoir,* "it is as if [Clifton] were showing us a cherished family album and telling us the story about each person which seemed to sum him or her up best," described a *New Yorker* contributor. Calling the book an "eloquent eulogy of [Clifton's] parents," Reynolds Price wrote in the *New York Times Book Review* that, "as with most elegists, her purpose is perpetuation and celebration, not judgment. There is no attempt to see either parent whole; no attempt at the recovery of history not witnessed by or told to the author. There is no sustained chronological narrative. Instead, clusters of brief anecdotes gather round two poles, the deaths of father and mother." Price believed that *Generations* stands "worthily" among the other modern elegies that assert that "we may survive, some lively few, if we've troubled to *be* alive and loved." However, a contributor to *Virginia Quarterly Review* thought that the book is "more than an elegy or a personal memoir. It is an attempt on the part of one woman to retrieve, and lyrically to celebrate, her Afro-American heritage."

In a review of Clifton's work for *Southern Literary Journal,* Hilary Holladay remarked about how Clifton addresses her "ancestral South." "Although she does not have the intimate knowledge of the region that her father and mother had, her feelings about the region are nevertheless complicated and passionate. The South we encounter in her poems is a conceit enabling her to address two subjects, the first concrete and the second abstract, that have been equally important to her poetry for many years: 1) slavery and its seemingly endless impact on American life, and 2) the all-powerful role of language in determining our knowledge of ourselves and others. In her poems with southern settings, we don't see much of the region's landscape, but we do see how language . . . can either obliterate or validate one's identity."

Clifton's books for children are designed to help them understand their world. *My Friend Jacob,* for instance, is a story "in which a black child speaks with affection and patience of his friendship with a white adolescent neighbor . . . who is retarded," observed Zena Sutherland in the *Bulletin of the Center for Children's Books.* "Jacob is Sam's 'very very best friend' and all of his best qualities are appreciated by Sam, just as all of his limitations are accepted. . . . It is strong in the simplicity and warmth with which a handicapped person is loved rather than pitied, enjoyed rather than tolerated." Critics felt that Clifton's characters and their relationships are accurately and positively drawn in *My Friend Jacob*. Ismat Abdal-Haqq noted in *Interracial Books for Children Bulletin* that "the two boys have a strong relationship filled with trust and affection. The author depicts this relationship and their everyday adventures in a way that is unmarred by the mawkish sentimentality that often characterizes tales of the mentally disabled." And a contributor to *Reading Teacher* stated that, "in a matter-of-fact, low-keyed style, we discover how [Sam and Jacob] help one another grow and understand the world."

Clifton's children's books also facilitate an understanding of black heritage specifically, which in turn fosters an important link with the past. *All Us Come 'cross the Water*, for example, "in a very straight-forward way . . . shows the relationship of Africa to Blacks in the U.S. without getting into a heavy rap about 'Pan-Africanism,'" stated Judy Richardson in the *Journal of Negro Education*. Richardson added that Clifton "seems able to get inside a little boy's head, and knows how to represent that on paper."

An awareness of one's origins figures also in *The Times They Used to Be*. Called a "short and impeccable vignette—laced with idiom and humor of rural Black folk," by Rosalind K. Goddard in *School Library Journal*, the book was described by Lee A. Daniels in the *Washington Post* as a "story in which a young girl catches her first glimpse of the new technological era in a hardware store window, and learns of death and life." "Most books that awaken adult nostalgia are not as appealing to young readers," maintained Sutherland in the *Bulletin of the Center for Children's Books*, "but this brief story has enough warmth and vitality and humor for any reader."

In addition to quickening an awareness of black heritage, Clifton's books for children frequently include an element of fantasy as well. In *Three Wishes*, for example, a young girl finds a lucky penny on New Year's Day and makes three wishes upon it. Christopher Lehmann-Haupt, in the *New York Times Book Review*, called the book "an urbanized version of the traditional tale in which the first wish reveals the power of the magic object . . . the second wish is a

mistake, and the third undoes the second." Lehmann-Haupt added: "Too few children's books for blacks justify their ethnicity, but this one is a winning blend of black English and bright illustration." *The Lucky Stone*, in which a lucky stone provides good fortune for all of its owners, was described by Ruth K. MacDonald in *School Library Journal* as "Four short stories about four generations of Black women and their dealings with a lucky stone. . . . Clifton uses as a frame device a grandmother telling the history of the stone to her granddaughter; by the end, the granddaughter has inherited the stone herself."

Barbara Walker wrote in *Interracial Books for Children Bulletin* that Clifton "is a gifted poet with the greater gift of being able to write poetry for children." But in a *Language Arts* interview with Rudine Sims, Clifton indicated that she does not think of it as poetry especially for children. "It seems to me that if you write poetry for children, you have to keep too many things in mind other than the poem. So I'm just writing a poem," she said.

Some of the Days of Everett Anderson is a book of nine poems, about which Marjorie Lewis observed in *School Library Journal*: "Some of the days of six-year-old 'ebony Everett Anderson' are happy; some lonely—but all of them are special, reflecting the author's own pride in being black." In the *New York Times Book Review*, Hoyt W. Fuller thought that Clifton has "a profoundly simple way of saying all that is important to say, and we know that the struggle is worth it, that the all-important battle of image is being won, and that the future of all those beautiful black children out there need not be twisted and broken." *Everett Anderson's Christmas Coming* concerns Christmas preparations in which "each of the five days before Everett's Christmas is described by a verse," observed Anita Silvey in *Horn Book*. Silvey added: "The overall richness of Everett's experiences dominates the text." Jane O'Reilly suggested in the *New York Times Book Review* that "Everett Anderson, black and boyish, is glimpsed, rather than explained through poems about him." *Everett Anderson's Year* celebrates "a year in the life of a city child . . . in appealing verses," according to Beryl Robinson in *Horn Book*. Robinson felt that "mischief, fun, gaiety, and poignancy are a part of his days as the year progresses. The portrayals of child and mother are lively and solid, executed with both strength and tenderness."

Language is important in Clifton's writing. In answer to Sims's question about the presence of both black and white children in her work, Clifton responded specifically about *Sonora Beautiful,* which is about the insecurities and dissatisfaction of an adolescent girl and which has only white characters: "In this book, I *heard* the characters as white. I have a tendency to *hear* the language of the characters, and then I know something about who the people are." However, regarding objections to the black vernacular she often uses, Clifton told Sims: "I do not write out of weakness. That is to say, I do not write the language I write because I don't know any other. . . . But I have a certain integrity about my art, and in *my* art you have to be honest and you have to have people talking the way they really talk. So all of my books are not in the same language."

In her interview with Sims, she was asked whether or not she feels any special pressures or special opportunities as a black author. Clifton responded: "I do feel a responsibility. . . . First, I'm going to write books that tend to celebrate life. I'm about that. And I wish to have children see people like themselves in books. . . . I also take seriously the responsibility of not lying. . . . I'm not going to say that life is wretched if circumstance is wretched, because that's not true. So I take that responsibility, but it's a responsibility to the truth, and to my art as much as anything. I owe everybody that. . . . It's the truth as I see it, and that's what my responsibility is."

In Clifton's 1991 title, *Quilting: Poems 1987-1990,* the author uses a quilt as a poetic metaphor for life. Each poem is a story, bound together through the chronicles of history and figuratively sewn with the thread of experience. The result is, as Roger Mitchell in *American Book Review* described it, a quilt "made by and for people." Each section of the book is divided by a conventional quilt design name such as "Eight-pointed Star" and "Tree of Life," which provides a framework within which Clifton crafts her poetic quilt. Clifton's main focus is on women's history; however, according to Mitchell, her poetry has a far broader range: "Her heroes include nameless slaves buried on old plantations, Hector Peterson (the first child killed in the Soweto riot), Fannie Lou Hamer (founder of the Mississippi Peace and Freedom Party), Nelson and Winnie Mandela, W. E. B. DuBois, Huey P. Newton, and many other people who gave their lives to [free] black people from slavery and prejudice."

Enthusiasts of *Quilting* included critic Bruce Bennett in the *New York Times Book Review,* who praised Clif-

ton as a "passionate, mercurial writer, by turns angry, prophetic, compassionate, shrewd, sensuous, vulnerable and funny. . . . The movement and effect of the whole book communicate the sense of a journey through which the poet achieves an understanding of something new." Pat Monaghan, in *Booklist,* admired Clifton's "terse, uncomplicated" verse, and judged the poet "a fierce and original voice in American letters." Mitchell found energy and hope in her poems, referring to them as "visionary." He concluded that they are "the poems of a strong woman, strong enough to . . . look the impending crises of our time in the eye, as well as our customary limitations, and go ahead and hope anyway."

Clifton's 1993 poetry collection, *The Book of Light,* examines "life through light in its various manifestations," commented Andrea Lockett in a *Belles Lettres* review of the collection. Among the poetic subjects of the collection are bigotry and intolerance, epitomized by a poem about controversial U.S. Senator Jesse Helms; destruction, including a poem about the tragic bombing by police of a MOVE compound in Philadelphia in 1985; religion, characterized by a sequence of poems featuring a dialogue between God and the devil; and mythology, rendered by poems about figures such as Atlas and Superman. "If this poet's art has deepened since . . . *Good Times,* it's in an increased capacity for quiet delicacy and fresh generalization," remarked *Poetry* contributor Calvin Bedient. Bedient criticized the poems in the collection that take an overtly political tone, taking issue with "Clifton's politics of championing difference—except, of course, where the difference opposes her politics." However, Bedient commended the more personal poems in *The Book of Light,* declaring that when Clifton writes without "anger and sentimentality, she writes at her remarkable best." Lockett concluded that the collection is "a gift of joy, a truly illuminated manuscript by a writer whose powers have been visited by grace."

Political messages are present in other Clifton works, including "Jasper Texas 1998," about an African-American man who was dragged to death from the back of a truck by three white men in Texas, and "Stop," which calls on people to take action. Clifton recited and discussed these poems at a Folger Shakespear Library reading, which Adrienne Ammerman reviewed for *Off Our Backs.* Ammerman noted, as did Sims, that Clifton has a desire to be truthful, "even if it's not currently the 'correct' thing to do." Responding to a critic who was disappointed that Clifton "played the race card," the writer remarked, "It's not a game and I'm not playing." "Stop" is about Nkosi Johnson, the noted twelve-year-old South African victim of AIDS, in which Clifton "calls for people to stop what they are doing, to stop what they are not doing, to pay attention, and to act." Ammermen noted that Clifton takes you to that "sticky place where we are scared to face an exhausting reality, but where we know we can't reconcile ourselves to ignorance." Citing great respect for Clifton's work, the reviewer indicated that the poet "defies the mores of political correctness and is candid about her feelings on race in many of her poems. By putting voice to her experiences, Clifton creates a public space within which politics may take place. By putting voice to the experience of others, she exercises her verbal privilege as a talented writer by enabling others to weld their personal lives with the lives of those different from themselves."

The Terrible Stories and *Blessing the Boats: New and Selected Poems, 1988-2000* shed light upon women's survival skills in the face of ill health, family upheaval, and historic tragedy. *Blessing the Boats* is a compilation of four other Clifton books, plus nineteen new poems, which, Becker noted in her review for *American Poetry Review,* "shows readers how the poet's themes and formal structures develop over time." Among the pieces collected in these volumes are several about the author's breast cancer, but she also deals with juvenile violence, child abuse, biblical characters, dreams, the legacy of slavery, and a shaman-like empathy with animals as varied as foxes, squirrels, and crabs. She also speaks in a number of voices, as noted by Becker, including "angel, Eve, Lazarus, Leda, Lot's Wife, Lucifer, among others . . . as she probes the narratives that undergird western civilization and forges new ones."

In a *Booklist* review of *Blessing the Boats,* Donna Seaman found the poems "lean, agile, and accurate, [with] a beauty in their directness and efficiency." A *Publishers Weekly* reviewer likewise concluded that the collection "distills a distinctive American voice, one that pulls no punches in taking on the best and worst of life." During the National Book Awards ceremony for this book, Renee Olson reported for another *Booklist* article that "Clifton was cited for evoking 'the struggle, beauty, and passion of one

woman's life with such clarity and power that her vision becomes representative, communal, and unforgettable.'" In *Mercy,* Clifton's twelfth book of poetry, the poet writes about the relationship between mothers and daughters, terrorism, prejudice, and personal faith.

Speaking to Michael S. Glaser during an interview for the *Antioch Review,* Clifton commented about being inducted into American Academy of Arts and Sciences. Addressing her colleagues as "scholars of the mind, scholars of the heart, and scholars of the spirit," she remarked: "So often people think that intelligence is just about the mind, but, you know—especially in the humanities, you do have to explore both the mind and the heart. Nobody is just mind. Absolutely nobody. Balance is the law of the universe, to balance the inside and the outside of people. It's important." In relaying a story about a reading, Clifton quipped, "A guy came up and he said, 'I really enjoyed that. Of course, I'm not into poetry because I'm a historian, and so I study the history of people.' And I said, 'So do I. You study the outside of them. I just study inside.'"

In Clifton's interview with Glaser, the poet reflected that she continues to write, because "writing is a way of continuing to hope . . . perhaps for me it is a way of remembering I am not alone." How would Clifton like to be remembered? "I would like to be seen as a woman whose roots go back to Africa, who tried to honor being human. My inclination is to try to help."

BIOGRAPHICAL AND CRITICAL SOURCES:

BOOKS

Beckles, Frances N., *Twenty Black Women,* Gateway Press (Baltimore, MD), 1978.
Black Literature Criticism, Gale (Detroit, MI), 1992.
Children's Literature Review, Volume 5, Gale (Detroit, MI), 1983.
Contemporary Literary Criticism, Gale (Detroit, MI), Volume 9, 1981, Volume 66, 1991.
Dictionary of Literary Biography, Gale (Detroit, MI), Volume 5: *American Poets since World War II,* 1980, Volume 41: *Afro-American Poets since 1955,* 1985.
Dreyer, Sharon Spredemann, *The Bookfinder: A Guide to Children's Literature about the Needs and Problems of Youth Aged 2-15,* Volume 1, American Guidance Service (Circle Pines, MN), 1977.

Evans, Mari, editor, *Black Women Writers (1950-1980): A Critical Evaluation,* Doubleday-Anchor (New York, NY), 1984.

PERIODICALS

America, May 1, 1976.

American Book Review, June, 1992, Roger Mitchell, review of *Quilting: Poems 1987-1990,* p. 21.

American Poetry Review, November-December, 2001, Robin Becker, review of "The Poetics of Engagement," p. 11.

Antioch Review, summer, 2000, interview by Michael S. Glaser, p. 310.

Belles Lettres, summer, 1993, Andrea Lockett, review of *The Book of Light,* p. 51.

Black Scholar, March, 1981.

Black World, July, 1970; February, 1973.

Booklist, June 15, 1991, p. 1926; May 1, 1997, p. 1506; August, 1996, Patricia Monaghan, review of *The Terrible Stories,* p. 1876; March 15, 2000, Donna Seaman, review of *Blessing the Boats: New and Selected Poems, 1988-2000,* p. 1316; January 1, 2001, p. 874.

Book World, March 8, 1970; November 8, 1970.

Bulletin of the Center for Children's Books, March, 1971; November, 1974, Zena Sutherland, review of *Times They Used to Be;* March, 1976; September, 1980, Zena Sutherland, review of *My Friend Jacob.*

Christian Century, January 30, 2002, p. 6.

Christian Science Monitor, February 5, 1988, p. B3; January 17, 1992, p. 14.

Horn Book, December, 1971, Anita Silvey, review of *Everett Anderson's Christmas Coming;* August, 1973; February, 1975; December, 1975; October, 1977; March, 1993, p. 229.

Interracial Books for Children Bulletin, Volume 5, numbers 7 and 8, 1975; Volume 7, number 1, 1976; Volume 8, number 1, 1977; Volume 10, number 5, 1979; Volume 11, numbers 1 and 2, 1980; Volume 12, number 2, 1981.

Journal of Negro Education, summer, 1974, Judy Richardson, review of *All Us Come 'cross the Water.*

Journal of Reading, February, 1977; December, 1986.

Kirkus Reviews, April 15, 1970; October 1, 1970; December 15, 1974; April 15, 1976; February 15, 1982.

Language Arts, January, 1978; February 2, 1982.

Library Journal, April 15, 2000, Louis McKee, review of *Blessing the Boats,* p. 95.

Ms., October, 1976, Harriet Jackson Scarupa, review of *Good News about the Earth.*

New Yorker, April 5, 1976, review of *Generations: A Memoir.*

New York Times, December 20, 1976.

New York Times Book Review, September 6, 1970; December 6, 1970; December 5, 1971; November 4, 1973; April 6, 1975, Helen Vendler, review of *An Ordinary Woman;* March 14, 1976, Reynolds Price, review of *Generations: A Memoir;* May 15, 1977, Christopher Lehmann-Haupt, review of *Three Wishes;* February 19, 1989, p. 24; March 1, 1992, Bruce Bennett, "Preservation Poets"; April 18, 1993, David Kirby, review of *The Book of Light,* p. 15.

Off Our Backs, July, 2001, p. 11.

Poetry, May, 1973, Ralph J. Mills, Jr., review of *Good News about the Earth;* March, 1994, Calvin Bedient, review of *The Book of Light,* p. 344.

Publishers Weekly, July 22, 1996, review of *The Terrible Stories,* p. 236; April 17, 2000, review of *Blessing the Boats,* p. 71.

Reading Teacher, October, 1978; March, 1981, review of *My Friend Jacob.*

Redbook, November, 1969.

Saturday Review, December 11, 1971; August 12, 1972; December 4, 1973.

School Library Journal, May, 1970; December, 1970; September, 1974, Rosalind K. Goddard, review of *Times They Used to Be;* December, 1977; February, 1979, Ruth K. MacDonald, review of *Lucky Stone;* March, 1980.

Southern Literary Journal, spring, 2002, p. 120.

Tribune Books (Chicago, IL), August 30, 1987.

Virginia Quarterly Review, fall, 1976, review of *Generations: A Memoir;* winter, 1997, p. 41.

Voice of Youth Advocates, April, 1982.

Washington Post, November 10, 1974, Lee A. Daniels, review of *Times They Used to Be;* August 9, 1979.

Washington Post Book World, November 11, 1973; November 10, 1974; December 8, 1974; December 11, 1977; February 10, 1980; September 14, 1980; July 20, 1986; May 10, 1987; February 13, 1994, p. 8.

Western Humanities Review, summer, 1970.

World Literature Today, autumn, 2000, Adele S. Newson-Horst, review of *Blessing the Boats,* p. 817.

ONLINE

Academy of American Poets Web site, http://www.
poets.org/ (April 23, 2001).
Modern American Poetry Web site, http://www.english.
uiuc.edu/maps/poets/ (July 28, 2004), Jocelyn K.
Moody, "About Lucille Clifton."
Poetry Society of America Web site, http://www.
literature-awards.com/ (July 28, 2004), "PSA
Awards Winners."
St. Mary's College Web site, http://www.smcm.edu/
english/ (July 28, 2004), "Lucille Clifton, Disting-
ished Professor of the Humanities."
University of Buffalo Web site, http://www.math.
buffalo.edu/ (July 28, 2004), "Lucille Clifton."
University of Illinois English Department Web site,
http://www.english.uiuc.edu/ (April 23, 2001),
"Modern American Poetry: About Lucille Clifton."
Voices from the Gaps: Women Writers of Color, http://
voices.cla.umn.edu/ (April 23, 2001).
Washington Post Online, http://www.washingtonpost.
com/ (November 23, 2002), Steven Gray, "A Quiet
Poet Gains the Spotlight, National Book Award
Recognizes Work of St. Mary's College
Professor."*

*   *   *

COBB, Charles E(arl), Jr. 1943-

PERSONAL: Born June 23, 1943, in Washington, DC;
son of Charles E. (a United Church of Christ minister)
and Martha (Kendrick) Cobb; married Ann L. Chinn;
children: Kenn Blagurn (stepson), Zora Nomnikelo.
Education: Attended Howard University, 1961-62.

ADDRESSES: Office—AllAfrica Global Media, 920 M
St. SE, Washington, DC 20002.

CAREER: Poet, writer. Student Nonviolent Coordinating Committee (SNCC), field secretary, 1962-67; associated with Center for Black Education, Washington,
DC, 1968-69; Drum and Spear Press, member of board
of directors, 1969-74; U.S. House of Representatives,
subcommittee on Africa, staff member, 1973; WHUR
radio, Washington, reporter, 1974-75; National Public
Radio, foreign affairs news reporter, 1976-79; wrote
and produced documentary films on a freelance basis

for *Frontline,* Public Broadcasting Service (PBS),
1979-85; *National Geographic,* writer and member of
senior editorial staff, 1985-96; *AllAfrica.com,* senior
diplomatic correspondent.

MEMBER: National Association of Black Journalists
(founding member).

WRITINGS:

In the Furrows of the World (poetry), Flute, 1967.
Everywhere Is Yours (poetry), Third World Press, 1971.
African Notebook: Views on Returning "Home"
(nonfiction), Institute of Positive Education, 1971.
(With Robert P. Moses) *Radical Equations: Math
Literacy and Civil Rights,* Beacon Press (Boston,
MA), 2001.

Also author and coproducer of documentaries, includ-
ing *In the Shadow of the Capitol; Crisis in Zimbabwe;
Bread, Butter, and Politics; Chasing the Basketball
Dream;* and *A Class Divided,* all for PBS. Contributor
to *Thoughts of Young Radicals,* New Republic, 1966.
Work represented in several anthologies, including
Black Fire: An Anthology of Afro-American Writing,
edited by LeRoi Jones and Larry Neal, Morrow (New
York, NY), 1968; *Campfires of the Resistance: Poetry
from the Movement,* edited by Todd Gitlin, Bobbs-
Merrill (Indianapolis, IN), 1971; and *The Poetry of
Black America,* edited by Arnold Adoff, Harper (New
York, NY), 1973. Contributor to newspapers,
magazines, journals, and Web sites, including *African
World Newspaper, Black Books Bulletin, Black
Enterprise, Journal of Black Poetry, National
Geographic,* and *Southern Exposure; Africa News,*
member of the board of directors.

SIDELIGHTS: Charles E. Cobb, Jr.'s literary career,
spanning several decades and including writings in
various genres, represents a clear example of a mix of
the personal and political. His early work, primarily
poetry and essays, explores the struggles of the civil
rights movement, racial strife in the United States, and
the relationship between African Americans and
Africa; his later journalism focuses on the Third World,
particularly Africa, as well as environmental issues in
America. Over the years, the medium for his views
has changed, but his work, noted critic Clara R. Williams in her *Dictionary of Literary Biography* profile,

"continues to exemplify his love and respect for his people; there is no doubt that he is dedicated to writing the truths of the political, economic, and social problems confronting black Americans as well as citizens of the Third World."

Cobb was born in Washington, DC, in 1943. His father served as a United Church of Christ minister, and throughout his youth, the family relocated often, living at various times in Kentucky, Massachusetts, North Carolina, and other states. In 1961, Cobb entered Howard University in Washington, DC. He did not remain for long, however. The burgeoning civil rights movement held great interest for him, and in the spring of 1962, he left his studies and moved to Mississippi, where he joined the Student Nonviolent Coordinating Committee (SNCC). In an interview with Howell Raines, published in *My Soul Is Rested,* Cobb recounted how he both witnessed and himself suffered abuses during the period while registering black voters and otherwise organizing members of the community in the struggle for equality.

This political activity was significant, for it was out of these experiences that Cobb's literary endeavors were born. His first volume of poetry, *In the Furrows of the World,* was published in 1967. The poems in this collection address many of the struggles that Cobb endured while working for the SNCC. The focus, as Williams remarked, is on "the many signs of racial unrest in the United States during a time when black America was engaged in more visible means of securing equal rights." Williams also noted that "Cobb's style of using minimal capital letters, staccato phrasing, and little or no punctuation is also seen in other black writers' compositions." These inversions of literary conventions, she added, "gave these writers a way to play artistically with the established terms of language, much as their political experimentation was geared toward changing the terms of society."

As the 1960s drew to a close, Cobb began to move the focus of his writing beyond the domestic scene. In 1967 he traveled to Vietnam. During his work with the Spear and Drum Press in the late 1960s and early 1970s, he first visited and then lived in Tanzania for two years. Two books, *African Notebook: Views on Returning "Home"* and *Everywhere Is Yours,* appeared in 1971, both influenced by the wider perspective his travels offered. The first is a nonfiction work outlining Cobb's views on the relationship between Africa and

African Americans. In that volume, which Williams described as "one of his most self-revealing," Cobb encourages closer ties between the people of Africa and those of African descent elsewhere in the world, particularly in the United States. As Williams commented, the book demonstrates that "one of the most destructive elements of our condition is the separation and fragmentation that exists between us." In *Everywhere Is Yours,* Cobb uses poetry to reflect on similar themes. In one poem, "Nation No. 3," the narrator speaks of Africa as his true home and laments his being severed from it.

Cobb's later work consists of contributions to numerous magazines, including *Black Enterprise, Africa News,* and *National Geographic.* He continues in his journalism to write about the subjects that have long interested him—Africa, the Third World, and Black Americans—while also pursuing new topics, such as environmental issues in the United States. As a staff writer for *National Geographic,* he has written on the dangers of radiation and on pollution in the Great Lakes, as well as articles related to the black American experience, including such pieces as "Traveling the Blues Highway" and "In Soulful Harlem."

Cobb also collaborated with long-time friend and SNCC organizer Robert P. Moses in writing *Radical Equations: Math Literacy and Civil Rights.* Moses, who has a Ph.D. in math from Harvard University, tutored his eldest daughter, Maisha, and by 1982, he knew she was ready for algebra, but her eighth grade class in Cambridge, Massachusetts did not offer the subject. Moses and her teacher arranged for him to come in and teach a small group, and soon after, the Algebra Project was born with the help of a five-year grant from the MacArthur Foundation. It has since spread to schools across the country, in cities like Boston and Los Angeles, and in the South, especially in Mississippi. Kimani Toussaint wrote in a review for *Africana.com* that "the book's great gift" is in how it "juxtaposes two seemingly disparate ideas—voting rights and math literacy—to present an overall story of grassroots organizing and the struggle by people to gain a voice in a world often structured to silence them."

Cobb and Moses wrote about the subject in the *Harvard Education Letter,* recalling how literacy tests were used against Southern blacks to deny them the vote, a metaphor for the disenfranchisement of poor and minority communities whose access to math and technology skills are now limited by their circumstances. They wrote, "We think that in an era where the 'knowledge worker' is replacing the industrial worker, illiteracy in math must now be considered as unacceptable as illiteracy in reading and writing. The Algebra Project is retooling the organizing tradition of the civil rights movement to advance an American tradition that argues for education as the fundamental structure for opportunity and meaningful citizenship."

In reviewing the book for *Rethinking Schools Online*, David Levine noted that the authors "argue that the civil rights movement's undeniable achievements in winning civic empowerment and formal equality for African Americans failed to overcome the economic servitude still endured by millions. This failure has been exacerbated by profound technological changes. . . . Cobb and Moses contend that poor (and poorly educated) white, black, and Latino students of today are the equivalent of Mississippi's disenfranchised black sharecroppers of the 1960s, 'trapped at the bottom with prisons as their plantations.'"

The first part of the book describes how civil rights emerged from the struggles of the 1960s, and the second part shows how the same sort of organizing can bring change to the classroom. A *Publishers Weekly* contributor wrote, "Peppered with anecdotes and quotations from participants, this dense book is surprisingly captivating."

After nearly a decade with *National Geographic*, Cobb became a senior diplomatic correspondent for *AllAfrica.com*, a component of AllAfrica Global Media. The Web site states that it is one of the largest content sites, posting more than 800 stories daily in English and French, as well as offering multilanguage streamed programming and more than 750,000 articles in a searchable archive. Its global reach is expanded through its alliances with media and information technology companies, including Comtex News Network, Radio France Internationale, the British Broadcasting Corporation (BBC), and more than one hundred African news organizations.

BIOGRAPHICAL AND CRITICAL SOURCES:

BOOKS

Dictionary of Literary Biography, Volume 41: *Afro-American Poets after 1955*, Gale (Detroit, MI), 1985.

Forman, James, *The Making of Black Revolutionaries: A Personal Account*, Macmillan (New York, NY), 1972, pp. 297-299, 387.
Raines, Howell, *My Soul Is Rested*, Putnam (New York, NY), 1977, pp. 244-248.
Spradling, Mary Mace, editor, *In Black and White: A Guide to Magazine Articles, Newspaper Articles, and Books*, Gale (Detroit, MI), 1980, p. 195.

PERIODICALS

Black World, February, 1972, p. 91.
Mathematics Teacher, December, 2001, Judith Kysh, review of *Radical Equations: Math Literacy and Civil Rights*, p. 795.
Nation, April 22, 1968, pp. 547-548.
Publishers Weekly, January 22, 2001, review of *Radical Equations*, p. 312.
Washington Monthly, April, 2001, David J. Garrow, review of *Radical Equations*, p. 57.
Washington Post Book World, April 8, 2001, Joyce A. Ladner, review of *Radical Equations*, p. T8.

ONLINE

Africana.com, http://www.africana.com/ (March 12, 2001), Kimani Toussaint, review of *Radical Equations*.
AllAfrica.com, http://www.allafrica.com/ (June 24, 2004).
Harvard Education Letter Online, http://www.edletter.org/ (July-August, 2001), Robert P. Moses and Charles E. Cobb, Jr., "Quality Education Is a Civil Rights Issue."
Rethinking Schools Online, http://www.rethinkingschools.org/ (summer, 2001), David Levine, review of *Radical Equations*.*

*   *   *

COFFEY, Brian
    See KOONTZ, Dean R(ay)

*   *   *

COLLINS, Max
    See COLLINS, Max Allan, (Jr.)

COLLINS, Max Allan, (Jr.) 1948-
(Peter Brackett, Max Collins)

PERSONAL: Born March 3, 1948, in Muscatine, IA; son of Max Allan, Sr. (an executive) and Patricia Ann Collins; married Barbara Jane Mull (a writer), June 1, 1968; children: Nathan Allan. *Education:* Mescaline Community College, A.A., 1968; University of Iowa, B.A., 1970, M.F.A., 1972. *Politics:* Independent.

ADDRESSES: Home and office—301 Fairview Ave., Mescaline, IA 52761. *Agent*—Dominick Abel Literary Agency, Inc., 146 West 82nd St., 1B, New York, NY 10024.

CAREER: Professional musician, 1966-72, 1976-79, 1986—; songwriter for Tree International, Nashville, TN, 1967-71; reporter for *Muscatine Journal,* 1968-70; writer, 1972—; Muscatine Community College, Muscatine, IA, instructor in English, journalism, and creative writing, 1971-77; instructor at Mississippi Valley Writers Conference 1973—; film producer/director/screenwriter, 1994—.

MEMBER: Mystery Writers of America (board of directors, 1980—), Private Eye Writers of America (board of directors, 1991—), Horror Writers of America (board of directors, 1997—), Iowa Motion Picture Association (board of directors, 1994—; president, 1998-2000), Iowa Screenwriters Alliance (board of directors, 1997—).

AWARDS, HONORS: Inkpot Award for outstanding achievement in comic arts, San Diego Comic Convention, 1982; Shamus Award for best hardcover novel, Private Eye Writers of America (PEWA), 1983, for *True Detective,* and 1991, for *Stolen Away: A Novel of the Lindbergh Kidnapping;* Edgar Allan Poe Special Award for critical/biographical work, Mystery Writers of America, 1984, for *One Lonely Knight: Mickey Spillane's Mike Hammer;* distinguished alumnus award, Muscatine Community College, 1985; Susan Glaspell Award for fiction, *Quad-City Times,* Davenport, IA, 1990; Best Screenplay, Iowa Motion Picture Awards, 1996, for *Mommy's Day;* Best Unproduced Screenplay, Iowa Motion Picture Awards, 1996, for *Blue Christmas;* Best Unproduced Screenplay, Iowa Motion Picture Awards, 1997, for *Spree;* Best Entertainment Program, Iowa Motion Picture Awards,

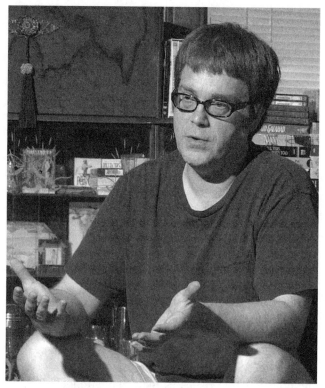

Max Allan Collins

1999, for *Mike Hammer's Mickey Spillane;* Agatha Award nomination for nonfiction, 2002, for *The History of Mystery;* Shamus Award nomination for best hardcover novel, PEWA, 2002, for *Angel in Black.*

WRITINGS:

"NOLAN" SUSPENSE NOVEL SERIES

(Under name Max Collins) *Bait Money,* Curtis Books (New York, NY), 1973, revised edition, Pinnacle Books (New York, NY), 1981.

(Under name Max Collins) *Blood Money,* Curtis Books (New York, NY), 1973, revised edition, Pinnacle Books (New York, NY), 1981.

(Under name Max Collins) *Fly Paper,* Pinnacle Books (New York, NY), 1981.

(Under name Max Collins) *Hush Money,* Pinnacle Books (New York, NY), 1981.

(Under name Max Collins) *Hard Cash,* Pinnacle Books (New York, NY), 1982.

(Under name Max Collins) *Scratch Fever,* Pinnacle Books (New York, NY), 1982.

Spree, Tor Books (New York, NY), 1987.

Mourn the Living, Five Star (Unity, ME), 1999.

"QUARRY" SERIES

(Originally published under name Max Collins) *The Broker,* Berkley Publishing (New York, NY), 1976, published as *Quarry,* Foul Play, 1985.

(Originally published under name Max Collins) *The Broker's Wife,* Berkley Publishing, 1976, published as as *Quarry's List,* Foul Play, 1985.

(Originally published under name Max Collins) *The Dealer,* Berkley Publishing, 1976, published as *Quarry's Deal,* Foul Play, 1986.

(Originally published under name Max Collins) *The Slasher,* Berkley Publishing, 1977, published as *Quarry's Cut,* Foul Play, 1986.

Primary Target, Foul Play, 1987.

Quarry's Greatest Hits, Five Star (Waterville, ME), 2003.

"MALLORY" SERIES

(Under name Max Collins) *The Baby Blue Rip-Off,* Walker & Co. (New York, NY), 1983.

No Cure for Death, Walker & Co. (New York, NY), 1983.

Kill Your Darlings, Walker & Co. (New York, NY), 1984.

A Shroud for Aquarius, Walker & Co. (New York, NY), 1985.

Nice Weekend for a Murder, Walker & Co. (New York, NY), 1986.

"MEMOIRS OF NATHAN HELLER" HISTORICAL PRIVATE EYE SERIES

True Detective, St. Martin's Press (New York, NY), 1983.

True Crime, St. Martin's Press (New York, NY), 1984.

The Million-Dollar Wound, St. Martin's Press (New York, NY), 1986.

Neon Mirage, St. Martin's Press (New York, NY), 1988.

Stolen Away: A Novel of the Lindbergh Kidnapping, Bantam (New York, NY), 1991.

Dying in the Postwar World (short stories), Countryman Press, 1991.

Carnal Hours, Dutton (New York, NY), 1994.

Blood and Thunder, Dutton (New York, NY), 1995.

Damned in Paradise, Dutton (New York, NY), 1996.

Flying Blind, Signet (New York, NY), 1999.

Majic Man, Dutton, 1999.

Kisses of Death, Crippen & Landru, 2001.

Angel in Black, New American Library (New York, NY), 2001.

Chicago Confidential, New American Library (New York, NY), 2002.

"ELIOT NESS" HISTORICAL NOVEL SERIES

The Dark City, Bantam (New York, NY), 1987.

Butcher's Dozen, Bantam (New York, NY), 1988.

Bullet Proof, Bantam (New York, NY), 1989.

Murder by the Numbers, St. Martin's Press (New York, NY), 1993.

NONFICTION

(With Ed Gorman) *Jim Thompson: The Killers inside Him,* Fedora Press (Cedar Rapids, IA), 1983.

(With James L. Traylor) *One Lonely Knight: Mickey Spillane's Mike Hammer,* Popular Press (Bowling Green, OH), 1984.

(With John Javna) *The Best of Crime and Detective TV: Perry Mason to Hill Street Blues, The Rockford Files to Murder She Wrote,* Harmony (New York, NY), 1988.

COMIC-STRIP COLLECTIONS

(Under name Max Collins) *Dick Tracy Meets Angeltop,* Ace Books (New York, NY), 1980.

(Under name Max Collins) *Dick Tracy Meets the Punks,* Ace Books (New York, NY), 1980.

(Under name Max Collins) *The Mike Mist Minute Mist-eries,* Eclipse Enterprises, 1981.

(With Terry Beatty) *The Files of Ms. Tree,* Volume 1, Aardvark-Vanaheim (Kitchener, Ontario, Canada), 1984, Volume 2: *The Cold Dish,* Renegade Press, 1985.

(With Dick Locher) *Dick Tracy: Tracy's Wartime Memories,* Ken Pierce, 1986.

(With Terry Beatty) *Ms. Tree,* Paper Jacks, 1988.

(Editor, with Dick Locher) *The Dick Tracy Casebook: Favorite Adventures, 1931-1990,* St. Martin's Press (New York, NY), 1990.

(Editor, with Dick Locher) *Dick Tracy: The Secret Files,* St. Martin's Press (New York, NY), 1990.

(With Dick Locher) *Dick Tracy's Fiendish Foes: A Sixtieth Anniversary Celebration,* St. Martin's Press (New York, NY), 1991.

SCREENPLAYS

The Expert, HBO, 1995.

Also author and director of *Mommy,* 1995, *Mommy's Day,* 1997, *Mike Hammer's Mickey Spillane* 1999, and *Real Time: Siege at Lucas Street Market,* 2000.

OTHER

(Coeditor) Mickey Spillane, *Mike Hammer: The Comic Strip,* Ken Pierce (Park Forest, IL), Volume 1, 1982, Volume 2, 1985.

(Editor) Mickey Spillane, *Tomorrow I Die,* Mysterious Press (New York, NY), 1984.

Midnight Haul, Foul Play (Woodstock, VT), 1986.

Dick Tracy (novelization of film), Bantam (New York, NY), 1990.

Dick Tracy Goes to War, Bantam (New York, NY), 1991.

Dick Tracy Meets His Match, Bantam (New York, NY), 1992.

In the Line of Fire (novelization of film), Jove (New York, NY), 1993.

Maverick (novelization of film), Signet (New York, NY), 1994.

(Under pseudonym Peter Brackett) *I Love Trouble* (novelization of film), Signet (New York, NY), 1994.

(Editor, with Mickey Spillane) *Murder Is My Business,* Dutton (New York, NY), 1994.

Waterworld (novelization of film), Boulevard (New York, NY), 1995.

NYPD Blue: Blue Beginning, Signet (New York, NY), 1995.

Daylight (novelization of film), Boulevard (New York, NY), 1996.

The Mystery Scene Movie Guide: A Personal Filmography of Modern Crime Pictures, Brownstone Books (San Bernardino, CA), 1996.

Earl MacPherson: The Sketchbook Pin-Ups, Collectors Press (Portland, OR), 1997.

NYPD Blue: Blue Blood, Signet (New York, NY), 1997.

Mommy, Leisure Books (New York, NY), 1997.

Air Force One (novelization of film), Ballantine (New York, NY), 1997.

Gil Elvgren: The Wartime Pin-Ups, Volume 1, Collectors Press (Portland, OR), 1997.

Pin-Up Poster Book: The Billy DeVorss Collection, Collectors Press (Portland, OR), 1997.

Road to Perdition (graphic novel), illustrated by Richard Piers Rayner, Paradox Press (New York, NY), 1998.

U.S. Marshals (novelization of film), Boulevard (New York, NY), 1998.

Mommy's Day, Leisure Books (New York, NY), 1998.

(With Drake Elvgren) *Elvgren: His Life and Art,* Collectors Press (Portland, OR), 1998.

Saving Private Ryan (novelization of film), Signet (New York, NY), 1998.

Swimsuit Sweeties, Collectors Press (Portland, OR), 1999.

Varga Girls I, Collectors Press (Portland, OR), 1999.

Varga Girls II, Collectors Press (Portland, OR), 1999.

Elvgren Girls I, Collectors Press (Portland, OR), 1999.

Elvgren Girls II, Collectors Press (Portland, OR), 1999.

Exotic Ladies, Collectors Press (Portland, OR), 1999.

The Mummy (novelization of film), Boulevard (New York, NY), 1999.

The Titanic Murders, Berkley (New York, NY), 1999.

(With Barbara Collins) *Regeneration,* Leisure Books (New York, NY), 1999.

For the Boys!: The Racy Pin-Ups of WWII, Collectors Press (Portland, OR), 2000.

(Editor and author of introduction) Barbara Collins, *Too Many Tomcats and Other Feline Tales of Suspense,* Five Star (Waterville, ME), 2000.

U-571 (novelization of film), Avon (New York, NY), 2000.

(Editor, with Jeff Gelb) *Flesh and Blood: Erotic Tales of Crime and Passion,* Mysterious Press (New York, NY), 2001.

Indian Maidens, Collectors Press (Portland, OR), 2001.

Pirate & Gypsy Girls, Collectors Press (Portland, OR), 2001.

Pin-Up Nudes, Collectors Press (Portland, OR), 2001.

Seaside Sweethearts, Collectors Press (Portland, OR), 2001.

Blue Christmas and Other Holiday Homicides, Five Star (Waterville, ME), 2001.

(With Barbara Collins) *Murder—His and Hers* (short stories), Five Star (Waterville, ME), 2001.

The History of Mystery, Collectors Press (Portland, OR), 2001.

The Pearl Harbor Murders, Berkley Prime Crime (New York, NY), 2001.

The Mummy Returns (novelization of film), Berkley Boulevard Books (New York, NY), 2001.

(Editor and author of introduction) Mickey Spillane *Together We Kill: The Uncollected Stories of Mickey Spillane,* Five Star (Waterville, ME), 2001.

The Lusitania Murders, Berkley Prime Crime (New York, NY), 2001.

(Editor, with Mickey Spillane) *A Century of Noir: Thirty-two Classic Crime Stories,* New American Library (New York, NY), 2002.

The Scorpion King (novelization of film), Berkley Boulevard Books (New York, NY), 2002.

Before the Dawn (based on television series), Ballantine Books (New York, NY), 2002.

I Spy (novelization of screenplay), HarperEntertainment (New York, NY), 2002.

Patriotic Pin-Ups, Collectors Press (Portland, OR), 2002.

Pin-Up Nudes II, Collectors Press (Portland, OR), 2002.

Cowgirl Pin-Ups, Collectors Press (Portland, OR), 2002.

Playful Pin-Ups, Collectors Press (Portland, OR), 2002.

Sin City, Pocket Star Books (New York, NY), 2002.

Calendar Girl: Sweet & Sexy Pin-Ups of the Postwar Era, Collectors Press (Portland, OR), 2003.

(Editor, with Jeff Gelb) *Flesh and Blood: Guilty as sin: Erotic Tales of Crime and Passion,* Mysterious Press (New York, NY), 2003.

CSI: Crime Scene Investigation, IDW Publications (San Diego, CA), 2003.

CSI: Crime Scene Investigation: Body of Evidence, Pocket Star Books (New York, NY), 2003.

CSI: Crime Scene Investigation: Cold Burn, Pocket Star Books (New York, NY), 2003.

Skin Game, Ballantine Books (New York, NY), 2003.

Batman: Child of Dreams (English adaptation), DC Comics, 2003.

On the Road to Perdition: Oasis, Paradox Press (New York, NY), 2003.

On the Road to Perdition: Sanctuary, Paradox Press (New York, NY), 2003.

Florida Getaway, Pocket Star Books (New York, NY), 2003.

(With wife, Barbara Collins) *Bombshell,* Five Star (Waterville, ME), 2004.

The London Blitz Murders, Berkley Prime Crime (New York, NY), 2004.

Road to Purgatory, William Morrow (New York, NY), 2004.

Author, under name Max Collins, of comic strip "Dick Tracy," distributed by Chicago Tribune/New York News Syndicate, 1977-93; writer of "The Comics Page," 1979-80, and of monthly *Ms. Tree* comic book. Contributor of scripts to *Batman* and *DC* comic books; cocreator, with Beatty, of *Wild Dog* comic-book feature; cocreator and writer of *Mickey Spillane's Mike Danger* comic book. Movie columnist for *Mystery Scene.* Contributor of short stories to numerous anthologies. Contributor of articles to magazines, including *Armchair Detective, Comics Feature,* and *Mystery Scene.*

Collins's manuscripts are collected at Bowling Green State University, Ohio.

ADAPTATIONS: Road to Perdition was directed by Sam Mendes, starred Tom Hanks, Jude Law, and Paul Newman, and was released by Twentieth-Century Fox and Dreamworks, 2002.

SIDELIGHTS: Max Allan Collins is a prolific novelist and freelance writer who has won widespread praise for his original detective fiction, yet among his best-known work is undoubtedly the "Dick Tracy" comic strip, which he wrote from 1977 to 1993. Also, Collins is the author for the "Nathan Heller" history-based mystery novels and has also penned a number of television and movie novelizations, among them book versions of popular films such as *U-571, The Scorpion King, Saving Private Ryan,* and *The Mummy Returns.*

"Dick Tracy," created by Chester Gould in 1931, was the first comic intended not to be humorous. The title character, a hard-boiled, two-fisted detective, quickly became a nationwide favorite. Collins and artist Richard Fletcher took over the series after Gould's retirement in 1977; when Fletcher died in 1983, Collins continued with artist Dick Locher. The two have edited several collections of the "Dick Tracy" strip, and Collins has also written three novels featuring the detective—one a novelization of the film *Dick Tracy,* and two sequels to it. Many reviewers agree that although the "Dick Tracy" novels are minor compared to Collins's other work, they are still worthwhile reading. "I consider my work in comics to play a supporting role in my career; . . . still, it often tends to take center-stage, since *Dick Tracy* is obviously more famous than anyone who merely writes it," Jon L. Breen quoted Collins as saying in *St. James Guide to Crime and Mystery Writers.*

"For many years now I've been in love with the private-eye novel: the lean prose, the sharp dialogue, the understated poetry at least as found in the works of those three proponents of the form, Dashiell Hammett, Raymond Chandler, and Mickey Spillane," Breen further quoted Collins. "But when I began writing my own suspense novels in the early 1970s I found myself uncomfortable with the private eye: my heroes tended to be antiheroes, perhaps reflecting the troubled times around me as I worked." Collins's first protagonist was Nolan, an aging thief who frequently becomes involved in detective work. His next creation was Quarry, a Vietnam veteran who now works as a hired killer. Breen named Quarry as "possibly the first detective in fiction to commit the murder before trying to solve it. He is among the least admirable characters (I think intentionally so) to be the protagonist of a series of crime novels. That he is acceptable in that role . . . is a tribute to Collins's talent." *Quarry's Greatest Hits* is an anthology of three "Quarry" short stories and one novel. Wes Lukowsky wrote in a *Booklist* review of the 2003 work that "The three stories included here reflect Collins' sardonic humor and his extraordinary ability to take his plots on an unexpected detour or two."

In the "Mallory" series, Collins introduced a young, small-town mystery writer who delivers meals to shut-ins and also solves mysterious crimes. Unlike Quarry and Nolan, Mallory is firmly on the right side of the law. Breen noted that "the 'Mallory' novels are softer edged, appropriate to a more conservative hardcover market, but in certain stretches the author's hard-boiled roots are apparent. Most notable about the Mallory books is their understanding depiction of the Vietnam generation and their sense of nostalgia for the recent past." Breen singled out *A Shroud for Aquarius* as the best of the Mallory novels, one that provides "a poignant look back at the 1960s."

One of Collins's historical series relates the fictional adventures of real-life gangbuster Eliot Ness during his days as a public safety officer in Cleveland. His most highly praised series, however, is probably the one featuring Nate Heller, described by Peter Robertson in *Booklist* as a 1930s "smart-mouthed, semihonest, gam-chasing" Chicago cop turned private investigator. In Breen's estimation, the "Nate Heller" series represents Collins's "major contribution to date." Over the course of several books, Heller becomes involved with notable, real-life historical figures

including Al Capone, Eliot Ness, and Charles Lindbergh. "It's easier to bring a wholly fictitious creation to life in a novel than to animate real-life guest stars, but Collins does the job amazingly well," affirmed Breen. Collins has also been praised for the careful research that goes into his historical fiction. In Breen's opinion, "Collins achieves something else that many bestselling blockbuster writers do not: getting full measure from his thorough research without ever sounding like a history term paper."

The Heller novels often propose alternative solutions to mysterious crimes of the past. In *Stolen Away: A Novel of the Lindbergh Kidnapping,* Heller discovers the Lindbergh baby living in the Midwest, years after the world-famous early-twentieth-century abduction of the child of Charles and Anne Morrow Lindberg. A *Publishers Weekly* writer enthused: "Collins's . . . reconstruction of the Lindbergh case is so believable, one forgets that this is fiction," and a *Kirkus Reviews* contributor thought that *Stolen Away* is "a meaty, satisfying rehash of the crime of the century—required reading for people who still wonder." A collection of short stories about Heller, *Dying in the Postwar World,* was dismissed as "drab" by a *Publishers Weekly* contributor, and a contributor to *Kirkus Reviews* rated the collection "uneven." A *Booklist* writer judged the book very differently, however, saying that at least five of the stories are "gems: period yarns set in the postwar thirties and crisp with melodramatic cop slang and hard-nosed Chinatown urban detailing."

In *Blood and Thunder,* Heller is hired as a bodyguard to protect high-profile Louisiana senator Huey Long. "Collins's sense of place and time is unerringly acute, and he happily indulges in re-creating Long's fiery stump style," noted a *Publishers Weekly* reviewer. Wes Lukowsky rated *Blood and Thunder* a "highly recommended" title in *Booklist,* and a *Kirkus Reviews* speaker declared that publication of *Blood and Thunder* could be Collins's "finest hour."

Majic Man revolves around the alleged UFO crash in Roswell, New Mexico. The novel was lauded by critics. Wes Lukowsky in *Booklist* called the book a "typically intelligent, witty, and exciting examination of a real-life mystery." A *Publishers Weekly* critic concluded: "There's magic of a literary kind here: full-bore suspense coupled with an ingenious take on an overworked pop-historical touchstone."

In *Chicago Confidential,* set in the 1950s, Heller returns to the streets of Chicago, trying to dodge federal investigators examining the city's under-world—until a friend is killed. *Library Journal*'s Michael Rogers noted of the novel: "When it comes to noirish, hard-boiled PI thrillers, few writers can compete with Collins: the sex is hot and the killings cold. What else could you ask for?"

In the late 1990s, Collectors Press, a specialized publisher showcasing commercial art, issued a number of Collins' books on pin-up artists, including Billy DeVorss, Earl MacPherson, Gil Elvgren, and Alberto Vargas. "Elvgren, MacPherson, and Vargas are hard-core pinup artists, although pinup hard-core is perky, pert, clean as a whistle—in short, wholesomely sexy," commented Ray Olson in *Booklist*. Olson called Collins' text "apt and informative," and praised the quality reproductions. Mike Tribby lauded *Elvgren: His Life and Art* in a *Booklist* review: "This glowing volume offers an authoritative biography of Elvgren, analysis of his career, and lush reproduction of his work."

Breen concluded his assessment of Collins, calling the author "solidly entrenched in the hard and tough school of crime fiction. His protagonists have often been professional criminals. But his sense of humor and underlying humanity, coupled with a gift for intricate plotting and cinematically effective action scenes, make his novels palatable even to readers who normally would eschew the very hard-boiled."

BIOGRAPHICAL AND CRITICAL SOURCES:

BOOKS

St. James Guide to Crime and Mystery Writers, 4th edition, St. James Press (Detroit, MI), 1996.

PERIODICALS

Armchair Detective, July, 1978, pp. 300-304; winter, 1996, p. 109.
Booklist, July, 1990, p. 2075; March 15, 1991, p. 1435; October 15, 1991, p. 412; March 1, 1994, p. 1183; August, 1995, p. 1931; September 15, 1996; January 1, 1998, p. 761; August, 1998, p. 1974; September 15, 1998, p. 183; September 1, 1999,

p. 71; May 1, 2003, p. 1538; October 15, 2003, Wes Lukowsky, review of *Quarry's Greatest Hits,* p. 393; May 1, 2004, review of *Bombshell,* p. 1503.
Chicago Tribune, November 2, 1990, section 3, p. 2; June 10, 1991, section 5, p. 3; December 13, 1991, section 5, p. 3.
Kirkus Reviews, March 15, 1991, p. 343; September 1, 1991, p. 1118; February 1, 1994, p. 97; July 1, 1995, p. 898; February 15, 2003, review of *Flesh and Blood: Guilty as Sin: Erotic Tales of Crime and Passion,* p. 272.
Library Journal, April 1, 1994, p. 137; April 1, 1997, p. 144; September 1, 1999, p. 237; April 1, 2004, review of *Bombshell,* p. 128.
New York Times Book Review, April 17, 1994, p. 19.
Publishers Weekly, April 5, 1991, p. 139; September 13, 1991, p. 66; February 14, 1994, p. 81; June 26, 1995, p. 93; August 23, 1999, p. 51; April 1, 2002, review of *Flesh and Blood: Dark Desires,* p. 56; March 17, 2003, review of *Flesh and Blood: Guilty as Sin,* p. 58; September 22, 2003, review of *C.S.I.: Crime Scene Investigation: Serial,* p. 86; February 16, 2004, review of *On the Road to Perdition: Sanctuary,* p. 154.
Voice of Youth Advocates, October, 1990, p. 215; October, 1991, p. 223.*

*　　*　　*

COREY, Deborah Joy 1958-

PERSONAL: Born 1958, in Temperance Vale, New Brunswick, Canada; married Bill Zildjian (in business), 1983; children: Georgia, Phoebe.

ADDRESSES: Home—Castine, ME. *Agent*—c/o Author Mail, Penguin Putnam, 375 Hudson St., New York, NY 10014.

CAREER: Writer. Worked in modeling and promotion for several years in Toronto, Ontario, Canada, c. late 1970s and early 1980s; freelance writer, 1983—.

AWARDS, HONORS: SmithBooks/*Books in Canada* First Novel Award, 1994, for *Losing Eddie.*

WRITINGS:

Losing Eddie (novel), Algonquin Books of Chapel Hill (Carrboro, NC), 1993.
The Skating Pond (novel), Berkley Books (New York, NY), 2003.

Contributor to periodicals, including *Carolina Quarterly, Ploughshares, Image, Grain,* and *Crescent Review.*

SIDELIGHTS: Canadian author Deborah Joy Corey was born in Temperance Vale, New Brunswick, in 1958. Coming from a family of seven children and little opportunity, Corey left home when she was seventeen to attempt a modeling career in New York City. Although Corey was eventually successful, it was not in New York, but mostly in Toronto, Ontario, Canada. After seven years in the business, however, she came down with rheumatic fever and mononucleosis. On a trip home to Temperance Vale to recover, Corey met Bill Zildjian of the Zildjian cymbal-manufacturing family, and the two eventually married. Following the wedding, according to John Bemrose in *Maclean's,* the couple traveled in Switzerland for a year, and in an apartment they rented there Corey discovered an abandoned copy of Joyce Carol Oates's short fiction collection, *The Wheel of Love.* Corey told Bemrose, "I'd never read stories like that. I decided then that I wanted to write." She managed to get her short fiction accepted by magazines, and her first novel, *Losing Eddie,* was published in 1993. *Losing Eddie* went on to garner the following year's SmithBooks/*Books in Canada* First Novel Award.

Though the narrator of *Losing Eddie* remains unnamed until the end of the novel, she is Laura, a nine-year-old girl growing up in conditions similar to those of Corey's own youth. Corey, however, never suffered through the death of a sibling; the novel's title refers to the death of Laura's older brother in an alcohol-related car accident. But Eddie's death is not the only tragedy suffered by Laura's dysfunctional but loving family. Laura's brother-in-law beats her sister, her younger brother, Bucky, narrowly escapes death twice, her mother endures two periods in a sanitarium before she is able to deal with her grief over Eddie, and her father battles alcoholism following the loss of his son. The mother of one of Laura's friends dies, while another of Laura's friends commits willing incest with her brother. Nevertheless, Bemrose explained that "the overriding theme of the novel is love." He went on to assert that "*Losing Eddie* could well stand as a cautionary tale to anyone accustomed to talking blithely—and dismissively—of 'dysfunctional families.'"

Other critics have had complimentary things to say about *Losing Eddie* as well, though a *Kirkus Reviews* contributor wrote that Corey has "hobbled herself here by overdoing the disasters." The reviewer did concede, however, that the novel's "freshness of language and observation mark Corey as a promising newcomer." Kate Fitzsimmons, who discussed *Losing Eddie* in *Belles Lettres,* praised Corey's book-length debut, noting that the author's "brilliant metaphoric language, coupled with her compassionate flashes of insight, elevate the story out of the gritty, unpredictable world in which her narrator lives." Bemrose concluded that *Losing Eddie* "is one of the most confident debuts Canadian fiction has seen in some time."

Corey's second novel, *The Skating Pond,* focuses on fourteen-year-old Elizabeth Johnson, whose family is wrought with tragedy. First, her mother, a talented ice-skater, is hit in the head with a hockey puck while skating on a local pond—an injury that results in her disfigurement and, ultimately, her death. When Elizabeth's father leaves to pursue an art career with his new girlfriend, Elizabeth is left to fend for herself in the frozen Maine village. She falls into the arms of a much older man named Frederick, who though tender at first, eventually leaves her, pregnant and once again on her own. Elizabeth finds comfort with a neighbor named Michael. They marry and eventually have two children together. When Frederick returns after many years, however, the young mother finds herself longing for her first love once again.

A *Publishers Weekly* reviewer called *The Skating Pond* sensuous but overwrought and noted, "Corey's voluptuous descriptions of physical sensation carry the reader pleasantly along, but the characters' solemn pronouncements . . . grow tiresome, and it becomes difficult to overlook the improbabilities of the plot." *Library Journal's* Judith Kicinski, however, called the book "beautiful and harrowing." *Booklist's* Whitney Scott noted that *The Skating Pond* "resembles ice fragments, in that Corey intersperses dreams, flashbacks, and scenes set in the fictional present." Debby Waldman of *People* wrote, "Stories like these usually lead to salvation, but it isn't obvious that Elizabeth will get it: She follows every sensible decision with an awful one. Her complexity could easily sustain another book." Shanda Deziel of *Maclean's* noted, "Elizabeth stays with you after the novel is finished. She's a character that many women understand."

As an author, Corey attempts to tell those stories that are often neglected and overlooked. She told Deziel in *Maclean's,* "One of the things that interests me is people who choose what we perceive as a simpler life—and just how complex those lives actually are. The flashy stories are everywhere, but stories about the people I know are not always told."

BIOGRAPHICAL AND CRITICAL SOURCES:

PERIODICALS

Belles Lettres, summer, 1994, pp. 53, 55.

Booklist, September 15, 1993, Alice Joyce, review of *Losing Eddie,* p. 126; December 15, 2002, Whitney Scott, review of *The Skating Pond,* p. 731.

Boston Herald, January 5, 2003, Jessica Ullian, review of *The Skating Pond,* p. 58.

Kirkus Reviews, August 1, 1993, pp. 951-952; November 1, 2002, review of *The Skating Pond,* p. 1549.

Library Journal, September 1, 1993, Dawn L. Anderson, review of *Losing Eddie,* p. 220; January, 2003, Judith Kicinski, review of *The Skating Pond,* p. 152.

Los Angeles Times, January 5, 2003, Susan Salter Reynolds, review of *The Skating Pond,* p. R-15.

Maclean's, April 11, 1994, John Bemrose, review of *Losing Eddie,* p. 64; March 17, 2003, Shanda Deziel, review of *The Skating Pond,* p. 54.

New York Times Book Review, February 9, 2003, John Hartl, review of *The Skating Pond,* p. 24.

People, February 10, 2003, Debby Waldman, review of *The Skating Pond,* p. 49.

Publishers Weekly, August 16, 1993, review of *Losing Eddie,* p. 88; December 9, 2002, review of *The Skating Pond,* p. 61.

School Library Journal, February, 1994, Marguerite O'Connor, review of *Losing Eddie,* p. 136.

ONLINE

Idiot's Guide.com, http://www.idiotsguide.com/ (March 18, 2004), description of *The Skating Pond.*

Random House of Canada Web site, http://www.randomhouse.ca/ (March 18, 2004), review of *The Skating Pond.*

Reading Group Guides, http://www.readinggroup guides.com/ (March 18, 2004), description of *The Skating Pond.**

CRAFT, Robert 1923-

PERSONAL: Born October 20, 1923, in Kingston, NY; son of Raymond and Arpha (Lawson) Craft. *Education:* Juilliard School of Music, B.A., 1946; also studied at the Berkshire Music Center in Tanglewood, MA, and studied conducting with Monteux.

ADDRESSES: Home—1390 South Ocean Blvd., Pompano Beach, FL 33062-7151.

CAREER: Conductor of orchestras in Europe, Japan, and the United States, beginning 1952. Conducted the New York Brass and Woodwind Ensemble, 1947; conductor of Evenings-on-the-Roof and Monday Evening Concerts, Los Angeles, CA, 1950-68. Lecturer at Dartington School, England, 1957, and at Princeton Seminar for Contemporary Music, 1959; Lucas Lecturer, Carleton College, 1981-82. Conducted twenty-five record albums for Columbia Records. *Military service:* U.S. Army, 1943-44.

AWARDS, HONORS: National Institute and American Academy award in literature, 1976; received two Grand Prix du Disque awards; Edison Prize, for recordings by Varese and Stravinsky.

WRITINGS:

(With Allesandro Piovesan and Ramon Vlad) *Le Musiche religiose di Igor Stravinsky con il catalogo analitico completo di tutte le sue opere di Craft, Piovesan, Vlad,* Lombroso (Venice, Italy), 1957.

Table Talk, Doubleday (New York, NY), 1965.

Bravo Stravinsky, photographs by Arnold Newman, World Publishing (Iowa Falls, IA), 1967.

Stravinsky: The Chronicle of a Friendship, 1948-1971, Knopf (New York, NY), 1972, revised and expanded edition published as *Stravinsky: Chronicle of a Friendship,* Vanderbilt University Press (Nashville, TN), 1994.

Prejudices in Disguise: Articles, Essays, Reviews, Random House (New York, NY), 1974.

Current Convictions: Views and Reviews, Random House (New York, NY), 1977.

(With Vera Stravinsky) *Stravinsky: In Pictures and Documents,* Simon & Schuster (New York, NY), 1979.

(Translator) *Stravinsky: Selected Correspondence,* Knopf (New York, NY), Volume 1, 1981, Volume 2, 1984, Volume 3, 1985.

(Author of captions) *Igor and Vera Stravinsky: A Photograph Album, 1921 to 1971,* photographs selected by Vera Stravinsky and Rita McCaffrey, Thames & Hudson (New York, NY), 1982.

A Stravinsky Scrapbook, 1940-1971, illustrations chosen by Patricia Schwark, Thames & Hudson (New York, NY), 1983.

Present Perspectives, Critical Writings, Knopf (New York, NY), 1984.

(Editor) *Dearest Bubushkin: The Correspondence of Vera and Igor Stravinsky, 1921-1954, with excerpts from Vera Stravinsky's Diaries, 1922-1971,* translated from the Russian by Lucia Davidova, Thames & Hudson (New York, NY), 1985.

Small Craft Advisories: Critical Articles, 1984-1988: Art, Ballet, Music, Literature, Film, Thames & Hudson (New York, NY), 1989.

Stravinsky: Glimpses of a Life, St. Martin's (New York, NY), 1993.

A Moment of Existence: Music, Literature, and the Arts, 1990-1995, Vanderbilt University Press (Nashville, TN), 1996.

Places: A Travel Companion for Music and Art Lovers, Thames & Hudson (New York, NY), 2000.

An Improbable Life: Memoirs, Vanderbilt University Press (Nashville, TN), 2002.

Columnist, *World* magazine.

WITH IGOR STRAVINSKY

Conversations with Igor Stravinsky, four volumes, Doubleday (New York, NY), 1959, reprinted, University of California Press (Berkeley, CA), 1980.

Memories and Commentaries, Doubleday (New York, NY), 1960, reprinted, University of California Press (Berkeley, CA), 1981.

Expositions and Developments, Doubleday (New York, NY), 1962, reprinted, University of California Press (Berkeley, CA), 1981.

Dialogues and a Diary, Doubleday (New York, NY), 1963, revised edition published as *Dialogues,* University of California Press (Berkeley, CA), 1982.

Themes and Episodes (also see below), Knopf (New York, NY), 1966.

Retrospectives and Conclusions (also see below), Knopf (New York, NY), 1969.

Themes and Conclusions (contains excerpts from *Themes and Episodes* and *Retrospectives and Conclusions*), Faber (New York, NY), 1972.

SIDELIGHTS: For more than two decades, conductor Robert Craft enjoyed a rather unique position as resident house guest, collaborator, and confidant of composer Igor Stravinsky. Indeed, Craft is credited by many for having had a profound influence on Stravinsky's work. When the composer from the Ukraine came to America to live, it was Craft who helped to steer him away from the traditional schools of musical theory adhered to in Europe and toward a willingness to experiment; in fact, Craft persuaded Stravinsky to write music using the twelve-tone (dodecaphony) method that was so important in the composer's creative evolution. As Claudio Spies put it in a *Notes* review of *Stravinsky: Glimpses of a Life,* Craft had a definite role "in bringing about certain very crucial changes in Stravinsky's attitudes, in his musical concerns, and in his conscious efforts to adapt to American informality and relaxation." *Publishers Weekly* critic Sybil S. Steinberg described Craft as "Stravinsky's musical assistant, protégé and spiritual son." During his years with the composer, Craft recorded his impressions of life with him and his second wife, Vera Stravinsky, in a journal. Years later these impressions were the basis of several books written by Craft.

While Craft was the sole author of a number of these books, he wrote seven of his Stravinsky books in collaboration with Stravinsky himself; one was written with Stravinsky's widow, Vera. These books contain essays by and on the composer and his music, reviews, conversations with Stravinsky and other artists, and parts of Craft's journals. "Together, these collections of interviews, essays on music and reviews make up an extraordinary loose-leaf monument to the twentieth century's leading composer," explained a writer for *Time.* "Professionally speaking, Stravinsky has always been brilliant but baffling. A fierce and uncompromising pioneer who quite literally revolutionized the music of his century, he was also as modishly conscious of musical fashions as Picasso was addicted to changing taste in art and sculpture. Craft has made Stravinsky's one of the best-documented lives since Beethoven's, and his book [*Retrospectives and Conclusions*], music aside, presents some of the most lively and intelligent casual reading available." *New York Times* reviewer Anatole Broyard believed that "there are so many brilliant and moving things in Robert Craft's [*Stravinsky: The Chronicle of a Friendship, 1948-1971*] that one hardly knows where to begin in praising the book. In the last two decades of Stravinsky's life, Mr. Craft functioned as friend, sounding board, musical catalyst and stand-in conductor under Stravinsky's supervision. Having collaborated on six books with Stravinsky, Mr. Craft is a practiced writer: he is also an extremely good one."

Many critics pointed out that the truly inspired parts of these book collaborations were the sections written by Craft. Robert Evett explained in *New Republic* that "in their [*Retrospectives and Conclusions*] the authors have divided the book roughly in half: first, miscellaneous writings of Stravinsky, then a generous, but not-quite generous enough selection from the diaries of Robert Craft. The Stravinsky portion is entertaining but predictable. . . . The really valuable material is in the Craft diaries. . . . It is clear from his writing that he enjoys the company of the great and famous, feels honored to drop their names, and does not mind being known as side-kick in residence to an eminent man." And *Atlantic* reviewer Oscar Handlin said that Craft's contributions to *Themes and Episodes* "derive their interest not only from the unusual people and places visited but also from the perceptive and lively style in which they are recorded. . . . These are the reflections of a powerful personality. The sentences are struck off like the thought they express, without premeditation and with intense feeling."

Reviewers have also found these admirable qualities in the Stravinsky books that Craft wrote by himself. In a *New York Times Book Review* article on *Stravinsky: The Chronicle of a Friendship,* Simon Karlinsky wrote that "Stravinsky is the main subject of Craft's diary, but . . . we are in the presence of Robert Craft's own mind and personality throughout, and what a fascinating mind it is: uncompromising in its insistence on musical excellence, philosophically subtle, attuned to every manifestation of contemporary sensibility, open to complex new ideas and new experiences. There is a deep humanity in Craft's sympathetic accounts." Karlinsky went on to remark, "If we add Craft's awesome erudition on almost every conceivable subject and the enviable stylistic mastery of his writing, it becomes clear that he is the ideal chronicler of Stravinsky's life, times and ideas." Michael Steinberg made similar remarks in a *New York Times Book Review* article. "On music itself, though, Craft can be intensely interesting and stimulating," Steinberg observed, "and for two reasons especially: he has a way of writing about things as though his experience of them were very fresh . . . and brings to his writing a daunting wealth of book-learning and musical reference."

Craft's 1993 book about his composer friend, *Stravinsky: Glimpses of a Life,* differs from his earlier books on Stravinsky in that, as Spies explained, "rather than presenting a string of essays on relatively unrelated biographical, literary, critical, or autobiographical materials that had previously been published in a variety of journals, the current collection consists of revisions and amplifications of articles now presented together for the first time." The central theme that ties the essays together, as Spies saw it, has to do with Craft's influence on Stravinsky, which, now that Stravinsky has been dead for several decades, "has lost all traces of . . . self-serving implications. It is merely an accurate statement of fact." Now, it can clearly be seen that Craft, indeed, was the person who was primarily responsible for breaking down the wall of tradition that had hampered Stravinsky and showed him new possibilities simply by exposing the composer to music and composers previously unknown to him.

In 2002, Craft published *An Improbable Life: Memoirs,* in which he details much about his days with Stravinsky, as well as many other famous people he has met over the years as a result of his association with the composer. In a review of the memoir in *Opera News,* Robert Croan acknowledged Craft's "considerable accomplishments as a conductor, and his extraordinary verbal and musical facility," but the critic felt that the "most interesting portions of *An Improbable Life* are those dealing with Stravinsky and the celebrities Craft met through him," while the sections about the author's own life struck Croan as "flat and even tedious." Having grown up middle-class in New York City, Craft led a fairly ordinary life until he met Stravinsky, and the sections of the book not related to this friendship reflect this ordinariness in their "prosaic" style, according to Croan, who added that, "In all, we don't really get to know Craft as well as we should from such a personal memoir." Nevertheless, Craft's contributions to the music world through his relationship with Igor Stravinsky have earned him an important place in its history.

BIOGRAPHICAL AND CRITICAL SOURCES:

PERIODICALS

Atlantic, October, 1966.
Booklist, October 1, 2002, George Cohen, review of *Memories and Commentaries,* p. 295.
Chicago Tribune, January 28, 1979.
Economist, June 6, 1992, review of *Stravinsky: Glimpses of a Life,* p. 97.
High Fidelity, November, 1982, David Hamilton, review of *Igor Stravinsky: Selected Correspondence,* Volume 1, p. MA15.
Library Journal, August, 1982, Larry Lipkis, review of *Igor and Vera Stravinsky: A Photograph Album, 1921 to 1971,* p. 1464; February 15, 1986, Robert W. Richart, review of *Dearest Bubushkin: The Correspondence of Vera and Igor Stravinsky, 1921-1954, with excerpts from Vera Stravinsky's Diaries, 1922-1971,* p. 183; January, 1993, Timothy J. McGee, review of *Stravinsky: Glimpses of a Life,* p. 116.
Nation, June 15, 1970.
National Review, February 24, 1984, Terry Treachout, "Monologues in Disguise," p. 57; December 28, 1984, Terry Treachout, review of *Present Perspectives: Critical Writings,* p. 53; May 11, 1992, Ralph De Toledano, review of *Igor Stravinsky, 1882-1927* (sound recording), p. 54.
New Republic, January 10, 1970.
New Statesman, October 15, 1982, Andrew Clements, review of *Stravinsky: Selected Correspondence,* p. 30; September 21, 1984, Andrew Clements, review of *Stravinsky: Selected Correspondence,* Volume 2, p. 33.
New Yorker, October 11, 1982, Desmond Shawe-Taylor, "Stravinsky," p. 174; July 30, 1984, review of *Stravinsky: Selected Correspondence,* Volume 2, p. 87.
New York Times, June 15, 1972.
New York Times Book Review, July 2, 1972, October 16, 1977, January 28, 1979, May 23, 1982; December 5, 1982, "Stravinsky," p. 16; August 5, 1984, David Hamilton, review of *A Stravinsky Scrapbook: 1940-1971* and *Stravinsky: Selected Correspondence,* p. 11; January 13, 1985, Hubert Saal, review of *Present Perspectives,* p. 24; September 22, 1985, Leon Botstein, review of *Stravinsky: Selected Correspondence,* Volume 3, p. 18.

Notes, June, 1994, Claudio Spies, review of *Stravinsky,* p. 1408.
Opera News, November, 1994, Patrick J. Smith, review of *Stravinsky: The Rake's Progress* (sound recording), p. 48; January, 2003, Robert Croan, review of *Memories and Commentaries* and *An Improbable Life: Memoirs,* p. 88.
Publishers Weekly, January 15, 1979; December 3, 1982, "A Book about Stravinsky," p. 53; December 9, 1983, review of *Stravinsky: Selected Correspondence,* Volume 2, p. 42; January 13, 1984, review of *A Stravinsky Scrapbook, 1940-1971,* p. 58; February 3, 1984, review of *Present Perspectives: Critical Writings,* p. 392; July 5, 1985, Genevieve Stuttaford, review of *Stravinsky: Selected Correspondence,* Volume 3, p. 59; November 30, 1992, review of *Stravinsky,* p. 39; August 8, 1994, review of *Stravinsky: Chronicle of a Friendship,* p. 408.
Smithsonian, October, 1984, Alan Rich, review of *Stravinsky: Selected Correspondence,* Volume 2, p. 187.
Time, December 19, 1969.
Times Literary Supplement, February 27, 1980; January 31, 2003, David Schiff, "Probably Bob," p. 7.
Washington Post Book World, December 31, 1967, May 23, 1982.

ONLINE

Robert Craft Web Site, http://www.robertcraft.net/index.html (October 6, 2003).*

*   *   *

CROWLEY, John 1942-

PERSONAL: Born December 1, 1942, in Presque Isle, ME; son of Joseph B. (a doctor) and Patience (Lyon) Crowley; married Laurie Block, 1984; children: two daughters. *Education:* Indiana University, B.A., 1964.

ADDRESSES: Home—Box 395, Conway, MA 01341.

CAREER: Photographer and commercial artist, 1964-66; fiction writer and freelance writer for films and television, 1966—. Yale University, visiting professor of creative writing.

AWARDS, HONORS: American Book Award nomination, 1980, for *Engine Summer;* Hugo Award nomination, Nebula Award nomination, and World Fantasy Award, all 1982, all for *Little, Big;* American Film Festival Award, 1982, for *America Lost and Found;* World Fantasy Award, 1990, for *Great Work of Time;* American Academy of Arts and Letters Award for literature; *Locus* award, for short story "Gone"; Academy Award nomination, 1991, for *The Restless Conscience: Resistance to Hitler within Germany 1933-1945,* and 1992, for *The Liberators: Fighting on Two Fronts in World War II.*

WRITINGS:

NOVELS

The Deep (also see below), Doubleday (New York, NY), 1975.

Beasts (also see below), Doubleday (New York, NY), 1976.

Engine Summer (also see below), Doubleday (New York, NY), 1979.

Little, Big, Bantam (New York, NY), 1981.

Ægypt (first novel in tetralogy), Bantam (New York, NY), 1987.

Great Work of Time (novella), Bantam (New York, NY), 1991.

Love and Sleep (second novel in tetralogy), Bantam (New York, NY), 1994.

Three Novels, Bantam (New York, NY), 1994.

Dæmonomania (third novel in tetralogy), Bantam (New York, NY), 2000.

The Translator, Morrow (New York, NY), 2002.

Otherwise: Three Novels (contains *The Deep, Beasts,* and *Engine Summer*), Perennial (New York, NY), 2002.

OTHER

(Editor, with Howard Kerr and Charles L. Crow) *The Haunted Dusk: American Supernatural Fiction, 1820-1920,* University of Georgia Press (Athens, GA), 1983.

Novelty (short stories), Bantam (New York, NY), 1989.

Antiquities: Seven Stories, Incunabula (Seattle, WA), 1993.

Novelties and Souvenirs: Collected Short Fiction, Perennial (New York, NY), 2004.

Author of screenplays for documentaries, including *America Lost and Found,* 1979, *No Place to Hide,* 1982, *America and Lewis Hine,* 1985, *The World of Tomorrow,* 1985, *Are We Winning Mommy? America and the Cold War,* 1986, *The World of Tomorrow,* 1989, *Fit: Episodes in the History of the Body,* 1990, *The Restless Conscience: Resistance to Hitler within Germany 1933-1945,* 1991, *Pearl Harbor: Surprise and Remembrance,* 1991, *The Liberators: Fighting on Two Fronts in World War II,* 1992, *The Gate of Heavenly Peace,* 1995, and *A Morning Sun,* 2003.

Work represented in anthologies, including *Shadows,* Doubleday (New York, NY), 1977; and *Elsewhere,* Ace Books (New York, NY), 1981. Author of television scripts for *America Lost and Found* and *No Place to Hide,* Public Broadcasting System (PBS). Contributor to periodicals, including *Omni.*

SIDELIGHTS: Author John Crowley has been praised by critics for his thoughtful, finely wrought works of science fiction and fantasy, which include the novels *The Deep, Ægypt, Love and Sleep,* and *Dæmonomania.* A successful television writer who has never pandered to popular tastes, Crowley infuses his genre writings with literary quality and "mind-catching philosophical musings," according to a *Publishers Weekly* reviewer of *Dæmonomania.* Suzanne Keen reported in *Commonweal* that his characters "are psychologically convincing, an accomplishment that makes the historical and fantastic elements of his [novel *Love and Sleep*] all the more thrilling." Whether his work visits far planets or local neighborhoods, some critics have suggested, Crowley always challenges the accepted perceptions of things and offers multi-layered mysteries for his characters—and his readers—to explore. As a *Kirkus Reviews* contributor explained it in a review of *Dæmonomania,* "Crowley's work is a taste well worth acquiring, but you have to work at it."

In a *New York Times Book Review* piece on Crowley's first novel, *The Deep,* Gerald Jonas declared that "paraphrase is useless to convey the intensity of Crowley's prose; anyone interested in the risk-taking side of modern science fiction will want to experience it firsthand." Jonathan Dee noted, also in the *New York Times Book Review,* that Crowley "is an abundantly gifted writer, a scholar whose passion for history is matched by his ability to write a graceful sentence." Some reviewers observed that with his third novel,

Engine Summer, Crowley developed more complex plots and characters, and his themes began reflecting the influence of the fantasy genre. Charles Nicol wrote in *Saturday Review:* "A lyric adventure as concerned with the meaning of actions as with the actions themselves, [*Engine Summer*] presents a meditative world that should appeal to lovers of the great fantasies. Crowley has published some science fiction previously; here he has gone beyond his genre into that hilly country on the borderlands of literature." Similarly, Crowley's Nebula and Hugo Award nominee *Little, Big* was described by John Clute in the *Washington Post Book World* as a "dense, marvelous, magic-realist family chronicle about the end of time and the new world to come."

Novelist Carolyn See, in a review for the *Los Angeles Times,* commented that Crowley's fifth novel, *Ægypt,* contains "some extraordinary storytelling." Incorporating fantasy, satire, and philosophical romance, the novel centers on Pierce Moffett, a professor of Renaissance history whose desire to write a book about finding the meaning in life leads him to a mythical area and a mysterious woman. *Washington Post Book World* contributor Michael Dirda remarked that *Ægypt* "is clearly a novel where thought speaks louder than action, where people, places and events are at once actual and allegorical. . . . Crowley wants readers to appreciate his foreshadowings, echoes, bits of odd lore, multiple voices—in the evolution of complex pattern is his art." Dirda also noted, however, that Crowley's narrative is so complex that it can occasionally be confusing. Commenting on this complexity, John Clute, in a review for the *New York Times Book Review,* suggested that *Ægypt* provides "a dizzying experience." *Ægypt* is the first novel in an ambitious tetralogy centering upon the intellectual and personal journey of Moffett.

In *Love and Sleep,* Crowley continues the tale begun in *Ægypt.* While *Ægypt* tells of Moffett's life during the 1960s and 1970s, *Love and Sleep* frames that period, returning to the 1950s and allowing readers a glimpse of Moffett's Kentucky childhood, a time full of "minor incidents and wonders," according to *Washington Post Book Review* critic Lawrence Norfolk, before leaping ahead of *Ægypt* in true sequel fashion. In the novel, Norfolk explained, Crowley hangs his plot upon the speculation that "between the old world of things as they used to be, and the new world of things as they would be instead, there has always fallen

a sort of passage time, a chaos of unformed possibilities in which all sorts of manifestations could be witnessed." It has "an interim feel, a sense of its author treading water while the players are maneuvered into position" for the proposed third and fourth segments of the series, Norfolk continued. "As it stands, *Love and Sleep* is a collection of strange episodes, of hints and premonitions. The ultimate worth of this strange, teasing book hangs on the two yet to be written." Jonathan Dee offered a similar assessment of the work for the *New York Times Book Review:* while the first section of *Love and Sleep* "generates a true, expansive sense of human mystery . . . the novel's own vision, so crystal clear in that opening section, grows woollier and more diffuse" as Moffett's saga continues. Chicago *Tribune Books* contributor Robert Chatain maintained that the author's mixture of realism and fantasy "is not for every reader," yet the critic added: "to dislike fantasy is not to dismiss Crowley; he's one of the few writers who successfully crosses the razor-thin but definite line between genre fiction and literary fiction." Citing the author's "metaphysical conceits," Chatain concluded of Crowley, "there is no temptation to confuse [his novels] with other fictions; there's really nothing like them."

Dæmonomania continues the Pierce Moffett saga, as magic seeps further into the lives of Moffett and his acquaintances in Faraway Hills, New York. The title refers to a possible case of demonic possession, but the book portends even more massive shifts in what appears to be reality. For his part, Moffett comes to understand that magic once worked, that science has only temporarily halted the potency of magic, and that a "secret history," shared by a select few, actually directs the course of human actions. A *Kirkus Reviews* critic, while noting that the book will mean more to those who have read its two predecessors, called it "[d]eeply atmospheric, impressively learned, endlessly suggestive."

In 2002 Crowley went in a new direction with his writing, publishing *The Translator,* a work that "demonstrates to the reader . . . the escape that poetry and literature can provide in times of trouble," observed *Booklist* critic Ted Leventhal. Set in 1962, *The Translator* examines the relationship between Innokenti Falin, an exiled Russian poet, and Kit Malone, an American coed with a troubled past. The pair develop a close friendship, and Malone becomes Falin's translator. When the Cuban Missile Crisis erupts, their relationship is threatened by government officials who have been watching Falin. "Crowley's lovely, effortless writing and his accurate, earnest portraits of Russians make this a sad love story with an important piece of rhetoric at its heart," wrote a contributor in *Kirkus Reviews.* James Schiff, reviewing *The Translator* in *Book,* noted that "this simple and sincere novel, which masterfully renders a moment in history, possesses a certain beauty."

Novelties and Souvenirs: Collected Short Fiction, a 2004 work, contains fifteen tales of the fantastic. In an interview on *HarperCollins.com,* Crowley remarked that the stories "reflect matters . . . that have always been of deep interest to me. Among those is the malleability of reality, and what it would be like if it could be altered by human wishes; what goes on in the mind and heart of someone who makes such wishes . . . ; and the open-ended nature of the course of time, that produces unintended consequences, not always good or bad." A *Kirkus Reviews* contributor deemed *Novelties and Souvenirs* a "pleasing introduction to a very interesting writer's several 'worlds.'"

Crowley's works are noted for their lyrical, lucid style and diverse, provocative characters. In an interview with Gavin J. Grant on *Booksense.com,* the author was asked why he writes from such varied points of view. "I'm drawn to characters who seem to perceive the secret history of the world, or see a world-story proceeding, and don't trust themselves—and don't believe that they could know such a thing—but are drawn to it anyway," Crowley responded. "That's been a consistent direction all my writing has taken. I can think of people whose minds are active in that way in almost all the books I've written."

BIOGRAPHICAL AND CRITICAL SOURCES:

BOOKS

Contemporary Literary Criticism, Volume 57, Gale (Detroit, MI), 1990.

Dictionary of Literary Biography Yearbook 1982, Gale (Detroit, MI), 1983.

St. James Guide to Science Fiction Writers, 4th edition, St. James Press (Detroit, MI), 1996.

Turner, Alice K., and Michael Andre-Driussi, editors, *Snake's-Hands: The Fiction of John Crowley,* Cosmos Books (Canton, OH), 2003.

PERIODICALS

Analog: Science Fiction/Science Fact, June, 1977; August, 1987; December, 1989.

Atlantic, September, 1994, review of *Love and Sleep,* p. 112.

Berkshire Sampler, September 13, 1981.

Book, March-April, 2002, James Schiff, review of *The Translator,* p. 79.

Booklist, February 15, 2002, Ted Leventhal, review of *The Translator,* pp. 990-991.

Commonweal, December 2, 1994, Suzanne Keen, review of *Love and Sleep,* p. 26.

Extrapolation, spring, 1990.

Kirkus Reviews, June 15, 1994, review of *Love and Sleep;* June 15, 2000, review of *Dæmonomania,* p. 815; February 1, 2002, review of *The Translator,* p. 121; March 1, 2004, review of *Novelties and Souvenirs: Collected Short Fiction,* p. 194.

Library Journal, August, 2000, Rachel Singer Gordon, review of *Dæmonomania,* p. 168.

Locus, August, 1991; September, 1991; May, 2001, pp. 4-5, 66-67; February, 2002, Faren Miller, review of *The Translator.*

Los Angeles Times, May 4, 1987, Carolyn See, review of *Ægypt.*

Magazine of Fantasy and Science Fiction, April, 1980; December, 1987; January, 1992; June, 2002, Elizabeth Hand, review of *The Translator.*

New Statesman, November 20, 1987.

New York Review of Science Fiction, July, 1998, Jennifer Stevenson, "Memory and the World of John Crowley," pp. 1, 8-11; August, 1999, Alice K. Turner, "Deep Thoughts: John Crowley's Fifteenth-Century Game of Kings," pp. 1, 4-5, and Michael Andre-Driussi, "John Crowley's Great Blond Beasts," pp. 1, 6-12, and Alice K. Turner, "One Writer's Beginnings: John Crowley's *Engine Summer* as the Portrait of the Artist," pp. 17-18; October, 1999, Michael Andre-Driussi, "John Crowley," pp. 1, 4-7; January, 2000, Alice K. Turner, "Daily Alice's Childhood; *Little, Big* for Little Folk," pp. 9-10; October, 2000, Michael Andre-Driussi, "Off the Deep End," pp. 18-19; January, 2002, Sondra Ford Swift, "Pierce Moffett the Ass: Apuleian and Brunonian Theses in John Crowley's *Dæmonomania,*" pp. 1, 6-8; March, 2002, Bill Sheehan, "Life after *Ægypt,*" pp. 12-15.

New York Times Book Review, November 21, 1976, Gerald Jonas, review of *The Deep;* March 27, 1977; May 20, 1979; March 2, 1986; October 12,

1986; May 3, 1987, pp. 9, 11, John Clute, review of *Ægypt;* August 14, 1988; May 21, 1989; July 5, 1992; February 6, 1994, review of *Antiquities,* p. 22; September 4, 1994, Jonathan Dee, review of *Love and Sleep,* p. 9; September 17, 2000, Jeff Waggoner, review of *Dæmonomania,* p. 25; June 2, 2002, review of *The Translator,* p. 24.

Publishers Weekly, February 20, 1987; April 14, 1989; August 29, 1994, Robert K. J. Killheffer, "John Crowley: 'I Still Owe a Debt of Gratitude,'" p. 53; July 3, 2000, review of *Dæmonomania,* p. 53; January 14, 2002, review of *The Translator,* p. 38; May 24, 2004, p. 50.

Saturday Review, April 14, 1979.

Science Fiction and Fantasy Book Review, January-February, 1982.

Times Literary Supplement, May 28, 1982; November 20-26, 1987, p. 1274.

Tribune Books (Chicago, IL), October 18, 1981; June 18, 1989, p. 6; September 11, 1994, Robert Chatain, review of *Love and Sleep,* pp. 1, 13.

Village Voice, April 5, 2002, Elizabeth Hand, "Angels in America."

Voice Literary Supplement, September, 1994, p. 31.

Washington Post Book World, March 23, 1980; July 26, 1981; October 4, 1981; April 19, 1987, pp. 1, 7, Michael Dirda, review of *Ægypt;* March 19, 1989; December 6, 1992, review of *Little, Big,* p. 4; November 28, 1993, review of *Antiquities,* p. 8; July 10, 1994; August 14, 1994, Lawrence Norfolk, review of *Love and Sleep,* p. 5; March 24, 2002, Howard Norman, review of *The Translator.*

ONLINE

Booksense.com, http://www.booksense.com/ (August 17, 2004), Gavin J. Grant, "The Secret History of John Crowley."

HarperCollins Web site, http://www.harpercollins.com/ (August 20, 2004) "An Interview with John Crowley."

January Magazine Online, http://www.january magazine.com/ (April, 2002), David Dalgleish, "False Modesty."

Ransom Center Web site, http://www.hrc.utexas.edu/ (August 20, 2004), "John Crowley Papers."

Salon.com, http://www.salon.com/ (March 21, 2002), Laura Miller, review of *The Translator.**

D

DANN, Patty 1953-

PERSONAL: Born October 30, 1953, in New York, NY; married Willem Nooter, May, 1991 (deceased); children: Jacob Nooter. *Education:* University of Oregon, B.A.; Columbia University, M.F.A.

ADDRESSES: Agent—Malaga Baldi, Literary Agency, 233 West 99th St., Apt. 19-C, New York, NY 10025. *E-mail*—ptty86@aol.com.

CAREER: Summer Olympics, Los Angeles, CA, participant, 1984; West Side Young Men's Christian Association (YMCA), New York, NY, teacher, 1988—; Columbia University, New York, NY, thesis advisor to M.F.A. writing program. Also worked as manager of documentary programs, A&E Television Network.

WRITINGS:

Mermaids (novel), Ticknor & Fields, 1986.
The Baby Boat: A Memoir of Adoption, Hyperion (New York, NY), 1998.
Sweet & Crazy, St. Martin's Press (New York, NY), 2003.

Contributor to periodicals, including *New York Times, Chicago Tribune, More, Writer,* and *Redbook.*

Mermaids has been translated into six languages.

ADAPTATIONS: Mermaids was adapted for film by Orion Pictures, 1990.

WORK IN PROGRESS: A novel.

SIDELIGHTS: Patty Dann's novel *Mermaids,* published in 1986, was a first effort that scored a great success with reviewers and the public; it was eventually translated into six languages and was made into a 1990 hit movie by Orion Pictures that starred Cher, Bob Hoskins, and Winona Ryder. The novel's story is told from the perspective of its fourteen-year-old protagonist, Charlotte Flax, who has had eighteen different homes in her young life. Her mother, whom she refers to as "Mrs. Flax," has as much trouble settling on a town in which to live as she does a man to love; she is constantly on the move looking for both. Significantly, the only dishes Mrs. Flax is able to cook are hors d'oeuvres. The family, which includes Charlotte's younger sister Kate, is currently "settled" in Grove, Massachusetts, and the maturing girls are focused on some very specific goals: for Charlotte, joining a nunnery—one is located next door—for Kate, becoming the Olympic swimmer her father was not able to be, and for both girls, staying in Grove long enough for their father to find them.

The novel is full of endearingly quirky characterizations: Charlotte longs for the chaste life—the opposite of her mother's—despite the fact that she is Jewish and that she cannot help falling in love with, among others, the convent's young caretaker; Kate spends long hours training in the local pool and at home is most comfortable in the bathtub. Their mother tries out new recipes, but only for appetizers; and the stream of men through her bedroom door is fairly constant. But as Mary-Ann Tirone Smith wrote in her *New York Times* review, "All three members of the family are completely tolerant of one another's oddball behavior." Reviewers were taken with Charlotte and what a *Publishers Weekly* critic called the "charm and freshness" of Dann's writing. The same reviewer called Kate and Charlotte "sharply etched and recognizable" characters who exerted "strong demands on the reader's affection." Elke Liebs, writing in the *UNESCO Courier,* found some aspects of the novel unlikely: the fact that Mrs. Flax "takes a malicious delight in stealing her daughter's first love" and that "she does not even want to come into the house with the father whom her children long to see on his only visit." Liebs felt that the book shows "a distorted picture of emancipation, psychological neglect and sarcasm which prevents us from experiencing clear feelings." But Tirone Smith found the character of Charlotte to be "a magnificent voice . . . compelling and tender, touching and alive," and deemed the overall work "a radiant debut."

In 1998 Dann published *The Baby Boat: A Memoir of Adoption,* a book about the experience she and her husband had in adopting a Lithuanian child. Dann writes that the national bird of Lithuania is the stork, a hard irony considering the horrific bureaucracy that impedes the adoption process to the point that only a determined few adoptive parents can persevere. First, an infant girl the couple had hoped to adopt dies before they can meet her. Then, after numerous administrative foul-ups, the year-old boy they next choose to adopt becomes ill and is sent to a poorly staffed and ill-equipped hospital. The couple continue to pursue the adoption, including going to great lengths to secure hard-to-find items such as medicine and diapers for the child. Finally, Dann's husband, Willem, is able to convince a Lithuanian judge to let them adopt the boy with the statement, "I fell in love with my wife in one day as well."

Describing her 2003 novel, Dann told *CA:* "My book *Sweet & Crazy* is a poignant and bittersweet novel of a single mother coping with the extremes of life. Set in Ash Creek, Ohio, Hanna Painter and her son have just begun to patch together their lives, when the World Trade Center is attacked. Hanna struggles with the challenges of raising a son alone, romance, and racism as their once peaceful town faces a new century."

BIOGRAPHICAL AND CRITICAL SOURCES:

BOOKS

Dann, Patty, *The Baby Boat: Memoir of an Adoption,* Hyperion (New York, NY), 1998.

PERIODICALS

Booklist, September 1, 2003, Deborah Donovan, review of *Sweet & Crazy,* p. 53.

New York Times, October 12, 1986, Mary-Ann Tirone Smith, review of *Mermaids,* p. 50.

Publishers Weekly, September 29, 1986, review of *Mermaids;* September 8, 2003, review of *Sweet & Crazy,* p. 250.

UNESCO Courier, July-August 1997, Elke Liebs, review of *Mermaids,* pp. 16-19.

ONLINE

Readerville Web site, http://www.readerville.com/ (February 27, 2005).

*   *   *

DAOUST, Jean-Paul 1946-

PERSONAL: Born January 30, 1946, in Valleyfield, Quebec, Canada; son of Jules and Adrienne (Beausoleil) Daoust. *Education:* University of Montreal, M.A., 1976.

ADDRESSES: Home—151 chemin Champoux, St. Melanie, Quebec J0K 3A0, Canada. *E-mail*—mesanges@pandore.qc.ca.

CAREER: Writer, teacher, and editor. Cegep Edouard-Montpetit, Quebec, Canada, professor.

MEMBER: Union des Écrivains Québécois.

AWARDS, HONORS: Governor General's Literary Award in Poetry, Canada Council, 1990, for *Les cendres bleues.*

WRITINGS:

POETRY

Oui, cher: récit (title means "Yes, Dear: A Narrative"), Éditions Cul Q (Montreal, Quebec, Canada), 1976.
Chaise longues (title means "Lounge Chairs"), Éditions Cul Q (Montreal, Quebec, Canada), 1977.

Portrait d'intérieur (title means "Portrait of an Interior"), APLM, 1981.

Poèmes de Babylone (title means "Babylon Poems"), Écrits des forges (Trois-Rivieres, Quebec, Canada), 1982.

Taxi, Écrits des forges (Trois-Rivieres, Quebec, Canada), 1984.

Dimanche après-midi (title means "Sunday Afternoon"), Écrits des forges (Trois-Rivieres, Quebec, Canada), 1985.

La peau du cœur et son opera (title means "Heart Skin and its Opera"), Éditions du Noroît (Montreal, Quebec, Canada), 1985.

Les garçons magiques; récits (title means "Magic Boys"), VLB Éditeur (Montreal, Quebec, Canada), 1986.

Suite contemporaine (title means "Contemporary Suite"), Écrits de forges (Trois-Rivieres, Quebec, Canada), 1987.

Les cendres bleues, Écrits de forges (Trois-Rivieres, Quebec, Canada), 1990, translation by Daniel Sloate published as *Blue Ashes: Selected Poems 1982-1998*, Guernica (Buffalo, NY), 1999.

Rituels d'Amériques (title means "Rituals of the Americas"), Éditions Incidit, 1990.

Les poses de la lumière (title means "Poses of Light"), Éditions du Noroît (Montreal, Quebec, Canada), 1991.

Du dandysme (title means "On Dandyism"), Éditions Trois (Laval, Quebec, Canada), 1991.

Black Diva: Selected Poems, 1982-1986, translated by Daniel Sloate, introduction by André Roy, Guernica (Montreal, Quebec, Canada), 1991.

Les chambres de la mer, Éditions l'arbre à paroles (Brussels, Belgium), 1991.

(With Louise Desjardins and Mona Latif-Ghattas) *Poèmes faxés* (title means "Faxed Poems"), Écrits des forges (Trois-Rivieres, Quebec, Canada), 1994.

111, Wooster Street, VLB Éditeur (Montreal, Quebec, Canada), 1996.

Taxi pour Babylone, Écrits des forges (Trois-Rivieres, Quebec, Canada), 1996.

Les saisons de l'Ange, Éditions du Noroît (Montreal, Quebec, Canada), 1997, Volume 2, 1999.

L'Amérique, XYZ Éditeur (Montreal, Quebec, Canada), 1999.

Le poème déshabillé, Éditions l'Interligne (Ottawa, Ontario, Canada), 2000.

Les versets amoureux, Écrits des forges (Trois-Rivieres, Quebec, Canada), 2001.

Levres ourvertes, Lanctôt (Montreal, Quebec, Canada), 2001.

Roses labyrinthes, Castor Astral (Paris, France), 2002.

Also author of *Fusions*, 1994.

OTHER

Soleils d'Acajou (novel; title means "The Mahogany Suns"), Éditions Nouvelle optique (Montreal, Quebec, Canada), 1983.

Le désert Rose (novel), Stanké (Montreal, Quebec, Canada), 2000.

Member of editorial board, *Estuaire*.

SIDELIGHTS: Jean-Paul Daoust has had collections of French-language poetry published since 1976. His 1990 volume *Les cendres bleues* garnered him one of Canada's most prestigious literary prizes—the Governor General's Award in Poetry. Since then, some of the poetry that preceded *Les cendres bleues* has been translated for readers of English. The first such volume is *Blue Ashes: Selected Poems, 1982-1986*.

The poems in *Blue Ashes* contain a great deal of imagery surrounding young male adolescents; they reminded Erin Moure, critiquing the collection in *Books in Canada,* of the young male angels in Wim Wenders' motion picture, *Wings of Desire*. Citing a line from *Blue Ashes* that runs, "Because to be happy / You always do things / That make you tremble all over," Moure concluded: "The book does that. Makes me tremble all over, that is."

Another well-known volume of Daoust's work is *Poèmes de Babylone*. In this collection Daoust compares modern cities—ranging from Montreal to New York, Hollywood, and Las Vegas—to the ancient Biblical kingdom of Babylon. Sarah Lawall observed in the *French Review* that *Poèmes de Babylone* "is no celebration of pagan richness. Daoust's Babylon is—in the traditional image of militant Christian literature—a symbol of modern decadence and sterility." The collection is divided into three sections titled "Poème de nuit," "Poèmes de ville" and "Poèmes de voyage." Lawall expressed her belief that all three segments are bound together by common themes of "paralysis, sterility, and isolation." In the first segment, night is portrayed as mere negative space, a contrast to the day in which one can at least entertain illusions of meaning. The second segment focuses on the topic of current major cities—especially those of the United

States—and the frenetic but futile lives lived within them. The city is the fast-paced illusion Daoust opposes to night in the first segment; the second segment is thus filled with imagery of neon lights, television advertising, and people who use too much makeup. The "black champagne" used to describe the night of the first segment now becomes pink, but, according to Lawall, this transformation takes place "ominously." The poetic narrator is filled with despair, even in the daylight.

The third segment, though referring promisingly to trips, is in reality only the dreams of the narrator, who can escape from the cities of the second segment only through his imagination. Even his dreams of exotic locales such as Thailand and Egypt turn them into barren, desert places with no life. "Even the possibility of love," reported Lawall, "which is usually the poet's panacea for life's misery and the ills of society, is a parched, mummified, dead experience." The critic described *Poèmes de Babylone* as having "aggressively modern overtones."

BIOGRAPHICAL AND CRITICAL SOURCES:

BOOKS

Daoust, Jean-Paul, *Poèmes de Babylone,* Écrits des forges (Trois-Rivieres, Quebec, Canada), 1982.
Daoust, Jean-Paul, *Blue Ashes: Selected Poems, 1982-1986,* translated by Daniel Sloate, introduction by André Roy, Guernica (Buffalo, NY), 1991.

PERIODICALS

Books in Canada, December, 1991, Erin Moure, review of *Black Diva: Selected Poems, 1982-1986,* p. 52.
Canadian Book Review Annual, 2000, review of *Les cendres bleues,* p. 193.
French Review, December, 1984, Sarah Lawall, review of *Poèmes de Babylone,* pp. 306-307.
Kirkus Reviews, November 1, 1999, review of *Les cendres bleues,* p. 1680.
Translation Review Supplement, December, 1999, *Les cendres bleues,* p. 13.

University of Toronto Quarterly, winter, 2000, review by Roger Chamberland, p. 29; winter, 2000, review by Jane Koustas, p. 271.

*   *   *

DÁVILA, Arlene M. 1965-

PERSONAL: Born May 31, 1965, in San Juan, Puerto Rico; daughter of Diego (a cattle rancher and farmer) and Laura (a flower arranger; maiden name, Feliciano) Dávila. *Ethnicity:* "Puerto Rican." *Education:* Tufts University, B.A., 1987; New York University, M.A. and certificate in museum studies, both 1990; Graduate Center, City University of New York, Ph.D., 1996.

ADDRESSES: Office—Department of American Studies, New York University, 285 Mercer St., 8th Floor, New York, NY 10003. *E-mail*—ad62@nyu.edu.

CAREER: Harvard University, Cambridge, MA, curatorial intern at Peabody Museum of Archaeology and Ethnology, 1985-86; Brooklyn Museum, Brooklyn, NY, curatorial intern in Department of African, Oceanic, and New World Art, 1988; Museum of Contemporary Hispanic Art, New York, NY, director of education, 1989; El Museo del Barrio, New York, NY, curatorial assistant, 1990-93; City University of New York, adjunct lecturer in Puerto Rican studies at Herbert H. Lehman College, 1992-93; City University of New York—Hunter College, New York, NY, adjunct lecturer in anthropology, 1994-95; Syracuse University, Syracuse, NY, assistant professor of anthropology, beginning 1995; New York University, New York, NY, assistant professor of American studies. University of Connecticut, guest speaker, 1997; Colgate University, guest speaker, 1998; New York University, visiting research associate at Center for Media, Culture, and History, 1998—.

MEMBER: American Anthropological Association, Association of Latino and Latina Anthropologists, Association of Cultural Anthropology, Puerto Rican Studies Association, Latin American Studies Association.

AWARDS, HONORS: Grants from Wenner-Gren Foundation for Anthropological Research, National Science Foundation, and Ford Foundation, all 1998.

WRITINGS:

Sponsored Identities: Cultural Politics in Puerto Rico, Temple University Press (Philadelphia, PA), 1997.

(Editor, with Agustín Laó-Montes) *Mambo Montage: The Latinization of New York,* Columbia University Press (New York, NY), 2001.

Latinos, Inc.: The Marketing and Making of a People, University of California Press (Berkeley, CA), 2001.

Barrio Dreams: Puerto Ricans, Latinos, and the Neoliberal City, University of California Press (Berkeley, CA), 2004.

Contributor to books, including *Puerto Rican Jam: Colonialism and Nationalism,* edited by Frances Negron and Ramon Grosfoguel, University of Minnesota Press (Minneapolis, MN), 1997; and *Taíno Revival: Critical Perspectives on Puerto Rican Identity and Cultural Politics,* edited by Gabriel Haslip-Viera, Markus Wiener Publishers (Princeton, NY), 2001. Contributor of articles and reviews to scholarly journals, including *Cultural Anthropology, Latino Review of Books, Identities: Global Studies in Culture and Power, Studies in Latin American Popular Culture,* and *American Ethnologist.*

BIOGRAPHICAL AND CRITICAL SOURCES:

PERIODICALS

American Anthropologist, September, 1999, Laurie Kroshus Medina, review of *Sponsored Identities: Cultural Politics in Puerto Rico,* p. 671.

American Ethnologist, November, 2000, Kirk Dombrowski, review of *Sponsored Identities,* p. 974.

American Studies International, October, 2003, Patrick Frank, review of *Latinos, Inc.: The Marketing and Making of a People,* p. 116.

Bloomsbury Review, May-June, 2002, Cristian Salazar, review of *Mambo Montage: The Latinization of New York City.*

Choice, January, 2002, S. D. Clark, review of *Latinos, Inc.,* p. 926; February, 2002, R. Acuna, review of *Mambo Montage,* p. 1106.

Chronicle of Higher Education, September 28, 2001, Nina C. Ayoub, review of *Latinos, Inc.,* p. A34.

Current Anthropology, December, 1999, Rafael L. Ramirez, review of *Sponsored Identities,* p. 738.

Hispanic American Historical Review, August, 2000, Jose-Manuel Navarro, review of *Sponsored Identities,* p. 615.

Journal of Communication, September, 2003, Devorah Heitner, review of *Latinos, Inc.,* p. 557.

Los Angeles Times, December 9, 2001, Gregory Rodriguez, review of *Latinos, Inc.,* p. R7.*

*　　*　　*

de BECKER, Gavin

PERSONAL: Male.

ADDRESSES: Office—Gavin de Becker and Associates, 11684 Ventura Blvd., Suite 440, Studio City, CA 91604. *E-mail*—infoline@gavindebecker.com.

CAREER: Security consultant. Gavin de Becker and Associates (security consulting firm), Los Angeles, CA, founder and chief executive. University of California—Los Angeles, senior fellow at School of Public Policy and Social Research. U.S. Department of Justice, past member of President's Advisory Board; California Department of Mental Health, past member of Governor's Advisory Board; Domestic Violence Advisory Board, cochair; served at U.S. Department of State; General Services Administration/American Institute of Architects, featured speaker at Post 9-11 Forum; designer of MOSAIC threat assessment tool; principal advisor on a federal research project into mentally ill people who stalk public figures; also served as expert witness and trainer.

AWARDS, HONORS: Special award from the U.S. attorney general and director of the Federal Bureau of Investigation, 1985, for work in threat assessment; Director's Certificate of Appreciation, Central Intelligence Agency; award from International Association of Chiefs of Police; Distinguished Hoosier Award, governor of Indiana; Presidential Inaugural Certificate of Appreciation.

WRITINGS:

The Gift of Fear: Survival Signals that Protect Us from Violence, Little, Brown (Boston, MA), 1997.

Protecting the Gift: Keeping Children and Teenagers Safe (and Parents Sane), Dial Press (New York, NY), 1999.

Thinking Caps: Mind Puzzles for Sharper Intuition, Dell (New York, NY), 2001.

Fear Less: Real Truth about Risk, Safety, and Security in a Time of Terrorism, Little, Brown (Boston, MA), 2002.

Contributor to books, including author of forewords to *Surviving a Stalker: Everything You Need to Know to Keep Yourself Safe,* by Linden Gross, Marlowe and Co. (New York, NY), 1994; *Beauty Bites Beast: Awakening the Warrior within Women and Girls,* by Ellen Snortland, B3 Books, 1998; and *A Girl's Gotta Do What a Girl's Gotta Do: The Safety Chick's Guide to Living Safe and Smart,* by Kathleen Baty, Rodale Press (Emmaus, PA), 2003; author of introduction, *Raising Safe Kids in an Unsafe World: Thirty Proven Ways to Protect Your Child from Becoming Lost, Abducted, Abused, or Victimized,* by Jan Wagner, Yellow Dyno Publishing, 2003.

The Gift of Fear has been published in more than a dozen languages.

ADAPTATIONS: The book *The Gift of Fear: Survival Signals that Protect Us from Violence* has been adapted as an audio book.

SIDELIGHTS: Gavin de Becker is the head of his own security consulting firm. He has advised many international media figures, served as a presidential advisor, testified in high profile cases, and created a system to evaluate threats made to U.S. Supreme Court justices. In 1997 de Becker's first book, *The Gift of Fear: Survival Signals that Protect Us from Violence,* was published. The aim of the book is to help everyday citizens make themselves safer from the threat of crime. De Becker promoted his book with a guest spot on the television show of talk-show host Oprah Winfrey, which helped propel *The Gift of Fear* to its status as a nationwide best-seller. In addition, the television program *PrimeTime Live* aired three segments on the book, and interviewer Larry King spent two full hours with de Becker.

The main argument of *The Gift of Fear* is that people should follow their intuition when dealing with potentially dangerous situations. As Tom Morganthau

and Mark Miller noted in a review of *The Gift of Fear* for *Newsweek:* "Don't like the looks of that seedy-looking guy in the elevator? Wait for another car. Pay attention to your gut sense that something's not quite right." Yet, in the book, de Becker differentiates between true fear and ordinary anxiety—the latter caused by too much emphasis on the spectacular violent crimes characteristically depicted in media from movies to local television newscasts. "True fear," de Becker told *Newsweek,* "is a signal in the presence of danger, and it is based on your perception, your environment or your circumstances. . . . If it's not something you can smell, see, taste, hear, et cetera, [the fear is] likely to be unwarranted."

The Gift of Fear advises readers on situations including random crime, stalking, spousal abuse, disgruntled coworkers who might go on shooting rampages, and potentially abusive child care workers. De Becker also provides what David Van Biema described in *Time* as "a four-part test for assessing the possibility of violence," as well as a list of seventeen signs that a coworker might take violent action and thirty factors that can predict possible murder by a spouse. Somewhat unconventional advice from the author is that victims of domestic violence can avoid what Van Biema described as "the knee-jerk use of temporary restraining orders." In *The Gift of Fear* de Becker notes that restraining orders "work best on the person least likely to be violent anyway." Another tip, for the target of stalkers, is not to change one's phone number, because the stalker will most likely find out the new number anyway. Instead, de Becker recommends installing an additional phone line and placing an answering machine on the original line. "The stalker won't realize you've changed, and you'll have a record of his calls if you need it," the author states.

In addition to the attention from Winfrey, *The Gift of Fear* has had positive reviews from other sources. *Time* reviewer Van Biema praised de Becker's "practical advice" and predicted "he will probably make a lot of money and save a few lives." *Newsweek* contributors Morganthau and Miller noted that the author "has a lot to say about crime . . . and he says it persuasively." A *Kirkus Reviews* critic also commented that de Becker presents his case convincingly. According to Patricia Hassler in *Booklist, The Gift of Fear* is "written with consummate style." Gregor A. Preston commented in *Library Journal* that de Becker's book is "a valuable contribution on a timely topic." *Boston*

Globe reviewer Zachary R. Dowdy concluded, "A page-turner, *The Gift of Fear* is an empowering antidote in its reasoned response to an all-too-preventable epidemic." The book also appeared in the *New York Times* best-seller list for four months.

BIOGRAPHICAL AND CRITICAL SOURCES:

BOOKS

De Becker, Gavin, *The Gift of Fear: Survival Signals that Protect Us from Violence,* Little, Brown (Boston, MA), 1997.

PERIODICALS

America, September 18, 1999, review of *Protecting the Gift: Keeping Children and Teenagers Safe (and Parents Sane),* p. 24.
Booklist, June 1-15, 1997, Patricia Hassler, review of *The Gift of Fear: Survival Signals that Protect Us from Violence,* p. 1628; May 1, 1999, Ray Olson, review of *Protecting the Gift,* p. 1557.
Boston Globe, August 25, 1997, Zachary R. Dowdy, review of *The Gift of Fear.*
FBI Law Enforcement Bulletin, June, 2002, Julie R. Linkins, review of *The Gift of Fear,* p. 5.
Kirkus Reviews, May 1, 1997, review of *The Gift of Fear,* p. 711.
Library Journal, June 15, 1997, Gregor A. Preston, review of *The Gift of Fear,* p. 84.
Newsweek, July 21, 1997, Tom Morganthau and Mark Miller, review of *The Gift of Fear,* p. 78.
New York Times Magazine, December 12, 1999, Brett Forrest, "Risky Business," p. 47.
Publishers Weekly, April 26, 1999, review of *Protecting the Gift,* p. 61.
Time, July 28, 1997, David Van Biema, review of *The Gift of Fear,* pp. 34-35; June 21, 1999, Andrea Sachs, review of *Protecting the Gift,* p. 82K.

*   *   *

DHONDY, Farrukh 1944-

PERSONAL: Born 1944, in Poona, Bombay, India. *Education:* Wadia College (Poona, Bombay, India), B.Sc.; Cambridge University, B.A. (English), 1967; University of Leicester, M.A. (English).

ADDRESSES: Agent—c/o Nicky Lund, David Higham Associates, 5-8 Lower John St., Golden Square, London W1F 9HA, England.

CAREER: Henry Thornton Comprehensive School, Clapham, London, England, English teacher; Archbishop Temple School, Lambeth, London, English teacher, then head of department, 1974-80; Channel 4 Television, London, commissioning editor, 1985-97.

AWARDS, HONORS: Children's Rights Workshop Other award, 1977, for *East End at Your Feet,* and 1979, for *Come to Mecca, and Other Stories;* Collins/Fontana Award for books for multi-ethnic Britain, for *Come to Mecca, and Other Stories;* works represented in "Children's Fiction in Britain, 1900-1990" exhibition, British Council's Literature Department, 1990; Whitbread Literary Award for first novel nomination, 1990, for *Bombay Duck.*

WRITINGS:

East End at Your Feet (short stories), Macmillan (London, England), 1976.
Come to Mecca, and Other Stories, Collins (London, England), 1978.
The Siege of Babylon (novel), Macmillan (London, England), 1978.
Poona Company (short stories), Gollancz (London, England), 1980.
Trip Trap (short stories; contains "Herald," "The Bride" [also see below], "Homework," "The Mandarin Exam," "Batty and Winifred," "The Fifth Gospel," "Lost Soul," and "Under Gemini"), Gollancz (London, England), 1982.
(With Barbara Beese and Leila Hassan) *The Black Explosion in British Schools,* Race Today Publications, 1982.
Romance, Romance [and] *The Bride,* Faber (London, England), 1985.
Bombay Duck (adult novel), J. Cape (London, England), 1990.
(Compiler) *Ranters, Ravers, and Rhymers: Poems by Black and Asian Poets,* Collins (London, England), 1990.
Black Swan, Gollancz (London, England), 1992, Houghton (Boston, MA), 1993.
Janacky and the Giant, and Other Stories, Collins (London, England), 1993.

C. L. R. James: A Life, Orion, 1996.
C.L.R. James: Cricket, the Carribean, and World Revolution, Weidenfeld & Nicolson (London, England), 2001.

Contributor to Indian periodicals *Debonair* and *Economic and Political Weekly,* and to British periodicals, including *Granta, Race Today,* and *Listener.* Former editor, *Carcanet.*

PLAYS:

Mama Dragon, produced in London, England, 1980.
Trojans (adaptation of a play by Euripedes), produced in London, England, 1982.
Kipling Sahib, produced in London, England, 1982.
Vigilantes (produced in 1985), Hobo Press, 1988.
King of the Ghetto (television series), British Broadcasting Company (BBC1), 1986.
Split Wide Open (screenplay; based on the story by Dev Benegal), Adlabs/BMG Crescendo, 1999.

Also author of the stage plays *Shapesters, Film, Film, Film,* and, with John McGrath and others, *All the Fun of the Fair.* Author of television plays, including *Maids in the Mad Shadow,* 1981, *Good at Art,* 1983; *Dear Manju,* 1983; *Salt on a Snake's Tail,* 1983; *The Empress of the Munshi,* 1984; *To Turn a Blind Eye,* 1986; and *Prejudice and Pride.* Author of series of ethnic situation comedies for British television, including *No Problem* (with Mustapha Matura), 1983, and *Tandoori Nights,* 1985.

SIDELIGHTS: A native of India, Farrukh Dhondy came to Great Britain to be a schoolteacher, and also embarked on a career as an author, journalist, and playwright. Identifying with the growing number of non-white teens who were coming of age at that time, Dhondy has become known for works, such as the short-story collection *East End at Your Feet,* that show the confusion and anxieties of these young people. He has also been praised by critics for using accurate descriptions, dialect, and slang expressions to add emphasis to his tales.

Raised in Bombay, India, where his father was an officer in the army, Dhondy loved to read, but this habit was not encouraged, particularly the boy's love of American comic books. "To my dad it was bad language and imported American nihilism. He insisted that if [my sister and I] were to read comics we should go to the big booksellers in Madras and buy some educational ones," Dhondy recalled to a *Times Literary Supplement* contributor.

After finishing his secondary education, Dhondy moved to Bombay to study chemical technology, which his parents considered a worthwhile subject. Still, his fondness for reading continued, and he read what he could between solving mathematical equations. Eventually, the young student had second thoughts: "I was completely bored with the great prospect that yawned before me. An utterly predictable life: you know what kind of house you will have, what sort of person you will marry, where your children will go to school," he told Anwer Bati in the *Times Literary Supplement.* Quitting college, Dhondy instead began to travel throughout India; he also began to immerse himself in literature, reading works by British authors such as D. H. Lawrence, Rudyard Kipling and E. M. Forster. He also applied for a scholarship to study at Pembroke College, Cambridge. Moving to England, he became active as a playwright in the Black Theatre Cooperative, contributed articles to the literary magazine *Granta,* and edited a magazine called *Carcanet.*

After graduation, he became a teacher of English at a secondary school in London, England, but was fired from his job for being too radical in his thinking. Dhondy found a better fit at the Archbishop Temple School, where he eventually became head of the English and Humanities department. It was while teaching at the Temple School that Dhondy began to observe the lives of British teens and also study their slang and dialect.

Dhondy's first book, 1976's *East End at Your Feet,* profiles young adults in London's ethnically diverse East End neighborhood. In "Dear Manju" he chronicles the life of a traditional Indian family living in London. After his father dies, fourteen-year-old Bhupinder, now the oldest male in the family, is required to take care of his elder sister, Manju. However, Manju has other ideas: She chases after boys, is irreverent, and casts off her Indian upbringing in favor of British teen culture. In another story, "K.B.W. (Keep Britain White)," a white teen tries to make sense of the violence and racism that drove his friend's Bangladeshi family out of the neighborhood.

Come to Mecca, and Other Stories showed Dhondy's talent for dealing honestly and openly with the racial problems of Asian and West Indian teenagers in Great Britain. Neil Philip, writing in the *Times Educational Supplement,* praised the 1978 story collection and called its author "subtle, penetrating, witty: one of the few children's authors able adequately to reflect racial differences in the texture of his language." Written for a broader adult audience, *Poona Company* contains stories about the gossip-filled, spirited atmosphere of a Poona gathering place, where locals gather to catch up and tell tales. The result, according to some reviewers, is illuminating. According to Dervla Murphy in the *Times Literary Supplement,* in *Poona Company* "Dhondy is illuminating not merely a sliver of the Indian scene but a chunk of universal human nature." Gillian Welch also praised the volume, writing in *New Statesman* that the collection "is the work of a natural story-teller, entertaining and funny and truth-telling in a way that no lesson about other cultures could ever be."

In Dhondy's first young-adult novel, *The Siege of Babylon,* he focuses on three East Indian teenagers who are persuaded to rob a car rental store by Kwate, an older man who has been involved in political controversy. When the robbery goes awry, they decide to take hostages, but are ultimately captured. Margery Fisher, writing in *Growing Point,* praised *The Siege of Babylon* for its well-developed characters, "tight structure and the forceful, idiomatic dialogue which distinguish this book for the intelligent middle teens." A. R. Williams, reviewing *The Siege of Babylon* for the *Junior Bookshelf,* cited Dhondy's insightful social commentary and pronounced the novel "stimulating, if often uncomfortable or even disquieting."

Black Swan, Dhondy's second young-adult novel, tells a more intricate tale as it follows an aspiring actress named Rose. When Rose's mother becomes sick, Rose takes over her job as personal assistant to the mysterious Mr. B. On instructions from her employer, Rose begins translating a long and complicated document written in Elizabethan English, and for readers this document contains the story within Dhondy's story. The document, written by Elizabethan physician and amateur thespian Simon Forman, tells about a dark-skinned man named Lazarus who is involved in much intrigue, including faking his own death, and about Kit Marlowe, who also fakes his death and falls in love with Lazarus. Together, Marlowe and Lazarus

write several plays under the name William Shakespeare; Shakespeare himself, a mediocre and drunken actor in this tale, becomes a front for the pair's work.

Although Lucinda Lockwood, writing in the *School Library Journal,* dubbed *Black Swan* "a wobbly mystery with a very muddy solution," other reviewers differed. A *Junior Bookshelf* contributor found the book complicated but interesting, stating that "multilayered is for once an apt label for a work which should be thoroughly enjoyed by adult readers as well as budding literati." A *Kirkus Reviews* critic praised the novel's "intriguingly complicated construction" and added that *Black Swan* is "a fast-moving, idea-packed read that will stretch young minds." Praising the book as "Multilayered, challenging and filled with mysterious beauty," a *Publishers Weekly* reviewer cited Dhondy for revealing to sophisticated teen readers the "revolutionary power of the written and the spoken word."

While Dhondy has gone on to write for television, pen the adult novel *Bombay Duck,* and produce a highly regarded biography of athlete, writer, and Pan-Africanist C. L. R. James, his contribution to late-twentieth-century young-adult literature remains significant. Noting the dearth of children's books written by minority authors, David Rees commented in *Children's Literature in Education* that Dhondy filled that gap. "One of the reasons for his success is that, being coloured himself, he experienced and is able to present vividly some of the complexities of race relations that often escape the notice of white authors of children's books," noted Rees, concluding that Dhondy serves as a role model to newer multicultural writers for "showing the way."

BIOGRAPHICAL AND CRITICAL SOURCES:

BOOKS

Children's Literature Review, Volume 41, Gale (Detroit, MI), 1996, pp. 65-81.
St. James Guide to Young Adult Writers, St. James Press (Detroit, MI), 1999.

PERIODICALS

Booklist, February 15, 2002, p. 1001.
Book Report, May-June, 1994, Carol Jean Pingel, review of *Black Swan,* p. 43.

British Book News, October, 1990.

Bulletin of the Center for Children's Books, September, 1993, p. 8.

Children's Literature in Education, summer, 1980, pp. 91-97; spring, 1983, pp. 35-43.

Growing Point, July, 1978, pp. 3363-3364.

Junior Bookshelf, August, 1978, p. 200; August, 1992, p. 163.

Kirkus Reviews, July 15, 1993, p. 932.

New Statesman, November 28, 1980, review of *Poona Company,* p. 31; July 30, 2001, review of *C. L. R. James: Cricket, the Caribbean, and World Revolution.*

Publishers Weekly, June 28, 1993, review of *Black Swan,* p. 79.

School Librarian, March, 1983, pp. 53-54; August, 1991, p. 111.

School Library Journal, December, 1985, review of *Poona Company,* pp. 98-99; September, 1993, p. 248.

Sunday Times (London, England), May 13, 1990, Anwer Bati, "Exposing the Fraud Squad," p. H10.

Times Educational Supplement, January 18, 1980, p. 42; March 18, 1983, p. 35; July 15, 1983, p. 18; April 26, 1991, p. 24.

Times Literary Supplement, November 26, 1982, Dervla Murphy, review of *Trip Trap,* p. 1303; July 15, 1977, p. 866; April 7, 1978, p. 379; November 21, 1980, Dervla Murphy, review of *Poona Nights,* p. 1322; November 26, 1982, p. 1303; May 13, 1990, p. H10; June 1, 1990, review of *Bombay Duck,* p. 585.

Voice of Youth Advocates, December, 1993, p. 289.*

*   *   *

DILLON, Martin 1949-

PERSONAL: Born June 2, 1949, in Belfast, Northern Ireland; son of Gerard (a telephone engineer) and Mary Theresa (Clarke) Dillon; married Mildred Smyth (a general administrative officer), August 24, 1973. *Education:* Attended Montfort College, 1961, and Belfast College of Business Studies, 1968-70. *Politics:* "To be revealed." *Hobbies and other interests:* Reading, listening to music, and observing.

ADDRESSES: Office—c/o British Broadcasting Corp., Ormeau Ave., Belfast, Northern Ireland; c/o Carroll & Graf Publishers, Inc., 161 William St., New York, NY 10038.

CAREER: Full-time author and terrorism expert. Worked as reporter for *Irish News,* 1968-72; and for *Belfast Telegraph,* 1972-73, both in Belfast, Northern Ireland; British Broadcasting Corporation, Belfast, regional news assistant, 1973-74, talks producer, 1974—. Was the expert on terrorism for news outlets on SKY Television and Channel Four and has been featured on news shows in the British Isles and on U.S. networks, such as Cable News Network (CNN) and American Broadcasting Companies, Inc. (ABC).

MEMBER: National Union of Journalists.

WRITINGS:

(With Denis Lehane) *Political Murder in Northern Ireland,* Penguin (New York, NY), 1973.

"The Squad" (play), broadcast by BBC on radio and television, 1976.

(With Roy Bradford) *Rogue Warrior of the SAS: Lt-Col "Paddy" Blair Mayne, DSO, (3 Bars), Croix de Guerre, Legion D'Honneur,* J. Murray (London, England), 1987.

The Shankill Butchers: A Case Study of Mass Murder, Hutchinson (London, England), 1989.

(Editor) *Interfaces for Information Retrieval and On-line Systems: The State of the Art,* Greenwood Press (New York, NY), 1991.

Killer in Clowntown: Joe Doherty, the IRA, and the Special Relationship, Arrow Books (London, England), 1992.

Stone Cold: The True Story of Michael Stone and the Milltown Massacre, Hutchinson (London, England), 1992.

The Enemy Within, Doubleday (New York, NY), 1994.

The Serpent's Tail (novel), R. Cohen Books (London, England), 1995.

God and the Gun: The Church and Irish Terrorism, Routledge (New York, NY), 1998.

The Dirty War: Covert Strategies and Tactics Used in Political Conflicts, Routledge (New York, NY), 1999.

(With Thomas Gordon) *Robert Maxwell, Israel's Superspy: The Life and Murder of a Media Mogul,* Carroll & Graf (New York, NY), 2003.

Also author of plays for television and radio and author and producer of documentaries for Channel Four, the BBC, and RTE.

SIDELIGHTS: Martin Dillon is a former journalist for the British Broadcasting Corporation who has turned his investigations of terrorism and corruption in Northern Ireland into several critically acclaimed books, including a three-book series in which he investigates those responsible for the violence that plagues Northern Ireland. In *The Shankill Butchers: A Case Study of Mass Murder,* he reports on a Loyalist band of killers, named in the title of the book, who murdered many Catholics in Belfast. The sequel *Killer in Clowntown: Joe Doherty, the IRA, and the Special Relationship* "can be read at the level of an extraordinary adventure story," observed Esmond Wright in *Contemporary Review.* This book describes the life of Joe Doherty, an Irish-American hero who was arrested for a political murder, but then managed to escape from a high-security prison with the help of many civilians sympathizing with his cause. Wright dubbed *Killer in Clowntown* "an accurately assembled, chilling and fascinating book." *The Dirty War: Covert Strategies and Tactics Used in Political Conflicts,* the third book in the series, describes how the British security forces secretly murdered IRA operatives while the IRA bombed and murdered British troops.

In *God and the Gun: The Church and Irish Terrorism,* Dillon tackles the relationship between religion and violence in Northern Ireland. While most people believe the conflict in Northern Ireland is religious, Moore examines contributing factors, such as a violent labor struggle in the 1920s between Protestant elites and a Protestant-Catholic labor force and the nationalist struggle against the British army. By interviewing both Protestant and Catholic paramilitary and religious leaders, Dillon attempts to give a balanced portrayal of the conflict.

Writing about *God and the Gun* in *Bulletin of the Atomic Scientists,* Michael Flynn explained, "The notion that the IRA 'hijacked' the civil rights movement is not an altogether foreign sentiment on the Catholic side. However, as Dillon demonstrates through interviews with Catholic priests and former IRA members, the church's failure to address injustice was critical in enabling the IRA to capture 'the hearts and minds of Catholic nationalists.'" "There are many passages that make the book poignant and ironic as Dillon concludes that what should have been a civil rights struggle was manipulated into a religious war," Robert C. Moore observed in *Library Journal.* Moore felt, however, that "Dillon bogs down a bit at the end, reciting history to put his story in context," but

concluded that the book "is still essential for all Irish history collections."

Dillon and coauthor Gordon Thomas question whether the death of a media giant was really an accident in *Robert Maxwell, Israel's Superspy: The Life and Murder of a Media Mogul.* Maxwell supposedly drowned in a 1991 boating mishap off the coast of the Canary Islands. The authors contend that he was murdered by officials from Mossad, his former employer, after a failed extortion attempt. To back up their theory, Dillon and Thomas interview a former Mossad agent and a former Mossad assasin, who says he was involved in Maxwell's murder. They also interview Maxwell's widow, daughter, two former CIA directors, and three former prime ministers of Israel.

While most critics considered the book entertaining, they were not completely convinced that Maxwell was murdered. Dillon and Thomas "don't prove their case beyond a shadow of a doubt, but they do present a reasoned and well-supported argument," concluded *Booklist*'s David Pitt, who added, "Whether it's the startling truth or merely revisionist nonsense, it makes a thought-provoking and compelling book." A *Publishers Weekly* reviewer described the book as "somewhat over-reaching" but noted that "those interested in the world of international intrigue will find themselves engrossed."

BIOGRAPHICAL AND CRITICAL SOURCES:

PERIODICALS

Booklist, February 15, 2003, David Pitt, review of *Robert Maxwell, Israel's Superspy: The Life and Murder of a Media Mogul,* p. 1023.
Books Magazine, February, 1996, review of *Twenty-five Years of Terror,* p. 24.
Bulletin of the Atomic Scientists, July-August, 1998, Michael Flynn, review of *God and the Gun: The Church and Irish Terrorism,* pp. 57-60.
Choice, September, 1992, review of *Interfaces for Information Retrieval and Online Systems,* p. 96.
Contemporary Review, March, 1993, Esmond Wright, review of *Killer in Clowntown: Joe Doherty, the IRA, and the Special Relationship,* p. 160.
Daily Telegraph, January 4, 2003, Alan Dershowitz, "Was he pushed?: This tale of Maxwell's death is too incredible, insists Alan Dershowitz."

Guardian, December 11, 1997, review of *God and the Gun,* p. 12.

Guardian Weekly, July 8, 1990, review of *The Dirty War: Covert Strategies and Tactics Used in Political Conflicts,* p. 29.

Journal of Academic Librarianship, May, 1992, review of *Interfaces for Information Retrieval and Online Systems,* p. 122.

Kirkus Reviews, March 1, 1999, review of *The Dirty War,* p. 348; March 15, 1999, review of *The Shankill Butchers: A Case Study of Mass Murder,* p. 424; November 1, 2002, review of *Robert Maxwell, Israel's Superspy,* p. 1603.

Library Journal, April 1, 1999, Robert C. Moore, review of *God and the Gun,* p. 116; January, 2003, Daniel K. Blewett, review of *Robert Maxwell, Israel's Superspy,* p. 126.

Library Resources and Technical Services, January, 1993, review of *Interfaces for Information Retrieval and Online Systems,* p. 106.

Listener, October 12, 1989, review of *The Shankill Butchers,* p. 29.

M2 Best Books, October 29, 2002, review of *Robert Maxwell, Israel's Superspy.*

New Statesman and Society, October 13, 1989, Kevin Toolis, review of *The Shankill Butchers,* p. 35; February 23, 1996, review of *Twenty-five Years of Terror,* p. 45.

Publishers Weekly, March 2, 1998, review of *God and the Gun,* p. 50; January 6, 2003, review of *Robert Maxwell, Israel's Superspy,* p. 55.

Reference and Research Book News, review of *God and the Gun,* August, 1998, p. 24.

Times Literary Supplement, December 15, 1989, Sarah Nelson, review of *The Shankill Butchers,* p. 1394; March 3, 1995, Charles Townshend, review of *The Enemy Within,* p. 32; May 1, 1998, Eunan O'Halpin, review of *God and the Gun,* p. 28.

ONLINE

Ann Online, http://www.annonline.com/ (June 28, 2004), "Biography of Martin Dillon."*

*   *   *

DOKEY, Cameron 1956-

PERSONAL: Born August 14, 1956, in Stockton, CA; daughter of Richard (a writer and teacher) and Charron (a teacher; maiden name, Johnson) Dokey; married James F. Verdery (a theater manager), September 23, 1984. *Education:* University of Washington, B.A. (magna cum laude).

ADDRESSES: Agent—Fran Lebowitz, Writers House, Inc., 21 West 26th St., New York, NY 10010.

CAREER: Novelist. Oregon Shakespeare Festival, Ashland, actor, 1977-81; Pacific Science Center, Seattle, WA, exhibit copywriter, 1989-93; novelist, 1993—.

MEMBER: Romance Writers of America.

WRITINGS:

YOUNG ADULT NOVELS

Eternally Yours (horror), Kensington Publishing (Kalamazoo, MI), 1994.

The Talisman (horror), Kensington Publishing (Kalamazoo, MI), 1994.

(Editor and contributor, with Marie G. Lee, Anne Lemieux, and Dian Curtis Regan) *New Year, New Love,* Flare (New York, NY), 1996.

Graveside Tales (a "Fright Light" book), illustrations by Peter Georgeson, Andrews McMeel (Kansas City, KS), 1997.

Midnight Mysteries (a "Fright Light" book), illustrations by Peter Georgeson, Andrews McMeel (Kansas City, KS), 1997.

Together Forever, Bantam (New York, NY), 1997.

(With R. L. Stine) *Dance of Death* ("Fear Street Sagas," No. 8), Simon Pulse (New York, NY), 1997.

(With Kathryn Jensen, Jean Thesman, and Sharon Dennis Wyeth) *Be Mine* (story collection), Flare (New York, NY), 1997.

Hindenburg, 1937 (historical fiction), Pocket Books (New York, NY), 1999.

Washington Avalanche, 1910 (historical fiction), Pocket Books (New York, NY), 2000.

(With Cade Merrill) *The Prisoner* ("The Blair Witch Case Files," Case File No. 6), Bantam (New York, NY), 2001.

Beauty Sleep (fairy tale retelling), Simon Pulse (New York, NY), 2002.

The Storyteller's Daughter (fairy tale retelling), Simon Pulse (New York, NY), 2002.

How Not to Spend Your Senior Year, Simon Pulse (New York, NY), 2004.

Sunlight and Shadow, Simon Pulse (New York, NY), 2004.

"MYSTERY DATE" SERIES; YOUNG ADULT SUPERNATURAL ROMANCE NOVELS

Love Me, Love Me Not, Zebra Books (New York, NY), 1995.

Blue Moon, Kensington Publishing (Kalamazoo, MI), 1995.

Heart's Desire, Kensington Publishing (Kalamazoo, MI), 1995.

"HEARTS AND DREAMS" SERIES; YOUNG ADULT HISTORICAL FICTION NOVELS

Katherine, Heart of Freedom, Avon (New York, NY), 1997.

Charlotte, Heart of Fire, Avon (New York, NY), 1997.

Stephanie, Heart of Gold, Avon (New York, NY), 1998.

Carrie, Heart of Courage, Avon (New York, NY), 1998.

BOOKS BASED ON TELEVISION SERIES

Winning Is Everything (based on the television series *Full House*), Simon Spotlight (New York, NY), 1998.

Here Be Monsters (based on the television series *Buffy the Vampire Slayer*), Simon Pulse (New York, NY), 2000.

Haunted by Desire (based on the television series *Charmed*), Simon Pulse (New York, NY), 2000.

The Summoned (based on the television series *Angel*), Simon Pulse (New York, NY), 2001.

Truth and Consequences (based on the television series *Charmed*), Simon Pulse (New York, NY), 2003.

OTHER

Also author of book *Lost and Found* (1999). Contributor of two stories to *How I Survived My Summer Vacation, Volume 1,* based on the television series *Buffy the Vampire Slayer* (Simon Pulse, 2000). Coauthor of educational materials based on the cable television series *Beakman's World.*

SIDELIGHTS: Cameron Dokey has authored a number of books for young adults. Her writing is diverse—from historical fiction to novels based on popular television shows—but a common thread connects much of her work. The characters in Dokey's novels are strong, intelligent young women, who meet and defeat the challenges in their lives. Even in her horror novels, a genre known for its depiction of weak female characters, Dokey's young women emerge victorious with a better sense of who they are.

Dokey once told *CA,* "My own books reflect my personal interests, as well as a couple of publisher requests." Dokey explained that her first two books, horror novels titled *Eternally Yours* and *The Talisman,* "caused some people who know me to raise their eyebrows and throw up their hands in dismay. 'Why was I writing horror novels?,' they wondered. 'Weren't those always horribly violent, particularly toward young women? Didn't I want to write anything where good things happened? Didn't I want to write things that were uplifting and worthwhile?'"

Dokey defended her work, saying, "Read my books. . . . I think you'll find that they are not gratuitously violent. You'll find that my girls are strong characters who overcome great odds. They grow and change throughout the course of their stories. They become more self-aware. They refuse to become victims, and their words and actions say so. I am writing something where good things happen. I am writing something worthwhile, and I am particularly pleased to find my own views about my work reflected in special mentions by librarians."

Dokey's horror writings include *Eternally Yours,* in which Mercedes Amberson falls for Conner Egan, the lead singer of a local band, not realizing that Conner is actually a vampire looking for the eternal love of a woman in order to become human again. In *The Talisman,* an ancient pendant holds the key to the mystery of how Gina Serventi's best friend, Diane, wound up dead. Dokey published two "Fright Light" books called *Graveside Tales* and *Midnight Mysteries* and three "Mystery Date" books titled, *Love Me, Love Me Not, Blue Moon,* and *Heart's Desire.*

In *Love Me, Love Me Not,* Kristen is in a graveyard mourning the death of her twin sister when she unwittingly captures the eye—and the heart—of Death himself. Death takes over the identity of one of her classmates in order to get Kristen to fall in love with him. A *Publishers Weekly* critic noted, "Conveniently, the principal characters take an elective in world mythology, paving the way for numerous references to Hades's abduction of Persephone and thus glossing this enterprise with a veneer of respectability."

Dokey's young adult historical fiction novels abide by the same rules she applies to her horror novels. She told *CA*, "I want to be interested in the people I create. I want to watch them grow. If I really wanted to get cosmic about all this, I could say that I try to expect the same things of my characters as I do of myself. I need to grow and change as a writer. I need to take on new things."

In the "Hearts and Dreams" series, Dokey focuses on romance and the brave young women who inherit a hope chest as it is passed from one generation to the next. Each story is based on an actual event in history, and each young woman is faced with a challenge she must overcome. *Katherine, Heart of Freedom* is set during the American Patriot activities. After Katherine learns that her father is involved in the action, she disguises herself as a boy to help fight for freedom and finds love along the way. *Charlotte, Heart of Hope* is set during the War of 1812, when the Indiana Territory is being threatened by Indian attacks. Charlotte is sent to Baltimore to live with her aunt. Alone and in a new place, Charlotte is surrounded by people she is not sure she can trust. When she is kidnapped, Charlotte must figure out the truth. When Stephanie is separated from her true love by her father in *Stephanie: Heart of Gold,* she stows away on a ship headed to California in search of her beloved. The final novel in the series, *Carrie, Heart of Courage,* is set during the Great Chicago Fire. The shy, timid Carrie emerges as a heroine, saving herself and others from the devastating blaze.

Dokey's other historical fiction novels include *Hindenburg, 1937,* and *Washington Avalanche, 1910.* In *Hindenburg, 1937,* Anna fulfills her grandfather's dying wish and boards the ill-fated Hindenburg in order to escape to freedom in America. Once on board, Anna finds comfort with a stranger named Erik Peterson, but her comfort is short-lived when her former love, now a Nazi spy, boards the ship, and Anna must decide between the two men. In *Washington Avalanche, 1910,* Ginny Nolan boards a train headed to Seattle to escape the wrath of her stepbrother. She befriends Virginia Hightower, a woman on her way to marry a man she has never met. Ginny is unprepared for the love she finds with Nicholas Bennett (the man to whom Virginia is betrothed), and no one is prepared for the avalanche that engulfs their train in the middle of the night.

Some of Dokey's most critically acclaimed books are her retellings of traditional fairy tales. In *The Storyteller's Daughter,* Dokey reworks the tale, "The Thousand and One Nights," about a young woman named Shahrazad who is picked by the king, Shahrayar, to be his next wife. The problem is that Shahrayar was betrayed by his first wife, so he keeps each of his new wives for only one night before killing them in the morning. In order to save her life, Shahrazad tells an unending story, night after night, that keeps the king captivated. *School Library Journal*'s Connie Tyrrell Burns called "The Thousand and One Nights" "a delightful retelling, tweaked by the author to create a fresh, often quirky feminist who is not afraid to speak her mind." Burns continued, "Dokey's style blends just the right amount of old-fashioned phrases and figurative language that touches of contemporary tongue-in-cheek."

In *Beauty Sleep,* according to Angela J. Reynolds of *School Library Journal,* "Dokey has taken the familiar 'Sleeping Beauty' fairy tale and turned it into a fantastical romance guided by adventure and magic with humor and wordplay thrown in for good measure." A spell is cast on a baby Aurore that she will die at the age of sixteen, but another spell cast says she will sleep for one hundred years. When terrible things happen to her kingdom, Aurore sets out into the magical forest to try to figure out a way to stop them. In the forest, Aurore meets Prince Ironheart, in search of a princess who has been sleeping for one hundred years. *Kliatt*'s Stacey Conrad concluded, "this story will appeal to all who love a good fairy tale."

How Not to Spend Your Senior Year is Dokey's contemporary novel about a senior girl who must pick up her entire life and move away from her friends for the twentieth time since third grade. When Jo O'Connor questions her father, she learns that he is a witness in an important court case, and that their constant moving has something to do with her mother's death. Changing her appearance and her name, Jo must forget her past and move on. Lynne Marie Pisano of *Kliatt* called *How Not to Spend Your Senior Year* "an innovative, unusual, 'can't-put-this-down' story." She went on to describe the book as "a riveting, fast-paced, illuminating story of love at first sight, friendship and high-school survival techniques."

In addition to her many young adult fiction novels, Dokey has written several books based on popular television series such as *Full House, Charmed, Buffy the Vampire Slayer,* and *Angel.* She contributed two stories to a collection titled *How I Spent My Summer Vacation, Volume 1,* which is also based on the *Buffy* series. In a collection of romantic Valentine-themed stories titled *Be Mine,* Dokey penned a humorous tale of a tampon that accidentally flies through the air only to land right in the middle of the class hunk's textbook. A *Publishers Weekly* critic noted that the collection is laced with "spunky, offbeat characters" that "give well-worn plots new life."

Dokey once told *CA,* "I've always wanted to be a writer, even though I haven't always known what I wanted to write. When I was growing up, my father taught high school and my mother taught kindergarten. (The totally cool thing about having parents who were teachers was that all of us got the summers off. We'd go camping, which my father loved and my mother hated.) Every weekday evening during the school year, from eight o'clock to ten o'clock, my father would go to his study and write. I'm not sure I thought about it much at the time. It was just the way things worked at our house. Gradually, however, I began to realize that my father was doing something special. Once I'd realized that, the certainty began to grow upon me that, someday, I would be a writer, too.

"I did many things before I became a full-time writer. I worked as an actor in a professional repertory theater, and I worked at a lot of secretarial and retail jobs. The turning point came when I was hired to be the exhibit writer at the Pacific Science Center in Seattle, Washington. At last, I was fulfilling my dream of being a writer. Naturally, I began to look around to see what other kind of writer I could be.

"Friends from my acting days were writing young adult fiction. When I expressed an interest, they agreed to mentor me. . . . I've been writing young adult fiction ever since. In many ways, it makes a lot of sense that I've landed in the young people's corner. I was a voracious reader as a young person. Every two weeks, my mom and I would make the trip to the library. She would check out books for her class, and I'd check out as many books as I could for myself. I think the number was ten. Two weeks later, I'd return those ten books, all read, and go home with ten more. The librarians loved me (except when my books were overdue!)."

For the future, Dokey told *CA,* "I'd like to write something for someone over the age of sixteen. It would be a novel that takes three years to write and another two to revise. I would only write a paragraph a day, maybe (as compared to producing a complete new work in eight weeks or so). While I'm at it, I'd like to collaborate with an illustrator and do a children's book, and I'd like to write a cookbook that I can dedicate to my mom, who died when I was twenty-one. She never got to see me become a writer."

Dokey concluded, "Writing is a process. I'm interested in all of it."

BIOGRAPHICAL AND CRITICAL SOURCES:

PERIODICALS

Kirkus Reviews, November 15, 2002, review of *Beauty Sleep,* p. 1691.

Kliatt, March, 1998, review of *Charlotte, Heart of Hope,* p. 10, review of *Katherine, Heart of Freedom,* p. 10; November, 1999, review of *Hindenburg, 1937,* p. 16; November, 2002, Deborah Kaplan, review of *The Storyteller's Daughter,* p. 18; March, 2003, Stacey Conrad, review of *Beauty Sleep,* p. 32; January, 2004, Lynne Marie Pisano, review of *How Not to Spend Your Senior Year,* p. 16.

Publishers Weekly, July 3, 1995, review of *Love Me, Love Me Not,* p. 62; February 3, 1997, review of *Be Mine,* p. 107.

School Library Journal, December, 2002, Connie Tyrrell Burns, review of *The Storyteller's Daughter,* p. 136, Angela J. Reynolds, review of *Beauty Sleep,* p. 136; October, 2003, reviews of *The Storyteller's Daughter* and *Beauty Sleep,* p. S67.

Science Fiction Chronicle, February, 2002, review of *The Summoned,* p. 60; March, 2004, Lynn Evarts, review of *How Not to Spend Your Senior Year,* p. 208.

Voice of Youth Advocates, August, 1997, review of *Be Mine,* p. 177, review of *New Year, New Love,* p. 177.*

*   *   *

DOUGHTY, Robin W. 1941-

PERSONAL: Born January 3, 1941, in Swanland, Hull, England; immigrated to the United States, 1967; son of Walter K. (in business) and Mary (Whitaker) Doughty. *Education:* Vatican College, Baccalaurea in Philosophia, 1963; University of Reading, B.A. (with honors), 1966; University of California—Berkeley, Ph. D., 1971.

ADDRESSES: Office—Department of Geography, University of Texas—Austin, Austin, TX 78712.

CAREER: Smithsonian Institution, Washington, DC, research associate, 1970-71; University of Texas—Austin, Austin, assistant professor, 1971-73, associate professor of geography, 1974—, sponsor of Oxford Summer Exchange, 1985-86. Oxford University, visiting lecturer, 1976-77.

MEMBER: Association of American Geographers, Texas Institute of Letters.

WRITINGS:

Feather Fashions and Bird Preservation: A Study in Nature Protection, University of California Press (Berkeley, CA), 1975.
(With William E. deBuys, Jr.) *Future Landscapes of the Colorado Plateau: Impacts of Energy Development,* Center for Energy Studies, University of Texas—Austin (Austin, TX), 1982.
Wildlife and Man in Texas: Environmental Change and Conservation, Texas A & M University Press (College Station, TX), 1983.
(With Larry L. Smith) *The Amazing Armadillo: Geography of a Folk Critter,* University of Texas Press (Austin, TX), 1984.
At Home in Texas: Early Views of the Land, Texas A & M University Press (College Station, TX), 1987.

State Birds: The Mockingbird (monograph), University of Texas Press (Austin, TX), 1987.
(With Barbara M. Parmenter) *Endangered Species,* illustrated by Angelo Mitchell, Texas Monthly Press (Austin, TX), 1989.
Return of the Whooping Crane, University of Texas Press (Austin, TX), 1989.
The Eucalyptus: A Natural and Commercial History of the Gum Tree, Johns Hopkins University Press (Baltimore, MD), 2000.
(With Rob Fergus) *The Purple Martin,* University of Texas Press (Austin, TX), 2002.

Shorter works include "The English Sparrow in the American Landscape: A Paradox in Nineteenth Century Wildlife Conservation," Oxford Publishing (Oxford, England), 1978.

SIDELIGHTS: Robin W. Doughty once told *CA:* "I am interested in the interplay between culture and environment, most especially in the history of environmental change and our shift in attitudes toward places and resources. My travels and a childhood interest in ornithology have led me to be deeply curious about how we shape our world and how, often indirectly, our activities shape the destinies of a host of other co-inhabitants of the earth's surface."

Feather Fashions and Bird Preservation: A Study in Nature Protection is a history of the bird protection movement and its opponents, including the commercial interests whose huge profits in the late nineteenth century were responsible for the death of hundreds of millions of colorful birds. Stella Mary Newton wrote in the *Times Literary Supplement:* "In this book the story of the campaigns on both sides of the Atlantic is interestingly and objectively recorded."

BIOGRAPHICAL AND CRITICAL SOURCES:

PERIODICALS

Agricultural History, winter, 1989, Stanley W. Trimble, review of *At Home in Texas: Early Views of the Land,* p. 101.
American Historical Review, December, 1988, Kristine Fredriksson, review of *At Home in Texas,* p. 1396.

Annals of the Association of American Geographers, March, 1991, Ronald Bordessa, review of *Wildlife and Man in Texas: Environmental Change and Conservation,* p. 165.

Booklist, March 15, 1989, review of *State Birds: The Mockingbird,* p. 1229; June 1, 2002, George Cohen, review of *The Purple Martin,* p. 1655.

Bookwatch, April, 1989, review of *State Birds,* p. 2.

Book World, July 8, 1990, review of *Return of the Whooping Crane,* p. 13.

Canadian Geographic, April-May, 1990, Alex Mills, review of *Return of the Whooping Crane,* p. 86.

Choice, July, 1989, review of *State Birds,* p. 1862; May, 1990, review of *Return of the Whooping Crane,* p. 1528; September, 1994, review of *Wildlife and Man in Texas,* p. 49.

Historical Geography (annual), 2001, Daniel W. Gade, review of *The Eucalyptus: A Natural and Commercial History of the Gum Tree,* p. 185.

Journal of Historical Geography, October, 1989, John R. Wunder, review of *At Home in Texas,* p. 451.

Journal of Southern History, November, 1988, Albert E. Cowdrey, review of *At Home in Texas,* p. 653.

New Scientist, April 21, 1990, Alison Stattersfield, review of *Return of the Whooping Crane,* p. 60.

Publishers Weekly, December 9, 1988, Genevieve Stuttaford, review of *State Birds,* p. 52.

Quarterly Review of Biology, December, 1990, Mark Riegner, review of *Return of the Whooping Crane,* p. 515; June, 2001, Mark Adams, review of *The Eucalyptus,* p. 238.

Reference Services Review, February, 1993, review of *Endangered Species,* p. 56.

Science Books and Films, September, 1990, review of *Return of the Whooping Crane,* p. 39.

SciTech Book News, February, 1989, review of *State Birds,* p. 13; July, 1990, review of *Return of the Whooping Crane,* p. 18.

Southwestern Historical Quarterly, October, 1989, Joseph C. Porter, review of *At Home in Texas,* p. 251.

Times Literary Supplement, October 24, 1975, Stella Mary Newton, review of *Feather Fashions and Bird Preservation: A Study in Nature Protection.*

Tribune Books, December 2, 1990, review of *Return of the Whooping Crane,* p. 16.

University Press Book News, June, 1990, review of *Return of the Whooping Crane,* p. 38.

Western American Literature, summer, 1988, review of *At Home in Texas,* p. 188.

Western Historical Quarterly, August, 1988, review of *At Home in Texas,* p. 336.

ONLINE

E-Streams: Electronic Reviews of Science and Technology References, http://www.e-streams.com/ (February, 2001), review of *The Eucalyptus.**

*   *   *

DRUCKER, Johanna 1952-

PERSONAL: Born May 30, 1952, in Philadelphia, PA; daughter of Boris (a cartoonist) and Barbara Drucker; married Thomas Bradley Freeman (an artist), May 17, 1991 (divorced, June, 2004). *Education:* California College of Arts and Crafts, B.F.A. (printing), 1973; University of California—Berkeley, M.F.A. (visual studies), 1982, Ph.D. (interdisciplinary studies), 1986. *Hobbies and other interests:* Printing.

ADDRESSES: Home—110 Warren Ln., Charlottesville, VA 22904. *Office*—142 Cabell Hall, P.O. Box 400866, University of Virginia, Charlottesville, VA 22904-4866. *Agent*—Steve Clay, Granary Books, 307 Seventh Ave., Suite 1401, New York, NY 10001. *E-mail*—jrd8e@virginia.edu; jabbooks@earthlink.net.

CAREER: Educator and author. University of Texas—Dallas, assistant professor, 1986-88; Harvard University, Cambridge, MA, faculty fellow in art history, 1988-89; Columbia University, New York, NY, assistant professor of modern art, 1989-94; Yale University, New Haven, CT, associate professor of contemporary art, 1994-98; State University of New York—Purchase College, Binghamton, NY, professor of art history, 1998-99; University of Virginia, Charlottesville, VA, Robertson Professor of Media Studies, director of media studies, 1999—; cofounder, Speculative Computing Lab, 1999. Feminist Art and Art History Conference, coordinator, 1995-96; work represented in special collections in the United States and abroad, including Museum of Modern Art Library, Getty Center for the Humanities, National Museum of Women in the Arts, Sackner Archive of Visual Poetry, Franklin Furnace Archive, and Library of Congress.

MEMBER: College Art Association of America.

AWARDS, HONORS: National Merit Scholar, 1969; Regents' Fellowship, University of California—Berkeley, 1980-81, 1981-82, 1983-84; Fulbright fellow, 1984-85; Harvard Mellon Faculty fellow, Harvard University, 1988-89; humanities research grant, University of California—Berkeley, 1991; Getty Foundation fellow, 1992-93; Phillip and Ruth Hettleman Award for junior faculty teaching, Columbia University, 1994; Djerassi Foundation artists residency, 1998.

WRITINGS:

Dark, Druckwerk (New York, NY), 1972.

As No Storm, Rebis Press (Oakland, CA), 1975.

Twenty-Six '76 Let Hers, Chased Press (Berkeley, CA), 1976.

From A to Z: Our An (Collective Specifics) An Impartial Bibliography: Incidents in a Non-Relationship, or, How I Came to Not Know Who Is: The Politics of Language, Chased Press (Berkeley, CA), 1977.

Fragile, Chased Press (Berkeley, CA), 1977.

Surprise Party, Chased Press (Berkeley, CA), 1977.

Selected Writing, 1971, Chased Press (Berkeley, CA), 1977.

Experience of the Medium, Druckwerk (New York, NY), 1978.

Netherland: How (so) Far, Druckwerk (New York, NY), 1978.

Kidz, Druckwerk (New York, NY), 1979.

Jane Goes Out w' the Scouts, Druckwerk (New York, NY), 1980.

'S Crap 'S Ample, Druckwerk (New York, NY), 1980.

Italy, Figures (Berkeley, CA), 1980.

Dolls of the Spirit, Druckwerk (New York, NY), 1981.

It Happens Pretty Fast, Druckwerk (New York, NY), 1982.

Tongues, Druckwerk (New York, NY), 1982.

Just As, Druckwerk (New York, NY), 1983.

Against Fiction, Druckwerk (New York, NY), 1983.

Spectacle, Druckwerk (New York, NY), 1984.

Through Light and the Alphabet, Druckwerk (New York, NY), 1986.

(With Emily McVarish) *Sample Dialogue,* Druckwerk (New York, NY), 1989.

The Word Made Flesh, Druckwerk (New York, NY), 1989.

Simulant Portrait, Druckwerk (New York, NY), 1990.

The History of the/My Wor(l)d: Fragments of a Testimonial to History, Some Lived and Realized Moments Open to Claims of Memory, Druckwerk (New York, NY), 1990.

(With Brad Freeman) *Otherspace: Martian Ty/opography,* Druckwerk (New York, NY), 1993.

Books: 1970 to 1994, Druckwerk (New York, NY), 1994.

Theorizing Modernism: Visual Art and the Critical Tradition, Columbia University Press (New York, NY), 1994.

The Visible Word: Experimental Typography and Modern Art, 1909-1923, University of Chicago Press (Chicago, IL), 1994.

Narratology: Historical Romance, Sweet Romance, Science Fiction, Romantic Suspense, Supernatural, Horror, Sensual Romance, Adventure, Thriller, Glitz, Druckwerk (New York, NY), 1994.

Three Early Fictions, Potes and Poets Press (Berkeley, CA), 1994.

The Alphabetic Labyrinth: The Letters in History and Imagination, Thames and Hudson (New York, NY), 1995.

The Century of Artists' Books, Granary Books (New York, NY), 1995.

Dark Decade (fiction), Detour Press (Detroit, MI), 1995.

The Current Line, Druckwerk (New York, NY), 1996.

(Editor, with K. David Jackson and Eric Vos) *Experimental, Visual, Concrete: Avant-Garde Poetry since the 1960s,* Rodopi (Atlanta, GA), 1996.

(Essays, with William H. Gass) *The Dual Muse: The Writer as Artist, the Artist as Writer,* introduction by Cornelia Homburg, John Benjamins Publishing (Philadelphia, PA), 1997.

Prove before Laying, Druckwerk (New York, NY), 1997.

Figuring the Word: Essays on Books, Writing, and Visual Poetics, Granary Books (New York, NY), 1998.

The Next Word: Text and/as Image and/as Design and/as Meaning, Neuberger Museum of Art (Purchase, NY), 1998.

(With Brad Freeman) *Nova Reperta,* JAB Books (Charlottesville, VA), 1999.

(With Brad Freeman) *Emerging Sentience,* JAB Books (Charlottesville, VA), 2000.

Night Crawlers on the Web, Druckwerk (New York, NY), 2000.

Quantum, Druckwerk (New York, NY), 2001.

(With Susan Bee) *A Girl's Life,* Granary Books (New York, NY), 2002.

Damaged Spring, Druckwerk (New York, NY), 2003.

Sweet Dreams: Contemporary Art and Complicity, University of Chicago Press (Chicago, IL), 2005.

Also author of *Dark, the Bat Elf,* 1972, and *Experience of the Medium,* 1978. Contributor to *Typographically Speaking: The Art of Matthew Carter,* by

Margaret Re, University of Maryland (Baltimore, MD), 2002. Author of "unique books," one-print editions, including *Light and the Pork Pie,* 1974, *Rite Soft Passage,* 1975, *Mind Massage,* 1985, *Yellow Dog,* 1986, *Bookscape,* 1988, *Heavy Breathing,* 1991, and *Crisis Romance,* 1991. Work represented in anthologies, including *The Line in Postmodern Poetry,* edited by Robert Frank and Henry Sayre, University of Illinois Press (Champaign, IL), 1988. Contributor to periodicals, including *Central Park, Black Ice, Stifled Yawn, Generator,* and *ArtPapers.* Member of editorial board, *Art Journal* and *Journal of Artists' Books.*

SIDELIGHTS: Johanna Drucker once told *CA:* "Because I write both creative prose and work in a scholarly or critical mode, I am keenly aware of the differences between the restraints put on language that must be responsible to external references and language that is allowed to develop freely from a personal, highly subjective perspective. Each mode feeds the other for me. Research in the field of typography, design, alphabet history, or the visual arts often charges the imaginative spark plugs, racing the synaptic networks with the excitement of previously unthought possibilities.

"The alphabet exerted an early fascination over me, because of the contradiction I perceived between its finitude as a system and its potential for infinite combination and expression. The visual forms seemed fraught with power and character, if not explicit meaning. The elegant 'K' and 'R' and the imposing 'W' and 'M' with their massive presence, for instance, contrasted with the matronly 'B' and the boring but stable 'H.' Later I became involved in letterpress printing and came to enjoy language as a physical form that I could hold in my hands. From that experience, the graphic potential of format as an aspect of meaning took on new value in my creative work.

"The great prose writers from the eighteenth to the early twentieth centuries remain models for me, from Denis Diderot to George Eliot, Jane Austen, the Brontës, and Thomas Mann. As a scholar I have been drawn to the thoughtfully creative work of Erwin Panofsky, Meyer Schapiro, and Sigmund Freud. In a more contemporary frame I am drawn to popular writing—mysteries, science fiction, and tabloid language—while retaining my admiration for the subtle lucidity of Raymond Williams, the intensity of Susan Howe, the personal vision of H.D., and the flexible, eclectic precision of Charles Bernstein.

"I want my work—whether critical or creative—to have a certain immediacy in the language itself—an evident awareness of the material qualities of words, the generative impact of images, and the communicative potential of text. Some language massages the brain, some phrases or sentences slap the reader into consciousness, and some rhythms lull the perceiving intelligence into tranquility, and so on. As far as I am concerned, the textures of prose should be as varied and as specific as those of a geographical terrain, each as particular to itself, as richly revealing of its own character and qualities. In addition, the consciousness that illumines the field of letters on the page should be as various as the moods of the atmosphere—as ephemeral, as durable, as reliable, as fleeting, and as sublime. In the tenuous space between abstract self-involvement and communicative urgency, I write to make sense of the world and my experience of it."

"As both an art historian and a book artist, Drucker brings a unique combination of historical knowledge and practical experience to her writing," explained Buzz Spector in a review of Drucker's *The Century of Artists' Books* for *Art Journal. The Century of Artists' Books* is a comprehensive analysis of the development of artists' books, meaning books that are considered works of art. In the book's fourteen chapters, Drucker groups artists' books into the following themes: idea and form, democratic multiple, rare object, visual form, verbal exploration, sequence, agent of social change, conceptual space, and document.

The first four chapters of *The Century of Artists' Books* present a history of artists' books and identifies the social and philosophical issues associated with them. Spector remarked that Drucker's "'dual-citizenship' as historian and practitioner emphatically enriches the analysis of the works in these chapters, which deal with the book as both a physical structure and a mode of communication." Writing in *Afterimage,* Tom Trusky also felt that Drucker's background gave her a good foundation from which to write this book, saying "Drucker's first-hand experiences in printing, and her collaborations with printer/bookmaker Brad Freeman, provide her with a practical expertise we can trust as she explains the mysteries of 'split fountains,' 'stripping,' and 'overprinting,' as well as the economics of production." Trusky also observed, "One of the most irritating features of artists' books has been their unavailability. . . . Most people have not seen most artists' books and, therefore, have not been able to appreciate what they have not seen." Trusky felt that *The Century of Artists' Books* makes these books accessible.

In an interview by Steven Heller published in *Print,* Drucker admitted that while theory has a place in the study of art, it does not "make somebody better at creating a printed page, a Web page, an object, or anything else." She continued, "People who work from a theoretical perspective, whether it's in design or the visual arts, often do very stilted, self-conscious work that ultimately is only an illustration of the theoretical position."

Drucker contemplates the negative effect of theory on the interpretation of the futurist, Dadaist, and Cubist artists of the early twentieth century in *The Visible Word: Experimental Typography and Modern Art, 1909-1923.* These artists used typography in new and exciting ways that blended visual art and literature, so that their boundaries were less distinct. Drucker contends that the introduction of New Criticism and high modernism separated the genres to the extent that interpreting the art was no longer possible. She reviews significant theories in the book and analyzes the work of four artists: Ilia Zdanevich, Filippo Marinetti, Guillaume Apollinaire, and Tristan Tzara. In a review of the book for the *British Journal of Aesthetics,* Hugh Bredlin explained that although these four artists "were representative of the avant-garde at the start of the century, they drew on the earlier achievements of William Morris' arts and crafts movement, and on prior developments in commercial graphics and poster design. They were not themselves typographic artists, but they used typography as a method of innovation in poetry." Bredlin felt that Drucker's discussion of why experimental poetry fell out of favor "is not weighty enough" but concluded that the book "explores an important and hitherto neglected part of our intellectual history."

Drucker again contemplates the blurring of the boundaries of text and image in *The Next Word: Text and/as Image and/as Design and/as Meaning.* "One recoils from the heft of such an unwieldy title not to mention the reciprocity among these broad categories (as the title implies)," remarked Nola Tully in *Afterimage,* who went on to explain, "Drucker makes the point that cultural changes and technological advances have helped to blur the lines that once defined mediums and genres. She suggests it is the job of the viewer to maintain a distinction between these boundaries through looking, reading, and creating meaning." Tully felt that this juxtaposition of genres is a major strength of *The Next Word.*

BIOGRAPHICAL AND CRITICAL SOURCES:

BOOKS

Contemporary Poets, St. James Press (Detroit, MI), 2001.

PERIODICALS

Afterimage, July-August, 1997, Tom Trusky, review of *The Century of Artists' Books,* p. 19; January-February, 1999, Nola Tully, review of *The Next Word: Text and/as Image and/as Design and/as Meaning,* p. 17.
Art Journal, fall, 1997, Buzz Spector, review of *The Century of Artists' Books,* p. 95.
Bloomsbury Review, January, 1996, review of *The Alphabetic Labyrinth,* p. 13; November-December, 2002, review of *The Century of Artists' Books.*
British Journal of Aesthetics, Hugh Bredlin, review of *The Visible Word: Experimental Typography and Modern Art, 1909-1923,* pp. 198-200.
Library Journal, June 15, 1996, Paula Frosch, review of *The Century of Artists' Books,* p. 61.
Print, November-December, 1997, Steven Heller, "Johanna Drucker: Art and Design Theorist," p. 30.
School Arts, March, 2002, Kent Anderson, review of *The Alphabetic Labyrinth,* pp. 53-55.

ONLINE

Electronic Poetry Center, http://www.epc.buffalo.edu/ (August 27, 2004), Johanna Drucker, "A Chronology of Books from 1970 to 1994."

*   *   *

DWYER, Deanna
  See KOONTZ, Dean R(ay)

*   *   *

DWYER, K. R.
  See KOONTZ, Dean R(ay)

E

EDWARDS, Susan 1947-

PERSONAL: Born 1947, in York, PA; daughter of Fred (in business) and Jane (a homemaker; maiden name, Rothrock) Tabnau. *Ethnicity:* "Anglo." *Education:* Arizona State University, M.A. (education), 1971, M.A. (counseling), 1975, Ph.D., 1983; attended University of Minnesota—Twin Cities, 1978; postdoctoral fellow at Rutgers University, 1988-90. *Hobbies and other interests:* Horseback riding, drawing, writing poetry.

ADDRESSES: Home and office—515 Executive Dr., Princeton, NJ 08540.

CAREER: Counselor at elementary schools in Tempe, AZ, 1971-76; community mental health counselor in Phoenix, AZ, 1976-82; University of New England, Biddeford, ME, teacher of counseling and psychology, 1983-88, director of School/Health Psychology Program, 1985-88; private practice of psychology in Princeton, NJ, 1988—. University of Maine, teacher, 1983-88; consultant and trainer for schools, businesses, and clinics; guest on television and radio programs, including the British series *Men, Love, and Relationships Made Easy,* Live-TV.

MEMBER: Authors Guild, Authors League of America, National Federation of Press Women, American Counseling Association, American Psychological Association, New Jersey Press Women, Maine Media Women.

AWARDS, HONORS: Best Program Award, counseling and guidance, Arizona Guidance Association, 1976; first place award, Maine Media Women Communications Contest, Middlesex Community Newspapers of Farmingham, MA, and second place award for non-fiction books, general category, New Jersey Press Women Communications Contest, both 1996, both for *When Men Believe in Love: A Book for Men Who Love Women and the Women They Love.*

WRITINGS:

HISTORICAL ROMANCE NOVELS

White Wind, Dorchester Publishing (New York, NY), 1996.
White Wolf, Leisure Books (New York, NY), 1999.
White Flame, Leisure Books (New York, NY), 1999.
White Dreams, Leisure Books (New York, NY), 2000.
White Nights, Leisure Books (New York, NY), 2000.
White Dove, Leisure Books (New York, NY), 2001.
White Dusk, Leisure Books (New York, NY), 2002.
White Dawn, Leisure Books (New York, NY), 2002.
White Shadows, Leisure Books (New York, NY), 2003.
White Deception, Leisure Books (New York, NY), 2004.

OTHER

When Men Believe in Love: A Book for Men Who Love Women and the Women They Love, Element Books (Rockport, MA), 1995.
Dangerous Clients: How to Protect Yourself, Miller Freeman Books (San Francisco, CA), 1998.

Columnist for *Portland Business Journal,* 1985-88, *For Mothers Only,* 1990, and *Custom Builder.* Contributor to psychology and counseling journals.

SIDELIGHTS: Susan Edwards once told *CA:* "I knew in the fifth grade that I would write five books. What I didn't expect was that it would take so long. My first book was published in 1995, and it has been quite awhile since I was a fifth grader.

"Writing has always been a means of empowerment to me. As a child, I wrote stories and poems that helped me learn about myself. As a psychologist, I continue to write stories for children who experience hurt or loss. For adult readers, my work often provides new ways of looking at old issues: the perspective of a multimodal psychologist offers analyses seldom seen in today's psychology books. Over the years, it has been my experience that anything which facilitates true understanding can make a difference in a person's life. I have spent my career fostering that process.

"Along the way, I have learned from both my patients and my mentors. However, there is much yet to discover about understanding the complexities of human behavior. I hope to make a special contribution through my writing, whether my work helps to awaken one's own inner feelings, an understanding of others, or the value of love in a world of violence. Ultimately, I hope to strengthen the place where love lives."

BIOGRAPHICAL AND CRITICAL SOURCES:

PERIODICALS

Library Journal, November 15, 1998, Kristin Ramsdell, review of *White Wolf,* p. 58.

ONLINE

BookBrowser, http://www.bookbrowser.com/ (May 7, 2002), review of *White Dawn.*
Romance Reader, http://www.theromancereader.com/ (November 12, 1999).
Susan Edwards Home Page, http://www.susanedwards. com (September 9, 2004).*

EGGERS, Dave 1971(?)-

PERSONAL: Born c. 1971; married Vendela Vida (an author and magazine editor), 2003.

ADDRESSES: Office—c/o McSweeney's, 826NYC, 372 Fifth Ave. Brooklyn, NY 11215; 826 Valencia St., San Francisco, CA 94110

CAREER: Writer. *Might* magazine, founder and editor, beginning 1997. Also editor at *Esquire* and *Timothy McSweeney's Quarterly Concern.* Consultant for ESPN. Has appeared on various radio and television shows, including *This American Life,* for National Public Radio (NPR), and *The Real World,* for Music Television (MTV).

WRITINGS:

(And editor, with others) *For the Love of Cheese: The Editors of Might Magazine,* Boulevard Books (New York, NY), 1996.
A Heartbreaking Work of Staggering Genius (memoir), Simon & Schuster (New York, NY), 2000.
You Shall Know Our Velocity (novel), self-published, 2002.
(Editor, with Michael Cart) *The Best American Nonrequired Reading 2002,* Mariner Books, 2002.
(Editor, with Zadie Smith) *The Best American Nonrequired Reading 2003,* Houghton Mifflin, 2003.
(Editor) *The Best American Nonrequired Reading 2004,* Mariner Books, 2004.
(Editor, with others) *Created in Darkness by Troubled Americans: The Best of McSweeney's Humor Category,* Knopf, 2004.
Sacrament! (play; adapted from *You Shall Know Our Velocity,*) produced at the Campo Santo Company, San Francisco, CA, 2004.
How We Are Hungry (short stories), McSweeney's, 2004.

Contributor to numerous periodicals.

ADAPTATIONS: A Heartbreaking Work of Staggering Genius is being adapted as a screenplay by Nick Hornby and D. V. DeVincentis.

Dave Eggers

SIDELIGHTS: Founder in 1994 and former editor of *Might* magazine, writer Dave Eggers edits *Timothy McSweeney's Quarterly Concern,* a quarterly journal and Web site in existence since 1998. Jeff Daniel of the St. Louis *Post-Dispatch* likened Eggers to avant-garde pop musicians Radiohead and the movie-making Coen brothers, placing him among the "rare breed that has managed to marry commercial and critical success." Daniel called Eggers a "self-starter and self-promoter," praising him for his work ethic and writing talent. Daniel, too, noted that *McSweeney's* continues to be commended for promoting clever writing. Christopher Lydon, interviewer for *WBUR Boston,* commented that *McSweeney's* is a "quirky" Monty Python-style publication as well as a "postmodern examination of everything." Only a few years prior to the development and launch of *Might,* Eggers and his three siblings faced the grim reality of having seen both their parents die within weeks of each other. After two of Eggers' siblings moved to California, he decided to take on the task of raising his eight-year-old brother, Christopher, or Toph, on his own. That experience, as well as many others, prompted Eggers to write *A Heartbreaking Work of Staggering Genius.*

Daniel Handler, in *Voice Literary Supplement,* stated that "whether [Eggers is] discussing early *Might* meetings or parent-teacher conferences, he invariably finds a perfect tone and zeroes in on the triple paradox of . . . slacker days: you want to do something, preferably the right thing, but are paralyzed by self-awareness; despite self-awareness you do something anyway." Handler commented that Eggers "may end up becoming something he richly deserves and probably does not aspire to be: the voice of a generation." Mark Horowitz, reviewing *A Heartbreaking Work of Staggering Genius* for *New York,* praised Eggers' honest voice, noting that he "lays everything out in exquisite, excruciating detail." Horowitz called the book "a heart-wrenching yet often very funny memoir."

Sara Mosle, in the *New York Times Book Review,* commented on the humor in *A Heartbreaking Work of Staggering Genius,* calling the work "a book of finite jest, which is why it succeeds so brilliantly." Mosle commented that the book "goes a surprisingly long way toward delivering on its self-satirizing, hyperbolic title," and that it "is a profoundly moving, occasionally angry and often hilarious account of those odd and silly things, usually done in the name of Toph." Elise Harris described in *Nation* how "conviction and doubt, depth and humor, are placed side by side," and that "each is a style, and each is true and false at once." According to Harris, Eggers "won't let the reader make a choice between them—we don't know where he really falls. The result is exhausting and frustrating, but trustworthy." James Poniewozik, in *Time,* stated that in *A Heartbreaking Work of Staggering Genius* "literary gamesmanship and self-consciousness are trained on life's most unendurable experience, used to examine memory too scorching to stare at, as one views an eclipse by projecting sunlight onto paper through a pinhole." Grace Fill, a reviewer in *Booklist,* was another reviewer who commented on Eggers' use of humor, stating that his "piercingly observant style allows hilarity to lead the way in a very personal and revealing recounting of the loss of his parents." A reviewer in *Publishers Weekly* said that "literary self-consciousness and technical invention mix unexpectedly in this engaging memoir." Eric Bryant, a reviewer in *Library Journal,* "highly recommended" the book, calling the work "a surprisingly moving tale of family bonding and resilience."

Eggers' first novel, *You Shall Know Our Velocity,* concerns two young men on a week-long trip around the world with the goal of giving away an unexpected windfall of cash one of them received. Kyle Minor of the *Antioch Review* pointed out the plot is simply a way for Eggers to conduct a philosophical character analysis of the duo as they deal with feelings of guilt and attempt to come to grips with a friend's death. Minor felt the Eggers produced a "convincing book-length dialogue between them that works on multiple levels," remarking that, it is a "minor work, but it is a satisfying and meritorious effort." Benjamin Markovitz noted in the *New Statesman* that Eggers draws the title for his novel from "a lengthy anecdote about a harmless, foolish, and ambitious South American tribe who believed they could jump their way to heaven. Its relation to the story is clear, and explains why their failure and nobility appealed to Eggers." Markovits also commented that Eggers' writing is more "grown up in style" and the plot tighter than in his memoir, yet he still exhibits some of the irreverence shown in his first book. "He deserves his success," commented Markovitz. "He writes well and he practises what he preaches: he teaches literacy at his own foundation in San Francisco, while *McSweeney's,* the independent literary magazine and press that he founded, is now the place publishers look for new talent."

BIOGRAPHICAL AND CRITICAL SOURCES:

PERIODICALS

Antioch Review, spring, 2003, Kyle Minor, review of *You Shall Know Our Velocity,* p. 373.

Booklist, January 1, 2000, Grace Fill, review of *A Heartbreaking Work of Staggering Genius,* p. 860.

Entertainment Weekly, March 3, 2000, Clarissa Cruz, "His So-Called Life: Author du jour Dave Eggers' Crazy Existence Gets Even Crazier," p. 67.

Library Journal, November 15, 1999, Eric Bryant, review of *A Heartbreaking Work of Staggering Genius,* p. 77.

Nation, March 20, 2000, Elise Harris, "Infinite Jest," p. 45.

New Statesman, February 24, 2003, Benjamin Markovitz, review of *You Shall Know Your Velocity,* p. 53.

New York, January 31, 2000, Mark Horowitz, "Laughing through His Tearjerker," pp. 30-33.

New York Times Book Review, February 20, 2000, Sara Mosle, "My Brother's Keeper," p. 6.

Publishers Weekly, December 13, 1999, review of *A Heartbreaking Work of Staggering Genius,* p. 72.

St. Louis Post-Dispatch, July 17, 2003, Jeff Daniel, "Quirky Dave Eggers Comes to Town to Promote His New Book," p. 5.

Time, February 7, 2000, James Poniewozik, "Dave Eggers' Mystery Box: With a Curious Journal and an Ambitious New Memoir of Orphanhood, This Young Editor and Writer Opens a Package of Literary Surprises," p. 72.

U.S. News & World Report, February 7, 2000, Linda Kulman, "He's Ingenious and He Knows It," p. 62.

Voice Literary Supplement, February-March, 2000, Daniel Handler, "Reality Writes," p. 107.

ONLINE

Timothy McSweeney's Internet Tendency, http://www.mcsweeneys.net/ (August 14, 2004).

WBUR Boston Web site, http://www.wbur.org/ (February 22, 2000), Christopher Lydon, "Dave Eggers, Novelist and Editor of *McSweeney's.*"*

*   *   *

ERDRICH, (Karen) Louise 1954-
(Heidi Louise, a joint pseudonym, Milou North, a joint pseudonym)

PERSONAL: Born June 7 (one source says July 6), 1954, in Little Falls, MN; daughter of Ralph Louis (a teacher with the Bureau of Indian Affairs) and Rita Joanne (affiliated with the Bureau of Indian Affairs; maiden name, Gourneau) Erdrich; married Michael Anthony Dorris (a writer and professor of Native-American studies), October 10, 1981 (died, April 11, 1997); children: Reynold Abel (died, 1991), Jeffrey Sava, Madeline Hannah, Persia Andromeda, Pallas Antigone, Aza Marion. *Education:* Dartmouth College, B.A., 1976; Johns Hopkins University, M.A., 1979. *Politics:* Democrat. *Religion:* "Anti-religion." *Hobbies and other interests:* Quilting, running, drawing, "playing chess with daughters and losing, playing piano badly, speaking terrible French."

ADDRESSES: Agent—Andrew Wylie Agency, 250 West 57th St., Suite 2114, New York, NY 10107-2199.

CAREER: Writer. North Dakota State Arts Council, visiting poet and teacher, 1977-78; Johns Hopkins University, Baltimore, MD, writing instructor, 1978-

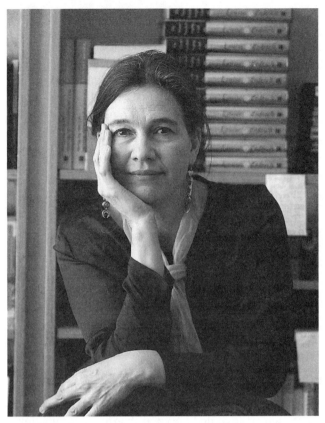

Louise Erdrich

79; Boston Indian Council, Boston, MA, communications director and editor of the *Circle,* 1979-80; Charles Merrill Co., textbook writer, 1980. Previously employed as a beet weeder in Wahpeton, ND; waitress in Wahpeton, Boston, MA, and Syracuse, NY; psychiatric aide in a Vermont hospital; poetry teacher at prisons; lifeguard; and construction flag signaler. Has judged writing contests.

MEMBER: International Writers, PEN (member of executive board, 1985-88), Authors Guild, Authors League of America.

AWARDS, HONORS: Johns Hopkins University teaching fellow, 1978; MacDowell Colony fellow, 1980; Yaddo Colony fellow, 1981; Dartmouth College visiting fellow, 1981; First Prize, Nelson Algren fiction competition, 1982, for "The World's Greatest Fisherman"; National Endowment for the Arts fellowship, 1982; Pushcart Prize, 1983; National Magazine Fiction awards, 1983 and 1987; Virginia McCormack Scully Prize for best book of the year dealing with Indians or Chicanos, National Book Critics Circle Award for best work of fiction, and *Los Angeles Times* Award for best

novel, all 1984, and Sue Kaufman Prize for Best First Novel, American Academy and Institute of Arts and Letters, American Book Award, Before Columbus Foundation, and named among best eleven books of 1985 by the *New York Times Book Review,* all for *Love Medicine;* Guggenheim fellow, 1985-86; *The Beet Queen* named one of *Publishers Weekly*'s best books, 1986; First Prize, O. Henry awards, 1987; National Book Critics Circle Award nomination; World Fantasy Award for Best Novel, World Fantasy Convention, 1999, for *The Antelope Wife;* National Book Award for fiction finalist, 2001, for *The Last Report on the Miracles at Little No Horse,* and 2003, for *The Master Butchers Singing Club.*

WRITINGS:

NOVELS

Love Medicine, Holt (New York, NY), 1984, expanded edition, 1993.
The Beet Queen, Holt (New York, NY), 1986.
Tracks, Harper (New York, NY), 1988.
(With husband, Michael Dorris) *The Crown of Columbus,* HarperCollins (New York, NY), 1991.
The Bingo Palace, HarperCollins (New York, NY), 1994.
Tales of Burning Love, HarperCollins (New York, NY), 1996.
The Antelope Wife, HarperFlamingo (New York, NY), 1998.
The Last Report on the Miracles at Little No Horse, HarperCollins (New York, NY), 2001.
The Master Butchers Singing Club, HarperCollins (New York, NY), 2003.
Four Souls, HarperCollins (New York, NY), 2004.

POETRY

Jacklight, Holt (New York, NY), 1984.
Baptism of Desire, Harper (New York, NY), 1989.
Original Fire: New and Selected Poems, HarperCollins (New York, NY), 2003.

FOR CHILDREN

Grandmother's Pigeon, illustrated by Jim LaMarche, Hyperion (New York, NY), 1996.

(And illustrator) *The Birchbark House,* Hyperion Books for Children (New York, NY), 1999.

The Game of Silence, HarperCollins (New York, NY), 2004.

OTHER

Imagination (textbook), C. E. Merrill (New York, NY), 1980.

Louise Erdrich and Michael Dorris Interview with Kay Bonetti, (sound recording), American Audio Prose Library, 1986.

(Author of preface) Michael Dorris, *The Broken Cord: A Family's Ongoing Struggle with Fetal Alcohol Syndrome,* Harper (New York, NY), 1989.

(Author of preface) Desmond Hogan, *A Link with the River,* Farrar, Straus (New York, NY), 1989.

(With Allan Richard Chavkin and Nancy Feyl Chavkin) *Conversations with Louise Erdrich and Michael Dorris,* University Press of Mississippi (Jackson, MS), 1994.

The Falcon: A Narrative of the Captivity and Adventures of John Tanner, Penguin (New York, NY), 1994.

The Blue Jay's Dance: A Birth Year, (memoir), Harper-Collins (New York, NY), 1995.

Books and Islands in Ojibwe Country, National Geographic (Washington, DC), 2003.

Author of short story, "The World's Greatest Fisherman"; contributor to anthologies, including *Norton Anthology of Poetry; Best American Short Stories of 1981-83, 1983, and 1988;* and *Prize Stories: The O. Henry Awards,* 1985 and 1987. Contributor of stories, poems, essays, and book reviews to periodicals, including *New Yorker, New England Review, Chicago, American Indian Quarterly, Frontiers, Atlantic, Kenyon Review, North American Review, New York Times Book Review, Ms., Redbook* (with her sister Heidi, under the joint pseudonym Heidi Louise), and *Woman* (with Dorris, under the joint pseudonym Milou North).

ADAPTATIONS: The Crown of Columbus has been optioned for film production.

SIDELIGHTS: The daughter of a Chippewa Indian mother and a German-American father, Louise Erdrich explores Native-American themes in her works, with major characters representing both sides of her heritage. In an award-winning series of related novels and short stories, Erdrich has visited and re-visited the North Dakota lands where her ancestors met and mingled, creating "a Chippewa experience in the context of the European American novelistic tradition," to quote P. Jane Hafen in the *Dictionary of Literary Biography.* Many critics claim Erdrich has remained true to her Native ancestors' mythic and artistic visions while writing fiction that candidly explores the cultural issues facing modern-day Native Americans and mixed heritage Americans. As an essayist for *Contemporary Novelists* observed: "Erdrich's accomplishment is that she is weaving a body of work that goes beyond portraying contemporary Native American life as descendants of a politically dominated people to explore the great universal questions—questions of identity, pattern versus randomness, and the meaning of life itself." In fact, as Hafen put it, Erdrich's "diverse imageries, subjects, and textual strategies reaffirm imperatives of American Indian survival."

A contributor to *Contemporary Popular Writers* credited Erdrich with a body of work that is "more interested in love and survival than in recrimination." The critic added: "Past wrongs and present hardships do figure in her work but chiefly as the backdrop against which the task of 'protecting and celebrating' takes on added force and urgency. . . . Erdrich's sense of loss never gives way to a sense of grievance; her characteristic tone is hopeful, not mournful, and springs from her belief in the persistence and viability of certain Native American values and the vision to which they give rise." The author's creative impulse has led to a significant accomplishment. Elizabeth Blair declared in *World and I:* "In an astonishing, virtuoso performance sustained over more than two decades, Erdrich has produced . . . interlinked novels that braid the lives of a series of fallible, lovable, and unpredictable characters of German, Cree, métis, and Ojibwe heritage." Blair concluded: "The painful history of Indian-white relations resonates throughout her work. In her hands we laugh and cry while listening to and absorbing home truths that, taken to heart, have the power to change our world. We listen because these truths come sinew-stitched into the very fabric of the tapestry she weaves so artfully."

Erdrich's first year at Dartmouth College, 1972, was the year the college began admitting women, as well as the year the Native-American studies department was established. The author's future husband and collaborator, anthropologist Michael Dorris, was hired to chair the department. In his class, Erdrich began the exploration of her own ancestry that would eventually inspire her novels. Intent on balancing her academic training with a broad range of practical knowledge, Erdrich told Miriam Berkley in an interview with *Publishers Weekly,* "I ended up taking some really crazy jobs, and I'm glad I did. They turned out to have been very useful experiences, although I never would have believed it at the time." In addition to working as a lifeguard, waitress, poetry teacher at prisons, and construction flag signaler, Erdrich became an editor for the *Circle,* a Boston Indian Council newspaper. She told *Writers Digest* interviewer Michael Schumacher: "Settling into that job and becoming comfortable with an urban community—which is very different from the reservation community—gave me another reference point. There were lots of people with mixed blood, lots of people who had their own confusions. I realized that this was part of my life—it wasn't something that I was making up—and that it was something I *wanted* to write about." In 1978, the author enrolled in an M.A. program at Johns Hopkins University, where she wrote poems and stories incorporating her heritage, many of which would later become part of her books. She also began sending her work to publishers, most of whom sent back rejection slips.

After receiving her master's degree, Erdrich returned to Dartmouth as a writer-in-residence. Dorris—with whom she had remained in touch—attended a reading of Erdrich's poetry there and was impressed. A writer himself—Dorris would later publish the best-selling novel *A Yellow Raft in Blue Water* and receive the 1989 National Book Critics Circle Award for his nonfiction work *The Broken Cord: A Family's Ongoing Struggle with Fetal Alcohol Syndrome*—he decided then that he was interested in working with Erdrich and getting to know her better. When he left for New Zealand to do field research and Erdrich went to Boston to work on a textbook, the two began sending their poetry and fiction back and forth with their letters, laying a groundwork for a literary relationship. Dorris returned to New Hampshire in 1980, and Erdrich moved back there as well. The two began collaborating on short stories, including one titled "The World's Greatest Fisherman." When this story won five thousand dollars in the Nelson Algren fiction competition, Erdrich and Dorris decided to expand it into a novel—*Love Medicine.* At the same time, their

literary relationship led to a romantic one and in 1981 they were married.

The titles Erdrich and Dorris chose for their novels—such as *Love Medicine* and *A Yellow Raft in Blue Water*—tend to be rich poetic or visual images, and was often the initial inspiration from which their novels were drawn. Erdrich told Schumacher, "I think a title is like a magnet: It begins to draw these scraps of experience or conversation or memory to it. Eventually, it collects a book." Erdrich and Dorris's collaborative process began with a first draft, usually written by whomever had the original idea for the book, the one who would ultimately be considered the official author. After the draft was written, the other person edited it, and then another draft was written; often five or six drafts would be written in all. Finally, the two read the work aloud until they agreed on each word. Although the author had the original voice and the final say, ultimately, both collaborators were responsible for what the work became. This "unique collaborative relationship," according to Alice Joyce in *Booklist,* is covered in *Conversations with Louise Erdrich and Michael Dorris,* a collection of twenty-five interviews with the couple. By 1997, when Dorris committed suicide, the pair had separated and were no longer actively collaborating. Erdrich alone is responsible for much of her work in the 1990s and all of her publications since the turn of the twenty-first century.

Erdrich's novels *Love Medicine, The Beet Queen, Tracks, The Bingo Palace,* and *Tales of Burning Love* encompass the stories of three interrelated families living in and around a reservation in the fictional town of Argus, North Dakota, from 1912 through the 1980s. The novels have been compared to those of William Faulkner, mainly due to the multi-voice narration and non-chronological storytelling which he employed in works such as *As I Lay Dying.* Erdrich's works, linked by recurring characters who are victims of fate and the patterns set by their elders, are structured like intricate puzzles in which bits of information about individuals and their relations to one another are slowly released in a seemingly random order, until three-dimensional characters—with a future and a past—are revealed. Through her characters' antics, Erdrich explores universal family life cycles while also communicating a sense of the changes and loss involved in the twentieth-century Native-American experience.

Poet Robert Bly, describing Erdrich's nonlinear story-telling approach in the *New York Times Book Review,* emphasized her tendency to "choose a few minutes or a day in 1932, let one character talk, let another talk, and a third, then leap to 1941 and then to 1950 or 1964." The novels' circular format is a reflection of the way in which the works are constructed. Although Erdrich is dealing with a specific and extensive time period, "The writing doesn't start out and proceed chronologically. It never seems to start in the beginning. Rather, it's as though we're building something around a center, but that center can be anywhere."

Erdrich published her first novel, *Love Medicine,* in 1984. "With this impressive debut," stated *New York Times Book Review* contributor Marco Portales, "Louise Erdrich enters the company of America's better novelists." *Love Medicine* was named for the belief in love potions which is a part of Chippewa folklore. The novel explores the bonds of family and faith which preserve both the Chippewa tribal community and the individuals that comprise it.

The story begins at a family gathering following the death of June Kashpaw, a prostitute. The characters introduce one another, sharing stories about June which reveal their family history and their cultural beliefs. Albertine Johnson, June's niece, introduces her grandmother, Marie, her grandfather, Nector, and Nector's twin brother, Eli. Eli represents the old way—the Native American who never integrated into the white culture. He also plays a major role in *Tracks,* in which he appears as a young man. The story of Marie and Nector brings together many of the important images in the novel, including the notion of "love medicine." As a teenager in a convent, Marie is nearly burned to death by a nun who, in an attempt to exorcise the devil from within her, pours boiling water on Marie. Immediately following this incident, Marie is sexually assaulted by Nector. Marie and Nector are later married, but in middle age, Nector begins an affair with Lulu Lamartine, a married woman. In an attempt to rekindle Nector and Marie's passion, their grandson Lipsha prepares "love medicine" for Nector. But Lipsha has difficulty obtaining a wild goose heart for the potion. He substitutes a frozen turkey heart, which causes Nector to choke to death.

Reviewers responded positively to Erdrich's debut novel, citing its lyrical qualities as well as the rich characters who inhabit it. *New York Times* contributor D. J. R. Bruckner was impressed with Erdrich's

"mastery of words," as well as the "vividly drawn" characters who "will not leave the mind once they are let in." Portales, who called *Love Medicine* "an engrossing book," applauded the unique narration technique which produces what he termed "a wondrous prose song." The novel won numerous awards, including the National Book Critics Circle Award for best work of fiction in 1984.

After the publication of *Love Medicine,* Erdrich told reviewers that her next novel would focus less exclusively on her mother's side, embracing the author's mixed heritage and the mixed community in which she grew up. Her 1986 novel, *The Beet Queen,* deals with whites and half-breeds, as well as American Indians, and explores the interactions between these worlds. The story begins in 1932, during the Depression. Mary and Karl Adare's recently-widowed mother flies off with a carnival pilot, abandoning the two children and their newborn brother. The baby is taken by a young couple who have just lost their child. Karl and eleven-year-old Mary ride a freight train to Argus, seeking refuge with their aunt and uncle. When they arrive in the town, however, Karl, frightened by a dog, runs back onto the train and winds up at an orphanage. Mary grows up with her aunt and uncle, and the novel follows her life—as well as those of her jealous, self-centered cousin Sita and their part-Chippewa friend Celestine James—for the next forty years, tracing the themes of separation and loss that began with Mary's father's death and her mother's grand departure.

The Beet Queen was well received by critics, some of whom found it even more impressive than *Love Medicine.* Many commented favorably on the novel's poetic language and symbolism; Bly noted that Erdrich's "genius is in metaphor," and that the characters "show a convincing ability to feel an image with their whole bodies." Josh Rubins, writing in *New York Review of Books,* called *The Beet Queen* "a rare second novel, one that makes it seem as if the first, impressive as it was, promised too little, not too much." Other reviewers had problems with *The Beet Queen,* but they tended to dismiss the novel's flaws in light of its positive qualities. *New Republic* contributor Dorothy Wickenden considered the characters unrealistic and the ending contrived, but she lauded *The Beet Queen*'s "ringing clarity and lyricism," as well as the "assured, polished quality" which she felt was missing in *Love Medicine.* Although Michiko Kakutani found the ending artificial, the *New York Times* reviewer called Erdrich "an immensely gifted young writer." "Even with its weaknesses," proclaimed Linda Simon in *Commonweal*, "*The Beet Queen* stands as a product of enormous talent."

After Erdrich completed *The Beet Queen,* she was uncertain as to what her next project should be. The four-hundred-page manuscript that would eventually become *Tracks* had remained untouched for ten years; the author referred to it as her "burden." She and Dorris took a fresh look at it, and decided that they could relate it to *Love Medicine* and *The Beet Queen.* While more political than her previous novels, *Tracks* also deals with spiritual themes, exploring the tension between the Native Americans' ancient beliefs and the Christian notions of the Europeans. *Tracks* takes place between 1912 and 1924, before the settings of Erdrich's other novels, and reveals the roots of *Love Medicine*'s characters and their hardships. One of the narrators, Nanapush, is the leader of a tribe that is suffering on account of the white government's exploitation. He feels pressured to give up tribal land in order to avoid starvation. While Nanapush represents the old way, Pauline, the other narrator, represents change. The future mother of *Love Medicine*'s Marie Lazarre, Pauline is a young half-breed from a mixed-blood tribe "for which the name was lost." She feels torn between her Indian faith and the white people's religion, and is considering leaving the reservation. But at the center of *Tracks* is Fleur, a character whom *Los Angeles Times Book Review* contributor Terry Tempest Williams called "one of the most haunting presences in contemporary American literature." Nanapush discovers this young woman—the last survivor of a family killed by consumption—in a cabin in the woods, starving and mad. Nanapush adopts Fleur and nurses her back to health.

Reviewers found *Tracks* distinctly different from Erdrich's earlier novels, and some felt that her third novel lacked the characteristics that made *Love Medicine* and *The Beet Queen* so outstanding. *Washington Post Book World* critic Jonathan Yardley stated that, on account of its more political focus, the work has a "labored quality." Robert Towers, in the *New York Review of Books,* found the characters too melodramatic and the tone too intense. Katherine Dieckmann, writing in the *Village Voice Literary Supplement,* affirmed that she "missed [Erdrich's] skilled multiplications of voice," and called the relationship between Pauline and Nanapush "symptomatic of the overall lack of grand orchestration and perspectival interplay that made Erdrich's first two novels polyphonic masterpieces." According to *Commonweal* contributor Christopher Vecsey, however, although "a reviewer might find some of the prose overwrought, and the two narrative voices indistinguishable . . . readers will appreciate and applaud the vigor and inventiveness of the author."

Other reviewers enjoyed *Tracks* even more than the earlier novels. Williams stated that Erdrich's writing "has never appeared more polished and grounded," and added, "*Tracks* may be the story of our time." Thomas M. Disch lauded the novel's plot, with its surprising twists and turns, in the *Chicago Tribune.* The critic added: "Erdrich is like one of those rumored drugs that are instantly and forever addictive. Fortunately in her case you can *just say yes.*"

Erdrich and Dorris's jointly authored novel *The Crown of Columbus* explores Native-American issues from the standpoint of the authors' current experience, rather than the world of their ancestors. Marking the quincentennial anniversary of Spanish explorer Christopher Columbus's voyage in a not-so-celebratory fashion, Erdrich and Dorris raise important questions about the meaning of that voyage for both Europeans and Native Americans today. The story is narrated by the two central characters, both Dartmouth professors involved in projects concerning Columbus. Vivian Twostar is a Native-American single mother with eclectic tastes and a teenage son, Nash. Vivian is asked to write an academic article on Columbus from a Native-American perspective and is researching Columbus's diaries. Roger Williams, a stuffy New England Protestant poet, is writing an epic work about the explorer's voyage. Vivian and Roger become lovers—parenting a girl named Violet—but have little in common. Ultimately acknowledging the destructive impact of Columbus's voyage on the Native-American people, Vivian and Roger vow to redress the political wrongs symbolically by changing the power structure in their relationship. In the end, as Vivian and Roger rediscover themselves, they rediscover America.

Some reviewers found *The Crown of Columbus* unbelievable and inconsistent, and considered it less praiseworthy than the individual authors' earlier works. However, *New York Times Book Review* contributor Robert Houston appreciated the work's timely political relevance. He also stated: "There are moments of genuine humor and compassion, of real insight and sound satire." Other critics also considered Vivian and Roger's adventures amusing, vibrant, and charming.

Erdrich returned to the descendants of Nanapush with her 1994 novel, *The Bingo Palace*. The fourth novel in the series that began with *Love Medicine, The Bingo Palace* weaves together a story of spiritual pursuit with elements of modern reservation life. Erdrich also provided continuity to the series by having the novel primarily narrated by Lipsha Morrissey, the illegitimate son of June Kapshaw and Gerry Nanapush from *Love Medicine*. After working at a Fargo sugar beet factory, Lipsha has returned home to the reservation in search of his life's meaning. He finds work at his uncle Lyman Lamartine's bingo parlor and love with his uncle's girlfriend, Shawnee Ray Toose. Thanks to the magic bingo tickets provided to him by the spirit of his dead mother, June, he also finds modest wealth. The character of Fleur Pillager returns from *Tracks* as Lipsha's great-grandmother. After visiting her, Lipsha embarks on a spiritual quest in order to impress Shawnee and learn more about his own tribal religious rites. Family members past and present are brought together in his pursuit, which comprises the final pages of the novel.

Reviewers' comments on *The Bingo Palace* were generally positive. While Lawrence Thornton, in the *New York Times Book Review,* found "some of the novel's later ventures into magic realism . . . contrived," his overall impression was more positive: "Erdrich's sympathy for her characters shines as luminously as Shawnee Ray's jingle dress." Pam Houston, writing for the *Los Angeles Times Book Review,* was especially taken by the character of Lipsha Morrissey, finding in him "what makes this her most exciting and satisfying book to date."

The Bingo Palace was also reviewed in the context of the series as a whole. *Chicago Tribune* contributor Michael Upchurch concluded, *The Bingo Palace* "falls somewhere between *Tracks* and *The Beet Queen* in its accomplishment." He added, "The best chapters in *The Bingo Palace* rival, as *Love Medicine* did, the work of Welty, Cheever, and Flannery O'Connor."

Erdrich turned to her own experience as mother of six for her next work, *The Blue Jay's Dance*. Her first book of nonfiction, *The Blue Jay's Dance* chronicles Erdrich's pregnancy and the birth year of her child. The title refers to a blue jay's habit of defiantly "dancing" towards an attacking hawk, Erdrich's metaphor for "the sort of controlled recklessness that having children always is," noted Jane Aspinall in *Quill & Quire*. Erdrich has been somewhat protective of her family's privacy and has stated the narrative actually describes a combination of her experience with several of her children. Sue Halpern, in the *New York Times Book Review,* remarked on this difficult balancing act between public and private lives but found "Erdrich's ambivalence inspires trust . . . and suggests that she is the kind of mother whose story should be told."

Some reviewers noted that Erdrich's description of the maternal relationship was a powerful one: "the bond between mother and infant has rarely been captured so well," commented a *Kirkus Reviews* contributor. While the subject of pregnancy and motherhood is not a new one, Halpern noted that the book provided new insight into the topic: "What makes *The Blue Jay's Dance* worth reading is that it quietly places a mother's love and nurturance amid her love for the natural world and suggests . . . how right that placement is." Although the *Kirkus Reviews* contributor found *The Blue Jay's Dance* to be "occasionally too self-conscious about the importance of Erdrich's role as Writer," others commented positively on the book's examination of the balance between the work of parenting and one's vocation. A *Los Angeles Times Book Review* reviewer remarked: "this book is really about working and having children, staying alert and . . . focused through the first year of a child's life."

Erdrich retained her focus on children with her first children's book, *Grandmother's Pigeon*. Published in 1996, it is a fanciful tale of an adventurous grandmother who heads to Greenland on the back of a porpoise, leaving behind grandchildren and three bird's eggs in her cluttered bedroom. The eggs hatch into passenger pigeons, thought to be extinct, through which the children are able to send messages to their missing grandmother. A *Publishers Weekly* reviewer commented, "As in her fiction for adults . . . , Erdrich makes every word count in her bewitching debut children's story."

Within the same year, Erdrich returned to the character of June Kasphaw of *Love Medicine* in her sixth novel, *Tales of Burning Love*. More accurately, it is the story of June's husband, Jack Mauser, and his five—including June—ex-wives. To begin the tale, Jack meets June while they are both inebriated and marries her that night. In reaction to his inability to consummate their marriage, she walks off into a blizzard and is found dead the next day. His four subsequent marriages share the same elements of tragedy and comedy, culminating in Jack's death in a fire in the house he built. The story of each marriage is told by the four ex-wives as they are stranded together in Jack's car during a blizzard after his funeral. Again, Erdrich references her previous work in the characters of Gerry and Dot Nanapush, Dot as one of Jack's ex-wives and Gerry as Dot's imprisoned husband.

Reviewers continued to note Erdrich's masterful descriptions and fine dialogue in this work. According to Penelope Mesic in the *Chicago Tribune,* "Erdrich's strength is that she gives emotional states—as shifting and intangible, as indefinable as wind—a visible form in metaphor." A *Times Literary Supplement* contributor compared her to Tobias Wolff—"[like him], she is . . . particularly good at evoking American small-town life and the space that engulfs it"—as well as Raymond Carver, noting her dialogues to be "small exchanges that . . . map out the barely navigable distance between what's heard, what's meant, and what's said."

Tales of Burning Love also focuses Erdrich's abilities (and perhaps Dorris's collaborative talents) on the relationship between men and women. As the *Times Literary Supplement* reviewer continued, "Erdrich also shares Carver's clear and sophisticated view of the more fundamental distance between men and women, and how that, too, is negotiated." However, Mark Childress in the *New York Times Book Review* commented that while "Jack's wives are vivid and fully realized . . . whenever [Jack's] out of sight, he doesn't seem as interesting as the women who loved him."

While Erdrich covers familiar territory in *Tales of Burning Love,* she seems, claim several critics, to be expanding her focus slightly. Roxana Robinson, in *Washington Post Book World,* remarked, "The landscape, instead of being somber and overcast . . . is vividly illuminated by bolts of freewheeling lunacy: This is a mad Gothic comedy." Or as Verlyn Klinkenborg noted in the *Los Angeles Times Book Review,* "this book marks a shift in [Erdrich's] career, a shift that is suggested rather than fulfilled . . . there is new country coming into [her] sight, and this novel is her first welcoming account of it."

The Antelope Wife was the first book Erdrich released following Dorris's suicide, and although the author disavowed any relationship between herself and her characters, the story does include a self-destructive husband who inadvertently kills his child in a botched suicide attempt. The episodic plot revolves around the history of Rozin, married to the suicidal Richard and in love with another man, and Richard's friends Klaus Shawano and Sweetheart Calico—the latter the "Antelope Wife" of the title. Intercut with the modern tale of these four are the stories of their ancestors, Native and European, who live out their lives and passions on the plains. Erdrich reveals how the Antelope Wife received her mystical powers and how a dog named Almost Soup cheats mortality. *People* reviewer V. R. Peterson called the novel "a captivating jigsaw puzzle of longing and loss."

New York Times Book Review correspondent Diana Postlethwaite suggested that the Native-American craft of beadwork serves as a metaphor for the linked narratives in *The Antelope Wife.* As Postlethwaite wrote: "Family—both immediate and ancestral—is a tensile bond that links the novel's characters, as much a hangman's noose as a lifeline." The critic concluded that reading *The Antelope Wife* "offers a . . . rich taste of the bitter and the sweet." In a *New York Times* review Michiko Kakutani described *The Antelope Wife* as "one of [Erdrich's] most powerful and fully imagined novels yet." Kakutani added: "Erdrich has returned to doing what she does best: using multiple viewpoints and strange, surreal tales within tales to conjure up a family's legacy of love, duty and guilt, and to show us how that family's fortunes have both shifted—and endured—as its members have abandoned ancient Indian traditions for a modern fast-food existence. . . . As for Ms. Erdrich's own storytelling powers, they are on virtuosic display in this novel. She has given us a fiercely imagined tale of love and loss, a story that manages to transform tragedy into comic redemption, sorrow into heroic survival. She has given us a wonderfully sad, funny and affecting novel."

Erdrich has also embarked upon a series of novels for children based on lives of Native-American young people at the time of white encroachment. *The Birchbark House,* published in 1999, tells the story of seven-year-old Omakayas, who lives with her extended family on an island in Lake Superior. In rich detail, Erdrich describes Omakayas's hardships and triumphs as she learns the lessons of her heritage and completes the routines of daily living. Heartache comes too, as Omakayas fails to nurse her beloved baby brother back to health when he contracts smallpox. *Booklist* contributor Hazel Rochman found the characters in *The Birchbark House* "wonderfully individualized, humane and funny," adding that readers of the "Little House" series by Laura Ingalls Wilder "will discover a new world, a different version of a story they thought they knew."

A peripheral character from Erdrich's previous novels, Father Damien, takes center stage in *The Last Report on the Miracles at Little No Horse.* Having served the parishioners of a North Dakota Indian reservation for eight decades, Father Damien is finally dying—and is revealed to be a woman named Agnes DeWitt who was once ousted from a convent for playing Chopin piano pieces in the nude. Agnes's passion finds an outlet amongst the families of the reservation, whose names and deeds are already familiar from other Erdrich novels. What this story provides is a stage upon which the author can address the collaboration between Native beliefs and Catholicism. "This is the miracle of Erdrich's writing," stated Ann-Janine Morey in the *Christian Century.* "She conveys the fluidity of meanings across religious systems and across time through her full, rich characters." Elizabeth Blair likewise noted: "In this tale of passion and compassion, a priest meets an elder possessing love medicine and under his tutelage constructs a hybrid religious life that abounds with mysteries and miracles."

Again the reviewers found much to praise in *The Last Report on the Miracles at Little No Horse.* Kakutani found the portrait of Father Damien "so moving, so precisely observed." The critic further commented: "By turns comical and elegiac, farcical and tragic, the stories span the history of this Ojibwe tribe and its members' wrestlings with time and change and loss. . . . Erdrich has woven an imperfect but deeply affecting narrative and in doing so filled out the history of that postage-stamp-size world in Ojibwe country that she has delineated with such fervor and fidelity in half a dozen novels." *New York Times Book Review* contributor Verlyn Klinkenborg maintained that in *The Last Report on the Miracles at Little No Horse* Erdrich "takes us farther back in time than she ever has, so far back that she comes, in a sense, to the edge of the reservation that has been her fictional

world. What makes it possible is the Ojibwa language, which is both as fresh and as ancient as rain. It is the leading edge of a discovery that will, one hopes, take Erdrich even farther." In the *New Leader* Lynne Sharon Schwartz declared: "*The Last Report . . .* comes from the 'dictates of a great love,' the author's for her land and her people. Love alone never produced a fine novel, but Erdrich's gifts are abundant enough to subsume melodrama and quash disbelief. She has made this improbable saga moving and luminous."

Although Erdrich continues to dedicate herself to her saga involving Native-American characters, she steps away from that world to touch on her German-American heritage with *The Master Butchers Singing Club,* the 2003 novel that made her a National Book Award finalist for the second time. The title is indicative of the inventive plot that does indeed include singing and intertwines the lives of a German World War I veteran and his wife with those of circus performers and other small-town residents. Erdrich's fans will find themselves in familiar territory, as this story is set in North Dakota like previous Erdrich novels; however this time there are few Native-American characters. The book was highly praised, a *Booklist* contributor commenting that, "Combining a cast of remarkable characters, a compelling plot, and an unforgiving North Dakota setting, Erdrich tells the story of indefatigable Fidelis Waldgovel, a butcher with a talent for singing."

With *Four Souls,* released in 2004, Erdrich picks up the thread of previous tales by returning to the story of Fleur Pillager from *The Last Report on the Miracles at Little No Horse.* Fleur wants revenge and her target is the man who swindled her out of her land, but this revenge not only takes its toll on the intended, but on Fleur as well. Critical reaction to *Four Souls* was mixed; the common complaint was Erdrich's lyrical style. The verdict from a *People* contributor was that while, "On occasion Erdrich's lyrical descriptions of Ojibwe beliefs run on and overwhelm the story," the author nonetheless "sustains a literary voice like no other." Noting the author's growing body of long fiction, in the *Dictionary of Literary Biography,* Peter G. Beidler ranked Erdrich among "the most important contemporary Native American writers," and maintained that "her novels, particularly, deserve to be read, discussed, and appreciated."

BIOGRAPHICAL AND CRITICAL SOURCES:

BOOKS

American Women Writers: A Critical Reference Guide from Colonial Times to the Present, 2nd edition, St. James Press (Detroit, MI), 2000.

Authors and Artists for Young Adults, Volume 10, Gale (Detroit, MI), 1993.

Chavkin, Allan, and Nancy Feyl Chavkin, editors, *Conversations with Louise Erdrich and Michael Dorris,* University Press of Mississippi (Jackson, MS), 1994.

Chavkin, Allan, editor, *The Chippewa Landscape of Louise Erdrich,* University of Alabama Press (Tuscaloosa, AL), 1999.

Concise Dictionary of American Literary Biography: Modern Writers, 1900-1998, Gale (Detroit, MI), 1998, pp. 44-55.

Contemporary Literary Criticism, Gale (Detroit, MI), Volume 39, 1986, Volume 54, 1989, Volume 120, 1999.

Contemporary Novelists, 7th edition, St. James Press (Detroit, MI), 2001.

Contemporary Poets, 6th edition, St. James Press (Detroit, MI), 1996.

Contemporary Popular Writers, St. James Press (Detroit, MI), 1997.

Contemporary Women Poets, St. James Press (Detroit, MI), 1998.

Cooperman, Jeannette Batz, *The Broom Closet: Secret Meanings of Domesticity in Postfeminist Novels,* Peter Lang (New York, NY), 1999.

Dictionary of Literary Biography, Gale (Detroit, MI), Volume 152: *American Novelists since World War II, Fourth Series,* 1995, Volume 175: *Native American Writers of the United States,* 1997, pp. 84-100, Volume 206: *Twentieth-Century American Western Writers, First Series,* 1999, pp. 85-96.

Erdrich, Louise, *Tracks,* Harper (New York, NY), 1988.

Erdrich, Louise, *Baptism of Desire,* Harper (New York, NY), 1989.

Jacobs, Connie A., *The Novels of Louise Erdrich: Stories of Her People,* Peter Lang (New York, NY), 2001.

Lyons, Rosemary, *A Comparison of the Works of Antonine Maillet of the Acadian Tradition of New Brunswick, Canada, and Louise Erdrich of the Ojibwe of North America with the Poems of Longfellow,* Edwin Mellen Press (Lewiston, NY), 2002.

Pearlman, Mickey, *American Women Writing Fiction: Memory, Identity, Family, Space,* University Press of Kentucky (Lexington, KY), 1989, pp. 95-112.

Peterson, Nacy J., *Against Amnesia: Contemporary Women Writers and the Crises of Historical Memory,* University of Pennsylvania Press (Philadephia, PA), 2001.

Scott, Steven D., *The Gamefulness of American Postmodernism: John Barth and Louise Erdrich,* Peter Lang (New York, NY), 2000.

Stookey, Lorena L., *Louise Erdrich: A Critical Companion,* Greenwood Press (Westport, CT), 1999.

PERIODICALS

America, May 14, 1994, p. 7.

American Indian Culture and Research Journal, 1987, pp. 51-73; winter, 1999, Peter G. Beidler, review of *The Antelope Wife,* p. 219; spring, 2001, Peter G. Beidler, review of *The Last Report on the Miracles at Little No Horse,* p. 179.

American Literature, September, 1990, pp. 405-422.

Atlantic, March, 2003, p. 108; July-August, 2004, p. 164.

Belles Lettres, summer, 1990, pp. 30-31.

Book, January-February, 2003, p. 67.

Booklist, January 15, 1995, p. 893; April 1, 1999, Hazel Rochman, review of *The Birchbark House,* p. 1427; February 15, 2001, Bill Ott, review of *The Last Report on the Miracles at Little No Horse,* p. 1085; January 1, 2002, p. 767; October 1, 2002, pp. 334-335; December 1, 2002, p. 629; May 1, 2003, p. 1568; September 15, 2003, p. 195; April 15, 2004, p. 1405.

Chicago Tribune, September 4, 1988, pp. 1, 6; January 1, 1994, pp. 1, 9; April 21, 1996, pp. 1, 9.

Christian Century, September 26, 2001, Ann-Janine Morey, review of *The Last Report on the Miracles at Little No Horse,* p. 36.

College Literature, October, 1991, pp. 80-95.

Commonweal, October 24, 1986, pp. 565, 567; November 4, 1988, p. 596.

Economist, May 15, 2001, p. 8.

Entertainment Weekly, June 25, 2004, p. 169.

Explicator, summer, 2002, pp. 241-243; summer, 2003, pp. 248-250; winter, 2003, pp. 119-121.

Horn Book, May, 1999, review of *The Birchbark House,* p. 329.

Kirkus Reviews, February 15, 1996, p. 244; April 15, 1996, p. 600; August 15, 2002, p. 1222; November 15, 2002, p. 1640; April 15, 2004, p. 347.

Library Journal, January, 2002, p. 49; December, 2002, p. 177; August, 2003, pp. 88-89; May 15, 2004, p. 114.

Los Angeles Times Book Review, October 5, 1986, pp. 3, 10; September 11, 1988, p. 2; May 12, 1991, pp. 3, 13; February 6, 1994, p. 1, 13; May 28, 1995, p. 8; June 16, 1996, p. 3.

MELUS, fall, 2002, pp. 113-132, 147-159.

Midwest Quarterly, summer, 2004, pp. 427-428.

Mothering, summer, 1997, Lisa Solbert-Sheldon, review of *The Blue Jay's Dance: A Birth Year,* p. 50.

Mother Jones, May, 2001, Josie Rawson, "Louise Erdrich: Cross-Dressing the Divine," p. 102.

Nation, October 21, 1991, pp. 465, 486-490.

New Leader, May, 2001, Lynne Sharon Schwartz, "Corporate Sinners and Crossover Saints," p. 35.

New Republic, October 6, 1986, pp. 46-48; January 6-13, 1992, pp. 30-40.

Newsday, November 30, 1986.

Newsweek, February 17, 2003, p. 66.

New York Review of Books, January 15, 1987, pp. 14-15; November 19, 1988, pp. 40-41; May 12, 1996, p. 10.

New York Times, December 20, 1984, p. C21; August 20, 1986, p. C21; August 24, 1988, p. 41; April 19, 1991, p. C25; March 24, 1998, Michiko Kakutani, "Myths of Redemption Amid a Legacy of Loss"; April 6, 2001, Michiko Kakutani, "Saintliness, Too, May Be in the Eye of the Beholder."

New York Times Book Review, August 31, 1982, p. 2; December 23, 1984, p. 6; October 2, 1988, pp. 1, 41-42; April 28, 1991, p. 10; July 20, 1993, p. 20; January 16, 1994, p. 7; April 16, 1995, p. 14; April 12, 1998, Diana Postlethwaite, "A Web of Beadwork"; April 8, 2001, Verlyn Klinkenborg, "Woman of the Cloth."

People, June 10, 1991, pp. 26-27; April 13, 1998, V. R. Peterson, review of *The Antelope Wife,* p. 31; July 19, 2004, p. 45.

Playboy, March, 1994, p. 30.

Progressive, April, 2002, pp. 36-40.

Publishers Weekly, August 15, 1986, pp. 58-59; April 22, 1996, p. 71; January 29, 2001, review of *The Last Report on the Miracles at Little No Horse,* p. 63, "PW Talks with Louise Erdrich," p. 64; July 2, 2001, review of *The Last Report on the Miracles at Little No Horse,* p. 31; September 9, 2002, p. 67; December 23, 2002, pp. 43-44; October 6, 2003, pp. 80-81; May 10, 2004, p. 33.

Quill & Quire, August, 1995, p. 30.

Time, February 7, 1994, p. 71; April 28, 1997, Elizabeth Gleick, "An Imperfect Union," p. 68.

Times Literary Supplement, February 14, 1997, p. 21.

Village Voice Literary Supplement, October, 1988, p. 37.

Washington Post Book World, August 31, 1986, pp. 1, 6; September 18, 1988, p. 3; February 6, 1994, p. 5; April 21, 1996, p. 3.

Western American Literature, February, 1991, pp. 363-364.

World and I, September, 2001, Elizabeth Blair, review of *The Last Report on the Miracles at Little No Horse,* p. 214.

World Literature Today, winter, 2000, Howard Meredith, review of "The Antelope Wife," p. 214.

Writer's Digest, June, 1991, Michael Schumacher, interview with Erdrich, pp. 28-31.

ONLINE

Bedford/St. Martin's Web site, http://www.bedford stmartins.com/ (August 23, 2004), "Louise Erdrich."

Carol Hurst's Children's Literature Site, http://www.carolhurst.com/ (December 2, 2001), review of *The Birchbark House.*

Salon.com, http://www.salon.com/ (August 23, 2004), interview with Erdrich.*

*   *   *

ESPINOSA, Maria 1939-

PERSONAL: Original name, Paula Cronbach; name changed June 6, 1966; born January 6, 1939, in New York, NY; daughter of Robert (a sculptor) and Maxine (Silver) Cronbach; married Mario Espinosa (a journalist), c. 1963 (divorced, 1965); married Walter Selig (a research chemist), c. 1975; children: (first marriage) Carmen. *Ethnicity:* "Jewish." *Education:* Attended Radcliffe College, c. 1957-58; Columbia University, B.A., 1962; San Francisco State University, M.A., 1981. *Religion:* Jewish.

ADDRESSES: *Home*—3396 Orchard Valley Ln., Lafayette, CA 94549. *E-mail*—paulamar99@earthlink.net.

CAREER: Writer, 1967—. New College of California, San Francisco, teacher of creative writing, 1986-90, co-coordinator of creative writing department, 1990; teacher of English in Tucson community colleges, 1990-92; also worked as a teacher of English as a second language. Worked at a variety of other jobs, including dishwasher in a restaurant in Patagonia, AZ.

AWARDS, HONORS: American Book Award, 1996, for *Longing.*

WRITINGS:

Love Feelings (poetry), Four Winds Press (San Francisco, CA), 1967, new edition published as *Night Music,* Tides (Sausalito, CA), 1969.
(Translator) George Sand, *Lelia,* Indiana University Press (Bloomington, IN), 1978.
Longing (fiction), Cayuse Press (Berkeley, CA), 1986, reprinted, Arte Público Press (Houston, TX), 1995.
Dark Plums (fiction), Arte Público Press (Houston, TX), 1995.
Incognito: Journey of a Secret Jew (fiction), Wings Press, 2002.

Translator of *Plain-Chant* [and] *L'Ange heurtebise* (bilingual edition), by Jean Cocteau, Sun and Moon Press; also translator of one chapter from George Sand's autobiography *Ma Vie,* edited by Thelma Jurgrau, State University of New York Press (Albany, NY), 1990. Work represented in anthologies, including *Alameda Poets' Anthology; Anthologies of Underground Poetry,* edited by Herman Berlandt; and *Bay Area Poets Coalition.* Contributor of poetry, articles, and short fiction to periodicals, including *Studies in Literary Imagination, Three Penny Review, Tidings, Voices of America,* and the online magazine *Tertulia.*

The fictional work *Longing* was translated into Greek.

WORK IN PROGRESS: Dying Unfinished, a novel.

SIDELIGHTS: Part of poet and novelist Maria Espinosa's motivation for writing, she explains in her *Contemporary Authors Autobiography Series (CAAS)* entry, comes out of her troubled family history. "The

psychiatrist R. D. Laing writes that schizophrenia is caused in part by double binds," Espinosa stated. "At home there were double and triple binds nearly choking me. My father never touched me casually or with tenderness. His embrace was furtive and passionate, so that I was a little afraid of his touch." "I needed my parents' approval and affection," she continued. "Since they were rarely direct, a mere word or gesture, discounting through silence or changing the subject would profoundly affect me. Hooked on people's words, naively believing them, nevertheless I was aware that they were often false." "During these years," Espinosa concluded, "I wrote and wrote and wrote in order to loosen the bindings. I wrote in a large, scribbling uneven hand, pages and pages of ramblings which have long since been lost or destroyed."

Although Espinosa's troubled childhood led to more difficulties as an adult—including hospitalization in a psychiatric hospital after she had been expelled from Radcliffe for taking part in a pornographic film—she was able to deal with some of her problems in her fiction. *Dark Plums,* her novel about a young woman's descent into sexual obsession and madness, was begun in the early 1960s while Espinosa was staying on the Greek island of Rhodes. "*Longing,*" she wrote in *CAAS,* "deals with my family, and I felt I had to write about things so long suppressed in order to keep—or regain—my own sanity."

Espinosa recently told *CA* that her novel *Dying Unfinished,* not yet published, also deals with her family.

BIOGRAPHICAL AND CRITICAL SOURCES:

BOOKS

Contemporary Authors Autobiography Series, Volume 30, Thomson Gale (Farmington Hills, MI), 1999.

ONLINE

Maria Espinosa Home Page, http://www.maria espinosa.com (February 21, 2005).

F

FAIRHOLM, Gil
See FAIRHOLM, Gilbert W(ayne)

*   *   *

FAIRHOLM, Gilbert W(ayne) 1932-
(Gil Fairholm)

PERSONAL: Born September 1, 1932, in Salt Lake City, UT; son of Leo Rex (a contractor) and Kate N. (Smith) Fairholm; married, November 21, 1956; wife's name, Barbara C.; children: Ann, Paul, Daniel, Scott, Matthew. *Ethnicity:* "Caucasian." *Education:* Brigham Young University, B.S., 1958; University of Pennsylvania, M.G.A., 1960; State University of New York—Albany, D.P.A., 1970. *Politics:* Conservative. *Religion:* Church of Jesus Christ of Latter-day Saints (Mormons). *Hobbies and other interests:* Building furniture, gardening.

ADDRESSES: Home—2810 Park Ridge Rd., Midlothian, VA 23113. *E-mail*—gfair@mail1.vcu.edu.

CAREER: State of New York, Albany, deputy director of Department of Motor Vehicles, 1965-75, and worked in Department of Transportation, Office of Community Affairs, and Division of the Budget; State of Wisconsin—Madison, Madison, director of state and local finance, 1975-77; Virginia Commonwealth University, Richmond, associate professor of political science and public administration, 1977-96, professor emeritus, 1996—. University of Richmond, adjunct associate professor, 1993—; Hampden-Sydney College,

visiting professor; University of Nigeria, professor of local government and consultant; Brookings Institution, conducted senior executive service training. Fairholm Associates (management consultants), president, 1960—; served as assistant city manager for Ogden City and Orem City, UT, and as city manager for Layton, UT; consultant to local and national government and public agencies. *Military service:* U.S. Air Force, 1954-56; became sergeant.

WRITINGS:

Values Leadership: Toward a New Philosophy of Leadership, Praeger (Westport, CT), 1991.

Organizational Power Politics: Tactics in Organizational Leadership, Praeger, 1993.

Leadership and the Culture of Trust, Praeger (Westport, CT), 1994.

Capturing the Heart of Leadership: Spirituality and Community in the New American Workplace, Praeger (Westport, CT), 1997.

Perspectives on Leadership: From the Science of Management to Its Spiritual Heart, Quorum Books (Westport, CT), 1998.

(Under name Gil Fairholm) *So You Have Been Called to Be a Leader: The Savior's More Excellent Leadership Way,* Three Questions Press (Midlothian, VA), 1999.

Mastering Inner Leadership, foreword by Herbert R. Tillery, Quorum Books (Westport, CT), 2001.

The Techniques of Inner Leadership: Making Inner Leadership Work, foreword by Natalie K. Houghtby-Haddon, Praeger (Westport, CT), 2003.

FELLOWS, Oscar L. 1943-

PERSONAL: Born October 5, 1943, in Del Rio, TX. *Ethnicity:* "Texan." *Education:* Brevard Community College, A.S., 1981; Park College, B.S., 1995. *Politics:* Independent. *Religion:* "Deist, with Christian leanings." *Hobbies and other interests:* Scientific research and experimentation.

ADDRESSES: Home—112 Clear Spring Rd., Georgetown, TX 78628. *E-mail*—frg@io.com.

CAREER: Writer. U.S. Government, worked as military engineer and operations manager, 1972-93; Fellows Research Group, Inc., Austin, TX, general manager, 1993-99. *Military service:* U.S. Marine Corps, 1962-66.

MEMBER: Austin Writers Guild.

WRITINGS:

Operation Damocles (suspense novel), Baen Books (Riverdale, NY), 1998.
Catalyst (suspense novel), iUniverse (Lincoln, NE), 2001.

WORK IN PROGRESS: Research on thermo-acoustic engines and related phenomena.

SIDELIGHTS: Oscar L. Fellows once told *CA:* "I think my primary motivation for writing is having something to say, whether it be a philosophical observation or a fictional scenario that pops into my head, and wanting to communicate it to someone. Each of us has a slant on life, and I think it's human nature to want to know what others think of our ideas, perceptions, and conclusions. I think this applies to all writers in some degree.

"If I had to pick a single writer whom I most admire, I would have to say Isaac Asimov. His nonfiction books on physics and chemistry are the most understandably written works in the fields, and they enlightened me. Jules Verne, H. G. Wells, Edgar Rice Burroughs, Silverberg, Heinlein, Bova, Pournelle, Niven, and others started me down the road in reading science fiction. As my interest in physical science grew, I came to admire Michael Crichton most, because his stories reflect real science in an exciting way, the way it should be depicted. Arthur C. Clark is another favorite. I like other genres, too. I like Ian Fleming's spy stories, and P. G. Wodehouse's wry sense of humor, and the mysteries of Martha Grimes and Arthur Conan Doyle. I liked Zane Grey and Louis Lamour. I think they all have influenced the way I look at the world: sadness for the changing times and loss of freedom; admiration for the real heroes of the past, the pioneers and inventors and doers; the excitement of discovery; the sense of honor that people once had.

"I don't have a writing process. I probably would get more done if I did. I love to write, once I get started, but I have to force myself to sit down and start.

"The uncommon perspective fascinates me, especially since it is usually the most logical. In 'Temblor Station No. 5' I write about a government agency that controls earthquakes. Since they do so much damage, shouldn't we prevent them? It seems logical to me, but, even though we have technology, it raises all sorts of legal questions about liability. So, we choose to let people die, rather than risk getting sued for breaking someone's crockery, or scaring a pregnant woman, or irritating the dairy cattle. The same is true of urban sprawl. We don't limit growth or plan it well, because that would irritate the developers. To me, human society is not sane. The common approach is not to solve problems, but to alleviate the immediate social pressures. Smoke and mirrors are always the forte of the incompetent, and rhetoric is easier than practical solutions. Fairy tales and propaganda are doled out to the passengers of our sinking ship; no one finds a competent person to plug the hole. I guess I would have to say that the things that inspire me to write are the things that irritate me. Writing is my attempt to influence others to think about things, and to see them the way I see them."

*   *   *

FIALKA, John J. 1938-

PERSONAL: Born October 5, 1938, in New Ulm, MN; son of J. Ray (an insurance sales manager) and Selma G. (a homemaker) Fialka; married, October 14, 1967; wife's name, Deborah R. (a writer); children: J. Wren,

Joseph A. *Education:* Loras College, B.A. (magna cum laude), 1960; Columbia University, M.S., 1962; Georgetown University, J.D., 1965. *Politics:* Democrat. *Religion:* Roman Catholic.

ADDRESSES: Office—Wall Street Journal, Ste. 800, 1025 Connecticut Ave. NW, Washington, DC 20036.

CAREER: Reporter and author. *Sun,* Baltimore, MD, reporter, 1965-76; *Washington Star,* Washington, DC, reporter on local and national desks, 1967-81; *Wall Street Journal,* Washington Bureau, Washington, DC, national security reporter, 1981-97, energy and environment reporter, 1997. Also legislative aide for the National Petroleum Association, 1962-65. Founder of SOAR!, a charity for retired religious people, primarily Roman Catholic nuns.

AWARDS, HONORS: Worth Bingham Award and Raymond Clapper Award, both for investigative journalism.

WRITINGS:

Hotel Warriors: Covering the Gulf War, Johns Hopkins University Press (Baltimore, MD), 1992.
War by Other Means: Economic Espionage in America, Norton (New York, NY), 1997.
Sisters: Catholic Nuns and the Making of America, St. Martin's (New York, NY), 2003.

SIDELIGHTS: A reporter specializing in national security issues for the *Wall Street Journal,* John J. Fialka has also written two books on military and intelligence topics, *Hotel Warriors: Covering the Gulf War* and *War by Other Means: Economic Espionage in America.*

In *Hotel Warriors* Fialka tells the story of how the American news media covered the Gulf War. Fialka himself was one of the reporters on the scene, and his account includes first-hand observations as well as interviews with many other reporters in the Gulf. Bernhard S. Redmont, in *Television Quarterly,* writes that Fialka's book "is packed with facts, anecdotes and reasonable conclusions, delineating in graphic detail military officers' totalitarian mentality, manipulation, censorship and sheer incompetence. In truth, the

journalists themselves were often ignorant and unprepared." In his review of the book for *Parameters,* Lieutenant Colonel Larry F. Icenogle notes that "for all the barbs directed at the Army, Fialka is just as tough on the press. . . . All the issues surfaced by Fialka are worthy of study, by *both* sides." Writing in the *Naval War College Review,* El Ahlwardt calls *Hotel Warriors* "a revealing look through experienced eyes at the relationship between the military and the media. . . . This work should be required reading for any professional in the military and the media."

Fialka turned to another kind of war with his second book, *War by Other Means: Economic Espionage in America.* In this study he examines the post-Cold War world and finds many remaining threats to American security, particularly involving the nation's economic strength. Citing examples where supposed allies have stolen industrial secrets and technological procedures, especially Asian nations like Japan, Fialka warns that such theft can steal away a nation's livelihood and he endorses the idea of limiting access to America's technological research. Fialka raises the possibility, according to Peter G. Gosselin in the *New York Times Book Review,* that "we are being drained of the brains and inventions necessary to maintain our living standards." Fialka informed *CA* that U.S. Secretary of Defense William S. Cohen described *War by Other Means* to its author in a letter: "The American people are certain to be both entertained and outraged by *War by Other Means.* The narrative flows smoothly, the tales of intrigue and espionage unfold smartly, and the conclusion that the U.S. is suffering massive economic losses to foreign bribery and espionage hits home hard. This is an important book that I hope will be widely read by government officials, business leaders, and the public."

In *Sisters: Catholic Nuns and the Making of America,* Fialka tells the story of America's Catholic nuns, whom he dubs "America's first feminists" because they made significant contributions in a male-dominated society. Discussing the sisters' many accomplishments is an incredible task, since they extended the faith through their hard work, which included establishing 800 hospitals and 10,000 parochial schools. To limit the book's size to one volume, Fialka focuses on one large order, the Sisters of Mercy, often called "the Mercies." Fialka's "approach makes a well-told history of these remarkable women from the time of their arrival in America to the present, when their numbers have dwindled considerably," remarked a *Publishers Weekly* contributor.

In what *Booklist*'s Margaret Flanagan called "an engrossing glance backward," Fialka chronicles the history of the Sisters of Mercy beginning in 1780 in Dublin when the order was founded by Catherine McAuley. At forty-two, McAuley inherited a fortune from her employer and established a parochial school and a home for servant girls. She worked for the Catholic Church for ten years before asking to be accepted into the convent, a move which most viewed as a huge step backward for McAuley. The Sisters of Mercy were known for their humility and poverty. They were revolutionary during their time, praying in public and establishing schools where there were none. After McAuley's death, the Sisters of Mercy were asked to help people on the American Frontier. For a time, the order grew, but then entered into a period of steady decline. While in 1968 there were about 180,000 sisters in the order, today there are merely 81,000 with an average age of sixty-nine. "Fialka sprinkles his account" of the order "with personal recollections and writes sympathetically of a group that has often been maligned and caricatured," explained a *Publishers Weekly* contributor, who went on to conclude, "Nuns will appreciate his treatment of their lives, as will Catholics pondering a church with diminishing numbers of the women who helped shape it." While a *Kirkus Reviews* contributor felt that "the narrative stumbles a bit at the end, when the reader is introduced to a whirlwind of nuns—all very interesting women, but the necessarily brief profiles begin to blend together," the same reviewer ultimately described the book as "a very readable history of the order" and felt that the "author deftly shows the staggering level of involvement of the nuns throughout the fields of education and health care."

BIOGRAPHICAL AND CRITICAL SOURCES:

PERIODICALS

Black Scholar, winter, 1993, p. 42.
Booklist, January 1, 1997, p. 793; December 15, 2002, Margaret Flanagan, review of *Sisters: Catholic Nuns and the Making of America,* p. 710.
Bulletin of the Atomic Scientists, September, 1993, pp. 52-54.

Business Week, February 10, 1997, p. 16.
Economic Journal, November, 1998, Terutomo Ozawa, review of *War by Other Means: Economic Espionage in America,* p. 1969.
Fortune, February 17, 1997, p. 136.
Issues in Science and Technology, winter, 1996, p. 93.
Journal of Military History, April, 1993, pp. 362-364.
Kirkus Reviews, November 15, 2002, review of *Sisters,* p. 1671.
Naval War College Review, spring, 1993, pp. 151-153.
New York Times Book Review, February 16, 1997, p. 17.
Orbis, winter, 1998, Mark T. Clark, review of *War by Other Means,* p. 121.
Parameters, winter, 1992, pp. 121-123; autumn, 1998, review of *War by Other Means,* p. 150.
Publishers Weekly, November 25, 1996, p. 62; December 23, 2002, review of *Sisters,* p. 62.
Security Management, February, 1998, Howard Keough, review of *War by Other Means,* pp. 92-94.
Television Quarterly, Volume 26, number 2, 1992, pp. 83-87.
Wall Street Journal, April 3, 1997, p. A16.
Washington Monthly, April, 1997, p. 46.*

*   *   *

FISHER, Humphrey J(ohn) 1933-

PERSONAL: Born September 20, 1933, in Dunedin, New Zealand; son of Allan G. B. and E. A. (Pope) Fisher; married Helga H. A. Kricke, 1958; children: Clemens, Duncan, Crispin, Thomas. *Education:* Attended Deep Springs Junior College, 1950-52; Harvard University, B.A. (magna cum laude), 1955; Oxford University, D.Phil., 1959. *Religion:* Quaker.

ADDRESSES: Home—66 Ormond Ave., Hampton, Middlesex, England. *Office*—School of Oriental and African Studies, University of London, London WC1, England.

CAREER: University of London, School of Oriental and African Studies, London, England, 1952—, began as lecturer, became reader in African history, became emeritus professor of history.

MEMBER: Association of University Teachers, African Studies Association, Phi Beta Kappa.

WRITINGS:

Ahmadiyyah: A Study in Contemporary Islam on the West African Coast, Oxford University Press (New York, NY), 1963.

(With father, Allan G. B. Fisher) *Slavery and Muslim Society in Africa: The Institution in Saharan and Sudanic Africa and the Trans-Saharan Trade,* C. Hurst (New York, NY), 1970, Doubleday (New York, NY), 1971, revised version published as *Slavery in the History of Muslim Black Africa,* New York University Prress (New York, NY), 2000.

(Editor and translator with father, Allan G. B. Fisher) Gustav Nachtigal, *Sahara and Sudan,* Volume IV: *Wadai and Darfur,* University of California Press (Berkeley, CA), 1972, Volume I: *Tripoli and Fezzan, Tibesti or Tu,* Barnes & Noble (New York, NY), 1974, Volume II: *Kawar, Bornu, Kanem, Borku, Ennedi,* C. Hurst (London, England), 1978, Volume III: *The Chad Basin and Bagirmi,* Humanities Press International (Atlantic Highlands, NJ), 1987.

(Editor, with Nehemia Levtzion) *Rural and Urban Islam in West Africa,* L. Rienner (Boulder, CO), 1987.

(Editor, with David Parkin and Lionel Caplan) *The Politics of Cultural Performance,* Berghahn Books (Providence, RI), 1996.

Contributor to *Journal of African History* and to other journals.

SIDELIGHTS: Humphrey J. Fisher is emeritus professor of history at the University of London's School of Oriental and African Studies. Born in New Zealand, Fisher has specialized in the religious history of pre-colonial Africa, and particularly in its Islamic roots. In collaboration and alone, he has also written, translated, or edited works about European travelers in Africa, such as Gustav Nachtigal, and about slavery in tropical Africa.

Working with his father, Allan G. B. Fisher, the author translated, edited, and wrote the introduction for Nachtigal's *Sahara and Sudan,* a "unique classic of mid-nineteenth-century travel in the Eastern Sahara and its southern borderlands," according to H. T. Norris in the *Bulletin of the School of Oriental and Africa*

Studies. The four-volume work spanned fifteen years of work by the Fishers, bringing this long out-of-print and rare book back to availability. Norris, reviewing Volume II, *Kawar, Bornu, Kanem, Borku, Ennedi,* commented, "One can readily see why this series of English translations . . . received favourable, even enthusiastic, comments from reviewers in several disciplines." The same contributor went on to note that "at least one reviewer has hailed the series as perhaps *the* major contribution to African history in the last decade." Norris also commented that the "excellence of the translation cannot be praised too highly." In a review of Volume III, *The Chad Basin and Bagirmi,* Dierk Lange, writing in the *Journal of African History,* found that the Fishers' "wide range of interests precluded them from merely supplying a translation of Nachtigal's German, though this is so carefully rendered into English that translation would certainly have been an admirable end in itself." Rather, according to Lange, the translators "enriched Nachtigal's own work" by supplying a more complete index and by adding footnotes and references to more contemporary publications.

Working with Nehemia Levtzion, Fisher edited *Rural and Urban Islam in West Africa,* a 1987 collection of nine essays centering on the relations between rural Islam and cities in West Africa. For Murray Last, writing in the *Journal of African History,* this was "overall, for the historian, . . . a useful collection which scotches, once again, the hoary notion that West African Islam is just an urban phenomenon." Reviewing the same title in the *Journal of Modern African Studies,* Jibrin Ibrahim wrote that the editors, rather than providing a "systematic analysis of either rural or urban Islam in West Africa," have instead presented "an interesting collection of case studies." Ibrahim also noted of Fisher's contribution to the collection, the final chapter titled "Liminality, *Hijira* and the City," that it "opens an important debate on the possibility of evolving a unified theoretical approach in the life-cycles of religions."

Fisher also served as editor, along with David Parkin, of *The Politics of Cultural Performance,* a collection dedicated to a long-time professor at the School of Oriental and African Studies, Abner Cohen. The essays in this volume deal with such cultural performance and ritual as the singing and dancing of Samburu boys to attain "moranhood," and cultural performance of British Pakistanis. For Mario I. Aguilar of the *Journal of the Royal Anthropological Institute,* "the strength of the volume comes . . . from the fact that it provides continuity to the study of ethnicity in social anthropology, and can serve as a solid collection of comparative ethnographies."

Fisher turns his attention to slavery in *Slavery in the History of Muslim Black Africa,* a book that explores the little-known aspect of slave trading by Muslims. While most focus has been placed on the Atlantic slave trade from West Africa to England and the United States, much less has been written about that which supplied slaves for the Near East and North Africa. Fisher sets out to shed light on that neglected history and, according to *Times Higher Education Supplement* contributor Peter Shinnie, is both "scholarly and detailed" in his account. An updated revision of *Slavery and Muslim Society in Africa: The Institution in Saharan and Sudanic Africa and the Trans-Saharan Trade,* a 1970 work written with his father, the book "examines with care the ambivalent Muslim attitude to slavery, in which taking slaves in *jihad* was not only permitted but encouraged, while taking fellow Muslims was forbidden," noted Shinnie. Fisher also details the use of such slaves for servants, concubines, soldiers, and agricultural workers, much of his anecdotal information coming from Nachtigal. Martin A. Klein, writing in the *Journal of African History,* felt that while Fisher's book "will be useful to students doing research on slavery," it was also disappointing. For Klein, the author "totally ignores most of what has been written about slavery in Muslim Africa over the last 25 years." Reviewing the book in the *Times Literary Supplement,* Gervase Clarence-Smith was more positive, calling the work the "culmination of a lifetime's academic study of Africa." As Clarence-Smith further commented, "The chapters are organized by theme, with an exhaustive examination of almost every aspect of slavery and the lives of slaves." Though Clarence-Smith faulted Fisher for "uneven coverage" and a "tendency to lose sight of Islam," he also noted that the "great strength of Fisher's book lies in the immediacy of his descriptions of slavery."

BIOGRAPHICAL AND CRITICAL SOURCES:

PERIODICALS

Bulletin of the School of Oriental and African Studies, Volume 44, number 44, 1981, H. T. Norris, review of *Sahara and Sudan,* pp. 428-429.

Journal of African History, Volume 28, number 3, 1987, Murray Last, review of *Rural and Urban Islam in West Africa,* p. 467; Volume 32, number 1, 1991, Dierk Lange, review of *Sahara and Sudan,* pp. 150-152; July, 2003, Martin A. Klein, review of *Slavery in the History of Muslim Black Africa,* pp. 346-347.

Journal of Modern African Studies, December, 1990, Jibrin Ibrahim, review of *Rural and Urban Islam in West Africa,* pp. 715-716.

Journal of the Royal Anthropological Institute, September, 1997, Mario I. Aguilar, review of *The Politics of Cultural Performance,* pp. 642-643.

Times Higher Education Supplement, August 23, 2002, Peter Shinnie, review of *Slavery in the History of Muslim Black Africa.*

Times Literary Supplement, June 28, 2002, Gervase Clarence-Smith, review of *Slavery in the History of Muslim Black Africa,* pp. 7-8.

ONLINE

School of Oriental and African Studies Web site, http://www.soas.ac.uk/ (February 8, 2004).*

* * *

FITZMAURICE, Gabriel 1952-

PERSONAL: Born December 7, 1952, in Moyvane, County Kerry, Ireland; son of John (a grocer) and Maud (a homemaker; maiden name, Cunningham) Fitzmaurice; married Brenda Downey (a primary schoolteacher), August 17, 1991; children: John, Nessa. *Education:* Mary Immaculate College of Education, primary teaching certificate. *Politics:* "Sort of a liberal." *Religion:* Roman Catholic.

ADDRESSES: Home—Applegarth, Moyvane, County Kerry, Ireland. *Office*—Moyvane National School, Moyvane, County Kerry, Ireland.

CAREER: Irish Department of Education, schoolteacher, beginning 1972. Singer and musician; recorded two albums of music; producer of the album *The Songs and Ballads of Kerry;* guest on Irish television and radio programs. Writers' Week, Listowel, County Kerry, Ireland, chair, 1982-85, 1991-92.

MEMBER: Comhaltas Ceoltoiri Eireann (past public relations officer for County Kerry branch).

AWARDS, HONORS: Award from Gerard Manley Hopkins Centenary Poetry Competition, 1989.

WRITINGS:

POETRY

Rainsong, Beaver Row Press (Dublin, Ireland), 1984.

Road to the Horizon, Beaver Row Press (Dublin, Ireland), 1987.

Nocht, Coiscéim (Baile Átha Cliath, Ireland), 1989.

Dancing Through, Beaver Row Press (Dublin, Ireland), 1990.

The Father's Part, Story Line Press (Brownsville, OR), 1992.

The Space Between: New and Selected Poems, 1984-1992, Cló Iar-Chonnachta (Indreabhán, Conamara, Ireland), 1993.

Ag síobshiúl chun an rince: dánta, Coiscéim (Baile Átha Cliath, Ireland), 1995.

The Village Sings: Poems, Story Line Press (Brownsville, OR), 1996.

Giolla ne namhrán: dánta nua agus rogha dánta, 1988-1998, Coiscéim (Baile Átha Cliath, Ireland), 1998.

A Wrenboy's Carnival: Poems, 1980-2000, Wolfhound Press (Dublin, Ireland), 2000.

I and the Village, Mercier (Dublin, Ireland), 2002.

FOR CHILDREN

The Moving Stair, Kerryman (Tralee, Ireland), 1989, revised edition, 1993.

(With Gabriel Rosenstock) *The Rhino's Specs,* Mercier (Dublin, Ireland), 2002.

Also author of *Nach Iontach mar atá Rainn do Pháistí,* 1994, *But Dad!,* 1995, *Puppy and the Sausage,* 1998, and *Dear Grandad,* 2001.

EDITOR

(With Declan Kiberd) *An Crann faoi bhláth—The Flowering Tree: Contemporary Irish Poetry with Verse Translations,* Wolfhound Press (Dublin, Ireland), 1991.

Between the Hills and Sea: Songs and Ballads of Kerry, Oidhreacht (Chorca Dhuibhne, County Kerry, Ireland), 1991.

Con Greaney, Traditional Singer, Oidhreacht (Chorca Chuibhne, County Kerry, Ireland), 1991.

An Alternative Anthology of Irish Poetry, Wolfhound Press (Dublin, Ireland), 1992.

Irish Poetry Now: Other Voices, Wolfhound Press (Dublin, Ireland), 1993.

Kerry through Its Writers, New Island Books (Dublin, Ireland), 1993.

The Listowel Literary Phenomenon: North Kerry Writers: A Critical Introduction, Cló Iar-Chonnachta (Indreabhán, Conamara, Ireland), 1994.

(And translator) *Poems I Wish I'd Written: Translations from the Irish,* Cló Iar-Chonnachta (Indreabhán, Conamara, Ireland), 1996.

(With Robert Dunbar) *Rusty Nails and Astronauts: A Wolfhound Poetry Anthology,* Wolfhound Press (Dublin, Ireland), 1999.

The Kerry Anthology, Marino (Dublin, Ireland), 2000.

Also editor of *Homecoming/An Bealah 'na Bhaile: Selected Poems of Cathal Ó Searcaigh,* 1993.

OTHER

(Translator) Michael Hartnett, *The Purge,* Beaver Row Press (Dublin, Ireland), 1989.

Kerry on my Mind: Of Poets, Pedagogues, and Place (essays), Salmon Publishing (Clare, Ireland), 1999.

Also author, with A. Cronin and J. Looney, of *"The Boro"* and *"The Cross:" The Parish of Moyvane-Knockanure,* 2000.

SIDELIGHTS: Gabriel Fitzmaurice once told *CA:* "I work as a teacher and have gained valuable insights from teaching—and being taught by—the children. I believe that poetry has lost much of its vitality in a maze of literary theory. I seek to give the life of music and rhythm to my poetry without accepting the straitjacket of a new formalism. I see the function of poetry, if indeed poetry has any function, to communicate with the literate reader. To this end I try to make my poetry as simple as my subject matter will allow, and as appealing as possible through my use of language. I do not believe in obscurity for obscurity's sake, believing such pseudo-profundity to be counterproductive. I seek the profound in the ordinary and try to translate that into poetry."

BIOGRAPHICAL AND CRITICAL SOURCES:

PERIODICALS

Academic Library Book Review, June, 1994, review of *Irish Poetry Now: Other Voices,* p. 18.

Booklist, March 15, 1994, Pat Monaghan, review of *Irish Poetry Now,* p. 1323; August, 1996, Ray Olson, review of *The Village Sings,* p. 1876; November 15, 2000, Ray Olson, review of *A Wrenboy's Carnival: Poems, 1980-2000,* p. 604; December 1, 2002, Ray Olson, review of *I and the Village,* p. 642.

Guardian, December 23, 2000, Giles Foden, review of *A Wrenboy's Carnival.*

Irish Literary Supplement, fall, 1992, review of *The Father's Part,* p. 36; spring, 1995, review of *Irish Poetry Now,* p. 36.

Library Journal, November 1, 1999, Denise J. Stankovics, review of *Kerry on My Mind: Of Poets, Pedagogues, and Place,* p. 81.

School Librarian, November, 1996, review of *The Village Sings,* p. 167.

Stand, autumn, 1994, review of *Irish Poetry Now,* p. 64.

Times Literary Supplement, June 21, 1991, p. 18.

World Literature Today, summer, 1994, Kieran Quinlan, review of *Irish Poetry Now,* p. 614.*

*   *   *

FORCHÉ, Carolyn (Louise) 1950-

PERSONAL: Surname is pronounced "for-*shay*"; born April 28, 1950, in Detroit, MI; daughter of Michael Joseph (a tool and die maker) and Louise Nada (a journalist; maiden name, Blackford) Sidlosky; married Henry E. Mattison (a news photographer), December 27, 1984; children: Sean-Christophe. *Education:* Michigan State University, B.A., 1972; Bowling Green State University, M.F.A., 1975.

ADDRESSES: Home—Maryland. *Office*—George Mason University, 4400 University Dr., Fairfax, VA, 22030-4444. *Agent*—Virginia Barber, 353 West 21st St., New York, NY 10011. *E-mail*—cforchem@osf1.gmu.edu.

CAREER: Justin Morrill College, Michigan State University, East Lansing, visiting lecturer in poetry, 1974; San Diego State University, San Diego, CA, visiting lecturer, 1975, assistant professor, 1976-78; journalist and human rights activist in El Salvador, 1978-80; University of Virginia, Charlottesville, visiting lecturer, 1979, visiting associate professor, 1982-83; University of Arkansas, Fayetteville, assistant professor, 1980, associate professor, 1981; New York University, New York, NY, visiting writer, 1983, 1985; correspondent for National Public Radio's *All Things Considered* in Beirut, 1983; Vassar College, Poughkeepsie, NY, visiting writer, 1984; Writer's Community, New York, NY, visiting poet, 1984; State University of New York—Albany, Writer's Institute, writer-in-residence, 1985; Columbia University, adjunct associate professor, 1984-85; University of Minnesota, visiting associate professor, summer, 1985; George Mason University, Fairfax, VA, associate professor, 1994—. Consultant on Central America and member of Commission on U.S.-Central American Relations.

MEMBER: Amnesty International, PEN American Center (member of Freedom to Write and Silenced Voices committees), Poetry Society of America, Academy of American Poets, Associated Writing Programs (president, beginning 1994), Institute for Global Education, Coalition for a New Foreign Policy, Theta Sigma Phi.

AWARDS, HONORS: Devine Memorial fellowship in poetry, 1975; First Award in Poetry, *Chicago Review,* 1975; Yale Series of Younger Poets Award, 1975, for *Gathering the Tribes;* Tennessee Williams fellowship in poetry, Bread Loaf Writers Conference, 1976; National Endowment for the Arts fellowships, 1977 and 1984; John Simon Guggenheim Memorial fellowship, 1978; Emily Clark Balch Prize, *Virginia Quarterly Review,* 1979; Alice Fay di Castagnola Award, Poetry Society of America, 1981; Lamont Poetry Selection Award, Academy of American Poets, 1981, for *The Country between Us;* H.D.L., Russell Sage College, 1985; Lannan Foundation Literary fellowship, 1992; *Los Angeles Times* Book Award for Poetry, 1994, for *The Angel of History;* Edita and Ira Morris Hiroshima Foundation Award (Japan) for her use of poetry as a "means to attain understanding, reconciliation, and peace within communities and between communities," 1997; National Book Critics Circle Award, 2003, for poem "Blue Hour."

WRITINGS:

(With Martha Jane Soltow) *Women in the Labor Movement, 1835-1925: An Annotated Bibliography,* Michigan State University Press (East Lansing, MI), 1972.

Gathering the Tribes (poetry), Yale University Press (New Haven, CT), 1976.

The Colonel, Bieler Press (St. Paul, MN), 1978.

(Editor) *Women and War in El Salvador,* Women's International Resource Exchange (New York, NY), 1980.

(Coauthor) *History and Motivations of U.S. Involvement in the Control of the Peasant Movement in El Salvador: The Role of AIFLD in the Agrarian Reform Process,* EPICA (Washington, DC), 1980.

The Country between Us (poetry), Copper Canyon Press (Port Townsend, WA), 1981.

(Translator) Claribel Alegría, *Flowers from the Volcano,* University of Pittsburgh Press (Pittsburgh, PA), 1982.

Carolyn Forché and George Starbuck Reading Their Poems, Library of Congress (Washington, DC), 1982.

(Author of text) *El Salvador: The Work of Thirty Photographers,* edited by Harry Mattison, Susan Meiselas, and Fae Rubenstein, Writers and Readers Publishing Cooperative (New York, NY), 1983.

"The Poet and the Poem" at the Library of Congress, (sound recording), Library of Congress (Washington, DC), 1990.

(Translator, with William Kulik) *The Selected Poems of Robert Desnos,* Ecco Press (New York, NY), 1991.

(Editor and author of introduction) *Against Forgetting: Twentieth-Century Poetry of Witness* (anthology of poetry), Norton (New York, NY), 1993.

The Angel of History (poetry), HarperCollins (New York, NY), 1994.

Colors Come from God—Just like Me! Abingdon Press (New York, NY), 1995.

(Author of introduction) Natalie Kenvin, *Bruise Theory: Poems,* Boa Editions (Brockport, NY), 1995.

The Angel of History, HarperPerennial (New York, NY), 1995.

(With others) *Lani Maestro/Cradle Cradle Ugoy* (exhibition catalog), Art in General (New York, NY), 1996.

(Author of introduction) George Trakl, *Autumn Sonata,* translated by Daniel Simko, Moyer Bell (Kingston, RI), 1998.

(With others) *Seven Washington Poets Reading Their Poems in the Coolidge Auditorium, Library of Congress* (sound recording), Library of Congress (Washington, DC), 1998.

(Translator) Claribel Alegría, *Saudade=Sorrow,* Curbstone Press (Willimantic, CT), 1999.

(Editor, with Philip Gerard) *Writing Creative Nonfiction: Instruction and Insights from Teachers of the Associated Writing Programs,* Story Press (Cincinnati, OH), 2001.

(Translator and editor, with Munir Akash, Sinan Antoon, and Amira El-Zein) Mahmoud Darwish, *Unfortunately, It Was Paradise: Selected Poems,* University of California Press (Berkeley, CA), 2003.

Blue Hour (poetry), HarperCollins (New York, NY), 2003.

Contributor to books, including *Martyrs: Contemporary Writers on Modern Lives of Faith,* edited by Susan Bergman, HarperSanFrancisco, 1996. Contributing editor, *The Pushcart Prize: Best of the Small Presses,* Volume 3; poetry coeditor of *The Pushcart Prize: Best of the Small Presses,* Volume 8. Work represented in anthologies, including *The Pushcart Prize: Best of the Small Presses,* Volume 6 and Volume 8; *The American Poetry Anthology;* and *Anthology of Magazine Verse: Yearbook of American Poetry.* Contributor of poetry, articles, and reviews to periodicals, including *Parnassus, New York Times Book Review, Washington Post Book World, Ms., Antaeus, Atlantic,* and *American Poetry Review.* Poetry editor of *New Virginia Review,* 1981; contributing editor of *Tendril.*

SIDELIGHTS: "Perhaps no one better exemplifies the power and excellence of contemporary poetry than Carolyn Forché, who is not only one of the most affecting . . . poets in America, but also one of the best poets writing anywhere in the world today," Jonathan Cott wrote in the introduction to his interview with Forché for *Rolling Stone.* Such praise was not new to Forché. Her first book of poetry, *Gathering the Tribes,* recounts experiences of the author's adolescence and young-adult life and won the 1975 Yale Series of Younger Poets Award; her second, *The Country between Us,* was named the 1981 Lamont Poetry Selection and became that most-rare publication: a poetry bestseller. In a critique for the *Los Angeles Times Book Review,* Art Seidenbaum maintained that the poems of the second volume "chronicle the awakening of a political consciousness and are themselves acts of commitment: to concepts and persons, to responsibility, to action." According to Joyce Carol Oates in the *New York Times Book Review,* Forché's ability to wed the "political" with the "personal" places her in the company of such poets as Pablo Neruda, Philip Levine, and Denise Levertov.

By the time she was twenty-four years old, Forché had completed *Gathering the Tribes,* described by Stanley Kunitz in the book's foreword as a work centering on kinship. In these poems, Forché "remembers her childhood in rural Michigan, evokes her Slovak ancestors, immerses herself in the American Indian culture of the Southwest, explores the mysteries of flesh, tries to understand the bonds of family, race, and sex," related Kunitz. "Burning the Tomato Worms," for example, deals with a young woman's sexual coming of age. But this poetic tale of "first sexual experience," Mark Harris stated in a *Dictionary of Literary Biography* essay, "is told against the larger backdrop of her grandmother's life and death and their meaning to a woman just grown."

If *Gathering the Tribes* "introduced a poet of uncommon vigor and assurance," as Oates wrote, then *The Country between Us* served as "a distinct step forward." A *Ms.* reviewer called the second collection "a poetry of dissent from a poet outraged." Forché herself told Cott: "The voice in my first book doesn't know what it thinks, it doesn't make any judgments. All it can do is perceive and describe and use language to make some sort of re-creation of moments in time. But I noticed that the person in the second book makes an utterance."

Forché's first two volumes of poetry were separated by a period of five years, during the course of which she was involved with Amnesty International and with translating the work of Salvadoran poets. In those years, she also had the opportunity to go to Central America as a journalist and human rights advocate where she learned firsthand of violations against life and liberty. While there, she viewed inadequate health facilities that had never received the foreign aid designated for them and discovered that sixty-three out of every thousand children died from gastrointestinal infections before age one; she saw for herself the young girls who had been sexually mutilated; she learned of torture victims who had been beaten, starved, and otherwise abused; and she experienced

something of what it was like to survive in a country where baby food jars are sometimes used as bombs.

Her experiences found expression in *The Country between Us.* As reviewer Katha Pollitt observed in the *Nation,* Forché "insists more than once on the transforming power of what she has seen, on the gulf it has created between herself and those who have seen less and dared less." The poet herself admitted to the compelling nature of her Central American experience. "I tried not to write about El Salvador in poetry, because I thought it might be better to do so in journalistic articles," she told Cott. "But I couldn't—the poems just came." El Salvador became the primary subject of *The Country between Us.* In these poems Forché "addresses herself unflinchingly to the exterior, historical world," Oates explained. She did so at a time when most of her contemporaries were writing poetry in which there is no room for politics—poetry, Pollitt stated, "of wistful longings, of failed connections, of inevitable personal loss, expressed in a set of poetic strategies that suit such themes."

Forché is considered particularly adept at depicting cruelty and the helplessness of victims, and in so doing, Paul Gray wrote in *Time,* she "makes pain palpable." More than one critic singled out her poem "The Colonel," centering on her now-famous encounter with a Salvadoran colonel who, as he made light of human rights, emptied a bag of human ears before Forché. The poem concludes: "Something for your poetry, no? he said. Some of the ears on the floor caught this scrap of his voice. Some of the ears on the floor were pressed to the ground." Pollitt remarked that "at their best, Forché's poems have the immediacy of war correspondence, postcards from the volcano of twentieth-century barbarism."

A dozen years passed between the publication of *The Country between Us* and Forché's editing of *Against Forgetting: Twentieth-Century Poetry of Witness,* an anthology collecting the works of poets addressing human-rights violations on a global level. The poems in this anthology present what Matthew Rothschild in the *Progressive* called "some of the most dramatic antiwar and anti-torture poetry written in this benighted century." The poems provide, Gail Wronsky pointed out in the *Antioch Review,* "irrefutable and copious evidence of the human ability to record, to write, to speak in the face of those atrocities." Building on the tradition of social protest and the antiwar poems of the late 1960s, Forché presents a range of approaches: "Many of the poems here are eyes-open, horrifyingly graphic portrayals of human brutality," observed Rothschild. "But others are of defiance, demonstrating resolve and extracting hope even in the most extreme circumstances."

Against Forgetting begins with poets who witnessed the Ottoman Turk genocide of one-and-a-half million Armenians between 1909 and 1918. In this section, the executed Armenian poet Siamento seems to speak for all the other poets in the collection: "Don't be afraid. I must tell you what I say / so people will understand / the crimes men do to men." Another section includes poems by Americans, Germans, and Japanese about the effects of World War II upon those who witnessed and recorded the events. There are also sections on the Holocaust, the Spanish Civil War, the Soviet Union, Central and Eastern Europe, the Mediterranean, the Middle East, Latin America, South Africa, and China.

Critics were divided upon both the selections in and the importance of *Against Forgetting*. Wronsky, for example, questioned why "women of all races and ethnicities are underrepresented here (124 male poets to 20 female)," while Phoebe Pettingell in the *New Leader* argued that the work's flaws are "outweighed by the anthology's breadth and scope, and by the excellence of most of its entries. *Against Forgetting*," Pettingell continued, "preaches the hope that humanity, after a century of unparalleled brutality met largely by helplessness, can finally learn to mend its ways." John Bayley, writing in the *New York Review of Books*, called the collection "a remarkable book. Not only in itself and for the poems it contains, but for the ideas that lie behind their selection as an anthology."

In an article in the *Mason Gazette*, Forché commented that "The poetry of witness reclaims the social from the political and in so doing defends the individual against illegitimate forms of coercion." The year following the publication of *Against Forgetting* saw Forché bring out her own book of witness, *The Angel of History*, which won the 1994 *Los Angeles Times* Book Award for poetry. The book is divided into five sections dealing with the atrocities of war in France, Japan, and Germany and with references to the poet's own experiences in Beirut and El Salvador. The title figure, the Angel of History—a figure imagined by German philosopher and critic Walter Benjamin—can

record the miseries of humanity yet is unable either to prevent these miseries from happening or from suffering from the pain associated with them. Kevin Walker, in the *Detroit Free Press*, called the book "a meditation on destruction, survival and memory." Don Bogen, in the *Nation*, saw this as a logical development, since Forché's work with *Against Forgetting* was "instrumental in moving her poetry beyond the politics of personal encounter. *The Angel of History* is rather an extended poetic mediation on the broader contexts— historical, aesthetic, philosophical—which include [the twentieth] . . . century's atrocities," wrote Bogen.

Critical response to *The Angel of History* was generally supportive. Calvin Bedient in the *Threepenny Review* claimed that *The Angel of History* is "instantly recognizable as a great book, the most humanitarian and aesthetically 'inevitable' response to a half-century of atrocities that has yet been written in English." Steven Ratiner, reviewing the work for the *Christian Science Monitor*, called it one that "addresses the terror and inhumanity that have become standard elements in the twentieth-century political landscape— and yet affirms as well the even greater reservoir of the human spirit."

While Forché is a poet of social and political conscience in an era when poetry is often criticized for being self-centered and self-absorbed, her verse does not always succeed, according to some critics. Pollitt noted an "incongruity between Forché's themes and her poetic strategies," and also commenting on a certain lack of "verbal energy" in her work. William Logan, critiquing for the *Times Literary Supplement*, explained that "in her attempt to offer a personal response to the horrors she has witnessed, Forché too often emphasizes herself at their expense. . . . Forché's work relies on sensibility, but she has not found a language for deeper feeling." Nevertheless, recognizing Forché's achievement, Pollitt commended the poet for "her brave and impassioned attempt to make a place in her poems for starving children and bullet factories, for torturers and victims." While some critics emphasize that she might not be a reassuring poet, in the words of Gray, "she is something better, an arresting and often unforgettable voice."

In 1997, Forché was presented with the Edita and Ira Morris Hiroshima Foundation Award for using her poetry as a "means to attain understanding, reconciliation, and peace within communities and between communities." Hope J. Smith commented in the *Madison Gazette* that while it was "surprising for a poet to receive recognition for her work outside of the usual genre prizes, . . . Forché's work is unusual in that it straddles the realms of the political and the poetic, addressing political and social issues in poetry when many poets have abandoned these subjects altogether. In recognizing the link Forché has made between these worlds, the Hiroshima Foundation recognizes her human rights work as much as it does her writing."

BIOGRAPHICAL AND CRITICAL SOURCES:

BOOKS

Contemporary Literary Criticism, Gale (Detroit, MI), Volume 25, 1983, Volume 83, 1994, Volume 86, 1995.
Contemporary Poets, 5th edition, St. James Press (Detroit, MI), 1991.
Dictionary of Literary Biography, Volume 5: *American Poets since World War II,* Gale (Detroit, MI), 1980.
Forché, Carolyn, *Gathering the Tribes,* Yale University Press (New Haven, CT), 1976.
Poetry Criticism, Volume 10, Gale (Detroit, MI), 1994.

PERIODICALS

American Poetry, spring, 1986, pp. 51-69.
American Poetry Review, November-December, 1976, p. 45; July-August, 1981, pp. 3-8; January-February, 1983, pp. 35-39; November-December, 1988, pp. 35-40.
Antioch Review, summer, 1994, Gail Wronsky, review of *Against Forgetting: Twentieth-Century Poetry of Witness,* p. 536.
Bloomsbury Review, September-October, 1994, p. 19.
Book Forum, annual, 1976, pp. 369-399.
Boston Globe, July 24, 1994, p. 42.
Centennial Review, spring, 1986, pp. 160-180.
Chicago Tribune, December 13, 1982, pp. 1-3.
Christian Science Monitor, April 20, 1994, Steven Ratiner, review of *The Angel of History,* p. 20.
Commonweal, November 25, 1977.
Detroit Free Press, May 27, 1982; May 22, 1994, Kevin Walker, review of *The Angel of History,* p. 8.

Detroit News, June 8, 1982.
Georgia Review, winter, 1982, pp. 911-922; summer, 1994, pp. 361-366.
Library Journal, May 1, 1993, p. 88.
Los Angeles Times, August 24, 1982; October 17, 1982; February 22, 1984.
Los Angeles Times Book Review, May 23, 1982; October 17, 1982.
Ms., January, 1980; September, 1982, review of *The Country between Us.*
Nation, May 8, 1982; October 16, 1982; December 27, 1993, pp. 809, 814; October 24, 1994, Don Bogen, review of *The Angel of History,* p. 464.
New England Review, spring, 1994, pp. 144-154.
New Leader, May 17, 1993, Phoebe Pettingell, review of *Against Forgetting,* pp. 23-24.
New York Review of Books, June 24, 1993, John Bayley, review of *Against Forgetting,* pp. 20-22.
New York Times Book Review, August 8, 1976; April 4, 1982; April 19, 1982; December 4, 1983.
Parnassus, spring-summer, 1982, pp. 9-21.
Progressive, October, 1993, Matthew Rothschild, review of *Against Forgetting,* pp. 45-46.
Publishers Weekly, February 1, 1993, review of *Against Forgetting,* p. 78; January 31, 1994, review of *The Angel of History,* p. 7.
Rolling Stone, April 14, 1983, Jonathan Cott, interview with Forché, pp. 81, 83-87, 110-111.
Text and Performance Quarterly, January, 1990, pp. 61-70.
Threepenny Review, summer, 1994, Calvin Bedient, review of *The Angel of History,* pp. 19-20.
Time, March 15, 1982.
Times Literary Supplement, June 10, 1983.
Triquarterly, winter, 1986, pp. 30, 32-38.
Village Voice, March 29, 1976.
Virginia Quarterly Review, autumn, 1994, p. 136.
Washington Post Book World, May 30, 1982.
Whole Earth Review, spring, 1996, p. 70.
Women's Review of Books, July, 1995, p. 3.

ONLINE

Daily Mason Gazette Online, http://gazette.gmu.edu/ (April 26, 2005).
George Mason University Web site, http://mason.gmu.edu/ (July 27, 2004), "Carolyn Forché."*

FRENCH, David 1939-

PERSONAL: Born January 18, 1939, in Coley's Point, Newfoundland, Canada; son of Edgar Garfield (a carpenter) and Edith (Benson) French; married Leslie Gray (a dance teacher), January 5, 1978 (one source says 1979). *Education:* Studied acting under Al Saxe in Toronto, 1958, at Pasadena Playhouse, 1959, and at Roy Lawler Acting School, Toronto, 1960.

ADDRESSES: Home—254 Brunswick Ave., Toronto, Ontario M5S 2M7, Canada. *Office*—c/o Tarragon Theatre, 30 Bridgman Ave., Toronto, Ontario M5R 1X3, Canada. *Agent*—Charles W. Northcote, Literary Agent, 3 Church St., Suite 507, Toronto, Ontario M5E 1M2, Canada.

CAREER: Canadian Broadcasting Corp. (CBC-TV and-Radio), Toronto, Ontario, Canada, actor in plays, 1960-65, writer of radio and television scripts, 1962-72; writer, 1972—; post office worker, 1967-68. Writer-in-residence, University of Western Ontario, 2002-03; has also been a writer-in-residence at Trent University.

MEMBER: Playwrights Union of Canada, Association of Canadian Television and Radio Artists, Dramatists Guild.

AWARDS, HONORS: Chalmers Award for best Canadian play from Ontario Arts Council, 1973, and Lieutenant Governor's Award, 1974, for *Of the Fields, Lately;* Canada Council grants, 1974 and 1975; Dora Mavor Moore award for outstanding play, Hollywood Drama-Logue Critics award, and Hollywood Drama League award, all 1985, Canadian Authors Association Literary Award for Drama, 1986, Governor General's Award for Drama finalist, all for *Salt-Water Moon;* Arthur Ellis Award nomination for best mystery play, for *Silver Dagger.* Inducted into the Newfoundland Arts Hall of Honour, 1989; named Officer of the Order of Canada, 2001; recipient, Golden Jubilee Medal.

WRITINGS:

PLAYS

Leaving Home (two-act; first produced in Toronto, Ontario, Canada, at Tarragon Theatre, 1972; produced in New York, NY, at Theatre of Riverside Church, 1974), New Press (Toronto, Ontario, Canada), 1972, Samuel French (New York, NY), 1976.

David French

Of the Fields, Lately (two-act; first produced in Toronto, Ontario, Canada, at Tarragon Theatre, 1973; produced on Broadway at Century Theatre, 1980), introduction by Urjo Kareda, Playwrights (Toronto, Ontario, Canada), 1973, Samuel French (New York, NY), 1975.

One Crack Out (three-act; first produced in Toronto, Ontario, Canada, at Tarragon Theatre, 1975; produced Off-Broadway at Phoenix Theatre, 1978), Playwrights (Toronto, Ontario, Canada), 1975.

(Translator) Anton Chekov, *The Seagull* (four-act; translation first produced in Toronto, Ontario, Canada, at Tarragon Theatre, 1977), Playwrights (Toronto, Ontario, Canada), 1977.

Jitters (three-act; first produced in Toronto, Ontario, Canada, at Tarragon Theatre, 1979; produced on Broadway, 1981), Talonbooks (Vancouver, British Columbia, and Los Angeles, CA), 1980.

The Riddle of the World, first produced in Toronto, Ontario, Canada, at the Tarragon Theatre, 1981.

Salt-Water Moon (first produced in Toronto, Ontario, Canada, 1984; produced in Costa Mesa, CA, 1985; produced in Edinburgh, Scotland, 1986), Playwrights (Toronto, Ontario, Canada), 1985, Dramatists Play Service (New York, NY), 1988.

(Adapter) *The Forest,* first produced in Toronto, Ontario, Canada, 1987.

1949 (first produced in Toronto, Ontario, Canada, by Canadian Stage Company, 1988), Talonbooks (Vancouver, British Columbia), 1989.

Silver Dagger (first produced in Toronto, Ontario, Canada, 1993), Talonbooks (Vancouver, British Columbia), 1993.

That Summer (first performed, 1999), Talonbooks (Vancouver, British Columbia, Canada), 2000.

Soldier's Heart (first performed in Toronto, Ontario, Canada, 2001), Talonbooks (Vancouver, British Columbia, Canada), 2002.

TELEVISION PLAYS

Beckons the Dark River, Canadian Broadcasting Corporation-TV (CBC-TV), 1963.

The Willow Harp, CBC-TV, 1964.

A Ring for Florie, CBC-TV, 1964.

After Hours, CBC-TV, 1964.

Sparrow on a Monday Morning, Westinghouse Broadcasting Corp., 1966.

A Token Gesture, CBC-TV, 1970.

A Tender Branch, CBC-TV, 1972.

The Happiest Man in the World (adaptation of the short story by Hugh Garner), CBC-TV, 1972.

RADIO PLAYS

Angeline, Canadian Broadcasting Corporation-Radio (CBC-Radio), 1967.

Invitation to a Zoo, CBC-Radio, 1967.

Winter of Timothy, CBC-Radio, 1968.

OTHER

A Company of Strangers, (novel), 1968.

(Editor, with Michael Richards) *Media Education across Europe,* Routledge, 1994.

(Editor, with Michael Richards) *Contemporary Television: Eastern Perspectives,* Sage Publications, 1996.

(Editor, with Michael Richards) *Television in Contemporary Asia,* Sage Publications, 2000.

Author of scripts for children's television series *Razzle Dazzle;* contributor to *In First Flowering,* edited by Anthony Frisch, Kingswood House, 1956. Contributor of short stories to magazines, including *Montrealer* and *Canadian Boy.*

SIDELIGHTS: Canadian playwright David French is an award-winning author often recognized for his series of plays featuring the Mercer family, a group of Irish immigrants who have settled in Newfoundland. These plays include *Leaving Home, Of the Fields, Lately, Salt-Water Moon, 1949,* and *Soldier's Heart. Leaving Home,* French's first stage play, concerns the family's frustration with moving from their recently-established home in Newfoundland to Toronto. Their sense of displacement aggravates normal family tensions, and bitter arguments result, especially between Jacob Mercer and his oldest son, Ben. Jacob sees in Ben his hopes for recapturing what he feels has been his own unsuccessful life, but Ben wants to break free of his traditionalist father's aspirations for him to work in a trade and instead go to university. Between the two warring men, Ben's mother, Mary, tries vainly to maintain the peace, while his younger brother, Billy, prepares to marry a Catholic woman whom he has gotten pregnant. It is the wedding the brings the family's tensions to a peak, ending in Ben finally leaving home.

French's next play, *Of the Fields, Lately,* continues the story of the Mercers with Ben's return to attend an aunt's funeral. He and his father renew their old quarrels, which end only with Jacob's death and Ben's complete feeling of alienation at the play's end. "The play is permeated with a sense of death," commented a *Contemporary Dramatists* essayist, "but the funeral device does not create as tight a dramatic unity as does the wedding in *Leaving Home.*" On the other hand, Michiko Kakutani maintained in a *New York Times* review: "This lyrical play is actually an extended flashback that meticulously traces the incidents that day by day, year by year have built up a wall between the two men." The play also shows what familial relations might have been if the father and son had reconciled their differences. Such a glimpse makes the son's concluding monologue all the more poignant.

Taking the Mercer family back before the time of the action in *Leaving Home,* French explores the early relationship between Jacob and his future wife, Mary, in *Salt-Water Moon.* The play "focuses narrowly on Jacob and Mary, their frustrated love, their poverty, and their poignant struggle in different ways to help their families," related the *Contemporary Dramatists* writer: "Mary to save her sister from the brutality of an orphan asylum, and Jacob to spare his father the humiliation of being 'in collar,' a pernicious employment system devised by the local fishing bosses." Theatergoers familiar with the earlier plays by French will know that Jacob and Mary eventually work out their problems and wed, so the main tension of the play arises from the question of how this resolution will come about.

The Mercer saga continues with *1949*, set in a year when Newfoundland is to solidify its political ties with the rest of Canada. The family greets the event with mixed emotions, feeling that it represents both the future of their adopted country and the loss of the unique culture of Newfoundland. With 2001's *Soldier's Heart* French explores the character of Jacob and his relationship with his father, Esau, by going back to the year when Jacob was sixteen and is preparing to enlist in the military and fight in World War II. Esau, who fought in the Great War, does not want his son to leave, and so he finally tells Jacob of the many horrible and traumatic experiences he had as a soldier, something he had been unable to do before this time. His opening up to Jacob finally mends the rift between father and son. Acknowledging the promising theme in this play, a *Maclean's* nevertheless found the piece weakened by sentimentality.

In addition to the Mercer plays, French has also written a number of other comedies, mysteries, and dramas for the stage. Among these is *One Crack Out*, which chronicles how Charlie, a has-been pool hustler, regains enough courage and confidence to meet Bulldog, a cruel, vindictive debt collector, in a poolgame showdown. Charlie's devoted wife and a reluctantly sympathetic pimp support him in his struggle against his tormentor. Noting that *One Crack Out* was French's first play not to include the Mercer's, the *Contemporary Dramatists* writer said, "Despite the fact that the play is less strong than French's first two, it marks a forward step in his development by moving away from the autobiographical into an invented, objective world."

Mercer's other works include the comedies *The Riddle of the World* and *Jitters*. The former, as it is described on the playwright's Web site, is a "comedy about the struggle between the flesh and the spirit"; the latter is a backstage comedy, a play within a play, which records the story of a group of actors who have the "jitters" four days before their play is to open. Excitement is also high as a big Broadway producer is expected to be in the audience. With both humor and sentimentality, French explores the personal aspirations and problems of each actor as the fateful day approaches.

Other more recent plays by French include the mystery *Silver Dagger* and the drama *That Summer. Silver Dagger* concerns mystery writer Steve Marsh, whose literary conceits soon become reality as he and his wife receive a series of threatening phone calls and are put in jeopardy by blackmail and murder. *That Summer* reacquaints audiences with the familiar ground of French's Newfoundland, where an elderly woman has returned with her granddaughter and reminisces about one fateful summer in her life. Although *Variety* critic Mira Friedlander found the plot of *That Summer* to be conventional, she conceded that "the play does deliver a potent dose of nostalgia which should appeal to audiences craving a simpler, kinder world where even death had dignity."

BIOGRAPHICAL AND CRITICAL SOURCES:

BOOKS

Anthony, Geraldine, *Stage Voices: Twelve Canadian Playwrights Talk About Their Lives and Work*, Doubleday, 1978, pp. 233-250.

Bryden, Ronald, and Boyd Neil, eds., *Whittaker's Theatre: A Critic Looks at Stages in Canada and Thereabouts 1944-1975*, Whittaker Project, 1985, pp. 158-161.

Contemporary Dramatists, sixth edition, St. James (Detroit, MI), 1999.

Zimmerman, Wallace and Cynthia, *The Work: Conversations with English-Canadian Playwrights*, Coach House Press, 1982, pp. 304-316.

PERIODICALS

Canadian Drama/L'Art Dramatique Canadien, fall, 1975, pp. 115-118; spring, 1976, pp. 58-66, 67-72; spring, 1980, pp. 30-42; spring, 1985, pp. 2-229.

Canadian Forum, March, 1974, pp. 26-27.

Canadian Literature, summer, 1980, pp. 62-69, 71-85.

Canadian Theatre Review, spring, 1980, pp. 30-43.

Fiddlehead, winter, 1974, pp. 61-66.

Maclean's, November 26, 2001, "Great War Wounds," p. 48.
New York Times, January 18, 1978; November 6, 1979; March 12, 1980; April 15, 1980.
Variety, August 9, 1999, Mira Friedlander, review of *That Summer,* p. 50.

ONLINE

David French Web Site, http://www.davidfrench.net (November 24, 2003).*

* * *

FROST, Gregory 1951-

PERSONAL: Born May 31, 1951, in Des Moines, IA; son of Dee Lloyd (a lawyer and banker) and Curtis Rosemary (Rice) Frost; married Mara L. Johnson, December 6, 1980 (divorced, August, 1985); remarried; wife's name, Barbara. *Education:* Attended Drake University, 1969-72, and Michigan State University, 1975; University of Iowa, B.L.A., 1977. *Politics:* Independent/progressive. *Religion:* "Nondenominational." *Hobbies and other interests:* Aikido, cycling, birding, yoga.

ADDRESSES: Agent—Martha Millard, 122 Kenilworth Rd., Merion Station, PA 19066. *E-mail*—gf@gregoryfrost.com.

CAREER: Science fiction and fantasy writer. Also worked as word processor, secretary, legal secretary, bookstore salesperson, drapery hanger, bookkeeper, record reviewer, and illustrator.

MEMBER: Science Fiction Writers of America, The Nameless Workshop Group.

AWARDS, HONORS: Hugo Award finalist, James Tiptree Award finalist, and Theodore Sturgeon Memorial Award finalist, best novelette category, 2003, for "Madonna of the Maquiladora"; World Fantasy and International Horror Guild Award finalist, best novel category, 2003, for *Fitcher's Brides.*

WRITINGS:

Lyrec (novel), Ace Books (New York, NY), 1984.
Tain (novel; first volume of the "Tales of Cu Chulainn"; also see below), Ace Books (New York, NY), 1986.

Remscela (novel; second volume of the "Tales of Cu Chulainn"; also see below), Berkley (New York, NY), 1988.
The Pure Cold Light (novel), Avon Books (New York, NY), 1993.
Crimson Spear: The Blood of Cu Chulainn (reprint of *Tain* and *Remscela* in one volume), Cascade Mountain Publishing, 1998.
Fitcher's Brides (part of "The Fairy Tale" series created by Terri Windling), Tor (New York, NY), 2002.
Attack of the Jazz Giants and Other Stories, Golden Gryphon Press (Urbana, IL), 2005.

Also author of the novelette "Madonna of the Maquiladora." Work represented in anthologies, including *Snow White, Blood Red,* Morrow, 1993; *Intersections: The Sycamore Hill Anthology,* Tor Books, 1996; *Mojo: Conjure Stories,* Warner Books, 2003; *Swan Sister,* Simon & Schuster, 2003; and *The Faery Reel,* Viking, 2004. Contributor of stories and articles to magazines, including *Asimov's, Fantasy and Science Fiction, Weird Tales,* and *Realms of Fantasy.*

SIDELIGHTS: Gregory Frost is the author of science-fiction, fantasy, and horror novels and short stories, including the critically acclaimed *Fitcher's Brides,* and the multi-nominated short story "Madonna of the Maquiladora." Frost's first novel-length work, *Lyrec,* is the story of two good travelers (a man and a cat) and an evil traveler from another universe. Together, the three descend upon a medieval world. Good battles evil in this novel to protect civilization from total destruction.

Frost's next novel, *Tain,* is the first in a two-volume collection involving the tales of Cu Chulainn, a character from Irish mythology. *Tain,* along with the second volume, *Remscela,* were combined into a single volume, titled *Crimson Spear: The Blood of Cu Chulainn.* Frost wrote, "*Tain* and *Remscela* took about eight years of my life to research, and this included a bicycle tour of original landscape in Ireland." *Tain* and *Remscela* are Frost's translation and telling of the Táin Bó Cúalnge (The Cattle-Raid of Cooley) saga. The books combine theology, history, and mythology to recount the Celtic tale.

In *The Pure Cold Light,* Frost presents readers with Thomasina Lyell, a journalist who uncovers a secret about mega-corporations' quest to take over the world.

Frost's next novel, *Fitcher's Brides,* is perhaps his most critically acclaimed. *Fitcher's Brides* is part of author Terri Windling's "Fairy Tale" series and retells the Bluebeard fairy tale. In the original legend, women are wary of marrying the wealthy Bluebeard because his wives seem to disappear. When he finally marries a young girl, he warns her not to open a secret closet with a special key while he is gone away. Curiosity gets the best of the young girl and she peeks into the room, only to discover the bodies of Bluebeard's murdered wives.

In Frost's retelling, Reverend Elias Fitcher convinces people that the world will end in 1843, and that he alone can lead them to heaven if they join his utopian community Harbinger. Among Fitcher's believers are the parents of Vernelia, Amy, and Katherine (Kate) Charter. The charismatic Fitcher takes Vern as his first bride, followed by Amy, and each in turn vanishes within Harbinger. When Fitcher finally weds Kate, she knows it is up to her to expose Fitcher's as the monster he really is. Paula Luedtke of *Booklist* dubbed Frost's tale a "superb retelling of Bluebeard," and noted the book was "well-researched and extremely well-written." Jackie Cassada of *Library Journal* offered a similar opinion, writing that Frost "blends dark fantasy and social commentary in an intriguing tale." A *Publishers Weekly* contributor called *Fitcher's Brides* "a fresh and highly readable spin on the classic Bluebeard tale."

BIOGRAPHICAL AND CRITICAL SOURCES:

BOOKS

Reginald, Robert, *Science Fiction and Fantasy Literature, 1975-1991,* Gale (Detroit, MI), 1992.

PERIODICALS

Analog Science Fiction and Fact, July, 1995, review of *The Pure Cold Light,* p. 303.
Booklist, December 15, 2002, Paula Luedtke, review of *Fitcher's Brides,* p. 740.
Book World, February 23, 1986, review of *Tain,* p. 12; June 26, 1988, review of *Remscela,* p. 12.
Fantasy Review, June, 1985; April, 1986, review of *Tain,* p. 22.
Kliatt, spring, 1986, review of *Tain,* p. 22.

Library Journal, April 15, 1993, Jackie Cassada, review of *The Pure Cold Light,* p. 130; December, 2002, Jackie Cassada, review of *Fitcher's Brides,* p. 184.
Locus, June, 1993, review of *The Pure Cold Light,* p. 53.
Magazine of Fantasy and Science Fiction, February, 1994, John Kessel, review of *The Pure Cold Light,* p. 39.
Publishers Weekly, November 18, 2002, review of *Fitcher's Brides,* p. 46.
Science Fiction Chronicle, July, 1993, review of *The Pure Cold Light,* p. 30.
Voice of Youth Advocates, April, 1994, review of *The Pure Cold Light,* p. 37.
Washington Post Book World, February 23, 1986.

ONLINE

Best Reviews Web site, http://www.thebestreviews.com/ (November 25, 2002), Harriet Klausner, review of *Fitcher's Brides.*
Gregory Frost Web site, http://www.gregoryfrost.com (February 5, 2004), biography and list of books.

*   *   *

FUENTES, Carlos 1928-

PERSONAL: Born November 11, 1928, in Panama City, Panama; Mexican citizen; son of Rafael Fuentes Boettiger (a career diplomat) and Berta Macias Rivas; married Rita Macedo (a movie actress), 1959 (divorced, 1969); married Sylvia Lemus (a television journalist), 1973; children: (first marriage) Cecilia; (second marriage) Carlos Rafael, Natasha. *Education:* National University of Mexico, LL.B., 1948; graduate study, Institute des Hautes Etudes (Geneva, Switzerland). *Politics:* Independent leftist. *Hobbies and other interests:* Reading, travel, swimming, visiting art galleries, listening to classical and rock music, motion pictures, the theater.

ADDRESSES: Home—Mexico City, Mexico; and London, England. *Agent*—c/o Alfaguara, S.A.-Grupo Santillana, Torrelaguna, 60, 28043 Madrid, Spain.

CAREER: Writer. International Labor Organization, Geneva, Switzerland, began as member, became secretary of the Mexican delegation, 1950-52; Ministry

Carlos Fuentes

of Foreign Affairs, Mexico City, Mexico, assistant chief of press section, 1954; National University of Mexico, Mexico City, Mexico, secretary and assistant director of cultural dissemination, 1955-56, head of department of cultural relations, 1957-59; Mexican ambassador to France, 1975-77; Cambridge University, Norman Maccoll Lecturer, 1977, Simon Bolivar Professor, 1986-87; Barnard College, New York, NY, Virginia Gildersleeve Professor, 1977; Columbia University, New York, NY, Henry L. Tinker Lecturer, 1978; University of Pennsylvania, professor of English, 1978-83; Harvard University, Cambridge, MA, Robert F. Kennedy Professor of Latin American studies, 1987. Fellow at Woodrow Wilson International Center for Scholars, 1974; lecturer or visiting professor at University of Mexico, University of California—San Diego, University of Oklahoma, University of Concepción in Chile, University of Paris, University of Pennsylvania, and George Mason University; Modern Humanities Research Association, president, 1989—; member of Mexican National Commission on Human Rights.

MEMBER: American Academy and Institute of Arts and Letters (honorary).

AWARDS, HONORS: Centro Mexicano de Escritores fellowship, 1956-57; Biblioteca Breve Prize, Seix Barral (publishing house, Barcelona, Spain), 1967, for *Cambio de piel;* Xavier Villaurrutia Prize (Mexico), 1975; Romulo Gallegos Prize (Venezuela), 1977, for *Terra Nostra;* Alfonso Reyes Prize (Mexico), 1979, for body of work; National Award for Literature (Mexico), 1984, for "Orchids in the Moonlight"; nominated for *Los Angeles Times* Book Award in fiction, 1986, for *The Old Gringo;* Miguel de Cervantes Prize, Spanish Ministry of Culture, 1987; Ruben Dario Order of Cultural Independence (Nicaragua) and literary prize of Italo-Latino Americano Institute, both 1988, for *The Old Gringo;* Medal of Honor for Literature, National Arts Club (New York, NY), 1988; Rector's Medal, University of Chile, 1991; Casita Maria Medal, 1991; Order of Merit (Chile), 1992; French Legion of Honor, 1992; Menedez Pelayo International Award, University of Santander, 1992; named honorary citizen of Santiago de Chile, Buenos Aires, and Veracruz, 1993; Principe de Asturias Prize, 1994; Premio Grinzane-Cavour, 1994; candidate for Neustadt International Prize for Literature, 1996; Ruben Dario Prize, 1998; nominated for the 2002 Impac Dublin Literary Award for *The Years with Laura Díaz;* Common Wealth Award for Distinguished Service, 2002; Chubb Fellowship, Yale, 2004; honorary degrees from Bard College, Cambridge University, Columbia College, Chicago State University, Dartmouth College, Essex University, Georgetown University, Harvard University, and Washington University.

WRITINGS:

NOVELS

La región más transparente, Fondo de Cultura Economica (Mexico City, Mexico), 1958, translation by Sam Hileman published as *Where the Air Is Clear,* Ivan Obolensky, 1960.

Las buenas consciencias, Fondo de Cultura Economica (Mexico City, Mexico), 1959, translation published as *The Good Conscience,* Ivan Oblensky, 1961.

La muerte de Artemio Cruz, Fondo de Cultura Economica (Mexico City, Mexico), 1962, translation by Sam Hileman published as *The Death of Artemio Cruz,* Farrar, Straus (New York, NY), 1964.

Aura (also see below), Era, 1962, reprinted, 1982, translation by Lysander Kemp, Farrar, Straus (New York, NY), 1965.

Zona sagrada, Siglo XXI, 1967, translation by Suzanne Jill Levine published as *Holy Place* (also see below), Dutton (New York, NY), 1972.

Cambio de piel, Mortiz, 1967, translation by Sam Hileman published as *A Change of Skin,* Farrar, Straus (New York, NY), 1968.

Cumpleaños, Mortiz, 1969, translation published as *Birthday* (also see below).

Terra Nostra (also see below), Seix Barral (Barcelona, Spain), 1975, translation by Jill Levine, afterword by Milan Kundera, Farrar, Straus (New York, NY), 1976.

La cabeza de hidra, Mortiz, 1978, translation by Margaret Sayers Peden published as *Hydra Head,* Farrar, Straus (New York, NY), 1978.

Una familia lejana, Era, 1980, translation by Margaret Sayers Peden published as *Distant Relations,* Farrar, Straus (New York, NY), 1982.

El gringo viejo, Fondo de Cultura Economica (Mexico City, Mexico), 1985, translation with Margaret Sayers Peden published as *The Old Gringo,* Farrar, Straus (New York, NY), 1985.

Cristóbal Nonato, Fondo de Cultura Economica (Mexico City, Mexico), 1987, translated as *Christopher Unborn,* Farrar, Straus (New York, NY), 1989.

La frontera de cristal, Alfaguara (Mexico City, Mexico), 1995, translated as *The Crystal Frontier: A Novel in Nine Stories.*

Diana, the Goddess Who Hunts Alone, introduction by Alfred J. Mac Adam, Farrar, Straus (New York, NY), 1995.

Años con Laura Díaz, Alfaguara (Mexico City, Mexico), 1999, translation by Alfred Mac Adam published as *The Years with Laura Díaz,* Farrar, Straus (New York, NY), 2000.

Instinto de Inez, Alfaguara (Mexico City, Mexico), 2001, translation by Margaret Sayers Peden published as *Inez,* Farrar, Straus (New York, NY), 2002.

La silla del águila, Alfaguara (Mexico City, Mexico), 2003.

Also author of *Holy Place & Birthday: Two Novellas,* Farrar, Straus (New York, NY).

SHORT STORIES

Los días enmascarados (also see below), Los Presentes, 1954.

Cantar de ciegos (also see below), Mortiz, 1964.

Dos cuentos mexicanos (title means "Two Mexican Stories"; previously published in *Cantar de ciegos*), Instituto de Cultura Hispanica de Sao Paulo, Universidade de Sao Paulo, 1969.

Poemas de amor: Cuentos del alma, Imp. E. Cruces (Madrid, Spain), 1971.

Chac Mool y otros cuentos, Salvat, 1973.

Agua quemada (anthology), Fondo de Cultura Economica (Mexico City, Mexico), 1981, translation by Margaret Sayers Peden published as *Burnt Water,* Farrar, Straus (New York, NY), 1980.

Constancia y otras novelas para vírgenes, Mondadori (Madrid, Spain), 1989, translation by Thomas Christensen published as *Constancia and Other Stories for Virgins,* Farrar, Straus (New York, NY), 1989.

Inquieta compañía, (title means "Uneasy Company"), Alfaguara (Mexico City, Mexico), 2004.

PLAYS

Todos los gatos son pardos (also see below), Siglo XXI, 1970.

El tuerto es rey (also see below; produced in French in 1970), Mortiz, 1970.

Los reinos originarios (contains *Todos los gatos son pardos* and *El tuerto es rey*), Seix Barral (Barcelona, Spain), 1971.

Orquídeas a la luz de la luna (produced in English as *Orchids in the Moonlight* at American Repertory Theater in Cambridge, MA, 1982), Seix Barral (Barcelona, Spain), 1982.

NONFICTION

The Argument of Latin America: Words for North Americans, Radical Education Project, 1963.

(Contributor) *Whither Latin America?* (political articles), Monthly Review Press, 1963.

París: La revolución de mayo, Era, 1968.

La nueva novela hispanoamericana, Mortiz, 1969.

(Contributor) *El mundo de José Luis Cuevas,* Tudor (Mexico City, Mexico), 1969.

Casa con dos puertas (title means "House with Two Doors"), Mortiz, 1970.

Tiempo mexicano (title means "Mexican Time"), Mortiz, 1971.

Cervantes; o, La crítica de la lectura, Mortiz, 1976, translation published as *Don Quixote; or, The Critique of Reading,* Institute of Latin American Studies, University of Texas at Austin (Austin, TX), 1976.

On Human Rights: A Speech, Somesuch Press (Dallas, TX), 1984.

Latin America: At War with the Past, CBC Enterprises, 1985.

Myself with Others: Selected Essays, Farrar, Straus (New York, NY), 1988.

Buried Mirror: Reflections on Spain in the New World, Houghton Mifflin (Boston, MA), 1992.

A New Time for Mexico, Farrar, Straus (New York, NY), 1996.

El Espejo Enterrado, Alfaguara (Mexico City, Mexico), 2001.

En esto creo, Seix Barral (Barcelona, Spain), 2002, translation by Kristina Cordero published as *This I Believe: An A to Z of a Life,* Random House (New York, New York), 2005.

Carlos Fuentes: viendo visions, Fondo de Cultura Económica (Mexico City, Mexico), 2003.

OTHER

(Editor and author of prologue) Octavio Paz, *Los signos en rotacion, y otros ensayos,* Alianza, 1971.

Cuerpos y ofrendas (anthology; includes selections from *Los días enmascarados, Cantar de ciegos, Aura,* and *Terra Nostra,*) introduction by Octavio Paz, Alianza, 1972.

(Author of introduction) Milan Kundera, *La vida está en otra parte* (Spanish translation of *Life Is Elsewhere*), Seix Barral (Barcelona, Spain), 1977.

(Author of introduction) Omar Cabezas, *Fire from the Mountain,* Crown (New York, NY), 1988.

Valiente Mundo Nuevo, Fondo de Cultura Economica (Mexico City, Mexico), 1990.

The Campaign, Farrar, Straus (New York, NY), 1991.

Geografía de la novela, Fondo de Cultura Economica (Mexico City, Mexico), 1993.

El naranjo, o los circulos del tiempo, Alfaguara (Mexico City, Mexico), 1993.

The Orange Tree, introduction by Mac Adam, Farrar, Straus (New York, NY), 1994.

The Writings of Carlos Fuentes, edited by Raymond L. Williams, University of Texas Press (Austin, TX), 1996.

Los cinco soles de México: Memoria de un milenio, Seix Barral (Barcelona, Spain), 2000.

(Author of introduction) Michael L. Sand, editor, *Witnesses of Time,* photographs by Flor Garduno, Aperture Foundation (New York, NY), 2000.

Contributor to *Juan Rulfo: México,* Lunwerg Editores (Barcelona, Spain), 2001, translation by Margaret Sayers Peden published as *Juan Rulfo's Mexico,* Smithsonian Institution Press, 2002, and *Nudes/Desnudos: The photographs of Manuel Alvarez,* edited by Ariadne Kimberly Huque, Distributed Art Publishers (New York, NY), 2002. Collaborator on several film scripts, including *Pedro Paramo,* 1966, *Tiempo de morir,* 1966, and *Los caifanes,* 1967. Work represented in numerous anthologies, including *Antología de cuentos hispanoamericanos,* Nueva Decada (Costa Rica), 1985. Contributor to periodicals in the United States, Mexico, and France, including *New York Times, Washington Post,* and *Los Angeles Times.* Founding editor, *Revista Mexicana de Literatura,* 1954-58; coeditor, *El Espectador,* 1959-61, *Siempre,* 1960, and *Politica,* 1960.

ADAPTATIONS: Two short stories from *Cantar de ciegos* were made into films in the mid-1960s; *The Old Gringo* was adapted into a film of the same title by Fonda Films, 1989.

WORK IN PROGRESS: A novel about the assassination of Emiliano Zapata.

SIDELIGHTS: "Carlos Fuentes," stated Robert Maurer in *Saturday Review,* is "without doubt one of Mexico's two or three greatest novelists." He is part of a group of Latin American writers whose writings, according to Alistair Reid's *New Yorker* essay, "formed the background of the Boom," a literary phenomenon Reid described as a period in the 1960s when "a sudden surge of hitherto unheard-of writers from Latin America began to be felt among [U.S.] readers." Fuentes, however, is singled out from among the other writers of the Boom in José Donoso's autobiographical account, *The Boom in Spanish American Literature: A Personal History,* in which the Chilean novelist called Fuentes "the first active and conscious agent of the internationalization of the Spanish American novel." Since the 1960s, Fuentes has continued his international influence in the literary world; his 1985 novel, *The Old Gringo,* for example, was the first written by a Mexican to ever appear on the *New York Times* best-seller list.

Although, as Donoso observed, early worldwide acceptance of Fuentes's novels contributed to the internationalization of Latin American literature, his work is an exploration of the culture and history of one nation, his native Mexico. Critics note the thematic presence of Mexico in nearly all Fuentes's writing. Robert Coover commented in the *New York Times Book Review* that in *The Death of Artemio Cruz*, for instance, Fuentes delineated "in the retrospective details of one man's life the essence of the post-Revolutionary history of all Mexico." Mexico is also present in Fuentes's novel *Terra Nostra*, in which, according to *Washington Post Book World* contributor Larry Rohter, "Fuentes probes more deeply into the origins of Mexico—and what it means to be a Mexican—than ever before." *Old Gringo*, published more than twenty years after *The Death of Artemio Cruz*, returns to the same theme as it explores Mexico's relationship with its northern neighbor, the United States.

Fuentes explained his preoccupation with Mexico, and particularly with Mexican history, in a *Paris Review* interview. "Pablo Neruda used to say," he told Alfred MacAdam and Charles Ruas, "that every Latin American writer goes around dragging a heavy body, the body of his people, of his past, of his national history. We have to assimilate the enormous weight of our past so that we will not forget what gives us life. If you forget your past, you die." Fuentes also noted that the development of the same theme in his novels unifies them so that they may be considered part of the same work. The author observed in the same interview, "In a sense my novels are one book with many chapters: *Where the Air Is Clear* is the biography of Mexico City; *The Death of Artemio Cruz* deals with an individual in that city; [and] *A Change of Skin* is that city, that society, facing the world, coming to grips with the fact that it is part of civilization and that there is a world outside that intrudes into Mexico."

Along with thematic unity, another characteristic of Fuentes's work is his innovative narrative style. In a *New Yorker* review, Anthony West compared the novelist's technique to "a rapid cinematic movement that cuts nervously from one character to another." Evan Connell stated in the *New York Times Book Review* that Fuentes's "narrative style—with few exceptions—relies on the interruption and juxtaposition of different kinds of awareness." Reviewers Donald Yates and Karen Hardy also commented on Fuentes's experimental style. In the *Washington Post Book World*, Yates called Fuentes "a tireless experimenter with narrative techniques and points of view." In *Hispania*, Hardy noted that in Fuentes's work "the complexities of a human or national personality are evoked through . . . elaborate narrative devices."

The Death of Artemio Cruz and *Terra Nostra* are especially good examples of his experimental techniques. The first novel deals with a corrupt Mexican millionaire who, on his deathbed, relives his life in a series of flashbacks. In the novel Fuentes uses three separate narrations to tell the story, and for each of these he uses a different narrator. *New York Review of Books* contributor A. Alvarez explained the three-part narration of the novel: "Cruz's story is told in three persons. 'I' is the old man dying on his bed; 'you' is a slightly vatic, 'experimental' projection of his potentialities into an unspecified future. . . . 'he' is the real hero, the man whose history emerges bit by bit from incidents shuffled around from his seventy-one years." In John S. Brushwood's *Mexico in Its Novel: A Nation's Search for Identity*, the critic praised Fuentes's technique, commenting: "The changing narrative viewpoint is extremely effective, providing a clarity that could not have been accomplished any other way. I doubt that there is anywhere in fiction a character whose wholeness is more apparent than in the case of Artemio Cruz."

Coover observed that in *Terra Nostra*, Fuentes once again uses a variety of narrators to tell his story. Commenting favorably on Fuentes's use of the "you" narrative voice in the novel, Coover wrote: "Fuentes's second person [narration] is not one overheard on a stage: the book itself, rather than the author or a character, becomes the speaker, the reader or listener a character, or several characters in succession." Spanish novelist Juan Goytisolo similarly stated in *Review*: "One of the most striking and most successful devices [in *Terra Nostra*] is the abrupt shift in narrative point of view (at times without the unwary reader's even noticing), passing from first-person narration to second . . . and simultaneously rendering objective and subjective reality in one and the same passage with patent scorn for the rules of discourse that ordinarily govern expository prose." In the *Paris Review*, Fuentes commented on his use of the second person narrative, calling it "the voice poets have always used and that novelists also have a right to use."

Fuentes's use of the second person narrative and other experimental techniques makes his novels extremely complex. In a *New York Times Book Review* interview with Frank MacShane concerning the structure of *Terra Nostra,* Fuentes described the intricacy of the work: "My chief stylistic device in *Terra Nostra* is to follow every statement by a counter statement and every image by its opposite." This deliberate duplicity by the author, along with the extensive scope of the novel, caused some reviewers to criticize *Terra Nostra* for being inaccessible to the average reader. Maurer, for instance, called the novel "a huge, sprawling, exuberant, mysterious, almost unimaginably dense work of 800 pages, covering events on three continents from the creation of man in Genesis to the dawn of the twenty-first century," and added that "*Terra Nostra* presents a common reader with enormous problems simply of understanding what is going on." *Newsweek's* Peter S. Prescott noted: "To talk about [*Terra Nostra*] at all we must return constantly to five words: excess, surreal, baroque, masterpiece, [and] unreadable."

Other critics, however, have written more positive reviews, seeing *Terra Nostra* and other Fuentes works as necessarily complex. *Village Voice* contributor Jonah Raskin found Fuentes is at his best when the novelist can "plunge readers into the hidden recesses of his characters' minds and at the same time allow language to pile up around their heads in thick drifts, until they feel lost in a blizzard of words that enables them to see, to feel, in a revolutionary way." Fuentes also defended the difficulty of his works in a *Washington Post* interview with Charles Truehart. Recalling his conversation with Fuentes, Truehart quoted him as saying: "I believe in books that do not go to a ready-made public. . . . I'm looking for readers I would like to *make.* . . . To *win* them . . . to *create* readers rather than to give something that readers are expecting. That would bore me to death."

In 1992 Fuentes produced *The Buried Mirror: Reflections on Spain in the New World,* a historical work that discusses the formation and development of the Latin American world. The title refers to polished rocks found in the tombs of ancient Mediterranean and Amerindian peoples, presaging, in Fuentes's view, the convergence of these distant cultures. Fuentes wrote that his book is "dedicated to a search for the cultural continuity that can inform and transcend the economic and political destiny and fragmentation of the Hispanic world." Attempting to disentangle the complex legacy of Spanish settlement in the New World, Fuentes first addresses the mixed ethnicity of the Spanish conquerors, whose progeny include Celts, Phoenicians, Greeks, Romans, Arabs, and Jews, and the consequent diversity produced in Latin America through war, colonization, and miscegenation.

Praising Fuentes's intriguing though broad subject, Nicolas Shumway wrote in the *New York Times Book Review,* "The range of the book is both its principal defect and its chief virtue. Beginning with the prehistoric cave paintings at Altamira in Spain and ending with contemporary street art in East Los Angeles, Mr. Fuentes seeks to cover all of Spanish and Spanish-American history, with frequent digressions on a particular artist, political figure, novel or painting." *The Buried Mirror,* according to David Ewing Duncan in a *Washington Post Book World* review, is "invigorated by the novelist's sense of irony, paradox and sensuality. Here is a civilization, he says, that defies whatever stereotypes we may hold, a society at once erotic and puritanical, cruel and humane, legalistic and corrupt, energetic and sad." Guy Garcia noted in *Time* that the book "represents an intellectual homecoming for Fuentes, who conceived of the project as 'a fantastic opportunity to write my own cultural biography.'"

Four years later Fuentes followed with *A New Time for Mexico,* a collection of essays on the internal injustice and international indignity suffered by Mexico. Viewed as a sequel to his 1971 publication, *Tiempo mexicano* (translated as "Mexican Time"), Fuentes addresses current events in his native country, including political reform, the Chiapas rebellion, social inequities, and the significance of the North American Free Trade Agreement (NAFTA) for Mexico and its perception in the United States. Though noting the bias of Fuentes's strong nationalism, Roderic A. Camp maintained in *Library Journal* that his "brief cultural vignettes" are "appealing and insightful." A *Publishers Weekly* reviewer commended Fuentes's "lapidary, lyrical meditations on Mexico as a land of continual metamorphosis."

The Orange Tree offers five novellas whose subjects span several centuries, each connected by the image of the orange. For Fuentes the orange tree signifies the possibilities of beauty, sustenance, transplantation, and rejuvenation. Its seeds were introduced to Spain through Roman and Moorish invaders, reached the New World with the conquistadors, and have flourished since. Fuentes illustrates various manifestations of violence, deception, and suffering by recounting episodes from the conquest of Roman Iberia and Mexico, a contemporary corporate takeover, and the death wish of an American actor.

"In all this intercourse between Old World and New, Rome and Africa and Spain, past and present," Alan Cheuse wrote in Chicago's *Tribune Books,* "Fuentes makes the older material resonate with all of the exotic and yet familiar attraction of compelling human behavior." Michael Kerrigan praised the work in a *Times Literary Supplement* review, noting that "The challenge and opportunity *The Orange Tree* presents its reader are those of escaping from 'a more or less protected individuality' into a wider existence of multiple possibility and a cyclical history that holds past and present in simultaneity and in ceaseless renewal." Kerrigan concluded, "What strikes the reader first in Fuentes' work may be his erudition and intellectual rigour, but what remains in the mind is his sympathy, his concern to commemorate the countless lives sacrificed in pain and obscurity so that we might live."

In 1995 Fuentes published *Diana, the Goddess Who Hunts Alone,* a semi-autobiographical novel that follows a love affair between an unnamed, married Mexican novelist and an American film actress, Diana Soren. The fictional romance, however, contains obvious parallels to the author's real-life affair with film actress Jean Seberg. Mirroring actual events surrounding the liaison between Fuentes and Seberg, the writer meets Soren at a New Year's Eve party in 1969 and follows her to a Santiago film location where they enjoy a passionate, albeit brief, relationship. After several months of literary conversation and tenuous intimacy, the self-absorbed writer is abandoned by the unstable actress, who maintains a second relationship via telephone with a Black Panther, and keeps a photograph of her last lover, Clint Eastwood, by her bed.

Though the book received mixed reviews, Rosanne Daryl Thomas observed in Chicago's *Tribune Books* that the novel reveals "the tensions between imagination, language and reality, between generosity born of love and the profound selfishness often found in artists." Thomas concluded, "Carlos Fuentes takes off the mask of literary creation and reveals a man nakedly possessed by a desperate passion. Then he

raises the mask to his face and tells a fascinating, frightening tale of heartbreak."

While Fuentes's innovative use of theme and structure has gained the author an international reputation as a novelist, he believes that only since *Terra Nostra* has he perfected his craft. "I feel I'm beginning to write the novels I've always wanted to write and didn't know how to write before," he explained to Philip Bennett in a *Boston Globe Magazine* interview. "There were the novels of youth based on energy, and conceptions derived from energy. Now I have the conceptions I had as a young man, but I can develop them and give them their full value."

Fuentes delivered a narrative history of twentieth-century Mexico and insightful commentary on his country's past in *The Years with Laura Díaz.* The novel turns on the life story of Laura Díaz, a woman whose passionate nature and dramatic love life place her close to many of the key people and events in recent Mexican history. The story is narrated by Laura's grandson, who has traveled to Detroit to photograph murals by Diego Rivera—paintings that feature Laura's image. As Laura's story unfolds for readers, her interactions provide a way for Fuentes to present discourses on political subjects such as the opposition between fascism and communism. "Fuentes's emotional commitment to his subject shows in the lucidity of the book's underlying intellectual dialogues," commented a *Publishers Weekly* reviewer, who added that the author animates his commentary "with a learned lyricism that should make this volume one of his most admired and memorable." Some reviewers voiced reservations about *The Years with Laura Díaz,* finding the book overburdened with social discourse and reflection. Richard Eder, writing in the *New York Times Book Review,* noted that the heroine was "not much more than an effigy." While acknowledging that the author "writes well of places, ideas, confrontations," Eder felt that "it is characters that defeat him." Emiliana Sandoval, a writer for *Knight-Ridder/Tribune News Service,* described Laura as frequently "maddeningly opaque, just a pair of eyes through which we look at Mexico." But while warning that *The Years with Laura Díaz* is "not light reading," Sandoval ultimately recommended it as "evocative and absorbing." And *Library Journal* contributor Jack Shreve stated, "this fictionalized memoir brilliantly recaptures the turbulent and exciting history of twentieth-century Mexico. . . . This roman fleuve of a novel can hardly fail to entertain and enlighten."

Describing his writing method to Caleb Bach for *Americas*, Fuentes said, "I work from seven to noon, when I go out on my walk. By then I feel I've said what I want to say and am at peace with myself. I am a Calvinist! That's my rhythm, I go right on through the weekend. When I get tired after three or four weeks, I go off on vacation to the beach, read novels, walk, see other things." Bach commented, "Any reader who has entered the Fuentian realm never fails to be astounded by the spectacular somersaults he makes through time and space, audacious games he plays with fact and fiction, the precarious balancing act he performs."

Part of the genius of Fuentes is his involvement in different worlds and his ability to bring them together. He does not separate art from politics. Officially he was Mexico's ambassador to France in the seventies, but his works have always taken on the role of ambassador as well. Fuentes continued to meditate on Mexico in many of the essays found in *En esto creo*, published in 2002 and in 2003 with the novel *La silla del águila*. These books use different genres, but both discuss Mexico's growing pains and its place in the world. In an article for *Financial Times*, John Authers and Sara Silver characterized *La silla del águila* as a "devastatingly accurate futuristic novel of politics," adding that "Fuentes' idea was to use a thriller set in the future to warn about the present. But he worries that his fantasies could turn into prophesies." These worries are not without merit, since some of his visions from *Cristóbal Nonato*, published in 1989, were quite accurate.

BIOGRAPHICAL AND CRITICAL SOURCES:

BOOKS

Authors in the News, Volume 2, Gale (Detroit, MI), 1976.

Brushwood, John S., *Mexico in Its Novel: A Nation's Search for Identity*, University of Texas Press (Austin, TX), 1966.

Conde Ortega, José Francisco and Arturo Trejo, editors, *Carlos Fuentes: 40 años de escritor*, Universidad Autónoma Metropolitana (Mexico City, Mexico), 1993.

Contemporary Literary Criticism, Gale (Detroit, MI), Volume 3, 1975, Volume 8, 1978, Volume 10, 1979, Volume 13, 1980, Volume 22, 1982, Volume 41, 1987, Volume 60, 1991.

Dictionary of Hispanic Biography, Gale (Detroit, MI), 1996.

Dictionary of Literary Biography, Volume 113: *Modern Latin American Fiction Writers, First Series*, Gale (Detroit, MI), 1992.

Donoso, José, *The Boom in Spanish American Literature: A Personal History*, Columbia University Press (New York, NY), 1977.

Encyclopedia of World Biography, second edition, seventeen volumes, Gale (Detroit, MI), 1998.

Faris, Wendy B., *Carlos Fuentes*, Frederick Ungar (New York, NY), 1983.

Feijoo, Gladys, *Lo fantástico en los relatos de Carlos Fuentes: aproximación teórica*, Senda Nueva de Ediciones (New York, NY), 1985.

García-Gutiérrez, Georgina, editor, *Carlos Fuentes desde la crítica*, Universidad Nacional Autónoma de México (Mexico City, Mexico), 2001.

García Núñez, Fernando, *Fabulación de la fe: Carlos Fuentes*, Universidad Veracruzana (Xalapa, Mexico), 1989.

González, Alfonso, *Carlos Fuentes; Life, Work, and Criticism*, York Press (Fredericton, New Brunswick, Canada), 1987.

Helmuth, Chalene, *The Postmodern Fuentes*, Associated University Press (Cranbury, NJ), 1997.

Herández de López, Ana María, *La obra de Carlos Fuentes: una visíòn múltiple*, Pliegos (Madrid, Spain), 1988.

Hispanic Literature Criticism, Gale (Detroit, MI), 1994.

Ibsen, Kristine, *Author, Text, and Reader in the Novels of Carlos Fuentes*, P. Lang (New York, NY), 1993.

Lindstrom, Naomi, *Twentieth-Century Spanish American Fiction*, University of Texas Press (Austin, TX), 1994.

Ordiz, Francisco Javier, *El mito en la obra de Carlos Fuentes*, Universidad de León (León, Spain), 1987.

Plimpton, George, editor, *Writers at Work: The Paris Review Interviews, Sixth Series*, Penguin, 1984.

Short Story Criticism, Volume 24, Gale (Detroit, MI), 1997.

Van Delden, Maarten, *Carlos Fuentes, Mexico and Modernity*, Vanderbilt University Press (Nashville, TN), 1998.

Williams, Raymond Leslie, *The Writings of Carlos Fuentes*, University of Texas Press (Austin, TX), 1996.

World Literature Criticism, Gale (Detroit, MI), 1992.

PERIODICALS

Americas (English edition), April, 2000, Caleb Bach, "Time to Imagine," p. 22; January-February 2002, Barbara Mujica, review of *Instinto de Inez,* p. 62.

Antioch Review, winter, 1998, review of *A New Time for Mexico,* p. 114.

Book, May-June 2002, Beth Kephart, review of *Inez,* p. 77.

Booklist, September 1, 2000, Veronica Scrol, review of *The Years with Laura Díaz,* p. 6; November 1, 2000, Brad Hooper, review of *The Vintage Book of Latin American Short Stories,* p. 519; April 1, 2002, Donna Seaman, review of *Inez,* p. 1283.

Boston Globe Magazine, September 9, 1984.

Financial Times, July 1, 2004, John Authers and Sara Silver, "A visionary approach: Mexican writer and democrat Carlos Fuentes' cautionary writing has a knack of predicting his country's political future," p. 26.

Foreign Policy, March-April, 2004, Christopher Dominguez Michael, "Mexico's former future," pp. 84-85.

Hispania, May, 1978.

Hispanic, June, 1998, review of *The Crystal Frontier,* p. 70.

Journal of Latin American Studies, Amit Thakkar, review of *Juan Rulfo's Mexico,* pp. 393-394.

Kirkus Reviews, April 15, 1996, p. 575; September 1, 1997, review of *The Crystal Frontier,* p. 1328; April 1, 2002, review of *Inez,* p. 441.

Knight-Ridder/Tribune News Service, November 15, 2000, Emiliana Sandoval, review of *The Years with Laura Díaz,* p. K24.

Library Journal, January, 1994, p. 96; January, 1995, p. 77; January, 1996, p. 81; May 1, 1996, p. 112; August, 1997, review of *The Crystal Frontier,* p. 137; July, 1999, review of *Los Años con Laura Díaz,* p. 76; October 1, 2000, Jack Shreve, review of *The Years with Laura Díaz,* p. 147; August, 2001, David Garza, review of *Instinto de Inez,* p. S33, Isabel Cuadrado, review of *Los cinco soles de México: Memoria de un milenio,* p. S48; May 15, 2002, Barbara Hoffert, review of *Inez,* p. 124.

London Review of Books, May 10, 1990, p. 26.

Los Angeles Times Book Review, April 10, 1994, p. 6; October 26, 1997, review of *The Crystal Frontier,* p. 9; December 14, 1997, review of *The Crystal Frontier,* p. 4.

Nation, February 17, 1992, p. 205.

New Perspectives, spring, 1994, p. 54.

New Statesman, August 26, 1994, p. 37; September 29, 1995, p. 57; July 17, 1998, review of *The Crystal Frontier,* p. 46.

Newsweek, November 1, 1976.

Newsweek International, May 17, 2004, Scott Johnson "Carlos Fuentes: A Tropical Stalinism," p. 72.

New Yorker, March 4, 1961; January 26, 1981; February 24, 1986; November 3, 1997, review of *The Crystal Frontier,* p. 109.

New York Review of Books, June 11, 1964.

New York Times Book Review, November 7, 1976; October 19, 1980; October 27, 1985, Earl Shorris, review of *The Old Gringo,* p. 1; October 6, 1991, p. 3; April 26, 1992, p. 9; October 22, 1995, p. 12; October 26, 1997, review of *The Crystal Frontier,* p. 20; December 7, 1997, review of *The Crystal Frontier,* p. 60; December 20, 1998, review of *The Crystal Frontier,* p. 28; November 12, 2000, Richard Eder, review of *The Years with Laura Díaz,* p. 8.

Observer (London, England), April 1, 1990, p. 67; November 28, 1999, review of *The Picador Book of Latin American Stories,* p. 14.

Paris Review, winter, 1981.

Publishers Weekly, April 15, 1996, p. 55; August 11, 1997, review of *The Crystal Frontier,* p. 381; November 10, 1997, review of *A New Time for Mexico,* p. 71; September 18, 2000, review of *The Years with Laura Díaz,* p. 85; November 6, 2000, "December Publications," p. 72; May 6, 2002, review of *Inez,* p. 35.

Review, winter, 1976.

Review of Contemporary Fiction, spring, 2001, Steve Tomasula, review of *The Years with Laura Díaz,* p. 191; fall, 2002, Christopher Paddock, review of *Inez,* p. 165.

Saturday Review, October 30, 1976.

School Library Journal, September, 2001, David Garza, "Inez's Instinct," p. 533; June, 2003, Bruce Jensen, review of *The Seat of Power,* p. SS36.

Time, June 29, 1992, p. 78.

Time for Kids, September 20, 2001, Ronald Buchanan, "Telling Mexico's story: Author Carlos Fuentes shares his unique view of Mexico with the world through his books, plays, stories and essays," p. 6.

Times Literary Supplement, June 10, 1994, p. 23; September 29, 1995, p. 27; February 20, 1998, review of *A New Time for Mexico,* p. 27; June 5, 1998, review of *The Crystal Frontier,* p. 24.

Translation Review Supplement, July, 1997, review of *A New Time for Mexico,* p. 14, review of *Diana: The Goddess Who Hunts Alone,* p. 38.

Tribune Books (Chicago, IL), April 19, 1992; April 11, 1994, p. 6; December 17, 1995, p. 3.

Village Voice, January 28, 1981; April 1, 1986.

Washington Post, May 5, 1988.

Washington Post Book World, October 26, 1976; January 14, 1979; March 29, 1992; October 19, 1997, review of *The Crystal Frontier: A Novel in Nine Stories,* p. 1.

World Literature Today, autumn, 1994, p. 794; spring, 1997, review of *La Frontera de Cristal,* p. 354.

ONLINE

Center for Book Culture Web site, http://www.centerfor bookculture.org/ (August 2, 2004), Debra A. Castillo, "Travailing Time: An Interview with Carlos Fuentes."

Librynth Web site, http://www.themodernworld.com (August 2, 2004), biography of Carlos Fuentes.

Mexico Connect Web site, http://www.mexconnect. com (1999), Jim Tuck, "Rebel, Internationalist, Establishmentarian: The Meadering Road of Carlos Fuentes."

Speakers Worldwide Web site, http://www.speakers worldwide.com (2000), biography of Carlos Fuentes.*

G

GARCIA-AGUILERA, Carolina 1949-

PERSONAL: Born July 13, 1949, in Havana, Cuba; immigrated to United States, 1959; daughter of Carlos Garcia-Beltran (an agricultural engineer) and Lourdes Aguilera de Garcia; divorced; remarried; children: Sara, Antonia, Gabriella. *Ethnicity:* "Hispanic (Cuban)." *Education:* Rollins College, B.A. (history and political science), 1971; attended Georgetown University, 1971; University of South Florida, M.B.A. (finance), 1983; completed coursework toward Ph.D. (Latin American affairs), University of Miami. *Religion:* Roman Catholic.

ADDRESSES: Home—1030 14th St., Miami Beach, FL 33139. *Agent*—Elizabeth Ziemska, c/o Nicholas Ellison, Inc., 55 Fifth Ave., New York, NY 10003. *E-mail*—4cubans@bellsouth.net.

CAREER: Private investigator and mystery novelist. C & J Investigations (private investigative firm), Miami, FL, president, 1986—; novelist, 1995—.

MEMBER: International Association of Crime Writers, Amnesty International (member of board), PEN American Center, Mystery Writers of America, Private-Eye Writers of America, Sisters in Crime, Authors Guild.

WRITINGS:

"LUPE SOLANO" MYSTERY NOVELS

Bloody Waters, Putnam (New York, NY), 1996.
Bloody Shame, Putnam (New York, NY), 1997.
Bloody Secrets, Putnam (New York, NY), 1998.
A Miracle in Paradise, Putnam (New York, NY), 1999.
Havana Heat, Morrow (New York, NY), 2000.
Bitter Sugar, Morrow (New York, NY), 2001.

OTHER

One Hot Summer, Rayo (New York, NY), 2002.
Luck of the Draw, Rayo (New York, NY), 2003.

Contributor to an anthology of Florida mystery writers, 1999.

SIDELIGHTS: Born in Cuba, novelist Carolina Garcia-Aguilera and her family immigrated to the United States in 1959, one year after Fidel Castro gained power over their homeland. The family lived in Palm Beach, Florida, for two years before finally settling in New York City. Early on in her life, Garcia-Aguilera was fascinated by detective literature, beginning with Nancy Drew novels she read as a child, and dreamed of one day writing her own mystery stories.

Garcia-Aguilera made a serious step toward making her dream a reality when, having moved to Miami, she applied for a State of Florida license to start a detective agency, with the goal of one day being able to write about private investigating with first-hand knowledge. While working as a private investigator, Garcia-Aguilera gained invaluable experience and a rich knowledge of the field. In 1996, Garcia published *Bloody Waters,* the first in her series of novels featuring Cuban-American detective Lupe Solano.

Set in Miami, *Bloody Waters* finds Lupe Solano investigating an illegal adoption business in which Cuban-born children are placed with Cuban families in Miami. Garcia-Aguilera's premier novel received favorable reviews, with most critics mentioning that the author's experience in investigative work and first-hand knowledge of Cuba and Cubans lends authenticity to the book. Writing in the *Christian Science Monitor*, for example, Amelia Newcomb deemed *Bloody Waters* a "lively and engaging read," and observed that "Garcia-Aguilera's experience gives *Bloody Waters* its air of authenticity." In another account, Catherine Crohan, writing in *Multicultural Review*, remarked that "Cuba becomes as much of a character as any of the people," and assessed *Bloody Waters* "a well-written detective novel."

Garcia-Aguilera's second "Lupe Solano" novel, *Bloody Shame*, was also well received. In this novel, Lupe is working to clear her client, a jeweler who has been charged with second-degree murder in the death of a man, Gustav Gaston. The jeweler, Alonso Arango, insists he killed the man in self-defense, but his story is uncorroborated by the evidence the police have gathered. While investigating the incident, Lupe experiences her own tragedy—her best friend is killed in a car accident. As Lupe digs deeper into the jeweler's case, however, she realizes there is a connection between Gaston's murder and her friend's death. Lupe then works to uncover the truth. *Bloody Shame* was applauded by reviewers, among them Harriet Klausner, who wrote in *Armchair Detective*, "With this second book the author goes one step further by giving her mystery a literary framework. This makes for a much more exciting and entertaining whodunit which provides a first-hand, insider look into the Cuban-American South Florida culture."

Garcia-Aguilera's third "Lupe Solano" mystery, *Bloody Secrets*, is again set in Miami. The story concerns Lupe's investigation of the prominent and respected de la Torre family, at the request of a Cuban refugee, Luis Delgado. Delgado claims the de la Torre family grew rich in America with money that belonged to Delgado's father. Critics again praised Garcia-Aguilera's ability to spin a mystery story, among them a *Publishers Weekly* critic who opined, "With sharp-edged characters and some profound probing of moral ambiguities, the latest Lupe Solano tale is suspenseful, provocative and satisfying."

A Miracle in Paradise, the fourth novel in the "Lupe Solano" series, ends the pattern of "bloody" titles.

This novel sends Lupe on an investigation into the Catholic Church and Cuban customs, where she explores the miracle of Virgin at Ermita de la Caridad, a holy statue that has been rumored to cry over the separation of her people in Cuba and the United States on October 10, Cuban Independence Day. Lupe must investigate the suspicious activities of a group of Yugoslavian nuns and seek the truth behind the "miracle." The "engaging plot" and "fiery heroine armed with sharp insights into Cuban and Catholic ways will lead readers into the sultry heat of Little Havana," observed a *Publisher's Weekly* reviewer.

In *Havana Heat*, Lupe Solano accepts three different cases regarding valuable Cuban art only to learn that all three cases are connected. Lupe must try to locate a famed unicorn tapestry, attempt to smuggle several Cuban paintings, and search for a stolen piece of Cuban art. Critics praised the novel's plot and inclusion of art history. Wrote *Booklist*'s Jenny McLarin, "Garcia-Aguilera combines a clever plot and an endearing protagonist with a fascinating portrayal of Cuba's turbulent history and vibrant culture." *Library Journal* reviewer Rex Klett deemed *Havana Heat* "a stunning mixture of art history" and "Cubans-in-exile politics," and described Lupe as "a uniquely classy Miami heroine."

Lupe investigates foreigners interested in purchasing unprofitable sugar mills in Cuba from her father's best friend, Ramone, in *Bitter Sugar*. When Ramone's nephew, co-owner of the sugar mills, ends up dead, Lupe's investigation escalates and the killings continue, with Lupe herself nearly indicted for murder. A *Kirkus Reviews* critic felt *Bitter Sugar*'s plot was not as coherent as Garcia-Aguilera's other novels, concluding, "Relentlessly glamorous meals, cars, outfits, and supporting characters can't hide the threadbare plotting in Lupe's sixth case, whose complications are still getting phoned in seconds before the fadeout." However, *Booklist*'s Carrie Bissey felt that "Lupe cracks the case with style and a sense of humor—and teaches readers a bit about Cuba in the process."

In an interview published on *Voices from the Gaps* Web site, Garcia-Aguilera confesses that she often thinks and acts like a man. "As a private investigator for the last eight years, I've worked in a field dominated by men. The men I've worked with, as well as the men I've been involved with, have always tried to ascertain who is the real Lupe Solano. Eventually they all discover that I have two sides: a gentle, feminine veneer that I display when I need to, and the ruthless heart and soul of a man underneath," she explained.

Garcia-Aguilera left behind the "Lupe Solano" series to pen her next two books, *One Hot Summer* and *Luck of the Draw*. *One Hot Summer* is Garcia-Aguilera's first attempt at a romantic novel. The book finds Margarita, the partner of a law firm, debating whether to return to her law practice or remain at home with her young son. Margarita begins an extramarital affair with her former college boyfriend, further complicating her situation. When Margarita learns she is pregnant, she is unsure if her baby's father is her husband or her lover. *One Hot Summer* was met with harsh reviews. *Library Journal* critic Samantha Gust maintained that the book had "unbelievable plotting," and a *Kirkus Reviews* contributor considered the novel "a tawdry romantic comedy about family and adultery among the upper echelons of Miami's expatriate Cuban community."

Garcia-Aguilera's *Luck of the Draw* was much better received. Señora Navarro dreams of resurrecting her family's casino, La Estrella, but to do so, she needs all of her daughters together. Esmerelda, Sapphire, Ruby, and Quartz are all available to help their mother, but the youngest sister, Diamond, a reporter in Las Vegas, is missing. Esmerelda journeys to Sin City in search of her sister, and finds herself tangled in a deadly mystery. A *Publishers Weekly* reviewer observed that *Luck of the Draw* had "plenty of twists and turns," and was "skillfully written and plotted." *Booklist* critic Mary Frances Wilkes commented, "Garcia-Aguilera . . . writes with both authenticity and style," and dubbed the book, "an entertaining romp."

BIOGRAPHICAL AND CRITICAL SOURCES:

PERIODICALS

Armchair Detective, spring, 1997, pp. 239-240.
Booklist, August, 2000, Jenny McLarin, review of *Havana Heat,* p. 2119; October 1, 2001, Carrie Bissey, review of *Bitter Sugar,* p. 301; May 1, 2003, Mary Frances Wilkens, review of *Luck of the Draw,* p. 1544.
Chicago Tribune Books, February 2, 1997, p. 4.

Christian Science Monitor, July 25, 1996.
Kirkus Reviews, September 1, 1999, review of *A Miracle in Paradise,* p. 1347; September 15, 2001, review of *Bitter Sugar,* p. 1326; May 1, 2002, review of *One Hot Summer,* p. 596.
Library Journal, September 1, 2000, Rex Klett, review of *Havana Heat,* p. 254; November 1, 2001, Rex Klett, review of *Bitter Sugar,* p. 136; May 15, 2002, Samantha J. Gust, review of *One Hot Summer,* p. 124; June 15, 2003, Amy Brozio-Andrews, review of *Luck of the Draw,* p. 100.
Multicultural Review, December, 1996.
New York Times, July 21, 2002, Mirta Ojito, "A Private Eye Prowls Little Havana," p. ST6.
New York Times Book Review, December 9, 2001, Marilyn Stasio, review of *Bitter Sugar,* p. 29.
Publishers Weekly, December 30, 1996, p. 58; December 8, 1997, p. 58; September 20, 1999, review of *A Miracle in Paradise,* p. 78; September 4, 2000, review of *Havana Heat,* p. 89; September 17, 2001, review of *Bitter Sugar,* p. 57; April 29, 2002, review of *One Hot Summer,* p. 41; May 26, 2003, review of *Luck of the Draw,* p. 44.
School Library Journal, December, 2002, Carmen Ospina, review of *Aguas Sangrientas (Bloody Waters),* p. S36.

ONLINE

Voices from the Gaps: Women Writers of Color Web site, http://www.voices.cla.umn.edu/ (March 15, 2003), "Carolina Garcia-Aguilera."*

*   *   *

GERDY, John R. 1957-

PERSONAL: Born January 25, 1957, in Paterson, NJ; married E. Follin Smith, December 22, 1989; children: Wallace, James. *Ethnicity:* "White." *Education:* Davidson College, B.A., 1979; Ohio University, M.A., 1983, Ph.D., 1986. *Hobbies and other interests:* Music.

ADDRESSES: Home and office—409 Sickman Mill Rd., Conestoga, PA 17516. *E-mail*—jrg331234@aol.com.

CAREER: National Collegiate Athletic Association, Overland Park, KS, legislative assistant, 1986-89, associate commissioner of Southeastern Conference, Birmingham, AL, 1989-95. Ohio University, visiting professor of sports administration.

WRITINGS:

The Successful College Athletic Program: The New Standard, Oryx (Phoenix, AZ), 1997.

(Editor and contributor) *Sports in School: The Future of an Institution,* Teachers College Press (New York, NY), 2000.

Sports: The All-American Addiction, University Press of Mississippi (Jackson, MS), 2002.

BIOGRAPHICAL AND CRITICAL SOURCES:

PERIODICALS

Black Issues in Higher Education, April 26, 2001, Karen A. Celestan, review of *Sports in School: The Future of an Institution,* p. 56.

Choice, September, 2001, review of *Sports in School,* p. 160; October, 2002, R. McGehee, review of *Sports: The All-American Addiction,* p. 316.

Publishers Weekly, February 18, 2002, review of *Sports,* p. 85.

Reference and Research Book News, February, 2002, review of *The Successful College Athletic Program: The New Standard,* p. 64.

Sociology of Sport Journal, December, 2000, Michael Sagas, review of *The Successful College Athletic Program,* p. 423.

*   *   *

GOULD, Lewis L(udlow) 1939-

PERSONAL: Born September 21, 1939, in New York, NY; son of John Ludlow (a journalist) and Carmen (Lewis) Gould; married Karen D. Keel (an art historian and author), October 24, 1970. *Education:* Brown University, A.B., 1961; Yale University, M.A., 1962, Ph.D. (history), 1966. *Politics:* Democrat.

ADDRESSES: Home—2602 La Ronde, Austin, TX 78731-5924. *Office*—Department of History, University of Texas, Austin, TX 78712.

CAREER: Yale University, New Haven, CT, instructor, 1965-66, assistant professor of history, 1966-67; University of Texas—Austin, assistant professor, 1967-

71, associate professor, 1971-76, professor of history, 1976-83, Eugene C. Barker Centennial Professor of American history, 1983-98, professor emeritus, 1998—, chairman of history department, 1980-84.

MEMBER: Organization of American Historians, American Historical Association, Southern Historical Association, Phi Beta Kappa.

AWARDS, HONORS: Carr P. Collins Prize, Texas Institute of Letters, 1973, for *Progressives and Prohibitionists;* Young Humanist fellowship, National Endowment for the Humanities, 1974-75.

WRITINGS:

Wyoming: A Political History, 1868-1896, Yale University Press (New Haven, CT), 1968.

(Editor, with James C. Curtis) *The Black Experience in America: Selected Essays,* University of Texas Press (College Station, TX), 1970.

Progressives and Prohibitionists: Texas Democrats in the Wilson Era, University of Texas Press (College Station, TX), 1973.

(Editor and contributor) *The Progressive Era,* Syracuse University Press (Syracuse, NY), 1974.

(With Richard Greffe) *Photojournalist: The Career of Jimmy Hare,* University of Texas Press (College Station, TX), 1977.

Reform and Regulation: American Politics, 1900-1916, Wiley (New York, NY), 1978, third edition published as *Reform and Regulation: American Politics from Roosevelt to Wilson,* Waveland Press (Prospect Heights, IL), 1996.

Reform Politics to the Depression (sound recording), Everett/Edwards (De Land, FL), 1979.

The Presidency of William McKinley, Regents Press of Kansas (Lawrence, KS), 1980.

The Spanish-American War and President McKinley, University Press of Kansas (Lawrence, KS), 1982.

Lady Bird Johnson and the Environment, University Press of Kansas (Lawrence, KS), 1988.

(With Craig H. Roell) *William McKinley: A Bibliography,* Meckler (Westport, CT), 1988.

Wyoming, from Territory to Statehood, High Plains Publishing (Worland, WY), 1989.

The Presidency of Theodore Roosevelt, University Press of Kansas (Lawrence, KS), 1991.

Progressives and Prohibitionists: Texas Democrats in the Wilson Era, Texas State Historical Association (Austin, TX), 1992.

1968: The Election That Changed America, Ivan R. Dee (Chicago, IL), 1993.

(Editor) *American First Ladies: Their Lives and Their Legacy,* Garland (New York, NY), 1996, second edition, Routledge (New York, NY), 2001.

(With Nancy Beck Young) *Texas, Her Texas: The Life and Times of Frances Goff,* Texas State Historical Association (Austin, TX), 1997.

(Editor, with Katherine J. Adams) *Inside the Natchez Trace Collection: New Sources for Southern History,* Louisiana State University Press (Baton Rogue, LA), 1999.

Lady Bird Johnson: Our Environmental First Lady, University Press of Kansas (Lawrence, KS), 1999.

America in the Progressive Era, 1890-1914, Longman (New York, NY), 2001.

(Editor) Jack Gould, *Watching Television Come of Age: The New York Times Reviews,* University of Texas Press (Austin, TX), 2002.

The Modern American Presidency, University Press of Kansas (Lawrence, KS), 2003.

Grand Old Party: A History of the Republicans, Random House (New York, NY), 2003.

SIDELIGHTS: Historian Lewis L. Gould has specialized in the history of American politics. His books have often focused on the American presidency, as well as First Ladies of the White House. In many cases Gould's books have contradicted conventional wisdom to offer a fresh historical viewpoint on his subject. For example, in his *1968: The Election That Changed America,* he maintains that Robert Kennedy, even if he had survived his assassin's bullet, did not pose a great threat to Richard Nixon's candidacy. Furthermore, the historian asserts that it was not the Vietnam War so much that determined the outcome of the race as it was the candidates'—Nixon, George Wallace, and Hubert Humphrey—position on race issues. To prove his point, Gould dug up information from previously unpublished papers at the Lyndon B. Johnson library to create what a *Publishers Weekly* reviewer called an "engrossing analysis" of the election. Nevertheless, *Historian* critic Robert S. La Forte complained that Gould "does not use voting statistics or public opinion polls to support" some of his arguments, and that, at times, his "statements . . . indirectly contradict his thesis." The reviewer concluded that the 1968 election was, indeed, a turning point in American politics, but not necessarily for the reasons Gould points out.

In addition to books with more narrow focuses, such as *1968* and his analyses of individual presidents like McKinley and Roosevelt, Gould has written broad histories of American politics. In *The Modern American Presidency,* for example, the historian covers the administrations of William McKinley through George W. Bush. His main thesis in tracing the evolution of the presidential office is that the head of state's responsibilities have become so broad over the years that it is nearly impossible for any one person to carry out the leadership role effectively, especially as the president has become more of a national symbol of the country. Gould also criticizes the cult of celebrity that has caused presidents to spend increasingly large amounts of time and energy campaigning for reelection, rather than focusing on their executive responsibilities. In a *Perspectives on Political Science* review of the book, R. E. Dewhirst noted that Gould's discussion of the Clinton presidency is particularly worthwhile, and observed that the "well-written narrative" would suit general readers. *Booklist* reviewer Jay Freeman concluded that "This is a valuable and provocative examination of the office and the men who have strived to be effective in it."

More recently, Gould completed a history of the Republican party in *Grand Old Party: A History of the Republicans,* tracing changes in the party's philosophy from Abraham Lincoln to the Reagan era. A *Library Journal* contributor called the beginning and ending of the book "engaging," but felt that the middle chapters made it an "uneven read" overall. In *New York Times,* Douglas Brinkley described the work as a "smart, sprawling, highly readable survey of the Republican Party from its origins in 1854 to George W. Bush" that is "surprisingly chock full of factoids . . . that will delight readers who embrace political history as a trivia sport." Gould notes, for example, that in the mid-1800s Republicans believed that the wealthy should pay higher income taxes than the poor, and that between 1940 and 1960 the Republican Party supported the Equal Rights Amendment.

Gould has received positive reviews for his studies of individuals in history. His *The Presidency of Theodore Roosevelt,* for one, in which he covers the accomplishments and failings of Roosevelt during the years 1901 to 1909, was praised as a "balanced, scholarly assessment" by a *Publishers Weekly* reviewer. Critics also enjoyed Gould's *Lady Bird Johnson: Our Environmental First Lady.* Here, the historian reveals how under-appreciated the former First Lady's efforts at environmentalism were because they were labeled as "beautification" initiatives, thus feminizing the issue and making it appear unimportant to the media and public at the time. "Gould's book is a very good introduction to the accomplishments of a woman whose modest demeanor and tenure during turbulent times has eclipsed her contributions to the role of First Lady and to the American environment," concluded June Sochen in *Journal of Southern History.*

As editor of *American First Ladies: Their Lives and Their Legacy,* Gould has also helped to bring more attention to the role presidents' wives have played in American politics. Although other books have been written on the subject, this up-to-date collection of short biographies is more thorough, according to reviewers, covering Laura Bush and Hillary Rodham Clinton. "This work provides the researcher with a thorough understanding of the role these women played in our country's history," asserted a *Booklist* critic.

BIOGRAPHICAL AND CRITICAL SOURCES:

PERIODICALS

Annals of the American Academy of Political and Social Science, May, 1983, review of *The Presidency of William McKinley,* p. 173.
Booklist, March 1, 1993, Gilbert Taylor, review of *1968: The Election That Changed America,* p. 1137; August, 1996, review of *American First Ladies: Their Lives and Legacy,* p. 1920; March 1, 2002, Mary Ellen Quinn, review of *American First Ladies,* second edition, p. 1170; April 15, 2003, Jay Freeman, review of *The Modern American Presidency,* p. 1444; September 15, 2003, Mary Carroll, review of *Grand Old Party: A History of the Republicans,* p. 184.
Book Report, January-February, 1997, Carol Fox, review of *American First Ladies,* p. 42.
Historian, winter, 1994, Robert S. La Forte, review of *1968,* p. 426.
Journal of American History, March, 1992, Evan Anders, review of *The Presidency of Theodore Roosevelt,* p. 1475; September, 1999, Dorothy D.

DeMoss, review of *Texas, Her Texas: The Life and Times of Frances Goff,* p. 860; December, 2000, Leah Rawls Atkins, review of *Inside the Natchez Trace Collection: New Sources for the Southern History,* p. 1035.
Journal of Southern History, August, 1989, Suellen Hoy, review of *Lady Bird Johnson and the Environment,* p. 523; November, 1992, Richard H. Collin, review of *The Presidency of Theodore Roosevelt,* p. 737; August, 1994, Myron I. Scholnick, review of *1968,* p. 621; November, 1998, Nancy Baker Jones, review of *Texas, Her Texas,* p. 774; November, 2001, June Sochen, review of *Lady Bird Johnson: Our Environmental First Lady,* p. 905.
Library Journal, March 15, 1993, Frank Kessler, review of *1968,* p. 91; April 1, 2003, Michael A. Genovese, review of *The Modern American Presidency,* p. 112; October 1, 2003, Grant A. Fredericksen, review of *Grand Old Party,* p. 99.
New York Times, November 12, 2003, Douglas Brinkley, "Republican Evolution, from Lincoln to Reagan," p. E7.
New York Times Book Review, July 24, 1988, Grady Clay, review of *Lady Bird Johnson and the Environment,* p. 14.
Perspectives on Political Science, summer, 2003, R. E. Dewhirst, review of *The Modern American Presidency,* p. 167.
Publishers Weekly, November 9, 1990, Genevieve Stuttaford, review of *The Presidency of Theodore Roosevelt,* p. 52; February 1, 1993, review of *1968,* p. 81.
School Library Journal, August, 1996, Linda A. Vretos, review of *American First Ladies,* p. 186.*

*   *   *

GRANDIN, Temple 1947-

PERSONAL: Born August 29, 1947, in Boston, MA; daughter of Richard McCurdy (a real estate agent) and Eustacia (a writer, singer, and actress; maiden name, Purves) Grandin. *Education:* Franklin Pierce College, B.A. (with honors), 1970; Arizona State University, M.S., 1975; University of Illinois—Urbana, Ph.D., 1989. *Politics:* Republican. *Religion:* Episcopalian. *Hobbies and other interests:* Star Trek.

ADDRESSES: Office—Department of Animal Science, Colorado State University, Fort Collins, CO 80523. *E-mail*—cmiller@ceres.agsci.colostate.edu.

CAREER: Arizona *Farmer Ranchman,* Phoenix, livestock editor, 1973-78; Corral Industries, Phoenix, equipment designer, 1974-75; Grandin Livestock Handline Systems, founder and consultant, 1975—; Colorado State University, Fort Collins, began as lecturer, became assistant professor of animal science, 1990—. Livestock Conservation Institute, Madison, WI, chair of handling committee, 1976-95; American Meat Institute, member of animal welfare committee, 1991—. Wood Gush Memorial Lecturer, International Society of Applied Ethology, 2001.

MEMBER: Autism Society of America (member of board of directors, 1988-92), American Society of Animal Science, American Society of Agricultural Consultants (member of board of directors, 1981-83), American Society of Agricultural Engineers, American Meat Institute (supplier member), American Registry of Professional Animal Scientists, National Institute of Animal Agriculture.

AWARDS, HONORS: Meritorious Service award, Livestock Conservation Institute, 1986; distinguished alumni award, Franklin Pierce College, 1989; Trammel Crow Award, Autism Society of America, 1989; named One of Processing Stars, National Provisioner, 1990; Industry Innovator's Award, *Meat Marketing and Technology* magazine, 1994; Golden Key award, National Honor Society, 1994; Industry Advancement Award, American Meat Institute, 1995; Animal Management Award, American Society of Animal Science, 1995; Harry Rowsell Award, Scientists' Center for Animal Welfare, 1995; Brownlee Award, Animal Welfare Foundation (Vancouver, Canada), 1995; Forbes Award, National Meat Association, 1998; Geraldine R. Dodge Foundation grant, 1998; named Woman of the Year in Service to Agriculture, *Progressive Farmer* magazine; Humane Award, American Veterinary Medical Association, 1999; honorary doctorate, McGill University, 1999; Industry Influential designation, *Meat Marketing and Technology,* 1999; Founders Award, American Society for the Prevention of Cruelty to Animals, 1999; Joseph Wood Krutch Medal, Humane Society of the United States, 2001; Knowlton Award for Innovation, *Meat Marketing and Technology,* 2001.

WRITINGS:

(With Margaret M. Scariano) *Emergence: Labeled Autistic* (autobiography), Arena Press (Novato, CA), 1986, Warner Books (New York, NY), 1996.

(Editor and contributor) *Livestock Handling and Transport,* CAB International (Wallingford, England), 1993, 2nd edition, CABI (New York, NY), 2000.

Thinking in Pictures, and Other Reports from My Life with Autism (autobiography), foreword by Oliver Sacks, Doubleday (New York, NY), 1995.

(Editor) *Genetics and the Behavior of Domestic Animals,* Academic Press (San Diego, CA), 1998.

(Author of commentary) Norm Ledgin, *Diagnosing Jefferson: Evidence of a Condition That Guided His Beliefs, Behavior, and Personal Association,* Future Horizons, 2000.

(Author of foreword) Michael D. Powers, editor, *Children with Autism: A Parents' Guide,* Woodbine House, 2000.

(With Kate Duffy) *Developing Talents: Careers for Individuals with Asperger Syndrome and High-Functioning Autism,* Austism Asperger (Shawnee Mission, KS), 2004.

(With Catherine Johnson) *Animals in Translation: Using the Mysteries of Autism to Decode Animal Behavior,* Scribner (New York, NY), 2005.

Also author of *Recommended Animal Handling Guidelines for Meat Packers;* coauthor of Food Industry Animal Welfare Report, 2002. Contributor to *Animal Welfare and Meat Science,* CABI (New York, NY), 1998; contributor of articles to periodicals and professional journals, including *Journal of Child and Adolescent Psychopharmacology, Meat and Poultry, Journal of Animal Science, Applied Animal Behavior Science, Journal of the American Veterinary Medical Association, Veterinary Medicine, Agri-Practice, Zoo Biology,* and *Beef.*

SIDELIGHTS: Highly accomplished inventor and animal scientist Temple Grandin has designed numerous pieces of livestock-handling equipment that provide for the humane treatment of livestock on farms and in slaughterhouses. Her inventions are used worldwide by farmers and meat packers, and in 2002 it was estimated that more than half of the cattle in North America were prepared for market through use of her "Stairway to Heaven" system of stress-free slaughter. What is remarkable about Grandin, other than the fact that she is an award-winning innovator in a male-dominated field, is that she has lived with autism since birth and has found ways to succeed not despite of it, but because of it. Her autobiographies *Emergence: Labeled Autistic,* which she wrote with

Margaret M. Scariano, and *Thinking in Pictures: And Other Reports from My Life with Autism* chronicle her life and shed light on the autistic mind. Grandin's other publications—more than 300 journal articles and several books—deal with livestock behavior and livestock facility design.

Diagnosed as autistic at the age of two and a half, Grandin, like many autistic children, hated to be held, and she would stiffen her body to fend off her mother's hugs; she shunned others, preferring solitude, and was given to fits of rage; she also was limited in her verbal skills and was easily startled by noise and keenly aware of odors. Fortunately, however, she was surrounded by nurturing parents, aunts, and teachers who devoted themselves to her instruction. Her mother enrolled her in private schools and coached her in reading while encouraging the girl's creativity and imagination.

As she grew older, Grandin's verbal skills improved, but she exhibited the obsessive behavior often exhibited by autistics, behavior she found tormenting. She became easily fixated, for example, on rotating objects. She once heard a minister quote the biblical passage: "I am the door: by me if any man enter in, he shall be saved," and from then on the literal-minded Grandin sought out special doors. Her penchant for doors brought her much-needed peace; when she found them, they led to places of comfort for her troubled mind. The author describes her chronic anxiety level as akin to that of a person being mugged in an urban subway.

One summer, while visiting her aunt's cattle ranch, Grandin experienced something that would determine her life's work. Grandin was fascinated by the squeeze chute that was used to hold animals still while they were inoculated. Desiring hugs, but fearful of the pain caused her by human touch, she tried out the machine on herself, while her aunt manned the controls. Grandin found this mechanical hug exhilarating and relaxing. She subsequently designed a similar machine for herself, which she keeps in her home to provide stimulation and relaxation. Schools and institutes for autistic children have since implemented Grandin's squeeze chute in their treatment programs. The machine has also proven beneficial to children with other anomalies, such as hyperactivity.

Grandin's experience in the squeeze machine also gave her insight into the way animals feel, for they, also, live in a visual world and retreat from human touch.

Such insights into the animals she has observed have caused her to feel most at home when with cattle and to become one of the foremost developers of gentle livestock-handling equipment. All of her designs are intended to lessen fear in animals and minimize their pain, and Grandin has been instrumental in the development of improved, animal-friendly dip-vats, stockyards, research laboratories, ramps at slaughter plants, and slaughter techniques, as well as numerous other products or methods dealing with cattle. Such industry giants as McDonald's and Burger King seek out her expertise, and even more remarkably, she has been cited for her work on animal welfare by People for the Ethical Treatment of Animals. *Forbes* contributor Ann Marsh declared: "Thanks to Temple Grandin, meat-eaters can be fairly certain the animals they consume met a placid death. . . . That one person—a woman—has won over so many players in the independenly managed and very male meat-processing industry is remarkable."

Grandin's accomplishments and autism are documented in her autobiographies. *Emergence* seeks to promote understanding of autism and its disturbing symptoms—especially the autistic's tendency to avoid touch—and describes Grandin's joy at her discovery of the squeeze machine. Commenting in *Psychology Today,* Paul Chance praised *Emergence,* writing that Grandin "has provided us with a fascinating look at autism from the inside."

Unlike *Emergence,* Grandin wrote *Thinking in Pictures* without the assistance of a professional writer, thus giving readers greater insight into her thought patterns. As the title indicates, *Thinking in Pictures* focuses greatly on the author's ability to visualize, which has resulted in her success as a livestock facility designer. Grandin's explanations of her visual techniques fascinated reviewer Stacey D'Erasmo, who wrote in *Voice Literary Supplement:* "Grandin has replaced the teleology of autobiography with something much closer to her heart: a diagram, in this case a diagram of her own mind. Slowly and patiently she explains it, taking care to be thorough: this is how it works, this is what caused how it works, here is the research, there are the consequences. She is a sober and literal architect. . . . Her great gift, as the title of her book suggests, is her ability to visualize, to think in pictures."

Grandin has achieved a remarkable renown for someone in her line of work. She is the subject of a documentary film, and a feature film about her life was planned by Home Box Office. *Time* magazine featured her in a cover story about autism in 2002. Since so few people with autism can effectively articulate what they feel and experience, Grandin's candid view of her situation has helped scholars studying the disorder. She has not been satisfied just to speak about autism, however, but is engaged in new projects and research. When asked for her advice to other functioning autistic persons, Grandin told the *Harvard Brain* online: "People respect talent. Make yourself so good at something that people will hire you to do it. It has to be something there's a need for."

BIOGRAPHICAL AND CRITICAL SOURCES:

BOOKS

Grandin, Temple, and Margaret M. Scariano, *Emergence: Labeled Autistic* (autobiography), Arena Press (Novato, CA), 1986, Warner Books (New York, NY), 1996.

Grandin, Temple, *Thinking in Pictures and Other Reports from My Life with Autism* (autobiography), foreword by Oliver Sacks, Doubleday (New York, NY), 1995.

Sacks, Oliver W., *An Anthropologist on Mars: Seven Paradoxical Tales,* Knopf (New York, NY), 1995.

PERIODICALS

Booklist, October 15, 1995, p. 374.
Canadian Veterinary Journal, August, 1995.
Daily Variety, March 13, 2002, Melissa Grego, "Animal Magnetism at HBO," p. 1.
Denver Post, March 1, 2000, "CSU Prof Gets Star Treatment," p. F1; July 21, 2002, "Austistic Prof Helps Improve Livestock's Lot," p. B1.
Feedstuffs, February 21, 2000, "Animal Handling in Packing Plants Shows Improvement," p. 10.
Forbes, July 6, 1998, Ann Marsh, "A Kinder, Gentler Abattoir: Thanks to Temple Grandin, Meat-Eaters Can Be Fairly Certain the Animals They Consume Meet a Placid Death," p. 86.
Journal of the American Veterinary Medical Association, Volume 205, no. 3, 1994, p. 463.
Library Journal, May 15, 1986, p. 71.
Los Angeles Times Book Review, May 4, 1986, p. 4.

New Scientist, December 23-30, 1995, pp. 70-71; June 2, 2001, Jon Copley, "Raging Bull," p. 16.
New Yorker, December 27, 1993, pp. 106-125.
Psychology Today, November, 1986, p. 86.
Publishers Weekly, October 30, 1995, p. 55.
Resource, July, 2002, "Temple Grandin," p. 20; August, 2002, "Animal Temperament and Bone Size Linked," p. 3.
Seattle Times, September 24, 2000, "Scientist Wins Respect from All Sides," p. A11.
Time, May 6, 2002, "Inside the World of Autism."
U.S. News and World Report, May 27, 1996, Joseph P. Shapiro, "Beyond the Rain Man: A Singular Woman Changes the Cattle Industry and Our Image of Autism," p. 78.
Voice Literary Supplement, November, 1995, p. 13.
Washington Times, November 26, 1995, p. 37.

ONLINE

Harvard Brain Online, http://hcs.harvard.edu/ (March 21, 2000), interview with Grandin.
Temple Grandin Web site, http://www.grandin.com/ (November 10, 2003).*

*   *   *

GRANT, Neil 1938-
(David Mountfield)

PERSONAL: Born June 9, 1938, in United Kingdom; son of Alastair and Margaret (Sims) Grant. *Education:* St. Johns College, Cambridge, B.A., 1961.

ADDRESSES: Home—Middlesex, England. *Office*—c/o Author Mail, McGraw-Hill Children's/Peter Bedrick Books, 8787 Orion Place, 4th Fl., Columbus, OH 43240.

CAREER: Author. *American People Encyclopedia,* New York, NY, associate editor, 1962-67.

WRITINGS:

Benjamin Disraeli: Prime Minister Extraordinary, F. Watts (London, England), 1969.
Charles V: Holy Roman Emperor, F. Watts (London, England), 1970.

Victoria: Queen and Empress, F. Watts (London, England), 1970.

English Explorers of North America, Messner (New York, NY), 1970.

The Renaissance: A First Book, F. Watts (New York, NY), 1971.

Munich, 1938: Appeasement Fails to Bring Peace for Our Time, F. Watts (London, England), 1971.

Cathedrals: A First Book, F. Watts (London, England), 1972.

Guilds: A First Book, F. Watts (London, England), 1972.

The Easter Rising: Dublin, 1916, F. Watts (London, England), 1972.

The Industrial Revolution, F. Watts (London, England), 1973.

The Partition of Palestine, 1947: Jewish Triumph, British Failure, Arab Disaster, F. Watts (London, England), 1973.

The New World Held Promise: Why England Colonized North America, Messner (New York, NY), 1974.

(Under pseudonym David Mountfield) *A History of Polar Exploration,* Dial (New York, NY), 1974.

(Under pseudonym David Mountfield) *A History of African Exploration,* Domus Books, 1977.

Diamonds: Myth, Magic, and Reality, Bonanza Books (New York, NY), 1980.

Life in the Rainforest, Rourke Enterprises (Vero Beach, FL), 1987.

Atlas of the World Today, Harper & Row (New York, NY), 1987.

United Kingdom, Silver Burdett Press (Englewood Cliffs, NJ), 1988.

Ireland, Silver Burdett Press (Englewood Cliffs, NJ), 1989.

Village London, Past and Present, Pyramid Books (London, England), 1990.

Heroes of World War II, Steck-Vaughn (Austin, TX), 1990.

James Dean in His Own Words, Hamlyn (London, England), 1991.

Marilyn: In Her Own Words, Hamlyn (London, England), 1991.

The Great Atlas of Discovery: A Pictorial Atlas of World Exploration, Knopf (New York, NY), 1992.

Chronicle of Twentieth-Century Conflict, Smithmark Publishers (New York, NY), 1993.

The Egyptians, Oxford University Press (New York, NY), 1996.

People and Places, Gareth Stevens (Milwaukee, WI), 1997.

The Vikings, Oxford University Press (New York, NY), 1998.

Hamlyn History: Literature, Hamlyn (London, England), 1998.

Eric the Red: The Viking Adventurer, Oxford University Press (New York, NY), 1998.

Scottish Clans and Tartans, Lyons Press (New York, NY), 2000.

Oxford Children's History of the World, Oxford University Press (New York, NY), 2000.

History of Theatre, Sterling Publishing (New York, NY), 2002.

Everyday Life of the Celts, illustrated by Manuela Cappon, Smart Apple Media (North Mankato, MN), 2003.

Everyday Life in Medieval Europe, Smart Apple Media (North Mankato, MN), 2003.

Everyday Life in Ancient Rome, Smart Apple Media (North Mankato, MN), 2003.

The Atlas of the Renaissance World, Peter Bedrick Books (Columbus, OH), 2003.

SIDELIGHTS: Neil Grant is the author of several historical nonfiction works, among them the *Oxford Children's History of the World, History of Theatre,* and *Everyday Life of the Celts.* Many of Grant's works are geared toward children, to be used as educational tools. "Clearly and succinctly written," according to Susan Shaver of *School Library Journal,* the *Oxford Children's History of the World* is an encyclopedia that "captures the essence of historical time periods in an easy-to-follow format."

In his *History of Theatre* Grant provides readers with a brief, yet informative glimpse into the history of world theatre, including varying cultural traditions and similarly related arts. Laura A. Ewald, in a review for *Library Journal,* stated that "Grant's analysis includes a mixture of literary, archaeological, and historical evidence, and his metaphorical prose provides a pleasurable and insightful discussion of theatre in a social context."

Included as part of the "Uncovering History" series, Grant's *Everyday Life of the Celts* provides younger readers with an informative look at one of the world's most intriguing cultures. The topics discussed range from clothing and household responsibilities to more complex social relationships involving religion and social customs. While the book's generalized approach was questioned by some critics, *Everyday Life of the Celts* nonetheless answers the basic questions of those American readers who are less-than-familiar with this ancient British culture.

BIOGRAPHICAL AND CRITICAL SOURCES:

PERIODICALS

Booklist, September, 1996, Cynthia Sturgis, review of *The Egyptians,* p. 214; December 1, 1998, April Judge, review of *The Vikings,* p. 663.
Library Journal, June 15, 2002, Laura A. Ewald, review of *History of Theatre,* p. 68.
Publishers Weekly, April 12, 1993, review of *Chronicle of Twentieth-Century Conflict,* p. 56.
School Library Journal, December, 1998, Eunice Weech, review of *Eric the Red,* p. 102; May, 2001, Susan Shaver, review of *Oxford Children's History of the World,* p. 86; February, 2004, Lynda S. Poling, review of *Everyday Life of the Celts,* p. 164.*

*   *   *

GRAVES, John (Alexander III) 1920-

PERSONAL: Born August 6, 1920, in Fort Worth, TX; son of John Alexander and Nancy (Kay) Graves; married Jane Marshall Cole, 1958; children: Helen, Sally. *Education:* Rice University, B.A., 1942; Columbia University, M.A., 1948. *Hobbies and other interests:* Natural history, the outdoors.

ADDRESSES: Home—P.O. Box 667, Glen Rose, TX 76043.

CAREER: Freelance writer. University of Texas—Austin, Austin, instructor in English, 1948-50; Texas Christian University, Fort Worth, adjunct professor of English, 1958-65; U.S. Department of Interior, Washington, DC, writer and consultant, 1965-68. *Military service:* U.S. Marine Corps, 1941-45; became captain; received Purple Heart.

MEMBER: PEN, Nature Conservancy, Audubon Society, Texas Institute of Letters (president, 1984), Phi Beta Kappa.

AWARDS, HONORS: Texas Institute of Letters, Collins Award, 1961, for *Goodbye to a River: A Narrative,* and Barbara McCombs/Lon Tinkle Memorial Award, 1983; Guggenheim fellow, 1963; Rockefeller fellow, 1972; Parkman Prize, Texas Institute of Letters, 1974, for *Hard Scrabble: Observations on a Patch of Land;* Distinguished Alumni Award, Rice University, 1983; D.Litt., Texas Christian University, 1983; Bookend Award, Texas Book Festival, 2000.

WRITINGS:

Home Place: A Background Sketch in Support of a Proposed Restoration of Pioneer Building in Fort Worth, Texas, Pioneer Texas Heritage Committee (Fort Worth, TX), 1958.
Goodbye to a River: A Narrative (first volume of "Brazos" trilogy), Alfred A. Knopf (New York, NY), 1960.
The Creek and the City: Urban Pressures on a Natural Stream, Rock Creek Park and Metropolitan Washington, Department of the Interior (Washington, DC), 1967.
The Nation's River, U.S. Government Printing Office (Washington, DC), 1968.
(With Robert Boyle and T. H. Watkins) *The Water Hustlers,* Sierra Club (San Francisco, CA), 1971, revised edition, 1973.
(With others) *Growing Up in Texas,* Encino Press (Austin, TX), 1972.
Hard Scrabble: Observations on a Patch of Land (second volume of "Brazos" trilogy), Alfred A. Knopf (New York, NY), 1974, reprinted with new introduction by Rick Bass and new afterword by the author, Southern Methodist University Press (Dallas, TX), 2002.
The Last Running, Encino Press (Austin, TX), 1974, published as *The Last Running: A Story,* illustrated by John Groth, Lyons & Burford (New York, NY), 1990.
(With Jim Bones, Jr.) *Texas Heartland: A Hill Country Year,* Texas A & M University Press (College Station, TX), 1975.
(Editor, with John Walsh) *The River Styx, Salt Spring Cave System,* Texas Cave Report Series (San Antonio, TX), 1976.
From a Limestone Ledge: Some Essays and Other Ruminations about Country Life in Texas (third volume of "Brazos" trilogy), Alfred A. Knopf (New York, NY), 1980.

(Editor) Gail W. Starr, *Mall,* Envision Communications of Albany (Albany, NY), 1980.

(With others) *The American Southwest, Cradle of Literary Art,* Southwest Texas State University (San Marcos, TX), 1981.

Blue and Some Other Dogs, Encino Press (Austin, TX), 1981.

A John Graves Reader, University of Texas Press (Austin, TX), 1996.

John Graves and the Making of Goodbye to a River: Selected Letters, 1957-1960, edited by Dave Hamrick, Taylor Wilson Publishing, 2000.

Texas Rivers, photographs by Wyman Meinzer, Texas Parks and Wildlife Press (Austin, TX), 2002.

Texas Hill Country (essay), photographs by Wyman Meinzer, University of Texas Press (Austin, TX), 2003.

Myself and Strangers: A Memoir of Apprenticeship, Alfred A. Knopf (New York, NY), 2004.

Work represented in anthologies, including *Prize Stories: The O. Henry Awards,* 1955 and 1962; *The Best American Short Stories, 1960,* Houghton Mifflin (Boston, MA), 1960; and *Of Birds and Texas,* illustrated by Stuart Gentling and Scott Gentling, Gentling Editions (Fort Worth, TX), 1986, revised edition, University of Texas Press (Austin, TX), 2002. Author of introduction, *Landscapes of Texas,* Texas A & M University Press (College Station, TX), 1980. Contributor to numerous magazines, including *Holiday* and *Texas Monthly.*

Collections of Graves's manuscripts are housed at the Humanities Research Center, University of Texas—Austin, and Southwest Texas State University.

SIDELIGHTS: A native Texan naturalist, John Graves writes primarily of his home state and of his experiences as the owner of Hard Scrabble Ranch, 400 acres of arid land near Fort Worth. He is best known for a trio of books called the "Brazos" trilogy: *Goodbye to a River: A Narrative, Hard Scrabble: Observations on a Patch of Land,* and *From a Limestone Ledge: Some Essays and Other Ruminations about Country Life in Texas.*

Goodbye to a River began as a magazine article for *Holiday* magazine, about a canoe trip the author took down the Brazos River. It is the third largest river in Texas and the largest between the Red River and the Rio Grande. Graves was inspired to take the trip in 1957, after learning that the Brazos was scheduled to be dammed by the federal government. After completing his magazine piece, Graves had so much material left over that he put together a book. It is, according to *Dictionary of Literary Biography Yearbook* contributor Timothy Dow Adams, "part autobiography, part history, part philosophy, and part woodlore, loosely tied to the erratic but steady flow of John Graves's canoe down twists of the river through both yellow-blue and rain-ruined November days and on into December snow and freezing northers." Adams deemed Graves's writing style "highly polished and literate, reflecting the wide variety of influence alluded to in chapter headings and in the body of the book itself, writers such as Thoreau, Yeats, Shakespeare, Thorstein Veblen, George Herbert, and the author of *Sir Gawain and the Green Knight.*" Adams added, however, that "for all his literary ancestors, Graves's style is peculiarly his own, his syntax characterized by rhythmic stops and starts, like a boat caught momentarily on an obstruction in the current, now catching and spinning backward, now speeding downstream."

Despite the highly favorable critical response to *Goodbye to a River,* more than a decade passed before Graves's next major book appeared. According to a reviewer in the *Atlantic Monthly, Hard Scrabble,* a book of essays, is "a rumination tinctured with [Graves's] love of history, his inquisitiveness about his neighbors, and his shrewd knowledge of the natural world." A *New Yorker* critic found that Graves's subjects, which include everything from "hired help [to] armadillos, . . . come to us reshaped and reenlivened by his agreeably individual . . . notions." Edward Hoagland called the book "galloping" and "spontaneous" in the *New York Times Book Review* and pointed out that "what the best [naturalists], like Graves, do have . . . and what can give their books exceptional staying power, is a tone that suits the book . . . a life, a grace, an impetus [that] is lent to their efforts" by their unique perspective.

In the third part of the "Brazos" trilogy, *From a Limestone Ledge,* Graves presents essays previously printed in *Texas Monthly* magazine. Many of these function as sequels to subjects introduced in *Hard Scrabble.* Referring to *From a Limestone Ledge,* Susan Wood of the *Washington Post* said that Graves "writes about Texas and Texans with full attention to the complex peculiarities that distinguish the region; but because he so lovingly particularizes, rather than generalizes, his thoughts come to us in larger terms, made universal by the art of language and feeling. Although permeated with a sense of place, Graves's writing translates Texas as though it were Anywhere." Bill Marvel, reviewing the book in the *Detroit News,* reported that the "ruminative essay on country life is a tradition in American letters, . . . and it is [here] that John Graves's *From a Limestone Ledge* takes its place."

Adams commented: "John Graves has outgrown his strong regional identification and emerged as an important American writer in the naturalist mode. To the list of recent writers such as Edward Hoagland, Annie Dillard, Noel Perrin, John McPhee, and Wendell Berry, who have inherited that particularly American combination of autobiography-natural history-philosophy handed down from Thoreau and William Bartram through Louis Bromfield, Joseph Wood Krutch, and John Muir, the name of John Graves should be added."

BIOGRAPHICAL AND CRITICAL SOURCES:

BOOKS

Bennett, Patrick, *Talking with Texas Writers: Twelve Interviews,* Texas A & M University Press (College Station, TX), 1981, pp. 63-88.
Dictionary of Literary Biography Yearbook: 1983, Gale (Detroit, MI), 1984.
Grover, Dorys Crow, *John Graves,* Boise State University (Boise, ID), 1989.
Twentieth-Century Western Writers, 2nd edition, St. James Press (Chicago, IL), 1991, essay by Timothy Dow Adams.

PERIODICALS

Atlantic Monthly, August, 1974, review of *Hard Scrabble: Observations on a Patch of Land.*
Detroit News, January 25, 1981, Bill Marvel, review of *From a Limestone Ledge: Some Essays and Other Ruminations about Country Life in Texas.*
Houston Chronicle, August 18, 2002, Wyman Meinzer, "Six Rivers in Three Years: Scenic Views of Six Texas Waterways Explored by Photographer Wyman Meinzer, Accompanied by Writer John Graves," p. 8.

Library Journal, November 15, 2002, Gregg Sapp, review of *Texas Rivers,* p. 97.
New Yorker, August 19, 1974, review of *Hard Scrabble;* December 29, 1980.
New York Times Book Review, May 19, 1974, Edward Hoagland, review of *Hard Scrabble.*
Texas Monthly, November, 2000, review of *John Graves and the Making of Goodbye to a River: Selected Letters, 1957-1960,* p. 122.
Washington Post, December 27, 1980, Susan Wood, review of *From a Limestone Ledge.**

*   *   *

GRAY, Spalding 1941-2004

PERSONAL: Born June 5, 1941, in Providence, RI; died, January, 2004, in New York, NY; son of Rockwell (a factory employee) and Margeret Elizabeth (a homemaker; maiden name, Horton) Gray; married Renee Shafransky (a writer and stage director), August, 1991 (divorced); married Kathleen Russo; children: three. *Education:* Emerson College, B.A., 1965.

CAREER: Actor and writer. Actor in Cape Cod, MA, and Saratoga, NY, 1965-67; actor with Alley Theater, Houston, TX, 1967; actor with Performance Group (experimental theater company), New York, NY, 1967-79; cofounder of Wooster Group (theater company), New York, NY, 1977; writer, beginning 1979. Actor in summer stock plays, including *The Curious Savage, Long Day's Journey into Night,* and *The Knack;* actor in *The Best Man,* 2000; actor in films, including *The Killing Fields,* 1983, *Swimming to Cambodia,* 1985, *True Stories,* 1987, *Stars and Bars,* 1988, *Clara's Heart,* 1988, *Beaches,* 1989, *Straight Talk,* 1992, *King of the Hill,* 1993, *The Paper,* 1994, *Diabolique,* 1996, *Drunks,* 1997, and *Kate and Leopold,* 2001. Visiting instructor at University of California, Santa Cruz, summer, 1978, and at Columbia University, 1985; artist-in-residence at Mark Taper Forum, Los Angeles, CA, 1986-87.

AWARDS, HONORS: Grants from National Endowment for the Arts, 1978, Rockefeller Foundation, 1979, and Edward Albee Foundation, 1985; fellowships from National Endowment for the Arts, 1978, and Rockefeller Foundation, 1979; Guggenheim fellowship, 1985; Obie Award, *Village Voice,* 1985, for *Swimming to Cambodia.*

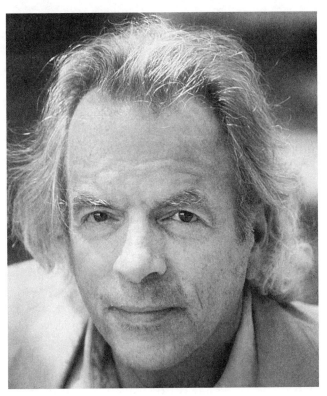

Spalding Gray

WRITINGS:

DRAMATIC MONOLOGUES

Sex and Death to the Age 14 (also see below), produced off-Broadway, 1979.

Booze, Cars, and College Girls (also see below) produced off-Broadway, 1979.

India (and After), produced off-Broadway, 1979.

A Personal History of the American Theatre, produced off-Broadway, 1980.

(With Randal Levenson) *In Search of the Monkey Girl* (produced off-Broadway, 1981), Aperture Press (New York, NY), 1982.

Swimming to Cambodia (produced off-Broadway, 1985; also see below), Theatre Communications Group (New York, NY), 1985.

Sex and Death to the Age 14 (collection; includes *Booze, Cars, and College Girls*), Random House (New York, NY), 1986.

Travels through New England, produced off-Broadway, 1986.

Terrors of Pleasure, produced in New York, NY, at Lincoln Center, 1986.

Swimming to Cambodia: The Collected Works of Spalding Gray (includes *Sex and Death to the Age 14, Booze, Cars, and College Girls, Forty-seven Beds,*

Nobody Wanted to Sit behind a Desk, Travels through New England, and *Terrors of Pleasure*), Picador (New York, NY), 1987.

Monster in a Box (produced in New York, NY, at Lincoln Center, 1990), Vintage (New York, NY), 1992.

Gray's Anatomy (produced in New York, NY, 1993), Vintage (New York, NY), 1994.

It's a Slippery Slope (produced in New York, NY, at Lincoln Center, 1996), Noonday Press (New York, NY), 1997.

Morning, Noon, and Night (produced in Chicago, IL, 1999), Farrar, Straus & Giroux (New York, NY), 1999.

Contributor of *Rivkala's Ring* (based on Anton Chekhov's short story "A Witch"; produced in Chicago, IL, 1986, as part of a production titled *Orchards*), to *Orchards* (anthology), Knopf (New York, NY), 1986.

OTHER

(With Elizabeth LeCompte) *Sakonnet Point* (one-act play), produced off-Broadway, 1975.

(With Elizabeth LeCompte) *Rumstick Road* (one-act play), produced off-Broadway, 1977.

(With Elizabeth LeCompte) *Nyatt School* (one-act play), produced off-Broadway, 1978.

(With Elizabeth LeCompte) *Three Places in Rhode Island* (play trilogy; includes *Sakonnet Point, Rumstick Road,* and *Nyatt School*), produced off-Broadway, 1979.

Point Judith (one-act play; epilogue to *Three Places in Rhode Island*), produced off-Broadway, 1979.

Seven Scenes from a Family Album (short stories), Benzene Press, 1981.

Impossible Vacation (novel), Knopf (New York, NY), 1992.

Also producer of improvisations, including "Interviewing the Audience," 1981, and "Art in the Anchorage," 1985. Contributor of articles to drama journals and periodicals, including *Elle, Rolling Stone, Gentleman's Quarterly, Performing Arts Journal,* and *Drama Review.*

ADAPTATIONS: Several of Gray's performances of *Swimming to Cambodia* were adapted by director Jonathan Demme for the 1987 film of the same title, with music by Laurie Anderson; *Terrors of Pleasure* was filmed as an HBO Comedy Special; *Monster in a Box* was released as a film by Fine Line Features in 1992, with music by Laurie Anderson; *Gray's Anatomy* was directed by Steven Soderberg and filmed in 1997.

SIDELIGHTS: Dubbed "our bard of self-absorption" by *Nation* critic Laurie Stone, actor and performance artist Spalding Gray was known for his critically acclaimed autobiographical dramatic monologues in which he drew upon some of the most intimate areas of his personal history in order to produce observant, humorous, and insightful stories of contemporary life. "Recycling negative experience is one of the things the monologues are about," Gray once explained to Don Shewey in the *New York Times.* "I go out and digest what could be disturbing situations and convert them into humor in front of an audience." As Stone further noted, Gray learned to see such self-absorption "with detachment, turning it into a subject, a hot tub big enough for a group soak." Many of these monologues, such as *Swimming to Cambodia, Monster in a Box, Gray's Anatomy, It's a Slippery Slope,* and *Morning, Noon, and Night* were adapted for books and some for popular movies. Writing in *Contemporary Literature,* Gay Brewer noted that Gray's "art is the autobiographic monologue, a composite of reality and artifice." According to Brewer, Gray's works "share adventures achieved in the pursuit of artistic expression and colored by an obsession with the unattainable—life as art, encapsulated and preserved." In 2004 Gray was at work on yet another monologue, "Black Spot," about a near-fatal car accident he had in Ireland, when he died in New York, an apparent suicide.

Born in Rhode Island to middle-class parents, Gray became interested in the theater as a teenager. He studied acting at Emerson College, and after his 1965 graduation he performed for two years in summer stock theater in New England and in New York state. In 1967 he traveled to Texas and Mexico, and upon his return several months later he learned his mother had committed suicide. The loss and subsequent family trauma caused him to suffer a prolonged depression that resulted in a nervous breakdown nine years later. Gray eventually used events from his childhood and college life as well as experiences as a struggling actor as material for his dramas and monologues.

In the late 1960s Gray moved to New York City, where he joined the Performance Group, an experimental off-Broadway theater company. There he composed his first autobiographical dramatic works, and in 1977 he founded the Wooster Group with Elizabeth LeCompte. Also with LeCompte, Gray wrote *Sakonnet Point* and *Rumstick Road,* two experimental dramas which explored his mother's mental illness and suicide and their effects on his youth and on his family, and *Nyatt School,* a satire of poet and dramatist T. S. Eliot's play *The Cocktail Party.* The three plays made up a trilogy titled *Three Places in Rhode Island,* which Gray produced collectively in 1979.

Gray became interested in the dramatic monologue's possibilities during his tenure as a summer workshop instructor at the University of California's Santa Cruz campus in 1978. As related by David Guy in the *New York Times Book Review,* Gray lamented what he foresaw as the demise of white middle-class life to a friend who replied, "During the collapse of Rome the last artists were the chroniclers." Gray consequently decided to "chronicle" his own life orally in dramatic monologue form; the performer felt that writing it down implied a faith in the future that he did not possess. In 1979 Gray performed *Sex and Death to the Age 14,* his first monologue, at SoHo's Performing Garage. This confessional account of Gray's boyhood experiences with family turmoil and sexuality was followed by an examination of his life at college titled *Booze, Cars, and College Girls* and then by *India (and After),* the story of his nervous collapse when he returned from a tour of India in 1976. "I'll never run out of material as long as I live," *Newsweek*'s Cathleen McGuigan quoted the actor describing his work's content. "The only disappointment is that I probably won't be able to come back after I die and tell that experience." After the success of these first monologues, Gray began giving performances across the country.

In the early-1980s Gray used the monologue form to produce *Interviewing the Audience* and *In Search of the Monkey Girl.* In the former Gray elicited stories from audience members, while the latter was the product of a trip that Gray, hoping to generate new material for his monologues, took to interview carnival members and sideshow freaks at the 1981 Tennessee State Fair. The resulting monologue was published as the text of a book of photographs by the same name in 1982. During this time Gray also published his first fictional work, *Seven Scenes from a Family Album,* a book of short, interrelated autobiographical sketches depicting, with satire as well as humor, the sexual tensions and complex emotional relationships in a suburban family.

Publicity from Gray's one-man performances resulted in his being cast as an American ambassador's aide in the 1983 feature film *The Killing Fields,* the story of the friendship between an American correspondent and his Asian assistant during the 1970s war in Cambodia. The two months Gray spent filming on location in Thailand became the subject of his next effort, *Swimming to Cambodia,* considered by many critics to be his masterpiece. The monologue premiered in 1985 and evolved improvisationally at New York City's Performing Garage. Gray, who performed the monologue sitting at a desk with only a glass of water, a notebook, and two maps of Southeast Asia as props, narrated anecdotes and observations from several levels of his own experience—as an individual coping with personal problems, as a professional actor in a large-scale movie production, as an American facing the aftermath of U.S. policy in Cambodia since the Vietnam War, and as a human being learning of the atrocities committed by the Khmer Rouge, a guerrilla group that terrorized the country in 1975. The monologue takes its title, as quoted by Janet Maslin in the *New York Times,* from Gray's remark in the piece that "explaining the upheaval in that country 'would be a task equal to swimming there from New York.'"

Swimming to Cambodia met with an enthusiastic reception. Critics admired the pace and fluidity of Gray's narrative, the numerous descriptive details in his recollections, and the honesty with which he presented his stories. "What really makes [*Swimming to Cambodia*] work is its shifting frames of reference, as Gray contracts and expands his point of view to move from meticulously described immediate experience to a detached global-historical vision," assessed Dave Kehr in the *Chicago Tribune. New York Times* writer Mel Gussow was similarly impressed, asserting that Gray's "stream of experience has the zestful, first-hand quality of a letter home from the front." And David Richards, writing for the *Washington Post,* called the actor "an original and disciplined artistic temperament at work," concluding that when Gray is "talking about himself—with candor, humor, imagination and the unfailingly bizarre image—he ends up talking about all of us."

Gray's stage success with *Swimming to Cambodia* inspired him to collaborate with future wife Renee Shafransky on a movie version of the monologue. The film version of *Swimming to Cambodia* was produced by Shafransky, directed by Jonathan Demme, and released in 1987 to widespread critical acclaim. Deemed by Kehr a "documentary on the face and voice of Spalding Gray," the movie was filmed in the Performing Garage and later embellished only with music and a few clips from *The Killing Fields.*

Gray published as well as performed his monologues. *Swimming to Cambodia,* issued in 1985, 1993's *Gray's Anatomy,* and a 1986 collection titled *Sex and Death to the Age 14* are among the transcriptions of Gray's many performances through which the printed form of each monologue evolved. "Almost all of my writing has grown out of speaking it in front of an audience," Gray once explained to *CA.* "Then, after a great number of performances, I take the best tape, get it transcribed, and rework it for print." Critical responses to Gray's monologues in book form, however, have been mixed: some readers, while admiring the author's storytelling ability, have questioned the literary merit of his material. Lisa Zeidner, for instance, wrote in the *New York Times Book Review* that *Swimming to Cambodia* "is surprisingly successful on the page—breezy and theatrical," while *New Statesman* reviewer Nick Kimberley complained that in the writing Gray "simply comes across as a cartoon version of the self-dramatising, all-American alternative culturist. . . . He lazily spews up the world in an endless burble of 'me-me-me.'"

Gray followed the popular *Swimming to Cambodia* with two more monologues: *Terrors of Pleasure,* which premiered at the Lincoln Center for the Performing Arts in New York City in 1986, and *Rivkala's Ring.* The story of Gray's purchase of a dilapidated house in New York's Catskill Mountains and his resultant frustration in learning that the structure's rotting foundations were causing it to sink, *Terrors of Pleasure* was praised by Gussow, who remarked that the "narrative has dramatic cohesiveness as well as comic insight." Gray was also commissioned in 1986 by the Juilliard Theater School's Acting Company to write a theatrical adaptation of a short story by Russian author and dramatist Anton Chekhov for a production called *Orchards.* For the project Gray penned *Rivkala's Ring*—a monologue to be performed by an actor other than Gray in which an insomniac, upon receiving a copy of Chekhov's short story "The Witch" in the mail, begins a winding narrative having little overt connection to the story. Some reviewers found Gray's contribution to the program too far removed from Chekhovian themes, but John Beaufort, in the *Christian Science Monitor,* called the monologue "a windy word-scape, effectively recited." Again Gussow admired Gray's work, describing his contribution to *Orchards* as "a stream of fascinating experience," and concluded that "even more clearly than before, one realizes the extent of Mr. Gray's creativity as dramatist as well as performance artist."

In line with his autobiographical bent, Gray also wrote an autobiographical novel. Titled *Impossible Vacation* and published in 1992, the novel had its genesis in the monologue *Monster in a Box,* which was first performed at New York's Lincoln Center in 1990. The monologue featured "a man who can't write a book about a man who can't take a vacation"; the "monster" of the title refers to the stack of handwritten manuscript pages that multiply—but to no conclusive "The End"—during the monologue's performance. In *Impossible Vacation* that man becomes Brewster North—a thinly disguised Gray—who cannot hold down a job because of his belief that something better is just around the corner, whose emotionally troubled mother eventually commits suicide, and whose own emotional and financial instability occasionally topples him into lulls of depression as well. The continuous frustration of each of North's goals is the lifeblood of the work; while David Montrose commented in the *Times Literary Supplement* that later portions of the novel are "without Gray's usual humour and charm," *Spectator* reviewer Cressida Connolly noted of *Impossible Vacation:* "Its hero spends many years trying to relax, hang out and enjoy life: his failure to do so makes hilarious reading." Meanwhile, *Monster in a Box,* which was a play, book, and movie, continued Gray's rise in the estimation of many critics. For Stanley Kauffmann, writing in the *New Republic,* it showed Gray as "earnestly funny and, above all else, articulate." Others were less impressed. For example, *National Review* critic Joe Queenan failed "to see what all the fuss is about." According to Queenan, Gray seems "not near as funny as the young Woody Allen or even the young Eddie Murphy. He is NPR's idea of what a comic should be: a Bob Newhart who has been to Europe." Lawrence O'Toole, reviewing the same movie for *Entertainment Weekly,* felt that Gray's second film effort lacks the punch of *Swimming to Cambodia.* Stone wrote, "this time self-reference has given way to self-fascination."

Throughout the 1990s Gray continued to mine personal experience and misadventure for his monologues,

including *Gray's Anatomy,* which explores his reactions to and treatment for an eye affliction; *It's a Slipper Slope,* detailing his attempts on skis and the breakup of his marriage when his current girlfriend became pregnant with his baby; and *Morning, Noon, and Night,* a very domestic day-in-the-life of the new Spalding family at their Long Island home. Reviewing the book publication of *Gray's Anatomy,* a critic for *Publishers Weekly* found Gray to be "always entertaining, and sometimes hilarious." Reviewing the movie version, Steve Hayes noted in *American Theatre* that the "film is a visual delight, a creative effort of a talented team." Kauffmann, however, writing in the *New Republic,* viewed the film as "padded," and that both "speaker and director are nervous about the material."

Robert Simonson, writing in *Back Stage,* found the stage version of *It's a Slippery Slope* an "engaging production," while Stone, writing in the *Nation,* was less laudatory in her assessment, complaining that the play is a "scrapbook of [Gray's] narcissism." Still Stone praised Gray's monologue as "bravura stand-up unreeled with grand minimalism." Reviewing the book version of the monologue, *Booklist*'s Benjamin Segedin called it the story of a "midlife crisis" and a "welcome addition to the Gray oeuvre." A reviewer for *Publishers Weekly* noted that the monologue looks at more "commonplace human crises" than Gray's previous works. Here the themes are "adultery, separation, fatherhood." The same *Publishers Weekly* critic concluded that *It's a Slippery Slope* is a "portrait of a man in the painful process of being disabused." *People*'s Jim Brown, however, found less to like, noting that in the book version "the vaunted Gray charm is for the most part lacking. He comes off here as a major worrywart."

Similar mixed reactions greeted both the stage and book versions of Gray's next work, *Morning, Noon, and Night.* Jonathan Abarbanel, writing in *Back Stage,* found the stage version a "day in the domestic life of Gray—horny house husband, homeowner, gardener, yoga master, bicyclist, day sailor, stepdad, and proud papa in his fifties, lover of children and small animals." For Abarbanel "something more affirming has taken hold" in this monologue. Abarbanel described this "something else" as "contentment and joy and living in the moment, rather than pondering the unanswerables." *Variety* critic Chris Jones, however, found the "newly cheery Gray" more suited to "the

Family Channel than Bravo," and opined that Gray "has gone soft and paternal in middle age." Reviewing the book of the monologue, a critic for *Publishers Weekly* described it as a "portrait of the artist as bemused dad," "by turns funny, meditative and self-absorbed." *Booklist*'s Jack Helbig allowed that Gray "remains a gifted storyteller," but also feared that the author/artist's "longtime fans will miss the hilarity of his earlier work."

Gray's domestic bliss suffered a setback with a car accident in Ireland in 2000 in which he was nearly killed. But true to form, he was in the process of turning this misfortune into his twentieth monologue when depression overcame him. He tried to commit suicide by jumping off a bridge but was talked down by a passerby. In January of 2004, he went missing in New York, and several months later his body was found in the East River, an apparent suicide.

BIOGRAPHICAL AND CRITICAL SOURCES:

BOOKS

Contemporary Dramatists, 6th edition, St. James Press (Detroit, MI), 1999.
Contemporary Literary Criticism, Gale (Detroit, MI), Volume 49, 1988, Volume 112, 1999.
Contemporary Theatre, Film, and Television, Gale (Detroit, MI), Volume 7, 1989, Volume 15, 1996, Volume 24, 2000, Volume 49, 2003.

PERIODICALS

American Theatre, November, 1996, Steve Hayes, "Gaze Anatomy," p. 70.
Back Stage, November 29, 1996, Robert Simonson, review of *It's a Slippery Slope,* p. 53; September 17, 1999, Jonathan Abarbanel, review of *Morning, Noon, and Night,* p. 71; March 12, 2004, p. 6.
Booklist, September 1, 1997, Benjamin Segedin, review of *It's a Slippery Slope,* p. 51; August, 1999, Jack Helbig, review of *Morning, Noon, and Night,* p. 1981.
Chicago Tribune, July 9, 1986; April 7, 1987; May 20, 1987.
Christian Science Monitor, April 30, 1986.

Contemporary Literature, summer, 1996, Gay Brewer, "Talking His Way Back to Life: Spalding Gray and the Embodied Voice," p. 23.
Daily Variety, March 9, 2004, p. 1.
Entertainment Weekly, January 29, 1993, Lawrence O'Toole, review of *Monster in a Box,* p. 63; October 1, 1999, Megan Harlan, review of *Morning, Noon, and Night,* p. 70.
Library Journal, July, 1997, Thomas E. Luddy, review of *It's a Slippery Slope,* p. 84; October 1, 1999, Barry X. Miller, review of *Morning, Noon, and Night,* p. 96.
Los Angeles Times, January 15, 1985; January 18, 1985; April 3, 1987; May 20, 1987; January 8, 1988.
Nation, April 18, 1987; December 23, 1996, Laurie Stone, review of *It's a Slippery Slope,* p. 33.
National Review, July 20, 1992, Joe Queenan, review of *Monster in a Box,* p. 43.
New Republic, July 6, 1992, Stanley Kauffmann, review of *Monster in a Box,* p. 26; April 7, 1997, Stanley Kauffmann, review of *Gray's Anatomy,* p. 26.
New Statesman, September 7, 1987.
Newsweek, July 28, 1986.
New York Times, November 16, 1984; March 28, 1986; April 23, 1986; May 11, 1986; May 15, 1986; March 7, 1987; March 13, 1987; March 22, 1987; April 24, 1987; November 11, 1996.
New York Times Book Review, January 12, 1986; May 4, 1986; May 22, 1992; July 12, 1992, pp. 9-10; October 12, 1997.
New York Times Magazine, March 8, 1987.
Observer (London, England), February 15, 1987.
People, October 13, 1997, Jim Brown, review of *It's a Slippery Slope,* p. 36; February 2, 2004, "Without a Trace," p. 86.
Publishers Weekly, January 20, 1992, p. 59; November 22, 1993, review of *Gray's Anatomy,* p. 58; July 7, 1997, review of *It's a Slippery Slope,* p. 56; August 23, 1999, review of *Morning, Noon, and Night,* p. 37; May 13, 2002, John F. Baker, "Spalding Gray and His 'Black Spot,'" p. 24.
Spectator, January 16, 1993, p. 30.
Time, April 27, 1987.
Times (London, England), February 7, 1987.
Times Literary Supplement, January 8, 1993, p. 17.
Variety, September 27, 1999, Chris Jones, review of *Morning, Noon, and Night,* p. 159.
Village Voice, January 27, 1982.
Washington Post, June 2, 1979; April 1, 1985; May 1, 1987.

OBITUARIES

PERIODICALS

American Theatre, July-August, 2004, Eric Bogosian, "Spalding Gray: 1941-2004; The Perfect Moment," p. 22, Mark Russell, *Spalding Gray: 1941-2004; One True Thing at a Time,* p. 23.
Back Stage West, March 11, 2004, p. 2.
Newsweek, March 22, 2004, p. 10.
Variety, March 14, 2004, Robert Hofler, "Gray Was Pithy Speaker," p. 57.
Village Voice, March 17-23, 2004, Mark Russell, "Spalding Gray 1971-2204."

ONLINE

CNN.com, http://www.cnn.com/ (March 9, 2004).
New York Times Online, http://www.nytimes.com/ (March 9, 2004).*

* * *

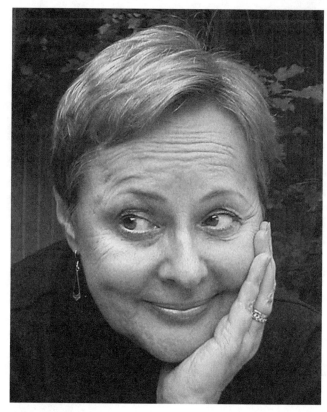

Valiska Gregory

GREGORY, Valiska 1940-

PERSONAL: Born November 3, 1940, in Chicago, IL; daughter of Andrej (a sign painter) and Stephania (a clerk; maiden name, Lascik) Valiska; married Marshall W. Gregory (a university professor), August 18, 1962; children: Melissa, Holly. *Education:* Indiana Central College, B.A. (cum laude), 1962; University of Chicago, M.A., 1966; postgraduate study at Vassar Institute of Publishing and Writing, 1984, and Simmons College Center for the Study of Children's Literature, 1986. *Politics:* Democrat.

ADDRESSES: Home—5300 Grandview Dr., Indianapolis, IN 46228. *Office*—Children's Literature Conference, Butler University, 4600 Sunset Ave., Indianapolis, IN 46228. *Agent*—Tracey Adams, McIntosh & Otis, Inc., 353 Lexington Ave., New York, NY 10016. *E-mail*—vgregory@butler.edu.

CAREER: White Oak Elementary School, Whiting, IN, music and drama teacher, 1962-64; Oak Lawn Memorial High School, Oak Lawn, IL, teacher, 1965-68; University of Wisconsin, Milwaukee, lecturer in English, 1968-74; University of Indianapolis, Indianapolis, IN, adjunct professor of English, 1974-83; Butler University, Indianapolis, adjunct professor of English, 1983-85, fellow at Butler Writers' Studio and founding director of Butler University Midwinter Children's Literature Conference, 1989—, writer-in-residence, 1993—. Speaker/workshop leader at schools, libraries, and conferences across the United States, 1983—.

MEMBER: Authors Guild, Authors League of America, American Association of University Women (creative writers president, 1984-86), Society of Children's Book Writers and Illustrators, National Book Critics Circle, Children's Reading Round Table, Society of Midland Authors.

AWARDS, HONORS: Illinois Wesleyan University Poetry Award, 1982; Billee Murray Denny National Poetry Award honorable mention, 1982; Hudelson Award for Children's Fiction Work-in-Progress, 1982; individual artist master fellowship, Indiana Arts Commission/National Endowment for the Arts, 1986, for artistic excellence and achievements; *Chicago Sun-*

Times Best of the Best selections, 1987, for *The Oatmeal Cookie Giant* and *Riddle Soup;* named State Art Treasure, *Arts Indiana,* 1989, for achievement in poetry and children's fiction; Parents' Choice Award, 1992, for *Through the Mickle Woods;* American Booksellers Association Pick of the List, 1992, for *Through the Mickle Woods,* and 1995, for *Looking for Angels;* Parents' Choice Honor Award, 1993, for *Babysitting for Benjamin;* Cooperative Children's Book Center best book designation, and New York Public Library notable book designation, both for *When Stories Fell like Shooting Stars;* Best Book Gold Award, Oppenheim Institute, for *Shirley's Wonderful Baby.*

WRITINGS:

FOR CHILDREN

Terribly Wonderful, illustrated by Jeni Bassett, Macmillan/Four Winds (New York, NY), 1986.

Sunny Side Up, illustrated by Jeni Bassett, Macmillan/Four Winds (New York, NY), 1986.

Riddle Soup, illustrated by Jeni Bassett, Macmillan/Four Winds (New York, NY), 1987.

The Oatmeal Cookie Giant, illustrated by Jeni Bassett, Macmillan/Four Winds (New York, NY), 1987.

Happy Burpday, Maggie McDougal!, illustrated by Pat Porter, Little, Brown (Boston, MA), 1992.

Through the Mickle Woods, illustrated by Barry Moser, Little, Brown (Boston, MA), 1992.

Babysitting for Benjamin, illustrated by Lynn Munsinger, Little, Brown (Boston, MA), 1993.

Stories from a Time Before, illustrated by Margot Tomes, Open Court (LaSalle, IL), 1995.

Kate's Giants, illustrated by Virginia Austin, Candlewick Press/Walker Books (New York, NY), 1995.

Looking for Angels, illustrated by Leslie Baker, Simon and Schuster (New York, NY), 1996.

When Stories Fell like Shooting Stars, illustrated by Stephano Vitale, Simon and Schuster (New York, NY), 1996.

A Valentine for Norman Noggs, illustrated by Marsha Winborn, HarperCollins (New York, NY), 1999.

Shirley's Wonderful Baby, illustrated by Bruce Degen, HarperCollins (New York, NY), 2002.

The Mystery of the Grindlecat, illustrated by Claire Ewart, Guild Press/Emmis Publishing (Cincinnati, OH), 2003.

Contributor to *On Her Way,* edited by Sandy Asher, Dutton (New York, NY), 2004. Contributor of stories and poems for children to *Cricket.*

OTHER

The Words like Angels Come (poetry for adults), Juniper Press (Bangor, ME), 1987.

Contributor of poetry and articles to periodicals, including *Publishers Weekly, Poetry Northeast, Spoon River,* and *Poet.* Contributor of children's book reviews to *Publishers Weekly.*

Author's poetry and adult book manuscripts are housed in the Juniper Press Collection, Rare Book Room, University of Wisconsin Library.

Author's books have been translated into seven languages.

WORK IN PROGRESS: Heroes, illustrated by Mike Wimmer, for Dutton.

SIDELIGHTS: Beginning her writing career in the mid-1980s, Valiska Gregory has become widely recognized in the children's literature field. Her books *Through the Mickle Woods* and *Babysitting for Benjamin* won Parents' Choice Awards in 1992 and 1993 respectively.

Gregory gained her insights into the world of children's literature from a combination of practical and scholarly experience. She learned to love stories from an early age. "I was lucky enough to grow up in a Czech neighborhood in Chicago where money was scarce but children were treasured, and where, always, my father told us stories," the author once commented. "I received my M.A. degree from the University of Chicago on a Ford Foundation fellowship," she also explained, "and I have taught every grade there is— from kindergarten children to seniors in college, with courses ranging from poetry and drama to music and American literature."

"I don't really choose the stories I write; they have a way of choosing me," Gregory noted. "I have long been fascinated by the creative process: how the experience we call life is woven into the pattern we call fiction. I try to save everything, the way some people save bits of string or pieces of cloth. This saving is important, because one never knows when a particular slant of light or glance of vermillion might be something from which a story grows."

It was an eighteen-pound pet rabbit belonging to her daughters that inspired Gregory's 1993 picture book, *Babysitting for Benjamin.* The book introduces young readers to Ralph and Frances, an old married mouse couple who decide to babysit a rabbit to put some zip back into their lives. They get more than they bargained for when Benjamin wreaks havoc upon their home. By the end of the story, however, Ralph and Frances have found a happy solution to keeping their wits without having to lose Benjamin's frolicsome company. "This wholesome message," praised a *Kirkus Reviews* critic, "is appealingly packaged with amusingly wry dialogue and disarming illustrations."

Another of Gregory's popular creations is *Happy Burpday, Maggie McDougal!,* in which Maggie faces the problem of getting her friend Bonkers a nice birthday present when she has no money. Cynthia, her snooty classmate, has spent tons of cash on a present, and Maggie is stumped at what to do until she finds some treasures in her grandmother's attic that Bonkers ends up liking more than Cynthia's gift. While *School Library Journal* contributor Maggie McEwen was uncomfortable with the coincidence that Maggie happens to find valuable issues of Bonkers' favorite comic book in the attic, she praised the "vivid images and neat turns of phrase"—especially the "delightfully funny" scenes portraying teacher Ms. Chumley's efforts to instruct Maggie's class—and concludes that the book is a "satisfying" work for "beginning chapter book readers."

Through the Mickle Woods is a much more serious work for Gregory; it has its genesis in a difficult time in the author's life and, as she once explained, "wove together all I had learned about despair and the healing power of love." The story tells of a king and his grief over his dying queen. Her last request to him is that he go into the "dark and mickle woods" and find a mysterious bear. When the king finds the bear, the animal turns out to be a wise creature whose stories about beauty and life eventually console the king. "The language and phrasing are as pleasing to the ear as the story is to the heart," declared *Horn Book* critic Elizabeth S. Watson.

Kate's Giants tells of a little girl who imagines terrible monsters in the darkness of her bedroom at night. Told by her parents that since she can think these monsters into existence, she can also think them away, Kate takes this a step further when she imagines friendly creatures into existence by story's end. "Inspiring self-reliance, this inventive story is just the ticket for children afflicted by a bogeyman," commented a critic in *Publishers Weekly.* "Even the youngest will appreciate Kate's imagined bears and giants," Linda Ward-Callaghan added of Gregory's work in *Booklist.*

In *A Valentine for Norman Noggs* Gregory recounts the story of young Norman, a hamster who loves Wilhelmina. But Norman is bullied by two larger boy hamsters who threaten to tear up the homemade valentine he plans to give his beloved. Ilene Cooper, in a *Booklist* review, maintained that "school children will recognize the ups and downs of young love and will like the nice twist at the end." Jackie Hechtkopf, in *School Library Journal,* called the book a "a warm-hearted confection."

A new baby in a hippo family is the subject of *Shirley's Wonderful Baby,* in which everybody loves Shirley's new brother Stanley . . . except for Shirley. Only when babysitter Ms. Mump pretends not to like children does Shirley come to appreciate her new sibling. A critic for *Publishers Weekly* praised Gregory for getting "the arch tone just right, and it grows warmer as Shirley's affection deepens." A *Kirkus Reviews* critic found that having "Ms. Mump serving as a foil to bring Shirley and Stanley close is a nice twist." Kristin de Lacoste, writing in *School Library Journal,* concluded: "Children with siblings will relate to this young hippo."

On her Web site, Gregory offered suggestions to writers regarding ideas for stories: "Make sure you do not miss a single thing. Find as many interesting things to put inside your head as you can, and you'll have plenty of interesting things to write about. . . . Save all the things you see and read and do and think about. Then ask yourself, what if . . . ?" Regarding her chosen career, she also commented: "If it is true that all of us write the stories of our own lives each day, as we live them, then books for children are important, because it is through books that children learn about the power of language, about joy and sorrow and laughter and action, about how they might weave together the disparate experiences and possibilities that will become the stories of their own lives."

More recently Gregory told *CA*: "Before I begin writing a story, I'm like a magpie, always collecting things. Generally, a phrase or image rattles around in my head until a story forms around it. I like to think of it as a grain of sand in an oyster, but it often feels more like a barnacle stuck to the bottom of a ship. For example, the phrase that began *Shirley's Wonderful Baby* came from the 'real' Shirley Mullin, owner of Kids Ink Children's Bookstores, who told me about her new grandson, Max. Each time I saw Shirley, I would ask, 'So how's Max?' Shirley would invariably light up like a Madonna with a halo on a Christmas card and answer 'He's wonderful!' Each time I asked about Max, Shirley would say the same thing, and her 'He's wonderful!' rattled around in my head for months. One day, the book Shirley tap danced on to my computer screen, and the story seemed to write itself."

BIOGRAPHICAL AND CRITICAL SOURCES:

PERIODICALS

Booklist, December 1, 1992, review of *Through the Mickle Woods,* p. 675; April 15, 1993, Hazel Rochman, review of *Babysitting for Benjamin,* p. 1523; October 15, 1995, Linda Ward-Callaghan, review of *Kate's Giants,* p. 411; June 1, 1996, Ilene Cooper, review of *Looking for Angels,* p. 1734; April 1, 1999, Ilene Cooper, review of *A Valentine for Norman Noggs,* p. 1420.

Bulletin of the Center for Children's Books, September, 1992, p. 11.

Horn Book, March-April, 1993, Elizabeth S. Watson, review of *Through the Mickle Woods,* pp. 202-203; September-October, 1993, Hanna B. Zeiger, review of *Babysitting for Benjamin,* pp. 585-586.

Kirkus Reviews, May 15, 1992, pp. 669-670; May 15, 1993, p. 660; August 15, 2002, review of *Shirley's Wonderful Baby,* p. 1224.

Publishers Weekly, July 25, 1986, pp. 183-184; May 17, 1993, review of *Babysitting for Benjamin,* p. 78; September 11, 1995, review of *Kate's Giants,* p. 84; April 22, 1996, review of *Looking for Angels,* p. 71; October 21, 1996, review of *When Stories Fell like Shooting Stars,* p. 82; December 14, 1998, review of *A Valentine for Norman Noggs,* p. 75; July 8, 2002, review of *Shirley's Wonderful Baby,* p. 48.

School Library Journal, March, 1987; February, 1988; June, 1992, Maggie McEwen, review of *Happy Burpday, Maggie McDougal!,* p. 93; June, 1993,

Rachel Fox, review of *Babysitting for Benjamin,* p. 76; December, 1995, Tana Elias, review of *Kate's Giants,* p. 81; March, 1996, Kate McClelland, review of *Looking for Angels,* p. 174; October, 1996, Rita Soltan, review of *When Stories Fell like Shooting Stars,* p. 94; January, 1999, Jackie Hechtkopf, review of *A Valentine for Norman Noggs,* p. 88; November, 2002, Kristin de Lacoste, review of *Shirley's Wonderful Baby,* p. 124.

ONLINE

Valiska Gregory Web site, http://www.valiskagregory.com (November 6, 2003).

*   *   *

GRIFFIN, Adele 1970-

PERSONAL: Born July 29, 1970, in Philadelphia, PA; daughter of John Joel Berg (a business manager) and Priscilla Sands Watson (a school principal); married Erich Paul Mauff (an investment banker). *Education:* University of Pennsylvania, B.A., 1993. *Politics:* Democrat. *Hobbies and other interests:* Movies.

ADDRESSES: Office—215 Park Ave. S., New York, NY 10003. *Agent*—Charlotte Sheedy, c/o Sterling Lord Literistic, 65 Bleecker St., New York, NY 10012.

CAREER: Writer. Clarion Books, New York, NY, assistant editor, 1996-98, freelance manuscript reader, 1996—.

MEMBER: Society of Children's Book Writers and Illustrators, "Young Penn Alum," Friends of the New York Public Library, 92nd Street Young Men's Christian Association (YMCA) of New York.

AWARDS, HONORS: National Book Award nomination, National Book Foundation, 1997, and Notable Book citation, American Library Association (ALA), 1997, both for *Sons of Liberty;* Books for the Teen Age, New York Public Library, 1997, and *Parenting Magazine* Award, 1997, both for *Split Just Right;* Blue Ribbon designation, *Bulletin of the Center for*

Adele Griffin

Children's Books, Best Books, *Publishers Weekly* and *School Library Journal,* Notable Book citation, ALA, Best Books for Young Adults, ALA, and One Hundred Titles for Reading and Sharing, New York Public Library, all 1998, all for *The Other Shepards;* Best Books, ALA and *Publishers Weekly,* both 2001, both for *Amandine.*

WRITINGS:

Rainy Season, Houghton Mifflin (Boston, MA), 1996.
Split Just Right, Hyperion (New York, NY), 1997.
Sons of Liberty, Hyperion (New York, NY), 1997.
The Other Shepards, Hyperion (New York, NY), 1998.
Dive, Hyperion (New York, NY), 1999.
Amandine, Hyperion (New York, NY), 2001.
Hannah, Divided, Hyperion (New York, NY), 2002.
Overnight, G. P. Putnam's Sons (New York, NY), 2003.
Where I Want to Be, G. P. Putnam's Sons (New York, NY), 2004.

"WITCH TWINS" SERIES

Witch Twins, Hyperion (New York, NY), 2001.

Witch Twins at Camp Bliss, Hyperion (New York, NY), 2002.
Witch Twins and Melody Malady, illustrated by Jacqueline Rogers, Hyperion (New York, NY), 2003.

SIDELIGHTS: Adele Griffin once commented: "One of my most treasured childhood memories is the excitement I felt going book shopping before summer vacation. I looked forward to our family's annual visit to New York City and trip to Brentano's, where I was allowed to purchase as many books as I wanted, a joyful extravagance. I knew what I liked: stories about princesses, tough heroines who, defying all odds, would rise from a garret or cottage adjacent to the requisite bog to become a mogul—usually of a department store. I did *not* like science fiction, fantasy, or books about boys.

"While my books are not science fiction or fantasy, I do like to write about both girls *and* boys. (Perhaps age and marriage have helped with that particular aversion.) The voices in my writing are those of the children I have listened to hear and have strained to remember, voices that speak from the secret world we too soon leave. My goal, as I continue my career, is to write books for all young people, even boys, who look forward to a trip to the library or bookstore with great joy, and who are companioned by the friendship of a favorite book."

Since the late 1990s Griffin has emerged as a novelist who explores teen behavior in all its variety, good and bad. Some of her novels, such as *Overnight* and *Amandine,* offer realistic portraits of manipulative, selfish young women and the friends they attract. Other books, including *Dive* and *Hannah, Divided* introduce unconventional young adults who must come to terms with their uniqueness. On the lighter side, Griffin's "Witch Twins" series wraps lessons on sibling rivalry and cooperation around stories of magic, spell-casting, and the supernatural. According to Ilene Cooper in *Booklist,* "Griffin elevates every genre she writes," whether it be fantasy or straight realistic fiction.

Griffin's well-received debut novel, *Rainy Season,* was lauded in a *Publishers Weekly* review as "ambitiously conceived and sharply observed." The story follows Lane Beck, a fearful twelve-year-old girl, and her belligerently bold younger brother Charlie through a single transformative day. The Beck family is living on an army base in the Panama Canal Zone in 1977, when resentment of American imperialism is at its peak. The story's setting is key mainly for its contribution of danger and suspense, but the history and politics relevant to the Canal Zone are also discussed in an author's note. *Horn Book* reviewer Nancy Vasilakis wrote that the Panama setting "adds a faint aura of decadence to the narrative." Janice M. Del Negro of the *Bulletin of the Center for Children's Books* maintained that the story's atmosphere is "strongly evoked but never intrusive," adding that "the politics are present but always in the background." In anticipation of a battle with the children on the opposite side of the Zone, the Beck children and their friends begin building a fort. Tensions escalating outside the family are paralleled by the strains existing within the family. Lane is prone to panic attacks, Charlie to bully-like behavior, and both children's problems are being deliberately ignored by their parents. Lane's concern for her brother forces her to break the family's pathological silence about the grief they feel over older sister Emily's death in a car accident. *School Library Journal* contributor Lucinda Lockwood commented favorably on Griffin's "evocative" writing and the author's ability to "capture the setting and the nuances of adolescent relationships." A *Publishers Weekly* critic commended the way Griffin "unfolds the events of the day and lets the reader make sense of them," revealing the nature of the tragedy "deep into her story without resorting to melodrama or otherwise manipulating the characterizations." Del Negro concluded that certain images in the work "will remain with readers long after the book is closed."

In an interview with Elizabeth Devereaux for *Publishers Weekly,* Griffin explained that *Rainy Season* was not an autobiographical novel. Griffin did, however, make frequent summer visits to Panama as a child, after her parents divorced and her father moved to Central America. She tackled the subjects of divorce and a girl's experience of life without her father in her next book, *Split Just Right. Horn Book* reviewer Nancy Vasilakis noted that the "sunny" tones of this novel "differ markedly from the somber, interior voice that characterized Griffin's first novel." *Bulletin of the Center for Children's Books* reviewer Janice M. Del Negro also commented on the "more relaxed, humorous tone" of *Split Just Right,* commending the "natural, easy flow" with which Griffin portrays central protagonist Danny's interpersonal relationships.

A well-grounded fourteen-year-old who enjoys writing, Danny (otherwise known as Dandelion Finzimer) lives with her flamboyant, single, part-time waitress/actress/drama-teacher mother. With no memory of her father, Danny is unsure whether she should trust her mother's view of him and longs to learn about—or perhaps even meet—him. By way of a mix-up, Danny does get to meet her father, and in the process discovers much about her parents, her work as a burgeoning writer, and the line between fact and fiction. *School Library Journal* contributor Carol A. Edwards asserted that in this work, Griffin "takes one of the most tired plots in current fiction and gives it fresh zip." *Booklist* correspondent Ilene Cooper praised the book for successfully tackling "a number of interesting issues, including class distinction and family relationships."

Griffin's next book, *Sons of Liberty,* again adopts the more serious tone of her first novel. Through seventh-grader Rock Kindle, Griffin seriously examines the complicated issues faced by members of a dysfunctional family. Rock has always looked up to his father, and in imitation of his father's behavior, has become a bully. Rock's older brother, Cliff, has lost patience with their father's warped sense of militancy, which prescribes regular doses of humiliation and such bizarre punishments as waking the boys up in the middle of the night to do chores and calisthenics. When the family shatters, no longer able to stand the strain, Rock is forced to choose between loyalty to his father and loyalty to his newly discovered sense of self. In a starred review, a *Publishers Weekly* critic praised Griffin's use of "pointedly jarring dialogue" and her "keen ear for adolescent jargon." *Horn Book* reviewer Kitty Flynn credited the development of Rock's character with providing "the tension in what could have been a superficial treatment of the issues."

With *The Other Shepards,* Griffin created a supernatural teen romance about a girl named Holland and her obsessive-compulsive sister Geneva. The two are passing their adolescent years in a world that is haunted by the memory of three older siblings who died before the two sisters were even born. In the guise of Annie, a mural painter, the spirit of the older sister breathes color into the Shepard family. A *Publishers Weekly* critic wrote that Griffin "spins a taut story of two girls . . . who must confront the unknown in order to liberate themselves. . . . Griffin's story offers a resounding affirmation that fears are to be faced, not denied, and life is to be lived, not mourned." In a *Booklist* review, Ilene Cooper lauded the way Griffin "paints Annie so carefully she seems as real as a kiss from a first boyfriend, and what can be more real than that?" Cooper concluded her positive assessment of *The Other Shepards* by asserting: "Carefully crafted both in plot and language, this book shows the heights that popular literature can scale."

Dive explores the difference between family ties forged by biology and those crafted from circumstance. When his irresponsible mother deserts the family, eleven-year-old Ben elects to stay with his well-grounded stepfather, Lyle. Ben's brother, Dustin, is more inclined to engage in daring behavior, so Dustin chafes under Lyle's rules. The brothers must sort out their problematic relationship after Dustin suffers a serious injury in a diving accident. Nancy Vasilakis in *Horn Book* called *Dive* "a wrenching tale of a young man struggling to find his voice in an unpredictable world."

In 2001 Griffin launched her "Witch Twins" series, introducing ten-year-old twins Claire and Luna. Although they look alike, Claire and Luna are distinct individuals with unique personalities. They must keep their magic a secret from most of their family members, with the exception of Grandy, the grandmother from whom they have inherited their witchy talents. The action in *Witch Twins* revolves around Claire and Luna's attempts to break up their father's impending marriage to a woman named Fluffy. "Griffin's modern tale bursts with everyday enchantment," noted Catherine T. Quattlebaum in her *School Library Journal* review of the book. The critic also lauded the work for its "breezy mixture of otherworldly witchcraft and ordinary activities." The twins attend summer camp in *Witch Twins at Camp Bliss,* once again proving their independence by pursuing different courses from the moment they arrive. Claire must overcome a rival to win the coveted "Camp Bliss Girl" trophy, and Luna cannot find the magic dust given to her by her grandmother. In *School Library Journal,* Debbie Whitbeck observed that in this sequel, Griffin "keeps the characters true to their personalities introduced in the first novel." Diane Foote in *Booklist* liked the "satisfying and convincing happy ending."

In their third adventure, *Witch Twins and Melody Malady,* the girls get an opportunity to meet their idol, film and television star Melody Malady. Tension erupts when Melody becomes friends with Claire, leaving Luna in the company of Melody's brainy but quiet sister, Dolores. Through a series of adventures, both

sets of siblings learn to appreciate their family ties. "Fans of the series will enjoy this offering," maintained Linda B. Zeilstra in *School Library Journal.*

Griffin tackles the difficult subject of teen friendships in two realistic novels, *Amandine* and *Overnight.* Both books frankly confront the way some teenaged girls seek to manipulate their peers and to exert power. Delia, the insecure narrator of *Amandine,* is drawn into an obsessive friendship with dramatic, artistic Amandine. When Amandine's behavior toward another girl takes a dangerous turn, Delia tries to break away. Only then does she discover the full force of Amandine's wrath. According to Anita L. Burkam in *Horn Book,* "Amandine's controlling nature and Delia's weak complicity are believably and subtly developed." Ilene Cooper, in *Booklist,* felt that Griffin "takes well-worn stereotypes . . . and . . . makes them seem much more: more real, more vulnerable, more scary." *School Library Journal* contributor Alison Follos called *Amandine* "a powerful story with real characters."

Overnight, published in 2003, "once again penetrates the cruelty inherent in female cliques," to quote a *Publishers Weekly* critic. Griffin introduces readers to the "Lucky Seven," a tightly-knit group of girls who gather for a sleepover on Friday the Thirteenth. Certain rifts have developed amongst the girls, and these conflicts become noticeable when one of their number, Gray, disappears during the party. The group's leader, Martha, is ready to assert her control, even if it means putting Gray's life in jeopardy. B. Allison Gray, in *School Library Journal,* deemed the novel an "insightful version of the universal story of ostracism and manipulation among preteens." The *Publishers Weekly* contributor felt that Griffin "expertly captures the pettiness of the Lucky Seven."

One of Griffin's most popular books is the novel *Hannah, Divided.* Set in Depression-era Pennsylvania, the story centers on Hannah, a farm girl who also happens to be a math genius and an obsessive-compulsive. Hannah loves living on a farm, helping her family with the chores and attending a one-room school with children she has known all her life. But her love of math just will not go away, and with the help of a wealthy Philadelphia patron, Hannah travels to the big city to try to win a scholarship. Once there, she is torn between her homesickness and her burning desire to work with numbers, even in an alien place full of automobiles, loud music, and strangers. "This portrait of a child struggling with symptoms of obsessive-compulsive disorder is sensitive and convincing," declared Barbara Scotto in *School Library Journal*. Scotto also found *Hannah, Divided* to be "a novel well worth savoring." A *Publishers Weekly* critic gave the book a starred review, particularly praising the way Griffin "makes inventive use of a third-person narration to demonstrate Hannah's computer-like brain and quirky personality." In her starred *Booklist* review of the work, Ilene Cooper concluded: "In other hands, this might have been a problem novel. Here it is a celebration."

In her 1996 *Publishers Weekly* interview, Griffin admitted, "I have no life. . . . I leave work, go to the gym, come home and have dinner, and I write, every night. I talk to my mother, and then I go to bed. . . . I don't even have a plant." Much has changed since those days. Griffin is now a full-time writer with numerous awards and commendations for her work—and she is married. Offering an outlook on her writing future, Griffin said in 1996: "I don't think I want to do this my whole life, but right now, while I still feel so passionate about putting all my spare time into writing, I'll do it." In a more recent interview with the *Embracing the Child* Web site, she said: "Writing is not something that just came naturally to me. There was lots of practicing—still is. So my advice would be not to feel embarrassed about playing other people's songs before you find your own style."

BIOGRAPHICAL AND CRITICAL SOURCES:

PERIODICALS

Booklist, June 1 and 15, 1997, Ilene Cooper, review of *The Other Shepards,* pp. 1702-1703; September 15, 1997, Carolyn Phelan, review of *Sons of Liberty,* p. 235; August, 1998, Ilene Cooper, review of *The Other Shepards,* p. 1999; April 15, 2001, Ilene Cooper, review of *Witch Twins,* p. 1552; September 15, 2001, Ilene Cooper, review of *Amandine,* p. 226; July, 2002, Diane Foote, review of *Witch Twins at Camp Bliss,* p. 1844; October 1, 2002, Ilene Cooper, review of *Hannah, Divided,* p. 323; September 15, 2003, Karin Snelson, review of *Witch Twins and Melody Malady,* p. 236.

Bulletin of the Center for Children's Books, February, 1997, Janice M. Del Negro, review of *Rainy Season,* p. 207; September, 1997, Janice M. Del Negro, review of *Split Just Right,* p. 11.

Horn Book, March-April, 1997, Nancy Vasilakis, review of *Rainy Season,* p. 198; July-August, 1997, Nancy Vasilakis, review of *Split Just Right,* p. 455; January-February, 1998, Kitty Flynn, review of *Sons of Liberty,* p. 72; November, 1999, Nancy Vasilakis, review of *Dive,* p. 739; September, 2001, Anita L. Burkam, review of *Witch Twins,* p. 583; November-December, 2001, Anita L. Burkam, review of *Amandine,* p. 748.

Plain Dealer (Cleveland, OH), April 13, 2003, Cheryl Stritzel McCarthy, "A Transplanted Savant Finds She Has Much to Learn off the Farm," p. J11.

Publishers Weekly, October 14, 1996, review of *Rainy Season,* p. 84; December 16, 1996, Elizabeth Devereaux, "Flying Starts: Six First-Time Children's Book Authors Talk about Their Fall," p. 32; September 8, 1997, review of *Sons of Liberty,* p. 77; September 21, 1998, review of *The Other Shepards,* p. 86; July 2, 2001, review of *Witch Twins,* p. 76; August 20, 2001, review of *Amandine,* p. 81; August 26, 2002, review of *Hannah, Divided,* p. 69; December 16, 2002, review of *Overnight,* p. 68.

San Francisco Chronicle, April 25, 1999, Susan Faust, "Haunting Novel Is Not Your Average Ghost Story," p. 9.

School Library Journal, November, 1996, Lucinda Lockwood, review of *Rainy Season,* pp. 104-105; June, 1997, Carol A. Edwards, review of *Split Just Right,* p. 117; July, 2001, Catherine T. Quattlebaum, review of *Witch Twins,* p. 82; November, 2001, Alison Follos, review of *Amandine,* p. 158; June, 2002, Debbie Whitbeck, review of *Witch Twins at Camp Bliss,* p. 96; December, 2002, Barbara Scotto, review of *Hannah, Divided,* p. 138; February, 2003, B. Allison Gray, review of *Overnight,* p. 141; July, 2003, Linda B. Zeilstra, review of *Witch Twins and Melody Malady,* p. 96.

ONLINE

Embracing the Child, http://www.embracingthechild.org/ (November, 2002), "An Interview with Adele Griffin" and synopses of the author's books.*

GRUEN, Erich S(tephen) 1935-

PERSONAL: Born May 7, 1935, in Vienna, Austria; immigrated to United States, 1939, naturalized citizen, 1946; son of Siegfried (an accountant) and Irma (Spalter) Gruen; married Joan Brannick (a university administrator), August 30, 1959; children: Bonnie, Keith, Jason. *Ethnicity:* "Caucasian." *Education:* Columbia University, B.A., 1957; Oxford University, M.A., 1960; Harvard University, Ph.D., 1964.

ADDRESSES: Office—Department of History, University of California, Berkeley, CA 94720; fax: 510-524-0353. *E-mail*—gruene@socrates.berkeley.edu.

CAREER: Writer. Harvard University, Cambridge, MA, instructor in history, 1964-66; University of California, Berkeley, assistant professor, 1966-68, associate professor, 1968-72, professor of history, 1972—, Gladys Rehard Wood Professor of History and Classics, 1987—. Institute for Advanced Study, Princeton, member, NJ, 1973-74; Oxford University, visiting fellow of Merton College, 1978; University of Colorado, distinguished visiting humanist, 1981; University of Cincinnati, Semple Classical Lecturer, 1985, Phi Beta Kappa Lecturer, 1985-86; Princeton University, visiting professor of classics, 1987-88; American Academy in Rome, resident in classics, 1990; Cornell University, Townsend Professor of Classics and History, 1991; Hebrew University of Jerusalem, member of Institute for Advanced Studies; consultant to Educational Development Corp.

MEMBER: American Historical Association, American Philological Association (member of board of directors, 1984-87; vice president, 1986-90; president, 1992), American Academy of Arts and Sciences (elected member), American Philosophical Society (elected member).

AWARDS, HONORS: Guggenheim fellow, 1969-70 and 1989-90; fellow of National Endowment for the Humanities, 1984, 1996; Distinguished Teaching Award from University of California, Berkeley, 1987; Austrian Cross of Honor for Arts and Letters, 1999.

WRITINGS:

Roman Politics and the Criminal Courts, 149-78 B.C., Harvard University Press (Cambridge, MA), 1968.

(Editor) *The Image of Rome,* Prentice-Hall (Englewood Cliffs, NJ), 1969.
(Editor) *Imperialism in the Roman Republic,* Holt (New York, NY), 1970.
The Last Generation of the Roman Republic, University of California Press (Berkeley, CA), 1974.
The Hellenistic World and the Coming of Rome, two volumes, University of California Press (Berkeley, CA), 1984.
Studies in Greek Culture and Roman Policy, E. J. Brill (Long Island City, NY), 1990.
Culture and National Identity in Republican Rome, Cornell University Press (Ithaca, NY), 1992.
(Editor) *Images and Ideologies,* University of California Press (Berkeley, CA), 1993.
(Editor) *Hellenistic Constructs,* University of California Press (Berkeley, CA), 1997.
Heritage and Hellenism: The Reinvention of Jewish Tradition, University of California Press (Berkeley, CA), 1998.
Diaspora: Jews amidst Greeks and Romans, Harvard University Press (Cambridge, MA), 2002.

Contributor to history and classical studies journals.

BIOGRAPHICAL AND CRITICAL SOURCES:

PERIODICALS

American Historical Review, October, 1969; October, 1975.
New York Times Book Review, September 23, 1984.
Times Literary Supplement, August 16, 1985.
Virginia Quarterly Review, autumn, 1974.

*   *   *

GUEST, Judith (Ann) 1936-

PERSONAL: Born March 29, 1936, in Detroit, MI; daughter of Harry Reginald (a businessman) and Marion Aline (Nesbit) Guest; married, August 22, 1958; husband's name, Larry (a data processing executive); children: Larry, John, Richard. *Education:* University of Michigan, B.A., 1958.

ADDRESSES: Home—4600 West 44th St., Edina, MN 55424. *Agent*—Patricia Karlan Agency, 3575 Cahvenga Blvd., Suite 210, Los Angeles, CA 90068; c/o Author Mail, Viking/Penguin, 375 Hudson St., New York, NY 10014.

Judith Guest

CAREER: Writer. Employed as teacher in public grade schools in Royal Oak, MI, 1964, Birmingham, MI, 1969, and Troy, MI, 1975.

MEMBER: Authors Guild, Authors League of America, PEN American Center, Detroit Women Writers.

AWARDS, HONORS: Janet Heidinger Kafka Prize, University of Rochester, 1977, for *Ordinary People.*

WRITINGS:

Ordinary People (novel), Viking (New York, NY), 1976.
Second Heaven (novel), Viking (New York, NY), 1982.
The Mythic Family: An Essay, Milkweed Press (Minneapolis, MN), 1988.
(With Rebecca Hill) *Killing Time in St. Cloud* (novel), Delacorte (New York, NY), 1988.
Errands (novel), Ballantine (New York, NY), 1996.
Icewalk (essay), Minnesota Center for the Book Arts (Minneapolis, MN), 2001.

Also author of a screenplay adaptation of *Second Heaven* and of three short stories by Carol Bly, titled *Rachel River, Minnesota.* Contributor to periodicals, including *The Writer.*

ADAPTATIONS: Ordinary People was filmed by Paramount in 1980, directed by Robert Redford, starring Mary Tyler Moore, Donald Sutherland, Timothy Hutton, Judd Hirsch, and Elizabeth McGovern; a stage version was published by Dramatic Publishing in 1983. *Errands* were adapted for audiobook.

SIDELIGHTS: Judith Guest achieved startling success with her debut novel *Ordinary People,* and continued writing novels with similar themes. Contrary to custom, Guest sent the manuscript to Viking Press without a preceding letter of inquiry and without the usual plot synopsis and outline that many publishing houses require. The manuscript was read by an editorial assistant who liked it well enough to send Guest a note of encouragement and pass the story along to her superiors for a second reading. Months passed. Then, in the summer of 1975, when Guest was in the midst of moving from Michigan to Minnesota, came the word she had been waiting for: Viking would be "honored" to publish *Ordinary People,* the first unsolicited manuscript they had accepted in twenty-six years. Guest's book went on to become not only a best-selling novel—selected by four book clubs, serialized in *Redbook,* and sold to Ballantine for paperback rights for $635,000—but also an award-winning film that captured the 1980 Oscar for best movie of the year. Since that time, Guest has published several other novels, including the family stories *Second Heaven,* and *Errands,* and the mystery *Killing Time in St. Cloud.*

The story of a teenage boy's journey from the brink of suicide back to mental health, *Ordinary People* shows the way that unexpected tragedy can destroy even the most secure of families. Seventeen-year-old Conrad Jarrett, son of a well-to-do tax lawyer, appears to have everything: looks, brains, manners, and a good relationship with his family. But when he survives a boating accident that kills his older brother, Conrad sinks into a severe depression, losing touch with his parents, teachers, friends, and just about everyone else in the outside world. His attempt to kill himself by slashing his wrists awakens his father to the depth of his problems, but it also cuts Conrad off from his mother—a compulsive perfectionist who believes that his bloody suicide attempt was intended to punish her. With the help of his father and an understanding analyst, Conrad slowly regains his equilibrium. "Above all," commented *New York Review of Books* contributor Michael Wood, "he comes to accept his mother's apparent failure to forgive him for slashing his wrists, and his own failure to forgive her for not loving him more. It is true that she has now left his father, because he seemed to be cracking up under the strain of his concern for his son, but Conrad has learned 'that it is love, imperfect and unordered, that keeps them apart, even as it holds them somehow together.'"

"The form, the style of the novel dictate an ending more smooth than convincing," according to Melvin Maddocks in *Time*. "As a novelist who warns against the passion for safety and order that is no passion at all, Guest illustrates as well as describes the problem. She is neat and ordered, even at explaining that life is not neat and ordered." While *Newsweek*'s Walter Clemons thought that *Ordinary People* "solves a little too patly some of the problems it raises," he also allowed that "the feelings in the book are true and unforced. Guest has the valuable gift of making us like her characters; she has the rarer ability to move a toughened reviewer to tears." *Village Voice* contributor Irma Pascal Heldman also had high praise for the novel, writing that "Guest conveys with sensitivity a most private sense of life's personal experiences while respecting the reader's imagination and nurturing an aura of mystery. Without telling all, she illuminates the lives of 'ordinary people' with chilling insight."

Guest's insights into her male protagonist are particularly keen, according to several reviewers, including Lore Dickstein, who wrote in the *New York Times Book Review:* "Guest portrays Conrad not only as if she has lived with him on a daily basis—which I sense may be true—but as if she has gotten into his head. The dialogue Conrad has with himself, his psychiatrist, his friends, his family, all rings true with adolescent anxiety. This is the small, hard kernel of brilliance in the novel." But while acknowledging that Guest's male characters are well-defined, several reviewers believe that Beth, the mother, is not fully developed. "The mother's point of view, even though she is foremost in the men's lives, is barely articulated," wrote Dorothea D. Braginsky in *Psychology Today*. "We come to know her only in dialogue with her husband and son, and through their portrayals of her. For some reason Guest has given her no voice, no platform for expression. We never discover what conflicts, fears and aspirations exist behind her cool, controlled facade."

Guest herself expressed similar reservations about the character, telling a *Detroit News* contributor that Beth

is "pretty enigmatic in the novel. The reader might have been puzzled by her." But Guest also believes that Mary Tyler Moore's portrayal of Beth Jarrett in the film adaptation of the novel did much to clarify the character. "[Mary Tyler Moore] just knocks me out," Guest told John Blades in a *Chicago Tribune* interview. "She's a terrific actress, a very complex person, and she brought a complexity to the character that I wish I'd gotten into the book. I fought with that character for a long time, trying to get her to reveal herself, and I finally said this is the best I can do. When I saw Mary in the movie, I felt like she'd done it for me."

Guest was also pleased with the movie's ending, which was more inconclusive than the book's ending. "The more things get left open-ended the better," Guest told Blades. "If you tie everything into a neat little bow, people walk out of the theater and never give it another thought. If there's ambiguity, people think about it and talk about it." She believes director Robert Redford's sensitive presentation "leaves the viewer to his own conclusions," which is how it should be.

In 1982 Guest published *Second Heaven,* a novel that shares many of its predecessor's concerns. "Again, a damaged adolescent boy stands at the center of the story; again, the extent of his wounds will not be immediately apparent," noted Peter S. Prescott in *Newsweek*. "Again, two adults with problems of their own attempt to save the boy from cooperating in his own destruction." In an interview with former *Detroit Free Press* book editor Barbara Holliday, Guest reflected on her fascination with what she calls this "crucial" period known as adolescence: "It's a period of time . . . where people are very vulnerable and often don't have much experience to draw on as far as human relationships go. At the same time they are making some pretty heavy decisions, not necessarily physical but psychological decisions about how they're going to relate to people and how they're going to shape their lives. It seems to me that if you don't have sane sensible people around you to help, there's great potential for making irrevocable mistakes."

The way that signals can be misinterpreted, leading to a breakdown in communication between people who may care deeply for one another, is a theme of both her novels and a topic she handles well, according to novelist Anne Tyler, who is also known for her ability to accurately portray human relationships. "[Guest] has a remarkable ability to show the unspoken in human relationships—the emotions either hidden or expressed so haltingly that they might as well be hidden, the heroic self-control that others may perceive as icy indifference," Tyler wrote in the *Detroit News.*

In *Second Heaven,* it is Gale Murray, abused son of a religiously fanatic father and an ineffectual mother, who hides his feelings behind a facade of apathy. After a brutal beating from his father, Gale runs away from home, seeking shelter with Catherine "Cat" Holzmann, a recently divorced parent with problems of her own. When Gale's father tries to have his son institutionalized, Cat enlists the aid of Mike Atwood, a disenchanted lawyer who is falling in love with Cat. He takes on the case, largely as a favor to her. According to Norma Rosen in the *New York Times Book Review,* "Cat and Michael must transcend their personal griefs and limits in order to reach out for this rescue. In saving another's life they are on the way to saving their own."

Because of the story's clear delineation of good versus evil and its melodramatic courtroom conclusion, *Second Heaven* struck some critics as contrived. "Everything in the book is so neat and polished; so precisely timed and calibrated," suggested *New York Times* reviewer Christopher Lehmann-Haupt, "the way the newly divorced people dovetail, conveniently providing a surrogate mother and a fatherly counselor for battered Gale Murray. . . . The reader continually gets the feeling that Mrs. Guest is working with plumb line and level and trowel to build her airtight perpendicular walls of plot development." Or, as Rosen puts it: "On the one hand there are the clear evils of control, rules, order. They are associated with inability to love, fanaticism, brutality. Clutter and lack of organization are good. . . . Yet in the context of the author's anti-neatness and anticontrol themes, the technique of the novel itself appears at times to be almost a subversion: the quick-march pace, the click-shot scenes, the sensible serviceable inner monologues unvaried in their rhythms."

While acknowledging the book's imperfections, Jonathan Yardley maintained in the *Washington Post* that "the virtues of *Second Heaven* are manifold, and far more consequential than its few flaws. . . . Neither contrivance nor familiarity can disguise the skill and, most particularly, the sensitivity with which Guest tells her story. She is an extraordinarily perceptive

observer of the minutiae of domestic life, and she writes about them with humor and affection." Concluded *Tribune Books* contributor Harry Mark Petrakis: "By compassionately exploring the dilemmas in the lives of Michael, Catherine, and Gale, Judith Guest casts light on the problems we often endure in our own lives. That's what the art of storytelling and the craft of good writing are all about."

With *Errands* Guest continues to examine the contemporary American family with adolescent children in crisis, though this novel was based in fact. Guest was inspired by her own family history as recounted in a diary that told of her grandfather's premature death and the fate of his widow and five children in Detroit during the 1920s. As Guest told Joanne Kaufman of *People,* she did not simply want to base the story on her ancestors, who repressed their feelings. "I needed to make it my story. . . . I never heard about the sadness and anger you feel when you lose your father at age ten, as my father did," she said, adding, "I wanted to write a story to find out what it felt like."

Thus readers first meet the Browner family of *Errands,* a word that has the more serious connotation of "mission," as they begin their annual vacation. They are a likable, normal family except that Keith, the father, must begin chemotherapy as soon as they return. But the treatment is not successful; his wife, Annie, and three young children, Harry, Jimmy, and Julie, must carry on without him. Life without Keith is a struggle for each of them, and they are each in a state of crisis when Jimmy has a dangerous accident that almost blinds him. But Jimmy's accident requires them to support each other and begins the rebuilding process for this troubled family. The work caught the attention of reviewers. Writing in the *New York Times Book Review,* Meg Wolitzer admired the "natural cadences and rhythms" spoken by the children but suggested that the adults "never fully come to life" and that overall "the novel, while appealing, seems slightly sketchy and meditative." Although *Entertainment Weekly*'s Vanessa V. Friedman found the characters stock treatments and "unsympathetic" at that, others praised Guest's portrayal of family dynamics during a crisis. For example, *Booklist*'s Brad Hooper noted that "Guest is perfectly realistic in her depictions of family situations; her characters act and react with absolute credibility." And Sheila M. Riley of *Library Journal* declared *Errands* "true, touching, and highly recommended."

BIOGRAPHICAL AND CRITICAL SOURCES:

BOOKS

Contemporary Literary Criticism, Gale (Detroit), Volume 8, 1978; Volume 30, 1984.

Szabo, Victoria and Angela D. Jones, *The Uninvited Guest: Erasure of Women in Ordinary People,* Popular Press (Bowling Green, OH), 1996.

PERIODICALS

Billboard, January 18, 1997, Trudi Miller Rosenblum, review of *Errands* (audio version), p. 74.

Booklist, October 15, 1996, Brad Hooper, review of *Errrands,* p. 379.

Chicago Tribune, November 4, 1980.

Detroit Free Press, October 7, 1982, review of *Second Heaven.*

Detroit News, September 26, 1982, review of *Second Heaven;* October 20, 1982, review of *Second Heaven.*

Entertainment Weekly, February 14, 1997, Vanessa V. Friedman, review of *Errands,* pp. 56-57.

Library Journal, May 1, 1976, Victoria K. Musmann, review of *Ordinary People,* p. 1142; July 1, 1982, Michele M. Leber, review of *Second Heaven,* p. 1344; April 15, 1983, "Lorain, Ohio, Public Library Invites Judith Guest for Tea," p. 786; October 15, 1996, Sheila M. Riley, review of *Errands,* p. 90; March 1, 1997, Carolyn Alexander and Mark Annichiarico, review of *Errands* (audio version), p. 118.

Ms., December, 1982, review of *Second Heaven.*

Newsweek, July 12, 1976, review of *Ordinary People;* October 4, 1982, review of *Second Heaven.*

New Yorker, July 19, 1976, review of *Ordinary People;* November 22, 1982, review of *Second Heaven.*

New York Review of Books, June 10, 1976, review of *Ordinary People.*

New York Times, July 16, 1976, review of *Ordinary People;* October 22, 1982, review of *Second Heaven;* January 12, 1997, Meg Wolitzer, "Ordinary Loss," review of *Errands,* p. 18.

New York Times Book Review, July 18, 1976, review of *Ordinary People;* October 3, 1982, review of *Second Heaven;* January 12, 1997, Meg Wolitzer, "Ordinary Loss," review of *Errands,* p. 18.

People, February 10, 1997, Joanne Kaufman, "Family Matters," review of *Errands,* p. 33.

Psychology Today, August, 1976, review of *Ordinary People.*

Publishers Weekly, April 19, 1976, review of *Ordinary People;* October 28, 1996, Sybil S. Steinberg, review of *Errands,* p. 56.

Redbook, January, 1997, Judy Koutsky, "Red Hot Books," review of *Errands,* p. G-4.

Saturday Review, May 15, 1976, review of *Ordinary People.*

School Library Journal, September, 1976, Jay Daly, review of *Ordinary People,* p. 143; December, 1982, Priscilla Johnson and Ron Brown, review of *Second Heaven,* p. 87; August, 1983, Hazel Rochman, "Bringing Boys Books Home," review of *Ordinary People,* pp. 26-27; July, 1997, Carol Clark, review of *Errands,* p. 116.

Sunday Times (London, England), February 16, 2003, Marianne Gray, review of *Ordinary People,* p. 29.

Time, July 19, 1976, review of *Ordinary People;* October 25, 1982, review of *Second Heaven.*

Tribune Books (Chicago, IL), October 3, 1982, review of *Second Heaven.*

Village Voice, July 19, 1976, review of *Ordinary People.*

Washington Post, September 22, 1982, review of *Second Heaven.*

Washington Post News Feed, February 24, 1997, Reeve Lindbergh, review of *Errands,* p. D4.*

H

HAIKEN, Elizabeth

PERSONAL: Female.

ADDRESSES: Agent—c/o Author Mail, Johns Hopkins University Press, 2715 N. Charles St., Baltimore, MD 21218-4319.

CAREER: Writer and corporate communications specialist.

WRITINGS:

Venus Envy: A History of Cosmetic Surgery, Johns Hopkins University Press (Baltimore, MD), 1998.

SIDELIGHTS: In *Venus Envy: A History of Cosmetic Surgery* author Elizabeth Haiken takes a look at the Western world's obsession with the pursuit of beauty through cosmetic surgery. Haiken outlines the historical evolution of plastic surgery without making suggestions about its future implications and directions. But according to *Sunday Times* book reviewer Zoe Heller, Haiken does her readers a service by going beyond the traditional treatment of the subject. Instead of railing against plastic surgery from a feminist standpoint, the author admits that women have been more than passive victims in the growth of the industry since the early twentieth century. Haiken looks at the history of the phenomenon that has been dominated by male surgeons and has catered largely to female patients. Heller found Haiken's treatment not that of an irritable feminist, but of a historian reporting on her troubling and sad research results.

Elective cosmetic surgery was practiced in the early 1900s sparingly; most reputable doctors reserved these efforts for victims of wars or accidents. But a few individuals, who were considered quacks, offered what were the beginning face lift efforts. Other doctors could not escape noticing the demand for these services or the potentially lucrative trend that was developing. As the number of doctors practicing elective cosmetic surgery grew, these doctors also started to focus on other parts of the body such as breasts or thighs. According to Haiken, the perception of cosmetic surgery has traveled further from being perceived as narcissism, making it easier for those who desire it and can afford it to justify it in their minds. Between 1982 and 1992, people who said that they approved of plastic surgery increased by fifty percent and disapproval ratings fell by sixty-six percent.

While Haiken makes no predictions about the future of cosmetic surgery, she does offer some suggestions for combating the trend. Women should take "collective action," says the author, and a standard that defines beauty internally. Haiken suggests that women contribute their annual cosmetic budget to women's social causes instead. But Haiken also acknowledges the deep roots that contribute to a woman's feelings of inferiority about her appearance. These feelings come, not only from society, but from formative interactions that people (particularly women) have in adolescence when they are busy measuring themselves up to the so-called beauty of others. It is particularly important, suggests Haiken, for fathers to help instill confidence in their daughters in regard to appearance.

Taking examples from real life, Haiken uses the stories of two well known celebrities to illustrate her points about Western society's comfort, or discomfort, with their personal looks. Barbra Streisand is presented as an example of a person confident enough to live with her nose, even while living in appearance-obsessed southern California. Michael Jackson went the other way to advance his career and presents a picture of what Joan Jacobs Brumberg of the *Nation* called "racial discomfort." Brumberg noted that Haiken also describes another interesting aspect of cosmetic surgery; it has gained face in the late twentieth century by attaching itself to the self-help and self-improvement movements. Southern California appears to be a leader in this area, where many children are routinely shuffled to plastic surgeons in an attempt to improve their self-esteem. Brumberg cited instances in southern California of widely available and massively advertised plastic surgery opportunities. She called southern California the future of plastic surgery and a place that propagates the "cult of beauty and youth." A reviewer in the *Economist* declared Haiken's treatment of cosmetic surgery "entertaining," but warned that the trend is not likely to "go away" soon.

BIOGRAPHICAL AND CRITICAL SOURCES:

PERIODICALS

Booklist, November 1, 1997, p. 443.
Economist, February 14, 1998, review of *Venus Envy: A History of Cosmetic Surgery,* pp. R15-R16.
Entertainment Weekly, January 23, 1998, p. 58.
Journal of the American Medical Association, July 24, 1998, p. 2006.
Lancet, January 31, 1998, p. 377.
Library Journal, October 1, 1997, p. 110.
London Review of Books, November 27, 1997, pp. 11-12.
Nation, December 29, 1997, Joan Jacobs Brumberg, review of *Venus Envy,* pp. 38-40.
Sunday Times, June 28, 1998, Zoe Heller, review of *Venus Envy,* pp. 1-2.

ONLINE

Salon.com, http://www.salon.com/ (November 21, 1997), Michelle Goldberg, review of *Venus Envy.*
Wisconsin Public Radio—To the Best of Our Knowledge: The Quest for Beauty, http://www.wpr.org/book/980111c.htm (April 8, 1999).

HAMPSON, Norman 1922-

PERSONAL: Born April 8, 1922, in Leyland, Lancashire, England; son of Frank (in local government) and Elizabeth Jane (Fazackerley) Hampson; married Jacqueline Gardin (a teacher), April 22, 1948; children: Françoise, Michele. *Education:* University College, Oxford, B.A., 1941, M.A., 1947; University of Paris, D.Univ., 1955. *Hobbies and other interests:* Gardening.

ADDRESSES: Home—305 Hull Rd., York, Yorkshire YO10 3LU, England.

CAREER: University of Manchester, Manchester, England, lecturer, 1948-62, senior lecturer in French history, 1962-67; University of Newcastle upon Tyne, Newcastle upon Tyne, England, professor of modern history, 1967-74; University of York, Yorkshire, England, professor of history, 1974-89, professor emeritus, 1989—. *Military service:* Royal Navy, 1941-45, including two years as liaison officer with Free French Navy; became lieutenant.

MEMBER: British Academy (fellow), Royal Historical Society (fellow).

AWARDS, HONORS: D.Litt., University of Edinburgh, 1989.

WRITINGS:

La Marine de l'an II: Mobilisation de la flotte de l'Océan, 1793-1794, M. Riviére (Paris, France), 1959.
A Social History of the French Revolution, Routledge & Kegan Paul (London, England), 1963.
A Cultural History of the Enlightenment, Pantheon (New York, NY), 1968, published as *Pelican History of European Thought,* Volume 4: *The Enlightenment,* Pelican (Harmondsworth, England), 1969.
The First European Revolution, 1776-1815, Harcourt (New York, NY), 1969.
The Life and Opinions of Maximilien Robespierre, Duckworth (London, England), 1974.
A Concise History of the French Revolution, Thames & Hudson (London, England), 1975.

Danton, Holmes & Meier Publishers (New York, NY), 1978.

The Terror in the French Revolution, Historical Association (London, England), 1981.

Will and Circumstance: Montesquieu, Rousseau, and the French Revolution, University of Oklahoma Press (Norman, OK), 1983.

Prelude to Terror: The Constituent Assembly and the Failure of Consensus, 1789-1791, Blackwell (New York, NY), 1988.

Saint-Just, Blackwell (Cambridge, MA), 1991.

The Perfidy of Albion: French Perceptions of England during the French Revolution, St. Martin's Press (New York, NY), 1998.

Not Really What You'd Call a War (memoir), Whittles Publishing (Caithness, Scotland), 2001.

Contributor to history journals.

BIOGRAPHICAL AND CRITICAL SOURCES:

BOOKS

Crook, Malcolm, William Doyle, and Alan Forrest, editors, *Enlightenment and Revolution: Essays in Honour of Norman Hampson,* Ashgate (Burlington, VT), 2004.

Hampson, Norman, *Not Really What You'd Call a War,* Whittles Publishing (Caithness, Scotland), 2001.

PERIODICALS

Albion, fall, 1999, review of *The Perfidy of Albion: French Perceptions of England during the French Revolution,* p. 507.

American Historical Review, February, 1977, review of *The Life and Opinions of Maximilien Robespierre,* p. 20; December, 1979, review of *Danton,* p. 1394; October, 1984, R. Emmet Kennedy, Jr., review of *Will and Circumstance: Montesquieu, Rousseau, and the French Revolution,* p. 1084; October, 1990, David P. Jordan, review of *Prelude to Terror: The Constituent Assembly and the Failure of Consensus, 1789-1791,* p. 1210; February, 2000, Orville T. Murphy, review of *The Perfidy of Albion,* p. 296.

Books and Bookmen, November, 1978, review of *Danton,* p. 54.

British Book News, October, 1983, review of *Will and Circumstance,* p. 654.

Choice, March, 1979, review of *Danton,* p. 134; December, 1983, review of *Will and Circumstance,* p. 627; May, 1989, review of *Prelude to Terror,* p. 1575; July, 1991, review of *Saint-Just,* p. 1829.

Economist, September 16, 1978, review of *Danton,* p. 124.

Eighteenth-Century Studies, summer, 1987, review of *Will and Circumstance,* p. 488.

English Historical Review, April, 1980, review of *Danton,* p. 430; April, 1986, review of *Will and Circumstance,* p. 516; June, 1994, Alan Forrest, review of *Saint-Just,* p. 749.

European History Quarterly, July, 1993, Frank Tallett, review of *Saint-Just,* p. 450.

Guardian Weekly, October 16, 1988, review of *Prelude to Terror,* p. 28.

History: Journal of the Historical Association, June, 1992, Irene Collins, review of *Saint-Just,* p. 330.

History: Reviews of New Books, March, 1979, review of *Danton,* p. 96; winter, 1990, review of *Prelude to Terror,* p. 71; winter, 1992, review of *Saint-Just,* p. 84.

History Today, February, 1982, review of *A Cultural History of the Enlightenment,* p. 52; December, 1989, Nigel Aston, review of *Prelude to Terror,* p. 54; May, 1991, T. C. W. Blanning, review of *Saint-Just,* p. 56.

Journal of Military History, July, 2002, Arthur L. Funk, review of *Not Really What You'd Call a War,* p. 896.

Journal of Modern History, June, 1977, review of *The Life and Opinions of Maximilien Robespierre,* p. 283; March, 1980, review of *Danton,* p. 148; September, 1986, review of *Will and Circumstance,* p. 726; September, 1993, David P. Jordan, review of *Saint-Just,* p. 624; June, 2000, James Livesey, review of *The Perfidy of Albion,* p. 503.

London Review of Books, August 4, 1983, review of *Will and Circumstance,* p. 10; April 4, 1991, review of *Saint-Just,* p. 22; December 10, 1998, review of *The Perfidy of Albion,* p. 11.

New Statesman, September 22, 1978, review of *Danton,* p. 365.

New Statesman and Society, February 22, 1991, Brian Morton, review of *Saint-Just,* p. 33.

New York Review of Books, June 28, 1984, Robert Darnton, review of *Will and Circumstance,* p. 32.

Observer, January 1, 1989, review of *Prelude to Terror,* p. 38; February 10, 1991, review of *Saint-Just,* p. 55.

Reference and Research Book News, February, 1999, review of *The Perfidy of Albion,* p. 22.

Social Science Quarterly, June, 1985, review of *Will and Circumstance,* p. 467.

Spectator, September 3, 1983, review of *Will and Circumstance,* p. 18; December 17, 1983, review of *Will and Circumstance,* p. 52; November 19, 1988, review of *Prelude to Terror,* p. 31.

Times Educational Supplement, January 6, 1984, review of *Will and Circumstance,* p. 34.

Times Literary Supplement, January 20, 1989, review of *Prelude to Terror,* p. 65; February 15, 1991, Eugen Weber, review of *Saint-Just,* p. 3; December 6, 1991, review of *Saint-Just,* p. 12; September 4, 1998, Gwynne Lewis, review of *The Perfidy of Albion,* p. 24.

ONLINE

H-Net: Humanities and Social Sciences Online, http://www.h-net.msu.edu/ (March, 1999), review of *The Perfidy of Albion.**

* * *

HANDLER, David 1952-
  (Russell Andrews, a joint pseudonym)

PERSONAL: Born September 14, 1952, in Los Angeles, CA; son of Chester (a salesperson) and Ruth Handler. *Education:* University of California—Santa Barbara, B.A., 1974; Columbia University, M.S., 1975.

ADDRESSES: Home—7 Library Lane, Old Lyme, CT 06371. *Agent*—Dominick Abel Literary Agency, 146 West 82nd St., New York, NY 10024.

CAREER: Writer, ghostwriter, screenwriter, and producer. Also worked as a syndicated columnist and Broadway critic.

MEMBER: International Association of Crime Writers, Mystery Writers of America, Writers Guild of America.

AWARDS, HONORS: Edgar Allan Poe Award for best original paperback, Mystery Writers of America, and American Mystery Award, both 1991, both for *The Man Who Would Be F. Scott Fitzgerald.*

WRITINGS:

NOVELS

Kiddo, Ballantine (New York, NY), 1987.
Boss, Available Press (New York, NY), 1988.
(With Peter Gethers under joint pseudonym Russell Andrews) *Gideon,* Ballantine Books (New York, NY), 1999.

"STEWART HOAG" MYSTERY NOVELS

The Man Who Died Laughing, Bantam (New York, NY), 1988.
The Man Who Lived by Night, Bantam (New York, NY), 1989.
The Man Who Would Be F. Scott Fitzgerald, Bantam (New York, NY), 1990.
The Woman Who Fell from Grace, Doubleday (New York, NY), 1991.
The Boy Who Never Grew Up, Doubleday (New York, NY), 1992.
The Man Who Canceled Himself, Doubleday (New York, NY), 1995.
The Girl Who Ran off with Daddy, Doubleday (New York, NY), 1996.
The Man Who Loved Women to Death, Doubleday (New York, NY), 1997.

"BERGER & MITRY" MYSTERY NOVELS

The Cold Blue Blood, Thomas Dunne Books/St. Martin's Minotaur (New York, NY), 2001.
The Hot Pink Farm House, Thomas Dunne Books/St. Martin's Minotaur (New York, NY), 2002.
The Bright Silver Star, Thomas Dunne Books (New York, NY), 2003.
The Burnt Orange Sunrise, Thomas Dunne Books (New York, NY), 2004.

OTHER

Also author of screenplays, including scripts for television series *Kate and Allie* and *The Saint;* contributor to *TV Guide.*

SIDELIGHTS: David Handler's earliest novels are coming-of-age stories set in the author's native Los Angeles, California. His first novel, *Kiddo,* takes place in 1962 and records the adolescent tribulations of Danny Levine, a confused thirteen-year-old who struggles with his Jewish identity, his weight, and his relationships with girls. He latches on to another thirteen-year-old, Newt Biddle, an anti-Semitic preppie who teaches Danny the joys of smoking, shoplifting, and frustrating his parents' efforts to make him learn to play the violin. Eventually Danny makes decisions about his own character and his friends and gives up his rebellious ways, even resuming his violin lessons. David Freeman, writing in the *New York Times Book Review,* concluded that Handler "has great affection for his characters." Danny reappears as the protagonist of Handler's second novel, *Boss,* which is set not in the rebellious 1960s of *Kiddo* but in the more cautious 1970s. Danny is still confused, bumbling, and fighting his waistline; however, a year in Europe has endowed him with a newfound wisdom that allows him to marry and begin working at his father's business.

In his third novel, *The Man Who Died Laughing,* Handler introduces Stewart "Hoagy" Hoag, who is also the protagonist of several of Handler's later novels. Hoag is a writer whose career has gone flat, so he becomes a ghostwriter and is hired to pen the memoirs of Sonny Day, a famous comic. Soon, however, he is caught in the middle of a murder and begins investigating—with the help of his dog, Lulu—the mysterious break-up of Knight and Day, the most famous comedy team of the fifties, which occurred years before the novel begins. The transcripts of his interviews with family, friends, and enemies provide a nostalgic tour through Hollywood, Las Vegas, and the Jewish resort area in the Catskill Mountains known as the Borscht Belt.

In Handler's 1990 book, *The Man Who Would Be F. Scott Fitzgerald,* Hoag is hired by the literary agent of Cameron Sheffield Noyes, a bratty young New York author with writer's block, to help Noyes write a bestselling autobiography. But what Noyes dictates under Hoag's coaching is instead an exposé of the New York celebrity publishing scene. The work in progress prompts anonymous threats that could have come from a variety of unscrupulous characters, each with a motive for wanting to see the project halted. When both Noyes's publisher and ex-lover are murdered and

Noyes disappears, Hoag again turns from writer to sleuth. A *Wall Street Journal* contributor wrote of *The Man Who Would Be F. Scott Fitzgerald:* "Charming lead characters and good breezy writing are among this book's strong suits."

In *The Woman Who Fell from Grace* Handler spoofs the real-life sensation aroused by the publication of the sequel to Margaret Mitchell's landmark novel *Gone with the Wind. Oh, Shenandoah* is Alma Glaze's sweeping romantic saga of the American Revolution that has sold over thirty million copies since its publication in 1940. When the heirs to her estate negotiate a deal for what is hyped as the most eagerly awaited book sequel of all time, they hire Hoag to take over the writing duties from Glaze's daughter. Hoag quickly finds himself tangled in a mystery. It is well known that Alma Glaze had been accidentally killed right after the film version of *Oh, Shenandoah* was completed. But the housekeeper turns up dead after suggesting that the death of one of the film's stars at the same time was murder. Hoag investigates while preparations for a gala anniversary celebration of the novel go on around him. Sybil Steinberg, writing in *Publishers Weekly,* commented: "Handler's breezy, unpretentious and warm-hearted hero provides a breath of fresh air in a world of investigative angst." *New York Times Book Review* contributor Marilyn Stasio noted that Handler "writes a mean plot, full of crises that ingeniously spoof the melodramatic events of the original potboiler saga."

The Man Who Canceled Himself finds Hoag hired to ghostwrite a memoir of Uncle Chubby, a television comedy star whose career took a nosedive after he was arrested for public indecency in a Times Square pornography theater. But Uncle Chubby—whose real name is Lyle Hudnut—proves to be a difficult subject, possibly even psychotic. Hoag's research for Chubby's book leads to a bombing on the set of Hudnut's television show, a poisoning of the program's cast and crew, and eventually, murder. Handler's own background in the television industry gives the ring of authenticity to his novel, in the estimation of *Booklist* reviewer George Needham, who called *The Man Who Canceled Himself* "a thoroughly satisfying mystery that offers a cynical look at the economics, politics, and sociology of a TV sitcom." A *Publishers Weekly* critic also thought that the book is "great fun," largely because of the "gimlet-eyed observations of the fierce, delicious and dizzy infighting in Sitcom Land."

The Girl Who Ran off with Daddy "satisfies both as a mystery and as light comedy," judged Emily Melton in *Booklist*. In this adventure, Hoag's ghostwriting career is floundering, but he hardly cares, as he has plenty of money in savings and the rest of his life is working out nicely. He has a new baby with his live-in ex-wife and a comfortable life as a gentleman farmer in Connecticut. This peaceful interlude is disturbed when an old friend, Thor Gibbs, turns up on Hoag's doorstep. With Gibbs is his new girlfriend, who is young enough to be Thor's granddaughter; and she is, in fact, his stepdaughter. When Thor is murdered, the suspects include his rejected wife, his girlfriend's father, the father's gay lover, and the girlfriend's ex-boyfriends. "Handler controls his material masterfully, delivering newsy verisimilitude and domestic repartee worthy of Nick and Nora Charles," noted a *Publishers Weekly* contributor. Melton further described the book as "breezy, funny, and debonair." Melton also gave her approval to *The Man Who Loved Women to Death*, in which Hoag chases a serial killer who may in fact be one of his old friends. Reviewing that book, she declared: "Handler has written a sleek, sophisticated, over-the-top story that's filled with red herrings, laugh-aloud humor, and plenty of suspense."

In 2001 Handler introduced a new mystery series featuring film critic and author Mitch Berger and the beautiful Lt. Desiree "Des" Mitry. Writing in *Booklist*, Jenny McLarin commented that "Handler's Berger and Mitry series stands out from the crowd in a couple of ways. First, its romantically involved protagonists are a genuine odd couple: chubby Jewish film critic Mitch Berger and gorgeous African American state trooper Desiree Mitry. Second, the series' setting—Connecticut's Gold Coast shoreline—is hardly a common locale for crime fiction." The detective duo met in the first installment of the series, *The Cold Blue Blood*. Renting an old carriage house on a private island off the southern Connecticut shore, Berger finds himself living among the "blue bloods" as he tries to get over his wife's death from cancer. He soon discovers that his landlady's missing second husband is buried in the garden, and Mitry arrives on the scene to investigate. Not only do the two solve the crime, but also discover their mutual attraction in the process. GraceAnne A. DeCandido, writing in *Booklist*, noted that the "New York color is perfectly rendered, as is the Connecticut salt." Critics also praised the use of numerous movie stories told by Berger in the novel. "Film references, unique characterizations, and focused prose bode well for this new series," wrote Rex E. Klett in *Library Journal*.

In the *The Hot Pink Farm House*, Berger continues the Berger-Mitry romance as the two begin to investigate another murder case, this one involving land developers, an eccentric sculptor, and his daughters, one of whom ends up murdered. DeCandido, once again writing in *Booklist*, thought the book has too much melodrama and does not focus enough on Berger and Mitry. In another *Library Journal* review, Klett felt that *The Hot Pink Farm House* "will not leave readers wanting." A *Publishers Weekly* contributor commented that, despite some familiar plot devices, "the author's skill at depicting everyone from young children to aging adults and investing his characters with delightful quirks or grievous flaws makes this a superior read."

In the third outing of Handler's "Berger-Mitry" series, *The Bright Silver Star*, a beautiful movie star comes to the small Connecticut coastal enclave, along with her Latin heartthrob husband, who ends up falling off a cliff. Although initially thought to be a suicide, foul play is soon suspected, and Berger becomes a prime suspect when he pens a terrible review of the Latin movie star's last film and it is learned that he had a subsequent fistfight with the deceased. A *Publishers Weekly* contributor noted that Handler is particularly adept at handling the scenes in which Berger returns to New York to come to terms with his late wife's memory. The reviewer added, "With its vivid setting, quirky and unusual characters, and fast-paced plot skillfully interwoven with movie trivia, this cozy with attitude is sure to satisfy Handler's many committed fans and attract new ones."

BIOGRAPHICAL AND CRITICAL SOURCES:

PERIODICALS

Booklist, January 15, 1995, George Needham, review of *The Man Who Canceled Himself*, p. 899; April 1, 1996, Emily Melton, review of *The Girl Who Ran off with Daddy*, p. 1346; May 1, 1997, p. 1483; August, 2001, GraceAnne A. DeCandido, review of *The Cold Blue Blood*, p. 2096; October 15, 2002, GraceAnne A. DeCandido, review of *The Hot Pink Farmhouse*, p. 391; November, 2003, Jenny McLarin, review of *The Bright Silver Star*, p. 304.
Library Journal, April 1, 1997, Rex E. Klett, review of *The Man Who Loved Women to Death*, p. 133; October 1, 2001, Rex E. Klett, review of *The Cold*

Blue Blood, p. 146; November 1, 2002, Rex E. Klett, review of *The Hot Pink Farmhouse,* p. 131; September 1, 2003, Rex Klett, review of *The Bright Silver Star,* p. 214.
Los Angeles Times, March 5, 1987.
New York Times Book Review, May 3, 1987, p. 37; November 3, 1991, p. 27.
Publishers Weekly, September 21, 1990, Penny Kaganoff, review of *The Man Who Would Be F. Scott Fitzgerald,* p. 69; August 2, 1991, review of *The Woman Who Fell from Grace,* p. 66; July 13, 1992, review of *The Boy Who Never Grew Up,* p. 48; December 5, 1994, review of *The Man Who Canceled Himself,* p. 68; March 24, 1997, review of *The Man Who Loved Women to Death,* p. 62; January 15, 1996, review of *The Girl Who Ran off with Daddy,* p. 447; September 10, 2001, review of *The Cold Blue Blood,* p. 64; October 14, 2002, review of *The Hot Pink Farmhouse,* p. 67; September 1, 2003, review of *The Bright Silver Star,* p. 67.
Wall Street Journal, November 5, 1990, p. A13.

*   *   *

HARRIS, Christine 1955-

PERSONAL: Born August 5, 1955, in South Australia, Australia; daughter of Glenn (a carpenter) and Martha (a homemaker; maiden name, Gallacher) Brown; married David William Harris (a writer), July 6, 1989; children: Samuel Reynolds, Jennifer Reynolds. *Education:* Graduated from Dover Gardens Girls' Technical High School; College of Technical and Further Education, certificate (creative writing). *Hobbies and other interests:* Cottage gardening, swimming, bushwalking, shi ba shi.

ADDRESSES: Office—P.O. Box 478, Mt. Barker, South Australia 5251, Australia. *Agent*—Lyn Tranter, Australian Literary Management, 2-A Booth St., Balmain, New South Wales 2041, Australia. *E-mail*—christine@christineharris.com.

CAREER: Warooka Community Hall, Warooka, Australia, caretaker, 1985-86; Jenny Piper Promotions, staff member, 1986-87; Myer Bookstore, Adelaide, South Australia, Australia, sales assistant, 1990-94; writer, 1995—. Also works occasionally as a

photographer, with work published in newspapers including *Australian, Herald Sun,* and *Australian Airways* magazine.

MEMBER: Australian Society of Authors, South Australian Writers' Centre, Ekidnas (children's book writers' group), Royal Geographical Society.

AWARDS, HONORS: Golden Gateway Literary Award; Australia Council Literature Board grant, 1991, for *Trees in My Ears,* and 2004; Department for Arts and Cultural Development grants, 1993, for *Strike!,* 1995, for *Baptism of Fire;* Children Rate Outstanding Writers (CROW) Awards, shortlist, 1993, for *Outer Face,* and 1994, for *Buried Secrets;* Notable Book designation, Children's Book Council, for *Outer Face, Strike!, Party Animals, Baptism of Fire,* and *Sleeping In;* KROC Award runner-up, 1996; Western Australian Young Readers Book Award shortlist, 1997, for *Party Animals;* ArtSA grant, 1997, for *Foreign Devil;* Christian Schools Award nomination, 1998, for *Baptism of Fire;* Aurealis Award shortlist, 2000, for *Omega,* and 2002, for *Hairy Legs;* Children's Peace Literature Award shortlist, Psychologists for the Promotion of World Peace, 2001, for *Omega;* South Australia Kanga Award Focus Book designation, 2003, for *Jamil's Shadow.*

WRITINGS:

SHORT STORY COLLECTIONS

Outer Face, Random House (New York, NY), 1992.
Buried Secrets, Random House (New York, NY), 1993.
Widdershins, Random House (New York, NY), 1995, published as *Party Animals,* 1997.
(With Clare Carmichael and Margaret Clark) *Deadly Friends,* Random House (New York, NY), 1997.
Fortune Cookies, Random House (New York, NY), 1998.
Warped, Random House (New York, NY), 2000.

NOVELS; FOR YOUNG ADULTS

Strike!, Random House (New York, NY), 1994.
Countdown, Omnibus, 1995.
Baptism of Fire, Random House (New York, NY), 1996.

Pitt Man, Random House (New York, NY), 1996.

Torture Chamber, Random House (New York, NY), 1997.

Slime Time, Hodder (Sydney, Australia), 1997.

Foreign Devil, Random House (New York, NY), 1999.

Omega, Random House (New York, NY), 2000.

Hairy Legs, Random House (New York, NY), 2001.

Halfway 'round the World, Rigby (Orlando, FL), 2001.

Jamil's Shadow, Penguin (New York, NY), 2001.

Headspace, Penguin (New York, NY), 2004.

Author's work has been translated into French and Italian.

"SPY GIRL" SERIES; FOR YOUNG ADULTS

Secrets, Scholastic (New York, NY), 2004.

Fugitive, Scholastic (New York, NY), 2004.

Nighttime, Scholastic (New York, NY), 2005.

Danger, Scholastic (New York, NY), 2005.

"HOTSHOT" SERIES; FOR YOUNG ADULTS

Brain Drain, illustrated by Gus Gordon, Hodder Headline (Sydney, Australia), 2001.

Windbag, Hodder Headline (Sydney, Australia), 2001.

Psycho Gran, Hodder Headline (Sydney, Australia), 2001.

"VIBES" SERIES; SCIENCE-FICTION NOVELS

Suspicion, Hodder Headline (Sydney, Australia), 1998.

Masks, Hodder Headline (Sydney, Australia), 1998.

Jigsaw, Hodder Headline (Sydney, Australia), 1998.

Shadows, Hodder Headline (Sydney, Australia), 1998.

EDITOR; NONFICTION

No Bed of Roses, Wakefield Press, 1993.

Old Yanconian School Daze, Wakefield Press, 1995.

What a Line! ("History of Hills Hoists" series), Hills Industries, 1995.

In Looking-Glass Land, Seaview Press, 1996.

OTHER

Trees in My Ears: Children from around the World Talk to Christine Harris, Wakefield Press, 1992.

A Real Corpse, HarperCollins (New York, NY), 1997.

Sleeping In (picture book), illustrated by Craig Smith, Random House (New York, NY), 1997.

Odd Balls: Jokes and Funny Stories, illustrated by David Mackintosh, Random House (New York, NY), 1998.

I Don't Want to Go to School (picture book), illustrated by Craig Smith, Random House (New York, NY), 1999.

The Little Book of Elephants (humor and nonfiction), Hodder Headline (Sydney, Australia), 1999.

Also author of play *Break a Leg,* 2001.

ADAPTATIONS: Several of Harris's short stories were adapted as the dance performance *Second Hand,* produced by Outlet Dance, for performance at the space theatre and in South Australian schools, 1995.

WORK IN PROGRESS: An adult nonfiction work, titled *What the Hell Are We Doing Here?,* with husband David William Harris; a book in the "My Story" series, titled *Flying Doctor: The Diary of Jimmy Porter.*

SIDELIGHTS: Australian author Christine Harris has drawn upon her highly developed imagination, as well as her skills as a writer and her sense of fun, to create a body of short stories and novels that have gained a large following in her native country. Reviewing Harris's collection *Outer Face* in *Magpies,* Kevin Steinberger maintained: "While acknowledging the established appeal of bizarre humour and ironic twists, [Harris] is also analytical, descriptive, and reflective. There is something for everyone in her . . . stories." In addition to writing fiction, Harris has also edited several volumes of short fiction, and has served as the compiler of *Trees in My Ears,* a collection of narrations by children living in a variety of countries. The subjects covered in the book range from family life, friendship, school, and pets to heroes and aging. *Trees in My Ears* "provides a quite remarkable insight into how young minds and hearts interpret and respond to life as it unfolds around them," stated *Magpies* contributor Cathryn Crowe.

Born in South Australia in 1955, Harris grew up with a love of books. "As a child I escaped into other worlds via the written page and pretended I was a character in the story," she commented. "I still do this, but now I write down my own versions of what that character does. For many years, it seemed to some of my relatives that I had a book welded to my hands, whatever I was doing: cooking, ironing (yes, I actually used to iron once), in the bath, and even when walking (but keeping half an eye open for potholes and vehicles)."

After graduating from an all-girls technical high school near her home, Harris knew she wanted to advance her writing skills, but living in the country limited her options. So she enrolled in a home-study course with South Australia's College of Technical and Further Education, eventually earning a certificate in their creative writing program. She worked for several years in a bookstore in Adelaide, South Australia, before the success of such short story collections as *Outer Face* and the young adult novel *Strike!* gave her the confidence to devote full-time attention to writing.

Outer Face served as a book-buyer's introduction to Harris's work. A collection of fourteen short stories, *Outer Face* features such selections as "Knocked Out," about a young man who finds his newly acquired ability to read minds is a mixed blessing; "Mirror Door," in which a young woman enters a ghostly dimension through a portal that opens only on Halloween; and "A Bad Year," which showcases a farming family forced to lose its stock of sheep because of a severe drought. *Outer Face* "announces a new talent that will find a comfortable place" in the children's short story genre, noted *Magpies* reviewer Steinberger.

The short stories in the collection *Buried Secrets* help to establish a Harris trademark: each features a likeable teen protagonist, a slightly off-beat problem, and a dash of bizarre humor. Here the author introduces a wide variety of new characters, including a boy who sees through people's clothes, a woman who takes on the personality of the ruthless Black Widow spider, and even a young man who suspects his date of being a horrible monster. Praising the volume as being suitable for even reluctant teen readers, *Magpies* contributor Alf Mappin called *Buried Secrets* entertaining and asserted that "Harris's style, with its lightness and, one suspects, tongue-in-cheek attitude to what is being related, works well."

While Harris does write for her young readers with an eye toward entertainment, she occasionally uses her writing to make a point. "Sometimes I feel strongly about something and want to highlight a message through the medium of a story," Harris once explained. "Among the themes I have chosen are freedom of thought (*Baptism of Fire*), loyalty (*Strike!*), [and] communication and understanding of other cultures (*Fortune Cookies*)."

When she is writing, Harris becomes completely absorbed in her fictional world to the point that she even dreams about her characters. "For example, when I was halfway through writing *Baptism of Fire,* I was about to write a scene involving a fire when I dreamt the fire. I heard the crackle of flames on the thatched Fijian roofs, felt the heat and smelt the smoke. When I woke, I was sure that I could still smell smoke. I went straight to the computer and wrote that scene in one passionate sitting."

Harris frequently suffers from insomnia, so a great deal of her writing is accomplished during sleepless nights, particularly in the quiet hours between midnight and 3 a.m. "But on days when I write in daylight hours, I clean up, get dressed, and switch on the computer by 9 a.m., just as if I was going out to an office to work," Harris explained.

Having become familiar with many of the books available to young readers through her work in a local bookstore, Harris maintains that a great deal of quality writing exists for young readers. "And that's good," she related, "because we compete with television, the Internet, computer games, sport and all the other activities that fill and enrich children's lives. But [writers] have to be good, entertaining, and thought-provoking if we are to keep a place for books."

What is Harris's advice to young students thinking about becoming writers someday? "I would say read, read, and then read some more. Don't give up. It is not always the best writers who are published. Sometimes, it is the most determined. Train yourself to be observant, keep instincts. Keep your eye on market trends and listen to readers when they speak about the kinds of stories they like to read. Make time. Follow your heart. And be prepared to rewrite, take advice and keep polishing until the story is the best it can be. And hope for a bit of luck."

BIOGRAPHICAL AND CRITICAL SOURCES:

PERIODICALS

Lollipops, July-August, 1998, p. 15.
Magpies, July, 1992, p. 4; July, 1993, p. 4; September, 1993, p. 4; March, 1997, p. 33.

ONLINE

Christine Harris Web site, http://www.christineharris. com (February 20, 2005).

*   *   *

HAYS, Peter L. 1938-

PERSONAL: Born April 18, 1938, in Bremerhaven, Germany; son of Eric (a grocer) and Elsa (Nussbaum) Hays; married Myrna Mantel (a teacher), September 14, 1963; children: Melissa Anne, Eric Lee, Jeffrey Michael. *Education:* University of Rochester, A.B., 1959; New York University, M.A., 1961; Ohio State University, Ph.D., 1965.

ADDRESSES: Home—Davis, CA. *Agent*—c/o Author Mail, University of Idaho Press, Moscow, ID 83844. *E-mail*—plhays@ucdavis.edu.

CAREER: Writer. Ohio State University, Columbus, instructor in English, 1965-66; University of California, Davis, assistant professor, 1966-72, associate professor, 1972-77, professor of English and comparative literature, 1977-2004, department chair, 1974-77; retired, 2004. Fulbright lecturer in Mainz, West Germany (now Germany), 1977-78. University of California, Berkeley, instructor; chair, department of German and Russian, 1997-98. *Military service:* U.S. Army, 1959-60; U.S. Army Reserve, 1960-66.

MEMBER: Modern Language Association of America, Hemingway Society, Wharton Society, F. Scott Fitzgerald Society.

WRITINGS:

The Limping Hero, New York University Press (New York, NY), 1971, reprinted, Senivenety Press (Houston, TX), 2000.

A Concordance to Hemingway's "In Our Time," G. K. Hall (Boston, MA), 1990.
Ernest Hemingway, Continuum (New York, NY), 1990.
(Editor and contributor) *Teaching Hemingway's "The Sun Also Rises,"* University of Idaho Press (Moscow, ID), 2003.

Contributor of numerous articles to literature journals.

SIDELIGHTS: Peter L. Hays's book *Ernest Hemingway* was described by several reviewers as a concise, insightful introduction to the life and work of the man many people consider one of the greatest American authors. Hemingway's life was full and complicated, and his writing moved through several distinct stages. Hays divided his study of the author into seven sections. One focused on biographical facts; another presented a description of Hemingway's style and its influence on the writing that followed it; and there were also notes on his greatest successes, a chronology of his publishing history, and an extensive bibliography. His remarks covered classics such as *To Have and Have Not* and *Green Hills of Africa;* later efforts including *Men at War, Over the River and into the Trees,* and *The Old Man and the Sea;* and works published posthumously, such as *The Garden of Eden, The Dangerous Summer,* and *A Moveable Feast.*

Roland Wulbert, a reviewer for *Booklist,* noted that the book broke no new critical ground and commented that the historical portion of the book was "sketchy," but he concluded that "all in all," it was "a concise and serviceable introduction to Hemingway's crowded life and oeuvre." *Choice* contributor F. L. Ryan also noted that "there is not much that is new for the Hemingway scholar or the veteran reader," but he approved of Hays's commentary as "refreshingly brief but provocative." Ryan concluded: "Strongly recommended for anyone, particularly the undergraduate or community college student who needs a handbook that is both informative and lively."

Hays once told *CA:* "Although faculty may be paid only for their teaching and promoted . . . largely for their publications, publication, for me, is not separate from teaching, but rather, extends the podium offered in the classroom and allows professors further scope 'to profess' their views, to educate more widely."

BIOGRAPHICAL AND CRITICAL SOURCES:

PERIODICALS

American Literature, March, 1991, p. 176.

American Reference Books Annual, 1991, p. 468.

Booklist, April 15, 1990, Roland Wulbert, review of *Ernest Hemingway,* p. 1602.

Choice, December, 1990, F. L. Ryan, review of *Ernest Hemingway,* p. 628.

Hemingway Review, spring, 2004, Ann Putnam, review of *Teaching Hemingway's "The Sun Also Rises."*

*   *   *

HILL, John
    See KOONTZ, Dean R(ay)

*   *   *

HILTS, Philip J(ames) 1947-

PERSONAL: Born May 10, 1947, in Chicago, IL; son of Edward L. (a writer) and Katharine (Bonn) Hilts; married Mary Donna McKeown (a writer and editor), April 26, 1974; children: Benjamin, Alexis. *Education:* Attended Georgetown University, 1965-67 and 1969.

ADDRESSES: Office—New York Times, 229 West 43rd St., New York, NY 10036. *Agent*—Georges Borchardt, Inc., 136 East 57th St., New York, NY 10022.

CAREER: Reiss Coal, Manitowaca, WI, merchant sailor on SS *John A. Kling,* 1967-68; bookstore clerk in Washington, DC, 1968-69; *Washington Daily News,* Washington, DC, reporter, 1970-72; *Rocky Mountain News,* Denver, CO, reporter, 1972; freelance writer, 1972-80; *Washington Post,* Washington, DC, national reporter, 1980-89; *New York Times,* New York, NY, health and science reporter, 1989—.

AWARDS, HONORS: Two Front Page awards from Newspaper Guild, both 1982; National Media Award, American Psychological Association, 1983; National Book Award finalist, c. 1983, for *Scientific Temperaments: Three Lives in Contemporary Science.*

WRITINGS:

Behavior Mod, Harper's Magazine Press, 1974.
Scientific Temperaments: Three Lives in Contemporary Science, Simon & Schuster (New York, NY), 1982.

Memory's Ghost: The Strange Tale of Mr. M and the Nature of Memory, Simon & Schuster (New York, NY), 1995.
Smokescreen: The Truth behind the Tobacco Industry Cover-up, Addison-Wesley (Reading, MA), 1996.
Protecting America's Health: The FDA, Business, and One Hundred Years of Regulation, Knopf (New York, NY), 2003.

Contributor of more than one hundred articles to magazines, including *Omni* and *Science 83.*

SIDELIGHTS: In over twenty years as a reporter for the *Washington Post* and *New York Times,* Philip J. Hilts has covered many important health and science issues. He has brought his expertise to several nonfiction volumes as well, including the National Book Award finalist *Scientific Temperaments: Three Lives in Contemporary Science.* In this book he profiles a physicist, a molecular biologist, and a computer scientist, each prominent in his field, and explores how their personalities interact with their scientific work. "Hilts understands how scientists feel about their work, capturing the side they usually keep hidden beneath professionally cool exteriors," Lynn Hall observed in *Technology Review.* While the critic felt that the three "colorful" scientists Hilts profiles are not typical of all scientists, she concluded that "*Scientific Temperaments* is elegantly and gracefully written, colorful without being flashy, and precise without resorting to jargon. The progression of ideas, and the way in which biographical materials are interwoven with scientific information, is so natural that the style always serves the material."

Hilts was working at *New York Times* when he received an extraordinary package from a whistleblower at the Brown and Williamson tobacco company. It contained documents demonstrating that the company knew more about the dangers of cigarette smoking than they had admitted, and Hilts covered this growing scandal in more than twenty front-page stories. His 1996 book *Smokescreen: The Truth behind the Tobacco Industry Cover-Up* "is less a single investigation than a fast-paced, rewarding tour . . . through the recent revelations that have Big Tobacco on the run," a *Publishers Weekly* critic noted. The author uses the Brown and Williamson documents and other research to show how tobacco companies have carefully controlled the levels of addictive nicotine in their products, as well as how they deliberately target teens. The result is "an excellent analysis of recent regulatory, political, and legal developments affecting the tobacco industry," according to E. Ripley Forbes in *Public Health Reports*. The critic added that "Hilts is at his best in explaining how tobacco advertising affects the young and sustains his points with documents straight from the industry's own files." *New Republic* contributor Malcolm Gladwell, however, found an "intemperance and righteousness" in parts of Hilts's book, particularly "the incredible moral and analytical simplification, the obliteration of notions of responsibility, that is required to compare the act of selling people cigarettes to the act of herding people into a gas chamber." "The issue of smoking aside, Hilts' is a troubling look at the abuses of corporate power," *Booklist* reviewer David Rouse stated, while Stephen D. Sugarman concluded in *Science*, "Most readers are likely to experience a growing outrage at the industry, and especially its lawyers and friendly scientists, as they read along."

Hilts takes on another subject of national importance in 2003's *Protecting America's Health: The FDA, Business, and One Hundred Years of Regulation*. He traces the various approaches government has taken towards safeguarding America's food and drug supply, from the Pure Food and Drug Act of 1906 to recent attempts to weaken the Food and Drug Administration (FDA) by deregulating drug companies. The author reminds readers of the tragedies that spurred the government into action, from a 1930s antibiotic sold in a toxic solution to the Thalidomide babies of the 1960s. Hilts "writes both with a historian's attention to piecemeal dissection and analysis and with the flourish and vividness of an experienced journalist aware of the drama inherent in the story he is telling," Sherwin B. Nuland remarked in *New York Times Book Review*. John Crey similarly observed in *Business Week* that Hilts's book "is compelling, and it comes with a powerful message: that Americans are hugely in debt to the reformers who gave the 'FDA' its powers—and to the usually unappreciated bureaucrats toiling away in the trenches." Other reviewers hailed the author's defense of the FDA; as Noemie Maxwell concluded in *Library Journal*, Hilts "offers an important perspective" on the FDA's role in protecting the public, as well as "profound insight into issues emerging at the intersection of science, business, and ethics."

BIOGRAPHICAL AND CRITICAL SOURCES:

PERIODICALS

Booklist, August, 1995, Donna Seaman, review of *Memory's Ghost: The Strange Tale of Mr. M. and the Nature of Memory,* p. 1920; May 1, 1996, David Rouse, review of *Smokescreen: The Truth behind the Tobacco Industry Cover-Up,* p. 1466; April 15, 2003, David Siegfried, review of *Protecting America's Health: The FDA, Business, and One Hundred Years of Regulation,* p. 1431.

Business Week, July 28, 2003, John Crey, "The Hundred Years' War at the FDA," p. 20.

Library Journal, April 1, 2003, Noemie Maxwell, review of *Protecting America's Health,* p. 121.

Los Angeles Times, December 17, 1982, Carolyn See, review of *Scientific Temperaments: Three Lives in Contemporary Science,* sec. V-A, p. 1.

New Republic, November 4, 1996, Malcolm Gladwell, review of *Smokescreen,* p. 27.

New York Review of Books, July 11, 1996, Michael Massing, review of *Smokescreen,* p. 32.

New York Times Book Review, January 2, 1983, Peter Engel, review of *Scientific Temperaments,* p. 11; August 13, 1995, Howard Gardner, review of *Memory's Ghost,* p. 12; April, 27, 2003, Sherwin B. Nuland, "Don't Eat This Page," p. 17.

Public Health Reports, November-December, 1996, E. Ripley Forbes, review of *Smokescreen,* p. 556.

Publishers Weekly, July 3, 1995, review of *Memory's Ghost,* p. 43; May 6, 1996, review of *Smokescreen,* p. 61; February 4, 2003, review of *Protecting America's Health,* p. 60.

Reason, December, 1996, Jacob Sullum, review of *Smokescreen,* p. 46.

Science, August 9, 1996, Stephen D. Sugarman, review of *Smokescreen,* p. 744.

Technology Review, July, 1983, Lynn Hall, review of *Scientific Temperaments,* p. 66.

Washington Post, June 3, 1997, Mary Davis Suro, review of *Smokescreen,* p. WH11.

ONLINE

Frontline, http://www.pbs.org/wgbh/pages/frontline (February 20, 2004), interview with Philip J. Hilts.*

HOBAN, Russell (Conwell) 1925-

PERSONAL: Born February 4, 1925, in Lansdale, PA; son of Abram T. (an advertising manager for the *Jewish Daily Forward*) and Jeanette (Dimmerman) Hoban; married Lillian Aberman (an illustrator), January 31, 1944 (divorced, 1975); married Gundula Ahl (a bookseller), 1975; children: (first marriage) Phoebe, Abrom, Esme, Julia; (second marriage) Jachin Boaz, Wieland, Benjamin. *Education:* Attended Philadelphia Museum School of Industrial Art, 1941-43. *Hobbies and other interests:* Stones, short-wave listening.

ADDRESSES: Home and office—Fulham, London, England. *Agent*—David Higham Associates Ltd., 5-8 Lower John St., Golden Sq., London WlR 4HA, England.

CAREER: Artist and illustrator for magazine and advertising studios, New York, NY, 1945-51; Fletcher Smith Film Studio, New York, NY, story board artist and character designer, 1951; Batten, Barton, Durstine & Osborn, Inc., New York, NY, television art director, 1952-57; J. Walter Thompson Co., New York, NY, television art director, 1956; freelance illustrator for advertising agencies and magazines, including *Time, Life, Fortune, Saturday Evening Post,* and *True,* 1957-65; Doyle, Dane, Bembach, New York, NY, copywriter, 1965-67; novelist and author of children's books, beginning 1967. Art instructor at the Famous Artists Schools, Westport, CT, and School of Visual Arts, New York, NY. *Military service:* U.S. Army, Infantry, 1943-45; served in Italian campaign; earned the Bronze Star.

MEMBER: Authors Guild, Authors League of America, Society of Authors, PEN.

AWARDS, HONORS: American Library Association nomination for notable books, for *The Sorely Trying Day, The Mouse and His Child, How Tom Beat Captain Najork and His Hired Sportsmen,* and *Dinner at Alberta's;* Library of Congress Children's Book selection, 1964, for *Bread and Jam for Frances;* Boys' Club Junior Book Award, 1968, for *Charlie the Tramp; School Library Journal*'s Best Books, 1971, Lewis Carroll Shelf Award and Christopher Award, both 1972, all for *Emmet Otter's Jug-Band Christmas;* Whitbread Literary Award, 1974, and International

Board on Books for Young People Honor List, 1976, both for *How Tom Beat Captain Najork and His Hired Sportsmen;* John W. Campbell Memorial Award for the best science fiction novel of the year, Science Fiction Research Association, 1981, National Book Critics Circle nomination and Nebula Award nomination, 1982, all for *Riddley Walker;* Recognition of Merit, George G. Stone Center for Children's Books, 1982, for contributions to books for younger children.

WRITINGS:

CHILDREN'S NONFICTION

(Self-illustrated) *What Does It Do and How Does It Work?: Power Shovel, Dump Truck, and Other Heavy Machines,* Harper (New York, NY), 1959.
(Self-illustrated) *The Atomic Submarine: A Practice Combat Patrol under the Sea,* Harper (New York, NY), 1960.

CHILDREN'S FICTION

Bedtime for Frances, illustrated by Garth Williams, Harper (New York, NY), 1960, new edition, HarperTrophy (New York, NY), 1995.
Herman the Loser, illustrated by Lillian Hoban, Harper (New York, NY), 1961.
The Song in My Drum, illustrated by Lillian Hoban, Harper (New York, NY), 1961.
London Men and English Men, illustrated by Lillian Hoban, Harper (New York, NY), 1962.
(With Lillian Hoban) *Some Snow Said Hello,* Harper (New York, NY), 1963.
The Sorely Trying Day, illustrated by Lillian Hoban, Harper (New York, NY), 1964.
A Baby Sister for Frances, illustrated by Lillian Hoban, Harper (New York, NY), 1964, new edition, HarperTrophy (New York, NY), 1993.
Nothing to Do, illustrated by Lillian Hoban, Harper (New York, NY), 1964.
Bread and Jam for Frances, illustrated by Lillian Hoban, Harper (New York, NY), 1964, revised edition, HarperCollins (New York, NY), 1993.
Tom and the Two Handles, illustrated by Lillian Hoban, Harper (New York, NY), 1965.
The Story of Hester Mouse Who Became a Writer and Saved Most of Her Sisters and Brothers and Some of Her Aunts and Uncles from the Owl, illustrated by Lillian Hoban, Norton (New York, NY), 1965.

What Happened When Jack and Daisy Tried to Fool the Tooth Fairies, illustrated by Lillian Hoban, Scholastic (New York, NY), 1965.

Henry and the Monstrous Din, illustrated by Lillian Hoban, Harper (New York, NY), 1966.

The Little Brute Family, illustrated by Lillian Hoban, Macmillan (New York, NY), 1966, reprinted, Farrar, Straus and Giroux (New York, NY), 2002.

(With Lillian Hoban) *Save My Place,* Norton (New York, NY), 1967.

Charlie the Tramp, illustrated by Lillian Hoban, Four Winds (New York, NY), 1967, book and record, Scholastic (New York, NY), 1970.

The Mouse and His Child, illustrated by Lillian Hoban, Harper (New York, NY), 1967, new edition illustrated by David Small, 2001.

A Birthday for Frances, illustrated by Lillian Hoban, Harper (New York, NY), 1968, reprinted, Harper-Trophy (New York, NY), 1994.

The Stone Doll of Sister Brute, illustrated by Lillian Hoban, Macmillan (New York, NY), 1968.

Harvey's Hideout, illustrated by Lillian Hoban, Parents' Magazine Press (New York, NY), 1969.

Best Friends for Frances, illustrated by Lillian Hoban, Harper (New York, NY), 1969, new illustrated edition, HarperCollins (New York, NY), 1994.

Ugly Bird, illustrated by Lillian Hoban, Macmillan (New York, NY), 1969.

The Mole Family's Christmas, illustrated by Lillian Hoban, Parents' Magazine Press (New York, NY), 1969.

A Bargain for Frances, illustrated by Lillian Hoban, Harper (New York, NY), 1970, reprinted, Harper-Festival (New York, NY), 1999.

Emmet Otter's Jug-Band Christmas, illustrated by Lillian Hoban, Parents' Magazine Press (New York, NY), 1971.

The Sea-Thing Child, illustrated by son, Abrom Hoban, Harper (New York, NY), 1972, new edition illustrated by Patrick Benson, Candlewick Press (Cambridge, MA), 1999.

Letitia Rabbit's String Song (Junior Literary Guild selection), illustrated by Mary Chalmers, Coward (New York, NY), 1973.

La Corona and the Tin Frog (originally published in *Puffin Annual,* 1974), illustrated by Nicola Bayley, J. Cape (London, England), 1978, Merrimack Book Service, 1981.

How Tom Beat Captain Najork and His Hired Sportsmen, illustrated by Quentin Blake, Atheneum (New York, NY), 1974.

Ten What?: A Mystery Counting Book, illustrated by Sylvie Selig, J. Cape (London, England), 1974, Scribner (New York, NY), 1975.

Crocodile and Pierrot: A See the Story Book, illustrated by Sylvie Selig, J. Cape (London, England), 1975, Scribner (New York, NY), 1977.

Dinner at Alberta's, illustrated by James Marshall, Crowell (New York, NY), 1975.

A Near Thing for Captain Najork, illustrated by Quentin Blake, J. Cape (London, England), 1975, Atheneum (New York, NY), 1976.

Arthur's New Power, illustrated by Byron Barton, Crowell (New York, NY), 1978.

The Twenty-Elephant Restaurant, illustrated by Emily Arnold McCully, Atheneum (New York, NY), 1978, illustrated by Quentin Blake, J. Cape (London, England), 1980.

The Dancing Tigers, illustrated by David Gentlemen, J. Cape (London, England), 1979, Merrimack Book Service, 1981.

Flat Cat, illustrated by Clive Scruton, Philomel (New York, NY), 1980.

Ace Dragon Ltd., illustrated by Quentin Blake, J. Cape (London, England), 1980, Merrimack Book Service, 1981.

They Came from Aargh!, illustrated by Colin McNaughton, Philomel (New York, NY), 1981.

The Serpent Tower, illustrated by David Scott, Methuen/Walker (London, England), 1981.

The Great Fruit Gum Robbery, illustrated by Colin McNaughton, Methuen (London, England), 1981, published as *The Great Gum Drop Robbery,* Philomel (New York, NY), 1982.

The Battle of Zormla, illustrated by Colin McNaughton, Philomel (New York, NY), 1982.

The Flight of Bembel Rudzuk, illustrated by Colin McNaughton, Philomel (New York, NY), 1982.

Big John Turkle, illustrated by Martin Baynton, Walker, 1983, Holt (New York, NY), 1984.

Jim Frog, illustrated by Martin Baynton, Walker, 1983, Holt (New York, NY), 1984.

Lavinia Bat, illustrated by Martin Baynton, Holt (New York, NY), 1984.

Charlie Meadows, illustrated by Martin Baynton, Holt (New York, NY), 1984.

The Rain Door, illustrated by Quentin Blake, J. Cape (London, England), 1986, HarperCollins (New York, NY), 1987.

The Marzipan Pig, illustrated by Quentin Blake, J. Cape (London, England), 1986.

Ponders, illustrated by Martin Baynton, Walker (London, England), 1988.

Monsters, illustrated by Quentin Blake, Scholastic (New York, NY), 1989.

Jim Hedgehog and the Lonesome Tower, illustrated by Betsy Lewin, Clarion Books (New York, NY), 1990.

Jim Hedgehog's Supernatural Christmas, illustrated by Betsy Lewin, Clarion Books (New York, NY), 1992.

M.O.L.E.: Much Overworked Little Earthmover, J. Cape (London, England), 1993.

The Court of the Winged Serpent, illustrated by Patrick Benson, Trafalgar Square (New York, NY), 1995.

Trokeville Way, Knopf (New York, NY), 1996.

Trouble on Thunder Mountain, illustrated by Quentin Blake, Orchard Books (New York, NY), 2000.

Jim's Lion, illustrated by Ian Andrew, Candlewick Press (Cambridge, MA), 2001.

CHILDREN'S VERSE

Goodnight, illustrated by Lillian Hoban, Norton (New York, NY), 1966.

The Pedaling Man, and Other Poems, illustrated by Lillian Hoban, Norton (New York, NY), 1968.

Egg Thoughts, and Other Frances Songs, illustrated by Lillian Hoban, Harper (New York, NY), 1972.

NOVELS

The Lion of Boaz-Jachin and Jachin-Boaz, Stein & Day (New York, NY), 1973.

Kleinzeit, Viking (New York, New York), 1974.

Turtle Diary, J. Cape (London, England), 1975, Random House (New York, NY), 1976.

Riddley Walker, J. Cape (London, England), 1980, Summit Books (New York, NY), 1981, expanded edition with new foreword, Indiana University Press (Bloomington, IN), 1998.

Pilgermann, Summit Books (New York, NY), 1983.

The Medusa Frequency, edited by Gary Fisketjohn, Atlantic Monthly (New York, NY), 1987.

Fremder, J. Cape (London, England), 1996.

Mr Rinyo-Clacton's Offer, J. Cape (London, England), 1998.

Amaryllis Night and Day, Bloomsbury (London, England), 2001.

Angelica's Grotto, Carroll & Graf (New York, NY), 2001.

Her Name Was Lola, Arcade (New York, NY), 2003.

OTHER

(Illustrator) W. R. Burnett, *The Roar of the Crowd: Conversations with an Ex-Big-Leaguer,* C. N. Potter, 1964.

The Carrier Frequency (play), first produced in London, England, 1984.

Riddley Walker (stage adaptation of his novel), first produced in Manchester, England, 1986.

(Author of introduction) Wilhelm K. Grimm, *Household Tales,* illustrated by Mervyn Peake, Schocken, 1987.

A Russell Hoban Omnibus, Indiana University Press (Bloomington, IN), 1999.

Also author of *Come and Find Me* (television play), 1980. Contributor of articles to *Granta, Fiction Magazine,* and *Holiday.* Hoban's papers are included in the Kerlan Collection at the University of Minnesota.

ADAPTATIONS: The Mouse and His Child was made into a feature-length animated film by Fario-Lockhart-Sanrio Productions, 1977, and featured the voices of Cloris Leachman, Andy Devine, and Peter Ustinov (who also read an abridged version of the novel for a Caedmon recording in 1977); Glynis Johns recorded selections from *Bedtime for Frances, A Baby Sister for Frances, Bread and Jam for Frances,* and *A Birthday for Frances* in a sound recording entitled "Frances," as well as selections from *A Bargain for Frances, Best Friends for Frances,* and *Egg Thoughts, and Other Frances Songs* in a sound recording entitled "A Bargain for Frances and Other Stories," both by Caedmon in 1977; *Turtle Diary* was adapted for the screen by United British Artists/Brittanic in 1986, featuring a screenplay by Harold Pinter and starring Glenda Jackson and Ben Kingsley; *Riddley Walker* was staged by the Manchester Royal Exchange Theatre Company, 1986.

WORK IN PROGRESS: A novel titled *Come Dance with Me.*

SIDELIGHTS: "Russell Hoban is a writer whose genius is expressed with equal brilliance in books both for children and for adults," wrote Alida Allison in *Dictionary of Literary Biography.* Largely self-educated, Hoban has moved masterfully from being an artist and illustrator to writing children's fables and adult allegorical fiction. Praising his "unerring ear for dialogue," his "memorable depiction of scenes," and his "wise and warm stories notable for delightful plots and originality of language," Allison considered Hoban to be "much more than just a clever and observant writer. His works are permeated with an honest, often painful, and always uncompromising urge toward self-identity." Noting that "this theme of identity becomes more apparent, more complex as Hoban's works have become longer and more penetrating," Allison stated, "Indeed, Hoban's writing has leaped and bounded—paralleling upheavals in his own life."

In an interview with Rhonda M. Bunbury in *Children's Literature in Education,* Hoban indicated that as a child he was "good with words and good with drawing. It just happened my parents more or less seized on the drawing and thought that I'd probably end up being a great painter. I did become an illustrator, but I think that the drawing formula was always a little bit poisoned by the expectations that were laid on me, while the writing was allowed to be my own thing." He wrote poetry and short stories in school, and won several prizes. Having attended the Philadelphia Museum School of Industrial Art, Hoban worked as a freelance illustrator before he began writing children's stories. He would drive throughout Connecticut, occasionally stopping at construction sites and sketching the machinery being used. A friend saw his work and suggested that it might make a good children's book; Hoban's first published work was about construction equipment—*What Does It Do and How Does It Work?: Power Shovel, Dump Truck, and Other Heavy Machines.*

Although Hoban has since originated several well-known characters in children's literature, including *Charlie the Tramp, Emmet Otter, The Mouse and his Child,* and *Manny Rat,* he is especially recognized for a series of bedtime books about an anthropomorphic badger named Frances. Reviewers generally concurred that these stories depict ordinary family life with much humor, wit, and style. Benjamin DeMott suggested in the *Atlantic Monthly* that "these books are unique, first, because the adults in their pages are usually humorous, precise of speech, and understandingly conversant with general life, and second, because the author confronts—not unfancifully but without kinky secret garden stuff—problems with which ordinary parents and children have to cope." *Bedtime for Frances,* for instance, concerns nighttime fears and is regarded by many as a classic in children's literature; and according to a *Saturday Review* contributor, "The exasperated humor of this book could only derive from actual parental experience, and no doubt parents will enjoy it."

"Hoban has established himself as a writer with a rare understanding of childhood (and parental) psychology, sensitively and humorously portrayed in familiar family situations," noted Allison. He and his first wife, Lillian, also an illustrator and author of books for children, collaborated on many successful works, including several in the Frances series. Allison added that although their work together was usually well-received, "there were pans as well as paeans." While some books have been faulted for "excessive coziness, for sentimentality, and for stereotyped male-female roles," Allison said that a more general criticism of their work together is that "it tends toward repetition." However, commenting in *Children and Books,* May Hill Arbuthnot and Zena Sutherland found that all of Hoban's stories about Frances show "affection for and understanding of children" as well as "contribute to a small child's understanding of himself, his relationships with other people, and the fulfillment of his emotional needs." Further, they said, "These characters are indeed ourselves in fur." Yet as a *Times Literary Supplement* contributor observed, "Excellent as [the Frances books] are, they give no hint that the author had in him such a blockbuster of a book as *The Mouse and His Child.*"

Revered in England as a modern children's classic, *The Mouse and His Child* was described in the *New York Times Book Review* by Barbara Wersba as a story about two wind-up toy mice who are discarded from a toyshop and are then "buffeted from place to place as they seek the lost paradise of their first home—a doll house—and their first 'family,' a toy elephant and seal." Ill-equipped for the baffling, threatening world into which they are tossed, the mouse and his child innocently confront the unknown and its inherent treachery and violence, as well as their own fears. The book explores not only the transience and inconstancy of life but also the struggle to persevere. "Helpless when they are not wound up, unable to stop when they *are,* [the mice] are fated like all mechanical things to breakage, rust and disintegration as humans are to death," writes Margaret Blount in her *Animal Land: The Creatures of Children's Fiction.* "As an adult," said Blount, "it is impossible to read [the book] unmoved." Distressed, however, by the "continuing images of cruelty and decay," Penelope Farmer remarked in *Children's Literature in Education* that *The Mouse and His Child* is "like Beckett for children." But assessing whatever cruelty and decay there is in the novel as the "artful rendering of the facts of life," Allison affirmed, "If there is betrayal, there is also self-sacrifice. If there is loss, there is also love. If there is homelessness, there is also destination. The mouse child gets his family in the end; children's literature gets a masterpiece."

"Like the best of books, [*The Mouse and His Child*] is a book from which one can peel layer after layer of meaning," said the *Times Literary Supplement* contributor. Some critics, however, questioned the book's suitability for children. Hoban responded to these critics in an essay for *Books for Your Children*: "When I wrote [*The Mouse and His Child*] I didn't think it was [a children's book]. I was writing as much book as I was capable of at the time. No concessions were made in style or content. It was my first novel and . . . it was the fullest response I could make to being alive and in the world." Hoban indicated to Bunbury that the book has become his favorite book for children, the one that has given him the most satisfaction, "Though it may not be the best of my novels, it is the closest to my heart because of that." Believing the book reveals "an absolute respect for its subject—which means its readers as well," Isabel Quigley added in the *Spectator*, "I'm still not sure just who is going to read it but that hardly seems to matter. . . . It will last." Hoban felt that within its limitations, the book is suitable for children, though. "Its heroes and heroines found out what they were and it wasn't enough, so they found out how to be more," he says in his essay. "That's not a bad thought to be going with."

Nominated as the most distinguished book of fiction by the National Book Critics Circle and for the Nebula Award by the Science Fiction Writers of America, *Riddley Walker* imagines a world and civilization decades after a nuclear holocaust; the story of what remains is narrated in a fragmented, phonetical English by a twelve-year-old boy struggling to comprehend the past so that its magnificence might be recaptured. "Set in a remote future and composed in an English nobody ever spoke or wrote," wrote Benjamin DeMott in the *New York Times*, "this short, swiftly paced tale juxtaposes preliterate fable and Beckettian wit, Boschian monstrosities and a hero with Huck Finn's heart and charm, lighting by El Greco and jokes by Punch and Judy. It is a wrenchingly vivid report on the texture of life after Doomsday."

Detecting similarities in *Riddley Walker* to other contemporary works such as Anthony Burgess's *A Clockwork Orange*, John Gardner's *Grendel*, and the complete works of William Golding, DeMott believed that "in vision and execution, this is an exceptionally original work, and Russell Hoban is actually his own best source." *Riddley Walker* "is not 'like' anything," noted Victoria Glendinning in the *Listener*. As A. Alvarez observed in the *New York Review of Books*, Hoban has "transformed what might have been just another fantasy of the future into a novel of exceptional depth and originality."

Critically lauded and especially popular in England, *Riddley Walker* has been particularly commended for its inventive language, which Alvarez thought "reflects with extraordinary precision both the narrator's understanding and the desolate landscape he moves through." Reviewing the book in the *Washington Post Book World*, Michael Dirda commented that "what is marvelous in all this is the way Hoban makes us experience the uncanny familiarity of this world, while also making it a strange and animistic place, where words almost have a life of their own." "What Hoban has done," suggested Barbara A. Bannon in a *Publishers Weekly* interview with Hoban, "is to invent a world and a language to go with it, and in doing both he remains a storyteller, which is the most significant achievement of 'Riddley Walker.'"

Alvarez called *Riddley Walker* an "artistic tour de force in every possible way," but Natalie Maynor and Richard F. Patteson suggested in *Critique* that even more than that, it is "perhaps the most sophisticated work of fiction ever to speculate about man's future on earth and the implications for a potentially destructive technology." Eliot Fremont-Smith maintained in the *Village Voice* that "the reality of the human situation now is so horrendous and bizarre that to get a hold on it requires all our faculties, including the imaginative. We can't do it through plain fact and arms controllers' reasoning alone . . . [r]ead *Riddley*, too." Although Kelly Cherry referred to the novel in the *Chicago Tribune Book World* as a "philosophical essay in fictional drag," DeMott thought that Hoban's focus on what has been lost in civilization "summons the reader to dwell anew on that within civilization which is separate from, opposite to, power and its appurtenances, ravages, triumphs." *Riddley Walker,* said DeMott, is "haunting and fiercely imagined and—this matters most—intensely ponderable."

An American by birth but an Englishman at heart, Hoban has made his home in London for much of his adult life. In a 1998 *Pure Fiction Reviews* online interview with the author, John Forsyth declared that Hoban's enthusiasm for his adopted city "remains undiminished, decades after moving here . . . and that this affection places him in a whole tradition of English writing." As Hoban told Forsyth, "I came here because I was a great admirer of British ghost stories and supernatural stories. . . . I've been at great pains to have [my narrators] speak in an English manner, and to make their background a credible English background."

During the same interview Hoban revealed one more attraction of London—its subway system, the Underground. "I hate buses, you know; they never turn up, people rush ahead of you and all that," he elaborated. "At most Tube stations it tells you how long it's going to be till the next Wimbledon train or whatever. And then there's the perpetual nocturnal mood of the Underground; it never seems like daytime down there, it always seems like night. I'm a nocturnal kind of person, and I like to work at night."

The Underground plays a role in Hoban's 1998 adult novel, *Mr Rinyo-Clacton's Offer.* The story follows one Jonathan Fitch as he is approached in the Piccadilly Circus subway station by the title character, an eccentric aristocrat. The offer of the title is of the Faustian variety: Rinyo-Clacton offers Fitch a million pounds in exchange for his life in one year. "What kind of weirdo are you?," asks Fitch. "The kind with lots of money," is the reply. The book then goes on to examine the tragic circumstances that impel Fitch to consider the fateful deal.

For all their suspense, though, "in my books there aren't characters who are simply bad or simply good," Hoban told Fred Hauptfuhrer in *People.* "Nothing in life is that simple." Writing for adults has added both breadth and depth to Hoban's work; and as his work has grown in complexity, he has commented upon the

process by which an idea evolves into a book. As he explained to Bannon: "There always seems to be something in my mind waiting to put something together with some primary thought I will encounter. It's like looking out of the window and listening to the radio at the same time. I am committed to what comes to me, however it links up."

Hoban's mind turned to questions about how humans perceive the world, time, and the reality of dreams with his next adult book. Writing in the *Economist* about Hoban's 2001 novel, *Amaryllis Night and Day,* a reviewer commented, "Readers without training in higher mathematics will need all the mental agility they can muster to follow him into the realm of pure geometry, which has inspired his . . . novel." The narrator is painter Peter Diggs, who meets a woman in his dreams named Amaryllis. Diggs eventually encounters the real-life Amaryllis, and the couple finds out that they share not only a dream life but also common real experiences and guilt. In addition to his strange relationship with Amaryllis, the narrator ponders the nature of labyrinths and Klein bottles (a type of glass that is twisted in a way that makes it difficult to distinguish the inside from the outside), which leads, as noted by James Hopkin in the *New Statesman,* "to meditations on the nature of time and perception." The *Economist* contributor found the novel's "characters stilted and the story contrived." Hopkin noted that Hoban's flaws in the novel were making the female characters too talented, beautiful, and irresistibly drawn to the narrator and said that "the mock-Hollywood happy ending is annoying, regardless of any ironic intent." Nevertheless, he also noted, "Yet Hoban has a gift for being almost inadvertently contemporary. He follows his own obsessions, but cannot help revealing aspects of a society that refuses to 'achieve grown-upness.'"

Hoban's next novel, *Angelica's Grotto,* is a dark, comic look at art connoisseur Harold Klein who wanders onto a pornographic Web site and ultimately an erotic odyssey. As noted by Christopher L. Reese in *World Literature Today,* the novel "explores a wide variety of issues and ideas, from dealing with old age to the relationships between art and pornography and between individuals and society." In his seventies, Klein has a strange problem in that the loss of his "inner voice" causes him to be totally uninhibited in all his utterances. When Klein meets the much younger Melissa Bottomley, the sex researcher who runs the

Web porn site, they begin to act out their sexual fantasies. Reese found that the novel did not offer answers to the many questions it raises concerning "the individual concept of self and how it is created, and what we expect from art/pornography." Reese went on to note, "Overall, what Hoban has produced here is a comic piece of writing that considers several serious issues in a humorous light." A *Publishers Weekly* contributor commented, "Hoban . . . has fashioned an intensely conceived coda to the verities of desire and fulfillment—not to mention trust, honesty and pornography—and Klein is a sharp, funny and intelligent protagonist whom readers will find it hard not to like." Carrie Bissey, writing in *Booklist,* noted that "those willing to follow his [Hoban's] meandering thoughts will be rewarded by an intelligently bizarre novel."

Although focusing more on adult literature, Hoban has not forsaken his children's writings, such as his oversized picture book for older children called *Jim's Lion,* published in 2001. A story about an extremely sick boy who is worried about being anesthetized for an operation, the book describes Jim's relationship with South African nurse Bami and how she helps him face his fears. A *Publishers Weekly* contributor felt that the story was perhaps too frightening for children and commented that with "its complicated plot and its convoluted theme, this tale may perplex rather than soothe its intended audience." Cynthia Turnquest, writing in *Booklist,* called the book a "complex, touching story that will make a good springboard for discussing difficult questions about hospitalization and mortality." Faith Brautigan noted in *School Library Journal,* "Critically ill children, a population largely absent from the picture-book world, will now have a hero in Jim."

Hoban's adult novel *Her Name Was Lola* appeared on bookshelves in 2003. Once again, Hoban reveals his penchant for black comedy in a story about a struggling London writer named Max Lesser who has a series of successful children's books but is facing writer's block with his adult novel. Max soon meets two women and conducts a simultaneous affair with them. Lola, who Max declares to be his destined love, finds out about the other woman, Lula Mae, and leaves him. Lula Mae, a transplanted Texan who works in technology, eventually decides that Max is not the right man for her, even though she is carrying his child, and moves back to Texas. The story is told primarily in flashbacks as Max goes about trying to overcome his desolation at losing both women and being unable to finish his novel. Despite the fact that he felt that "Lola and Lula Mae aren't quite flesh and blood," Hugo Barnacle, writing in the *New Statesman,* noted, "Hoban apparently wants to see how much outrageous artifice and willful exposure of literary technique he can get away with while still working his magic on the reader. The answer is plenty. Far from being an arid exercise, the novel has great charm and grace." A *Publishers Weekly* contributor called the story a "quirky, tender tale" but noted that "some readers will enjoy the journey, while others will find that Hoban's form trumps his content." In a review in *Booklist,* Jennifer Baker stated that the novel was a "wonderfully funny, refreshing, and compelling love story."

BIOGRAPHICAL AND CRITICAL SOURCES:

BOOKS

Allison, Alida, editor, *Russell Hoban/Forty Years: Essays on His Writings for Children,* Garland Publishing (New York, NY), 2000.

Arbuthnot, May Hill, and Zena Sutherland, *Children and Books,* 4th edition, Scott, Foresman (Chicago, IL), 1972.

Blount, Margaret, *Animal Land: The Creatures of Children's Fiction,* Morrow (New York, NY), 1974.

Children's Literature Review, Volume 3, Gale (Detroit, MI), 1978.

Contemporary Literary Criticism, Gale (Detroit, MI), Volume 7, 1977, Volume 25, 1983.

Dictionary of Literary Biography, Volume 52: *American Writers for Children since 1960: Fiction,* Gale (Detroit, MI), 1986, pp. 192-202.

Hoban, Russell, *The Thorny Paradise: Writers on Writing for Children,* edited by Edward Blishen, Kestrel (Harmondsworth, England), 1975.

Hoban, Russell, *Mr Rinyo-Clacton's Offer,* J. Cape (London, England), 1998.

Twentieth-Century Children's Writers, 3rd edition, St. James Press (Detroit, MI), 1989.

Wilkie, Christine, *Through the Narrow Gate: The Mythological Consciousness of Russell Hoban,* Fairleigh Dickinson University Press (Rutherford, NJ), 1989.

PERIODICALS

American Artist, October, 1961.

Antioch Review, summer, 1982.

Atlantic Monthly, August, 1976, pp. 83-84; December, 1983.

Booklist, May 15, 2001, Carrie Bissey, review of *Angelica's Grotto,* p. 1731; January 1, 2002, Cynthia Turnquest, review of *Jim's Lion,* p. 865; June 1, 2004, Jennifer Baker, review of *Her Name Was Lola,* p. 1700.

Books for Your Children, winter, 1976, p. 3.

Chicago Tribune Book World, July 12, 1981, Kelly Cherry, review of *Riddley Walker.*

Children's Literature in Education, March, 1972; spring, 1976; fall, 1986, pp. 139-149.

Critique, fall, 1984.

Economist, January 27, 2001, review of *Amaryllis Night and Day,* p. 4.

Educational Foundation for Nuclear Science, June, 1982.

Encounter, June, 1981.

Globe and Mail (Toronto, Ontario, Canada), March 29, 1986.

Harper's, April, 1983.

Junior Bookshelf, July, 1963.

Library Journal, July, 2004, Robin Nesbitt, review of *Her Name Was Lola,* p. 70.

Listener, October 30, 1980, Victoria Glendinning, review of *Riddley Walker,* p. 589.

Los Angeles Times, February 14, 1986.

New Statesman, May 25, 1973; April 11, 1975; January 29, 2001, James Hopkin, review of *Amaryllis Night and Day,* p. 54; November 3, 2003, Hugo Barnacle, review of *Her Name Was Lola,* p. 55.

Newsweek, March 1, 1976; June 29, 1981; December 7, 1981; May 30, 1983; February 17, 1986.

New Yorker, March 22, 1976; July 20, 1981; August 8, 1983.

New York Review of Books, November 19, 1981, pp. 16-18.

New York Times, November 1, 1981; June 20, 1983; February 14, 1986.

New York Times Book Review, February 4, 1968; March 21, 1976; June 6, 1982; May 29, 1983; November 27, 1983.

Observer (London, England), March 13, 1983.

People, August 10, 1981.

Publishers Weekly, May 15, 1981, Barbara A. Bannon, interview with author; June 4, 2001, review of *Angelica's Grotto,* p. 57; November 12, 2001,

review of *Jim's Lion,* p. 59; May 24, 2004, review of *Her Name Was Lola,* p. 42.

Saturday Review, May 7, 1960; May 1, 1976; December, 1981.

School Library Journal, January, 2002, Faith Brautigam, review of *Jim's Lion,* p. 101.

Spectator, May 16, 1969, pp. 654-655; April 5, 1975; March 12, 1983.

Time, February 16, 1976; June 22, 1981; May 16, 1983.

Times (London, England), January 7, 1982; March 24, 1983.

Times Literary Supplement, April 3, 1969, p. 357; March 16, 1973; March 29, 1974; October 31, 1980; March 7, 1986; April 3, 1987; September 4, 1987.

Village Voice, June 15, 1982, Eliot Fremont-Smith, review of *Riddley Walker.*

Washington Post, February 28, 1986.

Washington Post Book World, June 7, 1981, pp. 1, 14; June 27, 1982; May 29, 1983;' July 12, 1987; October 14, 1990.

Wilton Bulletin, September 26, 1962.

World Literature Today, autumn, 2001, review of *Angelica's Grotto,* p. 162.

ONLINE

Pure Fiction Reviews, http://www.purefiction.com/ (October 2, 2001), interview with Russell Hoban.*

*   *   *

HOFFMAN, Alice 1952-

PERSONAL: Born March 16, 1952, in New York, NY; married Tom Martin (a writer); children: Jake, Zack. *Education:* Adelphi University, B.A., 1973; Stanford University, M.A., 1975.

ADDRESSES: Home—Brookline, MA. *Agent*—Elaine Markson Literary Agency, 44 Greenwich Ave., New York, NY 10011.

CAREER: Writer, 1975—.

AWARDS, HONORS: Mirelles fellow, Stanford University, 1975; Bread Loaf fellowship, summer, 1976; Notable Books of 1979 list, *Library Journal,* for *The Drowning Season.*

WRITINGS:

NOVELS

Property Of, Farrar, Straus (New York, NY), 1977.
The Drowning Season, Dutton (New York, NY), 1979.
Angel Landing, Putnam (New York, NY), 1980.
White Horses, Putnam (New York, NY), 1982.
Fortune's Daughter, Putnam (New York, NY), 1985.
Illumination Night, Putnam (New York, NY), 1987.
At Risk, Putnam (New York, NY), 1988.
Seventh Heaven, Putnam (New York, NY), 1990.
Turtle Moon, Berkley (New York, NY), 1993
Second Nature, Putnam (New York, NY), 1994.
Practical Magic, Putnam (New York, NY), 1995.
Here on Earth, Putnam (New York, NY), 1997.
The River King, Putnam (New York, NY), 2000.
Blue Diary, Putnam (New York, NY), 2001.
The Probable Future, Doubleday (New York, NY), 2003.
Blackbird House, Doubleday (New York, NY), 2004.

FOR CHILDREN

Fireflies, illustrated by Wayne McLoughlin, Hyperion (New York, NY), 1997.
Horsefly, illustrated by Steve Johnson, Hyperion (New York, NY), 2000.
Aquamarine, Scholastic (New York, NY), 2001.
Indigo, Scholastic (New York, NY), 2002.
Green Angel, Scholastic (New York, NY), 2003.
(With Wolfe Martin) *Moondog,* illustrated by Yumi Heo, Scholastic (New York, NY), 2004.

OTHER

Independence Day (screenplay), Warner Bros., 1983.
Local Girls (short stories), Putnam (New York, NY), 1999.

Also author of other screenplays. Contributor of stories to *Ms., Redbook, Fiction, American Review,* and *Playgirl.*

ADAPTATIONS: Practical Magic was adapted by Robin Swicord, Akiva Goldsman, and Adam Brooks into a film directed by Griffin Dunne, starring Sandra Bullock, Nicole Kidman, and Aidan Quinn, and released by Warner Bros. in 1998; a sound recording was produced of *Local Girls.*

SIDELIGHTS: Through the course of numerous novels, Alice Hoffman's work has been characterized by "a shimmering prose style, the fusing of fantasy and realism, [and] the preoccupation with the way the mythic weaves itself into the everyday," Alexandra Johnson summarized in the *Boston Review.* "Hoffman's narrative domain is the domestic, the daily. Yet her vision—and voice—are lyrical," the critic continues. "She is a writer whose prose style is often praised as painterly, and, indeed, Hoffman's fictional world is like a Vermeer: a beautifully crafted study of the interior life." Hoffman's characters "tend to be rebels and eccentrics," Stella Dong stated in a *Publishers Weekly* interview with the author. Hoffman explained that she writes about such people "because they're outsiders and to some extent, we all think of ourselves as outsiders. We're looking for that other person—man, woman, parent or child—who will make us whole." As the author once told *CA:* "I suppose my main concern is the search for identity and continuity, and the struggle inherent in that search."

The protagonist of Hoffman's first novel, *Property Of,* for instance, is an unnamed seventeen-year-old girl enamored of McKay, the leader of an urban gang involved in violence and drugs; the story of their year-long relationship is what *Times Literary Supplement* contributor Zachary Leader called "a sort of punk or pop-gothic *Jane Eyre.*" Despite the "harsh and gritty" quality of the world it portrays, *Property Of* is nevertheless "a remarkably envisioned novel, almost mythic in its cadences, hypnotic," Richard R. Lingeman observed in the *New York Times.* "McKay and the heroine are like tragic lovers in a courtly romance played out in candy stores, clubhouses and mean streets. . . . Hoffman imbues her juvenile delinquents with a romantic intensity that lifts them out of sociology." Edith Milton offered a similar assessment, commenting in the *Yale Review* that "the narrative is engrossing because Hoffman creates characters touched by legend." The critic further elaborated that Hoffman is able to balance "parody and sentiment, cutting her own flights of panting prose with acid self-mockery."

While the writing in *Property Of* "had speed, wit, and a mordant lyricism," Margo Jefferson remarked in *Ms.* that "*The Drowning Season* has extravagance and generosity as well." Tracing "a legacy of lovelessness from frozen White Russia to modern New York," as *Newsweek* contributor Jean Strouse described it, *The Drowning Season* follows Esther the White and Esther the Black, a grandmother and granddaughter who overcome a past of failed communication to slowly establish a relationship. Like Hoffman's first novel, *The Drowning Season* functions on two levels, as Susan Wood suggested in the *Washington Post:* "The *Drowning Season,* just as hypnotic and mythic in its language and rhythms, reverberates with situations and characters that suggest ancient myths and European folk tales and seems on one level to function as a symbolic, allegorical tale in a modern setting. Yet it is very much a novel about believable and imperfect human beings, as concrete and individualized as the family next door." Barry Siegel found Esther the White in particular "a truly compelling character," writing in the *Los Angeles Times Book Review* that while "she is the source of her family's malaise . . . Hoffman sees in her something much more complex than a villain." The critic concluded that Hoffman "is a superb writer who brings us to understand and to care about all her characters. . . . Hoffman at all times remains in control of her fine narrative."

Hoffman followed *The Drowning Season* with *Angel Landing,* a romance set near a nuclear power plant, and *White Horses,* the story of a young girl's obsession with her older brother. Teresa, the protagonist of *White Horses,* has been brought up hearing the family legend of the *Arias,* dangerous and beautiful young outlaws who carry women off to exciting lives; this legend led Teresa's mother into an unhappy marriage, and Teresa herself into an incestuous love for Silver, whom she sees as her ideal *Aria.* "Incest may be the most difficult theme for a novelist to undertake," stated *Newsweek* reviewer Peter S. Prescott, "yet Hoffman here makes it tolerable by the mythic mold in which she has cast her story." *New York Times Book Review* contributor Anne Tyler likewise saw a mythic dimension in the novel: "*White Horses* combines the concrete and the dreamlike. Its characters are people we think we recognize at first; but then on second thought we're not so sure." The critic continued, "There's an almost seamless transition from the real to the unreal, back and forth and back again." Stephanie Vaughn, however, faulted the novel's symbolism as "ask[ing] us to see an epic dimension that the story does not quite deliver," as she remarked in her *Washington Post* review. And while Tyler also thought that the novel is at times "burdened by the very musicality

that was so appealing in the beginning," she admitted that "these are quibbles, and very minor quibbles at that. The overall impression is one of abundant life, masterfully orchestrated by the author." *White Horses,* Tyler concluded, "is a satisfying novel, at the same time mysterious and believable, and it marks a significant advance for Alice Hoffman."

While *Fortune's Daughter,* in the vein of Hoffman's earlier novels, "has the quality of folk tale—of amazing events calmly recounted," Perri Klass asserted in the *New York Times Book Review* that unlike *White Horses* it has "no . . . explicit myth. Instead, the sense of magic and elemental force arises from the central mystery of childbirth." Klass continued, "This novel's great strength lies in its two heroines, who both find themselves drawn, without plans, hopes or full understanding, into the inevitably mythological process of pregnancy and childbirth." Rae, pregnant with her first child, has just been deserted by the man for whom she left her home and traveled across a continent. Seeking reassurance, she finds Lila, a fortune teller who reads a child's death in Rae's tea leaves. Against Lila's wishes, Rae enlists the older woman's assistance with her pregnancy, evoking Lila's memories of the child she gave up for adoption over twenty years ago. The result, observed Robin Hemley in the *Chicago Tribune Book World,* is "an elegant and evocative novel that conjures up a kind of modern-day female mythology."

Some critics, however, such as *Boston Review* contributor Patricia Meyer Spacks, felt the plot of *Fortune's Daughter* verges on "soap-opera sentimentalities." Nevertheless, they acknowledge, as Klass wrote, that "the peculiar offbeat humor keeps the narrative from drifting into melodrama." The critic elaborated, "It is in its juxtaposition of the mythic, the apocalyptic, with the resolutely ordinary, in its portrait of eccentric characters living in a very familiar world, that this novel finds its unique voice. It is beautifully and matter-of-factly told, and it leaves the reader with an almost bewildered sense that this primal mythological level does exist in everyday reality, and that there is no event, from the standard miracle of childbirth to the most bizarre magic imaginable, that cannot occur in a setting of familiar, everyday details."

"*Illumination Night,* Hoffman's sixth novel, is in many ways her most subtle," Johnson claimed, describing it as "a powerful if often disturbing look at the interior lives, domestic and emotional, of a young family and the teenage girl set on destroying them all." Andre and Vonny are a young couple concerned about their son's lack of growth and the tension in their marriage caused by the unwanted attentions of Jody, a neighboring sixteen-year-old, towards Andre. "This may sound like soap opera," *New York Times* critic Christopher Lehmann-Haupt declared, but Hoffman "has enough power of empathy to make her characters matter to us. Daringly mixing comedy with tragedy, and the quotidian with the fabulous, she has created a narrative that somehow makes myth out of the sticky complexities of contemporary marriage." Hoffman "has a penchant for finding a near-gothic strangeness and enchantment on the edges of everyday experience," Jack Sullivan likewise commented in the *Washington Post Book World.* Throughout the book "is the sure sense that magic and spirituality infuse our lives, and that this magic is as readily available to the poor as to the rich," *Los Angeles Times* critic Carolyn See similarly reported.

"Subtle touches here and there make this intelligent novel shine," Gwyneth Cravens maintained in the *New York Times Book Review.* "Ms. Hoffman knows how to tell a story in clear language and how to avoid subordinating the meanderings of temperament to logic or plot. The characters suddenly, and believably, change their behavior toward one another in the presence of the irrational." Other critics have also remarked on the quality of the author's characterizations. Lehmann-Haupt, for example, observed that "Hoffman writes so simply about human passions that her characters are branded onto one's memory," while London *Times* reviewer Philip Howard stated that Hoffman "hits bull's eyes on the incomprehensions between the young and the old, on the magic and pain of ordinary life." As Candice Russell noted in her *Chicago Tribune* review, the author's "omniscient voice . . . explores the underpinnings of her characters, who become increasingly connected and interdependent." Sullivan similarly praised Hoffman's narrative for its "unusually fluid form of subjectivity that becomes a kind of total omniscience . . . without breaking the rhythm of her prose or storyline. From a technical as well as emotional standpoint," the critic concluded, "this is an impressive, stirring performance."

With *At Risk,* the story of a young girl whose AIDS precipitates a family crisis, Hoffman "is mainstreaming a refined literary talent," *Time* writer R. Z. Shep-

pard recounted. By taking as her subject such a topical social concern, however, Hoffman has drawn criticism from some reviewers for letting the issue of AIDS overcome the story. *Washington Post* writer Jonathan Yardley, for example, contended that the novel "is very much wrought from material offered by the headlines, yet it fails to shape that material into anything approximating life." But Lehmann-Haupt believed that *At Risk* "does succeed in overcoming these obstacles [of topicality]. From its opening sentence, we know we are in a world that is specific and alive."

Because the issues in *At Risk* are more self-evident than in the author's other work, some reviewers have suggested that the novel does not contain as much of a "magical" element as do her other books. But *Newsweek* critic Laura Shapiro contended that "this wonderful book isn't markedly different in style or imagination from Hoffman's last novel." As Chicago *Tribune Books* contributor Michele Souda observed, the novel contains many "dark and bizarre experiences that remind us how much Hoffman has always trusted her characters' dreams and how well she has invented them." And, as the author explained to London *Times* writer Catherine Bennett, "part of the reason [for the diminished emphasis on magic] is that AIDS took the place of that, that was the inexplicable part of it. AIDS is like something you'd invent, it's bizarre, it's horrible, it's kind of like a spaceship—this disease just landing. I felt that anything else I was going to add was going to reduce it." The result, concluded Souda, is that Hoffman "has taken the nightmare of our time, stripped it of statistics and social rhetoric, and placed it in the raw center of family life."

In *Seventh Heaven* Hoffman returns again to the illusive quiet of suburbia, this time in 1959—the cusp of a new, noisier era. Into a seemingly idyllic New York community comes Nora Silk, a divorced woman whose unconventional manner disturbs the peaceful facade of the neighborhood. Nora is struggling to begin a new life and be a good mother to her children; she has little concern for what her neighbors think of her, giving her a freedom others resent. But as she gradually adjusts to her surroundings, so does the community begin to accept her and overcome their own inhibitions. "Hoffman is out to remind us that all those suburban stereotypes, creaky facades though they may often be, are propped up by some very real, and very basic, hopes and fears," Alida Becker remarked in the

New York Times Book Review. The novel contains "many of the plot twists you'd expect from a late-fifties's melodrama," the critic continued, adding that "what's unexpected, though, is the wonderful blend of humor, shrewdness and compassion that Ms. Hoffman brings to these familiar scenes."

Detroit News contributor Alice Vachss likewise praised the author's writing: "Hoffman's usual abilities—her enchanting storytelling and her gift for interweaving magic and realism—are even more finely honed than in her previous novels." Hoffman's mystical elements are effectively incorporated into *Seventh Heaven,* according to some critics. As *People* reviewer Ralph Novak commented, the author "makes greater use of the supernatural—or the allure of the supernatural—without compromising her insight into human behavior." This insight is considerable, for "Hoffman has intuitive grasp of the thoughts and feelings that are masked by conventional behavior," a *Publishers Weekly* critic noted, commending in particular the author's "unerring understanding of people of nearly every age and across a broad social spectrum." *Seventh Heaven,* asserted Shapiro, "is one of the rare novels so abundant with life it seems to overflow its own pages. . . . Hoffman has always enjoyed a coterie of devoted fans, but her immensely winning novels deserve a much wider readership. *Seventh Heaven,* her eighth and best, confirms her place as one of the finest writers of her generation."

Turtle Moon and *Second Nature,* Hoffman's next two novels, again feature single women struggling to define life on their own terms. The novels are also infused with Hoffman's trademark use of magic and heightened realism. *Turtle Moon* is set in a sleepy Florida town with a large population of divorced women and follows the exploits of Bethany, a woman who has fled with her infant daughter from a child-custody fight; Lucy Rosen, a single mother; her son, Keith, a mean boy who bullies his peers and who steals at will; Julian Cash, an acerbic, taciturn policeman; and Julian's dog, Arrow, who shares his owner's temperament. The story revolves around the disappearance of Keith with Bethany's baby and the quest to solve a local murder. Reviewing the work in the *New York Times Book Review,* Frederick Busch averred that "Hoffman writes quite wonderfully about the magic in our lives and in the battered, indifferent world. I don't know that she's written better." *New York Times* daily reviewer Michiko Kakutani had a less enthusiastic view of the

book, however, saying that it "showcases Hoffman's assurance as a writer, and her less admirable penchant for situating her characters in a slick, tricked-up plot that's decorated with pointlessly whimsical asides."

Second Nature is a tale about a wild man raised by wolves who brings love and joy to a lonely woman's suburban world. *New York Times Book Review* contributor Howard Frank Mosher called the novel "magical and daring" and commented that the book is written "with grace and beauty, making it at once [Hoffman's] richest and wisest, as well as her boldest, novel to date." Christopher Lehmann-Haupt, another critic for the daily *New York Times,* thought *Second Nature*'s premise about the conflict between nature and so-called civilization "familiar almost to the point of cliche," but liked some aspects of the story, "many of whose complications are richly ambiguous."

Hoffman's eleventh novel, *Practical Magic,* is set in a small Massachusetts town and features a matriarchal dynasty, the Owenses. Specifically, the novel focuses on two Owens sisters, Gillian and Sally, and the aunts who raise them. As children, Gillian and Sally sneak down from bed to listen as their aunts prescribe love potions for the town women. Determined not to suffer from any such lovesickness when they grow older, the girls take differing paths. Gillian becomes a promiscuous vagabond who never marries or has children, while dutiful Sally survives the death of her husband and subordinates her own desires to those of her daughters. Terming *Practical Magic* "a particularly arch and dexterous example of [Hoffman's] narrative powers," *Times Literary Supplement* reviewer Lorna Sage concluded that "Hoffman spins out the intrigue with show-off skill." Writing in the *New York Times Book Review,* Mark Childress noted that "Hoffman's trademark narrative voice is upbeat, breathless and rather bouncy. She creates vivid characters, she keeps things moving along, and she's not above using sleight of hand and prestidigitation to achieve her considerable effects."

Here on Earth deals with a married woman, March Murray, who becomes involved with an old lover, Hollis, when she comes back from California to her native Massachusetts for a funeral. It has echoes of Emily Bronte's *Wuthering Heights.* Hollis, for instance, resembles Bronte's dark, brooding Heathcliff. *New York Times Book Review* contributor Karen Karbo found it implausible that a smart, modern woman like

March would resume a relationship with Hollis, and thought the course of their affair sadly predictable. "The madness of being madly in love is one of the most difficult subjects to write about convincingly," Karbo observed. "And you've got to give Hoffman points for trying. Unfortunately, just as March is too good for Hollis, Hoffman is too good for a story like this."

Local Girls is Hoffman's first collection of short stories, which are linked by their characters, members of a dysfunctional Long Island family, the Samuelsons. They follow the key character, Gretel, over roughly a decade of her life, beginning in her teen years. As she grows to womanhood, the intelligent, observant Gretel has to cope with troubles, including her parents' bitter divorce, her brother's drug addiction, and her mother's serious illness. Like many of Hoffman's other works, *Local Girls* has a strong element of female bonding—Gretel's best friend, Jill, and cousin Margot are her main sources of emotional support—and touches of magical realism. *Redbook* contributor Rose Martelli observed that Hoffman "turns [the Samuelsons'] trials into a celebration of family, revealing what it takes to brave real crises together." A *Publishers Weekly* reviewer noted that Hoffman's "disarming wit" keeps the tales from becoming depressing, adding, "she indicates that the human spirit can survive despite the cruel workings of fate." "These stories sometimes have a sketchy feel," noted *Library Journal* critic Barbara Hoffert. *New York Times Book Review* commentator Sarah Ferguson stated, "The stories suffer from a debilitating overlap when they're read as a collection. As in a soap opera, where any episode may be the viewer's first, background information is repeated and characters are reintroduced ad nauseam."

Hoffman again used interconnected stories in *Blackbird House,* a book in which the common bond of the stories is a Cape Cod farmhouse. For reviewer Ellen Shapiro, writing for *People,* this was problematic, "When all the dust settles, it is the house itself that emerges as the book's enduring—and inspiring—character." Other reviews, such as the one in *Publishers Weekly* praised the book: "Hoffman's lyrical prose weaves an undeniable spell."

The River King revolves around Haddan School, an exclusive preparatory academy in a picturesque small town in Massachusetts. The plot turns on an investigation into the death of a student named Gus Pierce, a "Holden Caulfield-like misfit," as *Entertainment Weekly* reviewer George Hodgman put it. Local police officer Abel Grey suspects that Gus's drowning was no accident or suicide, but murder, and in the course of his detective work he becomes attracted to photography teacher Betsy Chase, who is engaged to another Haddan faculty member. Meanwhile, Carlin Leander, a scholarship student who had befriended Gus, encounters what she believes to be his ghost. "The puzzle of the drowning helps propel Hoffman's at times meandering narrative, but she's more interested in the mysteries of love, the crimes of the heart," observed Nancy Pate in the *Orlando Sentinel.* A *Publishers Weekly* reviewer praised *The River King* as "a many-layered morality tale" and Hoffman as "an inventive author with a distinctive touch," while *Booklist* contributor Donna Seaman credited the author with "illuminating the power of emotion and the exquisite mysteries of life." Hodgman, however, was less impressed, finding some of the characters sketchily drawn, "basic romantic types," although he felt Hoffman "does a nice job of weaving together a meandering tapestry of plots." Amanda Fortini, writing in the *New York Times Book Review,* had a similar take, applauding Hoffman's "good old-fashioned storytelling" but deeming her characters "so numerous that she rarely has time to develop them beyond mere tag lines." *Library Journal* critic Reba Leiding deemed the novel a bit too atmospheric: "One wishes Hoffman had pared down the precious local descriptions and allowed the plot, which has some unexpected twists, to shine through." Pate, though, concluded that Hoffman "is a writer who can cast a spell."

BIOGRAPHICAL AND CRITICAL SOURCES:

BOOKS

Contemporary Literary Criticism, Volume 51, Gale (Detroit, MI), 1989.

PERIODICALS

Belles Lettres, summer, 1992, p. 20.
Book, May-June 2003, Kristin Kloberdanz, review of *Green Angel,* p. 31; May-June 2003, Chris Bohjalian, "Girl Power," pp. 69-71.
Booklist, March 15, 1999, Brad Hooper, review of *Local Girls,* January 1, 2000, review of *Local Girls,* p. 819; March 15, 2000, Mary McCay, review of

Local Girls, Practical Magic, and *Angel Landing,* pp. 1396-1397; April 15, 2000, Donna Seaman, review of *The River King,* p. 1500; March 1, 2003, Donna Seaman, review of *The Probable Future,* pp. 1107-1108 April 15, 2003, Gillian Engberg, review of *Green Angel,* pp. 69-71; May 15, 2004, Donna Seaman, review of *Blackbird House,* p. 1519; June 1, 2004, Ilene Cooper, review of *Mondog,* pp. 1742-1743.

Boston Review, September, 1985; October, 1987.

Chicago Tribune, August 31, 1987, Candice Russell, review of *Illumination Night.*

Chicago Tribune Book World, May 5, 1985, Robin Hemley, review of *Fortune's Daughter.*

Cosmopolitan, February, 1994.

Detroit News, September 5, 1990, Alice Vachss, review of *Seventh Heaven.*

Entertainment Weekly, October 23, 1998, review of film *Practical Magic,* p. 47; July 16, 1999, p. 62; August 4, 2000, George Hodgman, "Alice's Wonders," p. 78; June 27, 2003, Amy Feitelberg, "The Probable Future: Anne Hoffman Mystical Fiction," p. 142; July 23, 2004, Henry Goldblatt, review of *Blackbird House,* p. 81.

Globe and Mail (Toronto, Ontario, Canada), August 25, 1990.

Horn Book, March-April, 2003, Lauren Adams, review of *Green Angel,* pp. 211-213.

Journal of Adolescent and Adult Literacy, November, 2003, Jean Boreen, review of *Green Angel,* pp. 271-273.

Kirkus Reviews, September 1, 1997, review of *Fireflies;* March 15, 2003, review of *The Probable Future,* p. 418; May 15, 2004, review of *Blackbird House,* p. 461; July 1, 2004, review of *Moondog,* p. 631.

Kliatt, July, 2003, Lesley S. J. Dr. Farmer, "Water Tales, two novels; Aquamarine and Indigo," p. 32; July, 2004, Janet Julian, review of *The Probable Future,* p. 19.

Library Journal, May 15, 1999, Barbara Hoffert, review of *Local Girls,* p. 130; December, 1999, Rochelle Ratner, review of *Local Girls,* p. 205; April 1, 2000, Joyce Kessel, review of *Angel Landing,* p. 150; May 15, 2000, Reba Leidling, review of *The River King,* p. 124; March 15, 2003, Starr E. Smith, review of of *The Probable Future,* p. 114.

London Review of Books, August 6, 1992, p. 19.

Los Angeles Times, December 5, 1980; May 28, 1982; May 9, 1985; August 24, 1987; June 30, 1988.

Los Angeles Times Book Review, August 19, 1979; July 10, 1988; August 5, 1990; May 28, 1995, p. 1.

Magazine of Fantasy and Science Fiction, April, 1994; December, 1995, p. 46.

Ms., August, 1979; May, 1982; June, 1985.

Nation, November 26, 1990.

Newsweek, May 23, 1977; April 12, 1982; August 1, 1988; August 20, 1990.

New Yorker, May 3, 1982; July 15, 1985; July 27, 1992; April 11, 1994.

New York Times, July 14, 1977; July 25, 1987; July 4, 1988; August 10, 1990; April 21, 1992, Michiko Kakutani, "Books of The Times: A Killer Strikes as Sea Turtles Fill the Streets"; February 10, 1994, Ruth Reichl, "At Home with Alice Hoffman: A Writer Set Free by Magic"; February 24, 1994, Christopher Lehmann-Haupt, "Books of The Times: A Wilderness Child Confronts Civilization," p. C19.

New York Times Book Review, July 15, 1979; November 9, 1980; March 28, 1982; March 24, 1985; August 9, 1987; July 17, 1988; August 5, 1990; April 26, 1992, Frederick Busch, "The Soul Is Part of the Action"; February 6, 1994, p. 13; June 25, 1995, p. 25; September 14, 1997, Karen Karbo, "Heathcliff Redux"; June 13, 1999, Sarah Ferguson, "Islanders," p. 31; July 16, 2000, Amanda Fortini, "The Spirit Moves Him."

Orlando Sentinel, August 2, 2000, Nancy Pate, review of *The River King.*

People, September 3, 1990; September 5, 1994, p. 34; July 3, 1995, p. 31; August 14, 2000; July 26, 2004, p. 47; August 11, 2003, p. 41; July 26, 2004, p. 47.

Ploughshares, fall, 2003, Maryanne O'Hara, *About Alice Hoffman; a profile by Maryanne O'Hara,* pp. 194-198.

Publishers Weekly, April 12, 1985; June 1, 1990; February 3, 1992; November 29, 1993; January 2, 1995, p. 30; March 20, 1995, p. 40; April 22, 1996, p. 67; May 3, 1999, review of *Local Girls,* p. 1259; July 5, 1999, review of sound recording of *Local Girls,* p. 35; June 5, 2000, review of *The River King,* p. 71; July 31, 2000, Daisy Maryles, "Women, Women, Women," p. 21; August 14, 2000, review of *Horsefly,* p. 355; May 15, 2003, review of *The Probable Future,* p. 196; November 10, 2003, review of *Green Angel,* p. 37; June 21, 2004, review of *Blackbird House,* p. 42.

Redbook, July, 1999, Rose Martelli, "What Makes Families Strong?," p. G1.

School Library Journal, November, 1995, p. 138; July 2003, Pam Johnson, review of *The Probable Future,* p. 152

Time, July 18, 1988; August 6, 1990.

Times (London, England), November 28, 1985; October 1, 1987; October 1, 1988.

Times Literary Supplement, April 21, 1978; March 11, 1988; March 25, 1994, p. 21; July 5, 1996, p. 23.

Tribune Books (Chicago, IL), June 26, 1988; August 5, 1990; April 26, 1992, p. 6; February 20, 1994; August 6, 1995.

Vogue, July, 1992.

Washington Post, August 2, 1979; April 13, 1982; June 29, 1988, Jonathan Yardley, review of *At Risk.*

Washington Post Book World, December 21, 1980; August 2, 1987; June 4, 1995, p. 8.

Yale Review, winter, 1978, Edith Milton, review of *Property Of.*

ONLINE

Alice Hoffman Web site, http://www.alicehoffman.com (August 25, 2004).

BookBrowse.com, http://www.bookbrowse.com/ (August 25, 2004), "Alice Hoffman."

BookPage.com, http://www.bookpage.com/ (August 6, 2004), Ellen Kanner, "Making Believe: Alice Hoffman Takes Her Practical Magic to the River."

BookReporter.com, http://www.bookreporter.com/ (August 6, 2004), interview with Hoffman.

RomanceReader.com, http://www.romancereader.com/ (August 6, 2004), Susan Scribner, review of *Practical Magic.**

*　　*　　*

HOOD, Lynley (Jane) 1942-

PERSONAL: Born November 14, 1942, in Hamilton, New Zealand; daughter of Horace Everton (a wine and spirits merchant) and Flora Eveline (Preston) Calcott; married James Alfred Alexander Hood (a dentist and university professor), 1965; children: David, Christina, Lyndon. *Education:* University of Otago, B.Sc., 1965, M.Sc., 1968. *Politics:* "Socialistic tendencies." *Religion:* "Atheist."

ADDRESSES: Home and office—16 Marewa St., Kew, Dunedin, New Zealand. *Agent*—Richards Literary Agency, Box 31240, Milford, Auckland, New Zealand.

CAREER: University of Otago, Dunedin, New Zealand, research physiologist at medical school, 1965-68; freelance writer, 1973—. University of Otago, Robert Burns fellow, 1991. La Leche League, member.

MEMBER: International PEN, Oral History Association of New Zealand, New Zealand Federation of University Women.

AWARDS, HONORS: Goodman Fielder Wattie Book of the Year Award, 1989, Best First Book of Prose Award, New Zealand PEN, 1989, and selection as talking book of the year, New Zealand Foundation for the Blind, all for *Sylvia! The Biography of Sylvia Ashton-Warner;* Montana Medal for Non-Fiction, history category, 2002, for *A City Possessed: The Christchurch Civic Creche Case.*

WRITINGS:

Sylvia! The Biography of Sylvia Ashton-Warner, Viking (New York, NY), 1988.

Who Is Sylvia? The Diary of a Biography, J. McIndoe (Dunedin, New Zealand), 1990.

Minnie Dean: Her Life and Crimes, Penguin (Auckland, New Zealand), 1994.

A City Possessed: The Christchurch Civic Creche Case—Child Abuse, Gender Politics, and the Law, Longacre Press (Dunedin, New Zealand), 2001.

Contributor to magazines and newspapers.

SIDELIGHTS: Lynley Hood once told *CA:* "The four obsessive years that I spent writing my biography of the creative and controversial educational writer Sylvia Ashton-Warner were the most challenging, extending, and enjoyable years of my life. They transformed me from a sociable, part-time scribbler to a full-time writer with all the changes of philosophy, lifestyle, and self-image that such a transformation implies."

BIOGRAPHICAL AND CRITICAL SOURCES:

PERIODICALS

Child Abuse and Neglect, May, 1996, Karen Zelas, review of *Minnie Dean: Her Life and Crimes,* p. 467.

New Zealand Law Journal, October, 2001, Ian Freckelton, review of *A City Possessed: The Christchurch Civic Creche Case—Child Abuse, Gender Politics, and the Law,* pp. 359-361.

Otago Law Review (annual), 2002, Megan Henaghan, review of *A City Possessed,* pp. 271-274.

Times (London, England), May 4, 1989.

ONLINE

Lynley Hood Web site, http://www.lynleyhood.org (May 17, 2004).*

*   *   *

HOROWITZ, David (Joel) 1939-

PERSONAL: Born January 10, 1939, in New York, NY; son of Philip (an activist) and Blanche (Brown) Horowitz; married Elissa Krauthamer, June 14, 1959 (divorced); children: Jonathan, Sarah, Benjamin, Anne. *Education:* Columbia University, A.B., 1959; University of California—Berkeley, M.A., 1961, graduate study, 1962; London School of Economics and Political Science (London, England), graduate study, 1964.

ADDRESSES: Office—c/o Center for the Study of Popular Culture, 4401 Wilshire Dr., 4th Fl., Los Angeles, CA 90010.

CAREER: Writer. Bertrand Russell Peace Foundation, London, England, former director of research and publications; *Ramparts* (magazine), Berkeley, CA, editor, 1969-74; Second Thoughts Project, Washington, DC, founder and codirector, beginning 1986; Center for the Study of Popular Culture, president and codirector. Republican Party National Convention, alternate delegate, 1996.

WRITINGS:

Student, Ballantine (New York, NY), 1962.

Shakespeare: An Existential View, Hill & Wang (New York, NY), 1965.

The Free World Colossus, Hill & Wang (New York, NY), 1965, revised edition, 1971, published as *From Yalta to Vietnam: American Foreign Policy in the Cold War,* Penguin (London, England), 1967.

Hemispheres North and South: Economic Disparity among Nations, Johns Hopkins University Press (Baltimore, MD), 1966.

Empire and Revolution: A Radical Interpretation of Contemporary History, Random House (New York, NY), 1969, published as *Imperialism and Revolution,* Allen Lane (London, England), 1969.

The Enigma of Economic Growth: A Case Study of Israel, Praeger (New York, NY), 1972.

The Fate of Midas and Other Essays, Ramparts Press (Palo Alto, CA), 1973.

The First Frontier: The Indian Wars and America's Origins, 1607-1776, Simon & Schuster (New York, NY), 1978.

(With Peter Collier) *The Kennedys: An American Drama,* Summit Books (New York, NY), 1984.

(With Peter Collier) *The Fords: An American Epic,* Summit Books (New York, NY), 1987.

The Rockefellers: An American Dynasty, Summit Books (New York, NY), 1989.

(With Peter Collier) *Destructive Generation: Second Thoughts about the Sixties,* Summit Books (New York, NY), 1989.

(With Peter Collier and David Lee) On the Edge: A History of America since World War II, West (St. Paul, MN), 1989.

(With Peter Collier and David Lee) *On the Edge: A History of America from 1890 to 1945,* West (St. Paul, MN), 1990.

(With Peter Collier) *Deconstructing the Left: From Vietnam to the Persian Gulf,* Second Thoughts Books (Lanham, MD), 1991.

(With Peter Collier) *The Roosevelts: An American Saga,* Simon & Schuster (New York, NY), 1994.

Radical Son: A Generational Odyssey (autobiography), Free Press (New York, NY), 1997.

The Politics of Bad Faith: The Radical Assault on America's Future, Free Press (New York, NY), 1998.

Hating Whitey: And Other Progressive Causes, Spence Publishing (Dallas, TX), 1999.

The Art of Political War: And Other Radical Pursuits, Spence Publishing (Dallas, TX), 2000.

How to Beat the Democrats: And Other Subversive Ideas, Spence Publishing (Dallas, TX), 2002.

Uncivil Wars: The Controversy over Reparations for Slavery, Encounter Books (San Francisco, CA), 2002.

Columnist for the online magazine *Salon.* Contributor to periodicals, including *Nation* and *Studies on the Left.*

EDITOR:

Containment and Revolution, Beacon Press (Boston, MA), 1967, published as *Containment and Revolution: Western Policy towards Social Revolution, 1917 to Vietnam,* Anthony Blond (London, England), 1967.

Marx and Modern Economics, Monthly Review Press (New York, NY), 1968.

Corporations and the Cold War, Monthly Review Press (New York, NY), 1970.

Issac Deutscher: The Man and His Work, Macdonald and Co. (London, England), 1971.

Radical Sociology: An Introduction, Canfield Press (San Francisco, CA), 1971.

(With Michael Lerner and Craig Pyes, and contributor) *Counterculture and Revolution,* Random House (New York, NY), 1972.

(With Peter Collier) *Second Thoughts: Former Radicals Look Back at the Sixties,* Madison Books (Lanham, MD), 1989.

(With Peter Collier) *Second Thoughts about Race in America,* Madison Books (Lanham, MD), 1991.

(With Peter Collier) *The Heterodoxy Handbook: How to Survive the PC Campus,* Regnery (Lanham, MD), 1994.

(With Peter Collier) *The Race Card: White Guilt, Black Resentment, and the Assault on Truth and Justice,* Prima Publications (Rocklin, CA), 1997.

(With Peter Collier) *The Anti-Chomsky Reader,* Encounter Books (San Francisco, CA), 2004.

Past editor, *Heterodoxy;* editor in chief, *FrontPage Mag.com.*

ADAPTATIONS: Some of Horowitz's books have been adapted as audio books, including *Hating Whitey: And Other Progressive Causes.*

SIDELIGHTS: David Horowitz and his collaborator Peter Collier are best known in political circles as the founders of the Second Thoughts Project, an association of former sixties radicals who have since denounced the agenda of the New Left. Perhaps no other conservative writers are more ideally suited for this task: Horowitz and Collier began their association while on the editorial board of the radical *Ramparts* magazine in the late 1960s, and they were avowed left wingers who wrote numerous books and magazine articles in the service of radical causes. Journeying to the opposite end of the political spectrum, the two became equally enthusiastic about conservatism and a free market economy, and have presented their ideas in such works as *Destructive Generation: Second Thoughts about the Sixties* and *Deconstructing the Left: From Vietnam to the Persian Gulf. National Review* correspondent Joseph Sobran observed that Horowitz and Collier are producing "must reading" about the lasting national effects of sixties radicalism, "and they write about it with intelligence, gossipy intimacy, and a sort of savage introspection." Sobran concluded: "There's not a trace of sentimentality about the Left's 'idealism,' which they correctly interpret as malicious fantasizing."

Horowitz's unconventional childhood prepared him for left wing politics and socialist idealism. He was born and raised in Queens by parents who belonged to the Communist Party, and his childhood memories include comic-book burnings at a communist-run summer camp for children. Later, both of Horowitz's parents lost their teaching jobs in the McCarthy era. Their travails were not lost on young David, who began writing political commentary in the early 1960s. "As members of a new radical generation, our political identity was virginal," the author recalls in his autobiography, *Radical Son: A Generational Odyssey.* "We had the benefit of everybody's doubt. We could position ourselves as radical critics of American society without having to defend the crimes committed by the Soviet bloc. . . . And we could express our moral outrage at Communist excesses."

Moral outrage defined the tenor of much of Horowitz's writing. In *The Free World Colossus,* his first widely-read book, he denounces the United States as the architect of the Cold War in its pursuit of a monopoly on international power. "The heaviest price exacted by the cold war has been the moral contamination of people," wrote Arnold S. Kaufman in the *Nation.* "Perhaps one should accept the toll with reflective calm. David Horowitz has refused to do so. The result is a book that describes and interprets the history of the cold war in a way that challenges, excites, provokes, angers and inspires. Horowitz has written a sincere and important book, which says much that desperately needs saying in these times of madness."

In 1968 Horowitz established himself in Berkeley, California, and began working as an editor of *Ramparts,* a radical magazine that served as a forum for the political views of the New Left. Among the other causes championed by *Ramparts* was the Black Panther Party, and Horowitz became personally acquainted with many of the most important Panther leaders. His eventual disillusionment with the New Left began with his realization that Black Panther violence was being overlooked by left-wing journalists in the same way that Josef Stalin's crimes had been overlooked by an earlier generation of committed revolutionaries. "Like all radicals, I lived in some fundamental way in a castle in the air," Horowitz recalled in his autobiography. "Now I had hit the ground hard, and had no idea how to get up."

In fact, Horowitz did not flounder for long. He formed a partnership with Collier, and the two wrote three well-received family biographies: one about the Kennedys, one about the Rockefellers, and one about the Henry Ford dynasty.

Far more provocative are the political writings Horowitz produced since becoming a conservative in the early 1980s. With Collier, or on his own, Horowitz challenged both the left-wing politics of the 1960s and what he saw as the lasting ill effects of those politics in American society. *Destructive Generation: Second Thoughts about the Sixties* was widely reviewed in the nation's political magazines, with opinions on the work varying according to the reviewer's own ideology. Not surprisingly, Saul Landau in the leftist *Progressive* labeled Horowitz and Collier "defective defectors" and characterized their book as "disconnected and bilious." Paul Berman presented a different approach in the *New Republic* when he noted that the authors "have produced pieces of lasting value. These chapters go to the heart of the matter, to the explosive quality of the New Left, to the notion, so crucial to the New Left's appeal, that you can batter down your own limitations, that conventions are oppressions, that an existential choice can turn you into something better, more heroic, more powerful."

In *Leaders from the 1960s,* Thomas R. West stated that Collier and Horowitz may have broken from left-wing politics, but their new right-wing views have proven equally strident. *Destructive Generation,* the critic declared, "is the report of a conversion. Collier and Horowitz discovered human imperfection, but this did not make them humble. Instead, they insisted, with an aggressive self-righteousness, that everyone should be judged by their new standards. . . . Even if the reader is not convinced, however, the book does il-

lustrate something about the uses of critical introspection in the forming of a politics that is at once personal and responsible."

Horowitz gives more personal details about his political conversion in his autobiography, *Radical Son.* "Many intellectuals have made the voyage from Left to Right in recent decades," observed Christopher Caldwell in *Commentary.* "But few have come from as deep inside the hard Left as Horowitz, and none has retained more of the sixties style. . . . *Radical Son,* his memoir, charts a trek from one political commitment to something approaching its opposite, and the events that propelled him on his way." *Reason* magazine correspondent Steven Hayward noted: "Taken as a whole, *Radical Son* is a compelling story, because it goes farther than many of the previous narratives in conveying how deeply radicalism cuts into one's character and psychology. The supposedly redemptive power of radical ideology, Horowitz makes clear, reaches into every corner of the soul, thus making a break from radicalism a desperate and personally devastating matter." In *Commonweal,* Julia Vitullo-Martin stated: "This is an American journey of sorts— traveling the short road from authoritarian left to demagogic right. But does the journey, excruciatingly detailed in *Radical Son,* have anything to tell the rest of us? The answer is yes, in part because the story of a red-diaper American childhood has seldom been told, and perhaps never so well." Hayward concluded of the former radical: "Horowitz has not changed that much since the 1960s; he is still at war with the dominant culture. So in the end he is in harmony with his essential political being."

BIOGRAPHICAL AND CRITICAL SOURCES:

BOOKS

Horowitz, David, *Radical Son: A Generational Odyssey,* Free Press (New York, NY), 1997.
Leaders from the 1960s, Greenwood Press (Westport, CT), 1994, pp. 349-353.

PERIODICALS

American History, April, 1995, p. 27.
American Spectator, December, 2000, Mark Hemingway, review of *The Art of Political War: And Other Radical Pursuits,* p. 69.

Booklist, January 1, 1997, pp. 9-10; October 15, 1998, review of *The Politics of Bad Faith: The Radical Assault on America's Future,* p. 394; August, 2000, Ray Olson, review of *The Art of Political War,* p. 2085.

Commentary, October, 1984, p. 66; March, 1988, pp. 78-82; June, 1997, Christopher Caldwell, review of *Radical Son: A Generational Odyssey,* pp. 64-67; April, 2002, Jacob Heilbrunn, review of *Uncivil Wars: The Controversy over Reparations for Slavery,* p. 68.

Commonweal, May 23, 1997, Julia Vitullo-Martin, review of *Radical Son,* pp. 26-27.

Cosmopolitan, June, 1994, p. 18.

Detroit News, June 4, 1997; October 4, 1997.

Dissent, winter, 1998, review of *Radical Son,* p. 118.

Entertainment Weekly, July 8, 1994, p. 50.

Guardian (London, England), May 30, 2001, Duncan Campbell, "Portrait: Right Turn," p. 6.

Human Events, May 15, 1998, review of *Radical Son,* p. 20; February 19, 1999, review of *The Politics of Bad Faith,* p. 21.

Insight on the News, November 13, 2000, Stephen Goode, review of *The Art of Political War,* p. 14.

Journal of American History, June, 1995, p. 284.

Kirkus Reviews, September 1, 1998, review of *The Politics of Bad Faith,* p. 1260; October 1, 1999, review of *Hating Whitey: And Other Progressive Causes,* p. 1547.

Library Journal, December, 1996, p. 104; July, 1998, review of *The Politics of Bad Faith,* p. 114; October 15, 1999, review of *Hating Whitey,* p. 87; August, 2000, Jack Forman, review of *The Art of Political War,* p. 130; July, 2002, Michael A. Genovese, review of *How to Beat the Democrats: And Other Subversive Ideas,* p. 101.

Los Angeles Times, June 2, 1992, p. E1; April 14, 1993, p. B1; February 28, 1997, p. E1.

Los Angeles Times Book Review, March 19, 1989, p. 2; October 11, 1998, review of *The Politics of Bad Faith,* p. 4.

Maclean's, July 16, 1984, p. 50.

Mother Jones, August-September, 1984, p. 56; January, 1988, p. 10.

Nation, February 21, 1966, Arnold S. Kaufman, review of *The Free World Colossus,* pp. 214-216; April 6, 1985, p. 388; October 31, 1987, p. 475; November 27, 1989, pp. 630-632; February 17, 1997, pp. 30-33.

National Review, March 24, 1989, Joseph Sobran, review of *Destructive Generation: Second Thoughts about the Sixties,* pp. 43-44; June 13,

1994, pp. 65-68; March 24, 1997, pp. 50-51; August 9, 1999, review of *The Politics of Bad Faith,* p. 56; September 30, 2002, Michael Potemra, review of *How to Beat the Democrats,* p. 52.

New Leader, December 16, 1996, pp. 5-8.

New Republic, August 27, 1984, pp. 31-34; April 24, 1989, Paul Berman, review of *Destructive Generation,* pp. 26-34; June 26, 1989, pp. 38-42.

Newsweek, July 2, 1984, p. 25.

New York Times, April 23, 1989, p. 18; June 1, 1989, p. C19; July 16, 1989.

New York Times Book Review, March 4, 1979, p. 11; June 19, 1994, p. 13; February 16, 1997, p. 34; June 14, 1998, review of *Radical Son,* p. 32.

People, August 29, 1994, p. 29.

Progressive, May, 1985, p. 4; August, 1989, Saul Landau, review of *Destructive Generation,* pp. 37-38.

Publishers Weekly, December 30, 1996, p. 49; May 5, 1997, p. 188; October 25, 1999, review of *Hating Whitey,* p. 57; August 14, 2000, review of *The Art of Political War,* p. 340.

Reason, March, 1997, Steven Hayward, review of *Radical Son,* pp. 62-63.

Time, July 25, 1994, p. 67; November 22, 1999, review of *Hating Whitey,* p. 101.

Times Literary Supplement, September 9, 1965, p. 773.

Wall Street Journal, August 13, 1996, p. A14; February 3, 1997, p. A12.

Washington Monthly, May, 1989, p. 44.

Washington Post Book World, June 5, 1994, p. 3; February 9, 1997, p. 3.

Whole Earth Review, fall, 1989, p. 102.*

*   *   *

HOUGH, John T., Jr. 1946-

PERSONAL: Surname rhymes with "puff"; born January 31, 1946, in York, PA; son of John T. and Mary (Kurtz) Hough. *Education:* Haverford College, B.A., 1968. *Politics:* "Farthest left edge of the Democratic Party." *Religion:* Episcopalian.

ADDRESSES: Home—15 Inman St., Apt. 1, West Tisbury, MA 02139.

CAREER: Falmouth Enterprise, Falmouth, MA, reporter, summers, 1966, 1967; Volunteers in Service to America (VISTA), tutor and counselor in junior high school, Detroit, MI, 1968-69; member of staff of Senator Charles McC. Mathias, Jr., of Maryland, 1969-70; Massachusetts Correctional Association, Boston, writer and social worker (as conscientious objector, in lieu of military service), 1970-72; speech writer for Senator Charles McC. Mathias, Jr., 1976-77; *New York Times,* New York, NY, assistant to James Reston, Washington Bureau, beginning 1977; *Falmouth Enterprise,* columnist.

WRITINGS:

A Peck of Salt: A Year in the Ghetto, Little, Brown (Boston, MA), 1970.
A Two Car Funeral (novel), Little, Brown (Boston, MA), 1973.
The Guardian (novel), Little, Brown (Boston, MA), 1975.
The Conduct of the Game, Harcourt Brace Jovanovich (San Diego, CA), 1986.
(With Gary Carter) *A Dream Season,* Harcourt Brace Jovanovich (San Diego, CA), 1987.
A Player for the Moment: Notes from Fenway Park, Harcourt Brace Jovanovich (San Diego, CA), 1988.
The Last Summer (a novel), Simon & Schuster (New York, NY), 2002.

WORK IN PROGRESS: A Matter of Time, for Simon & Schuster.

SIDELIGHTS: John T. Hough, Jr., is a writer with a special bent for baseball stories. He has written nonfiction books on the topic, such as his *A Dream Season* and *A Player for the Moment: Notes from Fenway Park.* However, it was his 1986 novel, *The Conduct of the Game,* that caught the eye of *Sports Illustrated* reporter Jeremiah Tax. The novel conveys the story of Lee Malcolm, a young man who dreams of a professional career in sports but is one day pushed behind the plate in the role of umpire, a position that he grows to like and decides to pursue. By his mid-twenties, he is umpiring major league baseball rather successfully when a series of catastrophes hit him. He has a fight with one of the big superstar players, a dispute with some of the members of his umpire crew, a conflict with the women in his life, and a fateful encounter with a fellow umpire who is gay. Tax applauded Hough for handling all these challenges without becoming too

melodramatic about them in his writing. However, the critic stated that there were moments when he wished that "Malcolm [the protagonist] were a bit brighter or more sophisticated than Hough's creation." Overall, Tax enjoyed the reading, stating that Hough "convincingly" develops his story and that "the finish to which he leads us is eminently satisfactory."

In 2002, Hough dropped the sports theme and wrote a love story, *The Last Summer.* The setting of the story is the late 1960s, and Hough touches on such real-life events as Robert Kennedy's murder and the riotous Democratic Convention in Chicago. He also incorporates a murder mystery theme, in which his female protagonist, ex-Senator Clair Malek, becomes involved.

Beth Warrell, for *Booklist,* found that Hough's writing was "quiet and lyrical;" while a critic from *Kirkus Reviews* thought that despite some overall "formulaic" plotting, the story was "spiced up" by Hough's incorporation of historic events and his ability to provide "real suspense."

According to a *Publishers Weekly* article by John F. Baker, Hough is working on a new novel to be titled *A Matter of Time.* It is another bittersweet romance set in the 1960s.

BIOGRAPHICAL AND CRITICAL SOURCES:

PERIODICALS

Best Sellers, October 15, 1970.
Booklist, June 1, 2002, Beth Warrell, review of *The Last Summer,* pp. 1683-1684.
Kirkus Reviews, May 15, 2002, review of *The Last Summer,* p. 686.
Publishers Weekly, April 29, 2002, review of *The Last Summer,* p. 38.
Sports Illustrated, May 19, 1986, Jeremiah Tax, review of *The Conduct of the Game,* p. 5.*

*   *   *

HUBBELL, Sue 1935-

PERSONAL: Born January 28, 1935, in Kalamazoo, MI; daughter of B. LeRoy (a landscape architect) and Marjorie (a homemaker; maiden name, Sparks) Gilbert; married Paul Hubbell (an engineer), October 31, 1955 (divorced, 1983); married Arne Sieverts (spokesperson for the U.S. Senate Foreign Relations committee), 1988; children: (first marriage) Brian; stepchildren: (second marriage) Michael, Lisa. *Education:* Attended Swarthmore College, 1952-54, and University of Michigan, 1954-55; University of Southern California, A.B., 1956, Drexel Institute, M.S., 1963.

ADDRESSES: Home—Missouri and Washington, DC. *Agent*—Liz Darhansoff, 1220 Park Ave., New York, NY 10128.

CAREER: The Book Shelf, Moorestown, NJ, manager, 1960-63; Trenton State College, Trenton, NJ, acquisitions librarian, 1963-67; elementary school librarian in Peacedale, RI, 1967-68; Brown University, Providence, RI, serials librarian, 1968-72; commercial beekeeper in Missouri, beginning 1973; writer, 1985—.

AWARDS, HONORS: Nomination for Walter Sullivan prize, 1991, for "Earthquake Fever" (magazine piece).

WRITINGS:

A Country Year: Living the Questions, illustrated by Lauren Jarrett, Random House (New York, NY), 1986.
A Book of Bees: . . . and How to Keep Them, illustrated by Sam Potthoff, Random House (New York, NY), 1988.
On This Hilltop, Ballantine (New York, NY), 1991.
Broadsides from the Other Orders: A Book of Bugs, illustrated by Dimitry Schidlovsky, Random House (New York, NY), 1993.
Far Flung Hubbell (collected essays and articles), Random House (New York, NY), 1995.
(Author of introduction) Rachel Carson, *The Edge of the Sea,* Houghton Mifflin (Boston, MA), 1998.
Waiting for Aphrodite: Journeys into the Time before Bones, Houghton Mifflin (Boston, MA), 1999.
Shrinking the Cat: Genetic Engineering before We Knew about Genes, illustrated by Liddy Hubbell, Houghton Mifflin (Boston, MA), 2001.
From Here to There and Back Again, University of Michigan Press (Ann Arbor, MI), 2004.

Contributor to magazines and newspapers, including *New Yorker, Smithsonian, New York Times Magazine, Time, Harper's, Sports Illustrated,* and *Discover.* Contributor to anthologies, including *Best Essays of the Year,* 1990.

Author's works have been translated into French and Japanese.

WORK IN PROGRESS: Research for a book on North Africa; magazine articles.

SIDELIGHTS: Writer and beekeeper Sue Hubbell's *A Country Year: Living the Questions* is a collection of forty-one essays describing Hubbell's reflections on life and her experiences with nature over the course of one year. Lauded by critics for her vivid descriptions of nature, Hubbell tells about her trips to her Missouri beehives in her thirty-year-old pickup truck and about making her own shingles in preparation for shingling a barn on her Ozark Mountain property. Doris Betts, writing in the *Los Angeles Times Book Review,* called *A Country Year* "a record of mysteries questioned, then embraced." According to Jeremiah Tax in *Sports Illustrated,* the essays in *A Country Year* "are filled with the wonders and surprise that the diligent, empathetic observer finds in the behavior of wild things." He added that "one's reaction when finishing many of the essays is likely to be an entrancement brought on by the softness and innocence of Hubbell's prose." Betts also praised Hubbell's writing, declaring that "like a pane of glass, her prose reveals without distortion or sentimentality." Dubbing the author a "sunny naturalist who writes stimulating prose," *Booklist* contributor Donna Seaman praised Hubbell's more recent book, *Waiting for Aphrodite: Journeys into the Time before Bones,* and noted that, "as philosophical as she is descriptive" in her nature writing, Hubbell brings to each of her works an "astute attention and fluid sense of wonder."

With *A Book of Bees: . . . and How to Keep Them* and *Broadsides from the Other Orders: A Book of Bugs,* Hubbell earned a reputation as "one of the two or three best writers-about-bugs now living," in the words of Noel Perrin, in the *Washington Post Book World. A Book of Bees* can be read as a primer in beekeeping: Hubbell educates readers on how hive frames are built to allow beekeepers get at the honey, how to calm angry bees, and how to peacefully integrate two warring colonies with just a piece of newspaper. But as David Quammen noted in the *New York Times Book Review,* even readers who have no interest in taking up beekeeping can appreciate her fascinating account of her mutually dependent relationship with the bees. "Strictly speaking," Hubbell admonishes in her book, "one never 'keeps' bees—one comes to terms with their wild nature."

The appeal of *Broadsides from the Other Orders,* according to Christopher Lehmann-Haupt in his *New York Times* review, is that while many writers would not be able to describe thirteen insect orders without falling into numbing repetition, Hubbell takes a refreshingly wide variety of approaches in her thirteen chapters. She goes to California to learn about the multi-million-dollar ladybug business; recounts the mating activities of camel crickets observed in her home terrarium; and explains the hundred-year history of humankind's attempts to eradicate the destructive gypsy moth. Lehmann-Haupt concluded that "given Ms. Hubbell's graceful prose and observant eye, she makes an excellent ambassador from [the insect] world to us."

In *Shrinking the Cat: Genetic Engineering before We Knew about Genes,* Hubbell discusses the largely controversial issue of genetic engineering, with some intriguing case studies. She clearly explains the effects of engineering efforts throughout the decades "in plain English, with no confusing scientific terminology to bore or distract readers," according to Irwin Weintraub in *Library Journal.* Discussing such topics as silk worms, apples, and even the common housecat, Hubbell explains the dependency that has evolved alongside genetic engineering and some of the evolutional drawbacks that have come to pass. A reviewer for *Publishers Weekly* called Hubbell's *Shrinking the Cat* a "fresh and personalized take on genetics," while Gilbert Taylor commented in *Booklist* that the work is "An engaging synthesis of material that will appeal to Hubbell's well-established audience."

BIOGRAPHICAL AND CRITICAL SOURCES:

BOOKS

Hubbell, Sue, *A Book of Bees: . . . and How to Keep Them,* illustrated by Sam Potthoff, Random House (New York, NY), 1988.

PERIODICALS

Booklist, April 1, 1999, Donna Seaman, review of *Waiting for Aphrodite: Journeys into the Time before Bones,* p. 1373; September 15, 2001, Gilbert Taylor, review of *Shrinking the Cat: Genetic Engineering before We Knew about Genes,* p. 172.
Library Journal, October 15, 2001, Irwin Weintraub, review of *Shrinking the Cat,* p. 104.
Los Angeles Times Book Review, April 13, 1986.
New York Review of Books, February 16, 1989.
New York Times, June 24, 1993.
New York Times Book Review, April 13, 1986; October 30, 1988; July 11, 1993.
Publishers Weekly, September 10, 2001, review of *Shrinking the Cat,* p. 76.
Sports Illustrated, April 21, 1986.
Washington Post Book World, April 27, 1986; August 8, 1993.*

I

ILLICK, Joseph E. 1934-

PERSONAL: Born November 15, 1934, in Bethlehem, PA; son of Joseph E., Jr. (a building contractor) and Margaret (Flexer) Illick; married Shirley Anthony, June 4, 1956; children: three, including Joseph Edward, IV. *Education:* Princeton University, B.S.E., 1956; University of Pennsylvania, A.M., 1957, Ph.D., 1961. *Politics:* Liberal.

ADDRESSES: Office—Department of History, San Francisco State University, 1600 Holloway Ave., San Francisco, CA 94132-1740. *E-mail*—illick@sfsu.edu.

CAREER: Kalamazoo College, Kalamazoo, MI, instructor, 1961-62; Lafayette College, Easton, PA, instructor, 1962-63; San Francisco State College (now San Francisco State University), San Francisco, CA, assistant professor, 1963-67, associate professor, 1967-71, professor of history, 1971—. San Francisco Psychoanalytic Institute, professor, 1974-75, 1978-79; visiting summer lecturer at Lehigh University, 1964, and New York University, 1965, 1966; University of California—Berkeley, visiting associate professor, 1968.

MEMBER: American Historical Association.

WRITINGS:

William Penn the Politician, Cornell University Press (Ithaca, NY), 1965.
(Editor) *America and England, 1558-1776,* Appleton-Century-Crofts (New York, NY), 1970.

Colonial Pennsylvania: A History, Scribner (New York, NY), 1976.
At Liberty: The Story of a Community and a Generation; The Bethlehem, Pennsylvania, High School Class of 1952, University of Tennessee Press (Knoxville, TN), 1989.
American Childhoods, University of Pennsylvania Press (Philadelphia, PA), 2002.

Contributor to books, including *Anglo-American Political Relations, 1675-1775,* edited by Alison Gilbert Olson and Richard Maxwell Brown, Rutgers University Press (New Brunswick, NJ), 1970; *The Colonial Legacy,* 1971; and *History of Childhood,* Harper (New York, NY), 1974. Contributor to *San Francisco Chronicle* and *Examiner* and to historical and popular periodicals, including *Pennsylvania Magazine of History and Biography.*

BIOGRAPHICAL AND CRITICAL SOURCES:

PERIODICALS

American Historical Review, April, 1977, review of *Colonial Pennsylvania: A History,* p. 430.
Best Sellers, September, 1976, review of *Colonial Pennsylvania,* p. 203.
Choice, October, 1976, review of *Colonial Pennsylvania,* p. 1044; February, 2003, E. W. Carp, review of *American Childhoods,* p. 1043.
Chronicle of Higher Education, March 28, 1990, Peter Monaghan, review of *At Liberty: The Story of a Community and a Generation; The Bethlehem, Pennsylvania, High School Class of 1952,* p. A3.

Educational Studies, winter, 1980, review of *Colonial Pennsylvania,* p. 418.

History: Reviews of New Books, September, 1976, review of *Colonial Pennsylvania,* p. 219; winter, 1991, review of *At Liberty,* p. 59.

Journal of American History, June, 1977, review of *Colonial Pennsylvania,* p. 119; March, 1991, Joseph M. Hawes, review of *At Liberty,* p. 142.

Library Journal, May 1, 1976, review of *Colonial Pennsylvania,* p. 1118.

Pacific Historical Review, February, 1978, review of *Colonial Pennsylvania,* p. 134.

Times Literary Supplement, November 8, 2002, Ashley Brown, review of *American Childhoods,* p. 35.

William and Mary Quarterly, April, 1977, review of *Colonial Pennsylvania,* p. 334.*

* * *

INKPEN, Mick 1952-

PERSONAL: Born December 22, 1952, in Romford, England; married, 1973; wife's name, Deborah; children: Simon, Chloe.

ADDRESSES: Office—c/o Author Mail, Hodder and Stoughton Ltd., 338 Euston Rd., London NW1 3BH, England.

CAREER: Graphic designer, 1970-86. Greeting card designer; TV AM, England, writer for series "Rub-a-Dub-Tub"; freelance writer and illustrator of children's books, 1986—.

AWARDS, HONORS: Acorn Award, Nottinghamshire Libraries (England), and Children's Book Award, Federation of Children's Book Groups (England), both 1991, both for *Threadbear;* Acorn Award, Nottinghamshire Libraries, 1992, for *Kipper;* Best Illustrated Children's Book of the Year runner-up, British Book Awards, 1992, for *Penguin Small,* and award, for *Lullabyhullaballoo!;* award for best animated children's film, British Academy of Film and Television Arts, 1998, for *Kipper;* Smarties Prize Silver Medal, 2001, for *Kipper's A to Z.*

WRITINGS:

ILLUSTRATOR, WITH NICK BUTTERWORTH

Elizabeth Lawrence and Noreen Wetton, *Can You Do This?,* Nelson (Nashville, TN), 1986.

Elizabeth Lawrence and Noreen Wetton, *Come up and Play,* Nelson (Nashville, TN), 1986.

Elizabeth Lawrence and Noreen Wetton, *Do You Like My Hat?,* Nelson (Nashville, TN), 1986.

Elizabeth Lawrence and Noreen Wetton, *Do You Like My House?,* Nelson (Nashville, TN), 1986.

Elizabeth Lawrence and Noreen Wetton, *I Am Going to Hide,* Nelson (Nashville, TN), 1986.

Elizabeth Lawrence and Noreen Wetton, *It Is Too Big,* Nelson (Nashville, TN), 1986.

Elizabeth Lawrence and Noreen Wetton, *Look What I Can Do,* Nelson (Nashville, TN), 1986.

Elizabeth Lawrence and Noreen Wetton, *May I Come In?,* Nelson (Nashville, TN), 1986.

Elizabeth Lawrence and Noreen Wetton, *May I Play with You?,* Nelson (Nashville, TN), 1986.

Elizabeth Lawrence and Noreen Wetton, *Where Is Monster?,* Nelson (Nashville, TN), 1986.

Elizabeth Lawrence and Noreen Wetton, *Where Is the Mouse?,* Nelson (Nashville, TN), 1986.

Elizabeth Lawrence and Noreen Wetton, *Mrs. Rabbit Gets Locked Out,* Nelson (Nashville, TN), 1987.

Elizabeth Lawrence and Noreen Wetton, *Lolli and Pop in Trouble,* Nelson (Nashville, TN), 1987.

Malcolm and Meryl Doney, *Who Made Me?,* Marshall Pickering (London, England), 1987, Zondervan (Grand Rapids, MI), 1992.

WITH NICK BUTTERWORTH; SELF-ILLUSTRATED

The Nativity Play, Little, Brown (Boston, MA), 1985.

The House on the Rock, Multnomah Press (Portland, OR), 1986.

The Precious Pearl, Multnomah Press (Portland, OR), 1986.

The Lost Sheep, Multnomah Press (Portland, OR), 1986.

The Two Sons, Multnomah Press (Portland, OR), 1986.

Nice and Nasty: A Book of Opposites, Hodder and Stoughton (London, England), 1987, published as *Nice or Nasty: A Book of Opposites,* Little, Brown (Boston, MA), 1987.

I Wonder at the Zoo, Zondervan (Grand Rapids, MI), 1987.

I Wonder in the Garden, Zondervan (Grand Rapids, MI), 1987.

I Wonder in the Country, Marshall Pickering (London, England), 1987, Chariot Victor Books (Colorado Springs, CO), 1994.

I Wonder at the Farm, Marshall Pickering (London, England), 1987, published as *I Wonder on the Farm,* Chariot Victor Books (Colorado Springs, CO), 1994.

Who Made . . . In the Country, HarperCollins (New York, NY), 1987.

Who Made . . . On the Farm, HarperCollins (New York, NY), 1987.

Who Made . . . At the Zoo, HarperCollins (New York, NY), 1987.

Who Made . . . In the Garden, HarperCollins (New York, NY), 1987.

Sports Day, Hodder and Stoughton (London, England), 1988.

The Magpie's Story: Jesus and Bacchaeus, Marshall Pickering (London, England), 1988.

The Mouse's Story: Jesus and the Storm, Marshall Pickering (London, England), 1988.

The Cat's Story: Jesus at the Wedding, Marshall Pickering (London, England), 1988.

The Fox's Story: Jesus Is Born, Marshall Pickering (London, England), 1988.

The Good Stranger, Marshall Pickering (London, England), 1989.

Just like Jasper!, Little, Brown (Boston, MA), 1989.

The Little Gate, Marshall Pickering (London, England), 1989, HarperCollins (New York, NY), 1992.

The Rich Farmer, Marshall Pickering (London, England), 1989, HarperCollins (New York, NY), 1992.

Ten Silver Coins, Marshall Pickering (London, England), 1989.

The School Trip, Delacorte (New York, NY), 1990.

Wonderful Earth!, Hunt and Thorpe (Alresford, England), 1990.

Field Day, Delacorte (New York, NY), 1991.

Jasper's Beanstalk, Hodder and Stoughton (London, England), 1992, Bradbury Press (New York, NY), 1993.

Opposites, Hodder and Stoughton (London, England), 1997.

Stories Jesus Told (includes *The House on the Rock* and *The Precious Pearl*), Zonderkidz (Grand Rapids, MI), 2002.

Animal Tales, Zonderkidz (Grand Rapids, MI), 2002.

SELF-ILLUSTRATED

One Bear at Bedtime: A Counting Book, Little, Brown (Boston, MA), 1987.

If I Had a Pig, Little, Brown (Boston, MA), 1988.

If I Had a Sheep, Little, Brown (Boston, MA), 1988.

Jojo's Revenge, Walker (London, England), 1989.

The Blue Balloon, Hodder and Stoughton (London, England), 1989, Little, Brown (Boston, MA), 1990.

Gumboot's Chocolatey Day, Macmillan (London, England), 1989, Doubleday (New York, NY), 1991.

Threadbear, Hodder and Stoughton (London, England), 1990, Little, Brown (Boston, MA), 1991.

Billy's Beetle, Hodder and Stoughton (London, England), 1991, Harcourt (San Diego, CA), 1992.

Penguin Small, Hodder and Stoughton (London, England), 1992, Harcourt (San Diego, CA), 1993.

Anything Cuddly Will Do!, Orchard Books (London, England), 1993.

Crocodile!, Orchard Books (London, England), 1993.

The Very Good Dinosaur, Orchard Books (London, England), 1993.

This Troll, That Troll, Orchard Books (London, England), 1993.

Lullabyhullaballoo!, Hodder and Stoughton (London, England), 1993, Artists and Writers Guild Books (New York, NY), 1994.

Nothing, Hodder and Stoughton (London, England), 1995, Artists and Writers Guild Books (New York, NY), 1996.

Don't Do That, Hodder and Stoughton (London, England), 1996, Intervisual Books (New York, NY), 1997.

Bear, Hodder and Stoughton (London, England), 1997.

Little Spotty Thing, Intervisual Books (New York, NY), 1997.

Say "Aaah"!, Intervisual Books (New York, NY), 1997.

Silly Billies, Intervisual Books (New York, NY), 1997.

Arnold, Hodder and Stoughton (London, England), 1998.

Honk!, Hodder and Stoughton (London, England), 1998.

Sandcastle, Hodder and Stoughton (London, England), 1998.

Splosh!, Hodder and Stoughton (London, England), 1998.

The Great Pet Sale, Orchard Books (New York, NY), 1999.

Hissss!, Harcourt (San Diego, CA), 1999.

In Wibbly's Garden, Viking (New York, NY), 2000.

Meow!, Harcourt (San Diego, CA), 2000.

Rocket, Harcourt (San Diego, CA), 2001.

Skates, Harcourt (San Diego, CA), 2001.

Inkpen Treasury, Hodder and Stoughton (London, England), 2003.

Blue Nose Island: Ploo and the Terrible Gnobbler, Hodder and Stoughton (London, England), 2003.

Blue Nose Island: Beachmoles and Bellvine, Hodder and Stoughton (London, England), 2004.

"KIPPER" SERIES

Kipper, Hodder and Stoughton (London, England), 1991, Little, Brown (Boston, MA), 1992.

Kipper's Toybox, Harcourt (San Diego, CA), 1992.

Kipper's Birthday, Harcourt (San Diego, CA), 1993.

Kipper's Book of Colours, Hodder and Stoughton (London, England), 1994, published as *Kipper's Book of Colors,* Harcourt (San Diego, CA), 1995.

Kipper's Book of Counting, Hodder and Stoughton (London, England), 1994, published as *Kipper's Book of Numbers,* Harcourt (San Diego, CA), 1995.

Kipper's Book of Opposites, Hodder and Stoughton (London, England), 1994, Harcourt (San Diego, CA), 1995.

Kipper's Book of Weather, Hodder and Stoughton (London, England), 1994, Harcourt (San Diego, CA), 1995.

Where, Oh Where, Is Kipper's Bear?: A Pop-up Book with Light!, Hodder and Stoughton (London, England), 1994, Harcourt Books (San Diego, CA), 1995.

Kipper's Snowy Day, Harcourt (San Diego, CA), 1996.

Kipper's Christmas Eve, Hodder Children's Books (London, England), 1999, Harcourt Books (San Diego, CA), 2000.

Kipper's A to Z: An Alphabet Adventure, Harcourt (San Diego, CA), 2000.

Kipper and Roly, Harcourt (San Diego, CA), 2001.

Kipper and the Egg, Harcourt (San Diego, CA), 2001.

Kipper's Rainy Day, Harcourt (San Diego, CA), 2001.

Kipper's Sunny Day, Harcourt (San Diego, CA), 2001.

Kipper's Sticky Paws, Harcourt (San Diego, CA), 2001.

Kipper's Basket, Harcourt (San Diego, CA), 2002.

Kipper's Kite, Harcourt (San Diego, CA), 2002.

Kipper's Lost Ball, Harcourt (San Diego, CA), 2002.

Kipper's Monster, Harcourt (San Diego, CA), 2002.

Kipper's Tree House, Harcourt (San Diego, CA), 2002.

Kipper's Surprise, Hodder and Stoughton (London, England), 2002.

Kipper's Balloon, Hodder and Stoughton (London, England), 2002.

Kipper's Beach Ball, Hodder and Stoughton (London, England), 2003.

"LITTLE KIPPER" SERIES

Arnold, Harcourt (San Diego, CA), 1998.

Honk!, Harcourt (San Diego, CA), 1998.

Sandcastle, Harcourt (San Diego, CA), 1998.

Splosh!, Harcourt (San Diego, CA), 1998.

Butterfly, Harcourt (San Diego, CA), 1999.

Swing!, Harcourt (San Diego, CA), 2000.

Picnic, Harcourt (San Diego, CA), 2001.

Thing!, illustrated by Stuart Trotter, Harcourt (San Diego, CA), 2001.

"WIBBLY PIG" SERIES

Wibbly Pig Is Happy!, Hodder and Stoughton (London, England), 1995, Viking (New York, NY), 2000.

Wibbly Pig Is Upset, Golden Books (New York, NY), 1995.

Wibbly Pig Can Dance!, Golden Books (New York, NY), 1995.

Wibbly Pig Can Make a Tent, Golden Books (New York, NY), 1995.

Wibbly Pig Likes Bananas, Golden Books (New York, NY), 1995.

Wibbly Pig Makes Pictures, Golden Books (New York, NY), 1995.

Wibbly Pig Opens His Presents, Golden Books (New York, NY), 1995.

Everyone Hide from Wibbly Pig, Viking (New York, NY), 1997.

In Wibbly's Garden, Viking (New York, NY), 2000.

Is It Bedtime Wibbly Pig?, Hodder and Stoughton (London, England), 2004.

ADAPTATIONS: Kipper was adapted as a television series by ITV, 1997, and broadcast in the United States on Nickelodeon. Many of Inkpen's stories about Kipper are also available on videocassette, including *Kipper,* Lyrick Studios, 1998, and *Kipper's Snowy Day,* Hallmark Home Entertainment, 1997.

SIDELIGHTS: Mick Inkpen is a British graphic artist-turned children's book writer and illustrator who is best known for such award-winning titles as *Kipper,*

Threadbear, and *Penguin Small.* His picture book characters include charming pigs, raucous mice, sleepy bears, and of course the playful puppy called Kipper. "I entered the world of children's books relatively late," Inkpen once commented, "after twelve years in graphic design." Quickly making up for lost time, he created several children's books with his long-time graphics partner, Nick Butterworth. Beginning publishing projects of his own in 1987, Inkpen has developed a distinctive writing and illustrating style marked by his unique humor and expressive characters.

Born in Romford, England, in 1952, Inkpen grew up in a "very suburban estate with white concrete roads all named after Scottish rivers," as the writer-illustrator told Stephanie Nettell in *Books for Keeps.* As Nettell noted, "English and Art marched side by side in Mick's affections" during his early schooling, but a job taken during his late teens preempted his decision to study English at Cambridge University. Friend Nick Butterworth had set up a graphic design studio, and offered Inkpen a temporary job. "After twelve months the temporary job became permanent," Inkpen expressed. "It was an excellent grounding—a kind of informal apprenticeship where I learned as much about dealing with stroppy printers and difficult clients as about the finer points of typography." Inkpen told Nettell that those years at the design studio were "marvelous for learning all the stuff that usually takes so long: Nick was an extremely good teacher—I'd choose that informal teaching over a college course every time—and I think I'm a good learner."

Initially, times were tough while the firm built a client base, and the partners were anything but good businessmen. Soon, however, things began to pick up. At age twenty-one, the now-married Inkpen found himself illustrating everything from bra packages to banking cartoons. Soon he and Butterworth turned their attention to children's books, creating a series based on a *Sunday Express* cartoon strip about a gang of mice that live in a deserted railway station called Upney Junction. There was also a brief excursion into television, with Inkpen writing "thirty or so stories about a pink haired punk character called Steve which Nick [Butterworth] narrated and illustrated live on camera," as he recalled. In addition to the Upney Junction mice books, Inkpen created a number of popular children's titles with Butterworth, including *Just like Jasper, Jasper's Beanstalk,* and *Nice and Nasty.* By 1986, however, he was ready to have a go at writing and illustrating his own books.

One of Inkpen's early titles, *One Bear at Bedtime,* is a counting book in which, according to *Booklist's* Barbara Elleman, "a young boy's imagination takes flight as he readies for bed." A pair of "what-if" books followed: *If I Had a Pig* and *If I Had a Sheep,* in which a boy and girl imagine they have been sent a pig and a sheep respectively and then wonder about all the things they would do with their new friend. Patricia Pearl, writing in *School Library Journal,* noted that the watercolor illustrations of "round-faced, dot-eyed, pink-cheeked children" are enhanced by "warm color tones and a gentle sense of humor," and concluded that these two books "are sure to have appeal to young children." Moira Small wrote in *Books for Keeps* that the pair of books by Inkpen are "truly delightful."

In *The Blue Balloon,* Inkpen indulges his love of balloons as "wonderful graphic objects with an endless list of properties," according to Nettell, by telling the story of a dog who brings home a soggy blue balloon. In this fold-out book, the balloon turns out to have wonderful form-changing powers that delight the dog's young owner. "Both boy and dog have wonderfully expressive faces as they react to the balloon's extraordinary feats," noted a critic in a *Publishers Weekly* review. A congenial pig is the star of *Gumboot's Chocolatey Day,* wherein the porker in question gets the last centimeter of delight from a chocolate bar his aunt has given him. A *Publishers Weekly* reviewer concluded that "Inkpen's droll illustrations do not disappoint," while a *Kirkus Reviews* critic found both story and illustrations effective: "Like his sympathetically humorous, deftly phrased text, Inkpen's watercolor illustrations are guilelessly engaging."

Inkpen's award-winning *Threadbear* refers to the patched-up old teddy-bear protagonist of the story. Threadbear decides to find Santa Claus in hopes of getting the squeaker in his stomach repaired. Even though young Ben loves his stuffed toy, squeaker or no, the bear sets off on a journey to the North Pole. A *Publishers Weekly* contributor called the picture book "a real charmer throughout," while in a *Junior Bookshelf* review, Marcus Crouch noted that Inkpen "has given his tubby hero a pleasing image supported by some suitably chilly night colours."

Another award-winning title from Inkpen is *Penguin Small,* the story of a little penguin who, with the help of a snowman and a whale, makes a miraculous journey to join his friends at the South Pole. In Inkpen's version, penguins actually hailed from the North Pole, but, tired of being eaten by polar bears, they swam south. All but Penguin Small, who is afraid of water. In a *Junior Bookshelf* review, Marcus Crouch dubbed the book a "neat story . . . enriched with the author's deadpan pictures and helped a little by some bibliographical tricks—folding pages which open to a four-page whale or a panoramic tropical island." *School Librarian* contributor Sarah Reed maintained that "this is a book that will be enjoyed by children of all ages. It's worth every penny."

In *Nothing,* Inkpen explores the themes of loneliness and loss. Toby, an old stuffed cat, forgets his name and who he is because he has been separated from his owners for so many years. Thinking his name is Nothing, he is finally reunited with his family and restored to his old glory by Grandpa. "Inkpen's familiar, unadorned watercolors animate this simple and fetching story," noted a *Publishers Weekly* reviewer. Liz Waterland, writing in *Books for Keeps,* was also enthusiastic about the work, asserting "I don't think Mick Inkpen has written anything I like better than this lovely book," while a *Kirkus Reviews* critic concluded that readers "searching for deep meanings will find plenty to ponder, especially in the perfect balance between the profoundness of Nothing's mission and the humor of the text."

In *Bear,* Inkpen delivers an engaging tale about a bear that falls from the sky. "Surely *Bear* will become a modern classic," wrote Ricki Blackhall in *Magpies.* In a combined review of Inkpen's *Splosh!, Honk!, Arnold,* and *Sandcastle,* Margaret Phillips, writing in *Magpies,* noted that "The very clever thing about the books is their child-centered approach—total absorption in the task at hand, the simple illustrations enhancing the concentration by the way in which they focus on the key element of the story line." *The Great Pet Sale* focuses on a boy in a pet store and his guide, an irascible and talkative rat. A reviewer for *Publishers Weekly* called the tale "beguiling" and noted that "funny text, an amiable menagerie, sturdy pages and some inventive extras . . . make this paper-over-board volume almost as irresistible as its fast-talking protagonist."

Perhaps Inkpen's most popular creation to date has been the young dog, Kipper, in his many incarnations. The initial title, *Kipper,* recounts the story of a puppy who has grown tired of his old blanket and basket and decides to search among the animals outdoors for a new place to sleep. George Delalis, in *School Library Journal,* noted particularly Inkpen's "deceptively simple" watercolor illustrations, both "playful and humorous," and concluded that "children will adore" Inkpen's new character. Marcus Crouch, writing in *Junior Bookshelf,* observed that this "delightful picture-book . . . should find favour with play-groups and story-tellers," while *School Librarian* contributor Richard Brown dubbed Kipper "an engaging little character, . . . a type from which series are made."

Brown's comments were indeed prophetic; Inkpen has followed the original "Kipper" title with several sequels, and his playful pup has even inspired a television series. In *Kipper's Toybox* the little dog's life changes when he discovers why there is a hole in his toybox. Dumping out the toys, he counts one too many; putting them back in the box there are two too many noses. Inkpen uses the clever device of a pair of mice to develop a subtle counting book. A *Kirkus Reviews* critic called the puppy "charming" and concluded that *Kipper's Toybox* is "an elegantly simple, satisfying story with a lot of opportunities for counting." *School Librarian* contributor Elizabeth Hormann wrote that "Inkpen has created a gentle tale to delight pre-schoolers, tickle their funnybones and charm the adults who read it to them."

The fun continues in *Kipper's Birthday,* in which a delay in sending out invitations causes Kipper's friends to come to his birthday party on the wrong day. "Just right for small people intrigued by the concepts of 'yesterday' and 'tomorrow,'" concluded a *Kirkus Reviews* critic. In *Kipper's Snowy Day* the puppy spends the day enjoying the snow with his best friend, Tiger, leaving paw prints and shapes all over the garden. Fiona Waters, in *Books for Keeps,* wrote that in this book Inkpen "captures perfectly the real magic and excitement of snow for very young children." *School Library Journal* contributor Martha Topol declared *Kipper's Snowy Day* "fun, pleasurable, and pleasant" and "Perfect for group sharing." Kipper has also made an appearance in the pop-up book *Where, Oh Where, Is Kipper's Bear?,* as well as in concept books such as *Kipper's Book of Numbers, Kipper's Book of Colors,* and *Kipper's Book of Weather.*

Kipper's Sunny Day and its companion work, *Kipper's Rainy Day,* employ simple questions to guide young readers through the text; the readers lift flaps to uncover the answers. In *Kipper's Sunny Day,* the pup spends a day at the beach with Tiger, and in *Kipper's Rainy Day,* he finds that his friends enjoy rain showers as much as he does. Reviewing *Kipper's Sunny Day,* a *Kirkus Reviews* critic noted that Inkpen's "cheery, uncluttered drawings are toddler-perfect," and *School Library Journal* contributor Karen Scott remarked that both titles are "great tools for creative thinking and stimulating the imagination."

Kipper and Tiger receive a bad scare in *Kipper's Monster.* Tiger is eager to try out his new flashlight, and he convinces Kipper to spend the night camping in the woods. As it grows dark, scary noises fill the air and the menacing shadow of a "monster" appears on the tent. Kipper discovers the shadow was actually caused by a tiny snail, but the two campers nonetheless head home to spend the rest of the night in comfort and safety. According to *School Library Journal* contributor Anne Knickerbocker, Inkpen's "bright, simple illustrations" give the work a "light, airy, uncomplicated quality." In *Kipper and Roly,* the sprightly pup decides on the perfect birthday present for his friend Pig: a new pet. After Kipper purchases Roly the hamster, however, he falls in love with Roly's antics and has trouble giving him away. Pig senses Kipper's discomfort and, in a show of friendship, asks Kipper to care for Roly. *Kipper and Roly,* provides "opportunities to discuss the qualities of good friends," observed *Booklist* reviewer Ellen Mandel.

Kipper's A to Z: An Alphabet Adventure garnered a Smarties Silver Medal in 2001. In the work, Kipper and his pal Arnold embark on an alphabet search, encountering a variety of creatures and objects along the way. According to a *Publishers Weekly* reviewer, Inkpen "introduces the letters in inventive ways, giving this volume a rollicking spontaneity and a story line." An overly enthusiastic zebra, for example, makes several appearances before his turn actually arrives, and Kipper and Arnold ask the reader for help with the letter "K." *School Library Journal* reviewer Judith Constantinides deemed *Kipper's A to Z* an "appealing concept book with childlike humor."

Another popular Inkpen series features Wibbly Pig, "a naked little pig with a round tummy who runs around with his big ears flopping," according to a *Kirkus Reviews* contributor. Wibbly appears in titles such as *Wibbly Pig Can Make a Tent, Wibbly Pig Is Happy!,* and *Wibbly Pig Makes Pictures.* In these simple stories,

the gleeful pig explores single activities, painting or dancing or putting up a tent. "Each volume is short and sweet," noted a critic in *Kirkus Reviews. In Wibbly's Garden* is a retelling of the "Jack and the Beanstalk" tale featuring the cuddly pig. While searching for a missing toy, Wibbly discovers a magic bean which grows into an enormous beanstalk. After climbing to the top, Wibbly meets a gentle giant who has also lost something important: his magic hen. The giant and Wibbly join forces to locate their missing items. *School Library Journal* contributor Joyce Rice called the "Wibbly Pig" books "an entertaining series that's sure to hold the attention of the toddler set."

Inkpen explained his illustrating and writing techniques to *Books for Keeps* interviewer Nettell: "I find it fairly easy to visually create characters that people find sympathetically real," he said. Such characters tend to be more impressionistic than photographically precise, created by round lines and soft colors. Surprisingly for this draftsman-turned-children's writer, he also told Nettell that he enjoys writing more than illustrating his books, "because there's less craft between you and the idea. You put the words down and there's the reality on the page." Inkpen also mentioned the danger in children's literature of people mistaking simplicity for lack of substance. "It's not easy to be simple," he noted.

BIOGRAPHICAL AND CRITICAL SOURCES:

PERIODICALS

Booklist, March 15, 1988, Barbara Elleman, review of *One Bear at Bedtime,* p. 1259; January 1, 1989, p. 788; April 1, 1992, Ilene Cooper, review of *Kipper,* p. 1457; April 15, 1992, Linda Callaghan, review of *Billy's Beatle,* p. 1537; October 15, 1992, Ilene Cooper, review of *Kipper's Toybox,* p. 440; January 15, 1993, Stephanie Zvirin, review of *Jasper's Beanstalk,* p. 920; March 15, 1998, Hazel Rochman, review of *Nothing,* p. 1248; April 15, 1999, Linda Perkins, review of *The Great Pet Sale,* p. 1535; October, 1999, Olga R. Barnes, review of *Kipper's Book of Colors, Kipper's Book of Opposites,* and *Kipper's Book of Weather,* p. 116; September 15, 2000, Kathy Broderick, review of *Kipper's Christmas Eve,* p. 248; September 15, 2001, Ellen Mandel, review of *Kipper and Roly,* p. 231.

Books for Keeps, March, 1992, Moira Small, review of *If I Had a Pig* and *If I Had a Sheep,* p. 6; November, 1996, Fiona Waters, "A Christmas Round-up," p. 21; November, 1996, Liz Waterland, review of *Nothing,* p. 6; November, 1997, Stephanie Nettell, "Authorgraph No. 107," p. 12.

Books for Your Children, spring, 1993, p. 19; autumn-winter, 1993, p. 8.

Bulletin of the Center for Children's Books, March, 1998, p. 247.

Christian Parenting Today, January, 2001.

Junior Bookshelf, April, 1988, p. 84; February, 1991, Marcus Crouch, review of *Threadbear,* p. 12; October, 1991, Marcus Crouch, review of *Kipper,* p. 202; October, 1992, p. 191; April, 1993, Marcus Crouch, review of *Penguin Small,* p. 60; October, 1996, pp. 184-185.

Kirkus Reviews, April 1, 1988, review of *One Bear at Bedtime,* p. 539; March 1, 1991, review of *Gumboot's Chocolatey Day,* p. 326; February 15, 1992, p. 256; March 15, 1992, p. 395; September 1, 1992, review of *Kipper's Toybox,* p. 1130; April 1, 1993, review of *Kipper's Birthday,* p. 457; April 1, 1995, p. 470; September 1, 1995, review of *Wibbly Pig Makes Pictures,* p. 1282; January 15, 1998, review of *Nothing,* p. 112; January 15, 1999, review of *The Great Pet Sale,* p. 146; August 1, 2001, *Kipper's Sunny Day,* p. 1125; April 1, 2002, review of *Kipper's Monster,* p. 493.

Magpies, March, 1998, Ricki Blackhall, review of *Bear,* p. 27; May, 1998, pp. 16-19; July, 1998, Margaret Phillips, review of *Splosh!, Honk!, Arnold,* and *Sandcastle,* p. 26.

New York Times Book Review, July 1, 1990, p. 19.

Publishers Weekly, April 29, 1988, review of *One Bear at Bedtime,* p. 75; August 26, 1988, reviews of *If I Had a Pig* and *If I Had a Sheep,* p. 85; December 22, 1989, review of *The Blue Balloon,* p. 56; January 18, 1991, review of *Gumboot's Chocolatey Day,* p. 58; June 28, 1991, review of *Threadbear,* p. 101; January 20, 1992, review of *Billy's Beatle,* p. 65; January 27, 1992, review of *Kipper,* p. 95; February 1, 1993, review of *Jasper's Beanstalk,* p. 93; September 25, 1995, review of *Where, Oh Where, Is Kipper's Bear?,* p. 55; January 19, 1998, review of *Nothing,* p. 376; April 27, 1998, review of *Wonderful Earth!,* p. 61; December 21, 1998, review of *The Great Pet Sale,* p. 66; May 22, 2000, "Seek and Ye Shall Find," p. 95; February 12, 2001, review of *Kipper's A to Z,* p. 120; July 16, 2001, "True Companions," p. 183; April 8, 2002, pp. 229-230.

Reading Time, November, 1997, pp. 19-20; February 12, 2001, review of *Kipper's A to Z: An Alphabet Adventure,* p. 210.

School Arts, December, 1995, Ken Marantz, review of *Kipper's Book of Colors,* p. 39.

School Librarian, February, 1991, p. 19; August, 1991, Richard Brown, review of *Kipper,* p. 101; February, 1992, p. 16; November, 1992, Elizabeth Hormann, review of *Kipper's Toybox,* p. 142; February, 1993, Sarah Reed, review of *Penguin Small,* p. 16; November, 1997, p. 186.

School Library Journal, June-July, 1988, Barbara S. McGinn, review of *One Bear at Bedtime,* p. 91; December, 1988, Patricia Pearl, review of *If I Had a Pig* and *If I Had a Sheep,* p. 88; July, 1990, p. 60; May, 1991, Luann Toth, review of *Gumboot's Chocolatey Day,* p. 80; May, 1992, George Delalis, review of *Kipper,* p. 90; August, 1992, Ruth Semrau, review of *Billy's Beetle,* p. 138; January, 1993, Kathy Piehl, review of *Kipper's Toybox,* p. 78; April, 1993, Denise Furgione, review of *Jasper's Beanstalk,* p. 90; June, 1993, review of *Kipper's Birthday,* p. 78; January, 1994, Julie Tomlianovich, review of *Penguin Small,* p. 91; January, 1995, Claudia Cooper, review of *Lullabyhullaballoo!,* p. 87; August, 1995, Helen Rosenberg, review of *Kipper's Book of Counting,* p. 124; December, 1996, Martha Topol, review of *Kipper's Snowy Day,* p. 94; December, 1997, Sally R. Dow, review of *Everyone Hide from Wibbly Pig,* p. 93; June, 1998, Sue Norris, review of *Nothing,* p. 109; July, 1999, Lisa Grangemi Krapp, review of *The Great Pet Sale,* p. 74; October, 2000, review of *Kipper's Christmas Eve,* p. 60; October, 2000, Joyce Rice, reviews of *Wibbly Pig Can Make a Tent, Wibbly Pig Is Happy!, Wibbly Pig Likes Bananas,* and *Wibbly Pig Opens His Presents,* p. 127; June, 2001, Judith Constantinides, review of *Kipper's A to Z,* p. 120; October, 2001, Karen Scott, review of *Kipper's Sunny Day* and *Kipper's Rainy Day,* pp. 120-121; July, 2002, Anne Knickerbocker, review of *Kipper's Monster,* p. 93.

ONLINE

Jubilee Books Web site, http://www.jubileebooks.co.uk/ (September 25, 2004), "Mick Inkpen."

Mick Inkpen Web site, http://authorpages.hoddersystems.com/MickInkpen (September 25, 2004).*

J

JENKINS, Jerry B(ruce) 1949-

PERSONAL: Born September 23, 1949, in Kalamazoo, MI; son of Harry Phillip (a police chief) and Bonita Grace (Thompson) Jenkins; married Dianna Louise Whiteford, January 23, 1971; children: Dallas Lawrence, Chadwick Whiteford, Michael Bruce. *Education:* Attended Moody Bible Institute, 1967-68, Loop College, 1968, and William Rainey Harper College, 1968-70. *Politics:* Independent. *Religion:* "Jesus Christ." *Hobbies and other interests:* Photography, tournament table tennis, Scrabble club.

ADDRESSES: Home—Three-Son Acres, 40542 Cornell St. N, Zion, IL 60099. *Office*—820 North LaSalle Dr., Chicago, IL 60610.

CAREER: WMBI-FM-AM-Radio, Chicago, IL, night news editor, 1967-68; Day Publications, Mt. Prospect, IL, assistant sports editor, 1968-69; Des Plaines Publishing Co., Des Plaines, IL, sports editor, 1969-71; *Tri-City Herald,* Kennewick, WA, sportswriter, 1971; Scripture Press Publications, Wheaton, IL, associate editor, 1971-72, managing editor, 1972-73; Inspirational Radio-Television Guide, Chicago, IL, executive editor, 1973-74; *Moody Monthly* (magazine), Chicago, managing editor, 1974-75, editor, 1975-81, director, 1978-81; Moody Press, Chicago, director, 1981-83; Moody Bible Institute, Chicago, manager of Publishing Division, 1983-85, vice president of Publishing Branch, 1985-88, writer-in-residence, 1988—. Visiting lecturer in advanced journalism, Wheaton Graduate School, 1975.

MEMBER: Evangelical Press Association, Christian Booksellers Association, Evangelical Christian Publishers Association, U.S. Table Tennis Association.

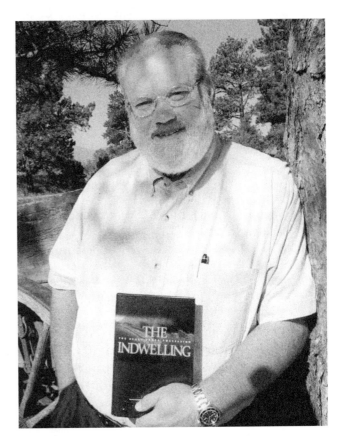

Jerry B. Jenkins

AWARDS, HONORS: Novel of the Year nomination, *Campus Life* magazine, for *Margo;* Religion in Media Angel Award, for *Meaghan* and *Margo's Reunion;* Biography of the Year award, *Campus Life* magazine, 1980, for *Home Where I Belong;* Evangelical Christian Publishers Association Gold Medallion nomination, for *The Night the Giant Rolled Over* and *Rekindled: How to Keep the Warmth in Marriage.*

WRITINGS:

You CAN Get thru to Teens, Victor Books (Wheaton, IL), 1973.

Sammy Tippit: God's Love in Action, as Told to Jerry B. Jenkins, Broadman (Nashville, TN), 1973.

VBS Unlimited, Victor Books (Wheaton, IL), 1974.

(With Hank Aaron and Stan Baldwin) *Bad Henry,* Chilton (Radnor, PA), 1974.

The Story of the Christian Booksellers Association, Nelson (Nashville, TN), 1974.

(With Pat Williams) *The Gingerbread Man: Pat Williams Then and Now,* Lippincott (Philadelphia, PA), 1974.

Stuff It: The Story of Dick Motta, Toughest Little Coach in the NBA, Chilton (Radnor, PA), 1975.

(With Sammy Tippit) *Three behind the Curtain,* Whitaker House (New Kensington, PA), 1975.

(With Paul Anderson) *The World's Strongest Man,* Victor Books (Wheaton, IL), 1975, expanded edition published as *A Greater Strength,* Revell (Old Tappan, NJ), 1990.

(With Madeline Manning Jackson) *Running for Jesus,* Word (Dallas, TX), 1977.

(With Walter Payton) *Sweetness,* Contemporary Books (Chicago, IL), 1978.

(With Sammy Tippit) *You, Me, He,* Victor Books (Wheaton, IL), 1978.

(With B. J. Thomas) *Home Where I Belong,* Word (Dallas, TX), 1978.

Light on the Heavy: A Simple Guide to Understanding Bible Doctrines, Victor Books (Wheaton, IL), 1978.

(With Sammy Tippit) *Reproduced by Permission of the Author,* Victor Books (Wheaton, IL), 1979.

The Luis Palau Story, Revell (Old Tappan, NJ), 1980.

The Night the Giant Rolled Over, Word (Dallas, TX), 1981.

(With Pat Williams) *The Power within You,* Westminster (Philadelphia, PA), 1983.

(With Robert Flood) *Teaching the Word, Reaching the World,* Moody (Chicago, IL), 1985.

(With Pat Williams) *Rekindled: How to Keep the Warmth in Marriage,* Revell (Old Tappan, NJ), 1985.

(With Meadowlark Lemon) *Meadowlark,* Nelson (Nashville, TN), 1987.

(With Pat Williams and Jill Williams) *Kindling: Daily Devotions for Busy Couples,* Nelson (Nashville, TN), 1987.

The Operative (novel), Harper & Row (New York, NY), 1987.

A Generous Impulse: The Story of George Sweeting, Moody (Chicago, IL), 1987.

Carry Me: Christine Wyrtzen's Discoveries on the Journey into God's Arms, as Told to Jerry B. Jenkins, Moody (Chicago, IL), 1988.

(With Larry and Diane Mayfield) *Baby Mayfield,* Moody (Chicago, IL), 1989.

(With Deanna McClary) *Commitment to Love,* Nelson (Nashville, TN), 1989.

(With Orel Hershiser) *Out of the Blue,* Wolgemuth & Hyatt (Brentwood, TN), 1989.

Hedges: Loving Your Marriage Enough to Protect It, Wolgemuth & Hyatt (Brentwood, TN), 1989, expanded edition, Moody (Chicago, IL), 1993.

(With Pat Williams and Jill Williams) *Just Between Us,* Revell (Tarrytown, NY), 1991.

(With Joe J. Gibbs) *Joe Gibbs: Fourth and One,* Nelson (Nashville, TN), 1991.

Twelve Things I Want My Kids to Remember Forever, Moody (Chicago, IL), 1991.

The Rookie (novel), Wolgemuth & Hyatt (Brentwood, TN), 1991.

(With Nolan Ryan) *Miracle Man: Nolan Ryan, the Autobiography,* Word (Dallas, TX), 1992.

(With William Gaither) *I Almost Missed the Sunset: My Perspectives on Life and Music,* Nelson (Nashville, TN), 1992.

The Deacon's Woman and Other Portraits (fiction), Moody (Chicago, IL), 1992.

(Editor) *Families: Practical Advice from More than Fifty Experts,* Moody (Chicago, IL), 1993.

(With George J. Thompson) *Verbal Judo: The Gentle Art of Persuasion,* Morrow (New York, NY), 1993.

Winning at Losing, Moody (Chicago, IL), 1993.

Life Flies When You're Having Fun, Victor Books (Wheaton, IL), 1993.

(With Sammy Tippit) *No Matter What the Cost: An Autobiography,* Nelson (Nashville, TN), 1993.

As You Leave Home: Parting Thoughts from a Loving Parent, Focus on the Family (Colorado Springs, CO), 1993.

(With Gary Almy and Carol Tharp Almy) *Addicted Recovery,* Harvest House (Eugene, OR), 1994.

Still the One: Tender Thoughts from a Loving Spouse, Focus on the Family (Colorado Springs, CO), 1995.

And Then Came You: The Hopes and Dreams of Loving Parents, Focus on the Family (Colorado Springs, CO), 1996.

The Neighborhood's Scariest Woman, ("Toby Andrews and the Junior Deputies" series), Moody (Chicago, IL), 1996.

The East Side Bullies ("Toby Andrews and the Junior Deputies" series), Moody (Chicago, IL), 1996.

(With Brett Butler) *Field of Hope: An Inspiring Autobiography of a Lifetime of Overcoming Odds,* Nelson (Nashville, TN), 1997.

(With William Gaither) *Homecoming: The Story of Southern Gospel Music through the Eyes of Its Best-Loved Performers,* Zondervan (Grand Rapids, MI), 1997.

'Twas the Night Before, Viking (New York, NY), 1998.

Though None Go with Me (novel), Zondervan (Grand Rapids, MI), 2000.

Hometown Legend, Warner Books (New York, NY), 2001.

(With Tim F. LaHaye) *Perhaps Today: Living Every Day in the Light of Christ's Return,* Tyndale House (Wheaton, IL), 2001.

The Youngest Hero, Warner Books (New York, NY), 2002.

"MARGO MYSTERY" SERIES

Margo, Jeremy Books, 1979, published as *The Woman at the Window,* Nelson (Nashville, TN), 1991.

Karlyn, Moody (Chicago, IL), 1980, published as *The Daylight Intruder,* Nelson, (Nashville, TN), 1991.

Hilary, Moody (Chicago, IL), 1980, published as *Murder behind Bars,* Nelson (Nashville, TN), 1991.

Paige, Moody (Chicago, IL), 1981, published as *The Meeting at Midnight,* Nelson (Nashville, TN), 1991.

Allyson, Moody (Chicago, IL), 1981, published as *The Silence Is Broken,* Nelson (Nashville, TN), 1991.

Erin, Moody (Chicago, IL), 1982, published as *Gold Medal Murder,* Nelson (Nashville, TN), 1991.

Shannon, Moody (Chicago, IL), 1982, published as *Thank You, Good-Bye,* Nelson (Nashville, TN), 1991.

Lindsey, Moody (Chicago, IL), 1983, published as *Dying to Come Home,* Nelson (Nashville, TN), 1991.

Meaghan, Moody (Chicago, IL), 1983.

Janell, Moody (Chicago, IL), 1983.

Courtney, Moody (Chicago, IL), 1983.

Lyssa, Moody (Chicago, IL), 1984.

Margo's Reunion, Moody (Chicago, IL), 1984.

"JENNIFER GREY MYSTERY" SERIES

Heartbeat, Victor Books (Wheaton, IL), 1983.

Three Days in Winter, Victor Books (Wheaton, IL), 1983.

Too Late to Tell, Victor Books (Wheaton, IL), 1983.

Gateway, Victor Books (Wheaton, IL), 1983.

The Calling, Victor Books (Wheaton, IL), 1984.

Veiled Threat, Victor Books (Wheaton, IL), 1984.

"THE BRADFORD FAMILY ADVENTURE" SERIES

Daniel's Big Surprise, Standard Publishing (Cincinnati, OH), 1984.

Two Runaways, Standard Publishing (Cincinnati, OH), 1984.

The Clubhouse Mystery, Standard Publishing (Cincinnati, OH), 1984.

The Kidnapping, Standard Publishing (Cincinnati, OH), 1984.

Marty's Secret, Standard Publishing (Cincinnati, OH), 1985.

Blizzard!, Standard Publishing (Cincinnati, OH), 1985.

Fourteen Days to Midnight, Standard Publishing (Cincinnati, OH), 1985.

Good Sport/Bad Sport, Standard Publishing (Cincinnati, OH), 1985.

In Deep Water, Standard Publishing (Cincinnati, OH), 1986.

Mystery at Raider Stadium, Standard Publishing (Cincinnati, OH), 1986.

Daniel's Big Decision, Standard Publishing (Cincinnati, OH), 1986.

Before the Judge, Standard Publishing (Cincinnati, OH), 1986.

"DALLAS O'NEIL AND THE BAKER STREET SPORTS CLUB" SERIES

The Secret Baseball Challenge, Moody (Chicago, IL), 1986.

The Scary Basketball Player, Moody (Chicago, IL), 1986.

The Mysterious Football Team, Moody (Chicago, IL), 1986.

The Weird Soccer Match, Moody (Chicago, IL), 1986.

The Strange Swimming Coach, Moody (Chicago, IL), 1986.

The Bizarre Hockey Tournament, Moody (Chicago, IL), 1986.

The Silent Track Star, Moody (Chicago, IL), 1986.

The Angry Gymnast, Moody (Chicago, IL), 1986.

Mystery of the Phony Murder, Moody (Chicago, IL), 1989.

Mystery of the Skinny Sophomore, Moody (Chicago, IL), 1989.

"TARA CHADWICK" SERIES

Time to Tell, Moody (Chicago, IL), 1990.
Operation Cemetery, Moody (Chicago, IL), 1990.
Scattered Flowers, Moody (Chicago, IL), 1990.
Springtime Discovery, Moody (Chicago, IL), 1990.

"LEFT BEHIND" SERIES, WITH TIM F. LAHAYE

Left Behind: A Novel of the Earth's Last Days, Tyndale House (Wheaton, IL), 1995.
Tribulation Force: The Continuing Drama of Those Left Behind, Tyndale House (Wheaton, IL), 1996.
Nicolae: The Rise of Antichrist, Tyndale House (Wheaton, IL), 1997.
Soul Harvest: The World Takes Sides, Tyndale House (Wheaton, IL), 1998.
Apollyon: The Destroyer Is Unleashed, Tyndale House (Wheaton, IL), 1999.
Assassins: The Great Tribulation Unfolds, Tyndale House (Wheaton, IL), 1999.
The Indwelling: The Beast Takes Possession, Tyndale House (Wheaton, IL), 2000.
Desecration: Antichrist Takes the Throne, Tyndale House (Wheaton, IL), 2001.
The Mark: The Beast Rules the World, Tyndale House (Wheaton, IL), 2001.
The Remnant: On the Brink of Armageddon, Tyndale House (Wheaton, IL), 2002.
Armageddon, Tyndale House (Wheaton, IL), 2003.
Glorious Reappearing: The End of Days, Tyndale House (Wheaton, IL), 2004.

"GLOBAL AIR TROUBLESHOOTERS" SERIES:

Terror in Branco Grande, Multnomah Books (Sisters, OR), 1996.
Disaster in the Yukon, Multnomah Books (Sisters, OR), 1996.
Crash at Cannibal Valley, Multnomah Books (Sisters, OR), 1996.

"LEFT BEHIND—THE KIDS" SERIES; WITH TIM F. LAHAYE:

The Vanishings, Tyndale House (Wheaton, IL), 1998.
Second Chance, Tyndale House (Wheaton, IL), 1998.
Through the Flames, Tyndale House (Wheaton, IL), 1998.
Facing the Future, Tyndale House (Wheaton, IL), 1998.
(And with Chris Fabry) *The Underground,* Tyndale House (Wheaton, IL), 1999.
Nicolae High, Tyndale House (Wheaton, IL), 1999.
(And with Chris Fabry) *Death Strike,* Tyndale House (Wheaton, IL), 2000.
(And with Chris Fabry) *Busted!,* Tyndale House (Wheaton, IL), 2000.

OTHER:

Also author of *Off the Map,* 1991. Contributor to periodicals, including *Moody Monthly, Power, Contact, Coronet, Saturday Evening Post,* and *Campus Life.*

ADAPTATIONS: Left Behind: A Novel of the Earth's Last Days was adapted for a feature film by Cloud Ten Pictures, 2001. Books in the "Left Behind" series have been adapted to audio cassette, interactive computer games, mugs, T-shirts, and other marketing merchandise.

WORK IN PROGRESS: A prequel and sequel, volumes thirteen and fourteen, to the "Left Behind" series.

SIDELIGHTS: Jerry B. Jenkins is the author of over one hundred titles, most of them religious and inspirational works. The best known of these are the dozen titles of the "Left Behind" series, penned with Tim F. LaHaye. With over sixty-two million copies of that series in print, the Jenkins-LaHaye team is, according to *Newsweek*'s David Gates, "arguably, the most successful literary partnership of all time." Gates further noted that "their Biblical techno-thrillers about the end of the world are currently outselling Stephen King, John Grisham, and every other pop novelist in America." The books in the hugely popular series are "old-time religion with a sci-fi sensibility," wrote Gates; they combine "the ultimate certainty the Bible offers with the entertainment-culture conventions of rock-jawed heroism and slam-bang special effects." Yet Jenkins continues to describe himself in interviews as "the most famous writer no one's ever heard of." Part of the reason for this lack of name recognition is the fact that over seventy per cent of the sales of the "Left Behind" series are from the South and Midwest, only six percent from the urban Northeast. A full eighty-five per cent of the readership of the series terms themselves "born again" Christians. As Gates put it, the typical buyer of the books is a "forty-four-year-old born-again Christian woman, married with kids, living in the South."

A native of Michigan, Jenkins worked as a journalist and publishing executive before turning to authorship in the 1970s. He wrote in a variety of nonfiction genres, but all his books were grounded in his evangelical Christian faith. The author also earned a reputation as the writing talent behind celebrity memoirs; his "as told to" autobiographies include those of sports heroes Henry Aaron, Orel Hershiser, and Brett Butler. But Jenkins told a *Marriage Partnership* interviewer, "fiction was always my first love. I wrote nonfiction to pay the bills, in the hopes that the fiction would hit."

The fiction did hit—first with a set of youth-oriented mysteries, then with the debut of the "Left Behind" books. The books were conceived by LaHaye, a well-known evangelical minister who left the pulpit in 1981 to devote time to writing and politics. According to a *People* article by Thomas Fields-Meyer, LaHaye was inspired to storytelling during his travel days: "Sitting on airplanes and watching the pilots," he commented to Fields-Meyer, "I'd think to myself, 'What if the Rapture occurred on an airplane'?" LaHaye searched for three years for someone to shape his idea into a novel, and fellow evangelical Jenkins was his selection. Though nearly twenty-five years apart in age, the two were comfortable working together. "It's like a father-son thing," Jenkins said in *People*. Jenkins is the author of the novels; LaHaye serves as consultant for prophetic accuracy.

In 1995 *Left Behind* was published by Tyndale House. True to LaHaye's vision, the novel opens on an airplane en route to London. Pilot Rayford Steele, who is contemplating an extramarital affair with flight attendant Hattie Durham, is surprised when Hattie bursts into the cockpit with startling news: several of the passengers have disappeared in an instant, leaving only their clothes and other possessions piled on their seats. Making an emergency landing in his hometown

of Chicago, Rayford returns home to find his wife and son, both recently born-again Christians, vanished as well. The conclusion: Christian true-believers have been spirited to heaven (the Rapture) while those back on Earth are faced with the biblical prophesy of war and pestilence leading to the Apocalypse, as heralded by the rise of the Antichrist.

Among those "left behind" is crusading journalist Cameron "Buck" Williams, who takes on the story for his magazine. His investigation leads to a charismatic Romanian politician, Nicolae Carpathia, who quickly rises to power by advocating a one-world government. Nicolae, appointed secretary general of the United Nations, has the power to control all but the unsaved; he reconstructs the nations of the Earth as the Global Community and plans to reign supreme over the world. When it becomes apparent that Nicolae is the Antichrist incarnate, it is up to Rayford, Buck, and their band of believers, who dub themselves the Tribulation Force, to defend their world. As the last line of *Left Behind* puts it, the rebels' task was clear: "their goal was nothing less than to stand and fight the enemies of God during the seven most chaotic years the planet would ever see."

Left Behind was followed by a steady stream of sequels, one every six months, all advancing the Apocalyptic plot. While few mainstream critics praised the stylistic aspects of the novels, many acknowledged that Jenkins's tales had value as thought-provoking page-turners. "I found [the first novel] rattling good reading, professionally terse yet fluid," commented J. C. Furnas of *American Scholar.* "Suppose the late Ian Fleming [of James Bond fame] had got End-Times religion and built on it a portentous Scripture-based epic in 007 style, only with a certain paucity of toothsome women." While *Atlantic Monthly* reviewer Joseph Gross noted Jenkins' reliance on easy characterization—"everyone in the books is above average. The characters' brains and physical beauty are sometimes described with clumsy cultural references"—*National Review* contributor Matthew Scully had a different view. He thought Jenkins had "a gift for plot and dialogue" which would serve the author well through the book series.

Some criticism of the "Left Behind" books focused on the way non-evangelicals were portrayed. "The authors' perception of the Jews as a great people gone wrong streaks the books with a queasy, forced amiability teetering on contempt," stated *Commonweal* writer Richard Alleva. The Catholic church "takes its lumps, too," Alleva continued. "The latest pope is raptured, but that is because he had stirred up controversy in the church with a new doctrine that seemed to coincide more with the 'heresy' of Martin Luther than with historic orthodoxy." "Catholics' chances of making the Rapture are slim," noted Teresa Malcolm in a *National Catholic Reporter* piece, but in her opinion the saving of the fictional pope reflected that "overt anti-Catholicism was deliberately toned down to give the novels a wider appeal."

But the books' severest barbs are aimed at the United Nations, "which practically hands itself over to the Antichrist and becomes the arm of his will," according to Alleva. "And what is his will? A world government, a world capital called New Babylon, a world army, and a world religion—all the usual suspects placed at the service of Satan's minion. In a country like ours, where fear of centralization and government interference has led to bombings, mass slaughter, and the creation of various thug militia-groups, how could the 'Left Behind' series fail?"

The timing of a tale about the Rapture coincided with the end-of-the-millennium mood in the United States. Worldwide political unrest and "Y2K" technological concerns fueled the interest in end-times literature, and the "Left Behind" series played into that interest. Jenkins and LaHaye's books, promotional items and Web site have drawn massive attention, leading a *Publishers Weekly* editor to tell *People*'s Fields-Meyer that the stories comprise "the most successful Christian-fiction series ever." "Left Behind is truly newsmaking stuff," remarked Alleva. Still, Jenkins maintains that money is not the primary force propelling the series, even though it has been reported that each author has earned over fifty million dollars on the series. "Neither [LaHaye] nor I grew up in families where success was defined by money," he said in the *Marriage Partnership* interview. His ministry, he said, was always more important. And he takes pleasure in writing the novels: "Discovering what happens is as much fun for me as it is for readers. I don't kill my characters off; I find them dead."

Any thought that the "Left Behind" series was simply a manifestation of millennial fever was put to rest with the continued success of the series after the year 2000. And with the terrorist attacks of 2001 in New York and Washington, and the ensuing war in Iraq, many of the fans of the series felt that the world in fact was entering the last days as prophesied in the Book of Revelation. The series came to its final volume—though a prequel and sequel are planned—with volume twelve, *Glorious Reappearing: The End of Days,* in which Jesus reappears. That book sold over two million copies even before its publication date.

It has been noted, especially with the George W. Bush White House, that the series functions not just as fiction but also as a subtle form of propaganda for the conservative Christian interpretation of the Bible. According to Gates, "The many critics of the series see a resonance between its apocalyptic scenario and the born-again President Bush's apocalyptic rhetoric and confrontational Mid East policies." These same critics see a LaHaye's far-right political agenda in topics in the books such as the United Nations acting as an evil institution. Other criticism continues to come from Christians themselves who "find the books more interested in God's wrath than God's love—as well as scripturally questionable," as Gates further observed. Critics also point to the "pedestrian writing and . . . gruesome violence" in the books, as Malcolm Jones pointed out in *Newsweek*. According to Jones, "Characterization is minimal and when Christ isn't spouting Scripture, he sounds like a traffic cop."

Yet detractors aside, the success of the series is its own justification. As Melani McAlister commented in a *Nation* article on the "Left Behind" franchise, "The astonishing success of the . . . series suggests that the conservative obsession with biblical prophecy is increasingly shaping our secular reality." Responding to critics of the vengeful God presented in their books, however, Jenkins noted to Gates that he and LaHaye read the Bible with this interpretation and "we sort of have a responsibility to tell what it seems to say to us." Speaking with David D. Kirkpatrick of the *New York Times,* Jenkins also acknowledged that his warrior, judgmental, vengeful Jesus "might not please everyone." However, Jenkins concluded, "that is the way it is in the Bible."

BIOGRAPHICAL AND CRITICAL SOURCES:

PERIODICALS

American Scholar, winter, 2000, J. C. Furnas, "Millennial Sideshow," p. 87.

Atlantic Monthly, January, 2000, Joseph Gross, "The Trials of Tribulation," p. 122.

Booklist, February 1, 1992, review of *Off the Map,* p. 1005; November 1, 1995, John Mort, review of *Left Behind: A Novel of the Earth's Last Days,* p. 455; October 1, 1996, John Mort, review of *Tribulation Force: The Continuing Drama of Those Left Behind,* p. 304; March 1, 1997, John Mort, review of *The Rookie,* p. 1111; July, 1997, John Mort, review of *Nicolae: The Rise of Antichrist,* p. 1775, Ray Olson, review of *Home-coming: The Story of Southern Gospel Music through the Eyes of Its Best-Loved Performers,* p. 1788; June 1, 1998, John Mort, review of *Soul Harvest: The World Takes Sides,* p. 1669; October 15, 1998, Toni Hyde, review of *'Twas the Night Before,* p. 374; February 1, 1999, John Mort, review of *Apollyon: The Destroyer Is Unleashed,* p. 940; August, 1999, John Mort, review of *Assassins: The Great Tribulation Unfolds,* p. 1987; January 1, 2000, John Mort, review of *Though None Go with Me,* p. 874; December 15, 2000, Bonnie Smothers, review of *The Mark: The Beast Rules the World,* p. 763; July, 2001, John Mort, review of *Hometown Legend,* p. 1951, Jeanette Larson, review of *The Indwelling: The Beast Takes Possession,* p. 2029; November 15, 2001, Judy Morrissey, review of *The Vanishings,* p. 591.

Christianity Today, September 1, 1997, Michael Maudlin, review of *Left Behind,* p. 22.

Christian Reader, September, 2000, review of *The Indwelling,* p. 7; November, 2000, review of *The Mark,* p. 6.

Commonweal, January 12, 2001, Richard Alleva, "Beam Me Up: A Repackaged Apocalypse," p. 17.

Electronic News, November 28, 1994, Grace Zisk, review of *Verbal Judo: The Gentle Art of Persuasion,* p. 34.

Free Inquiry, spring, 2001, Edmund Cohen, "Turner Diaries Lite," p. 58.

Insight on the News, August 26, 2002, Sheila R. Cherry, "Tour Guides to the Tribulation," pp. 36-39.

Kirkus Reviews, December 1, 1991, review of *Off the Map,* p. 1514; September 15, 1998, review of *'Twas the Night Before,* p. 1330.

Library Journal, June 1, 1996, Henry Carrigan, Jr., review of *Left Behind,* p. 92; September 1, 1996, Henry Carrigan, Jr., review of *Tribulation Force,* p. 164; October 1, 1997, Michael Colby, review of *Homecoming,* p. 84; June 1, 1998, Melissa Hudak, review of *Soul Harvest,* p. 94; November 1, 1998, review of *'Twas the Night Before,* p. 127; May 15, 1999, Melissa Hudak, review of *Left Behind,* p. 147; September 1, 1999, Melanie Duncan, review of *Assassins,* p. 172; November 1, 2000, Melanie Duncan, review of *The Mark,* p. 62.

Los Angeles Times Magazine, April 25, 2004, Nancy Shepherdson, "Waiting for Godot; the Bible Foretold It," p. 16.

Marriage Partnership, fall, 2000, review of *The Indwelling,* p. S4; summer, 2000, "Riding the Wave," p. S1; fall, 2001, review of *Desecration: Antichrist Takes the Throne,* p. S4; spring, 2002, review of *Desecration,* p. S4.

Nation, September 22, 2003, Melani McAlister, "An Empire of Their Own," p. 31.

National Catholic Reporter, June 15, 2001, Teresa Malcolm, "Fearful Faith in End Times Novel," p. 13.

National Review, December 21, 1998, Matthew Scully, "Apocalypse Soon," p. 62.

Newsweek, April 12, 2004, Malcolm Jones, "The Twelfth Book of Revelation," p. 60; May 24, 2004, David Gates, "Religion: The Pop Prophets," p. 44.

New York Review of Books, October 12, 1989, Wilfred Sheed, review of *Out of the Blue,* p. 49.

New York Times, February 11, 2002, David D. Kirkpatrick, "A Best-Selling Formula in Religious Thrillers," p. C2; March 29, 2004, David D. Kirkpatrick, "In the Twelfth Book of Best-Selling Series, Jesus Returns," p. A1; April 4, 2004, David D. Kirkpatrick, "The Return of the Warrior Jesus," p. D1.

New York Times Book Review, June 4, 1989, Charles Salzberg, review of *Out of the Blue,* p. 23.

People, December 14, 1998, Thomas Fields-Meyer, "In Heaven's Name," p. 139.

Publishers Weekly, September 14, 1998, review of *'Twas the Night Before,* p. 50; November 15, 1999, review of *Though None Go with Me,* p. 56; November 13, 2000, review of *The Mark,* p. 88; May 7, 2001, Cindy Crosby, "Left Behind Fuels Growth at Tyndale House," p. 18; July 16, 2001, review of *Hometown Legend,* p. 156; August 20, 2001, Daisy Maryles and Dick Donahue, "Making a Mark," p. 23; April 21, 2003, Daisy Maryles and Dick Donahue, "Armageddon Has Arrived," p. 16.

Today's Christian Woman, November, 2000, "Five Minutes with Jerry B. Jenkins," p. 78; March, 2001, "Down the Fiction Aisle," p. S4; September, 2001, review of *Desecration,* p. S4.

Voice of Youth Advocates, December, 1991, review of *The Rookie,* p. 312.

Wall Street Journal, July 14, 2000, Susan Lee, "Something of a Revelation," p. W11.

West Coast Review of Books, February, 1991, review of *The Rookie*, p. 7.

ONLINE

Official Jerry Jenkins Web site, http://www.jerry jenkins.com (March 15, 2002).*

*   *   *

JONES, Elinor 1930-

PERSONAL: Born February 28, 1930, in New York, NY; daughter of Hamilton (a businessman) and Caroline (a homemaker and political activist; maiden name, Norton) Wright; married Tom Jones (in theatre), June 1, 1963 (divorced, December, 1982). *Education:* Studied at Pasadena Playhouse, Pasadena, CA, 1948, and Cleveland Playhouse, Cleveland, OH, 1949-50.

ADDRESSES: Home—7 West 96th St., New York, NY 10025. *Agent*—Peter Franklin, William Morris, 1350 Sixth Ave., New York, NY.

CAREER: Playwright, producer, and actor. Barter Theatre, Abingdon, VA, attendant, 1951-52; acted in television productions for Kraft Playhouse and Philco Playhouse, New York, NY; acted on Broadway in *A Thurber Carnival*, 1960; assistant to producers Herman Shumlin, Courtney Burr, and Lewis Allen, and to film director Peter Brooks on *Lord of the Flies*, 1962; coproducer (with Robert Benton) of short film *A Texas Romance, 1909*, 1964.

MEMBER: Circle Repertory Theatre, League of Professional Theater Women, Dramatists Guild.

AWARDS, HONORS: First Prize for short subject (with Peter Brooks), San Francisco Film Festival, 1964, for *A Texas Romance, 1909.*

WRITINGS:

PLAYS

Colette, produced in New York, NY, 1970.

A Voice of My Own (produced in New York, NY, 1979), Dramatist Play Service (New York, NY), 1979.

What Would Jeanne Moreau Do?, Samuel French (New York, NY), 1982.

Three Short Plays (includes *6:15 on the 104*, *If You Were My Wife, I'd Shoot Myself*, and *Under Control*), Dramatists Play Service (New York, NY), 1989.

Out of Season, produced at Caldwell Theatre, Boca Raton, FL, 2002.

Also author of *Box Office*, produced in New York City.

OTHER

Coauthor of film screenplays *Fancy Strut* and *Norfleet.*

SIDELIGHTS: Elinor Jones' career in the dramatic arts has ranged from acting to producing to writing plays. Her husband of nearly twenty years, Tom Jones, is also a theatre person, best known for writing the book and lyrics for the long-running off-Broadway hit *The Fantasticks.* Jones' work in film production has included working as an assistant to director Peter Brook on the highly regarded *Lord of the Flies* and as a coproducer, with Robert Benton, for *A Texas Romance, 1909*, which won first prize at the San Francisco Film Festival for a short subject in 1964.

A number of Jones' plays have been produced and published, and her *A Voice of My Own* is frequently performed at colleges and universities. One of her major productions, *Colette*, was first produced in 1970 and starred Zoë Caldwell and Mildred Dunnock. The play is based on the collection of the French writer Colette's autobiographical writings titled *This Earthly Paradise*, edited and translated into English by Robert Phelps and published in 1966. Colette was born Sidonie Gabrielle Claudine Colette in the French provinces in 1873. She married at age seventeen and moved to Paris with her first husband at the turn of the twentieth century. At that young age she began performing as a mime dancer and, according to a review of the play in *Variety*, "shocked contemporary audiences by actually being kissed onstage" by a woman. An intriguing and controversial figure throughout her life, Colette was also a prodigious producer of a great variety of writing, including novels, plays, memoirs, essays, and theater critiques.

Colette, is constructed in two acts, which are episodic rather than closely plotted; the *Variety* reviewer described them as a "series of low-keyed, loosely linked scenes" based on Colette's life. Many of the scenes include Sido, Colette's mother, a warm and creative spirit who was a dominant force throughout her daughter's life. M. Willy, Colette's first husband and the first promoter of her acting and writing, figures prominently as well. The first act is much longer than the second and more diverse; the shorter second act is presented in the form of an interview of the aged Colette by two journalists.

Reviews of the 1970 production of *Colette* were varied. Stanley Kauffman, writing in the *New Republic,* had reservations about Jones's script, stating that it "includes some things and leaves out others. Not much more can be said of it, except that only the homosexuality of others gets mention, not Colette's lesbian activities, which—as against the protean truth of her life—thins her out." The critic in *Variety* found some fault with the play's structure but also stated that "*Colette* does justice to both the subject's life and art." Haskel Frankel, reviewing Jones' play for the *National Observer,* felt that "its virtues far outweigh its hurts" and declared that the work offered "a chance to hear

the written thoughts of a wise and witty woman." And Marilyn Stasio wrote in *Cue* that Jones' adaptation "overflows with the wondrously lyrical prose of the French novelist." Reviewer James Davis of the New York *Daily News* called *Colette* "a full, rich—and thoroughly enjoyable—dramatization of the life of Colette," adding that the play "makes for a charming and often beautiful evening. . . . [Y]ou will love all the characters, they are drawn and acted so well."

BIOGRAPHICAL AND CRITICAL SOURCES:

PERIODICALS

Cue, May 16, 1970, Marilyn Stasio, review of *Colette.*
Daily News (New York, NY), May 7, 1970, review of *Colette.*
National Observer, May 11, 1970, review of *Colette.*
New Republic, June 13, 1970, Stanley Kauffman, review of *Colette.*
Variety, May 13, 1970, review of *Colette.*

K

KARODIA, Farida 1942-

PERSONAL: Born 1942, in Aliwal North, Republic of South Africa; immigrated to Canada, 1969; daughter of Ebrahim and Mary Elizabeth Karodia; married (divorced, c. 1966); children: one daughter. *Education:* University of Calgary, B.Ed.

ADDRESSES: Agent—c/o Author Mail, Penguin Books, P.O. Box 9, Parklands 2121, Johannesburg, South Africa; c/o Author Mail, David Philip Publishers, P.O. Box 23408, Claremont 7735, 208 Werdmuller Centre, Newry St., Claremont, Cape Town 7700, South Africa.

CAREER: Short story writer, novelist, and scriptwriter for radio. Also worked as a teacher.

AWARDS, HONORS: Special mention, Banff Film Festival, for television drama *Midnight Embers,* 1992.

WRITINGS:

NOVELS

Daughters of the Twilight, Women's Press (London, England), 1986.
A Shattering of Silence, Heinemann (Portsmouth, NH), 1993.
Other Secrets, Penguin (Johannesburg, South Africa), 2000.
Boundaries, Penguin (Johannesburg, South Africa), 2003.

OTHER

Coming Home and Other Stories (short stories), Heinemann (London, England), 1988.
Against an African Sky and Other Stories(short stories), D. Philip (Cape Town, South Africa), 1995.

Work represented in numerous anthologies, including *Her Mother's Ashes,* Tsar (Toronto, Canada), 1998, and *Opening Spaces,* Heinemann (London, England), and *Seeds of Discontent,* both published in 1999, and *South African Indian Writings in English,* Madiba Publishers (South Africa), 2000. Wrote a children's book with Danish illustrator Maikki Harjanne that was distributed to schools in South Africa. Author of *Midnight Embers,* a half-hour drama for television. Also author of radio dramas for Canadian Broadcast Corporation (CBC).

WORK IN PROGRESS: A novel set in India and Canada.

SIDELIGHTS: Farida Karodia was born and raised in the Eastern Cape, but spent much of her adult life in Canada. Most of her fiction is set in South Africa, where she returned in 1994. Karodia told *CA,* "My writing is slowly moving beyond the South African settings, which feature so prominently in all of my work. Part of *Other Secrets* is set in London and in *Boundaries* a substantial part of the book is set in Canada. The book I am currently working on is set in India and Canada."

Karodia explained her writing process to *CA:* "A main character 'arrives' in my head, usually very clearly defined. I then set about developing this character, providing a setting and a problem. By this time I might know the ending, but not necessarily the story line or how the story will begin and it often takes several false starts for me to find the right voice. The rest, of course, is hard work—at least four to five hours a day, sometimes twelve to fifteen hours of writing, until I have the first draft of the story—usually a skeletal draft which is much more than an outline."

Karodia's novel *Daughters of the Twilight* follows the plight of an Indian family of shopkeepers living in South Africa. The oldest daughter of the family receives a good education, but after the Group Areas Act passes, the younger daughter finds herself classified as a "coloured" person, so she cannot receive the same education as her sister. This is only one of the family's problems. When the area in which they live is designated a "whites only" area, they must relocate and rebuild their lives from scratch. Michelene Wandor, writing in the *British Book News*, noted that *Daughters of the Twilight* "is a most assured piece of work, riveting and moving."

Karodia followed the novel with a collection of short stories, *Coming Home and Other Stories*. The stories have a variety of narrators—black, white, and "coloured"—and many of them have violent underpinnings in their discussions about South Africa. "Racists and sadists roam through these pages with impunity," wrote J. R. Moehringer in a review of the book in the *New York Times Book Review*, noting that "what remains is Ms. Karodia's clear vision of the South African tragedy."

In Karodia's novel *A Shattering of Silence,* a middle-aged white woman returns to Mozambique, where she had spent her youth as a revolutionary in the country's decades-long war. Much of the story is told in flashback and the woman eventually comes to terms with her past. In a *World Literature Today* review of *A Shattering of Silence,* Sheila Roberts observed sections of the book where "the writing loses its liveliness and color," but found that "the depictions of the effects of war on populations, towns, and villages are compelling."

Karodia has produced another collection of short stories. Like *Coming Home and Other Stories, Against an African Sky and Other Stories* features a collection of multicultural narrators speaking about (and reacting to) life in South Africa. Reviewer Adele S. Newson, in a *World Literature Today* review, described this collection of five stories as "an exciting commentary on post-apartheid South Africa" and concluded that it offers "a convincing mosaic of the country."

Karodia received much critical acclaim for her novel *Other Secrets,* the first part of which is a reworking of her earlier novel *Daughters of Twilight. Other Secrets* focuses on the tumultuous relationships between sisters and mothers and daughters. The brazen and beautiful Yasmin captures most of her mother's attention, leaving sister Meena feeling as if she lives in her shadow. Yasmin later leaves the small town of her childhood, casting off her elderly family and a child conceived out of rape. Meena proves herself strong and capable as she takes charge of her family's care. *Sunday Times* reviewer Penny Sukhraj praised Karodia's characterization, saying, "It has been a long time since I have come across a novel where the storyteller draws the reader into the lives of her characters so intimately." Sukhraj described the story as "unpredictable in the way it unfolds, unravels and again binds together the lives of the main players." Writing in the *Pretoria News,* reviewer Orielle Berry termed *Other Secrets* a "multi-faceted book," and explained, "When you read it, it's like peeling off the many layers of an onion, with each layer revealing a different aspect, not only of a tightly knit family, but of the comings and goings of a small town." "The only criticism of *Other Secrets* is that Karodia spends too much time exploring mundane scenes of everyday life, and too little time on life-changing events such as the hostility of local Afrikaner girls to Yasmin's obvious charm and beauty," noted Sukhraj.

Yasmin and Meena grow up in South Africa during the apartheid years. Observed *Sunday Tribune* reviewer Vasantha Angamuth, "Refreshingly, *Other Secrets* makes comment of the features of apartheid but is not overwhelmed by it." Sukhraj felt that South Africa's political situation "serves indirectly to steer Meena and Yasmin to strive for more—a life of equality and freedom."

In an interview published on the *Africa News Service,* Karodia explained that, as an only child, *Other Secrets* is not autobiographical. Karodia drew from her experiences with extended family and friends to create her characters. "Most of the women I knew as a child, while growing up in South Africa during the apartheid era, were strong and determined women and I often draw inspiration from them and use them as role models in my stories," Karodia told *CA.*

Most of *Boundaries* takes place in sleepy Vlenterhoek, a South African town with exceptional air and water that has remained untouched by the country's new democracy. Town clerk Danie Venter feels that the town's assets are strong enough to turn it into a tourist attraction. The development of a major health spa is planned and a film company may use the town's surroundings as the background of a documentary. "All of this hangs together fairly loosely and with good humour. It's a gentle, rather than sharp, satirical take on an easily-recognisable place peopled with the usual suspects," remarked Beverley Roos Muller in a review published on the *Cape Argus* Web site.

BIOGRAPHICAL AND CRITICAL SOURCES:

BOOKS

Blain, Viginia, Patricia Clements, and Isobel Grundy, *The Feminist Companion to Literature in English: Women Writers from the Middle Ages to the Present,* Yale University Press (New Haven, CT), 1990.
Buck, Claire, editor, *The Bloomsbury Guide to Women's Fiction,* Prentice Hall (New York, NY), 1992.

PERIODICALS

Africa News Service, September 8, 2000, Dr. Rajendra Chetty, "Mother of Invention: Farida Karodia's New Book Updates Her First Novel."
British Book News, December, 1986, p. 711.
Choice, September, 1991, p. 41.
New Statesman, October 31, 1986, p. 31.
New York Times Book Review, February 19, 1989, p. 20.
Observer (London, England), October 19, 1986, p. 27.
Pretoria News, September 27, 2000, Orielle Berry, "Multi-Faceted Book Attempts to Break Down Walls."
Sunday Times, September 24, 2002, Penny Sukhraj, "The Intimate Story of a Favoured Daughter."

Sunday Tribune, August 10, 2000, Vasantha Angamuthu, "Family Secrets."
World Literature Today, winter, 1990, pp. 182-183; spring, 1994, p. 416; spring, 1998, Adele S. Newson, review of *Against an African Sky and Other Stories,* pp. 445-447.

ONLINE

Cape Argus Web site, http://www.capeargus.vo.za/ (December 19, 2003), Beverley Roos Muller, "Gently Satirical Tale Is Idea for the Holidays."

*   *   *

KENDALL, Katherine
    See APPLEGATE, Katherine (Alice)

*   *   *

KILLIAN, Kevin 1952-

PERSONAL: Born December 24, 1952, in Long Island, NY; son of Raymond (an engineer), and Catherine (a teacher and union activist; maiden name, Doyle) Killian; married Dodie Bellamy (a novelist and editor), 1986. *Ethnicity:* "White." *Education:* Fordham University, B.A., 1974; State University of New York—Stony Brook, M.A., A.B.D., 1975-80. *Politics:* "Predictably left." *Religion:* Roman Catholic. *Hobbies and other interests:* Collecting autographs.

ADDRESSES: Home—1020 Minna St., San Francisco, CA 94103. *E-mail*—kevinkillian@earthlink.net.

CAREER: Novelist and playwright. Able Building Maintenance Co., San Francisco, CA, secretary, 1982—; *Mirage #4/Period[ical],* editor (with Dodie Bellamy), beginning 1985; Jack Kerouac School of Disembodied Poets, Naropa Institute, Boulder, CO, workshop instructor, 1997, 2000, 2002. Actor in plays and stage productions, including *Memory Play* and *Scenes from Goya's L.A.,* both produced in San Francisco, CA, 1994; *Blood Pact against the World* (also known as *The Poet-Killer*), *Cheap Speech,* and *Young Skulls II,* all produced in San Francisco, CA, 1995; *Horror Tape Script,* produced in San Francisco,

CA, 1997; *Cliff & Co.,* produced in San Francisco, CA, 1998; *Blood on My Neck* and *Dianne,* both produced in San Francisco, CA 2002; *Manual for a Block* and *The Seventh Game of the World Series,* both produced in San Francisco, CA, 2003; and *Troilus* and *Hamlet Variations,* both produced in San Francisco, CA, 2004. Actor in video projects *At Home with the Stars, Featuring Denton Welch,* 1995; *Sunset* and *Video 97,* both produced in San Francisco, CA, 1997; and *Nightfall,* produced in San Francisco, CA, 1998. Appeared in music video "Butyric Acid," 1994. Also appeared in films. Sponsor of poetry events. Also appeared as a performer, panelist, speaker, and lecturer at various venues.

AWARDS, HONORS: Lambda Literary Award nomination, 1990, for *Shy;* Award for Fiction, California Arts Council, 1991; Fund for Poetry grants, 1995 and 1996; Josephine Miles Award, PEN/Oakland, 1997, for *Little Men;* Award for Poetry, California Arts Council, 1997.

WRITINGS:

NOVELS

Shy, Crossing Press (Freedom, CA), 1989.
Arctic Summer, Hard Candy (New York, NY), 1997.

SHORT STORIES

Desiree (chapbook), e.g. Press (Berkeley, CA), 1986.
Santa, Leave Books (Buffalo, NY), 1995.
Little Men, Hard Press (West Stockbridge, MA), 1996.
I Cry like a Baby, Hard Press, 2000.

Contributor of short stories to books, including *Discontents: New Queer Writers,* edited by Dennis Cooper, Amethyst Press (New York, NY), 1992; *The Lizard Club,* by Steve Abbott, Autonomedia (New York, NY), 1993; *Sick Joke: Bitterness, Sarcasm, and Irony in the Second AIDS Decade* (exhibition catalogue), Kiki Gallery (San Francisco, CA), 1993; *Wrestling with the Angel: Faith and Religion in the Lives of Gay Men,* edited by Brian Bouldrey, Riverhead Books (New York, NY), 1995; *Best American Gay Fiction 1996,* edited by Brian Bouldrey, Little, Brown (Boston, MA), 1996; *Happily Ever After: Erotic Fairy Tales for Men,* edited by Michael Thomas Ford, Richard Kasak Books (New York, NY), 1996; *Sons of Darkness: Tales of Men, Blood, and Immortality,* edited by Michael Rowe and Thomas Roche, Cleis Books (Pittsburgh, PA), 1996; *Switch Hitters: Lesbians Write Gay Male Erotica and Gay Men Write Lesbian Erotica,* edited by Carol Queen and Lawrence Schimel, Cleis Books, 1996; *2000 and What?,* edited by Karl Roeseler and David Gilbert, Trip St. Press (San Francisco, CA), 1996; *Best American Gay Fiction 2,* edited by Brian Bouldrey, Little, Brown, 1997; *Best Gay Erotica 1997,* edited by Richard Labonte, Cleis Books, 1997; *Flesh and the Word 4,* edited by Michael Lowenthal, Plume (New York, NY), 1997; *Noirotica 2: Pulp Friction,* edited by Thomas Roche, Rhinoceros Books (New York, NY), 1997; and *Eros ex Machina: Eroticizing the Mechanical,* edited by M. Christian, Rhinoceros Books, 1998. Contributor of short stories to periodicals, including *Archive Newsletter, Avec, Bimbox, Blithe House Quarterly, Boo, Farm Farm Boys, Five Fingers Review, Framework, Front, Gerbil, Holy Titclamps, Ink, Interruptions, James White Review, Libido, Masquerade, New Langton Arts Catalogue of Programs, Red Wheelbarrow, Res, River City Sentinel USA, Some Weird Sin, Talisman,* and *Taste of Latex.*

PLAYS

That, produced in San Francisco, CA, 1988.
Return to Sender, produced in Seattle, WA, 1993, produced in San Francisco, CA, 1994.
Island of Lost Souls, produced in San Francisco, CA, 1993.
Flophouse: The First Sixty Years of the Lab, produced in San Francisco, CA, 1994.
Three on a Match, produced in San Francisco, CA, 1994.
(Author of program notes) Philip Horvitz, *Being Alive* (musical), produced in San Francisco, CA, 1995.
(With Wayne Smith) *Diamonds & Rust,* produced in San Francisco, CA, 1995.
(With Leslie Scalapino) *Stone Marmalade* (produced in Vancouver, British Columbia), Singing Horse Press (Philadelphia, PA), 1996.
Wet Paint, produced in San Francisco, CA, 1996.
Political Animals, produced in San Francisco, CA, 1997.
(With Scott Hewicker) *The Schwimmer Effect,* produced in San Francisco, CA, 1997.

Cut, produced in New York, NY, 1998.

(With Rex Ray) *The Vegetable Kingdom,* produced in Oakland, CA, 1999.

(With Jocelyn Saidenberg) *Capriccio,* produced in San Francisco, CA, 1999.

(With Wayne Smith) *The Shakers,* produced in San Francisco, CA, 2000.

(With Kota Ezawa) *White Rabbit,* produced in San Francisco, CA, 2001.

(With Rex Ray) *The Vegetable Kingdom,* (revival), produced in Buffalo, NY, 2001.

(With Brian Kim Stefans) *The American Objectivists,* produced in San Francisco, CA, 2001.

(With Norma Cole) *Art Colony Survivor,* produced in San Francisco, CA, 2002.

(With Wayne Smith) *Fascination,* produced in San Francisco, CA, 2002.

Flamingo Road, produced in San Francisco, CA, 2002.

(With Karla Milosevich) *Love Can Build a Bridge,* produced in San Francisco, CA, 2003.

(With Brian Kim Stefans) *The American Objectivists* (revival), produced in Santa Cruz, CA, 2003.

Seeing Red, Mantis 3: Poetry and Performance, produced at Stanford University, CA, 2003.

(With Craig Goodman) *The Smith Family,* produced in San Francisco, CA, 2003.

The Big Keep, produced in San Francisco, CA, 2003.

Cupid and Psyche, produced in San Francisco, CA, 2004.

Also author of *The House of Forks* and dramatic monologue *Who Is Kevin Killian?*

POETRY

Argento Series (serial poem), Krupskaya Books (San Francisco, CA), 2001.

Contributor of poetry to books, including *An Ear to the Ground: An Anthology of Contemporary American Poetry,* edited by Marie Harris and Kathleen Aguerro, University of Georgia Press (Athens, GA), 1988; *The American Poetry Archives Videotape Catalogue 1974-1990,* San Francisco State University (San Francisco, CA), 1991; *Gildzen at Fifty: A Celebration,* Toucan Books (Kent, OH), 1993; *This Is Not Her* (exhibition catalogue), Kiki Gallery, 1995; and *On Your Knees, Citizen: A Collection of "Prayers" for the "Public,"* edited by Rod Smith, Lee Ann Brown, and Mark Wallace, Edge Books (Washington, DC), 1996.

Contributor of poems to periodicals, including *Angle, Angles Apex of the M, B-City, Black Bread, Bloo, Capilano Review, Chain, Die Young, Errant Bodies, Jack of Diamonds, James White Review, Kevin Magee's Newsletter, Kiosk, Lyric & Non-Object Permanence Open 24 Hours, Prosodia, Sentinel USA, Shiny International, Sink, Situation, Soundings, Sulfur, Tinfish, Torque/Object, Writing 22, ZYZZYVA, Fence, Second Avenue, The Poker, Berkeley Poetry Review, Germ, Gargoyle,* and *Commonweal.*

NONFICTION

Bedrooms Have Windows (autobiography), Amethyst Press, 1989.

(With Lewis Ellingham) *Poet Be like God: Jack Spicer and the San Francisco Renaissance* (biography), Wesleyan University Press (Middletown, CT), 1998.

Contributor of nonfiction to books, including *Lighting the Corners on Art, Nature and the Visionary: Essays and Interviews,* American Poetry Book (Albuquerque, NM), 1993; *Gay and Lesbian Literature,* edited by Sharon Malinowski, St. James Press (Detroit, MI), 1994; and *The Gay and Lesbian Literary Heritage,* edited by Claude J. Summers, Holt (New York, NY), 1995. Contributor to periodicals, including *ACTS, Advocate Men, Archive Newsletter, Arshile, Artforum, Artweek, Bay Area Reporter, Chicago Review Contact, Court Green, Dear World, East West, Electronic Poetry Review, Field Reporter Five Fingers Review, Food for Life, Hole, Impercipient Lecture Series, Ink, James White Review, Lambda Book Report, Last Call, Life Style Lift, Lower Limit Speech, Narrativity, Nest, New Review of Literature, NYFA Quarterly, Our Stories, Poetics Briefs, Poetry Flash Poetry Project Newsletter, RIF/T, Rusty Word, Sentinel USA, Shark, Suffle Boil, Sodomite Invasion Review Soup, Stranger, Stranger Books, Sulfur, Talisman, Temblor, Traffic, Trepan, Tripwire, Tyuonyi, Visions Art Quarterly, West Coast Line,* and *Witz.*

OTHER

Brother and Sister Retold from the Brothers Grimm (artist's book), pictures by Brett Reichman, Jonathan Hammer Studios (San Francisco, CA), 1994.

The Kink of Chris Komater (monograph), Patricia Sweetow Gallery (San Francisco, CA), 1999.

EDITOR

"The Train of Thought": *Chapter Three of a Detective Novel,* Zasterle Press (Tenerife, Canary Islands, Spain), 1994.

Millennium Coming: The New Degenerate Art Show (exhibition catalog), curated by Chris Komater and Michelle Rollman, the Lab, 1995.

WORK IN PROGRESS: Spread Eagle, a novel; *Bachelors Get Lonely,* a memoir; *Argento Series,* an ongoing series of poems relating to the AIDS epidemic; *Duets,* stories written with other authors; an untitled New Narrative anthology with Canadian novelist Gail Scott; editing *Collected Poems of Jack Spicer,* with Peter Gizzi; *Action Kylie,* a book of poems.

SIDELIGHTS: Kevin Killian was born in Long Island, New York, on December 24, 1952, and grew up there. He received a bachelor's degree from Fordham University and a master's degree from the State University of New York—Stony Brook, where he completed all but the dissertation towards a Ph.D. Killian moved to the San Francisco Bay Area in the early 1980s, where his writing career flourished.

Killian has had his poetry, fiction, and various nonfiction works published in books and periodicals. He continues to write verse for the *Argento Series,* a serial poem about AIDS published in part in 1997. As Killian told *CA:* "Meow Press published a selection of some of the poems in this long, long serial poem I've been writing since the beginning of the AIDS epidemic. But there are many more poems to come in this, I'm afraid."

In *Strategies of Deviance: Studies in Gay Male Representation,* Earl Jackson, Jr. discusses two of Killian's works: the novel *Shy* and the memoir *Bedrooms Have Windows.* The critic examined the delineation between Killian and his characters, writing: "Killian's typical first-person narrator is constituted as an act of appearing as oneself, in both the philosophical and show business senses of that phrase. Killian has literally appeared as himself (in the role of 'Kevin Killian') in his own plays, such as *The House of Forks,* and his dramatic monologue *Who Is Kevin Killian?* He also performs in the work of other playwrights, filmmakers, and videographers, and his characteriza-

tions are informed with the 'Kevin Killian' persona developed from playing himself." Jackson continued that there are "mutually implicating tensions between 'self' and 'character' and 'reality' and 'representation'" in Killian's performances and writings.

Jackson's comments indicate how Killian's work does not include firm distinctions between character and author, or between novel and memoir. Instead, Killian ironically highlights and subverts the supposed differences that many other writers explicitly define and reinforce. His work also contains a conversational quality that can be both emotional and playful. For example, a short story from Killian's collection *Little Men* features a character named Kevin Killian having a poignant conversation with a dead friend's mother, but then gives humorous instructions on how to discourage telephone solicitors. Killian won the Josephine Miles Award from PEN/Oakland for the collection.

With Lewis Ellingham, Killian wrote *Poet Be like God: Jack Spicer and the San Francisco Renaissance,* a biography of San Francisco beat generation poet Jack Spicer and a chronicle of other poets of the period. This work is the first biography of Spicer, who has not received the same amount of attention as other beat poets such as Allen Ginsberg, Gary Snyder, and Lawrence Ferlinghetti. Spicer died at the age of forty in 1965 of acute hepatitis brought on by alcoholism. According to Bernard Welt in the *Lambda Book Report,* the poet "sat (frequently on a barstool) at the center of the San Francisco poetry scene." Similarly, *Library Journal* contributor David Kirby described Spicer as "a key player in the San Francisco poetry and gay cultures." The biography includes interviews from Spicer's contemporaries, including author Lewis Ellingham, himself a poet and a friend of Spicer, and other acquaintances of the poet. In his *Lambda Book Report* review, Welt wrote that "the interviews in the book have a freshness and immediacy unusual in literary biography."

Also reviewing *Poet Be like God,* a *Kirkus Reviews* contributor wrote that "Ellingham and Killian tread too lightly on their subject's more troublesome personality traits," but observed that the book is a "well-researched and readable biography." Welt called *Poet Be like God* "delicious" and "fabulous," adding that "this is what we like in literary biography—a fine balance between the tell-all approach we expect with less elevated celebrities like movie stars and a prissy, spoilsport academic reserve." He concluded, "Spicer will be remembered and this biography will be the means of his memorial."

Killian told *CA:* "I started writing when I was a little boy, pecking out stories on my mother's black upright 1940s typewriter with the two-colored ribbon that fascinated me. Stupid stories, horse stories, romances, spy thrillers, school epics, and finally the sex writing which has more or less preoccupied me ever since. I kept writing and writing but, while I loftily told everyone I was a 'writer,' I never really got anything done till I was thirty or so, so busy was I with alcohol, drugs, and indiscriminate sex, pleasure—oh, and graduate school, which I wasn't good at.

"When I lived in New York I had a lot of excitement but it was in San Francisco that I met my compadres—the other novelists in the 'New Narrative' movement—and it was here that I 'found myself' as a writer. In quick succession I became a poet, novelist, critic, playwright, and a coterie writer. I won't ever have the success or wide readership of Stephen King or Anne Rice, but I hope to continue to entertain and work with a smaller audience of interested readers. I'm a very slow writer. *Shy* and *Arctic Summer* each took over ten years to write, and I worked on the life of Jack Spicer for eight years. It's because I write many different things at once, and in addition attend (or sponsor) dozens of poetry events a year, hoping to keep my brain open for new developments on the front. And also, because I work with a lot of different people on writing projects, I keep their schedules too. Issuing *Mirage #4/Period[ical]* every month with the novelist Dodie Bellamy has kept me busy.

"I have written on the Bay Area art scene for *Artforum, Artweek, Framework,* etc., and though not a natural 'sub,' I've labored mightily in video and theatre work for Abigail Child, Cecilia Dougherty, Carla Harryman, Sue Marcoux, Camille Roy, Leslie Scalapino, Sarah Schulman, Leslie Singer, Laurie Weeks, et al. I like acting and getting my picture taken. And collecting autographs. That's why I became a writer, I suppose—to meet other writers and get their autographs and to sleep with them."

BIOGRAPHICAL AND CRITICAL SOURCES:

BOOKS

Jackson, Earl, Jr., *Strategies of Deviance: Studies in Gay Male Representation,* Indiana University Press (Bloomington, IN), 1995.

PERIODICALS

Kirkus Reviews, April 1, 1998, review of *Poet Be like God: Jack Spicer and the San Francisco Renaissance.*
Lambda Book Report, July, 1996; August, 1997; April, 1998, Bernard Welt, review of *Poet Be like God,* p. 9.
Library Journal, April 15, 1998, review of *Poet Be like God,* p. 80.

*   *   *

KINNELL, Galway 1927-

PERSONAL: Born February 1, 1927, in Providence RI; son of James Scott and Elizabeth (Mills) Kinnell; married Ines Delgado de Torres; children: Maud, Fergus, Natasha. *Education:* Princeton University, A.B. (summa cum laude), 1948; University of Rochester, M.A., 1949.

ADDRESSES: Home—Sheffield, VT 05866; 432 Hudson St., New York, NY 10014. *Office*—New York University, Department of English, New York, NY 10003.

CAREER: Poet and translator, 1949—. Alfred University, Alfred, NY, instructor in English, 1949-51; University of Chicago, Chicago, IL, supervisor of liberal arts program at downtown campus, 1951-55; University of Grenoble, Grenoble, France, American lecturer, 1956-57; University of Nice, Nice, France, lecturer in summer session, 1957; University of Iran, Teheran, Iran, Fulbright lecturer, 1959-60; Columbia University, New York, NY, adjunct associate professor, 1972, adjunct professor, 1974, 1976; University of Hawaii at Manoa, Honolulu, Citizens' Professor, 1979-81; New York University, New York, NY, director of writing program, 1981-84, Samuel F. B. Morse Professor of Arts and Sciences, Erich Maria Remarque Professor of Creative Writing. Poet-in-residence, Juniata College, 1964; Reed College, 1966-67; Colorado State University, 1968; University of Washington, 1968; University of California—Irvine, 1968-69; University of Iowa, 1970; and Holy Cross College, 1977. Resident writer, Deya Institute (Mallorca, Spain), 1969-70. Visiting professor, Queens College of

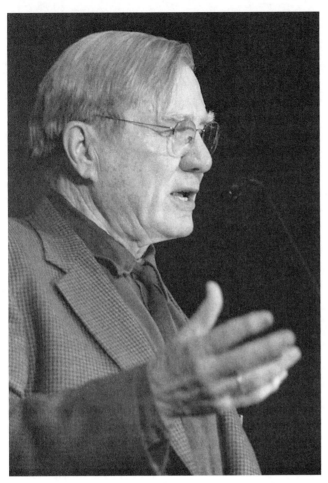

Galway Kinnell

the City University of New York, 1971; Pittsburgh Poetry Forum, 1971; Brandeis University, 1974; Skidmore College, 1975; and University of Delaware, 1978. Visiting poet, Sarah Lawrence College, 1972-78; Princeton University, 1976; and University of Hawaii. Visiting writer, Macquarie University (Sydney, Australia), 1979. Director, Squaw Valley Community of Writers, 1979—. Field worker for Congress of Racial Equality (CORE), 1963. Recorded poetry to sound and video cassette, including *Galway Kinnell Reading His Poems with Comment in New York City* (audio cassette), 1959; *Poetry Breaks I, Galway Kinnell,* (video cassette), 1988; and *Galway Kinnell and Sharon Olds Reading Their Poems in the Montpelier Room* (audio cassette), 1996. Chancellor, Academy of American Poets, 2001—. Advisory Board Member, Red Hen Press (Granada Hills, CA). *Military service:* U.S. Navy, 1944-46.

MEMBER: PEN, National Academy and Institute of Arts and Letters, Corporation of Yaddo.

AWARDS, HONORS: Ford grant, 1955; Fulbright scholarship, 1955-56; Guggenheim fellowships, 1961-62, 1974-75; National Institute of Arts and Letters grant, 1962; Longview Foundation award, 1962; Rockefeller Foundation grants, 1962-63, 1968; Bess Hokin Prize, 1965, and Eunice Tietjens Prize, 1966, both from *Poetry* magazine; Cecil Hemley Poetry Prize from Ohio University Press, 1968, for translation of Yves Bonnefoy's work; special mention by judges of National Book Awards for poetry, 1969, for *Body Rags;* Ingram Merrill Foundation award, 1969; Amy Lowell traveling fellowship, 1969-70; National Endowment for the Arts grant, 1969-70; Brandeis University Creative Arts Award, 1969; Shelley Prize, Poetry Society of America, 1974; Medal of Merit, National Institute of Arts and Letters, 1975; London Translation Prize, 1979; National Book Award for poetry (co-recipient) and Pulitzer Prize for Poetry, both 1983, both for *Selected Poems;* National Book Award for poetry finalist, 1996, for *Imperfect Thirst;* MacArthur fellow, 1984; National Book Critics Circle Award, 1986, for *The Past;* appointed Vermont State Poet, 1989-93.

WRITINGS:

POETRY

What a Kingdom It Was, Houghton (Boston, MA), 1960, revised, 2002.

Flower Herding on Mount Monadnock, Houghton (Boston, MA), 1964, revised, 2002.

Body Rags (also see below), Houghton (Boston, MA), 1968.

Poems of Night, Rapp & Carroll (London, England), 1968.

The Hen Flower, Scepter Press (Frensham, England), 1969.

First Poems: 1946-1954, Perishable Press (Mt. Horeb, WI), 1970.

The Shoes of Wandering, Perishable Press (Mt. Horeb, WI), 1971.

The Book of Nightmares, Houghton (Boston, MA), 1971.

The Avenue bearing the Initial of Christ into the New World: Poems 1946-1964, Houghton (Boston, MA), 1974, revised, 2002.

St. Francis and the Snow, Ravine Press (Chicago, IL), 1976.

Three Poems, Phoenix Book Shop (New York, NY), 1976.

Fergus Falling, Janus Press (Newark, VT), 1979.

There Are Things I Tell to No One (single poem), Nadja (New York, NY), 1979.

Two Poems, Janus Press (Newark, VT), 1979.

Mortal Acts, Mortal Words (also see below), Houghton (Boston, MA), 1980.

The Last Hiding Place of Snow, Red Ozier (New York, NY), 1980.

Selected Poems, Houghton (Boston, MA), 1982.

The Fundamental Project of Technology (single poem; also see below), Ewert (Concord, NH), 1983.

The Geese, Janus Press (Newark, VT), 1985.

The Seekonk Woods, with photographs by Lotte Jacobi, Janus Press (Newark, VT), 1985.

The Past (includes *The Fundamental Project of Technology; also see below),* Houghton (Boston, MA), 1985.

When One Has Lived a Long Time Alone, Knopf (New York, NY), 1990.

Three Books (includes *Body Rags, Mortal Acts, Mortal Words,* and *The Past,* Houghton (Boston, MA), 1993.

Imperfect Thirst, Houghton (Boston, MA), 1994.

A New Selected Poems, Houghton Mifflin (Boston, MA), 2001.

Also author of poem *When the Towers Fell,* 2002; poems have been anthologized in *Contemporary American Poetry,* Penguin (New York, NY), 1962; *Where Is Vietnam?: American Poets Respond,* Doubleday (New York, NY), 1967; Scott Walker, editor, *Buying Time,* Graywolf Press (Minneapolis, MN), 1985; Robert Hass, editor, *Best American Poetry of 2001,* Scribner (New York, NY), 2001; and *Pocket Book of Modern Verse.* Contributor of poetry to numerous journals and periodicals, including *New Yorker, Hudson Review, Poetry, Nation, Choice, Harper's,* and *New World Writing.*

TRANSLATOR

Rene Hardy, *Bitter Victory,* Doubleday (New York, NY), 1956.

Henri Lehmann, *Pre-Columbian Ceramics,* Viking (New York, NY), 1962.

The Poems of François Villon, New American Library (New York, NY), 1965, new edition, University Press of New England (Hanover, NH), 1982.

Yves Bonnefoy, *On the Motion and Immobility of Douve,* Ohio University Press (Athens, OH), 1968, reprinted, Bloodaxe Books (Newcastle upon Tyne, England), 1992.

Yvan Goll, *Lackawanna Elegy,* Sumac Press, 1970.

(With Richard Revear) Yves Bonnefoy, *Early Poems,* Ohio University Press (Athens, OH), 1991.

(With Hannah Liebmann) Rainer Maria Rilke, *The Essential Rilke,* Ecco Press (New York, NY), 1999.

OTHER

Thoughts Occasioned by the Most Insignificant of All Human Events (essay; first published in *Pleasures of Learning,* 1958), Ewert (Concord, NH), 1982.

Black Light (novel), Houghton (Boston, MA), 1966, revised edition, North Point Press (San Francisco, CA), 1980.

The Poetics of the Physical World (lecture), Colorado State University, 1969.

Walking down the Stairs: Selections from Interviews, University of Michigan Press (Ann Arbor, MI), 1978.

How the Alligator Missed Breakfast (juvenile), illustrated by Lynn Munsinger, Houghton (Boston, MA), 1982.

Remarks on Accepting the American Book Award, Ewert (Concord, NH), 1984.

(Author of postscript) Paul Zweig, *Eternity's Woods,* Wesleyan University Press (Middletown, CT), 1985.

(Editor and author of introduction) Walt Whitman, *The Essential Whitman,* Ecco Press (New York, NY), 1987.

Poetry Breaks I, Galway Kinnell, (video reading), Leita Hagemann and WGBH Educational Foundation (Boston, MA), 1988.

SIDELIGHTS: Galway Kinnell is an award-winning poet whose work over four decades has sought to establish the significance of life through daily human experience: the poetic, the cosmic, the social, the cultural, and the individual. *New York Times Book Review* essayist Morris Dickstein called Kinnell "one of the true master poets of his generation and a writer whose career exemplifies some of what is best in contemporary poetry." Dickstein added: "There are few others writing today in whose work we feel so strongly the full human presence." Robert Langbaum observed in the *American Poetry Review* that Kinnell, "at a time when so many poets are content to be skillful and trivial, speaks with a big voice about the whole of life." As Al Haley noted of Kinnell on the *Abiline University* Web site, "His poetry is understandable, and at the same time amazingly lyrical, energetic, and inventive. He has lived long enough to have produced a significant body of work that makes a lasting contribution to American poetry."

According to Charles Frazier in the *Dictionary of Literary Biography*, Kinnell's poetry "has been devoted to a remarkably consistent, though by no means limited, range of concerns. The subjects and themes to which he has returned again and again are the relation of the self to violence, transience, and death; the power of wilderness and wildness; and the primitive underpinnings of existence that are disguised by the superstructure of civilization. Kinnell's approach to these topics is by way of an intense concentration on physical objects, on the constant impingement of the other-than-human on our lives." *Hudson Review* contributor Vernon Young wrote: "By turn and with level facility, Kinnell is a poet of the landscape, a poet of soliloquy, a poet of the city's underside and a poet who speaks for thieves, pushcart vendors and lumberjacks with an unforced simulation of the vernacular."

The theme of death's inevitability permeates Kinnell's poetry as he seeks to derive understanding of the total life experience. To Charles Molesworth, writing in *Encyclopedia of World Literature in the Twentieth Century,* Kinnell's early poems "revolved around questions of suffering and death, using an essentially religious consciousness to question the human condition. Yet the religious fervor of the poetry never inhibited a full acceptance of the secular notions of pleasure and joy." Frazier contended that much of the poet's work "is a ritual filled with the dual awareness of the regrettability and the necessity of death." Kinnell's verse is sometimes harsh and violent—and sometimes bleak—but at the core is the notion that, as death looms, one must live with great intensity. *Partisan Review* essayist Alan Helms stated: "Kinnell's willed choice and his one necessity are to explore the confusion of a life beyond salvation, a death beyond redemption. The result is often compelling reading." In the *Washington Post Book World*, Robert Hass offered a similar assessment. "It is increasingly clear," Hass concluded, "that Kinnell's ambition all along has been to hold death up to life, as if he had it by the scruff of the neck, and to keep it there until he has extracted a blessing from it."

Kinnell often uses fire as a key image to signify cyclical phenomena: consumption by flame leads to death, which in turn allows rebirth. According to Richard Howard in his *Alone with America: Essays on the Art of Poetry in the United States since 1950,* Kinnell's poetry "is an Ordeal by Fire. . . . It is fire—in its constant transformations, its endless resurrection—which is reality, for Kinnell. . . . The agony of that knowledge—the knowledge or at least the conviction that all must be consumed in order to be reborn, must be reduced to ash in order to be redeemed—gives Galway Kinnell's poetry its astonishing resonance." In *The Fierce Embrace: A Study of Contemporary American Poetry,* Molesworth concluded: "The persistence of fire and death imagery throughout Kinnell's poetry forces us to disregard, or at least to minimize, the habitual expectation of ironic distance that we bring to much modern poetry. His obviously attempts to be a poetry of immersion into experience rather than of suspension above it."

To further illustrate his themes, Kinnell chooses earthy, natural elements: animals, blood, stars, skeletons, insects. Jerome McGann suggested in the *Chicago Review* that Kinnell finds solace in the regenerative power of nature, evident in even the least promising situations. In Kinnell, said McGann, "we see that the idea of paradise gets reborn in the cultivation of waste places. . . . Life is found in death, fountains in deserts, gain in loss, spring in winter, light in darkness. All these matters are the recurrent subjects of Kinnell's verse."

Kinnell does not think of himself as a "nature poet," per se, however. In an interview with Daniela Gioseffi for *Hayden's Ferry Review,* he noted: "I don't recognize the distinction between nature poetry and, what would be the other thing? Human civilization poetry? We are creatures of the earth who build our elaborate cities and beavers are creatures of the earth who build their elaborate lodges and canal operations and dams, just as we do. The human is unique in that it's taken over, but that's no reason to say that the human is of a different kind, a kind created in the image of some god while all the others are created in the image of mere lumps of dirt. . . . Poems about other creatures may have political and social implications for us."

Indeed, Kinnell achieved major recognition with the publication *Body Rags,* a collection that contains some of his best-known animal poems, in which the author explores himself through the subjective experiences of a fly, a crow, a porcupine, and a bear. In "The Bear," for instance, Kinnell "seeks entrance into a primitive state of identification with the nonhuman," according to Frazier. In *Modern Poetry Studies,* John Hobbs related how "The Bear" originated: "Speaking of the origins of 'The Bear' in an interview Kinnell said, 'I guess I had just read [e. e. cummings'] poem on Olaf. . . . And then I remembered this bear story, how the bear's shit was infused with blood, so that the hunter by eating the bear's excrement was actually nourished by what the bear's wound infused into it.'" The poem extrapolates the incident and follows the hunter as his identity merges with that of the bear he stalks. Hobbs added: "To the question of a conflict between the sacredness of all life and killing the bear, we can see that the hunter slowly becomes the bear, even after its death. . . . In a sense, the hunter hunts and kills himself."

Kinnell weaves this kind of pointedly unlovely imagery into many of his poems in order to present a balanced depiction of life. The author told the *Los Angeles Times:* "I've tried to carry my poetry as far as I could, to dwell on the ugly as fully, as far, and as long, as I could stomach it. Probably more than most poets I have included in my work the unpleasant because I think if you are ever going to find any kind of truth to poetry it has to be based on all of experience rather than on a narrow segment of cheerful events." *New Statesman* reviewer Alan Brownjohn praised the "precise, Roethke-ish sense of the natural processes," he saw in *Body Rags.* In a review for *Nation,* John Logan predicted that with the publication of *Body Rags,* "we can single out Kinnell as one of the few consummate masters in poetry."

Like his contemporaries, Kinnell "has attempted to develop the poetic explorations of Robert Lowell and Theodore Roethke in order to learn how the breakthroughs of these poets could form a basis for a poetry that served the needs of the final third of the twentieth century," stated a contributor to *Contemporary Poets.* "His own innovations have led [Kinnell] to abandon the intricate, allusive, and sometimes dense structures that characterized works of the school of [T. S.] Eliot and [Ezra] Pound. His poems have avoided studied ambiguity, and he has risked directness of address, precision of imagery, and experiments with surrealistic situations and images."

Yet Kinnell's verse does pay homage to numerous great poets, including Pound, Eliot, Robert Frost, William Carlos Williams, William Black, cummings, and Lowell. Critics most often compare his work to that of Walt Whitman, however, because of its transcendental philosophy and personal intensity, and Kinnell himself edited *The Essential Whitman.* As Robert Langbaum observed in *American Poetry Review:* "Like the romantic poets to whose tradition he belongs, Kinnell tries to pull an immortality out of our mortality." In *Western Humanities Review,* Molesworth noted a poetic legacy in Kinnell's writing from Pound, Blake, and Whitman. Yet the critic also perceived an ultimate difference from these poets in terms of Kinnell's poetic direction, claiming: "Kinnell became a shamanist, rather than a historicist, of the imagination." In seeing Whitman as the primary influence on Kinnell, Frazier wrote: "In developing his sense of the potentiality of free verse to correspond not to some external pattern but to what he calls 'the rhythm of what's being said,' Kinnell points most often to Walt Whitman. . . . Whitmanesque roughness and colloquiality make themselves felt not only in the longer, looser poems, . . . but also in the shorter, more personal lyrics."

His pushcart vendors, lumberjacks, animal images, and surrealism notwithstanding, Kinnell's is an intensely personal poetry, mining his own experiences of love, fatherhood, anxiety, joy, and spirituality. Said Kinnell of his work in his Gioseffi interview, "Self-knowledge is always helpful to our well being—but if we divide humankind into the good and the bad—and put ourselves among the good and others among the bad or poor slobs, we can never write truthful poetry. It's all false, if based on that erroneous premise—that we are the pure poet and the stupid rabble is all to blame. No doubt some people are morally better or worse than some others, but it is necessary to see that there's no absolute classification. . . . Knowing that what we call evil in others also exists in ourselves makes it more possible to write something that has authenticity."

Yet as Stephen Yenser noted in the *Yale Review,* Kinnell's best work is "a poetry that, however personal in its references, continually expands into larger statements." These "larger statements" surfaced early for Kinnell, taking advantage of opportunities to work for the civil rights movement, "instead of merely stewing about it," as he told Gioseffi, and to protest the Vietnam War.

Kinnell was born and raised in Rhode Island. He began to study poetry seriously as a teenager at the Wilbraham Academy in Massachusetts, and he continued his studies at Princeton University. There he came under the influence of his roommate, W. S. Merwin—who introduced him to the work of William Butler Yeats—and the poet Charles G. Bell, who recognized and encouraged his talent. After graduating from Princeton with highest honors, he received his master's degree from the University of Rochester and embarked on a teaching career that would carry him to France, Spain, Hawaii, and Iran. Soon after publishing his first book of poems, *What a Kingdom It Was,* Kinnell realized he could be more productive outside the academic environment. For much of the early 1960s he worked odd jobs, and, for a time, helped to register Southern black voters with the Congress of Racial Equality (CORE), because, as he told Gioseffi, he found it "unbearable to live in a segregated society."

All his experiences—world travel, city life, harassment as a member of CORE and an anti-Vietnam war demonstrator—eventually found expression in his poetry, and critics were quick to observe the immediacy and impact of his voice. The *Dictionary of Literary Biography* essayist quoted Ralph Mills, who noted that Kinnell's early writings signaled "decisive changes in the mood and character of American poetry as it departed from the witty, pseudo-mythic verse, apparently written to critical prescription, of the 1950s to arrive at the more authentic, liberated work of the 1960s." As Kinnell told Gioseffi, "There's this thing about political poems—one must learn something from them, learn something about the political event, and if possible in the best poems, about oneself as well."

Other well-known Kinnell works include *The Book of Nightmares,* published in 1971, and *The Avenue bearing the Initial of Christ into the New World: Poems 1946-1964.* In a review of the latter work, Williamson asserted that the title poem "is still arguably as good as anything [Kinnell] has written." The critic added that the work, which explores life on Avenue C in New York City's Lower East Side, "reminds one of Crane and early Lowell in its sonority, but more of [T. S. Eliot's] 'The Waste Land'—if, indeed of anything in literature in its ability to include a seething cauldron of urban sensations, of randomness and ugliness, yet hold its own poetic shape." James Atlas of *Poetry* offered a similar opinion of Eliot's influence on the work: *The Avenue bearing the Initial of Christ into the*

New World "is one of the most vivid legacies of [*The Waste Land*] in English, building its immense rhetorical power from the materials of several dialects, litanies of place, and a profound sense of the spiritual disintegration that Eliot divined in modern urban life. And, like Eliot's, Kinnell's is a religious poem. . . . Since it is impossible to isolate any single passage from the magnificent sprawl of this poem, I can only suggest its importance by stressing that my comparison of it to [*The Waste Land*] was intended to be less an arbitrary reference than an effort to estimate the poem's durable achievement."

Comparing *The Book of Nightmares* to *Body Rags,* Marjorie Perloff found the latter work "somewhat uneven. . . . As in his earlier poems," she commented in *Contemporary Literature,* "Kinnell uses images of nature in its most elemental forms . . . to discover the deeper instincts of the submerges self." To Langbaum, however, *The Book of Nightmares* "emerges as one of the best long poems of recent years. . . . [It] is, like so many poems, autobiographical and confessional." Langbaum cited Kinnell's use of free verse, adding: "but he universalizes his experience through an imagery that connects it with cosmic process." The critic concluded that "even with its weak spots, its few lapses in intensity, *The Book of Nightmares* is major poetry." *Western Humanities Review* correspondent Fred Moramarco, described *The Book of Nightmares* as "simply a stunning work, rich in its imagery, haunting in its rhythms, evocative and terrifyingly accurate in its insights."

While the poems in the more recent *Mortal Acts, Mortal Words* and *The Past* maintain the balance and intensity of *The Book of Nightmares,* some critics discerned a change in Kinnell's orientation. As Michiko Kakutani of the *New York Times* observed: "Human mortality, as ever, [remains] Mr. Kinnell's great subject, but one [senses] that his perspective has begun to shift. Whereas the earlier works focused on the skull beneath the skin," or the hidden horror of life, "the later ones dwell, however tentatively, on the undying spirit, on the possibility that death may mean not mere extinction, but a reconciliation with the universe's great ebb and flow." *Times Literary Supplement* contributor Mark Ford found the poems in *The Past* "more relaxed and meditative, less obsessively physical," with a "growing awareness of the domestic that has begun to infiltrate Kinnell's poetry in recent years."

Selected Poems, for which Kinnell won the Pulitzer Prize and was cowinner of the National Book Award in 1983, is, to quote Dickstein, "more than a good introduction to Galway Kinnell's work. It is a full scale dossier." The collection, published in 1982, contains works from every period in the poet's career and was released just shortly before he won a prestigious MacArthur foundation grant. In his review of the book, Hass concluded that Kinnell is "widely read by the young who read poetry. If this were a different culture, he would simply be widely read. . . . The common reader—the one who reads at night or on the beach for pleasure and instruction and diversion—who wants to sample the poetry being written in [his] part of the twentieth century could do very well beginning with Galway Kinnell's *Selected Poems.*"

Subsequently, Kinnell has published *When One Has Lived a Long Time Alone,* a collection of poems that closely examines loneliness. In the sequence of eleven poems that gives the book its title, each poem consists of thirteen lines and begins and ends with the words "when one has lived a long time alone." Noted Anthony Thwaite in the *Washington Post:* "I was glad to see Kinnell showing not only a sense of humor, something he has shown flickeringly before, but—in 'Oatmeal'—a fully-fledged sense of the marvelously ridiculous." Richard Calhoun took a more serious approach to *When One Has Lived a Long Time Alone,* writing in *Reference Guide to American Literature* that this collection specifies "the need for love, or at least for the presence of another creature, any creature, to negate loneliness. More than lonely immersion of self into nature is now required; lovers, friends, some kind of companionship, as well as the order and form that song and poems bring into life, all are now integral."

In *Imperfect Thirst* Kinnell reasserts his position as a latter-day romantic. As David Baker wrote in *Poetry:* "Kinnell's gift has always been to mediate between the visible, substantial world and the inutterably spiritual or mystical, and his approach in his greatest poems, like 'The Bear,' 'The Last River,' or any of the *Nightmares,* requires giving over the body's self to the regions of mystery and otherness he identifies in 'There Are Things I Tell to No One': 'I believe, / rather, in a music of grace / that we hear, sometimes, / playing to us / from the other side of happiness.'" The volume is symmetrically structured in five sections

containing five poems each, and Thomas M. Disch maintained in the *Hudson Review* that it offers further evidence that "among contemporary poets few can rival Galway Kinnell for sheer amiability."

A New Selected Poems, a retrospective collection, focuses on the poetry of the 1960s and 1970s, eras when, according to a *Publishers Weekly* contributor, Kinnell's poetry "typically [developed] . . . numbered sections full of dark imagery." Bernard Dick, in *World Literature Today,* noted the inclusion of the eleven related poems from *When One Has Lived a Long Time Alone* as the "real triumph" of this collection, saying that "never has loneliness been so seductive, so strangely inviting, so desirable, and at the same time so horrifying." Of Kinnell's later poetry, Ned Balbo, writing in *Antioch Review,* characterized them as "more relaxed and idiomatic, more apt to very tone, and frequently erotic." Balbo pointed to "Last Gods" as an example, saying that in this verse Kinnell "discovers the sacred element in a sexual encounter."

"It strikes me that Kinnell's is an utterly healthy poetry," noted Susan B. Weston in the *Iowa Review.* "It is healthy precisely because it confronts horrors—drunks dying of cirrhosis; war and destruction; the communal nightmare of a failing culture; the individual nightmare of the failure of love—along with all that is lovely and loving. These facets of the single gem, the human condition, are examined with a jeweler's sense not only of their beauty but also of their dimension. . . . Kinnell's gift is a cursed awareness of time—not just of individual mortality but of geological time that lends special poignance to even the most hostile of human encounters." In the *Boston Review,* Richard Tillinghast commented that Kinnell's work "is proof that poems can still be written, and written movingly and convincingly, on those subjects that in any age fascinate, quicken, disturb, confound, and sadden the hearts of men and women: eros, the family, mortality, the life of the spirit, war, the life of nations. . . . [Kinnell] always meets existence head-on, without evasion or wishful thinking. When Kinnell is at the top of his form, there is no better poet writing in America."

One topic Kinnell faced head-on was the tragedy of September 11, 2001, in his poem, *When the Towers Fell.* As he told Alice Quinn in an interview for the *New Yorker Online,* which published the work: "I wanted to make my account true to my own feelings, but I also felt I should protect the [victims'] families from any tendencies I might have to depict things in extreme ways. I didn't feel constrained so much as wary of going too far. At the same time, I believe that a poem that goes too far is ipso facto preferable to one that falls short." Said Quinn of *When the Towers Fell:* "The poem has a definite dramatic structure. Each section rises to a crescendo, a sort of fearful apprehension that will be confirmed. And there's a tentative, probing, investigative quality to the way it moves forward, seeking and searching." Responding to Quinn's comments about the qualities of this poem, Kinnell noted, "They were not the result of art but of my struggle to visualize and to understand. I wrote the poem in sections, and I tried to put these sections, or moments, into a clear narrative order, so that I wouldn't have to spell out the connectives between them and could focus entirely on the moments themselves."

In an interview with Elizabeth Lund for the *Christian Science Monitor Online,* Kinnell noted: "It's the poet's job to figure out what's happening within oneself, to figure out the connection between the self and the world, and to get it down in words that have a certain shape, that have a chance of lasting." But the terrorist attacks were "so huge that it [was] difficult to write about them directly." "Kinnell fans have long loved his work for its intelligence and honesty, his keen eye for detail, and the subtle connections between people and their environment," Lund added. "There is an authenticity, a humanity to his work that few of his contemporaries can match. . . . Kinnell never seems to lose his center, or his compassion. He can make almost any situation, any loss, resonate. Indeed, much of his work leaves the reader with a delicious ache, a sense of wanting to look once more at whatever scene is passing."

BIOGRAPHICAL AND CRITICAL SOURCES:

BOOKS

Calhoun, Richard James, *Galway Kinnell,* Macmillan (New York, NY), 1992.

Cambon, Glauco, *Recent American Poetry,* University of Minnesota (Minneapolis, MN), 1962.

Contemporary Literary Criticism, Gale (Detroit, MI), Volume 1, 1973, Volume 2, 1974, Volume 3, 1975, Volume 5, 1976, Volume 13, 1980, Volume 29, 1984.

Contemporary Poets, seventh edition, St. James Press (Detroit, MI), 2001.

Dickey, James, *Babel to Byzantium,* Farrar, Straus (New York, NY), 1956, new edition, 1968.

Dictionary of Literary Biography, Volume 5: *American Poets since World War II,* Gale (Detroit, MI), 1980.

Dictionary of Literary Biography Yearbook, 1987, Gale (Detroit, MI), 1988.

Encyclopedia of World Literature in the Twentieth Century, Volume 2, St. James Press (Detroit, MI), 1999.

Galway Kinnell: A Bibliography and Index of His Published Works and Criticism of Them, Frederick W. Crumb Memorial Library, State University College (Potsdam, NY), 1968.

Guimond, James, *Seeing and Healing: The Poetry of Galway Kinnell,* Associated Faculty Press (Gaithersburg, MD), 1988.

Howard, Richard, *Alone with America: Essays on the Art of Poetry in the United States since 1950,* Atheneum (New York, NY), 1965, new edition, 1969.

Kinnell, Galway, *Walking down the Stairs: Selections from Interviews,* University of Michigan Press (Ann Arbor, MI), 1978.

Mills, Ralph, *Cry of the Human: Essays on Contemporary American Poetry,* University of Illinois Press (Champaign, IL), 1975.

Modern American Literature, fifth edition, St. James Press (Detroit, MI), 1999.

Molesworth, Charles, *The Fierce Embrace: A Study of Contemporary American Poetry,* University of Missouri Press (Columbia, MO), 1979.

Nelson, Howard, editor, *On the Poetry of Galway Kinnell: The Wages of Dying,* University of Michigan Press (Ann Arbor, MI), 1987.

Poulin, A., Jr., editor, *Contemporary American Poetry,* Houghton (New York, NY), 1985.

Reference Guide to American Literature, fourth edition, St. James Press (Detroit, MI), 2000.

Shaw, Robert B., editor, *American Poetry since 1960: Some Critical Perspectives,* Dufour (Chester Springs, PA), 1974.

Thurley, Geoffrey, *The American Moment: American Poetry in Mid-Century,* St. Martin's Press (New York, NY), 1977.

Tuten, Nancy L., editor, *Critical Essays on Galway Kinnell,* G. K. Hall (New York, NY), 1996.

Zimmerman, Lee, *Intricate and Simple Things: The Poetry of Galway Kinnell,* University of Illinois Press (Champaign, IL), 1987.

PERIODICALS

American Book Review, March, 1987.

American Poetry Review, March-April, 1979.

Antioch Review, winter, 2001, Ned Balbo, review of *A New Selected Poems,* p. 121.

Atlantic, February, 1972.

Beloit Poetry Journal, spring, 1968; fall-winter, 1971-72.

Boston Review, February, 1983.

Carleton Miscellany, spring-summer, 1972.

Chicago Review, Volume 25, number 1, 1973; Volume 27, number 1, 1975.

Chicago Tribune Book World, June 8, 1980; February 2, 1986.

Commonweal, November 4, 1960; December 24, 1971; August 15, 1986.

Contemporary Literature, winter, 1973, Marjorie Perloff, review of *The Book of Nightmares;* autumn, 1979.

Explicator, April, 1975.

Hayden's Ferry Review, fall-winter, 2002-03, Daniela Gioseffi, interview with Kinnell.

Hudson Review, summer, 1968; autumn, 1971; winter, 1974-75; spring, 1986; summer, 1995.

Iowa Review, winter, 1979.

Kenyon Review, summer, 1986.

Literary Review, spring, 1981.

Los Angeles Times, June 16, 1983.

Massachusetts Review, summer, 1984.

Modern Poetry Studies, winter, 1974; number 11, 1982.

Nation, September 16, 1968, John Logan, review of *Body Rags,* p. 244.

New Republic, July 27, 1974; August 3, 1974.

New Statesman, September 12, 1969, Alan Brownjohn, review of *Body Rags,* p. 347.

New York Times, September 1, 1971; November 2, 1985; August 21, 1989.

New York Times Book Review, July 5, 1964; February 18, 1968; November 21, 1971; January 12, 1975; June 22, 1980; September 19, 1982; March 2, 1986.

Parnassus, fall-winter, 1974; annual, 1980.

Partisan Review, winter, 1967; Volume XLIV, number 2, 1977.

Perspective, spring, 1968.

Poetry, February, 1961; February, 1967; November, 1972; February, 1975; July, 1991, p. 217; April, 1996, p. 33.

Princeton University Library Chronicle, autumn, 1963.

Publishers Weekly, September 26, 1994, p. 57; December 5, 1994, p. 56; March 6, 2000, review of *A New Selected Poems,* p. 106.

Shenandoah, fall, 1973.

Times Literary Supplement, September 21, 1969; March 1, 1985; November 6, 1987; November 12, 1987.

Tribune Books (Chicago, IL), February 3, 1991.

Village Voice, April 1, 1986.

Virginia Quarterly Review, autumn, 1995, p. 656.

Washington Post Book World, September 5, 1982; January 5, 1986; December 30, 1990.

Western Humanities Review, spring, 1972; summer, 1973.

World Literature Today, autumn, 2000, Bernard Dick, review of *A New Selected Poems,* p. 819.

Yale Review, autumn, 1968; October, 1980.

ONLINE

Abilene Christian University Web site, http://www.acu.edu/events/news/ (January 23, 2003),"Pulitzer Prize-Winning Poet to Read in Major Literary Event."

Christian Science Monitor Online, http://www.csmonitor.com/ (October 25, 2001), Elizabeth Lund "Galway Kinnell Searches for the Real Beauty."

Cortland Review Online, http://www.cortlandreview.com/ (June 13, 2002), Daniela Gioseffi, interview with Kinnell.

New Yorker Online, http://www.newyorker.com/ (August 3, 2004), Alice Quinn, "Writing for the Dead, an Interview with Galway Kinnell."

Rambles.net, http://www.rambles.net/ (June 13, 2002), Daina Savage, review of *Imperfect Thirst.*

Salon.com, http://www.salon.com/ (August 5, 2002).

University of Illinois Department of English Web site, http://www.english.uiuc.edu/maps/poets/ (August 3, 2004) "Modern American Poetry, Galway Kinnell."*

*   *   *

KLAGSBRUN, Francine (Lifton)

PERSONAL: Born in Brooklyn, NY; daughter of Benjamin (a businessman) and Anna (Pike) Lifton; married Samuel C. Klagsbrun (a psychiatrist), January 23, 1955; children: Sarah Devora. *Education:* Brooklyn

College (now the City University of New York), B.A. (magna cum laude), 1952; Jewish Theological Seminary of America, B.H.L., 1952; New York University, M.A., 1959.

ADDRESSES: Home and office—1010 Fifth Ave., New York, NY 10028. *Agent*—c/o Crown Publicity, 1745 Broadway, New York, NY 10019.

CAREER: Author. Field Enterprises Educational Corp., Chicago, IL, assistant editor, 1957-59, subject editor, 1959-61, senior editor, 1961-64; Grolier, Inc., New York, NY, executive editor of *Encyclopedia Americana,* 1964-65; Cowles Book Co., New York, NY, executive editor, 1965-68; editorial director, U.E. C., Inc., 1969-73. Member of board of governors, Melton Research Foundation.

MEMBER: Authors League of America, Authors Guild, Jewish Publication Society of America, Phi Beta Kappa.

WRITINGS:

Sigmund Freud, F. Watts (New York, NY), 1967.
First Book of Spices, F. Watts (New York, NY), 1968.
The Story of Moses, F. Watts (New York, NY), 1968.
(Editor, with D. C. Whitney) *Assassination: Robert F. Kennedy,* Cowles (New York, NY), 1968.
Psychiatry—What It Is, What It Does: A Book for Young People, F. Watts (New York, NY), 1969.
(With husband, Samuel C. Klagsbrun) *Your Health: Nutrition,* F. Watts (New York, NY), 1969.
Read about the Teacher, F. Watts (New York, NY), 1970.
Read about the Librarian, F. Watts (New York, NY), 1970.
Read about the Parkman, F. Watts (New York, NY), 1971.
Read about the Sanitation Man, F. Watts (New York, NY), 1972.
Freedom Now! The Story of the Abolitionists, Houghton (Boston, MA), 1972.
(Editor) *The First Ms. Reader,* Warner Paperback (New York, NY), 1973.
(Editor, with others) *Free to Be . . . You and Me,* McGraw (New York, NY), 1974.
(Editor and compiler) *Words of Women,* Doubleday (New York, NY), 1975.

Too Young to Die: Youth and Suicide, Houghton (Boston, MA), 1976.
(Compiler) *Voices of Wisdom: Jewish Ideals and Ethics for Everyday Living,* Pantheon Books, (New York, NY), 1980, D. R. Godine, (Boston, MA), 1990.
Married People: Staying Together in the Age of Divorce, Bantam Books, (Toronto; New York, NY), 1985.
Mixed Feelings: Love, Hate, Rivalry, and Reconciliation among Brothers and Sisters, Bantam Books, (New York, NY), 1992.
Jewish Days: A Book of Jewish Life and Culture around the Year, illustrated by Mark Podwal, Farrar, Straus, Giroux, (New York, NY), 1996.
The Fourth Commandment: Remember the Sabbath Day, Harmony Books, (New York, NY), 2002.

Contributor to *World Book Encyclopedia,* 1964; contributor to *Ms.*

SIDELIGHTS: Francine Klagsbrun is known for her work on topics involving the Jewish faith, modern youth, sociology, and feminism. Klagsbrun began her career as a published author in 1967 and within a decade had written or contributed to fifteen highly diverse titles, including biographies of Sigmund Freud and Moses, informative pieces on nutrition, psychiatry, and suicide, and a series of young adult books designed to introduce children to career options.

Klagsbrun has received the most acknowledgement and acclaim for her more recent titles, including *Mixed Feelings: Love, Hate, Rivalry, and Reconciliation among Brothers and Sisters,* a study of sibling relationships inspired, she said, by her competitive relationship with her brother, Robert. For this book, Klagsbrun interviewed over one hundred families and interpreted what she learned about brothers and sisters and how they interact. Her conclusion: the bond between a child and his or her sibling is just as influential as between the child and his or her parents, and can have a marked impact on the child's life decisions far into adulthood. One *Publishers Weekly* reviewer called *Mixed Feelings* an "illuminating study of the complex sibling bond."

Klagsbrun's next two books were explorations into the mores of Judaism. *Jewish Days: A Book of Jewish Life and Culture around the Year* shares history of and insight into the religion's holidays, such as Yom Kippur and Passover, as well as other noteworthy dates from ancient times up to Israel Independence Day. Ilene Cooper from *Booklist* described it as "readable and stimulating." She went on to call it: "A useful and unique meditation on the nature of time."

The Fourth Commandment: Remember the Sabbath Day "presents a gentle introduction for anyone who, like Klagsbrun, desires a weekly mini-vacation from the 'infinite cacophony, competition and commotion of the world around us,'" said a *Publishers Weekly* reviewer. This "mini-vacation" is the Sabbath Day, which, Klagsbrun writes, is a sacred time during which people should "re-connect" with family, friends, and themselves. Klagsbrun backs up this both welcome and hard-to-accept revelation using references to her own life as well as the Bible, Talmud, Kabbalah, and thinkers from all eras in history. *The Fourth Commandment* is "an indispensable guide to a fuller comprehension of the Sabbath," wrote George Cohen in *Booklist*.

BIOGRAPHICAL AND CRITICAL SOURCES:

PERIODICALS

Best Sellers, February, 1977, review of *Too Young to Die: Youth and Suicide,* p. 375.
Booklist, May 1, 1980, review of *Voices of Wisdom: Jewish Ethics and Ideals for Everyday Living,* p. 1236; May 15, 1985, review of *Married People: Staying Together in the Age of Divorce,* p. 1283; October 15, 1996, Ilene Cooper, review of *Jewish Days: A Book of Jewish Life and Culture around the Year,* p. 381; September 15, 2002, George Cohen, review of *The Fourth Commandment: Remember the Sabbath Day,* p. 182.
Bookwatch, October, 1998, review of *Jewish Days,* p. 9.
Book World, August 4, 1985, review of *Married People,* p. 3.
Catholic Library World, March, 1977, review of *Too Young to Die,* p. 358.
Christian Century, August 28, 1985, review of *Married People,* p. 778.
Curriculum Review, February, 1979, review of *Too Young to Die,* p. 27.
Guardian Weekly, September 1, 1985, review of *Married People,* p. 18.

Horn Book, April, 1977, review of *Too Young to Die,* p. 183.
Journal of Marriage and the Family, November, 1993, review of *Mixed Feelings: Love, Hate, Rivalry, and Reconciliation among Brothers and Sisters,* p. 1055.
Kirkus Reviews, June 1, 1985, review of *Married People,* p. 523; July 1, 1992, review of *Mixed Feelings,* p. 829.
Kliatt Paperback Book Guide, winter, 1978, review of *Youth and Suicide,* p. 33; winter, 1982, review of *Too Young to Die,* p. 44; winter, 1985, review of *Too Young to Die,* p. 43.
Library Journal, March 1, 1980, review of *Voices of Wisdom,* p. 623; August, 1985, review of *Married People,* p. 102; September 15, 1996, review of *Jewish Days,* p. 73.
Los Angeles Times Book Review, December 22, 1985, review of *Too Young to Die,* p. 9.
New Age Journal, January, 1993, review of *Mixed Feelings,* p. 47.
New York Times Book Review, February 6, 1977, review of *Too Young to Die,* p. 10; November 3, 1985, review of *Too Young to Die,* p. 46; January 3, 1993, review of *Mixed Feelings,* p. 14.
People Weekly, October 14, 1985, Lee Powell, "Thirty years a wife and not embarrassed to say so, a feminist explains why good marriages last." pp. 75-79; September 28, 1992, Jane Sugden, "The ties that bind: effects of sibling rivalry on relationships." pp. 65-68.
Publishers Weekly, July 25, 1977, review of *Too Young to Die,* p. 70; May 31, 1985, review of *Married People,* p. 48; June 1, 1992, review of *Mixed Feelings,* pp. 43-45; September 30, 1996, review of *Jewish Days,* p. 76; August 12, 2002, review of *The Fourth Commandment,* p. 296.
School Library Journal, August, 1986, review of *Too Young to Die,* p. 114.
Tribune Books (Chicago, IL), September 21, 1986, review of *Married People,* p. 5.
Voice of Youth Advocates, December, 1981, review of *Too Young to Die,* p. 58; April, 1985, review of *Too Young to Die,* p. 76.

ONLINE

Lilith, The Independent Jewish Women's Magazine Web site, http://www.lilithmag.com/ (January 15, 2003), review of *Jewish Days.*

Miami Herald Web site, http://www.miami.com/ (January 15, 2003), Linda Brockman, "Klagsbrun featured in 'People of the Book' weekend at the Miami book fair."

Spirituality & Health Web site, http://www. spiritualityhealth.com/ (May 28, 2004), Frederic and Mary Ann Brussat, review of *Jewish Days.**

*   *   *

KLEEBLATT, Norman L(eslie) 1948-

PERSONAL: Born November 7, 1948, in Bridgeton, NJ; son of Karl and Frances (Aaron) Kleeblatt; married Nancy Polsky, June 24, 1971 (divorced, November, 1975). *Education:* Rutgers University, A.B., 1971; New York University, M.A. and diploma in conservation, both 1975.

ADDRESSES: Home—330 East 63rd St., New York, NY 10021. *Office*—Jewish Museum, 1109 Fifth Ave., New York, NY 10128-0118.

CAREER: Jewish Museum, New York, NY, conservator, 1975-94, curator of collections, 1981-87, Susan and Elihu Rose Curator of Fine Arts, 1995—. Museum of the Art and History of Judaism, member of scientific council. Guest lecturer at numerous institutions in the United States and abroad, including Columbia University, Princeton University, Georgetown University, University of Leeds, Smithsonian Institution, and National Foundation for Jewish Culture; consultant on art exhibitions and ecclesiastical art commissions.

MEMBER: International Association of Art Critics (American section), American Association of Museums, College Art Association of America.

AWARDS, HONORS: Nomination for Henry Allen Moe Prize, 1985, for *Jewish Heritage in American Folk Art,* and 1988, for *The Dreyfus Affair: Art, Truth, and Justice;* fellow, National Endowment for the Arts, 1996.

WRITINGS:

(Compiler, with Jørgen H. Barfod and Vivian B. Mann) *Kings and Citizens: The History of the Jews in Denmark, 1622-1983,* two volumes, Jewish Museum (New York, NY), 1983.

(Compiler, with Gerard C. Wertkin) *The Jewish Heritage in American Folk Art,* Universe Books (New York, NY), 1984.

(With Vivian B. Mann) *Treasures of the Jewish Museum,* Universe Books (New York, NY), 1986.

(Editor and contributor) *The Dreyfus Affair: Art, Truth, and Justice,* University of California Press (Berkeley, CA), 1987.

(Editor, with Susan Chevlowe) *Painting a Place in America: Jewish Artists in New York, 1900-1945; A Tribute to the Educational Alliance Art School,* Indiana University Press (Bloomington, IN), 1991.

(Editor) *Too Jewish? Challenging Traditional Identities,* Rutgers University Press (New Brunswick, NJ), 1996.

(With Kenneth E. Silver) *An Expressionist in Paris: The Paintings of Chaim Soutine,* Prestel (New York, NY), 1998.

(Editor) *John Singer Sargent: Portraits of the Wertheimer Family,* Jewish Museum (New York, NY), 1999.

(Editor and contributor) *Mirroring Evil: Nazi Imagery/ Recent Art,* Rutgers University Press (New Brunswick, NJ), 2001.

Shorter works include (with Anita Friedman) "Larry Rivers' History of Matzah: The Story of the Jews," Jewish Museum (New York, NY), 1984. Contributor to books, including *Diaspora and Modern Visual Culture: Representing African and Jewish Diaspora,* 1998, and *Encyclopaedia of American History and Culture.*

SIDELIGHTS: Norman L. Kleeblatt once told *CA:* "The underlying theme of many of my publications and exhibitions is the convergence of art history and cultural history. I generally explore areas of neglected artists and art historical movements which likewise elicit a consideration of the definitions of art."

BIOGRAPHICAL AND CRITICAL SOURCES:

PERIODICALS

American Book Review, January-February, 2003, Corinne Robins, review of *Mirroring Evil: Nazi Imagery/Recent Art,* pp. 21, 23.

Burlington, July, 1998, review of *An Expressionist in Paris: The Paintings of Chaim Soutine,* p. 502.

Choice, November, 1996, review of *Too Jewish? Challenging Traditional Identities*, p. 528; March, 1999, review of *An Expressionist in Paris*, p. 1254.

Journal of American Ethnic History, fall, 1994, Selma Berrol, review of *Painting a Place in America: Jewish Artists in New York, 1900-1945; A Tribute to the Educational Alliance Art School*, p. 115; fall, 1998, Selma Berrol, review of *Too Jewish?*, p. 140.

Library Journal, May 15, 1996, review of *Too Jewish?*, p. 66; November 15, 1998, review of *An Expressionist in Paris*, p. 64.

Los Angeles Times Book Review, March 31, 2002, review of *Mirroring Evil*, p. 8.

MultiCultural Review, January, 1992, review of *Painting a Place in America*, p. 58.

New York Times Book Review, July 26, 1998, review of *An Expressionist in Paris*, p. 18.

Reference and Research Book News, February, 2002, review of *Mirroring Evil*, p. 186.

ONLINE

H-Net: Humanities and Social Sciences Online, http://www.h-net.org/ (March, 1998), review of *Too Jewish?*

Jewish Post of New York Online, http://www.jewishpost.com/ (July 24, 2003), "Mirroring Evil: Nazi Imagery-Recent Art."*

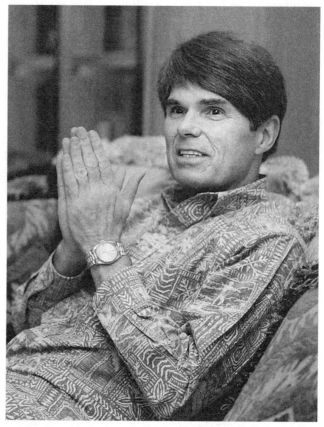

Dean R. Koontz

*   *   *

KOONTZ, Dean R(ay) 1945-
(David Axton, Brian Coffey, Deanna Dwyer, K. R. Dwyer, John Hill, Leigh Nichols, Anthony North, Richard Paige, Owen West)

PERSONAL: Born July 9, 1945, in Everett, PA; son of Ray and Florence Koontz; married Gerda Ann Cerra, October 15, 1966.

ADDRESSES: Agent—Robert Gottlieb, Trident Media Group, 488 Madison Ave., 17th Floor, New York, NY 10022.

CAREER: Teacher-counselor with Appalachian Poverty Program, 1966-67; high school English teacher, 1967-69; writer, 1969—.

AWARDS, HONORS: Atlantic Monthly college creative writing award, 1966, for story "The Kittens"; Hugo Award nomination, World Science Fiction Convention, 1971, for novella *Beastchild*; Litt.D., Shippensburg State College, 1989.

WRITINGS:

NOVELS, EXCEPT AS INDICATED

Star Quest, Ace Books (New York, NY), 1968.

The Fall of the Dream Machine, Ace Books (New York, NY), 1969.

Fear That Man, Ace Books (New York, NY), 1969.

Anti-Man, Paperback Library (New York, NY), 1970.

Beastchild, Lancer Books (New York, NY), 1970.

Dark of the Woods, Ace Books (New York, NY), 1970.

The Dark Symphony, Lancer Books (New York, NY), 1970.

Hell's Gate, Lancer Books (New York, NY), 1970.

The Crimson Witch, Curtis Books (New York, NY), 1971.

A Darkness in My Soul, DAW Books (New York, NY), 1972.

The Flesh in the Furnace, Bantam (New York, NY), 1972.

Starblood, Lancer Books (New York, NY), 1972.

Time Thieves, Ace Books (New York, NY), 1972.

Warlock, Lancer Books (New York, NY), 1972.

A Werewolf among Us, Ballantine (New York, NY), 1973.

Hanging On, M. Evans (New York, NY), 1973.

The Haunted Earth, Lancer Books (New York, NY), 1973.

Demon Seed, Bantam (New York, NY), 1973.

(Under pseudonym Anthony North) *Strike Deep,* Dial (New York, NY), 1974.

After the Last Race, Atheneum (New York, NY), 1974.

Nightmare Journey, Putnam (New York, NY), 1975.

(Under pseudonym John Hill) *The Long Sleep,* Popular Library (New York, NY), 1975.

Night Chills, Atheneum (New York, NY), 1976.

(Under pseudonym David Axton) *Prison of Ice,* Lippincott (Philadelphia, PA), 1976, revised edition under name Dean R. Koontz published as *Icebound* (also see below), Ballantine (New York, NY), 1995.

The Vision (also see below), Putnam (New York, NY), 1977.

Whispers (also see below), Putnam (New York, NY), 1980.

Phantoms (also see below), Putnam (New York, NY), 1983.

Darkfall (also see below), Berkley (New York, NY), 1984, published as *Darkness Comes,* W. H. Allen (London, England), 1984.

Twilight Eyes, Land of Enchantment (Westland, MI), 1985.

(Under pseudonym Richard Paige) *The Door to December,* New American Library (New York, NY), 1985.

Strangers (also see below), Putnam (New York, NY), 1986.

Watchers (also see below), Putnam (New York, NY), 1987, reprinted, Berkley Books (New York, NY), 2003.

Lightning (also see below), Putnam (New York, NY), 1988, reprinted, Berkley Books (New York, NY), 2003.

Midnight, Putnam (New York, NY), 1989, reprinted, Berkley Books (New York, NY), 2004.

The Bad Place (also see below), Putnam (New York, NY), 1990.

Cold Fire (also see below), Putnam (New York, NY), 1991.

Three Complete Novels: Dean R. Koontz: The Servants of Twilight; Darkfall; Phantoms, Wings Books (New York, NY), 1991.

Hideaway (also see below), Putnam (New York, NY), 1992.

Dragon Tears (also see below), Berkley (New York, NY), 1992, also published in a limited edition, Putnam (New York, NY), 1993.

Dean R. Koontz: A New Collection (contains *Watchers, Whispers,* and *Shattered* [originally published under pseudonym K. R. Dwyer; also see below]), Wings Books (New York, NY), 1992.

Mr. Murder (also see below), Putnam (New York, NY), 1993.

Winter Moon, Ballantine (New York, NY), 1993.

Three Complete Novels: Lightning; The Face of Fear; The Vision (*The Face of Fear* originally published under pseudonym Brian Coffey), Putnam (New York, NY), 1993.

Three Complete Novels: Dean Koontz: Strangers; The Voice of the Night; The Mask (*The Voice of the Night* originally published under pseudonym Brian Coffey; *The Mask* originally published under pseudonym Owen West), Putnam (New York, NY), 1994.

Dark Rivers of the Heart (also see below), Knopf (New York, NY), 1994.

Strange Highways (also see below), Warner Books (New York, NY), 1995.

Intensity (also see below), Knopf (New York, NY), 1995.

TickTock, Ballantine (New York, NY), 1996.

Three Complete Novels (contains *The House of Thunder, Shadowfires,* and *Midnight*), Putnam (New York, NY), 1996.

Santa's Twin, illustrated by Phil Parks, HarperPrism (New York, NY), 1996.

(Author of text) David Robinson, *Beautiful Death: Art of the Cemetery,* Penguin Studio (New York, NY), 1996.

Sole Survivor: A Novel, Ballantine (New York, NY), 1997.

Fear Nothing, Bantam (New York, NY), 1998.

Seize the Night (sequel to *Fear Nothing*), Bantam Doubleday Dell (New York, NY), 1999.

False Memory, Bantam (New York, NY), 2000.

From the Corner of His Eye, Bantam (New York, NY), 2000.

The Book of Counted Sorrows (e-book), bn.com, 2001.

One Door Away from Heaven, Bantam (New York, NY), 2002.

By the Light of the Moon, Bantam (New York, NY), 2003.

The Face, Bantam (New York, NY), 2003.

Odd Thomas, Bantam (New York, NY), 2004.

Robot Santa: The Further Adventures of Santa's Twin, HarperCollins (New York, NY), 2004.

The Taking, Bantam Books (New York, NY), 2004.

UNDER PSEUDONYM BRIAN COFFEY

Blood Risk, Bobbs-Merrill (Indianapolis, IN), 1973.

Surrounded, Bobbs-Merrill (Indianapolis, IN), 1974.

The Wall of Masks, Bobbs-Merrill Indianapolis, IN), 1975.

The Face of Fear, Bobbs-Merrill (Indianapolis, IN), 1977.

The Voice of the Night, Doubleday (New York, NY), 1981.

Also author of script for *CHiPS* television series, 1978.

UNDER PSEUDONYM DEANNA DWYER

The Demon Child, Lancer Books (New York, NY), 1971.

Legacy of Terror, Lancer Books (New York, NY), 1971.

Children of the Storm, Lancer Books (New York, NY), 1972.

The Dark of Summer, Lancer Books (New York, NY), 1972.

Dance with the Devil, Lancer Books (New York, NY), 1973.

UNDER PSEUDONYM K. R. DWYER

Chase (also see below), Random House (New York, NY), 1972.

Shattered (also see below), Random House (New York, NY), 1973.

Dragonfly, Random House (New York, NY), 1975.

UNDER PSEUDONYM LEIGH NICHOLS

The Key to Midnight, Pocket Books (New York, NY), 1979.

The Eyes of Darkness, Pocket Books (New York, NY), 1981.

The House of Thunder, Pocket Books (New York, NY), 1982.

Twilight, Pocket Books, 1984, revised edition under name Dean R. Koontz published as *The Servants of Twilight,* Berkley (New York, NY), 1990.

Shadowfires, Avon (New York, NY), 1987.

UNDER PSEUDONYM OWEN WEST

(With wife, Gerda Koontz) *The Pig Society* (nonfiction), Aware Press (Granada Hills, CA), 1970.

(With Gerda Koontz) *The Underground Lifestyles Handbook,* Aware Press (Granada Hills, CA), 1970.

Soft Come the Dragons (story collection), Ace Books (New York, NY), 1970.

Writing Popular Fiction, Writer's Digest (Cincinnati, OH), 1973.

The Funhouse (novelization of screenplay), Jove (New York, NY), 1980.

The Mask, Jove (New York, NY), 1981.

How to Write Best-Selling Fiction, Writer's Digest (Cincinnati, OH), 1981.

OTHER

Contributor to books, including *Infinity 3,* edited by Robert Haskins, Lancer Books, 1972; *Again, Dangerous Visions,* edited by Harlan Ellison, Doubleday, 1972; *Final Stage,* edited by Edward L. Ferman and Barry N. Malzberg, Charterhouse, 1974; *Night Visions IV,* Dark Harvest, 1987; *Stalkers: All New Tales of Terror and Suspense,* edited by Ed Gorman and Martin H. Greenberg, illustrated by Paul Sonju, Dark Harvest, 1989; and *Night Visions VI: The Bone Yard,* Berkley, 1991.

ADAPTATIONS: Demon Seed was filmed by Metro-Goldwyn-Mayer/Warner Bros., 1977; *Shattered* was filmed by Warner Bros., 1977; *Watchers* was filmed by Universal, 1988; *Hideaway* was filmed by Tri-Star, starring Jeff Goldblum, 1994; *Mr. Murder* was filmed by Patchett Kaufman Entertainment and Elephant Walk Entertainment, 1999. Many of Koontz's works were recorded unabridged on audiocassette, including *Cold Fire, Hideaway,* and *The Bad Place,* Reader's Chair (Hollister, CA), 1991; *Mr. Murder* and *Dragon Tears,*

Simon and Schuster Audio; *Dark Rivers of the Heart, Icebound,* and *Intensity,* Random House Audio; and *Strange Highways* and *Chase,* Warner Audio.

SIDELIGHTS: Dean R. Koontz is one of popular fiction's most successful novelists. Originally a science fiction writer, Koontz branched out from the genre in 1972, focusing mainly on suspense fiction. His novels, many of which have been bestsellers, are known for tightly constructed plots and rich characters—often combining elements of horror, science fiction, suspense, and romance.

While a prolific writer early in his career, with regard to sales and mainstream popular success, Koontz's breakthrough was his 1980 novel *Whispers.* According to Michael A. Morrison in *Sudden Fear: The Horror and Dark Suspense Fiction of Dean R. Koontz, Whispers* seems at first to be "a simple genre novel of the psychopathic-madman-assaults-woman variety." The novel revolves around Bruno Frye and his obsession with Hilary Thomas, a Hollywood screenwriter. But, Morrison argues, the parallels between the two characters become evident: "Both are victims of parental abuse, and both carry deep-seated neuroses as a consequence. Indeed, all the main figures of Koontz's novel reflect the constricting influence of childhood on adult life—the sins of the fathers and mothers." Elizabeth Massie, also a contributor to *Sudden Fear,* pointed out that Hilary emerges as a much stronger character than she initially appears after surviving the second attack and apparently killing Frye. For Massie, this "allow[s] the story to take off flying. It allows the tale to spend the majority of its energy with . . . Frye, which it is well advised to do. Having seen Hilary in action against Frye, the reader can know that, regardless of peril, Hilary will put up the good fight." Morrison concluded that Frye ranks "as one of the most original psychological aberrations in horror fiction."

Critical reaction to *Whispers* was mixed. A *Publishers Weekly* reviewer argued that readers will need "strong stomachs to tolerate the overheated scenes of rape and mayhem." While the reviewer praised Koontz's portrait of Frye, it was also noted that the mystery is too easy to solve because the author gives too many clues. *Library Journal* contributor Rex E. Klett viewed Koontz edging "dangerously close to a ruinous occultism" with *Whispers,* but also found the novel a smooth read. Denis Pitts, reviewing the novel in *Punch,* called *Whispers* a "superior crime read." Pitts advises: "*Whispers* is not a book to be read by women of a nervous disposition living alone in a country house. Or men, come to think of it."

Strangers, published in 1986, is the story of a group of people connected only by a weekend each spent at a motel in Nevada two years prior—a weekend none of them remember. The characters begin to experience nightmares, unusual, intense fears, and even supernormal powers, driving each toward uncovering the mystery and conspiracy that joins them all. Deborah Kirk, in the *New York Times Book Review,* found some of the characters unconvincing but concluded that *Strangers* is "an engaging, often chilling, book," while *Library Journal's* Eric W. Johnson dubbed the novel an "almost unbearably suspenseful page-turner." A *Booklist* reviewer deemed Koontz a "true master," and found *Strangers* "a rich brew of gothic horror and science fiction, filled with delectable turns of the imagination."

Dark Rivers of the Heart, published in 1994, is a suspense thriller and political parable revolving around Spencer Grant, an ex-policeman who "confronts a maniacally fascistic secret government agency, an underground web of computer espionage and his own hideous past," summarized Curt Suplee in the *Washington Post Book World.* As Edward Bryant noted in *Locus,* Spencer has ample paramilitary and cyberspace navigational skills himself, which "is lucky, since the bad guys are *so* bad and so well-equipped with high-tech surveillance gadgets and weaponry." Spencer becomes involved with Valerie Keene, a waitress and computer hacker, and finds that federal agents are soon pursuing them both. Suplee commented that this familiar ground, in which "boy can't get girl until the nefarious father/superego figures are adequately purged," is offset by Koontz's narrative, which is replete with "so much novelty and so many odd asides, new characters and screwball sub themes that there's a fresh surprise on virtually every page." Suplee argued that readers may be put off by Koontz's implausible character motivations and "uneconomical" prose style, but concluded that, with regard to "narrative pace and incessant invention, Koontz delivers." Bryant viewed *Dark Rivers* as reflecting Koontz's trust in his readers, finding that the narrative "flows better than many of Koontz's other recent novels because the characters spend less time explaining important issues to each other at length," and in conclusion called the novel "enormously entertaining."

The prolific Koontz published two works in 1995, *Strange Highways* and *Intensity,* the former a collection of short stories, novellas, and two novel-length pieces. A *Publishers Weekly* reviewer argued that a few of the stories in *Strange Highways* are "slight, but none is a failure," and concluded that Koontz's collection is "well crafted and imaginative." Brad Hooper commented in *Booklist* that Koontz's "legion of fans won't be let down." Koontz's best-selling novel *Intensity* is the story of Chyna Shepherd, a psychology student who must combat Edgler Vess, a killer obsessed with intensity of sensation, be it pleasure or pain. Colin Harrison, in a *New York Times Book Review* piece on *Intensity,* lamented that, despite Koontz's "gift for gruesome storytelling," his villain, Vess, is a pop-culture cliché. A *Publishers Weekly* reviewer, however, found *Intensity* "masterful, if ultimately predictable," and lauded Koontz's racing narrative, calling it a contender for the most "viscerally exciting thriller of the year."

In the 1997 work *Sole Survivor,* readers are introduced to former crime reporter Joe Carpenter, a man devastated by the death of his wife and two children in a plane crash. Unemployed and living on insurance money, Carpenter is reduced to derelict status. Then why, Carpenter wonders, does he appear to be under surveillance? The plot thickens when Carpenter encounters a strange woman while visiting the graves of his family. The woman claims to be a survivor of the airplane crash, although there were officially no survivors. Carpenter sets out to unravel the mystery and find out what brought the plane down. In the course of his investigations, he comes upon strange suicides, an esoteric cult, and a cover-up that is much more far reaching than the plane crash. Reviewing *Sole Survivor* for the *New York Times Book Review,* Charles Salzburg dubbed Koontz "a master of his trade." Although faulting the novelist's prose style as excessively flowery and his "paranoid perspective" as "often unbelievable and downright annoying," Salzburg nevertheless concludes that Koontz "does know how to tell an exciting story."

Two of Koontz's novels from the late 1990s, *Fear Nothing* and *Seize the Night,* have the same protagonist and setting. Poet-surfer Christopher Snow lives in the California beach town of Moonlight Bay. Born with a genetic mutation that makes him sensitive to light, Snow can go outside only after dark. In *Fear Nothing,* Snow discovers that the body of his recently deceased father has vanished and been replaced by that of a murdered hitchhiker. With the help of his dog, a Labrador mix named Orson, his surfer-friend Bobby, and local disc jockey Sasha, Snow tries to get to the bottom of things and recover his father's corpse. Commenting on the book in the *New York Times Book Review,* Maggie Garb characterized *Fear Nothing* as an "overwrought narrative," maintaining that Koontz's detective trio "seem more like the stuff of adolescent fantasy than fully believable sleuths." Garb also criticized Koontz's "surfer lingo and literary pretension," as detrimental to the suspense of the book.

In *Seize the Night* Snow makes his second appearance. A reviewer for *Entertainment Weekly* describes the novel as "either an utterly zany thriller or the first really cool young-adult novel of 1999 . . . or Koontz without tears, sadism, or even much bloodshed." The actions starts when seven children are abducted from their homes. Snow is soon on the trail of the kidnappers along with his friends, which now include, in addition to Sasha and Bobbie, a mind-reading cat and a biker. The chase takes them to a supposedly abandoned military base, Fort Wyvern, where genetic experiments are being conducted. Among the strange, mutated creatures Snow and his cohorts uncover are wormlike creatures that can devour just about anything. At one point Snow becomes trapped by a malfunctioning "temporal locator" that sends him both into the future and the past. An *Entertainment Weekly* reviewer noted that *Seize the Night* is "that holy-cow kind of novel— park your brains, don't ask why, tighten your seat belt." David Walton of the *New York Times Book Review* characterized the novel as "a bros-and-brew backslapper in which characters refer to Coleridge and T. S. Eliot as often as to genetic mutation."

A *Publishers Weekly* reviewer states of *False Memory* that "Koontz offers a standalone that's less thematically ambitious but more viscerally exciting" than the "Snow" novels that preceeded it. *False Memory* is the story of a woman who suffers from the mental disorder of autophobia, or fear of self. Marty Rhodes, successful at work and in her marriage, takes her agoraphobic friend Susan to therapy sessions with psychiatrist Mark Ahriman twice each week. Suddenly, Marty begins to develop a fear that she will inflict harm upon herself or her loved ones. Meanwhile, Marty's husband, Dusty, a painting contractor, finds himself having to save his half-brother Skeet from making a suicidal leap off a rooftop. After Dusty places Skeet in rehab, he returns home to find that Marty has removed all the sharp objects from the house. Soon Dusty begins to develop signs of paranoia. There are no coincidences here: all four of the novel's disturbed protagonists are victims of psychiatrist Mark Ahriman, who has used hypnosis to control their lives. Ray Olsen of *Booklist* called *False Memory* "a tale that is remarkably engaging, despite having so many pages and so little plot." Jeff Ayers expressed a similar viewpoint in *Library Journal* when he suggests that the book "could have been trimmed by 200 pages and not lost any impact. Still, the characters are rich, and the main story compelling." A *Publishers Weekly* reviewer commented that with "the amazing fertility of its prose, the novel feels like one of Koontz's earlier tales, with a simple core plot, strong everyman heroes (plus one deliciously malevolent villain) and pacing that starts at a gallop and gets only faster."

In *The Taking* Koontz offers up a "gripping, blood-curdling, thought-provoking parable," according to Ray Olsen in *Booklist*. Novelist Molly Sloan and her husband are at their home in the San Bernardino Mountains in California, when everything starts to come apart. In addition to a mysterious glowing acid raid, the power is off, but somehow appliances run and clocks start spinning out of control. Before long the couple realizes that the country is under attack by a malevolent alien race. "Mixing a hair-raising plot with masterly story telling and a subtle network of well-placed literary allusions, this deservedly popular author has written a tour de force," stated Nancy Mc-Nicol in *Library Journal,* while a reviewer for *Publishers Weekly* commented that "Koontz remains one of the most fascinating of contemporary popular novelists," with *The Taking* marking "an important effort, but not his best, though its sincerity and passion can't be denied."

Koontz's fictional characters are often pitted against unspeakable evil and amazing odds but nonetheless emerge victorious. Concerning this optimism Koontz once commented: "For all its faults, I find the human species—and Western culture—to be primarily noble, honorable, and admirable. In an age when doomsayers are to be heard in every corner of the land, I find great hope in our species and in the future we will surely make for ourselves. I have no patience whatsoever for misanthropic fiction, of which there is too much these days. In fact, that is one reason why I do not wish to have the 'horror novel' label applied to my books even

when it is sometimes accurate; too many current horror novels are misanthropic, senselessly bleak, and I do not wish to be lumped with them. I am no Pollyanna, by any means, but I think we live in a time of marvels, not a time of disaster, and I believe we can solve every problem that confronts us if we keep our perspective and our freedom. Very little if any great and long-lasting fiction has been misanthropic. I strongly believe that, in addition to entertaining, it is the function of fiction to explore the way we live, reinforce our noble traits, and suggest ways to improve the world where we can."

BIOGRAPHICAL AND CRITICAL SOURCES:

BOOKS

Kotker, Joan G., *Dean Koontz: A Critical Companion,* Greenwood Press (Westport, CT), 1996.

Munster, Bill, editor, *Sudden Fear: The Horror and Dark Suspense Fiction of Dean R. Koontz,* Starmont House (Mercer Island, WA), 1988.

Munster, Bill, *Discovering Dean Koontz: Essays on America's Best-Selling Writer of Suspense and Horror Fiction,* Borgo Press (San Bernardino, CA), 1998.

Ramsland, Katherine M., *Dean Koontz: A Writer's Biography,* HarperPrism (New York, NY), 1997.

PERIODICALS

Analog, January, 1984.

Armchair Detective, summer, 1995, p. 329.

Booklist, March 1, 1986, p. 914; April 15, 1995, p. 1452; December 15, 1999, Ray Olsen, review of *False Memory,* p. 739; May 1, 2004, Ray Olsen, review of *The Taking,* p. 1483.

Entertainment Weekly, January 12, 1996, p. 50; January 15, 1999, "'Night' Stalker," p. 56.

Library Journal, May 15, 1980, p. 1187; April 15, 1986, p. 95; January, 2000, Jeff Ayers, review of *False Memory,* p. 160; April 15, 2004, Kristen L. Smith, review of *The Face,* p. 146; June 15, 2004, Nancy McNicol, review of *The Taking,* p. 58.

Locus, February, 1989, p. 21; March, 1992, p. 62; September, 1994, p. 29; October, 1994, p. 21; December, 1994, p. 58; January, 1995, p. 49; February, 1995, p. 39.

Los Angeles Times, March 12, 1986.

Los Angeles Times Book Review, January 31, 1988; January 21, 1990; November 13, 1994, p. 14; May 21, 1995, p. 10.

New York Times Book Review, January 12, 1975; February 29, 1976; May 22, 1977; September 11, 1977; June 15, 1986, p. 20; November 13, 1994, p. 58; February 25, 1996, p. 9; April 20, 1997, Charles Salzberg, review of *Sole Survivor;* February 8, 1998, Maggie Garb, review of *Fear Nothing;* February 7, 1999, David Walton, review of *Seize the Night.*

Observer (London, England), February 12, 1995, p. 22.

People, April 13, 1987; April 24, 1989; January 19, 2004, Rob Taub, review of *Odd Thomas,* p. 45.

Publishers Weekly, April 4, 1980, p. 61; March 7, 1986, p. 82; December 18, 1987; December 19, 1994, p. 52; April 24, 1995, p. 60; November 6, 1995, p. 81; February 5, 1996, p. 41; December 13, 1999, review of *False Memory,* p. 67; May 10, 2004, review of *The Taking,* p. 37.

Punch, July 15, 1981, p. 109.

Rapport, April, 1994, p. 27.

School Library Journal, May, 2004, Katherine Fitch, review of *Odd Thomas,* p. 175.

Science Fiction and Fantasy Book Review, October, 1983, pp. 25-26.

Science Fiction Chronicle, March, 1995, p. 39.

Time, January 8, 1996.

Times Literary Supplement, September 11, 1981.

Tribune Books (Chicago, IL), April 12, 1981.

Washington Post Book World, December 11, 1994, p. 8.

ONLINE

Bookreporter.com, http://www.bookreporter.com/ (March 2, 2001), "Author Profile: Dean Koontz."

Books@Random, www.randomhouse.com/ (August 2, 2004), "Dean Koontz: The Official Web Site."*

*   *   *

KURALT, Charles (Bishop) 1934-1997

PERSONAL: Born September 10, 1934, in Wilmington, NC; died of complications of lupus, July 4, 1997, in New York, NY; son of Wallace Hamilton (a social worker) and Ina (a teacher; maiden name, Bishop) Kuralt; married Sory Guthery, 1957 (divorced); mar-

Charles Kuralt

ried Suzanna Folsom Baird, June 1, 1962; children: (first marriage) Lisa Catherine, Susan Guthery. *Education:* University of North Carolina, B.A., 1955.

CAREER: Charlotte News, Charlotte, NC, reporter and columnist, 1955-57; Columbia Broadcasting System, Inc. (CBS) News, New York, NY, writer, 1957-59, host of *Eyewitness to History,* 1959, correspondent for Latin American bureau, 1960-63, chief correspondent for U.S. West Coast, 1963, overseas correspondent until 1967, feature reporter for "On the Road" segments, broadcast on *CBS Evening News* 1967-80, anchor of *CBS News Sunday Morning,* 1979-94. Also hosted weekly television show *Mornings with Charles Kuralt,* 1980-81; anchor of *America Tonight,* 1992; WELY-AM-FM, Ely, MN, owner, 1995; host, syndicated show *American Moment* and CBS-TV cable show *I Remember,* 1997.

MEMBER: Players Club (New York, NY).

AWARDS, HONORS: Ernie Pyle Memorial Award, Scripps-Howard Foundation, 1959; George Foster Peabody Broadcasting Awards, University of Georgia, 1969, 1976, and 1979; Media Award, Odyssey Institute, 1979; named Broadcaster of the Year, International Radio and Television Society and received George Polk Memorial Award for national television reporting, both 1985; Fourth Estate Award, National Press Club, 1994; Spirit of Liberty Award for the American Way, 1994; Award DuPont-Columbia, 1995; named to Hall of Fame, Academy TV Arts and Sciences, 1996; thirteen Emmy Awards, National Academy of Television Arts and Sciences.

WRITINGS:

To the Top of the World: The Adventures and Misadventures of the Plaisted Polar Expedition, March 28-May 4, 1967, Holt (New York, NY), 1968.

Dateline America, Harcourt (New York, NY), 1979.

On the Road with Charles Kuralt, Putnam (New York, NY), 1985.

Southerners: Portrait of a People, Oxmoor House (Birmingham, AL), 1986.

(With Louis McGlohan) *North Carolina Is My Home,* East Woods (Charlotte, NC), 1986.

A Life on the Road, Putnam (New York, NY), 1990.

Charles Kuralt's America, Putnam (New York, NY), 1995.

Charles Kuralt's American Moments, edited with a preface by Peter Freundlich, Simon & Schuster (New York, NY), 1998.

Charles Kuralt's People, Kenilworth Media (Asheville, NC), 2002.

Contributor to periodicals, including *Saturday Review, Field and Stream, TV Guide,* and *Reader's Digest.*

SIDELIGHTS: Charles Kuralt was known nationwide as the CBS News correspondent who combed the back roads of America in search of off-beat human interest stories. In *Quill* Bill Wright described Kuralt as "the last of a fading breed: a wordsmith and storyteller of first rank."

Kuralt's "On the Road" feature was part of the *CBS Nightly News* for over a decade. The feature added "for many the unexpected, cheerful footnote to the evening news," to quote *Saturday Review* correspondent Peter Quinn Hackes. The affable Kuralt took to the road to find an antidote to the invariably grim fare that comprises most nightly newscasts. Margaret Engel noted in the *Washington Post Book World* that, in the process of compiling his "On the Road" sketches, Kuralt became "a reporter who devised a whole genre of journalism. He helped spawn a fascination with

roadside America that one sees in newly issued books about diners, movie houses, gas stations, motels, rural artists and down-home restaurants."

The stories Kuralt reported translated easily into the print medium as well. Such books as *On the Road with Charles Kuralt* and *A Life on the Road* chronicle Kuralt's methods of obtaining his film vignettes and offer profiles of some of the interesting people he met during his travels. Engel wrote of *A Life on the Road:* "Armchair travelers should be grateful that for thirty-three years, their pioneer has been someone with the discipline, intelligence and compassion of Charles Kuralt. . . . This book is a welcome lift, an episodic discovery of the strengths and resourcefulness of people who achieved greatness in large and small ways." Both *On the Road with Charles Kuralt* and *A Life on the Road* spent numerous weeks on the best-seller lists in 1985 and 1990, respectively.

Kuralt was born and raised in North Carolina. He spent most of his childhood on his grandparents' tobacco farm, and there he satisfied his yen for travel by reading *National Geographic* magazine. As a high school student he won a national essay award from the American Legion in its "Voice of Democracy" contest. The award included a visit to the White House to meet then-president Harry S. Truman as well as the honor of hearing Edward R. Murrow read the essay over the radio.

In college at the University of North Carolina, Kuralt served as editor of the campus newspaper, the *Daily Tar Heel.* He earned a bachelor's degree in 1955 and took a job as a reporter at the *Charlotte News* in North Carolina. It was there that he began his lifelong pursuit of human interest stories, in this case for a daily column in the newspaper.

At the tender age of twenty-three, Kuralt became a news writer for the Columbia Broadcasting System, Inc. (CBS) in New York City. He joined CBS in 1957 as a copywriter for the radio division, but the following year he moved into television as a writer for the fifteen-minute CBS evening news show. By 1959 he was promoted to correspondent, and after covering the 1960 presidential campaigns he was sent to the Latin America bureau. After three years based in Rio de Janeiro, he returned to America as manager of the Los Angeles news bureau. Kuralt reported on news from all over the globe, including Cuba, Vietnam, Asia, Africa, and Europe. He also prepared pieces for a documentary series called *CBS Reports.*

Eventually Kuralt began to question his own dedication to "hard news." He once told Arthur Unger of the *Christian Science Monitor:* "I was always worried that some NBC man was sneaking around behind my back getting better stories." A major career change came in 1967. Kuralt said: "I got the idea . . . one night in an airplane as I looked down at the lights in the countryside and wondered . . . what was going on down there. There are a lot of Americans who don't live in cities and don't make headlines. I was interested in finding out about them." From that idea "On the Road" was born. Kuralt convinced CBS management that he could find off-beat tales in America's back waters and small towns. He was given use of a second-hand motor home and the services of a cameraman and a sound technician. Together the three men set out to explore the country. "Turned out he was best suited to talking to real people who wouldn't know a sound bit from a mosquito bite," recalled Terry Jackson in an article published in *Knight Ridder/Tribune News Service.*

In *A Life on the Road,* reports Willie Morris of Chicago's *Tribune Books,* Kuralt wrote, "'On the Road' seemed to work best when I went slow and took it easy. I found that while it helped to have a story in mind up the road somewhere . . . I might find something more interesting along the way. When I finally shook off the tempo of daily journalism and fell into the rhythms of the countryside, I didn't have to worry about finding stories any longer. They found me." Kuralt celebrated the ordinary from all over America in segments that "manage to charm and move the viewer without stooping to tricks or pressing the CUTE button," to quote *Washington Post Book World* contributor Dennis Drabelle. Over time, Kuralt's "On the Road" segments won several Emmy Awards and three George Foster Peabody awards for broadcast news reporting.

In the *Christian Science Monitor,* Kuralt once said: "I have come to believe that it is useful to just once in awhile acknowledge that the whole country is not in flames and that everything going on in America is not represented by those big black headlines on page one." In the course of his travels, Kuralt has interviewed lumberjacks and cowpokes, fishermen and inventors, free spirits and philanthropists—many of whom have

helped him confirm America's strengths as a nation. Quinn Hackes called Kuralt simply "the bard of the byways."

Kuralt's best-known books are companions to his television pieces. *On the Road with Charles Kuralt* collects some of the more intriguing "On the Road" segments from the 1970s and 1980s. *A Life on the Road* is Kuralt's memoir of his discoveries great and small through two decades of almost constant travel. In a *Chicago Tribune* review of *A Life on the Road,* Morris wrote: "Kuralt's prose is clean, flexible and incisive, its context his own generous humanity. He himself is the best testimony to the quiet civilization that lies beneath our many layers."

Kuralt began serving as anchorman for the *CBS News Sunday Morning,* a program that offered his human-interest topics as well as the breaking stories of the day, in 1979. Reflecting on his four-decade career with CBS—and the success of "On the Road"—Kuralt once told Charles Champlin of the *Los Angeles Times:* "Covering Congress is a life-absorbing job. But I'd rather do the small things. . . . Kids, cops, dogs, that kind of thing." He concluded: "I get to choose all my own stories. It's still the best job in television."

Kuralt retired in 1994, telling his viewers that he wanted to spend more time writing and traveling. The following year, his book *Charles Kuralt's America* was published. Kuralt spent one month in each of the locations discussed in the book, beginning in New Orleans in January and ending in New York City in December. Critics expressed mixed views about the book. "The trouble is, while the previous book unpacked a lifetime's full of adventures, the new volume delivers a mere year's worth of journeying," explained Bret Watson in *Entertainment Weekly.* Watson added that "not a heckuva lot happens" in the book. Kuralt "takes full advantage of his privilege and ease in the world, partaking in good food, beautiful scenery, and an inordinate amount of stimulating conversation," noted Donna Seaman, writing her praise for the book in *Booklist.*

Kuralt's health deteriorated after retirement. He suffered from lupus and was hospitalized with chest pains a year before his death. He refused to give up smoking because he said it was something he enjoyed. He passed away suddenly on the fourth of July in 1997.

People across the nation mourned the man who took them off-the-beaten path across America. Upon hearing of his death, President Clinton was quoted in *Broadcasting and Cable* as saying, "Kuralt's extraordinary imagination and skill gave America a unique view of itself. He helped us see the beauty and strength of our small town and countryside. In doing so, he brought all members of the American family closer together." Jackson observed that Kuralt's "most fitting epitaph lies in the stories he told us—about Nickey the Chicken Man with his live chicken store in downtown Hartford, Connecticut, about Francis Johnson and his thirteen-foot-tall ball of twine in Darwin, Minnesota, and about Alice Huyler Ramsey, who was the first woman to drive a car coast-to-coast in 1909."

Shortly after his death, Kuralt made headlines once again when it was revealed that for twenty-nine years he apparently kept a mistress and maintained a second family in Montana, where he claimed to take fishing trips each year. His mistress sued for the estate in Montana and won, claiming that Kuralt left her the property in a letter he had written to her. "While his wife remained at their home in the concrete canyons of New York City, he nurtured a second family. The celebrated journalist was, in effect, husband and father to them, as well as breadwinner, friend and hero," explained Bob Anez in a *Salon.com* article.

Kuralt published two books posthumously: *Charles Kuralt's American Moments* and *Charles Kuralt's People*. The first is a compilation of vignettes from Kuralt's television programs. The book is divided into ten sections that include some of Kuralt's favorite people and sights, including a giant-bug sculptor and the librarian of the world's largest library. *Charles Kuralt's American Moments* was compiled and edited by Kuralt's long-time friend and producer Peter Freundlich. "Each brief taste of American life includes an illustration or photograph, although with Kuralt's creative language, the reader's imagination is enough," noted Kay Bowes in *Library Journal*. "This may be a different format from Kuralt's other books, but it is just as powerful, capturing these moments that Americans hold dear" Bowes observed.

Charles Kuralt's People is a compilation of columns Kuralt published at the beginning of his career. The columns are about people living in a North Carolina town. Writing in *Booklist*, Vanessa Bush said that

"Kuralt fans will enjoy this collection of 169 essays, in which his highlighting of the obscure and ordinary shows the early development of his distinctive style and his particular interests."

BIOGRAPHICAL AND CRITICAL SOURCES:

BOOKS

Encyclopedia of Television News, Oryx Press (Phoenix, AZ), 1999.

PERIODICALS

Booklist, May 15, 1994, review of *Charles Kuralt: A Life on the Road,* p. 1700; September 15, 1995, Donna Seaman, review of *Charles Kuralt's America,* p. 114; May 15, 1998, review of *Charles Kuralt's Autumn,* p. 246; September 15, 1998, review of *Charles Kuralt's America,* p. 246; October 1, 1998, Ray Olsen, review of *Charles Kuralt's American Moments,* p. 275; December 1, 2002, Vanessa Bush, review of *Charles Kuralt's People,* p. 630.
Book World, November 19, 1995, review of *Charles Kuralt's America,* p. 3.
Broadcasting and Cable News, July 14, 1997, "Charles Kuralt, 1934-1997," p. 72.
Chicago Tribune, June 18, 1987; November 4, 1990.
Christian Science Monitor, July 24, 1974.
Entertainment Weekly, October 13, 1995, Bret Watson, review of *Charles Kuralt's America,* p. 69.
Kirkus Reviews, October 1, 1998, review of *Charles Kuralt's American Moments,* p. 1447.
Knight Ridder/Tribune News Service, July 4, 1997, Terry Jackson, "Kuralt Took the Road Rarely Traveled."
Library Journal, November 1, 1995, review of *Charles Kuralt's America,* p. 117; January 1999, Kay Bowes, review of *Charles Kuralt's American Moments,* p. 116; June 1, 1999, Mark Pumphrey, review of *Charles Kuralt's American Moments,* p. 208.
Los Angeles Times, June 17, 1987; October 14, 1988.
Los Angeles Times Book Review, November 17, 1996, review of *Charles Kuralt's America,* p. 14.
Newsweek, July 4, 1983.
New York Times, January 7, 1986.

New York Times Book Review, October 28, 1990; December 22, 1996, review of *Charles Kuralt's America,* p. 20.

Publishers Weekly, September 18, 1995, review of *Charles Kuralt's America,* pp. 117-119; September 9, 1996, review of *Charles Kuralt's America,* p. 81; October 26, 1998, review of *Charles Kuralt's American Moments,* p. 59.

Quill, October, 1997, Bill Wright, "Wrought Iron Storytelling," p. 8.

Saturday Review, September-October, 1985.

Southern Living, review of *Charles Kuralt's America,* p. 70.

Time, April 2, 1984.

Washington Post, August 25, 1979; April 28, 1981; June 26, 1983.

Washington Post Book World, October 13, 1985; October 28, 1990.

ONLINE

Denver Post Online, http://63.147.65.175/books/book457.htm (November 12, 2003) J. Sebastian Sinisi, review of *Charles Kuralt's American Moments.*

Hall of Public Service, http://www.achievement.org/ (November 12, 2003), "Charles Kuralt."

Historic Personalities, http://www.cmhpf.org/personalities/ (November 12, 2003), "Charles Kuralt, 1934-1997."

Salon.com, http://www.salon.com/ (June 8, 1999) Bob Anez, "Charles Kuralt's Secret Life."

OBITUARIES

PERIODICALS

Chicago Tribune, July 5, 1997, section 1, p. 4.
Christian Science Monitor, July 24, 1974.
Los Angeles Times, July 5, 1997, p. A1.
New York Times, July 5, 1997, p. 24.
Washington Post, July 5, 1997, p. B4.

ONLINE

CNN Interactive http://www.cnn.com/ (July 4, 1997), "Charles Kuralt, CBS—Poet of Small-Town America, Dies at 62."

MSNBC, http://www.msnbc.com/ (July 5, 1997).

USA Today Online, http://www.usatoday.com/ (July 4, 1997).*

L

LETHEM, Jonathan (Allen) 1964-

PERSONAL: Born February 19, 1964, in New York, NY; son of Richard Brown (an artist) and Judith Frank (an activist) Lethem. *Education:* Attended Bennington College, 1982-84.

ADDRESSES: Agent—Richard Parks Agency, 138 East 16th St., No. 5B, New York, NY 10003.

CAREER: Writer. Brazen Head Books, New York, NY, bookseller, 1977-80; Gryphon Books, New York, bookseller, 1982-84; Pegasus Books, Berkeley, CA, bookseller, 1985-90; Moe's Books, Berkeley, bookseller, 1990-94.

AWARDS, HONORS: Theodore Sturgeon Memorial Award, third place, and Nebula Award finalist, both 1991, both for novella "The Happy Man"; best first novel, *Locus* magazine, 1994, for *Gun, with Occasional Music;* World Fantasy Award for Best Collection, World Fantasy Convention, for *The Wall of the Sky, the Wall of the Eye: Stories;* National Book Critics Circle Award for Fiction, 1999, for *Motherless Brooklyn; New York Times* Editor's Choice, 2003, for *The Fortress of Solitude.*

WRITINGS:

Gun, with Occasional Music (novel), Harcourt (San Diego, CA), 1994.
Amnesia Moon (novel), Harcourt (San Diego, CA), 1995.

Jonathan Lethem

The Wall of the Sky, the Wall of the Eye: Stories, Harcourt (San Diego, CA), 1996.
As She Climbed across the Table (novel), Doubleday (New York, NY), 1997.
Girl in Landscape (novel), Doubleday (New York, NY), 1998.
Motherless Brooklyn, Doubleday (New York, NY), 1999.

(Editor) *The Vintage Book of Amnesia: An Anthology,* Vintage Books (New York, NY), 2000.

This Shape We're In, McSweeney's Books (San Francisco, CA), 2001.

(Author of introduction) Paula Fox, *Poor George,* W. W. Norton (New York, NY), 2001.

The Fortress of Solitude, Doubleday (New York, NY), 2003.

Men and Cartoons: Stories, Doubleday (New York, NY), 2004.

The Disappointment Artist and Other Essays, Doubleday (New York, NY), 2005.

Contributor of short fiction to periodicals, including *Interzone, Journal Wired, Asimov's Science Fiction,* and *Pulphouse.*

SIDELIGHTS: Jonathan Lethem has gained a reputation as a writer whose works cross the borders of many literary genres. For example, his novel *Girl in Landscape* "exists somewhere in the previously uncharted interstices between science fiction, western, and coming-of-age novels," noted Elizabeth Gaffney in a *Publishers Weekly* profile of the author. And of the short story collection *The Wall of the Sky, the Wall of the Eye,* a *Publishers Weekly* reviewer commented that, "Although Lethem is claimed by the science fiction community as one of its own [his] work is really extra-genre, in the manner of Borges or William Burroughs."

Lethem once explained that "Everything I write is informed by genre traditions, which I love deeply. At the same time, I don't think I've written without straining against genre boundaries, and I've often violated them outright. I think my work reveals traces of an extremely eclectic reading history, and my narrative is also particularly informed by film. But my dearest models are nearly all twentieth-century Americans pursuing high art through popular forms: Shirley Jackson, Philip K. Dick, John Ford, Charles Willeford, George Herriman, and Patricia Highsmith, for instance." To Gaffney he expressed his disdain for the tendency to pigeonhole writers by genre and his sympathy for those "who had embattled careers because of genre prejudice, something I've had the good fortune to be spared. I sort of feel [science fiction writer] Philip K. Dick died for my sins."

Lethem's debut novel, *Gun, with Occasional Music,* brought him comparisons to Philip K. Dick as well as to crime novelist Raymond Chandler. In *Gun,* which combines futuristic and hard-boiled motifs, the hero is Conrad Metcalf, a Private Inquisitor or P.I., as detectives are known in Lethem's twenty-first-century society. Only P.I.s and the police are licensed to ask questions in this somewhat constricted world of the near-future; uttering one query in the course of everyday conversation will net the average citizen points on his or her "karma card." Lethem creates other bizarre elements in his vision of the next century: the government hands out drugs with names such as Acceptrol, Forgettol, and Regrettol to keep the citizenry under control. And, a disastrous experiment called "evolutionary therapy" has turned children into "babyheads"—overevolved, cynical humans who pass their lives in bars, while drinking, smoking, and speaking a language that only they can understand. In a botched attempt to replace the population doomed to "babyhead" status, animals have been genetically altered, but this too has gone awry, and some of the talking creatures have been given quasi-human status.

Gun, with Occasional Music begins as Metcalf is hired by a doctor to investigate the physician's wife. However, the practitioner is murdered and a peripheral character is wrongly accused. In trying to uncover the real perpetrator, Metcalf encounters some nefarious characters and an obvious cover-up, possibly involving the authorities and some underworld criminal elements. A trenchcoat-clad kangaroo named Joey Castle, in the employ of mobsters, proves especially troublesome. Metcalf's questions eventually lead to his imprisonment—six years in cold storage. When he awakens, Metcalf manages to solve the mystery by connecting the remaining clues, even though all memory has now been officially outlawed. In a *Newsweek* review, Malcolm Jones, Jr., called *Gun, with Occasional Music* "an audaciously assured first novel" and termed Lethem's storyline "merely an excuse for nailsplitting dialogue between the wisecracking Metcalf and a gaudy array of nemeses." Jones also praised Lethem's blend of science fiction and mystery, asserting that "Lethem conflated the two genres to fabricate a future that is frightening and funny and ultimately quite sad." A contributor to *Axcess* called the novel "a classy science fiction mystery that bristles with wit and imagination, turning both genres on their heads and inside out."

Amnesia Moon, Lethem's second novel, steers away from the conventions of noir mysteries to present a dystopic vision of the United States. Focusing on a character named Chaos, the narrative unfolds as a road trip. In search of his past identity—he was once known as Everett Moon—Chaos travels across post-apocalyptic America with a companion named Melinda. In each town they visit along their journey to San Francisco, the pair encounter a type of madness endemic to that locale, "with mass symptoms ranging from an imaginary blinding green mist to an obsession with luck," according to Carl Hays in *Booklist*. Lethem portrays "each stop on Chaos's journey with care . . . bringing to life all the horror and confusion inherent in his future world," remarked a contributor to *Publishers Weekly*. In a *Newsweek* review of *Amnesia Moon*, Jones stated that Lethem has emerged from the "shadow" of such influences as Dick to "deliver a droll, down-beat vision that is both original and persuasive."

Girl in Landscape is the story of Pella, a thirteen year old coping with the death of her mother and her family's move from a nearly uninhabitable Earth to a planet just being settled by humans. Her father, a politician, is trying to create a civilization in which humans coexist peacefully with the planet's earlier residents, the "arch-builders," of whom only a few are left. He meets an antagonist in Ephram Nugent, a settler who is prejudiced against the arch-builders but is drawn to Pella. Ephram is "a maverick John Wayne-type character," according to Gaffney in *Publishers Weekly*; indeed, she reported, one of Lethem's influences was "his obsession with the John Ford film *The Searchers*, in which the John Wayne character tries to rescue a young girl who has been abducted by Indians." She quoted Lethem as saying, "It's an obsessive quest, and he's an anti-heroic, racist, angry figure. I wanted to explore what it was like to have your sexual coming-of-age watched over by this bullying man." A *Publishers Weekly* reviewer opined that *Girl in Landscape* "affectingly chronicles Pella's tumultuous journey through puberty and loss and the knockabout society of children thrown together by their homesteading parents." *Library Journal* contributor Starr E. Smith deemed the novel "well constructed and plotted" but thought it "breaks no new literary ground stylistically."

In his 1999 novel *Motherless Brooklyn* Lethem presents readers with a work of crime fiction not quite like any other. As a *Publishers Weekly* contributor noted, "Hard-boiled crime fiction has never seen the likes of Lionel Essrog, the barking, grunting, spas-

modically twitching hero of Lethem's gonzo detective novel that unfolds amidst the detritus of contemporary Brooklyn." Lionel has Tourette's syndrome, a condition that causes uncontrollable verbal outbursts accompanied by a twisting of the language in startling, original ways. When his boss, small-time mobster Frank Minna is killed while Essrog and his coworkers in Minna's detective agency wait outside a meeting for him, the twitching minion sets out to solve the murder. Lethem takes full artistic advantage of Essrog's illness by making him the novel's narrator. As pointed out by Frank Caso in *Booklist*, Essrog's "description of the investigation—complete with Tourette tics and observations—is a tour de force of language." Starr E. Smith, writing in *Library Journal*, noted that the novel's "plot twists are marked by clever wordplay, fast-paced dialog, and nonstop irony."

After the appearance of his fifty-five-page story titled *This Shape We're In*, Lethem's next novel appeared in 2003. *The Fortress of Solitude* is a coming-of-age novel based on Lethem's own experience growing up as a white boy in a multiracial neighborhood. The story focuses on Dylan Ebdus and Mingus Rude. The white Dylan and the black Mingus grow up together in a tough environment, where Dylan learns from Mingus about life on the streets, complete with gang turf wars and graffiti. In adulthood, Mingus becomes a criminal and crack addict who ends up in prison while Dylan, who has gone to college, is a failed music journalist. Yet the bond between the two remains, not in any small part due to the bizarre fact that a vagrant gave Dylan a magic ring when he was a boy. Growing up together, the two boys shared the ring, which enabled them to fly and fight crime. Other powers of the ring include the ability to breathe underwater and to become invisible. Although the boys only use the ring sparingly, it ultimately comes into play when Dylan tries to get the ring to Mingus so he can use it to escape from jail.

In *Entertainment Weekly* Mark Harris described *The Fortress of Solitude* as "a flawlessly evoked, original, and vividly imagined (or is it remembered?) account of two boys, white and black, growing up in not-yet-gentrified Brooklyn in a decade of both freedom and urban rot." *Commentary* contributor Sam Munson was less engaged by the novel, especially the character of Dylan. "Dylan remains without shape," Munson maintained, "and so, for all of Lethem's strenuous protestations, does the world he inhabits." Max Watman had a similar objection in his *New Criterion* review, commenting that "Lethem wants it both ways: he wants to write a big novel and still be quirky—and I think he should be able to. I do not think he's done it. He has foiled his ambition with low metaphors, and he has foiled his fun with ambition. He has evaded his characters, and rested on their interactions, their society." Nevertheless, other reviewers gave the novel abundant praise. Writing in the *New Statesman*, Peter Bradshaw called *The Fortress of Solitude* "maddeningly readable and utterly baffling" and noted that, although "At the end, I didn't believe a man can fly. . . . Lethem's writing certainly does."

In addition to novels, Lethem has continues to broaden his writing to include a volume of short stories as well as essays. Nevertheless, as noted by Steven Zeitchik in *Publishers Weekly*, "there are some common threads, especially the shimmering chasm between reality and memory, between things as they were and as we wanted them to be." As Lethem explained to Zeitchik, "If you look at my books, they all have this giant howling missing center. Language has disappeared, or someone has disappeared, or memory has disappeared. I'm usually writing around a void."

BIOGRAPHICAL AND CRITICAL SOURCES:

PERIODICALS

Axcess, Volume 2, number 3, review of *Gun, with Occasional Music*, p. 106.

Book, September-October, 2003, Jerome V. Kramer, "Home Boy: Motherless Brooklyn's Jonathan Lethem Returns to the Street Where He Grew up for His New Novel, *The Fortress of Solitude*," p. 58, and Don McLeese, review of *The Fortress of Solitude*, p. 77.

Booklist, August, 1995, Carl Hays, review of *Amnesia Moon*, p. 1933; September 1, 1996, p. 69; July, 1999, Frank Caso, review of *Motherless Brooklyn*, p. 1895; June 1, 2003, Keir Graff, review of *The Fortress of Solitude*, p. 1710.

Commentary, November, 2003, Sam Munson, review of *The Fortress of Solitude*, p. 68.

Entertainment Weekly, April 11, 1997, p. 81; September 19, 2003, Mark Harris, review of *The Fortress of Solitude*, p. 89.

Kirkus Reviews, January 1, 1994, p. 23.

Library Journal, February 15, 1994, p. 188; April 1, 1998, Starr E. Smith, review of *Girl in Landscape*, p. 123; July, 1999, Starr E. Smith, review of *Motherless Brooklyn*, p. 133; July, 2003, Nathan Ward, review of *The Fortress of Solitude*, p. 123.

Locus, July, 1995, pp. 23, 52.

New Criterion, November, 2003, Max Watman, review of *The Fortress of Solitude*, p. 59.

New Leader, July-August, 2003, Evan Hughes, review of *The Fortress of Solitude*, p. 27.

New Statesman, January 19, 2004, Peter Bradshaw, review of *The Fortress of Solitude*, p. 51.

Newsweek, April 18, 1994, Malcom Jones, Jr., review of *Gun, with Occasional Music*, pp. 62-63; October 2, 1995, Malcom Jones, Jr., review of *Amnesia Moon*, p. 92; September 15, 2003, Malcom Jones, "Books: The Next Jonathan?," p. 13.

People, Kyle Smith, review of *The Fortress of Solitude*, p. 55.

Publishers Weekly, January 17, 1994, pp. 414, 416; November 7, 1994, p. 41; June 12, 1995, review of *Amnesia Moon*, p. 44; July 15, 1996, p. 54; February 9, 1998, review of *Girl in Landscape*, p. 71; March 30, 1998, Elizabeth Gaffney, "Jonathan Lethem: Breaking the Barriers between Genres," p. 50; August 6, 1999, review of *Motherless Brooklyn*, p. 57; October 25, 1999, Judy Quinn, "Lethem's Leap," p. 20; June 16, 2003, review of *The Fortress of Solitude*, p. 47; September 15, 2003, Steven Zeitchik, "A Brooklyn of the Soul," p. 37.

Time, October 11, 1999, Nadya Labi, review of *Motherless Brooklyn*, p. 90; September 15, 2003, Lev Grossman, review of *The Fortress of Solitude*, p. 77.*

* * *

LIGHTMAN, Alan P(aige) 1948-

PERSONAL: Born November 28, 1948, in Memphis, TN; son of Richard (owner of a movie theater chain) and Jeanne (a dancing teacher; maiden name, Garretson) Lightman; married Jean Greenblatt (a painter), November 28, 1976; children: Elyse, Kara. *Education:* Princeton University, A.B., 1970; California Institute of Technology, Ph.D., 1974.

ADDRESSES: Office—c/o Program in Writing and Humanistic Studies, Room 14E-303, Massachusetts Institute of Technology, Cambridge, MA 02139.

Alan P. Lightman

CAREER: Cornell University, Ithaca, NY, postdoctoral fellow in astrophysics, 1974-76; Harvard University, Cambridge, MA, assistant professor of astronomy, 1976-79, lecturer in astronomy and physics, 1979-89; Smithsonian Astrophysical Observatory, Cambridge, staff astrophysicist, 1979-89; Massachusetts Institute of Technology, Cambridge, professor of science and writing and senior lecturer in physics, 1989-95, John E. Burchard Professor of Humanities, 1995-2001, head of program in writing and humanistic studies, 1991-97, adjunct professor of humanities, 2001—.

MEMBER: American Physical Society, American Academy of Arts and Sciences (fellow), American Association for the Advancement of Science (fellow), American Astronomical Society, Society for Literature and Sciences.

AWARDS, HONORS: Award for best book in physical science, Association of American Publishers, 1990, for *Origins: The Lives and Worlds of Modern Cosmologists;* Critics' Choice award for the best ten nonfiction books of the year, *Boston Globe,* 1991, for *Ancient*

Light: Our Changing View of the Universe; PEN New England/*Boston Globe* Winship runner-up for *Einstein's Dreams,* 1993; named a Literary Light by Boston Public Library, 1995; Andrew Gemant Award, American Institute of Physics, 1996; Gyorgy Kepes Prize, MIT Council for the Arts, 1998; National Book Award finalist, 2000, for *The Diagnosis;* Distinguished Alumnus Award, California Institute of Technology, and Distinguished Arts and Humanities Medal for Literature, Germantown Arts Alliance (TN), both 2003; Massachusetts Book Award finalist, 2004, for *Reunion.*

WRITINGS:

Problem Book in Relativity and Gravitation (textbook), Princeton University Press (Princeton, NJ), 1975.

Radiative Processes in Astrophysics (textbook), Wiley (New York, NY), 1979.

(Editor, with James Cornell) *Revealing the Universe: Prediction and Proof in Astronomy,* MIT Press (Cambridge, MA), 1982.

Time Travel and Papa Joe's Pipe: Essays on the Human Side of Science, Scribner (New York, NY), 1984.

A Modern-Day Yankee in a Connecticut Court, and Other Essays on Science, Viking (New York, NY), 1986.

(With Roberta Brawer) *Origins: The Lives and Worlds of Modern Cosmologists,* Harvard University Press (Cambridge, MA), 1990.

Ancient Light: Our Changing View of the Universe, Harvard University Press (Cambridge, MA), 1991.

Time for the Stars: Astronomy in the 1990s, Viking (New York, NY), 1992.

Great Ideas in Physics: The Conservation of Energy, the Second Law of Thermodynamics, the Theory of Relativity, and Quantum Mechanics, McGraw (New York, NY), 1992, 3rd edition, 2000.

Einstein's Dreams (novel), Pantheon (New York, NY), 1993.

Good Benito (novel), Pantheon (New York, NY), 1995.

Dance for Two: Selected Essays, Pantheon (New York, NY), 1996.

The Diagnosis (novel), Pantheon (New York, NY), 2000.

(Editor, with Robert Atwan) *The Best American Essays 2000,* Houghton (Boston, MA), 2000.

The World Is Too Much with Me: Finding Private Space in the Wired World, Hart House, University of Toronto (Toronto, Ontario, Canada), 2002.

Reunion (novel), Pantheon (New York, NY), 2003.
(Editor, with Daniel Sarewitz and Christina Dressler) *Living with the Genie: Essays on Technology and the Quest for Human Mastery,* Island Press (Washington, DC), 2003.
A Sense of the Mysterious: Science and the Human Spirit, Pantheon (New York, NY), 2005.

Columnist for *Science 86,* 1982-86. Contributor to periodicals, including *Harper's, New Yorker, Daedalus, New York Times, Science, Atlantic, New York Review of Books, World Monitor, Granta, Discover, Smithsonian,* and *Washington Post.*

SIDELIGHTS: Alan P. Lightman is a physicist who has produced scientific writings of interest to the general reader as well as to the specialist. Praised for nonfiction works that include the award-winning *Origins: The Lives and Worlds of Modern Cosmologists,* Lightman began a new chapter in his writing career in 1993, with the publication of *Einstein's Dreams,* his first work of imaginative fiction.

In his book *Time Travel and Papa Joe's Pipe: Essays on the Human Side of Science,* Lightman addresses such complex subjects as astronomy, cosmology, and particle physics. Sarah Boxer, writing in the *New York Times Book Review,* credited Lightman with "leading a good-humored tour into unfamiliar, perhaps even unfriendly, territory."

In Lightman's 1986 work, *A Modern-Day Yankee in a Connecticut Court, and Other Essays on Science,* he reflects upon topics ranging from darkness to space exploration and from snowflakes to the more mundane aspects of life as a scientist. *Chicago Tribune* reviewer Patrick Reardon, describing a science writer's task as attempting "to explain complicated scientific information in simple and entertaining terms," noted that Lightman "communicates the beauty, mystery, elegance, danger, fulfillment, frustration, irony and potential of science." *Washington Post* contributor Gregory Benford was particularly impressed with Lightman's more personal reflections and said that with these, Lightman "is pointed and savvy with a light touch."

Lightman is also the author, with Roberta Brawer, of *Origins: The Lives and Worlds of Modern Cosmologists,* an ambitious work distilled from interviews the coauthors conducted with twenty-seven cosmologists. Through these scientists' discussions of their personal lives, ideas, and opinions about recent developments in science, *Origins* explores the nonscientific factors that shape the scientific enterprise. Dennis Overbye wrote in the *New York Times Book Review* that *Origins* "should prove invaluable" to scholars and writers pondering current scientific perspectives.

Among Lightman's other works are *Ancient Light: Our Changing View of the Universe,* which traces science's evolving perspective on the universe, and *Time for the Stars: Astronomy in the 1990s,* a book that aims to render astrophysics accessible to the lay reader. Donna Seaman commented on his edited collection, 2003's *Living with the Genie: Essays on Technology and the Quest for Human Mastery,* in *Booklist,* noting: "The premise for this stellar essay collection is the observation that although technology is clearly a double-edged sword, an exponentially increasing force rich in promise and rife with peril, we rarely question the necessity or consider the consequences of technological innovations. Lightman reminds us of our deep need for silence, solitude, and stillness."

In addition to his nonfiction, Lightman has also embarked on a second career as a novelist, beginning with a free-wheeling contemplation of time titled *Einstein's Dreams.* As the author once commented: "I have always been interested in both science and the humanities, especially writing and literature. As a child, I built rockets and I also wrote poetry. It has not been easy to pursue both of these directions, and for a long time I put my literary interests on the back burner. In the early 1980s, I began writing essays on science. This versatile form of writing was a good bridge connecting my two halves. My early role models in science were Lewis Thomas and Stephen Jay Gould, and I also read every essay written by the master, E. B. White. Other science and naturalist writers that I read and admired include John McPhee, Annie Dillard, Barry Lopez, David Quammen, James Gleick, and Richard Preston. I have continued to work as a professional scientist while writing.

"In 1991 I turned to fiction. My favorite contemporary fiction writers include Gabriel García Márquez, Jorge Luis Borges, R. K. Narayan, Italo Calvino, Primo Levi (a scientist), Salman Rushdie, and Michael Ondaatje. I especially like writers whose writing distorts reality in order to see reality more clearly. I also admire writers whose writing is not only beautiful but also crosses cultures, conveying a foreign world and its mentality. I hope in my writing to convey the culture of science, which is as foreign to most readers as India is to an American."

Lightman's fiction attempts to cross cultures, illustrating a scientist's take on the world at large to lay readers. In *Einstein's Dreams* the world-renowned physicist falls asleep at his Swiss office and dreams about time itself, each dream becoming a separate "chapter." Overbye, in the *New York Times Book Review,* called this work "a kind of post-modern hybrid of science writing and fantasy . . . [that] owes much to fabulists like Italo Calvino, whose book *Invisible Cities* seems to be [its] model." The thirty brief fables that comprise Lightman's novel are stories "grounded in precise crystalline prose," of a quality comparable to Calvino's writings, according to Michiko Kakutani in the *New York Times.* Kakutani went on to note that "The dreams Mr. Lightman has given the fictional Einstein also deal with the mysteries of space and time, but they have little to do, for the lay reader anyway, with the technicalities of quantum theory and everything to do with the human condition and its time-ridden existence." Lee Lescaze concluded in the *Wall Street Journal* that within in the various worlds Lightman has created—worlds with sometimes vastly altered states of time—his characters lose personal freedoms. In the world where everyone is immortal, "everyone forever has a father, a mother, a grandfather, a grandmother, and so on. No one comes into his own. All questions provoke endless deliberation. There is no individual freedom." Simpson Garfinkel echoed these points in *Voice Literary Supplement:* "Each story is a psychological investigation of how people would be changed by distortions in the way time flows."

Voice Literary Supplement reviewer Carol Anshaw also compared Lightman, "in his best moments," to Italian literary master Calvino, deeming *Einstein's Dreams* a "small, well-crafted piece of fabulism." As Lescaze noted, the novel "is a meditation, a fable, a pleasure. Its appeal is a tribute to the enduring power of the mystery of time—even in a post-Einstein world." But for its author, the novel also captures the connection between scientific meditation and artistic creation. In an interview with David L. Wheeler for *Chronicle of Higher Education,* Lightman explained: "When a scientific idea is emerging in the mind of a scientist and before it gets distilled into an equation, that process is very similar to any creative process, artistic or literary."

Lightman's second novel, *Good Benito,* received mixed reviews from critics. The novel details the experiences of protagonist Bennett Lang, a young physicist from Memphis, Tennessee, who embarks on a career in science. The title comes from Lang's childhood pal, John Lerner, who remarks, "Nice coils, Good Benito." Garfinkel, writing in the *Christian Science Monitor,* characterized *Good Benito* as "a novel that's more conventional and aimed squarely at a nonscientific reader. Where *Einstein's Dreams* was a whimsical exploration into scientific fantasy, *Good Benito* is a straightforward attempt at portraying a physicist as a young man." Garfinkel continued by saying that Lightman's work "is built upon well-worn cliches that will be familiar to anyone who has spent time around a big-university physics department." But despite its conventionality, James Idema, in the *Chicago Tribune,* maintained that *Good Benito*'s "best passages are charged with a similar exultation [to *Einstein's Dreams*]." Those exultations are contained in Lightman's ability to reveal science in poetic ways as seen in his first novel, Idema contended.

In his review of the work for the *Washington Post Book World,* Richard Grant called *Good Benito* "a brief novel of breathtaking delicacy and grace." Commenting on his own prose style in an interview with Smith, Lightman added that it is deliberately spare. "I like to let the readers do much of the writing for me," he noted. "Readers are so good at visualizing things, and when you say too much, you block the reader's invitation to participate in the imaginary experience." In this delicate and spare style Lightman creates his world as "an endeavor to construct a human equation, using the events of an individual's biography as his factors," according to John Tague in the *Times Literary Supplement.* "Scientists remark with some regularity that a certain idea, often a flash of insight, was so beautiful that they knew at once it must be the truth," Grant noted at the conclusion of his review, thus capturing the essence of Lightman's fictional writings. "The same can be said of Lightman's novel. I suggest reading *Good Benito* at one sitting (it's short enough to do so comfortably), late on a winter's night perhaps, while listening to Mahler."

Lightman's third novel, *The Diagnosis,* features Bill Chalmers, a businessman in the information industry who lives his life via the Internet, cell phones, pagers, computers, and other electronic communication devices. Most of his contacts with other people—including his own son—come through such things as e-mail. One day Chalmers, overwhelmed by the amount of information he is taking in, suddenly realizes he has forgotten who he is. Although the malady lasts only a short time, it leaves him confused and sluggish and he becomes a burden to his family, as he loses his job and his will to live. "To Lightman's credit," wrote Eric Wieffering in the Minneapolis *Star Tribune,* "he avoids taking the easy way out. This is no tale of triumph over physical adversity." "Lightman's evocation of the growth of Chalmers's interior life, as set against the disappearance of his normal outward life, is both luminous and dark," wrote David Dodd in *Library Journal.* Keith Miller, in the *Times Literary Supplement,* called *The Diagnosis* "a powerful critique of a barbarously accelerated society," while in the *San Francisco Chronicle,* Floyd Skloot found Lightman's book to be "a funny, troubling story about our culture's devotion to technology at the expense of humanity." According to Donna Seaman in *Booklist,* *The Diagnosis* is "a work of vivid sensuousness, sparkling intelligence, and poignant beauty." James Hynes, writing in the *Washington Post Book World,* called the novel "original and grimly unsentimental, by any measure a major accomplishment, written in austerely beautiful prose." Abraham Verghese, a reviewer in the *New York Times Book Review,* said that Lightman "reveals himself to be a highly original and imaginative thinker."

Lightman's novel *Reunion* concerns Charles, a once-promising poet who, in middle age, finds himself working as a professor at a small college, leading a comfortable but dreary life. When Charles uncharacteristically decides to attend his thirtieth college reunion, he vividly recalls an intense love affair he had as a college student. Remembering contradictory versions of the affair forces Charles to confront himself as a young man, and eventually his reality and self-identity dissolve into a haze of illusion. Lightman "has a Proustian concern for the manipulations of time and memory, . . . the infinite present of youth, the eternal regret of midlife," wrote Gail Caldwell in a review of *Reunion* for the *Boston Globe.* In the *New York Times Book Review,* Jonathan Wilson dubbed the novel "elegant," and added that it is "spare, charged with meaning." Praising the book as "a profoundly human story, rich in depth and nuance," Toronto *Globe and Mail* reviewer Robert Wiersema added that "Lightman writes with a lightness, a lyrical understatedness that belies the underlying depths and complexities of the novel."

Lightman sums up the dichotomy of his work and life in his *A Sense of the Mysterious: Science and the Human Spirit,* wherein he writes: "Ever since I was a young boy, my passions have been divided between science and art. I was fortunate to make a life in both, as a physicist and a novelist, and even to find creative sympathies between the two, but I have had to live with a constant tension in myself and a continual rumbling in my gut."

BIOGRAPHICAL AND CRITICAL SOURCES:

PERIODICALS

Alaska Quarterly, fall-winter, 1996, interview with Lightman.
Atlantic, September, 1991.
Baltimore Sun, September 24, 2000.
Booklist, August, 2000, Donna Seaman, review of *The Diagnosis,* p. 2111; October 1, 2000, Donna Seaman, review of *The Best American Essays 2000,* p. 312; June 1, 2003, review of *Reunion;* December, 2003, Donna Seaman, review of *Living with the Genie: Essays on Technology and the Quest for Human Mastery,* p. 638.
Boston Globe, March 4, 1982; December 20, 1992; December 27, 1993, interview with Lightman; September 10, 2000; July 20, 2003, review of *Reunion.*
Boston Herald, October 5, 2000, interview with Lightman.
Caltech News, fall, 2003.
Charlotte Observer (Charlotte, NC), November 26, 2000, Jack Harville, "Dark Humor Helps Leaven Stark Horror in *Diagnosis,*" p. F6.
Chicago Sun-Times, January 3, 1993.
Chicago Tribune, February 17, 1987; April 2, 1995, sec. 14, p. 6; October 17, 2000, interview with Lightman; September 24, 2000.
Christian Science Monitor, January 31, 1995, p. 12.
Chronicle of Higher Education, April 14, 1993, pp. A6, A13; September 22, 2003.
Cleveland Plain Dealer, October 1, 2000.
Concord Journal (Concord, MA), October 19, 2000, interview with Lightman.
Economist, January 16, 1993.
Globe and Mail (Toronto, Ontario, Canada), September 30, 2000; August 16, 2003, Robert Wierseba, review of *Reunion.*

Independent (London, England), November 26, 2000, Edward Stern, review of *The Diagnosis,* p. 54.

Library Journal, September 15, 2000, David Dodd, review of *The Diagnosis,* p. 113; October 1, 2000, Nancy P. Shires, review of *The Best American Essays 2000,* p. 94.

Los Angeles Times, January 10, 1993; September 10, 2000.

Nature, March 4, 1993.

Newsday, September 10, 2000; October 29, 2000, interview with Lightman.

Newsweek, December 7, 1992.

New Yorker, June 3, 1991, p. 104; November 20, 2000.

New York Review of Books, May 16, 1991; February 22, 2001.

New York Times, January 5, 1993, p. C16; September 24, 2000, Abraham Verghese, "Crashed"; November 20, 2000, interview with Lightman; January 28, 2003, *Lab Coat Chic: The Arts Embrace Science,* p. F1.

New York Times Book Review, May 13, 1984, p. 16; September 16, 1990, p. 23; January 3, 1993, p. 10; September 24, 2000; June 27, 2003, review of *Reunion.*

Observer (London, England), January 31, 1993.

People, June 14, 1993, interview with Lightman.

Physics Today, February, 1997, interview with Lightman.

Publishers Weekly, January 9, 1995, interview with Lightman, pp. 47-48; July 3, 2000, review of *The Diagnosis,* p. 45; September 18, 2000, review of *The Best American Essays 2000,* p. 100.

San Francisco Chronicle, September 17, 2000.

San Francisco Examiner, March 31, 1993, interview with Lightman.

Seattle Post Intelligencer, March 29, 1993.

Seattle Times, October 10, 2000.

Star Tribune (Minneapolis, MN), January 28, 2001, Eric Wieffering, "Grim *Diagnosis* Gains Strength as Its Protagonist Weakens," p. F14.

Time, January 18, 1993.

Times (London, England), October 25, 2000.

Times Literary Supplement, June 23, 1995, p. 27; October 13, 2000.

Voice Literary Supplement, April, 1993, pp. 22-23.

Wall Street Journal, February 1, 1993, p. A8; February 2, 1993.

Washington Post, January 26, 1987; June 9, 1993, interview with Lightman; August 10, 2003, review of *Reiunion.*

Washington Post Book World, September 2, 1990, p. 4; February 6, 1995, p. 9; April 23, 2000, interview with Lightman; November 26, 2000.

ONLINE

Alan Lightman Home Page, http://www.alanlightman. com (July 24, 2004).

Massachusetts Institute of Technology Web site, http://web.mit.edu/ (July 24, 2004), "Alan Lightman."*

*   *   *

LINCOLN, Bruce 1948-

PERSONAL: Born March 5, 1948, in Philadelphia, PA; son of William D. (a real estate agent) and Geraldine (a clinical psychologist; maiden name, Kovsky) Lincoln; married Louise Gibson Hassett (a curator and art historian), April 17, 1971; children: Rebecca, Martha (twins). *Education:* Haverford College, B.A. (with high honors), 1970; University of Chicago, Ph.D. (with distinction), 1976. *Politics:* "Unaffiliated Marxist, leaning to anarcho-syndicalism."

ADDRESSES: Home—3232 Bryant Ave. S., Minneapolis, MN 55408. *Office*—Department of Cultural Studies and Comparative Literature, 350 Folwell Hall, University of Minnesota—Twin Cities, Minneapolis, MN 55455; Department of History of Religion, University of Chicago, 1025 East 58th St., Chicago, IL 60637.

CAREER: History of Religions, Chicago, IL, editorial assistant, 1973-75; University of Minnesota—Twin Cities, Minneapolis, assistant professor, 1976-79, associate professor, 1979-1984, professor of humanities, religious studies, and South Asian studies, and chair of religious studies program, 1979-86, professor of comparative studies in discourse and society, beginning 1986, scholar of the college, 1990-93; University of Chicago, Chicago, professor of history of religions and anthropology, beginning 1993. Visiting professor, Universita degli Studi di Siena, Italy, 1984-85, University of Uppsala, Sweden, 1985, Novosibirsk State Pedagogical Institute, Russia, 1991.

MEMBER: Phi Beta Kappa.

AWARDS, HONORS: American Council of Learned Societies, grant, 1979, citation for best new book in the history of religion, 1981, for *Priests, Warriors, and Cattle: A Study in the Ecology of Religions;* grants from Rockefeller Foundation, 1981, Guggenheim Memorial Foundation, 1982-83, and National Endowment for the Humanities, 1986; citation for outstanding academic book, *Choice,* 1989, for *Discourse and the Construction of Society: Comparative Studies of Myth, Ritual, and Classification.*

WRITINGS:

Priests, Warriors, and Cattle: A Study in the Ecology of Religions, University of California Press (Berkeley, CA), 1981.

Emerging from the Chrysalis: Studies in Rituals of Women's Initiation, Harvard University Press (Cambridge, MA), 1981, revised edition, Oxford University Press (New York, NY), 1991.

(Editor) *Religion, Rebellion, Revolution: An Interdisciplinary and Crosscultural Collection of Essays,* St. Martin's Press (New York, NY), 1985.

Myth, Cosmos, and Society: Indo-European Themes of Creation and Destruction, Harvard University Press (Cambridge, MA), 1986.

Discourse and the Construction of Society: Comparative Studies of Myth, Ritual, and Classification, Oxford University Press (New York, NY), 1989.

Death, War, and Sacrifice: Studies in Ideology and Practice, University of Chicago Press (Chicago, IL), 1991.

Authority: Construction and Corrosion, University of Chicago Press (Chicago, IL), 1994.

Theorizing Myth: Narrative, Ideology, and Scholarship, University of Chicago Press (Chicago, IL), 1999.

Holy Terrors: Thinking about Religion after September 11, University of Chicago Press (Chicago, IL), 2003.

Contributor to books, including *Soteriology of the Oriental Cults in the Roman Empire,* edited by Ugo Biancho, E. J. Brill (Long Island City, NY), 1982; *Critical Essays on Mircea Eliade,* edited by Hans-Peter Duerr, Syndikat, 1983; *Proto-Indo-European: The Archeology of a Linguistic Problem; Festschrift for Marija Gimbutas,* edited by Susan Skomal and Edgar Polome, Institute for the Study of Man; and *Festschrift for Edgar Polome,* edited by M. A. Jazayery, University of Texas Press (Austin, TX); also contributor to encyclopedias. Contributor to scholarly journals. Coeditor of special issues of *History of Religions,* May, 1977, and *Cultural Critique,* spring, 1989.

Some of Lincoln's books have been translated into Italian and Spanish.

SIDELIGHTS: Bruce Lincoln once told *CA:* "I tend to view religion as the desperate attempt to invest an otherwise meaningless existence with some sense of purpose and worth. It thus has its origins in the human imagination, not in some divine sphere, and proper study of religion begins with the external factors which condition the exercise of the imagination within any given culture, including such factors as geography, climate, and patterns of social, political, and economic organization. In some measure, religion is a valorization and legitimation of those givens, being an attempt to endow the world in which one must live with a sense of transcendent meaning. On the other hand, religion can become a reaction against those same givens and an attempt to flee them for another level of existence beyond this life and world.

"I find myself simultaneously fascinated and utterly repelled by religious phenomena—myths, rituals, cosmologies, soteriologies, and the like. I suppose this is part of my family legacy, my great-grandfather having been a Russian anarchist and atheist, my great-grandmother (his wife) an orthodox Jew."

Lincoln is competent in Sanskrit, Avestan, Greek, Latin, Old Norse, Anglo-Saxon, Old Persian, Pahlavi, French, German, Italian, and Spanish, and has some knowledge of Hittite, Russian, Old Irish, Welsh, and Portuguese.

BIOGRAPHICAL AND CRITICAL SOURCES:

PERIODICALS

Times Literary Supplement, June 20, 2003, David Martin, review of *Holy Terrors: Thinking about Religion after September 11,* pp. 10-12.*

*   *   *

LITTLEFIELD, Holly 1963-

PERSONAL: Born April 6, 1963, in OH; daughter of Charles (a counselor) and Marilyn (a university administrator; maiden name, Hughes; present surname, Scamman) Littlefield; married John Enright, October 22, 1988; children: Patrick, Brennan. *Education:*

University of Minnesota—Twin Cities, B.A., 1985, M.A., 1992, Ph.D., 1999. *Hobbies and other interests:* Reading, movies, sailing, travel.

ADDRESSES: Home—15212 65th Place N., Maple Grove, MN 55311. *Office*—1-105 Carlson, University of Minnesota, Minneapolis, MN 55455. *E-mail*—hlittlefield@csom.umn.edu.

CAREER: High school teacher in Osseo, MN, 1985-92; University of Minnesota—Minneapolis, researcher and teacher of managerial communication, 1992—.

MEMBER: Modern Language Association of America, National Council of Teachers of English, Phi Beta Kappa.

WRITINGS:

Fire at the Triangle Factory (fiction), illustrated by Mary O'Keefe Young, Carolrhoda (Minneapolis, MN), 1996.
(With Lillian Bridwell-Bowles and Kathleen Sheerin DeVore) *Identity Matters: Rhetorics of Difference,* Prentice Hall (Upper Saddle River, NJ), 1998.

"COLORS OF THE WORLD" SERIES

The Colors of Germany, Carolrhoda (Minneapolis, MN), 1997.
The Colors of Japan, illustrated by Helen Byers, Carolrhoda (Minneapolis, MN), 1997.
Colors of Ghana, illustrations by Barbara Knutson, Carolrhoda (Minneapolis, MN), 1999.
Colors of India, illustrations by Janice Lee Porter, Carolrhoda (Minneapolis, MN), 2000.

"PICTURE THE AMERICAN PAST" SERIES

Children of the Trail West, Carolrhoda (Minneapolis, MN), 1999.
Children of the Orphan Trains, Carolrhoda (Minneapolis, MN), 2001.
Children of the Indian Boarding Schools, Carolrhoda (Minneapolis, MN), 2001.

SIDELIGHTS: Children's writer Holly Littlefield's first book, *Fire at the Triangle Factory,* is a fictional account of the 1911 fire that consumed the Triangle Shirtwaist Company in the garment district of New York City, which was located on the top three floors of a ten-story building. Of the 500 hundred workers, mostly female Jewish immigrants, some as young as fourteen, 146 died in less than fifteen minutes, a tragedy that was attributed to the fact that the exit doors had been locked to keep the workers at their sewing machines. The owners were acquitted of manslaughter charges and later ordered to pay damages of $75 to each of the victims' families. As a result of the fire, the City of New York initiated safety programs within the fire department, and the organizational efforts of the International Ladies Garment Workers Union intensified, a first step in the ongoing campaign for workplace safety. Littlefield offers the history of the fire through the eyes of two girls, Jewish Minnie, and Irish-Catholic Tessa, coworkers in the factory, imparting lessons in friendship and responsibility at the level of the younger reader.

Littlefield wrote several titles for Carolrhoda's "Colors of the World" series, introducing children to the cultures and images of countries that include Germany, Japan, Ghana, and India. She also wrote for that publisher's "Picture the American Past" series. *Children of the Trail West* is an account of the youngest of the family members who rode wagon trains across the country to the Western frontier. *Children of the Orphan Trains* tells how, from 1854 to 1929, thousands of homeless or orphaned children were sent West, some to loving families who made a place for them, but others to people who were merely looking for a servant or farmhand.

Children of the Indian Boarding Schools is a history of how, beginning in 1879, the United States government took Native-American children from their parents and reservations and put them in boarding schools to learn English and Christianity. They were stripped of their culture, forced to cut their hair and wear "modern" clothing, as depicted in before-and-after pictures of three young men, first in their native dress, then in the mandated attire. Each page of the volume contains a sepia-toned print. *School Library Journal*'s Barbara Buckley commented that the section of the book titled "Understanding Historical Photographs" is "one of the most valuable" and felt that it alone "could be fodder for hours of discussion." *Booklist*'s Hazel

Rochman noted that Littlefield "ends with excellent suggestions for further reading and classroom projects."

Littlefield once commented: "I really love the challenge of writing for children. When I was a child I read constantly, and I would like to think that I am writing the kinds of books that I would have enjoyed then and that my own children will like. I also like to do the research that goes with writing these books. So much of history is about what the adults did and said. I try to find and tell the children's stories."

BIOGRAPHICAL AND CRITICAL SOURCES:

PERIODICALS

Arts and Activities, December, 2001, Jerome J. Hausman, review of *Colors of India,* p. 8.
Booklist, May 15, 2001, Hazel Rochman, review of *Children of the Orphan Trains,* and *Children of the Indian Boarding School,* p. 1748.
School Library Journal, January, 1998, review of *Colors of Japan,* p. 102; June, 1998, review of *Colors of Germany,* p. 130; July, 2001, Barbara Buckley, review of *Children of the Indian Boarding Schools,* p. 95.*

*   *   *

LOUISE, Heidi
See ERDRICH, (Karen) Louise

*   *   *

LOW, Setha M. 1948-

PERSONAL: Born March 14, 1948, in Los Angeles, CA; daughter of Seth and Marilyn (maiden name, Maxon; present surname, Rudley) Low; married Joel Lefkowitz (a professor), June 26, 1994; stepchildren: Melanie, Jared. *Education:* Pitzer College, B.A., 1969; University of California—Berkeley, M.A., 1971, Ph. D., 1976; attended Eastern Pennsylvania Psychiatric Institute, 1979-80, and University of Pennsylvania, 1981-82. *Hobbies and other interests:* Park and garden design, historic preservation, swimming, tennis, skiing, swing dancing.

ADDRESSES: Home—Brooklyn, NY. *Agent*—c/o Author Mail, Routledge, 29 West 35th St., New York, NY 10001.

CAREER: San Francisco State College (now University), San Francisco, CA, instructor in anthropology, 1971; University of Pennsylvania, Philadelphia, assistant professor, 1976-82, associate professor of landscape architecture and regional planning, anthropology, and city planning, 1982-88, associate faculty of Center for the Study of Aging, 1982-87, and Leonard Davis Institute of Health Economics, 1984-87; Graduate School and University Center of the City University of New York, New York, NY, professor of environmental psychology and anthropology, beginning 1987, director of Public Space Research Group, beginning 1988. Universidad de Costa Rica, honorary professor, 1986-87; York University, Toronto, Ontario, Canada, visiting professor, 1991; University of Pennsylvania, visiting lecturer, 1992-95; New York University, visiting professor, 1995; speaker at Yale University and Columbia University. Pinelands Commission of New Jersey, member of Historical Preservation Resource Management Committee, 1983-84; Municipal Arts Society of New York City, member of Committee on Historical and Cultural Landmarks, 1992—; Parks Council of New York, member of Design Committee, 1992—; supporter of National Heritage Areas Coalition and Citizens Committee for New York City, Inc. Conducted anthropological field work in Costa Rica, El Salvador, Guatemala, Japan, Spain, Mexico, France, Cuba, Venezuela, and the United States; consultant to National Park Service, American Folklife Center, and National Trust for Historic Preservation. Gordon & Breach (publisher), member of medical anthropology editorial board, 1992—.

MEMBER: American Anthropological Association (fellow; member of executive board, 1993-96), Society for Urban Anthropology (member of council, 1992-95), Society for Applied Anthropology (fellow; member of executive board, 1993-96), Society for Cultural Anthropology (fellow), Environmental Design Research Association (vice chair, 1987-88; chair, 1988-89; member of board of directors, 1987-90), Society for Latin American Anthropology, Society for Medical Anthropology (member of executive board), American Ethnological Society, Society for Psychological Anthropology, Latin American Studies Association, Columbia University Seminar on the City (associate).

AWARDS, HONORS: Grant for El Salvador, Hunter-Grubb Foundation, 1968-69; fellow, Center for Latin American Studies, 1972-74; National Institute of Mental Health, fellow in Costa Rica, 1972-74, grant, 1976-78; grant from Center for Environmental Design and Planning, 1981-82; grant for Guatemala, Canada's International Development Research Centre, 1981-83; honorary M.A., University of Pennsylvania, 1983; Fulbright fellow in Costa Rica, 1986-87; grants for Spain and Italy from Wenner-Gren Foundation for Anthropological Research, 1987-88, 1994-96; National Science Foundation grant for Yugoslavia, 1988; fellow at John Carter Brown Library, National Endowment for the Humanities, 1989-90.

WRITINGS:

Culture, Politics, and Medicine in Costa Rica, Gordon & Breach (Philadelphia, PA), 1985.
(Editor, with E. Chambers) *Housing, Culture, and Design: A Comparative Perspective,* University of Pennsylvania Press (Philadelphia, PA), 1989.
(Editor, with D. David) *Gender, Health, and Illness: The Case of Nerves,* Hemisphere Publishing (Washington, DC), 1989.
(Editor, with I. Altman) *Place Attachment,* Plenum (New York, NY), 1992.
(With F. Johnston) *Children of the Urban Poor: The Sociocultural Environment of Growth, Development, and Malnutrition in Guatemala City,* Westview (Boulder, CO), 1995.
(Editor) *Theorizing the City: The New Urban Anthropology Reader,* Rutgers University Press (New Brunswick, NJ), 1999.
On the Plaza: The Politics of Public Space and Culture, University of Texas Press (Austin, TX), 2000.
Behind the Gates: Life, Security, and the Pursuit of Happiness in Fortress America, Routledge (New York, NY), 2003.

Editor of "Medical Anthropology Series," State University of New York Press (Albany, NY), beginning 1983; associate editor, "Advances in Environmental, Behavior, and Design Series," 1989-91. Contributor to books, including *Embodiment and Experience: The Existential Ground of Culture and Self,* edited by T. Csordas, Cambridge University Press (Cambridge, England), 1994; *Conserving Culture: A New Discourse on Heritage,* edited by M. Hufford,

University of Illinois Press (Urbana, IL), 1994; and *Setting Boundaries,* edited by D. Pellow, Bergen & Garvey (Amherst, MA), 1996. Contributor of articles and reviews to scholarly journals, including *American Ethnologist, Cultural Resources Management, Social Text, Landscape Journal, Human Organization,* and *City and Society. Medical Anthropology Quarterly,* corresponding editor, 1976-82, member of editorial board, 1994—; corresponding editor, *Practicing Anthropology,* 1977-86; editor, *Cultural Aspects of Design Newsletter,* 1985—; associate editor, *Medical Anthropology Journal,* 1986—; editor of special issues, *Architecture and Behavior,* 1988, and *Health Care for Women International,* 1989; member of editorial board, *City and Society,* 1995—.

BIOGRAPHICAL AND CRITICAL SOURCES:

PERIODICALS

Library Journal, May 15, 2003, Janet Ingraham Dwyer, review of *Behind the Gates: Life, Security, and the Pursuit of Happiness in Fortress America,* pp. 110-111.*

*   *   *

LUCAS, Robert Emerson, Jr. 1937-

PERSONAL: Born September 15, 1937, in Yakima, WA; son of Robert Emerson and Jane (Templeton) Lucas; married Rita Cohen, 1959; children: Stephen, Joseph. *Education:* University of Chicago, B.A., 1959, Ph.D., 1964.

ADDRESSES: Home—5441 South Hyde Park Blvd., Chicago, IL 60615. *Office*—Department of Economics, University of Chicago, 1126 East 59th St., Chicago. IL 60637.

CAREER: University of Chicago, Chicago, IL, lecturer in economics, 1962-63; Carnegie-Mellon University, Pittsburgh, PA, assistant professor, 1963-67, associate professor, 1967-70, professor of economics, 1970-74; University of Chicago, Ford Foundation visiting research professor, 1974-75, professor of economics and vice chair of department, beginning 1975, John

Dewey Distinguished Service Professor of Economics, beginning 1980. Northwestern University, visiting professor, 1981-82; Cambridge University, Marshall Lecturer.

MEMBER: American Economic Association (member of executive committee), Econometric Society, American Academy of Arts and Sciences, National Academy of Sciences, Phi Beta Kappa.

AWARDS, HONORS: Guggenheim fellowship, 1981-82; Nobel Prize in Economics, 1995.

WRITINGS:

(Editor, with Thomas J. Sargent) *Rational Expectations and Econometric Practice,* University of Minnesota Press (Minneapolis, MN), 1981.

Studies in Business-Cycle Theory, MIT Press (Cambridge, MA), 1981.
Lectures on Economic Growth, Harvard University Press (Cambridge, MA), 2003.

Editor, *Journal of Political Economy;* associate editor, *Journal of Economic Theory* and *Journal of Monetary Economics.*

BIOGRAPHICAL AND CRITICAL SOURCES:

PERIODICALS

New York Review, March 13, 2003, Robert Sidelsky, review of *Lectures on Economic Growth,* p. 28.*

M

MacCLANCY, Jeremy 1953-

PERSONAL: Born October 16, 1953, in London, England; son of John Roderic (a doctor) and Gwendoline (a homemaker; maiden name, Holcombe) MacClancy. *Education:* Oxford University, M.A., 1976, M.S., 1977, M.Litt. 1978, D.Phil., 1993.

ADDRESSES: Office—School of Social Sciences and Law, Brookes College, Oxford, Gipsy Lane, Oxford OX3 0BP, England. *Agent*—Bill Hamilton, A. M. Heath & Co. Ltd., 79 St. Martin's Ln., London WC2N 4AA, England. *E-mail*—jvmacclancy@brookes.ac.uk.

CAREER: Oxford University, Oxford, England, tutor, 1986—; Brookes College, Oxford, 1991—, began as lecturer, became professor of anthropology.

MEMBER: Association of Social Anthropologists.

AWARDS, HONORS: Fellow, Royal Anthropological Institute.

WRITINGS:

To Kill a Bird with Two Stones: A History of Vannatu, Vannatu Cultural Centre, 1981.
Consuming Culture: Why You Eat What You Eat, Chapmans, 1992, Henry Holt (New York, NY), 1993.
The Decline of Carlism: History and Anthropology in Northern Spain, 1939-1989, Oxford University Press (New York, NY), 1994, ("Basque" series), University of Nevada Press (Reno, NV), 2000.

(Editor and contributor) *Sport, Identity, and Ethnicity* ("Ethnic Identity" series), Berg (Herndon, VA), 1996.
(Editor, with Chris McDonaugh) *Popularizing Anthropology,* Routledge (New York, NY), 1996.
(Editor) *Contesting Art: Art, Politics, and Identity in the Modern World* ("Ethnic Identity" series), Berg (New York, NY), 1997.
(Editor) *Exotic No More: Anthropology on the Front Lines,* University of Chicago Press (Chicago, IL), 2002.
(Editor, with Helen Macbeth) *Researching Food Habits: Methods and Problems,* (Volume five of the "Anthropology of Food and Nutrition" series), Berghahn Books (New York, NY), 2004.

Contributor to academic journals, including *Journal of the Royal Anthropological Institute.*

SIDELIGHTS: Jeremy MacClancy once told *CA:* "Tired by the seemingly endless qualifications of academic prose and excited by the challenge of producing a 'popular' book of anthropology, I, at the suggestion of a friend, began work on an academically respectable, yet not always academically serious, survey of the literature on the anthropology of food. The result, *Consuming Culture: Why You Eat What You Eat,* has been published in the United Kingdom and the United States." MacClancy advises on the eating habits of various cultures, including feral children and the Japanese who very carefully eat the deadly blowfish. He studies what different groups consider edible and inedible, and foods that are considered taboo, such as the cow by Hindus. A *Publishers Weekly* contributor commented, "This altogether entertaining book's message? Eating is wonderful, but people are very silly about it."

Sport, Identity, and Ethnicity is an anthology to which editor MacClancy makes a contribution of four essays. In the opening chapter, he writes that sports "are vehicles of identity, providing people with a sense of difference and a way of classifying themselves and others, whether latitudinally or hierarchically." "Sport," he continues, "may not be just a marker of one's already established social identity but a means by which to create a new social identity for oneself" and "cannot be comprehended without reference to relations to power: who attempts to control how a sport is to be organized and played, and by whom; how it is to be represented; how it is to be interpreted." These are themes that carry through the volume. MacClancy addresses the linking of sport and ethnic identity in his chapter on Basque soccer. Kevin Young wrote in the *Canadian Ethnic Studies Journal* that the anthology "is informative, readable, and jammed with absorbing examples from all corners of the world on ways in which sport is inscribed with what the editor calls a 'plurality of identities,' both ethnically speaking and beyond."

Popularizing Anthropology, written with Chris McDonaugh, studies the "point" of anthropology and some of the debates of current approaches. It asks for whom the science is conducted and whether it should be approached in a style that is accessible to all, even to those studied. *Sociology*'s Sharon Macdonald wrote that *Popularizing Anthropology* "tackles an area which is justly deserving of anthropological attention, and does so by providing a range of contrasting perspectives and interesting cases."

The essays of *Contesting Art: Art, Politics, and Identity in the Modern World* develop "the idea that the arts offer a primary means of access to the values of social groups," wrote William Washabaugh in *Journal of the Royal Anthropological Institute.* "This book reflects the growing awareness that material objects and processes of artistic reproduction are profoundly tied to social relations and that, therefore, art and discourses about art influence and reflect social life. The range of questions here is astonishing and the controversies endlessly provocative."

Anthropology as a science has evolved since its beginnings in the nineteenth century. While it was then used to study primitive and exotic peoples, it is now ap-

plied to the study of many of the ills and controversies of contemporary life, including immigration, drug use, child labor, human rights, and environmentalism. *Exotic No More: Anthropology on the Front Lines* examines these, but also more upbeat subjects, including art, music, and the media. MacClancy's introduction "points to a number of features that characterize the discipline," noted James G. Carrier in *Journal of the Royal Anthropological Institute,* "including field work, a concern with local manifestations of global processes and forces, and taking seriously local people's lives and concerns." Carrier described the collection as "a presentation and celebration of the discipline aimed at a general, educated readership. It seeks to show that the discipline is much more than pith helmets and grass huts; rather, it is full of people who are working on topics that bear on important matters of public interest and debate."

MacClancy told *CA:* "My main advice to would-be 'popularizers' in academic positions is to expect the opprobrium of most of your colleagues (except close friends). It's best to have produced a 'serious' academic work before a 'popular' one. Otherwise you will be branded as a 'popularizer' forevermore. At the same time, your popular work will bring you a different, broader, audience. And some academics might consider that as important as writing books only for their colleagues."

BIOGRAPHICAL AND CRITICAL SOURCES:

BOOKS

MacClancy, Jeremy, editor and contributor, *Sport, Identity, and Ethnicity,* Berg (Herndon, VA), 1996.

PERIODICALS

American Anthropologist, September, 1998, Alexander Alland, Jr., review of *Contesting Art: Art, Politics, and Identity in the Modern World,* p. 835.
Canadian Ethnic Studies Journal, spring, 1998, Kevin Young, review of *Sport, Identity, and Ethnicity,* p. 165.
Choice, July, 2001, N. Greene, review of *The Decline of Carlism,* p. 2028.

Journal of Sociology, March, 1998, Ray Hibbins, review of *Sport, Identity, and Ethnicity,* p. 99.

Journal of the Royal Anthropological Institute, June, 1998, I. M. Leis, review of *Popularizing Anthropology,* p. 372; June, 2000, William Washabaugh, review of *Contesting Art,* p. 346; September, 2003, James G. Carrier, review of *Exotic No More: Anthropology on the Front Lines,* p. 610.

Publishers Weekly, May 31, 1993, review of *Consuming Culture: Why You Eat What You Eat,* p. 34.

Sociology, November, 1998, Sharon Macdonald, review of *Popularizing Anthropology,* p. 875.

Times Higher Education Supplement, December 6, 2002, Christopher Pinney, review of *Exotic No More,* p. 25.*

* * *

MARGALIT, Avishai 1939-

PERSONAL: Born 1939. *Education:* Hebrew University of Jerusalem, Ph.D., 1970.

ADDRESSES: Office—Department of Philosophy, Hebrew University of Jerusalem, Jerusalem, Israel 91905. *E-mail*—avishai@rsage.org.

CAREER: Hebrew University of Jerusalem, lecturer, 1970-72, senior lecturer, 1973-79, associate professor, 1980-97, professor, beginning 1998, currently Schulman Professor of Philosophy. Other academic positions include visiting scholar at Harvard University, Oxford University, Free University, and Max Planck Institute.

WRITINGS:

(Editor) *Meaning and Use,* Reidel (Boston, MA), 1979.

(Editor, with Edna Ullmann-Margalit) *Isaiah Berlin: A Celebration,* Hogarth Press (London, England), 1991.

(With Moshe Halbertal) *Idolatry,* translated by Naomi Goldblum, Harvard University Press (Cambridge, MA), 1992.

The Decent Society, translated by Naomi Goldblum, Harvard University Press (Cambridge, MA), 1996.

Views in Review: Politics and Culture in the State of the Jews, Farrar, Straus and Giroux (New York, NY), 1998.

The Ethics of Memory, Harvard University Press (Cambridge, MA), 2003.

(With Ian Buruma) *Occidentalism: The West in the Eyes of Its Enemies,* Penguin (New York, NY), 2004.

With Gabriel Motzkin, author of "The Uniqueness of the Holocaust," an article for *Philosophy and Public Affairs,* winter, 1996.

SIDELIGHTS: Avishai Margalit is a professor of philosophy at the Hebrew University of Jerusalem. Margalit's body of literary work covers such weighty topics as the nature of the best society and the nature of idolatry. His *Meaning and Use,* which was published in 1979, is a collection of essays by philosophers and other scholars on epistemological topics. Epistemology is the study of the nature and grounds of knowledge. Many of the authors who contributed to *Meaning and Use* examine human perception and the language that is used to describe human perception. One author discusses the notion that words spoken with a certain mood do not always have a certain force behind them. Another contributor looks at anti-realism and its construction of truth, and others explain the thought process behind such statements as "this (wooden) table might have been made of stone." Simon Blackburn, writing for *Philosophical Review,* called *Meaning and Use* a "worthwhile and thought-provoking volume."

Margalit collaborated with Moshe Halbertal to write *Idolatry,* which was translated from the Hebrew by Naomi Goldblum and published in 1992 by Harvard University Press. Margalit and Halbertal deliver a thorough account of religious idolatry in the book. They begin by asking what idolatry is and why it is considered "an unspeakable sin." Margalit and Halbertal note that the accusation of idolatry has historically come in two different forms. The first type is the worship of gods other than a "true" God. "The ban on idolatry is an attempt to dictate exclusivity," write Margalit and Halbertal, "to map the unique territory of the one God." Organized religions, such as Judaism, Christianity, and Islam, are monotheistic. That is, they forbid the idolizing of gods other than their own declared "true" God. This form of idolatry is used by monotheistic religions to establish a boundary between paganism, which is the worship of the "wrong" god or gods, and non-paganism. The second form of idolatry places a ban on manners of worship that are at odds with the particular religion. When a religion bans the worship of certain physical images, Margalit and Halbertal observe, it presents itself as the only way to worship.

The policy behind forbidding idolatry has changed throughout the centuries. In biblical accounts, idolatry was viewed as a form of sexual betrayal. In the Old Testament the Jews thought of God as human and themselves as married to God. The worship of the wrong god or a "false" physical idol was considered tantamount to adultery. Because religion and politics were so intertwined, idolatry was also considered a form of political betrayal.

In the twelfth century, Moses Maimonides (1135-1204) wrote of a God who was abstract, and not a tangible human entity. To Maimonides, the idea that God could be human was itself a form of idolatry, and this kind of idolatry transformed idolatry from a sexual sin to, in the words of Margalit and Halbertal, "the sin of the great error." The sin of idolatry became less about the performance of strange, unsanctioned rituals and more about the "harboring of alien beliefs."

As the centuries passed, idolatry became widely understood as either the worship of the wrong god or the belief in wrong religious principles and practices. The development of societies has added nuances to the notion of idolatry, making idolatry a fluid concept. As humans worship other idols, such as money, secular institutions, and even football teams, the accusation of idolatry must expand to thwart the new idols. *New York Review of Books* critic Wendy Doniger commented that the book "teaches us both why monotheistic religions have thought that they were right and everyone else was wrong." *Idolatry,* according to Doniger, is "a remarkable book, which tells us, more thoroughly and persuasively than anyone has done so far, why and in what ways religions hate one another."

The Decent Society is another ambitious book about a complex topic. The book discusses optimal society, but it does not attempt to outline the nature of a utopian society. Instead, it works within recognizable reality to suggest a paradigm for the best possible society. Theorists have long opined on the nature of the best society. More often than not, such endeavors revolve around ideas of justice, civility, tolerance, or fairness. The most important recent thoughts on the subject are in John Rawls's trend-setting 1971 book *A Theory of Justice,* in which Rawls seeks to explain the best society in terms of justice. According to Rawls, the best society is one that focuses on economic fairness and equal liberty. Margalit offers an alternative to Rawls in *The Decent Society.* For Margalit, the best society is one in which institutions avoid humiliating people—such a society, writes Margalit, would be a "decent" society.

Margalit does not endorse a particular theory, but explores the concept of "society" and its potential. Margalit notes that when Rawls talks about justice in society, he is, in a way, concerned in part with decency. In promoting the broad concepts of decency and respect, Margalit seeks to shift the focus away from the Rawlsian notion of justice toward preserving the dignity of social beings. Margalit asserts that a society may be civilized without being decent if it humiliates its members. Furthermore, a society may be civilized or just to its own members, but not to members outside of that society. Margalit, who is Jewish, observes that Arabs living in Israel demand equal rights not just to gain equal distribution of goods and services: "The fact that they are denied these goods, even by a society they do not identify with, is perceived not only as injustice but also as humiliation."

Margalit recognizes that it may be impossible to eradicate humiliation between individuals, so he concentrates on humiliation inflicted by institutions. He also recognizes that injustice may exist in a decent society; people may be exploited in a decent society, whereas exploitation may not exist in a just society. Margalit also recognizes the difference between a civilized society, where all individuals treat one another with respect, and a decent society, where only institutions are required to treat persons with respect. Rather than design a utopia, writes Margalit, he seeks to suggest "a utopia through which to criticize reality."

An analysis of dignity, self-respect, and humiliation lies at the heart of *The Decent Society.* Humiliation, to Rawls, occurs whenever someone's self-respect is damaged. Anarchists insist that a decent society is impossible to achieve because all institutional power is designed to humiliate. Stoics, conversely, argue that decency is irrelevant to persons who have sufficient self-esteem. Margalit questions these theories and points out their various vulnerabilities.

Margalit's book on the optimal society is considered by many critics to be the best answer to Rawls's arguments. Margalit's book, commented Michael Ignatieff in *Times Literary Supplement,* "is a model of how philosophers, using only a fine attention to distinctions between similar-sounding moral terms, can help to clarify, and by doing so, purify our moral language." "Compared to the sloppiness of so many 'virtue' books," remarked Alan Wolfe in *New Republic,* "Margalit's book offers a great deal, especially an opportunity to argue with someone who is really thinking. A decent society would have more books like *The Decent Society.*" *New York Review of Books* critic Alan Ryan commented that it "is serious without being ponderous, it is unassuming but ambitious, and it is engagingly unorthodox, both in its concerns and in the way it pursues them."

Views in Review: Politics and Culture in the State of the Jews is a collection of previously published essays by Margalit. The essays deal with a variety of political and social topics in Israel, such as the Shimon Peres legacy, the work of philosopher Martin Buber, the cultural and political oversight of the Israeli kitsch, and Palestinians. Critics praised *Views in Review*. *Library Journal* contributor Sanford R. Silverburg called the work "a pleasant read, offering a warm and sympathetic review of the humanity inherent in the Israeli national soul." A *Publishers Weekly* reviewer commented that *Views in Review* will "appeal to readers who want to improve their knowledge of Israel's complex reality."

Six lectures by Margalit are collected in *The Ethics of Memory,* which examines the question of whether there is an obligation to remember, whether it be atrocities of war or a person's name. Key concepts in this discussion are the distinction between morality and ethics, the existence of communities of memory, the role of moral witnesses, and the effects of forgiving and forgetting. Margalit says morality influences "thin" human relations, those between people with only remote awareness of each other, and calls ethics part of "thick" human relations, which exist between those whom people know and love. In concluding that memory is ethical not moral, he suggests that democratic societies, which typically focus on the individual

and shaping the future, would benefit from a greater awareness of the past.

Reviewers noted that *The Ethics of Memory* is not a specialist's work for other specialists. Margalit himself comments in the book that he is an "e.g." philosopher, not an "i.e." philosopher; he would rather make his points through real life examples rather than definitions and hypothetical situations. Reactions to the book included questions about its completeness and individual assertions, but critics generally found favor with Margalit's line of inquiry and purpose. In the *Los Angeles Times,* Lee Siegel said Margalit had crafted "a novel illumination of memory's moral implications" but added, "he traverses such difficult, boundless terrain that he has a hard time balancing his restless inquiries with full examinations." In the *Guardian* Gale Strawson challenged the author's suggestion that everyone wants to be remembered after death, yet characterized his work as "a lovely and often brilliant book." Commenting on the importance of Margalit's ideas in the aftermath of September 11, 2001, Jonathan Lear wrote in the *New York Times Book Review:* "Margalit is an astonishingly humane thinker. His philosophy is always tied to making sense of us humans in all our complexity. And yet he is committed to making sense of us in ways that will make us better." And in the *New Republic,* Michael Walzer was relieved to find that this "fashionable subject" was not dealt with in the usual "sentimental or cynical" way. Walzer described *The Ethics of Memory* as "a wonderfully effective antidote to both the marketing of memory and the 'discourse' of memory, a gift to all of us who are engaged by the contemporary arguments and who are radically unhappy about them."

BIOGRAPHICAL AND CRITICAL SOURCES:

BOOKS

Margalit, Avishai, *The Decent Society,* translated by Naomi Goldblum, Harvard University Press (Cambridge), 1996.

Margalit, Avishai, and Moshe Halbertal, *Idolatry,* translated by Naomi Goldblum, Harvard University Press, 1992.

PERIODICALS

Guardian (Manchester, England), January 4, 2003, Gale Strawson, "Blood and Memory: Do We Have a Duty of Remembrance to the Dead?," p. 8.

Library Journal, October 15, 1998, Sanford R. Silverburg, review of *Views in Review: Politics and Culture in the State of the Jews,* p. 84.

Los Angeles Times, April 20, 2003, Lee Siegel, "The Morality of Remembering," p. R12.

New Republic, May 27, 1996, Alan Wolfe, review of *The Decent Society,* p. 33; January 20, 2003, Michael Walzer, "The Present of the Past," p. 36.

New York Review of Books, April 21, 1994, Wendy Doniger, review of *Idolatry,* pp. 55-58; July 13, 1996, Alan Ryan, review of *The Decent Society,* pp. 17-20.

New York Times Book Review, February 9, 2003, Jonathan Lear, "Anger Management," p. 22.

Philosophical Review, January, 1982, Simon Blackburn, review of *Meaning and Use,* pp. 128-131.

Publishers Weekly, September 21, 1998, review of *Views in Review,* p. 36.

Times Literary Supplement, March 7, 1997, Michael Ignatieff, "The Necessary Sting," pp. 10-11.

ONLINE

Avishai Margalit home page, http://www.socrates.huji.ac.il/Prof_Avishai_Margalit.htm (November 15, 2003). *

*   *   *

MASSIE, Robert K(inloch) 1929-

PERSONAL: Born January 5, 1929, in Lexington, KY; son of Robert Kinloch and Mary (Kimball) Massie; married Suzanne Rohrbach (a writer), December 18, 1954 (divorced, 1990); married Deborah L. Karl, 1992; children: (first marriage) Robert Kinloch, Susanna, Elizabeth; (second marriage) Christopher. *Education:* Yale University, B.A., 1950; Oxford University, B.A. (Rhodes scholar), 1952. *Hobbies and other interests:* Sailing.

ADDRESSES: Home—60 West Clinton Avenue, Irvington, NY 10533.

CAREER: Collier's, New York, NY, reporter, 1955-56; *Newsweek,* New York, NY, writer and correspondent, 1956-62; *USA-1,* New York, NY, writer, 1962; *Satur-*day *Evening Post,* New York, NY, writer, 1962-65; freelance writer, 1965—. Princeton University, Ferris Professor of Journalism, 1977, 1985; Tulane University, Mellon Professor of Humanities, 1981. *Military service:* U.S. Naval Reserves, 1952-55; became lieutenant, junior grade.

MEMBER: Authors Guild (vice president, 1985-87, president, beginning 1987), Authors League of America, PEN, Society of American Historians.

AWARDS, HONORS: Christopher Award, 1976, for *Journey;* American Book Award nomination, American Library Association Notable Book citation, and Pulitzer Prize for Biography, all 1981, all for *Peter the Great: His Life and World.*

WRITINGS:

Nicholas and Alexandra (biography), Atheneum (New York, NY), 1967, reprinted, Ballantine Books (New York, NY), 2000.

(With Suzanne Massie) *Journey,* Knopf (New York, NY), 1975.

Peter the Great: His Life and World, Knopf (New York, NY), 1980.

(Author of introduction) Jeffrey Finestone, *The Last Courts of Europe: A Royal Family Album, 1860-1914,* Dent (London, England), 1981, Crown (New York, NY), 1983.

Dreadnought: Britain, Germany, and the Coming of the Great War, Random House (New York, NY), 1991.

The Romanovs: The Final Chapter, Random House (New York, NY), 1995.

Castles of Steel: Britain, Germany, and the Winning of the Great War at Sea, Random House (New York, NY), 2003.

Massie's works have been translated into Spanish and German.

ADAPTATIONS: Nicholas and Alexandra was adapted into a motion picture by James Goldman and Edward Bond and released by Columbia, 1971; *Peter the Great* was adapted for television as a four-part miniseries for National Broadcasting Company, Inc. (NBC), 1986, and has been recorded as an audiobook by Books on Tape.

SIDELIGHTS: A journalist turned historian, Robert K. Massie is the author of the acclaimed works *Peter the Great: His Life and World, Dreadnought: Britain, Germany, and the Coming of the Great War,* and *Nicholas and Alexandra.* As *Booklist* critic Brendan Driscoll noted of Massie in a review of the author's *Castles of Steel: Britain, Germany, and the Winning of the Great War at Sea,* Massies's major gift is a talent for creating "narrative histories so engaging that readers, losing themselves in the romance-novel story style, forget that they're reading nearly 1,000 pages of nonfiction."

Massie worked as a journalist for ten years before the circumstances of his personal life led him to the serious examination of Russian history. Soon after joining *Newsweek* as a book reviewer, Massie and his wife Suzanne discovered that their six-month-old son Bobbie suffered from hemophilia, a hereditary and incurable blood disease. Investigating his son's condition led Massie to spend many hours in the New York Public Library where he became caught up in the story of Alexei Romanov, heir of the last ruling family of Russia, who had been stricken with hemophilia through his mother, the Empress Alexandra. Familiarity with the devastating effects resulting from such a family tragedy prompted Massie to study the short, tragic reign of Alexei's father, Czar Nicholas II, from a unique perspective. Massie once commented: "When something unusual happens in your life, you are curious to see what has happened before. We were busy trying to find out how to deal with this disease, talking to a lot of other families, to doctors and social workers and people like that about hemophilia in mid-twentieth-century America. But I knew a bit of the story of the Tsarevich Alexis and I was curious to find out how his family had dealt with it, what was all this business about hypnotism and so forth."

Massie said he had no thoughts of writing a book: He was simply curious to find out what eventuated. While reading all he could find about the family, he began to notice discrepancies between accounts. "The general narrative historians swept pretty quickly by this whole business of the boy's illness with a sentence or two. I found that it was much more complicated than that. The links that even I could find, with very little background in the field, between the illness and what was happening politically were very much in evidence and were important," he commented. *Nicholas and Alexandra* was published ten years later to much critical acclaim. Robert Payne praised the book in the *New York Times Book Review:* "Massie's canvas is the whole of Russia, the Czar and Czarina merely the focal points. . . . What emerges is a study in depth of the reign of Nicholas, and for perhaps the first time we meet the actors in the drama face to face in their proper setting." The profits from *Nicholas and Alexandra,* along with royalties from the film that would later be based upon it, provided Massie with sufficient funds to help his son cope with life as a hemophiliac.

In 1975, Massie and his wife coauthored *Journey,* chronicling their young son's courage in facing his condition and describing how the disease affected their own lives as parents. "The substance of the book shifts from the mastery of pain to the mastery of life, and it is done in part by a turning outward in contrast to the Romanovs' [*Nicholas and Alexandra*] secretiveness and withdrawal," commented *New York Times Book Review* critic Elizabeth Hegeman. *Journey* contains a harsh indictment of America's "pitifully inadequate health plans, the workings of hospitals and the politics of the Red Cross which, charged the Massies, places the welfare of drug companies above that of hemophilia victims," according to *Newsweek* reviewer Margo Jefferson. Hegeman echoed the authors' frustration in describing "the grotesque folly of trying to raise enough money for the Hemophilia Society through charity balls and premieres and the inadequacy of the 'patchwork' of uncoordinated charities and agencies set up to help special need groups." She added that Massie's impassioned criticism should not be construed as self-serving: "It is the statement of a father who feels guilty over using so much of the precious blood derivative *even though he pays for it,* because he has carefully thought out his connection to society and he knows that something is deeply wrong with our social policy if blood is treated as a commodity to be exchanged for money."

After completing *Journey,* Massie once again turned his attention to the lush panorama of the Russian past. Although now familiar with the time period encompassing the life of the Tsarevich, there were still many areas of history with which Massie was unfamiliar. "While I was working on *Nicholas and Alexandra,* I was giving myself a course and reading as much as I could," Massie remembered. "I was fascinated by Peter [I]. There were glimpses of his character, stories and legends about him, but I couldn't find any biography which really captured him. After thinking about it for a while, I thought I could try one." Massie made frequent trips to Russia to do research for *Peter the Great.* He was fortunate in receiving a great deal of both official and scholarly assistance from the Soviet people who continue to have great reverence for Peter as one of the greatest of Russian heroes.

Considered the architect of modern Russia, Peter the Great was an imposing figure obsessed with forcing a backward Russian society into step with seventeenth-century Europe. Off came the flowing beards, gone were the long robes with their drooping sleeves; the monarch abolished such traditional emblems of the old order in favor of a "German" style of dress that allowed for the freedom of movement necessary for an active, forward-thinking people. Peter the Great went on to establish Russia as a major power. Flooding his homeland with Western technology through the importation of thousands of craftsmen and military personnel, raising the educational standards of his fellow Russians by setting up schools and sending young men abroad to study arts and sciences yet unknown in Russia, and defeating longtime opponent Charles XII of Sweden in the battle of Poltava in 1709, Peter crowned his growing empire with the city of St. Petersburg, capital of the new Russia and his "window into Europe," which he commanded be built upon the northern marshes bordering the Gulf of Finland.

A London *Times* critic felt that Massie's obvious admiration for his subject tends to color his view of the facts and remarked that "the urge to show Peter in the best light must spring partly from the relief of writing about a monarch who could, and did, do everything for himself, after devoting so many years to Peter's descendants who, between them, barely seemed able to tie up a ribbon or fasten a stud." John Leonard of the *New York Times* criticized Massie for the fact that "there is, in [*Peter the Great*], no thesis. . . . Peter's spotty education, his voracious curiosity, his epileptic convulsions, his talent with his hands, his ignorance of literature, his humor and his terror—all are merely reported and forgiven, like the weather." However, while noting in the *New York Times Book Review* the book's somewhat daunting length, Kyril Fitzlyon hailed *Peter the Great* as "an enthralling book, beautifully edited, with a first-rate index and excellent illustrations," and later added: "It would be surprising if it did not become the standard biography of Peter the Great in English for many years to come, as fascinating as any novel and more so than most."

"I had done enough about Russia," Massie acknowledged in an interview with Joseph A. Cincotti for the *New York Times Book Review,* "so I decided to come home from Russia by way of western Europe." End-of-the-century western Europe was the route that Massie chose to travel and the one that provided the subject for his next book, *Dreadnought.* Nine years in the writing, the book is a narrative account of Britain's retreat from "splendid isolationism" after the crisis at Fashoda, the battle that resulted in France's cessation of efforts towards building a rival colonial empire after 1898, *Dreadnought* covers the period from 1897 to August, 1914, when Britain came to France's aid in World War I. Taking its title from the name given to the heavily armored and gunned battleship H.M.S. *Dreadnought,* designed by the British to render all other navies obsolete, Massie's lengthy volume uses the naval antagonism between Britain and Germany as a point of departure. Organizing such a broad range of cataclysmic events into a comprehensive format is no easy task, and some reviewers found fault with the book's areas of concentration. Stanley Weintraub commented in the *New York Times Book Review:* "Since Massie uses the lens of the British-Germany rivalry, the picture that emerges of the European powder keg and its multiple fuses, all sputtering at different speeds, is out of focus, although dramatic nevertheless."

However, *Dreadnought* was praised for the characteristically engaging narrative style of its author. Commending Massie's sharp eye for detail and his ability to vividly portray characters, Geoffrey Moorhouse observed in the *Los Angeles Times Book Review,* "one will not forget . . . Bismarck working in his office, watched by his dog Tiras, who terrorized all visitors . . . or Lord Salisbury, who 'treated his children like small foreign powers: not often noticed, but when recognized, regarded with unfailing politeness.'" "*Dreadnought* is a saga elegantly spun out in palaces and cabinet rooms, on the decks of royal yachts and the bridges of battleships, in Europe's spas and rambling country houses," wrote Douglas Porch in *Washington Post Book World.* "Massie traces the development of naval forces and the calculations of European diplomats with clarity and humor," he added. "He has a subtle appreciation for interplay of personalities in an era when the ruling houses of England and Germany were blood relations, and their political leaders shared a strong sense of cultural communality."

In 2003 Massie completed his equally well-researched sequel to *Dreadnought.* In *Castles of Steel* he studies the rise of the German U-boats, which through their effectiveness at travelling undetected prompted advances in sonar technologies, as well as Germany and Great Britain's battle for supremacy at sea. The assumptions undergirding the initial war strategies of both sides in the war quickly proved faulty, and Massie follows the efforts of both Germany's Kaiser Wilhelm II—grandson of England's Queen Victoria and a man who believed he could quickly gain a well-mannered victory—and the British admiralty to reassess the strengths and weaknesses of their opponents. Praising Massie's work as "readable and dramatic" as well as well researched, David A. Smith noted in the *Naval War College Review* that *Castles of Steel* gives readers "a clear sense of how important the clash of British and German navies was to the war's eventual outcome, and it illustrates how Winston Churchill's dramatic description of Admiral John Jellicoe, commander in chief of the British Grand Fleet, as 'the only commander who could lose the war in an afternoon' could be an accurate one." Massie argues that it was Germany's decision to engage in unrestricted U-Boat attacks, sinking not only British battleships but also neutral merchant ships and passenger liners. "The tactic worked in the sense that Britain, like Germany, started to run out of food and fuel," explained an *Economist* reviewer. "But it was also in Mr. Massie's view the colossal misjudgment that ensured Germany's defeat by bringing an entirely new enemy with unlimited resources into the war: the United States." Praising Massie's history as "imposing in both size and quality," a *Publishers Weekly* contributor noted that the historian "describes his cast of characters with the vividness of a novelist."

With the collapse of communism in Russia in the early 1990s, Massie was able to continue his story of Nicholas and Alexandra. Records formerly hidden were revealed, and this new information allowed the author to complete his 1995 volume, *The Romanovs: The Final Chapter*. Beginning with the execution of the Russian royal family, Massie traces the events of the burial of their bodies in Ekaterinburg, their discovery almost half a century later, their exhumation in 1991, and the genetic analysis of the bones that determined conclusively that all seven members of the Romanov family—including the Tsarevich and Anastasia—had been executed in 1918. "Although no specialist in Russian history, and clearly dependent on translated sources, Massie tells the story with the same narrative skill that he displayed in his bestselling *Nicholas and Alexandra*," wrote *Times Literary Supplement* contributor Orlando Figes. Characterizing the book as "a tale of jealousy . . . ; bureaucratic fighting . . . ; false claims by impostors; endless legal hearings; and quarrelling between clans of the Romanovs," Figes added that "the prize of the imperial bones has brought out the worst in all those who would gain by laying claim to them," particularly most of the few surviving members of the Romanov family. Including a thorough discussion of the sixty-five-year-long deception by a woman claiming to be the Grand Duchess Anastasia, Massie's volume also traces the fate of other members of the Romanov family, seventeen of whom were killed within days of the Tsar. Calling the work "masterful" and "enthralling," *Washington Post Book World* contributor Joseph Finder praised *The Romanovs* as "a narrative as gripping as a well-wrought murder mystery, told in vividly realized, densely atmospheric scenes, rich with moments of grim fascination." While Massie subtitled his book "The Final Chapter," Finder noted that there are still mysteries left to be solved regarding this Russian chronicle, which may find the author returning to Mother Russia yet again in the future.

BIOGRAPHICAL AND CRITICAL SOURCES:

PERIODICALS

American Spectator, December, 1989, p. 32; September, 1992, p. 65.

Booklist, September 15, 2003, Brendan Driscoll, review of *Castles of Steel: Britain, Germany, and the Winning of the Great War at Sea*, p. 178.

Economist (U.S.), January 10, 2004, review of *Castles of Steel*, p. 73.

Kirkus Reviews, September 1, 2003, review of *Castles of Steel*, p. 1114.

Library Journal, October 1, 2003, Danile K. Blewett, review of *Castles of Steel*, p. 95.

Los Angeles Times Book Review, December 8, 1991, Geoffrey Moorhouse, review of *Dreadnought*, pp. 4, 15.

Naval War College Review, spring, 2004, David A. Smith, review of *Castles of Steel*, p. 185.

Newsweek, August 28, 1967; May 26, 1975; October 20, 1980, Walter Clemons, review of *Peter the Great*, p. 90.

New York Review of Books, March 26, 1992, p. 15.

New York Times, October 7, 1980, John Leonard, review of *Peter the Great*, section C, p. 8.

New York Times Book Review, August 20, 1967, pp. 1, 26; May 11, 1975, pp. 5-6; November 10, 1991, Joseph A. Cincotti, review of *Dreadnought: Britain, Germany, and the Coming of the Great War,* pp. 7, 9, and Stanley Weintraub, review of *Dreadnought,* p. 7.

Publishers Weekly, September 22, 2003, review of *Castles of Steel,* p. 97.

Punch, April 1, 1981, pp. 534-535.

Time, November 10, 1980, pp. 107-108; November 11, 1991, p. 90.

Times (London, England), February 5, 1981.

Times Literary Supplement, April 28, 1981, p. 467; April 17, 1992, p. 10; August 9, 1996, p. 26.

Tribune Books (Chicago, IL), December 15, 1991, p. 5; December 3, 1995, p. 3.

Washington Post Book World, November 24, 1991, Douglas Porch, review of *Dreadnought,* p. 5; October 22, 1995, Joseph Finder, review of *The Romanovs: The Final Chapter,* p. 5.*

*   *   *

MATTHIESSEN, Peter 1927-

PERSONAL: Surname is pronounced "*Math*-e-son"; born May 22, 1927, in New York, NY; son of Erard A. (an architect) and Elizabeth (Carey) Matthiessen; married Patricia Southgate, February 8, 1951 (divorced, 1958); married Deborah Love, May 16, 1963 (deceased, 1972); married Maria Eckhart, November 28, 1980; children: (first marriage) Lucas, Sara C.; (second marriage) Rue, Alexander. *Education:* Attended Sorbonne, University of Paris, 1948-49; Yale University, B.A., 1950.

ADDRESSES: Home—Bridge Lane, Box 392, Sagaponack, Long Island, NY 11962. *Agent*—Candida Donadio Associates, Inc., 231 West 22nd St., New York, NY 10011.

CAREER: Writer, 1950—; *Paris Review,* New York, NY (originally Paris, France), cofounder, 1951, editor, 1951—. Former commercial fisherman; captain of deep-sea charter fishing boat, Montauk, Long Island, NY, 1954-56; member of expeditions to Alaska, Canadian Northwest Territories, Peru, Nepal, East Africa, Congo Basin, Siberia, India, Bhutan, China, Japan, Namibia, Botswana, and Outer Mongolia and

Peter Matthiessen

of Harvard-Peabody Expedition to New Guinea, 1961; National Book Awards, judge, 1970. *Military service:* U.S. Navy, 1945-47.

MEMBER: American Academy and Institute of Arts and Letters, American Academy of Arts and Sciences, New York Zoological Society (member of board of trustees, 1965-78).

AWARDS, HONORS: Atlantic Prize, 1951, for best first story; permanent installation in White House library, for *Wildlife in America;* National Institute/American Academy of Arts and Letters grant, 1963, for *The Cloud Forest: A Chronicle of the South American Wilderness* and *Under the Mountain Wall: A Chronicle of Two Seasons in the Stone Age;* National Book Award nominations, 1966, for *At Play in the Fields of the Lord,* and 1972, for *The Tree Where Man Was Born;* Christopher Book Award, 1971, for *Sal Si Puedes: Cesar Chavez and the New American Revolution;* elected to National Institute of Arts and Letters,

1974; "Editor's Choice" citation, *New York Times Book Review,* 1975, for *Far Tortuga;* Brandeis Award and National Book Award for contemporary thought for *The Snow Leopard,* both 1979; National Book Award, general nonfiction, 1980, for paperback edition of *The Snow Leopard;* John Burroughs Medal and African Wildlife Leadership Foundation Award, both 1982, both for *Sand Rivers;* gold medal for distinction in natural history, Academy of Natural Sciences, Philadelphia, PA, 1985; Ambassador Award, English-Speaking Union, 1990, for *Killing Mister Watson;* John Steinbeck Award, Long Island University, Southampton, elected to Global 500 Honour Roll, United Nations Environment Programme, and designated fellow, Academy of Arts and Science, all 1991.

WRITINGS:

FICTION

Race Rock, Harper (New York, NY), 1954.
Partisans, Viking (New York, NY), 1955.
Raditzer, Viking (New York, NY), 1961.
At Play in the Fields of the Lord, Random House (New York, NY), 1965.
Far Tortuga, Random House (New York, NY), 1975.
On the River Styx, and Other Stories, Random House (New York, NY), 1989.

"WATSON" TRILOGY

Killing Mister Watson, Random House (New York, NY), 1990.
Lost Man's River, Random House (New York, NY), 1997.
Bone by Bone, Random House (New York, NY), 1999.

NONFICTION

Wildlife in America, Viking (New York, NY), 1959, revised edition, 1987.
The Cloud Forest: A Chronicle of the South American Wilderness, Viking (New York, NY), 1961.
Under the Mountain Wall: A Chronicle of Two Seasons in the Stone Age, Viking (New York, NY), 1962.
Oomingmak: The Expedition to the Musk Ox Island in the Bering Sea, Hastings House (New York, NY), 1967.

The Shorebirds of North America, paintings by Robert Verity Clem, Viking (New York, NY), 1967, published as *The Wind Birds,* illustrated by Robert Gillmor, 1973.
Sal Si Puedes: Cesar Chavez and the New American Revolution, Random House (New York, NY), 1970, published as *Sal Si Puedes (Escape if You Can),* University of California Press (Berkeley, CA), 2000.
Blue Meridian: The Search for the Great White Shark, Random House (New York, NY), 1971.
Everglades: With Selections from the Writings of Peter Matthiessen, edited by Paul Brooks, Sierra Club-Ballantine (New York, NY), 1971.
The Tree Where Man Was Born, photographs by Eliot Porter, Dutton (New York, NY), 1972, revised edition, Penguin Books (New York, NY), 1995.
Seal Pool (juvenile), illustrated by William Pene Du Bois, Doubleday (Garden City, NY), 1972, published as *The Great Auk Escape,* Angus & Robertson (London, England), 1974.
The Snow Leopard, Viking (New York, NY), 1978.
Sand Rivers, photographs by Hugo van Lawick, Viking (New York, NY), 1981.
In the Spirit of Crazy Horse, Viking (New York, NY), 1983.
Indian Country, Viking (New York, NY), 1984.
Men's Lives: The Surfmen and Baymen of the South Fork, Random House (New York, NY), 1986.
Nine-Headed Dragon River: Zen Journals 1969-1982, Shambhala (Boulder, CO), 1986.
African Silences, Random House (New York, NY), 1991.
Shadows of Africa, illustrated by Mary Frank, Abrams (New York, NY), 1992.
Baikal, photographs by Boyd Norton, Sierra Club Books (San Francisco, CA), 1992.
East of Lo Monthang, Shambhala (Boulder, CO), 1995.
Tigers in the Snow, Farrar, Straus & Giroux (New York, NY), 2000.
The Peter Matthiessen Reader, Vintage (New York, NY), 2000.
The Birds of Heaven: Travel with Cranes, Harvill Press, 2002.
End of the Earth: Voyages to the White Continent, National Geographic Society (Washington, D.C.), 2003.
Arctic National Wildlife Refuge: Seasons of Life and Land: A Photographic Journey, photographs by Subhankar Banerje, foreword by Jimmy Carter, Mountaineers Books (Seattle, WA), 2003.
(Editor and author of introduction) *North American Indians,* Penguin Books (New York, NY), 2004.

OTHER

Contributor to *The American Heritage Book of Natural Wonders,* edited by Alvin M. Josephy, American Heritage Press, 1972. Contributor of numerous short stories, articles, and essays to popular periodicals, including *Atlantic, Audubon, Conde Nast Traveler, Esquire, Geo, Harper's, Nation, Newsweek, New Yorker, New York Review of Books,* and *Saturday Evening Post.*

ADAPTATIONS: At Play in the Fields of the Lord was produced as a motion picture by Saul Zaentz, directed by Hector Babenco, starring Aidan Quinn, Tom Berenger, Tom Waits, Kathy Bates, and John Lithgow, and released by Metro-Goldwyn-Mayer, 1992; *Men's Lives* was adapted by Joe Pintauro and was performed on Long Island at the Bay Street Theater Festival on July 28, 1992. *Adventure: Lost Man's River—An Everglades Journey with Peter Matthiessen* was produced by the Public Broadcasting System (PBS) in 1991.

SIDELIGHTS: Peter Matthiessen is widely considered one of the most important wilderness writers of the twentieth century. In fiction and nonfiction alike, he explores endangered natural environments and human cultures threatened by encroaching technology. As Conrad Silvert noted in *Literary Quarterly,* Matthiessen "is a naturalist, an anthropologist and an explorer of geographies and the human condition. He is also a rhapsodist who writes with wisdom and warmth as he applies scientific knowledge to the peoples and places he investigates. Works of lasting literary value and moral import have resulted." Matthiessen also writes of the inner explorations he has undertaken as a practitioner of Zen Buddhism. His 1979 National Book Award-winning memoir *The Snow Leopard* combines the account of a difficult Himalayan trek with spiritual autobiography and contemplations of mortality and transcendence. According to Terrance Des Pres in the *Washington Post Book World,* Matthiessen is "a visionary, but he is very hardminded as well, and his attention is wholly with abrupt detail. This allows him to render strangeness familiar, and much that is menial becomes strange, lustrous, otherworldly." *Dictionary of Literary Biography* contributor John L. Cobbs noted: "In fiction and in nonfiction, Peter Matthiessen is one of the shamans of literature. He puts his audience in touch with worlds and forces which transcend common experience."

Critics contend that despite his pessimistic forecasts for the future of natural areas and their inhabitants, Matthiessen imbues his work with descriptive writing of high quality. According to Vernon Young in the *Hudson Review,* Matthiessen "combines the exhaustive knowledge of the naturalist . . . with a poet's response to far-out landscapes. . . . When he pauses to relate one marvel to another and senses the particular merging into the general, his command of color, sound and substance conjures the resonance of the vast continental space." *New York Times Book Review* contributor Jim Harrison wrote that Matthiessen's prose has "a glistening, sculpted character to it. . . . The sense of beauty and mystery is indelible; not that you retain the specific information on natural history, but that you have had your brain, and perhaps the soul, prodded, urged, moved into a new dimension." Robert M. Adams offered a similar assessment in the *New York Review of Books.* Matthiessen, Adams wrote, "has dealt frequently and knowingly with natural scenery and wild life; he can sketch a landscape in a few vivid, unsentimental words, capture the sensations of entering a wild, windy Nepalese mountain village, and convey richly the strange, whinnying behavior of a herd of wild sheep. His prose is crisp, yet strongly appealing to the senses; it combines instinct with the feeling of adventure."

Although Matthiessen was born in New York City, he spent most of his youth in rural New York state and in Connecticut, where he attended the Hotchkiss School. His father, an architect, was a trustee of the National Audubon Society, and Matthiessen took an early interest in the fascinations of the natural world. "I had always been interested in nature," he remembered in *Publishers Weekly.* "My brother and I started with a passion for snakes, and he went into marine biology, while I took courses in [zoology and ornithology] right up through college." After service in the U.S. Navy, Matthiessen attended Yale University, spending his junior year at the Sorbonne in Paris. Having realized that a writing vocation drew him strongly, he began writing short stories, one of which won the prestigious *Atlantic* Prize in 1951. His short fiction would be collected in *On the River Styx, and Other Stories,* published in 1989. Matthiessen received his B.A. degree in 1950, and after teaching creative writing for a year at Yale, he returned to Paris.

When *Race Rock* was published in 1954, Matthiessen returned to the United States, where he continued to write while eking out a livelihood as a commercial fisherman on Long Island. Reflecting on the early stages of his writing career in the *Washington Post*, Matthiessen said: "I don't think I could have done my writing without the fishing. I needed something physical, something non-intellectual." The friendships Matthiessen formed with Long Island's fishermen enabled him to chronicle their vanishing lifestyle in his book *Men's Lives: The Surfmen and Baymen of the South Fork.*

Matthiessen embarked on his first lengthy journey in 1956. Loading his Ford convertible with textbooks, a shotgun, and a sleeping bag, he set off to visit every wildlife refuge in the United States. He admitted in *Publishers Weekly* that he brought more curiosity than scientific expertise to his quest. "I'm what the nineteenth century would call a generalist," he said. "I have a lot of slack information, and for my work it's been extremely helpful. I've always been interested in wildlife and wild places and wild people. I wanted to see the places that are disappearing." Nearly three years of work went into Matthiessen's encyclopedic *Wildlife in America*, published in 1959 to high critical acclaim. A commercial success as well, *Wildlife in America* initiated the second phase of Matthiessen's career, a period of two decades during which he undertook numerous expeditions to the wild places that captured his curiosity. Since 1959, he has supported himself solely by writing.

The popularity of Matthiessen's nonfiction somewhat overshadows his equally well-received fiction. Three of his first four books were novels, and critics found them commendable and promising works. In a *New York Herald Tribune Book Review* piece about *Race Rock*, Gene Baro commented: "Mr. Matthiessen's absorbing first novel, apart from being a good, well-paced story, offers the reader some depth and breadth of insight. For one thing, *Race Rock* is a vivid but complex study of evolving character; for another, it is a narrative of character set against a variously changed and changing social background. Mr. Matthiessen has succeeded in making from many strands of reality a close-textured book." *New York Times* contributor Sylvia Berkman observed that with *Race Rock*, Matthiessen "assumes immediate place as a writer of disciplined craft, perception, imaginative vigor and serious temperament. . . . He commands also a gift of flexible taut expression which takes wings at times into a lyricism beautifully modulated and controlled." Cobbs wrote in *Dictionary of Literary Biography* that

although *Race Rock* "does not anticipate the experimental techniques or exotic subject matter of Matthiessen's later fiction, the novel shows the author's early concern with fundamental emotions and with the tension between primitive vitality and the veneer of civilization."

Partisans and *Raditzer*, Matthiessen's second and third novels, garnered mixed reviews. According to M. L. Barrett in the *Library Journal*, the action in *Partisans*, "notable for its integrity and dramatic quality, is realized in real flesh-and-blood characters." *New York Times* contributor William Goyen stated: "The characters [in *Partisans*] seem only mouthpieces. They are not empowered by depth of dramatic conviction—or confusion. They do, however, impress one with this young author's thoughtful attempt to find answers to ancient and serious questions." Critics were more impressed with the title character in *Raditzer*, a man Cobbs found "both loathsome and believable." In the *Nation*, Terry Southern described *Raditzer*'s anti-hero as "a character distinct from those in literature, yet one who has somehow figured, if but hauntingly, in the lives of us all. It is, in certain ways, as though a whole novel had been devoted to one of [Nelson] Algren's sideline freaks, a grotesque and loathsome creature—yet seen ultimately, as sometimes happens in life, as but another human being." Cobbs concluded: "A skillful ear for dialect and an immediacy in sketching scenes of violence and depravity saved *Raditzer*'s moral weightiness from being wearisome, and the novel proved Matthiessen's ability to project his imagination into worlds far removed from that of the intellectual upper-middle class."

At Play in the Fields of the Lord enhanced Matthiessen's reputation as a fiction writer when it was issued in 1965; the novel would increase his renown still further after it was filmed as a motion picture directed by Hector Babenco in 1992. Set in a remote jungle village in the Amazon region, the work is, in the words of *New York Times Book Review* contributor Anatole Broyard, "one of those rare novels that satisfy all sorts of literary and intellectual hungers while telling a story that pulls you along out of sheer human kinship." The story recounts the misguided efforts of four American missionaries and an American Indian mercenary to "save" the isolated Niaruna tribe. Cobbs suggested that the book shows "a virtuosity and richness that few traditional novels exhibit. There is immense stylistic facility in shifting from surreal dream and drug sequences to scrupulous realistic descriptions of tropical nature." *Nation* contributor J. Mitchell Morse voiced some dissatisfaction with *At Play in the Fields of the Lord,* claiming that Matthiessen "obviously intended to write a serious novel, but . . . he has unconsciously condescended to cheapness." Conversely, Granville Hicks praised the work in the *Saturday Review:* "[Matthiessen's] evocation of the jungle is powerful, but no more remarkable than his insight into the people he portrays. He tells a fascinating story, and tells it well. . . . It is this firm but subtle evocation of strong feeling that gives Matthiessen's book its power over the imagination. Here, in an appallingly strange setting, he sets his drama of familiar aspirations and disappointments."

Matthiessen's 1975 novel, *Far Tortuga,* presents a stylistic departure from his previous fictional works. As Cobbs described it, "the deep penetration of character and psychology that characterized *At Play in the Fields of the Lord* yields to an almost disturbing objectivity in *Far Tortuga,* an absolute, realistic reproduction of surface phenomena—dialogue, noises, colors, shapes." In *Far Tortuga* Matthiessen creates a fictitious voyage of a Caribbean turtling schooner, using characters' conversations and spare descriptions of time, weather and place. "The radical format of *Far Tortuga* makes the novel a structural tour de force and assured a range of critical reaction," Cobbs noted. Indeed, the novel's use of intermittent blank spaces, wavy lines, ink blots, and unattributed dialogue has elicited varying critical responses. *Saturday Review* contributor Bruce Allen called the work an "adventurous failure. . . . It exudes a magnificent and paradoxical radiance; but beneath the beautiful surface [it lacks] anything that even remotely resembles a harmonious whole." Most reviewers expressed a far different opinion, however. *Newsweek*'s Peter S. Prescott praised the book as "a beautiful and original piece of work, a resonant, symbolical story of nine doomed men who dream of an earthly paradise as the world winds down around them. . . . This is a moving, impressive book, a difficult yet successful undertaking." And *New York Review of Books* contributor Thomas R. Edwards felt that the novel "turns out to be enthralling. Matthiessen uses his method not for self-display but for identifying and locating his characters. . . . What, despite appearances, does *not* happen in *Far Tortuga* is a straining by literary means to make more of an acutely observed life than it would make of itself."

Killing Mister Watson details, through the linked recollections of ten individuals, life in the Florida Ever-

glades a century ago. Basing his story on actual events, Matthiessen novelizes the life of Edgar J. (Jack) Watson, who settled in the area in 1892 and became a successful sugar-cane farmer. Tales of a dark past begin to circulate among his neighbors: tales of murder, of past wives, of illegitimate children. People are mysteriously murdered, and Watson's volatile temper and mean streak are common knowledge. Despite, or perhaps because of, his wealth, strong physical charisma, and the golden tongue of a born politician, Watson eventually becomes the object of resentment and even fear in his community; he is a man approached with submission. Eventually, Watson is killed by a group of his neighbors—shot with thirty-one bullets—upon returning to town after the hurricane of 1910. "Aggressive and gregarious, without ethics or introspection, both hugely talented and dangerously addicted to untamed power, Edgar Watson finally seems to represent great potential gone awry, or America at its worst," noted Ron Hansen in the *New York Times Book Review.* But the act of his murder remains incomprehensible: "since accounts of the man differ so radically, we are left, like the detective-historian, with more questions than answers, and with a sense of frustration," remarked Joyce Carol Oates in the *Washington Post Book World.* "The more we learn about Watson, this 'accursed' figure, the less we seem to know."

Lost Man's River picks up on the story of Edgar Watson and forms the second installment in the "Watson" trilogy. While *Killing Mr. Watson* approached the tale of the central figure through patching together many documentary sources, *Lost Man's River* retraces this forceful man's life and his death through the single perspective of his son Lucius. Lucius, an academic and self-proclaimed failure, is haunted by his father's legacy, and fifty years later he begins to research the circumstances surrounding his death and comes across a new piece of evidence. The quest leads him into a dark and complicated family past and a tragic history, which is tied, as always, to the exploitation of the wilderness. The *New York Times Book Review*'s Janet Burroway, while praising Matthiessen for his "perfect ear for the cadences of Southern speech," suggested that the complex maze of familial connections and impostures is "hard on the reader. . . . Our involvement depends very much on our sharing Lucius's determination to thread this maze, and *Lost Man's River* does not entirely persuade us to do so." However, Kit Miniclier, a critic for the *Denver Post,* commented that Matthiessen "pulls his readers through the darkness of those human souls occupying the morose, flickering light of the deep Florida Everglades." And a *Kirkus Reviews* writer described Matthiessen's accomplishment in these glowing terms: "Interweaving a lament for the lost wilderness, a shrewd, persuasive study of character, and a powerful meditation on the sources of American violence, Matthiessen has produced one of the best novels of recent years."

Matthiessen's novel *Bone by Bone,* published in 1999, completed the trilogy, with the brawling Florida planter telling his story in his own words. This time the novel also explores Watson's youth back in Civil War days with a vicious father who beats both him and his mother. "The roots of Watson's violence aren't just familial but societal, however, which is evident in the first pages of the book as the boy observes a murdered runaway slave with a mix of sorrow and cool indifference," wrote Barbara Hoffert in *Library Journal.* As Watson recounts his tale, readers see how Watson dreamed of recovering the family plantation after the Civil War and his success as a gifted planter. Also portrayed are the violence of the times and how Watson is ultimately brought down by both his own failings and the failings of those around him. A *Publishers Weekly* contributor called Watson "a monumental creation, and in bringing him and his amazing period to life with such vigor Matthiessen has created an unforgettable slice of deeply true and resonant American history." Not all reviewers praised the novel. John Skow, writing in *Time,* felt that *Bone by Bone* and its predecessor in the trilogy were "two novels too many." Hoffert, however, commented, "A rich, provocative novel, sometimes overwritten, but who cares?" Peter Filkins, writing in *World and I,* commented "that the two powers grappling for control of *Bone by Bone,* if not the trilogy as a whole, are history and psychology, two very different approaches to the interpretation of individual experience." Filkins went on to note, "In the end, this urge to regenerate oneself and the freedom to do so, even in its most reckless state, are at the core of both the American spirit and Matthiessen's ambitious effort to capture that spirit."

Human victims form the core of Matthiessen's later writings about the United States. In *Sal Si Puedes: Cesar Chavez and the New American Revolution,* Matthiessen chronicles the efforts of migrant worker Cesar Chavez to organize farm laborers in California. In a review for the *Nation,* Roy Borngartz expressed the opinion that in *Sal Si Puedes* Matthiessen "brings a great deal of personal attachment to his account of Chavez and his fellow organizers. . . . He makes no pretense of taking any objective stand between the farm workers and the growers. . . . But he is a good and honest reporter, and as far as he was able to get the growers to talk to him, he gives them their say. . . . Matthiessen is most skillful at bringing his people to life."

A similar sympathy for oppressed cultures provides the focus for *Indian Country* and *In the Spirit of Crazy Horse. New Republic* contributor Paul Zweig noted that the author "has two subjects in *Indian Country:* the destruction of America's last open land by the grinding pressure of big industry, in particular the energy industry; and the tragic struggle of the last people on the land to preserve their shrinking territories, and even more, to preserve the holy balance of their traditions, linked to the complex, fragile ecology of the land." According to David Wagoner in the *New York Times Book Review,* what makes *Indian Country* "most unusual and most valuable is its effort to infuse the inevitable anger and sorrow with a sense of immediate urgency, with prophetic warnings. . . . Few people could have been better equipped than Mr. Matthiessen to face this formidable task. He has earned the right to be listened to seriously on the ways in which tribal cultures can teach us to know ourselves and the earth."

The focus of *In the Spirit of Crazy Horse,* while still directed toward the historic treatment of Native Americans, is more journalistic in nature than *Indian Country.* In fact, the book itself was the subject of much press when it became the subject of a lawsuit the year after its publication. Claiming that they were libeled in the book, both an FBI agent and then-governor of South Dakota, William Janklow, sued Matthiessen and Viking, the book's publisher, for a combined forty-nine-million dollars. While the two lawsuits were eventually thrown out by a federal appeals court, the actions of the two men effectively kept the book out of circulation for several years. A reading of the work makes their efforts understandable. *In the Spirit of Crazy Horse* presents an effective indictment of the FBI and other government offices in crushing the efforts of the American Indian Movement (AIM) to recover sacred Sioux lands illegally confiscated by the U.S. government. The discovery of uranium and other mineral deposits on the land prompted federal officials to go to desperate lengths, including, Matthiessen claims, framing AIM activist Leonard Peltier for murder. *In the Spirit of Crazy Horse* was reissued by Matthiessen in 1991, after new evidence came to light further reinforcing the author's contentions.

The Snow Leopard is perhaps the book that best integrates many of Matthiessen's themes—the abundance and splendor of nature, the fragility of the environment, the fascinations of a foreign culture—with contemplations of a more spiritual sort. The book is an autobiographical account of a journey Matthiessen took, in the company of wildlife biologist George Schaller, to a remote part of Nepal. *New York Times* columnist Anatole Broyard wrote of Matthiessen: "On this voyage he travels to the outer limits of the world and the inner limits of the self. . . . When he looks in as well as outward, the two landscapes complement one another." Jim Harrison likewise noted in a review in the *Nation:* "Running concurrent to the outward journey in *The Snow Leopard* is an equally torturous inward journey, and the two are balanced to the extent that neither overwhelms the other." As part of that "inward journey," Matthiessen remembers his second wife's death from cancer and opens himself to the spiritual nourishment of Zen. Terrance Des Pres, in the *Washington Post Book World,* suggested that as a result of these meditations, Matthiessen "has expressed, with uncommon candor and no prospect of relief, a longing which keeps the soul striving and alert in us all."

The Snow Leopard elicited wide critical respect, earning a second National Book Award for general nonfiction in 1980. In the *Saturday Review,* Zweig commented that the book "contains many . . . passages, in which the naturalist, the spiritual apprentice, and the writer converge simply and dramatically." *Atlantic Monthly* contributor Phoebe-Lou Adams concluded of the work: "It is as though [Matthiessen] looked simultaneously through a telescope and a microscope, and his great skill as a writer enables the reader to share this double vision of a strange and beautiful country." As a conclusion to his review, Des Pres called *The Snow Leopard* "a book fiercely felt and magnificently written, in which timelessness and 'modern time' are made to touch and join."

Though Matthiessen writes about Zen in *The Snow Leopard* and in *Nine-Headed Dragon River: Zen Journals 1969-1982,* he still expresses reservations

about offering his personal philosophies for public perusal. "One is always appalled by the idea of wearing your so-called religion on your sleeve," he told *Publishers Weekly.* "I never talked about Zen much. . . . If people come along and want to talk about Zen, that's wonderful, but I don't want to brandish it. It's just a quiet little practice, not a religion . . . just a way of seeing the world. . . . And I find myself very comfortable with it." He elaborated briefly: "Zen is a synonym for life, that's all. Zen practice is life practice. If you can wake up and look around you, if you can knock yourself out of your customary way of thinking and simply see how really miraculous and extraordinary everything around you is, that's Zen."

Matthiessen has focused his more recent writings primarily on nature and the human relationship with the surrounding environment. In *Tigers in the Snow,* the author explores the realm of the Siberian tiger while recounting a research project that began in 1990 with photographer Maurice Hornocker, director of the Hornocker Wildlife Institute. The research was conducted as a joint Russian-American venture, and Matthiessen's account of the effort to save this endangered species is accompanied by Hornocker's photographs. Edelle Marie Schaefer, writing in *Library Journal,* pointed out that the book has a "very readable, engaging text" and called it "essential reading for everyone interested in wildlife and the preservation of endangered species." *Booklist* contributor Nancy Bent noted that Matthiessen "brings his lyrical eye to an account of the plight of the Amur (or Siberian) tiger."

In *The Birds of Heaven: Travel with Cranes,* published in 2002, the author turns his focus on cranes as he journeys on five continents in search of the fifteen known species of cranes. Matthiessen discusses the growing threats to these birds' existence by an increasingly industrialized world. Nevertheless, as pointed out by a reviewer writing in *Whole Earth,* "This isn't just a litany of losses. Matthiessen celebrates scientists and conservationists struggling to save the cranes." Kevin Krajick, writing in the *Smithsonian,* commented, "The real intrigue of this, Matthiessen's twenty-eighth book, is in his evocation of people and landscapes." The reviewer went on to note, "The crane connection is not always obvious, but with Matthiessen questions of life and death are sources of eloquent meditations." *Time International* contributor Bryan Walsh said, "In addition to the marvelous flow of his prose, Matthiessen's greatest gift as a writer may be his ability to combine precise observation with a radiant sense of spiritual wonder. Despite a lifetime of globe-trotting, his remarkable talent for conveying the freshness of encounters with new places is undiminished."

Despite being in his seventies, Matthiessen showed no signs of slowing down as he traveled to Antarctica and wrote about his voyage through the islands surrounding Antarctica in *End of the Earth: Voyages to the White Continent,* published in 2003. In addition to describing the wildlife and environment that he encountered, Matthiessen also recounted much of the region's history, including stories about the pioneers and adventurers of the past who traveled to the region. Matthiessen and the crew also encountered their own adventure as they suddenly found themselves in the midst of an unrelenting hurricane that battered their ship and injured, in some way, everybody on board. A *Publishers Weekly* contributor found Matthiessen's descriptions to be "antiseptic." Donna Seaman, however, noted in *Booklist* that the author "describes with arresting lyricism the spiritual cleansing one experiences in this pristine, wind-scoured kingdom of ice." In a review in *Sports Illustrated,* Stephen J. Bodio commented, "*End of the Earth* is a splendid book, a celebration of Antarctica and an eloquent evocation of its appeal."

BIOGRAPHICAL AND CRITICAL SOURCES:

BOOKS

Contemporary Literary Criticism, Gale (Detroit, MI), Volume 7, 1977, Volume 11, 1979, Volume 32, 1985, Volume 64, 1991.

Dictionary of Literary Biography, Volume 6: *American Novelists since World War II,* second series, Gale (Detroit, MI), 1980.

Dowie, William, *Peter Matthiessen,* Twayne (Boston, MA), 1991.

Nicholas, D., *Peter Matthiessen: A Bibliography,* Orirana (Canoga Park, CA), 1980.

Parker, William, editor, *Men of Courage: Stories of Present-Day Adventures in Danger and Death,* Playboy Press, 1972.

Styron, William, *This Quiet Dust and Other Writings,* Random House (New York, NY), 1982.

PERIODICALS

Atlantic Monthly, June, 1954; March, 1971; November, 1972; June, 1975; September, 1978, Phoebe-Lou Adams, review of *The Snow Leopard;* March, 1983.

Birder's World, August, 2002, Christopher Cokinos, review of *The Birds of Heaven: Travels with Cranes,* p. 58.

Bloomsbury Review, September-October, 1990, pp. 22, 24.

Booklist, January 1-15, 1996, p. 779; February 15, 1999, Benjamin Segedin, review of *Bone by Bone,* p. 1004; December 1, 1999, Nancy Bent, review of *Tigers in the Snow,* p. 660; September 15, 2003, Donna Seaman, review of *End of the Earth: Voyages to the White Continent,* p. 179.

Chicago Tribune Book World, April 5, 1981; March 13, 1983; June 24, 1990, pp. 1, 5; July 28, 1991, pp. 6-7.

Christian Science Monitor, March 11, 1983.

Denver Post, December 7, 1997, Kit Miniclier, "Killing 'gators, running guns, smuggling drugs," review of *Lost Man's River,* p. G5.

Hudson Review, winter, 1975-76; winter, 1981-82.

Kirkus Reviews, September 15, 1997, review of *Lost Man's River.*

Library Journal, August, 1955, M. L. Barrett, review of *Partisans;* March 15, 1999, Barbara Hoffert, review of *Bone by Bone,* p. 110; January, 2000, Edell Marie Schaefer, review of *Tigers in the Snow,* p. 152.

Literary Quarterly, May 15, 1975.

Los Angeles Times, March 22, 1979; November 16, 1990, p. E4; May 30, 1991, p. E1; November 8, 1992, p. L9.

Los Angeles Times Book Review, May 10, 1981; March 6, 1983; May 18, 1986; August 24, 1986; May 14, 1989, pp. 2, 11; July 8, 1990, pp. 1, 5; July 28, 1991, p. 4; December 6, 1992, p. 36.

Maclean's, August 13, 1990, p. 59; July 22, 1991, p. 41.

Nation, February 25, 1961, Terry Southern, review of *Raditzer;* December 13, 1965, J. Mitchell Morse, review of *At Play in the Fields of the Lord;* June 1, 1970, Roy Borngartz, review of *Sal Si Puedes: Cesar Chavez and the New American Revolution;* May 31, 1975; September 16, 1978, Jim Harrison, review of *The Snow Leopard.*

New Republic, June 7, 1975; September 23, 1978; March 7, 1983; June 4, 1984; November 5, 1990, Paul Zweig, review of *Indian Country,* pp. 43-45.

Newsweek, April 26, 1971; May 19, 1975, Peter S. Prescott, review of *Far Tortuga;* September 11, 1978; December 17, 1979; April 27, 1981; March 28, 1983; August 11, 1986; June 11, 1990, p. 63.

New Yorker, May 19, 1975; April 11, 1983; June 4, 1984.

New York Herald Tribune Book Review, April 4, 1954, Gene Baro, review of *Race Rock.*

New York Review of Books, December 23, 1965; January 4, 1968; August 31, 1972; January 25, 1973; August 7, 1975, Thomas R. Edwards, review of *Far Tortuga;* September 28, 1978; April 14, 1983; September 27, 1984; January 31, 1991, p. 18.

New York Times, April 4, 1954, Sylvia Berkman, review of *Race Rock;* October 2, 1955, William Goyen, review of *Partisans;* November 8, 1965; April 23, 1971; August 24, 1978; March 19, 1979; May 2, 1981; March 5, 1983; June 19, 1986; October 11, 1986; July 7, 1990, p. A16; August 22, 1991; July 26, 1992.

New York Times Book Review, April 4, 1954; October 2, 1955; November 22, 1959; October 15, 1961; November 18, 1962; November 7, 1965, Anatole Broyard, review of *At Play in the Fields of the Lord;* December 3, 1967; February 1, 1970; November 26, 1972; May 25, 1975; May 29, 1977; August 13, 1978; November 26, 1978; May 17, 1981; March 6, 1983; July 29, 1984; June 22, 1986; May 14, 1989, David Wagoner, review of *Indian Country,* p. 11; June 24, 1990, Ron Hansen, review of *Killing Mister Watson,* p. 7; August 18, 1991, p. 3; December 6, 1992, p. 52; December 3, 1995, p. 49; November 23, 1997, Janet Burroway, review of *Lost Man's River,* p. 16.

New York Times Magazine, June 10, 1990, pp. 30, 42, 94-96.

Progressive, April, 1990, pp. 28-29.

Publishers Weekly, May 9, 1986; September 1, 1989, p. 8; November 9, 1990, p. 12; March 15, 1999, review of *Bone by Bone,* p. 47; September 1, 2003, review of *End of the Earth,* p. 79.

Saturday Review, April 10, 1954; November 6, 1965, Granville Hicks, review of *At Play in the Fields of the Lord;* November 25, 1967; March 14, 1970; October 28, 1972; June 28, 1975, Bruce Allen, review of *Far Tortuga;* August, 1978, Paul Zweig, review of *The Snow Leopard;* April, 1981.

Smithsonian, March, 2002, Kevin Drajick, review of *The Birds of Heaven: Travels with Cranes,* p. 108.

Spectator, June 13, 1981; May 23, 1992, p. 34.

Sports Illustrated, December 22, 2003, Stephen J. Bodio, review of *End of the Earth,* p. A10.

Time, May 26, 1975; August 7, 1978; March 28, 1983; July 7, 1986; July 16, 1990, p. 82; January 11, 1993, pp. 42-43; May 17, 1999, John Skow, review of *Bone by Bone,* p. 89.

Time International, March 11, 2002, Bryan Walsh, review of *The Birds of Heaven: Travels with Cranes,* p. 52.

Times Literary Supplement, October 23, 1981; March 21, 1986, p. 299; September 22, 1989, p. 1023; August 31, 1990; July 17, 1992, p. 6.

Vanity Fair, December, 1991, p. 114.

Washington Post, December 13, 1978.

Washington Post Book World, August 20, 1978; April 19, 1981; March 27, 1983; May 20, 1984; June 29, 1986; June 24, 1990, Joyce Carol Oates, review of *Killing Mister Watson,* p. 5; July 14, 1991, p. 1.

Whole Earth, spring, 2002, review of *The Birds of Heaven: Travels with Cranes,* p. 95.

Wilson Library Bulletin, March, 1964.

World and I, October, 1999, review of *Bone by Bone,* p. 276.*

*   *   *

MAYS, John Bentley 1941(?)-

PERSONAL: Born c. 1941, in Louisiana; son of John B. (a plantation owner) and Anne (Smith) Mays; married Margaret Cannon (a writer and columnist); children: Erin. *Education:* Attended University of Rochester, 1967-68. *Religion:* Anglican. *Hobbies and other interests:* Rooftop gardening, architecture, the music of Richard Wagner.

ADDRESSES: Office—Calumet College, York University, 4700 Keele St., North York, Ontario M3J 1P3, Canada. *Agent*—Jan Whitford, Westwood Creative Artists, 94 Harboard St., Toronto, Ontario M5S 1G6, Canada.

CAREER: York University, Calumet College, North York, Ontario, Canada, teacher, beginning 1971.

MEMBER: International PEN, Toronto Wagner Society.

AWARDS, HONORS: Canadian National Newspaper Award, 1983, for criticism; Canadian National Magazine Awards Foundation, gold medal for science and medicine reporting, silver medal for personal journalism, and president's medal for best article to appear in a Canadian periodical, all 1993, for the article "In the Jaws of the Black Dogs," and gold medal for critical writing, 1995, for the article "Night and Day: David Urban"; prize from Toronto Historical Board, 1994, for *Emerald City: Toronto Visited;* award for talking book of the year, nonfiction category, Canadian National Institute for the Blind, 1995, for *In the Jaws of the Black Dogs: A Memoir of Depression.*

WRITINGS:

The Spiral Stair, Coach House Press (Toronto, Ontario, Canada), 1977.

Emerald City: Toronto Visited, Vintage (Toronto, Ontario, Canada), 1994.

In the Jaws of the Black Dogs: A Memoir of Depression, Vintage/Penguin (Toronto, Ontario, Canada), 1995.

Power in the Blood: Land, Memory, and a Southern Family, HarperCollins (New York, NY), 1997.

Arrivals: Stories from the History of Ontario, Penguin (Toronto, Ontario, Canada), 2003.

Visual arts critic and columnist, *Globe and Mail* (Toronto, Ontario, Canada), 1980—; cultural critic-at-large for newspapers. Contributing editor, *Open Letter,* 1975-80.

SIDELIGHTS: John Bentley Mays, a longtime resident of Toronto, is an American whose recent books have dealt with the themes of place, person, and roots. A man of wide interests, Mays has taught at Calumet College in York University and is a visual arts critic for the Toronto *Globe and Mail.*

In *Emerald City: Toronto Visited,* Mays collected and extended seventy-four essays originally written as newspaper columns. Reviewer Brian Fawcett, in *Books in Canada,* said that, with this book, Mays had invented a new literary genre, "somewhere between urban travel writing and criticism." The essays consider abandoned industrial parks, rooftop gardens, rundown alleyways, buried waterways, and the imprint glaciers have left on the land, among other things. In the *Canadian Book Review Annual,* Steve Pitt commented that the book is "a fine guide for people who have a hard time seeing the city for the buildings."

Lisa Schmidt declared in *Quill and Quire* that *Emerald City* transforms Toronto "into an old friend one comes to know again, after a separation of many years."

In 1993 Mays wrote a candid magazine article about his experience with depression. The large number of responses from readers prompted him to write *In the Jaws of the Black Dogs: A Memoir of Depression.* According to *Quill and Quire* contributor Martha Harron, the title comes from Winston Churchill's characterization of the depression which hounded him as "the black dog." Mays interweaves excerpts from thirty years worth of journal entries and contemporary reflections on his life at the time of the entries. He traces his feelings of numbness and isolation, the hallmarks of depression, to his father's death when he was six and his mother's when he was eleven. Seeing, as Mays described in his book, his mother at the end, lying "in a stench of cancerous rot," he found her death so shocking that he felt no sorrow.

Much of *In the Jaws of the Black Dogs* describes Mays' various therapies. He notes his different attempts to cure his depression, and his final discovery of Prozac. At first, Mays thinks it banishes his depression, but later he realizes that for him, its effects are less than absolute. His continuing struggle with the disease makes him wary of therapists who enthusiastically promote Prozac as the answer, and Mays is critical of writers who suggest that depression is a sign of moral decay. Scott McKeen of the *Edmonton Journal Online* quoted Mays as saying that at the end, "a certain way of negotiating one's way through and around depression is possible; but that is all."

Mays' long residence in Toronto was interrupted when his elderly aunt Vandalia died in Louisiana, passing on to him his memorabilia-and memory-filled childhood home. Once there, Mays decided to rediscover his southern roots. The book resulting from this quest, *Power in the Blood: Land, Memory, and a Southern Family,* traces his American—but not necessarily "southern"—lineage back to 1609 when an Anglican minister named William Mays arrived at Chesapeake Bay. Mays' searches took him to Virginia, South Carolina, Mississippi, and Louisiana, where he found significance in tombstone epitaphs and family snapshots. Of Mays' writing, Phyllis Grosskurth, in *Books in Canada,* said, "He has often opened my eyes . . . I look forward to his views on many things."

BIOGRAPHICAL AND CRITICAL SOURCES:

BOOKS

Mays, John Bentley, *In the Jaws of the Black Dogs: A Memoir of Depression,* Vintage/Penguin (Toronto, Ontario, Canada), 1995.

PERIODICALS

Books in Canada, November, 1994, Brian Fawcett, review of *Emerald City: Toronto Visited,* pp. 42-43; September, 1995, Phyllis Grosskurth, review of *Power in the Blood: Land, Memory, and a Southern Family,* pp. 28-30; March, 2003, Clara Thomas, review of *Arrivals: Stories from the History of Ontario,* pp. 13-14.
Canadian Book Review Annual, 1994, Steve Pitt, review of *Emerald City.*
Maclean's, October 23, 1995, p. 69.
Quill and Quire, January, 1995, Lisa Schmidt, review of *Emerald City,* p. 31; September, 1995, Martha Harron, review of *In the Jaws of the Black Dogs: A Memoir of Depression,* p. 63.

ONLINE

Bookpage, http://www.bookpage.com/ (January 26, 1998).
Edmonton Journal Online, http://www.southam.com/edmontonjournal/archives (January 26, 1998), Scott McKeen, review of *In the Jaws of the Black Dogs: A Memoir of Depression.**

*   *   *

McCOURT, Frank 1930-

PERSONAL: Born August 19, 1930, in Brooklyn, NY; son of Malachy and Angela (a homemaker; maiden name, Sheehan) McCourt; married; wife's name, Alberta (marriage ended); second marriage ended; married Ellen Frey (a television industry publicist); children (first marriage): Margie. *Education:* New York University, B.A., M.A.

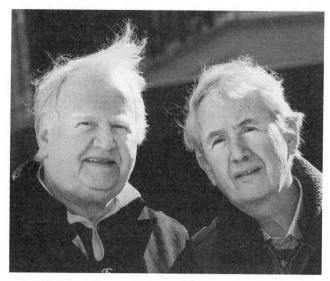

Frank McCourt (right) with his brother Malachy

ADDRESSES: Home—Roxbury, CT. *Agent*—c/o Author Mail, Simon & Schuster, 1230 Avenue of the Americas, New York, NY 10020.

CAREER: Writer. New York Public School system, teacher at various schools, including McKee Vocational and Technical on Staten Island and Peter Stuyvesant High School. Worked in Ireland and New York, NY, as a messenger, houseman, barkeeper, and laborer; costarred (with his brother) in vaudeville act; member of Irish Repertory Theatre; performer in plays, including *A Couple of Blaguards* and *The Irish . . . and How They Got That Way. Military service:* U.S. Army; served in Germany during the Korean War.

AWARDS, HONORS: Los Angeles Times Book Award, National Book Critics Circle Award in biography/autobiography, *Salon* Book Award, American Library Association Award, and *Boston Book Review*'s Anne Rea Jewell Nonfiction Prize, all 1996, Pulitzer Prize in biography, and American Booksellers Association Book of the Year, both 1997, all for *Angela's Ashes;* named Irish American of the Year, *Irish American Magazine,* 1998.

WRITINGS:

Angela's Ashes: A Memoir, Scribner (New York, NY), 1996.
The Irish . . . and How They Got That Way (play), produced by Irish Repertory Theatre, 1997.

'Tis: A Memoir (sequel to *Angela's Ashes*), Scribner (New York, NY), 1999.

(With others) *Yeats Is Dead: A Mystery by Fifteen Irish Writers,* Knopf (New York, NY), 2001.

(With Malachy McCourt) *Ireland Ever,* photographs by Jill Freedman, Harry N. Abrams (New York, NY), 2003.

Also author, with brother, of musical review *A Couple of Blaguards.*

ADAPTATIONS: Angela's Ashes was adapted by Laura Jones and Alan Parker into a film of the same name, directed by Parker, Paramount Pictures, 1999. *'Tis* was recorded on audiocassette.

SIDELIGHTS: Frank McCourt taught writing in the New York Public School system for several years, but waited until he had retired to pen his first book, 1996's award-winning *Angela's Ashes: A Memoir,* which tells the story of McCourt's poverty-stricken childhood in Ireland. The critically acclaimed volume remained on bestseller lists for more than two years, and garnered McCourt both a National Book Critics Circle Award and the Pulitzer Prize. Three years later, McCourt followed up with a sequel, *'Tis: A Memoir.* Robert Sterling Gingher, who described McCourt in *World* as "a consummate storyteller," noted of the author's autobiographical books: "We rarely acknowledge the magical power and mystery of the word, spoken or written, but McCourt's memoirs show that in nearly unimaginable seasons of extreme need, stories can keep us and our very souls alive."

McCourt was born in 1930 in Brooklyn, New York, to parents who had recently immigrated from Ireland. When McCourt was about four years old, his father, Malachy, decided to move the family back to Ireland. As outlined in *Angela's Ashes,* the elder McCourt had experienced difficulties keeping a job in the United States due to a drinking problem. He had even greater difficulties once he returned to his native country. Malachy occasionally found work as a laborer in the economically-depressed Irish town of Limerick, but would often spend an entire Friday night drinking in a pub. As a result, he would be too sick to show up for work on Saturday; ultimately he would be fired.

Between Malachy's sporadic jobs, the family would exist on the scant Irish version of welfare, but Malachy would often spend this meager amount entirely upon

alcohol. In his book, McCourt recounts all of this, as well as his mother Angela's efforts to keep the family alive and together by economizing, borrowing from family, and begging from local Catholic parish charity. He describes how his baby sister and two twin brothers died of disease because their family was too poor to ensure proper sanitation and adequate medical care. McCourt himself contracted typhoid as a child and had to be hospitalized for several weeks. There, from the books available in the hospital, he first encountered the works of English playwright William Shakespeare, and he developed a love of literature that would later guide his work.

Several critics reviewing *Angela's Ashes* concluded that McCourt rightfully placed the blame for his family's poverty upon his father. However, McCourt also details his father's sobriety during the work week. "I'm up with him early every morning with the whole world asleep," McCourt recalls in *Angela's Ashes.* "He lights the fire and makes the tea and sings to himself or reads the paper to me in a whisper that won't wake up the rest of the family." Michiko Kakutani of the *New York Times* surmised that "there is not a trace of bitterness or resentment in *Angela's Ashes.*" Devon McNamara reported in the *Christian Science Monitor* that "what has surprised critic and reader alike is how a childhood of poverty, illness, alcoholism, and struggle, in an environment not far removed from the Ireland of [eighteenth-century English writer Jonathan] Swift's 'A Modest Proposal,' came to be told with such a rich mix of hilarity and pathos." McCourt himself told McNamara: "I couldn't have written this book fifteen years ago because I was carrying a lot of baggage around . . . and I had attitudes and these attitudes had to be softened. I had to get rid of them, I had to become, as it says in the Bible, as a child." He explained further: "The child started to speak in this book. And that was the only way to do it, without judging."

Angela's Ashes also discusses McCourt's return to the United States at the age of nineteen, with one of his surviving brothers. The pair made a living with their own vaudeville show for a time, before Frank McCourt turned to teaching. "The reader of this stunning memoir can only hope," declared Kakutani, "that Mr. McCourt will set down the story of his subsequent adventures in America in another book. *Angela's Ashes* is so good it deserves a sequel." Denis Donoghue, discussing the book in the *New York Times Book*

Review, asserted: "For the most part, his style is that of an Irish-American raconteur, honorably voluble and engaging. He is aware of his charm but doesn't disgracefully linger upon it. Induced by potent circumstances, he has told his story, and memorable it is." John Elson, in *Time,* wrote favorably of *Angela's Ashes* as well, observing that "like an unpredicted glimmer of midwinter sunshine, cheerfulness keeps breaking into this tale of Celtic woe." Paula Chin, in *People,* hailed it as "a splendid memoir," while Mc-Namara concluded it to be "a book of splendid humanity."

Angela's Ashes ends with McCourt's return to the United States on the boat *Irish Oak.* The last word of the book is nineteen-year-old McCourt's statement "'Tis," a response he made to a crew member remarking on the greatness of America. Thus, *'Tis,* McCourt's 1999 memoir, begins exactly where *Angela's Ashes* leaves off. The book chronicles the author's struggles and successes during his first years in the United States. McCourt describes his first jobs, including cleaning at the Biltmore Hotel, hauling cargo, and cleaning toilets at a diner, gradually moving on to his time in the military during the Korean War and his unconventional education at New York University. Malcolm Jones described *'Tis* in *Newsweek:* "Superficially, *'Tis* is the classic immigrant's tale. . . . [A] melting-pot story where nothing melts. . . . But more than that, it is the story of a man finding two great vocations—teaching and storytelling—and he wins our trust by never touching up his memories."

L. S. Klepp concluded in *Entertainment Weekly* that, although unequal to *Angela's Ashes* in "concentrated power," *'Tis* "has the same clairvoyant eye for quirks of class, character, and fate, and also a distinct picaresque quality. It's a quest for an America of wholesome Hollywood happiness that doesn't exist, and it's about the real America—rendered with comic affection—that McCourt discovers along the way." Similarly, *Library Journal* reviewer Gordon Blackwell asserted, "McCourt's entertaining *'Tis* . . . recounts candidly, and with humor where appropriate, his return to the United States." "In *'Tis,* [McCourt] must live between the tormenting reality of [the American] dream and the sad past of his soul's memory," stated Gingher in *World,* adding: "The book's lyrical power of reclamation has everything to do with its author's ability to live between these worlds, which in some profound way are only vivid and intelligible in terms

of each other." John Bemrose related in *Maclean's* that "McCourt ultimately clambers up the ladder of success. But much of *'Tis*'s charm lies in his account of how he almost didn't make it." Mary Ann Gwinn complimented in a *Seattle Times Online* review, "With *Angela's Ashes* and [*'Tis*] McCourt establishes himself a Dickens for our time, a writer who can peel the many layers of society like an onion and reveal the core. . . . *'Tis* seldom loses its woeful tone, but it never loses its mordant humor, and it's struck through with a memory undimmed by the golden forgetfulness of nostalgia."

In addition to his memoirs, McCourt has written and performed in stage productions. He and one of his brothers created a musical review called *A Couple of Blaguards.* The duo has also spearheaded *The Irish . . . and How They Got That Way,* a play first produced in September, 1997, at the Irish Repertory Theatre. *Back Stage* contributor Elais Stimac described *The Irish . . . and How They Got That Way* as "a patchwork quilt of songs, stories, and celebration of the history of Irish in America." Its coverage of "all the major events over the past several centuries, as well as anecdotal sidebars . . . are sure to enlighten; and entertain."

BIOGRAPHICAL AND CRITICAL SOURCES:

BOOKS

McCourt, Frank, *Angela's Ashes,* Scribner (New York, NY), 1996.
McCourt, Frank, *'Tis: A Memoir,* Scribner (New York, NY), 1999.

PERIODICALS

Back Stage, January 14, 2000, Elais Stimac, review of *The Irish . . . and How They Got That Way,* p. 37.
Booklist, August, 1999, Donna Seaman, review of *'Tis,* p. 1981; April 1, 2000, Karen Harris, review of *'Tis* (audio recording), p. 1482.
Christian Science Monitor, December 4, 1996, p. 13; March 21, 1997, p. 4.
Commonweal, June 19, 1998, Daniel M. Murtaugh, review of *Angela's Ashes,* p. 28; October 22, 1999, Molly Finn, "Two for Two," p. 24.

Economist, February 27, 1999, review of *'Tis,* p. 83.

Entertainment Weekly, January 22, 1999, Andrew Essex, review of *'Tis,* p. 35; September 24, 1999, L. S. Klepp, "'Tis a Beaut: *Angela's Ashes* Is a Pretty Tough Act to Follow but Frank McCourt Dazzles Us Once Again in *'Tis,* the Enchanting Story of His Adventures—and Misadventures—in America," p. 139.

Irish Literary Supplement, spring, 2000, Vivian Valvano Lynch, "Ashes through a Glass Not Darkly," pp. 23-24.

Kirkus Reviews, July 1, 1996, review of *Angela's Ashes.*

Library Journal, October 15, 1999, Robert Moore, review of *'Tis,* p. 78; February 1, 2000, Gordon Blackwell, review of *'Tis* (audio recording), p. 132; May 1, 2000, Gloria Maxwell, review of *'Tis* (audio recording), p. 168.

Maclean's, October 18, 1999, John Bemrose, "From Emerald Isle to Green with Envy: A Dreamer Tussles with the American Dream," p. 93.

McCall's, September, 1998, Donna Boetig, "Frank McCourt's Lessons for Parents," p. 110.

Nation, July 27, 1998, Patrick Smith, "What Memoir Forgets," p. 30.

National Review, October 26, 1998, p. 40; September 27, 1999, Pete Hamill, review of *'Tis,* p. 54.

New Criterion, December, 1999, Brooke Allen, review of *Angela's Ashes* and *'Tis,* p. 71.

New Republic, November 1, 1999, R. F. Forester, "'Tisn't the Million-Dollar Blarney of the McCourts," p. 29.

Newsweek, August 30, 1999, review of *'Tis,* p. 58; September 27, 1999, Malcolm Jones, "An Immigrant's Tale: In *'Tis* Frank McCourt Finds America and Himself," p. 66.

New York, September 27, 1999, Walter Kirn, review of *'Tis,* p. 82.

New York Review of Books, May 25, 2000, Julian Moynahan, "Not-So-Great Expectations," pp. 51-53.

New York Times, September 17, 1996, Michiko Kakutani, review of *Angela's Ashes.*

New York Times Book Review, September 15, 1996, Denis Donoghue, review of *Angela's Ashes,* p. 13; September 14, 1999; Michiko Kakutani, "For an Outsider, It's Mostly Sour Grapes in the Land of Milk and Honey."

People, October 21, 1996, Paula Chin, review of *Angela's Ashes,* p. 42; October 4, 1999, Kim Hubbard, review of *'Tis,* p. 51.

Publishers Weekly, October 4, 1999, review of *'Tis* (audio recording), p. 37; October 4, 1999, Daisy Maryles and Dick Donahue, "McCourt Leads the Court," p. 19; November 1, 1999, review of *'Tis,* p. 51.

Time, September 23, 1996, John Elson, review of *Angela's Ashes,* p. 74; October 4, 1999, Paul Gray, "Frank's Ashes: The Sequel to a Beloved Best Seller Is Glum Going," p. 104.

Wall Street Journal, September 17, 1999, Hugh Kenner, "Alas, 'Taint," p. W11; June 6, 2000, Joseph T. Hallinan, "Whose Life Is It, Anyway? *Angela's Ashes* Suit May Help to Decide; Financial Backers of Old Play by the McCourt Brothers Say They're Due Royalties," p. B1.

World, April, 2000, Robert Sterling Gingher, "Out of the Ashes: The Voice of a Child in Limerick Returns Transformed into That of a Young Man Finding His Place in New York City," pp. 255-261.

World of Hibernia, winter, 1999, John Boland, review of *'Tis,* p. 156.

Writer's Digest, February, 1999, Donna Elizabeth Boetig, "Out of the Ashes," p. 18.

ONLINE

Independent, http://www.independent.co.uk/ (September 18, 1999), Mary Flanagan, "From a Town of Ashes to a City of Gilt."

Newshour Online, http://www.pbs.org/ (March 17, 1999), Terence Smith, interview with McCourt.

Salon.com, http://www.salon.com/ (August 31, 1999), Andrew O'Hehire, "In His Follow-up to Angela's Ashes Frank McCourt Confronts the Indignities of Immigrant Life."

Seattle Times Online, http://www.seattletimes.com/ (September 19, 1999), Mary Ann Gwinn, review of *'Tis.**

*   *   *

MEARS, Walter R(obert) 1935-

PERSONAL: Born January 11, 1935, in Lynn, MA; son of Edward Lewis and Edythe Emily (Campbell) Mears; married Sally Danton, December 28, 1956 (died, December, 1962); married Joyce Marie Lund, August 4, 1963 (divorced, 1983); children: (first marriage) Pamela (deceased), Walter Robert (deceased); (second marriage) Stephanie Joy, Susan Marie. *Education:* Middlebury College, B.A., 1956.

ADDRESSES: Agent—c/o Author Mail, Andrews McMeel Universal, 4520 Main St., Kansas City, MO 64111-7701.

CAREER: Associated Press, New York, NY, journalist in Boston, MA, 1956, correspondent in Montpelier, VT, 1956-60, state house correspondent in Boston, 1960-61, journalist in Washington, DC, 1961-69, chief political writer, 1969-72, assistant chief of Washington bureau, 1973-74, special correspondent, 1975, chief of Washington bureau, 1977-83, vice president, beginning 1978, executive editor, beginning 1983; retired.

MEMBER: National Press Club, Phi Beta Kappa, Delta Kappa Epsilon, Burning Tree Club, Gridiron Club.

AWARDS, HONORS: Pulitzer Prize for national reporting, 1977, for coverage of 1976 presidential campaigns; Litt.D., Middlebury College, 1977.

WRITINGS:

(With John Chancellor) *The News Business,* Harper (New York, NY), 1983.
(With John Chancellor) *The New News Business: A Guide to Writing and Reporting,* HarperPerennial (New York, NY), 1995.
Deadlines Past: My Forty Years of Presidential Campaigning; A Reporter's Story, Andrews McMeel Universal (Kansas City, MO), 2003.

SIDELIGHTS: Walter R. Mears is one of the communication field's most respected journalists. He has many years of experience covering political events in Washington, DC, and received a Pulitzer Prize in 1977 for coverage of the 1976 presidential campaigns. His book, *The News Business,* written with fellow journalist John Chancellor, is a step-by-step account of how news is processed from an actual occurrence to its presentation in the media. Harrison E. Salisbury, reviewing the book in the *Los Angeles Times Book Review,* declared: "Nothing could be more common-sensical, more enlightening than this simple, short book. Nor could anything be more effective than this

straight-arrow, anecdote-laden account in laying to rest the dark, portentous images of those who believe the media to be the devil's kitchen." He praised Mears and Chancellor for their "coolly understated" points.

BIOGRAPHICAL AND CRITICAL SOURCES:

BOOKS

Mears, Walter R., *Deadlines Past: My Forty Years of Presidential Campaigning; A Reporter's Story,* Andrews McMeel Universal (Kansas City, MO), 2003.

PERIODICALS

Christian Science Monitor, April 27, 1983.
Library Journal, July, 2003, review of *Deadlines Past: My Forty Years of Presidential Campaigning; A Reporter's Story,* pp. 105-106.
Los Angeles Times Book Review, March 27, 1983, Harrison E. Salisbury, review of *The News Business.*
National Review, March 7, 1980.*

*   *   *

MÉNDEZ, Miguel 1930-

PERSONAL: Born June 15, 1930, in Bisbee, AZ; son of Francisco Méndez Cardenas (a farmer and miner) and Maria Morales; married Maria Dolores Fontes; children: Miguil Fontes, Isabel Cristina. *Education:* Attended schools in El Claro, Sonora, Mexico, for six years.

ADDRESSES: Office—Department of Spanish and Portuguese, University of Arizona, Modern Languages, Tucson, AZ 85721.

CAREER: Writer. Went to work as an itinerant farm laborer along the Arizona-Sonora border at the age of fifteen; bricklayer and construction worker in Tucson, AZ, 1946-70; Pima Community College, Tucson, AZ, served as instructor in Spanish, Hispanic literature, and creative writing, beginning 1970; University of Arizona, Tuscon, AZ, instructor in Chicano literature, professor emeritus, Spanish and Portuguese.

MEMBER: Association of Teachers of Spanish and Portuguese.

AWARDS, HONORS: Honorary Doctor of Humanities, University of Arizona, 1984; Jose Fuentes Mares National Award of Mexican Literature, Universidad Autonoma de Ciudad Juarez, 1991; Creative Writing fellowship, Arizona Commission on the Arts, 1992.

WRITINGS:

(With others) Octavio I. Romano and Herminio Rios-C., editors, *El Espejo/The Mirror,* Quinto Sol, 1969.

Peregrinos de Aztlan (novel), Editorial Peregrinos, 1974, translation by David W. Foster published as *Pilgrims in Aztlan,* Bilingual Press/Editorial Bilingue (Tempe, AZ), 1992.

Los criaderos humanos y Sahuaros (poem; title means "The Human Breeding Grounds and Saguaros"), Editorial Peregrinos, 1975.

Cuentos para ninos traviesos: Stories for Mischievous Children (short stories; bilingual edition), translations by Eva Price, Justa (Berkeley, CA), 1979.

Tata Casehua y otros cuentos (short stories; bilingual edition; title means "Tata Casehua and Other Stories"), translations by Eva Price, Leo Barrow, and Marco Portales, Justa (Berkely, CA), 1980.

Critica al poder politico, Ediciones Universal (Miami, FL), 1981.

De la vida y del folclore de la frontera (short stories; title means "From Life and Folklore along the Border"), Mexican-American Studies and Research Center, University of Arizona (Tuscon, AZ), 1986.

El sueno de Santa María de las Piedras (novel), Universidad de Guadalajara, 1986, translation by David W. Foster published as *The Dream of Santa María de las Piedras,* Bilingual Press/Editorial Bilingue (Tempe, AZ), 1989.

Que no mueran los suenos, Era (Mexico), 1991.

Los Muertos También Cuentan, Universidad Autonoma de Ciudad Juarez (Chihuahua, Mexico), 1995.

Entre letras y ladrillos: autobiografia novelada, Bilingual Press/Editorial Bilingue (Tempe, AZ), 1996, translation by David William Foster published as *From Labor to Letters: A Novel Autobiography,* 1997.

Río Santacruz, Ediciones Osuna (Armilla, Granada), 1997.

El Circo que se perdió en el Desierto de Sonora, Fondo de Cultura Económica (Mexico), 2002.

Also author of *El Hombre vibora; Pasen, lectores, pasen. Aqui se hacen imagenes* (poems); *Cuentos para ninos precoces* (short stories); and *Cuentos y ensayos para reir y aprender* (title means "Stories and Essays for Laughing and Learning"), 1988. Contributor to periodicals, including *La Palabra* and *Revista Chicano-Riquena.* The spring-fall, 1981, issue of *La Palabra* is entirely devoted to Méndez' work.

SIDELIGHTS: Miguel Méndez has attracted the admiration of many critics with his richly poetic prose, his erudite language, and his depictions of the poor members of an uprooted society at odds with the Anglo-American culture that threatens their heritage. His first novel, 1974's *Peregrinos de Aztlan* (translated as *Pilgrims in Aztlan* in 1992), is considered a landmark in Chicano literature for its experimental use of Spanglish (a mixture of Spanish and English), its blending of mythology with social realism, and its attention to poor, itinerant farm workers who formed the bulk of early Mexican immigration to the United States.

Much of the author's work uses elements from his Spanish and Yaqui Indian heritages. The name Aztlan in *Peregrinos de Aztlan,* for instance, is taken from the mythic northern homeland of the Aztec Indians of Mexico, and is believed to have been somewhere in the southwestern United States. Loreto Maldonado, the main character of *Peregrinos de Aztlan,* who now wanders the streets of Tijuana, Mexico, making a living by washing cars, was once a revolutionary and served under Pancho Villa. The title character in "Tata Casehua," found in the short-story collection *Tata Casehua y otros cuentos,* is actually the hero warrior Tetabiate, and the story details his search for an heir to whom he can pass on his tribe's history. And Timoteo, a key character in the novel *El sueno de Santa María de las Piedras,* ventures across the United States in search of the earthly god Huachusey, apparently with success, as he is repeatedly told "What you say?" by Americans in answer to his questions about the creator of things he encounters.

Méndez also draws upon his personal past, growing up in a Mexican government farming community and later working in agriculture and construction, for his stories. "During my childhood," he told Juan D. Bruce-Novoa in *Chicano Authors: Inquiry by Interview,* "I heard many stories from those people who came from different places, and, like my family, were newcomers to El Claro. They would tell anecdotes about the [Mexican] Revolution, the Yaqui wars, and innumerable other themes, among which there was no lack of apparitions and superstitions. Those days were extremely dramatic. I learned about tragedy, at times in the flesh." When at the age of fifteen Méndez left Mexico to find work as an agricultural laborer in the United States, he met the exploited people who appear in his fiction—indigent workers, prostitutes, and Hispanics looking for jobs in the North, among others.

Another major component of the author's work is the oral tradition handed down by these poor people; indeed, Méndez sees their plight as one symptom of the loss of that tradition. "Familial, communal, ethnic, and national heritage, which once was preserved by word of mouth, is disappearing into silence," explained Bruce-Novoa. "At the same time, written history represents only the elite classes' vision of the past, ignoring the existence of the poor. Thus, as the poor abandon the oral preservation of their heritage and simultaneously embrace literacy, alienation and a sense of diaspora possess them. Méndez counterattacks through his writing, not only by revealing the threat to the oral tradition, but also by filling his written texts with oral tradition." The author's interest in reclaiming this lost tradition is evidenced in *El sueno de Santa María de las Piedras,* in which he "employs the narrative voice of five old Mexicans . . . in order to unfold the historical fragments of a fictitious, yet universal Mexican town in the Sonora desert between 1830 and 1987," remarked Roland Walter in *Americas Review.*

In 1997, the author's autobiography was published and translated into English as *From Labor to Letters: A Novel Autobiography.* In it Méndez recounts his extraordinary life, going from six years of grade school to manual labor to a university professor and acclaimed writer. Writing in *Melus,* Marco Portales noted, "Presenting himself as the subject of a Cinderella life that he alternately eschews and suggests, Méndez skillfully weaves a narrative from the warp and woof of this consciousness on the experiences he has amassed and imagined, everything in life serving as useful material for the ever-creating Chicano author." In his autobiography, Méndez weavers together pas-

sages that read like a diary with other sections that are written in stream-of-consciousness style. He ponders the hardships he experiences and his own doubts about his status as an author. He also talks about his love of life and academia. Portales praised Méndez as a "natural-born writer, an author who has worked and sacrificed to develop the talents with which he is endowed for writing stories and for detailing the seldom recorded and hard lives that Chicanos daily face in the Arizona-Mexico border region of the Mexican-American Southwest." The reviewer also noted that the author's "intuition and legacy is that time will continue to bring out the truth in his writings about the inner feelings and lives of Chicanos, and I believe his book hits the necessary target again."

BIOGRAPHICAL AND CRITICAL SOURCES:

BOOKS

Anaya, Rodolfo A., and Francisco A. Lomeli, editors, *Aztlan: Essays on the Chicano Homeland,* Academia/El Norte (Albuquerque, NM), 1989.

Bruce-Novoa, Juan D., *Chicano Authors: Inquiry by Interview,* University of Texas Press (Austin, TX), 1980.

Martinez, Julio A., *Chicano Scholars and Writers: A Bio-Bibliographical Directory,* Scarecrow Press (Metuchen, NJ), 1979.

Rodriguez del Pino, Salvador, *Interview with Miguel Méndez M.,* Center for Chicano Studies, University of California, Santa Barbara, 1976.

Tatum, Charles M., *Chicano Literature,* Twayne (Boston, MA), 1982.

PERIODICALS

America, July 18, 1992, p. 42.

Americas Review, spring, 1990, Roland Walter, pp. 103-112.

Bloomsbury Review, March-April, 1994, pp. 3, 5.

Booklist, December 15, 1992, p. 719.

Denver Quarterly, fall, 1981, pp. 16-22; spring, 1982, pp. 68-77.

La Palabra, spring-fall, 1981, pp. 3-17, 50-57, 67-76.

Library Journal, March 15, 1993, p. 108.

Melus, spring, 1998, Marco Portales, review of *From Labor to Letters: A Novel Autobiography.*

Publishers Weekly, February 8, 1993, p. 83.*

MEYERS, Maan
  See MEYERS, Martin

*   *   *

MEYERS, Martin 1934-
  (Maan Meyers)

PERSONAL: Born December 26, 1934, in New York, NY; son of Joseph (a waiter) and Sara (a cook; maiden name, Goldberg) Meyers; married Annette Brafman (a writer), August 19, 1963. *Education:* Attended New York High School for the Performing Arts, 1948-49, Seward Park High School, 1950-52, and American Theatre Wing, 1957-59.

ADDRESSES: Agent—c/o Author Mail, iUniverse Book Publishing Co., 2021 Pine Lake Rd., Ste. 100, Lincoln, NE 68512. *E-mail*—marty@meyersmysteries. com.

CAREER: Actor and writer. Has appeared in numerous plays on Broadway, including *Zorba;* appeared in such feature films as *The Incident;* television roles included Stan Perlo, *One Life to Live. Military service:* U.S. Army, 1953-55; became corporal.

MEMBER: Mystery Writers of America; Sisters in Crime; Private Eye Writers of America; Screen Actors Guild; International Association of Crime Writers, North America.

WRITINGS:

"PATRICK HARDY" SERIES

Kiss and Kill, Popular Library (New York, NY), 1975.
Hung Up to Die, Popular Library (New York, NY), 1976.
Red Is for Murder, Popular Library (New York, NY), 1976.
Reunion for Death, Popular Library (New York, NY), 1976.
Spy and Die, Popular Library (New York, NY), 1976.

"DUTCHMAN" SERIES; WITH WIFE, ANNETTE MEYERS, UNDER JOINT PSEUDONYM MAAN MEYERS

The Dutchman, Doubleday (New York, NY), 1992.
The Kingsbridge Plot, Doubleday (New York, NY), 1993.
The High Constable, Doubleday (New York, NY), 1994.
The Dutchman's Dilemma, Bantam (New York, NY), 1995.
The House on Mulberry Street, Bantam (New York, NY), 1996.
The Lucifer Contract, Bantam (New York, NY), 1997.

OTHER

A Federal Case, Scholastic Publications (New York, NY), 1978.
Suspect, Bantam (New York, NY), 1987.

Contributor of short stories to numerous books, including *Marilyn: Shades of Blonde,* Forge, 1997; *The Private Eyes,* Signet, 1998; *Flesh & Blood, Dark Desires,* Mysterious Press/Warner, 2002; and *Flesh & Blood: Guilty as Sin,* Mysterious Press/Warner, 2003. Contributor to periodicals, including *Argosy.* Also author of song lyrics for the television show *Captain Kangaroo,* Columbia Broadcasting System, Inc. (CBS).

SIDELIGHTS: The "Dutchman" series, written by Martin Meyers and his wife, Annette, under the joint pseudonym Maan Meyers, began with Annette Meyers' idea for the character of the Dutchman: a large blond lawman in a black hat, leather jacket, loose-fitting shirt, and boots who lived during the time when New Amsterdam became New York. Martin Meyers conducted preliminary research on New Amsterdam and discovered Pieter Tonneman, who was a Schout (sheriff) in New Amsterdam in 1664, and who fit his wife's criteria. The Meyers thoroughly researched the history of the region of modern-day Manhattan that was once New Amsterdam, as well as the history of the people who lived there, in order to create a narrative that accurately portrayed life during the period.

The "Dutchman" series traces the history of the Tonneman family over some 200 years, with each volume presenting a mystery set in a different period of New

York City's history. The books are, according to Emily Melton in *Booklist,* "well written, deftly plotted, and carefully researched." A critic for *Publishers Weekly,* reviewing *The Lucifer Contract,* which concerns a plot by Confederates to burn New York City during the Civil War, finds that the novel contains "a wealth of surprising and entertaining historical tidbits . . . and the city comes alive in all its glorious, noisy mid-nineteenth century diversity."

Meyers told *CA:* "In the years it took us to research and write *The Dutchman,* we spent hours at the New York Historical Society and in the New York Public Library, reading as much as we could about the Dutch, English, Jews, Africans, and Native Americans who walked the five hundred yards of lower Manhattan that was New Amsterdam.

"We pored over maps and read about food and clothing, weapons, the flora and fauna, and the furniture. We wandered those five hundred yards at the tip of Manhattan, once bordered on three sides by water and on the fourth by a wooden wall that is now Wall Street.

"The most amazing thing we discovered was that New Amsterdam then, and New York City now, in terms of its people and what moves them, are strikingly similar."

BIOGRAPHICAL AND CRITICAL SOURCES:

PERIODICALS

Booklist, September 15, 1994, p. 117; July, 1995, p. 1864.
Publishers Weekly, June 14, 1993, p. 63; July 18, 1994, p. 238; July 17, 1995, p. 224; October 20, 1997, p. 57.

*   *   *

MIÉVILLE, China 1973(?)-

PERSONAL: Male. Born c. 1973, in London, England. *Education:* Degree from Cambridge University; London School of Economics, master's degree with distinction.

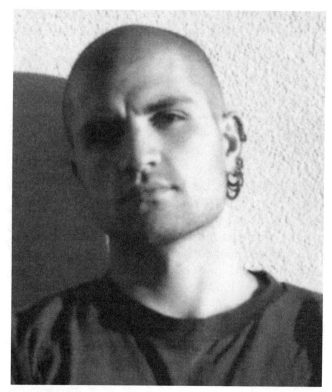

China Miéville

ADDRESSES: Office—c/o Del Rey Books, 1540 Broadway, New York, NY 10036.

CAREER: Writer.

AWARDS, HONORS: Nebula Award nomination in novel category, 2002, for *Perdido Street Station;* Philip K. Dick Award special citation, Philadelphia Science Fiction Society, 2002, Hugo Award nomination in best novel category, World Science Fiction Society, Arthur C. Clarke Award shortlist, and World Fantasy Award nomination in best novel category, and British Fantasy Society Award, all 2003, all for *The Scar.*

WRITINGS:

King Rat, Macmillan (New York, NY), 1998.
Perdido Street Station, Del Rey (New York, NY), 2001.
The Scar, Del Rey (New York, NY), 2002.
(With Michael Moorcock, Paul de Fillipo, and Geoff Ryman) *Cities,* Gollancz (London, England), 2003.
Iron Council, Del Rey (New York, NY), 2004.

SIDELIGHTS: China Miéville's debut novel, *King Rat,* was hailed by some critics as an updated take on the urban-gothic fable. In London, after an unknown intruder kills a man, the man's son, Saul, is wrongly convicted of the crime. Put in jail, Saul escapes, helped by a mysterious stranger who claims to be King Rat, a subterranean ruler. What is more, King Rat declares himself the deposed leader of a rodent army and reveals that Saul's mother is also of rat-kind. Now aware of his inborn abilities, Saul discovers he can "eat garbage, move soundlessly and unseen, squeeze through impossibly tiny openings, and climb vertical walls," as a *Kirkus Reviews* contributor described them.

In a variation of the Pied Piper theme, magical hip-hop music also enters into the story, leading to a showdown between King Rat and his young disciple. *King Rat* marks an "auspicious debut," according to a reviewer in *Publishers Weekly,* overcoming a "predictable plot" by pulling "the reader into the story through the kinetic energy" of Miéville's prose. To *Booklist* critic Roland Green, if the book lacks the balance of other works by noted urban-goth authors, those flaws are countered by Miéville's sense of "folkloric expertise . . . his depiction of the grungier side of urban life is vivid and extensive, not to mention well-worded."

Miéville's second book, *Perdido Street Station,* is a fantasy/horror tale set in New Crobuzon, a city full of gangsters, revolutionaries, and assorted human and non-human species. Isaac Dan der Crimnebulin and his lover, Lin, an insect-like creature, inadvertently release a flying monster on the city. Isaac and Lin must chase down the monster before the authorities find it, or them. Jackie Cassada, reviewing the novel in *Library Journal,* wrote that Miéville tells a "powerful tale about the power of love and the will to survive." A reviewer for *Publishers Weekly* called the novel "breathtakingly broad" and "an impressive and ultimately pleasing epic."

In Miéville's third book, *The Scar,* published in 2002, fugitives of New Crobuzon find more dangers await them when pirates take them to the floating city of Armada, which is ruled by a devious pair called The Lovers. Some critics have expressed dismay at the plot twists as well as with Miéville's writing style. Others found more to like; Jane Halshall, reviewing *The Scar* for *School Library Journal,* characterized

Miéville's writing as "something akin to Lewis Carroll's use of portmanteau."

Iron Council, Miéville's next work, takes readers on a return trip to the city of New Crobuzon, where revolt stirs in the minds of the residents living under a repressive capitalist regime that doles out inhumane reconstructive surgery as punishment. A reviewer for *Publishers Weekly* maintained that "Miéville represents much of what is new and good in contemporary dark fantasy, and his work is must reading for devotees of that genre."

BIOGRAPHICAL AND CRITICAL SOURCES:

PERIODICALS

Booklist, September 15, 1999, review of *King Rat,* p. 239; February 15, 2001, Roland Green, review of *Peridido Street Station,* p. 1122; July, 2002, Regina Schroeder, Jackie Cassada, review of *The Scar,* p. 1833; June 1, 2004, Ray Olson, review of *Iron Council,* pp. 1670-1671.

Bookseller, December 12, 2003, p. 29.

Extrapolation, spring, 2000, Scott Maisano, "Reading Underwater; or, Fantasies of Fluency from Shakespeare to Mieville and Emshwiller," pp. 76-88; fall, 2003, John Reider, "Symposium: Marxism and Fantasy," pp. 375-380; winter, 2003, Carl Freedman, "Toward a Marxist Urban Sublime: Reading China Mieville's *King Rat,*" pp. 395-408.

Kirkus Reviews, August 1, 1999, review of *King Rat,* p. 1181; May 1, 2002, review of Jackie Cassada, review of *The Scar,* p. 625; June 1, 2004, review of *Iron Council,* p. 522.

Library Journal, February 15, 2001, Jackie Cassada, review of *Perdido Street Station,* p. 204; July, 2002, Jackie Cassada, review of *The Scar,* p. 259; July, 2004, Jackie Cassada, review of *Iron Council,* p. 75.

Publishers Weekly, August 23, 1999, review of *King Rat,* p. 53; January 8, 2001, review of *Perdido Street Station,* p. 52; May 20, 2002, review of *The Scar,* p. 51; July 5, 2004, review of *Iron Council,* p. 42.

School Library Journal, March, 2003, Jane Halshall, review of *The Scar,* p. 259.

Spectator, May 6, 2000, Michael Moorcock, review of *Perdido Street Station,* pp. 33-34.

Times Literary Supplement, September 1, 2000, Edward James, review of *Perdido Street Station,* p. 11.

ONLINE

3 am Magazine Online, http://www.3ammagazine.com/ (August 18, 2004), Richard Marshall, "The Road to Perdido: An Interview with China Mieville."

BBC Web site, http://www.bbc.co.uk/ (August 18, 2004), "China Mieville."

Fantastic Fiction Web site, http://www.fantasticfiction. co.uk/ (August 18, 2004), "China Mieville."

Pan Macmillan Web site, http://www.panmacmillan. com/ (August 18, 2004).

Strange Horizon Web Site, http://www.strangehorizon. com/ (August 18, 2004), Cheryl Morgan, interview with Mieville.*

*   *   *

MOORE, Alan 1953-
(Curt Vile)

PERSONAL: Born November 18, 1953, in Northampton, England; son of Ernest (a brewery worker) and Sylvia (a printer) Moore; married, 1974; wife's name, Phyllis; children: Amber, Leah.

ADDRESSES: Home—Northampton, England. *Office*—America's Best Comics, 7910 Ivanhoe St., No. 438, La Jolla, CA 92037.

CAREER: Comics illustrator and writer. Cartoonist for *Sounds* (magazine; under the name Curt Vile), 1979. Founder of Mad Love Publishers, Northampton, MA, 1988, and America's Best Comics, La Jolla, CA, 1999.

AWARDS, HONORS: Eagle Award for Best Comics Writer, 1982 and 1983, for *V for Vendetta,* and for *Swamp Thing;* Jack Kirby Comics Industry Award, for *Swamp Thing;* Jack Kirby Best Writer Award, 1987, Hugo Award, 1988, and *Locus* award, 1988, all for *Watchmen;* Harvey Award for best writer, 1988, for *Watchmen,* 1989, for best story and for best graphic album, both for *The Killing Joke,* 1995 and 1996, both for *From Hell,* 1998, for body of work, 2000, for

League of Extraordinary Gentlemen, 2001, 2003, and 2004, for *Promethea,* 2003, for best writer for *ABC,* for best continuing series for *League of Extraordinary Gentlemen* Volume 2, and for best single issue or story, for *League of Extraordinary Gentlemen,* Volume 2, number 1; Will Eisner Comic Industry Award, 1988, for best finite series, best graphic album, best writer, and best writer/artist, all for *Watchmen,* 1989, for best graphic album and best writer, both for *The Killing Joke,* 1994, for best new graphic album, for *A Small Killing,* 1995, 1996, and 1997, all for best writer, all for *From Hell,* 2000, for best new series, for *Top Ten,* for best graphic album—reprint, for *From Hell,* and for best writer, for *League of Extraordinary Gentlemen,* 2001, for best single issue, for *Promethea,* number 10, for best continuing series, for *Top Ten,* for best writer, for *League of Extraordinary Gentlemen,* 2003, for best limited series, for *League of Extraordinary Gentlemen* Volume 2, and 2004, for best writer, for *League of Extraordinary Gentlemen, Promethea, Smax, Tom Strong,* and *Tom Strong's Terrific Tales.*

WRITINGS:

GRAPHIC NOVELS; EXCEPT AS NOTED

Shocking Futures, Titan (London, England), 1986.

Twisted Times, Titan (London, England), 1987.

Watchmen, illustrated by Dave Gibbons, DC Comics/ Warner (New York, NY), 1987.

(With others) *Swamp Thing,* DC Comics (New York, NY), 1987.

Batman: The Killing Joke, illustrated by Brian Bolland and John Higgins, DC Comics (New York, NY), 1988.

Brought to Light, illustrated by Bill Sienkiewicz, Titan (London, England), 1989.

V for Vendetta, illustrated by David Lloyd, Titan (London, England), 1990.

Miracleman (published in England as *Marvelman*), Eclipse Books (Forestville, CA), 1990–1992.

The Complete Ballad of Halo Jones, Titan (London, England), 1991.

Big Numbers, illustrated by Bill Sienkiewicz, Mad Love (Northampton, MA), 1990.

A Small Killing, illustrated by Oscar Zarate, Victor Gollancz (London, England), 1991.

From Hell, illustrated by Eddie Campbell, Mad Love/ Kitchen Sink Press (Northampton, MA), 1991–96.

The Complete Bojefferies Saga, illustrated by Steve Parkhouse, Kitchen Sink Press (Northampton, MA), 1994.

Lost Girls, illustrated by Melinda Gebbie, Kitchen Sink Press (Northampton, MA), 1995.

Voice of the Fire (novel), Victor Gollancz (London, England), 1996.

(With others) *Superman: Whatever Happened to the Man of Tomorrow?,* DC Comics (New York, NY), 1997.

Voodoo, Dancing in the Dark, Wildstorm Productions (La Jolla, CA), 1999.

(With others) *Bloodfeud,* Titan (London, England), 1999.

(With others) *Saga of the Swamp Thing,* DC Comics (New York, NY), 2000.

Top Ten, illustrated by Gene Ha and Zander Cannon, America's Best Comics (La Jolla, CA), 2000.

(With others) *Swamp Thing: The Curse,* DC Comics (New York, NY), 2000.

Love and Death, illustrated by John Totleben, Titan (London, England), 2000.

The League of Extraordinary Gentlemen, illustrated by Kevin O'Neill, America's Best Comics (La Jolla, CA), 2001.

Tom Strong Book 1, illustrated by Chris Sprouse, Titan (London, England), 2001.

Promethea Book 1, illustrated by J. H. Williams III, Titan (London, England), 2001.

Promethea Book 2, illustrated by J. H. Williams, Titan (London, England), 2001.

(With others) *Swamp Thing: A Murder of Crows,* Titan (London, England), 2001.

The Complete D. R. & Quinch, illustrated by Alan Davis, Titan (London, England), 2001.

(With others) *Tom Strong Book 2,* Titan (London, England), 2002.

Captain Britain, illustrated by Alan Davis, Marvel (New York, NY), 2002.

Skizz, illustrated by Jim Baikie, Titan (London, England), 2002.

Tomorrow Stories, America's Best Comics (La Jolla, CA), 2002.

(With others) *Mr. Majestic,* Wildstorm (La Jolla, CA), 2002.

(With others) *Swamp Thing: Earth to Earth,* DC Comics (New York, NY), 2002.

Supreme: The Story of the Year, Checker Book Pub. Group (Centerville, OH), 2002.

Judgement Day, Checker Book Pub. Group (Centerville, OH), 2003.

Supreme: The Return, Checker Book Pub. Group (Centerville, OH), 2003.

The Mirror of Love, illustrated by José Villarubia, Top Shelf Productions (Portland, OR), 2003.

America's Best Comics, America's Best Comics (LA Jolla, CA), 2004.

Also author of *1963.* Contributor to *The Starry Wisdom,* edited by D. M. Mitchell, Creation Books, 1994; and *Doctor Who Weekly;* created comic series, including "The Ballad of Hal Jones," "Skizz," and "D. R. & Quinch" for *2000 A.D.* and "Marvelman" and "V for Vendetta" series for *Warrior* (English anthology magazine). Contributor to comics series, including "Saga of the Swamp Thing" and "Tales of the Green Lantern Corps," DC Comics; to "The League of Extraordinary Gentlemen," "Promethea," "Tom Strong," "Tomorrow Stories," and "Top Ten," for America's Best Comics; and to "Supreme." Also performer on spoken word albums, including *The Birth Caul, Brought to Light, The Moon and Serpent Grand Egyptian Theatre of Marvels, Highbury Working* and *Angel Passage,* as well as the musical albums *The Sinister Ducks* and *The Emperors of Ice Cream.*

ADAPTATIONS: From Hell was adapted for a movie of the same title, starring Johnny Depp, directed by Albert and Allen Hughes, Twentieth Century-Fox, 2002; *The League of Extraordinary Gentlemen* was adapted for a movie of the same title, starring Sean Connery, directed by Stephen Norrington, Twentieth Century-Fox, 2002.

SIDELIGHTS: Dubbed the "Orson Welles of comics" by Steve Rose in the *Guardian,* Alan Moore is one of a handful of people who transformed the comic book industry in the 1980s, showing that "comic book scripts can have the subtlety of prose fiction, especially when they use their access to the rich potential subject matter of our fascination with heroes," as a contributor to *St. James Guide to Science Fiction Writers* noted. Moore's twelve-part comic-book serial "Watchmen" "changed the genre forever," according to Sridhar Pappu in *Salon.com.* In that series Moore transformed the old superhero model into "rapists, racists and flunkies of Richard Nixon . . . [to be] hunted down in the days before World War III," Pappu wrote. This deconstructing of the comic book hero was hailed a "sci-fi detective masterpiece," as Rose observed, making Moore "the comic industry's de facto leader." According to Rose, for comic fans, Moore is "the undisputed high priest of the medium, whose every word is seized upon like a message from the ether."

Moore has continued to amaze and confound his readers since the mid-1980s, writing series comics as well as graphic novels. For ten years he worked in the murky world of serial killers and madmen, writing his "From Hell" series about Jack the Ripper, the book of which was adapted for a 2002 film starring Johnny Depp. From works such as "V for Vendetta" and "Miracleman," to "The League of Extraordinary Gentlemen," Moore has created a large and significant body of work. As a critic on *Comicon.com* remarked, Moore "was the first modern writer to approach the medium of comics with the same intent and thoughtfulness . . . of any successful novel, screenplay, or theatrical production." Employing both playfulness and deadly earnestness, Moore "created an intoxicating mix of high and low; a nexus where readers could embrace some of the deepest aspirations of humankind while wallowing in the muckiest of trash culture." And writing in *Time,* Andrew D. Arnold declared that Moore "has written the best mainstream books of the last fifteen years while maintaining artistic credibility."

Moore himself is of two minds about his genre-bending "Watchmen," as he confided to Tasha Robinson in an *Onion AV Club* online interview: "In the fifteen years since 'Watchmen,' an awful lot of the comics field [has been] devoted to these very grim, pessimistic, nasty, violent stories which kind of use *Watchmen* to validate what they are, in effect, often just some very nasty stories that don't have a lot to recommend them. . . . It's almost become a genre. The gritty, deconstructivist postmodern superhero comic, as exemplified by *Watchmen,* also became a genre. It was never meant to. It was meant to be one work on its own. I think to that degree, it may have had a deleterious effect upon the medium since then."

Born in Northampton, England, in 1953, Moore grew up in a working-class family. His father was a brewery worker and his mother a printer; their flat was rented from the town council. Indoor plumbing was missing at one grandmother's house while electric lights were absent from the home of his other grandmother. "Looking back on it," Moore told Pappu, "it sounds like I'm describing something out of Dickens. I mean, I'm talking 1955, but 1955 in England. I've seen 'Happy Days' on television. Maybe the American fifties were

like that, but that wasn't what the British fifties were like. It was all sort of monochrome, and it was all indoors."

Moore grew up loving imaginative literature, from the Greek and Norse myths to children's books about Robin Hood. The first comics in his youth were British ones, done in black and white, full of school stories. Then he finally got his hands on a "Superman" comic. "I got my morals more from Superman than I ever did from my teachers or peers," Moore told Pappu. "Because Superman wasn't real—he was incorruptible. You were seeing morals in their pure form. You don't see Superman secretly going out behind the back and lying and killing, which, of course, most real-life heroes tend to be doing." At age seventeen Moore was thrown out of his conservative secondary school for dealing drugs, and thereafter took laboring jobs in and around Northampton, working at a sheep-skinning plant and cleaning toilets at a hotel. He finally moved up to an office job at the local gas company, but knew he had to make an effort to do something more creative.

Eventually finding himself married and with a child on the way, Moore quit his job, went on public assistance, and spent a year trying to make a living with his own imagination. One of his ultimately aborted projects during this time was a twenty-part space opera. Eventually he found a cartooning job for the rock weekly *Sounds.* In that magazine he published a comic detective story called "Roscoe Moscow" under the pen name of Curt Vile, but soon decided he was a better writer than artist. Thereafter he contributed works to British magazines such as *Doctor Who Weekly* and *2000 A.D.* In the latter publication, he created several popular comic-strips, including "The Ballad of Halo Jones"—which had one of the first feminist heroes in comics as Halo searches for her proper place in the galaxy—"Skizz," and "D. R. & Quinch," a darkly humorous—some might say deranged—look at college students who take readers through tales of slime wars and psychotic girlfriends.

Moore then began contributing to the British anthology magazine *Warrior,* where he initiated two series which would prove to be breakthroughs for him: "Marvelman"—titled "Miracleman" in the United States—and "V for Vendetta." With these tales, Moore's writing began to take on more of the multi-layered feeling of a novel. "With *Marvelman* there were some bits of cleverness creeping in there but with *V for Vendetta* I think that was where I started to realize that you could get some incredible effects by putting words and pictures together or leaving the words out for a while," Moore told Barry Kavanagh in a *Blather.net* online interview. "I started to realize what you could do with comic storytelling and the . . . layering, the levels of meaning that you could attach to the story. I think that certainly *V for Vendetta* was one of the first real major breakthroughs I made in terms of my own personal style."

With "Marvelman" Moore treats the stereotypical superhero in tights with a new sensitivity, and by the end the hero has become "genuinely godlike," according to the *St. James Guide to Science Fiction Writers* essayist "and graciously offers other humans the chance to join him. He is puzzled by the refusal of some, such as his former wife, to be converted into superhumanity; that failure of imagination, Moore implies, is Marvelman's ultimate limitation." "V for Vendetta," on the other hand, is set in a near-future, fascist Britain, where the only opposition to the government is the Guy Fawkes-masked vigilante known only as "V," a lone vigilante who is killing all the government officials once connected with a concentration camp. Illustrated in black and white by David Lloyd, the series has a gritty, noir feel that attracted readers on both sides of the Atlantic. "V" earned Moore his first awards as well; he received the Eagle Award for Best Writing in both 1982 and 1983.

"When we started to do *V*," Moore told Kavanagh, "the entirety of the idea was that we would have a dark, romantic, noirish adventurer and then we thought we'd set him in the future and then the details slowly came together and yeah, somewhere out of this we realized we were doing something about the contrast between anarchy and fascism, that there were lots of moral questions being asked and that yes, it was very much centered upon the world of ideas as being in some ways more important than the material world." Moore further told Kavanagh that "V" was also a breakthrough in terms of characters. "I was very pleased with the characterizations in *V*. There's quite a variety of characters in there and they've all got very distinctive characteristics. They've all got different ways of talking, different agendas and I think they're all credible because, well, they felt emotionally credible to me because there's none of them that I absolutely hate."

Moore's work in England did not go unnoticed by American comics publishers and fans, and in 1984 he began working for DC Comics, revamping the character of Swamp Thing for "The Saga of Swamp Thing." Taking over the nearly defunct series at number twenty, he stuck with it through the next forty issues. "It was the first time that I'd got colour and twenty-four pages to play with," Moore related to Kavanagh. "So I was able to kind of splash out and do a few things that I'd only been able to dream about doing with black and white material." Moore appreciated the opportunities as he noted in his introduction to "Saga of the Swamp Thing," the first of the issues he wrote: "The continuity-expert's nightmare of a thousand different super-powered characters co-existing in the same continuum can, with the application of a sensitive and sympathetic eye, become a rich and fertile mythic background with fascinating archetypal characters hanging around, waiting to be picked like grapes on the vine."

Moore depicts the Swamp Thing not as a man who became plantlike, but with all the memories of the man. "Shocked by the discovery that he was not human," explained the reviewer for *St. James Guide to Science Fiction Writers,* "the character first tries to sink into unconsciousness. When he is roused by the need to fight another man-plant being who wants to destroy all humans for their crimes against the vegetable world, Swamp Thing begins to care for some humans." In the end, Swamp Thing becomes able to share his world with them and, in the climax to actually love one human woman.

"Unconventional and serious, [Moore] turned the book into a tool for exploring social issues, using it to discuss everything from racism to environmental affairs," remarked Pappu. Soon Moore had increased monthly circulation of "Swamp Thing" from 17,000 to 100,000 copies by, as Rose commented, transforming the featured creature "from a walking vegetable into a ground-breaking gothic eco-warrior." Also working for DC, Moore penned "Tales of the Green Lantern Corps."

Meanwhile, Moore was also collaborating with Dave Gibbons on an idea for a type of new superhero story with a reconstructed gang of heroes thrown into new situations. Working off characters in the defunct Charlton comics, such as the Question, Mister A, Blue Beetle, and Captain Adam, in "Watchmen" Moore and

Gibbons came up with their own super heroes, including Dr. Manhattan with his nuclear powers, Rorschach, Adrian Veit and others. In Moore's take, these superheroes are all plagued by their human emotions and weaknesses. In an alternate America of 1985, super heroes have in fact existed for several decades. They have fought gangsters and then Nazis in World War II, have been purged in the McCarthy era, helped the country win the war in Vietnam, and have become hitmen for the CIA. One such superhero, Comedian, supposedly killed the Watergate journalists Woodward and Bernstein in 1972, thus stabilizing Richard M. Nixon's threatened presidency, and Comedian's own death in October of 1985 becomes the kick-off point for Moore's dark tale. Soon it becomes clear that someone is trying to kill off the second generation of super heroes, and as a nuclear threat becomes more and more urgent, the remaining super heroes know that they must stop this anonymous assassin before time runs out.

The twelve issues of the original "Watchmen" each include notes and end matter, supposedly "documentary" material of the time that is "wittily crafted and weirdly interesting," according to Fredric Paul Smoler in the *Nation.* The series quickly became a cult classic, appealing to adult and teenage readers alike. Rose noted that the series "was a dense, meticulous deconstruction of the whole superhero game that received mainstream 'literary' acclaim," and also became the symbol of a new genre—the graphic novel. *Watchmen* is a "formidably complex work, demanding that readers connect many references in text and art," noted the contributor for *St. James Guide to Science Fiction Writers.*

Before leaving DC Comics to found his imprint Mad Love Publishers, Moore published a Batman story, "The Killing Joke," about the relationship between Batman and Joker, though he came to view this particular venture as a "well-intentioned failure." His more recent projects have often resembled massive, unfinished monoliths. *Brought to Light,* with illustrations by Bill Sienkiewicz, is based on a lawsuit brought against the government for drug-smuggling and arms-dealing. The "1963" series appears to be a fairly genial spoof of early Marvel super heroes, but the series broke off just as Moore was bringing those more-innocent characters into the present, to face contemporary issues in the company of today's scruffier brand of superhero. Only two issues of "Big

Numbers" appeared, juxtaposing personal and big-business desires. *A Small Killing,* illustrated by Oscar Zarate, tells the story of Timothy Hole, an advertising man in New York, who is followed by a mysterious little boy.

Far and away Moore's most important project during the 1990s was "From Hell," a fictional account of the 1888 Jack the Ripper crimes, all based on thorough research. A "big, black, monumental work," is how Moore described "From Hell" to Kavanagh. "Victorian. I'm very proud of it." In Moore's version of the Ripper story, Prince Albert, heir to the British throne, has secretly married a woman from the London slums. To save the throne, all evidence of this must be removed, including the other slum women who know. Dr. William Gull, sincere defender of official morality, sets about this task at the request of his sovereign, Queen Victoria. He views himself as a masked vigilante, but history knows him as Jack the Ripper. But Gull is also an enigma: is he a real historical persona or a golem-like creation brought to life by royalty and the Freemasons?

Reviewing the graphic-novel publication of *From Hell* in *Booklist,* Gordon Flagg noted that Moore's "meticulous research . . . helps him evoke Victorian London convincingly, and his . . . storytelling skills make the story grippingly harrowing." Kenneth Turan, reviewing the movie adaptation of the book in the *Los Angeles Times,* noted that Moore's work is "no mere comic book. It's a massive, graphic novel published over the course of a decade and so fiendishly researched and detailed it has more than forty pages of footnotes in small print." And writing in the London *Observer,* Iain Sinclair called *From Hell* a "celebrated graphic novel."

After being imitated for so long as the progenitor of the deconstructed superhero, Moore set out with a new imprint in 1999, America's Best Comics (ABC), to resurrect the old-fashioned super hero. Beginning the practice when in his forties, Moore found a renewed joy in his craft, and his output rose after completion of *From Hell.* One of the turnaround incidents for him was a reclamation project in 1996 of a "very, very, very, very, very lame" superhero, as Moore recalled to Pappu. With Supreme, Moore re-fashions a down-at-heels super hero and had such fun doing it that he figured he could use that model to help breathe new life into a flagging comics industry. His ABC titles include "Promethea," about a mythic warrior woman, "Tom Strong," featuring a very straightforward, moral superhero, and "Top Ten," set in a police precinct where all the officers have superhuman powers.

With "The League of Extraordinary Gentlemen," Moore gathers nineteenth-century fictional personages such as Allan Quatermain from H. Rider Haggard's *King Solomon's Mines,* Captain Nemo from Jules Verne's *20,000 Leagues under the Sea,* Edward Hyde and Dr. Henry Jekyll from Robert Louis Stevenson's novel, Mina Murray from Bram Stoker's *Dracula,* and Hawley Griffin from H. G. Welles's *Invisible Man.* Reviewing the collection *The League of Extraordinary Gentlemen,* a contributor for *Publishers Weekly* called it a "delightful work" that features a "grand collection of signature nineteenth-century fictional characters, covertly brought together to defend the empire." The same reviewer concluded that Moore has created a "Victorian era Fantastic Four, a beautifully illustrated reprise . . . packed with period detail, great humor and rousing adventure."

Moving into his publishing venture, Moore has abandoned his bleak, noirish plot-lines in favor of a lighter touch in his books for ABC. "I feel good about this century," he told Joel Meadows in a *Tripwire* interview. "I feel that we're going somewhere in our minds and our minds are evolving into something. I think that imagination and the world of the imagination are at a premium in these coming times."

In the *Advocate,* Andy Mangels highlighted another passion of Moore's: a poem titled *The Mirror of Love,* which originally appeared in 1988 in a publication called *AARGH!* (Artists against Rampant Government Homophobia). "Moore's *Mirror of Love,*" explained Mangels, "is an epic poem that compresses gay history into a few thousand words, covering the dawn of humanity and ancient Sapphic and Spartan love up through the AIDS crisis and the gay-baiting media of the modern world." Moore, a heterosexual, told Mangels that the poem is "sweeping—melodramatic," and "It's got a very Shakespearean tone to it, but it felt like a big story that deserved to be spoken of in epic tongues. Some of the men and women that we mentioned in it—these are titans. They are the pillars of human culture, let 'alone gay culture.'" Moore and friends published the comic book to benefit the fight against a piece of British legislation that he deemed homophobic. As Moore explained to Mangels: "When-

ever any of our countries take these sudden, nasty fascist lunges, then I think it's down to all of us to actually stand up and say something about it."

BIOGRAPHICAL AND CRITICAL SOURCES:

BOOKS

Parkin, Lance, *Alan Moore,* Pocket Essentials, 2001.
St. James Guide to Science Fiction Writers, 4th edition, St. James Press (Detroit, MI), 1996.

PERIODICALS

Advocate, March 16, 2004, Andy Mangels, "From Queer to Eternity: Comic Master Alan Moore Tackles the History of Homosexuality in the Epic Poem *The Mirror of Love,*" p. 52.
Analog: Science Fiction-Science Fact, May, 1988, p. 184; January, 1991, pp. 308-309.
Booklist, June 1, 2000, Gordon Flagg, review of *From Hell,* p. 1830; November 1, 2003, Gordon Flagg, review of *Judgment Day,* p. 487.
Guardian (Manchester, England), February 2, 2002, Steve Rose, "Moore's Murder."
Library Journal, March 15, 1990, pp. 53-55; March 1, 2001, Stephen Weiner, review of *The League of Extraordinary Gentlemen,* p. 82; January, 2004, Steve Raiteri, review of *Across the Universe: The DC Universe Stories of Alan Moore,* p. 79; March 1, 2004, Steve Raiteri, review of *The League of Extraordinary Gentlemen,* Volume 2, p. 62.
Los Angeles Times, October 19, 2001, Kenneth Turan, "Violence Cuts like a Knife in the Jack the Ripper Tale," p. F4.
Nation, October 10, 1987, Fredric Paul Smoler, review of *Watchmen,* pp. 386-387; March 19, 1990, Pagan Kennedy, "P.C. Comics," pp. 386-389.
New Statesman, July 10, 1987, pp. 28-29; December 4, 1987, p. 30; December 18, 1987, p. 41.
Newsweek, January 18, 1988, pp. 70-71.
New York Times, October 19, 2001, Elvis Mitchell, "A Conspiracy Shrouded in London Fog," p. E16.
Observer (London, England), January 27, 2002, Iain Sinclair, "Jack the Rip-Off," p. 8.
Publishers Weekly, February 17, 1989, p. 73; June 14, 1999, p. 62; January 8, 2001, review of *The League of Extraordinary Gentlemen,* p. 49;

December 15, 2003, review of *Tom Strong: Book Two,* p. 56; February 9, 2004, review of *The League of Extraordinary Gentlemen,* Volume 2, p. 60.

Rolling Stone, February 11, 1988, pp. 103-108.

Time, December 8, 2000, Andrew W. Arnold, "Best Comics 2000."

ONLINE

Blather.net, http://www.blather.net/ (October 17, 2000), Barry Kavanagh, "The Alan Moore Interview."

Comicon.com, http://www.comicon.com/ (June 2, 2002), "Alan Moore."

Onion AV Club, http://www.theonionavclub.com/ (October 24, 2001), Tasha Robinson, interview with Moore.

Salon.com, http://www.salon.com/ (October 18, 2000), Sridhar Pappu, "We Need Another Hero."

Tripwire, http://www.human-computing.com/Tripwire/ (June 2, 2002), Joel Meadows, interview with Moore.*

*   *   *

MORROW, James (Kenneth) 1947-

PERSONAL: Born March 17, 1947, in Philadelphia, PA; son of William (a clerk) and Emily (a secretary; maiden name, Develin) Morrow; married Jean Pierce (a teacher), September 11, 1972 (divorced); married Kathryn Ann Smith; children: Kathleen Pierce Morrow and a son. *Education:* University of Pennsylvania, B.A., 1969; Harvard University, M.A.T. (visual studies), 1970. *Politics:* "Thomas Jefferson meets G. B. Shaw." *Religion:* "Pantheist."

ADDRESSES: Home and office—810 North Thomas St., State College, PA 16803. *Agent*—Writers House, 21 West 26th St., New York, NY 10010. *E-mail*—jim.morrow@sff.net.

CAREER: Cambridge Pilot School, Cambridge, MA, English teacher, 1970-71; Chelmsford Public Schools, Chelmsford, MA, instructional materials specialist, 1972-1974; Ordadek Productions, Westford, MA, motion picture writer, director, and editor, 1975-1978; Tufts University, Medford, MA, visiting lecturer in

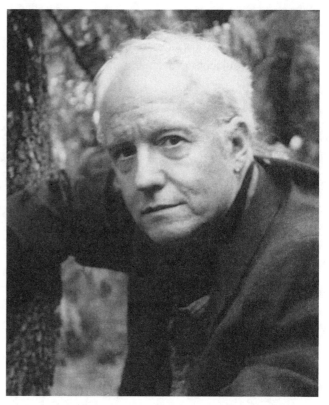

James Morrow

media and communications, 1978-1981; freelance fiction writer, 1980—. Children's book author, Learningways Corporation, Cambridge, 1982-87; visiting lecturer in fiction writing, Pennsylvania State University, University Park, 1990.

MEMBER: National Council of Teachers of English Science Fiction, Fantasy Writers of America, Westford Committee to Halt the Arms Race.

AWARDS, HONORS: Pennsylvania Council of the Arts fellowship, 1988; Nebula Award for best short story, Science Fiction and Fantasy Writers of America, 1988, for "Bible Stories for Adults, No. 17: The Deluge," and for best novella, 1992, for *City of Truth;* World Fantasy Award for best novel, 1991, for *Only Begotten Daughter,* and 1995, for *Towing Jehovah. Blameless in Abaddon* was named a *New York Times* Notable Book of the Year.

WRITINGS:

FICTION

The Wine of Violence, Holt (New York, NY), 1981.

The Adventures of Smoke Baily, (novelization of computer game), Spinnaker, 1983.

The Continent of Lies, Holt (New York, NY), 1984.

This Is the Way the World Ends, Holt (New York, NY), 1986.

Only Begotten Daughter, Morrow, 1990.

Swatting at the Cosmos (short stories), Pulphouse, 1990.

City of Truth (novella), Legend, 1991, St. Martin's (New York, NY), 1992.

Towing Jehovah (first book of the "Godhead Trilogy"), Harcourt (New York, NY), 1994.

Bible Stories for Adults (short stories), Harcourt (New York, NY), 1995.

Blameless in Abbadon (second book of the "Godhead Trilogy"), Harcourt (New York, NY), 1996.

The Eternal Footman (third book of the "Godhead Trilogy"), Harcourt (New York, NY), 1999.

The Cat's Pajamas & Other Stories, Tachyon Press, 2004.

CD-ROM; FOR CHILDREN

The Quasar Kids, Collamore, 1987.

What Makes a Dinosaur Sore, Collamore, 1987.

(With Marilyn Segal) *The Lima Bean Dream,* Collamore, 1987.

(With Marilyn Segal) *Not Too Messy, Not Too Neat,* Collamore, 1988.

The Best Bubble-Blower, Collamore, 1988.

OTHER

(With Murray Suid) *Moviemaking Illustrated: The Comicbook Filmbook* (textbook), Hayden, 1973.

(With Joe Adamson) *A Political Cartoon* (screenplay), published in *Scripts I,* Houghton (Boston, MA), 1973.

(With Murray Suid) *Media and the Kids: A Real-World Learning in the Schools* (textbook), Hayden, 1977.

(With Jean Morrow) *The Grammar of Media* (textbook), Hayden, 1978.

(With Murray Suid) *Creativity Catalogue: Comic Book Guide to Creative Projects* (textbook), Fearon, 1981.

(Editor) *Nebula Awards: SFWA's Choices for the Best Science Fiction and Fantasy of the Year,* numbers 26-28, Harcourt (New York, NY), 1992–1994.

Contributing editor, *Media and Methods,* 1978-80; contributing writer to *A Teacher's Guide to NOVA.* Creator of "Suspicion," a board game, for TSR Hobbies, 1977. Freelance fiction reviewer, *Philadelphia Inquirer,* 1986-90. Morrow's books have been translated into many languages, including French, German, Chinese, Czech, and Hungarian.

WORK IN PROGRESS: A novel, *The Last Witchfinder,* about the birth of the scientific worldview.

SIDELIGHTS: "If there is such a thing as an anti-science-fiction writer," declared *New York Times Book Review* contributor David McDonough, "it is James Morrow." "Since the publication of his first novel in 1981," wrote F. Brett Cox in the *St. James Guide to Science Fiction Writers,* Morrow has "produced a substantial body of high-quality work that rates as one of the field's best. While most of his novels and stories are recognizably science fiction, Morrow is not interested in rigid technological and sociological extrapolation; instead, he uses stock science-fictional devices as a means for examining moral and philosophical issues. Morrow's fiction is notable for its rich, often dazzling prose style, as well as for its strongly comic elements. All of these traits place Morrow squarely within a tradition marked variously by such writers as Ray Bradbury, Kurt Vonnegut, Philip K. Dick, and Robert Sheckley."

Morrow's first novel, *The Wine of Violence,* presents a utopian society, Quetzalia, in which violence has been obliterated through ritualized, technologically assisted purging of aggressive fantasies. As the story unfolds, the Quetzalians, despite years of conditioning, engage in a grisly battle of self-defense against a neighboring tribe of cannibals. "Although the plot is driven by a high level of action, culminating with the explorers convincing the Quetzalians to go to war against the Brain-Eaters," Cox explained, "the central concern is more abstract: are the Quetzalians heroes for having conquered the dark side of human nature, or hypocrites whose murderous fantasies belie their professed pacifism? The author's sympathies reveal themselves when one of the Quetzalians realizes that, by fighting the Brain-Eaters, he is acting in the tradition of his Earth ancestors and is now a part of history: 'History, he decided, was a terrible idea.'" The novel, Morrow told *Library Journal,* is "pro-science: the evil comes not from the engineers who built the machine, nor from any inherent flaw in the machines themselves, but from a terrible and arrogant choice regarding their use."

This Is the Way the World Ends offers a satiric attack on the nuclear arms race during the presidency of Ronald Reagan. The unthinkable war occurs, and a group of Americans—each of whom bears some responsibility for the failure of deterrence—awakens on a submarine crewed by the survivors' own ghostly descendants: the "unadmitted" multitudes who will never be born because humanity is extinct. Hauled to Antarctica, the six bewildered men are placed on trial for "crimes against the future." In Cox's view, "Although the novel is, among other things, a scathing critique of the Cold War mentality, Morrow never lets it become a one-sided polemic. The trial is a deliberate presentation of both sides of the deterrence debate, while the 'unadmitted' reveal themselves to be out not for justice, but for revenge." Writing in the *Philadelphia Inquirer*, Jay Neugeboren noted that *This Is the Way the World Ends* "begins where *Dr. Strangelove* ends. . . . [Morrow] deals seriously and intelligently with large issues—moral choice, global survival—within the most unlikely contexts, and in strangely captivating modes."

Often Morrow's satire takes aim at the foibles of organized religion. *Only Begotten Daughter,* which won the World Fantasy Award for best novel in 1991, tells of the immaculate conception and birth of Julie Katz, who is born in New Jersey in 1974 from sperm obtained from an Atlantic City sperm bank. She finds life just as difficult as Jesus had in Judea in the first century: she gets little or no heavenly guidance, and she is opposed by fundamentalist forces rooted in her native New Jersey. "The novel is a savage indictment of the potential evils of organized religion," wrote Cox. "It combines Swiftian satire, black humor, warmly sympathetic characters, with a clear yet eloquent prose style. However one wishes to label it, *Only Begotten Daughter* is one of the most impressive novels of the past decade." Jack Butler of the *New York Times Book Review* likened the novel's form to that of Kurt Vonnegut's works, commending its "dense, hyperkinetic plotting" and "brilliantly funny vignettes."

In *Bible Stories for Adults, Towing Jehovah,* and *Blameless in Abaddon,* Morrow expands his interest in satirizing organized religion. *Bible Stories,* a collection of twelve "dark, funny tales of spirituality,"

explained McDonough, shows how God interacts with the world he created, often in ways that people misinterpret and misunderstand. The book McDonough concluded, "will be advertised as irreverent," though McDonough himself disagrees, saying that despite Morrow's "biting humor," his writing displays respect for humankind's "place in the great cosmic joke." Gregory Feeley of the *Washington Post Book World* complimented Morrow's stories, saying they are "crisp and readable but they run in the danger of being glib."

In *Towing Jehovah,* God is dead—literally. His corpse has fallen from the heavens, and the Vatican has to contract with an unemployed oil tanker captain, Anthony Van Horne, to tow it to its final resting place in the Arctic. "The bizarre details actually work in context even if . . . they may seem extreme," wrote Joe Mayhew in the *Washington Post Book World.* "It is important, however, to remember that Morrow is writing about the vices of *man.* His novel attacks only the cartoons of religion, not the real thing."

Blameless in Abaddon, the sequel to *Towing Jehovah,* is a modern-dress retelling of the Book of Job. Devastated by a series of personal losses, a small-town magistrate named Martin Candle drags the comatose Corpus Dei before the World Court in The Hague. A *New York Times* notable book of the year, *Blameless in Abaddon* is "diverting and entertaining, sober and demanding, all at once," according to Peter Landry of the *Philadelphia Inquirer.*

The Eternal Footman, the third novel of the "Godhead" trilogy and Morrow's final word on "the post-theistic world," appeared late in 1999. Commenting on the increasingly popular genre of science fiction, Morrow told a reviewer *Library Journal:* "If I could eventually help fuse mainstream fiction's apprehension of human nature with science fiction's comprehension of human knowledge, I wouldn't mind dying one day."

BIOGRAPHICAL AND CRITICAL SOURCES:

BOOKS

St. James Guide to Science Fiction Writers, 4th edition, St. James Press, 1996.

PERIODICALS

Christian Science Monitor, July 31, 1992, p. 13.

Denver Post, November 28, 1999, review of *Blameless in Abaddon,* p. F2.

FermiNews, February 15, 2002, Mike Perricone, "Talk of the Lab."

Library Journal, June 15, 1981; April 15, 1992, p. 125.

Locus, June, 1994, pp. 23, 62.

New York Review of Science Fiction, March, 1994, pp. 1, 8-11.

New York Times Book Review, March 18, 1990; March 10, 1996, p. 8; September 15, 1996, p. 40.

Philadelphia Inquirer, August 24, 1986; August 25, 1996.

Pittsburgh Post-Gazette, February 26, 2000, Ken Chiacchia, "Sci-Fi Writers Urged 'To Think Until It Hurts,'" p. B-8.

Publishers Weekly, April 6, 1992, p. 55; March 21, 1994, pp. 69-70; April 4, 1994, p. 61.

San Diego Union Tribune, July 17, 1994; October 10, 1996.

Science Fiction Studies, March, 2003, Fiona Kelleghan, "War of World-Views: A Conversation with James Morrow," p. 1.

Utopian Studies, January 1, 1999, David N. Samuelson, "Overview of Science Fiction Literature in the 1980's and 1990's," p. 198.

Washington Post Book World, October 25, 1981; April 24, 1994, p. 10; March 31, 1996, p. 8.

ONLINE

SF Site, http://www.sfsite.com/ (November, 2000), Nick Gevers, "A Conversation with James Morrow."*

*   *   *

MOSS, Norman 1928-

PERSONAL: Born September 30, 1928, in London, England; son of Benjamin and Lydia Moss; married Hilary Sesta (an actress); children: Paul, Antony. *Education:* Attended Hamilton College (Clinton, NY), 1946-47.

ADDRESSES: Agent—c/o Author Mail, Houghton Mifflin Co. Trade Division, Adult Editorial, 8th Floor, 222 Berkeley St., Boston, MA 02116-3764.

CAREER: Reuter's News Agency, reporter and copy editor, 1952-56; Associated Press, London Bureau, London, England, reporter and copy editor, 1956-59; Radio Press International, foreign correspondent, 1962-65; *Sunday Times,* London, reporter, 1965-66; Metromedia Radio News, chief European correspondent, 1968-72; writer and broadcaster in London, beginning 1972.

WRITINGS:

Men Who Play God: The Story of the Hydrogen Bomb and How the World Came to Live with It, Harper & Row (New York, NY), 1968, revised edition, Penguin (Harmondsworth, England), 1972.

What's the Difference?: A British-American Dictionary, Harper & Row (New York, NY), 1973, published as *What's the Difference?: An American-British, British-American Dictionary,* Hutchinson (London, England), 1973, new and updated edition published as *British/American Language Dictionary: For More Effective Communication between Americans and Britons,* Passport Books (Lincolnwood, IL), 1991.

The Pleasures of Deception, Reader's Digest Press (New York, NY), 1977.

The Politics of Uranium, Universe Books (New York, NY), 1982.

The Travel Guide to British/American English, National Textbook Company (Chicago, IL), 1986.

Klaus Fuchs: The Man Who Stole the Atom Bomb, St. Martin's (New York, NY), 1987.

(Editor) *The Hutchinson Paperback Guide to the World,* Helicon (Baltimore, MD), 1990.

Managing the Planet: The Politics of the New Millennium, Earthscan (London, England), 2000.

Nineteen Weeks: America, Britain, and the Fateful Summer of 1940, Houghton Mifflin (Boston, MA), 2003.

Contributor to British and American magazines.

SIDELIGHTS: Norman Moss is a British journalist and freelance writer who has published a number of books on historical subjects, many of which concern military and political issues. His first book, *Men Who Play God: The Story of the Hydrogen Bomb and How the World Came to Live with It,* concerns the collaboration between scientists and politicians in the development of the hydrogen bomb. Originally published in

1968, Moss revised the book four years later to include extra material on the moral issues concerning nuclear weaponry. *Military Affairs* contributor S. L. Harrison felt that audiences with an interest in the military would appreciate the author's analysis of how the "evolution of new weaponry often becomes a tenuous process." *The Politics of Uranium,* published in 1972, is similar in some ways to *Men Who Play God* in that Moss relates the partnership between government and another potentially dangerous prospect: nuclear energy. The author touches on such points as safety issues and the international views about this energy source. Although John Abbotts, writing in *Business & Society Review,* felt that Moss asks more questions than he answers, the critic attested that Moss is interesting when he "describes the formation of the uranium producers' cartel from corporations and governments representing industrialized nations. Later, he recounts the Pakistani Government's efforts to construct a uranium enrichment plant by purchasing individual components through a chain of dummy corporations."

The dangers of nuclear technology also figure in Moss' much-reviewed book *Klaus Fuchs: The Man Who Stole the Atom Bomb,* which is a look at the British physicist who confessed in 1950 to giving information to the Soviets about the Manhattan Project. The Klaus case was an infamous chapter in the early history of the Cold War, helping to stir up what became the "Red Scare" of the 1950s in America and causing serious diplomatic problems between the United States and Great Britain, since the Americans had difficulty trusting British security after it was revealed Fuchs had been a spy for almost a decade without anyone noticing. Reviewers of *Klaus Fuchs* often compared it to Robert Chadwell Williams' *Klaus Fuchs, Atom Spy,* which was published at the same time. Williams' work, however, takes a broader look at Fuchs' spying within the context of surrounding historical events, while Moss is more interested in analyzing Fuchs the man. The result is a more biographical look that helps explain the psychological aspects of this quiet scientist who had deep-seeded beliefs in communism. *Science* writer Robert Bothwell felt that Moss does not do as well on the context of the situation as Williams, but that, overall, Moss is the "better writer . . . and he has the advantage of greater familiarity with British life and nomenclature." M. J. Heale, writing in *Reviews in American History,* similarly believed that Moss' book is the better of the two: Moss "has perhaps spent less time in archives and libraries than Williams, but seems to make more extensive use of interviews with

Fuchs's associates. In his pages Fuchs come[s] alive." Attesting that these books, taken together, complement each other well, *Los Angeles Times Book Review* critic Peter Goodchild nevertheless concluded that his preference was for Moss' more biographical approach because of its "more rounded portrayal of the man himself backed up as it is with an adequate perspective on both the politics and the espionage."

With *Nineteen Weeks: America, Britain, and the Fateful Summer of 1940,* Moss completed an ambitious project that delves into little-documented events in Britain that had major ramifications in the war against Adolf Hitler. The nineteen weeks of the title refers to a period in 1940 when the British government was considering a number of possible courses of action; these included everything from political deals with Ireland and France to secure stronger military resistance against Germany to accepting a speculative offer from Hitler himself to declare an armistice. Meanwhile, on the other side of the Atlantic, President Roosevelt was making important decisions about America's intervention, decisions that would eventually bring the United States to the fore of World War II in events that would precipitate the end to the British Empire but bring an end to the Nazi threat. "Even those familiar with the historical chronology will enjoy Moss' engaging narrative," declared Brendan Driscoll in *Booklist. Library Journal* contributor Robert Moore, however, found flaws in the book that, the critic felt, were the result of Moss' background as a journalist instead of as a historian: "histrionics and heavily freighted anecdotes [detract from] otherwise legitimate research," Moore asserted. While a *Kirkus Reviews* critic similarly pointed out that professional historians will be able to discern Moss' shortcomings, "general readers will find this a lucid introduction to the days before the tide was turned."

In addition to his books of historical interest, Moss has written on topics such as the environment and a language guide to the differences between British and American English.

BIOGRAPHICAL AND CRITICAL SOURCES:

PERIODICALS

American Speech, fall-winter, 1973, Henry R. Stern, "British and American," p. 276.
Booklist, May 1, 2003, Brendan Driscoll, review of *Nineteen Weeks: America, Britain, and the Fateful Summer of 1940,* p. 1576.

Business & Society Review, fall, 1982, John Abbotts, "Atomic Power, Atomic Bombs," pp. 78-81.

Kirkus Reviews, March 15, 2003, review of *Nineteen Weeks,* p. 446.

Library Journal, July 1, 1977, A. J. Anderson, review of *The Pleasures of Deception,* p. 1497; April 15, 2003, Robert Moore, review of *Nineteen Weeks,* p. 103.

Los Angeles Times Book Review, November 29, 1987, Peter Goodchild, "The Spy Who Sold Russia the Bomb," p. 8.

Military Affairs, October, 1973, S. L. Harrison, "*Military Professionalization and Political Power; Men Who Play God: The Story of the Hydrogen Bomb; The University and Military Research: Moral Politics at M.I.T.,*" p. 113.

Reviews in American History, December, 1988, M. J. Heale, "Secrets of a Special Relationship," pp. 630-635.

Saturday Review, July 5, 1969.

Science, November 6, 1987, Robert Bothwell, "The Fuchs Case," p. 831.*

MOUNTFIELD, David
   See GRANT, Neil

*   *   *

NICHOLS, Leigh
   See KOONTZ, Dean R(ay)

*   *   *

NORTH, Anthony
   See KOONTZ, Dean R(ay)

*   *   *

NORTH, Milou
   See ERDRICH, (Karen) Louise

N-O

NUNES, Lygia Bojunga 1932-
(Lygia Bojunga-Nunes, Lygia Bojunga)

PERSONAL: Born August 26, 1932, in Pelotas, Brazil; married.

ADDRESSES: Home—26 Cressy Rd., London NW3 2LY, England; Rua Eliseu Visconti 425, 20251 Rio de Janeiro, RJ, Brazil.

CAREER: Writer, translator, and actor. Member of theatre troupe Theatre Duse and of Repertoire Theatre of Henriette Morineau; cofounder of rural school, TOCA. Presenter of dramatic monologues at libraries, universities, and cultural centers.

AWARDS, HONORS: Jabuti award, 1973; Hans Christian Andersen award, 1982, for body of children's books; Molière prize, Theatre Critics of Paris, and Mambembe Trophy, Ministry of Education and Culture, Brazil, both 1986, both for play *O pintor;* Rattenfänger Literaturpreis, 1986; Astrid Lindgren Memorial award, 2004.

WRITINGS:

Os colegas, Sabia (Rio de Janeiro, Brazil), 1972, translated by Ellen Watson as *The Companions,* illustrated by Larry Wilkes, Farrar, Strauss (New York, NY), 1989.

Angélica, illustrated by Vilma Pasqualini, Artes Graficas Industrias Reunidas (Rio de Janeiro, Brazil), 1975.

A bolsa amarela (title means "The Yellow Bag"), illustrated by Marie Louise Nery, Artes Graficas Industrias Reunidas (Rio de Janeiro, Brazil), 1976.

A casa de madrinha (title means "Godmother's House"), illustrated by Regina Yolanda, Artes Graficas Industrias Reunidas (Rio de Janeiro, Brazil), 1978.

Corda bamba (title means "Tightrope"), Civilizacão (Rio de Janeiro, Brazil), 1979.

O sofá estampado (title means "The Chintz Sofa"), illustrated by Elvira Vigna, Olympio (Rio de Janeiro, Brazil), 1980.

Tomie Ohtake, [Rio de Janeiro, Brazil], 1983.

Tchau (title means "Bye"), Artes Graficas Industrias Reunidas (Rio de Janeiro, Brazil), 1984.

Nós três (for children; title means "The Three of Us"; also see below), 1987.

O meu amigo pintor (for children; also see below), Olympio (Rio de Janeiro, Brazil), 1987, translated by Giovanni Pontiero as *My Friend the Painter,* illustrated by Christopher DeLorenzo, Harcourt (New York, NY), 1991.

Livro (autobiography; title means "Book"), Artes Graficas Industrias Reunidas (Rio de Janeiro, Brazil), 1988.

Fazendo Ana Paz (title means "Creating Ana Paz"), illustrated by Regina Yolanda, Artes Graficas Industrias Reunidas (Rio de Janeiro, Brazil), 1991.

Paisagem (collected works; title means "Landscape"), Artes Graficas Industrias Reunidas (Rio de Janeiro, Brazil), 1992.

Seis vezes Lucas, illustrated by Roger Mello and Regina Yolanda, Artes Graficas Industrias Reunidas (Rio de Janeiro, Brazil), 1996.

Feito à mão, Artes Graficas Industrias Reunidas (Rio de Janeiro, Brazil), 1996.

O rio e eu, illustrated by Roberto Magalhães, Salamandra (São Paulo, Brazil), 1999.

A cama, Artes Graficas Industrias (Rio de Janeiro, Brazil), 1999.

Retratos de Carolina, Editoria Casa Lygia Bojunga Ltd. (Rio de Janeiro, Brazil), 2002.

Also author of *O pintor* (play; based on *O meu amigo pintor*), 1989, and *Nós três* (play; based on book of the same title), 1989.

Nunes's works have been translated into several languages, including French, German, Spanish, Swedish, Norwegian, Danish, Finnish, Basque, Hebrew, Italian, Icelandic, Dutch, Czech, Bulgarian, Galician, and Catalan.

SIDELIGHTS: Winner of the 1982 Hans Christian Andersen award and the 2004 Astrid Lindgren Memorial award, Brazilian author Lygia Bojunga Nunes has written several children's books that have been translated into a variety of languages. Though her work is known in many countries, only two of her works have been translated into English: *The Companions,* originally published in 1972 and translated to English in 1989, and *My Friend the Painter,* published in 1987 and followed by an English translation in 1991.

Though Nunes's titles are usually directed to children, they are noted for containing social commentary. The author is a critic of the Brazilian school system; in fact, Nunes was concerned enough about illiteracy that she cofounded a school for rural children to help them better their education. Her titles have also focused on topics such as women's rights, poverty, and the desire for freedom and democracy. When Nunes began writing, her country's government was in turmoil; from 1959 until 1989, there were no democratic elections held in Brazil, and in that time, there were military coups and dictators running the country. Nunes turned to children's books for her social commentary because, as she explained, "Generals don't read children's books." This commentary does not bog down Nunes's work, in the opinion of critics and readers. On the *Astrid Lindgren Memorial Award Web site,* a biographer noted that Nunes "constantly offsets the serious with playfulness and absurd humor."

Nunes's work is also noted for its use of magical realism. Like many Brazilian writers, she does not establish a boundary between the fantastic and the realistic. Animals may become addicted to television—the problem of a cat in *O sofá estampado*—while a girl may have her dreams literally pricked by a safety pin—which happens in *A bolsa amarela.* And fighting cocks may have their brains sewed together so they can only think of fighting, which also occurs in *A bolsa amarela.* Nunes also uses symbolism that nearly crosses the boundaries into the fantastic: young Maria walks a tightrope in *Corda bamba,* opening the doors she encounters and opens up memories she has blocked, while Alexander of *A casa de madrinha* seeks his imaginary godmother's house through many adventures, hoping to find someplace where he can be safe.

Os colegas, or *The Companions,* was Nunes's first novel. In the book, a young rabbit is abandoned by his family and left to fend for himself. He befriends a bear who has escaped from the zoo and a pampered dog who ran away from home to be free. When the rabbit's two friends are captured, the frightened rabbit rescues the dog, who joins him to rescue the bear. On the *Astrid Lindgren Memorial Award Web site,* Mats Berggren stated that Nunes presents "a wide-ranging view of the contrasts between oppression and freedom" at a level that young readers can understand.

O meu amigo pintor, or *My Friend the Painter,* is aimed at older elementary and middle-grade readers. In the book young Claudio must cope with the suicide of his adult friend, a painter who encouraged the boy's interest in art. The story is told in a realistic fashion, though Claudio's dreams are an important part of the grieving process. Berggren commented that Claudio comes to understand that he "needs to think of [the painter] . . . in his entirety, with all the details," in order to begin to comprehend his questions about the painter's death. According to some critics, Nunes's treatment of her subject is emotionally intense, while other reviewers found *My Friend the Painter* too abstract and subtle for young readers. A *Kirkus Reviews* critic praised the book as "a rich, poetic glimpse of universal feelings filtered through an unfamiliar culture," while in *Publishers Weekly* a reviewer described the writing as exhibiting "remarkable, sustained intensity." And a reviewer in the *Bulletin of the Center for Children's Books* called Nunes's conclusion "a lyrical celebration of a remembered friendship."

Nunes adapted *My Friend the Painter* as a play, and also dramatized her earlier novel, *Nós três.* She began utilizing playwriting as a medium with her second novel, *Angélica,* in which part of the story is told entirely as a play. The main characters—a pig, a stork, an elephant, and a crocodile—put on a play to show how people in power are able to make lies become popular thought. Throughout the course of the play, these characters defy the stereotypes other animals have against them and learn that by working together they can improve their own lives.

In other books the author uses short-story and episodic forms, such as in *Tchau* and *Seis vezes Lucas.* In the latter, Nunes illuminates six moments in Lucas's life, showing his fears of not living up to his father's expectations. In both *Tchau* and *Seis vezes Lucas* the author confronts the issue of marital infidelity through the eyes of a child hurt by the occurrence. *Retratos de Carolina,* like *Seis vezes Lucas,* focuses on moments in Carolina's life, from the time she is six years old until she is aged twenty-nine, at which point she encounters Nunes and asks the author to write her a happy ending.

Nunes once noted, "Since I was seven I began reading stories, and right from the beginning I fell in love with books. But it was a love of reading, not doing. My affair took me by surprise because it was so overwhelming, so much a part of me, that before I realized what was happening, I'd been taken over entirely by literature."

BIOGRAPHICAL AND CRITICAL SOURCES:

PERIODICALS

Bulletin of the Center for Children's Books, May, 1991, review of *My Friend the Painter,* p. 224.
Kirkus Reviews, May 1, 1991, review of *My Friend the Painter,* p. 607.
Publishers Weekly, April 19, 1991, review of *My Friend the Painter,* p. 66.
School Library Journal, January, 1990, Susan Helper, review of *The Companions,* p. 76; October, 1991, p. 125; February, 1998, Louise Yarian Zwick, review of *A bolsa amarela,* p. 93.

ONLINE

Astrid Lindgren Memorial Award Web site, http://www.alma.se/ (September 7, 2004), Mats Berggren, "Lygia Bojuna Nunes."*

OLIVER, Mary 1935-

PERSONAL: Born September 10, 1935, in Cleveland, OH; daughter of Edward William (a teacher) and Helen M. (Vlasak) Oliver. *Education:* Attended Ohio State University, 1955-56, and Vassar College, 1956-57.

ADDRESSES: Office—Bennington College, Bennington, VT 05201. *Agent*—c/o Molly Malone Cook Literary Agency, Box 619, Provincetown, MA 02657.

CAREER: Fine Arts Work Center, Provincetown, MA, chair of writing department, 1972-73, member of writing committee, 1984; Case Western Reserve University, Cleveland, OH, Mather Visiting Professor, 1980, 1982; Bucknell University, Lewisburg, PA, poet-in-residence, 1986; University of Cincinnati, Cincinnati, OH, Elliston Visiting Professor, 1986; Sweet Briar College, Sweet Briar, VA, Margaret Banister Writer-in-Residence, 1991-95; Bennington College, Bennington, VT, Catharine Osgood Foster Chair for Distinguished Teaching, 1996—.

MEMBER: PEN.

AWARDS, HONORS: First prize, Poetry Society of America, 1962, for "No Voyage"; Devil's Advocate Award, 1968, for "Christmas, 1966"; Shelley Memorial Award, 1972; National Endowment for the Arts fellow, 1972-73; Alice Fay di Castagnola Award, 1973; Guggenheim fellow, 1980-81; Award in Literature, American Academy and Institution of Arts and Letters, 1983; Pulitzer Prize, 1984, for *American Primitive;* Christopher Award and L. L. Winship Award, both 1991, for *House of Light;* National Book Award for Poetry, 1992, for *New and Selected Poems;* Lannan Literary Award for Poetry, 1998.

WRITINGS:

No Voyage, and Other Poems, Dent (New York, NY), 1963, expanded edition, Houghton Mifflin (Boston, MA), 1965.
The River Styx, Ohio, and Other Poems, Harcourt (New York, NY), 1972.
The Night Traveler, Bits Press, 1978.

Twelve Moons, Little, Brown (Boston, MA), 1978.

Sleeping in the Forest, Ohio Review Chapbook, 1979.

American Primitive, Little, Brown (Boston, MA), 1983.

Dream Work, Atlantic Monthly Press (Boston, MA), 1986.

Provincetown, Appletree Alley, 1987.

(Author of introduction) Frank Gaspar, *Holyoke,* Northeastern University Press, 1988.

House of Light, Beacon Press (Boston, MA), 1990.

New and Selected Poems, Beacon Press (Boston, MA), 1992.

A Poetry Handbook, Harcourt (San Diego, CA), 1994.

White Pine: Poems and Prose Poems, Harcourt (San Diego, CA), 1994.

Blue Pastures, Harcourt (New York, NY), 1995.

West Wind: Poems and Prose Poems, Houghton Mifflin (Boston, MA), 1997.

Rules for the Dance: A Handbook for Writing and Reading Metrical Verse, Houghton Mifflin (Boston, MA), 1998.

Winter Hours: Prose, Prose Poems, and Poems, Houghton Mifflin (Boston, MA), 1999.

The Leaf and the Cloud, Da Capo (Cambridge, MA), 2000.

What Do We Know, Da Capo (Cambridge, MA), 2002.

Why I Wake Early, Beacon (Boston, MA), 2004.

Boston Iris: Poems and Essays, Beacon (Boston, MA), 2004.

Long Life: Essays and Other Writings, Da Capo (Cambridge, MA), 2004.

New and Selected Poems, Volume Two, Beacon (Boston, MA), 2004.

Contributor of poetry and essays to periodicals in England and the United States.

ADAPTATIONS: Oliver's poems have been set to music for mezzo-soprano voice, violin, and piano by composer Augusta Read Thomas in *In Summer,* Theodore Presser (Bryn Mawr, PA), 1994, and for soprano voice and bassoon by composer Ann Kearns in *Six Poems of Mary Oliver,* Casia Publishing Co. (Bryn Mawr, PA), 1997.

SIDELIGHTS: Poet Mary Oliver is an "indefatigable guide to the natural world," wrote Maxine Kumin in *Women's Review of Books,* "particularly to its lesser-known aspects." Oliver's verse focuses on the quiet of occurrences of nature: industrious hummingbirds,

egrets, motionless ponds, "lean owls / hunkering with their lamp-eyes." Kumin noted of the poet: "She stands quite comfortably on the margins of things, on the line between earth and sky, the thin membrane that separates human from what we loosely call animal." The power of Oliver's poetry earned her numerous awards, including 1984's Pulitzer Prize for *American Primitive* and the National Book Award in 1992 for *New and Selected Poems.* Reviewing *Dream Work* for the *Nation,* critic Alicia Ostriker numbered Oliver among America's finest poets, as "visionary as [Ralph Waldo] Emerson."

American Primitive, according to *New York Times Book Review*'s Bruce Bennet, "insists on the primacy of the physical." Bennet noted that "recurring images of ingestion" figure throughout the volume, and "as we joyfully devour luscious objects and substances . . . we are continually reminded of our involvement in a process in which what consumes will be consumed." Bennet commended Oliver's "distinctive voice and vision" and asserts that the "collection contains a number of powerful, substantial works." Holly Prado of *Los Angeles Times Book Review* also applauded Oliver's original voice when she wrote that *American Primitive* "touches a vitality in the familiar that invests it with a fresh intensity."

Dream Work continues Oliver's search to "understand both the wonder and pain of nature" according to Prado in a later review for *Los Angeles Times Book Review.* Ostriker sounded this note more specifically when she considered Oliver "among the few American poets who can describe and transmit ecstasy, while retaining a practical awareness of the world as one of predators and prey." Colin Lowndes of the Toronto *Globe & Mail* similarly considered Oliver "a poet of worked-for reconciliations" whose volume deals with thresholds, or the "points at which opposing forces meet." Both Prado and Ostriker praised Oliver's lyrical gift. Ostriker described Oliver's verse as "intensely lyrical, flute-like, slender and swift . . . [riding] on vivid phrases," while Prado called the poetry of *Dream Work* "the best of the real lyrics we have these days." *Dream Work,* for Ostriker, is ultimately a volume in which Oliver moves "from the natural world and its desires, the 'heaven of appetite' . . . into the world of historical and personal suffering. . . . She confronts as well, steadily," Ostriker continued, "what she cannot change."

The transition from engaging the natural world to engaging the more personal is also evident in *New and*

Selected Poems. The volume contains poems from eight of Oliver's previous volumes as well as previously unpublished, newer work. Susan Salter Reynolds, in the *Los Angeles Times Book Review,* noticed that Oliver's earliest poems are almost always oriented towards nature, occasionally discuss relatives, but seldom examine her own self. In contrast, she appears constantly in her later works, such as *Long Life: Essays and Other Writings.* This is, as Reynolds noted, a good thing: "This self-consciousness is a rich and graceful addition." Just as the contributor for *Publishers Weekly* called particular attention to the pervasive tone of amazement—also the title of a poem—with regard to things seen in Oliver's work, Reynolds found Oliver's writings to have a "Blake-eyed revelatory quality." Oliver summed up her desire for amazement in her poem "When Death Comes" from *New and Selected Poems:* "When it's over, I want to say: all my life / I was a bride married to amazement. / I was the bridegroom, taking the world into my arms."

Oliver continues her celebration of the natural world in later collections, including *White Pine: Poems and Prose Poems, Blue Pastures, West Wind: Poems and Prose Poems,* and *Winter Hours: Prose, Prose Poems, and Poems.* Critics have compared her work to that of great American lyric poets and celebrators of nature, including Marianne Moore, Elizabeth Bishop, Edna St. Vincent Millay, John Muir, and Walt Whitman. "Oliver's poetry, pure as the cottony seeds of the dandelion," wrote *Poetry* contributor Richard Tillinghast in a review of *White Pine,* "floats above and around the schools and controversies of contemporary American poetry. Her familiarity with the natural world has an uncomplicated, nineteenth-century feeling." *America* reviewer David Sofield, in a critique of the same volume, called Oliver "an Emersonian rhapsode in full flight, but one with something like the canny vulnerability of Elizabeth Bishop when evoking the pathos of creatures great and small." "William Carlos Williams is alive in many of these poems," Sofield explained, as is the "late Wallace Stevens. . . . In putting her own stamp on poems about birds and trees and animals and seasons, and in her unyielding intensity," the *America* contributor concluded, ". . . this Mary Oliver provides serious pleasure."

In *Rules for the Dance: A Handbook for Writing and Reading Metrical Verse* Oliver returns to a subject she visited in *A Poetry Handbook.* Critics had celebrated the earlier volume as the work of "someone who has observed poems and their writing closely and who writes with unassuming authority about the work she and others do," according to a *Publishers Weekly* contributor. Oliver "starts in at poetry's real beginning, discussing the need for patient application: the need, in brief, to write and to do so regularly," explained Pat Monaghan in *Booklist.* "She so deeply knows her craft that she can describe it with perfect simplicity and concision." "Poetry is Oliver's lifeblood," declared *Booklist* contributor Donna Seaman in a review of *Rules for the Dance,* "and she writes about its creation with as much quiet ecstasy, acumen, and artistry as she writes poems themselves."

BIOGRAPHICAL AND CRITICAL SOURCES:

BOOKS

Contemporary Literary Criticism, Gale (Detroit, MI), Volume 19, 1981, Volume 98, 1998.
Contemporary Literary Criticism Yearbook 1984, Volume 34, Gale (Detroit, MI), 1985.
Contemporary Poets, 6th edition, St. James Press (Detroit, MI), 1996.
Dictionary of Literary Biography, Volume 5: *American Poets since World War II,* Gale (Detroit, MI), 1980.
Oliver, Mary, *New and Selected Poems,* Beacon Press, 1992.

PERIODICALS

America, January 13, 1996, David Sofield, review of *White Pine: Poems and Prose Poems.*
Booklist, July, 1994, Pat Monaghan, review of *A Poetry Handbook,* p. 1916; November 15, 1994, Donna Seaman, review of *White Pine,* p. 574; June 1, 1997, Donna Seaman, review of *West Wind: Poems and Prose Poems,* p. 1648; June 1, 1998, Donna Seaman, review of *Rules for the Dance: A Handbook for Writing and Reading Metrical Verse,* p. 1708; March 15, 1999, Donna Seaman, review of *Winter Hours,* p. 1279; September 1, 2000, Donna Seaman, review of *The Leaf and the Cloud,* p. 58; March 15, 2004, Donna Seaman, review of *Long Life: Essays and Other Writings,* p. 1259.
Globe & Mail (Toronto, Ontario, Canada), August 23, 1986.

Library Journal, July, 1997, Ellen Kaufman, review of *West Wind,* p. 87; August, 1998, Lisa J. Cihlar, review of *Rules for the Dance,* p. 104; December, 2000, Louis McKee, review of *The Leaf and the Cloud,* p. 145; December, 2003, Judy Clarence, review of *Owls and Other Fantasies: Poems and Essays,* p. 125; May 1, 2004, Kim Harris, review of *Long Life,* p. 107.

Los Angeles Times Book Review, August 21, 1983, p. 9; February 22, 1987, p. 8; August 30, 1992, p. 6.

Nation, August 30, 1986, pp. 148-150.

New York Times Book Review, July 17, 1983, pp. 10, 22; November 25, 1990, p. 24; December 13, 1992, p. 12.

Poetry, May, 1987, p. 113; September, 1991, p. 342; July, 1993, David Barber, review of *New and Selected Poems,* p. 233; August, 1995, Richard Tillinghast, review of *White Pine,* p. 289; August, 1999, Christian Wiman, review of *Rules for the Dance,* p. 286.

Publishers Weekly, May 4, 1990, p. 62; August 10, 1992, p. 58; June 6, 1994, review of *A Poetry Handbook,* p. 62; October 31, 1994, review of *White Pine,* p. 54; August 7, 1995, review of *Blue Pastures,* p. 457; June 30, 1997, review of *West Wind,* p. 73; March 29, 1999, review of *Winter Hours: Prose, Prose Poems, and Poems,* p. 100; August 28, 2000, review of *The Leaf and the Cloud,* p. 79; July 21, 2003, review of *Owls and Other Fantasies,* p. 188.

Washington Post Book World, February 1, 1987, p. 6.

Whole Earth Review, summer, 1995, Wade Fox, review of *A Poetry Handbook,* p. 30.

Women's Review of Books, April, 1993.*

*   *   *

OSBORN, Karen 1954-

PERSONAL: Born April 26, 1954, in Chicago, IL; daughter of Kenton Osborn (a chemist) and Lois (Mays) Osborn; married Michael Jenkins (an assistant athletic director), May 21, 1983; children: Kaitlynn, Shannon. *Ethnicity:* "White." *Education:* Hollins College, B.A. (cum laude), 1979; University of Arkansas—Fayetteville, M.F.A., 1983.

ADDRESSES: Home—Amherst, MA. *Agent*—Gelfman Schneider, 250 West 57th St., New York, NY 10107. *E-mail*—karenosborn@comcast.net.

CAREER: Novelist and poet. Arkansas Poetry in the Schools, poet, 1979-83, director, 1982-83; Clemson University, Clemson, SC, instructor in English, 1983-87; University of Kentucky, Lexington, part-time instructor in English, 1988-93. Technical writer, Clark Equipment, Inc., 1990; consultant, writing program adjunct for Engineering College, 1990-92. Has led writing workshops and given readings for numerous schools and organizations, including Writer's Voice, Augusta Round Table, Southern Festival of Books, Women Writer's Conference, and Bookfest.

AWARDS, HONORS: Hollins Literary Festival Awards for poetry and for fiction, both 1979; Nancy Thorp Prize for poetry, 1979; Mary Vincent Long Award, 1979, for distinguished literary achievement; McKean Award for poetry, 1981; Kentucky Foundation for Women grant, 1991, to fund work on *Between Earth and Sky;* Al Smith Artists Fellowship Award for fiction, Kentucky Arts Council, 1991; *New York Times* Notable Book Award, 1991, for *Patchwork.*

WRITINGS:

NOVELS

Patchwork, Harcourt Brace (New York, NY), 1991.
Between Earth and Sky, Morrow (New York, NY), 1996.
The River Road, Morrow (New York, NY), 2002.

OTHER

Work represented in numerous anthologies and collections, including *Jumping Pond: Poems and Stories from the Ozarks,* edited by Michael Burns and Mark Sanders, Southwest Missouri State University, 1983; *Cardinal: A Contemporary Anthology,* edited by Richard Krawiec, Jacar Press, 1986; and *Hollins Anthology,* 1991. Contributor of poems to numerous periodicals, including *Artemis, Mid American Review, Seattle Review, Tar River Poetry, Embers, Southern Review, Kansas Quarterly, Poet Lore, Passages North, Montana Review, Centennial Review,* and *Wisconsin Review.*

WORK IN PROGRESS: A fourth novel and a memoir.

SIDELIGHTS: Karen Osborn once told *CA,* "I started out as a poet, and I think the language of my fiction is still grounded in rhythm, image, and metaphor. I've moved so often in my life that it's hard to say that I'm from a particular region, although I've spent long periods of time in the South and feel an affinity with that part of the country. So far, each of my books takes place in a very different kind of location, and each has its own unique structure. As a writer, I like the challenge of taking on an unusual point of view or subject matter, so I've used techniques like letters and multiple points of views, and I've been drawn to characters who are very different from myself. For me, much of the excitement in writing comes from where that takes me and what I learn from having to stretch my own voice to meet it."

Praise for Osborn's first novel, *Patchwork,* included this statement from a *New York Times Book Review* critic: "Ms. Osborn, herself a poet, often renders rural Southern dialect into something close to poetry." A reviewer for *Atlanta Constitution Journal* also stated, "Many Southern writers have latched onto the quilt as a metaphor, but none has done a finer job of literary stitching than Kentucky poet Karen Osborn in *Patchwork,* a sensitive, unforgettable story of a South Carolina mill family." One *Publishers Weekly* reviewer called *Patchwork* an "engrossing, well-crafted, poignant first novel."

Osborn's second novel, *Between Earth and Sky,* spins a tale of the trials and triumphs of a remarkable pioneer woman's efforts to carve out a new life for her family in New Mexico. Told through letters, the book reflects the raw beauty of the Southwest in the period following the U.S. Civil War. Finding *Between Earth and Sky* rich in historical detail, a critic for *Kirkus Reviews* remarked that the book offers "an epistolary novel that, while not scanting the hardships and tragedies of pioneer life, luminously evokes a pristine northern New Mexico." Donna Seaman of *Booklist* noted that "Osborn is lyrical, focused, and enchanting."

The River Road, Osborn's next novel, was inspired by the tragic death of a student that occurred while Osborn was teaching. The book garnered the most critical attention of any of her works. In *The River Road,* brothers David and Michael Sanderson and their next-door neighbor Kay Richards have been friends all their lives. Kay knows she will marry one of the brothers,

and her affections finally settle upon David, the older brother, and they become lovers upon entering college. One night while on a break from school, the three travel to the French King Bridge in Northfield, Massachusetts, which stretches over the Connecticut River. Kay and David drop acid and climb out onto the bridge while Michael scowls on the shore. David believes that if he jumps he will live and swim to shore. After kissing Kay, he dives into the water . . . and dies.

Kevin, David and Michael's father, cannot accept what has happened. Several possibilities might explain the events of the night: David may have jumped truly believing he would live, he may have committed suicide, or he may have been murdered. Michael, who has always been jealous of Kay's relationship with David, suggests that Kay pushed his older brother into the river. Kevin accepts this as the only plausible explanation, and he proceeds to render Kay a sex-obsessed, drug-pushing temptress and murderer. The town stands behind Kevin and Michael, Kay is put on trial for David's murder, and many lives are destroyed. In a review of *The River Road* for *USA Today,* Susan Kelly wrote, "Osborn immerses us from the beginning in the hot and cold currents of love and hate that sustain, divide, and inexorably pull us all toward an uncertain fate."

The story is told through the oscillating perspectives of Kay, Michael, and Kevin. "Osborn's use of varied points of view is her masterstroke, showing compassion for all three characters and revealing their different experiences of David: the lover of danger, the competitive brother, the gifted son," suggested Kelly. "My intention in not using David's voice was to make his presence more palpable," Osborn revealed in an interview on the *HarperCollins* Web site. "He becomes a character or a person as remembered by the others, so that just as it's impossible to know what actually happened that night on the bridge, it's impossible to truly know who David was. . . . The identity or essence of an individual is a slippery thing, impossible to get one's hands around. Our many different sides are brought out by the complicated ways we relate to others."

One *Publishers Weekly* reviewer criticized Osborn's telling of the tragedy. "Osborn's prose is clean and neat," the reviewer wrote, "but the curious flatness of the narration—emotions blankly stated instead of evoked—robs the story of depth and power." This opinion, however, was in the minority. One *Kirkus Reviews* contributor stated that the novel was "carefully constructed and well told: a work of tremendous, quiet power." Carolyn See of the *Washington Post* also had much praise to offer Osborn. "There in no authorial ego exercised in *The River Road*. There is no obvious author, preening, trying and possibly failing to be smart. There is only an extraordinary effort to engage the American condition as we find it now," explained See, who applauded the author's ability to present the situation, "then adroitly slip away, leaving the reader to decide the meaning—which has nothing to do with arcane literary allusions and everything to do with the state of the human soul."

BIOGRAPHICAL AND CRITICAL SOURCES:

PERIODICALS

Atlanta Constitution Journal, July 14, 1991, review of *Patchwork,* p. N8.
Booklist, March 1, 1996, Donna Seaman, review of *Between Earth and Sky,* p. 1123; October 15, 2002, Elsa Gaztambide, review of *The River Road,* p. 388.
Kirkus Reviews, December 1, 1995, review of *Between Earth and Sky,* p. 1660; September 1, 2002, review of *The River Road,* p. 1257.
Library Journal, December, 2002, Christine Perkins, review of *The River Road,* p. 180.
New York Times Book Review, August 25, 1991, Judith Patterson, review of *Patchwork,* p. 11; May 12, 1996, p. 19.
Publishers Weekly, May 10, 1991, review of *Patchwork,* p. 274; November 27, 1995, review of *Between Earth and Sky,* p. 49; October 14, 2002, review of *The River Road,* p. 64.
USA Today, January 7, 2003, Susan Kelly, review of *The River Road,* p. D6.
Washington Post, November 8, 2002, Carolyn See, review of *The River Road,* p. C2.

ONLINE

HarperCollins Web site, http://www.harpercollins.com/ (March 23, 2004), "Karen Osborn."
Karen Osborn Web site, http://www.karenosborn.com (April 7, 2005).

Mostly Fiction Web site, http://mostlyfiction.com/ (March 23, 2004), excerpt from and synopsis of *The River Road.*

*   *   *

OZ, Amos 1939-

PERSONAL: Given name Amos Klausner; born May 4, 1939, in Jerusalem, Israel; son of Yehuda Arieh (a writer) and Fania (Mussman) Klausner; married Nily Zuckerman, April 5, 1960; children: Fania, Gallia, Daniel. *Education:* Hebrew University of Jerusalem, B.A., 1963; St. Cross College, Oxford, M.A., 1970.

ADDRESSES: Office—Ben Gurion University Negev, Beer Sheva, Israel. *Agent*—Mrs. D. Owen, 28 Narrow St., London E 14, England.

CAREER: Writer, 1962—. Hulda High School, Givat Brenner, Israel, teacher of literature and philosophy, 1963-86; visiting fellow, St. Cross College, Oxford University, 1969-70; writer-in-residence, Hebrew University of Jerusalem, 1975-76, and 1990, and Colorado College, 1985; University of California—Berkeley, visiting professor, 1980; visiting professor and writer-in-residence, Boston University, and Princeton University, both 1987; Ben Gurion University Negev, Beer Sheva, Israel, professor, 1986—. Has worked as a tractor driver, youth instructor, school teacher, and agricultural worker at Kibbutz Hulda, Israel. *Military service:* Israeli Army, 1957-60; also fought as reserve soldier in the tank corps in Sinai, 1967, and in the Golan Heights, 1973.

MEMBER: PEN, Peace Now, Academy of Hebrew Language, Catalan Academy of the Mediterranean.

AWARDS, HONORS: Holon Prize for Literature, 1965; Israel-American Cultural Foundation award, 1968; B'nai B'rith annual literary award, 1973; Brener Prize, 1978; Officier de l'Ordre des Art et des Lettres, 1984; Bialik Prize, 1986; Prix Femina, 1988; Wingate Prize, 1988; International Peace Prize, German Publishers Association, 1992; Chevalier de la Légion d'Honneur (France), 1997; Israel Prize for Literature, 1998; honorary degrees from Hebrew Union College, Western New England College, and Tel Aviv University.

Amos Oz

WRITINGS:

Artzot ha' tan (short stories), Massada (Tel Aviv, Israel), 1965, translation by Nicholas de Lange and Philip Simpson published as *Where the Jackals Howl, and Other Stories,* Harcourt (San Diego, CA), 1981.

Makom acher (novel), Sifriat Po'alim (Tel Aviv, Israel), 1966, translation by Nicholas de Lange published as *Elsewhere, Perhaps,* Harcourt (San Diego, CA), 1973.

Michael sheli (novel), Am Oved (Tel Aviv, Israel), 1968, translation with Nicholas de Lange published as *My Michael,* Knopf (New York, NY), 1972.

Ad mavet (two novellas), Sifriat Po'alim (Tel Aviv, Israel), 1971, translation with Nicholas de Lange published as *Unto Death,* Harcourt (San Diego, CA), 1975.

Laga'at ba'mayim, laga'at ba'ruach (novel), Am Oved (Tel Aviv, Israel), 1973, translation with Nicholas de Lange published as *Touch the Water, Touch the Wind,* Harcourt (San Diego, CA), 1974.

Anashim acherim (anthology; title means "Different People"), Ha'Kibbutz Ha'Meuchad (Tel Aviv, Israel), 1974.

Har he'etza ha'raah (three novellas), Am Oved (Tel Aviv, Israel), 1976, translation with Nicholas de Lange published as *The Hill of Evil Counsel,* Harcourt (San Diego, CA), 1978.

Soumchi (juvenile), Am Oved (Tel Aviv, Israel), 1978, translation with Penelope Farmer published as *Soumchi,* Harper (New York, NY), 1980, reprinted, Harcourt (San Diego, CA), 1995.

Be' or ha'tchelet he'azah (essays), Sifriat Po'alim, (Tel Aviv, Israel), 1979, translation by Nicholas de Lange published as *Under this Blazing Light: Essays,* Press Syndicate of the University of Cambridge (New York, NY), 1995.

Menucha nechonah (novel), Am Oved (Tel Aviv, Israel), 1982, translation by Hillel Halkin published as *A Perfect Peace,* Harcourt (San Diego, CA), 1985.

Po ve'sham b'eretz Yisra'el bistav 1982 (nonfiction), Am Oved (Tel Aviv, Israel), 1983, translation by Maurie Goldberg-Bartura published as *In the Land of Israel,* Harcourt (San Diego, CA), 1983.

(Editor, with Richard Flantz and author of introduction) *Until Daybreak: Stories from the Kibbutz,* Institute for the Translation of Hebrew Literature (Tel Aviv, Israel), 1984.

Mi-mordot ha-Levanon (essays), Am Oved (Tel Aviv, Israel), 1987, translation by Maurie Goldberg-Bartura published as *The Slopes of Lebanon,* Harcourt (San Diego, CA), 1989.

Black Box (novel), translation by Nicholas de Lange, Harcourt (San Diego, CA), 1988.

La-dat Ishah, Keter (Jerusalem, Israel), 1989.

To Know a Woman, Harcourt (San Diego, CA), 1991.

Ha-Matsav ha-Selishi, Keter (Jerusalem, Israel), 1991.

Fima, Harcourt (San Diego, CA), 1993.

Shetikat ha-Shamayim, Keter (Jerusalem, Israel), 1993.

Al Tagidu Layla, Keter (Jerusalem, Israel), 1994, translation by Nicholas de Lange published as *Don't Call It Night,* Harcourt (San Diego, CA), 1996.

Israel, Palestine, and Peace: Essays, Harcourt (San Diego, CA), 1995.

Panther in the Basement, Harcourt (San Diego, CA), 1997.

Kol ha-tokvot: Mahashavot 'al zehut Yi'sre'elit (title means "All Our Hopes"), Keter (Jerusalem, Israel), 1998.

The Story Begins: Essays on Literature, translated by Maggie Bar-Tura, Harcourt (San Diego, CA), 1999.

The Silence of Heaven: Agnon's Fear of God, translated by Barbara Harshay, Princeton University Press (Princeton, NJ), 2000.

The Same Sea, translated by Nicholas de Lange, Chatto & Windus (London, England), 2001.

Sipur 'al ahavah ve-hoshekh, Keter (Jerusalem, Israel), 2002, translation by Nicholas de Lange published as *A Tale of Love and Darkness,* Harcourt (Orlando, FL), 2004.

Be-'etsem yesh kan shete milhamot, Keter (Jerusalem, Israel), 2002.

(With Izzat Ghazzawi) *Enemies: A Love Affair,* Swirid-off (Künzelsau, Germany), 2002.

Editor of *Siach lochamium* (translated as "The Seventh Day"). Contributor of essays and fiction to Israeli periodicals, including *Davar,* and to journals such as *Encounter, Guardian,* and *Partisan Review.*

Oz's books have been translated into over fifteen languages, including Japanese, Dutch, Norwegian, and Romanian.

ADAPTATIONS: My Michael and *Black Box* were adapted into films in Israel.

SIDELIGHTS: Through fiction and nonfiction alike, Israeli author Amos Oz describes a populace under emotional and physical siege and a society threatened by internal contradictions and contention. According to Judith Chernaik in the *Times Literary Supplement,* Oz writes books that are "indispensable reading for anyone who wishes to understand . . . life in Israel, the ideology that sustains it, and the passions that drive its people." Immensely popular in his own country, Oz has also established an international reputation. In a *New Republic* assessment of the author's talents, Ian Sanders noted: "Oz is an extraordinarily gifted Israeli novelist who delights his readers with both verbal brilliance and the depiction of eternal struggles—between flesh and spirit, fantasy and reality, Jew and Gentile. . . . His carefully reconstructed worlds are invariably transformed into symbolic landscapes, vast arenas where primeval forces clash." *Times Literary Supplement* contributor A. S. Byatt observed that in his works on Israel, Oz "can write with delicate realism about small lives, or tell fables about large issues, but his writing, even in translation, gains vitality simply from his subject matter." *New York Review of Books* correspondent D. J. Enright called Oz Israel's "most persuasive spokesman to the outside world, the literary part of it at least."

"In a sense Amos Oz has no alternative in his novels but to tell us what it means to be an Israeli," wrote John Bayley in the *New York Review of Books.* Oz is a *sabra,* or native-born Israeli who has seen military service in two armed conflicts—the Six Day War and the Yom Kippur War—and has lived most of his adult life as a member of Kibbutz Hulda, one of Israel's collective communities. His fictional themes arise from these experiences and are often considered controversial for their presentations of individuals who rebel against the Israeli society's ideals.

The kibbutz provides Oz with a powerful symbol of the nation's aspirations, as well as serving as a microcosm of the larger Jewish family in Israel, suffocatingly intimate and inescapable, yet united in defense against the hostile forces besieging its borders. *New York Times Book Review* contributor Robert Alter declared that nearly all of Oz's fiction "is informed by the same symbolic world picture: a hemmed-in cluster of fragile human habitations (the kibbutz, the state of Israel itself) surrounded by dark, menacing mountains where jackals howl and hostile aliens lurk." According to *Jewish Quarterly* contributor Jacob Sonntag, the people of Oz's fiction "are part of the landscape, and the landscape is part of the reality from which there is no escape." If the landscape is inescapable, the bonds of family also offer little relief. *New York Times Book Review* correspondent Morris Dickstein wrote, "The core of feeling in Oz's work is always some sort of family, often a family being torn apart." *Los Angeles Times* correspondent Elaine Kendall similarly observed that Oz's fiction "confronts the generational conflicts troubling Israel today; emotional rifts intensified by pressure and privation. In that anguished country, the usual forms of family tension seem reversed; the young coldly realistic; the elders desperately struggling to maintain their belief in a receding ideal."

Alter contended that Oz's work is "symptomatic of the troubled connection Israeli writers increasingly feel with the realities of the Jewish state." Chernaik elaborated on this submerged "interior wilderness" that Oz seems compelled to explore: "The overwhelming impression left by his fiction is of the precariousness of individual and collective human effort, a common truth made especially poignant by a physical landscape thoroughly inhospitable to human settlement, and given tragic dimensions by the modern history of the Jews and its analogues in Biblical history." Oz himself explained in *New Republic* that he tries to tap his own turmoil in order to write. His characters, he said, "actually want two different things: peace and excitement, excitement and peace. These two things don't get along very easily, so when people have peace, they hate it and long for excitement, and when they have excitement, they want peace."

A central concern of Oz's fiction is the conflict between idealistic Zionism and the realities of life in a pluralistic society. As a corollary to this, many of his sabra characters have decidedly ambivalent feelings toward the Arab population, especially Palestinians. *Commentary* essayist Ruth R. Wisse wrote that in book after book, "Oz has taken the great myths with which modern Israel is associated—the noble experiment of the kibbutz, the reclamation of the soil, the wars against the British and the Arabs, the phoenix-like rise of the Jewish spirit out of the ashes of the Holocaust— and shown us their underside: bruised, dazed, and straying characters who move in an atmosphere of almost unalleviated depression." Nehama Aschkenasy offered a similar assessment in *Midstream:* "The collective voice is suspiciously optimistic, over-anxious to ascertain the normalcy and sanity of the community and the therapeutic effect of the collective body on its tormented member. But the voice of the individual is imbued with a bitter sense of entrapment, of existential boredom and nausea, coupled with a destructive surrender to the irrational and the antinomian." Dickstein noted that the author often "takes the viewpoint of the detached participant, the good citizen who does his duty, shares his family's ideals but remains a little apart, wryly skeptical, unable to lose himself in the communal spirit."

"Daytime Israel makes a tremendous effort to create the impression of the determined, tough, simple, uncomplicated society ready to fight back, ready to hit back twice as hard, courageous and so on," Oz told the *Partisan Review.* "Nocturnal Israel is a refugee camp with more nightmares per square mile I guess than any other place in the world. Almost everyone has seen the devil." The obsessions of "nocturnal Israel" fuel Oz's work, as Mark Shechner noted in *Nation.* "In [Oz's] fiction," Shechner wrote, "the great storms that periodically descend on the Jews stir up strange and possessed characters who ride the gusts as if in a dream: raging Zionists, religious fanatics poised to take the future by force, theoreticians of the millennium, strategists of the end game, connoisseurs of bitterness and curators of injustice, artists of prophecy and poets of doctrine."

This is not to suggest, however, that Oz's work is unrelentingly somber or polemical. According to Dickstein, the "glow of Oz's writing comes from the spare and unsentimental warmth of his own voice, his feeling for atmosphere and his gallery of colorful misfits and individualists caught in communal enterprises." Bayley likewise concluded: "One of the admirable things about Oz's novels is the humor in them, a humor which formulates itself in having taken, and accepted, the narrow measure of the Israeli scene. Unlike much ethnic writing his does not seek to masquerade as Weltliteratur. It is Jewish literature acquiescing amusedly in its new militantly provincial status."

My Michael, a novel about the psychological disintegration of a young Israeli housewife, was Oz's first work translated and published in English. *New Republic* contributor Lesley Hazleton called the book "a brilliant and evocative portrait of a woman slowly giving way to schizoid withdrawal" and "a superb achievement, . . . the best novel to come out of Israel to date." In *Modern Fiction Studies,* Hana Wirth-Nesher expressed the view that Oz uses his alienated protagonist "to depict the isolation and fear that many Israelis feel partially as a country in a state of siege and partially as a small enclave of Western culture in a vast area of cultures and landscapes unlike what they have known." Alter praised *My Michael* for managing "to remain so private, so fundamentally apolitical in its concerns, even as it puts to use the most portentous political materials."

Paul Zweig claimed in the *New York Times Book Review* that when *My Michael* was published in Israel, shortly after the Six Day War, it proved "extremely disturbing to Israelis. At a time when their country had asserted control over its destiny as never before, Oz spoke of an interior life which Israel had not had time for, which it had paid no heed to, an interior life that contained a secret bond to the Asiatic world beyond its border." Disturbing though it was, *My Michael* was a best-seller in Israel; it established Oz's reputation among his fellow Israelis and gave him entree into the international world of letters.

Oz's first novel, *Elsewhere, Perhaps,* was his second work to be translated and published abroad. Most critics felt that the book is the best fictional representation of kibbutz life to emerge from Israel. As Sonntag wrote, "I know of no other book that depicts life in the Kibbutz more vividly, more realistically or with greater insight." In *Nation* William Novak noted that the story of sudden, violent events in the lives of three kibbutz families "engages our sympathies because of the compelling sincerity and moral concerns of the characters, and because of the extent to which this is really the story of an entire society." *New York Times Book Review* correspondent A. G. Mojtabai stressed the realistic sense of conflict between military and civilian values portrayed in *Elsewhere, Perhaps*. According to Mojtabai, two perceptions of "elsewhere" are active in the story: "elsewhere, perhaps, the laws of gravity obtain—not here; elsewhere, perhaps in some kingdom by the sea exists the model which our kibbutz imperfectly reflects, a society harmonious, healthful, joyful, loving—not here, not yet." Novak concluded that the novel's publication in the United States "should help to stimulate American appreciation of contemporary Israeli literature and society."

Oz's novel *A Perfect Peace* revolves around two young kibbutzniks—one rebellious after a lifetime in the environment, the other an enthusiastic newcomer—and an aging politician, founder of the collective. According to Alter, the novel is "a hybrid of social realism and metaphysical brooding, and it gains its peculiar power of assertion by setting social institutions and political issues in a larger metaphysical context. There is a vivid, persuasive sense of place here . . . but local place is quietly evoked against a cosmic backdrop." *Times Literary Supplement* reviewer S. S. Prawer observed that the work holds the reader's attention by providing a "variety of boldly drawn characters who reveal themselves to us in and through their speech. . . . Oz's storytelling, with its reliance on journals and inner monologues, is pleasantly old-fashioned." In a *New York Times Book Review* piece, Grace Schulman contended that it is "on a level other than the documentary that this novel succeeds so well. It is concerned with inner wholeness, and with a more profound peace than respect between generations and among countries. . . . The impact of this novel lies in the writer's creation of characters who are outwardly ordinary but inwardly bizarre, and at times fantastic."

Oz began his literary career as an author of short fiction. He has since published several volumes of stories and novellas, including *Where the Jackals Howl and Other Stories*, *Unto Death*, and *The Hill of Evil Counsel*. "As a seamstress who takes different pieces of cloth and sews them into a quilt, Amos Oz writes short pieces of fiction which together form a quilt in the reader's consciousness," noted J. Justin Gustainis in *Best Sellers*. "Just as the quilt may be of many colors but still one garment, Oz's stories speak of many things but still pay homage to one central idea: universal redemption through suffering."

Aschkenasy suggested that the stories in *Where the Jackals Howl* "are unified by an overall pattern that juxtaposes an individual permeated by a sense of existential estrangement and subterranean chaos with a self-deceiving community collectively intent upon putting up a facade of sanity and buoyancy in order to deny—or perhaps to exorcise—the demons from without and within." Chernaik noted of the same book that the reader coming to Oz for the first time "is likely to find his perception of Israel permanently altered and shaped by these tales."

The novellas in *Unto Death* "take as their theme the hatred that surrounds Jews and that destroys the hated and the haters alike," to quote Joseph McElroy in the *New York Times Book Review*. *Midstream* contributor Warren Bargad found this theme one manner of expressing "the breakdown of the myth of normalcy which has been at the center of Zionist longing for decades: the envisioned State of Israel, with its promise of autoemancipation, which would make of the Jewish people a nation among nations. For Oz it is still an impossible dream."

Oz revisits similar themes in *Fima*, which portrays the paradoxical futility of the novel's eponymous character. Fima is a despairing divorcee who lives in solitary squalor and has long ago abandoned work as a poet for employment as a receptionist at an abortion clinic. Privately preoccupied with intractable ethical dilemmas and fantasies of running the government, he endures a pathetic, ordinary existence punctuated by public fulminations and interaction with his few friends, ex-wife, and ten-year-old albino son. Fima "is a breathing contradiction, a muddle-headed sage, a gentle buffoon who thinks about life very seriously indeed," wrote Michael Hayward in *Washington Post Book World*. Shechner similarly observed in *Chicago Tribune Books* that "For all his neurosis and ineffectuality, his self-absorption and lassitude, his petulance and his opinions, he is a true-blue peace advocate, like Oz himself." Hayward added, "one always senses that Oz is on the side of his hero's sanity. . . . Fima may not look like one, but he is a survivor."

Fima was well received by critics. According to Patricia Storace in the *New York Review of Books,* the novel's "insistent presentation of trivial daily events, of political discussions that faithfully reproduce recognizable arguments, its vignettes of Jerusalem life, make it seem, read from one angle, a work of talented, experienced and intelligent realism." Storace added that Oz "has made a thoroughly unconventional novel co-exist simultaneously with a work of more conventional realism. This world of whiskey-drinking and divorce, of newspaper-reading and passionate argument, is also the world of good and evil, of life and death."

The novel *Don't Call It Night* centers on the relationship of Theo and Noa, a childless couple who become involved in the establishment of a drug rehabilitation center in their small frontier town. The center is commissioned to honor the memory of one of Noa's former pupils, whose mysterious suicide lends an air of intrigue. Though the enterprise is originally presented to Noa, an idealistic teacher, her reluctance to involve Theo eventually succumbs to necessity. Theo is an experienced city planner and a realist whose expertise proves essential to bringing the task to completion. Despite their differences, as Tony Gould wrote in *Spectator,* "They are more alike than either cares to be, and what they have in common is their need. That is the one constant in a world where everything else is transient—relationships, commitments, even the new town itself, perched on the edge of a desert which is as metaphorical as it is real." Concentrating on atmosphere more than plot, Oz portrays the subtle variations of feeling and temperament that render a seemingly ordinary relationship complex.

Praising the novel in an *Observer* review, Kate Kellaway commented that "*Don't Call It Night* has a meditative confidence that a younger writer could not expect to achieve. It is daringly ambitious; it shows that non-events matter." Though critical of the novel's contrived action and digressions, *Times Literary Supplement* contributor Michael Hofmann believed that *Don't Call It Night* surpasses *Fima* and represents a major contribution to the literary canon of postwar Israel. "At its best," wrote Hofmann, "[the novel] has a kind of Dutch uneventfulness. Elements of nocturne, still life, portrait and landscape are blended to create . . . indelible images in the reader's mind: of the small town at the edge of the desert, of two people at night in their apartment, one asleep, the other musing and

pottering by the light of a fridge." Commenting on *Don't Call It Night* in a *New Statesman* interview with Christopher Price, Oz remarked, "Sociology does not interest me. I don't want to know how many people are like Theo and Noa. . . . I want to know what Theo and Noa are really like. This is why I am a storyteller and not a scientist."

In addition to his work as a storyteller, Oz assumes a position of objective detachment as an accomplished political observer and journalist. *In the Land of Israel,* a series of interviews Oz conducted with a wide variety of Israelis, is his best-known work of nonfiction. According to Shechner, the book "provoked an outcry in Israel, where many saw the portraits of Jews as exaggerated and tailored to suit Oz's politics." The study does indeed present a vision of a pluralistic, creatively contentious society, "threatened as much by the xenophobia and self-righteous tribalism within as by enemies without," according to Gene Lyons in *Newsweek.* Christopher Lehmann-Haupt offered a similar opinion in the *New York Times:* "All together, the voices of *In the Land of Israel* serve to elucidate the country's complex ideological cross-currents. And conducted as they are by Mr. Oz, they sing an eloquent defense of what he considers a centrist position, though some of his critics might call it somewhat left-of-center." Lyons felt that the work is most valuable for what it shows the reader about Oz and his belief regarding his country's future. Lyons concluded, "Eloquent, humane, even religious in the deepest sense, [Oz] emerges here—and I can think of no higher praise—as a kind of Zionist Orwell: a complex man obsessed with simple decency and determined above all to tell the truth, regardless of whom it offends."

Under This Blazing Light offers additional commentary on later-twentieth-century Israeli life in essays adapted from interviews and lectures conducted by Oz between 1962 and 1979. His main themes revolve around the necessity of compromise between Israel and the Palestinians and an examination of Hebrew language and literature. Regarding Oz's political analysis, Elizabeth Shostak wrote in *Wilson Library Bulletin,* "the author's principled determination to imagine the other side's point of view without giving up his own loyalty remains both convincing and attractive." On the function of literature in human affairs, Tova Reich wrote in the *New York Times Book Review,* "Oz answers with a refreshingly old-fashioned formulation: it is 'a circle of sorrow—protest—consolation.'" Shostak concluded, "Oz is a direct and lucid essayist."

Israel, Palestine, and Peace is a similar collection of Oz's writings devoted to Middle East politics. "The unusual aspect of Oz's viewpoint," noted Shelley A. Glantz in *Kliatt,* is that he "blames and credits Israeli and Palestinian leaders and citizens equally." Oz reaffirms his belief that peace cannot be achieved without compromise, which inevitably calls for moderation and reciprocal sacrifice. While asserting a two-state solution in which both could coexist without lingering on ceaseless accusation, Oz suggests that the first gesture of conciliation should be to erect "a monument to our mutual stupidity." According to *Washington Post Book World* reviewer Charles Solomon, Oz's essays represent "a compelling vision of tolerance and sanity." A *Kirkus Reviews* contributor similarly praised the volume as "a poignant and powerful collection." "Oz is one of those rare writers who is equally stimulating in fiction and essay," concluded a *Rapport* reviewer. Oz's position did not waver in the face of the escalation of terrorist violence in Israel and elsewhere in the wake of the terrorist attacks on Washington, D.C., and New York City on September 11th, 2001. "If we don't stop somewhere, if we don't accept an unhappy compromise, unhappy for both sides, if we don't learn how to unhappily coexist and contain our burned sense of injustice—if we don't learn how to do that, we end up in a doomed state," he explained to *NewsHour* interviewer Elizabeth Farnsworth in a televised discussion of the extension of the Israeli-Palestinian conflict into the twenty-first century.

In an assessment of Oz's nonfiction, Shechner described what he called the "two Amos Ozes." One, Shechner wrote, is "a fiction writer with an international audience, the other an Israeli journalist of more or less hometown credentials. . . . Oz's journalism would seem to have little in common with the crepuscular world of his fiction. A blend of portraits and polemics, it is straightforward advocacy journalism, bristling with editorials and belonging to the world of opinions, ideologies and campaigns." Despite his fiction's sometimes bleak portrayal of Israel, Oz believes in his homeland and expresses strong opinions on how he feels it should be run. Alter noted: "In contrast to the inclination some writers may feel to withdraw into the fastness of language, the Oz articles reflect a strenuous effort to go out into Israeli society and sound its depth." Furthermore, according to Roger Rosenblatt in the *New York Times Book Review,* as a journalist Oz establishes "that he is no ordinary self-effacing reporter on a quest, but a public figure who for years has participated in major national controversies and who

regularly gives his views of things to the international press, 'ratting' on his homeland." Schulman suggested in the *Washington Post Book World* that Oz's journalism "may be the way to an esthetic stance in which he can reconcile the conflicting demands of artistic concern and political turbulence."

Critics have found much to praise in Oz's portraits of the struggling nation of Israel. "Oz's words, his sensuous prose and indelible imagery, the people he flings living onto his pages, evoke a cauldron of sentiments at the boil; yet his human vision is capacious enough to contain the destruction and hope for peace," wrote Richard R. Lingeman in the *New York Times.* "He has caught a welter of fears, curses and dreams at a watershed moment in history, when an uneasy, restless waiting gave way to an upsurge of violence, of fearsome consequences. The power of his art fuses historical fact and symbol; he makes the ancient stones of Jerusalem speak, and the desert beyond a place of jackals and miracles." In the *Saturday Review,* Alfred Kazin stated that Oz's effect on him is always to make him realize "how little we know about what goes on inside the Israeli head. . . . To the unusually sensitive and humorous mind of Amos Oz, the real theme of Jewish history—especially in Israel—is unreality. When, and how can a Jew attain reality in the Promised Land, actually touch the water, touch the wind?" Chernaik felt that Oz is "without doubt a voice for sanity, for the powers of imagination and love, and for understanding. He is also a writer of marvelous comic and lyric gifts, which somehow communicate themselves as naturally in English as in Hebrew."

The Same Sea is a lyric novel, written partially in verse, with frequent allusions to the great poetry and prose of the Hebrew tradition. "This is vintage Mr. Oz, arguably his best work ever," Carol Herman observed in the *Washington Times,* although she noted that "those seeking the benefit of his political wisdom will find no explicit comfort here." Reading *The Same Sea* "is like being the guest at a dinner party of a wildly dysfunctional family that is not shy about airing its secrets," as *New York Times* reviewer William M. Hoffman described it. Albert, a recent widower; his son Rico, who is "finding himself" and experimenting with his sexuality in Asia; Dita, Rico's girlfriend, who moves in with Albert after she is cheated out of her money; and Bettine, a down-to-earth woman of Albert's own age who is the only character who consistently speaks in prose, all get to explain themselves.

Even Nadia, Albert's dead wife, speaks. "Some rhyme, some don't," Herman said of the characters, but "all breathe." *The Same Sea* "will doubtless be regarded as a defining work from a writer of major significance," Phillip Santo declared in *Library Journal.*

A Tale of Love and Darkness is a "moving, emotionally charged memoir of the renowned author's youth in a newly created Israel," wrote a critic in *Kirkus Reviews.* Focusing on Oz's childhood and adolescence, *A Tale of Love and Darkness* "deals frontally with an upbringing previously inferable only from his stories and novels," according to *Commentary* reviewer Hillel Halkin. The work also follows Oz's development as a writer during a time of great political upheaval. "In this heady, dangerous atmosphere . . . Oz comes of age, blossoming as a man of letters," wrote the *Kirkus Reviews* critic.

Oz is an unusual Israeli writer in that he has chosen to stay at the kibbutz throughout his career, even though the income from his royalties is substantial. Even when he was younger, he said in *Partisan Review,* the kibbutz "evoked and fed my curiosity about the strange phenomenon of flawed, tormented human beings dreaming about perfection, aching for the Messiah, aspiring to change human nature. This perpetual paradox of magnanimous dream and unhappy reality is indeed one of the main threads in my writing." Furthermore, he told the *Washington Post,* his fellow kibbutzniks react to his works in fascinating ways: "It's a great advantage, you know, to have a passionate, immediate milieu and not a literary milieu—a milieu of real people who tell me straight in my face what they think of my writing."

Hebrew is the language in which Oz chooses to write; he calls it a "volcano in action," still evolving rapidly into new forms. Oz likes to call himself the "tribal storyteller," as he explained in the *New York Times:* "I bring up the evil spirits and record the traumas, fantasies, the lunacies of Israeli Jews, natives and those from Central Europe. I deal with their ambitions and the powderbox of self-denial and self-hatred." In a *Washington Post* interview, he maintained that Israel would always be the source from which his inspiration would spring. "I'm fascinated," he said of his homeland. "Yes, indeed, I'm disgusted, appalled, sick and tired sometimes. Even when I'm sick and tired, I'm there. . . . It's my thing, if you will, in the same sense that William Faulkner belonged in the Deep South. It's my thing and my place and my addiction."

Married and the father of three children, Oz speaks and travels frequently, bringing his personal thoughts to television and lecture audiences in Israel and abroad. Describing his creative impulses, Oz told the *New York Times:* "Whenever I find myself in total agreement with myself, then I write an article—usually in rage—telling the government what to do. But when I detect hesitation, more than one inner voice, I discover in me the embryo of characters, the seeds of a novel."

BIOGRAPHICAL AND CRITICAL SOURCES:

BOOKS

Contemporary Literary Criticism, Gale (Detroit, MI), Volume 5, 1976, Volume 8, 1978, Volume 11, 1979, Volume 27, 1981, Volume 33, 1985, Volume 54, 1989.

Contemporary World Writers, 2nd edition, St. James Press (Detroit, MI), 1993.

Encyclopedia of World Biography, 2nd edition, Gale (Detroit, MI), 1998.

Encyclopedia of World Literature in the Twentieth Century, 3rd edition, St. James Press (Detroit, MI), 1999.

Hiro, Dilip, *Dictionary of the Middle East,* St. Martin's Press (New York, NY), 1996.

Legends in Their Own Time, Prentice Hall (New York, NY), 1994.

Magill, Frank N., editor, *Cyclopedia of World Authors II,* Salem Press (Pasadena, CA), 1997.

Murphy, Bruce, editor, *Benet's Reader's Encyclopedia,* 4th edition, HarperCollins (New York, NY), 1996.

Oz, Amos, *Israel, Palestine, and Peace: Essays,* Harcourt (San Diego, CA), 1995.

Reference Guide to Short Fiction, 2nd edition, St. James Press (Detroit, MI), 1999.

Short Story Criticism, Volume 66, Gale (Detroit, MI), 2004.

Wirth-Nesher, Hana, *City Codes: Reading the Modern Urban Novel,* Cambridge University Press (Cambridge, England), 1996.

PERIODICALS

Atlantic, December, 1983; May, 1988.

Best Sellers, October, 1978.

Book, May-June, 2002, Stephen Whited, review of *The Same Sea,* p. 80.

Booklist, February 15, 1999, review of *Kol Ha-Tokvot,* p. 1049; October 15, 2001, Donna Seaman, review of *The Same Sea,* p. 383.

Brick, summer, 2003, Ramona Koval, "An Interview with Amos Oz," pp. 68-80.

Chicago Tribune, December 7, 1989.

Commentary, July, 1974; April, 1984; April, 2004, Hillel Halkin, "Politics and the Israeli Novel," pp. 29-36.

Jewish Quarterly, spring-summer, 1974.

Kirkus Reviews, March 1, 1995, p. 304; July 1, 1995, p. 926; January 1, 1999, review of *The Story Begins,* p. 50; July 15, 2004, review of *A Tale of Love and Darkness,* p. 677.

Kliatt, January, 1996, p. 31; September, 1998, review of *Panther in the Basement,* p. 6; March, 1999, review of *Panther in the Basement,* p. 14.

Library Journal, January, 1999, Gene Shaw, review of *The Story Begins,* p. 97; August, 2001, Philip Santo, review of *The Same Sea,* p. 164; July, 2003, "Amos Oz Unto Death: Two Novellas—Crusade and Late Love"; June 1, 2004, Barbara Hoffert, review of *A Tale of Love and Darkness,* p. 104.

Los Angeles Times, May 21, 1981; June 24, 1985; December 25, 1989.

Los Angeles Times Book Review, December 11, 1983; May 29, 1988, p. 3; May 12, 1991, p. 2; September 3, 1995, p. 9.

Midstream, November, 1976; January, 1985; January, 2002, Leslie Cohen and Elvera Herbstman, review of *The Same Sea,* pp. 44-45.

Modern Fiction Studies, spring, 1978.

Nation, September 7, 1974; June 8, 1985; June 4, 1988, p. 796; November 11, 1996, John Leonard, "What Have We Come Here to Be?," pp. 25-30; January 21, 2002, Morris Dickstein, review of *The Same Sea,* p. 27.

National Review, April 20, 1984.

New Leader, January 6, 1975.

New Republic, November 29, 1975; October 14, 1978; June 27, 1981; July 29, 1985; October 28, 1991, p. 36-40; August 7, 2000, Hillel Halkin, review of *The Disappointments,* p. 39.

New Statesman, October 20, 1995, p. 20.

Newsweek, November 21, 1983; July 29, 1985.

New Yorker, November 18, 1974; August 7, 1978; August 19, 1985; January 31, 1994, p. 89.

New York Review of Books, February 7, 1974; January 23, 1975; July 20, 1978; September 26, 1985; August 18, 1988, p. 30; May 26, 1994, p. 17; June 25, 1995, p. 18; March 5, 1998, review of *Panther in the Basement,* p. 17.

New York Times, May 19, 1978; July 18, 1978; May 22, 1981; October 31, 1983; November 11, 1989; March, 1998, J. M. Coetzee, review of *Panther in the Basement,* pp. 17-18.

New York Times Book Review, May 21, 1972; November 18, 1973; November 24, 1974; October 26, 1975; May 28, 1978; April 26, 1981; March 27, 1983; November 6, 1983; November 25, 1984, p. 44; June 2, 1985; April 24, 1988, p. 7; March 19, 1989, p. 32; February 4, 1990; January 24, 1991, p. 32; June 9, 1991, p. 32; July 26, 1992, p. 24; October 24, 1993, p. 12; June 25, 1995, p. 18; January 11, 1998, review of *Don't Call It Night,* p. 20; December 27, 1998, review of *Panther in the Basement,* p. 20; July 4, 1999, Laurie Adlerstein, review of *The Story Begins,* p. 14; October 28, 2001, William M. Hoffman, "Thou Shalt Not Covet Thy Son's Girlfriend," p. 12.

Observer (London, England), July 7, 1985, p. 21; July 13, 1986, p. 27; June 26, 1988, p. 42; July 17, 1988, p. 42; February 4, 1990, p. 61; February 3, 1991, p. 54; September 12, 1993, p. 53; October 29, 1995, p. 16; May 29, 1999, review of *The Story Begins,* p. 11; February 18, 2001, review of *The Same Sea,* p. 15.

Partisan Review, number 3, 1982; number 3, 1986.

Publishers Weekly, May 21, 1973; September 6, 1993, p. 84; February 27, 1995, p. 92; June 17, 1996, p. 45; February 1, 1999, review of *The Story Begins,* p. 66; September 3, 2001, review of *The Same Sea,* p. 54.

Rapport, Volume 19, number 1, 1995, p. 39.

Saturday Review, June 24, 1972; November 2, 1974; May 13, 1978.

Spectator, January 9, 1982; December 17, 1983; August 10, 1985; April 22, 1995, p. 36; October 7, 1995, p. 54; February 17, 2001, review of *The Same Sea,* p. 39.

Studies in Short Fiction, winter, 1982.

Time, January 27, 1986.

Times (London, England), August 1, 1985.

Times Literary Supplement, July 21, 1972; February 22, 1974; March 21, 1975; October 6, 1978; September 25, 1981; July 27, 1984; August 9, 1985; June 24, 1988, p. 697; December 2, 1988, p. 1342; March 2, 1990; October 13, 1995, p. 24; December 1, 1995, p. 12; December 4, 1998, review of *Panther in the Basement,* p. 12; September 1, 2000, Morris Dickstein, "The Talking Dog of Jerusalem," pp. 12-13; February 9, 2001, review of *The Same Sea,* p. 21.

Tribune Books (Chicago, IL), November 14, 1993, p. 3.

Village Voice, February 14, 1984.

Washington Post, December 1, 1983.

Washington Post Book World, May 28, 1972; May 31, 1981; June 14, 1981; November 13, 1983; July 14, 1985; November 28, 1993, p. 6.

Washington Times, December 9, 2001, Carol Herman, "How Life Goes On in Israel," p. 6.

Whole Earth Review, spring, 1996, p. 77.

Wilson Library Bulletin, June, 1995, p. 104.

World Literature Today, spring, 1982; spring, 1983; summer, 1984; autumn, 1986; autumn, 1995, p. 862; spring, 1998, review of *Panther in the Basement,* p. 449; summer, 1999, review of *The Story Begins,* p. 589; summer-autumn, 2001, Eric Sterling, review of *The Same Sea,* pp. 110-111.

ONLINE

Department for Jewish Zionist Education Web site, http://www.jajz-ed.org.il/ (May 9, 2002), "Amoz Oz, Israeli Novelist."

Online NewsHour, http://www.pbs.org/newshour/ (January 23, 2002), Elizabeth Farnsworth, "Coping with Conflict" (televised interview transcript).*

P

PAGE, Robin 1943-

PERSONAL: Born 1943; female; married Steve Jenkins (an author/illustrator); three children. *Education:* Attended North Carolina State University.

ADDRESSES: Home—Boulder, CO. *Agent*—c/o Author Mail, Houghton Mifflin, 222 Berkeley St., Boston, MA 02116-3764.

CAREER: Graphic designer; illustrator and author.

AWARDS, HONORS: Caldecott Honor Book designation (with Steve Jenkins), 2004, for *What Do You Do with a Tail like This?*

WRITINGS:

(With husband, Steve Jenkins) *Animals in Flight,* Houghton Mifflin (Boston, MA), 2001.
(With husband, Steve Jenkins) *What Do You Do with a Tail like This?,* Houghton Mifflin (Boston, MA), 2003.

BIOGRAPHICAL AND CRITICAL SOURCES:

PERIODICALS

Booklist, December 15, 2001, Gillian Engberg, review of *Animals in Flight,* p. 735; February 15, 2003, Tim Arnold, review of *What Do You Do with a Tail like This?,* p. 1068.

Kirkus Reviews, October 15, 2001, review of *Animals in Flight,* p. 1485; January 15, 2003, review of *What Do You Do with a Tail like This?,* p. 142.
School Library Journal, November, 2001, Ellen Heath, review of *Animals in Flight,* p. 146; March, 2003, Wanda Meyers-Hines, review of *What Do You Do with a Tail like This?,* p. 220; April, 2004, review of *What Do You Do with a Tail like This?,* p. S20.

ONLINE

Children's Literature Web site, http://www.childrenslit. com/ (September 3, 2004), interview with Steve Jenkins.
Houghton Mifflin Web site, http://www.houghtonmifflin books.com/ (September 2, 2004), short author biography.*

*   *   *

PAIGE, Richard
See KOONTZ, Dean R(ay)

*   *   *

PALMER, Tim(othy) 1948-

PERSONAL: Born March 20, 1948, in Beaver, PA; son of James and Jane (Gremer) Palmer; married Ann Vileisis (an author). *Education:* Pennsylvania State University, B.S., 1971. *Politics:* Democrat.

ADDRESSES: Office—P.O. Box 1286, Port Orford, OR 97465. *E-mail*—tim@timpalmer.org.

CAREER: Author, photographer, public speaker. Chief county planner in Williamsport, PA, 1971-80; writer and photographer, 1980—. Consultant on river protection, 1986—.

AWARDS, HONORS: Independent Publisher Book Award, for *The Heart of America: Our Landscape, Our Future;* National Outdoor Book Award, 1998, for *The Columbia: Sustaining a Modern Resource;* Director's Award for outstanding publication of the year, National Park Service, 1996, for *Yosemite: The Promise of Wildness;* finalist, Ben Franklin Book Award, for *Pacific High: Adventures in the Coast Ranges from Baja to Alaska;* also received Lifetime Achievement Award from American Rivers, the River Conservationist of the Year Award from Perception, Inc., and the Peter Behr Award from Friends of the River.

WRITINGS:

Lycoming County . . . A Place in Which to Live, Lycoming County Planning Commission (Williamsport, PA), 1976.
Rivers of Pennsylvania, Pennsylvania State University Press (University Park, PA), 1980.
Stanislaus: The Struggle for a River, University of California Press (Berkeley, CA), 1982.
Youghiogheny: Appalachian River, University of Pittsburgh Press (Pittsburgh, PA), 1984.
Endangered Rivers and the Conservation Movement, University of California Press (Berkeley, CA), 1986, 2nd edition, Rowman & Littlefield (Lanham, PA), 2004.
The Sierra Nevada: A Mountain Journey, Island Press (Washington, DC), 1988.
The Snake River: Window to the West, Island Press (Washington, DC), 1991.
(Editor) *California's Threatened Environment: Restoring the Dream,* Island Press (Washington, DC), 1993.
The Wild and Scenic Rivers of America, Island Press (Washington, DC), 1993.
(Author of essay) *Yosemite: The Promise of Wildness,* photographs by William Neill, Yosemite Association (Yosemite Park, CA), 1994.

Lifelines: The Case for River Conservation, Island Press (Washington, DC), 1994, 2nd edition published as *Lifelines,* Rowman & Littlefield (Lanham, PA), 2004.
America by Rivers, Island Press (Washington, DC), 1996.
(And photographer) *The Columbia: Sustaining a Modern Resource,* The Mountaineers (Seattle, WA), 1997.
The Heart of America: Our Landscape, Our Future, Island Press (Washington, DC), 1999.
Pacific High: Adventures in the Coast Ranges from Baja to Alaska, Island Press (Washington, DC), 2002.
Oregon: Preserving the Spirit and Beauty of Our Land, photography by Terry Donnelly and Mary Liz Austin, foreword by John Daniel, Voyageur Press (Stillwater, MN), 2003.
California Wild: Preserving the Spirit and Beauty of Our Land, photography by Terry Donnelly and Mary Liz Austin, foreword by John Daniel, Voyageur Press (Stillwater, MN), 2004.

Also author of dozens of magazine articles, river studies, display packages, and brochures for conservation campaigns.

SIDELIGHTS: Author and photographer Tim Palmer has engaged readers with numerous books on rivers and the environment. Having canoed or rafted on over 300 different waterways and mountaineered extensively throughout North America, he brings his expertise and concern for conservation to his writings. In a review of *Lifelines: The Case for River Conservation, Booklist* critic Mary Carroll described this book as "an enlightening, energizing study" which "seeks to define the values of and threats to preservation of the nation's diminishing river legacy."

Palmer's nine-month excursion through the Pacific coast mountain ranges resulted in *Pacific High: Adventures in the Coast Ranges from Baja to Alaska.* Here he presents his travel escapades by foot, plane, boat, bicycle, and van—as well as insightful information on the interaction between mountains and their natural and human environment. *Library Journal* contributor John McCormick explained, "Interspersed throughout are Palmer's strong pro-environmental message and always amusing dialog between himself and those he meets along the way."

Palmer once told *CA:* "Nothing else really matters if we cannot learn to care for the earth, and the relationships involved in that challenge are the subjects of my writing. The dynamics between people and places are endless and fascinating, and my aim is to make my books convey an understanding of our times and our problems, of the extraordinary qualities in the landscapes and rivers of our earth, and of the fun of living in the natural world."

BIOGRAPHICAL AND CRITICAL SOURCES:

PERIODICALS

American Forests, July, 1987, review of *Endangered Rivers and the Conservation Movement,* p. 71.

Audubon, January, 1995, review of *Lifelines: The Case for River Conservation,* p. 115.

Booklist, March 15, 1987, review of *Endangered Rivers and the Conservation Movement,* p. 1081; November 15, 1988, review of *The Sierra Nevada: A Mountain Journey,* p. 521; August, 1991, review of *The Snake River: Window to the West,* p. 2084; May 15, 1993, review of *California's Threatened Environment: Restoring the Dream,* p. 1657; July, 1994, Mary Carroll, review of *Lifelines,* p. 1901. June 1, 1996, review of *America by Rivers,* p. 1656.

Bookwatch, July 24, 1988, review of *Endangered Rivers and the Conservation Movement,* p. 12; December 18, 1988, review of *The Sierra Nevada,* p. 10; October, 1991, review of *The Snake River,* p. 5.

Book World, November 13, 1994, review of *Lifelines,* p. 13; November 21, 1999, review of *The Heart of America: Our Landscape, Our Future,* p. 10.

Choice, February, 1987, review of *Endangered Rivers and the Conservation Movement,* p. 903; March, 1992, review of *The Snake River,* p. 1104; November, 1993, review of *The Wild and Scenic Rivers of America,* p. 478; September, 1994, review of *Endangered Rivers and the Conservation Movement,* p. 49; January, 1995, review of *Lifelines,* p. 812.

Earth Science, summer, 1990, review of *The Sierra Nevada,* p. 32.

Kirkus Reviews, April 1, 1996, review of *America by Rivers,* p. 513.

Library Journal, February 15, 1987, review of *Endangered Rivers and the Conservation Movement,* p. 155; March 1, 1993, review of *The Snake River,* p. 49; July, 1993, review of *The Wild and Scenic Rivers of America,* p. 105; June 15, 1994, review of *Lifelines,* p. 90; May 15, 1996, review of *America by Rivers,* p. 82; August, 2002, John McCormick, review of *Pacific High: Adventures in the Coast Ranges from Baja to Alaska,* p. 125.

New York Times Book Review, December 4, 1988, review of *The Sierra Nevada,* p. 18.

Pacific Historical Review, August, 1988, review of *Endangered Rivers and the Conservation Movement,* p. 378.

Publishers Weekly, October 21, 1988, review of *The Sierra Nevada,* p. 52; July 12, 1991, review of *The Snake River,* p. 61; April 1, 1996, review of *America by Rivers,* p. 61; October 4, 1999, review of *The Heart of America* p. 59.

Sierra, March, 1987, review of *Endangered Rivers and the Conservation Movement,* p. 94; May, 1989, review of *The Sierra Nevada,* p. 101.

Western Historical Society, October, 1987, review of *Endangered Rivers and the Conservation Movement,* p. 468.

Wilderness, spring, 1988, review of *Endangered Rivers and the Conservation Movement,* p. 68.

Workbook, spring, 1992, review of *The Snake River,* p. 39.

ONLINE

Tim Palmer Home Page, http://www.timpalmer.org (April 5, 2004), author's biographical information and information on titles.

*   *   *

PARFITT, Tudor (Vernon) 1944-

PERSONAL: Born October 10, 1944, in Porth, Wales; son of Vernon (a headmaster) and Margaret (Sears) Parfitt; married Jean Mac William (divorced); children: Justin, Natasha. *Education:* Oxford University, M.A., 1968, D.Phil., 1972; attended Hebrew University of Jerusalem, 1968-69.

ADDRESSES: Office—Department of Near and Middle East Studies, School of Oriental and African Studies, University of London, London WC1 7HP, England. *E-mail*—tp@soas.ac.uk.

CAREER: University of Toronto, Toronto, Ontario, lecturer, 1972-74; University of Southampton, Southampton, England, Parkes fellow, 1974; University of London, School of Oriental and African Studies, London, England, lecturer in Hebrew and Jewish studies, 1974—, currently chair of the Center for Jewish Studies.

WRITINGS:

(Translator, with Glenda Abramson) Yehuda Amichai, *The Great Tranquility: Questions and Answers,* Harper (New York, NY), 1983.

Operation Moses: The Untold Story of the Secret Exodus of the Falasha Jews from Ethiopia, Stein & Day (New York, NY), 1985.

The Thirteenth Gate: Travels among the Lost Tribes of Israel, Adler & Adler (Bethesda, MD), 1987.

The Jews in Palestine, 1800-1882, Boydell Press (Wolfeboro, NH), 1987.

The Jews of Africa and Asia: Contemporary Anti-Semitism and Other Pressures, Minority Rights Group (London, England), 1987.

Journey to the Vanished City: The Search for a Lost Tribe of Israel, Hodder & Stoughton (London, England), 1992, St. Martin's (New York, NY), 1993, revised and expanded edition, Phoenix, 1997.

The Road to Redemption: The Jews of the Yemen, 1900-1950, E. J. Brill (New York), 1996.

The Lost Tribes of Israel: The History of a Myth, Weidenfeld & Nicolson, 2002.

(With Emanuela Trevisan-Semi) *Judaising Movements: Studies in the Margins of Judaism in Modern Times,* Routledge (London, England)/Curzon (Surrey, England), 2002.

EDITOR

(With Glenda Abramson) *The Great Transition: The Recovery of the Lost Centers of Modern Hebrew Literature,* Rowman & Allanheld (Totowa, NJ), 1985.

(With Glenda Abramson) *The Academy: Essays on Jewish Education and Learning,* Harwood Academic (Langhorne, PA), 1994.

(With Glenda Abramson) *Jewish Education and Learning: Published in Honour of Dr. David Patterson on the Occasion of his Seventieth Birthday,* Harwood Academic (Langhorne, PA), 1994.

(With Steven Kaplan and Emanuela Trevisan-Semi) *Between Africa and Zion: Proceedings of the First International Congress of the Society for the Study of Ethiopian Jewry,* Ben-Zvi Institute (Jerusalem, Israel), 1995.

(With Emanuela Trevisan-Semi) *The Beta Israel in Ethiopia and Israel: Studies on Ethiopian Jews,* Curzon (Surrey, England), 1999.

Israel and Ishmael: Studies in Muslim-Jewish Relations, St. Martin's (New York), 2000.

(With Yulia Egorova) *Jews, Muslims and Mass Media: Mediating the "Other,"* Curzon (Surrey, England), 2004.

OTHER:

Also author and presenter of three British Broadcasting Corporation (BBC) radio programs about the founding of Israel and two programs about the Lemba tribe, 1992, and of Radio Four program *The Longest Exile,* 1994. Contributor to magazines and newspapers in England and the United States, including *Jewish Chronicle, London,* the London *Times, Poetry, Present Tense,* and *Moment.*

SIDELIGHTS: Tudor Parfitt is an acknowledged authority on the history of Israel in the nineteenth century, as well as being famous for his research in tracking down the mysteriously lost Ten Tribes of Israel. His studies have led him all around the world in search of ethnic communities in Africa, India, and even Japan that claim to have ties to the families of ten of the twelve sons of Jacob, whose people disappeared from history after the Assyrians conquered them in the eighth century B.C.E. Parfitt writes about his findings in such books as *Operation Moses: The Untold Story of the Secret Exodus of the Falasha Jews from Ethiopia, The Thirteenth Gate: Travels among the Lost Tribes of Israel,* and *The Lost Tribes of Israel: The History of a Myth.* Though these works have received much of the attention by critics, Parfitt is also interested in the history of the known Jewish peoples and of the Judaising movement in Africa.

Considering his fascination for the subject, it is interesting to note that Parfitt has no Jewish blood himself. He is, rather, the son of Welsh Baptists. He first became interested in the Jewish people at the age of nineteen, when he joined the Volunteer Service in Britain and was assigned to help Jews who had made it to Israel after the Holocaust in Europe. Becoming fascinated by their complex history and culture, when he returned to England he decided to study Jewish and Islamic history at Oxford, where he graduated in 1972 with a doctorate.

After teaching in Toronto, Canada, and Southampton, England, Parfitt joined the University of London faculty as a lecturer in Hebrew and Jewish studies. He began publishing books on his specialty in the mid-1980s, with his first major work being *Operation Moses,* the story of the black Jews of Ethiopia and their evacuation to new homes in Israel. Plagued by famine in their native land, oppressed by the hostility of their Christian neighbors and the brutality and corruption of government officials, the Falashas had dwindled to less than thirty thousand souls. In the face of international criticism and interference from other so-called relief efforts, the government of Israel managed to save some fourteen thousand Falashas in 1984. Though they speak no Hebrew and practice some religious laws that depart from traditional Judaism, an attempt has been made to assimilate them into the Israeli population. Parfitt not only tells their story, but as an eyewitness to events that occurred in Ethiopia and the Sudan in 1984, he charges the United Nations with procrastination and bowing to political pressure. He offers evidence of the negligence of the Sudanese government, unfair criticism by the international press of the Israeli rescue effort, and the ignorant interference of several other relief movements. Bernard Wasserstein wrote in the *Times Literary Supplement,* "The author . . . combines eyewitness reporting with academic understanding to produce a sympathetic and fair-minded account of the 'untouchables of Ethiopia.'"

With his next book, *The Thirteenth Gate,* Parfitt not only talks further about the Falashas, but also other ethnic groups in Africa and in Asia who claim a connection with Israel, including the Lemba of South Africa, the Baghdadi and Shinlung of India, and the Makuya and Beit Shalom of Japan. The title of the book comes from the old Jewish belief that people who ascend to heaven after they die but do not know to which of the twelve tribes they belong will enter through the thirteenth gate. It was the tale of how the Falashas were brought to Israel that led several of the Lemba tribesmen to contact Parfitt with their story. Parfitt was giving a talk about the Falashas at the University of Witwatersrand in South Africa when he noticed several black men wearing skullcaps. Curious,

he approached them, and they regaled him with a story of how their people were descended from a Jewish tribe that had originated in a city known as Sena and had made their way into southern Africa. At first, because of their obviously African appearance, Parfitt did not believe them, but he accepted an invitation to visit the Lemba homeland, a trip that would lead to a quest recorded in his book *Journey to the Vanished City: The Search for a Lost Tribe of Israel.*

The Lemba, Parfitt discovered, had a culture that was very un-African. It included Semitic customs, such as the sacrificial slaughter of animals, a disdain for gentiles, and a resistance to intermarriage, characteristics that had previously been identified by a Boer named Paul Kruger, which is why the Lemba had once been known in South Africa as "Kruger's Jews." Kruger's findings had not been definitive, however. But Parfitt's encounters bolstered his new suspicions that what the Lemba said might be true. Upon their request, he embarked on a journey to find where the city of Sena might be located. After much research, he believed he had located where the city might have been, in what is now southern Yemen.

But the most convincing evidence came when Parfitt combined anthropology with genetic science. He took DNA samples of from the Lemba and sent them to a lab. What the geneticists discovered was extraordinary. "There was the extraordinary finding of the Cohen modal haplotype," Parfitt told a *Nova* interviewer. "This is the element in the Y chromosome that appears to be a signature element . . . for the *Cohanim* or Jewish priesthood. The fact that we found this marker in such high concentrations in one of the Lemba subclans, the Buba—much higher, incidentally, than the general Jewish population—seemed finally to provide a real, useable link between the Lemba and Jews." Although their culture was definitely pre-Talmudic, and the Lemba's physical appearance was black because their members had married a number of native peoples, the Lemba could definitely claim Jewish ancestry.

This finding was quite stunning to many, and the BBC even filmed a documentary about Parfitt's discovery. But his *Journey to the Vanished City* is not just about resolving the mystery of the Lemba. As Jonathan Kirsch noted in his *Los Angeles Times* assessment, "Most of the time . . . Parfitt appears to be less interested in religious studies than in the human landscape of contemporary Africa. And his book is at its most engaging—and most illuminating—when Parfitt contemplates the sometimes breathtaking, sometimes comical manifestations of the clash between black and white." Nissim Rejwan, writing in the *Jerusalem Post,* similarly remarked that the book was part anthropology, part travelogue, part history. "In all three capacities," the critic asserted, "the book excels."

Parfitt readdresses the Lost Tribes concern in *The Lost Tribes of Israel.* Again discussing the various cultures claiming Jewish ancestry, this time the author is less interested in whether or not the connections are valid—and in some cases he is convinced they are not—than he is in answering the question *why* these people would want to be associated with one of the world's most oppressed minorities. Two conclusions, as David J. Wasserstein explained in his *Times Literary Supplement* article, are arrived at in the book: either the people wished "to differentiate themselves from other groups in the vicinity and to associate themselves more closely with alien rulers [the European colonists]," or the Europeans would arrive in a Third World land and identify the people they found with one of the Lost Tribes. Whether or not an association with a Lost Tribe was valid, however, Parfitt concludes in his book that the effects on those who believe they come from Jewish roots is profound, and many of them have ended up moving to Israel and/or converting to Judaism.

This has been true, too, with the Lemba tribe, and Parfitt has felt at least partially responsible for what has happened to them after he brought their story to the world's attention. Since the publication of *Journey to the Vanished City,* a number of Jews from North America have traveled to Africa to teach the Lemba the Talmud and other modern Jewish beliefs. "So as a result of my work," he told *Nova,* "though it was in no sense intended, they have become, if you like, properly Jewish and recognized as such by quite a number of people, particularly in America."

Parfitt has been continuing DNA studies in Africa and is finding more and more people there who believe they are descended from the Israelites. He has, for instance, traveled to Pakistan and Afghanistan, where the Pathan tribe, an ethnic group of about twenty million, practice Islam but believe themselves to actually be Jewish and whose culture has many Jewish traits. Parfitt and collaborator Neil Bradman have also

spent time in Asia conducting research on such Indian groups as the Bene Israel in Cochin, Kerala, and the Kukis of Manipur.

In addition to his extensive research on the spread of Jewish peoples through the Diaspora, Parfitt has written respected books about the Jews living in Palestine before the significant rise in Zionism, and on modern issues concerning such topics as current anti-Semitism and the relationship between Jews, Muslims, and Christians. *The Jews in Palestine, 1800-1882* has gained particular respect from critics, who generally acknowledge Parfitt as an authority on this period in Jewish history. Intended for scholars in the subject, the book includes valuable statistical data on demographics, insights into why populations fluctuated, and aspects of Jewish culture at the time. While *English Historical Review* critic Lionel Kochan noted that Parfitt limits his scope somewhat by admittedly bypassing such topics as economics, but he asserted that the book's value could be found in the scholar's analysis of immigration, the religious expectations of the Jews, and the "treatment of the Jews at the hands of Christians and Muslims." George Mandel, writing in *Bulletin of the School of Oriental and African Studies,* similarly felt the book could have been more comprehensive but concluded that "this book is essential, and often entertaining, reading for anyone concerned with Palestine in the nineteenth century and, indeed, the twentieth."

BIOGRAPHICAL AND CRITICAL SOURCES:

PERIODICALS

Bulletin of the School of Oriental and African Studies, Volume 52, number 1, 1989, George Mandel, review of *The Jews in Palestine, 1800-1882,* pp. 126-127.

English Historical Review, April, 1991, Lionel Kochan, review of *The Jews in Palestine, 1800-1882,* pp. 488-489.

Ethnic & Racial Studies, November, 2002, "Book Reviews," p. 1096.

Independent (London, England), May 16, 1998, Peter Popham, "British Experts Search India for Lost Jewish Tribe," p. 16.

Irish Times (Dublin, Ireland), January 3, 2004, Fergal Quinn, review of *The Lost Tribes of Israel: The History of a Myth,* p. 62.

Jerusalem Post, April 27, 1990, Helen Davis, "Tracking the Ten Tribes," p. 10; February 5, 1993, Nissim Rejwan, review of "Lost Tribe of Lemba," p. 27.

Journal of Religion in Africa, Volume 30, issue 1, 2000, J. Abbink, review of *The Beta Israel in Ethiopia and Israel,* p. 137.

Kirkus Reviews, March 1, 2004, review of *The Lost Tribes of Israel.*

Library Journal, October 15, 1985, David P. Snider and Janet Fletcher, review of *Operation Moses: The Untold Story of the Secret Exodus of the Falasha Jews from Ethiopia,* p. 91; December 1, 1987, Maurice S. Tuchman, review of *The Thirteenth Gate: Travels among the Lost Tribes of Israel,* p. 119; January 1, 1993, Ann E. Cohen, review of *Journey to the Vanished City: The Search for a Lost Tribe of Israel,* p. 142.

Los Angeles Times, November 12, 1987, Jonathan Kirsch, "Strange Encounters in the Search for the Lost Tribes," p. 38; March 10, 1993, Jonathan Kirsch, "Journey of Discovery Yields Magical Verse," p. E2.

New York Times, May 9, 1999, Nicholas Wade, "DNA Backs a Tribe's Tradition of Early Descent from Jews," section 1, p. 1; February 21, 2000, Walter Goodman, "DNA as Detective Again, but on a Biblical Case."

Observer (London, England), January 25, 1998, Melanie Phillips, "Solved: The Riddle of the African Jews," p. 17.

Times Literary Supplement, December 13, 1985, Bernard Wasserstein, review of *Operation Moses;* January 31, 2003, David J. Wasserstein, review of *The Lost Tribes of Israel.*

Transition, Volume 10, number 1, 2000, Seth Sanders, "Invisible Races," pp. 76-97.

ONLINE

Nova, http://www.pbs.org/wkbh/nova/ (May 11, 2004), "Tudor Parfitt's Remarkable Journey."*

                    *   *   *

PELKA, Fred 1954-

PERSONAL: Born October 16, 1954, in Patchogue, NY; son of Friedrich (a grocery store clerk) and Hilda (a homemaker) Pelka. *Ethnicity:* "German-American." *Education:* State University of New York—Buffalo, B.A.

ADDRESSES: Office—c/o 54 Burncolt Rd., Florence, MA 01062-1054; fax 413-586-1852.

CAREER: Hospital News, Boston, MA, reporter specializing in health care, health insurance, and finance, 1986-87; freelance writer. Boston Center for Independent Living, Boston, MA, cofounder and vice chairperson of transportation committee, 1984-86, member of board of trustees, 1990-93; Bancroft Library Regional Oral History Office, University of California, Berkeley, researcher and interviewer, Project on Disability Rights and Independent Living Movement, beginning 2000.

MEMBER: American Association of People with Disabilities, Society for Disability Studies, Justice for All.

AWARDS, HONORS: John Simon Guggenheim Memorial fellow, 2004.

WRITINGS:

The ABC-CLIO Companion to the Disability Rights Movement, American Bibliographical Center-CLIO Press (Santa Barbara, CA), 1997.

The Civil War Letters of Colonel Charles F. Johnson, Invalid Corps, University of Massachusetts Press (Amherst, MA), 2004.

Work represented in anthologies, including *SirS Researcher,* SirS, 1998; *The LRS Reader,* Library Reference Service-Verticomp, 1998; and *The Prose Reader,* Prentice-Hall (Englewood Cliffs, NJ), 1999. Contributor to magazines and newspapers, including *Mainstream, Americana, America's Civil War, Changing Men, Humanist, Nature and Health, Rural New England, Mouth, Boston Globe, Christian Science Monitor,* and *Threepenny Review.* Contributing editor, *On the Issues,* 1991-98; member of review board for *Review of Disability Studies.*

WORK IN PROGRESS: An essay on disability rights for *Social Issues: An Encyclopedia of Controversies, History, and Debates.*

                    *   *   *

PETERSON, Benjamin
    See ALLEN, Robert L(ee)

PICOULT, Jodi 1966-

PERSONAL: Surname is pronounced "*pee*-koe"; born May 19, 1966, in NY; daughter of Myron Michel (a securities analyst) and Jane Ellen (a nursery school director; maiden name, Friend) Picoult; married Timothy Warren van Leer (a technical sales representative), November 18, 1989; children: Kyle Cameron, Jacob Matthew, Samantha Grace. *Education:* Princeton University, B.A., 1987; Harvard University, M.Ed., 1990.

ADDRESSES: Home—P.O. Box 508, Etna, NH 03750. *E-mail*—c/o agent Laura Gross, lglitag@aol.com.

CAREER: Allyn & Bacon, Inc., Newton, MA, developmental editor, 1987-88; junior high school teacher of English and creative writing in Concord and Natick, MA, 1989-91; writer, 1991—.

AWARDS, HONORS: New England Book Award Winner for Fiction, New England Booksellers Association, 2003, for her entire body of work; Best Mainstream Fiction Novel designation, Romance Writers of America, 2003, for *Second Glance.*

WRITINGS:

NOVELS

Songs of the Humpback Whale, Faber & Faber (London, England), 1992.
Harvesting the Heart, Viking (New York, NY), 1994.
Picture Perfect, Putnam (New York, NY), 1995.
Mercy, Putnam (New York, NY), 1996.
The Pact: A Love Story, Morrow (New York, NY), 1998.
Keeping Faith, Morrow (New York, NY), 1999.
Plain Truth, Pocket Books (New York, NY), 2000.
Salem Falls, Pocket Books (New York, NY), 2001.
Perfect Match, Atria Books (New York, NY), 2002.
Second Glance, Atria Books (New York, NY), 2003.
My Sister's Keeper, Atria Books (New York, NY), 2004.

ADAPTATIONS: Picoult's novels *The Pact* and *Plain Truth* were adapted for television and aired on the Lifetime network, 2002 and 2004. *My Sister's Keeper* was optioned by Fine Line Films for theatrical release.

Jodi Picoult

WORK IN PROGRESS: Vanishing Acts, expected in 2005; *The Tenth Circle,* expected in 2006.

SIDELIGHTS: Since her first success with *Songs of the Humpback Whale* in 1992, novelist Jodi Picoult has produced several other books in quick succession, often working on two books simultaneously. While she did tell an interviewer for the *Allen-Unwin* Web site that "I moonlight as a writer. My daylight hours are spent with my three children," her writing time has become more constant since her husband chose to be a stay-at-home dad. Picoult's themes center on women's issues, family, and relationships. According to Donna Seaman in *Booklist,* the author is "a writer of high energy and conviction."

Picoult's second work, *Harvesting the Heart,* concerns Paige O'Toole, an Irish Catholic with some artistic talent. The product of an unhappy childhood and adolescence, Paige leaves home after high school and lands a job at a diner where she sketches customers. There she meets her future husband, the egocentric Nicholas Prescott, whom she eventually puts through medical school after his parents disown him. After their first child is born, Paige becomes frustrated with the pressures of motherhood and increasingly estranged from the busy Nicholas. At the end of her patience, she decides to leave her family and seek her own mother, who left her when Paige was only five. Paige's heartwrenching decision leads her to deal with her own identity as she discovers she is not like her irresponsible mother. A happy ending ensues, with Paige returning to her family and Nicholas learning to take on more family responsibilities. A *Kirkus Reviews* critic found that the book had "some good writing, but not enough to sustain a concept-driven and rather old-fashioned story."

After producing *Harvesting the Heart,* Picoult published *Picture Perfect,* a study of wife abuse, and *Mercy,* a story dealing with euthanasia. In 1998 she published *The Pact: A Love Story,* a legal thriller set in a New Hampshire town. The novel concerns the Hartes and the Golds, neighbors and close friends. Their teenaged children, Chris and Emily, who grew up almost as brother and sister, become romantically involved and enter into a suicide pact. However, Chris survives and is charged with murder. After an investigation, he is jailed, and the friendship between the two families dissolves. According to a *Kirkus Reviews* critic, the trial scenes in *The Pact* are "powerful," and the novel itself is "an affecting study of obsession, loss, and some of the more wrenching varieties of guilt." Seaman, writing in *Booklist,* dubbed Picoult's book "a finely honed, commanding, and cathartic drama."

The author's 1999 novel, *Keeping Faith,* also concerns characters in a small town struggling to maintain their concepts of honesty and faith. The protagonist, Mariah White, discovers that her husband has been unfaithful and subsequently sinks into depression. Her seven-year-old daughter, Faith, is upset by her mother's behavior and begins conversing with an imaginary friend, as well as acting as if she has newfound religious powers. Their lives enter a state of increasing upheaval as more and more of the faithful and the curious come to partake of Faith's supposed healing powers. Faith's father sues for custody of the girl, and an emotional court scene ensues. Margaret Flanagan, in *Booklist,* called the novel "a mesmerizing morality play."

Picoult's novel *Plain Truth* is set in the Pennsylvania Amish country. When a dead infant is discovered in the barn of an Amish farmer, a police investigation

suggests that the mother is an eighteen-year-old Amish girl and that the baby did not die of natural causes. Although the teen denies responsibility, she is arrested and charged with murder. She is defended by a Philadelphia attorney, Ellie Hathaway, who soon clashes both with the will of her client and with the cultural values of Amish society. In the process of building her client's difficult defense, Ellie discovers more and more about her own inner life and personal values, while also learning to appreciate the values of the "plain people." Many reviewers praised the novel's suspenseful plot, its characterization, and its skillful portrait of Amish culture. *Knight-Ridder/Tribune News Service* contributor Linda DuVal said that in *Plain Truth* Picoult writes with "clarity" and "depicts a simple, yet deceptively complex, society of people who share a sense of compassion and the unshakable belief in the goodness of their fellow men and women."

In *My Sister's Keeper,* Picoult uses her characters to explore the ramificiations of cloning and gene replacement therapy, asking whether birthing one child to save the life of another child makes one a good mother—or a very bad one. A *Kirkus Reviews* critic declared that in *My Sister's Keeper* the novelist "vividly evokes the physical and psychic toll a desperately sick child imposes on a family, even a close and loving one." Noting that there are "no easy outcomes in a tale about individual autonomy clashing with a sibling's right to life," the reviewer explained that "Picoult thwarts our expectations in unexpected ways" and dubbed *My Sister's Keeper* "a telling portrait" of a modern American family under stress.

Picoult once noted of her work: "I am particularly concerned with what constitutes the truth—how well we think we know the people we love and the lives we live. I also write about the intricacies of family ties and connections, which often unearth questions that have no easy answers."

BIOGRAPHICAL AND CRITICAL SOURCES:

PERIODICALS

Booklist, April 1, 1998, Donna Seaman, review of *The Pact: A Love Story;* May 15, 1999, Margaret Flanagan, review of *Keeping Faith;* December 15,

2002, Kristine Huntley, review of *Second Glance;* January 1, 2004, Kristine Huntley, review of *My Sister's Keeper.*

Kirkus Reviews, August 15, 1993, review of *Harvesting the Heart;* March 15, 1998, review of *The Pact;* April 15, 2002, review of *Perfect Match;* January 1, 2003, review of *Second Glance;* January 15, 2004, review of *My Sister's Keeper.*

Knight-Ridder/Tribune News Service, June 15, 2000, Linda DuVal, review of *Plain Truth,* p. K239.

Library Journal, May 1, 2002, Nancy Pear, review of *Perfect Match;* February 15, 2003, Diana McRae, review of *Second Glance;* March 15, 2004, Kim Uden Rutter, review of *My Sister's Keeper.*

Publishers Weekly, May 6, 2002, review of *Perfect Match;* February 16, 2004, review of *My Sister's Keeper.*

ONLINE

Allen-Unwin Web site, http://www.allen-unwin.com/ (October 2, 2000), interview with Picoult.

Jodi Picoult Web site, http://www.jodipicoult.com (August 23, 2004).*

*   *   *

PIEL, Gerard 1915-2004

PERSONAL: Born March 1, 1915, in Woodmere, NY; died September 5, 2004, in Woodmere, NY; son of William (a brewer) and Loretto (Scott) Piel; married Mary Tapp Bird (in publishing), February 4, 1938 (divorced, 1955); married Eleanor Virden Jackson (a lawyer), June 24, 1955; children: (first marriage) Jonathan Bird, Samuel Bird (deceased); (second marriage) Eleanor P. Womack. *Education:* Harvard University, A.B. (magna cum laude), 1937.

CAREER: Time, Inc., New York, NY, editorial trainee, 1937-39; *Life,* New York, science editor, 1939-44; Henry J. Kaiser Co. and Associated Companies, Oakland, CA, assistant to president, 1945-46; *Scientific American,* New York, president, 1946-84, publisher, 1948-84, chairman of the board, 1985-87. Overseer of Harvard University; trustee of Radcliffe College, Phillips Academy, American Museum of Natural History,

New York University, Foundation for Child Development, and Henry J. Kaiser Family Foundation.

MEMBER: American Philosophical Society, Council on Foreign Relations, American Academy of Arts and Sciences (president, 1985; chairman, 1986), Institute of Medicine of National Academy of Sciences, Phi Beta Kappa, Sigma Xi.

AWARDS, HONORS: Sc.D., Lawrence College, 1956, Colby College, 1960, University of British Columbia, 1965, Brandeis University, 1965; Litt.D., Rutgers University, 1961, Bates College, 1974; L.H.D., Columbia University, 1962, Williams College, 1966; LL.D., Tuskegee Institute, 1963, University of Bridgeport, 1964, Polytechnic Institute of Brooklyn, 1965, Carnegie-Mellon University, 1968. George K. Polk Award, 1961, for contribution to journalism; Kalinga Prize, UNESCO, 1962, Arches of Science Award, Pacific Science Center, 1969, and Rosenberger Medal, University of Chicago, 1973, all for contribution to public understanding of science; named publisher of the year, Magazine Publishers Association, 1980.

WRITINGS:

Science in the Cause of Man, Knopf (New York, NY), 1961, revised edition, 1962.

The Acceleration of History, Knopf (New York, NY), 1972.

Gerard Piel on Arms Control: Science and Economics (booklet), Miller Center on Arms Control, University of Virginia (Charlottesville, VA), 1987.

(Editor, with Osborn Segerberg, Jr.) *The World of René Dubos: A Collection from His Writings,* Henry Holt (New York, NY), 1990.

Only One World: Our Own to Make and to Keep, W. H. Freeman (New York, NY), 1992.

The Age of Science: What Scientists Learned in the Twentieth Century, illustrated by Peter Bradford, Basic Books (New York, NY), 2001.

Booklets published by the Center for the Study of Democratic Institutions (Santa Barbara, CA) include, *Consumers of Abundance,* 1961, and, with Ralph Helstein and Robert Theobald, *Jobs, Machines, and People: A Conversation,* 1964; contributor to a large number of periodicals, including *Bulletin of Atomic Scientists, Science, Foreign Affairs, Progressive, Amer-*

ican Heritage, Nation, Science Monthly, Saturday Review, Life, Science Digest, BioScience, and Atlantic Monthly.

SIDELIGHTS: Gerard Piel, a man who graduated from Harvard as a journalism major without taking a single science class, later nurtured and grew *Scientific American* until it was the model for science reporting, a magazine that appealed to scientists and lay readers with an interest in science. Because of Piel's high standards and journalistic ethics all during his career, scientists who generally refused to publish in popular magazines wrote for Piel, who, even during the Cold War, was one of the country's leading advocates for open science information and opponents of censorship.

Piel was the grandson of one of the founders of the Piel Brothers Brewery, and his own father worked in the business. Piel's first contribution to a major magazine was with *Life,* where he began sorting pictures and then became editorial assistant to managing editor John Billings. Prior to that time, he worked for the short-lived *Picture,* and he married Mary Tapp Bird, who had been his supervisor there. When Billings charged the twenty-four-year-old Piel with editing *Life*'s science department, Piel read science articles and convinced science writers to work with him, promising that their work would not be tampered with, that pictures would be added to enhance their writing, and that they could approve or change captions for the photographs. It was because of his consideration and professionalism that he built his reputation with writers.

His curious mind led Piel to develop stories and pictures that are remembered to this day, including an experiment for which he had a student of Massachusetts Institute of Technology's (MIT) Harold Edgerton use strobe lights to determine the path of a pitched curve ball. Piel soon realized that more than a science section was needed. A magazine devoted to science was his goal, but first, he needed more business experience. He arranged for a replacement at *Life* and went to work for Henry J. Kaiser, the wartime shipbuilder Piel had profiled several times in *Life.* After a year, the beginnings of a new magazine took shape, but before a single issue was published, McGraw-Hill came out with *Science Illustrated.* Piel and his partners and backers were correct in assuming that the competing magazine would be less scientific

and more general than their planned publication. McGraw's project failed, and, in fact, Piel was asked to salvage it. He refused and spent two more years raising half of what he needed. He sent out one hundred pleas to scientists for their support, and every one wrote back that he would write for the new magazine.

But instead of launching a new title, Piel bought the faltering *Scientific American,* offered great science stories, increased circulation, and received an offer from the American Academy of Arts and Sciences to take over the magazine. They were so impressed with Piel's content that they later ceased publication of their own *Scientific Monthly,* feeling that Piel was doing a better job of promoting science. The positive attention also drew in more investors and advertisers like General Electric, and reached the break-even point in 1951.

Piel's success was not without setbacks, however. In 1950, the Atomic Energy Commission forced the deletion of parts of articles about the creation of a hydrogen bomb, even though the information was in the public domain. In the same year, Piel resigned from the advisory board of a journal published by the Public Health Service after a loyalty check found that *Scientific American* had critiqued the evidence of the government in the Rosenberg spy trial, and when friends of Piel were questioned as to their loyalties.

Because of the growing circulation of *Scientific American,* advertising rates became prohibitive for most companies. When television became the new source for advertisers, the number of advertising pages dropped, although circulation continued to increase, and other competitors who tried to equal its popularity fell by the wayside. The Scientific American Library was created to publish science titles, and the circulation of the magazine exceeded one million copies, including international editions published in many languages.

Piel never wrote for his own magazine, using that space for contributors, but has written for many others. Following his retirement, he wrote *Only One World: Our Own to Make and to Keep,* in which he addresses the issues debated in the 1991 Rio de Janeiro *United Nations Conference on Environment and Development.*

Nathan Keyfitz reviewed the book in *Scientific American,* writing that "what gives *Only One World* vitality is its combining the healthy dissatisfaction of the young with a mature appreciation of the power of science and the industrial economy to move us to a more sustainable course than the one we have been following."

Piel described his *The Age of Science: What Scientists Learned in the Twentieth Century* as "what I have learned about what scientists learned in the twentieth century." Piel drew on fifty-three years worth of *Scientific American* in sections titled "Light and Matter," "Space and Time," "The Living Cell," "Earth History and the Evolution of Life," and "Tools and Human Evolution." "The resulting book," noted Loren Graham in the *New York Times Book Review,* "is somewhat similar to a text for general science at the advanced high school or elementary college level, but infinitely more interesting. As Piel observes, such texts usually have an author named 'Dull.' Piel is anything but dull."

A *Kirkus Reviews* critic noted that "true to the mission he mapped out for his magazine, Piel is always aware of the general reader's needs, and takes care to outline basic principles as well as the broader implications of the discoveries he describes." Piel's recurring theme is that technology must be used to address the problems of global inequity. An *Economist* reviewer wrote that *The Age of Science* "provides a satisfying sting in the tail by acknowledging the broader social context within which scientific research takes place."

Piel's emphasis was on pure science. Graham noted that in recent years, Americans have become "much more sophisticated" and that during the years Piel was with *Scientific American,* they "thought that science was an unproblematic positive force; the most difficult questions connected with it were the technical issues themselves." Graham said that public opinion polls now show that Americans "are still usually enthusiasts for science, but they no longer believe that the most difficult problems concerning science are in the body of science itself; those problems are in the ways in which science interacts with society. In a time of discussions of cloning, bioterrorism, global warming, stem cell research, nuclear energy, genetically modified crops, and euthanasia, educated citizens have learned that knowledge of the basic science involved is only a necessary, not a sufficient, condition for intelligent decisions."

Graham also felt that since scientists often disagree with each other, "citizens in the new millennium feel a need for a new kind of science journalism that will neither praise nor condemn science, but instead help them sort their way through these extremely difficult issues." Graham wrote that Piel "succeeded brilliantly" with *Scientific American* and offered the hope that "another such talented journalist of the sciences will emerge in the near future who will respond to the need of the new century."

BIOGRAPHICAL AND CRITICAL SOURCES:

BOOKS

Dictionary of Literary Biography: Volume 137: *American Magazine Journalists, 1900-1960,* Gale (Detroit, MI), 1994, pp. 232-241.

Piel, Gerard, *The Age of Science: What Scientists Learned in the Twentieth Century,* illustrated by Peter Bradford, Basic Books (New York, NY), 2001.

PERIODICALS

Booklist, October 15, 2001, Gilbert Taylor, review of *The Age of Science: What Scientists Learned in the Twentieth Century,* p. 364.

Economist, January 12, 2002, review of *The Age of Science.*

Kirkus Reviews, October 1, 2001, review of *The Age of Science,* p. 1406.

Library Journal, November 15, 2001, Wade M. Lee, review of *The Age of Science,* p. 95.

Nature, May 30, 2002, Zaheer Baber, review of *The Age of Science,* p. 489.

New Scientist, September 5, 1992, Eric Ashby, review of *Only One World: Ours to Make and to Keep,* p. 35.

New York Times Book Review, November 11, 2001, Loren Graham, review of *The Age of Science,* p. 29.

Publishers Weekly, March 30, 1992, review of *Only One World,* p. 94.

Quarterly Review of Biology, June, 2003, Nadine Weidman, review of *The Age of Science,* p. 212.

Scientific American, February, 1993, Nathan Keyfitz, review of *Only One World,* p. 114.

Times Higher Education Supplement, July 5, 2002, John Maddox, review of *The Age of Science,* p. 23.*

*   *   *

PINSKY, Robert 1940-

PERSONAL: Born October 20, 1940, in Long Branch, NJ; son of Milford Simon (an optician) and Sylvia (Eisenberg) Pinsky; married Ellen Jane Bailey (a clinical psychologist), December 30, 1961; children: Nicole, Caroline Rose, Elizabeth. *Education:* Rutgers University, B.A., 1962; Stanford University, Ph.D., 1966. *Religion:* Jewish.

ADDRESSES: Office—Department of English, Boston University, 236 Bay State Rd., Boston, MA 02215-1403. *E-mail*—rpinsky@bu.edu.

CAREER: University of Chicago, Chicago, IL, assistant professor of humanities, 1967-68; Wellesley College, Wellesley, MA, associate professor of English, 1968-80; University of California, Berkeley, professor of English, 1980-88; Boston University, Boston, MA, professor of English and creative writing, 1988—. Visiting lecturer, Harvard University, Cambridge, MA, 1979-80; Hurst Professor, Washington University, St. Louis, MO, 1981.

MEMBER: PEN, American Academy of Arts and Letters (appointed, 1999).

AWARDS, HONORS: Woodrow Wilson, Wallace Stegner, and Fulbright fellow, Stanford University; Massachusetts Council on the Arts grant, 1974; Oscar Blumenthal Prize, *Poetry* (Chicago, IL), 1978; American Academy of Arts and Letters Award, 1979; Saxifrage Prize, 1980; Guggenheim fellow, 1980; William Carlos Williams Prize, 1984; *Los Angeles Times Book Review* Award, Howard Morton Landon Prize for translation, both 1995, both for *The Inferno of Dante: A New Verse Translation;* Shelley Memorial Award, Poetry Society of America, 1996; Lenore Marshall Prize, and Pulitzer Prize nomination, both 1996, both for *The Figured Wheel: New and Collected Poems 1966-1996;* named Poet Laureate of the United

Robert Pinksy

States, 1997-2000; Harold Washington Literary Award, 1999; PEN/Voelcker Award for "an American poet at the height of his or her powers," 2004.

WRITINGS:

POEMS

Sadness and Happiness, Princeton University Press (Princeton, NJ), 1975.
An Explanation of America, Princeton University Press (Princeton, NJ), 1979.
History of My Heart, Ecco Press (New York, NY), 1984.
The Want Bone, Ecco Press (New York, NY), 1990.
(Translator) *The Inferno of Dante: A New Verse Translation,* illustrations by Michael Mazur, Farrar, Straus (New York, NY), 1994.
The Figured Wheel: New and Collected Poems, 1966-1996, Farrar, Straus (New York, NY), 1996.
Jersey Rain, Farrar, Straus (New York, NY), 2000.

OTHER

Landor's Poetry, University of Chicago Press (Chicago, IL), 1968.

The Situation of Poetry: Contemporary Poetry and Its Traditions, Princeton University Press (Princeton, NJ), 1976.

Robert Pinsky (recording), New Letters (Kansas City, MO), 1983.

(Translator, with Robert Hass) Czeslaw Milosz, *The Separate Notebooks,* Ecco Press (New York, NY), 1984.

Amy Clampitt and Robert Pinsky Reading Their Poems (recording), Archive of Recorded Poetry and Literature (Washington, DC), 1984.

Poetry and the World, Ecco Press (New York, NY), 1988.

Dorothy Barresi and Robert Pinsky Reading Their Poems (recording), Archive of Recorded Poetry and Literature (Washington, DC), 1992.

The Poet and the Poem from the Library of Congress: Robert Pinsky (recording), Archive of Recorded Poetry and Literature (Washington, DC), 1995.

Digital Culture and the Individual Soul (recording), Archive of Recorded Poetry and Literature (Washington, DC), 1997.

The Sounds of Poetry: A Brief Guide, Farrar, Straus (New York, NY), 1998.

(Collector) *The Handbook of Heartbreak: 101 Poems of Lost Love and Sorrow,* Rob Weisbach Books (New York, NY), 1998.

Poet Laureate Consultant in Poetry Robert Pinsky Reading His Poems in the Montpelier Room, Library of Congress, May 7, 1998, Archive of Recorded Poetry and Literature (Washington, DC), 1998.

Poetry and American Memory (recording), Archive of Recorded Poetry and Literature (Washington, DC), 1998.

Sharing the Gifts: Readings by 1997-2000 Poet Laureate Consultant in Poetry Robert Pinsky, 1999-2000 Special Poetry Consultants Rita Dove, Louise Glück, W. S. Merwin, 1999 Witter Bynner Fellows David Gewanter, Campbell McGrath, Heather McHugh (recording), Archive of Recorded Poetry and Literature (Washington, DC), 1999.

Robert Pinsky Reading Selections from the Anthology, "Americans' Favorite Poems, the Favorite Poem Project," and Discussing Them in the Mumford Room, Library of Congress, October 7, 1999 (recording), Archive of Recorded Poetry and Literature (Washington, DC), 1999.

The Poet and the Poem from the Library of Congress— Favorite Poets (recording), Archive of Recorded Poetry and Literature (Washington, DC), 1999.

(Author of introduction) David Noevich Goberman, *Carved Memories: Heritage in Stone from the Russian Jewish Pale,* Rizzoli (New York, NY), 2000.

(Editor, with Maggie Dietz) *Americans' Favorite Poems: The Favorite Poem Project Anthology,* Norton (New York, NY), 2000.

(Selector) Cate Marvin, *World's Tallest Disaster: Poems,* Sarabande Books (Louisville, KY), 2001.

(Editor, with Maggie Dietz) *Poems to Read: A New Favorite Poem Project Anthology,* W. W. Norton (New York, NY), 2002.

Democracy, Culture, and the Voice of Poetry, Princeton University Press (Princeton, NJ), 2002.

A Favorite Poem Reading with Frank Bidart, Louise Glück, and Robert Pinsky (recording), Recorded Sound Reference Center (Washington, DC), 2003.

(Editor) *William Carlos Williams: Selected Poems,* Library of America (New York, NY), 2004.

(Editor, with Maggie Dietz) *An Invitation to Poetry: A New Favorite Poem Project Anthology,* Norton (New York, NY), 2004.

Contributor of articles and poems to *American Review, American Poetry Review, Antaeus, Poetry, Shenandoah,* and *Yale Review.* Poetry editor, *New Republic,* 1978-86, and *Slate.com.*

SIDELIGHTS: Robert Pinsky is a poet and critic whose work reflects his concern for a contemporary poetic diction that nonetheless speaks of a wider experience. Elected Poet Laureate of the United States in 1997, Pinsky took his duties in that post quite seriously. His tenure as poet laureate was marked by ambitious efforts to prove the power of poetry, not just as an intellectual pursuit in the ivory tower, but as a meaningful and integral part of American life. "I think poetry is a vital part of our intelligence, our ability to learn, our ability to remember, the relationship between our bodies and minds," he told the *Christian Science Monitor.* "Poetry's highest purpose is to provide a unique sensation of coordination between the intelligence, emotions and the body. It's one of the most fundamental pleasures a person can experience." In a *New York Times Book Review* essay, Pinsky wrote: "Poetry is, among other things, a technology for remembering. But this fact may touch our lives far more profoundly than jingles for remembering how many days there are in June. The buried conduits among memory and emotion and the physical sounds of language may touch our inner life every day. . . . Poetry, a form of language far older than prose, is under our skins."

Pinsky once commented: "I would like to write a poetry which could contain every kind of thing, while keeping all the excitement of poetry." Pinsky's language, Willard Spiegelman stated in the *Dictionary of Literary Biography Yearbook,* "while obeying the idiomatic rules of [his] own age, is intelligible beyond the fashions of a given time." Calling Pinsky "a successful and assiduous poet laureate," *New York Times Book Review* correspondent Adam Kirsch added: "The tasks of the public poet usually suit him well, because his intelligence seems, at bottom, less lyrical than discursive, even didactic. This poetic mode is much less favored now than in the past, but as Pinsky proves, it is still able to give pleasure."

In his volumes of criticism, including *The Situation of Poetry: Contemporary Poetry in Its Traditions, Poetry and the World,* and *The Sounds of Poetry: A Brief Guide,* Pinsky presents his views on the nature of poetry. In *The Situation of Poetry,* he writes of the poet's need to "find a language for presenting the role of a conscious soul in an unconscious world." This emphasis on the actual leads Pinsky to see contemporary poetry as far more continuous with earlier poetry than many critics would believe. As Denis Donoghue remarked in the *New York Times Book Review,* Pinsky "believes, and is pleased to show, that contemporary poetry exhibits more continuity than change." Writing in the *Georgia Review,* Charles Molesworth commented that "given the pluralistic state of our poetry (and the jumbled social values it builds on), Pinsky's approach remains appropriate." Donoghue concluded that "the mind at work in *The Situation of Poetry* is lively, fresh and critical without being obsessed by the rigor of criticism."

In the essays of *Poetry and the World,* Pinsky expands on his concept of poetry and, in a series of essays, examines the impact words have had on his own life. "In his foreword," wrote John L. Brown in *World Literature Today,* "he claims that these various elements all concern 'the relation of poetry to its great, shadowy social context, the world.' They are also linked by a common tone, a tone of relaxed, unpretentious conversation comprehensible to the common reader." "Pinsky's criticism is far removed from that of his deconstructionist academic colleagues," Brown explained. "He proclaims his respect for literary tradition. . . . He has none of the urge to destroy the past which fired the avant-garde movements of this century." "Even the autobiographical digressions demonstrate a heartening sense of vocation," declared Amy Edith Johnson in the *New York Times Book Review.* "Mr. Pinsky's honorable practice confirms the dignity and creative dimension of . . . the function of criticism at the present time."

The Sounds of Poetry is a slim volume that can serve as a primer on the mechanics of poetry and also as a "treatise on the social functions of poetry," to quote James Longenbach in the *Nation.* The critic added that the work "is not only interesting but suspenseful to read. Without discussing the meaning of poems, Pinsky has created a keenly idiosyncratic account of the place of poetry in our time." *Atlantic Monthly* contributor David Barber noted that *The Sounds of Poetry* "is an achievement for which there is surprisingly little precedent: an authoritative yet accessible introduction to the tools of the poet's trade that can be read with profit by the serious student and the amateur alike." Barber characterized the volume as "less that of a solemn classroom lecture than that of a spirited audio tour, with Pinsky offering up various devices and motifs for inspection and providing a lively running commentary on how to fine-tune the ear to respond to the distinctive verbal energies that make poetry 'poetic.'" Longenbach concluded: "Whatever else it does, *The Sounds of Poetry* suggests why its author, who once wrote a poetry distinguished by subject matter, has become a poet of crotchety, gorgeous sounds. By showing us how to surrender ourselves to this bright confusion, Pinsky gives us the liberty to understand more than ever before."

In his own poetry, Pinsky has followed the principles set out in his criticism. "In Pinsky's poetry and criticism," explained Spiegelman, "there lies an abiding unity, of which the principal ingredients are ethical ambition, sanity, a sense of humor, and something to say." Critics of Pinsky's first collection, *Sadness and Happiness,* compared the work to Ranier Marie Rilke, James Wright, and Robert Lowell. "The feeling that, somehow, American poetry has entered a new era of confidence is borne out by . . . *Sadness and Happiness,*" declared *Yale Review* contributor Louis L. Martz. "Pinsky is the most exhilarating new poet that I have read since A. R. Ammons entered upon the scene. . . . The whole of the modern world is for Pinsky a region where the soul . . . has to face its mysteries; and the outer conditions for him are no worse or no better than they ever were for any generation."

Pinsky's book-length poem, *An Explanation of America,* examines the history of the United States in the same way that poet Robert Lowell had done, but, said Spiegelman, "his characteristic tone is less agonized and tense, more subdued than Lowell's." Although both poets draw on similarities between modern America and the ancient Roman Empire, the critic continued, "where Lowell's Rome is Juvenal's, Pinsky selects the earlier empire, Augustus's and Horace's, for his historical analogy to America." "Not the least remarkable thing about Robert Pinsky's remarkable [book]," stated Michael Hamburger in the *Nation,* "is that it seems to defy not only all the dominant trends in contemporary poetry but all the dominant notions—both American and non-American—of what is to be expected of an American poet." "In its philosophical approach, classical learning, and orderly structure," remarked *Hudson Review* contributor James Finn Cotter, *An Explanation of America* "resembles the work of William Cullen Bryant more than that of Hart Crane, but it is not old-fashioned. It is as American as Bryant's and Crane's long poems, as embedded in the past, and as identified with the woods and prairies."

Pinsky continues his examination of history— sometimes national, sometimes personal—in two later collections of poetry. "*History of My Heart,* which appeared in 1984," observed J. D. McClatchy in the *New Republic,* "was Pinsky's breakthrough, and my guess is that it will come to be seen as one of the best books of the past decade." McClatchy elaborated: "He might still use poetry as (in Emerson's phrase) 'a platform whence we may command a view of our present life, a purchase by which we may move it,' but he took his stand on the contradictions and desires of the self."

The best poems in Pinsky's 1990 collection, *The Want Bone,* according to McClatchy, "are more personal. They do not wrestle with religious angels or intellectual demons, the myths imposed on us by tradition. Instead, they address the self, those autobiographical myths we make out of memories." *Poetry* essayist Paul Breslin wrote: "In *The Want Bone,* Pinsky faces the limits of the pleasure principle that sustains *His-*

tory of My Heart. There, the erotic is the basis of the social, the drive that, not so much through sublimation as through cultivation, enables us to delight and sustain each other, and to delight in art. Here, desire is irreducible hunger."

The Figured Wheel: New and Collected Poems, 1966-1996 "will remind readers that here is a poet who, without forming a mini-movement or setting himself loudly at odds with the dominant tendencies of American poetry, has brought into it something new," maintained Katha Pollitt in the *New York Times Book Review.* Breslin felt that *The Figured Wheel* "signals a major turn in Pinsky's stylistic development. . . . [In] its hurling together of the apocalyptic and vast with the mundane and the particular, it fairly bristles with linguistic energy." The critic added: "The keen analytical intelligence of the earlier poetry does not disappear. But it is intellect in service to wonder, more ready to acknowledge the radical strangeness and intractability of the world it must try to comprehend." Pollitt claimed: "What makes Mr. Pinsky such a rewarding and exciting writer is the sense he gives, in the very shape and structure of his poems, of getting at the depths of human experience, in which everything is always repeated but also always new."

Pinsky's interest in a poetry of contemporary speech and wide-ranging subject matter led him in 1994 to publish a new translation of Dante's *Inferno.* He had been asked, with a group of nineteen other poets, to participate in a reading of the poem at the 92nd Street YMCA in New York City in May of 1993. Pinsky became fascinated with the work of the thirteenth-century Italian poet. "It just gripped me, like a child with a new video game," he told *New York Times* contributor Diana Jean Schemo. "I literally couldn't stop working on it." "I'm not fluent in Italian, but I love languages," Pinsky continued in an interview with *New York Times Book Review* contributor Lynn Karpen. "This was like being a child with a new toy. I called the translation a feat of metrical engineering, and I worked obsessively. It's the only writing I have ever done where it's like reading yourself to sleep each night. We have pillowcases stained with ink where my wife took the pen out of my hand at night."

Despite the fact that about fifty English-language translations of the *Inferno* have been published in the twentieth century alone, critics largely celebrated Pinsky's work. "The primary strength of this translation," declared *New Yorker* contributor Edward Hirsch, "is the way it maintains the original's episodic and narrative velocity while mirroring its formal shape and character. It is no small achievement to reproduce Dante's rhyme scheme and at the same time sound fresh and natural in English, and Pinsky succeeds in creating a supple American equivalent for Dante's vernacular music where many others have failed." "His skill and power as a poet inform every line of this splendid translation," stated John Ahern in the *New York Times Book Review*. "He shapes sinewy lines whose edges you can actually hear. This is true verse, not the typographical arrangement of poetic prose." The reviewer concluded: "From the beginning, his translation propels us through a gripping narrative whose drama is always in sharp focus and whose characters speak in distinctive voices. . . . [I]f he does not quite attain Dante's full symphonic range, no one has come closer."

Pinsky was named poet laureate in 1997 and served until 2000. The position carries a modest stipend, but its appeal lies in its visibility to the general public. Formerly a retiring person, Pinsky became a public figure, and he used the notoriety to promote a new project. Under his direction, ordinary Americans were invited to name their favorite poems—and some entrants were asked to read for a permanent audio archive at the Library of Congress. Pinsky set a goal of recording one hundred people, but he was inundated with letters and e-mails from all over the nation, and those participating represented all ages, all walks of life, and all levels of education. "The Favorite Poem Project is partly to demonstrate that there is more circulation of poetry and more life of poetry than there might seem with the stereotype," Pinsky explained in the *Progressive*. "I must say that the Favorite Poem readings, beyond my expectation, are very moving."

With Maggie Dietz, Pinsky edited a representative volume of reader responses called *Americans' Favorite Poems: The Favorite Poem Project Anthology*. A *Publishers Weekly* reviewer stated that "the selections are as diverse as the nation that chose them." *Americans' Favorite Poems* proved so popular that two subsequent collections have appeared: *Poems to Read: A New Favorite Poem Project Anthology* and *An Invitation to Poetry: A New Favorite Poem Project Anthology*. *Booklist* contributor Donna Seaman called *Poems to Read* "a graceful, sometimes jubilant, sometimes lyrical, sometimes brooding, but always welcoming and stirring collection."

Jersey Rain, published in 2000, was Pinsky's first collection of completely new work since *The Want Bone* appeared a decade earlier. Reviewing the work in *Library Journal*, Christian Graham observed that Pinsky's poems range from the mythic to the confessional. "Occasionally, his differing manners collide strangely," Graham stated, "but Pinsky delivers, as ever, intelligent, pensive poetry of great beauty." A critic in *Publishers Weekly* felt that the work's "lighter pieces will delight fans, but the poems with more profound aspirations lack a penetrating introspection." According to Lee Oser in *World Literature Today*, "the book holds interest both as a marker of poetry's development after modernism, and as the work of a fine and resourceful craftsman."

An *Atlantic Monthly* correspondent recognized Pinsky as "one of the most distinguished poets of his generation," and Breslin commented that Pinsky "has emerged as the finest American poet-critic since Randall Jarrell." For his own part, the last American poet laureate of the twentieth century told the *Progressive*: "I think the rhythms in a lot of my writing are an attempt to create that feeling of a beautiful, gorgeous jazz solo that gives you more emotion and some more and coming around with some more, and it's the same but it's changed, and the rhythm is very powerful, but it is also lyricism. I think I've been trying to create something like that in my writing for a long time."

BIOGRAPHICAL AND CRITICAL SOURCES:

BOOKS

Contemporary Literary Criticism, Gale (Detroit, MI), Volume 9, 1978, Volume 19, 1981, Volume 38, 1986.
Contemporary Poets, 7th edition, St. James Press (Detroit, MI), 2001.
Dictionary of Literary Biography Yearbook, 1982, Gale (Detroit, MI), 1983.
Poetry for Students, Volume 18, Gale (Detroit, MI), 2003.
Spiegelman, Willard, *The Didactic Muse*, Princeton University Press (Princeton, NJ), 1989.

PERIODICALS

American Poetry Review, July-August, 2003, Tony Hoaglund, "Three Tenors: Gluck, Hass, Pinsky, and the Deployment of Talent," pp. 37-42.

American Scholar, spring, 1999, Adam Kirsch, review of *The Sounds of Poetry,* p. 140.

Atlantic Monthly, March, 1999, David Barber, "What Makes Poetry 'Poetic?'," p. 114; October, 1999, p. 6.

Booklist, June 1, 2002, Donna Seaman, review of *Poems to Read: A New Favorite Poems Project Anthology,* p. 1670.

Christian Science Monitor, April 21, 1998, Marjorie Coeyman, "Poet Laureate's Request: Lend Me Your Voices," p. B8.

Georgia Review, spring, 1985.

Hudson Review, spring, 1980, pp. 131-145.

Library Journal, May 1, 2000, Graham Christian, review of *Jersey Rain,* p. 118; July 1, 2002, Daniel L. Guillory, review of *Poems to Read,* p. 85; October 15, 2002, Scott Hightower, review of *Democracy, Culture, and the Voice of Poetry,* p. 73.

Life, October, 1998, Melissa Faye Greene and Jillian Edelstein, "Poetry U.S.A.," p. 114.

Nation, January 26, 1980, pp. 86-87; September 21, 1998, James Longenbach, review of *The Sounds of Poetry,* p. 34.

New Republic, September 24, 1990, pp. 46-48; October 28, 2002, David Bromwich, "The Roughs and Beards," p. 25.

New Yorker, January 23, 1995, pp. 87-90.

New York Times, January 31, 1995, pp. B1, B2.

New York Times Book Review, February 20, 1977, Denis Donoghue, review of *The Situation of Poetry;* July 23, 1989, Amy Edith Johnson, review of *Poetry and the World,* p. 19; September 25, 1994, "A Man Goes Into a Bar, See, and Recites: 'The Quality of Mercy Is Not Strained,'" pp. 15-16; January 1, 1995, Lynn Karpen, "A Fear of Metrical Engineering," and John Ahern, "Vulgar Eloquence," p. 3; August 18, 1996, Katha Pollitt, "World of Wonders"; April 9, 2000, Adam Kirsch, "Vox Populi."

Poetry, October, 1990, pp. 39-41; July, 1997, Paul Breslin, review of *The Figured Wheel: New and Collected Poems 1966-1996,* p. 226; August, 1999, Christian Wiman, review of *The Sounds of Poetry,* p. 286.

Progressive, May, 1999, Anne-Marie Cusac, "Robert Pinsky," p. 35.

Publishers Weekly, October 25, 1999, "Home Grown," p. 77; March 6, 2000, review of *Jersey Rain,* p. 105.

TriQuarterly, winter, 1994, "A Conversation with Robert Pinsky," pp. 21-37.

Utne Reader, September-October, 1999, Anne-Marie Cusac, "Robert Pinsky's Grand Slam," p. 98.

World Literature Today, autumn, 1989, pp. 751-752; autumn, 2000, Lee Oser, review of *Jersey Rain,* p. 820.

Writer, November, 1999, Susan Kelly, "An Interview with Robert Pinsky," p. 18.

Yale Review, autumn, 1976.

ONLINE

Academy of American Poets Web site, http://www.poets.org/ (August 10, 2004), "Robert Pinsky."

Boston University Web site, http://www.bu.edu/ (October 17, 2003).

Favorite Poem Project Web site, http://www.favoritepoem.org/ (November 22, 2000).

Poetry & Literature Center of the Library of Congress Web site, http://www.loc.gov/poetry/poetry.html (August 9, 2004).*

*   *   *

POTTER, Lois 1941-

PERSONAL: Born February 20, 1941, in Oakland, CA; daughter of George Vernon (a physician) and Lois (Dorais) Potter. *Education:* Sorbonne, University of Paris, diploma, 1957; Bryn Mawr College, B.A., 1961; Girton College, Cambridge, Ph.D., 1965. *Politics:* "Vague." *Hobbies and other interests:* Attending theater and opera, travel, cats.

ADDRESSES: Office—Department of English, University of Delaware, Newark, DE 19716-2537.

CAREER: University of Aberdeen, Aberdeen, Scotland, assistant lecturer in English, 1964-66; University of Leicester, Leicester, England, lecturer, 1966-79, senior lecturer, 1979-89, reader in English, 1989-91; University of Delaware, Newark, Ned B. Allen Professor, 1991—. Broadcaster of drama reviews and other material on local radio station.

MEMBER: Modern Language Association of America, Shakespeare Association of America (member of board of trustees, 1999), Malone Society (honorary secretary), Medieval and Renaissance Drama Society, Renaissance English Text Society (member of council, 1997), Society for Theatre Research (England).

AWARDS, HONORS: Woodrow Wilson fellowship, 1961; Marshall scholarship, Cambridge University, 1961-64.

WRITINGS:

A Preface to Milton, Scribner (New York, NY), 1971.
Twelfth Night: Text and Performance, Macmillan (London, England), 1984.
Othello (study of the play in performance), Manchester University Press (Manchester, England), 2002.

Author of introduction to *The Dramatic and Poetical Works of the Late Lieutenant General J. Burgoyne: A Facsimile Reproduction,* Scholars' Facsimilies and Reprints, 1977. Also author and director of documentary programs for local radio and university theater broadcasts. Contributor to *Durham University Journal, Shakespeare Survey,* and *Times Educational Supplement.*

EDITOR

John Milton, *Paradise Lost,* Book III, Cambridge University Press (New York, NY), 1976.
(General editor) *The Revels History of Drama,* Methuen (London, England), Volume 1, 1981, (and contributor) Volume 4, 1983.
Francis Osborne, *The True Tragicomedy* (a formerly anonymous play manuscript from c. 1655), Garland Publishing (New York, NY), 1983.
Secret Rites and Secret Writing: Royalist Literature, 1641-1660, Cambridge University Press (New York, NY), 1989.
William Shakespeare and John Fletcher, *The Two Noble Kinsmen,* Routledge (New York, NY), 1996.
(And contributor) *Playing Robin Hood: The Legend as Performance in Five Centuries,* University of Delaware Press (Newark, DE), 1998.
(With Arthur F. Kinney, and contributor) *Shakespeare, Text, and Theater: Essays in Honor of Jay L. Halio,* University of Delaware Press (Newark, DE), 1999.

SIDELIGHTS: Lois Potter once told *CA:* "What I am proudest of, in an otherwise rather conventional academic career, is that I have sometimes managed to combine the creative and the scholarly. For example, in 1976 I wrote a musical documentary about the American Revolution from the point of view of General Burgoyne, and also contributed a scholarly introduction to a reprint of Burgoyne's plays and poems, published in 1977 in the 'Scholars' Facsimiles and Reprints' series; in 1981 I burrowed in the University Archives in order to write a dramatic documentary for Leicester's Jubilee year, which was broadcast with a cast of academics, students, and administrators. Attending courses on university teaching methods (especially DUET—Development of University English Teaching—at the University of East Anglia) made me much more aware of the possibilities for using my own and the students' creativity in teaching. Living in England but maintaining contacts with U.S. academic life was also a stimulus: it created the sense of uncertainty and restlessness which, for me, seems to be a precondition of effective thinking."

BIOGRAPHICAL AND CRITICAL SOURCES:

PERIODICALS

British Book News, July, 1985, review of *Twelfth Night: Text and Performance,* p. 435.
Comparative Drama, spring-summer, 2002, John R. Ford, review of *Shakespeare, Text, and Theater: Essays in Honor of Jay L. Halio,* p. 244.
Criticism, fall, 1991, review of *Secret Rites and Secret Writing: Royalist Literature, 1641-1660,* p. 547.
English Historical Review, January, 1993, Richard Ollard, review of *Secret Rites and Secret Writing,* p. 197.
Journal of English and Germanic Philology, January, 1992, review of *Secret Rites and Secret Writing,* p. 134.
Libraries and Culture, summer, 1992, review of *Secret Rites and Secret Writing,* p. 332.
Prolepsis: Tübingen Review of English Studies, December 20, 2000, William Fitzhenry, review of *Playing Robin Hood: The Legend as Performance in Five Centuries.*
Renaissance Quarterly, summer, 1991, review of *Secret Rites and Secret Writing,* p. 381; spring, 1999, review of *Playing Robin Hood,* p. 288.

Review of English Studies, May, 1991, review of *Secret Rites and Secret Writing,* p. 261.

Seventeenth-Century News, fall, 1991, review of *Secret Rites and Secret Writing,* p. 51.

Shakespeare Newsletter, spring-summer, 2001, Rachel Wifall, review of *Shakespeare, Text, and Theater,* p. 31.

Shakespeare Quarterly, spring, 1987, review of *Twelfth Night,* p. 111; summer, 2001, review of *Shakespeare, Text, and Theater,* p. 300.

Times Educational Supplement, May 3, 1985, review of *Twelfth Night,* p. 70.

Times Literary Supplement, November 19, 1982; January 3, 1986, review of *Twelfth Night,* p. 19; January 12, 1990, review of *Secret Rites and Secret Writing,* p. 42; October 25, 2002, Jonathan Bate, review of *Othello,* p. 13.*

* * *

PUTTFARKEN, Thomas 1943-

PERSONAL: Born December 19, 1943, in Hamburg, Germany; son of Franz Ferdinand (a dentist) and Traut Dorothea (Bruhn) Puttfarken; married Herma Zimmer, December 19, 1969 (divorced, 1981); married Elspeth Ann Crichton Stuart, October 10, 1981; children: (first marriage) Nathalie, Malte Ian. *Education:* University of Hamburg, D.Phil., 1969; attended University of Innsbruck, University of Munich, and Warburg Institute.

ADDRESSES: Office—Department of Art History and Theory, University of Essex, Wivenhoe Park, Colchester CO4 3SQ, England. *E-mail*—tomp@essex.ac.uk.

CAREER: Art history scholar. University of Essex, Colchester, England, lecturer, 1970-71, senior lecturer, 1974-78, reader, 1978-84, professor of art history and theory, 1984—, dean of students, 1978-81, dean of the School of Comparative Studies, 1984-86, pro vice chancellor, 1987—; lecturer at University of Hamburg, Hamburg, West Germany, 1971-74.

WRITINGS:

Roger de Piles' Theory of Art, Yale University Press (New Haven, CT), 1985.

(With others) *Falkland Palace and Royal Burgh,* National Trust for Scotland (Edinburgh, Scotland), 1995.

The Discovery of Pictorial Composition: Theories of Visual Order in Painting 1400-1800, Yale University Press (New Haven, CT), 2000.

Contributor to art magazines, including *Burlington, Art History,* and *Journal of the Warburg and Courtauld Institutes.*

SIDELIGHTS: Thomas Puttfarken's study *Roger de Piles' Theory of Art* was highly praised in the *Times Literary Supplement* by critic Richard Wollheim, who commented that the book "is an admirable contribution to the art-theoretical strand of art history. . . . It is also . . . an excellent example of how to retrieve the ideas of an interesting, if unsystematic, thinker for posterity." Wollheim considered it "a refreshing departure" that Puttfarken examined the seventeenth-century thinker "not so much for the light he can throw on a related body of painting, but in his own right." The critic particularly admired Puttfarken's own interpretation of illusion and his attention to de Piles's view that illusion and harmony are not only compatible, but mutually supportive of each other.

In *The Discovery of Pictorial Composition: Theories of Visual Order in Painting,* Puttfarken notes that prior to the seventeenth century, pictorial composition was not a factor, particularly since Italian artists and patrons concentrated on the representations and interactions of life-size saints depicted in large murals and altarpieces. He then goes on to study composition in theory and practice. David Topper, reviewing this volume for *Leonardo Digital Reviews* wrote, "I have often been disturbed by the incongruity between the foreground and background in most pictures by Leonardo da Vinci. This erudite and tightly argued book gives an answer to that puzzle." *London Review of Books* contributor Jules Lubbock called the art history "superb."

BIOGRAPHICAL AND CRITICAL SOURCES:

PERIODICALS

London Review of Books, October 31, 2002, Jules Lubbock, review of *The Discovery of Pictorial Composition: Theories of Visual Order in Painting 1400-1800,* p. 40.

Renaissance Quarterly, autumn, 2001, review of *The Discovery of Pictorial Composition,* p. 941.

Sixteenth Century Journal, spring, 2002, review of *The Discovery of Pictorial Composition,* p. 316.

Times Literary Supplement, March 28, 1986, Richard Wollheim, review of *Roger de Piles' Theory of Art.*

ONLINE

Leonardo Digital Reviews, http://mitpress2.mit.edu/e-journals/Leonardo/ldr.html (November, 2000), David Topper, review of *The Discovery of Pictorial Composition.**

R

RAMSDEN, John (Andrew) 1947-

PERSONAL: Born November 12, 1947, in Sheffield, England; son of Cyril and Mary (Brummitt) Ramsden; married Susan McKay (a lecturer in mathematics), July 19, 1980. *Education:* Corpus Christi College, Oxford, B.A., 1969; Nuffield College, Oxford, D.Phil., 1974. *Religion:* Christian.

ADDRESSES: Home—9 Daisy Rd., London E18, England. *Office*—Queen Mary College, University of London, Mile End Rd., London E1 4NS, England. *E-mail*—J.A.Ramsden@qmul.ac.uk.

CAREER: Educator and author. Queen Mary College, University of London, London, England, lecturer, 1972-80, reader in modern history, 1980-96, professor of modern history 1996—; chairman of London East End Constituency Conservative Council, 1978-80, and Wanstead and Woodford Conservative Association, 1980-82; member of council of London Borough of Redbridge, 1982—.

AWARDS, HONORS: Winston Churchill Memorial Trust fellow in New Zealand, 1999; Distinguished Academic Visitor at La Trobe University, Melbourne, 2001.

WRITINGS:

(With Chris Cook) *By-Elections in British Politics,* St. Martin's Press (London, England), 1973.
(With Chris Cook) *Trends in British Politics since 1945,* Macmillan (London, England), 1978.

The Age of Balfour and Baldwin, 1902-1940, Longman (London, England), 1978.
The Making of Conservative Party Policy: The Conservative Research Department since 1929, Longman (London, England), 1980.
(Editor and author of introduction) *Real Old Tory Politics: The Political Diaries of Sir Robert Sanders, Lord Bayford, 1910-35,* Historians' Press (London, England), 1984.
Ruling Britannia: A Political History of Britain 1688-1988, Longman (New York, NY), 1990.
The Age of Churchill and Eden, 1940-57, Longman (New York, NY), 1995.
The Winds of Change: Macmillan to Heath, 1957-75, Longman (New York, NY), 1996.
An Appetite for Power, HarperCollins (New York, NY), 1999.
(Editor) *The Oxford Companion to Twentieth-Century British Politics,* Oxford University Press (Oxford, England), 2002.
Man of the Century: Winston Churchill and His Legend since 1945, Columbia University Press (New York, NY), 2002.
The Dam Busters, Palgrove Macmillan (New York, NY), 2003.

SIDELIGHTS: John Ramsden, a professor of modern history at the University of London, is the author of a number of books that focus on the history of modern British politics. Commenting on Ramsden's *The Making of Conservative Party Policy: The Conservative Research Department since 1929,* a London *Times* reviewer stated that the author "has now handsomely filled the Conservative gap in a study of the Party's Research Department which will delight its many old boys and friends of every political persuasion. Dr. Ramsden's book contains a wealth of new material drawn from the Old Queen Street files. . . . His study shows convincingly that it would be difficult to write seriously about the Conservative Party, or even about modern British politics, without considering the contribution to both of the Research Department during its fifty years of sometimes eccentric but always influential history."

In *The Winds of Change: Macmillan to Heath, 1957-75* Ramsden evaluates the British Conservative Party from Harold Macmillan's rise to the office of prime minister through the election of Margaret Thatcher as party leader in 1975. The book is part of Longman's "History of the Conservative Party" series, which has established itself as the authoritative guide to the organization. A *Spectator* reviewer noted that *The Winds of Change* is "beautifully constructed, meticulous in [its] research and in [its] adamant, though courteous, resistance to the received idea. . . . High among the author's achievements is that he never allows himself to become, in fashionable parlance, judgmental, yet is never bland."

Ramsden delves further into the history of the British Conservative Party in his 1999 work, *An Appetite for Power*. In addition to covering most of the issues and accomplishments of the party from past to present, he also includes valuable statistical information such as general elections, a list of office holders since 1830, conferences of the National Union, and a glossary listing the party's dominant leaders. Robert S. Redmond maintained in *Contemporary Review* that *An Appetite for Power* will make "an excellent *vade mecum* for any student of politics," while in the *Independent*, Kenneth Morgan added, "as a calm and informative interpreter of events," Ramsden "is hard to beat."

Ramsden looks back at the influence of one of the most noted political leaders of the twentieth century in *Man of the Century: Winston Churchill and His Legend since 1945*. Remembered for his resolute leadership of Great Britain during World War II, during which his strongly worded speeches and frequent radio addresses shored up and gave confidence to an embattled nation, Churchill was also a complex person who, following the war, devoted great attention to establishing a worldwide reputation up until the time of his death in 1965. Beginning with Churchill's

funeral, the book tracks back through Churchill's career as a cold war-era statesman and orator, as well as noting the positive public relations generated from his six-volume World War II memoirs, which remained "largely unchallenged for twenty years," according to Michael F. Hopkins in *Contemporary Review*. Reviewing the study for *Library Journal*, Robert Moore noted that in *Man of the Century* Ramsden presents readers with "a wry, readable, and comprehensive study of the depth and roots of Churchill's legacy." *History Today* critic Geoffrey Best, noting in particular Ramsden's revelations concerning those who perpetuated the legend of Churchill as the "saviour" of Britain during the war years, praised the author for his even-handedness. "Ramsden is a good-tempered truth-seeker, not a malevolent muckraker," noted Best, adding that Churchill as presented in *Man of the Century* "is certainly no saint but he commands the author's admiration and amazement, plus a good deal of amusement."

The Oxford Companion to Twentieth-Century British Politics, edited by Ramsden in 2002, is a comprehensive reference guide to the politics of the years encompassing the two world wars as well as a host of social, cultural, and political changes. Ramsden marshaled over one hundred contributors to produce more than 3,000 essays which are organized alphabetically and cover a wide range of subjects, from institutions and people to television and other media. Michael Kerrigan wrote in a *Scotsman* review that "users will find entries here on such obscure historical figures as Brian Mawhinney, on such mythical prodigies as the 'flying picket' and on such arcane institutions as the Milk Marketing Board and Central Statistical Office. For the older and more cynical there is the pleasure of browsing through a book whose contributors, distinguished and authoritative though they are, aren't afraid to be irreverent." A *Booklist* contributor dubbed the work a "readable source" and praised the volume's contributors as "represent[ing] . . . a broad spectrum of experts including journalists, scholars, and former cabinet secretaries."

BIOGRAPHICAL AND CRITICAL SOURCES:

PERIODICALS

Booklist, November 1, 2002, review of *The Oxford Companion to Twentieth-Century British Politics*,

p. 541; September 1, 2003, George Cohen, review of *Man of the Century: Winston Churchill and His Legend since 1945,* p. 51.

Choice, November, 1979; October, 2002, p. 263.

Contemporary Review, September, 1980; May, 1999, review of *An Appetite for Power,* p. 267; July, 2003, Michael F. Hopkins, review of *Man of the Century,* p. 47.

Economist (U.K.), January 13, 1979.

English Historical Review, April, 1983, review of *The Making of Conservative Policy: The Conservative Research Department since 1929,* p. 469; June, 1997, review of *The Age of Churchill and Reason,* p. 691; April, 1999, review of *By-Elections in British Politics,* p. 514.

Financial Times, November 21, 1998, review of *An Appetite for Power,* p. 5.

Foreign Affairs, July, 1999, review of *An Appetite for Power,* p. 138.

History, February, 1980.

History Today, March, 1999, review of *An Appetite for Power,* p. 52; May, 2003, Geoffrey Best, review of *Man of the Century,* p. 87.

Independent, October 10, 1998, review of *An Appetite for Power,* p. 15.

Library Journal, September 15, 2003, Robert Moore, review of *Man of the Century,* p. 65.

Observer, January 21, 1979; October 3, 1999, review of *An Appetite for Power,* p. 16.

Perspective, April, 1981.

Scotsman, January 26, 2002, review of *The Oxford Companion to Twentieth-Century British Politics,* p. 11.

Spectator, January 13, 1979; April 13, 1996, review of *The Winds of Change,* p. 36; April 13, 1996, review of *The Age of Churchill and Reason,* p. 36; October 24, 1998, review of *An Appetite for Power,* p. 52; Raymond Carr, review of *Man of the Century,* p. 40.

Sunday Telegraph (London, England), February 3, 2002, review of *The Oxford Companion to Twentieth-Century British Politics,* p. 15.

Times (London, England), August 6, 1980.

Times Literary Supplement, November 23, 1979; March 15, 1996, review of *The Winds of Change,* p. 12; March 15, 1996, review of *The Age of Churchill and Reason,* p. 12; November 20, 1998, review of *An Appetite for Power,* p. 25; February 15, 2002, review of *The Oxford Companion to Twentieth-Century British Politics,* p. 7.*

RAVVIN, Norman 1963-

PERSONAL: Surname is pronounced like "raven;" born August 26, 1963, in Calgary, Alberta, Canada; son of Albert (in business) and Nan (Eisenstein) Ravvin; married Shelley Butler, September 3, 1995. *Education:* University of British Columbia, B.A. (with honors), 1985, M.A., 1986; University of Toronto, Ph. D., 1993. *Religion:* Jewish. *Hobbies and other interests:* Cycling, travel, gardening, old cars.

ADDRESSES: Office—Institute of Canadian Jewish Studies, Department of Religion, Concordia University, 1455 de Maisonneuve Blvd. W., Montreal, Quebec H3G 1M8, Canada. *E-mail*—ravvinbutler@sprint.ca.

CAREER: Screenwriter and freelance journalist in Toronto, Ontario, Canada, 1987-89; *Toronto Computes,* Toronto, staff writer, 1990; teacher of literature, beginning 1989; University of Toronto, Toronto, sessional lecturer in literature and creative writing, 1994-97; University of New Brunswick, Fredericton, New Brunswick, Canada, assistant professor of literature and creative writing, 1997-99; Concordia University, Montreal, Quebec, Canada, began as assistant professor, became professor and chair of Canadian Jewish Studies, 1999—. Red Deer Press, general editor of Hungry I Books, 2000—.

MEMBER: Association of Canadian College and University Teachers of English, Modern Language Association of America, Writers Guild of Alberta.

AWARDS, HONORS: Grant from Ontario Arts Council, 1989; Alberta Culture and Multiculturalism New Fiction Award, 1990, for *Café des Westens;* Morris Winemaker Prize for literary criticism; grants from Toronto Arts Council and Canada Council.

WRITINGS:

Café des Westens (novel), Red Deer Press (Red Deer, Alberta, Canada), 1991.

A House of Words: Jewish Writing, Identity, and Memory, McGill-Queen's University Press (Montreal, Quebec, Canada), 1997.

Sex, Skyscrapers, and Standard Yiddish: Stories, Paperplates Books (Toronto, Ontario, Canada), 1997.

(Editor) *Great Stories of the Sea,* Red Deer Press (Red Deer, Alberta, Canada), 1999.

(Editor) *Hidden Canada: An Intimate Travelogue,* Red Deer Press (Red Deer, Alberta, Canada), 2001.

(Editor and contributor) *Not Quite Mainstream: Canadian Jewish Short Stories,* Red Deer Press (Red Deer, Alberta, Canada), 2002.

Lola by Night, Paperplates Books (Toronto, Ontario, Canada), 2003.

The Canadian Jewish Reader, edited by Richard Menkis, Red Deer Press (Red Deer, Alberta, Canada), 2004.

Also author of *Lend Me Your Ear* (screenplay), 1988. Work represented in anthologies, including *Fresh Blood: New Canadian Gothic Fiction.* Contributor of articles and short stories to periodicals, including *Prism International, Wascana Review, Prairie Fire, Mosaic, Parchment, Western Living, West Coast Review,* and *English Studies in Canada.* Associate editor, *Books in Canada.*

SIDELIGHTS: Norman Ravvin once told *CA:* "*Café des Westens* is influenced by such central European fabulists as Kafka and Schulz, as well as by the writing of [folksinger] Leonard Cohen and the Beats. It is a portrait of generational conflict, set against the boom-and-bust backdrop of Calgary, Alberta. Jewish life in Canada and the local history of such western cities as Calgary and Vancouver are important in my fiction."

BIOGRAPHICAL AND CRITICAL SOURCES:

PERIODICALS

Books in Canada, February, 1992, review of *Café des Westens,* p. 55; December, 1997, review of *Sex, Skyscrapers, and Standard Yiddish: Stories,* p. 10; May, 2002, Michael Greenstein, review of *Not Quite Mainstream: Canadian Jewish Short Stories,* pp. 21-22.

Bookwatch, October, 2001, review of *Hidden Canada: An Intimate Travelogue,* p. 4.

Canadian Book Review Annual, 1997, review of *Sex, Skyscrapers, and Standard Yiddish,* p. 212; 1997, review of *A House of Words: Jewish Writing, Identity, and Memory,* p. 276; 2000, review of *Great Stories of the Sea,* p. 232.

Canadian Literature, autumn, 1992, review of *Café des Westens,* p. 158; summer, 1999, review of *A House of Words,* p. 235.

Canadian Materials for Young People, March, 1992, review of *Café des Westens,* p. 105.

Choice, April, 1998, review of *A House of Words,* p. 1373.

Essays on Canadian Writing, fall, 1998, review of *A House of Words,* p. 193.

Globe and Mail (Toronto, Ontario, Canada), April 11, 1992, p. C7.

Quill and Quire, December, 1991, review of *Café des Westens,* p. 17; April, 1997, review of *Sex, Skyscrapers, and Standard Yiddish,* p. 30.

ONLINE

Canadian Jewish News: Internet Edition, http://www.cjnews.com/ (February 28, 2002), review of *Not Quite Mainstream.**

*   *   *

REGIS, Ed
    See REGIS, Edward, Jr.

*   *   *

REGIS, Edward, Jr. 1944-
    (Ed Regis)

PERSONAL: Born January 7, 1944, in New York, NY; son of Edward J., Sr. (in business) and Doris (a homemaker; maiden name, Deloye) Regis; married Pamela Thompson (a college teacher), August 25, 1972. *Education:* Hunter College, B.A., 1965; New York University, M.A., 1969, Ph.D., 1972. *Politics:* Independent.

ADDRESSES: Home—Sabillasville, MD. *Office*—Western Maryland College, 2 College Hill, Westminster, MD 21157.

CAREER: Salisbury State College, Salisbury, MD, assistant professor of philosophy, 1971-72; Howard University, Washington, DC, assistant professor, 1972-

76, associate professor of philosophy, 1976-87; Western Maryland College, Westminster, MD, college scholar, 1988—; writer.

AWARDS, HONORS: Reason Foundation fellow, 1980 and 1982; Earhart Foundation research grant, 1980-81, for work in ethical theory; annual Philosophy Club symposium prize, 1982, for "The Moral Status of Multigenerational Interstellar Exploration."

WRITINGS:

(Editor) *Gewirth's Ethical Rationalism: Critical Essays with a Reply by Alan Gewirth,* University of Chicago Press (Chicago, IL), 1984.

(Editor) *Extraterrestrials: Science and Alien Intelligence,* Cambridge University Press (New York, NY), 1985.

(Under name Ed Regis) *Who Got Einstein's Office? Eccentricity and Genius at the Institute for Advanced Study,* Addison-Wesley (Reading, MA), 1987.

Great Mambo Chicken and the Transhuman Condition: Science Slightly over the Edge, Addison-Wesley (Reading, MA), 1990.

Nano: The Science of Nanotechnology: Remaking the World Molecule by Molecule, Little, Brown (Boston, MA), 1995.

Virus Ground Zero: Stalking the Killer Viruses with the Centers for Disease Control, Pocket Books (New York, NY), 1996.

The Biology of Doom: America's Greatest Germ Warfare Project, Holt (New York, NY), 1999.

The Info Mesa: Science, Business, and New Age Alchemy on the Santa Fe Plateau, W. W. Norton (New York, NY), 2003.

Contributor to *Interstellar Migration and the Human Experience,* edited by Eric M. Jones and Ben R. Finney, University of California Press, 1985; contributor of articles and reviews to periodicals, including *Air and Space, American Philosophical Quarterly, College English, Discover, Ethics, Journal of Critical Analysis, Journal of Philosophy, Metaphilosophy, New Scholasticism, Omni, Pacific Philosophical Quarterly, Religious Humanism, Review of Metaphysics, Science Digest, Smithsonian, Teaching Philosophy, Thomist,* and *Wired.*

SIDELIGHTS: In a handful of books, philosophy professor and science writer Edward Regis, Jr., has managed to explicate complex scientific and theoreti-

cal issues and products for the lay reader. Regis makes topics from nanotechnology to the functioning of viruses and the intricacies of complexity-theory computer programs accessible and even entertaining to readers with little science background. He explores the workings of some of the greatest theoretical minds of the twentieth century in his book *Who Got Einstein's Office? Eccentricity and Genius at the Institute for Advanced Study.* Funded by East Coast department store magnates Louis Bamberger and Caroline Bamberger Fuld and conceived by education expert Abraham Flexner, the Institute was designed to provide scientists with the ideal environment for purely theoretical pursuits. After reviewing the history of the Institute, Regis concentrates in his nonfiction study on the provocative theories and personalities of the scientists who have given the Institute its reputation as a refuge for eccentric geniuses. From the legendary quirks of physicist Albert Einstein to the flamboyant brilliance of Hungarian-born mathematician Johnny von Neumann, Regis creates an anecdotal chronicle of the scientists who have made the Institute a theoretical playground for more than fifty years.

Critics responded favorably to *Who Got Einstein's Office.* Jonathan Weiner, writing in *New York Times Book Review,* described the book as "entertaining" and praised the author's introductions to various scientific theories as being "among the best I have read." Though he felt that Regis might be "manipulating his material" and "reaching for effect," *Washington Post* contributor Robert Kanigel commended the author's competence as a science writer, adding that "readers grounded in science will be propelled through the text." And *Los Angeles Times Book Review* writer Malcolm C. MacPherson judged Regis a "science writer of the first magnitude" who has "a genius for bulldozing through dark thickets of scientific mumbo-jumbo."

In his next book Regis examines some of the more long-range possibilities of science and technology. *Great Mambo Chicken and the Transhuman Condition: Science Slightly over the Edge* derives the lead in its title from experiments conducted by Arthur Hamilton Milt in the early 1970s. Milt subjected chickens to increased gravity levels in centrifuges for months at a time. He discovered that the birds developed greater stamina and superior vascular and muscular systems. Some of the other scientists with speculative ideas that Regis portrays in his study include Princeton physicist Gerard K. O'Neill, who envisions cities in space; Freeman Dyson, who projects an artificial biosphere that will completely encompass the solar system; cryonics pioneer Bob Ettinger, who speculates on the possibilities inherent in freezing the human body after death; and Hans Moravec, a robotics expert, who thinks the contents of a human brain,—knowledge, memories, beliefs, feelings—could someday be downloaded onto computer disks. A reviewer from the *Futurist* noted: "With an informal and entertaining style, Regis explores the different scientists' far-out ideas and their commitment to turning science fiction into science fact." Howard Rheingold felt that Regis is "never condescending to his subjects." The *Whole Earth Review* writer adds: "Regis evokes humor, awe, and continued reflection on the sheer chutzpah of Homo sapiens in this informal but well-informed joyride through the territory of high-tech high-hubrists."

In *Nano: The Science of Nanotechnology: Remaking the World Molecule by Molecule,* Regis devotes an entire book to one of the future technologies he touches upon in *The Great Mambo Chicken.* The science of nanotechnology, still in its barest infancy, considers the possibility of engineering atoms and molecules into self-replicating machines, known as "nanobots." Stanford scientist Eric Drexler and other proponents of this technology predict that nanobots could accomplish a nearly endless variety of wondrous tasks: the terra-forming of Mars, an end to human disease and aging, and even the transformation of matter (changing dirt into sides of beef or rocket engines). Of course there are also dangers to consider, the possibility of renegade nanobots self-replicating uncontrollably and transforming the entire earth into "grey goo" in a few days. Critics of the movement, such as MIT professor Robert Silbey, feel that Drexler and his supporters are way ahead of themselves. Silbey points out that there exists no means to engineer atoms to perform specifics tasks, either now or in the foreseeable future. The behavior of atoms, as Heisenberg's uncertainty principle states, is unpredictable, and even slight changes in temperature could grossly deform the nanobots that Drexler envisions. Assessing *Nano* for *Technology Review,* Robert J. Crawford noted that Regis does not seriously consider such objections, but dismisses the critics of nanotechnology by accusing them of "'resisting' some new paradigm he never clearly defines." Further, Crawford dubbed Regis with the pejorative appellation of "techiecultest," and felt that his study represents "a tediously familiar formula: find a flamboyant researcher, broadcast that researcher's claims, explain a little about the technology behind

it, and then move on." In contrast, a *Publishers Weekly* critic described *Nano* as an "engaging report on what may be tomorrow's alchemy."

In *Virus Ground Zero: Stalking the Killer Viruses with the Centers for Disease Control,* Regis relates the history of the Centers for Disease Control (CDC) and its battles against infectious disease from its birth as a malaria-eradication agency in the 1940s to its contemporary world-wide role as the planet's central disease-fighting organization. Although he praises the CDC for swift responses that have prevented many epidemics, such as the early recognition of the hanta virus on a Navajo reservation in 1993, it is also Regis's contention that the CDC has engaged in "empire-building" by exaggerating the public health threat of many viruses (such as Ebola and Lassa, both of which can be easily combated with traditional methods) in an attempt to increase its own budget and importance. He also points out that the CDC has expanded its purview in recent years to include health problems that do not fall under the category of infectious disease, such as smoking, car crashes, and obesity. A *Publishers Weekly* writer reviewing *Virus Ground Zero* remarked: "This balanced report makes an impressive counterweight to more cautionary books such as Richard Preston's *The Hot Zone* and Laurie Garrett's *The Coming Plague.*" Jacob Sullum of *Reason* found Regis's account to be "fast-paced and absorbing . . . lively, engaging, and often amusing." Sullum also seconded the book's concerns about the CDC's self-aggrandizing use of its power.

In his 1999 study, *The Biology of Doom: America's Greatest Germ Warfare Project,* Regis explores another history, that of the U.S. government's biological warfare program. Begun in the 1930s in response to the threat posed by Nazi Germany, the program was formally terminated by Richard Nixon in 1969. Regis discusses a good deal of information that has only surfaced in recent years, such as accidental sheep kills and the experimental use of psychotropic agents on individuals who did not know they had become human "guinea pigs." He also delineates the different methods explored to deliver biological weapons, including sprays, fleas, and underwater bombs. A writer for *Publishers Weekly* observed: "Regis writes for the layperson, and he is careful to depict the human drama behind the science." Gilbert Taylor of *Booklist* called *The Biology of Doom* "an objectively handled summary."

Regis examines the high tech industry in his 2003 title, *The Info Mesa: Science, Business, and New Age Alchemy on the Santa Fe Plateau.* The author shows how the Southwest has become the new seedbed for cutting edge software development, replacing California's Silicon Valley. Partly energized by talent from the weapons lab at Los Alamos, New Mexico, the computer start-ups in the Sangre de Cristo Mountains of New Mexico focus on "simulation and complexity theory," according to Steven Levy, writing in *Newsweek.* In profiles of almost forty such scientists, Regis takes a look at how these companies are helping businesses and researchers in all sorts of ways: from tracking their cargoes to aiding in identification of the types of proteins in substances that could help to make new medicine. Among the notables included in Regis's book are Dave Weininger and Stuart Kauffman. A contributor for *Science News* felt that Regis "paints compelling portraits of these sometimes-eccentric personalities." Similarly, writing in *Booklist,* Bryce Christensen noted that Regis "tells the story of how these often eccentric innovators—partial to flying saucer music and New Age mysticism—are developing complexity-theory programs to solve daunting scientific and business problems." And according to Levy, "Regis knows how to spin a good yarn, and better yet, can untangle nontrivial scientific subjects."

Regis is a member of the Extropians, described by Gary Chapman of the *New Republic* as "a high-tech human potential cult based in California." In an article in *Wired,* Regis stated: "No ambition, however extravagant, no fantasy, however outlandish, can any longer be dismissed as crazy or impossible. . . . Suddenly, technology has given us powers with which we can manipulate not only external reality . . . but also, and much more portentously, ourselves."

Regis once noted, "I am a private pilot, and I live on a thirty-acre farm five miles from Camp David in rural Maryland."

BIOGRAPHICAL AND CRITICAL SOURCES:

PERIODICALS

Booklist, March 1, 1995, p. 1168; October 1, 1999, Gilbert Taylor, review of *The Biology of Doom: America's Greatest Germ Warfare Project,* p. 313;

May 1, 2003, Bryce Christensen, review of *The Info Mesa: Science, Business, and New Age Alchemy on the Santa Fe Plateau,* p. 1560.

Christian Science Monitor, October 13, 1987.

Futurist, May-June, 1991, review of *Great Mambo Chicken and the Transhuman Condition: Science Slightly over the Edge,* p. 43.

Los Angeles Times Book Review, September 13, 1987.

New Republic, January 9, 1995, Gary Chapman, review of *Wired,* p. 19.

Newsweek, September 29, 2003, Steven Levy, review of *The Info Mesa,* p. 34.

New York Times Book Review, September 27, 1987.

Publishers Weekly, February 6, 1995, review of *Nano: The Science of Nanotechnology: Remaking the World Molecule by Molecule,* p. 69; November 20, 1995, Paul Nathan, "On the World Stage," p. 21; October 28, 1996, review of *Virus Ground Zero: Stalking the Killer Viruses with the Centers for Disease Control,* p. 70; October 25, 1999, review of *The Biology of Doom,* p. 61.

Reason, June, 1997, Jacob Sullum, review of *Virus Ground Zero,* p. 62.

Science News, September 20, 2003, review of *The Info Mesa,* p. 191.

Technology Review, May-June, 1996, Robert J. Crawford, review of *Nano,* p. 69.

Washington Post, September 22, 1987.

Whole Earth Review, fall, 1993, Howard Rheingold, review of *Great Mambo Chicken and the Transhuman Condition,* p. 115.

ONLINE

Hotwired Web site, http://hotwired.wired.com/talk/club/special/transcripts/96-11-15-regis.html (July 29, 2004), Andy Rozmiarek, "Ed Regis."

Nanotechnology Now Web site, http://nanotech-now.com/ed-regis-interview-122001.htm (December, 2001), "Ed Regis Interview." *

*   *   *

RIBEIRO, Aileen 1944-

PERSONAL: Born April 15, 1944; married Robert Ribeiro (a lawyer). *Education:* King's College, University of London (London, England), B.A., 1965; Courtauld Institute of Art (London, England), M.A.,

1971, Ph.D., 1975. *Hobbies and other interests:* Art and image in eighteenth-century portraiture in Europe, costume and caricature.

ADDRESSES: Office—Courtauld Institute of Art, Somerset House, Strand, London WC2R 0RN, England. *E-mail*—aileen.ribeiro@courtauld.ac.uk.

CAREER: Courtauld Institute of Art, London, England, History of Dress Dept., lecturer, 1973—, head of department, 1975—. Governor of the Pasold Textile Fund, London.

WRITINGS:

A Visual History of Costume: The Eighteenth Century, Batsford (London, England), 1983.
(With Celina Fox) *Masquerade,* Museum of London (London, England), 1983.
The Dress Worn at Masquerades in England, 1730 to 1790, and Its Relation to Fancy Dress in Portraiture, Garland Publishing (New York, NY), 1984.
Dress in Eighteenth-Century Europe, 1715-1789, Batsford (London, England), 1984, Holmes and Meier (New York, NY), 1985, revised edition, Yale University Press (New Haven, CT), 2002.
Dress and Morality, Holmes and Meier (New York, NY), 1986.
The Female Face, Tate Gallery (London, England), 1987.
Dress and the French Revolution, Batsford (London, England), 1988.
Fashion in the French Revolution, Holmes and Meier (New York, NY), 1988.
(Editor) *The Earl and Countess Howe by Gainsborough: A Bicentenary Exhibition,* English Heritage (Ruislip, England), 1988.
(Compiler and editor, with Valerie Cumming) *The Visual History of Costume,* Drama Book Publishing (New York, NY), 1989.
The Art of Dress: Fashion in England and France, 1750 to 1820, Yale University Press (New Haven, CT), 1995.
Ingres in Fashion: Representations of Dress and Appearance in Ingres's Images of Women, Yale University Press (New Haven, CT), 1999.
The Gallery of Fashion, Princeton University Press (Princeton, NJ), 2000.
(With others) *Whistler, Women, and Fashion,* Yale University Press (New Haven, CT), 2003.

Author of foreword, *Fashions of the Past,* by Anna Buruma, Sterline (New York), 1999; contributor to works by others, including *Franz Xaver Winterhalter and the Courts of Europe, 1830-1870,* National Portrait Gallery (London, England), 1987, *Ingres's Images of Women,* Yale University Press (New Haven, CT), 1999, and *Goya: Images of Women,* edited by Janis A. Tomlinson, Yale University Press (New Haven, CT), 2002; editor of costume accessories series and visual history of costume series, both published by Batsford; contributor to periodicals, including the London *Times, Connoisseur, History Today, Apollo, Burlington, Connaissance des Arts,* and *Vogue.*

SIDELIGHTS: Aileen Ribeiro is an art historian specializing in the history of dress who "has taken the study of eighteenth-century dress several strides on in recent years," in the opinion of Pat Rogers of the *Times Literary Supplement.* Another *Times Literary Supplement* reviewer, Celina Fox, echoed Rogers, calling Ribeiro's *Dress in Eighteenth-Century Europe, 1715-1789* "an important book, certainly the most scholarly account of eighteenth-century dress ever to have been published," and praised its "richness of documentary evidence." In this work, Ribeiro focuses on fashion in Europe during the eighteenth century, or the "age of elegance," beginning with the ornate baroque dress of the early decades and concluding with the uncomplicated dress of the years prior to the French Revolution. She also assesses the role fashion played in society and the economy, eighteenth-century attitudes toward dress, and the relationship between fashion and social class.

According to Ribeiro in *Dress in Eighteenth-Century Europe,* the eighteenth-century upper classes often adopted certain forms of dress as an outward sign of their social standing. The Italian nobility wore black, in Russia the Empress Elizabeth demanded the women of her entourage to shave their heads and wear black wigs, and in France, Madame de Pompadour required that her guests wear gray. Yet with all its attention to beautiful clothing, the "age of elegance" had its myths, which Ribeiro dispels. She acknowledges that the styles of dress of the working classes and poor dated back to the Middle Ages in some cases and were put together strictly for usefulness and economy. Ribeiro also found that many people devised ingenious methods to conceal the physical signs, such as pockmarked skin and rotting teeth, of poor hygiene and diet. The author provides evidence that one woman dyed her teeth black so that they would appear to be lacquered. Even people most meticulous about their appearance failed to bathe regularly, and clothing—especially silks, which were almost impossible to clean—decayed in areas of heavy perspiration. The volume was reprinted nearly two decades later with slight revisions, and was newly praised, this time by *Library Journal*'s James F. DeRoche, who wrote that it "is a readable, thorough, and intelligent treatment of the excessively elaborate style of the day."

Ribeiro's *The Dress Worn at Masquerades in England, 1730 to 1790, and Its Relation to Fancy Dress in Portraiture* studies theatrical garb and costumes worn by men, women, and children during the greater part of the eighteenth century. Rogers was enthusiastic about Ribeiro's historic fashion discoveries that she presents in this work, saying that "first, she has brought together an immense amount of pictorial evidence, which shows the prevalence of the stock motifs in fashionable dress more clearly than ever before. . . . Second, Ribeiro advances our knowledge of the role played by pattern books. . . . In addition, Ribeiro advances our knowledge of the role played by drapery painters," whose works influenced later generations of artists who portrayed subjects in flowing costumes.

The Art of Dress: Fashion in England and France, 1750 to 1820 studies the relationship between fashion and portraiture, or as Ribeiro explains it, "the ways in which fashion acts as a link between life and art." Ribeiro treats England and France separately, noting styles could vary widely on either side of the English Channel, and examines clothing in paintings, drawings, and from letters and diaries.

In *Ingres in Fashion: Representations of Dress and Appearance in Ingres's Images of Women*, Ribeiro contends that nineteenth-century artist Jean-Auguste-Dominique Ingres's paintings can be more fully understood by knowing of his appreciation of fashion and of the costumes that inspired him as much as the subjects who wore them. Ingres arranged clothing and accessories to accentuate the lines of his female subjects' bodies, with velvet, lace, ribbons, and flowers. Suzy Menkes noted in a review for the *International Herald Tribune Online* that "as painstakingly as Ingres accumulated rich colors and tactile effects, Ribeiro builds up a portrait of an artist who was

fascinated with the surface of things—because of what they revealed. Here is a fashion book with luminous visuals and a lucid text. The details of a painting—a fleshy arm banded with pearl bracelets or a vividly embroidered cashmere shawl—is often the first introduction to a famous and familiar canvas. This not only makes the portraits seem fresh and intriguing, but unreels fashion history and the shifting notions of female allure." *Library Journal*'s Margarete Gross wrote that "whether one's interest is in Ingres, French history, or costuming, there is much to like about this book."

The Gallery of Fashion refers to the National Portrait Gallery in London, where images of the wealthy and famous reflect fashion through the ages down to Princess Diana. Ribeiro's text and commentary connect each portrait to its period of history and explain each artist's technique. *Booklist* reviewer Michael Spinella called the volume "fantastic" and said that it "should be seen by all fashionistas who want to see what people were wearing, and when."

Ribeiro is a coauthor of *Whistler, Women, and Fashion*, a study of James McNeill Whistler's (1834-1903) obsession with dress. Whistler himself sported a fur coat, cane, and monocle, and he went so far as to design the costumes of his subjects, one of whom was Frances Leland. He created a translucent gown for the woman whom it was rumored he loved. Lady Meux, who met her husband, the heir to a brewery fortune, in a tavern, commissioned several portraits by Whistler in an effort to establish herself as the lady she had become through marriage. The volume is enhanced by new material from the Centre for Whistler Studies, and follows the relationships between Whistler and his female subjects, including aristocrats, actresses, artists, family members, and mistresses, over fifty years. *New York Times Book Review* critic Hilarie M. Sheets called *Whistler, Women, and Fashion* "an engrossing study."

BIOGRAPHICAL AND CRITICAL SOURCES:

BOOKS

Ribeiro, Aileen, *The Art of Dress: Fashion in England and France, 1750 to 1820,* Yale University Press (New Haven, CT), 1995.

PERIODICALS

American Historical Review, June, 1997, Elizabeth Wilson, review of *The Art of Dress: Fashion in England and France, 1750-1820,* p. 810.

Booklist, December 15, 2000, Michael Spinella, review of *The Gallery of Fashion,* p. 777.

Eighteenth-Century Studies, summer, 1996, Sarah R. Cohen, review of *The Art of Dress,* p. 438.

Library Journal, June 15, 1999, Margarete Gross, review of *Ingres in Fashion: Representations of Dress and Appearance in Ingres's Images of Women,* p. 76; January 1, 2001, Stephan Allan Patrick, review of *The Gallery of Fashion,* p. 100; November 15, 2002, James F. DeRoche, review of *Dress in Eighteenth-Century Europe, 1715-1789,* p. 69.

New York Review of Books, May 20, 1999, James Fenton, review of *Ingres in Fashion,* p. 21; October 10, 2002, Richard Dorment, review of *Dress in Eighteenth-Century Europe, 1715-1789,* p. 6.

New York Times Book Review, July 27, 2003, Hilarie M. Sheets, review of *Whistler, Women, and Fashion,* p. 13.

TCI, February, 1997, Whitney Blausen, review of *The Art of Dress,* p. 54.

Times Higher Education Supplement, March 26, 1999, Rom Rosenthal, review of *Ingres in Fashion,* p. 28.

Times Literary Supplement, February 22, 1985, Pat Rogers, review of *The Dress Worn at Masquerades in England, 1730-1790;* January 10, 1986, Celina Fox, review of *Dress in Eighteenth-Century Europe, 1715-1789;* December 1, 1995, Claire Harman, review of *The Art of Dress,* p. 8; February 26, 1999, Robert Snell, review of *Ingres in Fashion,* p. 18.

William and Mary Quarterly, April, 1997, Patricia A. Cunningham, review of *The Art of Dress,* p. 430.

ONLINE

International Herald Tribune Online, http://www.iht.com/ (February 4, 1999), Suzy Menkes, review of *Ingres in Fashion.**

*　　　*　　　*

RICHARDSON, Anne
　　See ROIPHE, Anne (Richardson)

RIORDAN, James 1949-

PERSONAL: Born March 10, 1949, in Kankakee, IL; son of Clarence Joseph (a musician) and Nancy Ruth (a comedienne; maiden name, Kelly) Riordan; married Deborah Kay Griffin, February 14, 1974; children: Chris, Elicia Danielle, Jeremiah. *Education:* Attended Illinois State University, 1967-69. *Religion:* Christian.

ADDRESSES: Home—Malibu, CA. *Office*—Rock-Pop Syndications, 15445 Ventura Blvd., Suite 10, Box 5973, Sherman Oaks, CA 91413.

CAREER: Songwriter and record producer in Nashville, TN, 1969-71; WKAK-FM Radio, Kankakee, IL, record announcer, 1972-74; Rock-Pop Syndications, Kankakee, head writer in Kankakee and Malibu, CA, 1975—. Swordsman Press, Sherman Oaks, CA, publisher, 1980—; video producer at Platinum Rainbow Productions, 1982—. Former member of department of commercial music at Long Beach City College; member of advisory board of Professional Musicians Career Academy in Minneapolis; leader of band Hypnoises, c. 1996.

MEMBER: American Society of Authors, Composers, and Publishers.

AWARDS, HONORS: Service awards from Long Beach City College, 1982, and Boyd Hunt Enterprises, 1983.

WRITINGS:

(With Bob Monaco) *The Platinum Rainbow: How to Succeed in the Music Business without Selling Your Soul,* Swordsman Press (Sherman Oaks, CA), 1980, revised edition, Contemporary Books (Chicago, IL), 1988.

(Coauthor) *Recording Evaluation Directory,* Platinum Press, 1983.

Behind the Glass: The Producers (interviews), Swordsman Press (Sherman Oaks, CA), 1983.

(With Bob Monaco) *The New Music Business,* Swordsman Press (Sherman Oaks, CA), 1984.

Making It in the New Music Business, Writers' Digest Books (Cincinnati, OH), 1988, revised edition, 1991.

(With Jerry Prochnicky) *Break on Through: The Life and Death of Jim Morrison,* Morrow (New York, NY), 1991.

Stone: The Controversies, Excesses and Exploits of a Radical Filmmaker, foreword by Michael Douglas, Hyperion (New York, NY), 1995.

Also author, with Jason Miller, of *That Championship Season* (novel; adapted from the play by Miller). Contributor to *Songwriters Market, 1982,* Writer's Digest Books (Cincinnati, OH), 1982. Author of songs, with Michael Leppert, including "Cellophane Man" and "The Rainmaker." Author of "Rock-Pop," a newspaper column syndicated by Rock-Pop Syndications, 1976-83. Contributor to *American Song Festival.* Contributing editor of *Mix,* 1982-83.

SIDELIGHTS: James Riordan's first half-dozen books reflect his experiences in the music industry and dispense advice to those interested in songwriting, performing, and making records. He subsequently began a syndicated newspaper column that featured interviews with famous musicians, wrote biographies of Jim Morrison and Oliver Stone, and began fiction writing. Cowritten with the playwright, his first novel is *That Championship Season,* an adaptation of the Pulitzer Prize-winning play by Jason Miller.

Riordan's most widely reviewed books have been his biographies. *Break on Through: The Life and Death of Jim Morrison,* which was written with Jerry Prochnicky, examines the life of the lead singer for the Doors, who died in 1971 at age twenty-seven. The book covers Morrison's childhood, his experiences with the rock group including concerts, recording sessions, and groupies, and being charged with indecent exposure and profanity at a Miami concert. A *Publishers Weekly* reviewer felt that "the fan-club-style overstatement, redundancy and lyrics quoted for dramatic effect become tedious," while critic D. Hibbard commented in *Choice* that "The text is easily read and offers entertaining as well as informative reading."

Sex, drugs, and rock and roll are also prominent in *Stone: The Controversies, Excesses and Exploits of a Radical Filmmaker.* Riordan and Oliver Stone first had contact when Riordan served as a consultant for Stone's 1991 film *The Doors.* Among Stone's other films are *Platoon, Wall Street, JFK,* and *Nixon,*

examples of a body of work that is highly personal and often controversial. Riordan reveals what went on during the making of Stone's films, as well as providing background about the divorce of Stone's parents, voluntary service in the army during the Vietnam War, drug abuse, and infidelity. The biography is the first to be written about Stone and was done with his cooperation. Riordan gave the filmmaker permission to read and edit his quotes, and in turn was given access to many of Stone's friends and associates.

The lure of Stone's story outweighed concerns reviewers voiced about this arrangement. In *Entertainment Weekly,* writer Steve Daly suggested that "the often facile psychologizing aside, fans will appreciate the detailed, behind-the-scenes accounts of Stone's films." Similarly, in his review for the *Patriot,* John Anderson decided that "the information, as tainted as one presumes it to be, is fascinating. . . . What Stone gets from Riordan is a friendly, bordering-on-fawning treatment." According to William Leith in the London *Observer,* the book is decidedly satisfying: "It will brighten up a few afternoons or evenings. The writing is clear and unflashy. . . . [Riordan] understands Stone's class and generation, the first wave of educated people to get into dope and rock 'n' roll."

Riordan once told *CA* about other experiences: "Being a songwriter in Nashville was an adventure. I met some very interesting characters, who later formed the basis for the humorous stories in *The Platinum Rainbow,* my book about the music business. I learned a lot of valuable lessons about how not to approach a career in the music business. By making *all* the mistakes and totally confusing the reality with my own star fantasies, I had done the research for the book I was to write some ten years later.

"I began 'Rock-Pop,' the syndicated music column, from one tiny local paper and syndicated it myself, building it to millions of readers coast to coast in less than five years. I would contact the newspapers myself and persuade them that they needed a youth-oriented feature and that I could provide interviews with major artists—something a small local paper just couldn't do on their own. By going after these smaller papers I was able to build a network of them that had more readers than all but the largest metropolitan dailies. My readership allowed me to secure interviews with bigger and bigger artists, including George Harrison, the Doobie Brothers, Frank Zappa, Fleetwood Mac, Kenny Rogers, and others.

"I wrote *The Platinum Rainbow* because I wished I'd had something like it when I started down the yellow brick road of the music business. I am writing a sequel to it [which became *Making It in the New Music Business*] because the music business has changed and evolved into a do-it-yourself type of business for new artists and nothing has been written that details this process.

"I am also writing another novel, *Return of the Walrus*, because I loved the 1960's; I feel that a novel entailing the myths and romance of that period, based on the music of the era, could be very popular. It's a fiction, but one that those of us who grew up in the sixties all wanted to believe was true.

"I am a born-again Christian and, as unhip as it may sound, I believe that Jesus Christ is not only the answer but the one who is responsible for my success and more importantly my peace of mind. My life has radically changed from one of searching for fame and being constantly frustrated that my art was not universally recognized to one of contentment and peace. Being a Christian is not easy and the process of transformation is painful because it involves letting go of the ego, but it is well worth it. Naturally, this belief works into anything I write. I hope that my works are able to touch people and help them perceive hope and truth in this illusion-filled world."

BIOGRAPHICAL AND CRITICAL SOURCES:

PERIODICALS

Choice, November, 1991, D. Hibbard, review of *Break on Through: The Life and Death of Jim Morrison.*
Entertainment Weekly, December 1, 1995, Steve Daly, review of *Stone: The Controversies, Excesses and Exploits of a Radical Filmmaker,* p. 67.
Observer (London, England), October 20, 1996, William Leith, review of *Stone,* p. 16.
Patriot (Harrisburg, PA), January 1, 1996, John Anderson, review of *Stone,* p. C3.
Publishers Weekly, April 19, 1991, review of *Break on Through,* p. 52.*

* * *

ROBBINS, Jane Marla 1943-

PERSONAL: Born November 2, 1943, in New York, NY; daughter of Louis John (an attorney) and Mildred (an international development consultant; maiden name, Elowsky; later surname, Leet) Robbins. *Educa-*tion: Attended Bryn Mawr College, 1965; studied with Sonia Moore and Walter Lott in New York.

ADDRESSES: Home—22916 Portage Circle Dr., Topanga, CA 90290-4029.

CAREER: Actress, singer, dancer, writer, and producer, beginning 1967. Loyola-Marymount University, teacher at Esalen Institute. Film credits include appearances in *Rocky, Rocky II,* and *Coming Apart;* television credits include appearances in *79 Park Avenue, Remington Steele,* and *The Bob Newhart Show.* Worked with Martha Graham Dance Company; guest artist at Italy's Spoleto Festival; appeared in stage productions *Reminiscences of Mozart by His Sister,* John F. Kennedy Center for the Performing Arts, Washington, DC, 1995 and *Miriam's Dance,* Los Angeles, CA, and New York, NY, productions, 1998.

MEMBER: Screen Actors Guild, American Federation of Television and Radio Artists, Actors' Equity Association.

WRITINGS:

(With Terry Belanger) *Dear Nobody* (play), produced off-Broadway, 1968, aired as television program, Columbia Broadcasting System, Inc. (CBS), 1974.
Jane Avril (play), produced off-Broadway, 1982.
Acting Techniques for Everyday life: Look and Feel Self-Confident in Difficult, Real Life Situations, Marlowe (New York, NY), 2002.

Also author of *Copenhagen,* 1983, and the play, *Bats in the Belfry.*

SIDELIGHTS: Robbins speaks French, German, Italian, and Spanish and has traveled widely through Europe and the Middle East.

BIOGRAPHICAL AND CRITICAL SOURCES:

PERIODICALS

Publishers Weekly, November 11, 2002, review of *Acting Techniques for Everyday Life: Look and Feel Self-Confident in Difficult Real-Life Situations,* p. 48.*

ROIPHE, Anne (Richardson) 1935-
(Anne Richardson)

PERSONAL: Born Ann Roth, December 25, 1935, in New York, NY; daughter of Eugene (a lawyer) and Blanche (Phillips) Roth; married Jack Richardson, 1958 (divorced, 1963); married Herman Roiphe (a psychoanalyst), January 20, 1967; children: Emily, Kate, Becky; stepchildren: Margaret, Jean. *Education:* Sarah Lawrence College, B.A., 1957.

ADDRESSES: Home—285 Riverside Dr., New York, NY 10025. *Agent*—Carl Brandt, 101 Park Ave., New York, NY 10028.

CAREER: Writer.

WRITINGS:

NOVELS

(Under name Anne Richardson) *Digging Out,* McGraw (New York, NY), 1967.
Up the Sandbox!, Simon & Schuster (New York, NY), 1970.
Long Division, Simon & Schuster (New York, NY), 1972.
(Under name Anne Richardson) *Torch Song,* Farrar, Straus (New York, NY), 1977.
Lovingkindness, Summit Books (New York, NY), 1987.
The Pursuit of Happiness, Summit Books (New York, NY), 1991.
If You Knew Me, Little, Brown (Boston, MA), 1993.
Secrets of the City, Shaye Areheart/Crown (New York, NY), 2003.

NONFICTION

Generation without Memory: A Jewish Journey in Christian America (autobiographical essays), Simon & Schuster (New York, NY), 1981.
(With husband, Herman Roiphe) *Your Child's Mind: The Complete Book of Infant and Child Mental Health Care,* St. Martin's (New York, NY), 1985,

published as *Your Child's Mind: The Complete Book of Infant and Child Emotional Well-Being,* St. Martin's (New York, NY), 1986.
A Season for Healing: Reflections on the Holocaust, Summit Books (New York, NY), 1988.
Fruitful: A Real Mother in the Modern World, Houghton (Boston, MA), 1996.
1185 Park Avenue: A Memoir, Free Press (New York, NY), 1999.
For Rabbit, with Love and Squalor: An American Read, Free Press (New York, NY), 2000.
Married: A Fine Predicament, Basic Books (New York, NY), 2002.

OTHER

Also contributor to periodicals, including *Redbook, Glamour,* and *Family Circle.* Roiphe also writes a bi-weekly column in the *New York Observer.*

SIDELIGHTS: Anne Roiphe is a social commentator who is best known for her novel *Up the Sandbox!* Her works, which largely explore a woman's search for identity, also examine such topics as divorce, alienation, aging, marriage, and religious tradition. *Publishers Weekly* writer Sybil Steinberg judged the author's work to be of considerable significance. In Steinberg's opinion, "A sociologist seeking to understand some of the cultural and religious ferment of the last four decades of the twentieth century could do worse than read the . . . works of Anne Roiphe. With her thoughtful and often provocative appraisals of the zeitgeist, Roiphe has managed to offer impassioned insights into feminism, marriage, family and Jewish identity in books that draw on her personal life to explore larger social issues."

Roiphe's first book, *Digging Out,* presents the personal reflections of Laura Smith as she attends the bedside of her dying mother. Laura recalls the history of her large and rich Jewish family, interweaving its past with the details of her mother's illness. The story of Roiphe's next book, *Up the Sandbox!,* alternates the inner musings of Margaret Reynolds, as a young Manhattan mother who ministers to the needs of her two small children, and the Margaret Reynolds who envisions wild dream adventures, such as blowing up the George Washington Bridge with a group of black militants.

Lovingkindness explores the alienated relationship of secular Jewish feminist Annie Johnson, a widowed, financially successful writer, and her twenty-two-year-old daughter, Andrea, the rattlesnake-tattooed survivor of drug abuse and three abortions. When the girl finally phones her mother after five months of silence, she informs Annie she is in Jerusalem, having joined an ultra-Orthodox sect and changed her name to "Sarai" as a symbol of her newborn faith. Annie is concerned that her daughter is surrendering her free will for the rigidly defined dictates of a male-dominated, tightly structured religious system. Annie learns the Yeshiva has selected a husband for Sarai, a young American, Michael Rose, and she joins the intended spouse's parents when they travel to Israel in an attempt to halt the marriage by kidnapping their own son. Ultimately, Annie must decide whether to accept her daughter's decisions or to interfere.

Jane Blumberg, reviewing *Lovingkindness* in the *Times Literary Supplement*, described the work as "a beautifully constructed and restrained novel" and added, "If its presentation of a very specific Manhattan world of educated liberalism and disillusioned idealism is a bit rarified, not to say somewhat negligent of the new problems facing American Jews in regard to Israel, it is nonetheless powerful." However, Linsey Abrams of the *Los Angeles Times Book Review* wrote, "The human information in this novel calls for a profound sadness that is nowhere apparent. An impoverishment of vision and feeling on the part of the narrator does not do justice, either, to her own predicament as a woman and mother." Abrams concluded: "That love is to be found neither among individuals nor even in a nuclear family but only in religious community is the reactionary, perhaps inadvertent, message of this novel, its real moral center."

In *A Season for Healing: Reflections on the Holocaust*, Roiphe develops the theme that the impact of the Holocaust affects all people, not just Jews, and that failing to acknowledge the wrongs suffered by other groups and imputing guilt for its tragedy upon Christianity only leads to the renewal of anti-Semitism. She concludes that humankind should seek unity, not further divisiveness and anger. In the *New York Times Book Review*, Berel Lang commented, "Roiphe considers here the Jewish response to the Holocaust in the post-Holocaust world and especially a disproportion she finds in that response. This disproportion, she claims, has seriously harmed relationships between Jews and a number of groups to whom they are linked

by history or place. . . . It has also contributed to the rise of neoconservatism among American Jews, to the militaristic ethos of Israel and to the issue of dual loyalty which has been intensified for American Jews by events in Israel." Elaine Kendall, in the *Los Angeles Times Book Review*, asserted: "Appearing fifty years after *Kristallnacht*, Roiphe's book can be read as a reminder that humanity itself has become an endangered species."

The Pursuit of Happiness is an epic spanning five generations of the Gruenbaums, an immigrant Jewish family, who left Poland in 1880 to seek the American dream. The story begins in a Jerusalem hospital in 1990, where Hedy Gruenbaum Aloni awaits the outcome of her daughter Namah's head-wound surgery: the girl was shot during a conflict between Arabs and Jewish zealots. The narrative utilizes numerous flashbacks with a cast of dozens of family members, sharing their triumphs and losses in intimate detail.

There is an autobiographical tone to the work, noted Rita Kashner in her *Washington Post Book World* review: "The Gruenbaums are Roiphe's actual family of origin, with no attempt at veiling." In the *New York Times Book Review*, Amy Wallace commented: "We quickly grow fond of her sprawling family of sufferers and strivers," though she ultimately finds fault with "the plethora of characters—by the end it becomes confusing." Other critics offered similarly mixed opinions. Kashner stated that "the book is full of life, humor and insight" though "there are lapses. Some characters fail to rise above caricature. Roiphe overuses the arch address to 'Reader,' and there's a superfluous series of replays near the end." Frances Stead Sellers, in the *Los Angeles Times Book Review*, described the novel as "a somber chronicle of immigration, assimilation and eventual disillusionment." However, Sellers also observed: "The novel's ending and narrator are curious flaws in an otherwise polished, compelling and far-reaching story." Despite her reservations, Kashner declared: "The book is rich, sharp and touching—and full of stories, which are ultimately what one generation has to give another."

Up the Sandbox! marked Roiphe as an early feminist. In *Fruitful: A Real Mother in the Modern World*, she looks back at the feminist movement of the late twentieth century and offers some criticism of its more radical element. As in some of her other books, she illustrates her points with vignettes of her own life. According to Emily MacFarquhar in the *New York Times Book Review,* "Her riff on motherhood is passionate, lyrical, witty, insightful, commonsensical and off the wall. It will evoke shudders of recognition from anyone who has cared for a child." MacFarquhar noted that Roiphe questions if the term "mother-feminist" is an oxymoron and concluded: "*Fruitful* is her sometimes maddening, always engaging answer."

Andrew Billen gave a somewhat more complicated analysis of Roiphe's thesis in his London *Observer* review. He explained that, in Roiphe's view, "motherhood 'by definition' requires a 'sacrifice of self-wishes,' whereas feminism 'by definition insists on attention being paid to the self.'" Roiphe further suggests that by focusing on themselves, radical feminists have done serious damage to their children. Billen commented: "As a childless man, I suspect Roiphe has overestimated the damage feminist extremism has done to our psyches. . . . Yet the author is surely right when she says it is time for the astringent, corrective brand of feminist literature to be superseded by a pro-family domestic product that can be used by both sexes. . . . *Fruitful* is not only beautifully written; it is one of the most sensible things I have read for a while."

Roiphe turns from feminism to literary analysis in her year 2000 work *For Rabbit, with Love and Squalor: An American Read.* In this personal journey through the works of fiction that she has enjoyed, Roiphe spotlights writers and their fictional creations from J. D. Salinger and his fictional creation Holden Caulfield, to John Updike's Rabbit. She also relates these characters to her own life and experiences. For Mary Paumier Jones, writing in *Library Journal,* Roiphe "has done nothing less than invent a lively and original form of literary criticism" with her book. *Booklist*'s Donna Seaman also had praise for the book, noting that it "presents an electrifying paean to twentieth-century American literary heroes." And Diane Cole, writing in the *New York Times Book Review,* found the book a "chatty, informal memoir of one reader's lessons in literature."

With the 2002 work *Married: A Fine Predicament,* Roiphe "testifies to the rewards of the long-haul marriage," according to Noonie Minogue in the *Times Literary Supplement.* Just as she examined motherhood in *Fruitful,* she takes on social commentary relat-

ing to the idea of marriage in *Married,* blending "personal anecdotes with canny responses to trends, headlines, phobias," as *Booklist*'s Seaman commented. Roiphe examines cases of serial monogamy, the ups and downs of divorce, the trend toward the singles lifestyle, as well as the changing nature of marriage over the past half century to show, as Seaman noted, why, despite all the tough times in a marriage, "it's all worth it." A contributor for *Publishers Weekly* found the book "neither antiromantic nor hopelessly giddy." Nancy P. Shires, writing in *Library Journal,* called *Married* "thorough and readable," with Roiphe looking at both sides of the marriage debate. Lynda McDonnell, though, writing in *Washington Monthly,* felt that *Married* "is an incisive essay on marriage that seems padded to make a book," and Karen Dukess wrote in *USA Today* that Roiphe's book "is a rambling, probing and passionate defense of marriage." Writing in a similar critical vein, Jennifer Howard noted in the *Washington Post Book World* that Roiphe "prescribes marriage as the only cure for the loneliness that ails us even as she makes it sound like one bitter pill," and commented further that the book "suffers from a lack of focus." Yet for Martin Levin, writing in the *Weekly Standard,* this very hodgepodge of "gossip, grudges, small talk" was what made the book appealing. "I loved it," he wrote. "But one has to say, it comes a bit late in our cultural meltdown."

BIOGRAPHICAL AND CRITICAL SOURCES:

BOOKS

Contemporary Literary Criticism, Gale (Detroit, MI), Volume 3, 1975, Volume 9, 1978.
Dictionary of Literary Biography Yearbook: 1980, Gale (Detroit, MI), 1980.
Burstein, Janet Handler, *Writing Mothers, Writing Daughters: Tracing the Maternal in Stories by American Jewish Women,* University of Illinois Press (Urbana, IL), 1996.

PERIODICALS

Booklist, November 1, 2000, Donna Seaman, review of *For Rabbit, with Love and Squalor: An American Read,* p. 512; May 1, 2002, Donna Seaman, review of *Married: A Fine Predicament,* p. 1490.
Library Journal, October 15, 2000, Mary Paumier Jones, review of *For Rabbit, with Love and Squalor,* p. 71; April 1, 2002, Nancy P. Shires, review of *Married,* p. 128.

Los Angeles Times Book Review, September 6, 1987, Linsey Abrams, review of *Lovingkindness,* p. 6; November 27, 1988, Elaine Kendall, review of *A Season for Healing: Reflections on the Holocaust,* p. 1; August 11, 1991, Frances Stead Sellers, review of *The Pursuit of Happiness,* p. 7.

New York Times Book Review, November 13, 1988, Berel Lang, review of *A Season for Healing,* p. 7; July 21, 1991, Amy Wallace, review of *The Pursuit of Happiness,* p. 9; October 13, 1996, Emily MacFarquhar, review of *Fruitful: A Real Mother in the Modern World,* p. 23; February 11, 2001, Diane Cole, review of *For Rabbit, with Love and Squalor,* p. 21.

Observer (London, England), February 2, 1997, Andrew Billen, review of *Fruitful,* p. 17.

Publishers Weekly, August 2, 1993, Sybil Steinberg, "Anne Roiphe: Looking for Universal Truths in Personal Experiences Is This Writer's Goal," pp. 57-58; April 15, 2002, review of *Married,* p. 50.

Times Literary Supplement, May 6, 1988, Jane Blumberg, review of *Lovingkindness,* p. 500; September 5, 2003, Noonie Minogue, review of *Married,* p. 25.

USA Today, June 18, 2002, Karen Dukess, review of *Married,* p. D6.

Washington Monthly, July-August, 2002, Lynda McDonnell, review of *Married,* pp. 46-48.

Washington Post Book World, June 16, 1991, Rita Kashner, review of *The Pursuit of Happiness,* p. 1; May 19, 2002, Jennifer Howard, review of *Married,* p. 8.

Weekly Standard, June 10, 2002, Martin Levin, review of *Married,* p. 43.

ONLINE

Bloomsbury, http://www.bloomsbury.com/ (October 31, 2003), "Anne Roiphe."

Time Warner Bookmark, http://www.twbookmark.com/ (October 31, 2003), "Anne Roiphe."*

*　　*　　*

RYBCZYNSKI, Witold (Marian) 1943-

PERSONAL: Born March 1, 1943, in Edinburgh, Scotland; son of Witold K. (an engineer) and Anna (a lawyer; maiden name, Hoffman) Rybczynski; married Shirley Hallam, 1974. *Education:* McGill University, B.Arch., 1966, M.Arch., 1973.

ADDRESSES: Home—7801 Lincoln Dr., Philadelphia, PA 19118. *Agent*—Andrew Wylie, 250 West 57 St., New York, NY 10107.

CAREER: Worked as architect and planner for Moshe Safdie on Habitat 67 and as planner of housing and new towns in northern Canada, 1966-71; in practice as registered architect, 1970-82; McGill University, Montreal, research associate, 1972-74, assistant professor, 1975-78, became associate professor, 1978, professor of architecture until 1993; University of Pennsylvania, Philadelphia, Meyerson Professor of Urbanism, 1993—. Consultant to World Bank, United Nations, International Research Center, and Banco de Mexico in Nigeria, India, the Philippines, and Mexico, 1976—.

AWARDS, HONORS: Honorary fellow, American Institute of Architects, 1993; Alfred Jurzykowski Foundation Award, 1993; honorary M.A., University of Pennsylvania, 1994; Athanaeum of Philadelphia Literary Award, 1997 and 2001; Christopher Award, 2000; Anthony J. Lukas Prize, 2000, for *A Clearing in the Distance.*

WRITINGS:

(With Alexander Morse) *Patent Survey, 1859-1974: The Use of Elemental Sulphur in Building,* McGill University/Minimal Cost Housing Group, School of Architecture, McGill University (Montreal, Canada), 1974.

(Editor) *Use It Again, Sam,* McGill University/Minimal Cost Housing Group, School of Architecture, McGill University (Montreal, Canada), 1977.

Paper Heroes: A Review of Appropriate Technology, Doubleday (Garden City, NJ), 1980.

Taming the Tiger: The Struggle to Control Technology, Viking (New York, NY), 1983.

Home: A Short History of an Idea, Viking (New York, NY), 1986.

The Most Beautiful House in the World, Viking (New York, NY), 1989.

Waiting for the Weekend, Viking (New York, NY), 1991.

Looking Around: A Journey through Architecture, Viking (New York, NY), 1993.

A Place for Art: The Architecture of the National Gallery of Canada, National Gallery of Canada (Ottawa, Canada), 1993.

City Life: Urban Expectations in a New World, Scribner (New York, NY), 1995.

A Clearing in the Distance: Frederick Law Olmsted and America in the Nineteenth Century, Scribner (New York, NY), 1999.

One Good Turn: A Natural History of the Screwdriver and the Screw, Scribner (New York, NY), 2000.

The Look of Architecture, Oxford University Press (New York, NY), 2001.

The Perfect House: A Journey with the Renaissance Master Andrea Palladio, Scribner (New York, NY), 2002.

Member of the advisory board, *Encyclopedia Americana,* 1993—, the editorial board, *Open House International,* 1993—, and *Urban Design International,* 1995—; coeditor of *Wharton Real Estate Review,* 1996—.

SIDELIGHTS: In general, reviewers of *Home: A Short History of an Idea* conclude that architect Witold Rybczynski had two basic aims in mind: the first, to provide a survey of the gradual establishment of ease and comfort in the home over the centuries, and the second, to fault modernism with ignoring these past achievements and turning to aesthetics instead. With regard to Rybczynski's first aim, Jonathan Yardley noted in his *Washington Post Book World* article that "the idea of 'home' . . . may seem as old as the hills, but as . . . Rybczynski demonstrates in this exceptionally interesting and provocative book, it is a relatively modern notion that did not really begin until after the Middle Ages." As history would have it, living conditions in medieval times were sober, indeed; family members, as well as servants and visitors, had all of their activities confined to one room. According to Rybczynski, with the advent of both the separation of the workplace from the home in the seventeenth century and technological advances that were to flourish from that time on, a house started to take on the richness of a home. Privacy, intimacy, and comfort became increasingly possible and meaningful.

Rybczynski moves through the centuries recording the domestic changes that characterize this progression from public house to private home, and includes such highlights as the popularization of the extremely comfortable furniture of the Rococo movement in France in the eighteenth century and the Georgian tradition of the same time in England which consisted of a decor that was practical yet refined. In the opinion of Brina Caplan in the *Nation,* "as a historical survey, *Home* traces the technological and psychological changes that produced our modern sense of domestic ease. But while Rybczynski is explaining how we achieved comfort, he is also arguing that we are well on the way to losing it. He has a case to make against the 'fundamental poverty of modern architectural ideas.'" According to Wendy Smith in the *Village Voice,* Rybczynski felt the "fundamental poverty" of modern architecture is due to the failure of architects to learn from history; "unlike [Tom Wolfe's] *From Bauhaus to Our House,* however, *Home* is no hysterical polemic against modernism. Rybczynski's concern isn't with shouting condemnation from the rooftops a là Tom Wolfe, but with understanding how contemporary architects came to ignore 300 years of experience in arranging comfortable, convenient homes. . . . It's not the appearance of older buildings he misses . . . it's the attitude they reflected: an attention to human needs in the creation of spaces that were practical as well as pleasing to the eye. His closing chapter calls for a return to the idea of comfort in the home, an acknowledgement that houses are places for people to live, not forums for architects' aesthetic manifestos." Rybczynski, for example, criticizes the domestic deco of French architect and theorist Le Corbusier, describing it as cubelike, austere, and conducive to mass production, noted Christopher Lehmann-Haupt in the *New York Times.* Lehmann-Haupt further maintained that "Rybczynski knows the way out of the dilemma that he believes Modernism has led us into. It is, simply enough, to rediscover what is *comfortable,* and to do so not just by recapturing bourgeois styles of the past, but instead by re-examining bourgeois traditions."

When *Home* was published in 1986, Rybczynski "became an overnight authority on the subject of comfort," wrote *Globe & Mail* contributor Adele Freedman. As was the case with several other critics, William H. Gass for the *New York Times Book Review* felt that Rybczynski "tells the story of the development of the private dwelling from house to home . . . in a sensitive and balanced way." Additionally, remarks Gass, "Rybczynski's call for a reexamination of the bourgeois tradition is one that should be heeded, and when he remarks, for example, that the seventeenth-century Dutch interior can teach us a good deal about living in small spaces he is surely right." When it comes to Rybczynski's criticism of modern architecture, however, some critics disagree with his stance. As Gass saw it, "what remains a problem is

[Rybczynski's] basic opposition of art and comfort and the question whether an artist can really come to any kind of decent terms with the values of the middle class—because if living well remains a good revenge, living beautifully is yet better, indeed, best." Freedman likewise commented that "it was in the cards, but nonetheless wearisome, that a champion of intimacy, privacy, coziness, convenience and pragmatism would blame 'modernity' for banishing comfort in the name of esthetics." Yardley, however, viewed *Home* as "highly persuasive," and Lehmann-Haupt considered it a "delightful, intelligent book." Moreover, *New Yorker* contributor John Lukacs deemed it "exquisitely readable . . . a triumph of intelligence."

Rybczynski became Meyerson Professor of Urbanism at the University of Pennsylvania in the 1990s, and also published *City Life: Urban Expectations in a New World* mid-decade. The work was inspired by a friend's visit to Paris and her query upon her return as to why North American cities have failed to achieve the spectacular elegance of their European counterparts. In *City Life,* Rybczynski chronicles the history of urban development in North America from the first planned colonial towns like Philadelphia and Williamsburg to later metropolises noted for their daunting sprawl, like Los Angeles. Though he was examining a subject that had been well-dissected by other scholars of American and urban history, Rybczynski won praise for adding some fresh perspectives. "Threaded throughout the usual stories," wrote Brenda Scheer in her review of the tome for the *Journal of the American Planning Association,* "are lively descriptions of the attitudes that American city builders brought to their new world."

Rybczynski explains that American planners sought space, an obvious reaction to centuries of overcrowded conditions in European cities, and such desires were also blessed by an availability of land. *City Life* also shows how many cities that achieved greatness in the nineteenth century were built on the grid plan—among them New York and Chicago—which allowed for flexibility and quick expansion. He also reflects upon the importance of commerce to American cities. "Rybczynski points out that we have always viewed the city as a convenience, rather than as a timeless or monumental artifact," Scheer noted, and asserted in conclusion that the author "has offered not only a look at our past but an explanation for our current state of affairs." Paul Elie, reviewing the book for *Com-monweal,* faulted *City Life* for lacking a more critical approach, but termed the author "an uncommonly curious and nimble cultural critic. . . . Like many of the best cultural critics, Rybczynski doesn't state his case so much as give form to the virtues he espouses. Thus his book has the qualities that he most admires in urban life. It is orderly but not too planned. . . . Past and present are always jostling against each other."

For his next book, Rybczynski approached one of the giants of American urban history, a man whose genius was only truly appreciated well after his 1903 death. *A Clearing in the Distance: Frederick Law Olmsted and America in the Nineteenth Century* charts the life of America's greatest landscape architect. Olmsted was the designer of New York's Central Park, Prospect Park in Brooklyn, an estate in North Carolina for the Vanderbilt dynasty, and several other enduring marvels of what he considered "the three grand elements of pastoral landscape": meadows, forest, and water. Rybczynski writes about Olmsted's rather accidental path toward greatness: the son of a Connecticut dry-goods merchant, he found it difficult to settle on a profession for many years. He tried farming, became a sailor, and wrote about slavery for the *New York Times.* In 1857, a failed publishing venture spurred him to take a job as the superintendent for what New York City authorities had deemed "the Central Park." This was acreage set aside to serve as a public area, but it was not yet designed, and an architect by the name of Calvert Vaux suggested that Olmsted submit something. His plan won the competition, and Olmsted found that the gift for landscape architecture came naturally to him.

A Clearing in the Distance charts Olmsted's rise to eminence, but Rybczynski also chronicles the almost farcical struggles with local bureaucrats that plagued Olmsted's career. He was hired as the city planner of Buffalo, New York, and completed the design in less than a day's work, but for a park planned in the center, a local politician nearly won out in his bid to build a house in the middle of it. Rybczynski stresses that Olmsted was driven by personal conviction that public greenery was essential to the quality of life for all urban dwellers. Its restorative powers, he argued, should not be available just to the upper classes.

Rybczynski's biography reveals that Olmsted suffered from bouts of depression nearly all of his adult life and began to evidence signs of Alzheimer's disease in his early seventies. He handed over his business to his stepson and was confined in his last years to a sanitarium whose grounds he had designed but likely no longer recognized as his own handiwork. The biography won accolades for its author. "Like all fine biographers, Rybczynski has such a profound feeling for his subject that he is often at his best when the least is known and he is forced to impose his informed speculations upon the silent places in the life," remarked Robert Wilson in a review for *American Scholar. New York Times Book Review* critic Suzanna Lessard also praised *A Clearing in the Distance.* "The author has written a transparent book, in which he is a largely retiring but very pleasant guide," opined Lessard. "Every so often, he steps forward in a delightful, casual way"—in moments, as the critic noted, when the biographer recounts his own obstacles in researching Olmsted's life. Lessard described it as "a straightforward work, thorough and respectful, yet easeful in a way that is reminiscent of Olmsted himself."

In 1999, Rybczynski was invited by the *New York Times* to become a panelist for its "tool of the millennium" feature. The experience prompted him to write a short book on the history of his favorite tool. *One Good Turn: A Natural History of the Screwdriver and the Screw* was published in 2000, and discusses the screw and its companion at various points in history. It was crucial to some Renaissance weaponry, he finds, but advances in technology brought innovations and more widespread usage. "Siege engines . . . the precision lathe, door hinges and the great minds of ancient Greek geometry also figure among the threads of Rybczynski's tightly wound exposition," noted a *Publishers Weekly* reviewer.

The Look of Architecture, a short but succinct survey of style in architecture, came about as a result of a three-lecture series the author gave in the New York Public Library in 1999. In it, he discusses the ongoing relationship between architecture and style. He believes that, as does style, architecture mirrors the culture in which it exists and often imitates contemporary fashion. According to Michael Spinella of *Booklist,* he praises architects who build "with style and flair but also with firm foundations, grace, and the public interest at heart." A *Publishers Weekly* reviewer commented on Rybczynski's "ability to puncture [the architectural profession] pretensions without mean-spiritedness" and felt that, in this book, "the intimate, conversational tone he adopts manages to convey a lot of information in a very agreeable way."

BIOGRAPHICAL AND CRITICAL SOURCES:

BOOKS

Rybczynski, Witold, *Home: A Short History of an Idea,* Viking (New York, NY), 1986.

PERIODICALS

American Scholar, summer, 1999, Robert Wilson, review of *A Clearing in the Distance: Frederick Law Olmsted and America in the Nineteenth Century,* p. 142.
Atlantic, July 14, 1999.
Booklist, May 15, 1999, Donna Seaman, review of *A Clearing in the Distance,* p. 1659; June 1, 2001, Michael Spinella, review of *The Look of Architecture,* p. 1820.
Business Week, August 2, 1999, "The Man Who Brought Nature to the City," p. 12.
Chicago Tribune, July 28, 1986.
Commonweal, February 23, 1996, Paul Elie, review of *City Life,* p. 19.
Economist, July 17, 1999, "American City Parks," p. 7.
Fortune, June 21, 1999, Andrew Ferguson, "The Man Who Gave Us a Place to Relax," p. 48.
Globe & Mail (Toronto, Ontario, Canada), November 7, 1987.
Journal of the American Planning Association, fall, 1996, Brenda Scheer, review of *City Life,* p. 535.
Knight Ridder/Tribune News Service, October 23, 2002, Inga Saffron, review of *The Perfect House: A Journey with the Renaissance Architect Andrea Palladio,* p. K0125.
Library Journal, May 15, 1999, Grant A. Fredericksen, review of *A Clearing in the Distance,* p. 104; August, 2001, Paul Glassman, review of *The Look of Architecture,* p. 101.
Los Angeles Times Book Review, July 13, 1986.
Nation, December 20, 1986, Brina Caplan, review of *Home: A Short History of an Idea.*
Newsweek, August 18, 1986.
New Yorker, September 1, 1986.
New York Review of Books, December 4, 1986.
New York Times, July 14, 1986, Christopher Lehmann-Haupt, review of *Home.*
New York Times Book Review, November 6, 1983, August 3, 1986; June 13, 1999, Suzanna Lessard, "Scape Artist."

Planning, March, 1996, Harold Henderson, review of *City Life,* p. 33.

Public Interest, winter, 2000, David Brooks, "Designing the Cityscape," p. 99.

Publishers Weekly, May 31, 1999, review of *A Clearing in the Distance,* p. 76; June 12, 2000, review of *One Good Turn: A Natural History of the Screwdriver and the Screw,* p. 59; June 18, 2001, review of *The Look of Architecture,* p. 73.

Time, August 4, 1986.

Times Literary Supplement, May 6, 1988.

Village Voice, August 12, 1986, Wendy Smith, review of *Home.*

Washington Post, June 17, 1980, Jonathan Yardley, review of *Home.*

Washington Post Book World, September 25, 1983, July 6, 1986; December 5, 1999, p. X10.

Whole Earth, fall, 1999, Marianne Cramer, review of *A Clearing in the Distance,* p. 86.*

S

SAGAN, Dorion 1959-

PERSONAL: Born March 17, 1959, in Madison, WI; son of Carl Edward (an astronomer) and Lynn Petra (a biologist; maiden name, Alexander) Sagan; married Marjorie Lynn Baker, March 24, 1984 (divorced, 1987); children: Tonio Jerome. *Education:* University of Massachusetts—Amherst, B.A. (European history), 1981. *Politics:* Independent. *Religion:* "Gnostic-agnostic." *Hobbies and other interests:* Sleight of hand magic, basketball.

ADDRESSES: Home—P.O. Box 671, Amherst, MA 01004-0671. *Agent*—John Brockman Associates, Inc., 5 East 59th St., 8th Fl., New York, NY 10022. *E-mail*—gradientor@yahoo.com.

CAREER: Magician, freelance editor, teacher, consultant, speaker, trader, interviewer, appraiser, and indexer. Clerical worker in planetary biology and microbial ecology at National Aeronautics and Space Administration facility in San Jose, CA, 1984; technical writer for Applied Polymer Technology, 1985-86; general partner of Sciencewriters, Amherst, MA.

AWARDS, HONORS: Distinguished Achievement Award for excellence in educational journalism from Educational Press Association of America, 1986, for article "The Riddle of Sex."

WRITINGS:

(With mother, Lynn Margulis) *Microcosmos: Four Billion Years of Evolution from Our Microbial Ancestors,* Summit Books (New York, NY), 1986, University of California Press (Berkeley, CA), 1997.

(With Lynn Margulis) *Origins of Sex,* Yale University Press (New Haven, CT), 1986.

(With Lynn Margulis) *The Microcosmos Coloring Book,* Harcourt Brace Jovanovich (Boston, MA), 1988.

(With Lynn Margulis) *Garden of Microbial Delights: A Practical Guide to the Subvisible World,* Harcourt (Boston, MA), 1988.

(With Lynn Margulis) *Biospheres from Earth to Space,* Enslow (Hillside, NJ), 1989.

Biospheres: Metamorphosis of Planet Earth, McGraw-Hill (New York, NY), 1990.

(With Lynn Margulis) *Mystery Dance: On the Evolution of Human Sexuality,* Summit Books (New York, NY), 1991.

(With Lynn Margulis) *What Is Sex?,* Simon & Schuster (New York, NY), 1995.

(With Lynn Margulis) *What Is Life?,* University of California Press (Berkeley, CA), 1995.

(With Lynn Margulis) *Slanted Truths: Essays on Gaia, Symbiosis, and Evolution,* Copernicus (New York, NY), 1997.

(With Eric D. Schneider) *Cooking with Jesus: From the Primal Brew to the Last Brunch,* BookSurge (Charleston, SC), 2001.

(With Lynn Margulis) *Acquiring Genomes: A Theory of the Origins of Species* (includes sound recording), Basic Books (New York, NY), 2002.

(With John R. Skoyles) *Up from Dragons: The Evolution of Human Intelligence,* McGraw-Hill (New York, NY), 2002.

(With others) *Within the Stone: Nature's Abstract Rock Art,* photographs by Bill Atkinson, BrownTrout Press (San Francisco, CA), 2004.

(With Eric D. Schneider) *Into the Cool: Energy Flow, Thermodynamics, and Life,* University of Chicago Press (Chicago, IL), 2005.

Author of foreword to *Heretics: The Bloody History of the Christian Church,* by Sumner Davis, 1stBooks Library, 2002. Contributor to periodicals, including *Omni, Skeptical Inquirer, New York Times Book Review, Natural History, Wired, Cabinet, Sciences, Bostonian, Whole Earth Review, Environmentalist, Earthwatch,* and *Ecologist.*

SIDELIGHTS: Dorion Sagan is an accomplished science writer who has often aided his biologist mother, Lynn Margulis, to produce works that have intrigued readers. Sagan, the son of the renowned astronomer Carl Sagan, once told *CA* about his love of literature and the written word: "I want to apply my knowledge of sleight-of-hand to literature, both in the nonfiction relationship of perception to science and art, and in the fictional context of exploring point of view, metafiction, and 'magical' protagonists. Bernard De Voto's *World of Fiction* fascinates me: I can't wait to finish my nonfiction projects so that I can devote myself to what I consider to be fiction's superior latitude for exploring the truth, which after all is conditional—a species of lie. I am also interested in forcing a rapprochement between science writing and continental philosophy." Sagan has put his creative talents to work in his science writing, honing a style that has made for lively writing yet has sometimes exasperated the scientific establishment.

When asked how he became interested in writing, Sagan told *CA* that it "probably was a combination of my father's 'um-less' speech, which I first heard in the womb, and my young mother's beautiful voice, which regaled my child's mind with *The Jungle Book, Connecticut Yankee in King Arthur's Court,* the Greek myths, and other classics."

Reflecting on the sources of inspiration for his work, the author remarked to *CA,* "Everything: I see myself as a kind of lens. I am attuned to art, philosophy, and the perception/deception medium (i.e. magic). I'm a big fan of a large variety of books, from *The Gift of Death,* by Jacques Derrida, to the confessional fiction of Hamsun, Fante, and Bukowski. I tend to like books, whether fiction, philosophy, or other, that are 'true,' even if classified as nonfiction. I use art, history, and philosophy to multidimensionalize and 'place' science and science as an anchor and reality check for art."

In several works Margulis and Sagan discuss sex—that is, the mixing of genes, not just reproduction—by organisms. Each chapter of *What Is Sex?* contains "colorful insights, wild guesses, and just-so stories that are anchored in biological fact but allowed to float just out of reach of convincing proof," wrote *Boston Globe*'s Chet Raymo. "This may annoy some readers who will find it all a little gushy, but others will love it. Part science, part philosophy, occasionally poetic, *What Is Sex?* is a roller-coaster ride through the history of sex on earth." Calling the work "an exuberant meditation on life's place in the universe," *Washington Post* reviewer Susan Okie added, "This is science writing of a rare kind, a bold synthesis that draws on biology and physics."

The duo continued to write about this topic in their 1991 offering, *Mystery Dance: On the Evolution of Human Sexuality.* In this work the authors discuss the bacterial origin of sex and how the reproductive process varies in species and has led over time to different developments in the creatures under discussion. Reviews of the work varied, with a *Publishers Weekly* critic calling it an "eloquent, stimulating exploration" that sometimes "succumbs to reductionism," and W. Lener of *Choice* noting, "Although the book's information is generally accurate, there are errors." Paul S. Boyer had more serious criticism to offer in a *BioScience* review. He faulted the authors' use of "poetic imagery [that] obscures much of the scientific insight" and anthropomorphic imagery. While Boyer cited a few minor errors, such as incomplete or missing citations, his main complaint was the use of "unbridled speculation." According to Boyer, major points are couched in terms that make it difficult for the reader to discern known fact from supposition.

A professor and researcher, Margulis is a specialist in biology at the University of Massachusetts. Many of her works, coauthored with Sagan, deal with her area of specialization, including the 1989 title *Garden of Microbial Delights: A Practical Guide to the Subvisible World,* in which they introduce readers to the rich world of microbes. Praising this work as "fascinating, easy to read, deeply thorough," and "practical as a field guide" was *Whole Earth Review*'s Kevin Kelly. In *Microcosmos: Four Billion Years of Evolution from Our Microbial Ancestors,* they propose an alternative to the widely believed theory of evolution proposed by Charles Darwin. Margulis's theory is known as symbiosis-cooperation. In it, instead of using domination by the most fit, single-celled organisms gradually combine over time to create multi-celled organisms. "This provocative book will undoubtedly do much to disabuse readers of any anthropocentric notions," wrote William J. Hagan, Jr., in *Isis*. In the view of Lee Dembart of the *Los Angeles Times,* Margulis and Sagan's explanation of microbial evolution is "a fascinating, engrossing, superbly written account of how the conditions of the primitive Earth affected and were affected by the mechanisms of evolving forms of life and how those solutions remain with us today." Despite his enthusiasm for the work, Dembart also expressed some reservations: "This book's weakness is that it does not distinguish clearly between what is known and what the authors are filling in. They have put it all together in a virtually seamless web that makes most of their speculations sound like fact. For most of the book, this is merely annoying. In the last chapter, however, . . . they go off the deep end completely, but you wouldn't know it by the tone." "In their ambitious attempt to examine four billion years of evolution, Margulis and Sagan provide a compelling statement of the long-range goals of current research in the field," Hagan concluded. Margulis and Sagan defended this theory even more vigorously in their 2002 title, *Acquiring Genomes: A Theory of the Origins of Species,* which *Booklist*'s Gilbert Taylor called "polemical and provocative."

Beginning in the 1980s, Margulis joined James Lovelock in advancing the idea—dubbed the Gaia hypothesis—that the earth and its atmosphere together may be considered a self-regulating organism. Several works by Sagan and Margulis examine this thesis, including *Slanted Truths: Essays on Gaia, Symbiosis, and Evolution,* and *What Is Life?* In the first, a collection of essays "written in a lively and enthusiastic style," to quote *Choice*'s S. M. Paracer, the authors discuss the Gaia hypothesis. *What Is Life?* is a large format, highly illustrated book that demonstrates the wide variety of life on the planet, including one-celled organisms, plants, and animals. It simultaneously presents an alternate perspective on life and evolution, which, according to John D. Helmann writing in *Quarterly Review of Biology,* "will make interesting reading for those already familiar with the major themes of modern biological understanding. However, the complexity of the language, the frequent digressions, and the metaphysical and philosophical overtones will make much of the material quite difficult for the uninitiated."

In 2002 Sagan teamed up with John R. Skoyles to write *Up from Dragons: The Evolution of Human Intelligence,* an account of the evolution of human intelligence that forms a sequel to Carl Sagan's *The Dragons of Eden.* Alan Bilsborough of the *Times Higher Education Supplement* noted that the "book is generally clearly and engagingly written, though sometimes the anecdotes that begin the chapters are distracting and the work would have benefited from illustrations."

Hoping his books will "inform and enchant," Sagan described himself to *CA* as "one of those marked souls who can't not write. I have many unfinished projects all vying for my attention at various levels of obsessive compulsion. Sometimes I mine old projects, or 'cannibalize' them for new ones. But, although I have written mostly science books, I am more like an artist in that I prefer to always engage new material, or old material in new ways, rather than simply presenting information."

BIOGRAPHICAL AND CRITICAL SOURCES:

PERIODICALS

BioScience, September, 1992, Paul S. Boyer, review of *Mystery Dance: On the Evolution of Human Sexuality,* pp. 633-634.
Booklist, September 15, 1988, review of *Garden of Microbial Delights: A Practical Guide to the Subvisible World,* p. 107; June 15, 1989, review of *Biospheres from Earth to Space,* p. 1827; September 1, 1995, Gilbert Taylor, review of *What Is Life?,* p. 23; November 1, 1997, Gilbert Taylor, review of *What Is Sex?,* p. 443; June 1, 2002, Gilbert Taylor, review of *Acquiring Genomes: A Theory of the Origins of Species,* pp. 1655-1656.
Bookwatch, June, 1990, review of *Biospheres: Metamorphosis of Planet Earth,* p. 4.
Boston Globe, December 28, 1997, Chet Raymo, "The Itch of Ecstasy," review of *What Is Sex?,* p. L1.
Choice, September, 1990, F. F. Flint, review of *Biospheres;* April, 1992, W. Lener, review of *Mystery Dance;* March, 1996, W. Lener, review of *What Is Life?;* February, 1998, S. M. Paracer, review of *Slanted Truths: Essays on Gaia, Symbiosis, and Evolution,;* September, 1998, G. Stevens, review of *What Is Sex?;* January, 2003, S. I. Perloe, review of *Up from Dragons: The Evolution of Human Intelligence.*
Futurist, March, 1991, review of *Biospheres,* p. 38.

Isis, March, 1987, William J. Hagan, Jr., review of *Microcosmos: Four Billion Years of Microbial Evolution,* pp. 106-107.

Kirkus Reviews, February 1, 1990, review of *Biospheres,* p. 167; May 15, 2002, review of *Acquiring Genomes,* pp. 718-719.

Library Journal, March 15, 1990, review of *Biospheres,* p. 109.

Los Angeles Times, July 29, 1986, Lee Dembart, review of *Microcosmos,* p. 4; July 23, 1991, John Wilkes, "Stripping Down to the Core of Sexuality," review of *Mystery Dance,* p. 2.

New York Times Book Review, March 18, 1990, review of *Biospheres from Earth to Space,* p. 16.

Publishers Weekly, January 12, 1990, Genevieve Stuttaford, review of *Biospheres,* p. 57; June 14, 1991, review of *Mystery Dance,* p. 50; August 28, 1995, review of *What Is Life?,* p. 99; October 27, 1997, review of *What Is Sex?* p. 62; April 22, 2002, review of *Up from Dragons,* pp. 59-60.

Quarterly Review of Biology, March, 1988, Michael T. Ghiselin, review of *Origins of Sex: Three Billion Years of Genetic Recombination,* pp. 80-81; March, 1997, John D. Helmann, review of *What Is Life?,* pp. 62-63.

School Library Journal, January, 1989, review of *Garden of Microbial Delights,* p. 108; May, 1989, review of *Biospheres from Earth to Space,* p. 132.

Science Books & Films, May, 1989, review of *Biospheres from Earth to Space,* p. 291; September, 1990, review of *Biospheres from Earth to Space,* p. 38.

Science News, February 14, 1998, Cait Anthony, review of *What Is Sex?,* p. 98; October 26, 2002, review of *Acquiring Genomes,* p. 271.

SciTech Book News, October, 1988, review of *Garden of Microbial Delights,* p. 19.

Times Higher Education Supplement, July 3, 1998, Lewis Wolpert, "Gaian Takes on Darwin," review of *Slanted Truths;* April 25, 2003, Alan Bilsborough, "Why We Changed Our Minds," review of *Up from Dragons.*

Washington Post, March 29, 1998, Susan Okie, review of *What Is Sex?,* p. X06; October 20, 2002, Susan Okie, review of *Acquiring Genomes,* p. T10.

Whole Earth, fall, 1989, Kevin Kelly, review of *Garden of Microbial Delights,* p. 64; summer, 1997, Peter Warshall, reviews of *Slanted Truths* and *Gaia to Microcosm,* p. 73; fall, 1999, Stewart Brand, review of *What Is Life?* p. 71; fall, 2000, review of *Gaia to Microcosm,* p. 44.*

SALER, Benson 1930-

PERSONAL: Born May 2, 1930, in Philadelphia, PA; son of Samuel (in business) and Fannie (Weinberg) Saler; married Joyce E. Spivak, September 26, 1954; children: Michael T., Judith M., Bethel A. *Education:* Princeton University, B.A., 1952; University of Pennsylvania, M.A., 1957, Ph.D., 1960.

ADDRESSES: Home—393 Main St., Concord, MA 01742. *Office*—Department of Anthropology, Brandeis University, Waltham, MA 02454. *E-mail*—b4saler@aol.com.

CAREER: Writer. Brandeis University, Waltham, MA, professor of anthropology. *Military service:* U.S. Army, 1954-56.

MEMBER: American Anthropological Association (fellow).

WRITINGS:

Conceptualizing Religion, E. J. Brill (Long Island City, NY), 1993, 2nd edition, with new preface, Berghahn Books (New York, NY), 2000.

(With Charles A. Ziegler and Charles B. Moore) *UFO Crash at Roswell: The Genesis of a Modern Myth,* Smithsonian Institution Press (Washington, DC), 1997.

Contributor to books, including *Los aborigines de Venezuela,* Volume 3, Fundación La Salle (Caracas, Venezuela), 1988.

*   *   *

SEDARIS, David 1957-
(The Talent Family, a joint pseudonym)

PERSONAL: Surname pronounced "seh-*dar*-iss;" born 1957, in Raleigh, NC; son of Lou and Sharon Sedaris; partner of Hugh Hamrick (a painter). *Education:* Attended Kent State University; School of the Art Institute of Chicago, attained degree in 1987.

David Sedaris

ADDRESSES: Home—Kensington, London, England. *Agent*—Steven Barclay, 321 Pleasant St., Petaluma, CA 94952.

CAREER: Diarist, radio commentator, essayist, and short story writer. Has taught writing at the School of the Art Institute of Chicago, Chicago, IL; appeared on *Milly's Orchid Show,* Chicago; appeared on *The Wild Room,* WBEZ radio, Chicago; appeared on *This America Life,* National Public Radio; has held numerous part-time jobs, including employment as a performance artist, a moving company worker, an office worker, an elf in SantaLand at Macy's department store, a housepainter, an apple-picker, and an apartment cleaner; volunteered with English Language Library for the Blind in Paris, France, and Age Concern in London, England.

AWARDS, HONORS: Obie Award, *Village Voice,* 1995, for *One Woman Shoe;* Humorist of the Year, *Time* magazine, 2001; Thurber Prize for American Humor.

WRITINGS:

AUTOBIOGRAPHICAL ESSAYS

Origins of the Underclass, and Other Stories, Amethyst Press (Washington, DC), 1992.
Barrel Fever, Little, Brown (Boston, MA), 1994.
Naked, Little, Brown (Boston, MA), 1997.
Holidays on Ice, Little, Brown (Boston, MA), 1997.
Me Talk Pretty One Day, Little, Brown (Boston, MA), 2000.
Dress Your Family in Corduroy and Denim, Little, Brown (Boston, MA), 2004.

PLAYS

Jamboree, produced at Theatre for the New City (New York, NY), 1991.
Stump the Host, produced at La MaMa ETC (New York, NY), March, 1993.
(With sister, Amy Sedaris, as The Talent Family) *One Woman Shoe,* produced at La MaMa ETC (New York, NY), 1995.
(With Joe Mantello) *The SantaLand Diaries,* produced off-Broadway, November, 1996, published as *SantaLand Diaries and Seasons Greetings: Two Plays,* Dramatists Play Service (New York, NY), 1998.
(With sister, Amy Sedaris, as The Talent Family) *Little Freida Mysteries,* produced at La MaMa ETC (New York, NY), February, 1997.
(With sister, Amy Sedaris, as The Talent Family) *Incident at Cobbler's Knob,* produced at the Fiorello H. LaGuardia High School of Music and Art (New York, NY), 1997.
(With sister, Amy Sedaris, as The Talent Family) *The Book of Liz,* (produced at Greenwich House Theater, New York, 2001), Dramatists Play Service (New York, NY), 2002.

Also, with Amy Sedaris, author of the play *Stitches;* author of three plays produced in Chicago, IL, prior to 1991.

COMEDY ALBUMS

Barrel Fever and Other Stories, Time Warner Audio, 2001.

(With Amy Sedaris and Ann Magnuson) *The David Sedaris Box Set,* Time Warner Audio, 2002.

David Sedaris Live at Carnegie Hall, Time Warner Audio, 2003.

OTHER

Also author of commentaries for *This American Life* and other National Public Radio programs, 1992—. *This American Life* commentaries included in collections, including *This American Life: Lies, Sissies, and Fiascos,* Rhino Records, 1999, and *Crimebusters and Crossed Wires: Stories from This American Life,* Sony, 2003. Contributor to periodicals, including *Esquire.*

ADAPTATIONS: "Diary of a Smoker," an essay from *Barrel Fever,* was adapted by Matthew Modine into a thirteen-minute film shown at the Sundance Film Festival and on the Public Broadcasting System (PBS), 1994. Audiobook versions of *Naked* and *Holidays on Ice* were released by Time Warner Audio Books in 1997; an audiobook version of *Dress Your Family in Corduroy and Denim* was released by Time Warner Audiobooks in 2004.

SIDELIGHTS: "Thank God for the maladjusted lives of Lou and Sharon Sedaris," Hannah Sampson wrote in the *Miami Herald.* "Their home may have been frenzied and their six children destined for therapy, but they gave us the shrewd and unconventional David Sedaris, who has created a successful career of telling hilarious, heartbreaking stories about his dysfunctional family." Sedaris has published several books of essays about his life, including the *New York Times* best-sellers *Me Talk Pretty One Day* and *Dress Your Family in Corduroy and Denim.* Also, in collaboration with his sister Amy Sedaris (best known for her appearances on the cable show *Strangers with Candy*), Sedaris has written several satiric plays, including the Obie Award-winning *One Woman Shoe.* "No one puts the fun into function quite like Sedaris," Kim Harwell wrote in the *Dallas Morning News.*

Sedaris grew up in North Carolina and moved to Chicago while in his twenties, where he attended school and performed readings from his diaries for audiences. In the audience at one reading was Ira Glass, of the National Public Radio (NPR) programs *The Wild Room* and *This American Life.* After Sedaris

moved to New York in 1991, Glass called and asked him if he had any holiday-themed essays for a program Glass was putting together. Sedaris did—"SantaLand Diaries"—and this piece launched his career. Sedaris began reading excerpts from his diaries on the air, where his "nicely nerdy, quavering voice," in the words of *Newsweek* commentator Jeff Giles, delivered monologues praised for their acerbic wit and dead-pan delivery. Commenting about Sedaris's early commentaries in the *New York Times,* John Marchese wrote: "Sedaris has shown remarkable skill as a mimic and the ability to mix the sweet and the bitter: to be naive and vulnerable and at the same time, jaded and wickedly funny." Because of these radio pieces, Sampson continued, Sedaris has "become the closest thing public radio has to Elvis, so popular that his appearances at concert halls sell out."

Sedaris's comic, and often satirical, monologues draw primarily on his experiences in the odd day-jobs that he held before his work with NPR heated up his artistic career. Of his long-standing position as an apartment cleaner, Sedaris told Marchese in the *New York Times:* "I can only write when it's dark, so basically, my whole day is spent waiting for it to get dark. Cleaning apartments gives me something to do when I get up. Otherwise, I'd feel like a bum." As a result of his appearances on NPR, Sedaris has received numerous job offers, both for cleaning and for writing—as well as a two-book contract with Little, Brown, who in 1994, published *Barrel Fever,* a collection of Sedaris's essays and short stories.

Barrel Fever includes several pieces that brought Sedaris to national attention when he read them on the radio, including "Diary of a Smoker," in which the author declares that the efforts of nonsmokers to extend his life by not allowing him to smoke in front of them only gives him more time to hate nonsmokers, and "SantaLand Diaries," in which the author chronicles his amorous and aggravating experiences playing one of Santa's elves at Macy's one Christmas. Critics remarked on the humorously exaggerated self-delusion of Sedaris's narrators in the short stories, including a man who brags on talk-shows about his affairs with such stars as rock singer Bruce Springsteen and boxer Mike Tyson, and a gay man with a persecution complex who "bemoans his suffering at the hands of society in a style so over-the-top as to be laughable," according to a critic in *Kirkus Reviews.*

Critical response to *Barrel Fever* was generally positive, with reviewers appreciating Sedaris's humorous yet accurate portrayal of such American foibles as the commercialism of Christmas and the self-righteousness of health fanatics. "Without slapping the reader in the face with a political diatribe," wrote a critic for *Kirkus Reviews,* "the author skewers our ridiculous fascination with other people's tedious everyday lives." A contributor to *Publishers Weekly* commented: "Sedaris ekes humor from the blackest of scenarios, peppering his narrative with memorable turns of phrase and repeatedly surprising with his double-edged wit." And although *Newsweek* critic Giles found some of Sedaris's commentary relatively shallow, he nonetheless concluded: "This is a writer who's cleaned our toilets and will never look at us the same way."

Sedaris's second collection of essays, *Naked,* appeared in 1997. These essays, according to a reviewer for *Publishers Weekly,* reveal that "Sedaris can hardly be called a humorist in the ordinary sense. . . . Sedaris is instead an essayist who happens to be very funny." In his characteristic deadpan style, Sedaris tells stories "about nutty or bizarre experiences, like volunteering at a hospital for the insane," Craig Seligman observed in the *New York Times Book Review.* Other essays include Sedaris on hitchhiking, working in Oregon, his personal battle with his childhood nervous disorders, and the title piece, about his sojourn at a nudist colony. But, for Seligman, "the funniest [essays], and ultimately the saddest, have to do with the writer's family." In these autobiographical tales, wrote Margot Mifflin in *Entertainment Weekly,* "Sedaris covers an impressive emotional range. . . . from the comically corrosive title piece . . . to 'Ashes,' his account of his mother's death from cancer—a direct, unsentimental hit to the heart." As Ira Glass told Peter Ames Carlin in a *People* profile, "People come to his work because he's funny. . . . But there's a complicated moral vision there."

In *Me Talk Pretty One Day,* Sedaris tells more stories of his family, but also writes several essays about living in Paris with his partner, painter Hugh Hamrick. (Sedaris moved to Paris after becoming too recognizable in the United States. "It's harder to spy on people when someone is shouting 'Loved you on Letterman!,'" he told *Entertainment Weekly* reviewer Nancy Miller. Then, after he started to become famous in Paris as well, Sedaris moved on to London.) "Although amusing, Sedaris' tales of life in France now that he's happy don't have the bite of those in the first half of the book, many of them dealing with his eccentric father, an IBM engineer who ruins miniature golf with dissertations on wind trajectory," argued Nancy Pate in *Knight Ridder/Tribune News Service.* Lisa Schwarzbaum concluded in *Entertainment Weekly:* "These days Sedaris glitters as one of the wittiest writers around, an essayist and radio commentator who only appears to be telling simple then-what-happened anecdotes."

The trend towards a softer side in Sedaris's stories continued in *Dress Your Family in Corduroy and Denim,* many critics thought. "You get the sense that Sedaris is thinking, 'This is one screwed-up family, but it's my screwed-up family,'" commented *Knight Ridder/Tribune News Service* contributor David Tarrant. His late mother particularly benefits from Sedaris's new-found sympathetic side; in *Dress Your Family in Corduroy and Denim* she "emerges as one of the most poignant and original female characters in contemporary literature," declared a *Publishers Weekly* contributor. As Jason Rowan commented in *Lambda Book Report,* "It's moving to revisit their prickly relationship from a softer and more compassionate place." The fact that Sedaris "can see the ridiculousness in his family's misadventures, yet relate them with tenderness," Marta Salij wrote in the *Detroit Free Press,* makes *Dress Your Family in Corduroy and Denim* "an even richer pleasure than Sedaris' earlier books."

BIOGRAPHICAL AND CRITICAL SOURCES:

PERIODICALS

Advocate, February 25, 1992, Sarah Schulman, review of *Origins of the Underclass, and Other Stories,* pp. 82-84; December 10, 1996, Robert L. Pela, review of *The SantaLand Diaries,* p. 54; March 18, 1997, Robert L. Pela, review of *Naked,* pp. 76-77; June 20, 2000, Robert L. Pela, review of *Me Talk Pretty One Day,* p. 133.

American Theatre, July-August, 1993, Michael Broder, "David Sedaris: Welcome to the Talent Family," pp. 48-50.

Back Stage, June 23, 1995, David Sheward, review of *One Woman Shoe,* p. 29; November 29, 1996, Eric Grode, review of *The SantaLand Diaries,* p. 28; February 28, 1997, Robert Simonson, review of *The Little Frieda Mysteries,* p. 60; July 18, 1997, Robert Simonson, review of *Incident at Cobbler's Knob,* p. 40.

Berkshire Eagle (Berkshire County, MA), April 24, 1998, Seth Rogovoy, "David Sedaris: Just a Writer."

Book, September, 2000, Rochelle O'Gorman, review of *Me Talk Pretty One Day,* p. 85; March-April, 2003, review of *The David Sedaris Box Set,* p. 78, interview with Sedaris, p. 78.

Booklist, June 1, 1994, Benjamin Segedin, review of *Barrel Fever,* p. 1762; February 15, 1997, Donna Seaman, review of *Naked,* p. 996; May 1, 2004, Donna Seaman, review of *Dress Your Family in Corduroy and Denim,* p. 1482.

Chicago Tribune, February 2, 1996, sec. 7, p. 2.

Commonweal, June 15, 2001, Francis DeBernardo, review of *Me Talk Pretty One Day,* p. 24.

Dallas Morning News, June 29, 2004, Kim Harwell, "What We Like: David Sedaris."

Detroit Free Press, June 23, 2004, Marta Salij, review of *Dress Your Family in Corduroy and Denim.*

Entertainment Weekly, July 29, 1994, Margot Mifflin, review of *Barrel Fever,* p. 55; December 13, 1996, Kip Cheng, "Elf Awareness" (interview with Sedaris), p. S10; March 21, 1997, Margot Mifflin, review of *Naked,* p. 68; May 10, 2002, review of *Holidays on Ice,* p. 74; June 2, 2000, Lisa Schwarzbaum, review of *Me Talk Pretty One Day,* p. 72; January 23, 2004, review of *Dress Your Family in Corduroy and Denim,* p. 68; June 4, 2004, Augusten Burroughs, review of *Dress Your Family in Corduroy and Denim,* p. 84; June 11, 2004, Nancy Miller, "Where in the World Is David Sedaris? He Just Fled Paris for London, but America's Most Wanted Humorist Can't Outrun Success," p. 73.

Esquire, June, 2000, Ira Glass, review of *Me Talk Pretty One Day,* p. 38.

Fortune, June 12, 2000, review of *Me Talk Pretty One Day,* p. 358.

Gay and Lesbian Review, January, 2001, Lewis Whittington, review of *Me Talk Pretty One Day,* p. 46.

Independent (London, England), February 9, 2001, Steve Jelbert, "How to Take the World By Charm" (interview with Sedaris), section S, page 9.

Kirkus Reviews, April 1, 1994, p. 430; April 15, 2004, review of *Dress Your Family in Corduroy and Denim,* p. 384.

Knight Ridder/Tribune News Service, June 20, 2001, Nancy Pate, review of *Me Talk Pretty One Day,* p. K6846; July 18, 2001, Robert K. Elder, "Cult Writer David Sedaris Finds Mainstream Success with Acerbic Tales of the Absurd," p. K2674;

August 5, 2004, David Tarrant, review of *Dress Your Family in Corduroy and Denim,* p. K3038.

Lambda Book Report, September, 1997, David Tedhams, review of *Naked,* pp. 37-38; May, 2004, Jason Rowan, review of *Dress Your Family in Corduroy and Denim,* p. 8.

Library Journal, May 1, 1994, Thomas Wiener, review of *Barrel Fever,* p. 104; April 1, 1997, Mary Paumier, review of *Naked,* p. 93; July, 1997, Dana C. Bell-Russel, review of *Naked* (audiobook), p. 143; May 15, 2000, A. J. Anderson, review of *Me Talk Pretty One Day,* p. 95; October 15, 2000, Gloria Maxwell, review of *Me Talk Pretty One Day* (audiobook), p. 124; June 15, 2004, Robin Imhof, review of *Dress Your Family in Corduroy and Denim,* p. 72.

Los Angeles Times Book Review, October 16, 1994, p. 6; July 2, 1995, p. 11.

Miami Herald, June 13, 2004, Hannah Sampson, review of *Dress Your Family in Corduroy and Denim.*

Nation, September 8, 1997, Laurie Stone, review of *Incident at Cobbler's Knob,* pp. 32-33.

Newsweek, August 15, 1994, Jeff Giles, review of *Barrel Fever,* pp. 66-67.

New York Times, February 19, 1997, p. C14; March 2, 2001, Jesse McKinley, review of *The Book of Liz,* section B, page 2, section E, page 2; March 28, 2001, Ben Brantley, review of *The Book of Liz,* section B, page 1, section E, page 1.

New York Times Book Review, July 4, 1993, p. 5; March 16, 1997, p. 10; June 16, 2000, Michiko Kakutani, review of *Me Talk Pretty One Day;* June 20, 2004, Stephen Metcalf, review of *Dress Your Family in Corduroy and Denim,* p. 7.

Orlando Sentinel, June 28, 2000, Nancy Pate, review of *Me Talk Pretty One Day.*

O, The Oprah Magazine, June, 2004, Lisa Kogan, review of *Dress Your Family in Corduroy and Denim,* p. 148.

People, March 24, 1997, Paula Chin, review of *Naked,* pp. 35-37; October 20, 1997, Peter Ames Carlin, "Elf-Made Writer: Former Santa's Helper David Sedaris Turns His Odd Life into Literature," p. 129; June 26, 2000, review of *Me Talk Pretty One Day,* p. 20; June 7, 2004, Sean Daly, review of *Dress Your Family in Corduroy and Denim,* p. 50.

Publishers Weekly, April 25, 1994, review of *Barrel Fever,* p. 58; January 27, 1997, review of *Naked,* p. 88; April 7, 1997, p. 22; May 5, 1997, review of *Naked* (audiobook), pp. 40-41; November 24,

1997, review of *Holidays on Ice,* p. 55; May 8, 2000, review of *Me Talk Pretty One Day,* p. 212; June 19, 2000, Kathie Bergquist, interview with Sedaris, p. 54; August 7, 2000, review of *Me Talk Pretty One Day* (audiobook), p. 42; October 6, 2003, Shannon Maughan, "Him Talk Pretty on Audiobooks" (interview with Sedaris), pp. 26-27; December 1, 2003, review of *David Sedaris Live at Carnegie Hall,* p. 21; May 24, 2004, review of *Dress Your Family in Corduroy and Denim,* p. 56; June 14, 2004, Daisy Maryles, "Sedaris Scores," p. 24; July 5, 2004, review of *Dress Your Family in Corduroy and Denim* (audiobook), p. 18.

Sarasota Herald Tribune, December 14, 2001, Jay Handelman, review of *SantaLand Diaries,* p. 28.

South Florida Sun-Sentinel, August 11, 2004, Oline H. Cogdill, review of *The David Sedaris Box Set.*

Time, June 19, 2000, interview with Sedaris, p. 139; July 2, 2001, Belinda Luscombe, "That's Signing, Not Singing," p. 79; September 17, 2001, Walter Kirn, "Wry Slicer: Neurotic, Self-Absorbed and Laugh-Out-Loud Funny, David Sedaris Takes Readers on a Wild Ride Through His Improbable Life," p. 86; June 21, 2004, Josh Tyrangiel, "Ten Questions for David Sedaris," p. 8.

Variety, November 11, 1996, Greg Evans, review of *The SantaLand Diaries,* p. 66; April 2, 2001, Charles Isherwood, review of *The Book of Liz,* p. 30.

Wall Street Journal, June 2, 2000, Robert J. Hughes, review of *Me Talk Pretty One Day,* p. W10.

Washington Post, March 22, 1997, p. B1.

Whole Earth Review, winter, 1995, Allison Levin, review of *Barrel Fever,* p. 63.

ONLINE

Boston Phoenix Online, http://www.bostonphoenix.com/ (February, 1997), Robert David Sullivan, "Sedaris Gets Naked."

January Magazine, http://www.januarymagazine.com/ (August 12, 2004), Linda Richards, "January Interview: David Sedaris."

Stephen Barclay Agency Web Site, http://www.barclayagency.com/ (August 12, 2004), "David Sedaris."*

*   *   *

SHARP, Luke
    See ALKIVIADES, Alkis

SINGH, Simon 1964-

PERSONAL: Born September 19, 1964, in Somerset, England. *Ethnicity:* "Indian." *Education:* University of Cambridge, Ph.D. (particle physics), 1990.

ADDRESSES: Home—London, England. *Agent*—Patrick Walsh, Conville and Walsh Limited, 2 Ganton St., London W1F 7QL, England. *E-mail*—simon singh@visto.com.

CAREER: Author and science journalist. British Broadcasting Company (BBC), producer, 1990-96. Director, *Fermat's Last Theorem* (documentary, also released as *The Proof*); presenter, *The Science of Secrecy* (five-part series), Channel 4.

AWARDS, HONORS: British Academy of Film and Television Arts Award for Best Documentary, 1996, and Emmy nomination, both for *Fermat's Last Theorem;* shortlisted for Rhone-Poulenc Prize for Best Science Book, 1997, for *Fermat's Last Theorem;* named Member, Order of the British Empire, for contributions to science education and communication.

WRITINGS:

Fermat's Enigma: The Epic Quest to Solve the World's Greatest Mathematical Problem, Walker (New York, NY), 1997, published as *Fermat's Last Theorem: The Story of a Riddle That Confounded the World's Greatest Minds for 358 Years,* Fourth Estate (London, England), 1998.

The Code Book: The Evolution of Secrecy from Mary, Queen of Scots, to Quantum Cryptography (also see below), Doubleday (New York, NY), 1999, published as *The Code Book: The Evolution of Secrecy from Ancient Egypt to Quantum Cryptography,* Fourth Estate (London, England), 1999, published as *The Code Book: The Secret History of Codes and Code-Breaking,* Fourth Estate (London, England), 2000.

The Science of Secrecy: The Secret History of Codes and Codebreaking (associated with British television series), Fourth Estate (London, England), 2000.

The Code Book: How to Make It, Break It, Hack It, Crack It (for children; adaptation of *The Code Book*), Delacorte Press (New York, NY), 2001.

Simon Singh

Big Bang: The Origins of the Universe, Fourth Estate (London, England), 2004.

Contributor to journals and newpapers, including *New Statesman,* London *Daily Telegraph, Guardian, Observer, Sunday Telegraph, New Scientist,* and *Independent.*

SIDELIGHTS: *Fermat's Enigma: The Epic Quest to Solve the World's Greatest Mathematical Problem* by Simon Singh has been hailed as an appealing book for both a general audience and for mathematicians. Recounting the success of mathematician Andrew Wiles' proof of a theorem that had remained unproven for three hundred and fifty years, it is a dramatic tale that shows the personal side of such a quest. By detailing Wiles' nearly life-long interest in the theorem and the remarkable efforts of mathematicians before him, Singh provides a fascinating background to what is considered the most important mathematical event of the twentieth century.

The seventeenth-century judge and amateur mathematician Pierre de Fermat asserted that he had proven that the equation x to the nth power plus y to the nth power equals z to the nth power could not be solved using whole positive numbers when "n" is greater than two. This theorem was penciled into the margin of one of Fermat's books, along with the comment that there was not enough space to write down the proof. The absence of this proof has intrigued mathematicians ever since, and many have devoted themselves to solving it. Indeed, amateur mathematician Paul Wolfskehl even claimed that the theorem saved his life, when having intended to commit suicide at a specific hour the puzzle distracted him and his decision to kill himself was abandoned.

Singh began researching the subject of Fermat's theorem for a 1996 BBC television documentary in the *Horizons* series which he produced with John Lynch. Having spent many hours interviewing Wiles and gathering relevant mathematical history dating back to ancient Greece, Singh proceeded to turn his work into a more inclusive book. The result was a rare popular work on mathematics, one that *Library Journal* reviewer Gregg Sapp called a "mathematical page-turner." Sapp also compared *Fermat's Enigma* to another book, Amir Aczel's *Fermat's Last Theorem,* and found that "Singh's book has more perspective and builds to a truly engrossing climax." Likewise, Alan Clark noted in a *Lecturer* book review that "even though I knew the ending, I was captivated. This will join my (very small) collection of truly popular books on mathematics."

Other reviewers focused on the more academic merits of *Fermat's Enigma*. Richard Pinch, writing for *New Scientist,* expressed some reservations regarding Singh's presentation of mathematical theory, and noted "Singh makes a worthy effort at explaining the highly technical theory of elliptic curves. . . . But there are some decisions in the exposition that seem ill-judged." Specifically, Singh chose to use some non-standard terms in his explanations that might ultimately confuse a reader who sought additional information elsewhere. Pinch, however, concluded that "overall the presentation succeeds in conveying some of the flavour." Writing for the *New York Times Book Review,* Roger Penrose asserted that *Fermat's Enigma* is more than just an engaging story: "More important than Singh's accounts of individual mathematicians and particular mathematical events is his conveying of something of the mathematical ethos. . . . What motivates mathematicians is not the desire to solve practical problems, or even problems of science. The important drives are esthetic, coming from the internal appeal of mathematics itself." Penrose concluded, "I strongly recommend this book to anyone wishing to catch a glimpse of what is one of the most important and ill-understood, but oldest, cultural activities of humanity."

For his second book, Singh chose the subject of codes and secret languages, their impact on history, and their implications for the future. Reviewing *The Code Book: The Evolution of Secrecy from Mary, Queen of Scots, to Quantum Cryptography* for the *London Review of Books,* Brian Rotman found the work to be "a very readable and skillfully told history of cryptography." Robert Osserman of the *New York Times Book Review* commented that "The almost universal fascination with codes undoubtedly derives from the extraordinary feats of ingenuity that have gone into devising and breaking them, as well as their enormous impact on world events. Singh's book offers more than its share of both."

In the *Code Book,* Singh begins his discussion with one of the simplest codes or ciphers, known as "Caesar's Shift" because Julius Caesar was one of the first to employ it. This monoalphabetic cipher shifts a letter of the alphabet a given number of places, three in Caesar's case, and replaces the first letter with the second. By the ninth century, Arab philosopher-mathematicians al-Kindi discovered that codes such as this could be easily broken by recording the frequency of letters in a message. In English, the letter "e" occurs with greater frequency than any other letter, so it becomes the first key to deciphering an encrypted message. As Singh points out, the Caesar Shift was used by Mary, Queen of Scots, and her co-conspirators in 1586 while plotting to overthrow Elizabeth I and seize the British throne. Due at least in part to the efforts of cryptanalyst Thomas Phelippes, who cracked the code using the frequency approach, the plot failed.

The next advance in codes, a polyalphabetic cipher, was first formulated in the Renaissance and rediscovered in the sixteenth century by Blaise de Vigenere. Known popularly as the "Vigenere Cipher," this method varies the shifting factor by some prearranged method. Thus the first letter in a message might shift three letters in the alphabet, the second letter, seven, and so forth. Such codes were considered indecipherable until the nineteenth century when Prussian military officer Friedrich Kasiski and English inventor Charles Babbage hit upon a solution simultaneously.

Singh devotes a good deal of his discussion to the Enigma Code used by the Germans during World War II. This code, also considered unbreakable, was fashioned by a machine that changed the key to the code every day. The breaking of the Enigma Code, over a period of years, can be credited to the combined efforts of Polish mathematician Marian Rejewski and Englishman Alan Turing, who refined Rejewski's methods in response to a German refinement of the code.

In the last section of *The Code Book,* Singh explores modern developments in cryptography that are derived in large part from the studies of the English mathematician G. H. Hardy and his work with the theory of numbers. Hardy felt that his mathematical research was pure abstraction in the sense that it would never find a practical application. Yet, as Singh notes, Hardy's theories paved the way for public-key cryptography. First posited in 1976 by Whitfield Diffie and Martin Hellman, and later refined by mathematicians at the Massachusetts Institute of Technology and patented as the RSA—Rivest-Shamir-Adelman—algorithm, public-key cryptography has evolved into a two-hundred-million-dollar per-year business that is responsible for keeping information of all sorts secure in computer network environments. Singh argues that RSA programs produce codes that are for the first time truly unbreakable. Reviewing *The Code Book* for the *New York Times,* Richard Bernstein remarked: "Singh knows his subject and is a skillful popularizer of it. It would be hard to imagine a clearer or more fascinating presentation of cryptology and decryptology than nonspecialists will get in this book."

Singh tackles another major theory in his book *Big Bang: The Origins of the Universe.* He sets out to explain the science of the explosion which created the universe in terms that all can understand. In *Bookseller,* Singh is quoted as saying: "People use the phrase 'the Big Bang' all the time but it struck me that very few people understand what it is and why we should believe in it. At the same time I was aware that it's actually not that complicated. . . . With a little bit of effort, readers can understand one of the fundamental concepts we've developed over the past century."

BIOGRAPHICAL AND CRITICAL SOURCES:

PERIODICALS

Booklist, September 1, 1999, Gilbert Taylor, review of *The Code Book,* p. 5.

Bookseller, July 2, 2004, review of *The Big Bang,* p. 30.

Economist, August 26, 1999, review of *The Code Book: The Evolution of Secrecy from Mary, Queen of Scots, to Quantum Cryptography.*

Forbes, September 20, 1999, Susan Adams, "I've Got a Secret," p. 260.

Foreign Affairs, November-December, 1999, Eliot A. Cohen, review of *The Code Book.*

Kirkus Reviews, September 1, 1997, p. 1372.

Library Journal, October 15, 1997, p. 88; October 15, 1999, Dayne Sherman, review of *The Code Book,* p. 102.

London Review of Books, June 1, 1999, Brian Rotman, "Pretty Good Privacy," p. 15.

Maclean's, October 18, 1999, Brian Bethune, "A History of Secrecy," p. A11.

Nature, June 26, 1997, p. 868.

New Scientist, May 17, 1997, pp. 44-45.

New York Times, November 10, 1999, Richard Bernstein, "Crack a Communiqué, Shatter an Assumption."

New York Times Book Review, November 30, 1997, p. 12; November 7, 1999, Robert Osserman, "Cryptanalyze This."

Publishers Weekly, August 23, 1999, review of *The Code Book.*

School Library Journal, May 2002, Shauna Yusko, review of *The Code Book: How to Make It, Break It, Hack It, Crack It,* p. 176.

ONLINE

Simon Singh Web site, http://www.simonsingh.net (August 11, 2004).*

*　　　*　　　*

SMALLWOOD, Carol 1939-

PERSONAL: Born May 3, 1939, in Cheboygan, MI; daughter of Lloyd (a teacher) and Lucy (a teacher; maiden name, Drozdowska) Gouine; married, 1963 (divorced, 1976); children: Michael, Ann. *Education:* Eastern Michigan University, B.S. (history), 1961, M.A. (history), 1963; Western Michigan University, M.L.S., 1976.

ADDRESSES: Home—543 South Whiteville Rd., Mount Pleasant, MI 48858. *E-mail*—csmallwo@edcen. ehhs.cmich.edu.

CAREER: Teacher of English and history at schools in Flat Rock and Livonia, MI, 1961-64; Library Services and Construction Act Title-One program, library consultant, 1976-77; media director and English teacher at public schools in Pellston, MI, 1977-97. Northland Library System, assistant library director, 1977; developer of educational materials clearinghouse, 1981-83; adult education teacher for area schools, Cheboygan, MI, 1985-86; Saginaw Chippewa Tribal Library, Mount Pleasant, MI, library consultant, 1998; Central Michigan University, Mount Pleasant, instructor in CEC library classes, 1999—.

MEMBER: Humane Animal Treatment Society (founding member; officer, 1999—), Michigan Federation of Humane Societies, Cheboygan County Humane Society (founder; president and publicity chairperson, 1972-75), Friends of the University Libraries-Western Michigan University, Doris Day Animal Foundation.

AWARDS, HONORS: First prize, *Byline* magazine, for first chapter of a novel, 2004; first place in *Northern Lights* short story contest, 2004.

WRITINGS:

Free Michigan Material for Educators, Hillsdale Educational Publishers (Hillsdale, MI), 1980.

Exceptional Free Library Resource Materials, Libraries Unlimited (Littleton, CO), 1984.

Free Resource Builder for Teachers and Librarians, McFarland and Co. (Jefferson, NC), 1985, 2nd edition, 1992.

A Guide to Selected Federal Agency Programs and Publications for Librarians and Teachers, Libraries Unlimited, 1986.

Health Resources Builder, McFarland and Co. (Jefferson, NC), 1988.

Current Issues Builder, McFarland and Co. (Jefferson, NC), 1989.

An Educational Guide to the National Park System, Scarecrow Press (Metuchen, NJ), 1989.

Library Puzzles and Word Games for Grades 7-12, McFarland and Co. (Jefferson, NC), 1990.

Reference Puzzles and Word Games for Grades 7-12, McFarland and Co. (Jefferson, NC), 1991.

Helpful Hints for the School Librarian, McFarland and Co. (Jefferson, NC), 1993.

(Editor) *Michigan Authors,* 3rd edition, Hillsdale Educational Publishers, 1993.

Recycling for Librarians and Teachers, McFarland and Co. (Jefferson, NC), 1995.

An Insider's Guide to Libraries: Internet Resources and Tips, Linworth Publishing, 1997.

Free or Low-Cost Health Information, McFarland and Co. (Jefferson, NC), 1998.

(With Sharon McElmeel) *WWW Almanac: Making Curriculum Connections,* Linworth Publishing, 1999.

(Coauthor) *State Internet Sources: State-by-State Educational Sites,* McFarland and Co. (Jefferson, NC), 2005.

Columnist for *Detroit News,* 1983-85, *Entertainment News,* 1988-89, *Free Materials for Schools and Libraries,* 1996—, and newspapers, 2003—. Contributor of articles to periodicals, including *Instructor, School Library Media Activities Monthly,* and *Book Report.* Contributor of short stories, poetry, and essays to various literary magazines, including *Aurorean.*

WORK IN PROGRESS: Lily's Odyssey, a novel.

SIDELIGHTS: Carol Smallwood told *CA:* "Writing helps me think; it is a way of organizing. Writing *Michigan Authors* was very enjoyable because it allowed me contact with a great variety of writers. I am finding fiction is more difficult, much different, than nonfiction. Recent writing classes have helped some. I have been writing more poetry lately, exploring. It is something I never thought I could do and am enjoying the challenge. My aunt, Carolyn Andrews, was a talented writer, an accomplished storyteller, and a great inspiration as a child, and I am proud to have been named after her."

BIOGRAPHICAL AND CRITICAL SOURCES:

PERIODICALS

Academic Library Book Review, December, 1989, pp. 18-19.
Booklist, October 1, 1989.

*			*			*

SOBEL, Dava 1947-

PERSONAL: Born June 15, 1947, in New York, NY; daughter of Samuel H. (a physician) and Betty (a chemist; maiden name, Gruber) Sobel; married Arthur C. Klein (an author; divorced, December 14, 1995);

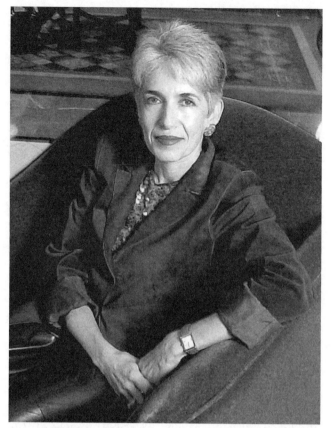

Dava Sobel

children: Zoe Rachel, Issac. *Education:* State University of New York—Binghamton, Bx.H.S. of Science, 1969. *Politics:* Democrat. *Religion:* Jewish. *Hobbies and other interests:* Ballroom dancing, amateur astronomy.

ADDRESSES: Agent—Michael Carlisle, William Morris Agency, 1325 Avenue of the Americas, New York, NY 10019-6011.

CAREER: Author. *New York Times,* New York, NY, science reporter, 1979-82; astronomy columnist for *East Hampton Independent,* East Hampton, NY, 1994—, and for the Discovery Channel Online, 1996—.

MEMBER: Planetary Society, National Association of Watch and Clock Collectors, American Association of University Women.

AWARDS, HONORS: American Psychological Foundation National Media Award, 1980; Lowell Thomas Award from Society of American Travel Writers, 1992;

gold medal, Council for the Advancement and Support of Education (CASE), 1994, for an article on longitude published in *Harvard Magazine*; *Los Angeles Times* Book Award for Science and Technology, 1999, for *Galileo's Daughter: A Historical Memoir of Science, Faith, and Love.*

WRITINGS:

(With Frank D. Drake) *Is Anyone Out There?: The Scientific Search for Extraterrestrial Intelligence,* Delacorte (New York, NY), 1992.

Longitude: The True Story of a Lone Genius Who Solved the Greatest Scientific Problem of His Time, Walker & Co. (New York, NY), 1995, new edition with William J. H. Andrewes published as *The Illustrated Longitude,* 1998.

Galileo's Daughter: A Historical Memoir of Science, Faith, and Love, Walker & Co. (New York, NY), 1999.

(Translator and annotator) Maria Celeste Galilei, *Letters to Father: Suor Maria Celeste to Galileo, 1623-1633,* Walker & Co. (New York, NY), 2001.

(Editor) *The Best American Science Writing 2004,* Ecco (New York, NY), 2004.

Contributor of articles to periodicals, including *Astronomy, Audubon, Discover, Harvard Magazine, Ladies Home Journal, Life, New York Times Magazine, New Yorker, New Woman, Omni, Redbook, Vogue,* and *Working Woman.*

WITH FORMER HUSBAND, ARTHUR C. KLEIN

Backache Relief: The Ultimate Second Opinion from Back-Pain Sufferers Nationwide Who Share Their Successful Healing Experiences, Times Books (New York, NY), 1985.

Arthritis: What Works, St. Martin's Press (New York, NY), 1989.

Arthritis: What Exercises Work, St. Martin's Press, 1993 (New York, NY), published with foreword by John Bland as *Arthritis: What Works; Breakthrough Relief for the Rest of Your Life, Even after Drugs and Surgery Have Failed,* St. Martin's Press (New York, NY), 1995.

Backache: What Exercises Work, St. Martin's Press (New York, NY), 1994.

ADAPTATIONS: Longitude was adapted for television.

WORK IN PROGRESS: A book about the solar system; a book of astronomical essays.

SIDELIGHTS: Former *New York Times* science reporter Dava Sobel has earned great critical recognition for the books *Longitude: The True Story of a Lone Genius Who Solved the Greatest Scientific Problem of His Time* and *Galileo's Daughter: A Historical Memoir of Science, Faith, and Love.* Both are highly unusual books that became international bestsellers. *Longitude* is the true story of the quest to devise a reliable navigational instrument for sailors; *Galileo's Daughter* creates a unique portrait of the famous astronomer Galileo Galilei, using letters from his cloistered daughter as its foundation. On the strength of these two books, *Entertainment Weekly* contributor Gillian Flynn praised Sobel as "a writer who has reached through the brambled, layered detritus of hundreds of years, retrieved a forgotten clock maker and a lost daughter, and gently restored these strangers to all their joyful, proud, petulant, toothachy genuineness."

Described as an "elegant history" by *New York Times* critic Christopher Lehmann-Haupt, *Longitude* is the story of an eighteenth-century clockmaker's persistence in developing a sea-worthy clock by which sailors might determine longitude, the distance east or west on the earth. Throughout history, without a tool or method for determining their positions, many sailors veered off-course. This at best delayed their deliveries of goods and frequently led to ships running aground on various hazards and sinking. In 1714, Sobel relates, England's parliament addressed the dire problem by promising a reward of 20,000 pounds (the equivalent of millions of dollars by modern standards) to anyone who could solve the problem of determining longitude. Scientists knew that every hour's time difference between a ship and its destination (or port of origin) equaled a change in longitude of fifteen degrees east or west; the solution, therefore, was to create an instrument that would withstand the erratic changes in climate and humidity aboard a ship so that sailors could determine their position by the time.

John Harrison, a self-educated clockmaker, accepted the challenge, devoting some forty-six years of his life to the building of weather-and motion-proof clocks.

His effort produced the chronometer and earned admiration and a monetary prize from King George III. Sobel relates many of the obstacles that Harrison had to overcome to create a working sea-clock, along with often amusing stories of solutions offered by others to the longitude problem, in her book, which, according to John Ellsworth, writing in the *New York Times Book Review*, "captures John Harrison's extraordinary character: brilliant, persevering and heroic in the face of adversity. He is a man you won't forget."

Longitude elicited further praise from critics, including Lehmann-Haupt, who lauded Sobel's "remarkable ability to tell a story with clarity and perfect pacing." Touched by Sobel's account of being reduced to tears upon visiting the maritime museum that houses Harrison's clocks, Lehmann-Haupt wrote: "Such is the eloquence of this gem of a book that it makes you understand exactly how she felt." Bruno Maddox expressed similar sentiments in his *Washington Post Book World* review: "*Longitude* is a simple tale, brilliantly told," Maddox wrote. "Perhaps one of the most impressive things about the book—given its subject matter—is the sheer simplicity of the whole thing. . . . She offers us no attack on the modern assumption that time is solid and objective; she wholly refrains from rubbing readers' noses in the artificiality of meaning, etc.; she offers us nothing, in short, but measured, nearly perfect prose and a magnificent story, an extraordinary book." *Longitude* spent forty weeks on the *New York Times* bestseller list and sold more than a million copies.

While researching *Longitude*, Sobel came across a letter written to the seventeenth-century astronomer Galileo—who supported Nicholas Copernicus's revolutionary theory that the earth moved around the sun instead of vice versa—from his daughter. She was surprised to know that he had a child at all; further investigation revealed that he had three illegitimate offspring. His two daughters, deemed unmarriageable due to their illegitimacy, had been placed in a convent during their teenage years. The elder of the pair, who took the name Sister Maria Celeste, was a truly remarkable woman who served as herbalist and accountant to the convent. Hundreds of letters to her father showed her great intelligence and devotion to her father, who returned her affection.

"Retelling the story of Galileo's famous battle with the Inquisition over geocentricism, [Sobel] brings it to life by concentrating on the everyday—his profes-

sional feuds, his own sincere religious beliefs and—most important—his intense relationship with his eldest daughter," noted Malcolm Jones in *Newsweek*, who deemed the book as portraying "an epic battle over our place in the cosmos." It is well known that Galileo's theories put him in opposition with the Roman Catholic Church; the Court of the Inquisition forced him to recant, but he cleverly succeeded in setting down his works for posterity by recasting them as a fictional dialogue. He is frequently portrayed as a defiant figure, "a scientific Martin Luther," in the words of *Library Journal* contributor Wilda Williams, but that image is incorrect. He was a true believer who experienced a real crisis within himself over the conflict between his work and the authority of the Church. Williams quoted Sobel as saying, "Galileo remained a good Catholic to his dying day. His scientific discoveries actually strengthened his faith."

Sobel has stated that as a Jew raised in the Bronx, she had a difficult time understanding the religious world of her story—particularly Maria Celeste's life as a member of the Poor Clares, a Franciscan order dedicated to poverty and seclusion. A rich correspondence with the mother abbess of a contemporary Poor Clares convent was so enlightening to her that she told Williams, "I could now understand why even today a young woman would enter a convent and live in poverty." Many reviewers credit *Galileo's Daughter* with providing a fascinating look into this kind of life, as well as providing a wonderful portrait of Galileo, his family, and his world. It is a "creative and compelling work" that reveals Sobel's "technical insight and originality," according to Hilary Burton in *Library Journal*. The author "has a remarkable ability to explain technical subjects without being simplistic or pedantic. There is a tremendous amount of fascinating detail in this work, and yet it reads as smoothly and compellingly as fiction."

Reading Sister Maria Celeste's letters so inspired Sobel that she translated all 124 surviving letters that the woman wrote to Galileo and published them, in a bilingual edition, as *Letters to Father: Suor Maria Celeste to Galileo, 1623-1633*. "Her letters show that, despite her cloistered and pious existance, she was exceptionally well-informed and open-minded," Jennifer Birriel commented in *Astronomy*. Sister Maria Celeste took responsibility for many of Galileo's domestic needs—mending and bleaching his shirts and collars, making cakes and candies for him—and much of their communication is about such "extremely mundane, domestic matters," Franco Mormando wrote in *America*. Yet "precisely because of their humble, domestic, utterly private nature, the letters help give true flesh and blood, an enlivening third dimension, to historical personages that more exalted, formal documentation—published treatises, papal bulls, inquisitorial reports—cannot supply." The letters also reveal Galileo's privileged place in society. Sister Maria Celeste frequently asked him for help in dealing with various problems around the convent, some of which required money and some which required favors from the authorities, and the evidence suggests that Galileo was always able and willing to assist the sisters. Sobel and her publisher donated all profits from the book to a Poor Clares convent in Roswell, New Mexico.

Sobel is also the coauthor, with her former husband Arthur C. Klein, of several books on back pain and arthritis, including 1989's *Arthritis: What Works*. Based on the authors' interviews with more than 1,000 arthritis sufferers, *Arthritis: What Works* discusses various methods of treatment that patients report have alleviated their pain, from traditional therapy offered by physicians and drugs, to less conventional treatments used by holistic healers. In addition, the authors share recipes and diet plans considered to be helpful in attacking arthritis through nutrition. A companion of sorts to *Arthritis: What Works* is *Arthritis: What Exercises Work*, in which Sobel and Klein describe and illustrate exercises that were reported by the arthritis sufferers they interviewed to relieve symptoms of arthritis. The authors issued a similar book, *Backache: What Exercises Work*, after speaking with some five hundred sufferers of back injury about activities that eased their pain and hastened their return to normal activity.

BIOGRAPHICAL AND CRITICAL SOURCES:

PERIODICALS

America, May 6, 2002, Franco Mormando, review of *Letters to Father: Suor Maria Celeste to Galileo, 1623-1633*, p. 30.

American Scientist, March, 2000, review of *Galileo's Daughter*, p. 173.

Analog: Science Fiction and Fact, September, 1993, Tom Easton, review of *Is Anyone Out There?: The Scientific Search for Extraterrestrial Intelligence*, p. 165.

Astronomy, June, 1993, Dave Bruning, review of *Is Anyone Out There?*, p. 92; December, 1995, review of *Longitude: The True Story of a Lone Genius Who Solved the Greatest Scientific Problems of His Time*, p. 103; March, 2000, review of *Galileo's Daughter*, p. 103; October, 2002, Jennifer Birriel, review of *Letters to Father*, p. 88.

Beaver: Exploring Canada's History, August-September, 1999, Thomas Sinclair, review of *Longitude*, p. 44.

Booklist, September 1, 1995, Gilbert Taylore, review of *Longitude*, p. 23; August, 1999, Gilbert Taylor, review of *Galileo's Daughter*, p. 1983; March 15, 2000, Whitney Scott, review of *Galileo's Daughter*, p. 1397; December 1, 2000, Karen Harris, review of *Galileo's Daughter*, p. 741; October 15, 2001, Gilbert Taylor, review of *Letters to Father*, p. 363.

Books and Culture, May, 2001, Virginia Stem Owens, review of *Galileo's Daughter*, p. 36.

Cross Currents, winter, 2000, John Daretta, review of *Galileo's Daughter*, p. 574.

Discover, December, 1999, Josie Glausiusz, review of *Galileo's Daughter*, p. 116.

Economist, October 19, 1996, review of *Longitude*, p. S13; November 13, 1999, "Heroes of Modern Science: Loyal Child" (review of *Galileo's Daughter*), p. 9.

Entertainment Weekly, December 11, 1998, David Hochman, review of *The Illustrated Longitude*, p. 71; November 19, 1999, Gillian Flynn, review of *Galileo's Daughter*, p. 91.

First Things, March, 2000, Elizabeth Powers, review of *Galileo's Daughter*, p. 76.

Forum for Applied Research and Public Policy, fall, 2000, Joshua A. Chamot, review of *Galileo's Daughter*, p. 107.

Geographical, November, 1996, Claire Hutchings, reivew of *Longitude*, p. 58; May, 2000, review of *The Illustrated Longitude*, p. 93.

Hindu, May 16, 2000, review of *Longitude*.

Kirkus Reviews, September 15, 2001, review of *Letters to Father*, p. 1337.

Kliatt, November, 2003, Jacqueline Edwards, review of *Galileo's Daughter* (audiobook), p. 55; May, 2004, Karen Reeds, review of *The Illustrated Longitude*, p. 42.

Library Journal, February 15, 1985, Laura Claggett, review of *Backache Relief*, p. 175; August, 1989, Frances Groen, review of *Arthritis: What Works*, p. 156; October 1, 1992, Gary D. Barber, review of *Is Anyone Out There?*, p. 113; November 15, 1993, Loraine F. Sweetland, review of *Arthritis:*

What Exercises Work, p. 94; September 15, 1995, James Olson, review of *Longitude,* p. 90; August, 1996, Carolyn Alexander, review of *Longitude* (audiobook), p. 136; February 1, 1999, Michael Rogers, review of *The Illustrated Longitude,* p. 126; October 1, 1999, Wilda Williams, "A Father of Science, A Daughter of God," p. 128, Hilary Burton, review of *Galileo's Daughter,* p. 131; October 1, 2001, Hilary Burton, review of *Letters to Father,* p. 137.

Los Angeles Times Book Review, November 22, 1992, p. 6.

Mercator's World, November, 1999, Cheri Brooks, review of *The Illustrated Longitude,* p. 54.

Natural Health, May-June, 1996, Kurt Tidmore, review of *Arthritis: What Exercises Work,* pp. 122-123.

New Statesman, August 9, 1996, Boyd Tonkin, review of *Longitude,* p. 45.

Newsweek, October 11, 1999, Malcolm Jones, "When the Earth Moved: Dava Sobel Pairs Galileo's Story with His Daughter's to Give Us Seventeenth-Century Italian Life in the Round" (review of *Galileo's Daughter*), p. 83.

New York Times, November 2, 1995, Christopher Lehmann-Haupt, review of *Longitude,* p. C 21.

New York Times Book Review, October 11, 1992, Anthony Aveni, review of *Is Anyone Out There?,* p. 18; November 26, 1995, John Ellsworth, review of *Longitude,* p. 15; October 17, 1999, p. 6.

New York Times Magazine, December 19, 1982, Josef H. Weissberg, "Short-Term Psychotherapy," p. 110.

Public Opinion Quarterly, spring, 1989, Howard Schuman, review of *Backache Relief,* p. 149.

Publishers Weekly, August 18, 1989, Molly McQuade, review of *Arthritis: What Works,* p. 60; September 7, 1992, review of *Is Anyone Out There?,* p. 89; June 27, 1994, review of *Backache: What Exercises Work,* p. 74; September 18, 1995, review of *Longitude,* p. 119; February 5, 1996, Paul Nathan, "Not in Our Stars," p. 24; July 19, 1999, review of *Galileo's Daughter,* p. 170; October 4, 1999, John F. Baker, "Dava Sobel: Matters of Science and Faith," p. 48; November 1, 1999, Daisy Maryles, "A Scientific Find," p. 24; November 29, 1999, Daisy Maryles, "A Father's Pride," p. 30; August 27, 2001, review of *Letters to Father,* p. 63; June 14, 2004, review of *The Best American Science Writing 2004,* p. 52.

Quadrant, April, 2000, Peter Slezak, review of *Galileo's Daughter,* p. 75.

School Library Journal, February, 1996, Judy McAloon, review of *Longitude,* p. 135.

Science, November 6, 1992, Ronald N. Bracewell, review of *Is Anyone Out There?,* p. 1012; October 8, 1999, review of *The Illustrated Longitude,* p. 248.

Scientific American, January, 1993, Philip Morrison, review of *Is Anyone Out There?,* p. 155.

Skeptical Inquirer, May, 2000, James C. Sullivan, review of *Galileo's Daughter,* p. 51.

Sky & Telescope, December, 1992, Frank White, review of *Is Anyone Out There?,* p. 650; July, 1996, Roger W. Sinnott, review of *Longitude,* p. 60.

Sunday Times, December 26, 1999, "Lucky Timing from the First Lady of Longitude," p. 11.

Systems Research and Behavioral Science, January, 2001, John P. van Gigch, review of *Galileo's Daughter,* p. 91.

Time, November 15, 1999, R. Z. Sheppard, "Footsteps No Longer: As Women's History Takes Root in the Canon, More Stories about the Past Take on a Female Voice," p. 108.

Washington Monthly, January-February, 1996, Gregg Easterbrook, review of *Longitude,* p. 53.

Washington Post Book World, November 26, 1995, p. 2.

World and I, April, 2000, Sara Schechner, review of *Galileo's Daughter,* p. 262.

ONLINE

Galileo's Daughter Web Site, http://www.galileos daughter.com (August 13, 2004).*

*   *   *

STEEL, Danielle (Fernande) 1947-

PERSONAL: Born August 14, 1947, in New York, NY; daughter of John and Norma (Stone) Schuelein-Steel; married Thomas Perkins, 1998; children: (first marriage) one daughter; (third marriage) two stepsons, four daughters, two sons. *Education:* Educated in France; attended Parsons School of Design, 1963, and New York University, 1963-67. *Religion:* Catholic.

ADDRESSES: Home—P.O. Box 1637, New York, NY 10156-1637. *Agent*—Janklow & Nesbit Associates, Inc., 445 Park Ave., New York, NY 10022.

Danielle Steel

CAREER: Writer. Supergirls, Ltd. (public relations firm), New York, NY, vice president of public relations, 1968-71; Grey Advertising, San Francisco, CA, copywriter, 1973-74; has worked at other positions in public relations and advertising; taught creative writing in English, 1975-76. National chair of the American Library Association. Founder of Nick Traina Foundation to benefit mental health.

AWARDS, HONORS: Order of Arts and Letters, the French government, 2002.

WRITINGS:

NOVELS

Going Home, Pocket Books (New York, NY), 1973.
Passion's Promise, Dell (New York, NY), 1977.
The Promise (based on a screenplay by Garry Michael White), Dell (New York, NY), 1978.

Now and Forever, Dell (New York, NY), 1978.
Season of Passion, Dell (New York, NY), 1979.
Summer's End, Dell (New York, NY), 1979.
The Ring, Delacorte (New York, NY), 1980.
Loving, Dell (New York, NY), 1980.
Remembrance, Delacorte (New York, NY), 1981.
Palomino, Dell (New York, NY), 1981.
To Love Again, Dell (New York, NY), 1981.
Crossings, Delacorte (New York, NY), 1982.
Once in a Lifetime, Dell (New York, NY), 1982.
A Perfect Stranger, Dell (New York, NY), 1982.
Changes, Delacorte (New York, NY), 1983.
Thurston House, Dell (New York, NY), 1983.
Full Circle, Delacorte (New York, NY), 1984.
Secrets, Delacorte (New York, NY), 1985.
Family Album, Delacorte (New York, NY), 1985.
Wanderlust, Delacorte (New York, NY), 1986.
Fine Things, Delacorte (New York, NY), 1987.
Kaleidoscope, Delacorte (New York, NY), 1987.
Zoya, Delacorte (New York, NY), 1988.
Star, Delacorte (New York, NY), 1989.
Daddy, Delacorte (New York, NY), 1989.
Message from 'Nam, Delacorte (New York, NY), 1990.
Heartbeat, Delacorte (New York, NY), 1991.
No Greater Love, Delacorte (New York, NY), 1991.
Mixed Blessings, Delacorte (New York, NY), 1992.
Jewels, Delacorte (New York, NY), 1992.
Vanished, Delacorte (New York, NY), 1993.
The Gift, Delacorte (New York, NY), 1994, Spanish-language version with Maria Jose Rodellar published as *El Regalo,* 1994.
Accident, Delacorte (New York, NY), 1994.
Wings, Delacorte (New York, NY), 1994.
Five Days in Paris, Delacorte (New York, NY), 1995.
Lightning, Delacorte (New York, NY), 1995.
Malice, Delacorte (New York, NY), 1996.
Silent Honor, Delacorte (New York, NY), 1996.
The Ranch, Delacorte (New York, NY), 1997.
Special Delivery, Delacorte (New York, NY), 1997.
The Ghost, Delacorte (New York, NY), 1997.
The Long Road Home, Delacorte (New York, NY), 1998.
The Klone and I: A High-Tech Love Story, Delacorte (New York, NY), 1998.
Mirror Image, Delacorte (New York, NY), 1998.
Now and Forever, Delacorte (New York, NY), 1998.
Bittersweet, Delacorte (New York, NY), 1999.
Granny Dan, Delacorte (New York, NY), 1999.
Irresistible Forces, Delacorte (New York, NY), 1999.
The House on Hope Street, Delacorte (New York, NY), 2000.
The Wedding, Delacorte (New York, NY), 2000.

Journey, Delacorte (New York, NY), 2000.

Leap of Faith, Delacorte (New York, NY), 2001.

Lone Eagle, Delacorte (New York, NY), 2001.

The Kiss, Delacorte (New York, NY), 2001.

The Cottage, Dell (New York, NY), 2002.

Answered Prayers, Delacorte (New York, NY), 2002.

Sunset in St. Tropez, Delacorte (New York, NY), 2002.

Dating Game, Delacorte (New York, NY), 2003.

Johnny Angel, Delacorte (New York, NY), 2003.

Safe Harbour, Delacorte (New York, NY), 2003.

Echoes, Delacorte (New York, NY), 2004.

Miracle, Delacorte (New York, NY), 2004.

Ransom, Dell (New York, NY), 2004.

Impossible, Delacorte (New York, NY), 2005.

FOR CHILDREN

Amando, Lectorum Publications, 1985.

Martha's Best Friend, Delacorte (New York, NY), 1989.

Martha's New Daddy, Delacorte (New York, NY), 1989.

Martha's New School, Delacorte (New York, NY), 1989.

Max and the Baby-Sitter, Delacorte (New York, NY), 1989.

Max's Daddy Goes to the Hospital, Delacorte (New York, NY), 1989.

Max's New Baby, Delacorte (New York, NY), 1989.

Martha's New Puppy, Delacorte (New York, NY), 1990.

Max Runs Away, Delacorte (New York, NY), 1990.

Max and Grandma and Grandpa Winky, Delacorte (New York, NY), 1991.

Martha and Hilary and the Stranger, Delacorte (New York, NY), 1991.

Freddie's Trip, Dell (New York, NY), 1992.

Freddie's First Night Away, Dell (New York, NY), 1992.

Freddie's Accident, Dell (New York, NY), 1992.

Freddie and the Doctor, Dell (New York, NY), 1992.

OTHER

Love Poems: Danielle Steel (poetry), Dell (New York, NY), 1981, abridged edition, Delacorte (New York, NY), 1984.

(Coauthor) *Having a Baby* (nonfiction), Dell (New York, NY), 1984.

His Bright Light: The Story of Nick Traina (biography/ memoir), Delacorte (New York, NY), 1998.

Contributor to *The Fabergé Case: From the Private Collection of Traina,* by John Traina. Contributor of articles and poetry to numerous periodicals, including *Good Housekeeping, McCall's, Ladies' Home Journal,* and *Cosmopolitan.* Many of Steel's titles have been translated into Spanish.

ADAPTATIONS: Numerous works have been adapted for film or television: *Now and Forever,* adapted into a movie and released by Inter Planetary Pictures, 1983; *Crossings,* made into an ABC-TV miniseries, 1986; *Kaleidoscope* and *Fine Things,* made into NBC television movies, 1990; *Changes, Daddy,* and *Palomino,* aired by NBC, 1991; *Jewels,* adapted as a four-hour miniseries, 1992; *Secrets,* 1992; *Heartbeat, Star,* and *Message from Nam,* 1993; *Once in a Lifetime, A Perfect Stranger,* and *Family Album,* 1994; *Mixed Blessings,* 1995; *Danielle Steel's "Zoya,"* made into a miniseries, 1996; and *No Greater Love, The Ring, Full Circle,* and *Remembrance,* 1996. Several of Steel's other novels, including *Wanderlust* and *Thurston House,* have also been optioned for television films and miniseries. Audio adaptations include *The Ranch,* Bantam Books Audio, 1997; *Echoes, Five Days in Paris, The Ranch, Second Chance,* and *The Gift,* all Random House Audio, 2004; *The Ghost, The Long Road Home, Malice,* and *Silent Honor,* all Random House Audio, 2005.

SIDELIGHTS: After producing a score of bestselling novels, Danielle Steel has distinguished herself as nothing less than "a publishing phenomenon," Jacqueline Briskin reported in the *Los Angeles Times Book Review.* Since the publication of her first hardcover in 1980, Steel has consistently hit both hardback and paperback bestseller lists; there are reportedly over 450 million of her books in print. Her popularity has also spilled over into television, where twenty-one film versions of her books have been produced and garnered good ratings.

Steel's fiction is peopled by women in powerful or glamorous positions; often they are forced to choose the priorities in their lives. Thus, in *Changes* a New York anchorwoman who weds a Beverly Hills surgeon must decide whether her career means more to her than her long-distance marriage does. *Jewels* tells of the struggles of an American-born noblewoman, the Duchess of Whitfield, to find peace and raise her children in pre-World War II Europe. And while reviewers seldom express admiration for the style of romantic novelists in general—*Chicago Tribune Book World* critic L. J. Davis claimed that *Changes* is written in "the sort of basilisk prose that makes it impossible to tear your eyes from the page even as your brain is slowly [turning] to stone"—some reviewers, such as a *Detroit News* writer, found that the author's "flair for spinning colorful and textured plots out of raw material . . . is fun reading. The topic [of *Changes*] is timely and socially relevant." Toronto *Globe & Mail* contributor Peggy Hill similarly concluded about 1988's *Zoya:* "Steel has the ability to give such formula writing enough strength to not collapse into an exhausted state of cliché. *Zoya* is a fine example of that achievement."

In addition to her contemporary fiction, Steel also confronts serious issues in her books. *Mixed Blessings* looks at issues of infertility in a work that a *Rapport* reviewer called "not only well written but extremely well researched." "On the whole," the reviewer concluded, "*Mixed Blessings* is definitely one of Steel's all-time best books." *Vanished* confronts the problem of kidnapped children in a story "set mainly in 1930's Manhattan," declared a *Kirkus Reviews* contributor. "The questions Steel raises about the tug-of-wars between guilt and responsibility . . . are anything but simple," stated Stuart Whitwell in *Booklist.* "The author of *Mixed Blessings* keeps her secrets well," stated a *Publishers Weekly* reviewer, "and . . . presents a strong portrait of a tormented young woman moving toward stability."

In *Accident* Steel offers a story about the stresses placed on a family after a serious car accident puts a couple's teenaged daughter in the hospital for a brain injury. Romance reenters protagonist Page Clark's life when she falls for the Norwegian divorced father of her daughter's friend—this after having learned that her husband has been having an affair with another woman. "Steel's good intentions—to show the resilience of the human spirit in the face of insurmountable odds—are obscured by her prose," stated Joyce R. Slater in the *Chicago Tribune.* "The ending is predictable but pleasant," declared a *Publishers Weekly* contributor, "bound to delight Steel's fans."

Malice is the story of Grace Adams's attempts to deal with her self-defense murder of her abusive father, while *The Gift* tells how a 1950s family slowly comes to accept the death of their youngest daughter and welcomes an unmarried expectant mother into their fold. "The narrative," stated a critic in a *Publishers Weekly* review of *The Gift,* has "well-meaning characters, uplifting sentiments and a few moments that could make a stone weep." A *Rapport* reviewer asserted that the most significant part of the story is "the affirmation of the grand design of tragedy and its transcendent message of purpose."

In 1998 Steel produced *The Klone and I: A High-Tech Love Story.* "While sticking to the typical Steel plot . . . this time around, she throws a bit of humor and weird sexual fantasy into the mix," commented Kathleen Hughes in *Booklist.* The story revolves around Stephanie, who, having been left by her husband, meets a new man, Peter, on a trip to Paris. Stephanie soon learns that Peter has cloned himself and Stephanie must decide between the two of them. Critics were largely positive in their assessment of *The Klone and I.* "Give Steel points for turning from her usual tearjerkers . . . and trying her hand at a playful romantic comedy with a twist," wrote a critic for *Kirkus Reviews.* A *Publishers Weekly* critic argued that although "the SF element is minimal (approximately one part Ray Bradbury to thirty-five parts Steel), Steel's speculative whimsy spices her romantic concoction to produce a light but charming read."

In 2000, the prolific Steel published three new novels, *House on Hope Street, The Wedding,* and *Journey.* Critics generally felt these novels gave Steel's fans exactly what they were looking for. In a *Booklist* review of *The Wedding,* for example, Patty Engelmann wrote, "All the key elements are here: a glamorous Hollywood setting along with the beautiful people and all their insecurities." Engelmann called the work "a good old-fashioned love story," claiming Steel is in "peak form." Engelmann felt similarly about *The House on Hope Street:* "Standard Steel fare and an excellent beach book, this will definitely please her readers." *Journey* received a similar reaction from critics. "Steel has her formula down pat, and she executes her story with her usual smooth pacing," concluded a critic for *Publishers Weekly.*

In *Second Chance,* Steel features a high-roller fashion editor who falls for a conservative businessman. Kathleen Hughes of *Booklist* remarked, "Steel's fans will enjoy the detailed descriptions of privileged lifestyles and the ultimate happy resolution." A *Publishers Weekly* reviewer noted that although some readers will dislike the fact that the heroine gives up her career, "others will enjoy the usual Steel frills: plenty of gorgeous outfits, fine dining and exquisite real estate."

Ransom was also released in 2004, amidst promises that it would be different from most of Steel's prior fiction. The story involves a kidnapping, and its characters include an ex-drug dealer, a widow, a shady businessman, and a police officer. In *Brandweek*, Ginger Danto suggested that the edgier flavor of the novel was a sign of the times. Danto wrote, "*Ransom* deals with crime, and apparently more violence than either writer or devoted reader are accustomed. As such, it is a deft reflection of the times, as movies and TV shore up more violence in the name of entertainment than ever before, perhaps to remain relevant alongside searing coverage of current events." In terms of the novel itself, a *Publishers Weekly* reviewer found the book disappointing: "The novel begins slowly . . . and never picks up speed, with Steel narrating as if from a distance, glossing over critical scenes and skimping on dialogue." Patty Engelmann of *Booklist* reached a similar conclusion: "This lackluster suspense novel and its plastic characters will have automatic appeal for Steel fans, but other readers may find it wanting."

In addition to her novels, children's fiction, and poetry, Steel ventured into biographical memoir in 1998 with *His Bright Light: The Story of Nick Traina*. The intensely personal memoir recounts the nineteen turbulent years of Steel's son's life—a life of manic depression, drugs, and ultimately suicide. Susan McCaffrey wrote in *Library Journal* that while Steel "is at times melodramatic and the pace is sometimes hampered by the inclusion of lengthy letters and poems, this is a compelling and surprisingly objective portrait of the devastating effects of mental illness." Steel founded the Nick Traina Foundation after her son's death to benefit mental health and other children's causes. Proceeds from *His Bright Light* went directly to the foundation.

Steel once told *CA:* "I want to give [readers] entertainment and something to think about."

BIOGRAPHICAL AND CRITICAL SOURCES:

BOOKS

Almanac of Famous People, sixth edition, Gale (Detroit, MI), 1998.

Bane, Vickie L. (with Lorenzo Benet), *The Lives of Danielle Steel: The Unauthorized Biography of America's Number One Best-Selling Author,* St. Martin's Press (New York, NY), 1994.
Bestsellers 89, Issue 1, Gale (Detroit, MI), 1989.
Bestsellers 90, Issue 4, Gale (Detroit, MI), 1991.
Contemporary Popular Writers, St. James Press (Detroit, MI), 1997.
Encyclopedia of World Biography, second edition, seventeen volumes, Gale (Detroit, MI), 1998.
Newsmakers, issue two, Gale (Detroit, MI), 1999.
Twentieth-Century Romance and Historical Writers, third edition, St. James Press (Detroit, MI), 1994.

PERIODICALS

Booklist, April 1, 1992, p. 1413; October 15, 1992, p. 380; June 1 & 15, 1993, p. 1735; October 15, 1994, pp. 372-373; April 15, 1995, p. 1453; October 15, 1995, p. 364; March 1, 1996, p. 1077; February 1, 1998, Kathleen Hughes, review of *The Long Road Home,* p. 877; April, 1998, Kathleen Hughes, review of *The Klone and I: A High-Tech Love Story,* p. 1278; October 15, 1998, Kathleen Hughes, review of *Mirror Image,* p. 371; March 1, 1999, Melanie Duncan, review of *Bittersweet,* p. 1104; February 1, 2000, Patty Engelmann, review of *The Wedding,* p. 997; March 15, 2000, Patty Engelmann, review of *The House on Hope Street,* p. 1294; August, 2000, Whitney Scott, review of *Journey,* p. 2076; January 1, 2004, Patty Engelmann, review of *Ransom,* p. 790; June 1, 2004, Kathleen Hughes, review of *Second Chance,* p. 1671.
Books, July, 1992, p. 18.
Brandweek, March 15, 2004, Ginger Danto, "A Literary Bandwagon," p. 25.
Chicago Tribune, September 26, 1993, pp. 6-7; March 27, 1994, p. 4.
Chicago Tribune Book World, August 28, 1983, L. J. Davis, review of *Changes.*
Detroit Free Press, December 1, 1989.
Detroit News, September 11, 1983, review of *Changes.*
Globe & Mail (Toronto, Ontario, Canada), July 9, 1988, Peggy Hill, review of *Zoya.*
Kirkus Reviews, October 1, 1992, p. 1212; June 1, 1993, p. 685; January 1, 1994, p. 16; April 15, 1994, p. 504; September 15, 1994, p. 1225; April 1, 1995, p. 422; October 1, 1995, pp. 1377-1378; March 1, 1996, pp. 328-329; April 1, 1998, review of *The Klone and I;* August 15, 2000, review of *Journey,* p. 1141.

Library Journal, September 1, 1993; October 15, 1993; October 15, 1994, p. 89; June 1, 1998, Kathy Ingels Helmond, review of *The Klone and I,* p. 161; December, 1998, Susan McCaffrey, review of *His Bright Light,* p. 172.

Los Angeles Times, January 6, 1988.

Los Angeles Times Book Review, April 14, 1985.

New York Times Book Review, September 11, 1983; August 19, 1984; March 3, 1985; July 9, 1995, p. 21.

People, October 3, 1994, p. 43.

Publishers Weekly, March 30, 1992, p. 88; October 26, 1992, pp. 55-56; June 7, 1993, p. 52; January 10, 1994, p. 41; May 23, 1994, p. 76; October 10, 1994, p. 60; December 12, 1994, p. 17; February 13, 1995, p. 21; May 1, 1995, p. 41; October 16, 1995, p. 44; March 25, 1996, p. 63; February 2, 1998, review of *The Long Road Home,* p. 78; April 20, 1998, review of *The Klone and I,* p. 44; June 1, 1998, review of *The Klone and I,* p. 34; October 26, 1998, review of *Mirror Image,* p. 45; March 15, 1999, review of *Bittersweet,* p. 46; May 24, 1999, review of *Granny Dan,* p. 65; February 14, 2000, review of *The Wedding,* p. 171; April 17, 2000, review of *The House on Hope Street,* p. 46; August 28, 2000, review of *Journey,* p. 50; March 5, 2001, review of *Lone Eagle,* p. 61; May 21, 2001, review of *Leap of Faith,* p. 82; January 12, 2004, review of *Ransom,* p. 36; May 31, 2004, review of *Second Chance,* p. 53.

Rapport, Volume 17, number 3, 1993, p. 23; Volume 18, number 1, 1994, p. 26; Volume 18, number 3, 1994, p. 23.

Saturday Evening Post, January, 1999, Patrick Perry, review of *His Bright Light,* p. 65.

Time, November 25, 1985.

Washington Post Book World, July 3, 1983; March 3, 1985.

ONLINE

Danielle Steel Home Page, http://www.randomhouse. com/features/steel (June 27, 2001).*

*   *   *

STEPHENSON, Neal 1959-

PERSONAL: Born October 31, 1959, in Fort Meade, MD; son of David Town (a professor) and Janet (a laboratory technician; maiden name, Jewsbury) Stephenson; married Ellen Marie Lackermann (a

Neal Stephenson

physician), June 28, 1985. *Education:* Boston University, B.A., 1981.

ADDRESSES: Agent—Liz Darhansoff, 1220 Park Ave., New York, NY 10128.

CAREER: Ames Laboratory, U.S. Department of Energy, Ames, IA, research assistant, 1978-79; Boston University, Boston, MA, teaching assistant in physics department, 1979; Corporation for a Cleaner Commonwealth (environmental group), Boston, researcher, 1980; University of Iowa, Iowa City, clerk in library, 1981-83; writer.

AWARDS, HONORS: Hugo Award for Best Novel, Mystery Writers of America, 1996, for *The Diamond Age;* Arthur C. Clarke Award, 2004, for *Quicksilver.*

WRITINGS:

NOVELS

The Big U, Vintage Trade (New York, NY), 1984.

Zodiac: The Eco-Thriller, Atlantic Monthly Press (New York, NY), 1988.

Snow Crash, Bantam (New York, NY), 1992.

The Diamond Age; or, A Young Lady's Illustrated Primer, Bantam (New York, NY), 1995.
Cryptonomicon, Avon (New York, NY), 1999.
In the Beginning . . . Was the Command Line, Perennial (New York, NY), 1999.

"BAROQUE CYCLE"; NOVELS

Quicksilver, Morrow (New York, NY), 2003.
The Confusion, Morrow (New York, NY), 2004.
The System of the World, Morrow (New York, NY), 2004.

OTHER

Contributor to the *Akron Beacon Journal.*

SIDELIGHTS: Neal Stephenson's first novel, *The Big U,* revolves around the American Megaversity, a huge, modern university, funded by a radioactive waste dump, and whose students arm themselves with machine guns. The satirical book, loaded with student pranks reminiscent of those in the 1978 film *National Lampoon's Animal House,* was deemed "a lot of fun" by Alan Cheuse in the *New York Times Book Review,* the critic noting that Stephenson's novel would appeal greatly to "alert and inquisitive students with a taste for campus comedy." Despite such positive reviews, however, *The Big U* did not find a large readership. Stephenson's second outing, *Zodiac: The Eco-Thriller,* was described by Steve Levy of *Newsweek* as "a tale of ecoactivism that won the hearts of tree huggers but didn't sell, either."

Stephenson's third novel, the widely acclaimed *Snow Crash,* proved to be the author's breakthrough book, bringing him cult status as one of the major cyberpunk novelists of his generation. According to *Entertainment Weekly* writer Chris Hashawaty, "The young and wired have turned . . . *Snow Crash* . . . into their dog-eared bible." Nadine Kolowrat, also writing in *Entertainment Weekly,* observed that 1992's *Snow Crash* "proved to be the pass-along favorite of sci-fi heads, hackers, and regular joes alike."

Snow Crash takes place partly in the Metaverse, a complex virtual-reality creation, and partly in the world that spawned it, a high-tech future dominated by corporations that are in turn opposed by renegade computer hackers. A similar setting was first made popular in William Gibson's seminal 1984 cyberpunk novel *Neuromancer* and has become the sine qua non of the genre. However, most reviewers find that Stephenson manages his own original and compelling take on what has become a cliché in the science-fiction field. John Leonard wrote in the *Nation* that no other cyberpunk writer has depicted virtual reality "so lyrically" as Stephenson, while Levy believed that, "when it comes to depicting the nerd mind-set, no one tops Stephenson." The "snow crash" of the book's title refers to a street drug/computer virus that has invaded the Metaverse, causing not only computer crashes in the virtual world but the physical collapse in the real world of those who encounter it. The central character of the novel, Hiro Protagonist—who has chosen his own name—employs information both from the Bible and ancient Summerian culture to track down the origins of snow crash. In the process he discovers a plot to take over and transform civilization. A writer for the *New York Times Book Review* noted that "Hiro's adventures . . . are brilliantly realized," and praised Stephenson as "an engaging guide to an onrushing tomorrow that is as farcical as it is horrific."

An *Entertainment Weekly* reviewer described Stephenson's follow-up to *Snow Crash, The Diamond Age; or, A Young Lady's Illustrated Primer,* as "equal parts Victorian novel, fairy tale, and sci-fi; a tantalizing peak into the twenty-first century that bogs down in its various subplots." Whereas virtual reality serves as the technological background for *Snow Crash, The Diamond Age* explores nanotechnology, the manipulation of atomic particles both to transform matter and to create submicroscopic machines. Though traversing several continents in the course of its action, the novel is set for the most part in a future Shanghai at a time when the nations of the world have been replaced by enclaves of individuals who share common cultural identities and beliefs. Computer engineer John Hackworth is hired by a rich and powerful neo-Victorian to write a primer to help educate his granddaughter. The plot of the book turns on the complications that arise when a stolen copy of the primer falls into the hands of a working-class girl who uses it for her own education.

"Building steadily to a wholly earned and intriguing climax," stated a reviewer for *Publishers Weekly, The*

Diamond Age "presents its sometimes difficult technical concepts in accessible ways." Noting that the book is a somewhat lengthy read, the reviewer nonetheless maintained that the science-fiction novel would also "appeal to readers other than habitual SF users." Kolowrat took a more critical stance, commenting that "reading about someone reading a book is about as riveting as watching an actor think." The critic also found Stephenson's use of a Victorian vocabulary in a science-fictional environment to be jarring, but granted that *The Diamond Age* "does have great riffs on a futuristic world and some mindbending settings."

Stephenson followed *The Diamond Age* with his fifth novel, the highly successful *Cryptonomicon.* The most mainstream of Stephenson's works, the 928-page *Cryptonomicon* centers on two major characters, mathematician Lawrence Waterhouse and his programmer grandson, Randy. The book moves back and forth in time between World War II, when Lawrence is employed deciphering German and Japanese military codes, and the present, when Randy is involved in the technological development of Southeast Asia. A hidden treasure in Japanese gold ties the two story lines together, as does their examination of the birth and development of information technology.

Lev Grossman, reviewing *Cryptonomicon* for *Entertainment Weekly,* cautioned: "don't write off Stephenson's novel as just another fast-paced, find-the-MacGuffin techno-thriller. It's an engrossing look at the way the flow of information shapes history—as well as a rare glimpse in the soul of a hardcore geek." Jackie Cassada, in *Library Journal,* called *Cryptonomicon* "a story of epic proportions," and concluded: "Stephenson's freewheeling prose and ironic voice lend a sense of familiarity to a story that transcends the genre and demands a wide readership among fans of techno thrillers as well as a general audience." Reviewing *Cryptonomicon* for the *New York Times Book Review,* Dwight Gardner made a general observation about Stephenson's novels: "Despite all the high-tech frippery, there's something old-fashioned about Stephenson's work. He cares as much about telling good stories as he does about farming out cool ideas. There's a strong whiff of moralism in his books, too. The bay guys in his fiction—that is, anyone who stands in a well-intentioned hacker's way—meet bad ends."

Readers of *Cryptonomicon* were also pleased with the publication of Stephenson's genre-defying and often

unwieldy historical trilogy the "Baroque Cycle," which features as a major character the ancestor of *Cryptonomicon*'s Waterhouses. The first installation of the trilogy, the almost 1,000-page *Quicksilver,* chronicles the adventures of a group of alchemists and vagabonds in the seventeenth and eighteenth century—some fictional, some not—including Daniel Waterhouse, Isaac Newton, and Samuel Pepys. A *Kirkus Reviews* critic commented on the book's "meandering, dense narrative," but called such a caveat "a trifle compared to [Stephenson's] awe-inspiring ambition and cheeky sense of humor." Grossman, writing for *Time,* noted that *Quicksilver* "will defy any category, genre, precedent or label," and praised Stephenson's ability to bring history to life: "he makes complex ideas clear, and he makes them funny, heartbreaking and thrilling."

The "Baroque Cycle" continues in the second volume, *The Confusion,* and the final installment, *The System of the World.* In the second book, Stephenson follows two parallel storylines that feature Jack Shaftoe and Eliza, characters from *Quicksilver.* A *Publishers Weekly* reviewer called *The Confusion* a "vast, splendid, and absorbing sequel," and while the reviewer noted that "one can't call anything about the Baroque Cycle 'brisk,'" the book's "richness of detail and language" received praise. A *Kirkus Reviews* critic summarized: "Packed with more derring-do than a dozen pirate films and with smarter, sparklier dialogue than a handful of Pulitzer winners, this is run-and-gun adventure fiction of the most literate kind."

BIOGRAPHICAL AND CRITICAL SOURCES:

Booklist, April 1, 1999, p. 1366.
Entertainment Weekly, January 27, 1995, p. 43; June 23, 1995, p. 60; March 15, 1996, p. 59; May 21, 1999, p. 24.
Kirkus Reviews, July 15, 2003, review of *Quicksilver,* p. 935; February 1, 2004, review of *The Confusion,* p. 107.
Library Journal, May 15, 1999, p. 130.
Los Angeles Times, September 7, 1984.
Nation, November 15, 1993, p. 580.
Newsweek, May 10, 1999, p. 90.

New York Times Book Review, September 30, 1984; December 14, 1992; March 12, 1995; May 23, 1999.

Publishers Weekly, March 16, 1992, p. 74; December 19, 1994, p. 49; March 22, 1999, p. 67; May 12, 1999, p. 24; August 25, 2003, review of *Quicksilver,* p. 39; March 29, 2004, review of *The Confusion,* p. 38.

Time, September 8, 2003, Lev Grossman, "Isaac Newton, Action Hero," p. 91.

ONLINE

Neal Stephenson Web site, http://www.nealstephenson.com (August 17, 2004).*

T

TALENT FAMILY, The
   See SEDARIS, David

* * *

TARROW, Sidney G. 1938-

PERSONAL: Born November 3, 1938, in New York, NY; son of Morris and Annette Tarrow; married Susan Fellows, 1965; children: Sarah Anne, Christopher Morris. *Education:* University of California—Berkeley, Ph.D., 1965.

ADDRESSES: *Home*—129 Burleigh Dr., Ithaca, NY 14850. *Office*—Cornell University, Department of Government, Ithaca, NY 14853. *E-mail*—sgt2@ cornell.edu.

CAREER: Currently Maxwell M. Upson Professor of Government and professor of sociology, Cornell University, Ithaca, NY.

MEMBER: American Political Science Association, American Association for the Advancement of Science, ASA, European Consortium of Political Research, European Community Studies Association.

AWARDS, HONORS: Fellowships from Guggenheim Foundation, Ford Foundation, German Marshall Fund, Fulbright Foundation, and Russell Sage Foundation.

WRITINGS:

Peasant Communism in Southern Italy, Yale University Press (New Haven, CT), 1967.

(With Fred I. Greenstein) *Political Orientations of Children; The Use of a Semi-projective Technique in Three Nations,* Sage Publications (Beverly Hills, CA), 1970.

Partisanship and Political Exchange in French and Italian Local Politics: A Contribution to the Typology of Party Systems, Sage Publications (Beverly Hills, CA), 1974.

(Editor, with Donald L. M. Blackmer) *Communism in Italy and France,* Princeton University Press (Princeton, NJ), 1975.

Between Center and Periphery: Grassroots Politicians in Italy and France, Yale University Press (New Haven, CT), 1977.

(Editor, with Peter J. Katzenstein and Luigi Graziano) *Territorial Politics in Industrial Nations,* Praeger (New York, NY), 1978.

(Editor, with Peter Lange) *Italy in Transition: Conflict and Consensus,* Cass (Ottawa, NJ), 1980.

Democracy and Disorder: Protest and Politics in Italy, 1965-1975, Oxford University Press (New York, NY), 1989.

Struggle, Politics, and Reform: Collective Action, Social Movements, and Cycles of Protest, Cornell University Press (Ithaca, NY), 1989.

(Editor, with Peter J. Katzenstein and Theodore Lowi) *Comparative Theory and Political Experience: Mario Einaudi and the Liberal Tradition,* Cornell University Press (Ithaca, NY), 1990.

Power in Movement: Social Movements, Collective Action, and Politics, Cambridge University Press (New York, NY), 1994, published as *Power in Movement: Social Movements and Contentious Politics,* Cambridge University Press, 1998.

(Coeditor, with David S. Meyer) *The Social Movement Society: Contentious Politics for a New Century,* Rowman and Littlefield (Lanham, MD), 1998.

(Coeditor, with Doug Imig) *Contentious Europeans: Protest and Politics in an Emerging Polity,* Rowman & Littlefield (Lanham, MD), 2001.

(Coauthor, with Douglas McAdam and Charles Tilly) *Dynamics of Contention,* Cambridge University Press (New York, NY), 2001.

(Coeditor, with Donnatella della Porta) *Transnational Protest and Global Activism,* Rowman & Littlefield (Lanham, MD), 2005.

SIDELIGHTS: Sidney G. Tarrow's long and illustrious career as a political science educator and scholar of social movements began in the 1960s, with the publication of his doctoral thesis *Peasant Communism in Southern Italy.* Reviewers admired the book for the thoroughness of its background, the clarity of its methodology, and the incisiveness of its analysis, no mean feats for a recent graduate. Denis Mack Smith, in the *New York Review of Books,* noted that Tarrow "shows how the structures and tactics of Communism in the peasant south of Italy depart radically from patterns familiar in the industrial north." Tarrow's book received a more polemical response in the *New Statesman,* where Jon Halliday complained of Tarrow's "insist[ence] on approaching [his] subject through the jaundiced undergrowth of bourgeois political theory." But he admired Tarrow's "astonishing clarity," adding that "this is a very important book which goes right to the heart of the absolutely basic problems of class, ideology, political education and organization facing the PCI throughout Italy."

Tarrow's next book to receive substantial notice was *Between Center and Periphery: Grassroots Politicians in Italy and France,* published in 1977. This work is based largely on long interviews with nearly 250 mayors from towns numbering less than 50,000 in four separate areas of each country, as well as on what a *Choice* reviewer called "aggregate data on the social, economic, electoral, and budgetary records of their municipalities." Tarrow's main argument here is that "grassroots politicians and the mechanisms of local national linkages they manipulate are crucial intervening variables between the economic marginality that marks much of the periphery in advanced societies and its ability to hold its own in the competition for resources at the center." According to John A. Armstrong of the University of Wisconson—Madison, in *Political Science Quarterly,* "Interview data, both coded and open-ended response form, is skillfully interwoven with aggregate data on the political

environments." By comparing data for the two countries, Tarrow was able to make generalizations for both, including the observation that "to citizens at the periphery the ideological drama at the top may seem like a fresco of baroque armies locked in futile combat above a stage in which the low comedy of political exchange is being played."

Between Center and Periphery was well received in academic and library reference journals. Armstrong wrote that "Sidney Tarrow's book is an impressive sign that behavioral science research has matured sufficiently to provide profound analyses of formally centralized systems." Armstrong's main critique of the book was that the situations Tarrow describes are so complex as to be difficult to summarize or draw generalizations from; but he noted too that "not the least of Sidney Tarrow's exceptional merits is that, while by no means timid in expressing his views, he is completely honest in presenting critical data that may suggest other conclusions." In the *Journal of Politics,* Robert H. Evans of the University of Virginia called *Between Center and Periphery* "a solid and challenging book, seven years in the works" and commented that "the book is well written with jargon' kept under reign and is enlivened by a discreet use of quotations from the interviews." Evans summed the book up as a "carefully conceived and pioneering study" in comparative politics.

Tarrow's next book was an editing collaboration with two other scholars titled *Territorial Politics in Industrial Nations.* A critic in *Choice* pointed out that it was a project in "observing center/periphery tensions" that came out of the Cornell University International Program. Tarrow introduced the book of essays in these words: "It is through the territorial units they live in that men (sic) organize their relations with the state, reconcile or fight out conflicts of interest, and attempt to adapt politically to wider social pressures." Case studies included areas of France, Poland, Israel, Australia, and Italy, and, in the United States, New York and Boston. A reviewer in *Choice* called it a "fine supplementary source containing recent information from the respective urban-industrial areas."

In 1989 Tarrow came out with the widely reviewed and acclaimed *Democracy and Disorder: Protest and Politics in Italy, 1965-1975.* This work brought in some of his earlier work on Italy, where the Europe-wide protests of the 1960s were quite severe, as well as new data and sources. According to Leonard Weinberg, who reviewed the book for the *American Political Science Review,* "Much of the book is focused on the diffusion of protest activity from one group to another—students to workers to white collar employees, and so on—as the [protest] cycle escalated and what the author refers to as the 'social movement center' expanded." Alice Kelikian noted in the *Times Literary Supplement* that Tarrow describes how "ordinary people participated increasingly in the collective action that came to characterize politics in the peninsula until 1972, when disruptiveness declined." Weinberg reported that, in Tarrow's view, this decline was due to the increasingly high costs placed on protestors by the "repressive apparatus of the state."

Weinberg's main critique of the book was that "by treating the cycle almost as a ballet of discontent that began in the mid-1960s and ended in the early 1970s, the author underestimates the extent to which mass protest has been a continuing feature of Italian politics in the postwar era." Nonetheless, Weinberg valued *Democracy and Disorder: Protest and Politics in Italy, 1965-1975* highly "if for no other reason" than that it "carefully chronicles and analyzes what may later come to be regarded as the last significant attempt to make a Marxist revolution in Western Europe."

One unusual element of Tarrow's argument, as noted by Kelikian, was to "keep the issues of student radicalism and political extremism separate," unlike the arguments of other scholars who have seen "the connection between the university ferment of the late 1960s and the tyranny of terrorism a decade later as axiomatic." "Tarrow boldly interprets the excesses of a desperate few as confirmation that the great majority of militants had been absorbed into the polity by 1975." Despite reservations on some points, Kelikian called *Democracy and Disorder* "an important and challenging book."

In 1989 Tarrow also published *Struggle, Politics, and Reform: Collective Action, Social Movements, and Cycles of Protest,* a book that broadens the idea of cycles of protest referred to in *Democracy and Disorder* as well as elsewhere in Tarrow's work. Here the author expands his view to encompass a theory about the history of social movements in general. In *Choice,* Pamela Oliver called the book a "'must read' . . . [for] everyone who studies social movements, reform,

or politics" and for graduates and undergraduates studying political sociology or social movements. She noted that the book "*starts* from the basics, so a novice can read it," but contains plenty of up-to-date material.

Tarrow's magnum opus is *Power in Movement: Social Movements, Collective Action, and Politics,* published first in 1994 and since revised and reissued. The book was greeted in the political science community as a work of great depth and penetration, a summation, in a sense, of Tarrow's scholarly work to date. Its scope is by far the broadest Tarrow has taken, as it covers two hundred years of selected social and political history, mostly in Europe and the United States. In the words of Robert D. Benford in the *American Journal of Sociology, Power in Movement* "develop[s] a general theory of collective action that accounts for the rise and fall of movements, the powers they derive and exercise, and their cultural and structural impacts."

Jeffrey N. Wasserstrom, appraising *Power in Movement* in the *American Historical Review,* wrote that "Tarrow highlights the long-term impact that social movements can have on both societies and individual participants. He succeeds in navigating a safe course between the Scylla of romanticization and the Charybdis of cynicism, suggesting sensibly that 'the most far-reaching impacts of cycles of protest' are often 'found in slow and incremental changes in political culture,' . . . rather than in dramatic transformations such as revolutions." Wasserstrom continued, "One pattern [Tarrow] stresses is the shift between the early modern and modern periods from 'segmentary' repertoires of contention to 'modular' ones." The first are characterized by "clear links between grievances and tactics," among other things. The "modular" form is marked by "groups with different social bases and ideologies using similar tactics (petition drives, barricade construction, demonstration) to pursue their goals." The growth of media, especially the television and computer media which link the globe, have sped this homogenization of tactics.

Although Wasserstrom complained about some of Tarrow's generalizations, especially in areas like China, with which Tarrow is not so familiar, the reviewer did deem the book "impressive," "noteworthy," and one that "provides enough in the way of insights and information to deserve a place of honor on many bookshelves."

BIOGRAPHICAL AND CRITICAL SOURCES:

BOOKS

Tarrow, Sidney G., Peter J. Katzenstein, and Luigi Graziano, editors, *Territorial Politics in Industrial Nations,* Praeger (New York, NY), 1978.

PERIODICALS

American Historical Review, April, 1995, pp. 472-474.
American Journal of Sociology, July, 1995, pp. 227-229.
American Political Science Review, December, 1990, pp. 1425-1426.
Choice, 1967, p. 267; October, 1977, p. 1127; October, 1978, p. 1129; June, 1990, p. 1748.
Contemporary Sociology, January, 1991, p. 40.
Journal of Politics, August, 1978, pp. 826-828.
New Statesman, February 16, 1968, pp. 211-212.
New York Review of Books, May 8, 1969, p. 31.
Political Science Quarterly, winter, 1977-78, pp. 753-755.
Times Literary Supplement, November 10, 1989, p. 1234.

*   *   *

TENNER, Edward 1944-

PERSONAL: Born August 1, 1944, in Chicago, IL; son of Irving (a professor) and Evelyn (a social worker; maiden name, Talmadge) Tenner. *Education:* Princeton University, B.A. (history), 1965; University of Chicago, A.M., 1967, Ph.D., 1972. *Hobbies and other interests:* Swimming, walking, bird watching, traveling.

ADDRESSES: Agent—c/o Alfred A. Knopf, Inc., 201 East 50th St., New York, NY 10022-7703. *E-mail*—tenner@clarity.princeton.edu.

CAREER: Senior research associate, Jerome and Dorothy Lemelson Center for the Study of Invention and Innovation, National Museum of American History. Editor for publications at the Institute for Advanced Study, Rutgers University, and Princeton University, 1975-91; Council of the Humanities, visiting lecturer, 1990; independent writer, editor, and speaker, 1991—; Institute for Advanced Study, visiting scholar, beginning 1991; visiting researcher at Princeton University's department of geological and geophysical sciences, and researcher for the university's English department. Has also served as a consultant for the Exxon Education Foundation Advisory Board.

MEMBER: Lemelson Center, National Museum of American History (Smithsonian Institution), Society for the History of Technology, History of Science Society, Society for Social Study of Science, American Historical Association.

AWARDS, HONORS: Junior fellow, Harvard Society of Fellows; Wadsworth Prize, *Harvard Magazine;* Guggenheim Memorial fellowship, 1991; Woodrow Wilson Center for Scholars fellow, 1995-96.

WRITINGS:

Tech Speak; or, How to Talk High Tech: An Advanced Post-Vernacular Discourse Modulation Protocol (humor), Crown (London, England), 1986.
Why Things Bite Back: Technology and the Revenge of Unintended Consequences (history of technology), Knopf (New York, NY), 1996.
Our Own Devices: The Past and Future of Body Technology, Knopf (New York, NY), 2003.

Contributor to periodicals, including *Harvard Magazine, Newsday, Princeton Alumni Weekly, U.S. News & World Report, Technology Review, Raritan Quarterly Review, American Heritage of Invention and Technology, Designer/Builder,* and *Wilson Quarterly.* Editorial board member, *Raritan Quarterly Review;* member of advisory board, *Knowledge, Technology and Policy;* contributing editor, *Wilson Quarterly* and *Harvard Magazine. Why Things Bite Back* has been translated into five languages.

WORK IN PROGRESS: Histories of the handshake and the top hat.

SIDELIGHTS: Edward Tenner, wrote Jackson Lears in a *New Republic* article, is "an American original, a historian of technology with an unparalleled fund of knowledge about ordinary things—from baby bottles to Barcaloungers—and how they work (or do not work) in everyday life." In his books *Why Things Bite Back: Technology and the Revenge of Unintended Consequences* and *Our Own Devices: The Past and Future of Body Technology,* Tenner explores the unintended consequences of technological advances. "Few historians have a better grasp of the ironies of technological progress," continued Learns, "or of the capacity of the material world to resist human manipulation, than Tenner."

Why Things Bites Back is a revealing look at the down side of scientific advancements that were meant to improve people's lives. The many examples Tenner gives of technology gone awry range from the obvious, such as the loss of jobs from the computer revolution, to the less so, such as how changes in agriculture may have led to more people needing to wear eyeglasses, how the development of chemicals used to break up oil spills actually results in killing more aquatic life, and how pesticides used to fight fire ants have caused their populations to explode by killing off other insect species unintentionally. As Edward Goldsmith described the book in an *Ecologist* review, "Its thesis is that our technological efforts to manage the world of living things are not working out too well. At first, they may seem magically successful, but then comes what Tenner calls their 'revenge effect' which at best transforms acute problems into chronic ones, at worst gives rise to all sorts of new problems, often more serious than whatever problem was targeted in the first place."

On rare occasions, admits Tenner, this revenge effect can have good results, such as when the *Titanic* disaster led to the creation of the International Ice Patrol. But people need to be more aware of the downside of science, the author insists, because trusting in it too much can have serious repercussions. "The growth of engineering as a profession has made a new type of error possible: overconfidence in the safety of a new design," writes Tenner. But *Why Things Bite Back* is, in the end, optimistic, according to Phillip Johnson in *Amicus Journal,* who noted that "Tenner believes that technological benefits do, on balance, outweigh technological burdens. Indeed, he is at bottom an optimist about progress. But he is saying that despite quantifiable improvements in health and safety, the anxiety and stress caused by technology's side effects are well-founded, and inescapable."

Reviewers of *Why Things Bite Back* found much of interest within its pages. "Whether you're a Luddite, a technophile, or a curious observer, this wide-ranging book, written in a literate and lucid style, will have you rethinking the conventional optimism that surrounds technological changes," asserted Martin H. Levinson in *Etc.: A Review of General Semantics.* However, *New Statesman* reviewer David Papineau wondered why Tenner "mentions global warming only in passing. . . . And he says nothing about overpopulation, which is surely the paramount example of things getting worse because they have got better." Nevertheless, other reviewers felt Tenner discusses sufficient examples to make his point. "Tenner covers an impressive range of 'revenge effects,'" wrote John Adams in *Scientific American,* "and shows convincingly that unintended and undesired consequences are the norm whenever new technologies are introduced."

Tenner's next book, *Our Own Devices,* though not as much an indictment on technology as his previous work, readdresses the effects of technology on people's lives. Specifically, he focuses on how science has changed human's bodies and physical behavior. "The new book might have been called 'Why Things Bite Back II: The Return of the Professor,'" according to David Pogue in the *New York Times Book Review.* "Once again, a recurring theme is how each new development affects us in unforeseen ways, and once again, Tenner proves himself to be a walking database of lively trivia, statistics and historical anecdotes." Some examples of unforeseen side effects include how chairs have had a negative impact on the human spine, how rubber baby bottle nipples have led to poorer nutrition for infants, and how the keyboard has had a negative impact on personal communications, music, literature, and the arts, while also leading to the demise of the art of handwriting. While Pogue was somewhat disappointed that Tenner did not extrapolate further as to how today's technologies might affect people tomorrow, the reviewer concluded that *Our Own Devices* "makes illuminating reading." A *Publishers Weekly* critic added that "Tenner's erudite yet approachable style and his way with telling details keep his potentially obscure subject from becoming dry and boring."

Tenner once told *CA:* "When I was six or seven, I wrote my first real essay, lamenting the decline of the wide, splashy ties in my father's closet and calling for their revival. Writing was what I always wanted to do for a living. It took me decades to become a real writer, but the detour was also the scenic route: it gave me the materials, the ideas, the techniques and the networks that made my new career possible.

"In humanities graduate school, I prepared to fill a projected college teacher shortage that soon proved nonexistent—a vivid early lesson in the value of expert predictions. When I changed from teaching history to acquiring and editing science books, I discovered what I really enjoyed: not refining a single specialty but reading into many different ones and connecting their ideas and findings with my own. Like other scientific editors I had to find men and women whose knowledge, taste, and good will could guide me. Their friendship and advice helped sustain me when I went independent.

"Understanding the patterns of the present in a historical way is a challenge. When I wrote *Why Things Bite Back: Technology and the Revenge of Unintended Consequences* I started with the question of why technology so often seems to be self-defeating despite the many gains it has brought. To reach my answer— that it tends to convert catastrophic problems into chronic ones—I monitored (and still follow) dozens of publications from scientific and medical journals to daily newspapers and commercial ephemera. I retained material from them not only on my immediate subjects but on dozens of others that might eventually become essays or books on their own. Then and now, I try to combine dense documentation with a personal outlook and distinctive style. One of my editors called the result the 'investigative essay'; I like the phrase.

"I've been looking at the history of headgear, footwear, seating, lighting, and other everyday objects—even bowling balls—to better understand how technology, values, and design work together, and sometimes against each other. And I'm still wondering about neckties."

BIOGRAPHICAL AND CRITICAL SOURCES:

BOOKS

Tenner, Edward, *Why Things Bite Back: Technology and the Revenge of Unintended Consequences,* Knopf (New York, NY), 1996.

PERIODICALS

Amicus Journal, winter, 1997, Phillip Johnson, review of *Why Things Bite Back: Technology and the Revenge of Unintended Consequences,* p. 43.

Booklist, April 15, 1996, Gilbert Taylor, review of *Why Things Bite Back,* p. 1400; June 1, 2003, Vanessa Bush, review of *Our Own Devices: The Past and Future of Body Technology,* p. 1720.

Computer Shopper, December, 1996, Chris O'Malley, review of *Why Things Bite Back,* p. 498.

Development & Change, June, 2000, Robbie Robertson, review of *Why Things Bite Back.*

Ecologist, September-October, 1998, Edward Goldsmith, review of *Why Things Bite Back,* p. 319.

Economist, July 20, 1996, review of *Why Things Bite Back,* p. S11.

Electronic News, March 10, 1997, Grace I. Zisk, "Books in Review."

Etc.: A Review of General Semantics, spring, 1997, Martin H. Levinson, review of *Why Things Bite Back,* p. 111.

Foreign Affairs, March-April, 1997, Eliot A. Cohen, review of *Why Things Bite Back,* p. 179.

Futurist, July-August, 1997, Andy Hines, review of *Why Things Bite Back,* p. 53; November-December, 2003, review of *Our Own Devices,* p. 59.

Kirkus Reviews, April 15, 2003, review of *Our Own Devices,* p. 599.

Library Journal, May 15, 1996, Gregg Sapp, "Book Reviews: Science & Technology," p. 82; June 15, 2003, Wade M. Lee, review of *Our Own Devices,* p. 97.

Magill Book Review, Philip McDermott, review of *Why Things Bite Back.*

New Republic, April 26, 2004, Jackson Lears, "The Resurrection of the Body: Medicine and the Pursuit of Happiness in America."

New Statesman, June 21, 1996, David Papineau, review of *Why Things Bite Back,* p. 48.

New York Times Book Review, August 18, 1996, Dick Teresi, "Not with a Whimper but a Bang"; July 6, 2003, David Pogue, "Smothered by Invention."

People Weekly, October 13, 1986, "Edward Tenner's Post-Vernacular Discourse Modulation Protocol Teaches You to Talk High Tech," p. 134; May 20, 1996, Mark Bautz, review of *Why Things Bite Back,* p. 32.

Print, January-February, 2004, Steven Heller, "Edward Tenner, Philosopher of Everyday Things."

Publishers Weekly, April 15, 1996, review of *Why Things Bite Back,* p. 57; May 19, 2003, review of *Our Own Devices,* p. 65.

School Library Journal, November, 2003, Paul Brink, review of *Our Own Devices,* p. 174.

Science, August 23, 1996, Langdon Winner, review of *Why Things Bite Back,* p. 1052.

Science News, July 12, 2003, review of *Our Own Devices,* p. 31.

Scientific American, October, 1996, John Adams, "Mistakes Were Made."

Social Studies, January-February, 1997, Ronald H. Pahl, review of *Why Things Bite Back,* p. 42.

Time, May 20, 1996, Julian Dibbell, "Everything that Could Go Wrong," p. 56.

Washington Post Book World, June 22, 2003, Jonathan Yardley, "Tales of Machines and Men and How They Interact to Their Mutual Benefit," p. 2.

Whole Earth, summer, 1997, J. Baldwin, review of *Why Things Bite Back,* p. 58.

Wilson Quarterly, summer, 1996, Jackson Lears, review of *Why Things Bite Back,* p. 86.

ONLINE

Edward Tenner Home Page, http://www.edwardtenner. com (May 18, 2004).

Princeton University Web site, http://www.princeton. edu/ (May 18, 2004), Jennifer Greenstein Altmann, "Unique Approach Opens Up Realm of Research."*

*   *   *

TROY, Nancy J. 1952-

PERSONAL: Born December 27, 1952, in New York, NY; daughter of William B. (a business executive) and Joanne (Joslin) Troy; married Wim de Wit. *Education:* Wesleyan University, B.A. (magna cum laude), 1974; Yale University, M.A., 1976, Ph.D., 1979.

ADDRESSES: Office—Department of Art History, University of Southern California, University Park Campus, Los Angeles, CA 90089. *E-mail*—ntroy@usc. edu.

CAREER: Waddington Galleries, London, England, gallery assistant, 1973; Johns Hopkins University, Baltimore, MD, assistant professor of history of art, 1979-83; Northwestern University, Evanston, IL, assistant professor, 1983-85, associate professor, 1985-92, professor of art history, 1992-93, department chair, 1990-92, AT&T research fellow, 1992-93; University of Southern California, Los Angeles, visiting professor, 1994-95, professor of art history, 1995—, department chair, 1997—. Solomon R. Guggenheim Museum, curatorial coordinator and special consultant, summers, 1972-74; National Gallery of Art, assistant to curator of French paintings, summer, 1975, member of board of advisors for Center for Advanced Study in Visual Arts, 1999-2002; Baltimore Museum of Art, member of committee on collections and fine arts accessions committee, both 1979-82. Yale University, research assistant, 1975, guest curator at Art Gallery, 1979; University of California—Los Angeles, visiting professor, 1994; Wesleyan University, member of board of trustees, 1994-97; guest lecturer at other institutions, including University of Brighton, University of London, University of Toronto, Mount Holyoke College, Tulane University, McGill University, Vassar College, and Royal College of Art, London, England. Institute for Advanced Study, fellow at School of Historical Studies, 1987; Getty Center for the History of Art and the Humanities, senior scholar, 1989-90, scholar in residence, 1993-96. Maryland Council on the Arts, member, 1981-82; National Committee for the History of Art, member of board of directors, 1998—. Art examiner and reviewer for colleges, universities, and grant programs; symposium chair; consultant to Art Institute of Chicago and Walter Art Center.

MEMBER: College Art Association of America (member of board of directors, 1992-97), Society of Architectural Historians.

AWARDS, HONORS: Kress Foundation travel grants, 1976, 1977; Fulbright-Hays fellow in the Netherlands, 1977-78, 1978; American Council of Learned Societies, fellowship, 1981, grants, 1991, 1998-99; fellow, National Endowment for the Humanities, 1982-83; grants from Graham Foundation for Advanced Studies in the Fine Arts, 1982, 1989; Lilly Endowment fellow, 1984-85; American Philosophical Society grant, 1986; grant, Zumberge Faculty Research and Innovation Fund, 1998-99; Guggenheim fellow, 1998-99; Raubenheimer Award for Excellence in Teaching,

Research, and Service, University of Southern California, 2001.

WRITINGS:

Mondrian and Neo-Plasticism in America (exhibition catalogue), Art Gallery, Yale University (New Haven, CT), 1979.
The De Stilj Environment, MIT Press (Cambridge, MA), 1983.
Modernism and the Decorative Arts in France: Art Nouveau to Le Corbusier, Yale University Press (New Haven, CT), 1991.
(Editor and author of introduction, with Eve Blau) *Architecture and Cubism,* MIT Press (Cambridge, MA), 1997.
Couture Culture: A Study in Modern Art and Fashion, MIT Press (Cambridge, MA), 2002.

Contributor to books, including *The Hudson River School: Nineteenth-Century American Landscapes in the Wadsworth Atheneum,* edited by Theodore Stebbins, Wadsworth Atheneum, 1976; *De Stilj, 1917-1931: Visions of Utopia,* edited by Mildred Friedman, Abbeville Press, 1982; and *The Historical Image: Essays on Art and Culture in France, 1750-1950,* Yale University Press (New Haven, CT), 1992. Coeditor of the series "Histories, Cultures, Contexts," Reaktion Book (London, England). Contributor to art and museum journals, including *Archithese, Arts, Studies in Art History, Design Book Review,* and *Journal of*

the Society of Architectural Historians. *Design Issues,* contributing editor, 1984-88, member of editorial board, 1993-97; *Art Bulletin,* member of editorial board, 1993-99, editor in chief, 1994-97; member of editorial board, *Grey Room,* 1998—.

WORK IN PROGRESS: The Visual Culture of Modernism and Modernity.

BIOGRAPHICAL AND CRITICAL SOURCES:

PERIODICALS

Architectural Review, April, 1998, Timothy Brittain-Catlin, review of *Architecture and Cubism,* p. 97.
Burlington, January, 1992, review of *Modernism and the Decorative Arts in France: Art Nouveau to Le Corbusier,* p. 42.
Chicago Tribune, September 15, 1991, section 10, p. 15.
Design Book Review, winter, 1992, review of *Modernism and the Decorative Arts in France,* p. 61.
Interior Design, September, 1998, Stanley Abercrombie, review of *Architecture and Cubism,* p. 171.
Journal of Modern History, December, 1993, review of *Modernism and the Decorative Arts in France,* p. 866.
Library Journal, November 1, 2002, Savannah Schroll, review of *Couture Culture: A Study in Modern Art and Fashion,* p. 88.*

V

VARLEY, John (Herbert) 1947-
(Herb Boehm)

PERSONAL: Born in 1947, in Austin, TX; son of John Edward (an oil worker) and Joan (Boehm) Varley; married Anet Mconel (a consumer advocate), October 10, 1970; children: Maurice, Roger, Stefan. *Education:* Attended Michigan State University, 1966. *Politics:* "Rational anarchist." *Religion:* "Lapsed Lutheran."

ADDRESSES: Home—2030 West 28th St., Eugene, OR 97405. *Agent*—Kirby McCauley, 432 Park Ave. S., Suite 1509, New York, NY 10016.

CAREER: Writer, 1973—.

MEMBER: Science Fiction Writers of America.

AWARDS, HONORS: Locus Award, 1976, special award for placing four novelettes in top ten, 1979, for novel *Titan,* 1980, for best single-author collection *The Barbie Murders* and a Hamilton Memorial Award for *Titan,* 1981, for best novella *Blue Champagne* and for best short story "The Pusher," and 1984, for novella *Press ENTER;* Jupiter Award, 1977, for novella *In the Hall of the Martian Kings;* Nebula Award nomination, Science Fiction Writers of America, 1975, for best novelette *Retrograde Summer,* 1977, for short story "Air Raid," 1979, for best novelette *Options,* 1979, for best novel *Titan,* 1980, for best novelette *Beatnik Bayou,* 1981, for best story "The Pusher"; Nebula Award, 1978, for story "The Persistence of

John Varley

Vision," and 1985, for *Press ENTER;* Prix Apollo (France), 1978, for *The Persistence of Vision;* Hugo Award nomination, World Science Fiction Convention, 1977, for novelette *The Phantom of Kansas* and *Gotta Sing, Gotta Dance,* 1978, for novella *In the Hall of the Martian Kings* and for short story "Air Raid," 1979, for novelette *The Barbie Murders,* 1980, for novelette *Options* and for novel *Titan,* 1981, for novelette *Beatnik Bayou* and for novel *Wizard,* 1982, for novella *Blue Champagne,* 1984, for novel *Millennium,* and 1993, for novel *Steel Beach;* Hugo Award, 1979, for novella *The Persistence of Vision,* 1982, for short story "The Pusher," and 1985, for *Press ENTER;* American Book Award nomination, 1980, for *The Persistence of Vision; Science Fiction Chronicle* award, 1982, for short story "The Pusher"; Genie Award (Canada) nomination, 1990, for best adapted screenplay; SF Con Hamacon Award (Japan), 1992, for *Tango Charlie and Foxtrot Romeo.*

WRITINGS:

"EIGHT WORLDS" SERIES; SCIENCE FICTION

The Ophiuchi Hotline, Dial (New York, NY), 1977.
The Persistence of Vision (stories), Dial (New York, NY), 1978, bound with *Nanoware Time* by Ian Watson, Tor Books (New York, NY), 1991, published as *In the Hall of the Martian Kings,* Sidgwick & Jackson (London, England), 1978.
Blue Champagne (stories), illustrated by Todd Cameron, Dark Harvest (Niles, IL), 1986.
Steel Beach, Putnam (New York, NY), 1992.
The Golden Globe, Ace Books (New York, NY), 1998.

"GAEA" TRILOGY; SCIENCE FICTION

Titan, illustrated by Freff, Berkley (New York, NY), 1979.
Wizard, Berkley (New York, NY), 1980.
Demon, Berkley (New York, NY), 1984.

OTHER

The Barbie Murders and Other Stories, Berkley (New York, NY), 1980, published as *Picnic on Nearside,* 1984.
Millennium (screenplay; based on "Air Raid"), Berkley (New York, NY), 1983.
Tango Charlie and Foxtrot Romeo (bound with *The Star Pit,* by Samuel Delany), Berkley (New York, NY), 1984.
Press ENTER (science fiction chapbook; bound with *Hawksbill Station,* by Robert Silverberg; originally published in *Isaac Asimov's Science Fiction Magazine*), illustrated by Bob Eggleton, Tor Books (New York, NY), 1990.

(Editor, with Ricia Mainhardt, and contributor) *Superheroes,* Ace Books (New York, NY), 1995.
Red Thunder (science fiction), Ace Books (New York, NY), 2003.
The John Varley Reader: Thirty Years of Short Fiction, Ace Books (New York, NY), 2004.

Also author of screenplays *Galaxy,* 1978, *The Phantom of Kansas* and *Have Spacesuit, Will Travel,* based on the Robert A. Heinlein novel. Contributor to anthologies, including *Orbit 18,* edited by Damon Knight, 1976; *Best Science Fiction of the Year Number 5,* edited by Terry Carr, Ballantine, 1976; *Best Science Fiction of the Year Number 6,* edited by Terry Carr, 1977; *The World's Best SF,* edited by Donald Wollheim, 1977; *The 1978 Annual World's Best SF,* edited by Donald Wollheim, 1978; *Best Science Fiction of the Year Number 7,* edited by Terry Carr, 1978; *Universe 9,* 1979; *The Best Science Fiction of the Year 9,* 1980; *Nebula Winners 14,* 1980; *The Best Science Fiction of the Year 10,* 1981; *The Best Science Fiction of the Year 11,* 1982; *The Road to Science Fiction 4: From Here to Forever,* 1982; *Nebula Award Stories 17,* 1983; *The Best from Universe,* 1984; *Terry Carr's Best Science Fiction of the Year 14,* 1984; *Nebula Awards 20,* 1985; *Great Science Fiction of the Twentieth Century,* 1987; *Terry Carr's Best Science Fiction and Fantasy of the Year 16,* 1987; *The Norton Book of Science Fiction,* 1993; *Simulations: Fifteen Tales of Virtual Reality,* 1993; *Strange Dreams,* 1993; *Nebula Award-winning Novellas,* 1994; *Reel Future,* 1994; *Tales in Space,* 1995; *Visions of Wonder,* 1996; *Timegates,* 1997; *Future on Ice,* 1998; *Not the Only Planet: Science Fiction Travel Stories,* 1998; *The Reel Stuff,* 1998; *Bangs and Whimpers: Stories about the End of the World,* 1999; *The Good New Stuff,* 1999; *Isaac Asimov's Solar System,* 1999; and *Explorers: SF Adventures to Far Horizons,* 2000. Author of introduction, *When Worlds Collide,* by Philip Wylie and Edwin Balmr, 2002. Contributor to science fiction magazines, including *Magazine of Fantasy and Science Fiction, Galaxy, Amazing Stories, Vertex,* and, under pseudonym Herb Boehm, to *Isaac Asimov's Science Fiction Magazine.* Varley's manuscript collection is maintained at Temple University, Philadelphia, PA.

SIDELIGHTS: John Varley is known especially for his inventive short stories and his three novels set on the living planet of Gaea, including *Titan, Wizard,* and *Demon.* He has often been compared to the early Robert A. Heinlein, whose science fiction adventures resemble Varley's own. The prolific inventiveness of Varley's stories has also been praised. "The man," as Algis Budrys once commented in the *Magazine of Fantasy and Science Fiction,* "has prodigies of imagination in him."

After dropping out of college in the middle 1960s, Varley traveled around the country for several years before settling in San Francisco, where he met and married his wife. When the couple's financial situation was particularly grim in the early 1970s, Varley looked around for ways to earn extra money. Because he had read science fiction for many years, Varley considered putting his imagination to work as a writer. He followed the guidance of Robert A. Heinlein, who once advised aspiring writers to begin a story, finish it, send it to a publisher, and keep on sending it out until it was finally accepted. The method worked for Varley. Within a year he was selling his work to the major science fiction magazines. These early stories treated such subjects as feminism, cloning, sexuality, and memory transfer. "Varley's rise to prominence," J. D. Brown commented in the *Dictionary of Literary Biography,* "was due in part to his mastery of the demanding short-story form." Particularly popular with science fiction fans, Varley's early stories won several awards as well, including the Jupiter Award and nominations for the Nebula and Hugo Awards. Varley's solid, workmanlike prose and his exuberant inventiveness were especially noted by the critics. Budrys, for one, claimed that Varley is best at "the depiction of exotic biologies. Since he also does a number of other things well, and few things outright clumsily, the total effect is first class."

Many of the authors early fans looked forward expectantly to his first novel, *The Ophiuchi Hotline,* published in 1977. Based in part on ideas previously explored in his short stories, the novel is set in a time when Earth has been invaded by aliens and humankind has been displaced to Mars and various satellites. A strong ecological message is apparent in the story, as the aliens save intelligent cetacean species from the humans and abolish our technology. However, the humans are not friendless; a mysterious alien source supplies the *homo sapiens* species with aid so that they will not become extinct. An "overcrowded but highly satisfying" tale, according to a *New York Times Book Review* critic, the story concerns a woman who has been condemned by a future government for conducting forbidden genetic experiments. To escape

prosecution, she clones herself several times throughout the course of the novel, changing her name and personality each time. Brown maintained that *The Ophiuchi Hotline* is "one of the finest science-fiction novels of the decade."

With the "Gaea" trilogy, Varley found bestseller status in a unique concept involving a living creature as large as a planet and shaped like a giant wheel called Gaea. Gaea orbits Saturn, and within her body live a host of creatures, including human beings. In god-like fashion, she is able to take on the shape of any creature she pleases and secretly join the population that lives within her. When Cirocco Jones and her spaceship crew become trapped on the planet in the first installment, *Titan,* they must make their way to Gaea's head in a symbolic and dangerous journey. In depicting this quest Varley combines, Brown explained, "the trappings of science fiction with those of a swashbuckling fantasy." Brown found *Titan* to be "a feminist space epic, readable, wildly inventive, complex in plot, [and] consistent in characterization." Budrys said he "liked it a great deal," and added that it is "endlessly inventive, full of the particularly attractive furnishings that Varley brings to SF."

Gaea appears again in *Wizard,* in which Cirocco and several other characters seek to free themselves from Gaea's overwhelming control. Their revolt fails, however, and Cirocco, in biblical fashion, is made into the devil of the planet. Displaying his imaginative skills, Varley includes such inventive tidbits as radio-transmitting plants, characters who speak only in song, and giant blimps who are living creatures. The author also reveals that the natives of Gaea, called Titanides, have multiple sexual abilities and can both conceive and carry a child. In fact, there are twenty-nine possible mating combinations between the dual-sexed creatures. Comparing *Wizard* to *Titan, Fantasy Review* contributor Michael E. Stamm called the novel "equally or more inventive and . . . an extraordinary feat of storytelling." *Demon* completes the story of Cirocco and tells of the final battle between Gaea and her inhabitants. "If you liked *Titan* and *Wizard,*" Budrys commented, "you'll like *Demon.* It has . . . boundless invention of landscapes and characters worthy of pre-War Disney."

Varley spent much of the 1980s writing movie screenplays in Hollywood, an occupation that, while profitable, proved very frustrating for the author and resulted in only one film, *Millennium,* that was actually produced. In *Millennium* Varley adapts the standard science fiction concept of time travel in his own way. The novel is self-consciously in the time-travel tradition: chapter titles are taken from old stories of the type, while Varley makes many references to the usual paradoxes found in such fiction. The story concerns a group of time-travelers who rescue passengers from doomed airliners. The rescued passengers are then given a chance at a new life in a far-future world. One such rescue is marred by the loss of an instrument. If the anomalous instrument is found by air crash investigators, it can mean a catastrophic disruption of the flow of time.

Several critics found *Millennium*'s ending to be disappointing, but judged the rest of the novel to be exceptional. "Time-travel narratives," Gerald Jonas wrote in the *New York Times Book Review,* "especially at book-length, are extraordinarily difficult to sustain. . . . Unfortunately for John Varley's novel, he brilliantly solves most of the problems inherent in the story and then throws away his achievement for the sake of cheap thrills." Similarly, Timothy Robert Sullivan said in the *Washington Post Book World* that "Varley could have done without the last few pages." Nonetheless, Sullivan believed that Varley's world of the far future "becomes as real as our own. This is Varley's considerable accomplishment, and he pulls it off with admirably lean prose, realistic dialogue, and the concise depiction of sympathetic characters."

After a long hiatus from novel writing, Varley returned to the "Eight Worlds" universe he created in *The Ophiuchi Hotline* with his 1992 novel, *Steel Beach.* Set two hundred years after the alien takeover of Earth, humans now enjoy a utopian existence where they are nearly immortal and have abundant resources; even their environmental climate is controlled to perfection. Although everyone should probably be happy and content with such a situation, tabloid reporter Hildy Johnson is having suicidal thoughts. But Hildy is not alone, there are other humans who feel the same way, and even the Central Computer that is the center of human civilization on Luna seems depressed to the point where it makes designs for itself that could lead to disaster on Luna. Varley's readers and critics alike were pleased with his return to science fiction novels. A *Publishers Weekly* critic, for example, wrote that this "long-awaited return is one of the best science fiction novels of the year."

Varley's *The Golden Globe* is a more recent installment of his "Eight Worlds" series, this time featuring the colorful character Sparky Valentine, a Shakespearean actor, criminal, and con man on the run from a dangerous Charonite assassin who has been physically enhanced to be almost invulnerable to attack. While trying to escape the clutches of the Charonite, Sparky still hopes to make it to Luna, where he plans to play the part of King Lear under the direction of one of the most famous directors in the solar system. On his way to Luna, Sparky recalls many memories and has dreams which reveal the character's past, including how he was abused by his father and the lethal confrontation that eventually evolved from that intolerable situation. "The story is really in the memories," commented Tom Easton in *Analog Science Fiction & Fact.* "Valentine Senior was a driven, egotistical SOB. Valentine Junior was a victim who loved his daddy and knew a bit about how to get around him but could not avoid the final, cataclysmic confrontation, nor the crippling aftereffects. The rest of the book is a guided tour of a civilization as chaotic and vital as our own, which as in *Steel Beach* still owes a great deal to Robert A. Heinlein's precedent." "Although a tad wordy . . . ," concluded a *Publishers Weekly* critic, "this is an engrossing novel by one of the genre's most accomplished storytellers."

More recently, Varley published *Red Thunder,* a story unconnected with either "Eight Worlds" or the "Gaea" trilogy. In a nod to the space race of the 1960s between the United States and Soviet Union, Varley pens a tale in which the Americans are pitted against the Chinese to reach Mars. It looks as if the Chinese are going to land first when Travis Broussard and his cousin Jubal learn that a design problem on the American spacecraft *Ares Seven* has put the life of Travis's astronaut wife in danger. Fortunately, Jubal is a brilliant scientist who has invented a new propulsion system that can get Travis, an ex-astronaut himself, to Mars in only three days. Building their own private spaceship, the *Red Thunder,* they must avoid detection by the government in order to achieve their daring mission. "With hilarious, well-drawn characters, extraordinary situations presented plausibly, plus exciting action and adventure, this book should do thunderously well," predicted a *Publishers Weekly* reviewer. Don D'Ammassa similarly remarked in his *Chronicle* assessment of the novel that "Varley matches a serious literary style with an outrageous plot and he's one of the few writers in the field who could make it work."

BIOGRAPHICAL AND CRITICAL SOURCES:

BOOKS

Dictionary of Literary Biography Yearbook, 1981, Gale (Detroit, MI), 1982.
St. James Guide to Science Fiction Writers, fourth edition, St. James Press (Detroit, MI), 1996.

PERIODICALS

Analog Science Fiction & Fact, February 2, 1981, Tom Easton, review of *Wizard,* p. 172; October, 1983, Tom Easton, review of *Millennium,* p. 164; November, 1984, Tom Easton, review of *Demon,* p. 164; April, 1999, Tom Easton, "The Reference Library," p. 131.
Booklist, July, 1992, Roland Green, review of *Steel Beach,* p. 1925; January 15, 1995, Carl Hays, review of *Superheroes,* p. 901; October 15, 1998, Roland Green, review of *The Golden Globe,* p. 407; March 15, 2003, Roland Green, review of *The Red Thunder,* p. 1286.
Chronicle, April, 2003, Don D'Ammassa, review of *The Red Thunder,* p. 40.
Extrapolation, spring, 1988, Judith J. Kollman, "John Varley's Women," p. 65; summer, 1991, Reinhold Kramer, "The Machine in the Ghost: Time and Presence in Varley's 'Millennium,'" p. 156.
Fantasy Review, August, 1984, Michael E. Stamm, review of *Wizard.*
Library Journal, June 15, 1978, Steve Lewis, review of *Persistence of Vision,* p. 1296; September 15, 1980, Rosemary Herbert, review of *Wizard,* p. 1664, and *The Barbie Murders and Other Stories,* p. 1883; March 15, 1990, Randy Pitman, review of *Millennium,* p. 130; June 15, 1992, Jackie Cassada, review of *Steel Beach,* p. 105; October 15, 1998, Jackie Cassada, review of *The Golden Globe,* p. 104.
Magazine of Fantasy and Science Fiction, October, 1980, Algis Budrys, review of *Wizard,* p. 59; October, 1983, Algis Budrys, review of *Millennium,* p. 26; December, 1984, Algis Budrys, review of *Demon,* p. 33.

New York Times Book Review, April 24, 1977, review of *The Ophiuchi Hotline;* July 31, 1983, Gerald Jonas, review of *Millennium,* p. 13; August 2, 1992, Gerald Jonas, review of *Steel Beach,* p. 19.
Omni, July, 1992, John Clute, "On the Steel Beach," p. 18.
Publishers Weekly, May 16, 1980, review of *Wizard,* p. 202; July 11, 1980, review of *The Barbie Murders and Other Stories,* p. 88; May 6, 1983, review of *Millennium,* p. 95; May 4, 1984, review of *Demon,* p. 54; May 3, 1985, "The 1985 Annual World's Best SF," p. 71; February 14, 1986, Sybil Steinberg, review of *Blue Champagne,* p. 73; May 25, 1992, review of *Steel Beach,* p. 42; September 21, 1998, review of *The Golden Globe,* p. 78; March 31, 2003, review of *Red Thunder,* p. 47.
St. Louis Post-Dispatch, July 20, 1992, J. Stephen Bolhafner, "Science-Fiction Writer Wilted in Hollywood," p. D1.
School Library Journal, September, 1978, Claudia Morner and Rose Moorachian, review of *Persistence of Vision,* p. 169; September, 1995, Pat Royal, "Book Review: Adult Book for Young Adults," p. 234.
Science Fiction Chronicle, October-November, 1998, Don D'Ammassa, review of *The Golden Globe,* p. 50.
Washington Post Book World, June 26, 1983, Timothy Robert Sullivan, review of *Millennium;* June 24, 1984, Craig Shaw Gardner, review of *Demon,* p. 6; January 25, 1987.
Wilson Library Bulletin, February, 1993, Gene LaFaille, review of *Steel Beach,* p. 91.

ONLINE

John Varley Home Page, http://www.varley.net (May 19, 2004).*

*   *   *

VILE, Curt
See MOORE, Alan

W

WALSH, Robb 1952-

PERSONAL: Born December 11, 1952, in NC; *Ethnicity:* "Irish Russian." *Education:* University of Texas—Austin, B.A., 1977. *Hobbies and other interests:* Golf.

ADDRESSES: Home—5908 Belfast Dr., Austin, TX 78723; fax 512-452-5850. *Agent*—Martha Casselman, Box 342, Calistoga, CA 94515. *E-mail*—robbwalsh@aol.com.

CAREER: Writer. Judge, Clicquot Wine Book of the Year Award, 1997-99; commentator, National Public Radio, 1998—. Food editor, *Austin Chronicle,* 1991-94; editor in chief, *Chile Pepper,* 1999-2000; *Houston Press* lead restaurant reviewer and food writer, 2000—. *Austin Chronicle* Hot Sauce Festival, founder and head judge.

MEMBER: International Association of Culinary Professionals.

AWARDS, HONORS: Journalism Award for best magazine feature writing with recipes, 1996, best radio segment on food, 1999, James Beard Foundation.

WRITINGS:

Kingdom of the Dwarfs, illustrations by David Wenzel, Centaur Books (New York, NY), 1980.
(With Jay McCarthy) *Traveling Jamaica with Knife, Fork, and Spoon,* Crossing Press (Trumansburg, NY), 1995.

(With David Garrido) *Nuevo Tex-Mex: Festive New Recipes from Just North of the Border,* foreword by Stephan Pyles, photographs by Manny Rodriquez, Chronicle Books (San Francisco, CA), 1998.
(With Grady Spears) *A Cowboy in the Kitchen: Recipes from Reata and Texas West of the Pecos,* Ten Speed Press (Berkeley, CA), 1998.
Legends of Texas Barbecue: Recipes and Recollections from the Pit Bosses, Chronicle Books (San Francisco, CA), 2002.
Are You Really Going to Eat That? Adventures of a Culinary Thrillseeker, Counterpoint Press (New York, NY), 2003.
The Tex-Mex Cookbook: A History in Recipes and Photos, Broadway (New York, NY), 2004.

Food columnist, *Natural History,* 1995-99. Contributor to periodicals, including *American Way, Chicago Tribune, Houston Chronicle,* and *Los Angeles Times.*

SIDELIGHTS: Robb Walsh is a food writer whose publications include works on recipes originating from the Texas-Mexico region of North America. In 1998, for example, Walsh collaborated with David Garrido in producing *Nuevo Tex-Mex: Festive New Recipes from Just North of the Border,* and he teamed with Grady Spears in publishing *A Cowboy in the Kitchen: Recipes from Reata and Texas West of the Pecos.* Four years later, Walsh issued *Legends of Texas Barbecue: Recipes and Recollections from the Pit Bosses,* which relates history and regional analysis while also serving as a cookbook. In the volume, Walsh charts the evolution of barbecue cooking in Texas, and he examines regional preferences, noting that east Texans favor pork while west Texans often cook goat and beef head.

Legends of Texas Barbecue has been acknowledged as a notable addition to the genre of regional cookbooks. Writing in the *Los Angeles Times,* Charles Perry noted that Walsh's book "stands out" among the slew of barbecue cookbooks that appeared during the summer of 2002. "It includes plenty of recipes," affirmed Perry, "but the best part is the fascinating lore about the history and folkways of Texas barbecue." Another critic, Dwight Garner, declared in the *New York Times Book Review* that *Legends of Texas Barbecue* is "worth knowing about," and he found it "pleasantly nostalgic."

In addition to writing cookbooks, Walsh has served as a food writer for such publications as *Natural History* and the *Houston Press.* He has also worked as an editor at both the *Austin Chronicle* and the *Chile Pepper,* and he has appeared as a judge at various cooking competitions.

BIOGRAPHICAL AND CRITICAL SOURCES:

PERIODICALS

Los Angeles Times, July 3, 2002, Charles Perry, "Cookbook Watch," p. H3.
New York Times Book Review, June 2, 2002, Dwight Garner, "Cooking."
Publishers Weekly, May 6, 2002, review of *Legends of Texas Barbecue: Recipes and Recollections from the Pit Bosses,* p. 51.

ONLINE

Robb Walsh Web site, http://www.robbwalsh.com (November 9, 2003).

*　　　*　　　*

WEIDEGER, Paula 1939-

PERSONAL: Born July 6, 1939, in New York, NY; daughter of Michael (a businessman) and Lillian (Topper) Weideger. *Education:* Attended Antioch College, 1956-58; New York University, B.A., 1968, M.A., 1971.

ADDRESSES: Home—London, England. *Agent*—Claire Smith, Harold Ober Associates, 22 East 49th St., New York, NY 10017.

CAREER: Center for Reproductive and Sexual Health, New York, NY, counselor, 1972; Women's Medical Center, New York, NY, lecturer in women's health, 1972-74; Healthright, Inc., New York, NY, staff associate, 1973; State University of New York College at New Paltz, instructor in women's studies, beginning 1975; writer.

MEMBER: Women's Ink, Passports for Pets.

AWARDS, HONORS: Fellowship, Macdowell Colony, 1973.

WRITINGS:

(With Geraldine Thorsten) *Travel with Your Pet,* illustrations by Ernie Pintoff, Simon & Schuster (New York, NY), 1973.
Menstruation and Menopause: The Physiology and Psychology, the Myth and the Reality, Knopf (New York, NY), 1976, revised edition, Dell (New York, NY), 1977.
Female Cycles, Women's Press (London, England), 1978.
History's Mistress: A New Interpretation of a Nineteenth-Century Ethnographic Classic, Viking (New York, NY), 1986.
Gilding the Acorn: Behind the Façade of the National Trust, Statesman and Nation Publishing (London, England), 1994.
Venetian Dreaming (memoir), Pocket Books (New York, NY), 2002.

Researcher, *Scientific American,* 1959-61; editor, *Excerpta Medica,* 1971.

SIDELIGHTS: Paula Weideger is a versatile writer whose publications include a study of women's issues, an investigative report, and a memoir. In 1976 she published *Menstruation and Menopause: The Physiology and Psychology, the Myth and the Reality,* and in 1994 she issued *Gilding the Acorn: Behind the Façade of the National Trust,* an examination into the practices of England's institution for the preservation of places holding historical interest or worth. In *Gilding the Acorn,* Weideger relates some of the National Trust's more controversial practices, and she illuminates what Alun Howkins, writing in *New Statesman and Society,* described as the institution's "distinct tendency to be lenient to the great and good and less caring for its smaller tenants and employees." Howkins called *Gilding the Acorn* "an extraordinary and naive account" and claimed that it constitutes "a series of loosely joined chapters with catchy titles." He added, however, that "there is something here, no matter how absurdly put."

Weideger is also the author of *Venetian Dreaming,* an account of her year spent as an apartment dweller in Venice. In the book Weideger relates difficulties ranging from the mere maintenance of her apartment—described in *Publishers Weekly* as "rundown"—to the linking of her computer to the Internet. In addition, she recounts the difficulties she encountered in communicating with others and finding her way about the labyrinthine city. The *Publishers Weekly* reviewer concluded that *Venetian Dreams* "appeals as a personal glimpse of one of Italy's most unusual cities," and a *Kirkus Reviews* critic affirmed that "on the level of the quotidian, Weideger's work transports and entertains."

BIOGRAPHICAL AND CRITICAL SOURCES:

PERIODICALS

Booklist, June 1, 2002, GraceAnne A. DeCandido, review of *Venetian Dreaming,* p. 1671.
Kirkus Reviews, April 15, 2002, review of *Venetian Dreaming,* p. 553.
Library Journal, June 1, 2002, Mari Flynn, review of *Venetian Dreaming,* p. 83.
New Statesman and Society, December 16, 1994, Alun Howkins, review of *Gilding the Acorn: Behind the Façade of the National Trust.*
Publishers Weekly, April 25, 2002, review of *Venetian Dreaming.*
Spectator, November 12, 1994, John Smith, review of *Gilding the Acorn,* p. 43.*

* * *

WEST, Owen
See KOONTZ, Dean R(ay)

WHITEHEAD, Neil L(ancelot) 1956-

PERSONAL: Born March 19, 1956, in London, England; immigrated to United States, 1993; son of Kenneth Lancelot and Irene Winifred (Dormer) Whitehead; married Theresa Margaret Murphy, June 7, 1986; children: Luke, Florence, Rose, Natalie. *Education:* Oxford University, B.A., 1977, M.A., 1978, D.Phil. (social anthropology), 1984, M.A., 1986.

ADDRESSES: Office—Department of Anthropology, University of Wisconsin, 1180 Observatory Dr., Madison, WI 53706. *E-mail*—nlwhiteh@wisc.edu.

CAREER: Oxford University, Oxford, England, tutor, 1990-92; University of Wisconsin, Madison, professor of anthropology, 1993—. Laboratoire d'Anthroplogie Sociale, École des Hautes Etudes, Paris, France, visiting professor, 2003. *Ethnohistory,* editor, 1997-2007.

MEMBER: American Anthropological Association, Royal Anthropological Institute, Koningslijk Institute, Hakluyt Society.

AWARDS, HONORS: University of London fellow, 1979-80; École de Haute Etudes fellow, 1980-81; Guggenheim Foundation fellow, 1985-90; Royal Anthropological Institute fellow; John Henry Breasted Prize, American Historical Association, 1998; National Endowment for the Humanities fellow, 2001; Rasputin Award, University of Wisconsin—Madison Center for the Humanities, 2002, for *Dark Shamans.*

WRITINGS:

Lords of the Tiger Spirit: A History of the Caribs in Colonial Venezuela and Guyana, 1498-1820, Foris Publications (Providence, RI), 1988.
(Editor, with R. Brian Ferguson) *War in the Tribal Zone: Expanding States and Indigenous Warfare,* School of American Research Press (Santa Fe, NM), 1992.
(Editor, with Peter Hulme) *Wild Majesty: Encounters with Caribs from Columbus to the Present Day: An Anthology,* Clarendon Press (Oxford, England), 1992.
(Editor) *Wolves from the Sea: Readings in the Anthropology of the Native Caribbean,* KITLV Press (Leiden, Netherlands), 1995.

(Transcriber and author of annotations and introduction) Sir Walter Raleigh, *The Discoverie of the Large, Rich, and Bewtiful Empyre of Guiana*, University of Oklahoma Press (Norman, OK), 1997.

(Author of foreword) Elsa M. Redmond, editor, *Chiefdoms and Chieftaincy in the Americas*, International Congress of Americanists, University Press of Florida (Gainesville, FL), 1998.

(With Blair Whitehead) *My Genes Made Me Do It!*, Huntington House, 1999.

(Editor, with Laura Rival) *Beyond the Visible and the Material: The Amerindianization of Society in the Work of Peter Rivière*, Oxford University Press (New York, NY), 2001.

Dark Shamans: Kanaimà and the Poetics of Violent Death, Duke University Press (Durham, NC), 2002.

(Editor) *Histories and Historicities in Amazonia* University of Nebraska Press (Lincoln, NE), 2003.

Nineteenth-Century Travels, Explorations, and Empires: Writings from the Era of Imperial Consolidation, 1835-1910; South America, Chatto & Pickering (London, England), 2004.

(Editor, with Robin Wright) *In Darkness and Secrecy: The Anthropology of Assault Sorcery and Witchcraft in Amazonia*, Duke University Press (Durham, NC), 2004.

(Editor) *Violence: Poetics, Performance, and Expression*, SAR Press (Santa Fe, NM), 2004.

(Editor, with Andrew Strathern and Pamela Stewart) *Terror and Violence: Anthropological Approaches*, Pluto Press (London, England), 2005.

Cannibal Conqueror: Hans Staden and the Spectacle of Anthropophagy in Brazil, Duke University Press (Durham, NC), 2005.

Contributor to periodicals, including *Current Anthropology*.

WORK IN PROGRESS: *Cultures of Violence and the Violence of Culture,* a nonfiction work addressing key aspects of human violence.

SIDELIGHTS: Anthropologist, editor, and author Neil L. Whitehead was born in England and attended Oxford University, where he served as a tutor. A professor of anthropology at the University of Wisconsin—Madison, Whitehead is the author of a number of books, among them *Lords of the Tiger Spirit: A History of the Caribs in Colonial Venezuela and Guyana, 1498-1820,* which was based on his doctoral thesis. Whitehead has also edited works about the indigenous people of eastern South America, including a group of people known as both the Caribs and the Karinyas. He also transcribed, introduced, and added notes to *The Discoverie of the Large, Rich and Bewtiful Empyre of Guiana,* a work by sixteenth-century English explorer Sir Walter Raleigh.

In *Lords of the Tiger Spirit* Whitehead describes the Venezuelan and Guyanan Caribs who managed to maintain their independence from the colonizing forces of the Spanish, the Dutch, and other European powers. *Journal of Historical Geography* contributor Peter Wade explained that the author "traces in great detail the history of the Carib Indians (now called Karinya) of this area and their staunch resistance to colonial domination until they were finally brought under missionary control in the eighteenth century." Reviewing the book in the *Hispanic American Historical Review,* Stephanie Wood declared that it "makes an admirable stab at capturing an elusive history of a valiant people which should interest historians of indigenous peoples and colonial experiences of the entire hemisphere."

With Peter Hulme, Whitehead edited the 1992 work *Wild Majesty: Encounters with Caribs from Columbus to the Present Day,* a collection of writings by European and American explorers and anthropologists. The writings included range from excerpts of explorer Christopher Columbus's journal penned in 1492 and 1493 to the observations of anthropologist Jose Barreiro in 1990. In between, a reader can find musings from seventeenth-century missionary Raymond Breton and Victorian-era birdwatcher Frederick Ober. In addition, Whitehead also edited *War in the Tribal Zone: Expanding States and Indigenous Warfare,* together with R. Brian Ferguson. This 1992 volume is a collection of articles by various anthropologists who argue that tribal conflicts have been greatly exacerbated by the influence of nationalism. According to *Science* contributor Bruce M. Knauft, topics in *War in the Tribal Zone* include discussions of the ancient Roman Empire, the West African slave trade, the Iroquois Confederacy in North America, and the impact of colonization on the highlands of Papua New Guinea. Knauft observed that "the editors tend to attribute all tribal warfare to the subsequent transformative effect of economic and political encroachment by Western and other states." Knauft continued that "as the book's best chapters amply demonstrate, the conflict dynamics of indigenous-state interaction need to be teased apart historically without sweeping either indigenous conflict patterns or the momentous and often horrendous effects of state political economies under the rug."

In *Wolves from the Sea: Readings in the Anthropology of the Native Caribbean* Whitehead assembles essays focusing on how previous anthropologists have categorized the Caribs and Arawaks, both indigenous people of the Caribbean islands. These categorizations often depict the Caribs as bloodthirsty cannibals, while they also state that the Arawaks are much more tractable. Although explorers and scholars created these labels centuries ago, they survive in some ways to this day. "In terms of clarifying Island Carib ethnicity, this book achieves mixed results," judged Peter O'B. Harris in the *Hispanic American Historical Review*. Harris also noted: "Despite the stress on ethnicity, the book is not addressed to Caribbean peoples of Amerindian descent," yet added that "in terms of defining Island Carib research strategy, however, this book makes a much-needed and major contribution." Reviewing *Wolves from the Sea* in *American Ethnologist*, Richard Price asserted that the authors "make clear that archaeologists, linguists, and ethnologists will need to collaborate closely and bring to bear their sharpest critical tools to piece together, out of diverse traces left by the Caribbean past, the larger interpretive puzzle" of Carib and Arawak history and anthropology, concluding that "this lively collection helps clear the path and provides numerous useful beacons."

Sir Walter Raleigh's *The Discoverie of the Large, Rich and Bewtiful Empyre of Guiana* was first published in 1596. Whitehead provides the introduction, transcription, and notes for an updated version of the text, publishing his edition of Raleigh's work in 1997. *The Discoverie* features Raleigh's accounts of his encounters with indigenous South American tribal leaders—people he termed "kings," the explorer's descriptions of the search for gold, and his accounts of "monster" sightings. While researching in preparation for updating Raleigh's text, Whitehead visited the regions Raleigh describes in *The Discoverie*. He incorporates these experiences as well as the writings of sixteenth-century authors contemporary to Raleigh, thereby providing additional perspectives on the famed explorer's text.

Whitehead told *CA:* "I am currently writing up research on the cultural practice of collective violence. Research to date has involved both the ethnographic study of a cult of ritual violence and the historical study of tribal warfare. I intend to use this ethnographic experience, in conjunction with a close examination of secondary literature on the cultural meaning of violence, and a global comparison of ethnographic case-studies to write a book-length work, *Cultures of Violence and the Violence of Culture*. This work will address key aspects of human violence that have often been ignored, principally how violence may be an expression of fundamental cultural practice and a sanctioned means of collective communication and exchange, such that the 'enemy' becomes integral to cultural identity. By offering a new framework for understanding the genesis and dynamics of ethnic violence and its burgeoning challenge to national and individual security it is hoped that anthropological debate will be stimulated and policy better informed with regard to the causes and development of collective conflict."

BIOGRAPHICAL AND CRITICAL SOURCES:

PERIODICALS

American Anthropologist, July, 1996, p. 615.
American Ethnologist, February, 1996, p. 187.
Australian Journal of Anthropology, August, 2004, Zeljko Jokic, review of *Dark Shamans: Knaìma and the Poetics of Violent Death,* p. 250.
Current Anthropology, April, 1996, pp. 339-341.
Hispanic American Historical Review, August, 1990, pp. 498-499; August, 1996, pp. 552-554.
Journal of Historical Geography, October, 1990, pp. 481-482.
Science, May 21, 1993, pp. 1184, 1186.

ONLINE

Isthmus Online, http://www.thedailypage.com (February 20, 2005), "Dark Sorcery" (interview with Whitehead).
University of Wisconsin Alumni Online, http://www.uwalumni.com/ (fall, 2003), "Kanaima as Unintended Consequence" (interview with Whitehead).

WILCOX, Stephen F. 1951-

PERSONAL: Born February 5, 1951, in Rochester, NY; son of Frederick Elias and Catherine (Holland) Wilcox; married Pauline Bennett (a project consultant), May 27, 1972; children: Bennett Elias. *Education:* Monroe Community College, A.S.; St. John Fisher College, B.A., 1978. *Hobbies and other interests:* Contemporary music, baseball, public-policy issues, home remodeling.

ADDRESSES: Home—25 Hulburt Ave., Fairport, NY 14450.

CAREER: Rochester Democrat and Chronicle, Rochester, NY, reporter, 1977-81; freelance writer, 1981—. *Military service:* U.S. Army, 1971-73; became private first class.

MEMBER: Mystery Writers of America.

WRITINGS:

"T. S. W. SHERIDAN" MYSTERIES

The Dry White Tear, St. Martin's Press (New York, NY), 1989.
The St. Lawrence Run, St. Martin's Press (New York, NY), 1990.
All the Dead Heroes, St. Martin's Press (New York, NY), 1992.
The Green Mosaic, St. Martin's Press (New York, NY), 1994.

"ELIAS HACKSHAW" MYSTERIES

The Twenty-Acre Plot, St. Martin's Press (New York, NY), 1991.
The Nimby Factor, St. Martin's Press (New York, NY), 1992.
The Painted Lady, St. Martin's Press (New York, NY), 1994.
The Jericho Flower: A Hackshaw Mystery, iUniverse (Lincoln, NE), 2002.

"THUMBPRINT" MYSTERIES

The Hard Time Cafe, Contemporary Books (Lincolnwood, IL), 1998.

Purgatory Prayers, Contemporary Books (Lincolnwood, IL), 1998.
The Hidden Men, Contemporary Books (Lincolnwood, IL), 1999.

SIDELIGHTS: Stephen F. Wilcox is the author of several mystery series. In his first novel, *The Dry White Tear,* he introduced protagonist T. S. W. Sheridan, a writer and amateur crime solver. In this story Sheridan learns that a past tragedy, in which bootleggers were responsible for a fire that claimed eighteen lives, may be related to a recent murder. Among the ensuing mysteries featuring sleuth Sheridan is *All the Dead Heroes,* in which the protagonist uncovers murder and corruption in the world of professional baseball. James Jay Gould, writing in the *Syracuse Herald-American,* reported that in *All the Dead Heroes* Wilcox succeeds in "deftly blending popular culture and history into a very credible and entertaining murder mystery."

Another of Wilcox's mystery series features Elias Hackshaw, a middle-aged reporter in rural New York State. Hackshaw first appeared in *The Twenty-Acre Plot,* in which he uncovers an unsavory land-development scheme. Hackshaw is also the hero of *The Nimby Factor,* where he becomes embroiled in a landfill controversy that leads to a murder.

Wilcox once told *CA:* "I write mysteries for the same reason that I and millions of others choose to read them: for the stimulation provided by a challenging plot (in this case, creating one rather than trying to figure out one); for the great variety to be found in the genre; for a comfortable escape to a world where right, at the very least, has a fighting chance to overcome wrong; and, perhaps most important, because mystery writing is a great medium for a storyteller.

"I must admit that, when I first left work as a newspaperman to try my hand at storytelling, it was so-called literary fiction I had in mind. But I soon found myself at a dead end, wrestling with pieces of a rather aimless and self-indulgent coming-of-age story that, I finally realized, wasn't something I wanted to read, let alone labor to write.

"Coincidentally—or maybe not—I'd just finished reading a mystery, so I set out to try my hand at a whodunit. The result was *The Dry White Tear.* But coincidence had no role in my decision to set each of the first three Sheridan mysteries in the small towns of upstate New York. To begin with, the sages advise to 'write about what you know,' and as one who has lived almost all his life in upstate New York, it wasn't a difficult decision to place my novels there. And there may have been a bit of reverse snobbery involved too. To most people who've never traveled to the state, 'New York' means tall buildings, Broadway, and street crime. I wanted to introduce readers to the other New York—the place of ancient mountains and small vineyards, farm communities and blue-collar cities, Great Lakes, deep forests, and the people who inhabit them.

"Of course, as much as I appreciate the charms of upstate life, I also have a sense of humor about it. I started a second mystery series, featuring a small-town newspaper editor, part-time house restorer, and full-time gadfly named Elias Hackshaw. Unlike Sheridan and other more traditional sleuths, Hackshaw hates mysteries, is repelled by violence, and wants only to be left alone to pursue his interests in old houses, youngish women, and friendly card games. Unfortunately for him, fate keeps leaving dead people in his path. But Hackshaw somehow manages to overcome the turmoil, keeping in mind that the first rule of preservation is self-preservation."

BIOGRAPHICAL AND CRITICAL SOURCES:

PERIODICALS

Kirkus Reviews, July 1, 1994, review of *The Green Mosaic,* p. 890.

Publishers Weekly, May 4, 1990; October 12, 1992, p. 66; January 10, 1994, review of *The Painted Lady,* p. 48; July 25, 1994, review of *The Green Mosaic,* p. 37; July 15, 2002, review of *The Jericho Flower: A Hackshaw Mystery,* p. 58.

San Francisco Chronicle, September 22, 1991.

Syracuse Herald-American, August 16, 1992, James Jay Gould, review of *All the Dead Heroes.*

ONLINE

Best Reviews Online, http://thebestreviews.com/ (June 13, 2002), Shadoe Simmons, review of *The Jericho Flower.*

Wilcox Gazette, http://stephenfwilcox.com/ (November 1, 2004).*

WOODS, Pamela 1938-

PERSONAL: Born January 30, 1938, in Reigate, England; daughter of John (a director) and Nora (a rug designer; maiden name, Cowell) Pearse; married Michael Woods (an artist), August 20, 1960 (divorced, 1975); children: Vanessa, Oliver, Geraldine. *Education:* Attended Nesta Brooking Ballet School, 1955-65, and London Central School of Theatrical Design; earned B.Sc. (with honors). *Religion:* Church of England.

ADDRESSES: Office—Gardens for the Soul, 512 Beech Lane, Brownshill, Gloucestershire GL6 8AJ, England. *E-mail*—pamela@gardensforthesoul.co.uk.

CAREER: Pamela Pearse Ballet School, Guildford, England, director, 1955-75; Pamela Woods Flowers Ltd., England, director, 1975-79; Pamela Woods Floral Agency and Design Studio, Bath, England, director, beginning 1979; Gardens for the Soul, Brownshill, Gloucestershire, England, principal, landscape designer, and presenter of seminars and training workshops. Lecturer at colleges; designer for Rayher Hobby; guest on British and American television programs.

AWARDS, HONORS: Silver Gilt Medal from Hampton Court Flower Show, 1999, for a feng shui garden design.

WRITINGS:

(With Peter Riva) *Paper Flowermaking,* Studio Vista (London, England), 1972.

(With Peter Riva) *Flowers from Feathers,* David & Charles (Newton Abbot, England), 1973.

(With Peter Riva) *Flowers from Fabrics,* David & Charles (Newton Abbot, England), 1974.

(With Peter Riva) *Party Decorations and Crackers,* Blandford (London, England), 1974.

(With Peter Riva) *Feathercraft,* Search Press, 1974.

(With Peter Riva) *Quilling,* Leisure Craft, 1975.

(With Peter Riva) *Christmas,* Blandford (London, England), 1975.

(With Peter Riva) *Creative Flowermaking,* Pan Books (London, England), 1975.

(With Peter Riva) *Part Works: Victorian Crafts Revived,* Batsford (London, England), 1976.

(With Peter Riva) *Crafts,* Lutterworth (London, England), 1977.

(With Peter Riva) *Crafts Encyclopedia,* Marshall Cavendish (Tarrytown, NY), 1977.

(With Peter Riva) *Papercraft,* Hamlyn (London, England), 1979, St. Martin's Press (New York, NY), 1980.

(With Peter Riva) *Ribbon Flowers,* Rayher Hobby (Laupheim, Germany), 1980.

Making Floral Designs, illustrated by Vanessa Woods, Batsford (London, England), 1984.

Gardens for the Soul: Designing Outdoor Spaces Using Ancient Symbols, Healing Plants, and Feng Shui, photographs by John Glover, Rizzoli (New York, NY), 2002.

Contributor to magazines, including *Womancraft* and *Family Circle.*

BIOGRAPHICAL AND CRITICAL SOURCES:

PERIODICALS

Booklist, October 1, 2002, Alice Joyce, review of *Gardens for the Soul: Designing Outdoor Spaces Using Ancient Symbols, Healing Plants, and Feng Shui,* p. 294.

ONLINE

Gardens for the Soul: Courses in the Sublime Art of Working with Nature, http://www.sacredgardens.u-net.com/ (May 18, 2004).*

*   *   *

WORCESTER, Robert
See WORCESTER, Robert M(ilton)

*   *   *

WORCESTER, Robert M(ilton) 1933-
(Robert Worcester)

PERSONAL: Born December 21, 1933; son of C. M. and Violet Ruth Worcester; married Joann Ransdell, 1958 (divorced); married Margaret Noel Smallbone, 1982; children: (first marriage) two sons. *Education:*

University of Kansas, B.Sc., 1955. *Hobbies and other interests:* Choral music, gardening, castles, scuba diving, skiing.

ADDRESSES: Office—Market and Opinion Research International (MORI), 6 Mori House, 79-81 Borough Rd., London SE1 1FY, England. *E-mail*—worc@mori. com.

CAREER: McKinsey and Co. (management consultants), Washington, DC, consultant, 1962-65; Opinion Research Corp., Princeton, NJ, controller and assistant to the chair, 1965-68; Market and Opinion Research International (MORI) Ltd., London, England, managing director, 1969—, chair, 1973—; chair and managing director, MORI Social Research Institute and MORI Australia. City University, London, England, honorary visiting professor of journalism. UNESCO International Social Science Council, vice president, member of council, and member of scientific activities committee; Ditchley Foundation, member of program committee; British Museum (Natural History) Development Trust, member of board of trustees; broadcaster, public speaker, and consultant.

MEMBER: World Association for Public Opinion Research (past president), British Institute of Management, Royal Society of Arts (fellow), Media Society (member of executive committee), Worldwide Fund for Nature (member of council), Democrats Abroad (member of executive committee), Pilgrims Society (member of executive committee), Reform Club, Hurlingham Club.

WRITINGS:

(Editor) *Consumer Market Research Handbook,* McGraw (New York, NY), 1971, 2nd edition, with John Downham, Van Nostrand Reinhold (New York, NY), 1978, 3rd edition, with John Downham, Elsevier Science (New York, NY), 1986.

(Editor, with Martin Harrop) *Political Communications: The General Election Campaign of 1979,* Allen & Unwin (London, England), 1982.

(Editor) *Political Opinion Polling: An International Review,* St. Martin's Press (New York, NY), 1983.

(With Lesley Watkins) *Private Opinions, Public Polls,* Thames & Hudson (London, England), 1986.

(With Eric Jacobs) *We British: Britain under the MORIscope,* Weidenfeld & Nicolson (London, England), 1990.

(As Robert Worcester, with Eric Jacobs) *Typically British? The Prudential MORI Guide,* Bloomsbury (London, England), 1991.

British Public Opinion: A Guide to the History and Methodology of Political Opinion Polling in Great Britain, Basil Blackwell (London, England), 1991.

(With Roger Mortimore) *Explaining Labour's Landslide,* Politico's Publishing (London, England), 1999.

(As Robert Worcester, with Roger Mortimore) *Explaining Labour's Second Landslide,* Politico's Publishing (London, England), 2001.

Also columnist for *Times* (London, England). Contributor to professional journals. Editor, *International Journal of Public Opinion Research;* member of editorial advisory board, *Electoral Studies, World Opinion Update, Index to International Public Opinion,* and *European Business Journal.*

SIDELIGHTS: Robert M. Worcester, expert on public opinion research in Britain, paired up with his colleague Roger Mortimore to write *Explaining Labour's Second Landslide. Times Literary Supplement* reviewer Peter Riddell described the book as being about "political history since 1997 as seen through MORI polls." Riddell commented on Worcester's "combative style" which he believes "can turn a difference of opinion into an argument, and a theoretical dispute into a personal feud." Riddell is able to overlook this, and comments that "Worcester and Mortimore provide a thoughtful and balanced account of public opinion . . . [the book shows] the strengths and limits of opinion polling, and show why the Tories never really had a chance." *Social and Behavioral Sciences* contributor M. Curtis stated, "this clearly written book will be useful for and amuse political pundits and psephologists." Curtis did note that it is "too specialized" for the general reader, however.

BIOGRAPHICAL AND CRITICAL SOURCES:

PERIODICALS

Choice, September, 2002, M. Curtis, review of *Explaining Labour's Second Landslide,* p. 179.

Journalism Quarterly, summer, 1992, review of *British Public Opinion: A Guide to the History and Methodology of Political Opinion Polling in Great Britain,* p. 510.

Social and Behavioral Sciences, September, 2002, M. Curtis, review of *Explaining Labour's Second Landslide.*

Times Literary Supplement, September 21, 1990; June 7, 2002, Peter Riddell, "The apathy landslide," pp. 11-12.

ONLINE

MORI Web site, http://www.mori.com/ (November 25, 2002), review of *Explaining Labour's Second Landslide.**

* * *

WORSWICK, Clark 1940-

PERSONAL: Born September 16, 1940, in Berkeley, CA; son of Wallace Burdette and Elizabeth (Benedict) Worswick; married Joan Mitchell (a teacher), September 19, 1970; children: Lucia, Nicholas. *Education:* Attended Visva Bharati, 1959, and Harvard University, 1966-70.

ADDRESSES: Home and office—Oak Summit Rd., Millbrook, NY 12545.

CAREER: Film director, 1960-86; Asia Society Gallery, guest director, beginning 1975; Japan Society Gallery, guest director, 1978-79; photographic historian and writer.

AWARDS, HONORS: Indo-American fellowship, Smithsonian Institution, 1979.

WRITINGS:

The Last Empire: Photographs of British India, Aperture (Millerton, NY), 1976.

Imperial China: Photographs 1850-1911, Crown (New York, NY), 1978.

An Edwardian Observer, Crown (New York, NY), 1978.

Japan: Photographs, 1854-1904, Knopf (New York, NY), 1979.

Princely India, Knopf (New York, NY), 1980.

The Camera and the Tribe, Knopf (New York, NY), 1982.

(With Belinda Rathbone) *Walker Evans: The Lost Work,* Arena Editions (Santa Fe, NM), 2000.

(Author of text) *Berenice Abbott and Eugène Atget* (photographs), Arena Editions (Santa Fe, NM), 2002.

FILM SCRIPTS

Family Honor, Cinerama/Abc Films, 1973.

(With Louis Pastore) *Agent on Ice,* Shapiro Entertainment, 1985.

Also author of feature film strips *The Second Raven,* and *A.N.T.,* both 1986, and documentary film strips *Changing Rains,* 1965, *California,* 1968, and *Kotah,* 1970.

SIDELIGHTS: Clark Worswick once commented: "When I was eighteen I went to India to university. At a certain moment in time I calculated that I had traveled 70,000 miles on Indian third-class trains—some sort of grotesque record, seeing the 'remains' of British India, archaeological sites, and tribal groups. Living in the Salvation Army hostels and the ashrams of the Maha Bodi society during the period I stayed in India affected me most as an artist; it was the last moment the 'white man' was held in (almost) universal esteem in Asia, the Middle East, and Africa. From the time I was eighteen until I was twenty-eight, over a ten-year period, I traveled more or less constantly in Asia, Africa, and the Middle East. I supported myself by doing freelance photography and films.

"Somewhere along the way I discovered the work of nineteenth-century photographers working in the same areas I was working in, and I brought together a collection of work done in India during the nineteenth century that resulted in an exhibition and a book, *The Last Empire: Photographs of British India.* It has always amazed me that photography managed, at the penultimate moment in Asia and the Middle East, to document the way traditional cultures were before they were radically, irrevocably changed by the onslaught of the European industrial revolution. This change has been so complete that at this moment Tehran is very similar to Tokyo in looks, Bombay looks like Rio, et cetera."

BIOGRAPHICAL AND CRITICAL SOURCES:

PERIODICALS

Library Journal, November 15, 2002, David Bryant, review of *Berenice Abbott and Eugène Atget,* p. 69.*

*   *   *

WUERTHNER, George 1952-

PERSONAL: Born June 11, 1952, in PA; son of George and Mildred Wuerthner; married Mollie Matteson (a wildlife biologist), 1987; children: Summer, Stratton. *Ethnicity:* "Mixture." *Education:* University of Montana, A.A., B.A.; attended Montana State University and University of Oregon, 1994-97; University of California—Santa Cruz, M.S.

ADDRESSES: Home—Richmond, VT. *Office*—P.O. Box 839, Richmond, VT 05477. *E-mail*—wuerthner@ gmavt.net.

CAREER: Freelance writer and photographer. Consulting ecologist and landscape photographer; natural history and wilderness guide; leader of photography workshops; partner in George Wuerthner Photography and Raventrails Tours. Instructor for Wildlands Studies Program, San Francisco State University, San Francisco, CA; staff ecologist for Predator Defense; researcher for Institute for Ecological Integrity; policy analyst for Wildlife Protection Institute; consultant to *National Geographic* books; associate and biological consultant with Conservation Science, Inc. Member of the board of directors of RESTORE, Forest Guardians, Oregon Natural Desert Association, Southern Plains Restoration Council, and Alliance for Wild Rockies.

WRITINGS:

Idaho Mountain Ranges, American Geographic Publishing (Helena, MT), 1986.

Oregon Mountain Ranges, American Geographic Publishing (Helena, MT), 1987.

(With Mollie Yoneko Matteson) *Vermont, Portrait of the Land and Its People,* American Geographic Publishing (Helena, MT), 1987.

Yellowstone and the Fires of Change, Haggis House Publications (Salt Lake City, UT), 1988.

The Adirondacks: Forever Wild, American Geographic Publishing (Helena, MT), 1988.

Alaska's Mountain Ranges, American Geographic Publishing (Helena, MT), 1988.

(And photographer) *The Maine Coast,* American Geographic Publishing (Helena, MT), 1989.

(And photographer) *Texas' Big Bend Country,* American Geographic Publishing (Helena, MT), 1989.

Southern Appalachian Country, American Geographic Publishing (Helena, MT), 1990.

Yellowstone: A Visitor's Companion, Stackpole Books (Harrisburg, PA), 1992.

(And photographer) *Nevada Mountain Ranges,* American & World Geographic Publishing (Helena, MT), 1992.

(And photographer) *California's Sierra Nevada,* American & World Geographic Publishing (Helena, MT), 1993.

Yosemite: A Visitor's Companion, Stackpole Books (Mechanicsburg, PA), 1994.

(And photographer) *North Idaho's Lake Country,* American & World Geographic Publishing (Helena, MT), 1995.

(And photographer) *Beautiful America's Alaska,* Beautiful America Publishing (Wilsonville, OR), 1995.

(And photographer) *California's Wilderness Areas: The Complete Guide,* Westcliffe Publishers (Englewood, CO), 1997.

Grand Canyon, Stackpole (Mechanicsburg, PA), 1998.

California Wilderness Areas, two volumes, Westcliffe Publishers (Englewood, CO), 1998.

(And photographer) *Olympic: A Visitor's Companion,* illustrations by Douglas W. Moore, Stackpole Books (Mechanicsburg, PA), 1999.

(And photographer) *Mount Rainier: A Visitor's Companion,* illustrations by Douglas W. Moore, Stackpole Books (Mechanicsburg, PA), 2000.

(And photographer) *Beautiful America's Washington,* Beautiful America (Woodburn, OR), 2000.

(And photographer) *Oregon's Best Wildflower Hikes: Northwest Region,* Westcliffe Publishers (Englewood, CO), 2001.

(And photographer) *Rocky Mountain: A Visitor's Companion,* illustrations by Douglas W. Moore, Stackpole Books (Mechanicsburg, PA), 2001.

Yosemite: The Grace and Grandeur, Voyageur (Stillwater, MN), 2002.

(Editor, with Mollie Yoneko Matteson) *Welfare Ranching: The Subsidized Destruction of the American West,* Island Press (Washington, DC), 2002.

(And photographer) *Oregon's Wilderness Areas: The Complete Guide,* Westcliffe Publishers (Englewood, CO), 2003.

(And photographer) *Great Smoky Mountains: A Visitor's Companion,* illustrations by Douglas W. Moore, Stackpole Books (Mechanicsburg, PA), 2003.

SIDELIGHTS: Photographer and ecologist George Wuerthner is the author and photographer of almost thirty books on American landscapes and wilderness areas. Wuerthner grew up in Pennsylvania and New Jersey, and became interested in the outdoors at an early age. In high school he began fly fishing and decided to become a fishery biologist. In pursuit of this goal, he attended the University of Montana, known for its proximity to some of the best fly fishing waters in the world, and earned degrees in liberal arts, botany, and wildlife biology. He also began practicing photography and increasing his photographic skills.

As an undergraduate, Wuerthner worked as a wilderness guide and instructor for the University of Montana Outdoor Program; a river ranger on the Fortymile River in Alaska; a backcountry ranger in the Gates of the Arctic National Park; a surveyor for the Bureau of Land Management in Alaska; a botanist and biologist for the Bureau of Land Management in Idaho; and a junior high school teacher in California. In addition, he worked as a wilderness guide in the Rocky Mountains and in Alaska. After earning a graduate degree at the University of California, Santa Cruz, Wuerthner began working full-time as a freelance photographer and writer.

Oregon's Best Wildflower Hikes: Northwest Region not only presents forty-nine day hikes chosen for their abundance of wildflowers, but allows readers to identify the flowers they see. In addition, all of the hikes are within three hours' driving time of Portland, Oregon, or the Willamette Valley.

Mount Rainier: A Visitor's Companion provides a thorough discussion of the mountain's history, geology, flora, fauna, and climate, illustrated with Wuerthner's photographs. In *Library Journal,* Joseph L. Carlson noted that the book goes beyond other tourist guides by giving readers a deeper understanding of the mountain, its ecosystem, and the various forces that created and still maintain it.

In *Yosemite: The Grace and Grandeur,* Wuerthner presents a photographic panorama of Yosemite National Park. The book earned high praise from Joseph L. Carlson in *Library Journal,* who compared Wuerthner's work to that of famed photographer Ansel Adams, and called Wuerthner a "gifted artist."

In addition to presenting photographs of Yosemite, the book also includes Wuerthner's passionate advocacy for preservation of the park, as well as the prevention of further development in or near it. As Carlson noted, Wuerthner backs up his arguments with his broad knowledge of natural history and ecological science.

In *Welfare Ranching,* Wuerthner and coeditor Mollie Yoneko Matteson present articles and photographs examining the practice of ranching in the American West and its effect on the environment. According to the book's publisher, ranching "has done more damage than the chainsaw and bulldozer combined."

Wuerthner maintains a library of over 220,000 images in a computer database, arranged by geographic region and topic. In addition to images of various North American locations, the library also includes photographs from Europe, South America, and Central America. He has also begun to document the activities of people, including children, in the wilderness.

BIOGRAPHICAL AND CRITICAL SOURCES:

PERIODICALS

Library Journal, March 15, 2000, Joseph L. Carlson, review of *Mount Rainier: A Visitor's Companion,* p. 117; June 1, 2002, Joseph L. Carlson, review of *Yosemite: The Grace and Grandeur,* p. 182.

ONLINE

George Wuerthner Photography Web site, http://www.wuerthnerphotography.com/ (August 21, 2002).

Z

ZAHN, Timothy 1951-

PERSONAL: Born September 1, 1951, in Chicago, IL; son of Herbert William (an attorney) and Marilou (an attorney; maiden name, Webb) Zahn; married Anna L. Romo (a computer programmer), August 4, 1979; children: Corwin. *Education:* Michigan State University, B.S. (physics), 1973; University of Illinois—Urbana-Champaign, M.S. (physics), 1975, further graduate study, 1975-80. *Hobbies and other interests:* Listening to classical music (particularly nineteenth-century romantic era), crossword puzzles, and martial arts.

ADDRESSES: Home—OR. *Agent*—Russell Galen, Scovil, Chichak, Galen Literary Agency, 381 Park Ave. S., Suite 1020, New York, NY 10016.

CAREER: Writer.

MEMBER: Science Fiction Writers of America.

AWARDS, HONORS: Hugo Award nominations, World Science Fiction Convention, 1983, for "Pawn's Gambit," and 1985, for "Return to the Fold"; Hugo Award for best novella, 1984, for *Cascade Point.*

WRITINGS:

SCIENCE FICTION

The Blackcollar, DAW Books (New York, NY), 1983.
A Coming of Age, Bluejay (New York, NY), 1984.

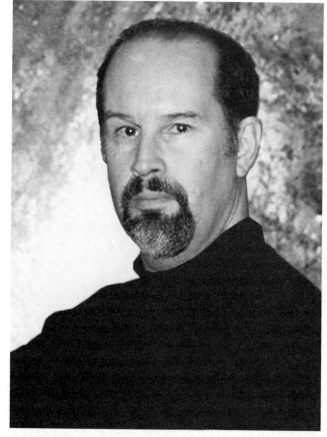

Timothy Zahn

Cobra, Baen (New York, NY), 1985.
Spinneret (first published serially in *Analog Science Fiction/Science Fact,* July-October, 1985), Bluejay (New York, NY), 1985.
Blackcollar: The Backlash Mission, DAW Books (New York, NY), 1986.

Cascade Point (stories), Bluejay (New York, NY), 1986, title novella published singly (bound with *Hardfought* by Greg Bear), Tor Books (New York, NY), 1988.

Cobra Strike, Baen (New York, NY), 1986.

Triplet, Baen (New York, NY), 1987.

Cobra Bargain, Baen (New York, NY), 1988.

Deadman Switch, Baen (New York, NY), 1988.

Time Bomb and Zahndry Others (stories), Baen (New York, NY), 1988.

Warhorse, Baen (New York, NY), 1990.

Heir to the Empire (first book in "Star Wars Thrawn" trilogy), Bantam (New York, NY), 1991.

Distant Friends and Others (stories), Baen (New York, NY), 1992.

Cobras Two, Baen (New York, NY), 1992.

Dark Force Rising (second book in "Star Wars Thrawn" trilogy), Bantam (New York, NY), 1992.

The Last Command (third book in "Star Wars Thrawn" trilogy), Bantam (New York, NY), 1993.

Conquerors' Pride, Bantam (New York, NY), 1994.

Conquerors' Heritage, Bantam (New York, NY), 1995.

Conquerors' Legacy, Bantam (New York, NY), 1996.

Specter of the Past (first book in "Star Wars: The Hand of Thrawn" series), Bantam (New York, NY), 1997.

Vision of the Future (second book in "Star Wars: The Hand of Thrawn" series), Bantam (New York, NY), 1998.

The Icarus Hunt, Bantam Books (New York, NY), 1999.

(With Michael A. Stackpole) *Star Wars: Mara Jade: By the Emperor's Hand* ("Star Wars" series graphic novel), illustrated by Carlos Ezquerra, Dark Horse Comics (Milwaukie, OR), 1999.

Angelmass, Tor (New York, NY), 2001.

Manta's Gift, Tor (New York, NY), 2002.

Star Song and Other Stories, Five Star (Waterville, ME), 2002.

Dragon and Thief: A Dragonback Adventure, Tor (New York, NY), 2003.

Dragon and Soldier: The Second Dragonback Adventure, Starscape (New York, NY), 2004.

The Green and the Gray, Tor (New York, NY), 2004.

Star Wars: Survivor's Quest, Ballantine/Del Rey (New York, NY), 2004.

The Cobra Trilogy (contains *Cobra, Cobra Strike*, and *Cobra Bargain*), Baen Books (Riverdale, NY), 2004.

Fool's Bargain (e-book), Ballantine (New York, NY), 2004.

Work included in anthologies, including *The 1983 Annual World's Best SF*, edited by Donald A. Wollheim, DAW, 1983, and *Alien Stars*, edited by Elizabeth Mitchell, Baen (New York, NY), 1985. Author of introduction, *The Star Wars Encyclopedia* by Stephen J. Sansweet, Ballantine (New York, NY), 1998. Contributor of numerous stories and novelettes to magazines, including *Analog Science Fiction/Science Fact, Ares, Fantasy and Science Fiction, Fantasy Gamer, Isaac Asimov's Science Fiction Magazine, Rigel*, and *Space Gamer*.

ADAPTATIONS: Star Wars: Heir to the Empire, read by Denis Lawson, is available on cassette from Bantam, 1991.

SIDELIGHTS: When Timothy Zahn decided to try his hand at writing, he had no idea how successful he would become, he just knew he enjoyed making up entertaining stories. Working towards a Ph.D. in physics at the University of Illinois, Zahn began writing science fiction as a hobby. In 1978, when he sold "Ernie," his first story, he considered taking a year off upon completion of his degree in order to write fiction full time. Zahn's plans changed completely in mid-1979, when his thesis advisor died suddenly and unexpectedly. Faced with the prospect of beginning a new project with another professor, the graduate student decided instead to take time off to write. The nine stories he sold that year convinced him to stick with writing science fiction.

Since that time, Zahn has become known for tales of complicated characters who face moral dilemmas, generally involving conflicts between human and alien cultures. He often focuses on seemingly impossible situations—uninhabitable planets, tyrannical alien rulers—and shows how ingenious, inventive, and determined individuals manage to find solutions. He presents readers with tightly constructed, fast-paced stories, and his tales have earned him both critical respect and popularity. Initially, Zahn limited himself to short stories, publishing many of them in the early 1980s. He became one of *Analog Science Fiction/Science Fact* magazine's regular contributors. In one of his early stories, "Hollow Victory," an alien ambassador has fallen seriously ill and two human biomedics must discover the cause of his sickness. To do this, they use clues about the Thrulmodi physiology and the Thrulmodi planet, where the first human-Thrulmodi conference is taking place. This is an early incidence of a common theme in Zahn's work: two cultures—generally, one human and one alien—must come to terms with each other.

The Blackcollar, his debut novel, combines science fiction with martial arts adventure. The book centers on the conflict between the Ryqril—a conquering alien race who have vanquished Earth and its worlds—and a group of their human subjects. Among these human revolutionaries are several people who remember a time when the humans had their own superwarriors, the Blackcollars, well-trained fighters whose reflexes were enhanced by drugs. Despite the fact that the Blackcollars were dissolved after the war with the Ryqril, a small band of them is known to still exist. Allen Caine leaves Earth to seek them out, highlighting one of Zahn's ongoing themes of the limits and strengths of human potency. *Analog Science Fiction/ Science Fact* reviewer Tom Easton complimented Zahn for not allowing the predictable triumph of humans to be total. He also made special mention of *Blackcollar's* originality: "There is more realism here, and hence more satisfaction." The writer uses the scenario again in a sequel titled *Blackcollar: The Backlash Mission.*

Telekinesis and social questions play key roles in Zahn's second novel, *A Coming of Age.* Zahn plays with the idea of a mutation whose effects bring both good and evil to humans. Because of a mutation that occurred some two hundred years before the novel begins, children on the planet Tigris develop psychic powers at five years of age. These powers enable them to fly and move objects with their minds, among other telekinetic skills, but the abilities disappear with the onset of puberty. During this eight-year interval, the children are more powerful than adults. Therefore, the society has developed several means by which to control the potent pre-teens and harness their powers. Once children reach puberty and lose their powers, they are allowed to go to school and are streamlined into adult society.

The characters in *Coming of Age* include a thirteen-year-old girl who dreads the loss of her special facility, an adult detective and his preteen assistant who are looking into a kidnapping, a scientist who is researching the biology of the telekinetic phenomenon, and a criminal who plans to use this research. By using the universal experience of adolescence and the ac-

companying gains and losses that everyone feels, Zahn shows that his concerns range beyond hard science and speculation of technological development to include social and psychological questions. *Analog's* Easton said he found *A Coming of Age* to be "a warm and sympathetic story very suitable for a broad range of ages," since it is "complex" enough to entertain older readers. A *Publishers Weekly* reviewer commended Zahn for writing "an entertaining science fiction police procedural that should especially appeal to teenagers."

While Zahn was branching out into more psychological themes, he maintained his ability to interest readers with space adventures. Despite the fact that Earth vessels can travel beyond the stars, no habitable worlds remain within reach as the author's 1985 novel *Spinneret* opens. All the potentially habitable areas have been colonized by other star-faring races. Zahn follows Colonel Lloyd Meredith's attempt to colonize Astra, a world no one wants because it has no metals—or so everyone thinks until its dormant volcano spews a metal thread into orbit shortly after Meredith's expedition lands. *Publishers Weekly* Sybil Steinberg pronounced this one of "Zahn's best novels."

Cobra, Cobra Strike, and *Cobra Bargain* deal with the theme of the superhuman warriors Zahn began to explore in the *Blackcollar* books. The Cobras (Computerized Body Reflex Armament) are technologically souped-up soldiers programmed to react lethally to anything their reflexes read as an attack. They are created after one of the colony worlds of the Dominion of Man is conquered by the Troft forces, whom they manage to subdue. Because the Cobras' indiscriminate responses make them dangerous for civilian life, they are sent to protect the colonists on the far side of Troft territory. Zahn focuses on Jonny Moreau, a twenty year old from a backwater planet who is one of the first people to sign up for the Cobra program. Moreau changes from a naive, idealistic young man into a savvy politician as he becomes a leader on his new home.

In *Cobra Strike,* second in the series, Jonny Moreau's three sons must contend with another threat. On the distant planet of Quasama, a paranoid race of humans lives in a mutually beneficial and dependent relationship with predatory birds called mojos. The formerly adversarial Trofts, now trading partners with the humans, want to use the Cobras as mercenaries to destroy this race, in return for five new worlds that can support human life.

The last installment of the "Cobra" series, *Cobra Bargain,* takes place after Jonny Moreau has passed away. Jonny's granddaughter, Jasmine, decides to buck the all-male tradition of the Cobras and join their ranks—she is a Moreau, after all. She successfully completes the training and proves herself to be a resourceful and independent young woman whose diplomatic and warrior abilities mirror or surpass those of her male predecessors.

Zahn gathered thirteen short fiction works for *Cascade Point and Other Stories,* including the Hugo Award-winning novella *Cascade Point. Booklist* reviewer Roland Green praised Zahn's "consistent intelligence in both the presentation and the resolution" of his stories, concluding that despite the traditional nature of Zahn's science fiction it is "certainly high-quality work." Gregory Frost remarked in the *Washington Post Book World* that "every story of Zahn's contains a novel idea" and that the stories center on scientific theories or possible advances in science. Frost did, however, take Zahn to task for failing to handle his ideas in an unusual way. He said that "Zahn is what is referred to as an 'idea' writer," someone whose stories "are often extrapolations from hard scientific data."

Zahn's *Triplet* takes its title from a strange planetary system where travelers from the Twenty Worlds land on Threshold in order to journey through a tunnel to reach the Hidden Worlds. These include Shamsheer, a world where technology is at such a high level that it appears like magic, and Karyx, where magic actually works but is dependent on summoning demons. Zahn's heroine is Danae mal ce Taeger, an heiress who uses her influence to get assigned to Ravagin, the most experienced courier to these worlds. Danae works hard to accomplish something for herself, to free herself of all the advantages that her father's wealth has afforded her, but ultimately she discovers that these too have their part in her success and that she can use them to her advantage. While *Publishers Weekly* John Mutter criticized the novel as one of Zahn's less successful efforts, the reviewer also said that "as usual he scores with a progressively enlarging perspective and gradual revelation of the hidden logic behind" his ideas.

In *Deadman Switch* the author explores possible permutations of the death penalty. The galactic society the novel describes uses its convicts as pilots for space travel to the world of Solitaire, which is surrounded by a mysterious cloud that can only be navigated by corpses. Ships that seek to enter or exit the system must kill a member of their crew to create a "zombi" pilot. When Gilead Benedar, who works for the magnate Lord Kelsey-Ramos as a human lie detector, is sent on an inspection tour of Kelsey-Ramos's newly acquired Solitaire-licensed ships, he discovers that one of the ship's two intended zombis is innocent. As well, he discovers that she, like Benedar, belongs to the Watchers, a Christian sect that is one of the last remnants of organized religion left in the galaxy. Watchers are trained to accurately, truly, and deeply observe the universe. Benedar's recognition—and subsequent search for a replacement zombi—leads to all sorts of problems with Solitaire's elite as well as the executives whose company his boss has taken over. *Analog* reviewer Easton chided the story for its "elementary" structure and theme, adding that the "plot is too largely predictable."

In *Warhorse,* the author imagines a conflict between an outwardly mobile human race and an alien species of sophisticated biological engineers. The "Tampies" have decided that all life is valuable and should be protected, a philosophy that often clashes with the violent realities of human society. Among the Tampies' weapons are living spaceships called "warhorses," which are more powerful than anything humanity has produced and could be used to destroy mankind if they proved a threat. Writing in *Booklist,* Green deemed *Warhorse* "Zahn at his best," making special mention of the author's mix of "hard science and social science extrapolation."

Sometimes a writer decides to rework a classic—a play by William Shakespeare, for example, or a myth—but very few do what Zahn did in 1991: take a popular and celebrated film series and resume the story where the creators left off. With *Heir to the Empire* the author picked up the *Star Wars* story five years after *The Return of the Jedi,* the last of George Lucas's original three films. Zahn's *Star Wars* books reawakened the immense interest in the film series and introduced several characters (including Mara Jade and Grand Admiral Thrawn) that now have as much legitimacy in the popular eye as the original ones who appeared in the first three movies. Zahn refuses to call himself the "savior" of *Star Wars;* he claims that he simply tapped into interest that was already present among science fiction fans. And the interest clearly was present; the books flew off the shelves and did much to further Zahn's career.

In *Heir to the Empire* Han Solo and Princess Leia are married and expecting twins. Luke Skywalker continues to learn the secrets of the Jedi, as well as to train Leia in the Jedi arts. Darth Vader and the Evil Empire have been defeated and the Republic is at peace. All appears to be well—until Grand Admiral Thrawn, former warlord of the empire, shows up and attacks the Republic. John Lawson noted in *School Library Journal* that while *Heir to the Empire* is "not on a par with Zahn's creative, powerful works" it is "well written." The book reached the top of the *New York Times* bestseller list and remained there for twenty-nine straight weeks.

Dark Force Rising, the second book in the series, joined *Heir to the Empire* on the bestseller list. The same characters are back, along with Grand Admiral Thrawn, who is preparing to crush the New Republic. To this end, he has enlisted the help of unsavory smugglers, political rivals, a well-placed snitch, and an insane Jedi Master. *Booklist*'s Green termed Zahn's adoption of the Star Wars characters "one of the more remarkable pastiches of recent years." He also praised Zahn's "real flair" for incorporating elements of science fiction into the *Star Wars* saga, while *Library Journal* contributor Jackie Cassada complimented Zahn's "snappy prose and cinematic style."

In the final volume of Zahn's trilogy, *The Last Command*, Grand Admiral Thrawn has been successful and is preparing to mount a final siege against the Republic using his clone soldiers. As Han and Leia struggle to keep up resistance—and await their twins at any moment—it becomes clear that the Empire has too many ships and clones for the rebels to have a chance in face-to-face combat. The only solution is the infiltration of Thrawn's stronghold by a small band of fighters led by Luke. Naturally, further dangers await them at Thrawn's headquarters. The book spent twelve weeks on the *New York Times* bestseller list.

Zahn returned to Star Wars to write another pair of books, *Specter of the Past* in 1997 and *Vision of the Future* in 1998; they comprise the "Hand of Thrawn" series. In *Specter of the Past* Luke, Han Solo, and Princess Leia fight the armies of the evil Grand Admiral Thrawn. Thrawn had been presumed dead,

but seems to have been mysteriously resurrected. In *Vision of the Future*, the heroes must once again keep the Empire at bay while preventing a civil war. Along the way, they engage in the intergalactic battles and intergalactic intrigue that has made the series so popular with readers.

After following this story line with a "Star Wars" graphic novel titled *Star Wars: Mara Jade: By the Emperor's Hand*, which he wrote with Michael A. Stackpole, Zahn completed *Survivor's Quest*. As expected given the burgeoning romance of the earlier books, Luke and Mara were meant for each other. They are married in *Survivor's Quest*, but despite this happy development there are many problems for them to face when the Outbound Flight, a fleet of once-lost ships carrying fifty thousand people, is discovered and shot-down by the Chiss, possibly by accident. Various alien species interested in the technology they might discover, set out to take advantage of the situation only to find out that there are survivors, and that they are not very friendly toward the New Republic. Luke and Mara are sent as ambassadors by the New Republic to meet with these people, but they quickly find themselves entangled in plenty of political intrigue and other entanglements. Critics of this installment of the "Star Wars" saga found it to be an exciting and intelligent addition. For example, Jackie Cassada called it a "first-rate" space opera in a *Library Journal* review, and *Booklist*'s Green declared it to be a "thoroughly absorbing story."

Returning to his military-themed tales, in *Conquerors' Pride* Zahn writes about an aggressive nonhuman species that suddenly appears and attacks several ships of the intergalactic Commonwealth Peacekeeper force. When a high-ranking Commonwealth official realizes that his son, Commander Pheylan Cavanagh, is the only human survivor and is now in alien captivity, he organizes a rescue mission along with another son and a daughter. However, the rescue mission may endanger the survival of the Commonwealth, which leads to troubling questions of family, duty, and patriotism. Zahn returned to the story line with *Conquerors' Heritage* and *Conquerors' Legacy*.

The 1999 novel *The Icarus Hunt* tells the tale of space smuggler Jordan McKell, who agrees to deliver an unidentified cargo to Earth aboard the spaceship *Icarus*. This cargo seems to be an alien star drive, which constitutes a serious threat to the Path, the dominant race of the galaxy. The Patth currently have the fastest star drive in existence, which lets them control all intergalactic trade, and they and their allies are in hot pursuit of the *Icarus*. They attack McKell several times and kill one of his crew members. McKell finally decides to fire up the star drive he is transporting, only to discover that it is in fact a star gate. This creates even more plot twists and excitement. Zahn does not shy away from the unpleasant but unavoidable aspects of life; in his world, wounds actually hurt and the living grieve for their dead friends. Green, reviewing the novel in another *Booklist* article, wrote that *The Icarus Hunt* "is one of the better novels in some time for readers moving from *Star Wars* and its clones to other sf, and, as such, is highly recommended."

In 2001 Zahn published *Angelmass*. The novel takes its name from an alien force that can control human behavior through its emissions, called "Angels," so named because they appear to encourage their users to be morally good. The Empyrean, the government of an interplanetary system, uses the Angelmass to help it govern. Empyrean's chief opponent, the Pax Comitus, is concerned about this practice. Zahn introduces a number of heroes, including a spy, a sixteen-year-old thief, and an Empyrean senator, all of whom question official governmental and scientific opinions. Zahn pays as much attention to ethics as he does to adventure. *Booklist*'s Green observed that the plot is the basic "good guys" against "bad guys" story that forms the classic mold of science fiction stories, and that the characters are broadly drawn. Nevertheless, he wrote, "the action is abundant and vivid, and there are absorbing subplots." In *Library Journal*, Jackie Cassada called *Angelmass* "a first-rate sf space adventure."

In the 2002 novel *Manta's Gift*, Zahn combines a coming-of-age tale with a vision of alien contact. Twenty-two-year-old Matt Raimey is a quadriplegic following an accident, so when he is offered the chance to escape his body in order to communicate with an alien race he jumps at the chance. The alien Qanska have been discovered in Earth's own solar system, living in Jupiter's atmosphere. After Matt's brain is transplanted into a Qanska's womb and he is reborn as one of the manta ray-like creatures, his new life is interrupted by an impending ecological disaster and the expectations of his human sponsors. "Zahn concentrates more on the psychological processes at work than on technological advances," a *Publishers Weekly* writer observed, concluding that the novel is "more than the usual SF action-adventure."

With *Dragon and Thief: A Dragonback Adventure* Zahn embarks on a new sci-fi series introducing fourteen-year-old Jack Morgan and his alien friend Draycos. Jack is an orphan whose caretaker, a con man named Uncle Virgel, has died, leaving him only with a computer program, also named Virgel, that simulates the original uncle's personality. Virgel's somewhat shifty life has left Jack in trouble with the law, and he is living on an uninhabited planet when Draycos's ship crash lands. Draycos's people, the K'da, are at war with the Valahgua, a species that has developed a horrifying weapon that threatens to wipe out the K'da and their allies. With both Draycos and Jack in trouble, they decide that they can help each other: Draycos needs Jack to be his symbiant or else he will die, and Jack could use the alien's help to save him from being punished for a crime he did not commit. Agreeing to Draycos's terms, Jack and the dragon-like alien embark on a fast-paced adventure that critics felt would be especially appealing to young adult audiences. *Booklist* contributor Sally Estes recommended it as a "romp of a space thriller, provided you don't take it too seriously," and a *Kirkus Reviews* writer felt it will prove to be "a palatable adventure for a young audience, well paced and smoothly narrated."

Zahn has become popular among readers and critics alike. Green, writing again in *Booklist*, has praised Zahn's "generally excellent military novels" as well as his "consistently acute eye for detail." And *Analog*'s Easton has pointed out that in the vein of most traditional science fiction, Zahn deals with a vast interplanetary system in his work. However, according to Easton, like many of his contemporaries, Zahn's ideas are "smaller, of lesser sweep" than those of older writers. But in Zahn's case, he concluded, "this is a consequence of more attention to character, to individuals, to matters of soul instead of destiny."

Zahn himself professes no deep motives to his writing other than to tell a good tale. "I consider myself primarily a storyteller and as such have no major pulpit-thumping 'message' that I always try to insert into each story or book," he once commented. "If any theme crops up more than any other, it is my strong belief that there is no prison—whether physical, social, or emotional—that can permanently trap a person who truly wishes to break free of the bonds."

BIOGRAPHICAL AND CRITICAL SOURCES:

BOOKS

Contemporary Popular Writers, St. James Press (Detroit, MI), 1997.

St. James Guide to Science Fiction Writers, fourth edition, St. James Press (Detroit, MI), 1996.

PERIODICALS

Analog Science Fiction/Science Fact, June 22, 1981, Jay Kay Klein, "Biog," p. 70; February, 1984, Tom Easton, review of *The Blackcollar,* p. 167; October, 1985, Tom Easton, review of *Cobra,* p. 182; November, 1985, Tom Easton, review of *A Coming of Age,* p. 182; August, 1986, Tom Easton, review of *Cobra Strike,* p. 178; November, 1986, Tom Easton, review of *Cascade Point and Other Stories,* p. 182; May, 1989, Tom Easton, review of *Deadman Switch,* p. 181; December, 1999, Tom Easton, review of *The Icarus Hunt,* p. 136; March, 2002, Tom Easton, "The Reference Library," p. 132; April, 2003, Tom Easton, review of *Manta's Gift,* p. 135, and *Star Song and Other Stories,* p. 137.

Booklist, January 1, 1986; May 1, 1986; August, 1987; March 15, 1990, Roland Green, review of *Warhorse;* April 1, 1992, Roland Green, review of *Dark Force Rising,* p. 1413; September 1, 1994, Roland Green, review of *Conqueror's Pride,* p. 28; September 1, 1995, Roland Green, review of *Conqueror's Heritage,* p. 48; September 15, 1997, Roland Green, review of *Specter of the Past,* p. 181; June 1, 1999, Roland Green, review of *The Icarus Hunt,* p. 1744; September 15, 2001, Green, review of *Angelmass,* p. 201; November 1, 2002, Roland Green, review of *Manta's Gift,* p. 481; December 1, 2002, Roland Green, review of *Star Song and Other Stories,* p. 652; February 15, 2003, Sally Estes, review of *Dragon and Thief: A Dragonback Adventure,* p. 1060; December 1, 2003, Roland Green, review of *Survivor's Quest,* p. 627.

Kirkus Reviews, June 15, 1999, review of *The Icarus Hunt,* p. 928; August 15, 2001, review of *Angelmass,* p. 1177; October 1, 2002, review of *Manta's Gift,* p. 1435; January 1, 2003, review of *Dragon and Thief,* p. 31.

Kliatt, March, 2004, Sherry Hoy, review of *Manta's Gift,* p. 28.

Library Journal, April 15, 1992, Jackie Cassada, review of *Dark Force Rising,* p. 125; February 1, 1995, Roxanna Herrick, review of *Conqueror's Pride,* p. 112; October 15, 1997, Susan Hamburger, review of *Specter of the Past,* p. 98; July, 1999, Jackie Cassada, review of *The Icarus Hunt,* p. 143; October 15, 2001, Jackie Cassada, review of *Angelmass,* p. 112; December, 2002, Jackie Cassada, review of *Manta's Gift,* p. 184, and *Death and the Librarian and Other Stories,* p. 185; February 15, 2004, Jackie Cassada, review of *Survivor's Quest,* p. 167.

New York Times, April 15, 2004, Cindy Dobrez and Lynn Rutan, "In the Dragon's Lair," p. 1454.

New York Times Book Review, March 2, 2003, Gerald Jonas, review of *Manta's Gift,* p. 19.

Publishers Weekly, December 14, 1984, review of *A Coming of Age,* p. 41; October 25, 1985, Sybil Steinberg, review of *Spinneret,* p. 61; March 21, 1986; July 3, 1987, John Mutter, review of *Triplet,* p. 58; July 5, 1991, review of *Heir to Empire* (sound recording), p. 46; March 23, 1992, review of *Dark Force Rising,* p. 64; September 29, 1997, review of *Specter of the Past,* p. 70; October 1, 2001, review of *Angelmass,* p. 43; October 7, 2002, review of *Manta's Gift,* p. 57; February 3, 2003, review of *Dragon and Thief,* p. 59; December 22, 2003, review of *Survivor's Quest,* p. 42.

School Library Journal, September, 1985, Penny Parker, review of *A Coming of Age,* p. 155; February, 1992, John Lawson, review of *Heir to Empire,* p. 122.

Washington Post Book World, May 25, 1986, Gregory Frost, review of *Cascade Point and Other Stories.*

ONLINE

Echo Station Web site, http://www.echostation.com/ (January 6, 2002), Jeff Carter, "Star Wars Per-Zahn-ified."

Scifi.com Web site, http://www.scifi.com/ (January 6, 2002), Mark Wilson, review of *Angelmass.**